THE OFFICIAL® PRICE GUIDE TO

ANTIQUES AND COLLECTIBLES

THE OFFICIAL® PRICE GUIDE TO

ANTIQUES AND COLLECTIBLES

EIGHTEENTH EDITION

RINKER ENTERPRISES, INC.

HOUSE OF COLLECTIBLES
THE BALLANTINE PUBLISHING GROUP • NEW YORK

Important Notice. All of the information, including valuations, in this book has been compiled from the most reliable sources, and every effort has been made to eliminate errors and questionable data. Nevertheless, the possibility of error, in a work of such immense scope, always exists. The publisher will not be held responsible for losses that may occur in the purchase, sale, or other transaction of items because of information contained herein. Readers who feel they have discovered errors are invited to write and inform us, so they may be corrected in subsequent editions. Those seeking further information on the topics covered in this book are advised to refer to the complete line of Official Price Guides published by the House of Collectibles.

Published by: House of Collectibles
The Ballantine Publishing Group
201 East 50th Street
New York, New York 10022

Distributed by The Ballantine Publishing Group, a division of Random House, Inc., New York, and simultaneously in Canada by Random House of Canada Limited, Toronto.

www.randomhouse.com/BB/

Manufactured in the United States of America

ISSN: 1050–6144

ISBN: 0–676–60185–5

Eighteenth Edition: April 2000
10 9 8 7 6 5 4 3 2 1

CONTENTS

Introduction

The antiques market is divided into three basic parts: (1) antiques, objects made before 1945, (2) collectibles, objects made between 1945 and the late 1970s, and (3) desirables, objects made between the late 1970s and the present. Antiques and collectibles have a stable secondary market. Desirables have a speculative secondary market. *The Official Price Guide to Antiques and Collectibles, 18th Edition,* provides coverage for all three segments.

This is a general price guide. It provides a sampling of objects commonly found in the antiques marketplace. A few highly desirable, scarce items are included in most category listings to show the category's high end.

Obviously, it is impossible in a general price guide to list every object available in a collecting category. Hopefully, this book provides you with sufficient comparable objects to value the one you own. If it does not, the category introductions include information on select reference books, periodicals, and collectors' clubs where you can find more detailed information.

The Official Price Guide to Antiques and Collectibles is a field guide, a place to find basic information and a reference source as to where to turn to next.

The antiques market is experiencing a major transition as it prepares to enter the twenty-first century. A new breed of young collectors, more me focused than past focused, the Internet, and a trendy market are three contributing factors. Traditionalist collectors watch with dismay as their favorite collecting categories stabilize or decline in value and with disgust as contemporary desirables such as Pokémon capture the public's imagination.

There will be a strong, vibrant antiques and collectibles market in the twenty-first century. However, it will be a different market in terms of what and how objects are collected. There are exciting times ahead. There is every reason to believe the changes will be positive.

While the computer will never replace traditional printed price guides such as this one, it continues to have an exponential impact on the antiques and collectibles field. Check out these auction (www.auctionuniverse.com and www.ebay.com), direct sale (www.antiqnet.com, www.collectoronline.com, www.kaleden.com, and www.tias.com), and periodical and specialty sites (www.mainantiquedigest.com and www.rinker.com). There is nothing you cannot find on the Internet, often at a bargain price. The problems are that it often takes a great deal of time to find it and the buying process can be troublesome. The Internet is in its infancy. Things will improve.

Finally, remember that the real joy of collecting is not found in the financial value of objects but the pleasure that comes from owning, living with, and enjoying the object.

COLLECTING TIPS

Condition is everything. The difference between very good and near mint can be the difference between $100 and $1000 or more!

Be a tough grader. Overgrading is a common mistake. If an item needs restoration, know what that will cost before you buy. Also remember that a restored antique is generally worth much less than an unrestored piece in pristine condition.

Just because something is scarce doesn't mean it is valuable. In today's trendy market, desirability is a major value key.

Do your homework! The information age has created an explosion of material on all subjects and topics. Taking advantage of a public library's book search service is well worth the time. Antiques and collectibles reference books are often expensive, but a $50 book can often save you from many $100 mistakes.

Learning the ordinary teaches about the extraordinary. Most pieces are far more common than people realize.

What goes up often comes down. The media loves reporting record prices. A market that is slowly ebbing away rarely receives attention.

Always ask the seller to provide a guarantee of authenticity. Get it in writing. If you do not ask for a guarantee, you had better know what you are buying.

AUCTION BUYING TIPS

Always thoroughly examine every piece before you bid on it. If you have not examined it, DO NOT BID.

Always set a dollar limit for yourself before you start bidding. Do not let auction frenzy drive your bidding, and do not forget to calculate in the buyer's penalty (premium).

Make certain the auctioneer sees your bidding. If you bid with just the nod of a head, the auctioneer may be selling to the person in front of you.

And yes, if your nose itches, you can scratch it without buying a fifteen–foot chandelier; just do not stare the auctioneer in the eye while you're doing it.

BUYING VERSUS SELLING PRICES

A dealer must make his profit to stay in business, and many businesses are expensive to run. The difference between a dealer's buying price and his selling price must cover the rent, the car, and everything else. Hence, the selling price of an item may be only a fraction of the price tagged in the window (or quoted in this guide!), especially for inexpensive items.

AUCTION SELLING TIPS

Choose your auction house by the service they offer, not the estimate they quote. You cannot deposit an estimate in the bank.

Do not be greedy. An item with a high estimate and/or a reserve scares away potential buyers. Once an item has failed to sell (or "bought in"), it is harder to sell the next time.

When evaluating the contract you are asked to sign, consider these points: (1) what is the condition? (2) who pays for photographs? (3) who pays for insurance? (4) what is the reserve (or minimum price) set at? and (4) when is payment made?

PRICES

The prices in this book represent the average price that an informed buyer will pay a knowledgeable and specialized dealer for these items.

Collecting is not the same as investing. The antiques and collectibles market is not the stock market. Prices do not tick up and down on a daily basis. If the value of your collection increases with time and rising markets, consider it a bonus. Most collections do not make money; they consume it.

SPOTTING PROBLEM PIECES

The ever–increasing availability of cheap labor and expensive machines has resulted in the production of countless fakes in all fields. Most dealers are honest, but many honest dealers get fooled. To beware, you need to be aware. Here are a few tips:

1. If it looks new, assume it is new.
2. Assume every object is bad. Make it prove to you that it is period.
3. Beware of bargains. They deserve a very careful second and third look.
4. Learn the styles of the times. Many fakes give themselves away because they just don't "feel right."
5. Learn to recognize tool marks and which tools were used when.
6. Visit museum gift shops and other places where high quality reproductions are sold.
7. Subscribe to *Antique & Collectors Reproduction News* (Box 71174, Des Moines, IA 50325). It is a great monthly report on fakes and reproductions.

USING THIS GUIDE

Sections are laid out by category. The term "sight" preceding a measurement refers to visible image size. Abbreviations used throughout this guide are:

c – circa	j – jewels	qt – quart
C – century	k – karat	sq – square
dia – diameter	l – long (length)	w – wide (width)
ea – each	pcs – pieces	w/ – with
h – high (height)	pt – pint	wo/ – without

COLLECTING–RELATED PUBLICATIONS

Hundred of periodicals on antiques and collectibles exist, some for specialized areas. Rinker Enterprises recommends the following general and regional periodicals:

Antique Gazette, 6949 Charlotte Pike, Suite 106, Nashville, TN 37209; (800) 660-6143; Fax: (615) 352-0941.

Antique Journal for California and Nevada, 2329 Santa Clara Avenue, Suite 207, Alameda, CA 94501; (800) 791-8592; Fax: (510) 523-5262; e-mail: antiquesjrl@aol.com.

Antique Review, 12 East Stafford Street, PO Box 538, Worthington, OH 43085; (614) 885-9757; Fax: (614) 885-9762.

The Antique Shoppe, PO Box 2175, Keystone Heights, FL 32656; (352) 475-1679; Fax: (352) 475-5326; web: www.antiquenet.com/antiqueshoppe; e-mail: EDSOPER@aol.com.

Antique Showcase, Trojan Publishing Corp., 103 Lakeshore Road, Suite 202, St. Catherines, Ontario, Canada L2N 2T6; (905) 646-0995; Fax: (905) 646-0995; e-mail: office@trajan.com.

The Antique Trader Weekly, PO Box 1050, Dubuque, IA 52004-1050; (800) 334-7165; Fax: (800) 531-0880; web: www.collect.com/antiquetrader; e-mail: traderpubs@aol.com.

Antique Trader's Collector Magazine & Price Guide, PO Box 1050, Dubuque, IA 52004-1050; (800) 334-7165; web: traderpr@mwci.net.

The Antique Traveler, PO Box 656, 109 East Broad Street, Mineola, TX 75773; (903) 569-2487; Fax: (903) 569-9080.

Antique Week (Central and Eastern Editions), 27 North Jefferson Street, PO Box 90, Knightstown, IN 46148; (800) 876-5133; Fax: (800) 695-8153; web: www.antiqueweek.com; e-mail: antiquewk@aol.com.

Antiques and the Arts Weekly, The Bee Publishing Company, PO Box 5503, Newtown, CT 06470-5503; (203) 426-8036; Fax: (203) 426-1394; web: www.thebee.com; e-mail: editor@thebee.com.

Antiques & Collectables, 500 Fensler, Suite 205, PO Box 12589, El Cajon, CA 92022; (619) 593-2930; Fax: (619) 447-7187.

Antiques and Collectibles Trader, PO Box 38095, 550 Eglinton Avenue West, Toronto, Ontario, Canada M5N 3A8; (416) 410-7620; Fax: (416) 784-9796.

Antiques & Collecting Magazine, 1006 South Michigan Avenue, Chicago, IL 60605; (800) 762-7576; Fax: (312) 939-0053; e-mail: lightnerpb@aol.com.

Antiques Trade Gazette, 17 Whitcomb Street, London WC2H 7PL, England; (0171) 930 4957; Fax: (0171) 930 6391; web: www.atg-online.com; e-mail: info@atg-online.com.

Arizona Antique News, PO Box 26536, Phoenix, AZ 85068; (602) 943-9137.

Arts & Antiques, 2100 Powers Ferry Road, Atlanta, GA 30339; (770) 955-5656; Fax: (770) 952-0669

Carter's Homes, Antiques & Collectables, Carter's Promotions Pty. Ltd., Locked Bag 3, Terrey Hills, NSW 2084, Australia; (02) 9450 0011; Fax: (02) 945-2532; web: www.carters.com.au; e-mail: michelle@carters.com.au.

Collectors' Eye, Woodside Avenue, Suite 300, Northport, NY 11768; (888) 800-2588; Fax: (516) 261-9684; web: www.collectorseye.com.

Collectors Journal, 1800 West D Street, PO Box 601, Vinton, IA 52349-0601; (800) 472-4006; Fax: (319) 474-3117; e-mail: antiquescj@aol.com.

Collectors News, 506 Second Street, PO Box 156, Grundy Center, IA 50638; (800) 352-8039; Fax: (319) 824-3414; web: collectors-news.com; e-mail: collectors@collectors-news.com.

Cotton & Quail Antique Trail, 205 East Washington Street, PO Box 326, Monticello, FL 32345; (800) 757-7755; Fax: (850) 997-3090.

Great Lakes Trader, 132 South Putnam Street, Williamston, MI 48895; (800) 785-6367; Fax: (517) 655-5380; web: GLTrader@aol.com.

The Magazine Antiques, 575 Broadway, New York, NY 10012; (800) 925-8059; Fax: (212) 941-2897; e-mail: brantpubs@aol.com.

Maine Antique Digest, 911 Main Street, PO Box 1429; Waldoboro, ME 04572; (207) 832-4888; Fax: (207) 832-7341; web: www.maineantiquedigest.com; e-mail: mad@maine.com.

MassBay Antiques, 254 Second Avenue, Needham, MA 02494; (800) 982-4023; e-mail: mbantiques@cnc.com..

MidAtlantic Antiques Magazine, Henderson Newspapers, Inc., 304 South Chestnut Street, PO Box 908, Henderson, NC 27536; (252) 492-4001; Fax: (252) 430-0125.

New England Antiques Journal, 4 Church Street, PO Box 120, Ware, MA 01082; (800) 432-3505; Fax: (413) 967-6009; e-mail:visit@antiquesjournal.com.

Old Stuff, VBM Printers, Inc., 336 North Davis, PO Box 1084, McMinnville, OR 97128; (503) 434-5386; Fax: (503) 435-0990; web: www.vbmpublishinng.com; e-mail: bnm@pnn.com..

The Old Times, 63 Birch Avenue South, PO Box 340, Maple Lake, MN 55358; (800) 539-1810; Fax: (320) 963-6499; web: www.theoldtimes.com; e-mail: oldtimes@lkdllink.net.

Renninger's Antique Guide, 2 Cypress Place, PO Box 495, Lafayette Hill, PA 19444; (610) 828-4614; Fax: (610) 834-1599; web: www.renningers.com.

Southern Antiques, PO Drawer 1107, Decatur, GA 30031; (888) 800-4997; Fax: (404) 286-9727; web: www.kaleden.com.

Treasure Chest, One Richmond Square, Suite 215E, Providence, RI 02906; (800) 557-9662; Fax: (401) 272-9422.

Unravel the Gavel, 14 Hurricane Road, #1, Belmont, NH 03220; (603) 524-4281; Fax: (603) 528-3565; web: www.the-forum.com/gavel; e-mail: gavel96@worldpath.net.

The Upper Canadian, PO Box 653, Smiths Falls, Ontario, Canada K7A 4T6; (613) 283-1168; Fax: (613) 283-1345; e-mail: uppercanadian@recorder.ca

Warman's Today's Collector, Krause Publications, 700 East State Street, Iola, WI 54990; (800) 258-0929; Fax: (715) 445-4087; web: www.krause.com; e-mail: todays-_collector@krause.com..

West Coast Peddler, PO Box 5134, Whittier, CA 90607; (562) 698-1718; Fax: (562) 698-1500; web: www.westcoastpeddler.com; e-mail: antiques@westcoastpeddler.com.

Yesteryear, PO Box 2, Princeton, WI 54968; (920) 787-4808; Fax: (920) 787-7381.

Advertising Memorabilia

The diversity of advertising is astounding. Collectors can concentrate on eras, products, companies, signs, tins, trade cards, watches, premiums, dolls, figural displays, toys, etc. In recent years interest has increased in post–World War II advertising. Adding these collectors to the pre-war collectors creates a huge and growing market. The prices listed below are for items in excellent or better condition. Although some wear is expected on older items it should not be substantial or interfere with the visual appeal of the item. Condition for newer items is near mint. The other section in this book that contains advertising and promotional material is Toys and Playthings.

For further reading see *America For Sale: A Collector's Guide to Antique Advertising* by Douglas Congdon-Martin (Schiffer, West Chester, PA, 1991), *Hake's Guide to Advertising Collectibles* by Ted Hake (Wallace Homestead, Radnor, PA, 1992), and *Huxford's Collectible Advertising, 4th Edition by* Sharon and Bob Huxford (Collector Books, Paducah, KY, 1998).

Left: Coffee Grinder, "Ever-Ready," litho tin, cast iron grinding base, 12" h, $880 at auction.

Right: Match Holder, Moxie, litho tin and wood, "Moxie Nerve Food," 7.25" x 2.5" x .875", $1265 at auction.

—Photos courtesy Wm. Morford.

	LOW	HIGH
Baseball Counter, Hires Root Beer, celluloid, changing score on 1 side changes face of Josh Slinger on other, 1915, 3" x 2.5"	$400	$700
Bottle, Moxie, glass, light aqua, porcelain stopper, embossed "Moxie Trade Mark Reg. U.S. Pat. Office" below neck, "Registered" around base, "A.B.G.O. 3DN" on bottom	20	60
Box, Bubble Gum Cigars, 5¢, Nixon's portrait inside lid and "Win With Dick," 8" x 4.5"	75	125
Box, Chiclets Gum, glass top, with original scalloped scoop, Frank H. Fleer & Co., 8" x 10"	100	150
Box, Frank Miller Blacking, dovetailed wood, inside label with Uncle Sam shaving using shiny boot as mirror, eagle attacks image of himself in other boot, factory vignette in upper left corner, 4.75" x 13.5" x 10.5"	200	400
Box, Hershey's Cocoa Butter Toilet Soap, brown and tan, "Soothing to the skin," with 3 wrapped bars, 7" x 3.5"	35	75
Box, Silver Top Chewing Gum, dovetailed wood, inside label with little boy holding full box of gum and spinning top, standing next to large advertisement for spinning top premium offer, patented July 16, 1878, 3.25" x 9.25" x 6.75"	150	300
Cabinet, Diamond Dyes, wood, embossed tin panel shows children playing with Maypole, 30" x 22.75" x 10.25"	450	900

	LOW	HIGH
Cabinet, Diamond Dyes, wood, embossed tin panel shows governess with children playing in park, ©1906, 23" x 30" x 9"	400	800
Cabinet, Humphrey's Remedies, wood, tin panel with list of remedies, 27.75" x 20" x 10.25"	300	600
Cabinet, Pratts Veterinary Remedies, oak, embossed tin panel with trademark horsehead logo and list of Pratt remedies, 33" x 16.5" x 7"	300	600
Cabinet, Zeno Gum, wood case with embossed marquee, glass front, mirrored back, 3 shelves, 18" h, 10.5" w	400	700
Calendar, Batchelder & Lincoln Company, "A Good Catch," pretty woman with fishing rod, metal rims at top and bottom, full calendar pad, 1908, 21.25" x 14.75"	125	250
Calendar, DuPont Explosives, cardboard, 2 bird dogs, artist signed Edm. H. Osthau, full calendar pad, 1937, 28" x 15"	250	500
Calendar, Harrington & Richardson Arms Co., oil cloth, hunter aiming rifle at caribou, framed, ©1907, 1908 calendar pad, 26.75" x 13.75"	2500	3500
Calendar, Hartney Machine & Motor Works, "Discovered," 2 dogs at point, full calendar pad, 1928, 16.5" x 10.5"	50	100
Calendar, Hercules Powder Co., "The Spirit of '46," 3 servicemen walking together, artist signed N.C. Wyeth, full calendar pad, 1946, 30.5" x 15"	100	200
Calendar, Libby, McNeill & Libby, cute young girl with sausage curls wearing straw hat, corned beef tin below, full 1906 calendar pad, 16.5" h, 10.75" w	75	150
Calendar, New York Central Railroad System, NY Central locomotive #4734, full calendar pad, 1951, 27.5" x 18.25"	75	125
Calendar, Peters Cartridges, oil cloth, mother pointer teaching pups, entitled "The First Lesson, 'Steady'," artist signed A. Muss Arnolt, metal rims at top and bottom, framed, ©1908, 1910 calendar pad, 27" x 13.75"	3000	4000
Calendar, Sharples Cream Separator, cardboard, "The Pride of the Ranch," western couple sharing glass of milk with Indian couple, calendar pad missing, 14" x 7"	50	100
Calendar, Winchester, paper, eagle attacking mountain goats on mountain cliff, artist signed Lynn Bogue Hunt, Forbes Litho Mfg. Co., 1915 calendar pad missing, framed, 29.5" x 14.5"	2000	3000
Chair, Piedmont Cigarettes, wood frame, 2-sided porcelain panel back, "For Cigarettes Virginia Tobacco is the Best"	100	150
Cigar Cutter, Kenteria Havana Cigars, cast iron top and embossed shield front with advertising for "Kenteria Havana Cigars Kent's Extra 5¢ Mac's Best," patented Aug. 7, 1906, 6" h	550	750
Cigar Cutter, New York Specials Havana Cigars, metal marquee with advertising above figural cast iron cigar cutter base, Brunhoff Mfg. Co., 7.5" h	600	800
Clock, Bulova, round clock with blue neon perimeter, "Meyerdi Jewelers" marquee on top, 20" h	200	350
Clock, Calumet Baking Powder, oak regulator, reverse-painted glass panel with "Time To Buy Calumet Baking Powder, 'Best by Test'," Sessions, complete with pendulum, 38.5" h, 16" w	1000	1500
Clock, Chevrolet emblem, Coopersburg, PA, dealership, round, neon rim, 19" dia	600	1200
Clock, Ever-Ready Safety Razor, diecut wood, trademark shaving man on round dial, original Wm. L. Gilbert Clock Co. label, varnished, 22" h not including replaced pendulum	1000	2000
Clock, Ever-Ready Safety Razor, embossed tin, rectangular, trademark shaving man on round dial, 8-day clock, 17.5" h, 12.5" w	1750	2500
Clock, Fleming Florist, cathedral shaped, wood front panel on sheet metal case, advertising on rotating drum in lower window, c1933, 21.5" h, 14" w	250	500

Display, Old Gold Cigarettes, cardboard, includes several early full packs, $413 at auction. —Photo courtesy Wm. Morford.

	LOW	HIGH
Clock, Ford, octagonal, neon rim, "Cars - Trucks - Parts - Accessories," 18" x 18"	600	1200
Clock, Friendship Cut Plug, animated, man's face on dial, mouth chews as clock ticks, patented Mar. 2, 1886, 4" h	400	800
Clock, Gruen Watches, octagonal with blue neon perimeter above marquee advertising "Williams Jewelry Co.," 15" w	350	700
Clock, Hires Root Beer, light-up, round, "Drink Hires Root Beer with root, barks, herbs," 15" dia	150	300
Clock, Longine's Watches, brass, round, "The world's most honored watch" on banner, 18.5" dia	200	400
Clock, Philadelphia Light and Electric, alarm clock, Reddy Kilowatt on dial, Westclox, 5" h	250	500
Clock, Wolf's Head Motor Oil, rectangular frame outlined with pink neon, motor oil can, round clock dial inside, 19" x 30"	500	1000
Dispenser, Buffalo Brand Salted Peanuts, glass globe embossed with buffalo and lettering mounted on metal support frame, with original Buffalo Peanut advertising bag, 21" h	1250	2500
Dispenser, Ginger Mint Julep, stoneware with fired-on lettering, "2599 Property of Emerson Drug Co. Baltimore Maryland. Made in U.S.A." on bottom	300	600
Dispenser, Iced Nestea, barrel-shaped glass globe, metal lid and base, 18.5" h	150	300
Display, Blue-Jay Corn and Bunion Plasters, 2 drawers, 2 hoboes walking along railroad tracks while passing billboard for Blue-Jay Plasters, "Make hard roads easy," ©1903, 6.5" x 9.25" x 10.25"	100	200
Display, Miller Locks, diecut cardboard, easel back, ship in Panama Canal, Gatun Locks displayed on wall of canal lock, missing 5 locks, Breuker & Kessler Co. Litho., patented 1905, 16" x 13"	200	300
Display, Moxie, wood, 3-dimensional soda bottle, paper label, tin cap, small doors in back, metal-lined, 36" h	1000	2000
Display, Occident Flour, tin over cardboard, 7 wheat samples at various stages of processing, 9" x 13.75"	150	300
Display, Red Goose Shoes, plastic red goose "lays" eggs, cardboard box base, 27" h, 22" w	300	500
Display, Yeast Foam, tin, wall mounted, cylindrical with image of stacked yeast tins depicting full rack, "Eat Yeast Foam" on sides, 27.25" x 2.5"	75	150
Dolls, Buster Brown and Tige, Buster with composition head and hands, stuffed Tige with composition head, 25" h Buster, 16.5" h Tige	1000	2000
Door Push, Pepsi-Cola, porcelain, Canadian, 3" x 31"	125	250
Festoon, Hires RJ Root Beer, diecut cardboard, winter motif with pretty woman holding snowshoes, reaching for soda bottle, 11" x 49.5"	400	800

Playing Cards, Planters Peanuts, linen finish, complete deck w/ Joker and box, 1920s, $1375 at auction. —Photo courtesy Wm. Morford.

	LOW	HIGH
Jar, Planters Peanuts, clear glass, embossed barrel shaped, 2 running and 2 standing Mr. Peanut figures, peanut finial, 12" h	200	300
Ledger Tin, Springfield Insurance Co. Mass., litho tin, Indian in shield, Wells & Hope Co., 12" h, 3" w	200	400
Ledger Tin, Western Assurance Co., Toronto, Canada, litho tin, company crest with unicorn, lion, and flags, 12.5" h, 3" w	200	400
Menu Board, Reid's Ice Cream, tin, top sign with pretty girl holding soda fountain glass, ice cream flavors listed below, c1915, 25" h, 11" w	1500	3000
Mug, Hire's Root Beer, ceramic, barrel shaped, trademark boy holding mug, Mettlach, 4.5" h	250	500
Paperweight, Armstrong Carriage, glass, round, horse-drawn carriage, 3" dia	200	400
Paperweight, A.T.A. Nelson Co., glass, naked woman standing behind leather hide, 2.5" x 4"	150	300
Paperweight, Donnelly Machine Co., glass, rectangular, scalloped edge, vintage factory, 3" x 4.5"	150	300
Paperweight, Fletcher Manufacturing Co., glass, oval, factory scene, 2.75" x 4.5"	150	300
Paperweight, Henry Hooker & Co. Carriage Manufacturers, glass, rectangular, horse-drawn carriage, 2.5" x 4"	150	300
Paperweight, Heywood Shoes, glass, rectangular, vintage shoe, "Heywood is in it," 2.5" x 4"	125	250
Paperweight, Lovell Diamond Cycles, glass, rectangular, vintage bicycle, 2.5" x 4"	100	200
Paperweight, New England Mutual Accident Association, glass, rectangular, man's portrait flanked by vintage train and paddle steamboat, 2.5" x 4"	200	400
Paperweight, New York Grand Central Station, glass, rectangular, vintage Grand Central Station, Barnes & Abrams Co., patented Sept. 5, 1882, 2.5" x 4"	800	1200
Paperweight, Oscar R. Boehne & Co., glass, rectangular, gold scale, 2.5" x 4"	150	300
Paperweight, Superior Putting-Out Machine, glass, rectangular, product image, 2.5" x 4"	100	200
Paperweight, White, Warner & Co., glass, rectangular, 2 men leaning against stove, 2.5" x 4"	150	300
Pin, Moxie, diecut tin, Moxie girl holding embossed soda glass and vintage bottle, 2" h	100	200
Plate, Dr. Pepper, girl holding large vase, Vienna Art, 10" dia	450	600
Pocket Mirror, Brotherhood Overalls, celluloid, round, bare-breasted lady wearing overalls, 2" dia	200	400
Pocket Mirror, Buster Brown Shoes, celluloid, round, Buster and Tige, "The little girl on the other side should wear Buster Brown Shoes," 1.75" dia	150	300

Left: Sign, Star Soap, porcelain, 28" h, 20" w, $429 at auction. —Photo courtesy Collectors Auction Services.

Right: Poster, Sunlight Soap, paper, 29.5" x 19.25", $853 at auction. —Photo courtesy Wm. Morford.

	LOW	HIGH
Pocket Mirror, Hires Root Beer, celluloid, oval, young lady with pink cheeks holding armful of roses, "Put Roses in your cheeks, Drink Hires Root Beer," 3" x 1.75"	200	400
Poster, Al G. Kelly & Miller Bros. Circus, giraffe, 28" x 21"	75	150
Poster, International Air Races, paper, biplanes racing over stadium, "Over 200 miles per hour, St. Louis-October 1-2-3," framed, 21" x 14"	400	700
Poster, Royal Baking Bowder, paper, gingerbread man pointing to baking powder tin and child's book entitled "The Little Gingerbread Man," 30" x 20.5"	150	300
Salesman's Sample, wood stove, "Little Eva N.S. Kate Boston Stove," cast iron	700	800
Sign, Admiration Cigars, tin, easel back, colonial lady gazing in mirror, 7.5" x 5.75"	300	500
Sign, Allied Mills, diecut porcelain, grain bag shape, silhouette of man on horseback in center, 32" x 24.5"	350	700
Sign, Ansco Film, diecut tin, 2-sided, film box shape, "Ansco Plenachrome Film," 10" x 24"	150	300
Sign, Beauty Shoppe, porcelain, 2-sided flange, profile of Art Deco lady w/ finger wave hairdo, 12" x 24"	300	600
Sign, Brown's Jumbo Bread, diecut tin, elephant shape, lettering on elephant's blanket, 12.75" x 15"	300	500
Sign, Buster Brown Bread, Golden Sheaf Bakery, embossed tin, Buster and Tige, 19.75" x 27.75"	200	400
Sign, Carter's Union Suits, tin, oval inset with man wearing union suit, framed, 10.75" x 6.75"	175	350
Sign, Colgate's Talc Powder, diecut cardboard, 2-sided, baby holding talcum powder tin, ©1913, 13.75" x 7.25"	100	200
Sign, Dad's Root Beer, embossed tin, soda bottle, 29" x 13.5"	150	300
Sign, Diamond Beverages, porcelain, 13.75" x 41.75"	150	300
Sign, Dutch Boy White Lead Paint, linen cloth, painter donning coveralls, smiling at Dutch Boy holding can of white lead paint, "Now for another *good* paint job," artist Rundle, Sweeny Litho Co., c1932, 49" x 26.5"	250	500
Sign, Eastern Airlines, laminated wood, winged logo shape, red hawk, gold lettering, blue ground, 8.5" h, 57" l	750	1250
Sign, Foster Hose Supporters, Pulveroid (celluloid competitor), corseted woman standing in front of oversized corset, F. Pulver Co., framed, 16.5" x 8.5"	350	600

	LOW	HIGH
Sign, GE Fans, tin, 2-sided flange, electric fan, "buy them here," 12" x 16"	200	400
Sign, Ghirardelli's Cocoa, diecut cardboard, baby in highchair, framed, 13" x 9.5"	400	800
Sign, Glendora Coffee, tin, coffee can image, 14" x 8.5"	50	100
Sign, Gooch's Sarsaparilla, paper, upper Thames river scene, "Gooch's Sarsaparilla - for the Blood," artist signed "Bowers," framed, 7.5" x 9.5"	250	500
Sign, Hills Bros. Coffee, diecut cardboard, easel back, 3-dimensional trademark man in robe drinking coffee, standing beside oversized coffee tin, c1949, 21" h, 19" w	200	400
Sign, Hy-Quality Coffee, diecut cardboard, 2-piece, lady holding cup of coffee, seated on swing suspended from sign with coffee tin, 36.5" h, 16" w	750	1250
Sign, Illinois Springfield Watches, tin, Observatory scene, original wood frame with lettering, 17.5" x 23.5"	250	450
Sign, Imperial Club Cigars, embossed tin, self-framed, full box of cigars, Sentenne & Green Litho., 10" x 13.5"	175	350
Sign, Imperial Suspenders, cardboard, policeman, fireman, and mechanic wearing suspenders, "Are good enough for us," framed, 15.5" x 10.5"	75	150
Sign, Independent Lock & Key Co., diecut tin, 2-sided, key shape, 14" x 32"	125	250
Sign, International Stock Food, paper, feed pail and before and after pictures of hog, "This hog gained 400 lbs in 100 days," framed, 27.75" x 20.5"	150	300
Sign, Ken-Wel Gloves, diecut cardboard, 2 baseball players using "Lou Gehrig Model" mitts, large baseball glove in background, 23.5" x 10.5"	300	600
Sign, Kinney Tobacco, paper, man flirting with woman while sitting on wall plastered with Kinney Brothers advertising, framed, 14.5" x 10.25"	400	800
Sign, Kis-Me Gum, diecut embossed cardboard, lady wearing diaphanous top, framed, ©1905, 18" x 13"	400	800
Sign, Lotus Flour, paper, boy dressed as chef, mixing ingredients for cake, framed, 15.25" x 11.5"	100	200
Sign, Marlin Firearms, paper, 2 hunters in canoe pursuing prey, artist signed Philip R. Goodwin, framed, ©1907, 24.25" x 13.75"	2000	3500
Sign, Mecca Cigarettes, paper, Art Deco woman looking over shoulder at viewer, Earl Christy illustration, original stenciled frame, 19.5" x 11"	200	400
Sign, Merkle's Blu-J Brooms, embossed tin, bird perched on broom, "Saves Rugs Carpets and Labor," framed, 13" x 9.5"	150	250
Sign, Monarch Paint, porcelain, 2-sided flange, hand holding paint brush, "100% Pure, Sold Here," 17" x 15.5"	250	500
Sign, Moxie, diecut cardboard, easel back, factory scene, "Drink Moxie, Frank Archer Invites you to Visit Moxieland," 28" x 39"	200	400
Sign, Moxie, diecut cardboard, easel back, trademark Moxie boy, 40" x 19.5"	150	250
Sign, Moxie, diecut tin, round, girl holding glass of soda, "I Like It," 6" dia	600	1200
Sign, New York Telephone Co., porcelain, round, trademark bell, 8" dia	200	400
Sign, Niagara Shoes, beveled tin over cardboard, waterfall vignette, American Art Works Litho, 19" x 8.75"	200	400
Sign, NuGrape, litho cardboard, "It's NuGrape, Imitation Grape Not Grape Juice, A Flavor You Cant Forget," hand pointing to bottle, yellow ground, 10.5" h, 13.5" w	20	50
Sign, Old Gold Cigarettes, diecut cardboard, Art Deco woman in flowing dress walking 2 borzois, "You can't improve on Nature, Not a cough in a carload," 38" x 49"	250	500
Sign, Oshkosh B'Gosh Overalls, porcelain, 10" x 30"	200	400
Sign, Peters Shoes, brass, debossed lettering, trademark diamond, 6" x 24"	125	250
Sign, Philip Morris, porcelain, pack of cigarettes and "Do you inhale - If so call for Philip Morris, Smoking pleasure without smoking penalties," 4" x 25.75"	250	500

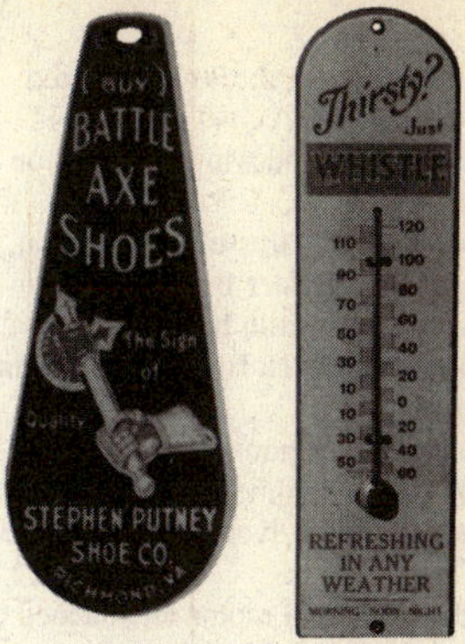

Left: Shoe Horn, Battle Axe Brand Shoes, litho tin, 4.5" x 1.75", $253 at auction.

Right: Thermometer, Whistle, painted wood, 1920s, 15" x 4", $550 at auction.

—Photos courtesy Wm. Morford.

	LOW	HIGH
Sign, Pioneer Baskets, cardboard, Art Deco lady stooping to retrieve item dropped from her shopping basket, "Then she bought a Pioneer Basket," 16" x 12.75"	100	150
Sign, Post Toasties, diecut cardboard, easel back, 3-dimensional, boy holding 2 cereal boxes, standing by begging dog, large cereal box in background, bowl of cereal in foreground, 30" h, 21" w	500	800
Sign, Public Service Company of Oklahoma, porcelain, white oval with lettering and running Reddy Kilowatt, green ground, 21.5" h, 71" l	300	500
Sign, Quaker Oats, paper, Dionne Quint pictures, "Today - The Dionne Quins Had Quaker Oats," 32" x 14.75"	150	250
Sign, Railway Express Agency, litho tin over cardboard, men unloading early railroad car while vintage truck drives by, H.D. Beach Co., 13.5" x 19.5"	400	700
Sign, Railway Express Agency, porcelain, yellow lettering and border, black ground, 12" x 71.5"	150	300
Sign, Roi Tan Cigars, tin over cardboard, debossed oval with loving couple at table, woman lights man's cigar, box of cigars on table, self-framed, c1910, 12" x 10"	500	900
Sign, Salvatine, paper, mountain scene with waterfall, "Salvatine will Cure Rheumatism & Neuralgia and also instant relief for all Pain," metal rims at top and bottom, 14.5" x 11"	400	800
Sign, Sherwin-Williams Paints and Varnishes, porcelain, 2-sided flange, tipped can pouring paint over world, "Sold Here," 16" x 22"	300	600
Sign, Smith Bros. Cough Drops, diecut cardboard, easel backs, 2 standing figures of Smith brothers, each figure 34.25" h	400	700
Sign, Sparkeeta Up, cardboard, attractive lady holding soda bottle, "California's Flavorite," framed, 1946, 29.5" x 23.5"	500	800
Sign, United States Savings Bonds, 2-sided, Lady Liberty and American flag, "for sale at This Window"	100	200
Sign, Van Houten's Cocoa, cardboard, country girl portrait, "Van Houten's Cocoa, Best and Goes Farthest," embossed "Van Houten's Cocoa" frame, 30" x 24"	250	500
Sign, Vel Volla Sponges, glitter over tin, horseshoe, "Quality - Kind," Baltimore Sign Co., 9.75" x 6.75"	150	300
Sign, Williams Ice Cream, tin, 2-sided flange, round with triange inside and "The Cream of Perfection," 13.5" dia	100	175
Sign, Winchester Repeating and Single Shot Rifles, paper, hunter in snowshoes pointing rifle at wolves, framed, ©1906, 29" x 15.25"	4000	8000

	LOW	HIGH
Sign, Winner Plug Tobacco, paper, race horses jumping through oversized stirrup, framed, 9.5" x 9.5"	50	100
Sign, Zenith "Long Distance" Radio, porcelain, blue and white lettering on red banner, yellow ground, 60" h, 18" w	400	500
Statue, Buster Brown and Tige, composition, Buster redressed in sailor hat, red jacket, and red-checked shorts, seated Tige, "Buster Brown" and vintage image of Buster and Tige playing tug-of-war on base	800	1000
Statue, Dutch Boy White Lead Paint, composition, Dutch Boy carrying paint can, 36" h	150	300
String Holder, Red Goose Shoes, cast iron, red figural goose, 11" h, 15" l	400	600
Thermometer, American Denatured Alcohol, tin, thermometer mounted in arrow pointing at company name, "Protect your Car, Non-Rust Anti-Freeze," 26.5" x 19.5"	125	250
Thermometer, Auto King, wooden, small glass bottle of motor oil attached at top, "Flows at 40° Below Zero, Turn Bottle, Prove It," 21" h	350	700
Thermometer, Mail Pouch Tobacco, porcelain, "Treat Yourself To The Best," framed, 72" h, 18" w	300	600
Tip Tray, Bettendorf Wagon, litho tin, rectangular, horse-drawn wagon in center, H. D. Beach Co., 3.25" x 5"	150	250
Tip Tray, Boston Herald, litho tin, round, vintage newsboy running with paper, "The Boston Herald, The Sunday Herald, On Sale Everywhere, A Newspaper Made For All," 3.5" dia	150	225
Tip Tray, C & B Line, litho tin, oval, steamship *Seeandbee* in center, "The largest and most costly passenger steamer on inland waters of the world," H. D. Beach Co., 4.5" x 6.25"	200	300
Tip Tray, Cortez Cigars, litho tin, round, Hernán Cortez portrait, "Cortez Cigars, Key West," 6" dia	250	400
Tip Tray, Evinrude, litho tin, round, "On a Crest of the Wave," woman in boat with vintage outboard motor, 4" dia	150	300
Tip Tray, Eye-Fix, litho tin, round, "The Great Eye Remedy," cherub putting eyedrops in woman's eye, H. D. Beach Co., 4.25" dia	200	275
Tip Tray, Fairy Soap, litho tin, round, little girl sitting on oversized bar of soap, "Have you a little 'Fairy' in your home?," 4.25" dia	75	150
Tip Tray, Gypsy Hosiery, litho tin, round, center vignette of dancing gypsy girl, gypsy camp in background, 6" dia	150	250
Tip Tray, Kenny's Teas & Coffees, litho tin, see no evil, hear no evil, speak no evil monkeys, Kaufmann & Strauss Co., 4.25" dia	175	250
Tip Tray, Lindquist's Crackers, litho tin, rectangular, scalloped rim, "Two Roosevelt Bears had a home out west. In a big ravine near a mountain crest.," teddy bears dressed as Roosevelt, ©1906, 5" x 3.75"	200	300
Tip Tray, Log Cabin Inn, litho tin, rectangular, scalloped rim, "I won't sleep upstairs; said Teddy G. I want a window, I want to see.," Teddy-G trying to descend from train's upper berth, ©1906, 5" x 3.75"	200	300
Tip Tray, Luden's Cough Drops, litho tin, round, product box in center, 3.5" dia	150	300
Tip Tray, Moxie, litho tin, round, "I Just Love Moxie Don't You?," girl holding soda glass, 6" dia	200	400
Tip Tray, National Cigar Stands Co., litho tin, round, woman holding daisies, 6" dia	125	175
Tip Tray, St. Louis World's Fair, litho tin, rectangular, Festival Hall and Cascades, c1904, 3.25" x 5"	75	100
Tip Tray, Success Manure Spreader, litho tin, rectangular, horse-drawn manure spreader at center, 3.5" x 4.75"	175	275
Tip Tray, Wrigley's Soap, litho tin, round, black cat sitting on bars of soap, Chas. W. Shonk Co., 3.5" dia	200	300

	LOW	HIGH
Trade Sign, Bernard Gloekler Co., Pittsburgh, PA, butcher, cast aluminum, painted silver, figural bull above base comprised of hacksaw, cleaver, and butcher knife, 20" h, 24" w	200	300
Tray, Jersey-Creme, pretty girl in green represents Jersey's "cream of the crop," entitled "The Perfect Drink," Chas. W. Shonk Co. Litho., 12" dia	175	350
Tray, Young's Ocean Pier, Atlantic City, NJ, scenic vignettes, C. W. Shonk Co. Litho., 12" dia	200	400
Trolley Sign, Beech-Nut Cough Drops, cardboard, oversized roll of cough drops beside display rack, "Delicious, Effective, 5¢," 11" x 21"	125	250
Trolley Sign, Crusoe Glue, Robinson Glue Co., paper, Robinson Crusoe with boiling kettle, making fish glue on beach, "It sticks everything but the buyer," matted and framed, 10" x 20"	150	250
Tumbler, 20th Century Waiters Club 1906, clear glass, white lettering, 4" h	50	60
Tumbler, Schiller Cigars, clear glass, acid-etched cigar, gold rim band, "Smoke Schiller," 3.75" h	75	125
Tumbler, Vernors Ginger Ale, clear glass, etched lettering, 4" h	100	150
Vending Machine, 1-2-3 Bluebird Gum, embossed tin marquee atop glass globe, metal base, dispenses 1 gumball for first penny, 2 for second penny, and 3 for third penny, c1915, 20" h	300	600
Vending Machine, Chic-Mint Gum, glass globe, sheet metal body with cast iron base plate and collar, c1915, 12" h	400	800
Vending Machine, E-Z, glass globe, cast iron base, dispenses gumball with hole drilled to hold lottery-type slip of paper, base repainted, Ad-Lee Co., patented Sept. 15, 1908, 16" h	400	800
Vending Machine, Magic Vendor, box shaped, glass panels, metal frame, "Al Hoff" embossed on coin door, repainted, Townsend Mfg. Co., c1939, 15" h	300	600
Vending Machine, Mansfield's Choice Pepsin Gum, 2-column vender, 5¢, bell rings when gum is dispensed, metal frame, "Automatic Clerk" etched on front glass panel, patented June 2, 1902, 16" h	700	1400
Vending Machine, Master Fantail, No. 77, penny/nickel, red and black porcelain frame, glass panels, Norris Mfg. Co., c1933, 16" h	1000	1500
Vending Machine, Master No. 2, gumball, penny/nickel, rectangular metal frame with glass panels, green porcelain base plate, Norris Mfg. Co., c1925, 16" h	325	650
Vending Machine, Postage Stamps, cast iron base, body, and back, glass top and sides, Schermack Stamp Machine Model 25, single unit, c1930, 13" h	75	150
Vending Machine, Rex Electrical Vender, bulb-shaped glass globe, white porcelain base, flash attachment, heating element, Hance Mfg. Co., c1920, 23" h	800	1200
Vending Machine, Sanitary, square glass globe, metal base, dispenses product in glassine bag, O. D. Jennings Co., repainted, c1934, 23" h	300	600
Vending Machine, Scup Matches, embossed cast iron, Art Nouveau filigree castings including 2 dolphins at bottom, Northwestern Corp, c1912, 13.5" h	750	1500
Vending Machine, Simpson Aristocrat, glass globe, embossed metal marquee, chrome base, "Delicious Boston Baked Beans," c1935, 16.5" h	300	600
Vending Machine, Teenie Weenies Prophylactics, sheet metal, 25¢, "For the man who has little," with full package of Midget Teenie Weenie Tickler Condems, Harmon Mfg. Co., reconditioned, c1962, 30.75" h	150	200
Vending Machine, U.S. Postage Stamps, sheet metal, 2-slot, 50¢ and 25¢, Parkway Machine Corp., 14.5" h	50	100

Advertising Tins

Collectors judge advertising tins by product, color, design and condition. A tin for expensive candy is more desirable than a tin for acne cream. Similarly, bright reds will generally outperform dull browns. Dents, paint loss and rust severely diminish the value of a tin. The majority of collected tins date from the late nineteenth and early twentieth centuries.

For more information, consult *Antique Tins* (1995, 1999 value update), *Book II* (1998), and *Book III* (1999) by Fred Dodge, Collector Books, Paducah, KY and *Encyclopedia of Advertising Tins, Vol. II,* by David Zimmerman, Collector Books, Paducah, KY, 1999.

Left: Krout's Baking Powder, litho paper label over cardboard canister, tin top and bottom, 6" h, $578 at auction.

Right: Favorite Tube Patch, cardboard sides, tin top and bottom, 4" h, $935 at auction.

—Photos courtesy Wm. Morford.

	LOW	HIGH
Apache Trail Cigars, mounted Indian surveying horizon, vertical box, 5.5" x 6" x 4.25"	$500	$1000
Big Buster Popcorn, parader beating bass drum, 10 lb canister, 9.5" h, 6.5" dia	200	400
Blue Bird Coffee, Stone-Ordean-Wells Co., blue bird both sides, American Can Co., 3 lb canister, slip lid, 9.25" h, 5.5" dia	300	600
Blue Jay Cigars, singing blue jay, vertical box, 6.25" x 5.5" x 4.25"	300	600
Buffalo Brand Salted Peanuts, standing buffalo, F. M. Hoyt & Co., 10 lb, 9" x 8.5"	200	300
Campfire Marshmallows, Campfire Kitchens, evening campfire scene, 2" h, 7.75" dia	100	150
Capitol Mills Coffee, Capitol building both sides, Lincoln, Seyms & Co., small top canister, 5.5" h, 5" dia	250	500
Dining Car Coffee, train dining car filled with passengers, 1 lb canister, key wind, 4" h, 5" dia	250	500
Dixie Queen Plug Cut, American Tobacco Co., small top canister, pretty girl, 6.5" h, 4.75" dia	300	500
Fast Mail Tobacco, Hasker & Marcuse, train, flat pocket tin, 3.75" x 2.25" x .5"	500	1000
Golden Shell Auto Oil, embossed shell on 4 sides, 5 gal, 13.75" x 9.25" x 9.25"	500	750
Golden Wedding Coffee, Ennis-Hanly-Blackburn Coffee Co., elderly couple at breakfast table, 1 lb canister, snap top, 3.75" h, 5.25" dia	100	200
Granulated 54 Sliced Plug, fat version, sample vertical pocket tin, litho top, 2" x 2.125" x 1"	150	250
Hoody's Peanut Butter, 2 girls seesawing over large peanut, 1 lb pail, 3.5" x 3.75"	200	300
Indian Head Hydraulic Brake Fluid, Permatex Co., Indian head profile	40	80
Jackie Coogan Peanut Butter, Coogan portrait, red ground, 12 oz pail, 3.25" x 3.75"	200	400
Jackie Coogan Salted Nut Meats, Jackie on elephant, Kelly Co., 7.25" x 7"	400	800

	LOW	HIGH
Mammoth Salted Peanuts, mammoth framed by peanut shells, Kelly Co., 10 lb, 11" x 7.5"	200	400
Maryland Club Mixture, club house, flip-top vertical pocket tin, 4" x 3.5"	200	400
Monarch Teenie Weenie Peanut Butter, embossed top, trademark shield, 1 lb pail, 3.75" x 3.5"	200	400
New York Coach Oil, Marshall Oil Co., vintage coach, spout top, 6.75" h	50	125
Old Judge Coffee, David G. Evans Coffee Co., 1 lb canister, 5.75" h, 4.25" dia	100	200
Pedro Smoking Tobacco, lunch box shape, 7.75" x 5.25" x 4"	100	200
Plaza Pipe Tobacco, embossed tobacco leaves, small top canister, 5" h, 4.75" dia	250	500
Pure As Gold Motor Oil, Pep Boys, 2 gal, 11.5" h, 8.5" w	75	150
Puritan Crushed Plug Mixture, Continental Tobacco Co., Puritan smoking pipe, vertical pocket tin, 4.5" x 3"	200	300
School Boy Peanut Butter, smiling boy's portrait, 1 lb pail, 3.75" x 3.25"	200	300
Scowcroft Peanut Butter, children picnicking and playing, 1 lb pail, 3.75" x 3.25"	400	800
Sunny Boy Peanut Butter, boy holding peanut butter sandwich, rayed sun in background, Brundage Bros. Co., Toledo, OH, 25 lb, 9.5" x 10"	200	400
Sunset Trail Cigars, 2 horseback riders, vertical box, dark blue version, 5.5" x 6" x 4.25"	300	600
Teddie Peanut Butter, John W. Leavitt Co, 1 lb pail, 3.5" x 3.75"	150	250
Three Feathers Plug Cut, 3 feathers, vertical pocket tin, 4" x 3.25"	250	350
Towle's Log Cabin Syrup, large size, log cabin shape, 7" x 4" x 6"	100	150
Toy Land Peanut Butter, marching band, E. K. Pond Co., 1 lb pail, 4" x 3.5"	200	300
Tuxedo Pipe Tobacco, smoking pipe, small top canister, 6.5" x 4" x 5"	200	300
Universal Coffee, E. B. Millar & Co., Uncle Sam, 1 lb, knob top, 6.5" h, 4" dia	200	400
Wampum Coffee, Stone-Ordean-Wells Co., Indian warrior both sides, American Can Co., 3 lb canister, slip lid, 9.25" h, 5.5" dia	400	800
Wedding Breakfast Coffee, 1 lb canister, 4" h, 5" dia	150	250
Yellow Cab Cigar Tin, vintage taxi, canister, missing lid, 5.5" h, 2.5" dia	750	1000

Tobacco Tins, pocket size. —Photo courtesy Gene Harris Antique Auction Center, Inc.

African-American Memorabilia

For the past century, the depiction of African Americans has been a reflection of this country's fitful growth as a free nation. Although many of the images are derogatory and degrading, both black and white collectors have found them historically interesting. A nation learning from its mistakes will find endless education here.

Refer to *Black Collectibles Sold in America* by P. J. Gibbs (Collector Books, Paducah, KY, 1987, 1996 value update) and *Images in Black: 150 Years of Black Collectibles, 2nd Edition* by Douglas Congdon-Martin (Schiffer, Atglen, PA, 1999) for additional information.

	LOW	HIGH
Advertising Display, Gillett's Lye, 3-dimensional life-size plaster figure of black boy wearing straw hat, seated on "Mammy Beverages" wooden crate and holding sign "Gillett's Lye Eats Dirt," 51" h	$2000	$3000
Advertising Tin, Dixie Kid Cut Plug, black child, lunch box, Nall & Williams Tobacco Co., 8" x 5.25" x 4"	500	1000
Advertising Tin, Niggerhair Tobacco, yellow version, black woman with nose ring and earrings, bail handle, 6.75" h, 5.5" dia	400	800
Advertising Tin, Pickaninny Brand Jumbo Salted Peanuts, black girl, F. M. Hoyt & Co., 9.5" h, 8.5" dia	200	400
Book, *Stride Toward Freedom: The Montgomery Story,* by Martin Luther King, autographed, hard cover, 1958	1200	2000
Broadside, "John Brown Still Lives," announces meeting held in Midwest w/ speakers' topics on "Brown's Invasion" and "Slavery Questions," 1859, 8.25" x 12"	1000	2000
Bust, Zulu tribesmen, ceramic, wire necklace, earrings, and hair wrap, 10" h	100	200
Carte de Visite, Sojourner Truth, close-up portrait, entitled "I Sell the Shadow to Support the Substance, Sojourner Truth," 1864	650	1250
Coin Operated Machine, The Jazz Band, 5¢, 66" h, 44" w	1000	2000
Dartboard, tin over cardboard, cartoon black boy wearing hat labeled "Sambo," Wyandotte Toy Mfg., 23" x 14"	50	100
Egg Timer, black chef holding swiveling glass sand timer, ceramic, 1930s, 3" h	75	150
Figure, black boy seated on stump, ceramic, late 1950s, 15.25" h	100	200
Film Poster, features black cowboy Bill Picket, *The Bull-Dogger,* linen-backed, 41" x 27"	3000	5000
Handbill, "Bill Robinson in Hot Mikado," single sheet, Broadway musical, 1940s, 5.5" x 8.75"	25	50
Mask, Al Jolson as Black Musician, painted papier-mâché, 12" h	300	600
Original Art, 4 pen and ink sketches depicting raccoon and black boy wearing coonskin cap, by Edwin Kemble, featured in Feb. 1913 *Cosmopolitan* magazine, framed size 9.5" h, 35" l	600	1200
Palm Puzzle, native boys and alligator, 1950s, 2.125" dia	50	75
Pillow Cover, black wedding scene, framed, 21.5" x 21.5"	250	450
Pinback Button, "De Berry For President," celluloid, De Berry portrait, 1964, 1.25" dia	10	20
Poster, "Colored Man Is No Slacker," black man going to war, saying goodbye to wife, black regiment marching in background, framed, ©1918, 19.5" x 15.5"	200	300
Poster, Ragtime Jubilee, cardboard, caricature black man w/ big red lips, "Big Time Minstrel Revue," 22" x 14"	50	100
Print, black family with father playing banjo, son dancing, log cabin in background, framed, 15.5" x 19.5"	200	400

	LOW	HIGH
Ribbon, "Colored Laundry Helpers Benevolent Association No. 1, Juvenile, Organized March 1st 1917, Mobile, Ala.," blue with gold letters and fringe, celluloid "Member" hanger, 6" h	125	200
Salt and Pepper Shakers, 2 black chefs, marked "Smokquee, The Royal, Boise Idaho," 3.75" h	300	500
Sign, Aunt Jemima Pancake Flour, diecut cardboard, Aunt Jemima holding plate of steaming pancakes, 15.5" x 12.5"	250	450
Sign, Ayers Pills, elderly black doctor with 2 black children, diecut cardboard, framed, 11.5" x 7"	400	800
Sign, Fairbank's Gold Dust Washing Powder, diecut cardboard, 2-sided, detergent box with Gold Dust Twins on label, letter "L" on top of box, 1 section of 8-piece hanging sign, 9.5" x 13.5"	50	100
Sign, Red Crow Cigars, paper, humorous rendition of black men playing poker, "5 Cent Limit," artist signed Van, framed, 22.5" x 19.5"	750	1250
Sign, Rochelle Club Beverages, paper, black boy holding soda bottle, framed, 22" x 14"	500	700
Slave Board, single log with 6 carved shallow bowls, 52" l	500	1000
Slave Collar, spiked, 6 sections	1000	2000
Slave Sale Receipt, blue lined paper, James King (Wash. Co., VA) sells 7 slaves (Jackson, Madison, Handy, and children Sharlotte, Ninez, Sarah, and Mary) to John King (Sulovan Co., TN) for $1, 5.75" x 8"	75	150
Slave Shackles, slip-knot type, 2 cuffs attached to 9.5" l chain	750	1250
Statue, chalkware, black boy stealing chicken, 2 friends watch from other side of fence, ©1898, 12" h	250	500
Stereoview Card, "Camp Wikoff, 10th US Cavalry (Colored) Playing Crap," 14 uniformed men, Spanish American War era	40	75
Tobacco Cards, framed set of 6, Sweet Lavender Tobacco, "A Sure Thing on a Possum"	750	1200
Token, "Am I Not a Woman & A Sister," bronze/copper, kneeling and praying black woman in chains, 1838, 1" dia	125	250
Vending Machine, Smiling Sam the Voo Doo Man, black man's face changes expressions when quarter is inserted, dispenses cardboard lucky charms, 76" h	1200	1800
Wall Plaque/Hot Pad Holder, black girl holding large umbrella, painted chalkware, 1950s, 5" x 7"	75	100

Wind-up Alarm Clocks, left to right: Luxor IV, Burke & James, Chicago, $220 at auction; "I'm on the Go," $231 at auction; "Shoe Shiner," No. 468, Lux Clock Mfg., $935 at auction. —Photos courtesy Collectors Auction Services.

Autographs

The personal mark of the famous and revered has always attracted collectors. The following abbreviations are used: *ALS*–Autograph Letter Signed (a letter handwritten by the person who signed it), *LS*–Letter Signed (a letter typed or written out by another person), *DS*–Document Signed (a signed document), *PhS*–Photo Signed, *Cut Sig.*–Cut Signature (a signature cut from a letter, autograph book, or other source).

For a comprehensive listing see *The Sanders Price Guide to Autographs, 4th Edition,* George Sanders, Helen Sanders and Ralph Roberts, Alexander Books, Alexander, NC, 1997.

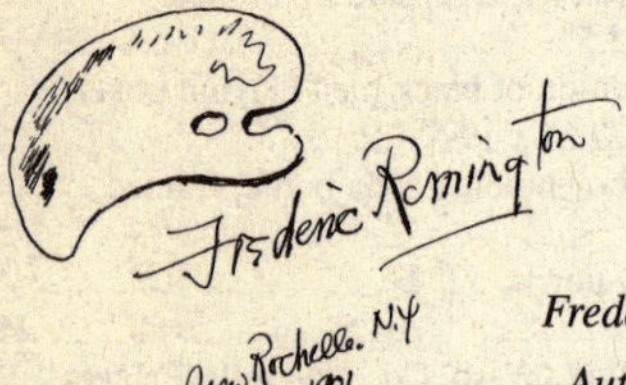

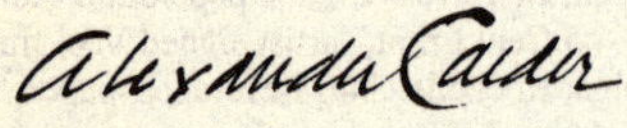

Frederic Remington and Alexander Calder.
—Autographs courtesy Robert F. Batchelder.

Artists

	ALS		Cut Sig.	
	Low	High	Low	High
Adams, Ansel	$450	$600	$75	$100
Audubon, John J.	2500	3250	600	750
Bellows, George	275	350	75	100
Bourke-White, Margaret	150	200	75	100
Brady, Mathew B.	1500	2000	180	250
Calder, Alexander	650	850	100	125
Cassatt, Mary	750	1000	150	200
Cellini, Benvenuto	8000	12,500	750	1000
Chagall, Marc	900	1200	200	275
Dali, Salvador	500	650	200	200
Daumier, Honore	1200	1500	150	250
Degas, Edgar	1500	2000	200	250
Eastlake, Sir Charles L.	650	850	35	50
Erté	275	350	55	75
Flagg, James Montgomery	200	275	35	50
Goya, Francisco	14,000	18,000	1500	2000
Homer, Winslow	850	1100	300	375
Israels, Jozef	275	350	35	50
Kent, Rockwell	225	300	30	40
Leech, John	125	175	60	75
O'Keefe, Georgia	750	975	200	250
Parrish, Maxfield	600	800	175	225
Remington, Frederic	2100	3000	450	600
Rodin, Auguste	450	600	115	150
Rubens, Peter Paul	17,500	22,000	1500	2000
Sargent, John Singer	275	350	75	100
Segal, George	25	35	20	25
Toulouse-Lautrec, Henri	4500	6000	750	1000
Wood, Grant	450	600	125	150
Wyeth, N.C.	1200	1500	125	150

Authors

Authors' letters have always been a favorite of collectors. But just like the novels and poems they wrote, content counts! A letter refusing a dinner invitation is worth a fraction of the value of a letter discussing alternative endings of a play.

	LS		ALS	
	Low	High	Low	High
Adams, Harriet	$35	$45	$40	$55
Alcott, A. Bronson	225	300	325	450
Alger, Horatio	175	225	250	350
Auel, Jean M.	5	10	20	25
Austen, Jane	1750	2250	6000	7500
Bacon, Francis	2750	3750	7500	10,000
Barlow, Jane	5	10	20	25
Baum, L. Frank	750	1000	900	1200
Beecher, Henry Ward	90	125	150	200
Bellamy, Edward	60	75	100	150
Black, Alexander	5	10	15	20
Bombeck, Erma	15	20	35	50
Bradbury, Ray	125	175	225	300
Bromfield, Louis	65	75	125	175
Brooke, Rupert	425	550	775	1100
Brooks, Philllips	100	125	100	150
Bryant, William Cullen	250	325	350	475
Buchwald, Art	10	15	20	25
Buck, Pearl S.	110	150	150	200
Burroughs, Edgar Rice	375	500	500	675
Cain, James	45	60	70	90
Caldwell, Erskine	115	150	150	200
Dahl, Roald	20	25	25	35
Eliot, T. S.	325	450	180	2400
Fitzgerald, F. Scott	1200	1625	2250	3000
Gibran, Kahlil	250	325	600	750
Hawthorne, Nathaniel	1000	1350	1500	2100
Hemingway, Ernest	2750	3675	3250	4350
Henry, O.	550	700	1000	1500
Hilton, Sir James	100	125	150	200
Howe, Julia Ward	120	150	250	350
Irving, Washington	275	375	750	1050
Jewett, Sarah Orne	150	200	225	300
Jong, Erica	8	12	12	20
Kerouac, Jack	2000	2500	3000	4000
King, Stephen	100	125	325	450
Kingsley, Charles	75	100	125	175
Lamb, Charles	275	350	600	750
Lindbergh, Anne Morrow	35	50	100	150
Longfellow, Henry W.	300	400	550	750
Lovecraft, H. P.	375	500	125	175
Luce, Clare Boothe	75	100	125	175
MacLeish, Archibald	100	125	100	150
Marx, Karl	1000	1500	10,000	15,000
Maugham, W. Somerset	200	250	250	325
Melville, Herman	1500	1900	7500	10,000

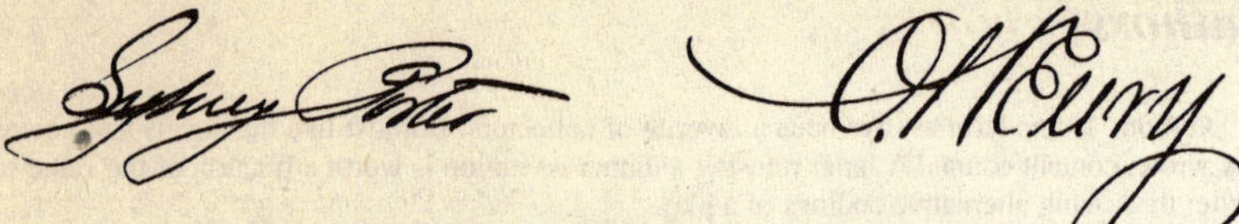

William Sydney Porter and pseudonym O. Henry

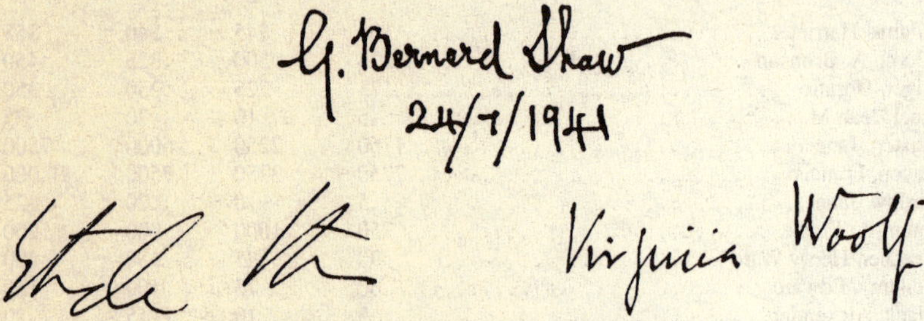

George Bernard Shaw, Gertrude Stein, and Virginia Woolf.
—Autographs courtesy Robert F. Batchelder.

	LS		ALS	
	Low	High	Low	High
Mencken, H. L.	200	250	275	375
Michener, James A.	175	275	275	350
Mitchell, Margaret	2000	2700	2250	3000
Nash, Ogden	60	75	75	100
Nietzsche, Friedrich	600	800	5000	7750
Norris, Kathleen	30	40	55	70
Oates, Joyce Carol	25	35	50	70
O'Casey, Sean	175	275	350	450
O'Neill, Eugene	225	375	300	400
Pope, Alexander	1500	2000	2000	2500
Porter, William Sydney (O. Henry)	600	850	1250	1700
Post, Emily	40	50	90	125
Potter, Beatrix	225	300	600	750
Pound, Ezra	600	800	800	1100
Rossetti, Christina	100	125	180	250
Santayana, George	125	175	275	350
Shaffer, Peter L.	20	25	30	40
Shaw, George Bernard	750	1000	1100	1500
Simon, Neil	60	75	110	150
Stein, Gertrude	375	500	600	750
Stoker, Bram	225	350	425	550
Swift, Jonathan	5750	7500	10,000	13,500
Tate, Allen	25	35	75	100
Thackeray, William Makepeace	300	400	500	650
Toklas, Alice B.	75	100	675	900
Uris, Leon	60	80	100	125
Voelker, John D.	5	10	10	15
Woolf, Virginia	1000	1250	1800	2250

Civil War Figures

Not everyone recognizes the officers and heroes of the Civil War. But a sharp eye can still pluck these nuggets from the piles of old letters and documents that still turn up in attics. Condition, content, and date can drive the value above (or below) the ranges noted here.

George A. Custer and Jefferson Davis. —Autographs courtesy Robert F. Batchelder.

	ALS		DS		Cut Sig.	
	Low	High	Low	High	Low	High
Alvord, Benjamin	$50	$75	$40	$50	$20	$25
Anderson, Robert	400	525	250	325	100	125
Barry, William Farquhar	150	200	100	150	60	75
Benjamin, Judah P.	900	1200	700	900	225	300
Bonham, M. L.	375	500	180	250	150	200
Booth, John Wilkes	3000	4000	2250	3000	1100	1500
Casey, Silas	135	175	75	110	35	50
Cooper, Samuel	400	500	200	250	100	125
Custer, Elizabeth	600	800	150	200	65	75
Custer, George A.	7500	9000	4500	8500	2300	3000
Davis, Jefferson	1800	2500	1250	1750	600	800
Dix, Dorothea	400	500	200	250	75	100
Douglas, Beverly, B.	45	60	35	50	20	30
Farragut, David G.	750	900	350	450	125	175
Forrest, Nathan Bedford	3750	5000	1600	2100	500	650
Franklin, William Buell	150	200	125	165	65	75
Fremont, John C.	900	1200	500	650	150	225
Gardner, Franklin	650	850	200	250	150	200
Hammond, Wm. A.	300	400	100	125	35	50
Hampton, Wade	750	1000	450	600	225	300
Hayes, Joseph	140	175	75	100	45	60
Hooker, Joseph M.	500	625	375	500	80	100
Jackson, William Hicks "Red"	180	250	150	200	75	100
Jones, Edward F.	135	175	100	125	35	50
Longstreet, James	1500	2000	1000	1250	300	425
Oglesby, Richard J.	80	110	65	85	30	40
Pope, John	325	300	95	125	80	100
Schurz, Carl	110	150	75	100	35	50
Sheridan, Philip H.	450	600	425	575	175	225
Slocum, Henry Warner	115	150	60	85	50	75
Stephens, Alexander Hamilton	375	500	300	400	150	200
Stuart, J. E. B.	10,000	13,000	4500	6000	3000	4000
Thatcher, Henry Knox	115	150	75	100	35	50
Thompson, Jacob	1000	1400	250	325	110	150
Whipple, Amiel Weeks	165	350	180	250	100	125
Wright, Horatio G.	150	200	125	175	40	50

Entertainers

Who signed that photo? As big stars received more requests for signed photos than they could supply themselves, they (or their studios) hired secretaries to sign photos for them. In the case of Jean Harlow, her mother signed most of the photos picturing this star.

	PS		Cut Sig.	
	Low	High	Low	High
Abbott, Bud	$325	$450	$150	$200
Abdul, Paula	60	75	20	25
Adams, Don	10	15	2	4
Adler, Stella	30	40	15	20
Aerosmith	75	100	35	50
Aherne, Brian	45	60	10	15
Aiello, Danny	25	30	7	10
Akins, Claude	25	35	8	10
Allen, Gracie	110	150	40	50
Allen, Woody	35	50	15	20
Alley, Kirstie	30	40	6	10
Alpert, Herb	20	25	5	10
Ameche, Don	45	60	15	20
Amos and Andy	185	250	75	100
Anderson, Loni	20	25	7	10
Andress, Ursula	25	35	10	15
Andrews, Dana	35	45	12	15
Anka, Paul	10	15	2	5
Anton, Susan	15	20	5	8
Arbuckle, Roscoe "Fatty"	600	800	275	350
Arden, Eve	30	45	15	20
Arlen, Richard	40	65	20	30
Armstrong, Louis	350	475	200	250
Arnaz, Desi	150	200	25	35
Arquette, Cliff	30	40	15	20
Arthur, Jean	225	300	100	125
Asner, Ed	10	15	2	5
Astaire, Fred	180	275	75	90
Astin, John	20	25	5	8
Attenborough, Richard	35	50	15	25
Autry, Gene	65	90	20	25
Ball, Lucille	375	500	110	150
Ballard, Kaye	20	25	10	15
Bancroft, Anne	25	30	5	8
Bankhead, Tallulah	185	275	75	90
Barbeau, Adrienne	10	15	3	6
Barker, Lex	150	200	50	75
Barr, Roseanne	45	60	15	20
Barrymore, Drew	35	50	12	20
Barrymore, Ethel	150	200	90	120
Baryshnikov, Mikail	150	200	55	75
Basinger, Kim	30	40	15	20
Baxter, Anne	30	45	15	20
Beatty, Clyde	100	150	35	50
Beck, Jeff	35	45	15	20
Belafonte, Shari	15	20	3	5

	PS		Cut Sig.	
	Low	High	Low	High
Bellamy, Ralph	30	40	12	15
Bennett, Tony	25	30	3	5
Benny, Jack	125	160	60	75
Benton, Barbi	12	15	3	5
Bergen, Candice	30	35	7	10
Bergen, Edgar	100	125	45	60
Bergman, Ingmar	90	125	25	35
Berle, Milton	25	35	10	15
Bernhardt, Sarah	800	1100	120	150
Bernstein, Leonard	190	250	115	150
Bertinelli, Valerie	20	30	4	6
Billingsley, Barbara	5	10	3	5
Bisset, Jacqueline	25	35	12	15
Bixby, Bill	25	30	3	5
Black, Karen	15	20	4	7
Blackstone, Harry, Jr.	10	15	2	5
Blake, Amanda	130	175	50	65
Blanc, Mel	125	160	45	60
Blondell, Joan	45	60	30	35
Bloome, Claire	15	20	3	5
Bogart, Humphrey	1900	2800	750	1000
Bogdonavich, Peter	15	20	7	10
Bow, Clara	375	500	125	175
Boy George	40	50	10	15
Boyle, Peter	10	15	6	8
Brolin, James	20	25	12	15
Brooks, Mel	15	25	8	10
Brown, Johnny Mack	100	125	40	50
Bruce, Nigel	250	325	115	150
Bryant, Anita	7	10	2	5
Cabot, Sebastian	60	75	20	25
Cage, Nicholas	35	50	10	15
Captain Kangaroo	18	25	5	8
Carson, Johnny	35	50	10	15
Caruso, Enrico	750	1000	200	275
Chakiris, George	20	25	6	10
Chandu the Magician	15	20	3	5
Chaplin, Charlie	800	1100	250	325
Chase, Chevy	30	35	3	5
Checker, Chubby	25	35	7	10
Clapton, Eric	70	85	25	30
Cliburn, Van	75	100	20	25
Clift, Montgomery	625	750	200	250
Coco, James	25	35	10	15
Colbert, Claudette	55	75	35	45
Collins, Judy	15	20	3	5
Costello, Lou	300	400	150	200
Crabbe, Buster	60	70	25	30
Crenna, Richard	10	15	3	5
Cugat, Xavier	75	100	20	25
Dafoe, Willem	30	35	7	10
Daltry, Roger	35	50	12	15

Stan Laurel and Oliver Hardy. —Autographs courtesy Robert F. Batchelder.

	PS		Cut Sig.	
	Low	High	Low	High
Day, Doris	30	40	7	10
DeCarlo, Yvonne	30	40	7	10
DeHavilland, Olivia	45	60	25	30
DeLuise, Dom	10	15	3	5
Dern, Bruce	12	15	4	7
Devo	45	60	25	30
Dietrich, Marlene	125	150	40	50
Diller, Phyllis	12	15	6	8
Douglas, Kirk	20	25	7	10
Douglas, Michael	30	40	10	15
Eastwood, Clint	45	60	15	20
Ebsen, Buddy	20	30	3	5
Elliott, Sam	30	35	7	10
Elvira	20	25	5	8
Evans, Dale	20	25	7	10
Evans, Linda	30	35	8	10
Fabares, Shelley	15	20	5	8
Fairbanks, Douglas, Sr.	225	300	100	125
Falk, Peter	20	25	3	5
Feldon, Barbara	30	35	3	5
Ferrigno, Lou	10	15	2	5
Fiedler, Arthur	40	50	25	35
Fields, W. C.	800	1200	225	300
Finch, Peter	125	175	65	75
Flagg, Fannie	10	15	3	5
Fogerty, John	40	45	10	15
Fonda, Henry	80	125	30	35
Forbes, Ralph	20	25	10	15
Ford, Glenn	45	60	25	30
Ford, Harrison	100	135	40	50
Francis, Connie	10	15	3	5
Furness, Betty	20	25	12	15
Furstenberg, Betsy von	7	10	3	5
Gable, Clark	900	1200	300	400
Gabor, Eva	15	20	20	25
Gabor, Zsa Zsa	12	15	3	5
George, Phyllis	8	10	2	5
Ghostley, Alice	10	15	3	5
Gillespie, Dizzy	60	75	40	50
Goldblum, Jeff	25	35	5	7
Graves, Peter	20	25	7	10
Guttenberg, Steve	18	25	3	5
Hackman, Gene	45	50	20	25

	PS		Cut Sig.	
	Low	High	Low	High
Hagar, Sammy	40	50	15	20
Hagman, Larry	20	25	5	8
Hamill, Mark	45	60	7	10
Hamilton, Margaret	135	175	60	75
Hampton, Lionel	45	65	30	40
Hanks, Tom	80	125	15	20
Hardy, Oliver	450	600	175	250
Harmon, Mark	20	25	7	10
Harris, Richard	30	40	10	15
Harrison, George	375	450	150	200
Harrison, Rex	75	100	30	45
Hartley, Mariette	10	15	3	5
Harvey, Lawrence	125	150	75	100
Haskell, James K.	20	25	6	10
Hawn, Goldie	30	40	7	10
Hayes, George "Gabby"	325	450	100	135
Hayward, Susan	450	550	110	150
Hayworth, Rita	475	575	115	150
Heflin, Van	75	100	25	35
Hemingway, Margaux	60	80	30	40
Hemingway, Mariel	35	50	8	10
Hemsley, Sherman	15	20	5	7
Henner, Marilu	20	25	4	6
Herman, Pee Wee	25	30	10	15
Hildegard	7	10	2	5
Hillerman, John	20	25	7	10
Hirsch, Judd	10	15	3	5
Hitchcock, Alfred	425	550	200	250
Hoffman, Dustin	30	35	15	20
Hogan, Paul	20	25	7	10
Holbrook, Hal	10	15	5	7
Holliday, Judy	300	350	90	125
Holly, Buddy	2500	3000	700	900
Holm, Celeste	10	15	3	5
Hope, Bob	40	65	7	10
Hopkins, Anthony	35	50	15	20
Hopper, Hedda	30	35	12	15
Horowitz, Vladimir	125	175	115	150
Houston, Whitney	60	75	30	35
Howard, Curley	750	1000	325	450
Howard, Ron	25	35	7	10
Howard, Shemp	450	600	450	600
Hudson, Rock	120	150	20	25
Humperdinck, Englebert	20	25	3	5
Hunt, Helen	45	60	15	20
Hunter, Tab	25	35	5	8
Hurt, William	45	60	20	25
Huston, John	60	80	30	40
Hutton, Lauren	20	25	6	10
Hyde-White, Wilfrid	30	35	10	15
Idol, Billy	20	25	7	10
Ireland, Jill	45	60	20	25

	PS		Cut Sig.	
	Low	High	Low	High
Jackson, Glenda	25	30	10	15
Jagger, Mick	110	150	35	50
Janssen, David	85	110	60	75
Jessel, George	75	95	25	30
Jethro Tull	60	75	25	35
Jett, Joan	40	50	15	20
Johnson, Don	35	45	10	15
Jolson, Al	375	450	120	175
Jones, Quincy	25	30	10	15
Jones, Shirley	20	25	7	10
Jones, Tommy Lee	30	35	15	20
Kahn, Madeline	10	15	3	5
Karloff, Boris	600	750	175	275
Kasem, Casey	10	15	3	5
Kaufman, Andy	40	65	110	150
Kazan, Elia	30	35	6	10
Keaton, Buster	300	400	150	200
Keaton, Diane	50	70	10	15
Keeler, Ruby	45	60	25	35
Keith, Brian	15	20	3	5
Kellerman, Sally	20	25	7	10
Kelly, Grace	325	450	150	200
Kennedy, George	35	45	3	5
Kerr, Deborah	20	25	10	15
Khan, Chaka	25	30	10	15
Kidder, Margot	20	30	7	10
King, Carole	20	25	10	15
Klemperer, Werner	20	25	10	15
Kline, Kevin	30	35	8	10
Klugman, Jack	20	25	7	10
Knight, Gladys	35	40	12	15
Knight, Ted	30	35	10	15
Knotts, Don	15	20	8	10
Korman, Harvey	10	15	3	5
Kristofferson, Kris	25	30	7	10
Kubrick, Stanley	45	60	12	15
Ladd, Alan	150	200	60	75
Lahr, Bert	450	575	225	300
Lamarr, Hedy	85	120	30	35
Lamas, Lorenzo	20	25	5	10
Lamour, Dorothy	30	35	7	10
Lancaster, Burt	60	70	25	30
Lane, Abbe	15	20	10	15
Lange, Hope	25	30	7	10
Lansbury, Angela	20	25	3	5
Lantz, Walter	100	125	50	65
Lanza, Mario	600	800	130	175
Larroquette, John	25	30	8	10
LaRue, Lash	20	25	3	5
Laughton, Charles	200	275	75	100
Laurel, Stan	300	400	110	150
Leachman, Cloris	15	20	7	10

	PS		Cut Sig.	
	Low	High	Low	High
Learned, Michael	20	25	7	10
Lee, Gypsy Rose	475	575	95	120
Leigh, Vivien	650	875	450	525
Lennon, John	850	1100	475	600
Letterman, David	30	40	15	20
Lewis, Huey	20	30	10	15
Lewis, Jerry Lee	65	75	25	35
Liberace	115	150	40	50
Linden, Hall	10	15	3	5
Linkletter, Art	12	15	5	8
Linville, Larry	20	25	7	10
Little, Cleavon	30	35	12	15
Little Richard	100	125	15	20
Lolobrigida, Gina	25	35	7	10
Lombard, Carole	600	800	250	350
Lombardo, Guy	90	120	15	20
Lord, Jack	10	15	6	8
Louise, Tina	20	25	7	10
Lucas, George	45	60	15	20
Lucci, Susan	15	20	5	7
Lupino, Ida	60	75	15	20
MacGraw, Ali	15	20	6	10
MacRae, Gordon	25	30	12	15
Madonna	200	250	40	50
Maharis, George	15	20	6	10
Malden, Karl	20	25	7	10
Mandell, Howie	10	15	3	5
Manilow, Barry	60	75	10	15
Mansfield, Jayne	325	450	125	160
Marceau, Marcel	75	100	15	20
Marchesi, Mathilde	125	175	40	50
Martin, Dean	65	85	20	25
Martin, Mary	40	50	30	35
Martinelli, Giovanni	50	70	25	30
Marx, Chico	250	350	85	125

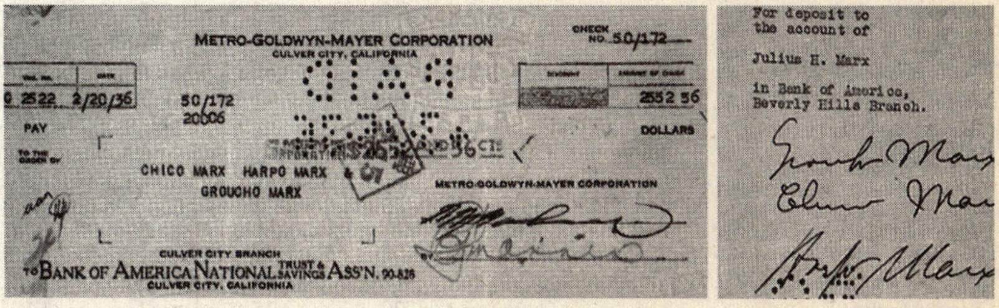

Front and back of MGM check made payable to Harpo, Chico, and Groucho Marx, endorsed by all 3, $1743 at auction. —Photo courtesy Mastro Fine Sports Auctions.

	PS		Cut Sig.	
	Low	High	Low	High
Marx, Groucho	275	350	180	250
Mason, Marsha	20	25	3	5
Massey, Raymond	45	60	20	25
Mastroianni, Marcello	40	50	15	25
Mathers, Jerry	40	50	15	20
Matthau, Walter	15	25	3	5
Mature, Victor	30	40	5	10
Maynard, Ken	140	175	100	125
McCartney, Paul	475	500	80	100
McDowell, Roddy	20	25	10	15
McNichol, Kristy	25	30	7	10
McQueen, Steve	265	350	185	225
Meara, Anne	10	15	3	5
Meeker, Ralph	35	45	20	25
Miranda, Carmen	300	400	90	125
Mitchell, Joni	10	15	3	5
Mitchell, Thomas	450	550	180	250
Mix, Tom	300	400	65	75
Mobley, Mary Ann	10	15	3	5
Monroe, Marilyn	5000	6500	1500	2000
Montalban, Ricardo	20	25	6	10
Moore, Clayton	40	50	12	15
Moore, Dudley	30	35	7	10
Moranis, Rick	15	25	2	5
Morita, Pat	20	25	7	10
Morris, Chester	60	75	45	50
Morrison, Jim	1200	1500	550	700
Morrison, Van	40	50	10	15
Mumy, Bill	10	15	3	5
Nabors, Jim	10	15	3	5
Nelson, Rick	225	300	75	100
Nero, Peter	10	15	5	8
Newhart, Bob	10	15	5	8
Newman, Paul	125	175	60	85
Newman, Randy	15	20	7	10
Newton-John, Olivia	40	50	10	15
Nicholson, Jack	45	60	12	15
Nicks, Stevie	40	50	20	25
Nielson, Leslie	20	25	8	10
Nimoy, Leonard	65	75	30	35
Norris, Chuck	30	40	5	10
Novak, Kim	60	80	7	10
Nugent, Ted	25	35	10	15
Nureyev, Rudolf	200	250	80	100
Oberon, Merle	80	100	40	50
O'Brien, Cubby	10	15	3	5
O'Connor, Carroll	15	20	6	8
O'Keefe, Dennis	10	15	3	5
Olson, Merlin	20	25	7	10
Osborne, Ozzy	35	45	20	25
Osmond, Donny	10	15	2	5
Osmond, Marie	20	25	3	5

	PS		Cut Sig.	
	Low	High	Low	High
O'Sullivan, Maureen	25	30	12	15
O'Toole, Peter	75	100	20	25
Ouspenskaya, Maria	300	400	120	150
Paar, Jack	15	20	3	6
Pacino, Al	40	50	8	12
Palance, Jack	40	60	10	15
Palmer, Robert	30	35	20	25
Parker, Fess	25	30	10	15
Parsons, Estelle	15	20	3	5
Pasternak, Joe	65	75	25	30
Paul, Les	60	75	20	25
Paulsson, Pat	10	15	3	5
Pavlova, Anna	450	600	275	350
Peck, Gregory	40	50	20	25
Peckinpah, Sam	40	50	20	25
Penn, Sean	25	35	5	8
Penner, Joe	15	20	7	10
Peppard, George	20	25	5	8
Perkins, Millie	20	30	8	10
Perlman, Rhea	10	15	3	5
Petty, Tom	75	100	30	40
Pflug, Jo Ann	8	12	1	3
Phillips, Lou Diamond	20	30	7	10
Pickens, Slim	150	200	80	100
Pickford, Mary	110	150	50	70
Pidgeon, Walter	60	75	20	25
Plant, Robert	75	100	30	40
Poitier, Sidney	35	45	10	12
Post, Markie	15	20	5	8
Power, Tyrone	200	250	75	100

Left: W. C. Fields, PS, "...with sincere good wishes from Bill Fields," 10" x 8", $1150 at auction; center: Elvis Presley, photo album signed "To Sharon from Elvis Presley," 16 pp, 8.5" x 11", $862 at auction; right: Frank Sinatra, PS, "To Helen, Sincerely Frank Sinatra," 10" x 8", $575 at auction. —Photos courtesy Swann Galleries, Inc.

	PS		Cut Sig.	
	Low	High	Low	High
Presley, Elvis	850	1200	500	650
Preston, Robert	75	100	45	60
Price, Vincent	65	75	40	50
Principal, Victoria	40	50	7	10
Prinze, Freddie	70	85	35	50
Pryor, Richard	18	25	7	10
Pyle, Denver	15	20	3	5
Quinn, Anthony	60	75	15	20
Raft, George	120	150	35	45
Rains, Claude	75	100	70	100
Rand, Sally	45	60	20	25
Rathbone, Basil	350	475	150	200
Ray, Aldo	10	15	2	5
Raye, Martha	35	45	15	20
Reddy, Helen	15	20	6	8
Redgrave, Vanessa	55	70	20	25
Reed, Rex	15	18	3	5
Reed, Robert	45	60	15	20
Reiner, Carl	20	25	7	10
Reiner, Rob	20	25	7	10
Reynolds, Debbie	15	20	5	8
Richards, Keith	85	120	20	25
Ringwald, Molly	65	75	15	25
Ritter, Tex	200	250	80	100
Roach, Hal, Sr.	140	175	70	100
Roarke, Hayden	35	50	20	25
Robards, Jason	25	30	10	15
Robinson, Smokey	35	50	20	25
Rogers, Buddy	30	40	10	15
Rogers, Ginger	110	150	40	50
Rogers, Roy	75	100	35	50
Romero, Cesar	60	75	20	25
Roth, Lillian	75	90	25	30
Rubens, Alma	125	175	65	75
Rush, Barbara	10	15	3	5
Russell, Jane	20	25	7	10
Sales, Soupy	10	15	3	5
Sargent, Dick	15	20	6	8
Saunders, Lori	10	15	3	5
Savales, Telly	35	45	12	15
Scaggs, Boz	30	35	10	15
Schreiber, Avery	8	12	2	4
Schwarzenegger, Arnold	80	100	25	35
Scofield, Paul	30	35	7	10
Stanwyck, Barbara	60	85	20	25
Tate, Sharon	475	575	190	250
Taylor, James	80	100	25	35
Townsend, Pete	65	75	25	30
Turner, Lana	75	100	20	25
Voight, Jon	15	25	3	5
Wagner, Robert	25	30	10	15
Youngman, Henny	10	15	5	8

Prince Rainier and Grace de Monaco (Grace Kelly), PS, signed by both, "Aboard the Constitution, *7 November 1956" on verso, 5" x 7", $316 at auction. —Photo courtesy Swann Galleries, Inc.*

Foreign Leaders

	ALS		Cut Sig.	
	Low	High	Low	High
Aga Khan IV	$85	$115	$10	$15
Akihito, Emperor of Japan	575	700	375	500
Alfonso XIII	550	650	100	150
Balfour, Arthur J.	75	100	40	50
Bismark, Otto von	750	950	200	250
Bolivar, Simon	4000	5000	300	400
Brandt, Willy	60	85	25	30
Camacho, Manuel	65	85	35	40
Castro, Fidel	900	1200	675	850
Churchill, Winston	2750	3500	600	800
Cromwell, Oliver	8500	10,500	1000	1250
Edward, Duke of Windsor	1500	2000	150	200
Elizabeth II	650	850	160	350
Faisal, King	75	100	20	25
Gladstone, William	425	500	60	75
Grace de Monaco (Grace Kelly)	325	450	150	200
Juan Carlos, King	185	250	45	60
Khruschchev, Nikita S.	475	600	250	325
Louis XIV	3000	3800	400	500
Mitterand, Francois	30	40	15	20
Mussolini, Benito	2500	3250	300	400
Noor, Queen	100	125	15	20
Pearson, Lester B.	140	175	30	40
Peel, Sir Robert	110	150	40	50
Pinochet, Augusto	200	250	25	30
Pompadour, Mme. J. A.	850	1200	110	150
Qaddafi, Muammar el	325	500	75	100
Rainier, Prince, III	150	200	60	75
Rowling, William E.	15	20	5	10
Stalin, Joseph	750	9000	1200	1500
Strauss, Franz Josef	80	125	10	15
Sun Yat-Sen	1200	1500	550	700
Talleyrand, Charles M. de	800	1000	150	200
Tito, Marshal J. Broz	200	275	60	80
Trotsky, Leon	2500	3200	750	1000

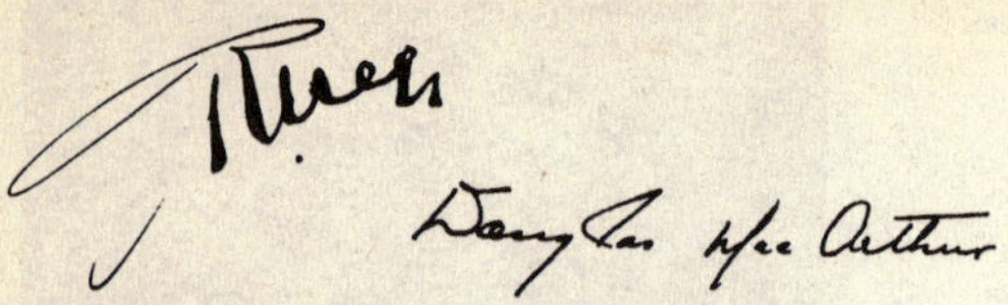

Above: Rudolf Hess and Douglas MacArthur.
—Autographs courtesy Robert F. Batchelder.

Left: Chester W. Nimitz, PS, 10" x 8", $690 at auction.
—Photo courtesy Swann Galleries, Inc.

Military

	ALS		Cut Sig.	
	Low	High	Low	High
Allen, Ethan	$2750	$3500	$500	$650
Arnold, Archibald	75	100	20	25
Baden-Powell, Sir Robert	300	375	90	125
Beatty, Admiral David	90	125	25	30
Bligh, Captain William	2000	2500	600	800
Blucher, Gebhard von	1750	2250	160	200
Brooke, Field Marshall Sir Alan	150	200	40	50
Bullard, Robert Lee	120	150	20	25
Calley, William	40	50	15	25
Chamberlain, S. J.	35	50	10	15
Clostermann, Pierre	100	125	40	60
Cook, Francis Augustus	45	60	55	75
Cornwallis, Charles	950	1250	130	175
Crockett, David	25,000	30,000	4500	6000
Devereux, James P. S.	80	100	30	40
Eichmann, Adolf	1000	1250	200	275
Gridley, Charles Vernon	750	900	180	250
Haig, Alexander M.	40	50	20	25
Hay, William Henry	20	30	3	5
Hess, Rudolf	600	825	120	150
Houston, Sam	2700	3500	450	600
Mac Arthur, Douglas	70	900	175	250
Marshall, George C.	450	600	150	200
McHenry, James	2000	2750	130	175
Mountbatten, Louis	250	325	100	125
Nimitz, Chester W.	300	400	100	125
North, Oliver	125	175	25	35
Patton, George S., Jr.	6000	7500	950	1250
Pershing, John J.	225	300	45	60
Powell, Ross E.	25	35	10	15
Quantrill, William C.	3500	4500	750	1000
Rusk, Thomas Jefferson	575	750	275	350
Santa Rosa, Annibale S., Count	120	150	20	25
Yamamoto, Isoroku	525	650	115	150

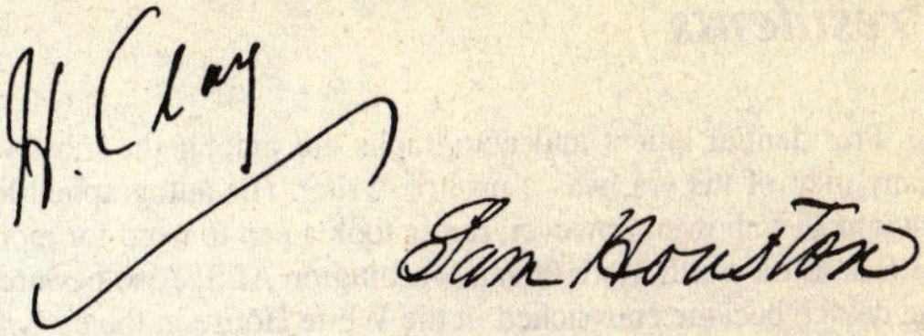

Above: Henry Clay and Sam Houston. —Autographs courtesy Robert F. Batchelder.

Left: Robert F. Kennedy, PS, 10" x 8", $1150. —Photo courtesy Swann Galleries, Inc.

Politicians

	ALS		Cut Sig	
	Low	High	Low	High
Agnew, Spiro	$140	$175	$25	$35
Benson, Ezra Taft	45	60	12	15
Blumenthal, W. Michael	10	15	3	5
Calhoun, John C.	375	475	120	150
Clay, Henry	1000	1350	120	150
Coolidge, T. Jefferson	20	25	3	5
Dearborn, Henry M.	450	600	85	110
Dodd, Thomas J.	60	70	15	20
Fowler, Henry	25	35	3	5
Garrett, Finis J.	18	25	7	10
Hamilton, Alexander	2750	3500	850	1200
Hamlin, Hannibal	250	325	75	90
Houston, Sam	2750	3500	450	650
Hufstedler, Shirley	10	15	3	5
Jenkins, Thornton Alexander	25	35	7	10
Jones, Jesse H.	10	15	10	15
Jordan, Hamilton	15	20	3	5
Kearny, Stephen	250	375	60	75
King, Preston	75	100	10	15
Lodge, Henry Cabot	150	200	40	50
Muskie, Edmund	35	45	7	10
Pickering, Timothy	1500	2000	200	250
Roberts, Owen	175	225	35	50
Rumsfeld, Donald	40	50	6	10
Rutledge, Wiley B.	200	275	25	30
Salinger, Pierre	35	50	35	50
Sargent, John G.	45	60	15	20
Seward, William H.	140	175	60	75
Sherman, John	75	100	80	100
Shriver, Sargent	20	25	3	5
Shultz, George P.	45	60	10	15
Summerfield, Arthur E.	25	30	8	15
Sumner, Charles	275	350	80	100
Sununu, John	20	25	10	15

Presidents

Presidential letters and autographs are among the most valuable. George Washington, like many men of his era, was a prolific writer. His autographed letters are often offered at auction. Dwight Eisenhower, however, rarely took a pen to hand for more than a signature. An Eisenhower ALS is often worth more than a Washington ALS! Also beware of auto-pen. This automatic signing device became entrenched in the White House in the early 1960s. It has signed a vast majority of letters coming from the presidents since that time.

ALS and DS

	ALS		DS	
	Low	High	Low	High
Adams, John	$14,000	$18,000	$4000	$6000
Adams, John Q.	7500	10,000	1500	2500
Arthur, Chester A.	1500	2000	1500	2500
Buchanan, James	1200	1800	750	900
Bush, George	800	1200	400	600
Carter, Jimmy	1000	1500	250	500
Cleveland, Grover	750	1000	400	600
Clinton, Bill	300	700	100	300
Coolidge, Calvin	1500	2000	400	800
Eisenhower, Dwight	2500	3500	500	800
Fillmore, Millard	2000	3000	1000	1500
Ford, Gerald	1000	1500	500	700
Garfield, James	1000	1500	750	1000
Grant, U. S.	4500	6000	800	1200
Harding, Warren G.	1500	2000	400	650
Harrison, Benjamin	3000	3500	1000	1500
Harrison, William H.	3000	3500	1200	1600
Hayes, R. B.	7500	1000	500	800
Hoover, Herbert	2000	3000	300	500
Jackson, Andrew	4500	6000	1500	2500
Jefferson, Thomas	16,000	22,000	5000	7000
Johnson, Andrew	6000	7500	1500	2000
Johnson, Lyndon	2000	3500	750	1000
Kennedy, John F.	6000	8000	2000	3000
Lincoln, Abraham	8000	12,000	5000	7500
Madison, James	3000	4500	1200	2100
McKinley, William	1500	2000	400	700
Monroe, James	2500	3200	1000	1500
Nixon, Richard M.	4500	6000	750	1000
Pierce, Franklin	1000	1500	800	1200
Polk, James K.	3000	4000	1300	2000
Reagan, Ronald	2000	3000	750	1000
Roosevelt, Franklin	1000	1500	750	1200
Roosevelt, Theodore	1500	2000	1000	1500
Taft, William H.	1500	2000	500	800
Taylor, Zachary	5000	6500	2000	2500
Truman, Harry	3500	5000	1000	1500
Tyler, John	2000	3000	1300	2000
Van Buren, Martin	750	1000	1200	1700
Washington, George	15,000	20,000	12,000	16,000
Wilson, Woodrow	1500	2000	500	800

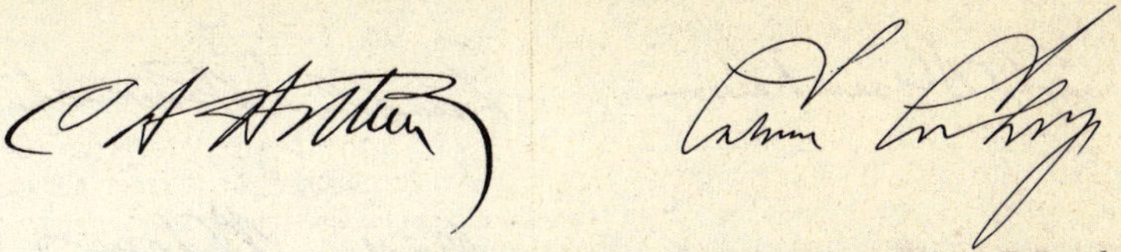

Chester A. Arthur and Calvin Coolidge. —Autographs courtesy Robert F. Batchelder.

PS and Cut Sig.

	PS		Cut Sig.	
	Low	High	Low	High
Adams, John	—	—	$1500	$2000
Adams, John Q.	—	—	300	500
Arthur, Chester A.	$400	$600	300	300
Buchanan, James	—	—	300	400
Bush, George	300	400	100	150
Carter, Jimmy	200	300	150	200
Clinton, Bill	300	400	100	150
Cleveland, Grover	500	800	200	300
Coolidge, Calvin	400	600	200	300
Eisenhower, Dwight	500	750	200	300
Fillmore, Millard	—	—	400	500
Ford, Gerald	200	300	200	300
Garfield, James	1500	2000	200	300
Grant, U. S.	2500	3800	600	900
Harding, Warren G.	7400	1000	200	300
Harrison, William H.	—	—	400	600
Harrison, Benjamin	700	1000	450	600
Hayes, R. B.	1000	1500	200	300
Hoover, Herbert	300	500	200	300
Jackson, Andrew	—	—	700	1000
Jefferson, Thomas	—	—	2500	4000
Johnson, Andrew	2000	2800	400	500
Johnson, Lyndon	300	500	150	200
Kennedy, John F.	1000	1500	600	800
Lincoln, Abraham	18,000	25,000	2500	3500
Madison, James	—	—	300	500
McKinley, William	800	1200	200	300
Monroe, James	—	—	300	500
Nixon, Richard M.	250	400	150	200
Pierce, Franklin	—	—	300	400
Polk, James K.	—	—	300	400
Reagan, Ronald	300	400	200	300
Roosevelt, Franklin	700	1000	300	400
Roosevelt, Theodore	1500	2000	400	500
Taft, William H.	300	500	150	200
Taylor, Zachary	—	—	500	800
Truman, Harry	400	700	200	300
Tyler, John	—	—	350	500
Van Buren, Martin	—	—	300	400
Washington, George	—	—	3500	5000
Wilson, Woodrow	500	800	200	300

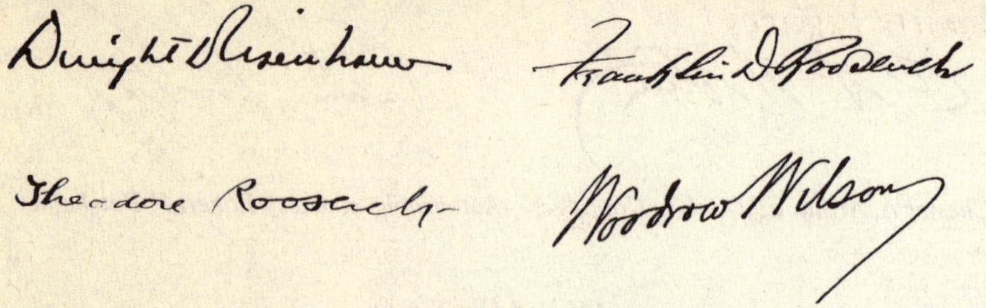

Presidents Dwight Eisenhower, Franklin Roosevelt, Theodore Roosevelt, and Woodrow Wilson. —Autographs courtesy Robert F. Batchelder.

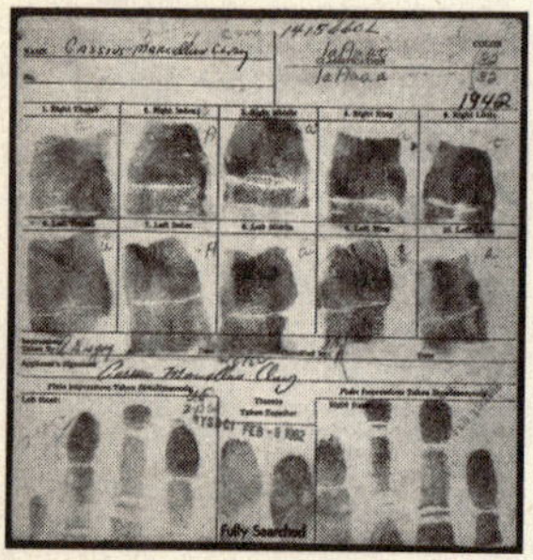

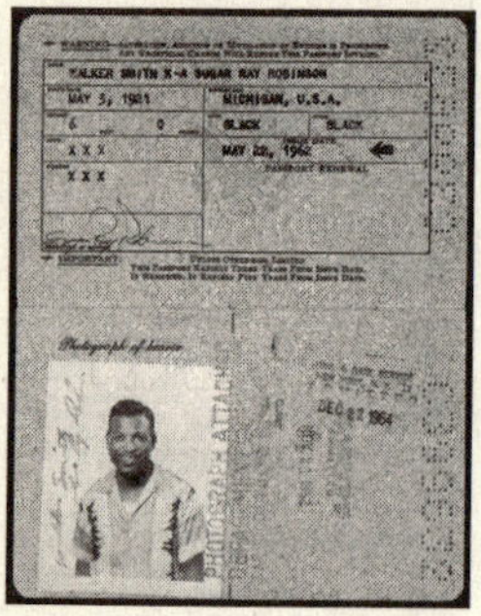

Left: Lou Gehrig, PS, 7.25" x 9.25", $14,790 at auction; center: Cassius Clay, boxing license application fingerprint card, $5372 at auction; right: Sugar Ray Robinson, passport, $3058 at auction. —Photos courtesy Mastro Fine Sports Auctions.

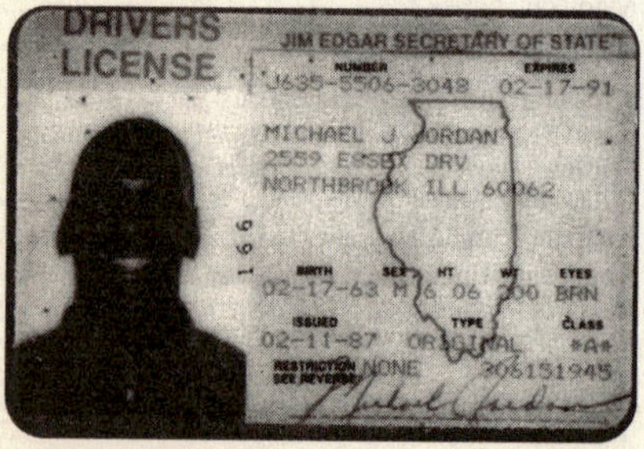

Left: Babe Ruth, PS, 8" x 10", $23,000 at auction; right: Michael Jordan, driver's license, $13,559 at auction. —Photos courtesy Mastro Fine Sports Auctions.

Sports Figures

	PS		Cut Sig.	
	Low	High	Low	High
Ali, Muhammad	$60	$75	$25	$35
Allison, Bobby	15	20	6	10
Anderson, George "Sparky"	10	15	4	8
Archibald, Nate	20	25	4	8
Baer, Max	225	300	125	175
Blanda, George	30	40	8	15
Boggs, Wade	15	20	5	10
Caras, Jimmy	5	10	3	5
Cauthen, Steve	30	40	10	15
Clay, Cassius M.	225	300	100	150
Clemens, Roger	10	15	4	8
Cooney, Gerry	10	15	5	10
Cooper, Wilbur	110	150	40	60
Corbett, James J.	650	850	375	500
Costas, Bob	5	10	2	5
Dean, Dizzy	200	250	75	100
Dempsey, Jack	150	200	75	100
Dorsett, Tony	5	10	2	5
Duran, Roberto	75	100	15	25
Dykstra, Lenny	5	10	2	5
Gehrig, Lou	3000	3750	750	1000
Gossage, Rich "Goose"	5	10	2	5
Griese, Bob	19	15	5	8
Henie, Sonja	125	175	40	50
Hexstall, Bryan	35	50	15	20
Hodges, Gil	225	300	80	100
Hogan, Ben	200	300	60	75
Jenner, Bruce	4	8	2	5
Johncock, Gordon	15	20	5	10
Jones, Deacon	12	18	4	8
Jordan, Michael	50	75	30	40
La Motta, Jake	30	40	10	15
Leonard, "Sugar Ray"	25	35	12	20
Lombardi, Vince	550	750	350	500
Maglie, Sal "The Barber"	45	60	20	30
Mancini, Ray "Boom Boom"	15	25	8	15
Mosconi, Willie	25	35	12	20
Nicklaus, Jack	65	85	30	40
Orr, Bobby	45	60	15	25
Payton, Walter	15	25	5	10
Pele	60	75	15	25
Plimpton, George	15	20	5	10
Robinson, Jackie	600	900	300	400
Robinson, Sugar Ray	185	250	85	110
Rose, Pete	15	20	5	10
Ruth, Babe	175	225	120	150
Salazar, Alberto	15	25	5	10
Shoemaker, Willie	40	65	20	30
Tarkenton, Fran	15	25	10	15
Weber, Dick	10	18	4	8
Yarborough, Cale	12	20	5	10

Baskets

There are several types of basket construction. Wickerwork, the most common and widely used technique, is an over-and-under pattern. Twining is similar; two strands are twisted as they are woven over and under, producing a finer weave. Plaiting gives a checkerboard effect in either a tight weave or left with open spaces. Twill work is similar, but with a diagonal effect achieved by changing the number of strands over which the weaver passes. Coiling is the most desirable weave for the collector. This technique has been refined since its conception around 7000 B.C. Fibers are wrapped around and stitched together to form the basket's shape. Most of these pieces were either used for ceremonial purposes or for holding liquids, since these tightly woven containers were leakproof.

Baskets are easy to care for but a few basic rules must be followed: Never wash an Indian basket, especially baskets made of pine needles, straw, grass or leaves. Dust them gently using a soft sable artist's brush. Willow, oak, hickory and rattan baskets may be washed in a mild solution of Murphy's Oil Soap and dried briefly in a sunny location. Baskets continuously exposed to the sun will fade.

	AUCTION	RETAIL	
		Low	High
Nantucket, splint, round, bentwood swivel handle, paper label "Lightship Basket made by Fred S. Chadwick Nantucket Mass. 4 Pine St.," 7.75" dia, 4.75" h plus handle	$920	$1200	$2000
Rye Straw, coiled, bound with splint, round with flat bottom and sides flaring toward rim, 2 woven-in rim handles, 19th C, 9.75" dia, 4.25" h	120	200	500
Rye Straw, round, large, bentwood rim handles, wear and rim damage, 20" dia, 9.75" h	605	1000	1500
Shaker, black ash, oval top, rectangular bottom, "C.S.C." painted on side, initialed "CSF" on shaped handle and bottom, single wrap rim, 1" w uprights, narrow weavers, 17" x 11.5", 5.75" h	475	750	1000
Splint, cheese basket, round, 6 shaped wooden fixed handles, 19th C, 17.75" dia, 6.5" h	850	600	1000

Left to right: Shaker Splint Basket, miniature bucket and melon basket pincushions, and 2 large painted melon baskets. — Photo courtesy Skinner, Inc., Boston, MA.

	AUCTION	RETAIL Low	RETAIL High
Splint, melon-shaped, egg or gathering basket, oval, arched bentwood stationary handle, 19th C, 7.75 x 7", 3.25" h plus handle	270	200	500
Splint, oblong, 49 ribs, 2 diamond designs and hand holds each end, stationary double-wide woven handle at center, made by Charles Shelton, 20th C, 19" x 27", 10.5" h plus handle	225	500	800
Splint, oval, bentwood handle, scrubbed finish, 10.5" x 12.5", 6" h plus handle	110	200	500
Splint, pitcher form, banded rim and base, ash handle, 19th C, 4.5" w, 7.75" h	862	700	1000
Splint, rectangular, 2 rim handles, painted pink and black, 19th C, 15" w, 5" h	489	300	500
Splint, rectangular, small, stationary bentwood handle, 5.75" x 7", 3.5" h plus handle	192	150	300
Splint, round, 33 ribs, old white paint, bentwood handle, 13" dia, 8" h plus handle	385	300	600
Splint, round, banded rim and base, shaped wood handle with flattened top, blue paint, 19th C, 13" dia, 13.25" h including handle	1380	1000	1500
Splint, round, small, flat bottom, stationary bentwood handle, 7.25" dia, 4.5" h plus handle	71	100	200
Splint, round, worn blue paint interior and exterior, swivel handle, 11" dia, 7.25" h	401	400	700
Splint, round, worn red paint exterior, bentwood swivel handle, 9.5" dia, 6.75" h	330	300	600

Nantucket Baskets, nesting set of 6 and 1 small basket, all by W. & J. Sayle, 1978-79; and a miniature Nantucket basket, $4025 at auction. —Photo courtesy Skinner, Inc., Boston, MA.

Beer-Related Memorabilia

For further reading consult *American Breweries II* by Dale P. Van Wieren (Eastern Coast Breweriana Assoc., West Point, PA, 1995) and *Collectible Beer Trays* by Gary Straub Schiffer, Atglen, PA, 1995).

	LOW	HIGH
Ashtray, Bartels Malt Extract, conical, man holding full beer mug aloft, removable match striker, 4" h, 4.75" dia	$200	$400
Bookmark, Erin Brew, Standard Brewing Co., Cleveland, diecut tin, bottle shape, 3" h	75	125
Bottle, Carib Lager Beer, Grenada Brewery, Grenada, WI, painted label, blue and yellow, 1940s	5	10
Bottle, Mohawk Special, Mohawk Prod. Co., Buffalo, NY, embossed, Indian, 1933	60	80
Bottle, Old Stock Porter, Philadelphia Brewing Co., Philadelphia, PA, paper neckband and label	5	10
Bottle, Pabst Extract, Pabst Brewing, Milwaukee, WI, paper label, original cap, 1933	30	50
Bottle, Rheingold, S. Liebmann's Brewing, New Nork, NY, embossed and paper label, late 1890s	65	85
Bottle, Stegmaier's Porter, Stegmaier Brewing, Wilkes-Barre, PA, paper neckband and label, 12 oz	10	15
Bottle Opener, Pilsener Brewing, cast metal, wall mount, original box	25	45
Can, ABC Beer, ABC Brewing, St. Louis, MO, instructional flattop, 1930s	125	150
Can, Altes Lager Beer, Tivoli Brewing, Detroit, MI, crowntainer	50	75
Can, Best Export Lager, Best Brewing, Chicago, IL, instructional flattop, 1930s	100	125
Can, Beverwyck Ale, Beverwyck Brewing, Albany, NY, low profile conetop	18	25
Can, Black Pride Lager Beer, West Bend Lithia, West Bend, WI, pulltab, 1970s	8	15
Can, Dakota Beer, Dakota Brewing, Bismark, ND, ziptop, 1960s	45	65
Can, Falstaff Beer, Falstaff Brewing, St. Louis, MO, high profile conetop	35	60
Can, Gibbons Beer, Lion, Inc., Wilkes-Barre, PA, high profile conetop	25	50
Can, Hoehler Select Beer, Erie Brewing, Erie, PA, high profile conetop	175	200
Can, Old Reading Beer, Old Reading Brewing, Reading, PA, high profile conetop	150	175
Can, Pfeiffer Famous Beer, Pfeiffer Brewing, Detroit, MI, ringtab, 1960s	5	10
Can, Reisch Gold Top Beer, Reisch Brewing, Springfield, IL, high profile conetop	40	60
Can, Star Beer, Great Western Brewing, Belleville, IL, high profile conetop	40	60
Clicker, Gunther's Beer, litho tin, red lettering, white ground, "Just Click For Gunther's Beer, The Beer That Clicks!"	20	25
Clock, Budweiser, electric, light-up, mantel-style clock above plastic case with 8 Clydesdale horses pulling wagon, "World's Champion Clydesdale Team," not working	100	200
Clock, Pearl Lager Beer, light-up, octagonal, red and white with blue neon rim, "Neon Products Inc. Lima Ohio," 18.5" w	200	600
Fly Swatter, Straub's Beer, plastic, 1950s	2	4
Foam Scraper, Marathon Lager Beer, 1950s	25	35
Playing Cards, Budweiser, beer label	8	12
Pocket Mirror, Buck-O Cereal Beverage, Lion Brewing Co., Wilkes-Barre, PA, round, ram's head, "It's A Good One"	100	150
Pocket Mirror, Congress Beer, Haberle Brewing Co., Syracuse, oval, beer bottle, red ground, 2.75" l	125	175

Sign, Columbia Brewing Co., Shenandoah, PA, vitrolite, curved, $7150 at auction. —Photo courtesy James D. Julia, Inc.

	LOW	HIGH
Sign, Acme Beer, neon, white and silver letters, with transformer, 20.5" x 10.5"	500	600
Sign, Anheuser-Busch, paper, Indians on raft, entitled "The Father of Waters," matted and framed, © August A. Busch, 13.25" x 19"	100	350
Sign, Anheuser-Busch, reverse painted on glass, trademark eagle and letter "A," red and gold, 9.5" dia	500	900
Sign, Bartels Beer, tin, trademark letters, Chas. W. Shonk Litho, 18.5" dia	100	200
Sign, Bavarian Brewing Co., stained glass window with dancing Bavarian holding full mug drawn from keg marked "Bavarian Brewing Company," framed, 39" x 31.5"	1500	3000
Sign, "Dewar's," neon, white and red, 22.5" l	75	175
Sign, Gluek Beer, curved vitrolite sign with trademark logo, tiger-striped copper frame, 23" x 17.5"	750	1500
Sign, Grace Bros. Beer, light-up, reverse painted on glass, "Has the flavor," red, cobalt blue, and silver letters on orange ground, silver-colored frame, 17" dia	1000	1200
Sign, Hudepohl Beer and Ale, Hudepohl Brewing Co., Cincinnati Ohio, cardboard, man with glass of beer sitting at table outdoors, hunting dog at his feet, matted and framed, 38" h, 29.5" w	300	400
Sign, Nutmeg Beer, wood, Uncle Sam and companion drinking beer by hearth, "Bottled at the Brewery for Family and Medicinal Use," Sentenne & Green Litho, 14" x 20"	750	1200
Sign, Pabst Blue Ribbon, paper, 2 vintage beer bottles and glass of beer next to tray of oysters, artist A. F. King, original wooden frame with Pabst tag, 22" x 26"	300	500
Sign, Ruppert's Bottled Beer, light-up, reverse painted on glass, red and green lettering, blue ground, black wood frame, 13.5" x 10.5"	150	250
Sign, Stegmaier's Beer, light-up, reverse painted on glass, "Stegmaier's Beer, Wilkes-Barre, Pennsylvania, est. 1857," shaded orange and silver lettering, black ground, chrome frame, 17.5" dia	750	900
Sign, Vic's Special Beer, Northern Brewing Co., Superior, WI, tin over cardboard, beer bottle, gold lettering, red ground, Scioto Sign Co., Kenton, 5.25" h, 11.25" l	50	150
Tap Knob Insert, Ballantine Ale, porcelain on metal	5	10
Thermometer, Regal Beer, embossed aluminum, beer bottle, 1950s	175	225
Tip Tray, J. Chr. G. Hupfel Brg. Co., factory scene with vintage truck and horse-drawn vehicle, Kaufmann & Strauss Co. Litho, 5" dia	300	500

	LOW	HIGH
Tip Tray, Peter Doelger Beer, American eagle atop first prize awards, "Expressly for the Home," 4.25" dia	125	225
Tip Tray, Rainier Beer, trademark Mt. Rainier, Chas. W. Shonk Co. Litho, 4.25" dia	125	150
Tip Tray, Tivoli Brewing Co., Altes Lager beer bottle, H. D. Beach Co. Litho., 4.25" dia	150	250
Tip Tray, Yengling's Beer, young lady with big hat, 4.25" dia	250	350
Tray, Anheuser-Busch, oval, large version, huge factory complex with early trains, trolleys, and horse-drawn vehicles, "America's Largest and Favorite Brewery," Standard Advertising Co. Litho, 15" x 18"	800	1500
Tray, Buffalo Brewing Co., children of the world paying homage to beautiful lady, "San Francisco Exposition 1915 The Nations Paying Homage to San Francisco," Kaufmann & Strauss Co. Litho, 12" dia	400	600
Tray, Burkhardt's Beer, Burkhardt Brewing Co., pretty girl holding glass of beer while looking back over her shoulder, Akron, OH, 1930s, 12" dia	150	200
Tray, Cream City Pelham Club Beer and Pilsener Beer, Cream City Brewing Co., Milwaukee, WI, company logo, "The Cream of Famous Milwaukee Beers," 1930s, 14" dia	225	300
Tray, Crescent Brewing Co., factory scene with horse-drawn carriages in foreground and crescent logo with hops background in sky, 12" dia	600	800
Tray, Effinger Fine Beer, Effinger Brewing, Baraboo, WI, saluting waiter holding tray with bottle and glass, 1940s, 12" dia	150	200
Tray, Frank's Old Fashioned Beer, M. Frank & Son Brewing, Mansfield, OH, rectangular, outdoor tavern scene, 1930s, 13.5" x 10.5"	100	150
Tray, Gesundheit Bottled Beer, Leidiger Brewing, Merrill, WI, square, long-haired maiden, stock design, 1910s, 13.25" sq	200	300
Tray, Grossvater Beer, Renner Brewing, Akron, OH, hand holding glass of beer, "It's Extra Good," 1930s, 14" dia	150	200
Tray, Grossvater Beer, Renner Brewing, Youngstown, OH, rectangular, distinguished white-haired gentlemen seated at table, drinking beer, "Grandfathers Drinking Grossvater Beer," 1910s	50	100
Tray, Hanley's Peerless Ale, James Hanley's Brewing, Providence, RI, bulldog resting on "Hanley's," "Brewed in Rhode Island's Largest Ale Brewery," 1940s, 12" dia	40	100
Tray, Hensler's Popular Beer - Ale, Joseph Hensler Brewing, Newark, NJ, woodgrain ground, "Since 1860," 1930s, 13.5" dia	35	75
Tray, Hull's Ale Lager, Hull's Brewing, New Haven, CT, company logo, 1930s, 13" dia	30	75
Tray, Iroquois Indian Head Beer and Ale, Indian in full headdress, "Iroquois Beverage Corp. Buffalo, N.Y., Am. Can Co. N.Y. & Chgo," 12" dia	100	250
Tray, Koehler's Beer - Ale - Porter, Erie Brewing Co., Erie, PA, eagle and beer keg logo, 1930s, 14" dia	80	150
Tray, Lebanon Valley Beer, Lebanon Valley Brewing, Lebanon, smiling lady's head, hand holding pilsener glass, "Pride of the Valley," 1940s, 13.5" dia	110	175
Tray, Mellet & Nichter Beer, Ale & Porter, Mellet & Nichter Brewing Co., Pottsville, PA, rectangular, stock design of smiling woman with roses drinking glass of beer, red drape background, 1910s, 10.5" x 13.25"	1200	1750
Tray, Miller High Life Beer, Miller Brewing, Milwuakee, WI, trademark girl on crescent moon, 1910s, 13" dia	200	350
Tray, Narragansett Lager & Ale, wheat and leaf border, Dr. Seuss illustration with Chief Gansett and cat, "Gangway For Gansett!, Too Good To Miss!," 12" dia	100	150

	LOW	HIGH
Tray, Olympia's Exquisite Butte Beer, stock image of gypsy woman, "Best in the West," Chas. W. Shonk Co. Litho, ©1907, 12"dia	250	400
Tray, Red Raven Splits, red raven with foot on vintage bottle, Chas. W. Shonk Co. Litho, 12" dia	200	400
Tray, Robert Smith Ale Brewing Co., oval, tiger head, "Tiger Head Brand, Ales and Stouts, established 1774," 23.5" x 19"	2000	4000
Tray, Schmidt's Beer, Schmidt's Brewing, Philadelphia, PA, pretty woman pouring beer from bottle into glass, "Quarts - Pints - Draught," red and black ground, 1930s, 12" dia	115	175
Tray, Seitz Beer, H. J. Osterstock trading as Seitz Brewery, Easton, PA, trademark eagle, c1933, 13" dia	150	200
Tray, Texas Pride, San Antonio Brewing, San Antonio, TX, rectangular, factory scene, 1930s, 13.25" x 10.5"	250	350
Tray, White Seal Beer, National Brewery Co., rectangular, factory scene with horse-drawn wagons, company logo, vintage blob-top bottle, Briesedieck Bros. Proprietors	500	1000
Tumbler, ABC Bohemian Beer, acid etched panel with "The ABC Bohemian, the American Brewing Co. St. Louis, MO" and eagle motif, 3.5" h	50	100
Tumbler, P. H. Zang Brewing Co., Denver, CO, acid etched with company emblem, gold rim band, 4" h	75	125

Trays, left to right: Excelsior Brewing Co., 13.75" x 13.75", $396 at auction; Fehr's Famous F.F.X.L. Beers, "Copyright 1910 by Frank Fehr Brewing Co. Inc.," 13" dia, $451 at auction. —Photos courtesy Collectors Auction Services.

Bottles

For information on bottles see *The Official Price Guide to Bottles, Twelfth Edition* by Jim Megura (House of Collectibles, New York, NY 1998), *Bottles, Second Edition* by Michael Polak (Avon Books, New York, NY, 1997), and *Kovels' Bottles Price List, 11th Edition* by Ralph and Terry Kovel (Three Rivers Press, New York, NY 1999).

Avon

David Hall McConnell founded The California Perfume Company in New York City at the end of the nineteenth century. The firm changed its name to Avon in 1939. A pioneer in home sales, most people recognize the company's figural decanters produced in the late 1960s to the early 1980s. Prices are for glass bottles in mint condition in original boxes of excellent to near mint condition. For further information see Bud Hastin's *Avon & C.P.C. Collector's Encyclopedia, 15th Edition,* published by author, 1998.

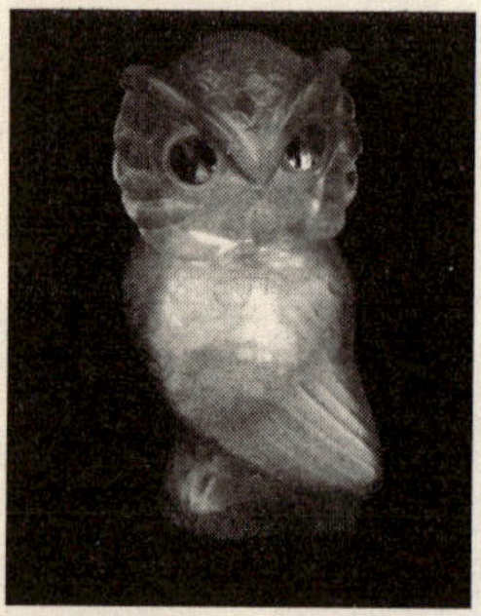

Snow Owl Powder Sachet II, frosted, 1979-80, 1.25 oz, $6-$10.

	LOW	HIGH
Aladdin's Lamp, green lamp, gold flame cap, 1971-73, 6 oz, 7.5" l	$6	$10
Alaskan Moose, amber body, cream-colored plastic antlers, 1974-75, 8 oz	5	8
Apothecary, light yellow apothecary bottle, gold cap, 1973-76, 8 oz	3	6
Athena Bath Urn, clear urn, 1975-76, 6 oz	2	4
Avon Calling For Men, gold-painted candlestick telephone, black mouthpiece, gold cap, 1969-70, 6 oz, 8.5" h	8	12
Bath Treasure Snail, clear snail, gold head cap, 1973-76, 6 oz	6	9
Beautiful Awakening, gold-painted alarm clock, paper dial, gold cap, 1973-74, 3 oz	3	6
Be My Valentine, clear heart, red cap, 1995, .5 oz	2	3
Big Game Rhino, green rhinoceros, green plastic head cap, 1972-73, 4 oz	5	8
Big Whistle Decanter, blue whistle, silver cap, 1972, 4 oz	4	7
Bon Bon, white milk glass poodle, white cap, 1972-73, 1 oz	4	7
Bucking Bronco, dark amber horse, bronze plastic cowboy cap, 1971-72, 6 oz	6	10
Butterfly, clear butterfly, gold cap, 1972-73, 1.5 oz, 3.5" h	5	7
Christmas Sparkler, purple-painted Christmas ball, gold cap, 1968, 4 oz	18	25
Christmas Surprise, green boot, silver cap	1	2
Cologne Royal, clear crown, gold cap, 1972-74, 1 oz	2	4
Country Charm, white milk glass pot-bellied stove w/ yellow window, green and white plastic flowered lamp shade cap, 1976-77, 4.8 oz	5	8
Dolphin, frosted dolphin, gold tail cap, 1968-69, 8 oz	6	9

	LOW	HIGH
Eiffel Tower, clear Eiffel Tower, gold cap, 1970, 3 oz, 9" h	6	9
Fashion Boot Pincushion, blue milk glass boot, pincushion top, 1972-76, 4 oz, 5.5" h	4	7
Fielder's Choice, dark amber baseball glove, white ball, black cap, 1971-72, 5 oz	5	8
Fragrance Hours, ivory grandfather clock, gold cap, 1971-73, 6 oz	5	8
French Telephone, white milk glass phone, clear receiver handle holds perfume, gold cap and trim, 1971, 6 oz	20	30
General 4-4-0, dark blue locomotive and cap, 1971-72, 5.5 oz	10	14
Golden Notes, light yellow-coated canary, yellow head, 1979-80, 1.75 oz	2	4
Golden Thimble, clear, gold thimble cap, 1972-74, 2 oz	3	5
Graceful Giraffe, clear body, gold head cap, 1976, 1.5 oz	4	6
Hammer on the Mark Decanter, amber handle, silver hammer head, 1978, 2.5 oz, 8.5" l	3	5
Heavenly Music, clear harp, gold cap, 1978-80, 1 oz	1	3
Honey Bear Baby, yellow-painted beehive, blue plastic bear on cap, 1974-76, 4 oz	2	4
Indian Head Penny, bronze-painted penny and cap, 1970-72, 4 oz, 4" h	6	10
King Pin, white milk glass bowling pin, white cap, red label, 1969-70, 4 oz, 6.5" h	4	7
Kodiak Bear, dark amber body and head, 1977, 6 oz	4	7
Little Dutch Kettle, orange-painted tea kettle, gold cap, 1972-73, 5 oz	4	7
Majestic Elephant, gray-painted African elephant, gray head cap, 1977, 5.5 oz	5	9
Packard Roadster, light amber auto, light amber plastic rumble seat cap, 1970-72, 6 oz, 6.5" l	7	10
Pear Lumiere, clear pear, 1975-76, 2 oz	3	5
Perfect Drive, golfer, green lower body, white plastic torso cap, 1975-76, 4 oz	5	8
Petti Fleur, clear flower, gold cap, 1969-70, 1 oz	4	7
Regal Peacock, blue peacock feathers, gold body cap, 1973-74, 4 oz	7	10
Right Connection Fuse, clear fuse, gold and brown cap, 1977, 1.5 oz	2	4
Royal Coach, white milk glass coach, gold cap, 1972-73, 5 oz	5	8
Royal Elephant, white milk glass elephant, gold snap-on houdah, 1977-79, .5 oz	4	6
Royal Swan, blue swan, gold crown cap, 1974, 1 oz	4	6
Sea Horse, clear sea horse, 1970-72, 6 oz	5	9
Sea Treasure, iridescent conch shell, gold cap, 1971-72, 5 oz	7	10
Sea Trophy, light blue leaping fish, blue plastic head cap, 1972, 5.5 oz	7	10
Short Pony Decanter, green horse head hitching post, gold cap, 1968-69, 4 oz	4	7
Silver Fawn, 2 fawns, silver coating over clear, 1978-79, .5 oz	1	3
Snoopy Surprise, white milk glass Snoopy, blue plastic cap w/ black ears, 1969-71, 5 oz, 5.5" h	5	9
Snow Bunny, clear body, gold head cap, 1975-76, 3 oz	4	6
Snug Cub Decanter, white milk glass bear, red cap, 1987, 1 oz	2	4
Stop 'n Go, green traffic light, green cap, 1974, 4 oz	4	7
Swiss Mouse, frosted cheese wedge, gold mouse cap, 1974-75, 3 oz	4	7
Victorian Lady, white milk glass body, white plastic cap, 1972-73, 5 oz	3	6
Victorian Manor, white-painted house, pink plastic roof, 1972-73, 5 oz	5	9
Whale Oil Lantern, green lantern, silver plastic cap and base, 1974-75, 5 oz	4	8
Whale Organizer, ivory milk glass whale's tooth, dark blue scrimshaw design, 1973, 3 oz	3	5
Wilderness Classic, silver-plated over clear leaping deer, silver plastic head cap, 1976-77, 6 oz	7	11
Wild West Bullet, bronze-plated bullet, silver cap, 1977-78, 1.5 oz	2	4

Barber

Clear, label under glass, "LeVarn's Shampoo and Hair Tonic," German silver spouts, 8.5" h, price for pair at auction, $125.

	LOW	HIGH
Amber, multicolored label under glass with floral decoration and "Hair Oil," smooth base, tooled lip, 7.25" h	$175	$250
Black Amethyst, white enameled ship on stormy seas, pontil scarred base, rolled lip, 6.5" h	250	350
Blue Milk Glass, Flute and Bead pattern, smooth base, tooled lip, 6.5" h	125	175
Brilliantine, white milk glass, yellow, red, orange, and blue enameled flowers and swags, smooth base, sheared and polished lip, 4.25" h	200	300
Clear, cut diamond pattern, smooth base, tooled lip, original sterling silver stopper with screw-off top, 8.5" h	75	125
Clear, cut floral design and "Bay Rum," polished pontil, tooled lip, original ground glass stopper, 7.25" h	100	150
Clear, light purple satin finish and silver overlay, smooth base, tooled lip, original hinged sterling silver cap, 7.75" h	100	150
Cobalt Blue, rib pattern, silver and yellow enameled Persian-style design, pontil scarred base, sheared lip, 6.75" h	125	175
Cobalt Blue, rib pattern, white and green enameled vines, pontil scarred base, sheared lip, 8.5" h	125	175
Deep Cobalt Blue, rib pattern, bell-form, white and gold enameled flowers and butterfly, pontil scarred base, sheared lip, 8" h	200	300
Deep Green, rib pattern, white enameled "Mary Gregory" decoration w/ girl pointing, pontil scarred base, rolled lip, 7.75" h	250	350
Frosted Grass Green, bell-form, white and gold Art Nouveau stylized vines, pontil scarred base, sheared lip, 8" h	375	500
Grass Green, rib pattern, white enameled flowers, pontil scarred base, sheared lip, 8.125" h	150	200
Honey Amber, melon-ribbed, Coin Spot pattern, smooth base, rolled lip, 6.75" h	75	100
Medium Cobalt Blue, rib pattern, multicolored floral decoration and gilt "Hair Tonic," pontil scarred base, rolled lip, 9" h	200	300
Medium Pink Amethyst, corseted waist, red and white enameled flowers and fleur-de-lis, pontil scarred base, sheared lip, 7.75" h	80	125
Medium Yellow-Green, rib pattern, yellow, red, and white enameled flowers, pontil scarred base, sheared lip, 7.5" h	125	175
Opalescent Cranberry, melon-ribbed, white daisy pattern, smooth base, rolled lip, 7.25" h	100	150

	LOW	HIGH
Opalescent Cranberry, white Hobnail pattern, ground pontil, polished lip, 8.125" h	125	160
Opalescent Milk Glass, pink wrap-around neck, gold and green arches, bellflowers, and lettering "Sea Foam, H.C. Shimp," pontil scarred base, applied mouth, 8.75" h	300	400
Opalescent Turquoise Blue, flat-sided, Spanish Lace pattern, polished pontil, rolled lip, 8.25" h	150	200
Opalescent Turquoise Blue, white swirl pattern, smooth base, rolled lip, 6.25" h	125	150
Pale Apple Green, Coin Spot pattern, yellow, orange, and white enameled flowers and trellises, pontil scarred base, rolled lip, 8.25" h	100	150
Pink Amethyst, rib pattern, red and white enameled flowers, vines, and swags, pontil scarred base, sheared lip, 7.25" h	120	165
Pale Green, rib pattern, multicolored floral decoration, smooth base, applied mouth, 7" h	80	125
Purple Amethyst, rib pattern, white enameled "Mary Gregory" decoration w/ cottage and "Witch Hazel," pontil scarred base, rolled lip, 7.75" h	350	450
Purple Amethyst, rib pattern, yellow, red, and white enameled flowers, pontil scarred base, rolled lip, 7.75" h	125	175
Red and White, vertical stripes, ground pontil, rolled lip, 8.75" h	175	275
Sapphire Blue, Coin Spot pattern, yellow, white, and orange enameled flowers, pontil scarred base, rolled lip, 8.25" h	175	250
Turquoise Blue, rib pattern, yellow, red, and white enameled flowers, pontil scarred base, sheared lip, 7.5" h	125	175
White Milk Glass, 6-sided, multicolored birds and "Witch Hazel," "E.W. Inc." on smooth base, rolled lip, 7.75" h	75	125
White Milk Glass, encased in shaded pink satin glass, polished pontil, flared and polished lip, 8.5" h	150	200
White Milk Glass, multicolored cherub decoration, pontil scarred base, sheared lip, 7.75" h	300	400
Yellow-Green, rib pattern, red and white enameled swags and flowers, pontil scarred base, sheared lip, 8" h	90	135

Barber Bottles. —Photo courtesy Glass-Works Auctions.

Bitters

Bitters Bottles. —Photo courtesy Glass-Works Auctions.

	LOW	HIGH
"Brady's Family Bitters," deep root beer amber, smooth base, applied sloping collar mouth, 1870-80, 9.375" h	$125	$175
"Dr. A. S. Hopkins Union Stomach Bitters," yellow w/ olive tone, smooth base, applied sloping collar mouth, 1870-80, 9.75" h	300	450
"Dr. Herbert John's Indian Bitters Great Indian Discoveries," reddish amber, smooth base, applied mouth, 1875-85, 8.5" h	175	250
"Dr. J. Hostetter's Stomach Bitters," deep olive green, smooth base, applied sloping collar mouth, bubbles throughout, 1855-70, 9.75" h	175	225
"Dr. Soule's Hop Bitters 1872," embossed hop berries and leaves, deep reddish amber, semi-cabin, smooth base, applied sloping double collar mouth, bubbles throughout, 1875-85, 9.375" h	150	200
"Edw Wilder's Stomach Bitters, (5-story building), Edw Wilder & Co. Wholesale Druggists, Louisville, KY," clear, semi-cabin, smooth base, tooled mouth, 1890-1910, 10.375" h	175	250
"Geo. Benz & Sons Appentine Bitters St. Paul, Minn.," reddish amber, ornate embossed scrollwork on paneled sides, "Pat. Nov. 23 1897" on smooth base, tooled mouth, 1897-1905, 8.25" h	350	550
"Geo. C. Hubbel & Co," aqua, semi-cabin, smooth base, applied sloping double collar mouth, 1865-75, 10.125" h	175	275
"German Tonic Bitters Boggs, Cottman & Co," aqua, iron pontil, applied sloping double collar mouth, 1845-65, 9.875" h	300	450
"John Moffat, New York, Phoenix, Bitters, Price $2.00," yellowish olive green, pontil scarred base, applied mouth, 1845-65, 6.875" h	2000	3000
"Kimball's Jaundice Bitters, Troy, N.H.," medium yellowish amber, iron pontil, applied sloping collar mouth, 1845-55, 7" h	500	700
"King's 25 Cent Bitters," aqua, smooth base, applied mouth, 1870-80, 6.625" h	80	125
"Morning (star) Bitters Inceptum, 5869 Patented 5869," amber, iron pontil, applied sloping collar mouth, original foil neck wrapping, 1865-75, 12.5" h	175	275
"Old Doctor C. W. Hufeland's German Bitters For Dyspepsia, Philada (bust of Dr. Hufeland)," bluish aqua, open pontil, applied sloping collar mouth, 1845-55, 7.5" h	800	1200
"Pepsin Calisaya Bitters, Dr. Russell Med. Co.," medium yellowish green, smooth base, tooled mouth, original label, contents, and foil neck seal, 1895-1910, 8" h	125	175
"S. Kaufman's Celebrated Anti Cholera Bitters, Patd 1865," deep amber, semi-cabin, smooth base, applied sloping collar mouth, 1865-75, 10" h	1500	2500
"St. Nicholas Stomach Bitters, Imported By Gentry & Otis, N.Y.," golden amber, pontil scarred base, applied sloping collar mouth, 1845-65, 7.5" h	1800	2800

Early American

Left to right: Blown three-mold toilet water bottle; Loaf-of-Bread demi-john; Midwestern globular. —Photos courtesy Glass-Works Auctions.

	LOW	HIGH
Blown Three-Mold, toilet water, deep brilliant cobalt blue, pontil scarred base, flared lip, original glass tam stopper, 1820-30, 5.375" h	$200	$300
Blown Three-Mold, toilet water, deep sapphire blue w/ purple tint, smooth base, flared and polished lip, 1855-65, 5.5" h	140	180
Blown Three-Mold, toilet water, medium purple amethyst, pontil scarred base, flared lip, 1820-30, 5.625" h	200	350
Blown Three-Mold, toilet water, smoky sapphire blue, smooth base, ground lip, 1820-30, 5.5" h	150	200
Club, Midwestern, deep bluish aqua, 24 broken rib pattern swirled to left, pontil scarred base, applied mouth, 1820-35, 8" h	175	275
Demi-John, medium cobalt blue, smooth base, applied sloping collar mouth, approx. 50 pimples around bottle made by mold's vent openings, 1860-80, 15.25" h	500	700
Demi-John, medium emerald green, smooth base, applied sloping collar mouth, blown in 4-pc mold, 1860-80, 15.25" h	150	250
Demi-John, medium pinkish amethyst, smooth base, applied sloping collar mouth, 1860-80, 15" h	400	600
Globular, amber, 24 rib pattern swirled to left, pontil scarred base, rolled lip, Midwestern, 1820-30, 8.25" h	375	550
Globular, golden yellowish amber, 24 vertical rib pattern, pontil scarred base, rolled lip, Midwestern, 1820-30, 7.75" h	1500	2200
Globular, light olive green w/ amber striations, pontil scarred base, rolled lip, bubbles throughout, 1790-1810, 8.75" h	140	185
Globular, medium amber, open pontil, rolled lip, Midwestern, 1820-30, 10.5" h	300	400
Globular, medium golden amber, 24 rib pattern swirled to right, pontil scarred base, rolled lip, Midwestern, 1820-30, 7.875" h	400	500
Globular, yellow w/ olive tone, 24 rib pattern swirled to right, pontil scarred base, rolled lip, Midwestern, 1820-30, 8.875" h	800	1200
Half-Size, toilet water, medium purple amethyst, 15 vertical rib pattern, pontil scarred base, rolled lip, original glass tam stopper, 1820-40, 4" h	700	900
Loaf-of-Bread Demi-John, bright yellowish olive green, smooth base, applied sloping collar mouth, bubbles and impurities throughout, 1855-75, 8.25" h	400	600
Ovoid Demi-John, deep yellowish green, pontil scarred base, applied sloping collar, blown in 4-pc. mold, 1850-75, 10.125" h	275	375
Pattern Molded, whiskey, medium amber, 26 rib pattern swirled slightly to right, pontil scarred base, applied double collar mouth, 1840-55, 9.75" h	275	375

Figural

Figural Bottles, left to right: Log Cabin; Indian Queen; Lady's Leg; Indian Queen; and Grape Cluster. —Photo courtesy Glass-Works Auctions.

Item	LOW	HIGH
Banjo, "Dingen's Napoleon Cocktail Bitters, Dingen Brothers, Buffalo, N.Y.," clear w/ grayish tint in pedestal base, iron pontil, applied sloping collar mouth, various size bubbles throughout, 1865-75, 10.125" h	$4000	$6000
Barrel, "Distilled in 1848, Old Kentucky 1849, Reserve Bourbon, A. M. Bininger & Co. 19 Broad St. N.Y.," medium amber, open pontil, applied double collar mouth, 1855-65, 8" h	175	250
Barrel, "Dr. C. W. Roback's Stomach Bitters, Cincinnati. O," medium amber, smooth base, applied sloping collar mouth, teardrop bubbles throughout, 1855-65, 9.375" h	150	250
Barrel, "Greeting, Theodore Netter, 1232 Market St., Philada, PA," cobalt blue, smooth base, long neck, tooled lip, 1890-1910, 6" h	275	375
Barrel, "Old Sachem Bitters And Wigwam Tonic," golden yellow w/ amber tone, smooth base, applied mouth, 1855-65, 9.325" h	300	400
Bust of George Washington, "Simon's Centennial Bitters Trade Mark," amber shading to yellow amber in arms, smooth base, applied double collar mouth, "V" shaped tooling imperfection on lip, 1865-80, 10" h	700	900
Cannon, "N.Y." (below arched and horizontal slug plates), golden yellow-amber, smooth base, sheared lip, 1865-70, 12.5" h	500	700
Clock Face, "Bininger's (clock face) Regulator, 19 Broad St New York," amber, pontil scarred base, applied double collar mouth, 1855-65, 6" h	300	400
Drum and Cannonballs, "McKeever's Army Bitters," medium amber, smooth base, applied sloping collar mouth, 1865-75, 10.5" h	1000	1500
Ear of Corn, "National Bitters," medium amber, "Patent 1867" on smooth base, applied mouth, 1867-75, 12.25" h	250	350
Ear of Corn, "National Bitters," yellow w/ olive tone, "Patented 1867" on smooth base, applied mouth, 1867-75, 12.5" h	1000	1500
Fish, "Doctor Fisch's Bitters, W. H. Ware, Patented 1866," golden amber, smooth base, applied mouth, 1866-75, 11.625" h	200	300
Fish, "The Fish Bitters, W. H. Ware, Patented 1866," medium yellow amber w/ olive tone, smooth base, applied mouth, 1866-75, 11.625" h	400	600
Fish, turquoise blue, smooth base, sheared lip, 1895-1915, 10.875" h	125	150
Indian Queen, "Brown's Celebrated Indian Herb Bitters, Patented 1868," medium amber, smooth base, tooled inward-rolled lip, 1868-75, 12.125" h	400	600
Klondike Nugget, opalescent white milk glass, smooth base, ground lip, original "Klondike" metal screw cap, 1890-1910, 5.625" h	75	100

	LOW	HIGH
Lady's Leg, "Brown & Drake Catawba Bitters, Binghampton N.Y.," yellowish root beer amber, iron pontil, applied mouth, 1855-60, 11.375" h	8000	12,000
Log Cabin, "Drake's Plantation Bitters, Patented 1862," yellow w/ amber tone, 4-log, smooth base, applied sloping collar mouth, 1862-70, 10" h	400	600
Log Cabin, "Holtzermann's Patent Stomach Bitters," amber, 4-roof, smooth base, tooled mouth, 9.875" h	200	300
Log Cabin, "Old Homestead Wild Cherry Bitters, Patent," medium amber, smooth base, applied sloping collar mouth, 1865-75, 9.625" h	275	375
Log Cabin, "Old Homestead Wild Cherry Bitters, Patent," yellow w/ olive tone, smooth base, applied sloping collar mouth, 1865-75, 9.75" h	1500	2200
Log Cabin, "Smokine, Imported and Bottled By Alfred Andersen & Co, The Western Importers, Minneapolis, Minn. And Winnipeg, Man., Smokine," reddish amber, smooth base, tooled lip, 1885-95, 6.625" h	275	375
Log Cabin, "St. Drake's 1860 Plantation X Bitters, Patented 1862," dark cherry puce, 6-log, smooth base, applied sloping collar mouth, 1862-70, 9.75" h	175	275
Log Cabin w/ Canoe, "H. H. Warner & Co - Tippecanoe," amber, "Pat. Nov 20 88, Rochester, N.Y." on smooth base, applied mouth, original tin "Warner's Safe Cure" loop, 1888-95, 9" h	75	100
Man on Barrel, turquoise blue, smooth base, tooled mouth, 20th C, 13.25" h	20	40
Moses, "Poland Water, Poland Mineral Spring Water (in banner around), PMSW (monogram), H. Ricker & Sons Proprietors," aqua, smooth base, applied sloping collar mouth, 1885-95, 11" h	125	175
Nightstick, yellow-olive, ground lip, original metal screw cap, 1885-1910, 10.5" h	125	150
Owl, clear, "Pat. Apd. For" on smooth base, tooled mouth, 1890-1910, 5" h	350	450
Pickle, medium emerald green, sheared and ground lip, 1890-1900, 4.5" l	75	125
Pig, "Good Old Bourbon In A Hogs" (arrow), golden amber, smooth base, tooled mouth, 1880-90, 6.75" l	200	300
Pineapple, bitters, medium amber, smooth base, applied double collar mouth, 1855-65, 8.875" h	150	200
Revolver, "Diamond Revolver" (on back of handle), medium amber, ground lip, original metal screw cap, 1890-1910, 8" l	50	75
Santa Claus, "M. C. Husted," clear, smooth base, tooled mouth, 1890-1910, 12.25" h	75	100
Shoe, black amethyst, smooth base, ground lip, original metal screw cap, original painted toe, 1890-1910, 3.625" h	100	130
Skull, "Poison, Pat. Appl'd For," deep cobalt blue, smooth base, tooled lip professionally repaired, 1890-1910, 4" h	700	900
Torpedo, "Eureka Spring Co., Saratoga, N.Y.," deep yellowish olive green, round bottom, smooth base, applied sloping double collar mouth, 1865-75, 9" l	700	900
Torpedo, "J. T. Brown, Chemist, Boston, Double Soda Water," deep sapphire blue, round bottom, smooth base, applied blob-type mouth, 1850-60, 8.75" l	600	900
Torpedo, "J. T. Brown, Chemist, Boston, Double Soda Water," teal blue-green, round bottom, smooth base, applied blob-type mouth, 1850-60, 9.125" l	250	350
Uncle Sam, clear, "Pat.' Apl'd For" on smooth base, ground lip, original metal high screw cap, 1890-1910, 9.5" h	50	75

Flasks

Glass flasks have a broad body and narrow neck, are usually for alcoholic beverages and are often fitted with a closure. Flask collectors search for examples from the early 1800s through the early 1900s. Before 1810, few glass containers were manufactured. Flasks with portraits of presidents or other politicians are highly sought. Many have been reproduced. Color is also an important consideration.

For a more extensive listing, see *American Bottles and Flasks and Their Ancestry* by Helen McKearin and Kenneth Wilson (Crown, NY, 1978), *The Official Price Guide to Bottles, Twelfth Edition,* by Jim Megura (House of Collectibles, Random House, New York, NY, 1998), and *Kovels' Bottles Price List, 11th Edition* by Ralph and Terry Kovel (Three Rivers Press, New York, NY, 1999).

	LOW	HIGH
Chestnut, bluish aqua, 10 diamond pattern, pontil scarred base, sheared lip, 1820-30, 4.625" h	$500	$700
Chestnut, deep tobacco amber, 10 diamond pattern, pontil scarred base, sheared lip, 1820-30, 5.75" h	700	900
Chestnut, medium amber, 24 broken rib pattern swirled to left, pontil scarred base, sheared lip, Midwestern, probably Zanesville, OH, 1820-30, 7.125" h	700	900
Chestnut, medium amber, 24 vertical rib pattern, pontil scarred base, sheared lip, Midwestern, 1820-30, 4.875" h	175	275
Chestnut, medium olive green, pontil scarred base, applied mouth, bubbles throughout, 1770-1800, 5.25" h	100	150
Chestnut, medium yellow-amber w/ olive tint, 10 diamond pattern, pontil scarred base, sheared lip, 1820-30, 4.875" h	1000	1500
Chestnut, olive yellow, 24 vertical rib pattern, pontil scarred base, sheared lip, Midwestern, 1820-30, 5.25" h	400	600
Chestnut, pale yellow-olive, 16 vertical rib pattern, pontil scarred base, sheared lip, Midwestern, 1820-30, 6" h	300	400
Chestnut, yellowish olive green, pontil scarred base, applied mouth, string of bubbles, small potstones, and impurities throughout, 1780-1800, 8.625" h	75	100
Corset Waist Scroll, bluish aqua, pint, pontil scarred base, sheared lip, Pittsburgh District, 1845-55	500	700
Flattened Chestnut, deep moss green, pontil scarred base, rolled lip, bubbles and paddle marks both sides, 1780-1820, 8.625" h	225	325
Flattened Chestnut, light straw yellow with olive tone, pontil scarred base, rolled lip, swirl lines throughout, 1780-1820, 8.625" h	200	300
Flattened Chestnut, medium yellowish olive amber, pontil scarred base, rolled lip, 1790-1830	150	185
Flattened Chestnut, medium yellow-olive, pontil scarred base, rolled lip, twisted misshapen neck and mouth, 1770-1800, 5.5" h	175	250
Flattened Chestnut, moss green, pontil scarred base, applied mouth, 1780-1820, 8.5" h	175	225
Grandfather Chestnut, orange amber, 24 vertical rib pattern, pontil scarred base, sheared and tooled lip, probably Zanesville, OH, 1820-30, 8.375" h	1000	1500
Historic, Cornucopia - Urn, medium olive amber, pint, pontil scarred base, sheared lip, 1825-35	75	100
Historic, Cornucopia - Urn, medium yellowish olive green, half pint, open pontil, sheared lip, 1825-35	300	400
Historic, Eagle - Cornucopia, pale citron, half pint, pontil scarred base, sheared lip, 1825-35	300	400
Historic, Eagle - Eagle, aqua, pint, pontil scarred base, sheared lip, Kensington Glassworks, 1820-30	175	275

	LOW	HIGH
Historic, Eagle - Eagle, deep blue-green, quart, pontil scarred base, sheared lip, pebbly w/ string of tiny bubbles and impurities throughout, 1825-35	700	900
Historic, Eagle - Eagle, eagle and "Pittsburgh PA" one side, eagle other side, medium emerald green, pint, smooth base, applied mouth, seedy, 1855-70	150	250
Historic, Eagle - Eagle, light yellow-green, pint, pontil scarred base, sheared lip, 1825-35	250	350
Historic, Eagle - Eagle, medium sapphire blue, pint, pontil scarred base, sheared lip, Louisville Glassworks, 1830-40	1800	2800
Historic, Eagle - Lyre, deep bluish aqua, pint, pontil scarred base, sheared lip, bold impression, 1.75" fold in glass on inside across lyre, 1825-35	600	900
Historic, Eagle - Masonic, "E. Pluribus Unum" in banner, eagle, and "IP" one side, Masonic arch other side, light blue-green, pint, pontil scarred base, sheared lip, 1815-25	275	375
Historic, Eagle w/ Banner, medium 7-Up green, calabash, iron pontil, applied sloping collar mouth, 1855-65	275	375
Historic, Hunter - Fisherman, copper puce, calabash, iron pontil, applied sloping collar mouth, 1855-65	200	300
Historic, Jenny Lind - Glass Works, "Jenny Lind" and bust of Jenny Lind one side, "Millfora G. Works" and glass works other side, aqua, calabash, pontil scarred base, applied sloping collar mouth, 1855-65	150	200
Historic, Lafayette - Clinton, "La Fayett," bust of Lafayette, and "T.S." one side, "De Witt Clinton," bust of Clinton, and "Coventry C.T." other side, yellowish olive amber, pint, pontil scarred base, sheared lip, 1825-35	375	475
Historic, Liberty Cap - Eagle, "B&W," aqua, pint, pontil scarred base, sheared lip, 1825-35	250	350
Historic, Pike's Peak - Eagle, "For Pike's Peak" and prospector one side, eagle and "Ceredo" other side, medium yellow-olive w/ amber tone, quart, smooth base, applied mouth, 1860-70	600	800
Historic, Sloop - Star, light blue-green, half pint, pontil scarred base, sheared lip, swirl lines (1 w/ string of unmelted sand), 1825-35	250	350
Historic, "Success to the Railroad" - Horse Pulling Cart, deep olive amber, pint, pontil scarred base, sheared lip, 1825-35	150	200
Historic, "Success to the Railroad" - Horse Pulling Cart, moss green, pint, pontil scarred base, sheared lip, bubbles throughout, 1825-35	275	375

Flasks, left to right: Eagle - Masonic Arch; Scroll; Jenny Lind - Glass Works Glasshouse calabash, Scroll, and Eagle - Masonic Arch. —Photo courtesy Glass-Works Auctions.

	LOW	HIGH
Historic, Taylor - Monument, "Genl. Taylor" and bust of Taylor one side, "Fell's Point" and monument other side, medium yellowish apple green, pint, pontil scarred base, sheared and slightly rolled-in lip, 1825-35	1500	1800
Historic, "Traveler's (star) Companion" - Sheaf of Wheat, medium amber, quart, smooth base, applied sloping collar mouth, whittle marks, 1855-70	150	250
Historic, Union - Eagle, "Union," clasped hands, and "Old Rye" one side, eagle, "A.&D.H.C." inside banner, and "Pittsburgh" other side, yellow-olive, quart, smooth base, applied mouth, 1860-70	500	700
Historic, Washington - Eagle, "General Washington," bust of Washington, and "Adams & Jefferson July 4 A.D. 1776, Kensington Glassworks Philadelphia, E. Pluribus Unum" one side, eagle and "T.W.D." other side, aqua, pint, pontil scarred base, sheared lip, 1820-30	200	300
Historic, Washington - Ship, "Albany Glass Works," bust of Washington, and "Albany N.Y." one side, ship on other side, bluish aqua, pint, pontil scarred base, applied double collar mouth, 1825-35	150	200
Historic, Washington - Taylor, "Bridgeton New Jersey" and bust of Washington one side, "Bridgeton New Jersey" and bust of Taylor other side, greenish aqua, quart, pontil scarred base, sheared lip, 1820-30	200	300
Historic, Washington - Taylor, "The Father of His Country" and bust of Washington one side, "Dyottville Glass Works Philada, Gen. Taylor Never Surrenders" and bust of Taylor other side, ice blue, pint, smooth base, applied mouth, 1850-60	50	75
Historic, Washington - Taylor, "The Father of His Country" and bust of Washington one side, "Dyottville Glass Works Philada, Gen. Taylor Never Surrenders" and bust of Taylor other side, light sapphire blue, pint, smooth base, sheared lip, 1850-60	300	400
Historic, Washington - Taylor, "The Father of His Country" and bust of Washington one side, "Genl. Taylor Never Surrenders" and bust of Taylor other side, deep cobalt blue, pint, open pontil, sheared lip, 1850-60	2500	3500
Letter "A" Scroll, bluish aqua pint, pontil scarred base, sheared lip, 1845-55	100	175
Pattern Molded Chestnut, aqua, 19 rib pattern swirled to right, pontil scarred base, applied string lip, seed bubbles throughout, 1800-20, 8" h	150	200
Pattern Molded Chestnut, medium amber, handled, 24 rib pattern swirled to right, pontil scarred base, applied lip ring and handle, 1840-50, 8.5" h	800	1200
Pitkin, light green, 30 broken rib pattern swirled to left, faint pontil scarred base, sheared lip, made in German half-post method, 1800-20, 5.875" h	300	400
Pitkin, medium emerald green, 16 broken rib pattern swirled to right, pontil scarred base, sheared lip, made in German half-post method, seed bubbles throughout, 1800-20, 6" h	375	475
Pitkin, smoky clear, 22 broken rib pattern swirled to right, pontil scarred base, sheared lip, made in German half-post method, 1800-20, 5.625" h	275	450
Scroll, deep root beer amber, pint, open pontil, sheared lip, 1845-55	375	475
Strapside, golden yellow-amber, quart, embossed safe in circle, smooth base, applied double collar mouth, light inside stain, 1885-95	100	175
Sunburst, deep bluish aqua, pint, pontil scarred base, sheared lip, 1820-30	175	275
Sunburst, deep yellowish root beer amber, pint, pontil scarred base, sheared lip, Baltimore, 1825-35	1500	2500
Sunburst, light bottle-glass green, pint, pontil scarred base, sheared lip, 1815-25	400	600
Sunburst, medium yellowish olive amber, half pint, "Keen - P&W," pontil scarred base, sheared lip, bubbles throughout, New England, 1810-20	300	400

Food and Beverage

	LOW	HIGH
"A. M. Bininger & Co, No 19 Broad St N.Y., Old London Dock Gin," root beer amber, smooth base, applied sloping collar mouth, 1855-65, 8" h	$125	$175
Autumn Whiskey, maple syrup, embossed cabin, tree, and cauldron w/ maple leaves around shoulder, clear, smooth base, tooled mouth, 1890-1910, 8.625" h	75	100
Berry, medium blue green, ribbed sides, smooth base, applied mouth, 1855-65, 11.25" h	200	300
"Blue Point Oysters American Oyster Co. New Haven, CT" paper label, clear, pint, smooth base, tooled mouth, 1905-15, 6.875" h	30	50
"Cooper Dairy, Half Pint Liquid," baby face milk bottle, clear, half pint, "Elmer, N.J." on smooth base, ABM lip with cap seat, 20th C	140	180
"Cop the Cream, Glenside Dairy, Deep Water, N.J., It Whips!," baby face milk bottle, clear, pint, smooth base, ABM lip w/ cap seat, 20th C	100	150
"E. N. Lewis Sarsaparilla Beer," deep bluish aqua, smooth base, applied mouth, 1870-80, 7" h	150	200
"Guilford Mineral, S. M. W. S. (inside circle) Guilford, VT, Spring Water," medium emerald green, quart, smooth base, applied sloping double collar mouth, tiny bubbles throughout, 1865-75	60	80
"John H. Gardner & Son, Sharon Springs N.Y., Sharon, Sulphur Water," teal blue, pint, smooth base, applied sloping double collar mouth, 1865-70	300	400
"Jumbo Brand (elephant) 2 Lbs, Peanut Butter, The Frank Tea & Spice Co, Cincinnati, O.," clear, smooth base, ABM lip, original wire bail handle and metal screw lid, 20th C, 5.875" h	35	50
"London Jockey Clubhouse Gin" (jockey running horse), dark olive amber, iron pontil, applied sloping collar mouth, 1855-65, 9.25" h	375	475
"M. B. Espy, Philada," aqua, iron pontil, rolled lip, 1850-60, 11.625" h	300	450
Peppersauce, deep aqua, roped corners, pontil scarred base, applied sloping collar mouth, 1845-55, 11" h	175	275
Peppersauce, yellow-green, 4-sided cathedral, smooth base, applied double collar mouth, 1855-65, 10.125" h	150	175
Petal, deep olive green, half gallon, iron pontil, applied mouth, 1855-65, 10.125" h	1800	2800
Pickle, deep blue-green, fluted shoulders and around base, large iron pontil, rolled lip, bubbles, 1845-65, 12.25" h	700	1000
Pickle, light apple green, 6-sided cathedral, smooth base, applied mouth, 1855-70, 13.5" h	250	350
"R. & F. Atmore," pickle, bluish aqua, 4-sided cathedral, smooth base, rolled lip, 1855-65, 11.375" h	200	300
"Saratoga Seltzer Water" around shoulder, deep teal blue, pint, smooth base, applied mouth, 1885-95	100	150
"Skilton, Foote & Co. Bunker Hill Pickles (around monument) Bunker Hill Brand," yellow-amber w/ hint of olive, 4-sided, smooth base, applied mouth, 1870-80, 6.625" h	125	175
"The American Ginger Ale, Coburn Lang & Co, Boston. Mass," aqua, smooth base, applied sloping collar mouth, 1865-75, 9.25" h	100	175
"Wells, Miller & Provost," deep aqua, open pontil, 1850-60, 12" h	400	550
"W. K. Lewis & Co, Boston," deep bluish aqua, iron pontil, applied mouth, 1850-60, 10.5" h	275	375

Ink Bottles, 2 umbrellas, 4 turtles, and "Harrison's Columbian Ink."

Fruit Jars, 3 Standard W. McC & Co. quarts and 3 Mason's pints.

Food Bottles, 3 cathedral pickles, another pickle bottle, and a peppersauce.
—Photos courtesy Glass-Works Auctions.

Fruit Jars

Nineteenth-century fruit jars for home canning are collected, especially those with the manufacturer's name or a decorative motif embossed on the jar. Before 1810, few glass containers were manufactured.

For further reading consult *The Collector's Guide to Old Fruit Jars: Red Book 8* by Douglas M. Leybourne, Jr. (published by author, North Muskegon, MI, 1997) and *The Guide to Collecting Fruit Jars, Vol. 3-1998* by Jerry McCann (published by author, Chicago, IL, 1997).

	LOW	HIGH
"American (eagle w/ flag) Fruit Jar," pale green, half gallon, smooth base, ground lip, original glass lid and lightning-type closure, 1885-95	$125	$175
"Atlas Strong Shoulder Mason," deep smoky cornflower blue, quart, smooth base and lip, original zinc screw lid, 1915-25	60	80
"Ball Perfect Mason," deep yellowish olive amber, quart, smooth base and lip, original zinc screw lid, 1915-25	55	75
"B.B.G.M. Co." (monogram), bluish aqua, quart, smooth base, ground lip, glass insert, zinc screw band	75	100
"Bloeser Jar," aqua, quart, smooth base, ground lip, original glass lid embossed "Pat Sept 27 1887," original metal closure, 1887-95	250	300
"Buckeye," bluish aqua, quart, smooth base, ground lip, original glass lid, reproduction metal closure, 1870-85	150	200
"Dexter" (inside wreath of fruit), aqua, midget, smooth base, ground lip, original glass insert, missing screw band, 1875-90	250	350
"Globe," medium golden amber, quart, "70" on smooth base, ground lip, "Patented May 25th 1886" on original glass lid, metal closure, 1886-90	50	75
"Griffin's Patent Oct 7 1862" on lid, bluish aqua, half gallon, smooth base, ground lip, original glass lid and metal closure, 1862-70	150	250
"Johnson & Johnson New York," deep cobalt blue, quart, smooth base, ground lip, "Made In U.S.A." on aqua glass lid, metal screw band, 1900-15	250	300
"Mason's (keystone in circle) Patent Nov 30th 1858," medium amber, quart, smooth base, ground lip, zinc screw lid, 1875-95	600	800
"Mason's Patent Nov 30th 1858," light sapphire blue, quart, smooth base, ground lip, zinc screw lid, 1875-95	150	250
"Mason's Patent Nov. 30th 1858," medium yellow green, oversized quart, smooth base, rough sheared and ground lip, zinc screw lid, 1875-95	125	175
"Mason's Patent Nov 30th 1858 N.C.L.," amber, quart, smooth base, ground lip, zinc screw lid, 1875-95	600	800
"Moore's Patent Dec 3d 1861," deep aqua, quart, smooth base, applied mouth, original "Patent, Dec. 3rd. 1861" glass lid and metal yoke, 1861-70	75	150
"Patd Dec 28th 1858 (eagle) Reisd June 16th 1858," aqua, quart, smooth base, ground lip, original glass lid and metal yoke, 1858-65	150	175
"Patd Feby 9th 1864 (banner) Reisd Jan 22D 1867," deep bluish aqua, quart, smooth base, ground lip, laid-on glass lid, 1867-75	175	225
"Stark Jar Patented," clear, quart, smooth base, smooth lip, original glass lid and spring-loaded metal closure, 1910-20	100	150
"The Ball Pat Apl'd For," aqua, quart, smooth base, ground lip, original metal lid and lightning-type closure, 1890-1900	275	375
"The Howe Jar Scranton PA," clear, quart, smooth base, ground lip, original glass lid embossed "Pat, Feby, 28 88" and wire closure, 1888-1900	60	80
"The King Pat. Nov. 2. 1860," aqua, quart, smooth base, ground lip, original glass lid and metal closure, 1860-70	200	300
"Trade Mark Lightning," yellow w/ hint of olive, quart, "Putnam" on smooth base, ground lip, original glass lid and lightning closure, 1877-90	200	300

Ink

	LOW	HIGH
Blown Three-Mold, olive amber, round, embossed geometric design all around, open pontil, applied disc mouth, 1820-35, 1.5" h	$200	$250
"Carter's" on base, medium cobalt blue, 6-sided, embossed clover leaf each side, smooth base, ABM lip, 1920-30, 3.875" h	150	200
Cone, medium amber, open pontil, rolled lip, 1845-55, 2.375" h	150	200
Cut Glass, canary yellow, polished base, 3 pen shelves, original brass hinged collar, probably Sandwich Glassworks, 1880-1900, 2.5" h	400	500
"David's," turtle, medium teal, smooth base, tooled lip, 1870-80, 1.75" h	350	450
"Dessauer's Jet Black Ink," turtle, bluish aqua, smooth base, ground lip, 1870-80, 2" h	150	200
"Harrison's Columbian Ink," aqua, 8-sided, pontil scarred base, rolled lip, 1845-55, 1.75" h	80	100
"Harrison's Columbian Ink," aqua, 12-sided, "Patent" on shoulder, pontil scarred base, applied mouth, 1845-55	200	275
"Hohenthal Brothers & Co Indelible Writing Ink, N.Y.," deep olive amber master ink, iron pontil, applied sloping collar mouth w/ pour spout, New England, 1845-55, 7" h	600	750
"J. & I. E. M.," medium yellow-olive, smooth base, tooled lip, 1870-80, 1.625" h	750	900
"N. J. Simond's, Lawrence, Mass" around shoulder, deep bluish aqua, pontil scarred base, applied sloping collar mouth w/ pour spout, bubbles throughout, 1845-55, 8" h	600	800
"Pat. March 1st 1870," barrel, smoky clear, smooth base, rolled lip, 1870-80, 2" h	70	90
Sandwich Type, clear w/ white and blue swirl pattern, inverted cup shape, pontil scarred base, original metal neck band and hinged lid, 1860-75, 3.625" h	1800	2000
"S. I. Comp," cottage, bluish aqua, smooth base, tooled mouth, 1885-95, 2.5" h	175	225
"S. O. Dunbar, Taunton, Mass.," aqua, pontil scarred base, applied sloping collar mouth, 1835-55, 5.625" h	80	100
Square, fiery opalescent powder blue milk glass, pontil scarred base, flared lip, 1810-20, 1.75" h	200	250
"Stafford's Ink," dark cherry puce, smooth base, applied mouth w/ pour spout, 1880-90, 7.75" h	850	1000
Umbrella, cobalt blue, 8-sided, pontil scarred base, rolled lip, 1845-55, 2.5" h	800	1000
Umbrella, deep bluish aqua, 12-sided, open pontil, rolled lip, 1845-55, 3" h	50	75
Umbrella, light blue-green, 12-sided, open pontil, rolled lip, 1845-55, 2.125" h	75	100
Umbrella, light emerald green, 8-sided, pontil scarred base, rolled lip, 1845-55, 2.5" h	125	150
Umbrella, medium blue-green, 8-sided, pontil scarred base, rolled lip, 1845-55, 2.25" h	100	150
"W. E. Boney," aqua, barrel, smooth base, applied mouth w/ pour spout, 1855-65, 5.125" h	150	175

Medicinal

	LOW	HIGH
"Alexanders Silameau," sapphire blue, pontil scarred base, applied mouth, 1845-55, 6.25" h	$700	$900
"Boswell & Warner's Colorific," opalescent milk glass, pontil scarred base, flared lip, 1855-65, 5.675" h	1200	1800
"Brown's Blood Treatment, Philadelphia," medium 7-Up green, "M. B. W. U.S.A." on smooth base, tooled lip, 1890-1910, 6.25" h	75	100
"By The King Royal Patent Granted To Robt Turlington For His Invented Balsam of Life, London, Jany 26 1754," bluish aqua, open pontil, rolled lip, 1835-45, 2.625" h	80	120
"C. Brinckerhoff's Health Restorative, Price $1.00, New York," medium olive green, pontil scarred base, applied sloping collar mouth, 1845-55, 7.25" h	400	600
"Craig's Kidney & Liver Cure Company," deep root beer amber, smooth base, applied double collar mouth, 1875-90, 9.625" h	150	200
"Dr. Eaton's Infantile Cordial, Church & Dupont, Sole Proprietors, New York," clear, open pontil, applied sloping collar mouth, 1845-55, 5" h	75	125
"Dr. Elmore's Rheumatine-Coutaline, The Only Remedy For Rheumatic Diseases, Best Remedy for Dyspepsia & Kidney, Liver, Bladder & Blood Disorders," medium amber, smooth base, tooled mouth, 1880-90, 9.75" h	175	250
"Dr. L. R. Parks Egyptian Anodyne," deep aqua, open pontil, rolled lip, 1845-55, 5.125" h	300	450
"Dr. Mitchell Ox Gall & Arnica Liniment," bluish aqua, open pontil, rolled lip, 1845-55, 4.625" h	100	175
"Dr. Perkins Syrup Albany," deep blue green, iron pontil, applied sloping collar mouth, seed bubbles throughout, 1845-55, 9.375" h	1000	1500
"Dr. Townsend's Sarsaparilla, Albany, N.Y.," deep emerald green, iron pontil, applied sloping collar mouth, 1845-55, 9.675" h	200	300
"E. Quirk's Inimitable Essence of Tyre For the Hair," clear, pontil scarred base, wide rolled lip, 1825-35, 4" h	150	200
"Gay's Compound Extract of Canchalagua, New York," bluish aqua, open pontil, flared lip, 1845-55, 6.25" h	150	200
"Holman's Natures Grand Restorative, J. B. Holman Prop, Boston Mass.," bluish aqua, pontil scarred base, applied mouth, 1845-55, 6.625" h	125	175
"I. Covert's Balm of Life," olive green, open pontil, applied sloping collar mouth, 1840-55, 6" h	1200	1600
"James Tarrant Druggist, New York," aqua, open pontil, applied sloping collar mouth, 1845-55, 5.5" h	75	100
"J. Grout," medium emerald green, pontil scarred base, rolled lip, 1845-55, 3.125" h	375	475
"L. Q. C Wishart's Pine Tree Tar Cordial, Phila, Patent (pine tree) 1859," medium blue-green, smooth base, applied mouth, 1860-70, 9.75" h	150	200
"Primley's Iron & Wahoo Tonic, Jones & Primley Co, Elkhart, Ind," yellowish olive green, "F. G. Mfg. Co" on smooth base, applied sloping double collar mouth, 1875-85, 9.5" h	500	700
"Rohrer's Expectoral Wild Cherry Tonic, Lancaster, PA," yellow amber, smooth base, applied sloping double collar mouth, 1855-65, 10.625" h	150	250
"Sanford's Radical Cure," cobalt blue, smooth base, applied mouth, 1875-85, 7.25" h	100	150
Swaim's Panacea, Philada," medium olive green shading to deeper at base, smooth base, applied sloping double collar mouth, 1855-65, 7.5" h	175	275
"U. S. A. Hosp. Dept.," medium cobalt blue, smooth base, flared lip, 1860-70, 4" h	400	600

Scent Bottles, left to right: Seahorse; Sunburst; Fleur-de-lis; Nailsea-type; Sunburst; Shield.

Poison Bottles, left to right: Cobalt blue coffin; Cobalt blue figural skull; and Golden amber w/ raised ridges.

Medicinal Bottles. —Photos courtesy Glass-Works Auctions.

Perfume

	LOW	HIGH
Atomizer, Lalique, frosted, "Danseuse Egyptiennes," black enameled molded frieze of dancing figures, c1930, 5" h	$550	$700
Cologne, light electric blue, 12-sided w/ sloped shoulders, smooth base, rolled lip, 1860-80, 6.125" h	70	100
Cologne, Nailsea type, smoky clear w/ white looping and deep aqua lip, pontil scarred base, sheared lip, applied rigaree, 1820-40, 3.25" h	250	300
Cologne, Sandwich, light smoky ice blue, herringbone corners, smooth base, tooled lip, 1855-75, 6.25" h	250	325
Cologne, white milk glass, vertical rib and star in banner pattern, smooth base, rolled lip, 1865-85, 5.75" h	100	150
Perfume, Czechoslovakian, clear, wide stepped base, elaborated oval stopper engraved and etched with kneeling woman gathering flowers, 8.25" h	175	250
Perfume, Guerlain, France, clear, "L'Heure Bleue," fluted and scroll design, paper label, fitted box, 2.75" h	50	80
Perfume, Lalique, clear and frosted, "Coeur Joie," heart-shaped bottle w/ embossed flowers, c1950, 5.75" h	300	400
Perfume, Schiaparelli, clear woman's torso form on frosted wave base, gold enameled stars, fringe, and ribbon, gilded stopper with green enameled "Zut," 4.75" h	200	300
Scent, aqua, pinwheel, pontil scarred base, rolled lip, 1845-55, 2.125" h	75	100
Scent, clear, sunburst, pontil scarred base, tooled lip, 3" h	75	100
Scent, medium cobalt blue, sunburst, pontil scarred base, tooled lip, 1850-60, 2.75" h	300	400

Poison

"16 oz," cobalt blue, fluted sides, smooth base, tooled mouth, 1890-1910, 8.375" h	$75	$100
"J. W. McBeath Kimberley Poison," cobalt blue, raised dots front and back, "W. T. & Co. U.S.A. Pat. Dec. 11. 1894" on smooth base, tooled lip, 5.375" h	250	350
"Poison," cobalt blue, 3-sided, raised hobnails, smooth base, sheared lip, 1910-12, 2.75" h	25	50
"Poison," cobalt blue, scalloped corners, smooth base, tooled lip, original label for "(skull and crossbones) Corrosive Sublimate Triangles," neck band, and cork, 1890-1910, 3.25" h	80	125
"Poison," yellow-amber, smooth base, tooled mouth, original label for "Antiseptic Disks, Sharpe & Dohme Baltimore," 1890-1910, 4.875" h	100	150
"Poison" embossed vertically, yellow-amber, "S & D" on smooth base, tooled lip, 1890-1910, 4.875" h	100	150
"Poison Mercury Bichloride Loeber Bros' New York (skull and crossbones)" on paper label, aqua, smooth base, tooled lip, 1885-1900, 2.25" h	75	100
"Poison - Poison," clear, smooth base, tooled lip, original label and contents for "Mercury Bichloride," 1890-1910, 2.625" h	70	90
"Poison (skull and crossbones) DP Poison," cobalt blue, coffin shape, scalloped corners, smooth base, tooled lip, 1890-1910, 3" h	700	900
"Poison (skull and crossbones) Poison," deep cobalt blue, smooth base, tooled lip, original label for "Antiseptic Tablets, Sharp & Dohme, Baltimore," 1910-20, 2" h	125	150

Whiskey, Collectible

Jim Beam bottle figural liquor containers were first issued in the 1950s. The company produces a variety of themes including the Executive Series, Regal China Series and Political Figures Series. Early Beam bottles made before the figural series are also collectible. In 1953, the company produced its first figural decanter. When the decanters sold well, Beam began producing decorative bottles on a large scale.

Ezra Brooks produces figural bottles with themes ranging from sports and transportation to antiques. The Antique Series includes an Edison phonograph and a Spanish cannon. Ezra Brooks rivals Jim Beam as one of the chief whiskey companies manufacturing figural bottles.

The Garnier Company began producing figural bottles in 1899. Those produced prior to World War II are scarce. Some of the better known include the Cat, 1930; Clown, 1910; Country Jug, 1937; and Greyhound, 1930.

	LOW	HIGH
Ballantine, Golf Bag	$3	$8
Ballantine, Seated Fisherman	5	10
Ballantine, Zebra	10	15
Ezra Brooks, Betsy Ross, 1975	10	15
Ezra Brooks, Brahma Bull, 1972	10	15
Ezra Brooks, Clown with Balloon, 1973	15	25
Ezra Brooks, Fireman, 1975	15	20
Ezra Brooks, Golden Eagle, 1971	20	25
Ezra Brooks, Great White Shark, 1977	10	15
Ezra Brooks, Harolds Club Dice, 1968	10	15
Ezra Brooks, Kachina Doll No. 8, 1979	50	75
Ezra Brooks, Keystone Cops, 1971	25	35
Ezra Brooks, Maine Lobster, 1970	15	20
Ezra Brooks, Moose, 1973	20	30
Ezra Brooks, North Carolina Bicentennial, 1975	10	15
Ezra Brooks, Red Fox, 1979	30	40
Ezra Brooks, Ski Boot, 1972	5	10
Ezra Brooks, Stagecoach, 1969	10	15
Ezra Brooks, West Virginia Mountaineer Lady, 1972	15	20
Garnier, Apollo, 1969	15	25
Garnier, Baby Trio, 1963	5	10
Garnier, Bluebird, 1970	10	15
Garnier, Christmas Tree, 1956	45	55
Garnier, Giraffe, 1961	15	25
Garnier, Grenadier, 1949	45	55
Garnier, Napoleon on Horseback, 1969	10	15
Garnier, Rocket, 1958	5	10
Garnier, Rolls Royce 1908, 1970	15	25
Garnier, Teapot, 1961	10	15
Garnier, Water Pitcher, 1965	5	10
Jim Beam, Barry Berish, Executive Series, 1985	65	85
Jim Beam, Boris Godinov, Opera Series, 1978	150	200
Jim Beam, Cable Car, Transportation Series, 1983	20	40
Jim Beam, Camaro, Automobile Series, silver, 1969	75	100
Jim Beam, Donkey Clown, Political Series, 1968	2	5
Jim Beam, Dusenburg Convertible Coupe, Automobile Series, gray	150	200
Jim Beam, French Cradle Telephone, Telephone Pioneers of America Series, 1979	15	25
Jim Beam, Golden Jubilee, Executive Series, 1977	8	12

Jim Beam Bottles, left to right: Duesenburg Roadster, 1935, $121 at auction; 1929 Model T Police Car, $66 at auction. —Photos courtesy Collectors Auction Services.

	LOW	HIGH
Jim Beam, Honga Hika, Maori Warriors, 1980	150	200
Jim Beam, Idaho, Regal China, 1963	30	50
Jim Beam, Kentucky Derby 97th Run for the Roses, 1971	5	10
Jim Beam, Mephistopheles, Opera Series, 1979	100	150
Jim Beam, Mercedes, Automobile Series, white, 1974	25	40
Jim Beam, Mr. Goodwrench, General Motors, 1978	25	30
Jim Beam, Nebraska Football, 1972	3	8
Jim Beam, Northern Pike, National Fresh Water Fishing Hall of Fame, 1977	10	15
Jim Beam, One Hundred First Airborne Division, Screaming Eagles, 1977	5	10
Jim Beam, Pennsylvania, Keystone State, Regal China, 1967	3	5
Jim Beam, Pony Express, 1968	5	10
Jim Beam, Presidential, Executive Series, 1968	5	10
Jim Beam, Ram, w/ calendar and thermometer, Regal China, 1958	50	75
Jim Beam, Robin, Regal China, 1969	5	8
Jim Beam, Short-Timer, armed forces commemorative, 1975	15	20
Jim Beam, Shriners Pyramid, El Kahir Temple of Cedar Rapids, IA, 1975	10	15
Jim Beam, Statue of Liberty, 1975	5	10
Jim Beam, St. Bernard, 1979	25	30
Jim Beam, Texas Rose, Executive Series, 1978	10	15
Jim Beam, Tiffany Poodle, 1973	10	18
Jim Beam, Trout Unlimited, Trout Unlimited Conservation Organization, 1977	10	15
Jim Beam, Wood Duck, Ducks Unlimited, 1975	30	50
J. W. Dant, California Quail	3	6
J. W. Dant, Indianapolis 500	5	10
J. W. Dant, Ring-Necked Pheasant	3	6
J. W. Dant, Washington Crossing the Delaware	2	5
J. W. Dant, Wrong-Way Charlie	10	15
Luxardo, Calypso Girl, 1962	10	15
Luxardo, Cherry Basket, 1960	10	15
Luxardo, Dolphin, 1959	30	40
Luxardo, Golden Fakir, 1961	15	25
Luxardo, Gondola, 1959	10	15
Luxardo, Pheasant, Murano, 1960	25	30
Luxardo, Puppy, Murano, 1960	15	20
Luxardo, Squirrel, 1968	30	40
Luxardo, Tower of Fruit, 1968	10	15
McCormick, Charles Lindbergh, Famous American Portrait Series	15	20
McCormick, Gambel's Quail, Bird Series, 1982	35	45

Left: Luxardo, Basket of Fruit, 1969, $15.

Right: Ski Country, Chukar Partridge, Game Birds, 1979, $20.

	LOW	HIGH
McCormick, Hank Williams Sr., Country and Western Series, 1980	50	75
McCormick, Huck Finn, Literary Series, 1980	15	20
McCormick, Hutchinson Kansas Centennial, 1972	15	25
McCormick, Iowa Hawkeyes, Football Mascots, 1974	60	75
McCormick, Jupiter Engine, Train Series, 1969	15	20
McCormick, Kansas City Royals, Sports Series, 1971	10	15
McCormick, Largemouth Bass, 1982	20	30
McCormick, Paul Bunyan, 1979	25	30
McCormick, Will Rogers, 1977	10	15
Old Commonwealth, Chief Illini No. 3, 1979	50	65
Old Commonwealth, Coal Miner No. 2, 1982	20	25
Old Commonwealth, Golden Retriever, 1979	25	30
Old Commonwealth, Modern Hero No. 1, Modern Firefighters Series, 1982	40	50
Old Commonwealth, Rebel Yell Rider, 1970	15	20
Old Commonwealth, South Carolina Tricentennial, 1970	10	15
Old Commonwealth, Western Boot, 1982	5	10
Old Fitzgerald, Blarney Castle, 1970	5	10
Old Fitzgerald, California Bicentennial, 1970	10	15
Old Fitzgerald, Hillbilly, 1954	40	50
Old Fitzgerald, Man O' War, 1969	2	5
Old Fitzgerald, Pilgrim's Landing, 1970	10	15
Ski Country, Black Swan, Birds, miniature	20	25
Ski Country, Bobcat Family, Animals	45	55
Ski Country, Bull Rider, Rodeo	30	35
Ski Country, Elephant on Drum, Circus	20	30
Ski Country, Holstein Cow, Domestic Animals	30	40
Ski Country, Mountain Sheep, Grand Slam, miniature	25	30
Ski Country, Osprey Hawk, Hawks, miniature	75	90
Ski Country, Penguin Family, Birds	30	45
Ski Country, Prairie Chicken, Game Birds	40	50
Ski Country, Rainbow Trout, Fish	40	50
Ski Country, Screech Owl Family, Owls	60	75
Ski Country, Scrooge, Christmas	30	40
Ski Country, Tom Thumb, Circus, miniature	15	20

Boxes

During the eighteenth and nineteenth centuries, Americans used boxes as utiltarian items. They made specialized boxes for a wide variety of purposes, from containers for food to storage of wedding dresses. Small boxes, for trinkets, matches or cigarettes, are some of the most collectible.

	LOW	HIGH
Book, carved pine, book-shaped, incised w/ hearts and geometric symbols, painted dark brown, 19th C, 7" l, 4.25" w, 1.5" d	$400	$500
Candle, pine w/ old dark red repaint over original green paint, double well, shaped crest with hole cut out for hanging, 14.25" w, 23.5" h	400	600
Comb, pine, hanging, trapezoidal w/ shaped backboard and wire loop hanger, early 19th C, 6" h, 5" w	1200	1500
Decorated, curly maple, dovetailed construction, academy-painted decoration w/ pink and green floral and seashell design, "Maria" in banner on back, bun feet, mid-19th C, 9.75" w, 3.5" h	3500	4500
Decorated, dovetailed construction w/ slide top, grain painted w/ yellow borders, stenciled fruit, mid 19th C, 8.25" l, 5.25" h	1750	2500
Decorated, walnut, hinged lid, scratch-carved design w/ 2 American flags flying upside down and inscription "J. C. Wettenmann, Union Box" on lid and "1874" on front panel, 13" l	300	400
Document, pine, paint decorated w/ red swags, red and black cardinal, and abstract foliate designs, light green ground, early 19th C, 11" w, 5" h	3500	5000
Jewelry, gilt cast white metal, Art Nouveau, hinged lid, embossed design w/ woman's head and flowers, scroll feet, fabric lining, 5.75" sq, 4.75" h	50	100
Knife, pine w/ traces of old red paint, dovetailed, cut out handle, 14" l	125	175
Sewing, tramp art, wooden, oblong, hinged lid, applied molding on lid and sides, brass tack decoration, removable tray w/ cutout handle and pincushions, c1900, 18.75" l, 6" h	150	300
Shaker, pine, oval, 3-finger construction, 10.5" l, 4" h	300	400
Tea Caddy, turned fruitwood, pear-shaped, original escutcheon, 18th C, 6.5" h	1200	1500
Trinket, inlaid wood veneer, landscape scene on hinged lid, ivory bun feet, signed in ink "C. A. Johansson," 6.75" l	150	225

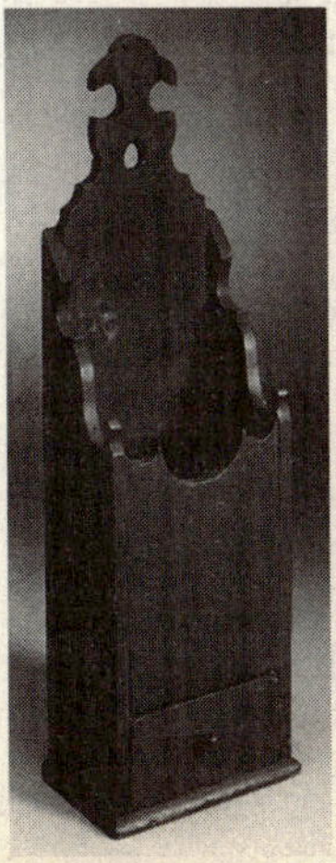

Left: Pipe Box, red-washed pine, early 19th C, 21.25" h, $2990 at auction.

Below: Shaker, maple and pine, nine-lap construction, mid-19th C, 19.75" l, $748 at auction.

—Photos courtesy Skinner, Inc., Boston, MA.

Cameras

Louis Daguerre invented the first commercial camera in 1839. For the next 30 years nearly all cameras were for professional studios. During the 1870s amateur photography bloomed. The cameras of the late nineteenth century were generally large and bulky box cameras and bellows cameras. But strange and sometimes bizarre novelty cameras also appeared, including cameras designed in the forms of pocket watches, canes, and even neckties. In 1888 the Eastman Dry Plate and Film Company introduced the first commercially available roll film camera, the Kodak. They followed it with the No. 1 Kodak the next year. Soon the Eastman Kodak Company came to dominate the American market. The hundreds of various cameras produced under the Kodak name outstrip any other maker's production record.

Collectors want cameras that are complete and in working order. Some allowance is made for the fragility of leather bellows and rubber parts. For further information see *The Price Guide to Antique and Classic Cameras, 1997–1998, 10th Edition,* edited by Jim and Joan McKeown (Centennial Photo Service, Grantsbury, WI, 1997).

Assorted

	LOW	HIGH
Accuraflex, 1950s	$75	$125
Acro	15	20
Adlake Repeater	50	75
Adox 300	150	250
Adox Golf	20	35
Adox Polomat	20	30
Adox Sport	25	50
Agfa-Ansco Captain	20	30
Agfa-Ansco Major	15	20
Agfa-Ansco Pioneer	15	20
Agfa-Ansco Shur-Shot Special	5	10
Agfa Autostar X-126	5	10
Agfa Billy	25	35
Agfa Billy Record 4.5	25	35
Agfa Box 24	30	40
Agfa Click I	5	10
Agfaflex I	75	125
Agfaflex 2000 Pocket	5	10
Agfa Isolar	50	75
Agfa Isolette I	20	30
Agfa Karat 4.5	30	40
Agfa Nitor	50	75
Agfa Paramat	30	40
Agfa Selecta	50	60
Agfa Standard	50	75
Agfa Synchro-Box	5	10
Agilux Agiflex I	75	125
Agilux Colt 44	5	10
Air King Aires 35-IIIC	50	75
Air King Airesflex Z	75	125
Air King Viscount	25	50

	LOW	HIGH
American Camera Mfg. Co., Buckeye No. 2	$75	$100
Ansco Admiral	5	10
Ansco Arrow	25	35
Ansco Bear Photo Special	75	125
Ansco Bingo No. 2	25	35
Ansco Buster Brown No. 2, folding	15	25
Ansco Cadet Flash	5	10
Ansco Century of Progress	75	125
Ansco Flash Champion	5	10
Ansco Folding No. 3	15	25
Ansco Goodwin, box	10	15
Ansco Junior Model A	25	40
Ansco Kiddie Camera	15	25
Ansco Panda	5	10
Ansco Pioneer	5	10
Ansco Readyflash	5	10
Ansco Rediflex	15	25
Ansco Royal No. 1A	25	50
Ansco Shur-Shot Jr.	5	10
Ansco Speedex Special R	50	75
Ansco Sundial	25	35
Ansco Vest Pocket No. 1	25	35
Ansco Viking Readyset	15	20
Anthony Bijou	250	400
Anthony Fairy	300	500
Anthony Klondike	75	125
Argus 75	5	10
Argus A, black	25	35
Argus A3	25	35

	LOW	HIGH
Argus C	.50	65
Argus FA	.35	50
Argus Model M	.50	75
Argus SLR	.75	100
Arnold Karma Sport	.500	750
Asahi Auto Takumar, 55mm, f2.0	.25	50
Asahi Letix	.75	100
Asahi Pentax Auto 110, brown	.300	500
Asahi Pentax K2	.100	150
Asahi Pentax ME Super	.100	150
Asahi Pentax MV-1	.75	100
Asahi Pentax S	.125	175
Asahi Super Takumar, 28mm, f3.5	.75	100
Balda-Werk Baldamatic II	.50	75
Balda-Werk Erkania	.25	40
Balda-Werk Glorina	.50	75
Balda-Werk Juventa	.25	50
Balda-Werk Lady Debutante	.15	20
Balda-Werk Micky Rollbox	.50	75
Balda-Werk Poka II	.25	35
Balda-Werk Springbox	.50	75
Balda-Werk Super Baldinette	.75	100
Beauty Super-L	.125	175
Belca-Werk Belmira	.25	50
Bell & Howell Autoload 340	.5	10
Bell & Howell Electric Eye 127	.15	20
Berning Robot I	.250	350
Berning Robot Junior	.150	200
Birdseye Flash	.5	10
Blair Baby Hawk-Eye	.250	350
Blair No. 3 Folding Hawk-Eye Model 3	.50	75
Blair No. 3 Weno Hawk-Eye	.25	50
Bolsey I	.150	250
Bolsey B2	.25	40
Bolsey Reflex Model G	.250	400
Bower 35	.25	50
Braun Gloria	.50	75
Braun Imperial Box 6x9	.25	35
Braun Norica III	.25	50
Braun Pax	.15	20
Braun Paxette IIB	.50	75
Braun Paxette Reflex	.50	75
Braun Reporter	.25	40
Brinkert Efbe	.75	125
Brückner Field Camera	.200	300
Burke & James 1A Rexo Jr.	.15	20
Burke & James Columbia 35	.50	75
Burke & James Cub	.15	20
Butcher Cameo	.50	75
Butcher Clincher	.25	50
Butcher Dandycam Automatic	.500	1000

	LOW	HIGH
Butcher Klimax	.25	50
Butcher Little Nipper	.75	100
Butcher Maxim No. 2	.25	50
Butcher Midget	.75	100
Butcher National	.300	500
Butcher Pilot No. 2	.50	75
Butcher Primus No. 1	.75	125
Butcher Watch Pocket Klimax	.75	125
Butler Cadet	.100	125
Butler Universal	.15	20
Camera Corp. Perfex DeLuxe	.50	75
Camera Corp. Perfex One-O-One	.50	75
Camera Corp. President	.15	20
Camera Corp. Silver King	.25	50
Canon 1950	.2000	3000
Canon AT-1	.100	150
Canon Canomatic C-30	.25	40
Canon Canomatic M70	.25	50
Canon Dial 35	.75	100
Canon EX-EE	.75	125
Canon F-1	.250	400
Canonflex RP	.100	150
Canon FP	.75	125
Canon IIA	.200	300
Canon IID2	.250	400
Canon IIS	.300	500
Canon L-1	.300	500
Canon P, black	.3000	4500
Canon P, chrome	.200	400
Canon Pellix QL	.150	200
Canon Snappy '84	.40	65
Canon TX	.75	100
Canon VL-2	.300	400
Capitol 120	.25	40
Capital MX-II	.5	10
Carl Ziess Jena Werra V	.75	100
Century Grand	.175	250
Century Petite	.150	200
Certex Digna	.25	40
Certo Certix	.15	35
Certo Dolly Vest Pocket	.75	125
Certo Durata	.25	50
Certoplat	.50	75
Certo Six	.75	125
Certosport	.50	65
Certo Super Dollina	.75	125
Certotrop, brown	.200	300
Chicago Mandelette	.75	125
Chiyodo Chiyoko	.50	75
Chuo Harmony	.25	35
CIA Stereo	.150	250
Cima 44	.25	40
Cima Luxette	.25	50
Cinex Deluxe	.5	10

	LOW	HIGH
Ciro 35	25	50
Ciroflex	40	60
Citex	10	15
Civica PG-1	15	25
Classic III, Japan	40	50
CMF Argo	25	50
CMF Delta	25	50
CMF Gabri	25	50
CMF Robi	20	35
Collegiate No. 3	50	75
Colorflash Deluxe	5	10
Columbia Pecto No. 5	125	175
Conley Kewpie Box No. 2	15	20
Conley Magazine	50	75
Conley Snap No. 2	25	50
Conley Truphoto No. 2	40	60
Contessa Adoro	50	80
Contessa Alino	50	75
Contessa Cocarette	25	50
Contessa Cocarette Luxus	250	350
Contessa Donata	75	100
Contessa Duchessa	250	350
Contessa Miroflex	300	450
Contessa Onito	50	75
Contessa Sonnar	75	100
Contessa Taxo	50	75
Contessa Tessco	50	80
Continental Insta-Load I	40	65
Coronet Ajax, black	15	25
Coronet Ajax, blue	50	75
Coronet Ambassador	15	20
Coronet Box	5	15
Coronet Cameo	75	125
Coronet Captain	15	20
Coronet Commander 2	2	6
Coronet Consul	20	30
Coronet Conway Super Flash	25	30
Coronet Cub	15	25
Coronet Eclair Box	15	20
Coronet Eclair Lux	35	50
Coronet Fildia	15	20
Coronet Flashmaster	15	20
Coronet Polo	15	20
Coronet Rapier	30	40
Coronet Rex	10	15
Coronet Twelve-20	15	20
Coronet Victor	15	20
Coronet Vogue	125	175
Crest-Flex	15	20
Crestline Empire-Baby	4	8
Crown Camera	25	50
Cruver-Peters Crystar	50	75
Cruver-Peters Sister	125	175
Dacora I	20	30

	LOW	HIGH
Dacora Daci Royal	15	20
Dacora Digna	4	8
Dacora Dignette	15	20
Dacora Royal	50	75
Dacora Super Dignette	15	25
Dai-Ichi Semi Primo	75	100
Dai-Ichi Waltax I	50	75
Dai-Ichi Waltax Acme	300	400
Dallmeyer Correspondent	300	400
Dallmeyer Snapshot	50	75
Dame, Stoddard & Kendall Hub	25	50
Dan 35 Model I	250	350
Dave Box	10	15
Defiance Auto Fixt Focus	50	75
DeJur-Amsco DeJur D-1	15	25
Dekon SR	100	150
Demaria Dehel	25	50
Demaria Telka II	75	100
Demaria Telka X	20	30
Detrola A	25	35
Detrola HW	25	50
Detrola KW	15	30
Diamond Jr.	75	100
Diana Deluxe	2	8
Dionne F2	2	8
Dover 620A	15	20
Drexel Jr. Miniature	25	35
Druopta Corina	20	30
Druopta Efekta	25	50
Druopta Vega II	50	75
Dufa Fit	25	50
Durst 66	25	50
Durst Duca	100	125
Eclipse 120	2	8
Eho-Altissa Altiflex	75	100
Eho-Altissa Altissa II	50	75
Eho-Altissa Altix IV	25	50
Eho-Altissa Eho Box	75	125
Eho-Altissa Super Altissa	75	100
Eiko Can Camera	40	60
Eiko-Do Ugein Model III A	75	100
Eiko Popular	25	50
Elbow Flex	75	100
Eldon	15	20
Elflex Deluxe	15	20
Elgin Miniature	2	8
Elmoflex	75	100
Emerald Box	15	20
Empire 120	2	8
Empire Scout	2	8
Emson	25	50
Encore De Luxe	25	50
Encore Hollywood	25	50
Enterprise Little Wonder	100	150

	LOW	HIGH
Ernemann Bob 0	50	75
Ernemann Bob I	50	75
Ernemann Bob II	50	75
Ernemann Bob III, vertical	25	50
Ernemann Bobette II	150	200
Ernemann Heag 0	40	60
Ernemann Heag III	50	75
Ernemann Heag VI	300	400
Ernemann Heag XII	50	75
Ernemann Heag XVI	175	250
Ernemann Liliput	75	100
Ernemann Rolf I	50	75
Ernemann Simplex Ernoflex	350	500
Ernemann Unette	175	250
Essex	2	8
Ettelson Mickey Mouse	100	150
Excella	25	50
Expo Easy Load	75	100
Falcon Miniature	10	15
Falcon Miniature Deluxe	25	40
Falcon Rocket	10	15
FAP Norca B	75	125
FAP Rower	50	75
Federal Fed-Flash	10	15
Fed Micron	50	75
Feinwerk Technik Mec 16 SB	75	125
Ferrania Alfa	25	35
Ferrania Box	40	60
Ferrania Condor Junior	75	125
Ferrania Elioflex	40	60
Ferrania Eura	10	15
Ferrania Lince 2	25	50
Ferrania Tanit	25	50
Fex 4.5	25	50

	LOW	HIGH
Fex Delta	20	30
Fex Graf	20	30
Fex Juni-Boy 6x6	15	20
Fex Rubi-Fex 4x4	15	20
Fex Sport-Fex	15	20
Fex Super-Boy, plastic	15	20
Fex Superfex	25	50
Fex Ultra-Fex	25	50
Fex Uni-Fex	15	20
Filma Box	25	50
Finetta-Werk Finetta 88	75	100
Finetta-Werk Finette	25	50
Fischer Nikette	150	200
Five Star Candid Camera	10	15
Flash Candid Flash	10	15
Foitzik Reporter	50	75
Folmer & Schwing Sky Scraper	300	450
Foster Swiftshot Model A	25	50
Foth Derby II	75	100
Foth-Flex	100	150
Fotima Reflex	50	75
Foto-Flex	10	20
Foto-Quelle Revue 3	40	60
Foto-Quelle Revue Mini-Star	50	75
Fototecnica Bandi	50	75
Fototecnica Eaglet	10	20
Fototecnica Rayelle	10	20
Franka-Werk Bonafix	25	50
Franka-Werk Frankarette	75	100
Franka-Werk Rolfix	25	50
Franke & Heidecke Rollei A26	75	100
Franke & Heidecke Rollei E110	125	175
Franke & Heidecke Rolleiflex Automat MX-EVS	175	250

Ernemann Heag VI

Leitz Leicaflex SL2

—Photos courtesy Auction Team Köln.

	LOW	HIGH
Franke & Heidecke Rolleiflex Grey Baby	200	300
Franke & Heidecke Rolleiflex Standard, new	125	175
Franke & Heidecke Rolleiflex Standard, old	100	125
Franke & Heidecke Rolleimagic	150	200
Franke & Heidecke Rollei Pocketline	15	25
Franke & Heidecke Rollei XF 35	40	60
Franks Presto	40	60
Frati 120	25	50
Fuji Fotojack	20	30
Fuji Fujicarex II	75	100
Fuji Rapid S	25	50
Fujita Classic 35 IV	50	75
Futura-P	75	100
Galter Hopalong Cassidy Camera	25	50
Genos Special	25	50
Gerlach Ideal Color 35	25	50
Gerlach Trixette	75	100
Ginrei Koki Vesta	75	125
Global	25	50
Gnome Baby Pixie	25	50
Gnome Pixie	15	20
Goerz Box Tengor	25	50
Goerz Coat Pocket Tenax	75	100
Goldstein Camping Box	15	20
Goldstein Goldty Metabox	15	30
Goldstein Olympic	25	50
Graflex 22	25	50
Graflex Graphic 35	25	50
Graflex Stereo Graphic	100	150
Hall Mirror Reflex	175	250
Hamco	25	50
Hamilton Super-Flex	15	20
Hanimex Standard 120 Box	15	20
Hanna-Barbera Yogi Bear	15	30
Herbert George Davy Crocket	50	75
Herbert George Flick-N-Flash	2	8
Herbert George Imperial Debonair	2	8
Herbert George Insta-Flash	2	8
Herbert George Official Scout	20	30
Houghton Autorange 220 Ensign	100	150
Houghton Coronet	200	350
Houghton Empress	400	500
Houghton Pocket Ensign	20	30
Houghton Vest Pocket Ensign	75	100
ICA Alpha	75	125
ICA Corrida	50	75
ICA Lloyd	50	75
ICA Reporter	125	175
ICA Teddy	50	75
ICA Trix	75	100
Ihagee Derby	25	50
Ihagee Exakta VX 1000	100	150
Ihagee Parvola	100	125
Ilford Sportsmaster	35	50
Imperial Deluxe Six-Twenty Twin Lens Reflex	2	8
Impulse Voltron Starshooter 110	25	50
Indo Impera	2	8
Indo Safari	15	20
Ising Isoflex I	25	35
Ising Puck	75	125
Kalimar A	25	50
Kalimar Six Sixty	125	175
Kemper Kenflex	50	75
Kershaw 110	15	25
Kershaw 450	25	50
Kershaw Raven	50	75
Kiddie Clown	50	75
Kiev 35A	75	100
Kigawa Kiko Semi	75	125
King Dominant	20	30
King Regula	50	75
King Regula Reflex SL	75	100
Kinn Kinax Baby	25	50
Kinon SC-1	2	8
Kochmann Reflex-Korelle	100	150
Konishiroku Baby Pearl	125	175
Konishiroku Konica II	75	125
Konishiroku Konica Auto S	50	75
Konishiroku Konilette 35	50	75
Konishiroku Rapid Omega 100	125	175
Konishiroku Snappy	175	225
Kowa SE	25	50
Krauss Rollette	50	75
Krauss Rollette Luxus	150	200
Krüeger Delta	125	175
Kuribayashi Petri 2.8 Color Super	10	20
Kuribayashi Petri Flex Seven	175	250
Kuribayashi Petri Push-Pull 110	25	50
Kuribayashi Petri RF	125	175
Kuribayashi Petri Seven S-11	15	30
K.W. Astraflex 35	100	125
K.W. Pilot 6	125	175
K.W. Praktica	50	75
K.W. Praktica IVBM	75	100
K.W. Prakticamat	50	75
K.W. Praktica Nova B	30	50
Leitz Leica If	300	400
Leitz Leicaflex SL2	1200	1800
Leitz Leica M3, olive	4000	5000
Leitz R3 Mot	400	500
Life-O-Rama III	20	30
Light Seagull No. 203	50	75

	LOW	HIGH
Lumiere Box No. 49	15	20
Lumiere Lumirex	25	35
Lumiere Optax	125	175
Lumiere Scout-Box	15	20
Macy M-16	15	20
Mansfield Automatic 127	10	15
Mar-Crest	2	8
Mason Companion	175	250
May Fair Box	15	25
Metropolitan Cardinal 120	15	20
Metropolitan Clix Deluxe	2	8
Minolta 16 Model I, fold	150	225
Minolta 16 Model P	25	50
Minolta 24 Rapid	75	100
Minolta A3	50	75
Minolta Autopress	250	400
Minolta Autowide	75	100
Minolta Baby Minolta	125	175
Minolta Electro Shot	40	60
Minolta Hi-Matic	50	75
Minolta Semi Minolta II	75	100
Minolta SR-1X	75	100
Minolta Uniomat III	50	75
Minolta XK	300	450
Minox III	200	300
Minox EC	150	200
Miranda Fv, chrome	75	125
Miranda Sensorex II	50	75
Monarch 620	15	25
Monroe No. 5	125	175
Monroe Sales Color-flex	50	75
Montgomery Ward Wardflex II	100	150
Nippon Nikkormat FT	75	125
Nippon Nikon FE	200	300
Nippon Nikon SP, black, motor drive	5000	6500

Nippon Nikon SP. —Photo courtesy Auction Team Köln.

	LOW	HIGH
Nishida Apollo 120	75	100
Nishida Mikado	50	75
Norton	25	50
Olympic Vest Olympic	125	175
Olympus 35 I	75	125
Olympus 35 IV	50	75
Olympus Auto	50	75
Olympus Chrome Six IV	150	200
Olympus Flex A3.511	100	150
Olympus OM-2 MD	150	225
Olympus Pen	75	100
Olympus Six	175	250
Orion No. 142	2	5
Pentacon Contax F	75	125
Pentacon FM	40	50
Pentacon Hexacon	125	175
Polaroid 110 Pathfinder	50	75
Polaroid 800	5	15
Polaroid Camel	125	175
Polaroid Swinger Model 20	1	2
Polaroid Swinger Sentinel M15	2	8
Remington Miniature	2	8
Revere Automatic-1034	2	8
Revere Eyematic EE 127	25	50
Ricoh 35	25	50
Ricoh Auto 35-V	25	50
Ricoh Auto Shot	25	50
Ricoh Singlex II	75	125
Ricoh Six	75	100
Ricoh Super 44	75	125
Rochester Cyclone Senior	40	50
Rochester Gem Poco	75	100
Rochester Ideal	200	300
Rochester Magazine Cyclone	75	100
Rochester Monitor	200	300
Rochester Pocket Premo	50	75
Rolls Picta Twin 620	15	25
Rolls Twin 620	15	25
Rondo Colormatic	25	35
Royal 35M	75	100
Royer A	20	30
Ruberg Little Wonder	75	100
Ruberg & Renner Baby Ruby	50	75
Ruberg & Renner Hollywood	25	50
Sears Delmar	25	50
Sears Marvel-flex	25	50
Sears Tower 23	200	300
Sears Tower 127EF	40	60
Sears Tower Junior	30	50
Sears Tower Phantom	2	8
Sears Tower Skipper	5	10
Sears Tower Snappy	10	15
Spartus 35F	15	20
Spartus Cinex	15	20

	LOW	HIGH
Spartus Super R-1	5	10
Spartus Vanguard	5	10
Spencer Majestic	2	8
Standard No. 2	25	50
Starflex	100	150
Star-Lite	25	50
Sunbeam Six Twenty	15	25
Thornton-Pickard Imperial Pocket	50	75
Thornton-Pickard Puck Special	75	125
Thornton-Pickard Royal Ruby	500	750
Thornton-Pickard Ruby Reflex	200	400
Tokyo Minion	125	175
Tokyo Topcon Auto 100	30	60
Tougodo Click	25	50
Tougodo Hobix Junior	40	60
Tougodo Kino-44	125	175
Tougodo Meikal EL	15	20
Tougodo Metraflex II	75	125
Tougodo Tougo	20	30
Underwood Instanto	200	400
Underwood Verax Superb	25	50
Universal Buccaneer	20	30
Universal Girl Scout Model AF Univex	250	350
Universal Iris Deluxe	25	50
Universal Meteor	2	8
Universal Roamer I	15	20
U.S. Camera Corp. Auto Fifty	50	75
U.S. Camera Corp Vagabond 120 Eveready Flash	2	8
Utility Falcon	15	20
Utility Falcon Model F	25	35
Utility Girl Scout Falcon	40	60
Varsity Model V	25	50
Voigt Junior Model 1	25	50
Voigtländer Bergheil, green	250	375

	LOW	HIGH
Voigtländer Bessa II, Apo-Lanthar	3000	4000
Voigtländer Box	30	50
Voigtländer Dynamatic	50	75
Voigtländer Heliar Reflex	250	350
Voigtländer Perkeo I	50	80
Voigtländer Ultramatic	200	300
Voigtländer Virtus	250	350
Voigtländer Vitessa 126 CS	20	35
Voigtländer Vito Automatic R	50	75
Voigtländer Vitoret Rapid D	25	50
Voss Diax Ib	75	125
Watson Argus Reflex	200	300
Yamato Pax Sunscope	40	60
Yashica C	75	100
Yashica Flash-O-Set II	25	50
Zeiss Ikon Colora	40	60
Zeiss Ikon Contaflex IV	75	100
Zeiss Ikon Contax III	200	300
Zeiss Ikon Contessa-35	175	250
Zeiss Ikon Contessamat	25	50
Zeiss Ikon Contina Ic	25	50
Zeiss Ikon Donata	50	75
Zeiss Ikon Ecarex 35, black	150	200
Zeiss Ikon Icarette	50	75
Zeiss Ikon Ikoflex IIa	100	150
Zeiss Ikon Simplex	75	125
Zeiss Ikon Super Ikonta C	150	200
Zeiss Universal Palmos	300	400
Zenith Winpro 35	20	30
Zenza Bronica ETRC	150	200
Zion Pocket Z	125	175
Zodiac	2	8

Zeiss Ikon Contarex Bullseye.

Voightländer Bessa II.

—Photos courtesy Auction Team Köln.

Eastman Kodak

	LOW	HIGH
Anniversary Kodak	$50	$75
Automatic 35	20	30
Autosnap	2	8
Baby Brownie	15	20
Baby Brownie Special	10	15
Baby Hawkeye	40	60
Bantam f8	15	25
Boy Scout Kodak	250	350
Brownie, original	700	1000
Brownie 44A	10	15
Brownie 127	10	15
Brownie Bullet	2	8
Brownie Bull's Eye, gold	15	30
Brownie Flash	15	30
Brownie Flash IV	25	50
Brownie Flash B	15	30
Brownie Hawkeye	10	15
Brownie Holiday	4	10
Brownie Model I	15	20
Brownie Reflex	10	15
Brownie Reflex Xynchro Model	2	8
Brownie Starflash, red	15	20
Brownie Starlet	2	8
Brownie Starmatic II	15	20
Brownie Starmeter	15	30
Brownie Vecta	20	30
Bullet, plastic	10	20
Camp Fire Girls Kodak	750	1000
Colorsnap 35 Model 2	15	30

Kodak Bantam Special.
—Photo courtesy Auction Team Köln.

	LOW	HIGH
Duo Six-20	$50	$75
Empire State	175	250
Ensemble	750	1000
Falcon	125	175
Flash Bantam	25	50
Girl Guide Kodak	200	300
Girl Scout Kodak	250	350
Happy Times Instant	125	175
Hawkette No. 2	75	100
Hawkeye Ace	25	50
Instamatic 250	50	75
Jiffy Kodak Six-16	15	20
Kodak Bantam Special, Compur Rapid	200	300
Kodak Ektra	600	800
Kodak Junior I	15	20
Kodak Junior 620	15	30
No. 0 Brownie	15	25
No. 0 Folding Pocket Kodak	75	100
No. 1 Autographic Kodak Special	40	50
No. 1 Kodak	1000	1500
No. 1 Pocket Kodak Junior, black	10	15
No. 1A Autographic Kodak	15	20
No. 2 Brownie, black	2	10
No. 2 Brownie, colors	40	60
No. 2 Bull's-Eye	40	50
No. 2 Folding Brownie	50	75
No. 2 Folding Bull's-Eye	150	250
No. 2 Folding Pocket Kodak	75	100
No. 2 Kodak	500	750
No. 2A Folding Autographic Brownie	15	20
No. 3 Autographic Kodak	20	30
No. 3 Cartridge Kodak	250	350
No. 3 Kodak	400	600
No. 3A Folding Cartridge Hawkeye	20	30
No. 4 Bullet	75	125
No. 4 Bullet Special	250	350
No. 4 Eureka	125	175
No. 4 Folding Pocket Kodak	100	150
No. 4 Kodak	350	500
No. 4 Kodak Jr.	400	600
No. 4 Panoram Kodak Model B	250	350
No. 4A Folding Kodak	150	200
Pony 135 Model B	10	15
Popular Brownie	15	20
Portrait Hawkeye A-Star-A	20	30
Premo No. 9	50	75
Signet 35	20	30
Six-20 Brownie B	20	30
Six-20 Brownie Junior	2	8
Six-20 Folding Brownie Model 2	15	30
Vest Pocket Rainbow Hawk-eye	125	175

Candy Containers

	LOW	HIGH
Airplane, "Spirit of St. Louis" clear glass body, metal wings, struts, undercarriage, wheels, axle rod, nose, and propeller, "Spirit of St. Louis" in red on wing tops, W. Glass Co., Jeannette, PA, 4.5" l	$450	$525
Amos and Andy Open Air Taxi, painted clear glass, embossed "Avor 1 oz, Victory Glass Co., Jeannette, Pa.," red tin snap-on closure, 4.5" l	500	650
Automobile, coupe w/ long hood, painted clear glass, tin slide-on closure, red stamped tin wheels, T. H. Stough Co., Jeannette, PA, 5.125" l	55	75
Automobile, electric coupe, clear glass, embossed "Pat Feb 18 1913," tin snap-on closure, Vail Bros., Philadelphia, PA, 3.375" l	65	80
Automobile, flat top w/ tassels, painted clear glass, unmarked, green tin snap-on closure, 4.125" l	325	400
Automobile, limousine w/ rear trunk and tire, painted clear glass, embossed "V G Co. Jenet Pa. U.S.A. Avor 3/4 oz," black tin snap-on closure, Victory Glass Co., Jeannette, PA., 4.875" l	100	150
Barney Google and Ball, painted clear glass, round base embossed "Barney Google, copyright 1927 King Features Syndicate, Inc.," tin threaded closure, 3.625" h	200	275
Bear on Circus Tub, clear glass, round base, attributed to Turney H. Stough Co., Jeannette, PA, 4.25" h	180	225
Camel, painted composition, glass eyes, Germany, 6.5" l, 5.5" h	300	400
Camera on Tripod, painted clear glass, tin closure marked "Pat App'l'd For," wooden bead bulb, wired and tin tripod, 5.25" h	350	425
Candlestick, red-flashed glass, gold-painted handles and top, silver-lettered "Souvenir of Pen Mar, Md.," tin threaded closure, 3.875" h	180	225
Cannon, clear glass cannon, red tin carriage and pierced wheels, open breech end w/ tin threaded closure, 4.5" l	200	250
Cannon, clear glass cannon, silvered tin carriage w/ gold pierced wheels, open breech w/ threaded metal closure, 5" l	475	600
Cannon, rapid fire gun, clear glass cannon, green enameled tin carriage w/ black pierced tin wheels, sliding lid closure stamped "West Bros. Co., Grapeville PA., U.S.A., Serial No. 2862, Net. Wt. 3/8 oz," 7.25" l	325	400
Charlie Chaplin, painted clear glass, embossed "Charlie Chaplin, Serial No. 2862, Net Wt 1 oz, Geo. Borgfeldt & Co. New York, Sole Licensees, Patent Applied For," mahogany wood-grained tin closure on glass barrel w/ coin slot, 3.75" h	135	180
Charlie Chaplin, painted clear glass, embossed "L. E. Smith Co., Net Wt. 1 1/2 oz," Chaplin standing next to straight-sided container w/ orange tin threaded top w/ coin slot, 4" h	325	400
Chick, painted composition, glass eyes, wire legs, Germany, 4.5" h	200	300
Chicken on Basket, painted clear glass, embossed "Avor 13/4 oz, U.S.A., V G Co J'Net PA," red tin snap-on closure, Victory Glass Co., Jeannette, PA, 3.5" l	50	65
Chick in Shell Auto, painted clear glass, embossed "U.S.A., Avor 1/2 oz," red wheels, blue tin snap-on closure, Victory Glass Co., Jeannette, PA, 4.625" l	250	300
Chick Nodder, painted composition, blue jacket, orange pants, Germany, 6" h	100	200
Chicks on Nest, painted composition, 2 chicks (1 hatching) and 2 eggs on wicker nest, Germany, 3.25" h	200	300
Dog by Barrel, painted clear glass, open barrel w/ orange tin threaded cap w/ coin slot, embossed "L. E. Smith Co. Net Wt 1 1/4 oz," 3.125" h	160	200
Duck, painted composition, spring-jointed wings, Germany, 6.25" h	100	150
Elephant, painted clear glass, embossed "G.O.P., U.S.A., V. G. Co.," red tin slide closure, 3.25" l	225	300

	LOW	HIGH
Elephant, painted composition, glass eyes, long tusks, Germany, 5.75" l	200	300
Fire Engine, Little Boiler, painted clear glass, embossed "U.S.A. (in lunette), Avor 3/4 oz, V. G. Co. Jnet PA," red tin snap-on closure, Victory Glass Co., Jeannette, PA, 4.375" l	35	50
Greyhound Bus, painted clear glass, embossed running greyhound and "V. G. Co., Je'n'et PA U.S.A., Avor 1 1/2 oz.," tin snap-on closure, metal axle, tin wheels, Victory Glass Co., Jeannette, PA, 5.125" l	250	310
Hen on Nest, painted papier-mâché, round removable cardboard base w/ straw around top, Germany, 4.75" h	150	200
House, painted clear glass, embossed details, tin slide closure	150	200
Jitney, clear glass body embossed "West Bros Co, Grapeville PA., Serial No. 2862, Net Wt 1/2 oz, Pat Apld For," painted tin top w/ 2 seats marked "Jitney Bus," 4" l	350	425
Liberty Bell, blue glass, w/ hanger, embossed "Liberty Bell, Pat Apld For," tin threaded closure	35	50
Mantel Clock, clear glass w/ gold-painted highlights, paper dials, embossed scroll designs, tin snap-on closure, unmarked, 3.875" h	110	150
Pheasant on Tree Stump, painted composition, polychrome-painted pheasant on spring legs, mica and painted stump, Germany, 3.75" h	150	250
Pumpkin Head Jr. Policeman, painted clear glass, threaded tin closure, 4.375" h	875	1100
Rabbit, painted composition, tan body w/ painted eyes, moss-covered base, Germany, 4" l	100	200
Rabbit, painted composition, wearing hat, turtleneck, and shorts, holding carrot, standing by 3 carrots on round container platform, Germany, 8" h	300	500
Rabbit, painted composition, white w/ black spots, glass eyes, seated w/ carrot in mouth, Germany, 7.25" h	150	250
Rabbit, white felt over composition, glass eyes, standing on hind legs, Germany, 10.75" h	100	200
Rabbit Pulling Cart, gray wool felt-covered composition rabbit w/ glass eyes, cane-woven cart w/ metal wheels, Germany, 12" l	250	400
Submarine, clear glass upper body, tin superstructure w/ periscope, hull painted green, "Geo. Borgfeldt & Co., New York, N.Y., Serial No. 2862, Net Wt. 1 1/2 oz, Pat. Applied For" paper label, 5.5" l	320	400
Uncle Sam Hat, painted milk glass, embossed stars and stripes, red tin push-in closure w/ coin slot, 2.5" h	60	75

German Composition Candy Containers. —Photo courtesy York Town Auction Inc.

Canes

Canes are either simple walking sticks or "gadget" canes that conceal a sword, pistol, musical instrument, or other device. The stylish canes of Europe came into vogue in the seventeenth and eighteenth centuries, while the nineteenth century saw gadget canes reaching their peak of popularity. When buying a cane or walking stick, examine it closely for indications of hidden compartments. Many devices go undiscovered for years.

Carved folk art canes are judged by their style and the skill of the carver. Many of the most desirable ones date from the mid-nineteenth century. We've seen many of varying quality in the auctions of New England.

"Good" examples are undamaged with simple carving or simple forming. "Best" examples have superior carving or forming and (if wood or metal) a fine patina.

For more information refer to Catherine Dike's *Cane Curiosa: From Gun to Gadget* (published by author, Geneva, Switzerland, 1983) and *Canes in the United States: Illustrated Mementoes of American History, 1607-1953* (Cane Curiosa Press, Ladue, MO, 1994).

	GOOD	BETTER	BEST
Ball Handle, rose quartz ball with faceted rock crystal band around center, silver collar, dark hardwood shaft w/ horn ferrule, English, c1900, 35.75" l	$800	$950	$1100
Cockatoo Head, carved elephant ivory bird's head w/ green glass eyes, crest painted yellow, beak and tongue painted black, ivory separator, octagonal silver and copper ferrule, Continental, c1860, 37" l	2000	2500	2750

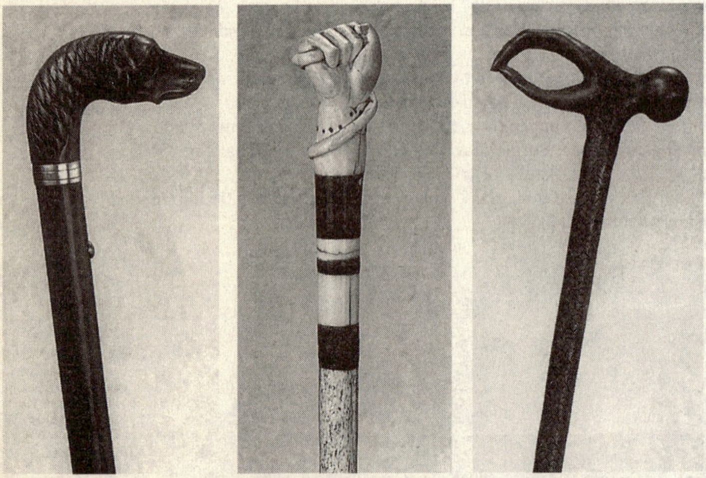

American Canes, left to right: Remington 32 cal. gun cane, molded gutta percha dog head handle, silver collar, brass and iron ferrule, c1875, 36.5" l, $7700 at auction (world's record high price for Remington large dog handle cane); Nautical cane w/ whale ivory handle carved as fist clutching snake, c1850, $2530 at auction; Folk art cane, carved hardwood w/ lady's hand and ball handle, fish scale design shaft, and brass ferrule, c1880, 34.75" l, $358 at auction. —Photos courtesy Tradewinds Antiques.

	GOOD	BETTER	BEST
Croquet Mallet, bamboo, cylindrical "T" handle w/ ebony end caps, 1 cap unscrews to reveal compartment w/ miniature croquet set w/ 2 mallets, 2 balls, and 2 brass wickets w/ ebony seats, mallets have leather handles and brass fittings to attach heads, ivory dot inlaid in each ball, cane has stepped bamboo shaft and narrow horn ferrule, English, c1870, 35.5" l	2000	2250	2500
Decorative Handle, pink gold flat knob above ivory-overlaid handle w/ 4 pink gold ovals inlaid w/ tortoiseshell, lower ring marked "W&D," dark malacca shaft w/ brass ferrule, American, 33.5" l	750	900	1100
Fishing Rod, carved bone knob handle, metal shaft painted brown, brass ferrule unscrews to reveal telescoping brass and bamboo fishing rod, English, c1880, 35" l cane extends to 8.5' l rod	1000	1250	1500
Folk Art, carved hardwood, plain crook handle above 14" l carved stylized lobster, American, c1900, 35.75" l	1750	1000	1200
Folk Art, carved hazelwood, handle is large stylized bird w/ black beak, round yellow eyes, and black feet perched on shaft w/ naturally twisted top, brass ferrule, English, c1890, 40" l	500	650	800
Gardener's Sickle, steel sickle handle incised w/ manufacturer's name and registration and design numbers, oak step-carved shaft w/ brass ferrule, English, c1900, 40" l	400	500	600
Glass Whimsey, crook handle, pale green w/ dark red and white twisted internal stripes, American, c1890, 37" l	300	400	500
Horse Head, silver w/ protruding veins, glass eyes, and partial mane, remainder of mane carved into macassar ebony shaft, silver collar, silver and iron ferrule, American, c1860, 36" l	500	650	800
Japanese Demon, elephant ivory handle carved as horned demon w/ bulging eyes and fangs, squatting on rock, wearing cloak and bands around arms and legs, sterling collar w/ 1895 London hallmark and "Brigg," malacca shaft w/ horn ferrule, 36.5" l	750	1000	1250
Man's Head, carved burl, smiling expression, muttonchop sideburns, sterling collar w/ 1900 London hallmark, hardwood shaft w/ speckle finish and light horn ferrule, 36" l	200	350	500
Natural Root, knob handle w/ encircling bronze snake extending 8.5" down shaft, brass and iron ferrule, Vienna, c1880, 36.5" l	175	250	350
Nautical, whale ivory knob above thin black baleen separator and free-turning sawtooth-carved ivory separator, whalebone shaft carved w/ 2 square chambers, 1 containing rope-carved cylinder w/ columns, other w/ fluted cylinder within columns, both chambers decorated w/ angled sawtooth designs and coin silver and abalone pins and dots, remainder of shaft carved in deeply incised twisting pattern, copper hand-wrought ferrule, American, c1840, 38" l	5000	7000	9000
Political Convention Souvenir, tin, working horn handle stamped w/ McKinley slogan "Prosperity, Protection and Patriotism," 1896, 33.5" l	400	550	700
Spaniel Head, carved elephant ivory, snarling expression, glass eyes, bowed ribbon collar, 2-toned lignum vitae shaft w/ round ivory eyelets and brass ferrule, Continental, c1870, 37.5" l	600	800	1000
Sunday Stick, mahogany handle carved as golf club driver w/ simulated foot plate and lead weight, black string whipping where handle connects to narrow hickory shaft, brass ferrule, American, c1900, 34.5" l	400	550	700

Cereal Boxes

The breakfast choice for youngsters in post-war America was a break from their parents' waffles, pancakes or eggs. Kids wanted cereal touted on radio, then television. The cereal box became the younger crowd's *New York Times* and *Wall Street Journal* rolled into one. After all, what else was there to do while consuming breakfast before the bus came? Boxes often contained contests, special offers and cutouts ("You have to finish it before you can have the box!"). Boomers are drawn to boxes that remind them of their childhood morning ritual and premium collectors are attracted to the information the boxes provide. Amazingly, boxes have survived and the prices below are for excellent, clean examples.

For further information see *Cereal Box Bonanza: The 1950's* by Scott Bruce (Collector Books, Paducah, KY, 1995).

	LOW	HIGH
Boo Berry, ad for Monster Erasers, Boo Berry Monster Beach Towel ad on side panel, w/ complete set of 6 erasers, ©1972 General Mills Inc.	$250	$350
Cap'n Crunch Crunchberries, back panel featuring state "Go-Go" stickers packaged 2 per box, includes Japan and Africa stickers, ©1963	125	175
Kellogg's Corn Flakes, baseball premiums including Bob Feller and Joe DiMaggio baseballs, Jerry Priddy and Pinky Higgins gloves, Louisville Slugger bats for Johnny Mize and Joe DiMaggio, bike reflector, and gold ore ring, Dec. 31, 1942 expiration date	200	300
Kellogg's Pep, "Havoc' Douglas U.S. Attack Bomber" model warplane punch-out and #19 and #20 cut-out "Plane Spotter Cards"	175	250
Kellogg's Pep Wheat Flakes, ad for miniature racing hot-rod vehicle on front, "Stereo Pix 3-Dimensional Panoramic Picture of Famous Train" on back featuring uncut #1 in series for "Santa Fe Super Chief," w/ red litho tin hot-rod, ©1954	50	100
Kellogg's Rice Krispies, includes complete Jungle Jump-Up Game premium consisting of jungle landscape target map and box w/ plastic animals, hunter w/ rifle, and bullets, English and French text, Canadian, 1965	150	250
Kellogg's Shredded Wheat, side panel ad for Fabri-Cal Hot Iron Transfers, 1950s	100	175
Kix, ad for set of 18 M-G-M movie star cards, includes Esther Williams sample card, 1955	75	125
Nabisco Wheat Honeys, w/ pair of 2" h soft plastic Breakfast Buddies, ads for "Buffalo Bee Breakfast Buddy" and "Jolly Clown Breakfast Buddy" on box, 1950s	200	300
Post Crispy Critters, w/ 32-pp "Linus the Lion Fun Book" premium, mailing envelope, Magic Color Sheet, and paint brush, ©1964 General Foods Corp.	150	250
Post Grape-Nut Flakes, #2 "Douglas A-4 D-2 Sky Hawk" jet fighter cut-out on back, 1960s	100	175
Post Sugar Crisp, w/ #3 and #6 Mighty Mouse Magic Mystery Pictures, ad for siren ring and Ford car premiums on side, ©1957	125	175
Quaker Puffed Rice, includes #16 and #17 Sgt. Preston "Yukon Adventure" cards, 1950	150	200
Quaker TinTin, comic character on front, two 3-dimensional hard plastic "Wiggly" figures pictured on back, English and French text, w/ blue plastic TinTin and Snowy figures sealed in cellophane, Canadian, 1966	125	175
Rice Honeys, ad for Little Orphan Annie, Smilin' Jack, Smitty, and Smokey Stover molded plastic premium patches, 2 patches included w/ box, ©1963	200	300
Wheaties, football player on front, ad for baseball stamp album w/ NY Yankees Tom Tresh photo and order blank, 1960s	100	150

Chalkware

Plaster of Paris figurines painted in bright colors are called chalkware. Originally produced as a cheap imitation of Staffordshire and Bennington wares during the middle and the late 1800s, American companies later manufactured examples as carnival prizes during the first half of the twentieth century. Animals with nodding heads are especially rare. Few were produced and even fewer have survived through the years. They are sometimes found in the Midwest.

Check closely for condition. Because of their fragility, many pieces are restored. Prices are for restored (R), minor paint loss (M), and perfect (P).

For additional listings of carnival chalkware, see *The Carnival Chalk Prize* (1985) and *Book II* (1994) by Thomas G. Morris (Prize Publishers, Medford, OR).

Carnival Chalkware.

Left: Horse, c1940-50, 10" h, $25-$35.

Right: Army Sgt. Bilko, bank, 1945-50, 12" h, $50-$75.

	R	M	P
Apache Babe, w/ cigarette, carnival prize, "©B. G. 1936," 14" h	$30	$65	$75
Bimbo/Bonzo Dog, carnival prize, "©J. Y. Jenkins, March 8, 1926," 1940s, 7" h	25	40	45
Bull, bank, brown and amber finish, 15.25" l	350	500	600
Cat, holding ball, carnival prize, 7" h	20	35	40
Cat, sleeping, painted gray w/ black stripes, blue ribbon, pink ears and nose, 12.25" l	250	375	450
Collie, sitting, carnival prize, c1935-45, 11.5" h	30	45	50
George Washington, carnival prize, marked "A. Incrocci, Pittsburgh, Pa, 1732-1932," 1940s, 12" h	30	45	50
German Shepherd, standing on rectangular base w/ oval ashtray insert, carnival prize, black and white body, glass jeweled eyes, 7" h	15	25	30
King Kong Gorilla, carnival prize, 1930-40, 13.5" h	60	85	100
Mae West, carnival prize, Jenkins, 14" h	70	100	125
Peach, bank, painted red and yellow, wooden stem, 19th C, 3.5" h	200	300	350
Pear, bank, painted red and yellow, replaced wooden stem, 19th C, 5.5" h	200	300	350
Popeye, carnival prize, c1940, 9.5" h	30	45	50
Scottish Lass, playing bagpipe, carnival prize, 1940-50, 15" h	35	55	65
Spaniel, seated, hollow, black and red highlights, 8.75" h	100	175	200
Spaniel, standing on stepped rectangular base, red and black highlights, 7.5" h	125	225	275
Staffordshire Dog, carnival prize, 11" h	20	35	40
Stag, reclining on oblong base, painted yellow w/ orange polka dots on body and orange band around base, black highlights, 9.75" h	450	675	750

Clocks

When buying a clock at auction, always factor in the cost of repair. Even if the clock was working during exhibition, by the time it has been moved from display to storage to you, it is often not. Be sure to check for all parts (pendulum, weights, etc.) both before you bid and when you pick it up. Buying from a dealer may cost more money, but can often save on headaches.

For further reading consult *American Clocks, Vol. 1* (1989) and *Vol. 2* (1995) by Tran Duy Ly (Arlington Book, Fairfax, VA) and *American Shelf and Wall Clocks* by Robert W. D. Ball (Schiffer, Atglen, PA, 1992).

Banjo Clocks. —Photos courtesy Gene Harris Antique Auction Center, Inc.

	LOW	AVG.	HIGH
Alarm, Double Bell Rotary No. 98, nickel-plated brass case, Parker Clock Co., c1904, 6.5" h	$75	$100	$125
Alarm, Princess Alarm No. 150, nickel-plated brass case, key wind, Parker Clock Co., c1912	85	125	175
Alarm, Watermill, nickel finish case, watermill scene on dial w/ animated waterwheel, Kroeber, c1900, 4" dial	3500	5000	6500
Banjo, No. 1, cherry case, enameled metal dial, Howard, c1875, 50" h	5500	7000	8500
Banjo, No. 2, pendulum movement, hour and half-hour dual chimetone strike, Ansonia, 1924, 40.5" h	1150	1500	1750
Banjo, No. 3, pendulum movement, Westminster quarter-hour chime, Ansonia, 1924, 40.5" h	1500	2000	2500
Banjo, No. 5, hardwood case, Howard, c1875, 29" h	2000	2500	3000
Banjo, No. 1500, mahogany case w/ brass trim, acorn finial, painted tablet w/ landscape, Waltham, c1930, 42" h	1500	2000	2500
Banjo, Ship's Bell No. 18, mahogany-finished case w/ polished brass trim, painted tablets w/ sailing ship and nautical scene, Waterbury, c1930, 22.5" h	350	450	550
Banjo, Willard No. 5, mahogany case w/ acorn finial and gilt trim, porcelain dial, convex glass, painted tablet w/ landscape, 8-day weight-driven movement, Waterbury, c1912, 42" h	900	1200	1500
Banjo, Willard No. 6, gilded mahogany case w/ flattened orb finial and gilt trim, porcelain dial, convex glass, painted tablet, 8-day spring-driven movement, Waterbury, c1912, 42.25" h	500	650	800
Carriage, Athens, gold-plated case, beveled glass panels, 7-jewel 8-day movement, Boston Clock Co., c1890, 6.5" h	375	500	650
Carriage, Bonanza, 8-day time, porcelain dial, Roman numerals, beveled glass, leather carrying case, Ansonia, 1901, 5.25" h	300	400	500

Crystal Regulators.

"Knight" Figural Clock.

	LOW	AVG.	HIGH
Crystal Regulator, Delphus, gold-plated case, beveled glass panels, 11-jewel 8-day movement w/ half-hour cathedral strike, Boston Clock Co., c1890, 10.5" h	600	750	900
Crystal Regulator, Donorah, 8-day movement, half-hour gong strike, porcelain visible escapement dial, Roman numerals, mercurial pendulum, beveled plate glass front, sides, and back, gold finish, jeweled sash and pendulum, Ansonia, 1901	350	500	650
Crystal Regulator, Earl, polished brass, Ansonia, 1920, 13" h	800	1200	1600
Crystal Regulator, No. 1, urn finial, floral decoration, Ansonia, 1906, 17.5" h	2000	2500	3000
Dome, Never-Wind No. 2000, gold-plated frame, glass dome, porcelain dial, Tiffany Electric Mfg. Co., c1920, 11" h	150	200	275
Figural, Poet, Japanese bronze figure and trim, porcelain dial w/ visible escapement, Ansonia, 1894, 22" h, 24" w	1250	1750	2250
Figural, Shakespeare, silvered figure and trim, porcelain dial w/ visible escapement, Ansonia, 1894, 15" h, 17.5" w	600	750	900

"Combatants" Figural Clock.

"Opera" Figural Clock.

—Photos courtesy Gene Harris Antique Auction Center, Inc.

Hanging Calendar Clocks. —Photos courtesy Gene Harris Antique Auction Center, Inc.

	LOW	AVG.	HIGH
Hanging, drop octagon, hardwood case w/ ebony and gilt trim, 8-day time and strike movement, Terry Clock Co., c1875, 19" h	750	900	1100
Hanging, drop octagon, walnut case, 8-day time and strike movement, Russell & Jones, c1890, 10" dial	275	350	450
Hanging, drop octagon calendar, oak case, 8-day time movement, Kroeber, c1898, 10" dial, 21" h	275	350	405
Hanging, figure-eight calendar, No. 34, double dial, oak case, 8-day time and strike movement, Waterbury, c1895, 12" time dial, 10" calendar dial, 29.5" h	1000	1250	1500
Hanging, figure-eight regulator, No. 9, black walnut case, enameled metal dial, Howard, c1875, 37" h	3800	5000	6200
Hanging, kitchen, Merchants Line, pressed oak case w/ floral and scroll decoration, 8-day time, half-hour strike, New Haven, 6" dial, 25.5" h	300	400	500
Hanging, locomotive, circular brass case, Roman numerals, 7-jewel 8-day movement, Boston Clock Co., c1890, 10" dia	325	450	600
Hanging, regulator, Admiral, quarter-sawn oak case, 8-day movement, half-hour gong strike, Waterbury, c1912, 32" h	300	400	500
Hanging, regulator, Capitol, mahogany finish, 8-day spring movement, half-hour gong strike, Ansonia, 1901	600	800	1000
Hanging, regulator, General, black walnut case, 8-day weight-driven movement, Ansonia, 1894, 68" h	2000	2750	3500
Hanging, regulator, No. 3, golden oak case, second hand, 3-day weight-driven movement, Chelsea Clock Co., c1910, 37" h	900	1250	1500
Hanging, regulator, No. 8, carved black walnut cabinet w/ gallery and columns, porcelain dial w/ sweep second hand, 8-day weight-driven movement, E. N. Welch, c1875, 66" h	3500	5000	6500
Hanging, regulator, No. 9, carved oak cabinet w/ fluted stiles, rope-turned brass railing, second hand, 8-day time and strike weight-driven movement, Waterbury, c1890, 76.25" h	3000	4000	5000
Hanging, regulator, No. 13, black walnut case, full-length pendulum, second hand, Howard, c1875, 56" h	3000	4000	5000
Hanging, regulator, No. 16, walnut veneered case w/ ebony trim, wooden rod pendulum, NY Standard Watch Co., c1900, 37" h	750	900	1100

Hanging Regulator Clocks. —Photos courtesy Gene Harris Antique Auction Center, Inc.

	LOW	AVG.	HIGH
Hanging, regulator, No. 18, black walnut case, 8-day weight-driven movement, Ansonia, 1894, 12" dial, 90" h	5500	7000	8500
Hanging, regulator, No. 21, carved cherry cabinet, arched pediment-turned finials and drops, turned half-columns, shaped apron, 8-day weight-driven movement, Waterbury, c1892, 55.5" h	1200	1500	1800
Hanging, regulator, No. 85, carved mahogany case, enameled zinc dial, Howard, c1890, 60" h	3500	5000	6500
Hanging, regulator, Senator, ornate oak cabinet w/ brass trim, 8-day movement, half-hour gong strike, silver dial, Ansonia, 1894, 22" h	1500	2000	2500
Hanging, Regulator Calendar No. 2, double dial, oak case, 8-day weight-driven movement, E. N. Welch, c1875, 12" time dial, 8" calendar dial, 34" h	1200	1500	1800
Hanging, Roman Gothic, walnut case, 8-day time and strike movement, Ansonia Brass & Copper Co., 1874, 30" h	750	900	1000
Mantel, Alhambra, gold-plated case w/ scrolled crest and fluted columns, beveled glass panels, 11-jewel 8-day movement w/ half-hour cathedral strike, Boston Clock Co., c1890, 13.5" h	1200	1500	1800
Mantel, Madeleine, black-enameled iron architectural case w/ verde bronze columns and trim, porcelain dial, 8-day movement, half-hour gong strike, Ansonia, c1905, 11.5" h, 16.5" w	225	300	400
Mantel, Newham, cabinet style, ornately carved oak case, 8-day half-hour slow-striking movement, cathedral gongs, Ansonia, 1901, 18.5" h	225	300	400
Mantel, octagon top, hardwood case w/ ebony and gilt trim, 8-day time and strike movement, Terry Clock Co., c1875, 19" h	750	900	1100
Mantel, papier-mâché, scrolled sides and feet, painted black w/ inlaid mother-of-pearl and painted gold floral decorations, painted zinc dial inscribed "C. Jerome," 8-day time and strike movement, Chauncey Jerome, 17" h	150	200	250
Mantel, Tambour No. 1, silvered metal dial, Chelsea Clock Co., c1910, 8" dial	800	1000	1200

Wooden Case Mantel Clocks. —Photos courtesy Gene Harris Antique Auction Center, Inc.

	LOW	AVG.	HIGH
Porcelain, No. 22, blue floral decoration and trim on white ground, 8-day eclipse movement, American dial, Kroeber, c1900, 18.5" h	275	350	450
Shelf, Aspen, pressed oak case w/ ornate crest and splats, glass door w/ painted geometric design, 8-day time and strike movement, half-hour gong, Ansonia, c1905, 6" dial, 22" h	225	300	400
Shelf, beehive case w/ rosewood veneer, painted tablet, paper label, painted zinc dial, 8-day time and strike movement, Jerome & Co., c1880, 19.25" h	150	200	250
Shelf, calendar, "$3^1/_2$ Parlour" Model Double Dial Calendar Clock, walnut case w/ carved and ebonized wooden trim, black paper upper dial and rollers, glass calendar dial and pendulum, silvered hands, 8-day movement w/ bell strike, Ithaca Calendar Clock Co., c1875, 20" h	2500	3000	3500
Shelf, calendar, Melrose No. 15, double dial, cherry case w/ ebony trim, beveled crystals, 8-day movement, half-hour strike, Ithaca Calendar Clock Co., c1880, 6" time dial, 8" calendar dial, 22" h	6000	7500	9000
Shelf, calendar, No. 44, double dial, carved walnut case, 8-day half-hour strike, Waterbury, c1891, 6" dials, 24" h	600	800	1000
Shelf, calendar, pressed oak case, ornate crest and sides, gold-painted tablet, barometer and thermometer mounted on sides, 8-day time and strike movement, c1885, 23" h	300	400	500
Shelf, calendar, Shelf Cottage No. 9, double dial, carved walnut case w/ turned finials, 8-day time and strike movement, Ithaca Calendar Clock Co., c1880, 7" time dial, 8" calendar dial, 23" h	750	1000	1250
Shelf, Chesterton, mahogany case w/ round top, inlaid fan, and ball feet, ivory dial, convex beveled glass, visible escapement, 8-day movement, half-hour gong strike, Waterbury, c1912, 9.5" h	200	250	300
Shelf, Conquest, carved walnut case w/ pierced crest and turned columns, illuminating dial, 8-day gong strike, Kroeber, c1900, 21.5" h	300	400	500
Shelf, cottage, grain-painted case, painted zinc dial, E. N. Welch, c1860, 12" h	225	300	400
Shelf, Doric, bronzed metal case, white porcelain dial, Chelsea Clock Co., c1910, 4.25" dial	300	400	500

	LOW	AVG.	HIGH
Shelf, Empire, double column, mahogany case w/ molded cornice, 4 turned columns, and painted table w/ sailing vessel, 30-hour time and strike brass movement by Union Clock Co., Sperry & Shaw, c1840, 26" h	150	200	250
Shelf, Empire, mahogany veneered case w/ cornice top, turned half-columns, 2 painted tablets w/ fruit designs, painted zinc dial, maker's label, 8-day time and strike brass movement, Seth Thomas, c1860, 32.5" h	225	300	400
Shelf, Empire style, double decker, gilt and tortoise gesso half-columns, gilt-stenciled wooden splat, original painted tablet, 8-day brass movement w/ escapement visible in dial cut-out, Eli Terry Jr., c1825-40, 31.25" h	600	750	900
Shelf, Empire style, mahogany case, cornice top, full columns, mirrored tablet, 8-day brass spring-operated movement, Seth Thomas, c1870, 16" h	150	200	250
Shelf, Empire style, mahogany veneered case, molded cornice, turned half-columns, upper tablet with styled floral design, lower tablet w/ landscape, flattened ball feet, 8-day wooden movement, Eli Terry Jr., 1835-40, 36" h	550	700	900
Shelf, Empire style, miniature, mahogany case w/ cornice top, turned half-columns, scrolled base, double doors w/ stenciled tablets, painted zinc dial, 8-day spring-driven movement, Sperry & Shaw, c1855, 20.5" h	500	650	800
Shelf, Empire style, rosewood case with octagonal half-columns, painted zinc dial, rectangular and octagonal gold-leafed reverse-painted tablets, 8-day lyre-shaped weight-driven movement, Seth Thomas, c1860, 31" h	550	700	900
Shelf, Gothic No. 43, carved hardwood case, 1-day time and strike movement, Terry Clock Co., c1875, 13" h	150	200	250

Double Dial Shelf Calendar Clocks. —Photo courtesy Gene Harris Antique Auction Center, Inc.

Shelf Clocks.
Left: Steeple.
Center: Pillar and Scroll.
Right: Column and Splat.
—Photos courtesy Gene Harris Antique Auction Center, Inc.

	LOW	AVG.	HIGH
Shelf, Gothic Pillar, black walnut case w/ peaked top and half-columns, 3-day time and strike movement, Waterbury, c1865, 15" h	150	200	250
Shelf, Gothic Steeple, 4-column, acid-etched tablet w/ flower and garland design, 8-day brass spring movement, marked "Brewster & Ingraham, original, Bristol, Ct. U.S." on face, c1845-50, 19" h	450	600	750
Shelf, kitchen, ornate pressed oak case, glass door w/ gold and black floral decoration, paper on zinc dial, 8-day time and strike brass movement, Sessions Clock Co., c1900, 24" h	275	350	450
Shelf, mahogany case w/ stenciled splat and quarter-columns, painted tablet, carved paw feet, 30-hour wooden weight-driven movement, E. Terry & Sons, 1825-30, 28.5" h	750	1000	1200
Shelf, mahogany veneered case w/ carved eagle crest, ornately carved columns, and carved paw feet, double doors, wooden dial w/ gilt decoration, 8-day wooden time and strike weight-driven movement, Atkins & Downs, c1830, 39" h	750	1000	1200
Shelf, mahogany veneered case w/ carved fruit basket crest, ornate half-columns, and paw feet, painted wooden dial and tablet, 30-hour wooden time and strike weight-driven movement, Langdon & Jones, c1835, 37.5" h	600	750	1000
Shelf, mahogany veneered case w/ cornice top, turned columns w/ carved capitals, and carved paw feet, painted wooden dial and reverse-painted tablet, 8-day wooden time and strike movement, Eli Terry & Sons, c1830, 33.5" h	600	800	1000
Shelf, miniature ogee case w/ rosewood veneer, painted zinc dial, maker's label, painted tablet w/ beehive, 8-day time and strike movement, New Haven Clock Co., c1860, 18.5" h	150	200	250
Shelf, pillar and scroll, mahogany veneered case, painted tablet, painted wooden dial, 30-hour wooden time and strike movement, Hugh Kearney, c1830, 28" h	375	500	650
Shelf, pillar and scroll, painting on glass tablet, 30-hour wooden movement, Seth Thomas, c1825, 31.25" h	750	1000	1250
Shelf, Scalchi, carved black walnut case w/ pierced gallery, fluted stiles, stepped base, arched glass door w/ gold decoration, 8-day "Patti" movement, cathedral bell strike, E. N. Welch, c1875, 19.5" h	750	1000	1200
Shelf, Ship's Bell No. 2, carved mahogany case, silvered metal dial, 8-day movement, Chelsea Clock Co., c1910, 4.5" dial	550	700	850

Parlor Clocks.

Kitchen Shelf Clocks, pressed oak cases.

Empire-Style Shelf Clocks.

—Photos courtesy Gene Harris Antique Auction Center, Inc.

	LOW	AVG.	HIGH
Shelf, Ship's Bell No. 17, polished brass case, silvered metal radium dial, 8-day jeweled movement, Waterbury, c1930, 8" h	375	500	650
Shelf, steeple, rosewood veneered case w/ painted tablet, paper label, and 8-day time and strike movement, New Haven Clock Co., c1860, 20" h	100	150	200
Shelf, stenciled half-columns and splat, 30-hour brass time-and-strike movement, Boardman & Wells, 1830-40, 32" h	350	450	550
Shelf, Texas, carved walnut case w/ rounded top and turned columns, 8-day gong strike, Kroeber, c1900, 23" h	275	350	500
Shelf, Yacht Wheel, silvered metal case, Chelsea Clock Co., c1910, 6" dial	750	1000	1250
Tall Case, Hall Clock No. 73, mahogany case w/ swan's neck pediment, ball finials, molded panels, and shaped bracket feet, arched gilt dial w/ moon phases, beveled plate glass center panel, 8-day weight-driven movement, half-hour tubular gong strike, Waterbury, c1912, 7'9" h	2500	3250	4000
Tall Case, No. 14, swan's neck pediment, urn finials, arched dial, fluted columns, eagle cartouche on lower case, carved paw feet, 9 tubes, Waltham, c1905, 8'7" h	8000	12,000	16,000
Tall Case, No. 35, rounded hood w/ urn finials and pierced crest, turned columns w/ carved capitals, paneled sides and base, time and strike movement, Waltham, c1905, 8'6" h	4000	5500	7500
Tall Case, No. 81, mahogany case, brass eagle and orb finials, scrolled crest, arched dial, fluted columns, hour and half-hour strike, Howard, c1890, 8'2" h	7500	9000	12,000

Left: Tall Case Clock w/ swan's neck pediment and arched dial w/ moon phases.

Right: Long Case Regulator Clock.

—Photos courtesy Gene Harris Antique Auction Center, Inc.

Clothing and Accessories

Clothing

Vintage clothing is collected by those who wish to add it to their wardrobes as well as by collectors who wish only to display it. Currently, most market activity is in clothes from the 1920s, 1930s and 1940s. Alterations and construction details are factors in determining price, while skilled workmanship or handmade trims often increase value. Clothing with beadwork is also a good investment.

Vintage clothing requires careful handling. Textiles are perishable: light, humidity, dust and body oil are potentially harmful. The acids in wood, cardboard and tissue paper can also hurt clothing. When storing pieces, it is best to wrap items in white sheets and use mothballs. Hang lightweight clothing on padded hangers, and store heavy clothing laid flat.

For further information refer to *Vintage Clothing: 1880–1980, 3rd Edition* by Maryanne Dolan (Books Americana, Florence, AL, 1995, available from Krause Publications) or *Collector's Guide to Vintage Fashions* by Kristina Harris (Collector Books, Paducah, KY, 1999) or contact The Costume Society of America, 55 Edgewater Dr., PO Box 73, Earleville, MD 21919.

Evening Ensemble, Valentino Regal, ivory w/ white mink collar, 1969, $6038 at auction. —Photo courtesy William Doyle Galleries.

	LOW	HIGH
Afternoon Dress, black crepe embroidered w/ allover folkloric pattern worked in chain stitch in gold metallic, orange, and green silk threads, chemise dress closing at side front, self-ties below waist, long sleeves, labeled "Made in France," size 10-12, early 1920s	$250	$400
Afternoon Gown, teal blue chiffon and satin, bodice embroidered w/ silk flowers and sewn w/ spotted net bretelles, skirt arranged w/ diagonal swath of satin in front ending in diagonal floating back panel decorated w/ woven straw oval buttons, labeled "7 Place Vendome Paris, Nice (maker illegible)," size 6, c1912	350	500
Afternoon Gown, Victorian, aubergine satin, bodice w/ low square neckline, velvet edging, crocheted buttons, circular passementerie and bead trim, skirt similarly trimmed, crenalated hemline, bustle, labeled "parcher," 1870s	250	400

	LOW	HIGH
Bathing Suit, wool, 1-piece w/ V neck, short skirt, and mid-thigh trunks, green w/ marigold trim and skirt stripes, 1920s	250	500
Christening Ensemble, Victorian, ivory silk rep w/ padded and quilted lining, high-waisted open front gown and detachable cape trimmed w/ wide bands of chemical lace and pleated China silk ruffles, 1890s	200	400
Coat, Fortuny, stenciled velvet, kimono cut w/ V at back neck, gold velvet stenciled w/ Persian-inspired patterns including a row of leafy trees above wide foliate band at hem, foliate roundels at shoulders and sleeves, vinery at front opening, celadon silk satin lining, round gray faille label "Mariano Fortuny Venise," 1920s	1500	2000
Cocktail Dress, Ceil Chapman, black taffeta, long sleeves, full skirt gathered at hip, neckline stands away from shoulders, rimmed self-buttons down front, labeled "Ceil Chapman," size 8, 1940s	125	300
Cocktail Dress, Lucien Lelong, black crepe, simple bodice w/ long cut-in-one gusseted sleeves and V neck, 2-layer skirt, top layer draped and gathered to form peplum effect at hips and irregular hemline revealing pleated underskirt, labeled "Lucien Lelong 16. Avenue Matignon. Paris," size 6, 1940s	600	800
Dress, Chanel, beige lace, long sleeves buttoning at wrist, square neckline, dress top comprised of bands of Alençon-style lace connected by hemstitching, solid lace skirt, chiffon slip attached at bodice, labeled "Chanel," size 6-8, late 1920s	1000	1500
Dress, Fortuny Delphos, rose pleated silk, sleeveless, glass beads on silk cord at sides, stenciled belt, 1920s	1500	2000
Evening Coat, black satin w/ beaded chinoiserie designs worked in blue silk, bugle beads, and gold metallic thread, cape collar, double-layered at back forming batwing sleeves, 2 large self-embroidered buttons, round cutaway front, labeled "Berthe Hermance, 91. Avenue des Champs Elysées," c1912	800	1200
Evening Coat, purple satin chinoiserie, cutaway front, 2 large self-buttons and square faux collar sewn w/ wide band of finely embroidered pink flowers and green dragons, extending to same length in back and sewn w/ 2 blond yak hair tassels, cuffs sewn w/ like bands, 1915-20	250	500
Evening Dress, chiffon, black printed w/ yellow roses, sleeveless, low round neck sewn w/ flowing panel, skirt hem arranged in flared panels, black slip, size 10, 1930s	150	300
Evening Dress, columnar gown of beige chiffon woven w/ gold metallic sprays, lace underbodice and cap sleeves, overskirt draped diagonally across front revealing gold lace underskirt, slightly raised waist encircled in green satin, beaded fringe and tassel trim, skirt back w/ center gold lace panel ending in square train, labeled "Dumay 32, Rue Godot de Mauroi Paris," size 4, c1912	500	700
Evening Dress, Lanvin, black silk velvet sewn w/ scooped flounces of cordonnet and net lace, squared-off V neckline trimmed w/ wide lace bertha forming deep points at back, double-tiered skirt finely gathered at dropped waist and gradually dipping to floor length in rear, labeled "Jeanne Lanvin Paris Unis France Été 1928," size 10, 1928	2500	3500
Evening Gown, Charles James, body-hugging strapless black velvet sheath sewn at bottom w/ immense ivory faille hooped panier flounce, cascades of gold and silver beads embroidered on flounce, hand-signed satin ribbon label "Charles James '54," size 4, 1954	10,000	15,000
Evening Gown, Halston, iridescent aquamarine metallic gauze, low round neck, bias-cut bodice body-hugging to hip, skirt arranged w/ multiple tiers descending in length from front to back, circular cape, labeled "Halston," size 4, 1970s	1000	1500

	LOW	HIGH
Evening Gown, pink tulle, bodice and skirt each decorated w/ garlands of ribbonwork flowers, bodice w/ puffed sleeves, satin waist belt, skirt w/ fine appliqué net flounce, waist size 22", c1905	1200	1500
Gentleman's Coat, camel vicuna, single-breasted, flapped pockets, labeled "Vicuna one hundred percent. Back seam length 42 inches, width across back 16 inches," 1950s	200	400
Gentleman's Dressing Gown, Hermès, blue silk printed w/ rope-tied lattice pattern, round lapels, patch pockets, self-belt, waist seam, labeled "Hermès Paris," large, 1970s	100	250
Gentleman's Dress Overcoat, black broadcloth w/ notched satin tuxedo lapels, raglan sleeves, turned back	100	200
Gentleman's Sport Shirt, Schiaparelli, raspberry slub silk or rayon printed w/ small white floral sprigs, pointed collar, short sleeves, labeled "Schiaparelli New York Paris," large, 1950s	100	250
Gown, Paul Poiret, ivory satin w/ sapphire blue chiffon tunic overdress embroidered in wool w/ row of green, black, and white palm trees above wide plush band, bodice and hem trimmed w/ strands of black beads and rhinestones which hang loosely as necklace in back, labeled "Paul Poiret à Paris," size 4, c1910	4000	6000
Jacket, Worth & Bobergh, black velvet, fitted at waist, narrow band collar, long sleeves, front and cuffs trimmed w/ double frills of faux Chantilly lace and passementerie, silk and braid dome-shaped buttons down front, stamped "Worth & Bobergh 7, Rue de la Paix 7, Paris," late 1860s	600	1000
Paper Dress, Yellow Pages pattern, sleeveless, A-line w/ V neck and rolled collar ending in bow, yellow printed w/ black entries from Yellow Pages, labeled "'Waste Basket Boutique' by Mars of Asheville, N.C. Do Not Wash. This material is fire resistant unless washed or dry cleaned. Then becomes dangerously flammable when dry," size 12-14, 1960s	250	500
Party Dress, beige georgette chemise w/ V neck and triple-tiered skirt, bodice sewn w/ pink, blue, and green sequins arranged in intricate floral vine pattern, tiers trimmed in sequined wave pattern, size 6, 1920s	100	300

Left: Gown, black net, Stern Bros., c1905, $2530 at auction.

Center: Afternoon Gown, paquin velvet, French, c1905, $3220 at auction.

Right: Evening Dress, Chanel, 1930s, $18,400 at auction.

Photos courtesy William Doyle Galleries.

Cocktail Dresses.

Left: Christian Dior, rose satin woven w/ velvet floral sprigs, labeled "Christian Dior Paris Automne-Hiver 1956 #83570," $1200-$1500.

Right: Traina-Norell, halter neck bodice, bare back, red satin hoop skirt, labeled "Traina-Norell New York, Bergdorf Goodman New York," 1959, $400-$600.

—Photos courtesy William Doyle Galleries.

	LOW	HIGH
Party Dress, machine-embroidered ivory net lace, straight sleeveless shift, central chiffon panel sewn full-length w/ crochet-covered buttons, filet lace pointed edging, size 10, 1920s	100	300
Party Dress, velvet dotted chiffon, black, each dot accented w/ a rhinestone, straight elbow-length sleeves ending in full slit flounce, low waist sewn with tiers, bodice sewn w/ 2 loose front panels, separate black silk slip w/ bottom self-band, size 14-16, 1920s	100	300
Shell Top, French, Art Deco, beaded, black chiffon sewn w/ swags and arcs pattern worked in silver bugle beads, sprinkled allover w/ same, size 10, 1920s	500	800
Suit, Jacques Fath, fine black and white flecked wool, double-breasted jacket w/ rounded shoulders, nipped waist, and padded peplum, sewn w/ pointed seaming at front and closely fitted at back waist, large black composition buttons, straight skirt, labeled "Jacques Fath Paris," size 8, c1950	900	1200
Sweater, black wool, edges outlined w/ black sequined disks and band, labeled "Laura Aponte V. Gesù E Maria. 7 Roma Made in Italy - Pure Wool 100%," 1950s	100	150
Walking Suit, morning style coat buttoning to waist, pointed hem and wide pleats, sleeves sewn w/ decorative tucks from elbow to wrist, tucking repeated on lower portion of flared skirt, side buttons sewn length of skirt, 2 separate cummerbunds, size 10, c1915	800	1200
Wedding Dress, Bonwit Teller, ivory satin w/ long tight sleeves, V neck, and triple-tiered skirt, knee-length front, tiers lengthen around back to form long broad train, labeled "Bonwit Teller New York," size 6-8, c1928	300	500
Wedding Dress, robe à la Française, trained and boned open robe of ribbed ivory damask w/ ruched and pinked faille robings, needlerun net lace engageantes, crochet-covered buttons, pleated lace dust ruffle, silk faille and embroidered organza lace petticoat, labeled "Mme. W. E. Thome, Modes, Daniels and Fisher, Denver, Colo.," early 1880s	450	600
Wedding Kimono, Japanese, off-white figured silk crepe worked allover w/ silver-embroidered sections of wave, tortoise, and lattice patterns, back embroidered w/ brilliant gold cranes, padded gold lamé hem and lining, mid-20th C	300	500

Accessories

For additional reading see *The Big Book of Buttons* by Elizabeth Hughes and Marion Lester (New Leaf, Sedgwick, ME, 1991), *The Collector's Encyclopedia of Buttons, Revised 3rd Edition* by Sally C. Luscomb (Schiffer, West Chester, PA, 1997), *Handbags* by Roseann Ettinger (Schiffer, West Chester, PA, 1991), *Antique Combs & Purses* by Evelyn Haertig (Gallery Graphics Press, Carmel, CA, 1983), and *Antique Purses, Revised Second Edition* by Richard Holiner (Collector Books, Paducah, KY, 1987, 1996 value update).

	LOW	HIGH
Afternoon Bag, burgundy alligator, rounded trapezoid w/ chain handle, red kid interior, labeled "Saks Fifth Avenue Made in France," 1950s	$300	$500
Afternoon Bag, Nettie Rosenstein, beige ostrich, tailored, w/ accordion gussets, fold-over flap, single handle, and taupe leather lining, 1950s	300	500
Belt, Hermès, black leather, gilt-metal H buckle, 1970s	75	100
Belt, Saint Laurent Rive Gauche, black faille waist cincher, labeled "Saint Laurent Rive Gauche Made in France," 1970s	125	175
Billfold, black alligator, tripartite, front set w/ Swiss watch, stamped "Genuine Alligator"	75	100
Boots, Hermès, brown leather, calf height, lace-up, medium heel, size $7\frac{1}{2}$, labeled "Hermès Paris"	150	200
Button, Bakelite, fruit, carved orange	20	30
Button, black glass, bird	6	12
Button, brass, rooster	12	18
Button, brass, stamped coat of arms	15	35
Button, calico, green on white	3	5
Button, celluloid, angel head, gold ground, gilt rims	35	45
Button, ceramic, cat	35	45
Button, cloisonné, fish	80	100
Button, enamel, floral design, 18th C	200	250
Button, gold, 18k, ball shape, 19th C	75	125
Button, ivory, painted Cupid	75	125
Button, porcelain, flowers and butterfly, 18th C	15	35
Button, steel, floral design	5	10
Button, turquoise, w/ 14k gold, button set w/ chain, 19th C	100	150
Button, Wedgwood, classical figure, white on royal blue, gilt rim, 18th C	225	275
Coolie Hat, straw, horizontal strips finely sewn w/ horizontal rows of stitching to basketweave underside, 1950s	100	250

Hermès Handbags at auction, black crocodile, left to right: Kelly Bag, $6325; Ring Bag, $1495; and Piano Bag, $1610. —Photo courtesy William Doyle Galleries.

	LOW	HIGH
Evening Bag, Elsa Peretti for Tiffany & Co., sterling silver worked in basketweave, flat and rectangular, lift-off top, labeled "Tiffany & Co. Sterling, Peretti"	1500	1800
Evening Bag, French, fine silver beads embroidered on front w/ gold metallic swag, gold metal spring frame embossed w/ flowers, labeled "Hand Made In France," 1950s	100	150
Evening Bag, Hobé, chinoiserie design, large rectangular clutch, deep blue silk brocade depicting cranes, pines, and mountains, center set w/ large ornament of carved bone figures framed in elaborate gold-filled and sterling silver floral surround, labeled "by Hobé," c1942	800	1200
Evening Bag, Mark Cross, forest green crocodile, small flat square bag w/ top handle, hinged sides, green kid lining and change purse, labeled on change purse "Mark Cross," 1960s	125	175
Evening Bag, Nettie Rosenstein, coral leather sewn allover w/ coral branches and beads and sprinkled w/ rhinestones, double leather handle, silk lining, signed "Nettie Rosenstein," 1950s	300	500
Evening Bag, Walborg, beaded, rigid springed flap, bag sewn allover w/ small white beads in aligned heart pattern, labeled "Made in France by hand, Walborg," 1950s	100	150
Gentleman's Boater, pinwheel design on crown, labeled "Subro Suntan," size 7, early 20th C	50	75
Gentleman's Riding Boots, English, tan leather, front lacing, labeled "Made in England Expressly For Saks Fifth Avenue New York"	100	125
Gloves, Renaissance style, black leather, slit tops, 1940s	50	75
Handbag, Art Deco style, sleek rectangle w/ green shagreen front and clasp, pebbled green leather back and sides, beige suede interior, 1920s	200	400
Handbag, Lucille de Paris, black crocodile, single top handle, soft side gussets, labeled "Lucille de Paris," 1950s	400	600
Handbag, Roberta Di Camerino, chocolate brown leather, double-handled w/ belt buckle trim at handle joints, labeled "Roberta Di Camerino, Italy, Genuine Leather"	200	300
Kelly Bag, Hermès, black crocodile w/ gilt-metal fittings, lock, and key sheath, labeled "Hermès - Paris 24 F^{G} ST Honoré," 36" w	2500	3000
Minaudière, Gucci, jeweled, patterned gilt-metal encrusted w/ faceted gold stones set in lattice pattern, ivory satin lining, labeled "Made in Italy Gucci," 1960s	150	200
Monk Puppet Beaded Bag, deep brown beaded robe and hood, painted wood head, hands, and feet, opening to pouch by lifting monk's head on string running through it	200	300
Ostrich Feather Hat, Hattie Carnegie, covered w/ froth of black feather, labeled "Hattie Carnegie Custom Made," w/ matching muff, c1920	100	125
Pill Box Hat, leopard skin, labeled "Macy's Little Shop"	100	250
Platform Shoes, beige lizard w/ high heels and ankle straps, decorated w/ straw dolls and gem-studded flowers, labeled "Gainsborough 1128 Lincoln Road Miami Beach, Fla.," 1950s	75	100
Portfolio, Pucci, flat envelope w/ oblique flap, cotton duck printed w/ geometric pattern in shades of brown, coral, and spring green, signed in gold "Emilio Pucci," 1960s	150	200
Purse, Gucci, bone leather, rounded fold-over flap, bamboo handle, bamboo pivot clasp, labeled "Made in Italy by Gucci 47," 1960s	200	300
Purse, Pucci, silk twill, white printed w/ yellow, pink, and red geometric pattern, gilt-metal chain handles, rigid frame w/ snap clasp in interior, labeled "Emilio Pucci by Jana Made In Italy," 1980s	150	200

	LOW	HIGH
Robe, Chinese, midnight blue gauze embroidered in gold metallic threads w/ dragons, scrolls, and diagonal wave border, horsehoof cuffs, 19th C	250	400
Scarf, Brooke Cadwallader, olive green silk printed in black w/ elaborate 17th-C town scene set in Amsterdam depicting public spectacle w/ armored horsemen, banners, etc.	100	150
Scarf, Hermès, rectangular, double-sided, silk twill printed w/ circus actors and animals, shades of yellow, gray, gold, and pink, signed "Hermès Paris"	350	450
Scarf, Salvador Dali, white silk twill printed w/ image of butterflies on faceless female bust, field splattered w/ black, butter yellow border, signed "Dali"	100	150
Shawl, French, paisley, woven w/ enormous swirling cones and black star center w/ 2 fleurs-de-lis, shades of red, blue, green, and gold, white woven signature, 1860s, 11'2" l, 64" w	800	1200
Shoulder Bag, Judith Leiber, navy leather w/ rounded tucked bottom and flap decorated w/ carved rock crystal lion's head set in gilt-metal, faille lining, signed "Judith Leiber," 1970s	400	600
Stiletto Heels, Raphael, black satin sewn w/ steel gray beads and faceted stones, labeled "Raphael Roma," size $9^{1}/_{2}$, 1950s	100	150
Stole, turquoise silk satin, fringed, 1950s	150	200
Straw Portrait Hat, Lilly Daché, small crown encircled w/ black grosgrain, broad brim squared off and trimmed w/ ribbon bow, labeled "Lilly Daché New York," 1940s	200	300
Summer Pumps, Manolo Blahnik, white leather w/ perforated toe design, high black patent leather spike heel, labeled "Manolo Blahnik," size 39	50	125
Sunbonnet, Christian Dior, white silk, topstitched in rows, broad brim gathered into crown, labeled "Christian Dior"	50	75
Sunglasses, leopard pattern, 1950s	200	300
Tie, Hermès, watermelon design, labeled	25	60
Tie-Dyed Shoes, Roger Vivier, shades of yellow, orange, and pink, square spike heel and rounded double strap attaching at covered button, labeled "Designed by Roger Vivier Paris," size $6^{1}/_{2}$ B, 1960s	100	150
Top Hat, beaver w/ faille edge, labeled "By Warrant to His Majesty The King, Henry Heath Limited, 105, 107, 109 Oxford St. W. London," w/ rectangular tan leather traveling case w/ burgundy quilted silk lining, lower portion fitted w/ straps, upper portion fitted for top hat, 19th C	100	150

Raphael Stiletto Heels, 1950s. —Photo courtesy William Doyle Galleries.

Coca-Cola Collectibles

The first batch of Coca-Cola was created by John Pemberton, an Atlanta pharmacist, in 1886. Mr. Pemberton was trying to create a tonic rather than a soft drink. The syrup was soon marketed to Willis Venable, an Atlanta soda fountain manager. As legend has it, a clerk mixed the syrup with soda and an empire was born. In 1894 Joseph Biedenhorn started bottling and distributing Coca-Cola in Vicksburg, MS. Coke became the world's favorite soft drink. With over 100 years of advertisements and promotional material, Coke collectors have an incredible breadth of material from which to draw. The firm has done a great job in promoting its product. One reason collectors love this material is that by viewing it you can draw a time line of our last 100 years. It begins with the Victorian elegance of the 1890s and travels through two World Wars, the Great Depression, Rock 'n' Roll, the country's struggle with the Vietnam War ("I'd Like to Teach the World to Sing"), to today's sports stars' endorsements. Coke ads are usually very appealing and reflective of their time. Since Coca-Cola is now a global entity, the material grows daily, and there are even Coke boutiques specializing in marketing new Coke clothing and products.

The only cautionary note is that there are also many reproductions and items that are done in the style of an earlier era. Such material is often offered as old with prices far beyond their value. Do your homework and deal with knowledgeable people that stand behind their products. The prices below are based on items in excellent or mint condition.

For further information see *Petretti's Coca-Cola Collectibles Price Guide, 10th Edition* by Allan Petretti (Antique Trader Books, Dubuque, IA 1997) and *Classic Coca-Cola Serving Trays* by Allan Petretti and Chris H. Beyer (Antique Trader Books, 1998). You may also wish to contact the Coca-Cola Collectors Club International, P.O. Box 49166, Atlanta, GA 30359.

Ice Box, wood w/ zinc lining, bottle opener on front, red stenciled letters on yellow ground, c1920s, 14" x 26" x 14", $220 at auction. —Photo courtesy Gary Metz's Muddy River Trading Co.

	LOW	AVG.	HIGH
Advertising Trade Card, folding, folded card shows girl in bathtub and "Appearances are sometimes deceiving but Coca-Cola can always be relied on as nourishing, refreshing and exhilarating," opens to same girl serving 2 men drinks and "When thirsty, tired or head-achy, or after a night out try a Coca-Cola High Ball," text on back, c1907, 6.25" x 3.5" closed size	$900	$1200	$1500
Bag Rack, tin marquee w/ 6-pack of bottles in yellow circle and "Take Home A Carton Of Coca-Cola" on red ground, wire rack, late 1930s, 16" h, 36" w	500	650	800
Billboard, 24 sheets dry-mounted on linen, World War II iron-worker enjoying a coke, "The rest-pause that refreshes, Welcome in peace…more welcome in war work," 1943, 8' x 20'	750	1000	1250
Calendar, barefoot boy eating sandwich and drinking Coke, dog watching, full pad and 1930 cover sheet, 1931	2000	2500	3000
Calendar, barefoot boy on stone well, begging dog at his feet, July page, 1932	300	350	400
Calendar, barefoot boy going fishing with dog, new old stock w/ full pad and cover sheet, 1937	1500	2000	2500

	LOW	AVG.	HIGH
Calendar, boy and girl building snowman, "Thirst knows no season," 6-sheet, 1942	350	450	550
Calendar, distributor's, lounging woman wearing gold slinky dress, November page, 1928	600	800	1000
Calendar, nurse holding bottle, pyramid in background, 1943	125	175	250
Calendar, pretty blonde holding skis and sunglasses, snowy background, 1947	375	500	650
Calendar, pretty girl, snowy background, "Coca-Cola, For the Pause that Refreshes, Thirst knows no Season," 1945	100	150	200
Calendar, pretty girl wearing Roaring '20s dress and string of beads, holding glass of Coke, partial pad, 1929	350	500	650
Calendar, pretty woman wearing elaborate flowered hat and drinking glass of Coke, "Drink Coca-Cola, Delicious and Refreshing," June-December pad, 1912, 12" x 31"	6000	8500	10,000
Calendar, woman wearing white gown w/ red ribbons, standing by dressing screen and ornate cooler, March page, 1904, 7.5" x 15" image	3500	5000	7500
Calendar, seated girl wearing summery dress and wide-brimmed hat, holding bottle, full pad, 1938	125	175	250
Calendar, southern belle holding bottle, Capitol in background, "The Gibson High-Sign, For the Pause that Refreshes," 1944	350	450	550
Calendar, white-haired southern gentleman and lady on veranda, full pad, 1934	250	350	450
Calendar Holder, metal, red button top and "Have A Coke" above calendar pad, 1950s, 19" h, 8" w	375	500	650
Calendar Top, girl holding glass and feather duster, w/ metal strip, 1923	500	650	800
Calendar Top, girl holding glass of Coke, bottle on table, title page featuring text about Coca-Cola and its history, w/ metal strip, 1924	600	750	900

Electric Clocks at auction, left to right: 1958 light-up w/ original box, 15" dia, $743; 1939, $825; 1948 restored, 36" l, $523; 1942 neon light-up w/ metal frame and glass front, 15.5" sq, $495; c1958 w/ Roman numerals, 15" dia, $440. —Photos courtesy Gary Metz's Muddy River Trading Co.

Sidewalk Signs at auction, tin, left to right: 1939, $688; 1941, $605; 1941, $495; 1952, $908; 1958, $853. —Photos courtesy Gary Metz's Muddy River Trading Co.

	LOW	AVG.	HIGH
Calendar Top, girl wearing wide-brimmed hat and pink lacy dress, holding glass of Coke, baseball game in background, w/ metal strip, 1922	2000	2500	3000
Case Insert, cardboard, Sprite Boy and "Take a case home Today, $1^{00} Plus Deposit," new old stock, 1947	100	150	200
Change Tray, Hilda Clark image of woman wearing white gown and holding glass of Coke and fan, gold rim, "Delicious, Refreshing," 1903, 4" dia	3000	3500	4200
Cooler, Lincoln Carton, coin-operated, w/ matching base, dry server dispenser, bottle opener, and cap catcher, chrome lid, 14" sq, 38" h	4000	5000	6500
Counter Sign, "Coca-Cola" on rectangular glass panel, mounted on wood base marked "Please Pay When Served," 1948, 8.5" h, 18" w	300	375	450
Door Bar, adjustable, wrought iron rails, "Drink Coca-Cola" on porcelain panel, 1930s	350	500	650
Festoon, 3-piece, cardboard, "All-Time Favorites," sports theme w/ Gene Tunney, Bobby Jones, Red Grange, Don Budge, Colonial Lady, Man O' War, Ty Cobb, and Helene Madison, Sprite boy with bottle and "Have A Coke" button, 1947	3500	5000	6500
Festoon, 5-piece, cardboard, pansies, center panel w/ girl holding glass, 1933	2000	2500	3000
Light Fixture, 2 bottles on Art Deco style brass and copper framework, 20" h acid-etched bottles w/ caramel-stained interior, 1930s	10,000	12,000	15,000
Matchbook Holder, brown leather, gold lettering "Compliments Coca-Cola Co., 'Coca-Cola Relieves Fatigue'," 1907	500	650	800
Menu, cardboard, 2-sided, Hilda Clark illustration on front, soda menu on back, 1903, 4" x 6"	2000	2500	3000
Mileage Meter, red plastic, white lettering, 1950s	1200	1500	1800
Pen and Pencil Set, miniature wooden baseball bats, marked "Chas. Gehringer, Detroit Tigers, Coca-Cola," original mailing box, 1930s	600	800	1000
Playing Cards, girl sipping soda from bottle through straw, green ground, red border, complete w/ Joker, bridge card, and original sleeve box, 1928	2000	2500	3000
Poster, girl skater taking break while enjoying bottle of Coke, "The year-round answer to thirst," 1940	1200	1500	1800
Poster, girl w/ umbrella standing beside cooler, "Talk about refreshing," 1942	375	500	650

Serving Trays, 10.5" x 13.25", left to right: 1926, $1000; 1928, $900; 1935 Madge Evans, $500; 1936, $450. —Photos courtesy Gene Harris Antique Auction Center, Inc.

	LOW	AVG.	HIGH
Pullmatch Ashtray, lamp-shaped, red shade w/ stick matches "fringe," chrome bottle, black Bakelite base, 1930s-40s	3250	4500	6000
Service Pins, set of 6, commemorating 5, 10, 15, 20, 25, and 30 years of service, diamond chip in 25- and 30-year pins, framed and mounted	300	450	600
Serving Tray, rectangular, girl wearing turban and stole gazing at glass of Coke, 1925	600	800	1000
Serving Tray, rectangular, sailor girl on dock holding bottle and fishing rod, "Drink Coca-Cola Delicious and Refreshing, 1940	550	750	1000
Sign, button, "Coca-Cola" and bottle, red ground, 1950s, 36" dia	600	800	1000
Sign, cardboard, bottle on iceberg, "Have a Coke," 1944, 20" h, 36" w	375	500	650
Sign, cardboard, woman pilot holding Coke bottle, prop plane in background, "Your thirst takes wings," 1940, 20" h, 36" w	1500	2000	3000
Sign, cardboard, woman wearing navy blue dress and hat, holding purse and 6-pack bottle carrier, "Take Home a Carton, Easy to Carry," 1937, 32" h, 14" w	1800	2400	3000
Sign, neon, round, red "Coca-Cola Classic" surrounded by white rim lettering "The Official Soft Drink of Summer," 1980s, 24" dia	750	1000	1250
Sign, porcelain, 2-sided, stainless steel rim, glass being filled from Coke dispenser, white ground, 1950s, 27" h, 28" w	1500	2000	2500
Sign, porcelain, diecut 6-pack of bottles, 1952, 11" h, 13" w	1200	1500	1800
Sign, porcelain, "Drink Coca-Cola, Fountain Service," words "Drink" and "Fountain Service" on white ribbon, yellow ground, 1950s, 12" h, 28" w	1200	1500	1800
Sign, porcelain, elongated shield shape, "Fountain Service" on green ground above "Drink Coca-Cola" in white on red ground, 1934, 14" h, 27" w	2500	3500	4500
Sign, reverse-painted glass, "Drink Coca-Cola," white lettering, red ground, original chain side hangers, chrome strips at top and bottom, and paper backing, Brunhoff Mfg. Co., 1938	800	1200	1600
Thermometer, embossed tin, red button top, red "Quality Refreshment" and blue border lines on white ground, 1950s, 9" h, 3" w	600	800	1000
Thermometer, masonite, "Drink Coca-Cola" button and soda bottle above "Thirst knows no season," 2-tone green ground, 1944, 17" h, 6.75" w	750	1000	1250
Tip Tray, litho tin, oval, woman wearing low-cut ruffled dress and holding glass, "Drink Coca-Cola, Relieves Fatigue, 5¢," 1907	600	750	900

Coins

The following ratings are from the American Numismatic Association grading system. For more detailed descriptions, write to the American Numismatic Association, 814 N. Cascade Ave., Colorado Springs, CO 80903.

Proof (PRF–65)—Refers to method of manufacture, distinguished by sharpness of detail and usually with brilliant mirror surface. Proof coins are in perfect mint state.

Uncirculated (MS–60)—No trace of wear but may show some contact marks; surface may be spotted or lack some luster.

About Uncirculated (AU–50)—Traces of light wear on many of the high points. At least half of mint luster is still present.

Extremely Fine (EF–40)—Design is lightly worn throughout, but all features are sharp and well defined. Traces of luster may show.

Very Fine (VF–20)—Shows wear on high points of design. All major details are clear.

Fine (F–12)—Moderate even wear; entire design is bold with pleasing appearance.

Very Good (VG–8)—Well worn; main feature clear and bold but rather flat.

Good (G–4)—Heavily worn; design visible but faint in areas; many details flat.

About Good (AG–3)—Very heavily worn with parts of lettering and date worn smooth.

Beware of altered coins. Some skilled fakers are able to change the date on an otherwise common coin to imitate a rare and valuable example. We have also seen totally fake coins coming from Asia.

For further information see *The Official 2000 Blackbook Price Guide to United States Coins, Thirty-Eighth Edition* by Marc Hudgeons (House of Collectibles, 1999) and *2000 North American Coins & Prices, 9th Edition* edited by David C. Harper (Krause Publications, Iola, WI, 1999).

Half Cents

Liberty Cap Type 1793–1797

	AG–3	G–4	VG–8	F–12	VF–20	EF–40
1793	$750.00	$1500.00	$2500.00	$3500.00	$5500.00	—
1794–97	80.00	250.00	325.00	600.00	1200.00	$2000.00

Draped Bust Type 1800–1808

	AG–3	G–4	VG–8	F–12	VF–20	EF–40
1800	$15.00	$30.00	$50.00	$75.00	$150.00	$325.00
1803–08	15.00	30.00	40.00	55.00	100.00	250.00

Classic Head Type 1809–1837

	G–4	VG–8	F–12	VF–20	EF–40
1809–26	$25.00	$35.00	$45.00	$80.00	$120.00
1828–35	20.00	25.00	35.00	50.00	75.00
1837 (copper)	25.00	40.00	50.00	100.00	150.00

Coronet Type 1840–1857

	G–4	VG–8	F–12	VF–20	EF–40
1849–57	$40.00	$45.00	$50.00	$65.00	$100.00

Large Cents

Draped Bust Type 1800–1807

	AG–3	G–4	VG–8	F–12	VF–20
1800–07	$15.00	$30.00	$60.00	$125.00	$300.00

Classic Head Type 1808–14

	AG–3	G–4	VG–8	F–12	VF–20
1808–14	$20.00	$40.00	$75.00	$200.00	$500.00

Coronet Type 1816–1857

	AG–3	G–4	VG–8	F–12	VF–20	MS–60
1816–25	$10.00	$15.00	$20.00	$30.00	$75.00	$400.00
1826–38	8.00	12.00	15.00	25.00	45.00	350.00
1839–57	5.00	10.00	12.00	15.00	30.00	250.00

Small Cents

Flying Eagle Type 1856–1858

	AG–3	G–4	F–12	VF–20	EF–40	MS–60
1856	$1500.00	$2500.00	$3000.00	$3500.00	$4000.00	$6000.00
1857–58	10.00	15.00	20.00	35.00	75.00	300.00

Indian Head Type 1859–1909

	AG–3	G–4	F–12	VF–20	EF–40	MS–60
1859–64	$3.00	$5.00	$12.00	$25.00	$30.00	$150.00
1865	3.00	5.00	7.00	15.00	25.00	60.00

	AG–3	G–4	F–12	VF–20	EF–40	MS–60
1866–68	7.00	20.00	40.00	60.00	80.00	175.00
1869–72	12.00	30.00	100.00	140.00	200.00	300.00
1873–76	4.00	15.00	25.00	35.00	55.00	100.00
1877	75.00	200.00	400.00	650.00	1000.00	2000.00
1878	8.00	15.00	30.00	40.00	50.00	150.00
1879	1.00	3.50	6.00	10.00	20.00	55.00
1880–84	1.00	2.00	3.50	6.00	15.00	40.00
1885–86	1.00	3.00	8.00	12.00	25.00	80.00
1887–1908	.50	.80	1.50	3.50	7.50	30.00

Lincoln Type, Wheat Sheaves 1909–1958

	AG–3	G–4	F–12	VF–20	EF–40	MS–60
1909 v.d.b.	$1.00	$2.00	$2.50	$3.00	$3.50	$500.00
1909S v.d.b.	150.00	300.00	350.00	400.00	450.00	500.00
1909–19	.10	.25	.35	.80	2.00	12.00
1920–34	.10	.15	.35	.65	1.50	8.00
1935–42	.05	.08	.10	.15	.25	2.00
1943 (steel)	.04	.08	.15	.25	.35	3.50
1944–58	.03	.05	.08	.12	.15	.75
Exceptions:						
1913S	2.00	7.00	9.00	12.00	25.00	100.00
1914D	25.00	75.00	100.00	175.00	400.00	800.00
1914S	4.00	8.00	12.00	20.00	35.00	175.00
1915S	3.50	7.00	10.00	12.00	25.00	120.00
1922D	1.50	5.00	7.50	10.00	20.00	85.00
1922 (plain)	85.00	165.00	275.00	450.00	2500.00	5000.00
1924D	4.00	9.00	15.00	25.00	50.00	225.00
1926S	1.50	3.00	4.50	7.00	12.00	100.00
1931D	1.00	2.00	3.50	4.50	8.00	50.00
1931S	10.00	30.00	35.00	40.00	45.00	65.00
1932	.50	1.50	2.00	2.50	3.00	18.00
1932D	.20	.60	1.20	1.80	2.50	15.00
1933	.20	.75	1.25	1.75	3.00	18.00
1933D	.50	1.50	2.25	3.00	4.00	25.00
1955 (double die)	—	—	250.00	375.00	450.00	1200.00

Lincoln Type, Lincoln Memorial 1959–date

	AG–3	G–4	F–12	VF–20	EF–40	MS–60
1960 (sm. date)	$.25	—	—	—	$1.00	$2.50
1970S (sm. date)	.20	—	—	—	.50	25.00
1972 (double die)	75.00	—	—	—	175.00	250.00

Two-Cent Pieces

1864–1873

	AG–3	G–4	F–12	VF–20	EF–40	MS–60
1864 (sm. motto)	$40.00	$50.00	$85.00	$150.00	$225.00	$550.00
1864–69	2.50	5.00	10.00	18.00	30.00	110.00
1870–71	4.50	10.00	20.00	35.00	60.00	225.00
1872	30.00	75.00	125.00	225.00	325.00	750.00

Three-Cent Pieces

Six-Point Star 1851–1873 (silver)

	AG–3	G–4	F–12	VF–20	EF–40	MS–60
1851–62	$5.00	$12.00	$20.00	$35.00	$75.00	$200.00
1863–72	250.00	—	—	—	—	550.00

Liberty Head Type 1865–1889 (nickel)

	AG–3	G–4	F–12	VF–20	EF–40	MS–60
1865–74	$2.50	$6.00	$8.00	$12.00	$20.00	$100.00
1875–76	3.00	8.00	15.00	20.00	30.00	150.00
1879–80	20.00	50.00	65.00	80.00	100.00	250.00
1881	2.50	6.00	7.50	12.00	20.00	95.00
1882	15.00	55.00	75.00	90.00	120.00	200.00
1883	35.00	110.00	150.00	180.00	250.00	350.00
1885	70.00	325.00	400.00	450.00	550.00	700.00
1887	80.00	225.00	250.00	325.00	425.00	500.00
1888–89	20.00	45.00	65.00	75.00	100.00	250.00

Nickel Five-Cent Pieces

Shield Type 1866–1883

	AG–3	G–4	F–12	VF–20	EF–40	MS–60
1866–67	$4.00	$12.00	$25.00	$45.00	$90.00	$250.00
1868–70	4.00	8.00	12.00	18.00	30.00	125.00
1871	12.00	30.00	40.00	60.00	90.00	275.00
1872–76	4.00	10.00	15.00	25.00	40.00	150.00
1879–80	85.00	215.00	325.00	400.00	500.00	600.00
1881	65.00	150.00	200.00	275.00	350.00	475.00
1882–83	3.50	8.00	12.00	18.00	30.00	125.00

Liberty Head Type 1883–1912

	AG–3	G–4	F–12	VF–20	EF–40	MS–60
1883–84	$2.00	$5.00	$12.00	$20.00	$35.00	$125.00
1885	65.00	175.00	325.00	400.00	600.00	950.00
1886	30.00	45.00	125.00	165.00	225.00	500.00
1887–96	2.00	4.00	15.00	20.00	35.00	100.00
1897–99	.50	1.50	6.00	10.00	20.00	100.00
1900–12	.30	.75	5.00	8.00	18.00	75.00
1912D	.50	1.20	5.00	15.00	45.00	200.00
1912S	20.00	35.00	60.00	225.00	375.00	500.00

Buffalo Type 1913–1938

	AG–3	G–4	F–12	VF–20	EF–40	MS–60
1913–15	$1.50	$4.00	$6.00	$10.00	$15.00	$45.00
1913D (high mound)	2.50	6.50	10.00	15.00	25.00	70.00
1913D (level ground)	12.00	30.00	50.00	60.00	85.00	200.00
1913S (high mound)	3.00	10.00	18.00	25.00	40.00	80.00
1913S (level ground)	30.00	75.00	125.00	150.00	200.00	350.00
1914D	8.00	20.00	50.00	75.00	120.00	300.00
1914S	3.00	5.50	10.00	18.00	35.00	175.00
1915D	2.00	6.00	20.00	35.00	55.00	200.00
1915S	4.00	10.00	25.00	50.00	125.00	400.00
1916–21	.50	.75	2.00	3.50	6.00	50.00
1916D, 1916S	2.50	5.00	10.00	20.00	45.00	150.00
1916 (double die)	600.00	1200.00	5000.00	6500.00	10,000.00	15,000.00
1917D, 1917S	3.00	4.50	15.00	40.00	90.00	250.00
1918D, 1918S	2.00	3.50	15.00	40.00	100.00	275.00
1919D, 1919S	1.50	3.75	15.00	50.00	140.00	425.00
1920D	1.00	3.50	12.00	50.00	175.00	375.00
1920S	.75	2.00	6.00	40.00	125.00	300.00
1921S	6.00	12.00	40.00	200.00	700.00	900.00
1923–24	.50	.75	1.75	3.00	8.00	40.00
1923S	1.00	1.50	8.00	45.00	175.00	300.00
1924D	1.00	2.50	8.00	40.00	125.00	250.00
1924S	2.50	5.00	25.00	125.00	900.00	1800.00

	AG–3	G–4	F–12	VF–20	EF–40	MS–60
1925–30	.30	.75	1.50	3.00	7.50	35.00
1925D, 1925S	1.75	3.00	12.00	60.00	150.00	350.00
1926D	1.25	2.00	12.00	50.00	125.00	200.00
1926S	2.00	5.00	30.00	200.00	700.00	2000.00
1927D	.50	1.00	5.00	18.00	40.00	110.00
1927S	.50	1.00	3.00	20.00	65.00	325.00
1928D–30D	.25	.50	.80	2.50	8.00	30.00
1928S	.25	.75	1.50	5.00	12.00	180.00
1929S–30S	.20	.60	1.15	3.50	10.00	45.00
1931S	1.15	3.00	5.00	7.50	15.00	40.00
1934–37	.15	.30	.75	1.25	4.00	20.00
1937D (3 legs)	—	50.00	125.00	175.00	250.00	400.00
1938D	.15	.40	.60	1.75	5.00	15.00

Jefferson Type 1938–date

	AG–3	G–4	F–12	VF–20	EF–40	MS–60
1938–39	$.12	$.15	$.30	$.50	$1.00	$3.00
1938D, 1938S	.40	.75	1.50	2.00	2.50	6.00
1939D	1.00	2.00	3.50	4.00	7.50	40.00
1939S	.25	.50	1.00	1.50	2.50	20.00
1940–42	—	—	—	—	.35	1.25
1942D	.20	.30	.65	1.00	2.00	20.00
1942P, 1942S (silver)	.20	.25	.50	.80	1.50	12.00
1943–45 (silver)	.20	.25	.50	.75	1.25	5.00
1946–49	—	—	—	—	.30	.65
1949 (double die)	—	—	25.00	35.00	75.00	200.00
1950–51	.10	.20	.40	.60	1.00	1.75
1952–58	—	—	—	—	.20	.45

Half Dimes

Flowing Hair Type 1794–1795

	AG–3	G–4	VG–8	F–12	VF–20	EF–40
1794	$400.00	$800.00	$1000.00	$1500.00	$2000.00	$2500.00
1795	375.00	650.00	850.00	1000.00	1200.00	1500.00

Draped Bust Type, Small Eagle 1796–1797

	AG–3	G–4	VG–8	F–12	VF–20	EF–40
1796–97	$400.00	$800.00	$950.00	$1200.00	$2000.00	$2500.00

Draped Bust Type, Heraldic Eagle 1800–1805

	AG–3	G–4	VG–8	F–12	VF–20	EF–40
1800–05	$300.00	$550.00	$700.00	$1000.00	$1400.00	$2000.00
1802	1800.00	10,000.00	15,000.00	20,000.00	30,000.00	50,000.00

Capped Bust Type 1829–1837

	G–4	VG–8	F–12	VF–20	EF–40	MS–60
1829–37	$12.00	$16.00	$25.00	$50.00	$110.00	$500.00
1837 (small 5¢)	20.00	30.00	45.00	90.00	160.00	2000.00

Seated Liberty Type 1837–1873

	G–4	VG–8	F–12	VF–20	EF–40	MS–60
1837	$25.00	$35.00	$50.00	$100.00	$210.00	$700.00
1838–40	7.00	9.00	12.00	25.00	60.00	400.00
1838O (no stars)	100.00	140.00	200.00	350.00	700.00	1800.00
1841–59	7.00	7.50	8.50	18.00	45.00	200.00
1842O	20.00	30.00	50.00	150.00	425.00	—
1846	125.00	175.00	300.00	500.00	1200.00	5000.00
1853 (no arrows)	25.00	35.00	60.00	100.00	200.00	650.00
1860–62	6.00	6.50	8.00	15.00	35.00	180.00
1863	90.00	120.00	190.00	250.00	375.00	700.00
1864	190.00	225.00	350.00	420.00	600.00	1300.00
1865	190.00	225.00	300.00	375.00	500.00	900.00
1866	150.00	180.00	250.00	300.00	450.00	750.00
1867	190.00	250.00	425.00	480.00	600.00	900.00
1868	30.00	45.00	75.00	120.00	215.00	500.00
1869	7.00	8.50	12.00	20.00	40.00	215.00
1870–73	5.00	6.00	8.50	12.00	30.00	175.00

Dimes

Draped Bust Type, Small Eagle 1796–1797

	AG–3	G–4	VG–8	F–12	VF–20
1796–97	$350.00	$850.00	$1100.00	$1500.00	$2400.00

Draped Bust Type, Large Eagle 1798–1807

	AG–3	G–4	VG–8	F–12	VF–20
1798–1801	$300.00	$500.00	$650.00	$900.00	$1500.00
1802	300.00	500.00	750.00	1200.00	2000.00
1803	300.00	450.00	700.00	1000.00	1500.00

	AG–3	G–4	VG–8	F–12	VF–20
1804	400.00	850.00	1200.00	2000.00	3200.00
1805–07	250.00	450.00	600.00	900.00	1200.00

Capped Bust Type 1809–1837

	G–4	VG–8	F–12	VF–20	EF–40	MS–60
1809–11	$75.00	$110.00	$200.00	$350.00	$850.00	$3000.00
1814 (small date)	50.00	60.00	90.00	175.00	350.00	1500.00
1814 (large date)	30.00	38.00	50.00	150.00	325.00	1000.00
1820–21	20.00	25.00	40.00	150.00	350.00	900.00
1822	150.00	300.00	700.00	1000.00	1800.00	6000.00
1823–24	12.00	18.00	30.00	75.00	275.00	1100.00
1825–27	20.00	25.00	40.00	150.00	350.00	900.00
1828	30.00	40.00	60.00	150.00	325.00	1400.00
1829–37	12.00	15.00	25.00	50.00	175.00	750.00

Seated Liberty Type 1837–1891

	G–4	VG–8	F–12	VF–20	EF–40	MS–60
1837	$25.00	$40.00	$60.00	$220.00	$450.00	$1000.00
1838 (large stars)	8.00	9.00	12.00	25.00	50.00	500.00
1838 (small stars)	15.00	24.00	40.00	75.00	150.00	1300.00
1838O	35.00	50.00	100.00	275.00	500.00	2000.00
1839–40	6.00	8.00	12.00	25.00	60.00	350.00
1840O	8.00	10.00	15.00	25.00	75.00	1000.00
1841–62	5.00	8.00	11.00	20.00	45.00	300.00
1841O	7.00	10.00	15.00	35.00	65.00	1200.00
1843O	35.00	70.00	100.00	200.00	550.00	1500.00
1844	30.00	65.00	90.00	200.00	500.00	2000.00
1845O	15.00	25.00	50.00	200.00	500.00	1500.00
1846	75.00	100.00	140.00	300.00	750.00	2000.00
1847	10.00	15.00	30.00	75.00	150.00	1000.00
1849O	10.00	20.00	30.00	100.00	300.00	2500.00
1850O	7.00	10.00	15.00	50.00	150.00	1200.00
1851O	10.00	15.00	25.00	70.00	170.00	1500.00
1852O	12.00	20.00	35.00	75.00	200.00	1500.00
1853O, 1854O	6.00	7.50	10.00	25.00	75.00	700.00
1856S	40.00	65.00	100.00	175.00	500.00	1500.00
1858O	10.00	15.00	35.00	60.00	150.00	800.00
1858S	40.00	75.00	125.00	200.00	450.00	1000.00
1859S	50.00	80.00	150.00	250.00	500.00	2500.00
1860O	300.00	425.00	650.00	1000.00	2000.00	—
1860S–1867S	15.00	25.00	40.00	100.00	200.00	1000.00
1863–65	100.00	150.00	250.00	350.00	500.00	1000.00
1866	110.00	175.00	400.00	550.00	750.00	1500.00
1867	200.00	300.00	450.00	550.00	700.00	2000.00
1868	7.00	8.50	12.00	30.00	70.00	450.00
1868S	10.00	15.00	25.00	50.00	125.00	400.00
1869	10.00	12.00	20.00	45.00	100.00	450.00
1870–72	5.00	7.00	10.00	18.00	40.00	250.00
1870S	50.00	80.00	150.00	220.00	400.00	2500.00
1871CC, 1872CC	350.00	500.00	800.00	1200.00	2500.00	—
1871S–1873S	10.00	15.00	30.00	60.00	125.00	800.00

	G–4	VG–8	F–12	VF–20	EF–40	MS–60
1873	5.00	8.00	12.00	20.00	40.00	600.00
1874	8.00	10.00	15.00	45.00	100.00	650.00
1874CC	1000.00	1500.00	2800.00	3500.00	6000.00	—
1874S	20.00	35.00	50.00	85.00	175.00	1000.00
1875–78	3.50	5.00	7.00	12.00	20.00	150.00
1875CC, 1875S	4.00	5.50	7.50	15.00	35.00	300.00
1878CC	30.00	50.00	75.00	110.00	200.00	650.00
1879	100.00	150.00	220.00	300.00	400.00	650.00
1880–81	75.00	100.00	150.00	200.00	325.00	550.00
1882–91	3.50	5.00	6.00	10.00	20.00	150.00
1884S, 1886S	12.00	15.00	20.00	30.00	65.00	500.00
1885S	125.00	160.00	300.00	400.00	650.00	2500.00
1889S	10.00	14.00	20.00	35.00	75.00	400.00
1890S	5.00	7.00	10.00	20.00	40.00	300.00

Barber or Liberty Head Type 1892–1916

	G–4	VG–8	F–12	VF–20	EF–40	MS–60
1892	$2.50	$5.00	$10.00	$12.00	$25.00	$115.00
1892O	4.50	6.00	12.00	18.00	30.00	150.00
1892S	25.00	35.00	75.00	100.00	150.00	350.00
1893	5.00	7.00	10.00	20.00	35.00	175.00
1893O	12.00	30.00	75.00	100.00	125.00	275.00
1894	30.00	60.00	125.00	175.00	300.00	950.00
1895	60.00	100.00	200.00	240.00	300.00	550.00
1895O	200.00	300.00	450.00	650.00	1200.00	2400.00
1896	6.00	12.00	25.00	35.00	50.00	175.00
1896O, 1896S	40.00	80.00	175.00	220.00	300.00	600.00
1897	3.00	3.50	4.00	10.00	25.00	150.00
1897S	7.00	18.00	40.00	55.00	75.00	325.00
1898–1916	1.50	2.25	4.00	10.00	20.00	125.00
1898O	4.00	20.00	45.00	70.00	110.00	400.00
1898S	4.00	8.00	15.00	24.00	35.00	300.00
1899O	3.00	10.00	40.00	60.00	110.00	350.00
1899S	3.00	6.00	12.00	20.00	35.00	250.00
1900O	4.00	15.00	45.00	75.00	150.00	500.00
1900S	3.00	4.00	6.00	12.00	25.00	150.00
1901O–1903O	2.00	3.50	7.50	18.00	45.00	300.00
1901S	30.00	65.00	130.00	180.00	350.00	750.00
1902S	3.00	8.00	20.00	35.00	60.00	300.00
1903S	25.00	65.00	175.00	350.00	600.00	800.00
1904S	20.00	30.00	75.00	150.00	250.00	550.00
1905O, 1905S	1.75	5.00	15.00	25.00	40.00	225.00
1906D	2.00	3.00	5.00	12.00	30.00	150.00

	G–4	VG–8	F–12	VF–20	EF–40	MS–60
1906O, 1906S	2.00	8.00	20.00	28.00	40.00	200.00
1907D, 1907O, 1907S	1.50	3.50	8.00	15.00	25.00	200.00
1908D	1.50	3.00	6.00	12.00	25.00	125.00
1908O	2.00	7.00	25.00	40.00	65.00	275.00
1908S	1.50	3.00	7.00	15.00	25.00	250.00
1909D	2.50	8.00	25.00	40.00	75.00	350.00
1909O	1.75	4.00	8.00	15.00	30.00	175.00
1909S	3.00	10.00	40.00	65.00	125.00	400.00
1910D	1.50	3.00	7.00	12.00	35.00	175.00
1910S	1.50	5.00	20.00	30.00	50.00	325.00
1911D–1914D	1.25	2.50	5.00	10.00	25.00	125.00
1911S	1.25	2.50	5.00	10.00	25.00	125.00
1912S	1.50	3.00	5.00	10.00	25.00	200.00
1913S	6.00	15.00	40.00	75.00	175.00	375.00
1914S	1.50	2.80	4.50	10.00	25.00	150.00
1915S	1.50	5.00	12.00	18.00	40.00	250.00
1916S	1.00	2.00	4.00	10.00	25.00	125.00

Mercury Type 1916–1945

	G–4	VG–8	F–12	VF–20	EF–40	MS–60
1916–28	$1.00	$2.00	$4.50	$7.50	$10.00	$30.00
1916D	350.00	600.00	1000.00	1500.00	2200.00	4000.00
1917D	2.50	5.00	7.50	15.00	35.00	115.00
1918	1.00	2.50	4.00	10.00	25.00	65.00
1919D, 1919S	2.00	3.50	5.00	15.00	35.00	130.00
1920D, 1920S	1.25	2.50	4.00	6.00	15.00	75.00
1921	20.00	40.00	75.00	175.00	400.00	1100.00
1921D	25.00	50.00	100.00	200.00	450.00	1200.00
1923S	1.25	2.50	4.00	7.50	30.00	100.00
1924D, 1924S	1.00	2.00	4.00	8.00	35.00	150.00
1925D	2.50	5.00	7.50	25.00	75.00	225.00
1925S	1.00	2.00	4.00	7.50	30.00	175.00
1926D	1.00	2.00	3.50	7.00	15.00	65.00
1926S	4.00	8.00	15.00	30.00	150.00	850.00
1927D, 1927S	1.75	2.50	5.00	12.00	40.00	165.00
1928D	2.00	3.50	5.00	12.00	30.00	125.00
1928S	1.25	2.00	3.00	5.00	12.00	75.00
1929–33	1.00	1.50	2.00	4.50	6.00	20.00
1929D	1.75	2.50	4.00	7.00	12.00	30.00
1929S	1.25	1.50	2.00	4.50	6.00	35.00
1930S	2.00	3.00	4.00	7.00	12.00	60.00

	G–4	VG–8	F–12	VF–20	EF–40	MS–60
1931D	4.50	6.00	10.00	18.00	30.00	75.00
1931S	3.00	4.00	5.00	7.50	12.00	60.00
1934–39	.75	1.25	2.00	3.50	5.00	15.00
1934D–1936D	.75	1.25	2.50	3.50	7.00	30.00
1940–45	.50	.60	.75	1.50	2.50	9.00

Roosevelt Type 1946–date

	G–4	VG–8	F–12	VF–20	EF–40	MS–60
1946–47	—	—	—	—	—	$1.00
1946D	—	—	—	—	—	1.50
1946S	—	—	—	—	—	2.00
1947D, 1947S	—	—	—	—	—	2.00
1948	—	—	—	—	—	5.00
1948D, 1948S	—	—	—	—	—	3.50
1949	—	—	—	—	—	11.00
1949D	—	—	—	—	—	5.00
1949S	—	—	—	—	—	20.00
1950	—	—	—	—	—	3.00
1950D	—	—	—	—	—	2.00
1950S	—	—	—	—	—	10.00
1951–55	—	—	—	—	—	1.15
1951S	—	—	—	—	—	6.00
1952S	—	—	—	—	—	3.00
1956–64	—	—	—	—	—	.75
1965–67	—	—	—	—	—	.40
1968–80	—	—	—	—	—	.30
1981	—	—	—	—	—	.20
1982	—	—	—	—	—	150.00
1982D, 1982P	—	—	—	—	—	.20
1983–87	—	—	—	—	—	.20

Twenty-Cent Pieces

1875–1878

	G–4	VG–8	F–12	VF–20	EF–40	MS–60
1875	$30.00	$50.00	$65.00	$90.00	$250.00	$900.00
1875S	20.00	40.00	60.00	90.00	175.00	700.00
1876	50.00	80.00	110.00	200.00	350.00	1200.00
1876CC	—	—	—	—	—	(very rare)
1877–78	—	—	—	—	—	(proof only)

Quarter Dollars

Draped Bust, Small Eagle 1796

	AG–3	G–4	VG–8	F–12	VF–20	MS–60
1796	$1000.00	$2000.00	$5000.00	$7000.00	$12,000.00	$25,000.00

Draped Bust, Heraldic Eagle 1804–1807

	AG–3	G–4	VG–8	F–12	VF–20	MS–60
1804	$350.00	$900.00	$1100.00	$2500.00	$4300.00	$21,000.00
1805–07	150.00	200.00	300.00	500.00	900.00	4800.00

Capped Bust Type 1815–1838

	AG–3	G–4	VG–8	F–12	VF–20	MS–40
1815–28	$25.00	$50.00	$65.00	$100.00	$300.00	$2500.00
1831–38	12.00	35.00	40.00	55.00	100.00	1000.00

Seated Liberty Type 1838–1891

	G–4	VG–8	F–12	VF–20	EF–40	MS–60
1838–40	$10.00	$15.00	$30.00	$75.00	$250.00	$1200.00
1841	50.00	65.00	100.00	130.00	250.00	1000.00
1841O	15.00	25.00	50.00	80.00	175.00	1000.00
1842	75.00	90.00	150.00	200.00	300.00	1400.00
1842O (large date)	12.00	20.00	35.00	80.00	180.00	—
1842O (small date)	400.00	550.00	800.00	1200.00	2400.00	—
1843–47	12.00	16.00	20.00	35.00	75.00	600.00
1843O	15.00	25.00	40.00	70.00	200.00	1000.00
1844O	12.00	20.00	40.00	60.00	200.00	1100.00
1847O	20.00	30.00	50.00	100.00	200.00	1200.00

	G–4	VG–8	F–12	VF–20	EF–40	MS–60
1848–53	20.00	30.00	45.00	75.00	140.00	1100.00
1849O	325.00	450.00	800.00	1200.00	3000.00	—
1851O	150.00	200.00	350.00	500.00	1000.00	2000.00
1852O	200.00	250.00	450.00	600.00	1100.00	2800.00
1854	10.00	14.00	20.00	35.00	75.00	750.00
1855	8.00	12.00	20.00	35.00	80.00	600.00
1855O, 1855S	40.00	55.00	80.00	140.00	300.00	1800.00
1856	10.00	12.00	15.00	28.00	60.00	400.00
1856O	10.00	15.00	30.00	45.00	100.00	750.00
1857–58	8.00	12.00	20.00	30.00	60.00	275.00
1857O, 1858O	8.00	12.00	20.00	35.00	70.00	850.00
1857S, 1858S	40.00	75.00	150.00	200.00	400.00	—
1859–60	8.00	12.00	20.00	30.00	60.00	500.00
1959O, 1860O	15.00	24.00	40.00	55.00	100.00	1000.00
1859S	50.00	85.00	175.00	225.00	400.00	—
1860S	70.00	140.00	300.00	375.00	650.00	—
1861–62	8.00	12.00	20.00	30.00	55.00	350.00
1861S	25.00	75.00	160.00	200.00	300.00	2300.00
1862S	25.00	65.00	125.00	175.00	325.00	—
1863–64	20.00	28.00	50.00	70.00	125.00	750.00
1864S	100.00	150.00	300.00	550.00	1100.00	1700.00
1865	35.00	60.00	100.00	130.00	250.00	1100.00
1865S	35.00	65.00	125.00	175.00	350.00	2000.00
1866	200.00	260.00	325.00	400.00	500.00	1800.00
1866S	100.00	140.00	250.00	350.00	700.00	2000.00
1867	100.00	135.00	200.00	275.00	450.00	1300.00
1867S	65.00	100.00	200.00	275.00	450.00	2000.00
1868	75.00	110.00	200.00	250.00	350.00	1200.00
1868S	40.00	60.00	100.00	150.00	275.00	2000.00
1869	100.00	140.00	275.00	350.00	500.00	1200.00
1869S	75.00	115.00	175.00	250.00	375.00	—
1870	40.00	50.00	75.00	120.00	200.00	900.00
1870CC	1200.00	1600.00	2500.00	3200.00	5500.00	—
1871	20.00	28.00	50.00	75.00	125.00	750.00
1871CC	600.00	900.00	1800.00	2500.00	3500.00	5800.00
1871S	200.00	250.00	375.00	500.00	800.00	2800.00
1872	20.00	30.00	60.00	90.00	125.00	1100.00
1872CC	225.00	350.00	700.00	1400.00	2800.00	—
1872S	200.00	275.00	500.00	650.00	1100.00	4500.00
1873–74	15.00	20.00	30.00	75.00	175.00	900.00
1873CC	600.00	900.00	1800.00	3000.00	5000.00	12,000.00
1873S, 1874S	30.00	35.00	50.00	150.00	275.00	1100.00
1875–78	10.00	15.00	25.00	35.00	75.00	300.00
1875CC	35.00	50.00	100.00	175.00	350.00	1500.00
1875S	30.00	40.00	60.00	90.00	125.00	600.00
1876CC–1878CC	10.00	18.00	30.00	40.00	75.00	550.00
1878S	50.00	65.00	125.00	160.00	275.00	1400.00
1879–89	85.00	100.00	150.00	185.00	275.00	650.00
1886	120.00	175.00	250.00	325.00	400.00	800.00
1888S	12.00	15.00	20.00	40.00	65.00	250.00
1890	45.00	60.00	85.00	120.00	160.00	550.00
1891, 1891S	8.00	12.00	20.00	30.00	50.00	300.00
1891O	100.00	140.00	200.00	300.00	500.00	2000.00

Barber or Liberty Head Type 1892–1916

	G–4	VG–8	F–12	VF–20	EF–40	MS–60
1892–1916	$3.00	$5.00	$15.00	$25.00	$65.00	$200.00
1892S	15.00	25.00	40.00	60.00	120.00	400.00
1893S	4.00	6.00	20.00	35.00	75.00	375.00
1894O, 1894S	3.50	7.00	18.00	30.00	65.00	300.00
1895O, 1895S	4.00	7.50	18.00	35.00	70.00	300.00
1896O	4.00	12.00	35.00	125.00	300.00	725.00
1896S	200.00	300.00	525.00	750.00	1100.00	3000.00
1897O	7.00	18.00	60.00	120.00	275.00	725.00
1897S	10.00	25.00	50.00	80.00	150.00	550.00
1898O	3.00	10.00	30.00	75.00	150.00	450.00
1898S	4.00	8.00	18.00	30.00	70.00	325.00
1899O, 1899S	5.00	10.00	20.00	35.00	70.00	325.00
1900O, 1900S	4.00	8.00	20.00	30.00	70.00	300.00
1901O	12.00	25.00	50.00	120.00	250.00	700.00
1901S	1150.00	1800.00	3000.00	4200.00	6000.00	9200.00
1902O, 1902S	4.00	8.00	20.00	35.00	75.00	325.00
1903O, 1903S	4.00	8.00	20.00	35.00	75.00	325.00
1904O	4.00	10.00	30.00	65.00	135.00	625.00
1905O, 1905S	5.00	10.00	20.00	45.00	90.00	300.00
1907S	3.50	8.00	25.00	45.00	85.00	300.00
1908S	6.00	12.00	40.00	100.00	200.00	600.00
1909O	7.00	15.00	35.00	80.00	175.00	550.00
1910D	2.50	7.00	20.00	35.00	75.00	250.00
1911D	2.75	15.00	65.00	120.00	250.00	500.00
1912S	2.75	8.00	20.00	35.00	75.00	300.00
1913	7.00	18.00	45.00	100.00	350.00	1000.00
1913S	300.00	600.00	1100.00	1700.00	2500.00	4000.00
1914S	40.00	65.00	115.00	220.00	325.00	800.00

Standing Liberty Type 1916–30

	G–4	VG–8	F–12	VF–20	EF–40	MS–60
1916	$900.00	$1200.00	$1400.00	$1800.00	$2400.00	$4200.00
1917	10.00	12.00	15.00	25.00	55.00	200.00
1918	14.00	16.00	20.00	30.00	50.00	150.00
1918D, 1918S	15.00	18.00	30.00	40.00	60.00	180.00
1919	20.00	30.00	40.00	50.00	65.00	165.00
1919D, 1919S	40.00	60.00	100.00	150.00	250.00	500.00
1920	12.00	16.00	20.00	27.00	35.00	165.00
1920D, 1920S	16.00	25.00	30.00	40.00	65.00	200.00
1921	50.00	75.00	100.00	140.00	215.00	450.00

	G–4	VG–8	F–12	VF–20	EF–40	MS–60
1923–24	12.00	15.00	20.00	27.00	35.00	150.00
1923S	100.00	125.00	175.00	250.00	350.00	600.00
1925–26	4.00	5.75	7.00	12.00	25.00	140.00
1926S	3.50	5.00	10.00	35.00	85.00	325.00
1927–30	3.50	4.00	6.00	12.00	25.00	150.00
1927D, 1927S	6.00	7.50	12.00	18.00	50.00	140.00

Washington Type 1932–date

	G–4	VG–8	F–12	VF–20	EF–40	MS–60
1932–40	$2.50	$3.50	$5.00	$6.50	$8.00	$25.00
1932D	32.00	35.00	45.00	65.00	140.00	525.00
1932S	30.00	32.00	36.00	45.00	65.00	350.00
1934D, 1935D	3.00	4.50	7.00	9.00	12.00	100.00
1935S	3.00	3.50	5.00	6.50	8.00	60.00
1936D	2.00	2.50	4.00	12.00	30.00	300.00
1936S	2.00	2.50	4.00	7.00	12.00	50.00
1937D	2.00	2.50	4.00	6.00	10.00	35.00
1937S	2.00	3.00	4.25	10.00	18.00	90.00
1938S	2.00	3.00	4.25	7.00	12.00	45.00
1939D	2.00	3.00	4.50	6.00	8.00	25.00
1939S	3.00	3.50	5.00	7.00	10.00	50.00
1940D	3.00	4.00	6.00	8.00	12.00	50.00
1940S	2.00	2.50	3.50	4.50	6.00	15.00
1941–48	1.00	1.25	2.00	3.00	4.00	7.00
1941D, 1941S	1.00	1.25	1.75	2.50	3.00	18.00
1942D	1.00	1.25	2.00	2.50	3.00	10.00
1942S	1.00	1.25	2.00	3.00	5.00	50.00
1943D	1.00	1.25	2.00	2.50	3.00	12.00
1943S	1.00	1.25	2.00	2.50	3.00	28.00
1944D, 1944S	1.00	1.25	1.50	1.75	2.00	9.00
1945D, 1945S	1.00	1.25	1.50	1.75	2.00	8.00
1946D, 1946S	1.00	1.25	1.50	1.75	2.00	4.25
1947D, 1947S	1.00	1.25	1.50	1.75	2.00	5.00
1948D, 1948S	1.00	1.25	1.50	1.75	2.00	4.50
1949	1.00	1.25	1.50	1.75	2.00	18.00
1949D	1.00	1.25	1.50	1.75	2.00	9.00
1950–53	.75	1.00	1.50	1.75	2.00	4.00
1951S	.75	1.00	1.25	1.50	1.75	10.00
1954–64	.65	.80	1.00	1.25	1.75	2.00

Half Dollars

Flowing Hair Type 1794–1795

	AG–3	G–4	VG–8	F–12	VF–20	EF–40
1794	$500.00	$1000.00	$1500.00	$2800.00	$4000.00	$8000.00
1795	250.00	400.00	500.00	750.00	1500.00	3500.00

Draped Bust, Small Eagle 1796–1797

	AG–3	G–4	VG–8	F–12	VF–20	EF–40
1796–97	$5000.00	$9000.00	$12,000.00	$15,000.00	$25,000.00	$45,000.00

Draped Bust, Heraldic Eagle 1801–1807

	AG–3	G–4	F–12	VF–20	EF–40	MS–60
1801–02	$75.00	$200.00	$500.00	$900.00	$2000.00	$9000.00
1803–06	45.00	125.00	350.00	600.00	900.00	6500.00
1807	35.00	75.00	125.00	350.00	600.00	4500.00

Capped Bust Type 1807–1839

	G–4	VG–8	F–12	VF–20	EF–40	MS–60
1807	$50.00	$75.00	$160.00	$300.00	$550.00	$3000.00
1808–11	30.00	45.00	80.00	125.00	250.00	1500.00
1812–23	30.00	40.00	75.00	85.00	100.00	1000.00
1824–36	25.00	30.00	50.00	75.00	100.00	750.00
1836 (reeded edge)	500.00	650.00	900.00	1200.00	2000.00	6500.00
1837	35.00	40.00	45.00	100.00	150.00	850.00
1838–39	40.00	45.00	50.00	90.00	150.00	900.00
1838O	—	—	—	—	—	50,000.00
1839O	125.00	160.00	200.00	400.00	700.00	3000.00

Seated Liberty Type 1839–1891

	G–4	VG–8	F–12	VF–20	EF–40	MS–60
1839	$20.00	$28.00	$40.00	$75.00	$150.00	$4000.00
1840, 1840O	20.00	30.00	35.00	55.00	100.00	500.00
1841	40.00	48.00	60.00	120.00	250.00	1200.00
1841O	25.00	35.00	50.00	70.00	125.00	850.00
1842	20.00	28.00	40.00	65.00	100.00	900.00
1842O (large date)	18.00	24.00	35.00	60.00	100.00	500.00
1842O (small date)	750.00	825.00	1000.00	2000.00	4200.00	—
1843–1847	15.00	22.00	35.00	60.00	100.00	500.00
1848	30.00	40.00	60.00	100.00	200.00	900.00
1848O	18.00	28.00	40.00	60.00	100.00	650.00
1849, 1849O	20.00	30.00	40.00	65.00	110.00	650.00
1850	50.00	70.00	110.00	210.00	450.00	1300.00
1850O	20.00	30.00	40.00	85.00	180.00	650.00
1851	50.00	120.00	200.00	275.00	450.00	1400.00
1851O	20.00	30.00	40.00	60.00	100.00	600.00
1852	75.00	125.00	250.00	400.00	650.00	1500.00
1852O	40.00	65.00	100.00	180.00	300.00	1200.00
1853, 1853O	15.00	25.00	40.00	80.00	250.00	2000.00
1854, 1854O	15.00	20.00	30.00	55.00	100.00	650.00
1855, 1855O	15.00	20.00	35.00	55.00	100.00	1200.00
1855S	250.00	350.00	600.00	1000.00	2500.00	6000.00
1856–58	15.00	20.00	30.00	50.00	75.00	400.00
1856S, 1857S	20.00	30.00	45.00	100.00	200.00	1300.00
1857O	15.00	20.00	30.00	50.00	80.00	700.00
1858S	20.00	30.00	35.00	75.00	125.00	850.00
1859–72	15.00	24.00	35.00	45.00	75.00	550.00
1859S	20.00	24.00	35.00	60.00	125.00	850.00
1870CC	325.00	600.00	1200.00	1800.00	3000.00	—
1871CC	80.00	100.00	150.00	300.00	800.00	3500.00
1872CC	40.00	65.00	100.00	200.00	400.00	2200.00
1873	15.00	24.00	35.00	80.00	150.00	800.00
1873CC	35.00	60.00	125.00	200.00	350.00	2200.00
1873S	35.00	42.00	65.00	180.00	250.00	1200.00
1874	25.00	30.00	35.00	80.00	225.00	900.00
1874CC	100.00	150.00	350.00	500.00	900.00	4000.00
1874S	30.00	35.00	45.00	100.00	250.00	1500.00
1875–78	15.00	24.00	30.00	50.00	75.00	500.00
1878CC	150.00	210.00	400.00	600.00	1100.00	4000.00
1878S	6000.00	6800.00	8000.00	10,000.00	14,000.00	29,000.00
1879–90	100.00	140.00	200.00	275.00	400.00	900.00
1891	20.00	30.00	50.00	80.00	150.00	600.00

Barber or Liberty Head Type 1892–1915

	G–4	VG–8	F–12	VF–20	EF–40	MS–60
1892	$14.00	$25.00	$35.00	$75.00	$175.00	$450.00
1892O, 1892S	75.00	110.00	175.00	250.00	400.00	900.00
1893–1915	7.00	20.00	30.00	75.00	150.00	400.00
1893S	50.00	65.00	100.00	175.00	350.00	950.00
1896O, 1896S	15.00	25.00	75.00	170.00	350.00	1100.00
1897O	40.00	100.00	200.00	350.00	700.00	1400.00
1897S	70.00	120.00	250.00	320.00	600.00	1200.00
1898O, 1898S	12.00	25.00	60.00	130.00	300.00	600.00
1901O	9.00	15.00	40.00	120.00	275.00	1200.00
1904O	10.00	18.00	40.00	120.00	300.00	1000.00
1904S	10.00	25.00	75.00	175.00	400.00	1400.00
1913	15.00	30.00	75.00	150.00	300.00	800.00
1914	20.00	70.00	150.00	210.00	400.00	700.00
1915	20.00	40.00	75.00	150.00	300.00	850.00

Liberty Walking Type 1916–1947

	G–4	VG–8	F–12	VF–20	EF–40	MS–60
1916	$18.00	$30.00	$50.00	$100.00	$150.00	$250.00
1916D	15.00	20.00	30.00	65.00	130.00	250.00
1916S	35.00	55.00	110.00	250.00	450.00	750.00
1917–18	5.00	8.00	12.00	25.00	35.00	120.00
1917D (obverse mint)	10.00	18.00	30.00	65.00	150.00	350.00
1917D (reverse mint)	7.50	12.00	20.00	50.00	125.00	550.00
1917S (obverse mint)	12.00	20.00	35.00	150.00	500.00	1300.00
1917S (reverse mint)	5.00	8.00	15.00	25.00	45.00	250.00
1919	12.00	17.00	35.00	120.00	375.00	850.00
1919D, 1919S	10.00	12.00	30.00	120.00	450.00	2000.00
1920	5.00	7.00	15.00	20.00	60.00	250.00

	G–4	VG–8	F–12	VF–20	EF–40	MS–60
1920D	7.00	12.00	20.00	75.00	300.00	1000.00
1920S	5.00	8.00	15.00	65.00	125.00	550.00
1921, 1921D	50.00	75.00	150.00	450.00	1200.00	2500.00
1921S	15.00	20.00	50.00	400.00	2400.00	7200.00
1923S	5.00	10.00	20.00	75.00	175.00	1000.00
1927S, 1928S	5.00	7.50	12.00	50.00	100.00	600.00
1929D, 1929S, 1933S	5.00	7.00	10.00	25.00	65.00	250.00
1934–39	4.00	4.50	6.00	8.00	12.00	40.00
1934D	4.00	4.50	6.00	12.00	25.00	100.00
1934S	4.00	4.50	6.00	12.00	25.00	200.00
1935D, 1935S	4.00	4.50	6.00	12.00	25.00	100.00
1936D, 1936S	3.00	3.50	5.00	10.00	20.00	90.00
1937D, 1937S	4.00	4.50	6.00	12.00	20.00	120.00
1938D	20.00	24.00	30.00	50.00	100.00	375.00
1939S	4.00	4.50	6.00	8.00	15.00	90.00
1940–47	3.00	3.50	5.00	6.00	7.00	30.00
1941S	2.50	3.25	4.50	5.50	7.00	80.00

Franklin Type 1948–1963

	VG–8	F–12	VF–20	EF–40	MS–60
1948	$1.50	$3.00	$4.50	$6.00	$16.00
1948D	1.50	3.00	4.00	6.00	10.00
1949–50	1.50	2.50	3.50	5.00	35.00
1949S	1.50	3.50	5.00	10.00	65.00
1950D	1.50	3.00	4.00	5.00	25.00
1951	1.50	3.00	3.50	4.00	12.00
1951D, 1951S	1.50	3.00	3.50	4.00	30.00
1952	1.50	3.00	3.50	4.00	10.00
1952S	1.50	3.50	4.00	5.00	30.00
1953	1.50	3.50	4.00	5.50	24.00
1953D, 1953S	1.50	3.00	3.50	4.50	10.00
1954–1957	1.50	4.00	4.50	5.50	7.00
1958–63	1.00	1.50	2.00	3.00	4.50

Kennedy Type 1964–date

	VG–8	F–12	VF–20	EF–40	MS–60
1964	$1.00	$1.25	$1.50	$2.00	$3.50
1965–69	.65	.75	.85	.95	1.50

Silver Dollars

Flowing Hair Type 1794–1795

	AG–3	G–4	VG–8	F–12	VF–20	EF–40
1794	$4000.00	$8500.00	$11,000.00	$16,000.00	$25,000.00	$50,000.00
1795	400.00	750.00	1000.00	1600.00	2600.00	5000.00

Draped Bust, Small Eagle 1795–1798

	AG–3	G–4	VG–8	F–12	VF–20	EF–40
1795–97	$300.00	$650.00	$800.00	$1100.00	$2000.00	$4000.00
1798	400.00	900.00	1200.00	1800.00	2500.00	5000.00

Draped Bust, Heraldic Eagle 1798–1804

	AG–3	G–4	VG–8	F–12	VF–20	EF–40
1798–1803	$150.00	$300.00	$400.00	$500.00	$800.00	$8000.00
1804	—	—	—	—	(extremely rare)	

Seated Liberty Type 1840–1873

	G–4	F–12	VF–20	EF–40	MS–60
1840–47	$125.00	$200.00	$275.00	$500.00	$2000.00
1846O	200.00	250.00	325.00	650.00	4000.00
1848	175.00	425.00	550.00	1000.00	2500.00
1849	125.00	200.00	275.00	500.00	1400.00
1850, 1850O	250.00	400.00	650.00	1200.00	4500.00
1851, 1852	2000.00	5500.00	7000.00	10,000.00	15,000.00
1853	175.00	250.00	375.00	750.00	1600.00
1854–55	500.00	1200.00	2300.00	3200.00	4500.00
1856–59	200.00	350.00	700.00	1200.00	2500.00
1858 (proof only)	—	—	—	—	—
1859O	100.00	175.00	300.00	600.00	1000.00
1860–70	150.00	300.00	500.00	800.00	1000.00
1861, 1862	275.00	500.00	1000.00	1600.00	2400.00
1870CC	200.00	450.00	1000.00	2000.00	4200.00
1871–73	80.00	160.00	300.00	600.00	1300.00
1871CC	1300.00	3000.00	8000.00	10,000.00	15,000.00
1872CC	700.00	1500.00	3200.00	7000.00	13,000.00

	G–4	F–12	VF–20	EF–40	MS–60
1872S	150.00	350.00	1000.00	4000.00	9000.00
1873CC	2300.00	4500.00	11,000.00	17,000.00	25,000.00

Trade Dollar 1873–1885

	F–12	EF–40	MS–60	PRF–65
1873–77	$100.00	$250.00	$1000.00	$3500.00
1873CC, 1873S	100.00	300.00	1200.00	—
1874CC	100.00	225.00	1000.00	—
1874S	100.00	200.00	500.00	—
1875CC, 1875S	100.00	175.00	750.00	—
1876CC, 1877CC	130.00	300.00	1100.00	—
1876S, 1877S	90.00	150.00	600.00	—
1878–1885	—	—	—	3000.00
1878CC	600.00	1300.00	5500.00	—
1878S	80.00	150.00	550.00	—

Liberty Head or Morgan Type 1878–1904, 1921

	F–12	EF–40	MS–60	PRF–65
1878	$12.00	$20.00	$40.00	$3500.00
1878CC	20.00	30.00	75.00	—
1878S	10.00	15.00	25.00	—
1879–80	10.00	12.00	25.00	3000.00
1879CC	35.00	175.00	1000.00	—
1879O	10.00	12.00	35.00	—
1879S	10.00	20.00	100.00	—
1880CC	40.00	80.00	150.00	—
1881–92	8.00	10.00	20.00	2400.00
1881CC	75.00	100.00	150.00	—
1882CC, 1883CC, 1884CC	25.00	40.00	60.00	—
1883S	10.00	25.00	30.00	—
1884S	12.00	35.00	3500.00	—
1885CC	150.00	180.00	225.00	—
1885S, 1886S, 1887S	12.00	20.00	75.00	—
1886O	10.00	20.00	200.00	—
1887O, 1888O	8.00	12.00	25.00	—
1889CC	200.00	650.00	6000.00	—
1889O, 1889S	18.00	25.00	80.00	—
1890CC, 1891CC	25.00	35.00	175.00	—

	F–12	EF–40	MS–60	PRF–65
1890O, 1890S, 1891O, 1891S	10.00	15.00	40.00	—
1892CC	35.00	80.00	300.00	—
1892O	12.00	20.00	100.00	—
1892S	15.00	125.00	9000.00	—
1893	40.00	70.00	250.00	3200.00
1893CC	70.00	300.00	900.00	—
1893O	65.00	150.00	1000.00	—
1893S	800.00	2500.00	20,000.00	—
1894	200.00	300.00	750.00	4500.00
1894O	20.00	30.00	450.00	—
1894S	25.00	70.00	300.00	—
1895	—	—	13,000.00	25,000.00
1895O	75.00	150.00	6000.00	—
1895S	125.00	325.00	1000.00	—
1896–1900	10.00	12.00	15.00	2000.00
1896O, 1896S, 1897O	12.00	30.00	550.00	—
1897S	10.00	12.00	35.00	—
1898S, 1899S, 1900S	10.00	25.00	100.00	—
1901	12.00	35.00	1100.00	3200.00
1901O	10.00	12.00	20.00	—
1901S	12.00	35.00	200.00	—
1902–04	10.00	12.00	35.00	2800.00
1902O, 1904O	10.00	12.00	20.00	—
1902S	20.00	50.00	125.00	—
1903O	100.00	125.00	175.00	—
1903S	20.00	175.00	1500.00	—
1904S	15.00	100.00	750.00	—
1921	7.00	9.00	12.00	—
1921D, 1921S	7.00	9.00	25.00	—

Peace Type 1921–1935

	F–12	VF–20	EF–40	MS–60
1921	$25.00	$30.00	$40.00	$140.00
1922–25	6.00	7.50	9.00	15.00
1924S	10.00	15.00	20.00	120.00
1925S	7.00	15.00	25.00	50.00
1926	7.00	8.50	12.00	25.00
1926D	10.00	12.00	15.00	45.00
1927	15.00	17.00	20.00	55.00

	F–12	VF–20	EF–40	MS–60
1927D	12.00	15.00	20.00	140.00
1927S	12.00	15.00	20.00	85.00
1928	100.00	110.00	120.00	175.00
1928S, 1934, 1934D	12.00	15.00	20.00	75.00
1934S	35.00	75.00	150.00	1000.00
1935	12.00	15.00	18.00	40.00
1935S	10.00	12.00	15.00	100.00

Eisenhower Type 1971–1978

	VF–20	EF–40	MS–60	PRF–65
1971, 1971D	—	—	$2.00	—
1971S	—	—	3.50	$6.00
1972, 1972D	—	—	1.80	—
1972S	—	—	3.00	6.00
1973, 1973D	—	—	4.00	—
1973S (copper clad)	—	—	3.50	7.00
1973S (silver clad)	—	—	7.00	24.00
1974, 1974D	—	—	1.80	—
1974S (copper clad)	—	—	1.80	6.50
1974S (silver clad)	—	—	5.50	7.00
1976, 1976D	—	—	1.80	—
1976S (copper clad)	—	—	—	7.00
1976S (silver clad)	—	—	—	10.00
1977, 1977D	—	—	1.85	—
1977S	—	—	—	7.00
1978, 1978D	—	—	1.80	—
1978S	—	—	—	7.00

Susan B. Anthony Type 1979–1981

	VF–20	EF–40	MS–60	PRF–65
1979D, 1979P	—	—	$1.45	—
1979S	—	—	1.85	$7.50
1980D, 1980P	—	—	1.50	—
1980S	—	—	1.60	9.50
1981D	—	—	3.00	—
1981P	—	—	3.25	—
1981S	—	—	3.00	8.00

Decoys

A decoy's value is detemined by the importance of the maker, how it looks and a detailed analysis of its condition. Most decoys are worth no more than a few hundred dollars, many less than $100. Decoys produced after the mid nineteenth century are most popular among collectors. Famous decoy carvers include Ira Hudson, Charles Wheeler, Albert Laing and Mark Whipple. Enthusiasts usually collect decoys by carver, species or fly-way (path of migration). Decoys made for actual use are more favored by collectors than those intended only for show. Original paint is extremely important to many collectors.

For further reading see *Collecting Antique Bird Decoys and Duck Calls, 2nd Edition* by Carl F. Luckey (Books Americana, Florence, AL, 1992), available through Krause Publications.

All decoys listed are carved wood unless noted otherwise.

Left to right, prices at auction: Dowitcher, John Dilley, Quoque, Long Island, NY, $9200; Canada Goose, A. Elmer Crowell, East Harwich, MA, $12,650; Yellow Legs, Elisha Burr, Hingham, MA, $2760. —Photo courtesy Skinner, Inc., Boston, MA.

	AUCTION	RETAIL	
		Low	High
Black Duck, Bob Morris, Churches Island, NC, oversized Battery bird, hand chopped, carved tail, original paint, boat keel design, weights and tie-eye intact, head repainted	$289	$400	$800
Black Duck, Mason Factory, Detroit, premier grade, snaky head style, glass eyes, hollow-carved, 80% original paint, lightly hit by shot, small chips to tail, dings in bill, weights removed to sit flat, missing some neck filler	520	400	800
Black Duck, Miles Hancock, Chincoteague, VA, hand chopped and painted, original paint, tack eyes, solid body construction, touch-up to head and bill, missing some neck filler, weights and tie-eye intact	289	400	800
Black Duck Drake, Capt. Jesse Urie, Rock Hall, MD, weights and tie-eye intact, reheaded and repainted, several cracks to back, 1930s	55	100	200
Blue Bill Drake, Doug Jester, Chincoteague, VA, hand chopped and painted, solid body construction, original paint w/ touch-up on back, painted eyes, carved bill, crack in neck	215	250	500

	AUCTION	RETAIL Low	RETAIL High
Blue Bill Drake, Doug Jester, Chincoteague, VA, hand chopped, old in-use repaint by Jester, solid body construction w/ weights intact, painted eyes, 1930s	174	200	400
Blue Bill Drake, Madison Mitchell, Havre de Grace, MD, 85% original paint, painted eyes, signed on bottom, crack in bottom, minor check to neck, dated 1948	440	200	400
Blue Bill Drake, Mason Factory, premier grade, hollow carved, original paint, glass eyes, head loose, weight missing	809	500	1000
Blue Bill Drake, ME or Canada, unknown maker, hand carved and painted, old in-use repaint, tack eyes, raised carved wings, lightly hit by shot, 1940s	105	50	100
Blue Bill Hen, Miles Hancock, Chincoteague, VA, hand chopped, original paint, tack eyes, old in-use repaint to bottom, weights removed	300	300	600
Blue Bill Hen, unknown carver, original paint, glass eyes, modern	30	40	80
Bufflehead Hen, Doug Snow, MI, carved primaries, original paint, glass eyes, weighted keel, unused, stamped "DS" on bottom, c1975	44	75	150
Canada Goose, Joe Lincoln, Accord, MA, hand carved and painted, tack eyes, solid body construction, carved bill, weight removed, minor wear	715	300	600
Canvasback Duck, NC, unknown maker, old in-use repaint, tack eyes, age cracks, c1900	231	100	200
Canvasback Hen, Dodge Factory, Detroit, MI, hollow carved, areas of repaint, 15" l, 6.75" h	748	800	1200
Coot, Madison Mitchell, Havre de Grace, MD, hand carved and painted, original paint, painted eyes, signed, dated 1974	440	200	400
Goldeneye Drake, Benjamin Schmidt, minor cracks, 14" l	633	300	500
Goose, Lloyd Tyler, Chrisfield, MD, hand chopped and painted, original paint, in-use wear, cracks in neck and body, repairs, chips to neck and tail, c1920s	191	300	600

Auction Prices, left to right, top row: Common Pintail Drake, Ward Bros., 1930, $1840; Wood Duck Decoy, A. Elmer Crowell, $7188; Black Duck, marked "BLTX Chas. Shang Wheeler Ken Peck 1920," $1955. Bottom row: Black-Bellied Plover, A. Elmer Crowell, East Harwich, MA, $6325; New Jersey style Herring Gull, $2760; Green Heron, A. Elmer Crowell, East Harwich, MA, $6325. —Photo courtesy Skinner, Inc., Boston, MA.

	AUCTION	RETAIL Low	RETAIL High
Long Bill Curlew, Chief Coffey, Long Island, NY, replaced bill, wear to wing tips, 15.5" l, 8" h	1380	1000	1500
Mallard Hen, Charles Perdew, Henry, IL, later varnish, paint imperfections, 17.5" l, 7" h	2013	1000	1500
Pintail Drake, Lloyd Tyler, Chrisfield, MD, old in-use repaint, cracks in neck and body, loose head, weights removed to sit flat, 1920s	331	300	600
Redhead Hen, Mason Factory, Detroit grade, solid body construction, original paint, glass eyes, minor touch-up to neck at replaced filler, weight replaced	336	200	400
Swan, Maryland Eastern shore, unknown maker, original paint, painted eyes, flat bottom, unused, 18.5" l, 12.5" h	56	100	200
Swan, Maryland Upper Bay, unknown maker, hand carved, flat bottom, original paint, unused, 23.5" l, 15.5" h	138	100	200
White-Winged Scoter Drake, Monhegan Island, unknown maker, cracks to base, minor losses, original patch, 17.5" l, 7.5" h	1495	1500	2500
Widgeon Drake, Joe Lincoln, Accord, MA, stamped "F.B. Rice" on base, old weathered surface, crack to base, chip to tail, 15.5" l, 7" h	1380	1500	2500
Widgeon Drake, Madison Mitchell, Havre de Grace, MD, very minor paint wear, chips to bill, 13.625" l, 6.75" h	316	300	500
Wood Ducks, Eastern Shore style, unknown maker, hand carved and painted, original paint, painted eyes unused, 1960s-70s, price for pair	770	300	600

Auction Prices, left to right, top: Flying Canvasback Drake, Tuveson Mfg. Co., Saint James, MN, 1927, $575. Center row: Monhegan Island style Red-Breasted Merganser Drake, $518; Eider Drake, $920; Red-Breasted Merganser Drake, $374. Bottom row: Merganser Drake, H. Keyes Chadwick, Martha's Vineyard, MA, $978; Barnacle Goose, $633; White-Winged Scoter Drake, Roswell Bliss, Stratford, CT, $288. —Photo courtesy Skinner, Inc., Boston, MA.

Firefighting Memorabilia

Firefighting collectibles run from the leather buckets kept in homes for fire emergencies to full hook and ladder trucks. Much equipment used by firemen received heavy use, so today many early items are scarce. This accounts for price variations and the high price often placed on small items.

For more information see *Firehouse Memorabilia* by James Piatti (Avon Books, New York, NY, 1994, out of print).

Fire Mark, cast iron, steamer, "United Firemen's Insurance Co. of Philadelphia," issued 1860, $125–$250. —Photo courtesy Gene Harris Antique Auction Center, Inc.

	LOW	AVG.	HIGH
Commemorative Shot Glass, "Little Giant Engine Company 1871, Chicago Fire Department," fire bucket shaped, silver plated, blue lettering w/ white badge w/ ladder, fire hydrant, and "six," Gorham Co., 2.75" h	$100	$150	$200
Fire Bucket, leather, decorated, leafy banner w/ "E. Sargent 1827" on green ground, black-painted rim and handle, 12.5" h	1250	1750	2250
Fire Bucket, leather, red lettering decals "F. F. D. 16," iron rings for handle, 12.5" h, 9.5" dia	125	200	275
Fire Grenade, aqua, quart, acanthus leaf and lion head pattern, smooth base, ground lip, American, 1875-95, 6.375" h	110	175	250
Fire Grenade, clear, pint, vertical rib pattern, smooth base, ground lip, French, 1880-95, 5.5" h	275	400	525
Fire Grenade, medium cobalt blue, quart, embossed "Manf'd by Fire Extinguisher M'F'G. Co., Babcock Hand Grenade, Non-Freezing, 325-331 S. Des. Plaines St. Chicago," smooth base, ground lip, 1875-95, 7.5" h	1000	1500	2000
Fire Grenade, medium cobalt blue, teardrop shaped, embossed "Rockford Kalamazoo Automatic and Hand Fire Extinguisher, Patent Applied For," smooth base, tooled mouth, 1890-1910, 11" l	300	450	600
Fire Grenade, medium orange-amber, pint, vertical rib pattern, embossed "Grenade UNIC Extenctrice," smooth base, ground lip, French, 1880-95, 5.5" h	200	300	400
Fire Grenade, medium yellowish amber, pint, embossed "Hayward's Hand Fire Grenade – S. F. Hayward, 407 Broadway N.Y. – Patented Aug 8 1871," smooth base, tooled mouth, original contents and stamped neck foil, 1871-85, 6.25" h	175	250	325
Fire Grenade, yellow-olive, pint, embossed "Hayward Hand Grenade Fire Extinguisher, No 407 Broadway New York" around neck and "Design H Patd" on smooth base, tooled mouth, 1875-90, 6" h	600	825	1100

	LOW	AVG.	HIGH
Fire Grenade, yellow-topaz shading to almost clear at shoulders and neck, pint, embossed "Systeme Labbe - Grenade Extingteur - L'Incombustibilite," smooth base, ground lip, French, 1875-95, 5.5" h	200	300	400
Fire Grenade, yellow w/ orange-amber tone, pint, embossed "Grenades du Progres - Grenades Extingtives," pontil scarred base, tooled mouth, French, 1875-90, 5.125" h	300	450	600
Firehouse Sign, "1 - HOSE - 1," gilt stencil lettering on black ground, signed "Evans," late 19th C, 112" l, 13" h	600	800	1000
Fireman's Belt, brown leather w/ "2nd Assistant" brass lettering, large "2" by buckle, 48" l	35	50	65
Fireman's Belt, leather w/ "Old Town" brass lettering, 1 side painted white, buckle stamped "Dirigo No. 1," 32" l	100	150	200
Fireman's Hat, leather, top hat style, painted black w/ gold lettering "Good Will 1802" on front, "G. W." on back, and "T. M. S." on top, 6" h, 13 x 11.75"	1750	2750	3750
Fireman's Hat, metal w/ hard leather rim, metal figural eagle's head projecting from top, 9.5" h, 15" x 10"	225	325	425
Fireman's Horn, brass, plain, 17" h	300	450	600
Fireman's Horn, brass, red-painted interior, inscribed "From Mrs. P H Bowman to G P Mason," 17" h	350	500	650
Fireman's Horn, silver plated, inscribed "Presented to E B Ackerman of Lafayette Co. No. 1," 18" h	500	700	900
Fireman's Horn, silver plated w/ repousse flowers, unsigned and unpresented, 23" h	500	700	900
Fireman's Uniform, white hat w/ "Liberty 5 J. C. W." panel and red interior, black coat w/ brass buttons embossed "F. D.," red shirt w/ black collar and brass buttons embossed "F. D.," white belt with "5" buckle, black trousers	275	400	525
Fire Mark, cast iron, "Baltimore Equitable Society, Baltimore, Maryland, 1794," clasped hands, salmon-colored paint, 10" l	500	750	1000
Fire Wagon Lantern, nickel-plated, "DeVoursney Bros. makers 389 Broome St. New York" w/ acid-etched and engraved blue, red, and clear glass panels depicting fire fighting equipment, geometric and foliate device, and "Prospect 4," removable oil font, 23.25" l	1200	1700	2200

Fire Grenades. —Photo courtesy Glass-Works Auctions.

Fishing Tackle

Rods, reels, flies and lures comprise the majoity of collectible fishing tackle. The manufacture of fishing tackle did not begin in the United States until around 1810.

Reels mde by J.F. and B.F. Meeks, B. Milam and Pfleuger are favored, as are rods made by Hiram Leonard. Flies—fake bait made by tying feathers, fur or other materials around the shaft of a hood—are also popular. There are over 5000 patterns and sizes of flies, each with its own name. The manufacturer, or tier, of individual flies is very difficult to discern, unless the fly is in its original marked container.

For additional reading refer to *Old Fishing Lures & Tackle, 5th Edition* by Carl F. Luckey (Krause Publications, Iola, WI, 1999), *Fishing Lure Collectibles* by Dudley Murphy and Rick Edmisten (Collector Books, Paducah, KY, 1995, 1997 value update), and *Fishing Tackle Antiques and Collectibles* by Karl T. White (Holli Enterprises, Luther, OK, 1990).

Creel, split willow, hand-tooled leather trim, stamped "4-A" on top, metal tag reads "Established 1857–The George Lawrence Co. Portland, Oregon," $2860 at auction. —Photo courtesy Lang's Sporting Collectables, Inc.

	LOW	AVG.	HIGH
Bait Tin, handmade, oval, copper hand-soldered bottom, hinged lid w/ screened cut-out heart, 2 tin belt loops on back, remnants of painted star and dots on side and bottom, old green paint, 4.25" l	$300	$450	$600
Book, *The Fly-Fisher's Entomology, 6th Edition,* Alfred Ronalds, 20 color plates, w/ 47-pocket leather fly wallet, 1862	275	400	525
Bootjack, maple, stamped "Thomas Rod Co., 170 Park Street, Bangor Maine," 2 swiveling wood legs, hole in end for hanging, 11" l	65	100	140
Bottle, Meek Reel Oil, cork stopper, partial contents	350	500	650
Calendar Print, "Off Limits," Ralph Crosby Smith, fisherman w/ leaping trout, mother bear and cubs watching, shrink-wrapped, 22" x 29"	65	100	140
Fish Grabber, spring loaded, marked "Norlund's Patent," 45" l	75	110	150
Fly Box, Hardy Neroda, w/ large clips and approx. 2 dozen flies, 4" x 6"	200	300	400
Lure, Abbey & Imbrie Glowbody Minnow, luminous glass tube body attached to spinning keels, original box, c1920	50	80	110
Lure, Hastings Weedless Rubber Frog, hand painted, hollow, external belly weight, 2 tail hooks, weed guard	300	450	600
Lure, Heddon Baby Vamp #7400, greenback scale finish, glass eyes, L-rig hardware, leaping bass box	180	275	375
Lure, Heddon Closed Leg Luny Frog, double belly hood, single tail hook, toilet seat hardware	100	150	200
Lure, Heddon Deep Diving Wiggler #1600, inch worm line tie, side mounted hooks, L-rig hardware, frog finish	100	150	200

	LOW	AVG.	HIGH
Lure, Heddon Musky Minnow #700, 3 hooks, cup hardware, marked props, glass eyes, green crackleback w/ hand-painted gill marks, 4 belly weights, 5" l	1750	2500	3250
Lure, Heddon Shrimpy Spook, green and red dots, 2-pc. hardware, black bead eyes	175	250	325
Lure, Heddon Spoony Fish, nickel finish, square barrel swivel, 1930-31, 4.25" l	150	225	300
Lure, Heddon Woodpecker, cup rig hardware, tail cap, white and red head finish, 4.625" l	550	775	1000
Lure, Kent Floater, large bulging eyes, neverfail hardware, frog finish, original box	1750	2500	3250
Lure, K & K Animated Minnow, jointed, large glass eyes, tin tail, 3 double hooks, 3.5" l	200	350	500
Lure, Klipon Minnow, Green-Wyle Co., Brooklyn, NY, glass eyes, marked diving plate, hook hanger, yellow w/ red horizontal stripes and red eye shadow, 3.75" l	80	120	160
Lure, Pepper Fish Spinner, 20th Century Wonder, wood, hand painted w/ black back and aluminum belly w/ 2 red gill marks, c1900, 2.5" l	225	350	525
Lure, Rhodes Mechanical Swimming Frog, Kalamazoo Fishing Tackle Co., original fitted box	3000	4200	5500
Lure, Rush Deluxe Tango, rainbow victory finish, metal head plate, 4" l	550	775	1000
Lure, Shakespeare Minnow, wooden, hand painted green and white w/ salmon-colored sides and 3 gill marks, glass eyes, gem clip hook hangers, original box, 3.625" l	1200	1800	2400
Lure, Woods Expert Minnow, dark green back blending to gray on belly, glass eyes, 5 hooks, 4" l	150	225	300
Minnow Bucket, Abbey & Imbrie, galvanized, lift-out liner, paper label w/ largemouth bass and "Abbey & Imbrie–Fishing Tackle–New York"	275	400	525
Minnow Trap, green glass, 6-sided jar w/ funnel opening 1 end, Mason jar lids both ends, 4" x 7"	180	275	380
Pitcher, Royal Doulton, "The Poacher, Copr. 1954," fisherman's head, trout handle, 7" h	200	300	400
Reel, B. F. Meek & Sons Blue Grass No. 3, bait casting reel, handmade, German silver, click and drag switches	250	375	500
Reel, B. F. Meek & Sons No. 44, first model "flat back" trout reel, German silver	3000	4500	6000
Reel, Heddon Pal P-41, silver finish, original papers and box dated 1949	110	175	225
Reel, Heddon's Dowagiac, level wind bait casting reel, German silver, lined leather case, signed wrench/screwdriver	200	300	400
Reel, Julius vom Hofe, trout reel, nickel-plated metal, narrow spool, click switch, 3.5 size	550	775	1000
Reel, McNeese Baby Trout No. 01-2.4N, black and gold anodized anti-reverse trout reel, under-handle drag adjusting ring, original labeled case	275	400	525
Reel, Pettingill Mohawk-2, side-mounted trout reel	100	140	180
Reel, Pflueger Buckeye, bait casting reel, 60 yd. size, large red bearing jewels, click and drag switches	50	75	100
Reel, Pflueger Golden West, trout reel, 60 yd. size, German silver, hard rubber and aluminum plates, click switch, gold on black bulldog medallion, 1903 and 1907 patent dates	375	500	625

	LOW	AVG.	HIGH
Reel, Shakespeare Standard professional 23053 – W. S. Jr., 1914 Model, German silver and hard rubber, non-level wind, 100 yds., wide spool, click and drag wheels, marked leather case	100	175	250
Reel, Winchester No. 1235, trout fly reel, raised pillar, bone handle, black finish	80	125	175
Rod, Carlson's Mount Carmel #7-5, trout, 2-pc., 2-tip, 5-weight line, 6-sided rod w/ aluminum slide band over cork, German silver butt cap reel seat, w/ bag and "Thomas Rod" tube, 7' l	1750	2500	3250
Rod, C. F. Orvis, Serial No. 380, trout, 3-pc., 2 midsections, 3-tip, Calcutta cane, intermediate winds, welted female ferrules, flat spring reel seat stamped "C. F. Orivs, Manchester, Vt.–Maker–Patented June 6, 1882," original bag, 9' l	700	1000	1300
Rod, Garrison 232 T-9-1, salmon, 2-pc., 2-tip, slide band over cork reel seat, cork extension butt, w/ bag and tube, 9' l	1800	2750	3750
Rod, Gary Howells #H006, trout, 2-pc., 2-tip, 4 1/8 oz., 5-weight line, screw up-locking reel seat, w/ bag and tube, 8' l	1250	2000	2750
Rod, Hardy "The Wye," salmon, 3-pc., 2-tip, rubbed ball butt button, sliding screw locking band reel seat, thread locking ferrules, agate stripper, turned walnut ferrules, plugs and intermediate winds, canvas case w/ reel seat wrench, 10' 6" l	275	400	525
Rod, Payne Model 198, trout, 3-pc., 2-tip, 4 1/8 oz., screw up-locking walnut reel seat, stamped "Made For Abercrombie & Fitch Co.," original bag, hanging tag, and tube, 7' 6" l	2500	3250	4000
Rod, Pinky Gillum, Serial No. 1-790, fly rod, 2-pc., 2-tip, screw up-locking reel seat, w/ bag and tube, 8' 9" l	800	1200	1600
Sign, "Fishing Tackle," painted yellow and black w/ orange trim, green frame, signed and dated "Herb Blackburn 1936," 25" x 37"	325	450	575
Tackle Box, mahogany, mortise and tenon construction, 4 divided lift-out trays, 2 brass-plated latches, worn leather handle, 20" x 12" x 10"	225	350	500

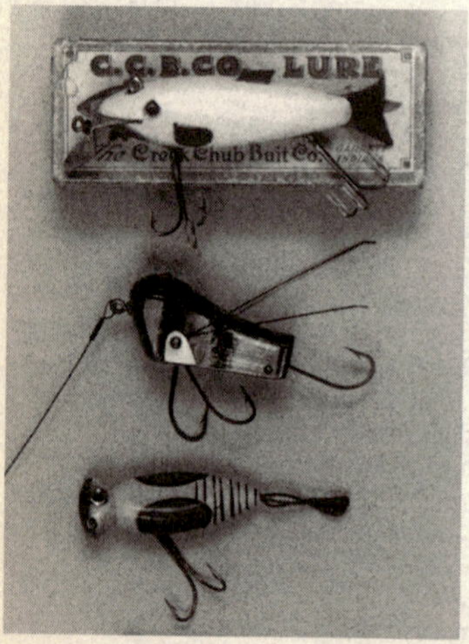

Above: Patent Reel, Lenard Atwood, Farmington Hills, ME, 1907, $1400 at auction.

Left, Creek Chub Bait Co. Lures at auction, top to bottom: Fin Tail Shiner, $1350; Wee Dee, $360; Creek Bug Wiggler, $440.

—Photos courtesy Lang's Sporting Collectables, Inc.

Folk Art

American folk art of the nineteenth and early twentieth centuries is a sophisticated field. Carvers such as Wilhelm Schimmel and John Bellamy have seen extremely high prices. But beware! Only pieces of the highest quality command the prices listed below. Many pieces are restored. Check closely for condition.

	LOW	AVG.	HIGH
Architectural Model, house, yellow clapboard sides, brown trim, turned porch posts, New England, 19th C, 13" h, 6.5" w, 12" d	$1500	$2500	$3500
Architectural Tile, cast terra cotta, classical urn w/ eagle handles holding floral arrangement, late 19th C, 20" h, 14.25" w, 4" d	350	500	650
Birdbath, painted and galvanized tin, square recessed top w/ cove-molded sides, square recessed paneled pedestal on stepped plinth, 19th C, 32.5" h, 17.75" sq top	2000	3000	4000
Bird Figures, carved and painted wood, glass eyes, 1 orange and black, the other yellow and black, both w/ metal legs and perched on wooden stands, late 19th/early 20th C, 4.5" h, 7" l, price for pair	4000	6000	8000
Fireboard, figural Papillon spaniel, painted sheet metal, 19th C, 12.25" h, 18.75" l	400	600	800
Fraktur, Christian Mertel (Dauphin and Lancaster Counties, born 1739, died 1802, known as "CM Artist"), taufschein (birth certificate), hand-drawn and hand-colored, center heart w/ text surrounded by chain of 12 small hearts, numbered and containing facial features surrounded by 5 small 8-pointed stars, rayed sunburst w/ facial features at top left corner, large stylized triple-tulip motif at bottom of heart, red, yellow, orange, green, blue, and brown birds on branches facing out from lower corners, 12.5" h, 15" w	3500	5000	6500
Fraktur, Ruben Kramer (Lancaster County, active 1849-51), heart-shaped paper w/ verse, hand-drawn and hand-painted, "Elisabeth Schimp" across top in red, yellow, and black lettering w/ bird-like designs and 3 red, yellow, and black lines below, 3 lines of German script text in blue ink w/ entwined line motif at base of heart, heart edges w/ blue undulating line design, modern frame, 6.375" x 7.125" heart	350	500	650
Grotesque Jug, Javan or Davis Brown, unglazed stoneware, applied facial features, horns, mustache, beard, and porcelain teeth, inscribed "Graham's Furniture and Hardware Store, Bakersvlle [*sic*], NC," c1940, 19" h	20,000	24,000	28,000
Grotesque Jug, Steve Abee, Lenoir, NC, green ash glaze, blue bulging eyes, stamped "SEA, N.C." on forehead, 12.5" h	175	250	350
Hooked Rug, charcoal gray dog w/ light brown ears and eye on cream and light brown background w/ red, blue, white, and cream geometric details, dated and titled "1901 Pointer," New England, 30" x 35.25"	2800	4200	5600
Hooked Rug, hen and rooster w/ 7 eggs, cream, indigo, red, and black, New England, 19th C, 23.75" x 40.75"	6000	9000	12,000
Painting, oil on board, portrait of a young lady, Prior/Hamblen School, Boston, unsigned, in period veneered frame under glass, 1800-50, 14" x 10.25"	3000	4500	6000
Painting, watercolor on paper, man and woman sharing a horse, American School, unsigned, framed, 19th C, 4.875" x 7.375"	350	500	650

Wood Carving, woman w/ outstretched arms holding towel bar, 20th C, 8.5" h, 14" w, $9775 at auction. —Photo courtesy Skinner, Inc., Boston, MA.

	LOW	AVG.	HIGH
Picture Frame, carved and painted wood, split baluster form, painted brown w/ black detail, 19th C, 20" x 16"	350	500	650
Scherenschnitte, cutwork paper, heart, birds and foliate designs, surmounted by ribbon-tied pair of love birds, mounted in gilt gesso frame, PA, 19th C, 7.5" x 4.5"	450	650	850
Scherenschnitte, taufschein (birth certificate), square w/ sawtooth edges, 8-pointed star in center surrounded by 8 small cutout hearts each w/ letter spelling "Nely Adams," surrounded by 8 larger cutout hearts each w/ text or picture, cutout arrows in corners, dated 1811, 12.75" sq	800	1250	1700
Sewerpipe Bank, sitting pig, hand-molded, incised details, greenish amber glaze, 9" h	400	600	800
Sewerpipe Figure, basset hound, hand-molded, incised details, 14" l	1000	1500	2000
Silhouette, attributed to August Deouart, full-length profile of Isaac T. Hopper in pastoral landscape, early 19th C, 10.75" h, 7.25" w	600	850	1100
Snake, textured body made from joined sections of wrought iron pipe, flattened head w/ open mouth, forked tongue, and brass screw eyes, 19th C, 66" l	8000	12,000	16,000
Statue, prone lion holding ball between front paws, carved stone, rectangular base, 2.75" h, 4.75" w	3500	5500	7500
Theorem, watercolor on paper, blue, green, and faded red basket of fruit and foliage, 14" h, 18" w	500	700	1000
Theorem, watercolor on paper, blue, green, brown, yellow, and faded red basket of flowers and strawberries, signed "W. P. Eaton, Boston, Oct. 1, 1843, W. P. E.," original frame w/ transfer portraits and gilded designs, 14.5" h, 15.75" w	1000	1500	2000
Theorem, watercolor on velvet, "A Still Life Basket of Fruit," framed, 12.25" x 13.625"	3000	4000	5000
Toy, Indian dancer, carved and painted wood figure w/ articulated arms and legs, wearing embroidered fabric dress w/ owl decoration, necklace, and bracelet, tattoo on lower back, mid-19th C, 13.5" h	9000	12,000	15,000
Whirligig, carved and painted wood, soldier, wearing red-painted uniform w/ white shoulder strap and belt and black pants, 19th C, 26.5" h	8000	12,000	16,000
Wood Valance, polychrome-painted and stenciled, central cartouche w/ farmhouse, horse, mountains, and sailboats painted in ivory, salmon, and mustard, gilt-decorated floral spandrels on either side, 1860-80, 8.375" h, 41.325" w	2500	3500	5000

Furniture

Antique

Antique furniture is a tricky field. The collector needs to be a connoisseur of proportions and alterations. Before the middle of the nineteenth century, cabinetmakers (not carpenters) made furniture by hand. Each piece was unique. The skill of the craftsman and the success of his design are important factors in evaluating furniture.

Alterations can reduce the value of a piece by over 75%. No collector will sweat over a piece of chipped veneer, but a replaced leg, no matter how skillfully executed, will kill the value of a piece. Also remember that American furniture of the eighteenth century is more valuable than an otherwise identical English piece.

Consult *Four Centuries of American Furniture* by Oscar P. Fitzgerald (Wallace-Homestead, Radnor, PA, 1995; available from Krause Publications) and *The Mirror Book: English American & European* by Herbert F. Schiffer (Schiffer, Exton, PA, 1983) for additional information.

All pieces listed are American unless noted otherwise.

	LOW	HIGH
Armchair, fruitwood, splayed rectangular spindle back flanked by outcurved arms, woven rush saddle seat, turned and tapered legs joined by turned box stretcher, possibly PA, mid-19th C	$100	$250
Armchair, horn, back and arms composed of latticework cattle horns, overstuffed seat upholstered in tan-colored hide, splayed horn legs	200	400
Armchair, painted, curving crest, raked terminals, vasiform splat, downward scrolling arms, block- and baluster-turned front legs ending in Spanish carved feet, boldly turned front medial stretcher, old splint seat, old red paint, New England, 1775-1800, 35.5" h	5000	8000
Armchair, painted, fancy, shaped crest above small urn panel flanked by turned spindles and pierced horizontal splat w/ 5 spindles below, scrolled arms on bamboo-turned supports, shaped seat, splayed bamboo-turned legs joined by stretchers, old black paint, New England, early 19th C, 34.75" h	300	500

Armchairs, left to right: Arts & Crafts, by David Wolcott Kendall, caned back and seat, $1840 at auction for pair; Art Deco, burgundy upholstery, wood trim, $3680 at auction for pair; Art Deco, Heywood Wakefield, rattan frames, gold Naugahyde upholstery, c1935, $805 at auction for pair. —Photos courtesy Skinner, Inc., Boston, MA.

	LOW	HIGH
Armchair, Victorian, carved walnut, shaped back w/ pierced foliate reserves, outcurved arms, padded serpentine-front seat, cabriole legs, late 19th C	100	150
Armchair, Windsor, chestnut and maple, crest w/ beaded edge continuing to shaped handholds, 12 tapered spindles, turned arm supports, shaped seat w/ extended piece in back to receive back bracing, deeply incised splayed legs joined by H-stretchers, branded "E. B. Tracy," Lisbon, CT, 1780-1803, 37" h	1000	1500
Armchair, Windsor, sack-back, bowed crest rail, 6 spindles, shaped handholds, carved saddle seat, splayed vase- and ring-turned legs joined by stretchers, old refinish, seat patched, New England, c1780, 37" h	400	600
Armchairs, Chippendale Style, wing-back, padded slightly arched back w/ shaped wings, loose cushion seat, overscrolled arms, square legs joined by H-stretcher, price for pair	500	750
Armchairs, Hitchcock Style, splayed rectangular spindle back, solid seat, turned and tapered legs joined by turned box stretcher, painted black w/ gilt highlights, price for set of 4	300	500
Bed, Art Deco, brass, stylized sunburst design on headboard and footboard, 42.5" h, 48.75" w	300	500
Bed, birch, tall pencil post, octagonal tapering posts continuing to square legs joined by molded peaked headboard and flat tester frame, New England, early 19th C, 81" h, 71" l, 51" w	2000	4000
Bed, brass, rectangular head- and footboards w/ rounded top corners, tubular frame w/ spindle latticework, lower footboard, double size, 59.5" h, 84.25" l, 54.5" w	200	400

Left: Empire Tester Bed, mahogany, molded ogee cornice, fluted posts, paneled headboard w/ high-relief fruit spray and foliate scrollwork, similarly decorated footboard and rails, stamped "C. Lee 1807," $12,650 at auction.

Below: Chippendale Blanket Chest, walnut, ogee-molded lid, lidded candle till, waist molding over 2 drawers, bracket feet, PA, 1775-1800, $3450 at auction.

—Photos courtesy Sloan's Washington DC Gallery.

	LOW	HIGH
Bed, Chippendale, mahogany, tall post, octagonal head posts w/ lamb's tongue detail continuing to square legs, angled headboard joined to fluted and stop-fluted foot post w/ lamb's tongue detailing, square legs joined by rails fitted for roping, accompanying tester frame and bed bolts, old refinish, RI, 18th C, 79" h, 85" l, 55" w	2500	5000
Bed, Federal Style, carved mahogany, 4 post, arched rectangular headboard raised on baluster-turned reeded posts w/ rice carving and urnform finials, short baluster-turned feet, 72.5" h, 86" l, 82.5" w	600	900
Bed, Federal Style, carved walnut, headboard w/ molded swan's neck pediment centered w/ urn, reeded baluster-turned posts topped w/ finials and carved w/ ribboned sheafs of barley, square tapered legs, molded block feet, king size, 86" h, 88.5" l, 80.5" w	400	600
Bed, Late Empire, tiger maple, low post, shaped overscrolled headboard, tulip-turned posts w/ ball finials, similar footboard w/ turned blanket rail, 1825-50, single size, 53.5" h, 51.5" w	500	800
Bed, Sheraton, carved mahogany, tall post, reeded tapered tall posts w/ carved wrapped leafage above stylized pineapple carving flanking serpentine headboard, square tapered fluted and stop-fluted legs joined to foot posts by molded rails fitted for roping, accompanying tester and some bed bolt covers, Southern, 19th C, 90" h, 78" l, 52.25" w	7000	10,000
Beds, painted butternut, low post, pedimented shaped headboard flanked by chamfered posts, scribed rails pierced for thonging, similarly chamfered foot posts, 19th C, single size, 34" h, 72.75" l, 40" w, price for pair	300	500
Billiard Table, carved oak, egg and dart-molded frieze over bombé apron w/ foliate-scroll molding, block supports similary molded, "Monarch Cushions, The Brunswick–Balke–Collender Co." maker's plaque, c1900, 109.5" l, 59" w	2000	4000
Blanket Chest, Chippendale, walnut w/ poplar and white pine secondary woods, rectangular top w/ ogee-molded edge and strap hinges, storage well w/ lidded candle till, front w/ waist molding over 2 drawers w/ overlapping molding, molded base w/ bracket feet, PA, 1775-1800, 29.75" h, 50" w, 23" d	3000	5000
Blanket Chest, painted white pine, molded rectangular top opening to interior w/ lidded till, molded base, turned ovoid feet, traces of red paint, 19th C, 21.5" h, 38" w, 19" d	300	500
Bookshelf, Queen Anne Style, hardwood, shelf w/ backboard, shaped sides and candle slides, each end support comprising paired columns raised on arched feet joined by turned pole stretcher, 26" h, 18.75" w, 16.5" d	150	300
Bookstand, mahogany, cradle-shaped w/ sloping sides, ends pierced for handles, paired ring-turned columnar supports joined by two shaped base shelves, late 19th/early 20th C, 27" h, 21.75" l, 11" w	50	100
Breakfast Table, Hepplewhite, mahogany and inlaid kingwood, drop-leaf top w/ large oval veneered central reserve banded in kingwood veneer and stringing and outlined w/ meandering inlaid vine w/ leaves and berries bordered by kingwood and stringing, square tapered legs topped by 12-point paterae above 6 graduated 3-point husks descending to cuff inlays over brass casters, old refinish, replaced brasses, Charleston, SC, 1790-1800, 28.5" h, 31.25" w, 19.625" d	200,000	250,000
Breakfast Table, oak, circular top w/ 2 leaves, ring-turned column w/ molded downswept legs ending in casters, late 19th/early 20th C, 29.5" h, 48" dia	600	800
Candlestand, cast iron and brass, 2-armed candlestand w/ 2 brass cups and drip pans fitted to horizontal sliding carrier and ending in tripod base, brass finial and standard decoration, 18th C, 48.25" h	2000	3000

	LOW	HIGH
Candlestand, cherry, circular tilt-top, vase- and ring-turned support, tripod base w/ cabriole legs ending in pad feet, CT, late 18th C, 28" h, 21" dia	1000	1500
Candlestand, cherry, octagonal top, vase- and ring-turned post, tripod base w/ cabriole legs, old varnish, Western MA, late 18th C, 25" h, 15.25" w, 15.125" d	1500	2500
Candlestand, Federal, cherry, rectangular top above single drawer and straight sides joined by corner posts ending in turned drops, vase- and ring-tuned post, arris cabriole legs, pad feet on platforms, refinished, CT, c1815-20, 25.5" h, 19" w, 19.5" d	500	750
Candlestand, Federal, cherry, square top w/ applied beaded edge, vase- and ring-turned post, tripod base w/ cabriole legs ending in pad feet, refinished, CT, c1790, 27.5" h, 18" w, 17" d	800	1200
Candlestand, Federal, inlaid mahogany, square top w/ string-inlaid edge, vase- and ring-turned support, tripod base w/ cabriole legs ending in pad feet, refinished, RI, c1790, 28" h, 17.75" w, 17.75" d	8000	1200
Card Table, Classical, carved mahogany and mahogany veneer, rectangular folding top, conforming frieze w/ beaded edge, carved support w/ acanthus leaves and basket of fruit, shaped concave platform, acanthus leaf-, scroll-, and paw-carved feet, refinished, Philadelphia, c1825, 30.25" h, 38" w, 18.5" d	3000	5000
Card Table, Hepplewhite, inlaid mahogany, hinged top w/ half-serpentine ends, elliptical front, and square corners, conforming base centering inlaid panel bordered by geometric stringing and crossbanding w/ cross-banded lower edge, square tapered legs w/ crossbanded panels in dies continuing to inlaid cuffs, refinished, MA, c1790, 30" h, 35.75" w, 17" d	2000	3000
Card Table, Sheraton, carved mahogany and flame birch veneer, serpentine top outlined in patterned inlay w/ ovolo corners, skirt w/ 2 rectangular inlaid panels flanking central oval, reeded and ring-turned legs topped by carved and veined leafage, old refinish, North Shore, MA, c1800, 30" h, 36" w, 16.875" d	5000	7500
Card Table, Sheraton, mahogany and inlaid bird's-eye maple, serpentine top w/ outset corners, conforming bird's-eye maple veneered skirt w/ central flame birch veneer oval reserve in mahogany veneered panel, reeded front legs stopped by colonettes and ending in ring-turned swelled feet, old refinish, Boston, 1790, 28.5" h, 36" w, 17.75" d	4000	6000
Chair Table, pine and maple, circular overhanging top, 4 square legs joined by seat and box stretchers, old refinish, New England, early 19th C, 29" h, 44" dia	800	1200
Chamber Stand, Classical, mahogany veneer, rectangular mirror on scrolled supports, 2 small drawers above single long drawer, ring-turned tapered legs, restored, New England, 1825-35, 63.5" h, 36.5" w, 19.25" d	1500	2500
Chamber Stand, Classical, paint-decorated and gilt-stenciled, scrolled splash-board above pierced top w/ bowed front and square corners, conforming skirt w/ flanking small drawers painted black w/ gilt cornucopia and Greek key designs, scrolled sides joining medial drawer, vase- and ring-turned legs, light blue-green ground w/ apple green striped borders, VT, c1825-35, 37.25" h, 18.5" w, 15" d	1500	2500
Chamber Stand, Federal, mahogany, shaped splashback w/ flanking quarter-round shelves above pierced top on turned supports joining valanced skirt, medial shelf and drawer on vase- and ring-turned legs, brass pull, refinished, New England, c1815-25, 42" h, 20.5" w, 16" d	1200	2000
Chest, blue-painted, 6-board, molded hinged lid opening to well w/ lidded till, molded straight skirt w/ shaped sides, early blue-green paint, New England, early 19th C, 25" h, 50" w, 19.75" d	1500	2000

	LOW	HIGH
Chest of Drawers, Chippendale, carved cherry, rectangular molded top, 4 thumb-molded graduated drawers, fluted lamb's tongue corners, bracket feet, replaced brasses, refinished, PA, c1770-80, 34" h, 41.5" w, 19.25" d	3500	5000
Chest of Drawers, Chippendale, carved mahogany, bow-front, overhanging top w/ inlaid edge, cockbeaded case w/ 4 graduated drawers, claw and ball feet, old refinish, replaced brasses, MA, c1780, 34.5" h, 37.75" w, 22" d	4000	6000
Chest of Drawers, Chippendale, carved mahogany, rectangular molded top, 4 cockbeaded graduated drawers, fluted quarter columns, ogee bracket feet, replaced bail brasses, old refinish, restored, PA, c1780, 35" h, 40" w, 19.5" d	4000	6500
Chest of Drawers, Chippendale, cherry, overhanging molded top, 2 thumb-molded short drawers and 4 graduated long drawers, ogee bracket feet, replaced brasses, old refinish, RI, c1770-80, 42" h, 36.5" w, 18.5" d	2000	3000
Chest of Drawers, Chippendale, maple, flat molded cornice above case w/ 2 thumb-molded graduated short drawers and 4 graduated long drawers, bracket feet, batwing brasses, old refinish, MA, 1770-80, 44.5" h, 36.75" w, 18" d	3500	4500
Chest of Drawers, Chippendale, maple, rectangular overhanging molded top, 4 graduated thumb-molded drawers, ogee bracket feet on casters, old brasses, old refinish, restored, MA, c1780, 31.5" h, 36" w, 19.5" d	1500	2500
Chest of Drawers, Chippendale Style, mahogany, molded rectangular top, 2 short drawers over 3 long drawers flanked by fluted quarter-column stiles, molded base, ogee bracket feet, 36.5" h, 46.5" w, 21.25" d	200	400
Chest of Drawers, Empire, mahogany, rectangular top, 2 swell-frieze drawers on outset scrolled stiles flanking 3 long recessed drawers, scroll feet, 1825-50, 43.5" h, 43.75" w, 22.75" d	400	600

Left to right: Chair Table, painted white pine, hinged oval top, scrolled arms, baluster-turned arm supports and legs, box stretcher, early 19th C, $978 at auction; Hepplewhite Cellaret, inlaid mahogany, hinged cockbeaded lid opening to well, front inlaid w/ tassled rope swags, molded stand w/ drawer, square tapered legs on casters, inlaid throughout w/ stringing, c1800, $1840 at auction. —Photos courtesy Sloan's Washington DC Gallery.

	LOW	HIGH
Chest of Drawers, Federal, cherry, overhanging rectangular top, 4 cock-beaded graduated drawers, flaring French feet, old brass pulls, old finish, New England, c1800-10, 36.5" h, 36.75" w, 19" d	4000	6000
Chest of Drawers, Federal, mahogany, rectangular top w/ reeded edge, 4 graduated cockbeaded drawers flanked by reeded stiles, spurred bracket feet, c1800, 27" h, 40.75" w, 21" d	1000	1500
Chest of Drawers, Federal, mahogany and bird's-eye maple veneer, bow-front, bowed top w/ inlaid edge, 4 cockbeaded drawers veneered w/ bird's- eye maple surrounded by crossbanded mahogany veneer, scrolled front skirt and sides, French feet, oval brasses, old refinish, NH, early 19th C, 37" h, 39.75" w, 22" d	5000	10,000
Chest of Drawers, Federal Style, pine, rectangular top, 3 drawers in outset molded base w/ bracket feet, 26.25" h, 33.25" w, 15.5" d	300	500
Chest of Drawers, grain-painted pine, 4 thumb-molded graduated drawers, shaped skirt, red and black graining simulating mahogany, replaced pulls, New England, early 19th C, 41" h, 39.5" w, 17.25" d	1000	1500
Chest of Drawers, painted and decorated birch and maple, rectangular back-board w/ molded edge, overhanging top drawer flanked by turned columns ending in ring-turned ball feet, recessed case w/ 3 long drawers, red paint and faux-grained drawers simulating mahogany, turned wooden pulls, Barre, VT, 1830s, 39.25" h, 43" w, 19.25" d	2000	3000
Chest of Drawers, Sheraton, mahogany and flame birch veneer, bowfront, bowed birch top, 4 graduated drawers veneered w/ flame birch surrounded by mahogany crossbanded veneer, flanked by colonettes and reeding and ending in ring-turned feet, shaped skirt outlined w/ stars burned into wood, replaced round brass pulls, Salem, MA, c1810, 37" h, 37.75" w, 20.25" d	12,000	18,000

Chests of Drawers, left: Empire, tiger maple, projecting long drawer above recessed drawers, scrolled pilasters, 1825-50, $978 at auction. —Photo courtesy Sloan's Washington DC Gallery; right: Country Hepplewhite, red-stained pine, bird's-eye maple drawer fronts, dovetailed drawers, $1100 at auction. —Photo courtesy Garth's Auctions, Delaware, OH.

Child's Rockers, left to right: Walnut comb-back; Walnut potty rocker; and Maple slat-back. —Photo courtesy Sloan's Washington DC Gallery.

	LOW	HIGH
Chest of Drawers, Victorian, walnut, gray-veined white marble on molded rectangular top w/ rounded front corners, 3 drawers w/ burr-walnut veneered fronts, molded stiles, 33.25" h, 39" w, 17" d	400	600
Chest of Drawers, walnut, 2 short drawers over 3 long drawers w/ tiger inlaid escutcheons, turned bulbous legs, some replaced pulls, refinished, PA, 49.5" h, 43" w, 20.25" d	400	600
Chest-on-Chest, Chippendale Style, pine, upper section w/ ogee-molded cornice, 2 short over 3 long graduated and molded drawers, outset molded lower section w/ 3 molded drawers, outset molded base w/ scrolled bracket feet, 67.5" h, 37.5" w, 19.75" d	1000	1500
Chest over Drawers, painted pine, hinged and molded top lifts to well, 2 thumb-molded drawers on straight front skirt w/ side shaping, replaced pulls, old red paint, New England, 18th C, 41.25" h, 43.75" w, 18.5" d	1200	1800
Chest over Drawers, painted pine, molded lift-top above deep well, double arch molded case w/ 2 false and 2 working drawers, applied molding at base on cutout ends, replaced brasses, repainted gray-brown, MA, early 18th C, 37" h, 39.5" w, 18" d	1000	1500
Child's Bureau, Empire, grained and painted, rectangular top and backsplash w/ 2 glove drawers, case w/ single overhanging drawer above 3 long drawers flanked by serpentine columns joined by shaped skirt, wooden pulls, 3 drawers fitted w/ compartments, pair of lovebirds painted on glove box top, yellow and pink roses on drawer fronts and case sides, sides and drawers banded w/ blue paint, 19th C, 12.5" h, 13.25" w, 8" d	500	800
Child's Chest, grain-painted, 6-board, molded hinged top, dovetailed box, slightly flaring bracket feet, mustard and brown paint resembles exotic wood, New England, late 18th C, 14" h, 20.5" w, 12" d	1500	2000
Child's Cradle, pine, splayed sides w/ vaulted hood and arched footboard, raised on segmental rockers, 19th C, 24.5" h, 37.75" l, 26" w	200	400
Child's Highchair, Windsor Style, painted, splayed rectangular fan back flanked by arms, shaped slab seat, turned and splayed legs joined by turned box stretcher, 19th C	100	200
Child's Potty Rocker, walnut, scalloped wings, pierced handle at top center of back, shaped skirt, 30" h	100	250
Child's Rocker, maple, slat-back, 3 shaped slats, acorn finials, shaped arms and rockers, woven rush seat, box stretcher, 27" h	150	300
Child's Rocker, rustic, intertwined twigs above solid splat, plank seat, square stretcher and rockers, old dark natural finish, NY, c1900, 9.75" h to seat	200	400
Child's Rocker, walnut, comb back, black painted and stenciled, shaped crest rail, 4-spindle back, scrolled arm, turned arm posts and front legs, box stretcher, 30.25" h	100	200

	LOW	HIGH
Child's Side Chair, Victorian, painted, open rectangular back w/ arched and shaped crest rail and crossbar, caned saddle seat, turned tapered and splayed legs joined by turned box stretcher, c1850	100	150
Child's Side Chair, Windsor, painted, bowed crest, 5 tapered spindles, shaped plank seat, swelled legs joined by H-stretchers, old black paint, cracks in seat, New England, early 19th C, 20.5" h	500	800
Child's Side Chairs, Classical, mahogany, paneled concave crest, horizontal splat, raked stiles, upholstered slip seat, saber legs, refinished, Boston, c1820, 28" h	500	800
Child's Side Chairs, Windsor Style, fruitwood, spindle back w/ curved crest rail, saddle seat raised on similary turned splayed legs joined by box stretcher, price for pair	100	150
Child's Stool, carved and painted, mushroom top, tree trunk pedestal, tripod legs, 9" h, 7.5" dia	300	500
Club Chairs, leather, button-upholstered back flanked by overscrolled arms, bow front seat w/ loose cushion, short turned legs, camel-colored close-nailed leather upholstery, price for pair	800	1200
Console Table, Empire Style, mahogany, rectangular top over outset ogee-molded frieze drawer raised on scrolled supports, platform stretcher w/ concave front and mirror backing, 34.5" h, 36" w, 30.75" d	800	1200
Corner Armchair, Victorian, oak, padded shaped rectangular back, outcurved spindle arms, serpentine front w/ loose cushion seat and molded rails, cabriole legs w/ casters, late 19th C	200	400

Left to right: Federal Style Clothespress, mahogany, molded cornice, doors opening to 2 sliding trays, 2 short over 2 long cockbeaded and crossbanded drawers, bracket feet, $3738 at auction; Corner Cupboard, various woods, molded cornice, glazed doors opening to shelves, frieze drawer, cupboard doors opening to shelf, molded base, bun feet, 19th C, $431 at auction. —Photos courtesy Sloan's Washington DC Gallery.

	LOW	HIGH
Corner Cabinet, Country Style, upper section w/ swan's neck pediment over glazed arched astragal door opening to shelves, lower section w/ pair of recessed panel doors opening to shelf, 80" h, 36.25" w, 17.5" d	400	600
Corner Cupboard, cherry and chestnut, upper section w/ outset ogee-molded cornice w/ canted corners and 9-pane door opening to 2 shelves, lower section w/ 2 doors over 2 recessed panel doors, canted stiles, and bracket feet, 19th C, 83" h, 48.25" w, 24.75" d	1000	1500
Corner Cupboard, painted white, upper section w/ outset molded cornice over pair of 8-pane astragal doors opening to shelves, lower section w/ paneled frieze centered by single drawer over pair of paneled doors opening to shelf, the whole centered by canted stiles continuing to stile feet, 19th C, 85" h, 47" w, 21.5" d	1800	3000
Cupboard, Federal, cherry, molded top above 2 beaded small drawers and glazed door, recessed panel sides, turned legs ending in small ball feet, refinished, PA or OH, c1830s, 25" h, 28" w, 13.5" d	1200	1800
Davenport, Victorian Eastlake, carved walnut, open shelf w/ shaped backboard raised on pierced supports atop hinged and molded slanted rectangular writing surface opening to fitted interior, all raised on similarly pierced columnar supports and base w/ 4 molded drawers on right-hand side and 4 opposing false drawers on left, block feet w/ casters, ring pulls, late 19th C, 46" h, 25.75" w, 24.75" d	500	700
Desk, Chippendale, birch, slant lid opening to shaped interior w/ 10 compartments and small drawers, cockbeaded case w/ 4 graduated drawers, bracket feet, replaced brasses, old refinish, MA, c1780, 44.25" h, 40" w, 21.25" d	1500	2000
Desk, Chippendale, mahogany, slant lid opening to interior w/ 8 valanced drawers above compartments and 4 small drawers w/ central shell-carved prospect door enclosing 2 valanced compartments and 2 blocked drawers, case w/ 4 thumb-molded graduated drawers on ogee bracket feet, replaced bail brasses, RI, c1770-80, 41.25" h, 38" w, 19" d	2000	3500

Slant Lid Desks. Left: William and Mary, walnut veneer, valanced interior, bulbous feet, early 18th C, $5175 at auction. —Photo courtesy Skinner, Inc., Boston, MA. Right: Hepplewhite, white cherry, fitted interior w/ vertical tambour doors and center document door, inlaid satinwood stringing and quarter-fan, bracket feet, late 18th C, $4025 at auction. —Photo courtesy Sloan's Washington DC Gallery.

	LOW	HIGH
Desk, Chippendale, mahogany, slant lid opening to interior w/ central concave fan-carved prospect door opening to 3 concave drawers flanked by baluster-fronted document drawers, 3 valanced compartments, blocked drawers, and fan-carved drawer above 2 concave drawers, case w/ 4 thumb-molded graduated drawers, and bracket feet, replaced brasses, old finish, Boston, c1770-80, 42.5" h, 39.5" w, 19.5" d	20,000	25,000
Desk, Federal, mahogany and birch, oxbow slant lid opening to interior w/ 7 drawers w/ inlaid stringing above 7 valanced compartments, cock-beaded case w/ 4 serpentine drawers, bracket feet, oval brasses, refinished, MA, c1780, 43.5" h, 40" w, 19.5" d	3000	5000
Desk, Federal, wavy birch, slant lid opening to valanced multi-drawer interior, 4 graduated drawers w/ incised cockbeading, cutout base, replaced brasses, old refinish, Southern New England, c1780-1800, 43.5" h, 39.25" w, 19.5" d	1500	2500
Desk, Heywood Wakefield, maple, rectangular top, long drawer flanked by 4 side drawers w/ shaped wooden pulls, medium finish, c1955, 29.5" h, 42" w, 19.5" d	300	500
Desk, shipping clerk's, grain-painted pine, rectangular top w/ canted sides above 2 short drawers, 2 long drawers, and lift top, centering a gallery w/ block-turned posts, all set in frame w/ square legs joined by straight skirt and box stretchers, grain-painted brown to resemble mahogany on dark green-painted base, New England, 1800-1850, 59" h, 61.5" w, 41" d	700	1000
Desk, table-top, Queen Anne, walnut, lid opens to interior w/ valanced compartments above 2 drawers and well, case w/ trunnels on molded dovetailed bracket base centering shaped pendant, refinished, restored, PA, c1740-60, 16.5" h, 23.5" w, 14.25" d	2000	3000
Desk Bookcase, Chippendale, carved cherry, molded scrolled cornice terminating in carved pinwheels above applied carved central ornament, spire and sphere finials, recessed panel doors open to 2-shelf interior w/ scrolled dividers, hinged slant lid opening to fitted interior w/ valanced compartments w/ scrolled dividers flanking pinwheel-carved drawer and smaller drawers arranged in 2 steps, case w/ graduated thumb-molded drawers flanked by fluted quarter columns above ogee bracket feet on platforms, batwing escutcheon and brasses, CT, 18th C, 91.5" h, 39" w, 20.5" d	25,000	35,000
Desk Bookcase, Classical, mahogany veneer, projecting cornice above veneered frieze, pair of glazed doors opening to 2 adjustable shelves above 3 small drawers, fold-out writing surface lifting to fitted well w/ 2 drawers and open compartments, 2 recessed panel doors opening to single-shelf interior, scrolled supports ending in leaf- and paw-carved front feet, replaced brasses, refinished, restored, New England, 1825-35, 81" h, 40" w, 23.25" d	1000	2000
Dining Chairs, Chippendale Style, carved walnut, comprising 2 armchairs and 6 side chairs, arched open back w/ shell-carved scroll crest over pierced tracery splat, saddle-shaped drop-in seat, molded rails, cabriole legs, claw and ball feet, acanthus foliage carved throughout, price for set of 8	600	1000
Dining Chairs, Empire, rectangular back w/ pierced and scrolled crest rail over shaped cross-bar, serpentine-fronted needlework seat w/ conforming rails, saber legs, mid-19th C	500	750
Dining Table, Federal Style, carved mahogany, 2-pedestal, extending, rectangular top w/ rounded corners, satinwood crossbanded edge and gadroon molding, each pedestal w/ baluster-form standard raised on tripod base w/ downswept legs ending in claw and ball feet, carved w/ foliage and coquillage throughout, 30.25" h, 114" l, 46" w	1000	1500

Dining Set, Leavens Co., oak, comprised of table w/ 4 leaves and 6 chairs, $2243 at auction. —Photo courtesy Skinner, Inc., Boston, MA.

	LOW	HIGH
Dining Table, gate-leg, walnut, 2 working drawers, gates swing to hold drop leaves, boldly turned legs ending in turned feet, PA, late 18th C, 27.75" h, 48.75" l, 55" d	5000	8000
Dining Table, Neoclassical, mahogany, 3-part pedestal base, hinged drop leaves on center section supported by 4 spiral-carved and ring-turned columns above shaped veneered platform w/ 4 reeded curving legs ending in brass paw feet on casters, 2 demilune flanking sections each w/ single hinged drop leaf above pedestal form identical to that of center section, skirt w/ rectangular dies above turned pendants, bottom edge outlined in veneer, refinished, NY, c1805, 30" h, 163.5" l, 53.75" w	50,000	75,000
Dining Table, Queen Anne, mahogany, square overhanging drop-leaf top, cutout apron, cabriole legs w/ arris knees continuing to pad feet, old refinish, New England, late 18th C, 27.375" h, 47" w, 46" d	2500	4000
Dining Table, Victorian, mahogany, extending, molded rectangular extension top w/ 2 leaves and swell apron, acanthus-capped squared cabriole legs w/ hairy-paw feet, late 19th C, 28.25" h, 71.25" l, 48" w	800	1200
Dough Box, Country, pine, removable rectangular top, box w/ everted sides, square splayed legs, 28" h, 25" w, 15.75" d	200	300
Dough Box, white pine, removable rectangular top, box w/ sloping sides, bead-and-quirk molded base w/ splayed square tapered legs, 1800-50, 27.25" h, 38.25" w, 23.75" d	400	600
Drawing Table, Victorian, cast iron and oak, molded rectangular tilt-top w/ paper ledge, telescopic-action extending standard, tripod base w/ downswept legs ending in molded cylinder feet, 1875-1900, 31.75" h, 26" w, 22" d	400	600
Dressing Table, Queen Anne, walnut, overhanging thumb-molded top w/ shaped front corners, case w/ single long drawer over 3 small drawers, center drawer w/ carved lunette, flat arched skirt w/ drop pendants, 4 cabriole legs ending in high pad feet, replaced batwing brasses, old refinish, Boston, 1730-50, 30.5" h, 34.5" w, 21" d	8000	12,000
Drinks Cabinet, Art Deco, grained oak, rectangular platform top, 2 doors each w/ 3 galleried shelves on reverse and opening to interior shelf, raised on plinth base, early 20th C, 40" h, 29.5" w, 15.5" d	100	250

	LOW	HIGH
Drop-Leaf Pedestal Table, Empire Style, mahogany, rectangular top w/ rounded corners, frieze w/ 2 convex drawers, baluster-form squared column on rectangular plinth w/ concave sides and canted scroll feet, 27.5" h, 31.75" l, 5.75" w	200	400
Drop-Leaf Table, Early Empire, cherry, rectangular top w/ rule-jointed leaves, twist-turned legs, turned feet, 1800-25, 29.25" h, 47.25" l, 36" w	400	600
Drop-Leaf Table, Federal, cherry, rectangular top w/ rule-jointed leaves and rounded corners, turned and tapered legs carved w/ spiral bands of foliage, 28.5" h, 44.5" l, 43.5" w	300	500
Drop-Leaf Table, Federal Style, poplar, rectangular top w/ demilune drop leaves, turned and ring-turned legs w/ toupie feet, 20.75" h, 31.25" l, 19" w	100	150
Drop-Leaf Table, Late Federal, mahogany, rectangular top w/ serpentine corners, frieze w/ drawer, tapered ring-turned legs w/ ball feet, 29" h, 47.25" l, 35.75" w	300	500
Drop-Leaf Table, Queen Anne, painted maple, scrubbed top w/ hinged leaves, straight skirt, ring-turned tapered legs ending in turned feet, faint gray-green painted surface, RI, late 18th C, 26.75" h, 42" l, 14.5" w	3500	5500
Easy Chair, Country, barrel-back, scrolling arms, cushion seat, chamfered front legs, rear raking square legs, old refinish, New England, 45.5" h	600	800
Easy Chair, Federal, mahogany, shaped crest, tight seat, scrolled arms, ring-turned tapered front legs, old refinish, New England, early 19th C, 46" h	1500	2000
Easy Chair, Victorian Eastlake, carved walnut, padded splayed rectangular back w/ architectural crest rail, serpentine-front overstuffed seat flanked by outcurved arms w/ elbow rests, turned and tapered legs w/ casters, 1875-1900	200	400
Footstool, Empire, mahogany, padded rectangular drop-in top, mirror-veneered battered sides, ogee bracket feet, mid-19th C	150	200

Left: Sheraton Dressing Table, mahogany and bird's-eye maple veneer, scrolled mirror supports, reeded stiles, c1810-20, $85,000 at auction.
—Photo courtesy Skinner, Inc., Boston, MA.

Below: Queen Anne Style Drop-Leaf Table, walnut, rule-jointed drop leaves, shaped frieze, turned and tapered legs w/ pad feet, $403 at auction.
—Photo courtesy Sloan's Washington DC Gallery.

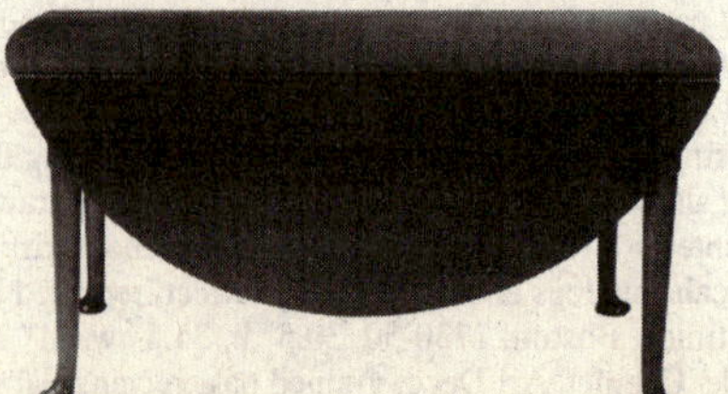

	LOW	HIGH
Hall Chair, Victorian, carved walnut, rectangular tracery back w/ padded panel surrounded by pierced foliate scrollwork, serpentine front w/ overstuffed seat and similarly carved rails, twist-turned legs w/ casters, late 19th C	200	400
Hall Rack, Art Deco, chromed metal framework w/ long hat shelf over center mirror and shelf, flanked by disk-shaped coat hooks over side storage racks, mirror replaced, 72" h, 42.75" w, 6.75" d	2500	3500
Highboy, Chippendale Style, mahogany, shell-carved, upper section w/ swan's neck pediment and 3 flaming-urn finials above 3 small drawers, 2 short drawers, and 3 long graduated drawers, all flanked by fluted quarter-column stiles, similar base w/ single long drawer over 3 short drawers, cabriole legs, claw and ball feet, 88.5" h, 42" w, 24.5" d	1800	2500
Highboy, Chippendale Style, mahogany, upper section surmounted by pierced foliate swan's neck pediment centered by urn and w/ arrangement of 5 short and 4 long cockbeaded drawers, lower section w/ 4 short drawers centered by shell- and leaf-carved drawer, molded scroll-carved skirt, and leaf-carved cabriole legs w/ claw and ball feet, 83.75" h, 40.5" w, 17" d	650	850
High Chest, Chippendale, carved cherry, scrolled top w/ sepentine cove molding, upper case w/ 3 small drawers above 5 graduated long drawers, lower case w/ single long drawer above 3 small drawers, upper and lower center small drawers w/ fan carving, skirt w/ shaped front and sides, cabriole legs ending in pad feet, some replaced brass, refinished, missing finials and pendants, New England, 18th C, 84" h, 38" w, 19.5" d	30,000	35,000
Joint Stool, William and Mary, maple, rectangular molded overhanging top, molded skirt, splayed block vase- and ring-turned legs continuing to turned feet and joined by stretchers, old refinish, MA, ealy 18th C, 23" h, 24" w, 16" d	5000	8000

Left: Chippendale Highboy, carved mahogany, swan's neck pediment, flaming-urn finials, fluted quarter-column stiles, cabriole legs, claw and ball feet, $2185 at auction.

Below: Queen Anne Lowboy, carved walnut, chamfered stiles, shaped skirt w/ carved scallop shell, cabriole legs, pointed pad feet, mid-18th C, $2990 at auction.

—Photos courtesy Sloan's Washington DC Gallery.

	LOW	HIGH
Occasional Table, Federal Style, walnut, rectangular molded top over frieze w/ 2 drawers, square tapered legs, 28.25" h, 16.5" w, 15.25" d	300	500
Occasional Table, painted satinwood, trefoil-form, molded top painted w/ sprays of flowers, triangular undercarriage w/ 3 baluster-turned legs joined by triangular base shelf and box stretcher, early 20th C, 20" h, 19.25" w, 19.25" d	300	500
Occasional Table, Victorian, walnut, gray-veined white marble top w/ inset serpentine corners, shaped conforming frieze, cluster-column standard w/ molded scroll legs and casters, late 19th C, 28.75" h, 26" l, 18" w	300	500
Occasional Table, Victorian, walnut, rectangular top w/ serpentine edges, conforming frieze w/ reel molding, bobbin-turned legs joined by shaped base shelf and similarly turned pole stretcher, arched feet, mid-19th C, 28" h, 30.75" l, 16.5" w	200	400
Occasional Table, Victorian, walnut, rectangular top w/ serpentine edges, shaped frieze w/ turned drops, bobbin-turned legs joined by rectangular base shelf and similarly turned pole stretcher, arched feet, late 19th C, 27" h, 26" l, 14.5" w	150	300
Overmantel Mirror, Renaissance Revival, gilt-gesso, rectangular plate w/ inset rounded upper corners, ogee-molded breakfront cornice centered by scrolled pediment w/ classical female bust in tympanum, outset ends w/ similar but smaller pediments raised on convex pilasters w/ strapwork capitals and anthemion-molded bases, inscribed "Jas Fitzgerald Manufacturer, 55 North Gay St., Baltimore Md, Dec 1875," 84" h, 68.25" w	1500	3000
Parlor Chair, Aesthetic Movement, mahogany, splayed rectangular back w/ arched and molded crest rail over vasiform splat, serpentine-front padded seat, turned tapered legs w/ splayed feet and turned box stretcher, c1900	100	200
Parlor Chair, Victorian Rococo Style, carved poplar, arched back w/ leaf-carved splat and crest, similarly carved cabriole legs, 20th C	100	150
Parlor Suite, Empire Style, carved walnut, 2-seat sofa w/ shaped and padded rectangular back, dipped crest rail carved w/ ribbon-tied laurel leaves, overstuffed seat flanked by overscrolled arms, reeded rail, and splayed lion's paw feet, carved throughout w/ acanthus foliage, 2 armchairs en suite, price for 3-pc set	800	1200
Parlor Suite, Victorian Eastlake, carved walnut, armchair w/ rectangular button back w/ shaped frame, bow-fronted overstuffed seat flanked by arms w/ elbow rests, and turned and tapered legs w/ casters, 2 side chairs en suite, 1875-1900, price for 3-pc set	300	500
Pembroke Table, Hepplewhite, inlaid mahogany, rectangular top w/ shaped drop leaves bordered by stringing, crossbanded skirt w/ working and false birch-veneered drawers bordered by stringing, square tapered legs inlaid w/ wavy birch panels in dies above stringing, refinished, NY, c1790-1800, 28.5" h, 20.5" w, 30.5" d	2000	3500
Pembroke Table, Sheraton, inlaid mahogany, rectangular overhanging top w/ rounded leaves, straight skirt w/ drawer and inlaid lower edge, vase- and ring-turned reeded tapered legs, old refinish, New England, c1810-15, 28.5" h, 36" w, 18.75" d	1000	2000
Piano Stool, Victorian, adjustable, circular molded seat raised on 4 baluster-turned legs w/ metal and glass claw and ball feet, cross stretcher similarly turned, late 19th C	100	200
Pier Glass, Neoclassical, giltwood, carved shell above leafage and cat-o'-nine-tails crest over spiral- and acanthus leaf-carved ring-turned columns w/ leaf-carved squares at each corner, early rectangular plate surrounded by molded black liner, Boston, c1815, 71" h, 36" w	18,000	22,000

	LOW	HIGH
Pole Screen, Federal Style, mahogany, screen embroidered w/ flowers and berries, molded frame, baluster-turned pole on tripod support w/ downswept legs and pad feet, 19th C, 56.5" h	200	400
Press Bed, red-painted, low-post, shaped headboard w/ rails hinged for folding attached to footposts w/ identical turned finials and legs, rails fitted for roping, New England, early 19th C, 35.5" h, 74" l, 49.75" w	600	800
Rocker, Country, rectangular ladder back w/ 4 graduated slats and outcurved arms, woven rush seat, turned legs joined by turned double-box stretcher, possibly CT, mid-19th C	100	250
Rocker, Victorian, walnut, arched, shaped, and padded rectangular back w/ foliate crest, arms w/ elbow rests and fretted supports, serpentine front w/ drop-in seat and conforming molded rails, curved squared legs	200	400
Roundabout Chair, Chippendale, walnut, shaped crest on scrolled arms, shaped splats, slip seat in molded frame, front cabriole leg ending in pad foot, 3 turned legs ending in small turned feet, old refinish, MA, 1770-1800, 30" h	5000	10,000
Roundabout Chair, Queen Anne, cherry, shaped crest rail continuing to scrolled arms on vase- and ring-turned supports flanking shaped splats on molded shoes, upholstered slip seat, 3 block and turned tapered legs joined by deep skirts to front cabriole leg ending in high pad foot, old finish, New England, c1740-60, 28" h	4000	6000
Secretary Bookcase, Empire, mahogany, upper section w/ molded cornice and 2 glazed and mullioned cupboard doors enclosing shelves and multiple drawers, lower section w/ hinged writing surface, single long drawer above 2 long recessed drawers flanked by turned pilasters, and bun feet, c1820, 76" h, 44.5" w, 22" d	3000	4000
Server, Classical, carved mahogany and mahogany veneer, rectangular top above 2 cockbeaded short drawers and single long drawer w/ banded borders flanked by applied gothic panels, vase- and ring-turned spiral-carved legs joined by medial shelf, cast brass casters, old refinish, replaced pulls, NY, c1825, 33.5" h, 30" w, 16.25" d	1000	2000

Left: Federal Secretary Bookcase, mahogany and flame mahogany veneer, c1810, $8050 at auction.

Right: Pie Safe, fruitwood, punched sheet metal doors, VA, 1850-1900, $748 at auction.

—Photos courtesy Sloan's Washington DC Gallery.

Left: Chippendale Style chair-back settee, carved mahogany, pierced ribbon and sheaf splats, needlework seats, $748 at auction. —Photo courtesy Sloan's Washington DC Gallery.

Right: Windsor comb-back rocker w/ bamboo turnings and yellow pinstriping, New England, c1810-15, $1380 at auction; Windsor fan-back side chair w/ vase- and ring-turned stiles and legs, grain-painted, yellow and green pinstriping, New England, c1790, $748 at auction. —Photo courtesy Skinner, Inc., Boston, MA.

	LOW	HIGH
Server, Classical, mahogany and mahogany veneer, rectangular top, ogee-molded drawer above 2 cupboard doors w/ flat mitered borders, flanking scrolls on scrolled legs, Boston, c1825, 34" h, 40" w, 18.5" d	1500	2000
Settee, Federal Style, mahogany, padded slightly arched rectangular back, downswept arms ending in scroll terminals raised on reeded baluster-form supports, 2-seat loose cushion seat, turned tapered fluted legs, 52.75" l	500	600
Settee, Victorian, carved rosewood, shaped and padded back w/ 2 arched end sections joined by dipped section, each w/ pierced foliate crest, serpentine front, overstuffed seat flanked by scrolled arms, conforming rails continuing to cabriole legs, frame leaf-carved throughout, c1870	500	800
Settee, Victorian, carved walnut, curved back w/ 3 oval button-upholstered panels, outcurved arms w/ elbow rests, serpentine front w/ overstuffed seat and shaped conforming rails continuing to cabriole legs, frame molded and leaf-carved, 1875-1900, 72.5" l	500	800
Settle Bench, painted pine, molded crest, shaped sides flanking paneled hinged doors opening to cupboard w/ shelves, fixed seat and sides, applied beaded board at bottom, old brown paint, England, c1800	1200	2500
Sewing Stand, Sheraton, mahogany and bird's-eye and tiger maple veneer, rectangular bird's-eye maple veneered top outlined w/ mahogany veneer and half-round molding, 2 bird's-eye maple veneered drawers w/ bone escutcheons, ring-turned tiger maple tapered legs ending in small ball feet, replaced pulls, old refinish, MA, c1790, 30.25" h, 20.5" w, 16.75" d	1500	3000

	LOW	HIGH
Shelves, walnut, 4 molded and graduated shelves w/ shaped backboards, molded, pierced, and shaped ends, c1900, 30" h, 22.25" w	200	300
Sideboard, Art Deco, figured walnut, shaped rectangular top backed by fan-shaped mirror in scrolled and fluted frame, conforming front w/ 2-door cupboard on left opening to 3 long drawers and single-door cupboard on right opening to shelf, doors w/ free-standing classical figures in arched niches, all raised on lotus-capped toupie feet, 1925-50, 73.75" h, 64.5" w, 24.25" d	1500	3000
Sideboard, Empire, gilt-bronze-mounted mahogany, molded rectangular top over swell frieze w/ 3 drawers, raised on 4 free-standing columns w/ gilt-bronze capitals and bases, latter dividing 4 paneled cupboard doors opening to shelf, all raised on 4 dramatically carved leaf-capped lion's paw feet, 1825-50, 42.5" h, 69.25" w, 21" d	1500	3000
Sideboard, Empire, mahogany, rectangular top w/ molded backboard, outset frieze w/ pair of drawers each w/ pyramidal front and raised on scrolled pilasters, recessed front w/ pair of paneled doors opening to shaped shelf, 1825-50, 50.75" h, 58.5" w, 25.5" d	700	900
Sideboard, Empire, various woods, molded rectangular top above outset frieze w/ 2 swell-fronted drawers on free-standing Ionic columns, pair of recessed doors opening to shelf, short turned feet, mid-19th C, 43" h, 40.25" w, 23" d	500	800
Sideboard, grain-painted, rectangular top, 2 short and 1 long drawer projecting over 2 recessed panel cupboard doors opening to single-shelf interior, black-painted turned columns continuing to turned feet, allover red and gold graining simulating mahogany, replaced hardware, VT, 1825-40, 50" h, 46.75" w, 21" d	1500	2500
Sideboard, Hepplewhite, inlaid mahogany, shaped top w/ inlaid edge, conforming case w/ single central drawer flanked by 2 small end drawers over 4 cupboard doors and 2 sectioned bottle drawers, facades outlined in stringing w/ 2 ovolo corners, 6 square tapered legs w/ cuff inlays, replaced oval brasses, refinished, some restoration, New England, c1800, 41" h, 67.5" w, 21" d	8000	12,000
Sideboard, Sheraton, inlaid mahogany, D-shaped top banded on edge w/ mahogany veneer between maple stringing, case w/ 3 cockbeaded drawers and 4 cupboard doors, turned and reeded legs topped by stringing in outline, replaced brasses, Boston area, 1795-1810, 29" h, 61.25" l, 23.25" d	6000	9000
Side Chair, beech, molded and carved crest over cane back panel, cane seat w/ serpentine front seat rail, horsebone front legs, raking rear legs ending in square elements, block-ended stretchers, 1730-32, 46" h	400	800
Side Chair, Chippendale, serpentine crest continuing to raked molded terminals, pierced splat, upholstered slip seat, square legs, front legs w/ molded outside edges, square-molded stretchers, old dark stain, Concord, MA, 1775-1800, 39" h	800	1200
Side Chair, Chippendale Style, mahogany, beech secondary wood, splayed rectangular back w/ pierced vasiform splat, shaped crest rail w/ over-scrolled ears, padded drop-in seat, square legs joined by H-stretcher, 19th C	300	400
Side Chair, Early American, cherry and hickory, open rectangular back w/ 3 arched and curved slats, turned posts w/ mushroom finials, woven-bark seat, baluster-turned legs joined by turned double-box stretcher, traces of red paint, early 18th C	100	300
Side Chair, black-painted, 6 spindles, bamboo turnings, branded "D. Abbot & Co.," Daniel Abbot, Newburyport, MA, 1809-11, 33" h	200	300

	LOW	HIGH
Side Chair, Queen Anne, walnut, double arched crest w/ central carved shell, vasiform splat, balloon-shaped over-upholstered seat, cabriole legs joined by block- and baluster-turned H-stretchers, padded disc front feet, old finish, Boston, 1740-65, 40.5" h	6000	8000
Side Chair, William and Mary, maple, block-, vase-, and ring-turned stiles, rectangular upholstered back, over-upholstered seat, block-, vase-, and ring-turned legs joined by stretchers, restored, New England, early 18th C, 47.5" h	400	600
Side Chair, Windsor, maple and ash, bowed beaded crest, 9 tapered incised spindles, incised shaped seat, incised swelled splayed legs joined by H-stretchers, refinished, branded "S. J. Tuck," Boston, 1790, 38" h	800	1200
Side Chairs, Chippendale, serpentine crest rail w/ central carved shell terminating in scrolled-back notched ears, interlaced splats w/ scrolled volutes, fluted stiles w/ rounded backs, trapezoidal seat frame w/ central carved shell, cabriole legs w/ foliate and leaf carving, claw and ball feet, old dark finish, PA, 1760-80, 39.5" h, price for pair	50,000	75,000
Side Chairs, Chippendale Style, oak, arched crest rail over pierced vasiform splat, drop-in seat, cabriole legs w/ paw feet, price for 3	300	500
Side Chairs, Hitchcock, painted black w/ gilt stenciling and polychrome-painted decoration, turned crest rails, wide slat w/ fox hunting scene, raked stiles, woven rush seat, ring-turned legs joined by stretchers and similarly turned front stretcher, Hitchcocksville, CT, c1825-30, 33.5" h, price for pair	1000	1200
Side Chairs, Hitchcock Type, open back w/ 2 paint-decorated curved slats, woven rush seat, turned legs and double-box stretchers, late 19th/early 20th C, price for pair	100	200
Side Chairs, maple and cane, spindle back w/ arched and wavy crest rail and slat, serpentine front, caned seat, restrained cabriole legs joined by turned U-stretcher and concave front stretcher, price for 3	300	500
Side Chairs, slat-back, graduated sepentine slats, turned stiles, woven rush seat, boldly turned medial stretcher, turned feet, refinished, Delaware River Valley, 19th C, 39" h, price for pair	500	800
Sofa, Country, upholstered, blue-painted frame w/ arched back, shaped arms, straight seat, block-turned legs, restored, New England, early 19th C, 30.5" h, 76" w, 26" d	1500	2000
Sofa, Federal Style, mahogany, padded rectangular back w/ reeded over-scrolled crest rail, overstuffed seat, reeded rails continuing to padded overscrolled arms, fluted scroll feet w/ casters and headed by paterae, 19th C, 90.5" l	600	1000

Empire Style Sofa, mahogany, overscrolled crest rail and arms, overstuffed seat w/ leaf-capped gadrooned rails, lion's paw feet w/ cornucopiae brackets, $805 at auction. —Photo courtesy Sloan's Washington DC Gallery.

Empire Table, mahogany, marble top w/ molded edge, squared pedestal w/ concave corners, quadruped base w/ downswept scrolled legs, 1825-50, $1610 at auction. —Photo courtesy Sloan's Washington DC Gallery.

	LOW	HIGH
Sofa Table, Classical, mahogany and mahogany veneer, rectangular overhanging top w/ rounded leaves, straight skirt w/ 2 short drawers, square tapered support on serpentine platform w/ canted corners and suppressed ball feet, old turned wooden pulls, refinished, Boston, c1825, 30" h, 57.25" w, 24" d	1500	2500
Stand, Federal, cherry, bird's-eye maple, and mahogany veneer, rectangular overhanging top w/ applied beaded edge, drawer w/ bird's-eye maple veneer and mahogany crossbanding, vase- and ring-turned legs continuing to tapering feet, old finish, RI, c1825, 27.75" h, 20" w, 19" d	700	900
Stand, Federal, cherry, overhanging square top w/ ovolo corners, square tapered legs joining straight skirt w/ drawer, old refinish, Southeastern New England, 26.5" h, 19" w, 18" d	600	800
Table, William and Mary, maple, gate-leg, oval drop-leaf top, 6 block-, vase-, and ring-turned legs joined by molded apron w/ drawer and similarly turned stretchers, refinished, MA, early 18th C, 22" h, 41.5" w, 52.25" d	7500	10,000
Tall Chest, Chippendale, carved maple and birch, flat molded cornice, 5 thumb-molded graduated drawers, top drawer w/ false 3-drawer facade centering carved fan, tall bracket feet, replaced brasses, refinished, MA or NH, 49.75" h, 38.25" w, 19.25" d	2500	3500
Tall Chest, Chippendale, cherry, flat molded cornice, 5 thumb-molded graduated drawers, bracket feet, replaced batwing brasses, refinished and stained to resemble tiger maple, MA, late 18th C, 52" h, 36.5" w, 17" d	4000	6000
Tall Chest, Chippendale, maple, flat molded cornice, 6 thumb-molded graduated drawers, tall bracket feet centering drop pendant, batwing brasses, refinished, NH, late 18th C, 58" h, 36.75" w, 18" d	6000	8000
Tall Chest, Empire Style, bow-front, carved mahogany, outset top w/ gadrooned edge, conforming front w/ 6 graduated drawers flanked by reeded twist-turned columns w/ Corinthian capitals, gadrooned base, claw and ball feet, 61.5" h, 50" w, 23" d	600	800
Tall Chest over Drawers, painted pine, molded lift-top above single-arch molded case w/ 2 false and 3 working drawers, base w/ applied molding, turned front feet, and cutout rear feet, replaced brasses, repainted gray-brown, New England, early 19th C, 49" h, 36" w, 18" d	1500	2500
Tea Cart, Art Deco, chrome and glass, oval chromed metal curvilinear framework w/ oblong smoky glass top and shelf, 25.75" h, 31.5" l, 18.5" w	500	800
Tea Table, Chippendale, mahogany, rotating circualr tilt-top on birdcage, swelled pedestal, tripod base w/ cabriole legs ending in pad feet, refinished, PA, c1760, 27.75" h, 21.75" dia	1500	2500
Tea Table, Queen Anne, maple, oval overhanging top, 4 block-turned tapered legs, straight skirt, pad feet, old refinish, 25.75" h, 32.5" w, 26" d	2000	3500

Wall Mirror, Federal, gilt gesso, c1820, $4715 at auction. —Photo courtesy Skinner, Inc., Boston, MA.

	LOW	HIGH
Terrace Table, Beaux-Arts Style, cast iron, molded circular top cast w/ pierced interlaced Moorish design enriched w/ foliate arabesques, cabriole legs headed by female masks and joined by conforming undertier, 26.5" h, 23.25" dia	600	800
Tilt-Top Table, Chippendale, mahogany, circular top, turned and tapered column w/ twisted knob, tripod base w/ molded downswept legs and pointed pad feet, 27.75" h, 33.5" dia	800	1000
Tilt-Top Table, Federal, inlaid mahogany, octagonal top bordered w/ inlaid geometric stringing and crossbanding, vase- and ring-turned post, 3 shaped legs inlaid w/ geometric banding, old refinish, MA, c1800, 29" h, 23.25" w, 16.25" d	1500	3000
Trunk, grain-painted, dome-top, exterior covered w/ yellow and burnt sienna fancy graining w/ green and yellow bordering simulating inlay, some hardware missing, New England, early 19th C, 12" h, 28" w, 14" d	300	500
Wall Cupboard, walnut and bird's-eye maple, hanging, outset molded top over pair of doors w/ lancet-shaped panes opening to shelves and flanked by reeded stiles, molded base, late 19th C, 28.5" h, 21.5" w, 7.5" d	300	500
Wall Mirror, Chippendale Style, walnut, rectangular plate within molded frame surmounted by fretted scroll crest and suspended similar skirt, 45" h, 23" w	200	400
Wall Mirror, Classical, giltwood, ring-turned half-column frame w/ square corners elaborated w/ foliate devices, 1830-40, 26.5" h, 30" w	400	600
Wall Mirror, Federal Style, carved mahogany, convex plate within cavetto-molded frame mounted w/ spherules, surmounted by eagle w/ outstretched wings perched on rocky outcrop flanked by acanthus scrolls, suspended foliate skirt, 38.5" h, 22.5" w	300	500
Wall Mirror, Federal Style, carved walnut, shaped oval plate within molded conforming frame surmounted by pierced crest centered by urn trailing bellflowers, 37.5" h, 26" w	100	250
Wall Mirror, Federal Style, gilt-composition, beveled rectangular plate within similar mirror border, composite frame w/ bands of beading and fluting, floral urn crest issuing wirework floral swags, 63" h, 42.75" w	500	750
Wall Mirror, Federal Style, inlaid mahogany, rectangular plate surmounted by verre-eglomise landscape, conforming frame w/ swan's neck pediment centered by floral urn and trailing floral garlands, suspended scrolled skirt, 56" h, 23.25" w	600	800
Wardrobe, poplar, outset top over 2-bay front, left side w/ mirrored cupboard door over 5 drawers, right side w/ full-length mirrored door opening to hanging space, short cabriole legs w/ casters, early 20th C, 69.25" h, 44.5" w, 21" d	300	500

	LOW	HIGH
Washstand, Federal, mahogany, rectangular top pierced for bowl, mounted w/ 2 turned receptacles and later added scrolled backboard, shaped frieze raised on square legs joined by square undertier suspending a drawer, shaped cross-stretcher, 1775-1800, 42.5" h, 14.5" w	300	500
Window Seat, Federal Style, padded overscrolled ends, overstuffed seat, molded square tapered legs	300	500
Wing Chair, Federal Style, ebonised, arched rectangular back flanked by shaped wings, overscroll arms w/ back-curved supports, serpentine front w/ overstuffed seat, square tapered legs, frame channeled throughout	200	300
Wing Chair, Queen Anne Style, walnut, arched and padded rectangular back w/ wings, overscrolled arms, loose cushion seat, cabriole legs w/ pad feet	200	400
Work Table, Empire, mahogany, white pine secondary wood, rectangular top w/ rule-jointed leaves and rounded corners, 2 ogee-molded drawers, square tapered column on conforming platform base w/ concave sides and canted scroll feet, 1825-50, 27.75" h, 36" w, 21" d	500	700
Work Table, Late Federal, mahogany, ovolo-molded rectangular top over 2 mirror-veneered drawers, columnar supports joined by rectangular platform stretcher w/ concave front, turned and tapered legs w/ casters, 1800-25, 30.25" h, 21.25" w, 16.75" d	700	900
Work Table, Sheraton, carved mahogany and mahogany veneer, projecting rectangular case w/ astragal ends and flanking hinged tops, cockbeaded compartmented drawer and deep drawer below, vase- and ring-turned legs ending in tapering feet, refinished, replaced brasses, NY or Philadelphia, c1815, 28.5" h, 24.5" w, 13.25" d	2000	3000
Work Table, Sheraton, mahogany veneer, rectangular top, 3 graduated drawers, reeded stiles and legs ending in casters, replaced brasses, refinished, restored, MA, c1815, 32.5" h, 22.25" w, 18.5" d	2000	3000
Work Table, Victorian, molded rectangular top w/ carved corners, paneled and molded frieze w/ drawer and pendant finials, baluster-turned supports joined by conforming under-tier, arched scroll feet, 1850-1900, 29.25" h, 24.25" w, 16.5" d	300	400
Writing Armchair, Windsor, curved rod back surmounted by scrolled crest rail, right-hand arm terminating in writing surface w/ suspended drawer, dished slab seat, baluster-turned splayed legs joined by H-stretcher, 19th C	300	500
Writing Table, Victorian, cherry, molded rectangular top surmounting a front w/ long frieze drawer over kneehole flanked by 2 small drawers, cabriole legs w/ claw and ball feet, 1850-1900, 30" h, 39.25" w, 20.5" d	300	600

Federal Work Tables, left to right: Tiger Maple and Bird's-Eye Maple, $805 at auction; Mahogany and Mahogany Veneer, $2070 at auction. —Photos courtesy Skinner, Inc., Boston, MA.

Mission

The name Stickley dominates the field of Mission furniture. Those items produced by Gustav Stickley with the "Als ich kann" (As I can) label are generally the most valuable. Unlike much Early American furniture, makers often labeled Mission pieces. Original finish is an important point in valuing Mission furniture.

Dover Publications and Turn of the Century Editions have reprinted various catalogs of Mission furniture. For further information see Bruce Johnson's *Arts and Crafts, Second Edition* (House of Collectibles, NY, 1992).

Lifetime

	LOW	HIGH
China Cabinet, overhanging through-tenon top and gallery, 2 glazed doors w/ fretwork, 3 shelves, triangular pulls, medium finish, unmarked, 54" h, 55" w, 16" d	$3000	$5000
Music Cabinet, flush top, keyed through-tenons, 9 shelves, dark finish, unmarked, 43" h, 24" w, 18.5" d	1000	1500
Sideboard, mirrored backsplash w/ plate shelf, 2 short drawers flanked by 2 recessed panel cabinet drawers w/ brass pulls, square legs w/ corbels, medium finish, Grand Rapids Chair Co. paper label, 57" h, 64" w, 20" d	1500	2500
Sideboard, recessed panel backsplash, overhanging top, arched sides w/ through-tenon stretchers, 2 short drawers flanked by 2 recessed panel cabinet doors above long linen drawer, medium finish, Lifetime paper label, 42.5" h, 60" w, 23" d	2500	3500

Limbert

China Cabinet, arched backsplash, 2 glass doors w/ arched top, tapered sides, arched toe-board, hammered copper hardware, medium finish, branded mark, 58" h, 31.5" w, 15" d	$3500	$4500
Desk, No. 727, arched gallery, drop-front writing surface, long drawer w/ square hammered copper pulls, plank legs, base shelf, through-tenon side stretchers, medium finish, branded mark, 40.5" h, 33" w, 16.5" d	1000	1500
Dining Chairs, comprising 1 armchair and 5 side chairs, arched crest rails, 3 vertical back slats, new tapestry seat cushions, medium finish, unmarked, price for set of 6	1200	2000
Dining Table, extending circular top on 4-sided pedestal base w/ corbels and leaf, medium finish, unmarked, 29.75" h, 48" dia	3000	4000
Library Table, rectangular flush top, 2 short drawers w/ square hammered copper pulls, long corbels, through-tenon base shelf, medium finish, branded mark, 29" h, 53" w, 31" d	2000	3000
Rocker, quarter-sawn oak, rounded crest rail, 4 vertical slats in back, flaring slat w/ cutout under broad flat arms, new upholstered seat cushion, arched skirt, medium finish, branded mark, 36" h, 29.5" w	800	1200
Settle Bench, quarter-sawn oak, rounded crest rail, 14 vertical slats in back, flaring slat w/ cutout under flat arms, arched skirt, loose seat cushion, medium finish, branded mark, 40.25" h, 72" w, 27" d	2000	3000
Sideboard, No. 1013¼, arched plate rail and toe-board, 2 short drawers above pair of cabinet doors w/ arched recessed panels above linen drawer, hammered copper hardware, medium finish, branded mark, 45" h, 44.5" w, 19.25" d	2500	3500

Above, left to right: Lifetime Sideboard, $1760 at auction; Lifetime China Cabinet, $4400 at auction. —Photos courtesy David Rago Auctions, Inc.

Left: Limbert Sideboard, No. 1453¼, $2185 at auction. —Photo courtesy Skinner, Inc., Boston, MA.

Below, left to right: Limbert Sideboard, $3575 at auction; Limbert Rocker, $880 at auction. —Photos courtesy David Rago Auctions, Inc.

Roycroft

	LOW	HIGH
Ali Baba Bench, half ash log on keyed through-tenon oak trestle base, dark finish, some restoration to bark, carved orb and cross mark, 19" h, 42" w, 15.25" d	$6000	$8000
Bookcase, open, overhanging top, 5 shelves, solid sides w/ cutout legs, chamfered back, bottom drawer w/ cast pulls, light finish, carved orb and cross mark, 65.25" h, 34" w, 9.25" d	6000	8000
Book Trough, curved sides, hand-cut dovetailed construction, dark finish, carved orb and cross mark, 4.5" h, 18" l, 5.75" d	750	1250
Child's Chair, 4 vertical back slats, tacked red leather seat, slightly tapered legs w/ Macmurdo feet, carved orb and cross mark, 24.5" h	1500	2500
Desk Chair, hourglass backsplat carved w/ initial "H," tacked-on Japan leather seat, tapered legs w/ Macmurdo feet, medium finish, carved orb and cross mark, 43.5" h	1200	1600
Hall Mirror, hanging, rectangular, 6 hammered hooks, dark finish, unmarked, 50" x 36"	1500	2500
Library Table, rectangular overhanging top, apron, slightly tapered legs w/ Macmurdo feet, flat side stretchers joining base shelf, skinned finish, carved orb and cross mark, 27.75" h, 30" w, 22" d	2500	5000
Magazine Stand, rounded top, solid tapered sides, 3 shelves, dark finish, carved orb and cross mark, 37.5" h, 14" w, 12" d	7500	9000
Sideboard, plate rack on overhanging top, single log drawer w/ oval pulls, 2 cabinet doors w/ leaded glass panels and round copper pulls, dark finish, carved orb and cross mark, 45" h, 42" w, 20.25" d	10,000	15,000
Side Chairs, ladder-back, 3 slats, tacked-on hard leather seat, tapered front legs, carved orb and cross mark, 36.5" h, price for pair	1000	1500
Writing Table, mahogany, slatted sides, 2 drawers w/ hammered copper pulls, lower shelf mortised w/ keyed through-tenons, tapered legs w/ Macmurdo feet, medium finish, carved orb and cross mark, 30" h, 48" w, 30" d	4500	5500

Left: Roycroft Chiffonier $1840 at auction. —Photo courtesy Skinner, Inc., Boston, MA.
Right: Roycroft Bookcase, $6500 at auction. —Photo courtesy David Rago Auctions, Inc.

Stickley Brothers

	LOW	HIGH
Armchair, 4 vertical slats in back, broad flat arms w/ 2 vertical slats and corbels, new brown leather seat cushion, unmarked, 39" h, 28" w, 24" d	$800	$1000
Bed, tapered posts, paneled headboard and footboard w/ decorative gallery panels inlaid w/ ebony and pewter Glasgow rose motif, medium finish, unmarked, 60" h, 56.5" w	5500	7500
Dining Chairs, comprising 1 armchair and 9 side chairs, arched crest rail, 2 vertical slats in back, drop-in seat w/ new brown leather upholstery, broad stretchers, medium finish, 37.5" h, price for set of 10	5000	6500
Dresser, rectangular swivel mirror on tapered posts, gallery top w/ tapered posts and 4 panels inlaid w/ ebony and pewter Glasgow rose motif, 2 short drawers over 3 long graduated drawers, medium finish, unmarked, 62.75" h, 44" w, 22" d	5000	7000
Liquor Cabinet, flush top, 2-door compartment w/ pull-out copper tray above single drawer w/ copper pulls and lower 2-door compartment, dark finish, unmarked, 51" h, 27.25" w, 16" d	2500	3500
Magazine Stand, gallery top, spindled sides, 3 shelves, dark finish, unmarked, 31" h, 26" w, 12.25" d	9000	1100
Nightstand, tapered posts w/ decorative gallery panels inlaid w/ ebony and pewter Glasgow rose motif, gallery, single drawer w/ arched apron, base cabinet, medium finish, unmarked, 38" h, 18" w, 13" d	6000	8000
Settle Bench, wide crest rail, 16 vertical slats in back, 4 vertical slats each side, new blue leatherette seat cushions, medium finish, Quaint metal tag, 31" h, 76.75" w, 29.5" d	2500	5000
Tabouret Table, flush square top, straight apron, tapered legs w/ Macmurdo feet, broad flat stretchers, medium finish, paper label, 18" h, 14" sq	300	400
Tea Cart, glass-lined tray top, slat sides, lower shelf, wood-spoke wheels missing rubber, branded mark, 33" h, 29" w, 17.25" d	1000	1200

Stickley Brothers Bedroom Suite, comprising bed, dresser w/ mirror, and nightstand. —Photo courtesy David Rago Auctions, Inc.

Stickley, Gustav

	LOW	HIGH
Armchair, 5 vertical backslats, broad flat arms w/ corbels, seat cushion w/ new brown leather upholstery, red decal, 37.25" h	$750	$1000
Bed, tapered posts, rounded top rail, headboard and footboard w/ 5 broad vertical slats, medium finish, red decal and paper label, full size, 48" h, 57.5" w	6000	9000
Bookcase, arched gallery top, through-tenon sides, single door w/ 16 glass panes and hammered copper pull, medium finish, red decal and Craftsman paper label, 56.25" h, 35" w, 13" d	5000	7500
Chest of Drawers, in the style of Harvey Ellis, rectangular swivel mirror on tapered supports, overhanging top, 2 short over 2 long drawers w/ oval pulls, arched toe-board, butterfly joints, light finish, red decal, 66" h, 48" w, 22" d	3500	5000
Chest of Drawers, in the style of Harvey Ellis, short backsplash, overhanging top, 6 short drawers above 3 long drawers w/ oval pulls, arched toe-board, medium finish, red decal and paper label, 50.5" h, 36" w, 20" d	15,000	18,000
Library Table, No. 636, circular top w/ tacked leather covering, arched apron, flaring plank legs, cross-stretchers mortised w/ keyed-through tenons, medium finish, large red box decal, 30" h, 48" dia	20,000	25,000
Library Table, overhanging rectangular top, trestle base, keyed through-tenon lower shelf, 28.75" h, 48" l, 29.5" d	1500	2000
Morris Chair, curved back w/ 4 horizontal slats, bowed arms w/ corbels, drop-in spring seat, arched seat rails, unmarked, 36.5" h, 30" w, 36.25" d	5000	7500
Sewing Rocker, 10-spindle back, low sling seat, side rails and stretchers joined by spindles, missing cusion, dark finish, red Stickley decal, 40" h, 19" w	2000	3000

Left: Gustav Stickley Dresser w/ Mirror, No. 905, branded mark, $9775 at auction.

Below: Gustav Stickley Library Table, No. 614, branded mark, $2070 at auction.

—Photos courtesy Skinner, Inc., Boston, MA.

Stickley, L. & J.G.

	LOW	HIGH
Bookcase, arched gallery top, keyed through-tenon sides, 3 doors each w/ 12 glass panes, medium finish, red decal, 55" h, 69.5" w, 12" d	$14,000	$16,000
China Cabinet, No. 728, arched gallery top, 2 doors each w/ 6 glass panes, arched apron, dark finish, unmarked, 55" h, 48" w, 15" d	5000	7500
Dining Chair, tall back w/ 8 spindles, tacked hard-leather seat, H-stretcher, dark finish, unmarked, 41.25" h, 17.5" w, 16" d	1000	1500
Dining Chairs, low back w/ 3 vertical slats, new woven rush seat, arched front stretcher, dark finish, Handcraft label, 36" h, 20" w, 16.5" d, price for set of 4	2500	3500
Drink Stand, circular top and lower shelf on cross-stretchers, 4 legs, skinned finish, "Work of..." decal, 29" h, 18" dia	1000	1500
Library Table, rectangular overhanging top, single long drawer w/ copper pulls above corbels, base shelf, dark finish, "The Work of..." label, 29" h, 42" l, 28" d	1000	2000
Magazine Stand, arched crest and side stretchers, 4 shelves, arched skirt, light finish, Handcraft decal, 45" h, 19" w, 12" d	2000	3000
Server, short backsplash, overhanging top, 2 lower shelves, dark finish, unmarked, 37" h, 40" w, 15" d	2000	3000
Settle Bench, No. 125/88½, quarter-sawn oak, tapered posts, back and sides w/ broad vertical slats each w/ carved panel, 6 back slats, 2 each side, cloud-lift stretchers, medium finish, stamped catalog number, 39" h, 58.75" w, 22.75" d	9000	12,000
Settle Bench, V-back, open arms w/ corbels, drop-in spring seat w/ new tan leather upholstery, red decal, 38" h, 76" w, 26" d	3000	5000
Sideboard, paneled backsplash w/ plate rack, overhanging top, 2 cabinet drawers flanked by 6 small drawers above long linen drawer, arched apron, medium finish, Handcraft decal, 48" h, 54" w, 22" d	4000	5000
Tabouret Table, octagonal tray top, 4 flat legs, shoe feet, remnants of paper label, 24.25" h, 19.75" w	1250	1750

L. & J.G. Stickley Bookcase, gallery top, through-tenon construction, 2 doors each w/ 12 glass panes, copper pulls, red decal, $6900 at auction. —Photo courtesy Skinner, Inc., Boston, MA.

Wallace Nutting

Wallace Nutting's legacy to collectors includes photographs, ironwares, furniture and an increased public awareness of American antiques. The reproductions of Early American furniture are now seriously collected in their own right, occasionally rising to values over and above some examples of the eighteenth-century originals that they copy.

Numbers in parentheses refer to Nutting's catalog numbers.

	LOW	HIGH
Armchair, Federal (438)	$2000	$3000
Armchair, ladderback (492)	2000	3250
Armchair, Windsor, comb back (415)	2500	3400
Bed, arched tester, turned feet, 68" h (846-B)	2500	4600
Bed, Sheraton, 4-post (846)	4200	7000
Bed, tester, Marlborough feet, 82" h (832-B)	2500	4600
Bookcase (927)	4200	6000
Brewster Chair (411)	3000	5000
Candlestand, Federal (644)	2000	3500
Candlestand, turned standard, cross base, 25" h, 14" dia (22)	700	1000
Candlestand, Windsor legs, 25" h, 14" dia (17)	700	1000
Chest, Gottard Townsend Style, 3-shell block front, 34.75" h, 39.5" w (979)	5500	10,000
Chest of Drawers (909)	6000	10,000
Corner Chair (430)	1400	2000
Day Bed (838)	4500	7600
Desk, Chippendale, slant front (701)	8000	14,000
Drop-Leaf Table, butterfly leaves, single drawer (624)	1000	1500
Gate-Leg Table (621)	2300	3400
Hat Rack (40)	700	1400
Highboy, Chippendale, broken swan's neck pediment, 85.5" h, 39.5" w (989)	7000	12,000
Library Table (637)	2300	4100
Refectory Table (601)	2300	3300
Secretary, Chippendale (729)	15,000	27,000
Settee, low back, Windsor turned legs, 87" l (533)	1500	2200
Settle Bench, wainscot, 3-panel, scroll arms, 57" l (589)	1200	1600
Side Chair, banister back, carved crest and rush seat, Spanish feet (380)	500	700
Side Chair, Chippendale, ribbon back (359-B)	700	900
Side Chair, Federal (338)	1200	2700
Side Chair, ladderback (374)	700	1100
Side Chair, Pilgrim (393)	500	900
Side Chair, Queen Anne, shell-carved (399)	1500	2200
Side Chair, Windsor, brace back (301)	900	1300
Side Chair, Windsor, comb/brace back (333)	1500	2500
Slipper Chair, Windsor (349)	1450	2500
Sofa, Chippendale, straight back (525)	3000	5000
Stand, Federal (608)	1500	2600
Stool, Gothic (292)	550	850
Stool, William & Mary (166)	800	1400
Table, William & Mary (653)	220	3500
Tavern Table, ball-turned, 30" h, 36" w (613)	1500	2500
Tea Table, Chippendale, piecrust tilt-top, 27.5" h, 33" dia (693-B)	3500	6000
Trestle Table, block- and ring-turned, 30" h, 50" w (615)	1400	2500
Tuckaway Table (616)	900	1300
Welsh Dresser (922)	6000	9000
Wing Chair, Chippendale (466)	5500	8000

Wicker

Wicker is the general term for pieces made of woven rattan, cane, dried grasses, willow, reed, or related material. The wicker heyday in the United States was from about 1860 to 1930. Cyrus Wakefield and the Heywood Brothers were the best known wicker manufacturers. They later joined to become the Heywood-Wakefield Company. Other companies include American Rattan Company and Paine's Manufacturing Company.

While nineteenth-century wicker is more valuable, pieces from the 1920s and 1930s are also desirable and easier to find. Natural finish wicker is preferred to painted pieces.

For more information see *Fine Wicker Furniture: 1870-1930* by Tim Scott (Schiffer, West Chester, PA, 1990).

Values quoted are for mid-nineteenth century (M–19), painted mid-nineteenth century (PM–19), late nineteenth century (L–19), painted late nineteenth century (PL–19), early twentieth century (E–20), painted early twentieth century (PE–20), machine made (M), and painted machine made (PM). Pieces described as ornate have features such as spooling, rolled arms and backs, unusual shapes, weaving between legs, etc.

Baby Carriage, $275 at auction. —Photo courtesy Collectors Auction Services.

	M–19	PM–19	L–19	PL–19	E–20	PE–20	M	PM
Armchair, ornate	$600	$350	$550	$350	$450	$350	—	—
Armchair, plain	360	210	350	250	270	200	$200	$150
Baby Carriage	770	460	670	440	520	410	460	400
Bassinet, all wicker	—	—	350	230	300	200	—	—
Birdcage	—	—	250	160	200	125	80	50
Chair, spider caning	830	500	700	450	—	—	—	—
Chaise Lounge, ornate	1100	700	900	600	—	—	—	—
Chaise Lounge, plain	800	500	600	500	500	450	380	320
Child's Rocker	420	250	370	240	260	200	150	130
Corner Chair, ornate	1430	850	1300	750	—	—	—	—
Corner Chair, plain	1100	700	1000	600	—	—	—	—
Crib	850	550	850	550	570	450	—	—
Crib, swinging frame	—	—	1000	680	850	650	—	—
Desk, oak top	860	510	750	500	600	450	—	—
Desk Chair	150	90	120	80	100	75	—	—
Dining Chair	—	—	150	100	130	100	90	70
Dining Table	—	—	1250	900	730	570	—	—
Dresser	3400	2000	3000	2500	2600	2000	700	500
Dresser, w/ mirror	4000	2400	3700	2400	3000	2300	—	—

	M–19	PM–19	L–19	PL–19	E–20	PE–20	M	PM
Étagère, 4 shelves	350	230	280	220	170	130	160	140
Highchair	510	300	530	340	310	240	230	190
Hourglass Chair	—	—	380	250	230	180	150	120
Library Table, all wicker	1000	800	850	600	520	400	270	220
Library Table, oak top	900	750	800	550	400	380	—	—
Lounge Chair	—	—	550	300	340	260	—	—
Loveseat, ornate	950	560	1170	760	800	600	—	—
Loveseat, plain	800	500	900	600	680	500	430	360
Magazine Rack	—	—	440	300	300	250	—	—
Magazine Stand	300	220	270	200	170	100	75	50
Music Cabinet	270	160	—	—	—	—	—	—
Photographer's Chair	1400	850	1300	700	—	—	—	—
Plant Table, ornate	550	320	500	300	310	240	—	—
Plant Table, plain	360	210	300	200	160	120	—	—
Platform Rocker, ornate	500	300	550	350	400	300	—	—
Platform Rocker, plain	450	260	380	250	340	260	—	—
Rocker, ornate	740	500	750	500	500	300	180	150
Rocker, plain	310	180	310	200	230	180	—	—
Rocker, upholstered, w/ pouch	450	260	450	300	360	280	—	—
Settee, ornate	1000	680	1000	680	700	400	—	—
Settee, plain	710	420	820	530	520	400	450	300
Side Chair, ornate	890	530	800	500	400	200	—	—
Side Chair, plain	600	350	410	270	160	120	110	100
Slipper Chair	510	300	500	320	—	—	—	—
Smoking Stand, ornate	420	250	500	300	300	175	—	—
Smoking Stand, plain	300	180	350	250	200	100	—	—
Sofa, ornate	800	650	800	600	550	430	—	—
Sofa, plain	—	—	640	420	440	340	360	300
Table, tilt-top	650	400	750	500	—	—	—	—
Tea Cart	—	—	580	380	550	430	—	—
Tête-à-Tête Chair	1670	990	1640	1000	1000	700	—	—
Vanity Bench	270	160	220	120	150	100	—	—

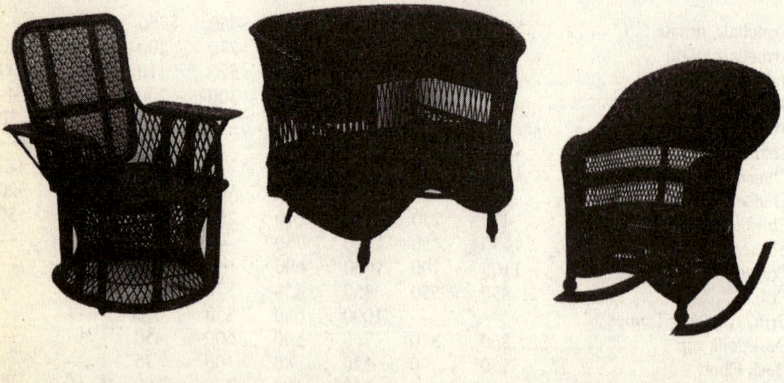

Wicker Furniture, left to right: Heywood Wakefield Armchair, 2-tone, $226 at auction; Settee, braced arm rests, brown and green, $523 at auction; Heywood Wakefield Rocker, 2-tone, wooden seat w/ brown wicker center, $825 at auction. —Photos courtesy Collectors Auction Services.

Glass

Art Glass

Art glass developed to satisfy middle-class Victorians' love for trinkets. In the late nineteenth century more Americans had more money to spend on beautifying the home. The decades surrounding the turn of the century produced much of the finest glass. Many of the firms famous then are still in business today. Some still manufacture designs created sixty years ago.

For all practical purposes, glass cannot be restored. A chip may be ground down, but this alters the shape and thus the value. A crack cannot be painted the way a skilled porcelain restorer can hide a small defect in pottery or porcelain. Glass can be damaged by water if it is allowed to sit in a vase or bowl for weeks on end.

For additional reading see *The Collector's Encyclopedia of American Art Glass* by John A. Shuman III (Collector Books, Paducah, KY, 1988, 1996 value update) and *Durand* by Edward J. Meschi (Glass Press, Marietta, OH, 1998). For information on glass in general, see *The Official Price Guide to Glassware, Second Edition* by Mark Pickvet (House of Collectibles, New York, NY, 1998).

Amberina

	LOW	HIGH
Beverage Set, consisting of pitcher and 10 tumblers, inverted thumbprint pattern, applied amber fluted handle, ground pontils, 6.5"	$800	$1000
Bud Vases, applied pinched ribbon amber snake, applied amber petal feet, 9" h, price for pair	200	300
Celery Vase, cylindrical w/ scalloped rim, twisted rib optic, ground pontil, attributed to Wheeling, 6.5" h	200	300
Celery Vases, cylindrical form, diamond quilted pattern, squared scalloped rim, late 19th C, 6.25" h, price for pair	400	600
Cologne Bottle, molded design of swirled pinwheels, silvered cap lifting to reveal clear hobnail-pressed stopper, Baccarat	250	500
Cruet, applied amber handle, cut stopper, inverted thumbprint pattern, 6.5" h	200	300
Juice Tumblers, tapered cylindrical form, applied reeded handles, late 19th C, 3.5" h, price for 10	600	800
Lily Vase, ribbed trumpet form w/ tricorn rim, disk base, late 19th C, 10.25" h	300	500
Pitcher, bulbous swirled body w/ applied reeded handle, 9" h	250	500
Tankard, 10-paneled, applied reeded handle, late 19th C, 6.625" h	300	500
Tumbler, thumbprint pattern, 3.75" h	75	100
Vases, swirled ribbing, applied amber crown and feet, delicate gilt butterflies and florals, 8" h, price for pair	500	700

Argy-Rousseau

Box, covered, pate-de-verre, cylindrical form, muted purple decorated w/ central red flower, amber and purple leaves on lid, and repeating leaf border around box, c1923, 5.25" dia	$4000	$5000
Lamp, "La Danse," pate-de-verre, broad oval illuminated body w/ deeply molded design of 3 classical dancing figures, strong colors of sienna orange, yellow amber, and accents of black and green, broad borders of stylized half-round blossoms at top and bottom, impressed molded mark "G. Argy-Rousseau" at side, gilt-metal reticulated lamp fittings, 29" h overall, 11.75" h pate-de-verre	18,000	20,000
Vase, short cylinder w/ flared rim, flambé decoration of dark to light amber w/ incised double snail design on base, marked "G. Argy-Rousseau," 4" h	800	1000

Left: Amberina Lily Vase. —Photo courtesy Skinner, Inc., Boston, MA.

Center: Bohemian Vase, blue and white overlay. —Photo courtesy William Doyle Galleries.

Right: Mount Washington Burmese Vase. —Photo courtesy Skinner, Inc., Boston, MA.

Bohemian

	LOW	HIGH
Basket, crimson shading to light green, optic rib pattern, 3 opalescent petals joined to form handle, 5.5" h	$100	$250
Beer Pitcher, clear w/ applied green wavy bands, hinged pewter lid, inscribed "Ehreagobe der Schutzengesellschaft Wallenfels 1910," attributed to Harrach, 9" h, 7" w	500	750
Center Bowl, broad dimpled form w/ ruffled rim, iridescent amber, early 20th C, 5" h, 8" l	200	400
Decanter, blue cut to clear w/ cut gilt-decorated scallops above and below rectangular panels, gilt bands around base, neck, and rim, tall spherical-shaped faceted stopper w/ alternating squiggle line decoration to facets in clear glass, 18.75" h	300	500
Goblet, mold-blown, cobalt blue w/ strong oil spot iridized exterior, acid-etched stamp "Czechoslovakia," 6.5" h	300	500
Jack-in-the-Pulpit Vase, bulbous, translucent lightly iridescent light blue body w/ amber spotting and light blue threading, early 20th C, 6.75" h	300	500
Plate, floriform w/ stylized petal rim, iridescent blue w/ oil spot decoration to underside, early 20th C, 8" dia	150	300
Rose Bowl, deep amber w/ dripped electric blue icicle rim and applied feet, attributed to Moser	200	300
Tumblers, embossed fish scale pattern, vaseline w/ pigeon blood foot, 5.5" h, price for pair	50	100
Vase, bulbous body w/ flared rim and applied elephant head handles, lightly iridized clear glass, applied fish decoration enhanced by enamel in blues, greens, and white, polished pontil, attributed to Harrach, c1890, 5.25" h	300	500
Vase, double bulbed vessel, green iridescent w/ vertical stripes interspersed w/ round spots, iridized overall, molded base, 5" h	200	400
Vase, elongated neck, ovoid body, clear, exterior w/ iridescent sand-finished surface, wheel-carved as delicate floral vine, 6.25" h	300	500
Vase, flared rim on ovoid body, red decorated internally w/ deep red spiral lines and dimples, polished pontil, 3.75" h	200	400
Vase, metal-mounted, tapered cylinder form, pale amber, dark metal mount of stylized flowers, 9.75" h	200	400

	LOW	HIGH
Vase, mold-blown pinched ovoid body w/ vine-like ribs and ruffled rim, overall light blue luster, polished pontil, 6.75" h	200	400
Vase, oviform body w/ squared rim, frosted pink and clear w/ pewter Art Nouveau-style blossom and leaf overlay extending from rim, centered w/ opalescent glass jewels, 4.75" h	200	400
Vase, ovoid, clear, layered in shades of cobalt blue, etched as frieze of men in classical costume leading bull and camel, facet cutting to rim, attributed to Moser, c1920, 10.5" h	500	700
Vase, stick form, pale green w/ lightly iridized surface, decorated in Egyptian motif w/ gold and multicolored enamel, applied disk foot, c1920, 12" h	300	400
Vase, tapered cylinder w/ ruffled rim, teal w/ 5 white and magenta pulled arches, overall iridescent luster, polished pontil, 4.25" h	200	400
Vase, tapered cylindrical form, maroon ground, etched w/ berries on hawthorn branches surrounded by ice-chip finish, enamel decorated w/ orange berries and green leaves, polished pontil, 12" h	300	500
Vase, tapered oval form, lightly crackled and iridized clear glass w/ applied handle and wrap at neck, enhanced by Art Nouveau foliate-style enameling in gold, white, green, blue, and red, large polished pontil, late 19th C, 11" h	150	350
Vase, tapered oviform, green clear glass ground w/ interior glitter-effect texture, etched and enameled to depict mauve and yellow iris, gilt accents, 8.75" h	400	600
Wine Bottles, ruby flash cut to clear, grape and vine design, 14" h, price for pair	200	400

Burmese

Bowl, triangular form, fish-in-net decoration all 3 sides, 5" w	$600	$900
Cabinet Vase, spherical w/ hexagonal neck, floral decoration, 3" h	300	500
Parlor Lamp, pink to yellow shading, handpainted and enameled font and domed shade w/ Egyptian motif of 5 ibis birds in flight in sunrise sky w/ pyramids and palm tree oasis scene overall, Burmese chimney, gilt metal mounts, Mount Washington, late 1890s, 20" h, 10" dia shade	9000	12,000
Vase, globular base w/ long flaring neck and ruffled rim, 3.75" h	300	500
Vase, globular w/ flaring quatreform neck, decorated w/ leafy berried branches, 3" h	300	500
Vase, goblet form w/ ruffled rim and foot, 4.5" h	300	500
Vase, lily form w/ quatrefoil rim, full-length handpainted fern frond, deep mahogany red rim and foot accents, Mount Washington, 12.25" h	700	900
Vase, oviform, handpainted Egyptian desert scene w/ pyramids and ibis in flight, gilt highlights, acid-finish, Mount Washington, late 19th C, 11.5" h	2000	3000
Vase, ovoid w/ pinched rim, polychrome Egyptian motif, attributed to Gunderson, 5" h	500	700
Vase, stick form w/ bulbous base, sparsely decorated w/ handpainted trailing roses in white, pink, gray, yellow, brown, and green, raised white dot border outlined in black, gilt line around rim, attributed to Mount Washington, late 19th C, 10.25" h	500	750
Vases, trumpet-form body w/ folded crimped rim, pastel pink shaded to yellow, raised on flat disk foot, Mount Washington, 14.5" h, price for pair	1200	1500
Vase, trumpet form w/ crimped rim, pastel pink shaded to yellow, flat disk foot, 14.5" h	600	800

Cameo

	LOW	HIGH
Biscuit Jar, citron ground layered in red, cameo-etched design of thistle and fern leaves, gilt-metal lid and bail handle, Harrach, 6" h	$700	$1000
Bowl, bulbous body, amber overlaid in orange and white, cameo-etched and carved w/ tasseled rope lattice, 3 applied frosted feet, English, 3.5" h, 4.5" dia	1000	1500
Cologne Bottle, cylindrical, transparent green overlaid in ruby red, double-etched w/ blossoms, swags, and gold accents, fitted w/ threaded rim and screw top w/ hallmarks at rim and within, attributed to Val St. Lambert, 5.25" h	300	500
Condiment Serving Jar, heavy-walled bowl form, aquamarine overlaid in blue-white, cameo-etched in criss-crossed foliate latticework, silvered metal rim, bail handle, and cover w/ blossom finial, English, 6" dia	500	700
Jar, covered, flattened ball shape, frosted clear cased to off-white and layered w/ enameled orange and black, cameo-etched as leaves and bellflower blossoms, black knob, cameo mark at side, Bohemian, 5.25" dia	500	700
Perfume, spherical body w/ raised rim, turquoise blue overlaid in bright white, cameo-etched w/ oriental flowering branch, gilt cap set w/ red and blue stones, Continental hallmarks, original fitted box, 4.5" h	1800	2500
Powder Jar, transparent green overlaid in ruby red, double-etched and decorated w/ blossoms, swags, and gold accents, fitted w/ beaded silver cover marked "Sterling 530," attributed to Val St. Lambert, 4.5" dia	600	800
Vase, baluster form, frosted cream overlaid in yellow, orange, brown, and dark blue, cameo-etched as bayou scene at sunset, "Michel" at lower side, 14.125" h	900	1200
Vase, baluster form, olive green layered in white, cameo-carved as blossoms on convoluted leafy stems, English, 8" h	3000	4500
Vase, bulbous, cameo-etched mottled white and clear w/ enameled stylized grape arbor border, signed "Legras" at side, 6" h	250	500
Vase, bulbous body, frosted red overlaid w/ white, cameo-etched w/ blossoms and leafy stems, 2 butterflies on reverse, English, 5" h	700	900
Vase, cylindrical w/ tapered raised rim, mottled shades of frosted orange layered in dark brown, etched as desert oasis scene w/ camels and palm trees, "Degue" in cameo on side, 5.5" h	700	900
Vase, elongated form, frosted clear etched and enameled w/ deep fuchsia trailing ivy vines, etched and enameled "Legras" among leaves, c1920, 9.125" h	400	600
Vase, flared cylindrical form, frosted clear enameled in brown and etched as tree-lined shore and rocky outcropping and distant hills, raised on gilt-metal pedestal w/ raised leaf pattern, signed "A. Delatte Nancy" on lower side, c1920, 6.125" h	500	700
Vase, flared elongated oval, white layered w/ orange and green under black, cameo-etched as lakeside scene w/ tall trees on shore and islands in background, signed "Muller" in cameo, 9" h	800	1000
Vase, flared oval form, acid-etched clear ground w/ mottled green overlay etched in Art Deco triangle motif, signed "Degue" at side, 18" h	800	1000
Vase, flattened oval bowl form w/ quatrefoil rim, transparent emerald green, acid-etched w/ lakeside scene of gilt-accented water lilies and pads among aquatic plants, European, 10.5" h	200	400
Vase, pinched rim on swollen and waisted vessel, clear etched and enameled as dark fuchsia ivy on textured and frosted surface, signed "Legras" on side, c1920, 5.625" h	300	500

Cased

	LOW	HIGH
Bride's Basket, blue cased to white, enameled w/ butterfly in flight among strawberries and fruit blossoms, satin ground, silver-plated winged cherub pedestal base w/ acanthus and scrolled floral relief, base marked "Poole Silver Co #1326," 4" h, 16" dia	$500	$750
Champagne Glasses, verre de soie, melon-shaped, decorated stems in pink cased glass, 5" h, price for pair	200	300
Epergne, 4 lily vases of various colors in bowl of red to white cased glass over vaseline, 14" h	400	600
Low Bowl, broad form, yellow shading to orange-red w/ streaks of maroon, cased to clear, base inscribed "Schneider France, Ovington New York," 3.5" h, 12" dia	300	500
Pitcher, pink w/ white opalescent interior under glossy finish, Guttate pattern, ground pontil, 9.5" h	200	500
Rose Bowl, white opaque w/ iridescent finish over geometric deeply angled blown-out surface, brass flower frog, 5.5" h	50	150
Vase, baluster form, cobalt blue cased to opalescent white, heavily layered and enameled overall w/ foliage decoration, Bohemian, 12.5" h	500	800
Vase, bulbous body w/ quatreform rim, opaque red w/ pulled and swirled black-green decorations throughout, polished pontil, attributed to Pallme Konig, 13" h	300	500
Vase, pinched and twisted elongated form, red cased to clear w/ pulled blue and green decoration and overall iridescence, Austrian, 12.25" h	250	500
Vase, shaded amber cased to white interior, satin finish, ground pontil, 10" h	200	350
Vase, squared folded rim on flared cylinder, gold luster exterior w/ green leaf and vertical vine decoration, iridescent gold interior, opal dot on base in Larson manner, 12" h	1500	2000
Vase, tapered cylinder w/ narrow neck, yellow rising to mottled orange cased to clear frosted exterior, decorated w/ flowering fuchsia branches in shades of green, red, and brown, enameled signature on side "Muller Fres Luneville," 7.75" h	700	900
Vase, waisted body w/ wide flaring quatreform rim, red satin exterior cased to opal and lined w/ stretched copper-colored interior, polished base, 10" h	200	400

Coraline

Condiment Serving Jar, blue mother-of-pearl satin, pink coraline decoration, silver-plated lid, 5.75" h, 3" dia	$150	$250
Pitcher, cranberry w/ coraline beaded decoration of blue bird on rose branch, applied clear handle, ground pontil, signed "W. L. Patent," 7.5" h	300	500
Pitcher, orange, coraline beading w/ white and green water lilies and leaves, applied amber handle, 8.5" h, 4" dia	250	350
Syrup, opalescent cranberry w/ enameled and coraline floral decoration, lidded tin spout, 6.5" h	300	500
Vase, bottle shaped w/ elongated neck, pink, diamond quilted pattern, later coraline floral decoration, 10" h	400	500
Vase, bulbous body w/ elongated neck, cut velvet, glossy finish of pink diamond quilting over white opalescent, later gold coraline and red jewel decoration, 11.5" h	100	200
Vase, bulbous body w/ ruffled rim, yellow coral on shaded pink ground, 3.25" h	200	300

Cranberry

	LOW	HIGH
Barber's Bottle, hobnail pattern w/ white opalescent hobs, ground pontil, 10" h	$150	$250
Biscuit Jar, covered, inverted thumbprint pattern w/ enameled florals, quadruple plate lid and rim w/ embossed flowers, 7.5" h	500	700
Bottle, gravic-cut designs of birds on floral branches layered in gold and silver, ground pontil, 9.5" h	150	250
Bowl, applied clear petal feet and pontil w/ applied prunt, 6" dia	50	100
Celery Vase, inverted thumbprint pattern w/ enameled decoration of birds and flowers, handled frame marked "Aurora Quad Plate," 8" h	800	1000
Creamer, applied clear handle, enameled florals and gilt swags, 5" h	50	100
Cruet, applied clear 3-ring neck, icicles, and wavy decoration, ground pontil, 9.5" h	300	500
Dresser Bottle, elongated neck above broad shoulder, footed base, applied and enameled game fish decoration, ball-shaped stopper, Harrach, 6.5" h	200	400
Jar, covered, cylindrical, enameled blue florals and gilt leaves, ball finial, 8" h	100	200
Muffineer, tapered cylinder w/ cut paneled sides and metal top, 6" h	100	150
Perfume, sterling overlay decoration, ground pontil, ball stopper, 3.25" h	200	300
Pitcher, applied clear handle, inverted thumbprint pattern, ground pontil, 7" h	75	150
Pitcher, applied clear twisted handle and collar, rosettes at base of handle, inverted thumbprint pattern, Sandwich, 7" h	150	300
Portrait Vase, flaring rim, pedestal foot, handpainted medallion of young countess, gold floral scrolling, Bohemian, 12.5" h	700	900
Stein, blown glass w/ inverted thumbprint pattern, highly decorated pewter mountings, handle, and lid, German, 10" h	300	500
Tankard, white-blue and stippled gold bands and foliage decoration, applied clear notched handle, 10.5" h	50	100
Vase, flared rim, slight twisted rib design, probably Morgantown, 6" h	40	80
Vase, tall cylinder w/ spreading foot, applied gilt and porcelain floral decoration, gilt band at foot, Bohemian, 12" h	400	600
Vase, wide tapered cylinder w/ ruffled rim, crystal Mat-Su-No-Ke appliqué and 3 large scrolled feet, crystal rosette applied to pontil, Hobbs, Brockunier, 8" h	400	600

Left to right: Legras Cameo Vase. —Photo courtesy Skinner, Inc., Boston, MA; Coraline Bottle. —Photo courtesy Gene Harris Antique Auction Center, Inc; English Cranberry Creamer; Crown Milano Vase. —Photo courtesy Skinner, Inc., Boston, MA.

Crown Milano

	LOW	HIGH
Biscuit Jar, handpainted floral and gold enamel decoration, signed "CM" and crown mark, silver-plated rim, bail, and cover marked "MW 4404," Mount Washington, late 19th C, 6.75" h	$600	$800
Vase, bulbous body w/ elongated neck, satin finish on creamy white beaded gold and bronze-shaded rose blossoms, buds, and thorny branches, purple "(crown) CM" mark over "565" on base, Mount Washington, 12.25" h	900	1200
Vase, bulbous body w/ elongated neck split at rim w/ 4 decorative points, satin white w/ delicate pink blossoms w/ gold leaves and tracery overall, base marked "(crown) CM" in purple, Mount Washington, 9.5" h	800	1000
Vase, elongated neck on oval opalescent body, decorated w/ flowering branches in muted blue, pink, yellow, and brown, elaborate scrolling gold enamel borders, base marked "CM 587" under crown in blue, Mount Washington, c1895, 17.25" h	800	1200
Vase, flattened globe w/ narrow neck, handpainted floral and medallions decoration, signed "(crown) CM 3606," 7" dia	600	800

D'Argental

Dresser Box, cylindrical, amber layered in burgundy red, cameo-etched w/ Art Deco stylized blossoms in overlapping design, similarly etched cover, marked on flower "D'Argental," 3.25" h, 3.5" dia	$500	$700
Vase, footed oval body, fiery golden amber layered in bright red and burgundy, cameo-etched overall w/ riverside scene w/ mountains beyond and tall trees in foreground, marked "D'Argental" in motif, 8" h	900	1200
Vase, oval bottle form w/ elongated neck, fiery golden amber layered in red-amber and maroon, cameo-etched w/ landscape and riverside scenes framed in scrolling arches, "D'Argental (cross)" etched in panel, 12" h	800	1000

Daum

Bowl, deep purple rising to mottled white and clear glass at quatreform pinched rim, etched, gilded, and enameled as gold, maroon, and dark green wheat stalks rising from ornate Art Nouveau border at base, polished pontil signed "Daum Nancy" in gold enamel, c1897, 2.75" h, 5.75" dia	$3000	$4000
Bowl, heavily ribbed form w/ flared rim, pale yellow-orange dispersed w/ acid-etched panels of ice crystals, polished pontil, foot inscribed "Daum (cross) Nancy France," 3.75" h, 8" dia	400	600
Bowl, pinched rim, mottled white, pink, purple, and yellow etched and enameled w/ Coreopsis daisies in shaded yellows w/ green foliage, signed in enamel "Daum Nancy France" on side, c1910, 3" h, 7.75" dia	1500	2500
Candy Dish, square form w/ heavy walls, mottled yellow and red layered in dark green, scenic cameo etching w/ trees by lake, signed "Daum Nancy" in cameo, c1910, 5.25" dia	600	800
Center Bowl, square form w/ heavy walls, crystal, molded decoration of ice formations at base, inscribed "Daum France," c1950, 3.375" dia	150	300
Figure, swimming dolphin w/ long sweeping tail, clear, inscribed "Daum France" on side, metal stand, 6.25" h, 18.5" l	350	500
Night Light, slender tapered form, frosted pale pink and green, cameo-etched and enameled in black as trees in rain, raised on illuminated patinated metal stand, 8.75" h	3000	4000

Left to right: D'Argental Cameo Vase; Daum Vase, w/ wrought iron base; Durand "King Tut" Ginger Jar. —Photos courtesy Skinner, Inc., Boston, MA.

	LOW	HIGH
Perfume, ovoid body, red ground, acid-etched and enameled as spray of daisies, highlighted in gold enamel, base and stopper mounted in chased silver, base signed "Daum (cross) Nancy" in gold enamel, 5" h	1000	1500
Salt, bucket form w/ 2 upright handles, frosted clear, cameo-etched and enameled in black as tree-lined shore w/ distant ruins, gilt rim, signed "Daum (cross) Nancy" on base, 1.375" h	500	700
Vase, elongated and swollen form, mottled yellow rising to white, etched and enameled in naturalistic greens and yellows as iris, signed "Daum Nancy (cross)" among leaves, c1900, 15.25" h	3500	5000
Vase, elongated bell form w/ slender and bulbed neck, pink overlaid in grass green, cameo carved and etched as flowering thistle on Martele ground, base inscribed "(cross), Daum Nancy," c1900, 9" h	1500	2000
Vase, footed bulbous form w/ flared rim, smoky blue etched w/ lady's hair fern, 4 applied medallions painted in tones of gray and depicting hunting and fishing scenes, signed "Daum (cross) Nancy," 5" h	4000	6000
Vase, trumpet form, light green and pink rising to clear glass, etched and enameled w/ purple and red cyclamen among green leaves, gilded highlights, "Daum Nancy" at side, c1905, 8.5" h	2500	3500
Wine Glass, slender form, opalescent and frosted sea green etched and enameled w/ violets in pale rose and green, gilded rim, base inscribed and enameled "Daum Nancy Rube 62 B2 Haussmann Paris," 7.75" h	800	1200

de Vez

Vase, baluster form, vaseline opalescent ground layered in midnight blue and red, cameo-etched scene of mountains and tall fir trees, signed "de Vez" in cameo 16" h	$1500	$2000
Vase, baluster form w/ narrow neck, shaded yellow and lavender ground layered w/ blue, cameo-etched mountain scene w/ large tree in foreground, signed "de Vez" in cameo, 6.25" h	800	1200
Vase, elongated oviform, frosted clear cased in amber, olive, and deep blue, cameo-etched as silhouetted trees overlooking water w/ distant villages and mountains, "de Vez" in cameo lower side, 10" h	1000	1200

	LOW	HIGH
Vase, oval body, maroon and fiery amber cameo-etched w/ cottages and mother and child under tall trees, polished rim, "de Vez" at side, 6" h	700	900
Vase, oval body w/ flared rim and broad shoulder, frosted clear layered in pink, cameo-etched w/ 5-petal flowers, marked "deVez" in cameo at side, 3.75" h	250	500
Vase, pear-shaped body, elongated neck w/ flaring rim, yellow overlaid w/ orange and blue, cameo-cut river scene, signed, c1910, 6" h	800	1000
Vase, semi-ovoid w/ wide rim, opalescent vaseline layered w/ deep burgundy, cameo-etched w/ Morrocan waterfront scene, signed "de Vez" in cameo, 4.25" h	600	800
Vase, squat body w/ flattened shoulder and long bulbous neck, opalescent vaseline ground layered in black and burgundy, cameo-etched mountain scene, signed "de Vez" in cameo, 7" h	800	1000
Vase, tall tapered cylinder w/ rolled rim and wide disk foot, yellow opalescent layered in cobalt blue w/ pink shaded neck and cobalt blue foot, cameo-etched w/ mountain lake scene w/ large flowering tree cut in foreground, signed "de Vez" in cameo, 14.5" h	1500	2000

Durand

Chandelier, baluster form central blue glass shaft w/ conforming iridescent threading, mounted to elaborate gilt-metal 6-light ceiling lamp, adjustable drop	$400	$600
Ginger Jar, covered, green w/ iridized gold King Tut decoration, applied amber decoration on cover, 7.25" h	2500	3500
Torchieres, trumpet form green and white striated glass w/ iridescent gold crackle decoration, mounted in bronze acanthus leaf electrified bases, c1926, 15.5" h, price for pair	1500	2000
Vase, Cluthra style, swirled green, yellow, and brown, paperweight finish, ground pontil, signed "Durand," 10.5" h	600	900
Vase, cylindrical body, blue iridescent, polished pontil, inscribed "Durand 1968-8," 8" h	650	850
Vase, flared mouth, iridescent cobalt blue w/ silver heart and vine motif, silver-blue iridescent interior, polished pontil inscribed "Durand 1707" in silver, c1925, 9.5" h	1500	2000
Vase, flared rim, ovoid form, light blue w/ overall blue iridescence, polished pontil w/ silver "Durand 1710-7" inscription, c1925, 7" h	500	700
Vase, flared rim tapering to squat base, gold iridescent interior and exterior, marked "V" and "Durand 1990 6" across pontil, 5.75" h	500	700
Vase, flattened globular body w/ elongated trumpet-form neck, green w/ undulating amber iridescent bands, signed, c1905-30, 12" h	1800	2500
Vase, Lady Gay, elongated neck on bulbous and footed body, rose pink w/ coiled iridescence, cased to white-yellow flared interior, silver enamel "Durand" over polished pontil, 12.5" h	2000	3000
Vase, oval body w/ broad shoulder, iridescent gold w/ green pulled and coiled King Tut decoration, gold interior over opal, base inscribed "Durand 1964-10," 10" h	2000	3000
Vase, ovoid body w/ flaring neck, blue iridescent, signed, 1905-25, 10.5" h	600	800
Vase, ribbed genie bottle shape w/ elongated slender neck, cobalt blue w/ iridescent blue-silver overall, mirror-bright near base, 15.5" h	2000	3000
Vase, stepped beehive shape 1978, amber w/ gold iridescent surface, polished pontil, unmarked, 1925, 13" h	800	1200
Vase, wide flared rim on oval body, iridescent blue w/ silvery blue threaded spider web overlay, unmarked, 7.25" h	800	1000

Gallé

	LOW	HIGH
Bowl, 8-sided oblong form, frosted purple and light blue overlaid in purple, cameo-etched as blossom clusters and leafy vines, "Gallé" in cameo at side, 4" h, 7" l	$1000	$1500
Bowl, cylindrical, pale blue layered in brown, cameo-etched as orchids in meadow, raised on applied flared foot, signed "Gallé" on side, 5.625" h	500	700
Bowl, tri-corner shape, frosted clear and pale yellow pinched bowl layered in lavender and blue etched as flowering myrtle vines, "Gallé" on side, 6" dia	800	1000
Box, covered, pale pink interior cased to frosted clear and layered in lavender and green, cameo-etched as blossoms on vine, marked "Gallé" on box and lid, 2.5" h, 4.5" dia	1000	1200
Decanter, flattened oval body w/ upturned rim and conical stopper, frosted clear and purple ground overlaid in deep purple, cameo-etched as iris, base engraved "Cristallerie de Galle Nancy modele et decor deposes," 10.25" h	2000	3000
Decanter, tapered barrel-form, frosted clear glass layered in orange cameo etched as grapes on vine w/ tendrils, stopper w/ applied curled handle, "Gallé" in cameo on side, 8.25" h	800	1200
Ewer, elongated oval body w/ organic spout, applied serpentine handle, and swollen disk foot, leaf green, etched and enameled w/ orchids, floral sprays, and mushrooms in shades of maroon, pink, blue, and green, etched and gold-enameled "Gallé" among mushrooms, c1880, 20.5" h	4500	6000
Flower Bowl, pale pink footed bowl w/ 4 pulled points, overlaid in light yellow-green and amber, cameo-etched as clusters of blossoms on leafy branches, signed in cameo "(star) Gallé" among leaves, c1904, 7.75" dia	700	1000
Vase, bulbous form w/ elongated neck of gray w/ pink streaks, layered in periwinkle and green, cameo-etched as stalk of stylized flowers, "Gallé" near base, 8" h	700	1000
Vase, elongated ovoid form w/ bulbed and flared neck, amber overlaid in leafy green, cameo etched as ferns, marked w/ star and "Gallé" among ferns, c1904, 6.5" h	500	700

Left to right: Gallé Cameo Vase; Schneider Le Verre Francais Cameo Vase; Loetz Silver-Overlaid Vase. —Photos courtesy Skinner, Inc., Boston, MA.

	LOW	HIGH
Vase, flattened ovoid form, shell pink layered in white, periwinkle, and green, cameo-etched as flowering hydrangea branch, "Gallé" in cameo on side, 6.5" h	.800	1000
Vase, ovoid body w/ raised flared rim, pale frosted blue cased in purple and olive green, cameo-etched as primrose among leaves, "Gallé" on side, 5" h	.400	600
Vase, raised neck on bulbous vessel, opaque pink cased to clear exterior and layered in olive green cameo etched as round berries among leaves, "Gallé" on side, 3.5" h	.500	700

Le Verre Francais

Center Bowl, tapered sides, orange layered w/ tortoiseshell brown, etched as 5 beetles alternating w/ geometric elements, lower edge inscribed "Le Verre Francais France, Ovington New York," 4.5" h, 10" dia	$600	$800
Ewer, mottled body of purples and pink w/ yellow and orange splashes on elongated spout, applied purple handle, bulbed disk foot, acid stamp "France" on base, c1925, 10.75" h	.300	500
Vase, baluster-form body, smoky topaz decorated at shoulder w/ acid-etched Art Deco band of overlaid leaves and 2 applied floral cluster prunts, signed "Schneider" near base, c1925, 13.75" h	.800	1000
Vase, bulbous, mottled orange and yellow overlaid in tango red shaded to aubergine, cameo-etched as stylized Art Deco flower-trees, base inscribed "Le Verre Francais," 9.5" h, 9" w	.1500	2000
Vase, flared elongated bulbous form, mottled white overlaid in tortoiseshell amber and browns shaded to orange, cameo-etched in abstract design of twisting ribbons and dots, pedestal foot inscribed "Le Verre France," 17" h	.900	1200
Vase, flared trumpet form, yellow shaded to red-orange overlaid in mottled green and brown, cameo-etched and cut as cascading flowers, pedestal foot signed "Le Verre Francais France," base signed "Ovington New York," 12.25" h	.800	1000
Vase, spherical form w/ raised rim, clear, etched to reveal band of stylized daisies flashed green at centers, inscribed "Charder Le Verre Francais," acid stamp "France Ovington" on base, c1925, 7.5" h	.600	800
Vase, swelled oval body, mottled orange, red, and yellow overlaid in glossy maroon, cameo-etched as stylized vines w/ grape clusters, pedestal foot inscribed "Le Verre Francais," 15.75" h	.1200	1800
Vase, teardrop-shaped body, mottled cream and clear overlaid in vitrified dark green and orange, acid-etched as leaves descending from flared neck, base drilled, c1925, 14.75" h	.700	900
Vase, trumpet-shaped, yellow overlaid in deep cobalt w/ variegated orange band, cameo-etched as stylized hollyhocks, pedestal foot inscribed "Le Verre Francais, 19" h, 13.5" dia	.3500	4000

Loetz

Ewer, flared cylindrical form, brilliant blue papillon decoration w/ silver overlay designed and engraved as entwined grapes on vines, applied silver handle, polished pontil, 10.5" h	.$5000	$7500
Vase, baluster form w/ pinched and ruffled rim, purple and yellow swirled w/ pulled iridized decoration to exterior, polished pontil, c1900, 5" h	.200	300
Vase, double bulbed and pinched form, pale green w/ iridescent gold papillon decoration to exterior, polished pontil, 6" h	.300	500
Vase, flared oval body, green w/ silver-blue oil spot iridescence, w/ Art Nouveau-styled clovers in silver overlay, polished pontil, c1900, 4.5" h	.700	900

	LOW	HIGH
Vase, mold-blown, cased green w/ pulled magenta and pearl iridescence rising to green bulbous top, c1905, 4.75" h	1000	1200
Vase, Persian bottle form, salmon pink w/ pulled silver leaves rising from base and descending from mouth, band of blue, amber, and white pulled swirls at base, polished pontil inscribed "Loetz Austria," c1900, 9" h	2000	2500
Vase, pinched oval vessel, amber decorated w/ pulled iridescent gold threads in scalloped drapery pattern, highlighted w/ opalescent blue luster, polished pontil, c1900, 5" h	500	700
Vase, ruffled rim on broad-shouldered vessel, clear w/ light blue papillon decoration on dark gold luster surface decorated overall w/ silver overlay of stylized iris, c1900, 7" h	1700	2000
Vase, tapered form, cased glass w/ swirled iridescent green rising to pearly blue, Art Nouveau stylized silver overlay, polished pontil, c1905, 6.5" h	700	900
Vase, waisted, clear w/ veils of gold iridescent papillon decoration over reddish gold iridescent surface, polished pontil, c1900, 10" h	1500	2000

Mary Gregory

Beverage Set, consisting of pitcher and 2 tumblers, forest green, enameled scenes w/ children, 6" h	$100	$200
Beverage Set, consisting of pitcher w/ ruffled rim and 2 tumblers, cranberry, enameled scenes w/ boy among trees, 9.5" h	200	400
Cruets, clear applied handles and stoppers, emerald green, enameled designs of boy and girl catching butterflies, 12" h, price for pair	300	500
Pitcher, applied clear handle, deep amber, enameled scene of woman in blue-trimmed dress watering flowers, ground pontil	300	500
Pitcher, inverted thumbprint pattern, applied clear handle, amber, polychrome scene of boy w/ butterfly net and girl w/ doll stroller, ground pontil, 8.5" h	200	400

Left to right: Mary Gregory Vase. —Photo courtesy Gene Harris Antique Auction Center, Inc.; Moser Rose Bowl, acid-etched decoration. —Photo courtesy Skinner, Inc., Boston, MA; Opalescent Barber Bottle, cranberry w/ white stripes. —Photo courtesy Glass-Works Auctions.

	LOW	HIGH
Tankard, electric blue, enameled scene of woman picking roses, ground pontil, 13.5" h	300	500
Vase, cylindrical, cranberry, enameled scene of woman picking flowers, probably Boston & Sandwich, 7.75" h	150	250
Vase, footed urn form, applied clear handles, cranberry, enameled outdoor scene w/ women, 12.5" h	300	500
Vases, tapered cylinder form, vaseline, enameled scene of boy on one, girl on other, 9" h, price for pair	200	300
Vases, urn form, applied pinched blue handles, amber, enameled scenes of children, 8.5" h, price for pair	200	400
Vases, waisted cylinder shape w/ pinched applied clear handles, electric blue, enameled man on one, woman on other, 11" h, price for pair	200	400

Moser

Center Bowl, ribbed, green w/ border of etched and gilded grapes on vine, acid-etched "Moser" within polished pontil, c1920, 7.5" h	$400	$600
Cordial Set, Alexandrite, decanter w/ elongated neck on broad angular base of dichroic ice blue to pink glass, entirely facet-cut, faceted spire stopper, 6 matching cordials w/ faceted flared cups on ball and disk bases, 10.25" h decanter, c1925, 2.5" h cordials, price for 7-pc. set	500	800
Dresser Set, consisting of 3 covered jars, dresser bottle, and tray, emerald green w/ elaborately enameled florals and gilt scrolls, each piece engraved "Moser" in script, 10.5" l tray	600	800
Lemonade Set, slightly ribbed pitcher and 4 glasses, amber w/ light blue handles, gilded and enameled w/ oriental floral motif, polished pontil, c1880, 10.5" h pitcher, 4.75" h glasses	500	800
Rose Bowl, spherical, smoke-colored glass, heavily acid-etched as stylized deer in garden setting, "Moser" acid-etched signature within polished pontil, c1920, 4.25" h, 5.5" dia	400	600
Vase, semi-ovoid, cranberry w/ enameled white flowers and scrolling heart-shaped frames w/ gilt interiors, "Moser" engraved on side, 9.5" h	250	400
Vase, tapered 8-paneled cylinder, amethyst shaded to clear, intaglio-engraved w/ long-stemmed tulip blossoms, 10" h	400	600
Vase, tapered cylinder w/ shaped rim, heavily enameled w/ florals, swags, and stippled gold accents, 10" h	400	600

Opalescent

Beverage Set, consisting of pitcher and 6 tumblers, blue, coin spot pattern, applied reeded handle, 9.5" h	$300	$500
Fruit Dish, rectangular w/ rolled rim and pulled and pierced handles, light green, 8" l	100	150
Miniature Lamp, blue, 3 pcs. consisting of blue font w/ clear petal feet, 4-fluted shade, and chimney, Brenner burner, 9.5" h	300	400
Miniature Lamp, white w/ cranberry windows, applied clear handle, Hornet burner, 3.75" dia	200	300
Pickle Castor, swirled pink and white, silvered frame w/ bail handle and tongs, 11" h	150	250
Pitcher, cranberry w/ white hobs and clear applied handle, ground pontil, 8" h	200	300
Spooner, white w/ platinum florals, Findlay Onyx, 6.5" h	150	250
Toothpick, white w/ platinum florals, Findlay Onyx, 2.5" h	100	200
Vase, bulbous body w/ elongated neck, cut velvet, white w/ fine vertical blue threaded ribs, 6" h	100	200

	LOW	HIGH
Vase, flared tricorn rim, opalescent w/ pastel green oil spot decoration, polished pontil, attributed to Loetz, Austrian, 6" h	200	400
Vase, flattened spherical form w/ raised neck, decorated w/ transfer image of cherubs in clouds, highlighted w/ raised gold enamel florals, 8.5" h	300	500
Vase, ribbed bulbous body w/ flaring neck, opalescent pink and white w/ iridized zippers, Nash, 5" h	300	500
Vase, ribbed gourd form w/ ruffled rim, applied pale amber surface shading to pale pink at top, decorated w/ elaborate gilt and enamel chrysanthemums in rose, light blue, white, and green, attributed to Mount Washington, 8.5" h	600	800

Overlay

Cabinet Vase, emerald green w/ fire-polished overlay, heavily enameled w/ stylized bellflowers in royal blue azure, yellow, ivory, and black, signed in enamel "Delatte Nancy," 5.75" h	$500	$700
Compote, burgundy cut to clear medallions w/ enameled roses and gold scrolling, pedestal foot w/ ground pontil, in the manner of Oertel, 11" h	300	500
Dish, covered, emerald green panels cut to clear, decorated w/ gilt florals and endless loops, Bohemian, 7" dia	100	200
Fan Vase, silver overlay in floral design w/ geometric pattern on black opaque glass, maker's mark, "Rockwell," and "no. 1371B," c1930, 8" h	200	400
Mantel Luster, white opaque cut to cranberry, handpainted medallions of portraits alternating w/ florals, bowl encircled w/ 10 cut crystal pendants, Bohemian, 12.25" h	400	600
Vase, amethyst overlaid w/ alternating bands of deep purple and cypriote-type finish, purple, gold, and green iridescence, Bohemian, c1900, 10.25" h	300	500
Vase, baluster form w/ flaring rim and pedestal foot, emerald green overlaid w/ white, white panels w/ enameled floral decoration and gilt scrolling, Bohemian, 13" h	250	500
Vase, bulbous base, elongated neck w/ shoulder ring and ruffled rim, cut velvet, white overlaid w/ yellow, diamond quilted pattern, 7" h	100	200
Vase, elongated neck flaring to squat base, mold-blown, iridescent green overlaid w/ glass threads meshed in patterns, Austrian, 10" h	50	150
Vase, footed broad ovoid form, frosted clear glass overlaid in amethyst etched and engraved w/ trailing nasturtium blossom, gilt highlights, elaborate gold enamel trademark on base, Burgun, Schverer, and Cie, Alsace-Lorraine, c1900, 7.25" h	2500	3000
Vase, goblet form, amber cut to clear, copper wheel-engraved florals around waist, blue enamel banded floral rim cut to clear, Novybor, 7.5" h	200	400

Peachblow

Goblet, flared rim, deep rose color, Gunderson Pairpoint, 7.25" h	$100	$200
Pitcher, quatreform rim, bulbous body, applied amber handle, Wheeling, late 19th C, 5.25" h	400	600
Shaker, cylindrical form tapering to neck, glossy finish w/ white opalescent glass lining, metal screw cap, Wheeling, c1890, 5.5" h	300	500
Syrup Pitcher, cased, offset handle, Gunderson Pairpoint, 2.75" h	100	200
Vase, bottle form, satin finish, stippled decoration w/ geometric designs of stars, florals, and birds, 10" h	200	400
Vase, melon-ribbed body w/ pinched rim, enameled rose buds, 11" h	100	200
Vase, quatreform mouth, deep raspberry rim on angular body, applied reeded handles, Gunderson-style, c1940, 4" h	500	750

	LOW	HIGH
Vase, stick form, 2-layered w/ acid finish, outer shell fading from deep purplish pink at top to white at base, white interior, gilt rim, English, 9.125" h	250	500
Vase, stick form, glossy finish w/ gilt-enameled vines and blossoms, 10" h	300	500
Vases, lily form w/ tricorn rim, Wild Rose decoration, New England, 6" h, price for pair	1000	1200
Vases, satin finish w/ gilt decoration of grape vines and blossoms w/ silvered highlights, 6" h, price for pair	600	800

Pomona

Bowl, etched second ground, amber ruffled rim w/ floral border, New England, 2.75" h	$50	$100
Cocktail Pitcher, etched first ground, diamond pattern, 12" h	100	200
Compote, etched first ground, amber ruffled rim, footed, New England, 3.5" h	150	300
Mustard Pot, etched second ground surface w/ scalloped border, hinged metal lid, no spoon, 3.25" h, New England, 2" dia	250	500
Pitcher, bulbous, quatreform rim, etched second ground, blue and amber pansy and butterfly decoration, amber rim and handle, New England, 7" h	200	400
Pitcher, etched first ground, amber ruffled rim, blue floral and gold leaf band, applied handle, New England, 5.5" w	75	150
Plate, ruffled, etched second ground, amber trim, New England, 6.75" dia	50	100
Punch Cups, etched first ground, amber leaf border, New England, price for 3	75	150
Toothpick, 2-handled, etched first ground, amber trim, New England, 2.75" h, 2.5" dia	50	100
Tumblers, etched first ground, amber tinted rims, 2 w/ floral bands w/ amber leaves, 2 w/ blue-tinted floral and amber leaf band, and 3 lemonades, New England, 4.75" h, 2.5" dia, price for 7	250	500
Vase, planter form, footed, etched first ground surface, amber-tinted crimped rim and feet, blue cornflower and gold leaf border, New England, 5.5" h, 5.25" dia	500	700
Vase, suppressed oval form, etched diamond pattern, Midwestern, 5" h	75	150
Wine Glass, etched second ground surface w/ floral border, amber stem, and scalloped rim, New England, 4.5" h, 2.5" dia	200	400

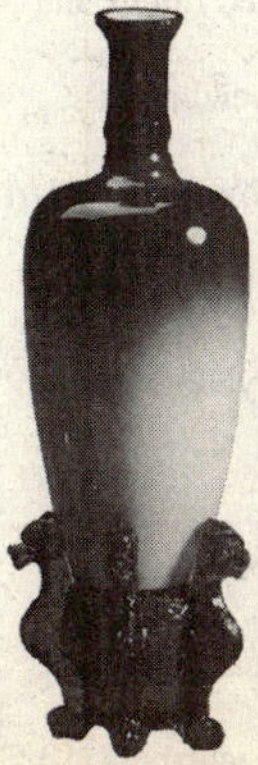

Left: Overlay Vase. —Photo courtesy Gene Harris Antique Auction Center, Inc.

Center: Wheeling Peachblow Vase.

Right: New England Glass Co. Pomona Vase.

—Photos courtesy Skinner, Inc., Boston, MA.

Quezal

	LOW	HIGH
Cabinet Vase, shouldered ovoid form, gold iridescent, signed, 2.75" h	$250	$500
Desk Lamp, heavy walled half-round opalescent shade lined w/ brilliant iridescent gold, exterior glossy surface w/ 5 broad pulled feather repeats, marked "Quezal" on inside top rim, mounted on 3-arm spider on black base w/ overlapping foliate devices, 19" h, 10.5" dia shade	1750	2000
Lamp Shades, squat, amber w/ gold iridescent luster, marked "Quezal" on rim, 3.25" h, 2.25" dia, price for pair	500	650
Vase, footed ovoid body w/ flared rim, cased w/ interior and exterior golden orange luster, base inscribed "Quezal," 8" h	500	700
Vase, green oval body w/ raised gold iridescent neck, decorated overall w/ pulled leaves in gold luster and brilliant iridescence, signed "Quezal" within polished pontil, 9" h	4000	5000
Vase, slightly ribbed form w/ bulbous base and flared neck, amber w/ strong overall gold iridescence, signed "Quezal I 866" within polished pontil, 3" h	500	700

Satin

Biscuit Jar, cranberry w/ pulled white ribbing, silvered bail handle and lid, Nailsea, 6" h	$600	$800
Bride's Basket, swirled ribs, pinched sides and rim, apricot w/ enameled floral design, ground pontil, attributed to Webb, 9.5" dia	200	400
Centerpiece Bowl, mottled orange, amber, and green bowl, wrought iron blackberry vine w/ leaves base, Verreries d'Art, signed "Lorrain," 8" dia	600	800
Cruet, blue mother-of-pearl w/ diamond pattern, clear satin stopper, applied twisted handle, ground pontil, 4" h	200	400
Dresser Box, covered, round, opaque white w/ handpainted floral decoration on lid, gilt-metal rims, Wavecrest trademark on base, late 19th C, 3" h	300	500
Jack-in-the-Pulpit Vase, shaded butterscotch w/ crimson interior, 7" h	150	250
Lamp Shades, square w/ fluted rim, cranberry mother-of-pearl satin finish, diamond quilt pattern, 4.5" sq, 2.5" fitter, price for pair	150	250
Pitcher, salmon-shaded mother-of-pearl, diamond quilted pattern, applied fluted handle, ground pontil, 8" h	200	300
Rose Bowl, blue shaded, applied white and pink mottled flowers, 5" h	100	200
Rose Bowl, pink mother-of-pearl, herringbone pattern, 4" h	100	200
Rose Bowl, shaded yellow, molded clamshell design, enameled florals and scrolls, ground pontil, 5" h	100	200
Tumblers, pink mother-of-pearl, diamond quilted pattern, ground pontils, 4" h, price for pair	100	150
Vase, globular body w/ elongated neck and ruffled rim, blue mother-of-pearl w/ diamond quilted pattern, ground pontil, 9.5" h	200	300
Vase, ovoid, pink w/ needlepoint enameled design of crane, florals, and dragonfly, 5.5" h	150	250
Vase, spherical w/ pinched rim, pink w/ polychrome red and yellow roses, 5" h	75	150

Spatter

Basket, purple, yellow, and white, applied thorn handle, Czechoslovakian, 5.5" h	$50	$100
Biscuit Jar, pink, green, yellow, purple, and white, applied clear handle on lid, 9" h	150	300
Vase, handled, red, pink, and white w/ silver foil flecks, vasa murrhina, 10.5" h	200	400

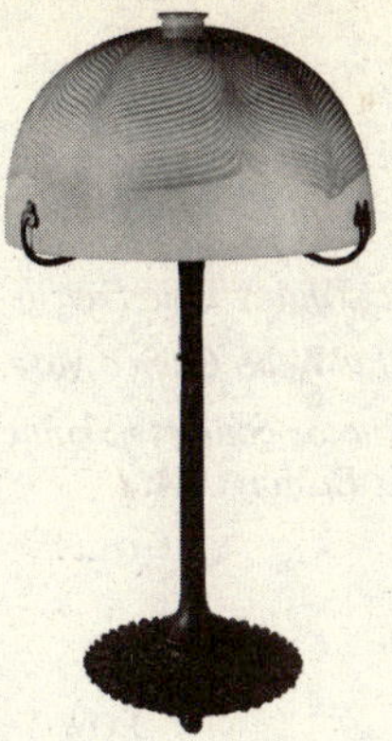

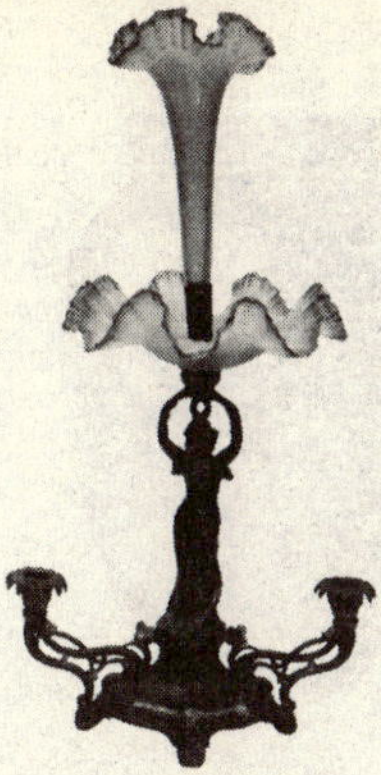

Left: Quezal Desk Lamp, iridescent shade w/ pulled feather design. —Photo courtesy Skinner, Inc., Boston, MA.

Right: Stevens & Williams Epergne, cased glass vase and bowl.

Stevens & Williams

	LOW	HIGH
Bowl, pink shading to white, applied florals and amber ribbon rim, ground pontil, 5" dia	$150	$250
Perfume, heat reactive dark amber shaded to green satin glass sphere w/ spiraled air-trap swirls, mounted w/ hallmarked and chased silver cap, c1890, 4.75" h	500	700
Vase, cylindrical, white cased to rose pink exterior, acid-etched as floral spray, c1880, 6.5" h	200	400
Vase, elongated and bulbed neck on ovoid body, deep red overlaid in white, cameo-etched and engraved as grosbeak on flowering branch w/ 2 butterflies, central stylized floral border, c1890	2000	2500
Vase, intaglio-cut, pale rose pink cased to transparent green, wheel-cut w/ foliate panels below horizontal stepped flared rim, 10" h	1500	2000
Vase, pink shading to white, applied fruit and blossoms, ground pontil, 10" h	100	300
Vase, quatreform cylinder w/ ruffled rim, pink shading to white, applied amber handles, feet, and florals, 13" h	200	400
Vase, satin glass, gourd-shaped body, bronze shaded to light blue cased to yellow interior, spiraled air-trap swirls, polished pontil, c1885, 7.125" h	300	500

Tiffany

Bowl, 10-ribbed body w/ ruffled rim, blue iridescent Favrile glass, base inscribed "L. C. T. Favrile," 2" h, 6" dia	$600	$900
Compote, cobalt blue w/ strong blue luster and stretched iridescence on broad rim, base signed "L. C. Tiffany Inc. Favrile X," 3" h, 9" dia	700	900
Lamp Shade, 10-ribbed dome, white exterior decorated w/ green swirls highlighted w/ trailing gold iridescent ribbons, rim inscribed "L. C. T. Favrile," 7" dia	3000	4000
Paperweight Vase, ovoid, pale aqua decorated internally w/ yellow, red, and black millefiori flowers among trailing heart leaves and vines of deep green w/ ocher swirls, base inscribed "L. C. Tiffany-Favrile 3527 P," partial paper label on button pontil, c1920, 7.25" h	6500	8000
Rose Bowl, 10-ribbed form w/ ruffled rim, cobalt blue w/ overall blue iridescence, base signed around polished pontil "L. C. Tiffany Favrile 1103-7725K," c1915, 3.75" h	700	900

Left: Tiffany Blue Favrile Vase.
Right: Webb Cameo Vase.
—Photos courtesy Skinner, Inc., Boston, MA.

	LOW	HIGH
Salt, open salt w/ broad shoulder, iridescent blue w/ 8 pulled prunts, base inscribed "L. C. T. Favrile X620," early 20th C, 2.125" dia	700	900
Vase, double bulbed form w/ elongated neck, ambergris w/ blue iridescent pulled feathers rising to red and gold luster at top, polished pontil, base signed "L. C. T. E550," paper label, c1895, 20.25" h	2500	3000
Vase, floriform, bulbous body w/ ruffled broad blossom rim enhanced by stretched gold iridescence, disk foot, base inscribed "L. C. Tiffany Favrile 8651 D," c1910, 4.25" h	1000	1500
Vase, floriform, cobalt blue bulbous body w/ wide flared and ruffled rim, stretch iridescence to rim, strong blue luster, short stem, applied disk foot, inscribed "L. C. Tiffany-Favrile 9041E," 5.5" h	800	1000

Webb

Jardiniere, peachblow, bulbous w/ extended rim, footed base, decorated in the manner of Jules Barbe, gilded and enameled in naturalistic colors w/ exotic plants, birds, butterflies, and insects, borders w/ flowers, oriental-style characters, and cross-hatched zig-zags, 10" h, 13" dia	$2000	$3000
Oil Lamp, frosted amber glass dome shade overlaid w/ white, cameo-etched and engraved as thorny branches of berries, supported by onyx and bronze electrified base designed as Ionic column, 19" h	2000	2500
Pitcher, flared bulbous body, red overlaid w/ white, cameo-etched flowering lilac branch and flying butterfly, applied foliate-decorated handle, 3.5" h	1000	1500
Vase, bulbous turquoise diamond-quilted body, pearl satin w/ layer of opaque white cameo-etched as wild roses on trailing thorny vine, 5" h	800	1000
Vase, elongated oval baluster form, sunset orange overlaid in white, cameo-etched as foxglove w/ stylized leaf border at rim, 12" h	2000	3000
Vase, flared oval form, clear overlaid in ruby red and opal white, cameo-etched and carved as narcissus and ornamental grasses, horseshoe-shaped "Tho^S Webb & Sons" mark on base, 7.5" h	2000	3000
Vase, flared urn-form body, diamond-quilted, red satin overlaid in opaque white, cameo-etched as iris and wild flowers, base marked "Webb," 8" h	500	750
Vase, flattened oval form, light amber overlaid in red and opal white, cameo-etched and carved as orchids and daisies, carved scrollwork gold ground, signed "Thomas Webb & Sons, Gem Cameo," 5.75" h	4000	5000
Vase, urn form, attributed to George Woodall, old ivory cameo-cut in intricate design w/ mythological bird-serpent creatures centered in arabesque frames and floral backgrounds, base marked "Thomas Webb & Sons," 8.5" h	4500	6000

Carnival Glass

The turn-of-the-century craze for iridescent art glass spawned the birth of Taffeta (or Carnival) glass in 1905. Using mass production and new chemical techniques, Carnival glass was widely produced toward the end of the Art Nouveau period. Tastes changed, however, ushering in the streamlined Art Deco period. Though produced until 1930, by 1925 Carnival glass was sold by the trainload to fairs and carnivals and given out as prizes (hence the name Carnival glass). Since the 1970s, Carnival glass has become a desired collectible.

For further information see *A Field Guide to Carnival Glass* by David Doty (Glass Press, Marietta, OH, 1998) and *Standard Encyclopedia of Carnival Glass, 6th Edition* by Bill Edwards and Mike Carwile (Collector Books, Paducah, KY, 1998)

	LOW	HIGH
Beverage Set, pitcher and 6 tumblers, Butterfly & Fern, Fenton, blue, 9.5" h pitcher, 4" h tumblers	$400	$600
Bowl, Dragon & Lotus pattern, Fenton, ruffled edge, blue, 9" dia	100	150
Bowl, Dragon & Lotus pattern, Fenton, ruffled edge, marigold, 9" dia	50	100
Bowl, Scroll Embossed pattern, Imperial, ruffled edge, purple, 9" dia	100	200
Candlesticks, Inverted Strawberry pattern, Cambridge, green, price for pair	800	1200
Console Bowl, Stag & Holly, 3 scrolled feet, marigold, 10.5" dia	50	100
Finger Lamp, Zippered Loop pattern, Imperial, marigold	1200	1600
Hatpin Holder, Grape & Cable pattern, Northwood, marigold	300	400
Hatpin Holder, Grape & Cable pattern, Northwood, purple	400	500
Ice Cream Bowl, Peacock at Urn pattern, Northwood, ice green, 10" dia	1000	1200
Loving Cup, Orange Tree pattern, Fenton, marigold	250	350
Plate, Horse Medallion pattern, Fenton, marigold, 7" dia	300	400
Plate, Peacock on Fence pattern, Northwood, marigold, 9" dia	400	500
Plate, Rose Show pattern, Northwood, cobalt blue, 9" dia	1600	1800
Rose Bowl, Beaded Cable, Northwood, amethyst, 4.5" dia	50	100
Vase, April Showers pattern, Fenton, marigold, 7.5" h	200	300
Vase, Plain Tornado pattern, Northwood, green, small size	400	600
Vase, Tree Trunk pattern, Northwood, green, 10.5" h	50	150

Carnival Glass Beverage Sets. —Photo courtesy Gene Harris Antique Auction Center, Inc.

Cut Glass

Cut glass features deep prismatic cutting in elaborate, often geometric designs. Developed during the sixteenth century in Bohemia, it remained popular until the invention of molded pressed glass in America about 1825. It enjoyed a revival during the Brilliant Period of cut glass in America from 1866–1916. The edges are sharp, refracting light clearly. It is thicker and heavier than most blown glass. Round shapes have a distinct bell tone when struck.

Making cut glass required patience and talent. Master craftsmen blew the finest 35%–45% lead crystal or poured it into molds producing a shaped piece called a blank. These blanks measured from .25" to .5" thick, necessary for the deep cutting which distinguished this glass from later periods. The resulting product was exceedingly heavy. Cutting and polishing required four steps. First, the desired pattern was drawn on the blank with crayons or paint. Next, the deepest cuts were made by rough cutting, pressing the blank on an abrasive cutting wheel lubricated by a stream of water and sand. In the third step, the rough cuts were smoothed with a finer stone wheel and water. Finally, the craftsman polished or "colored" the piece on a wooden wheel with putty powder or pumice to produce the gleaming finish.

For further information see *Identifying American Brilliant Cut Glass, Third Edition* by Bill and Louise Boggess (Schiffer, Atglen, PA, 1997), *American Cut and Engraved Glass* by Martha Louise Swan (Wallace-Homestead, Radnor, PA, 1986, 1994 value update, now available from Krause Publications), and *Evers' Standard Cut Glass Value Guide* by Jo Evers (Collector Books, Paducah, KY, 1975, 1998 value update).

	LOW	HIGH
Beverage Set, consisting of pitcher and 4 tumblers, No. 418 "Colias Design" w/ etched butterflies and cut floral and leaf sprays and spider webs, attributed to Pairpoint, 9.25" h pitcher, 4" h tumblers	$200	$400
Bowl, square faceted pyramids, alternating in amber and clear at rim above ribbed sections of same alternating colors, attributed to Hoffman, Austria, 3.5" h, 8" dia	400	600
Candleholders, cut crystal, wide flared bowl w/ copper wheel-cut Greek key and swag design w/ gold inlay, tall zippered stem, attributed to Hawkes, 8.25" h, price for set of 4	200	400
Candleholders, slightly bulging hollow stem w/ cut panels between faceted ball connectors, spreading foot, ground pontil, attributed to Val St. Lambert, 12" h, price for pair	150	300
Centerpiece, flared insert bowl w/ overall diamond pattern, supported by silver-plated putto holding flower and leaf swag motif mount, square marble and silver-plated base, marked "C1413," Pairpoint, 9.25" h	200	300
Chandelier, flared curved rim w/ diamond cutting above light bowl w/ floral wheel-cut design, suspended from 3 gilt-metal linked rods w/ central tripartite lighting devices, adjustable drop, American Brilliant Period, 12" dia bowl	500	800
Compote, Alhambra design, notched edges on rim and foot, attributed to Hawkes, 8" h	1000	1500
Humidor, cylindrical, strawberry diamond and fine-cut designs, conforming glass cover w/ elaborate star cutting on knob, rayed star-cut base, American Brilliant Period, 9" h	400	600
Picture Frame Panel, etched and engraved border w/ floral sprays, attributed to T. G. Hawkes & Co., 11.5" x 9.75"	50	100
Pitcher, tall flared cylinder form, notched applied handle, scalloped rim, hobstar and fan patterns, hobstar-cut base, American Brilliant Period, 11.5" h	700	900
Pitcher, tankard form, star, cane, fine-cut, and fan motifs, notched handle, American Brilliant Period, 14" h	600	800

	LOW	HIGH
Punch Bowl and Ladle, scalloped rim, star, fan, and fine-cut elements, silver ladle stamped "Pairpoint Mfg. Co." w/ cut glass knob, bowl signed "Hawkes," 7.5" h, 14.5" dia	1000	1500
Table Lamp, dome-shaped shade cut w/ leaves and daisies, raised on baluster-shaped standard and spreading scalloped sawtooth base w/ same pattern, w/ prisms, American Brilliant Period, 25" h, 12" dia shade	1000	1200
Table Lamp, dome-shaped shade cut w/ woven cane pattern, trumpet-shaped base w/ similar pattern, w/ prisms, American Brilliant Period, 27" h	1200	1500
Table Lamp, onion shade w/ hobstar and fan cuts, fan- and hobstar-cut shaft tapering to wide scalloped and notched base, w/ cut prisms, American Brilliant Period, 29.5" h, 11.5" dia shade	3000	4000
Vase, 2-handled, large hobstar design, American Brilliant period, 10" h	400	600
Vase, flattened trophy form w/ scalloped rim, applied notched handles, center star-cut design, pedestal base w/ wide star-cut and scalloped edge, American Brilliant Period, 10.25" h	1200	1500
Vase, goblet form w/ scalloped sawtooth rim, cut panels w/ hobstar and rosettes, horizontal step-cut standard, faceted ball connector, raised spreading star-cut sawtooth-edged base, attributed to Hawkes, American Brilliant Period, late 19th C, 13.5" h	800	1000
Vase, tall cylinder shape, iridized clear glass w/ cut and etched flowers, swags, and tassels, topped by sterling silver band w/ repeating swag and oval motifs, stamped "Hawkes" on base and "Hawkes Sterling 2262" on rim, 9.75" h, 3.75" dia	350	600
Vase, trumpet-shaped w/ ruffled and notched rim, star and fan motifs, American Brilliant Period, 14.25" h	400	600

American Cut Glass, Brilliant period. —Photo courtesy Skinner, Inc., Boston, MA.

Czechoslovakian Glass

	LOW	HIGH
Basket, black cased to green interior, decorated w/ silver mica flakes, 8.5" h	$200	$300
Console Bowl, oval form w/ flared rim, opalescent green, black rim wrap and 3 applied black flattened ball feet, attributed to Michael Powolny, 5" h, 10.5" d	250	350
Decanter Set, pitcher and 7 wines, Moorish-style heavily decorated w/ elaborate gold- and red-enameled borders and multicolored glass "jewels," 7.75" h decanter, 6" h wine	400	600
Perfumes, green malachite, molded w/ elaborate cherub and foliate design, conforming stopper w/ floral bouquet, polished base, unsigned, 6.25" h, price for pair	200	300
Rose Bowl, geometric deeply angled blown-out surface, white opaque cased glass w/ iridescent finish, brass flower frog, 5.5" h	75	150
Vase, baluster form, apple green w/ Chinese red and cobalt blue threading, marked "Czechoslovakia," 7.25" h	100	200
Vase, cylindrical, mottled white and purple cased to clear, enameled as stylized vignette of woman fishing, silver-mounted rim w/ English hallmarks, c1930, 6.25" h	100	200
Vase, fan-shaped, blue w/ yellow threading at top, 9.25" h	200	300
Vase, ovoid, malachite, mold-blown design w/ 4 female figures, 9.75" h, 6.5" dia	200	400
Vase, ovoid w/ tapered neck and flared mouth, mold-blown, black w/ furnace-decorated yellow-green to dark green winding ribbons, acid marked "Czechoslovakian" on base, c1930, 7.5" h	150	250

Left to right: Perfume, frosted clear w/ molded nude woman front and back, stopper w/ cherubs, 8" h, $230 at auction; Pair of Perfumes, blue heart-shaped cut crystal bottles, clear stoppers w/ intaglio portrait of woman picking bouquet (1 stopper frozen), 8.5" h, $633 at auction; Ice Bucket/Vase, press molded, flared trumpet form, transparent cornflower blue w/ Art Deco design, base marked "Czechoslov," 10.5" h, $374 at auction. —Photo courtesy Skinner, Inc., Boston, MA.

Depression Glass

Colored glassware was machine-made during the late 1920s and early 1930s. The glass was available in 10¢ stores, given away at filling stations and theaters and used for promotional purposes. More than eighty Depression glass clubs sponsor shows, with attendance in the thousands.

For more information on Depression glass see *Collector's Encyclopedia of Depression Glass, Thirteenth Edition* by Gene Florence (Collector Books, Paducah, KY, 1998). Gene Florence has authored several other books on Depression glass, all of which are available from Collector Books.

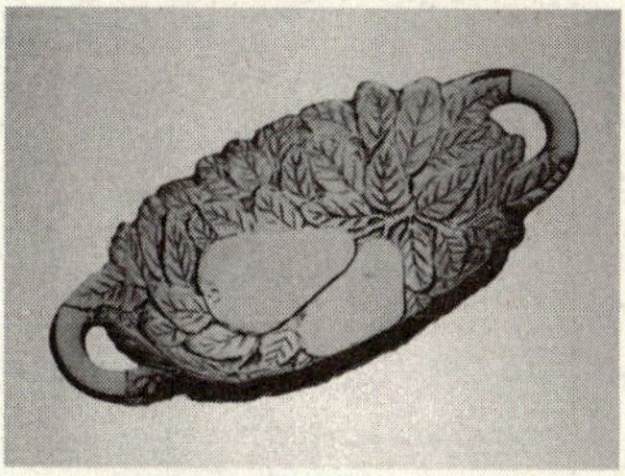

Avocado / No. 601.

Cube / Cubist.

Avocado / No. 601

	CRYSTAL	GREEN	PINK
Bowl, 1 handle, 7"	$8	$25	$20
Bowl, oval, 2-handled, 8"	12	30	22
Bowl, relish, footed, 6"	10	25	25
Bowl, salad, 7.5"	12	55	35
Cake Plate, 2-handled, 10.25"	15	55	35
Creamer, footed	12	35	30
Cup	—	32	30
Pitcher, 64 oz	350	1000	750
Plate, sherbet, 6.375"	5	17	15
Plate, luncheon, 8.25"	8	20	18
Saucer, 6.375"	—	25	22
Sherbet	—	60	50
Sugar, footed	12	35	32
Tumbler, footed	25	250	150

Cube / Cubist

	GREEN	PINK
Bowl, dessert, 4.5"	$8	$7
Bowl, salad, 6.5"	15	10
Butter, covered	65	65
Candy, covered, footed	33	30
Coaster	8	8
Creamer	8	7
Cup	9	8
Pitcher, 45 oz, 8.75"	225	200

	GREEN	PINK
Plate, luncheon, 8"	7	7
Plate, sherbet, 6"	5	4
Powder Jar, covered	28	28
Salt and Pepper, footed	35	35
Saucer	3	3
Sherbet, footed	8	8
Sugar, covered	22	20
Tumbler, 9 oz, 4"	75	70

Della Robbia

	CRYSTAL
Bowl, bell, 15"	$185
Bowl, footed, 12"	120
Candlesticks, pair, 2-lite, 4"	70
Candy, flat, chocolate	80
Compote, flanged, 13"	125
Creamer	15
Cup, punch	18
Goblet, 3.25 oz, cocktail	25
Goblet, 6 oz, champagne	25
Goblet, 8 oz, water, 6"	35
Nappy, heart shaped, 8"	135
Pitcher, 32 oz	200
Plate, bread and butter, 6.125"	12
Plate, dinner, 10.5"	75
Plate, luncheon, 9"	45
Plate, salad, 7.25"	20
Sherbet, 5 oz, low, footed, 3.5"	21
Sugar, footed	25
Tumbler, 8 oz, water	25
Tumbler, 12 oz, iced tea, footed	45

Dogwood / Apple Blossom / Wild Rose

	CREMAX	GREEN	MONAX	PINK
Bowl, berry, 8.5"	$38	$150	$38	$58
Bowl, cereal, 5.5"	5	40	5	30
Bowl, fruit, 10.25"	100	350	100	550
Cake Plate, 13"	175	120	175	160
Creamer, thick, footed, 3.25"	—	—	—	25
Creamer, thin, flat, 2.5"	—	60	—	20
Cup, thick	42	—	42	18
Cup, thin	—	42	—	17
Pitcher, 80 oz, decorated, 8"	—	550	—	235
Plate, bread and butter, 6"	24	12	24	8
Plate, dinner, 9.25"	—	—	—	36
Plate, grill, allover pattern, 10.5"	—	30	—	26
Plate, luncheon, 8"	—	12	—	8
Platter, oval, 12"	—	—	—	725
Salver, 12"	18	—	18	30
Saucer	20	12	20	7
Sherbet, low, footed	—	120	—	35

	CREMAX	GREEN	MONAX	PINK
Sugar, thick, footed, 3.25"	—	—	—	20
Sugar, thin, flat, 2.5"	—	60	—	20
Tumbler, 5 oz, juice, 3.5"	—	—	—	300
Tumbler, 11 oz, decorated, 4.75"	—	120	—	50
Tumbler, 12 oz, iced tea, decorated, 5"	—	125	—	75

Doric & Pansy

	CRYSTAL	GREEN	PINK	ULTRAMARINE
Bowl, berry, 4.5"	$10	$20	$10	$20
Bowl, berry, 8"	24	24	24	85
Butter, covered	—	450	—	450
Cup	10	20	10	20
Creamer	75	125	75	125
Plate, dinner, 9"	8	35	8	35
Plate, salad, 7"	—	40	—	40
Plate, sherbet, 6"	8	12	8	12
Salt and Pepper, pair	—	425	—	425
Saucer	5	5	5	5
Sugar, open	75	120	75	120
Sugar, child's	—	45	32	45
Tray, handled, 10"	—	40	—	40
Tumbler, 9 oz, 4.5"	—	125	—	125

Floral / Poinsettia

	DELPHITE	GREEN	PINK
Bowl, berry, 4"	$40	$25	$18
Bowl, salad, 7.5"	75	25	18
Butter, covered	—	120	110
Candlesticks, pair, 4"	—	110	75
Candy, covered	—	42	38
Coaster, 3.25"	—	11	13
Creamer, flat	90	20	15
Cup	—	14	15
Pitcher, 32 oz, cone, footed, 8"	—	36	35
Pitcher, 48 oz, lemonade, 10.25"	—	260	250
Plate, dinner, 9"	150	15	18

Doric & Pansy.

Floral / Poinsettia.

	DELPHITE	GREEN	PINK
Plate, grill, 9"	—	200	—
Plate, salad, 8"	—	15	12
Plate, sherbet, 6"	—	8	8
Platter, oval, 10.75"	165	21	17
Platter, rimmed, 11"	—	650	—
Relish, 2-part, oval	175	22	20
Salt and Pepper, pair, footed, 4"	—	45	50
Saucer	—	12	12
Sherbet	90	16	15
Sugar, flat	75	20	18
Sugar Lid	—	15	12
Tumbler, 7 oz, water, footed, 4.75"	200	17	18
Tumbler, 9 oz, lemonade, footed, 5.25"	—	60	60
Vegetable Bowl, oval, 9"	—	25	18

Homespun / Fine Rib

	CRYSTAL	PINK
Bowl, berry, closed handles, 4.5"	$10	$12
Bowl, cereal, closed handles, 5"	25	28
Butter, covered	55	60
Creamer, footed	10	12
Cup	10	12
Plate, dinner, 9.25"	18	20
Plate, sherbet, 6"	5	6
Saucer	4	5
Sherbet, low, flat	15	18
Sugar, footed	8	10
Tumbler, 6 oz, straight sided, 3.875"	20	24
Tumbler, 9 oz, water, flared rim, 4"	18	20
Tumbler, 13 oz, iced tea, 5.25"	30	32
Tumbler, 15 oz, footed, 6.25"	25	30

Homespun / Fine Rib.

Horseshoe / No. 612

	GREEN	YELLOW
Bowl, berry, 4.5"	$28	$24
Bowl, berry, 9.25"	50	55
Bowl, cereal, 6.5"	28	25
Bowl, salad, 7.5"	25	25
Butter, covered	800	—
Creamer, footed	20	20
Cup	12	15
Pitcher, 64 oz, 8.5"	275	400
Plate, grill, 10.375"	95	90
Plate, luncheon, 9.375"	14	15
Plate, salad, 8.375"	12	12
Plate, sherbet, 6"	9	10
Platter, oval, 10.75"	30	28
Relish, 3-part, footed	28	35
Saucer	6	8
Sherbet	15	16
Sugar, open	18	20
Tumbler, 9 oz, flat, 4.25"	160	—
Tumbler, 9 oz, footed, 4.25"	25	25
Tumbler, 12 oz, flat, 4.75"	160	—
Tumbler, 12 oz, footed, 4.75"	150	169
Vegetable Bowl, 8.5"	40	40
Vegetable Bowl, oval, 10.5"	25	30

Iris / Iris & Herringbone

	CRYSTAL	GREEN	IRIDESCENT	PINK
Bowl, berry, beaded, 4.5"	$50	—	$8	—
Bowl, berry, beaded, 8"	120	—	25	—
Bowl, cereal, 5"	150	—	—	—
Bowl, fruit, straight sided, 11"	80	—	—	—
Bowl, salad, ruffled, 9.5"	15	$100	12	$100
Bowl, sauce, ruffled, 5"	10	—	25	—
Bowl, soup, 7.5"	180	—	65	—
Butter, covered	48	—	42	—
Candlesticks, pair	42	—	42	—
Candy, covered	185	—	—	—
Coaster	120	—	—	—
Creamer, footed	12	120	10	120
Cup	15	—	14	—
Demitasse Cup	40	—	130	—
Demitasse Saucer	160	—	200	—
Goblet, 3 oz, wine, 4.5"	16	—	25	—
Goblet, 4 oz, 5.5"	25	—	125	—
Goblet, 4 oz, cocktail, 4.5"	25	—	—	—
Goblet, 8 oz, water, 5.5"	27	—	175	—
Nut Set, complete	100	—	—	—

	CRYSTAL	GREEN	IRIDESCENT	PINK
Pitcher, footed, 9.5"	38	—	36	—
Plate, dinner, 9"	60	—	38	—
Plate, luncheon, 8"	125	—	—	—
Plate, sherbet, 5.5"	15	—	11	—
Sandwich Plate, 11.75"	50	—	30	—
Saucer	12	—	11	—
Sherbet, footed, 2.5"	28	—	18	—
Sherbet, footed, 4"	25	—	150	—
Sugar, covered	22	120	22	120
Tumbler, flat, 4"	150	—	—	—
Tumbler, footed, 6"	18	—	16	—
Tumbler, footed, 6.5"	35	—	28	—
Vase	25	150	20	150

Manhattan / Horizontal Ribbed

	CRYSTAL	PINK
Bowl, berry, w/ handles, 5.375"	$15	$20
Bowl, berry, 7.5"	12	—
Bowl, cereal, wo/ handles, 5.25"	25	—
Bowl, salad, 9"	18	—
Bowl, sauce, w/ handles, 4.5"	8	—
Candy, covered	40	—
Candy, low, 3-footed	—	9
Coaster, 3.5"	12	—
Compote, 5.75"	45	48
Creamer, oval	10	12
Cup	15	150
Goblet, wine, 3.5"	4	—
Pitcher, 24 oz	30	—
Pitcher, 80 oz, tilted	40	75
Plate, dinner, 10.25"	20	130
Plate, salad, 8.5"	15	—
Plate, sherbet, 6"	6	55
Relish Tray, 4-part, 14"	15	—
Relish Tray, pink inserts, 14"	—	45
Relish Tray, red inserts, 14"	40	—
Salt and Pepper, pair	25	48
Sandwich Plate, w/ handle, 14"	18	—
Saucer	6	55
Sherbet	7	18
Sugar, oval	10	12
Tumbler, 10 oz, footed	15	18
Vase, 8"	15	—

Mayfair / Open Rose

	BLUE	FROSTED	GREEN	PINK	YELLOW
Bowl, cereal, 5.5"	$55	$25	$80	$28	$80
Bowl, cream soup, 5"	—	50	—	55	—
Bowl, fruit, scalloped, deep, 12"	100	60	50	65	225
Bowl, low, flat, 11.75"	80	65	45	70	200
Butter, covered	300	65	1250	70	1250

	BLUE	FROSTED	GREEN	PINK	YELLOW
Cake Plate, footed, 10"	85	35	100	40	—
Cake Plate, w/ handles, 12"	75	50	40	60	—
Candy Dish, covered	325	50	600	58	500
Cookie Jar, covered	300	48	600	55	850
Creamer, footed	85	25	225	30	200
Cup	55	15	150	18	150
Decanter and Stopper, 32 oz	—	175	—	225	—
Goblet, 3 oz, cocktail, 4"	—	90	390	120	—
Goblet, 3 oz, wine, 4.5"	—	85	450	105	—
Goblet, 9 oz, thin, 7.25"	200	175	—	250	—
Goblet, 9 oz, water, 5.75"	160	75	450	85	—
Pitcher, 37 oz, 6"	165	50	550	60	500
Pitcher, 60 oz, 8"	210	65	500	75	425
Pitcher, 80 oz, 8.5"	250	115	550	130	550
Plate, 5.75"	30	12	100	15	90
Plate, dinner, 9.5"	85	45	85	55	150
Plate, grill 9.5"	60	35	90	40	80
Plate, luncheon, 8.5"	55	25	85	30	85
Plate, off-center indent, 6.5"	32	25	125	28	—
Platter, oval, open handles, 12"	75	28	175	32	125
Relish, 2-part	—	32	—	37	—
Relish, 4-part, 8.375"	70	30	175	35	175
Salt and Pepper, pair, flat	295	60	1000	70	800
Sandwich Server, center handle	80	42	40	50	140
Saucer, w/ cup ring	—	30	—	37	150
Saucer, wo/ cup ring, 5.75"	30	12	100	15	90
Sherbet, footed, 3"	—	15	—	18	—
Sherbet, footed, 4.75"	85	16	150	18	150
Sugar, covered, footed	85	25	200	30	200
Tumbler, 1.5 oz, whiskey, 2.25"	—	80	—	100	—
Tumbler, 3 oz, juice, footed, 3.25"	—	125	—	160	—
Tumbler, 5 oz, juice, flat, 3.5"	140	55	—	65	—
Tumbler, 9 oz, water, flat, 4.25"	125	28	—	32	—
Tumbler, 10 oz, footed, 5.25"	135	40	—	45	200
Tumbler, 13 oz, iced tea, flat, 5.25"	250	65	—	75	—
Tumbler, 15 oz, iced tea, footed, 6.5"	275	35	250	45	—
Vase, Sweet Pea	125	180	300	225	—
Vegetable Bowl, 7"	65	25	140	32	150
Vegetable Bowl, 10"	75	25	—	30	130
Vegetable Bowl, covered, 7"	300	60	—	70	1250
Vegetable Bowl, covered, 10"	—	125	1250	145	1000
Vegetable Bowl, oval, 9.5"	75	30	125	38	125

Moondrops

	AMBER	AMETHYST	BLUE	GREEN	RED
Bowl, concave top, 3-footed, 8.375"	$25	—	$50	—	$50
Bowl, ruffled, 3-footed, 9.5"	—	—	70	—	70
Bowl, soup, 6.75"	—	—	90	$115	90
Bowl, winged, 13"	45	$175	125	50	125
Butter, covered	275	275	450	275	450
Candlesticks, pair, 3-lite, 5.25"	60	185	125	—	125
Creamer, 3.75"	10	10	18	12	18

	AMBER	AMETHYST	BLUE	GREEN	RED
Creamer, miniature, 2.75"	.12	—	18	—	18
Cup	.10	10	18	10	18
Decanter, 8.5"	.45	45	75	60	75
Decanter, 11.25"	.60	60	100	75	100
Goblet, 4 oz, wine, 4"	.15	15	24	18	24
Goblet, 9 oz, water, metal stem, 6.25"	.18	18	22	20	22
Plate, dinner, 9.5"	.18	18	28	20	28
Plate, luncheon, 8.5"	.15	15	15	15	15
Plate, salad, 7.125"	.12	12	15	15	15
Platter, oval, 12"	.25	25	40	30	40
Salt and Pepper, pair	.—	—	40	—	40
Saucer	.5	5	8	6	8
Sherbet, 2.625"	.12	12	18	15	18
Sugar, 3.75"	.10	10	18	12	18
Sugar, miniature, 2.75"	.12	12	15	15	15
Tumbler, 2 oz, whiskey, 2.75"	.12	12	18	12	18
Tumbler, 3 oz, juice, footed, 3.75"	.12	12	18	12	18
Tumbler, 5 oz, 3.625"	.12	12	15	12	15
Tumbler, 9 oz, 4.875"	.16	16	20	18	20
Tumbler, 9 oz, handled, 4.875"	.18	18	35	25	35

Newport / Hairpin

	AMETHYST	BLUE
Bowl, berry, 4.75"	.$16	$25
Bowl, berry, 8.25"	.40	65
Bowl, cereal, 5.25"	.45	55
Bowl, cream soup, 4.75"	.18	25
Creamer	.15	18
Cup	.12	15
Plate, dinner, 9"	.35	35
Plate, luncheon, 8.5"	.15	18
Plate, sherbet, 5.875"	.6	8
Salt and Pepper, pair	.45	50
Sandwich Plate, 11.75"	.35	45
Saucer	.5	5
Sherbet, footed	.12	15
Sugar	.14	18
Tumbler, 9 oz, 4.5"	.35	42

Old Colony / Lace Edge / Open Lace

	CRYSTAL	PINK
Bowl, cereal, 5.5"	.$8	$23
Bowl, plain, 9.5"	.—	26
Bowl, ribbed, 9.5"	.—	30
Bowl, salad, ribbed, 7.75"	.—	50
Candlesticks, pair	.—	270
Compote, open, 7"	.—	16
Cookie jar, covered	.—	85
Creamer	.—	23
Cup and Saucer	.—	30

	CRYSTAL	PINK
Flower Bowl, w/ crystal frog	—	26
Plate, dinner, 10.5"	—	32
Plate, grill, 10.5"	—	22
Plate, luncheon, 8.5"	—	20
Plate, salad, 7.75"	—	22
Platter, 5-part, oval, 12.75"	—	34
Relish, 3-part, 10.5"	—	20
Relish, 3-part, deep, 7.75"	—	75
Relish, 4-part, solid lace, 13"	—	70
Saucer	—	8
Sherbet	—	110
Tumbler, flat, 9 oz, 4.5"	—	25
Tumbler, footed, 10.5 oz, 5"	—	85

Parrot / Sylvan

	AMBER	GREEN
Bowl, berry, 5"	$18	$28
Bowl, berry, 8"	75	100
Bowl, soup, 7"	35	50
Butter, covered	1200	400
Creamer	65	55
Cup	40	45
Plate, dinner, 9"	40	65
Plate, grill, round, 10.5"	—	45
Plate, grill, square, 10.5"	35	—
Plate, salad, 7.5"	—	45
Platter, oblong, 11.25"	75	58
Salt and Pepper, pair	—	350
Saucer	15	20
Sherbet, cone, footed	24	30
Sugar, covered, footed	450	185
Tumbler, 10 oz, 4.25"	100	150
Tumbler, 12 oz, 5.5"	125	175
Tumbler, thick, footed, 5.75"	120	210
Vegetable Bowl, oval, 10"	70	65

Newport / Hairpin.

Old Colony / Lace Edge / Open Lace.

Petalware. —Photo courtesy Ray Morykan Auctions.

Petalware

	CREMAX	CRYSTAL	MONAX (Decorated)	MONAX (Plain)	PINK
Bowl, berry, 8.75"	$30	$10	$30	$20	$20
Bowl, cereal, 5.75"	15	4	17	11	10
Bowl, cream soup	15	5	17	14	12
Bowl, soup, 7.75"	75	—	75	60	—
Creamer, footed	15	5	10	6	10
Cup	7	4	9	4	8
Plate, dinner, 9"	18	5	20	8	12
Plate, salad, 8"	5	3	8	6	7
Plate, sherbet, 6.25"	6	3	8	3	4
Salver, 11"	12	6	18	12	15
Saucer	2	2	3	2	2
Sherbet, 4"	12	—	15	10	—
Sugar, footed	15	5	10	8	8

Royal Lace

	BLUE	CRYSTAL	GREEN	PINK
Bowl, berry, 5"	$55	$25	$32	$30
Bowl, cream soup, 4.75"	50	20	32	30
Bowl, rolled edge, 3-footed, 10"	320	200	80	100
Bowl, ruffled, 3-footed, 10"	450	40	70	95
Butter, covered	700	65	275	150
Candlesticks, rolled edge, pair	250	50	100	140
Candlesticks, straight edge, pair	160	35	85	65
Cookie Jar, covered	400	40	90	75
Creamer, footed	65	18	30	25
Cup	40	10	25	20
Nut Dish	1000	200	500	500
Pitcher, 48 oz, straight sided, ice lip	210	50	130	120
Pitcher, 64 oz, wo/ ice lip, 8"	275	60	135	125
Pitcher, 96 oz, w/ ice lip, 8.5"	300	75	160	150
Plate, dinner, 9.875"	55	20	30	40
Plate, grill, 9.875"	40	18	30	25
Plate, luncheon, 8.5"	38	12	20	20
Plate, sherbet, 6"	18	8	12	10

Swirl / Petal Swirl.

	BLUE	CRYSTAL	GREEN	PINK
Platter, oval, 13"	65	25	50	40
Salt and Pepper, pair	340	55	140	85
Saucer	15	7	10	8
Sherbet, footed, all glass	50	20	30	25
Sherbet, metal holder, 4"	28	10	—	—
Sugar, covered, footed	200	32	75	65
Toddy Set	285	—	—	—
Tumbler, 5 oz, juice, 3.5"	60	20	35	30
Tumbler, 9 oz, 4.125"	55	15	35	25
Tumbler, 12 oz, 5.375"	100	28	55	60

Swirl / Petal Swirl

	DELPHITE	PINK	ULTRAMARINE
Bowl, cereal, 5.25"	$18	$12	$16
Bowl, salad, 9"	35	20	27
Bowl, salad, rimmed, 9"	—	25	35
Bowl, soup, lug	—	30	40
Candy, covered	—	125	175
Coaster, 3.25"	—	10	15
Creamer, footed	15	12	18
Cup	12	10	18
Pitcher, 48 oz, footed	—	—	1750
Plate, dinner, 9.25"	18	15	20
Plate, salad, 8"	12	12	15
Plate, sherbet, 6.5"	8	6	8
Platter, oval, 12"	45	—	—
Salt and Pepper, pair	—	—	50
Sandwich Plate, 12.5"	—	18	35
Saucer	7	5	7
Sherbet, low, footed	—	15	25
Sugar, footed	18	15	20
Tray, w/ handles, 10.5"	32	—	—
Tumbler, 9 oz, flat, 4"	—	20	40
Tumbler, 9 oz, footed	—	24	45
Tumbler, 13 oz, iced tea, flat, 5.125"	—	50	180
Vase	—	20	30

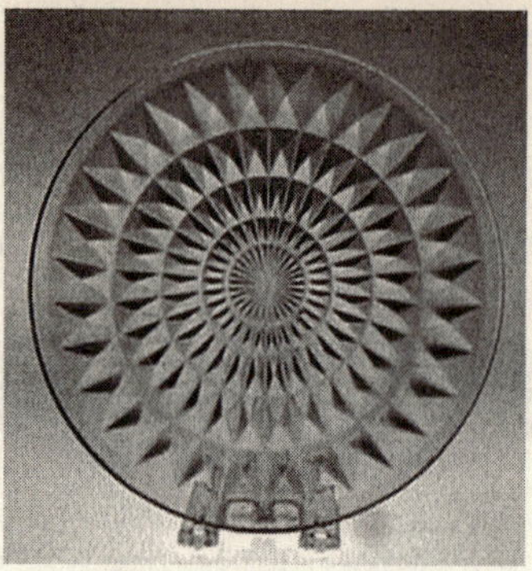

Windsor / Windsor Diamond.

Windsor / Windsor Diamond

	CRYSTAL	GREEN	PINK
Ashtray, 5.75"	$15	$50	$50
Bowl, fruit, 12.5"	28	—	120
Bowl, 3-footed, 7.125"	10	—	38
Bowl, berry, 4.75"	5	15	10
Bowl, boat shape, 7" x 11.75"	20	40	40
Bowl, cereal, 5.25"	10	25	25
Bowl, cream soup, 5"	8	30	25
Bowl, pointed edge, 5"	7	—	25
Bowl, pointed edge, 8"	10	—	65
Butter, covered	30	100	55
Candy, covered	18	—	—
Coaster	4	24	15
Creamer	6	15	12
Cup	5	15	12
Pitcher, 52 oz, 6.75"	15	70	32
Plate, chop, 13.625"	10	50	46
Plate, dinner, 9"	6	25	26
Plate, salad, 7"	5	24	20
Plate, sherbet, 6"	3	10	5
Platter, divided, 11.5"	12	—	225
Platter, oval, 11.5"	16	25	24
Salt and Pepper, pair	18	60	40
Sandwich Plate, open handle, 10.25"	8	20	20
Saucer	3	7	6
Sugar, covered, w/ lip	10	32	32
Sugar, covered, wo/ lip	15	—	125
Tray, w/ handles, 4.125" x 9"	6	18	18
Tray, w/ handles, 8.5" x 9.75"	8	40	25
Tray, wo/ handles, 4"	8	15	60
Tray, wo/ handles, 4.125 x 9"	10	—	70
Tray, wo/ handle, 8.5" x 9.75"	15	50	100
Tumbler, 5 oz, flat, 3.25"	10	50	25
Tumbler, 9 oz, flat, 4"	7	38	22
Tumbler, flat, 12 oz. 5"	10	55	35
Vegetable Bowl, oval, 9.5"	8	35	25

Drinking Glasses

For additional reading consult *Collectible Drinking Glasses* by Mark E. Chase and Michael J. Kelly (Collector Books, Paducah, KY, 1996, 1999 value update) and *Collector's Guide to Cartoon & Promotional Drinking Glasses* by John Hervey (L-W Book Sales, Gas City, IN, 1990, 1995 value update).

Drinking Glasses at Auction, left to right: Long-Billed Donald Duck, $186; 1948 Kentuck Derby, $165; 1980 Universal Monsters "Mutant," $150. —Photo courtesy Collectors Glass News.

	LOW	HIGH
Antique No. 1, brown, Swanky Swigs, 1954	$2	$4
Bad Witch, Wizard of Oz, Coca-Cola/Krystal, 1989	6	8
Barnum & Bailey Greatest Show on Earth, Circus Set, Pepsi-Cola, 1975	10	20
Betty and Veronica Give a Party, Archies, Welch's, 1973	1	2
Blue Fairy, Disney Pinocchio Series, 1940	15	20
Bugs Bunny in *Diving for Carrots,* Looney Tunes Adventures, Arby's, 1988	15	20
Camp Snoopy, "Civilization is Overrated!," McDonald's, 1983	1	2
Clarabell Tries Tiger Trick!, Kagran Howdy Doody, Welch's	15	20
Davy Crockett, "Steady Nerves...," yellow, Welch's	7	10
Elsie, Borden's, 1950s	10	5
Forget-Me-Not, yellow, Swanky Swigs, Kraft, 1948	2	4
Georgia, State Songs, Big Top Peanut Butter	2	4
Gone Fishing, Norman Rockwell Summer Scenes, Arby's, 1987	3	5
Hamburgers, Burger King Characters, 1978	12	15
Holly Hobbie "Happy Holidays!," American Greetings Corp.	2	4
Joanie, Happy Days Collector Series, Dr. Pepper/Pizza Hut, 1977	8	10
John Kennedy, Presidents and Patriots, Burger Chef, 1975	3	5
Pac-Man Speedy, Army and Air Force Exchange Service, 1980	4	6
Pebbles' Birthday Party, Hanna-Barbera Flintstones, Welch's, 1964	4	8
Put a Tiger in Your Tank, Esso Gasoline	3	5
Robin Hood, Libbey Classics	10	15
Rosie Tomato, Pizza Pete, late 1970s	30	40
Sadie Hawkins/Marryin' Sam, turquoise, Al Capp's Shmoos set, 1949	10	20
Scooby Doo, Pepsi-Cola, 1977	15	25
Steamboat, Currier & Ives, Kraft Cheese, 1970s	1	3
Sunday Afternoon, Old Time Series, Jewel Tea	2	4
Swee' Pea, Popeye's Famous Fried Chicken, 1979	10	20
The Locomotive, Transportation Series, Armour Peanut Butter	3	5
The Roaring '20s, Collector Series Limited Edition, Gulf Oil, early 1980s	3	5
Tony the Tiger, Kellogg's Collector Series, 1977	7	10
Tulips, blue, Swanky Swigs, Kraft, 1937	3	6
Ziggy, "Try to have a nice day...," Hardee's, 1979	5	8

Fostoria

Founded in Fostoria, Ohio, in 1887, Fostoria continues to produce at their Moundsville, West Virginia, factory. Many of their glassware lines are designated "elegant" Depression-era glass and are avidly sought by collectors. For more information see *Fostoria* (1997) and *Vol. II* (1997) by Ann Kerr (Collector Books, Paducah, KY) and *Fostoria Tableware: 1924-1943* by Milbra Long and Emily Seate (Collector Books, Paducah, KY, 1999).

Baroque Pattern – No. 2496 Line

	BLUE	CRYSTAL	PINK	YELLOW
Bon Bon, 3-toed, 7.375"	$40	$28	—	$35
Bowl, flared, 12"	70	50	$160	60
Bowl, rolled edge, 11"	130	60	—	85
Candlesticks, pair, 1-lite, 4"	60	34	—	65
Candlesticks, pair, 2-lite, 4.5"	125	60	—	130
Candlesticks, pair, 3-lite, 6"	175	75	—	150
Candy, covered, 3-part, 6.25"	75	40	—	80
Celery, 11"	80	35	—	75
Cheese and Cracker, 11"	90	75	—	90
Cocktail, 7 oz	25	12	—	15
Compote, 5.5"	50	18	—	45
Creamer and Sugar, individual size	65	28	—	50
Cream Soup, w/ liner	200	75	—	140
Cup and Saucer	35	12	—	26
Ice Bucket, w/ tongs, 4.375"	150	70	—	140
Jelly, covered, 7.5" h	200	65	—	170
Lustres, pair, 7.75"	250	155	—	250
Mayonnaise, 2-part, 6.5"	55	42	—	55
Mint, square, 4"	26	15	—	28
Nappy, flared, 5"	45	20	—	40
Nappy, round, 4.375"	32	20	—	24
Nappy, square, 4"	45	22	—	40
Nut Bowl, cupped, 3-toed, 6.25"	40	18	—	35
Oil Cruet, w/ stopper, 5.5"	400	100	—	240
Pickle Dish, 8"	55	25	—	50
Plate, 6"	12	6	—	10
Plate, 7"	15	8	—	12
Plate, 8"	20	12	—	20
Plate, 9"	75	25	—	60
Punch Bowl, footed	1350	425	—	—
Punch Cup	25	13	—	—
Relish, 3-part	60	25	—	42
Salt and Pepper, pair, 2"	300	125	—	300
Salt and Pepper, pair, 2.75"	170	75	—	150
Sauce Dish	95	35	—	80
Serving Dish, 2-handled, 8.5"	95	48	—	75
Sherbet	25	12	—	20
Tidbit, 3-toed, 8.25"	55	25	—	60
Torte Plate, 14"	100	60	—	85
Tumbler, 5 oz, juice, flat	45	15	—	30
Tumbler, 9 oz, water, footed	50	15	—	45
Tumbler, 12 oz, iced tea, footed	60	25	—	50
Tumbler, 14 oz, iced tea, flat	100	30	—	75

Coin Pattern – No. 1372 Line

	AMBER	BLUE	CRYSTAL	OLIVE	RUBY
Ashtray, #114, 4-coin, 7.5"	$25	$28	$20	$45	$20
Ashtray, #119, raised coin, 7.5"	16	20	12	—	25
Ashtray, #123, 5"	10	15	8	8	20
Ashtray, #124, 10"	35	90	30	30	—
Bowl, #179, round, 7.5"	65	80	35	60	70
Bowl, #189, oval, 9"	30	50	20	25	55
Bud Vase, #799, 8"	20	42	17	—	45
Cake Salver, #630	150	315	98	125	—
Candlesticks, #316, 4.5", pair	45	60	35	40	60
Candy, covered, #347, 6.5"	20	60	15	20	50
Candy, covered, #354, 4.125"	30	65	25	28	68
Cigarette Holder, #381, footed	35	48	25	30	40
Coach Lamp, #321, electric, 13.5"	120	250	75	—	—
Compote, #199, 8.5"	50	125	40	45	140
Courting Lamp, #310, oil, 9.75"	75	250	—	—	—
Courting Lamp, #311, electric, 10.125"	150	250	—	—	—
Creamer and Sugar, #680 and #673	40	80	25	35	80
Decanter, #400, w/ stopper	—	—	160	—	—
Goblet, #2, 10.5 oz, water	38	85	30	—	95
Goblet, #26, 5 oz, wine, 5.25"	35	80	25	—	90
Jelly, #448	30	75	25	25	80
Nappy, #499, handled, 5.375"	17	30	25	15	26
Patio Lamp, #466, electric, 16.625"	175	375	150	—	—
Salt and Pepper, pair, #652	30	65	25	20	60
Tumbler, #81, 9 oz, juice, 3.625"	—	—	30	—	—
Urn, covered, #829, 12.75"	68	115	65	68	130
Wedding Bowl, covered, #162, 8.5"	55	100	45	50	90

Navarre Pattern – Etching 327

	BLUE	CRYSTAL	PINK
Bowl, #2440, footed, 12"	—	$85	—
Bowl, #2470½, footed, 10.5"	—	75	—
Bowl, #2496, 2-handled, 4-toed, 10.5"	$65	80	—
Bowl, #2496, flared, 12"	—	65	—
Bowl, #2545, Flame, oval, 12.5"	100	100	—
Cake Plate, #2496, handled, 10"	—	55	—
Candlesticks, pair, #2472, 2-lite, 5"	—	95	—
Candlesticks, pair, #2482, 3-lite, 6.75"	—	150	—
Candlesticks, pair, #2496, 1-lite, 4"	30	45	—
Candlesticks, pair, #2496, 3-lite, 6"	—	125	—
Candy, covered, #2496, 3-part	—	175	—
Champagne, #6016, 5 oz, flute, 8.125"	125	120	$125
Champagne, #6016, 6 oz, saucer, 5.625"	45	25	45
Claret, #6016, 4.5 oz, 6"	65	40	65
Claret, #6016, 6.5 oz, 6.25"	70	50	70
Cocktail, #6016, 3.5 oz, 5.25"	—	25	—
Compote, #2400, 4.5"	—	60	—
Compote, #2496, 4.75"	—	45	—
Cracker Plate, #2496, 11"	—	55	—
Creamer and Sugar, #2496, individual size	—	40	—

Left: Coin Pattern. —Photo courtesy Ray Morykan Auctions.

Right: Navarre Pattern. —Photo courtesy Lenox, Inc.

	BLUE	CRYSTAL	PINK
Cup and Saucer, #2440	—	30	—
Magnum, #6016, 16 oz, 7.25"	160	130	—
Mayonnaise Set, #2375, 3 pieces	75	75	—
Nappy, #2496, handled, 4.375"	—	45	—
Oyster Cocktail, #6016, 4 oz, 3.625"	—	28	—
Pickle, #2496, 8"	—	75	—
Pitcher, #5000, 40 oz, footed	—	600	—
Plate, #2375, dinner, 9"	35	65	—
Plate, #2496, 2-handled, 10"	30	70	—
Relish, #2419, 5-part, 13.25"	—	130	—
Relish, #2496, 2-part, square, 6"	—	40	—
Relish, #2496, 3-part, 10" x 7.5"	—	75	—
Salad Dressing Bottle, #2083, 6.5"	—	490	—
Salt and Pepper, pair, #2364, flat, 3.25"	—	65	—
Salt and Pepper, pair, #2375, footed, 3.5"	160	140	—
Sauce Dish, #2496, 6.25" x 5.25"	—	90	—
Sauce Dish, #2496, divided, 6.5"	—	90	—
Sauce Dish, w/ liner, #2496, oval	—	180	—
Sherbet, #6016, 6 oz, 4.375"	—	25	—
Sherry, #6016, 6 oz, 6.25"	—	250	—
Sugar, #2440, footed, 3.625"	—	23	—
Tidbit, #2496, 3-toed, 8.25"	—	70	—
Torte Plate, #2496, 14"	50	70	—
Tumbler, #6016, 5 oz, juice, footed, 4.625"	—	28	—
Tumbler, #6016, 10 oz, water, footed, 5.375"	—	28	—
Tumbler, #6016, 12 oz, highball, 4.875"	60	90	—
Tumbler, #6016, 13 oz, double old fashioned, 3.625"	—	85	—
Tumbler, #6016, 13 oz, iced tea, footed, 5.875"	60	35	60
Water Goblet, #6016, 10 oz, 7.625"	50	36	50
Wine, #6016, 3.25 oz, 5.5"	—	55	—

Heisey Glass

A partnership including George Duncan and Daniel C. Ripley established the A.H. Heisey Glass Co. in the 1860s in Newark, Ohio. Cut and pressed glasswares were manufactured. Heisey glass is high quality. Many patterns are called "elegant Depression glass."

The Heisey Collectors of America, Inc. (169 W. Church St., Newark, OH 43055) publishes *Heisey News,* a newsletter with information on patterns, history of Heisey, and advertisements. For additional reading see *The Collector's Encyclopedia of Heisey Glass: 1925-1938* by Neila Bredenoft (Collector Books, Paducah, KY, 1986, 1999 value update) and *Collector's Guide to Heisey and Heisey by Imperial Glass Animals* by Frank L. Hahn and Paul Kikeli (Golden Era Publications, Lima, OH, 1991, 1994 value update).

Animal Figurines

	AMBER	COBALT	CRYSTAL	SULTANA
Elephant, 4"	$1500	—	$300	$1500
Gazelle, 11"	—	—	1500	—
Giraffe, 11"	—	—	200	1500
Goose, wings down, 2.75"	—	—	425	—
Goose, wings half way, 4.5"	—	—	80	—
Goose, wings up, 6.5"	—	—	100	—
Plug Horse, 4"	500	$1200	115	—
Pony, balking, 3.75"	5000	1200	200	—
Pony, kicking, 4.125"	450	1000	175	—
Pony, standing, 5"	500	1000	95	—
Rooster, 5.625"	1750	—	500	—
Rooster, fighting, 8"	—	—	120	—
Wood Duckling, standing, 2.625"	—	—	150	—

Empress Pattern – No. 1401

	CRYSTAL	FLAMINGO	MOONGLEAM	SAHARA
Bon Bon, 6"	$15	$35	$38	$30
Bowl, salad, 10"	30	65	75	50
Bowl, salad, square, 10"	45	65	75	60
Celery, 13"	20	45	60	40
Champagne, 4 oz, saucer	25	65	75	65
Creamer, footed	20	50	60	40
Creamer and Sugar, individual size	40	100	100	70
Cup and Saucer	18	42	45	40
Nappy, 8"	22	35	48	32
Oyster Cocktail, 2.5 oz	15	28	40	25
Plate, 6"	8	15	18	12
Plate, 8"	12	30	35	25
Plate, 9"	12	20	25	18
Plate, square, 10.5"	75	140	135	130
Platter, oval, 14"	32	50	75	48
Salt and Pepper, pair	45	100	125	100
Sandwich Plate, 2-handled, 12"	28	50	55	45
Sherbet, 4 oz	18	35	45	32
Sugar, 3-handled, footed	25	55	65	40
Tumbler, 8 oz	18	65	70	65
Vegetable Bowl, oval, 10"	25	40	50	40

New Era Pattern – No. 4044

	COBALT	CRYSTAL
Candlesticks, pair, 2-lite	—	$180
Celery, 13"	—	40
Champagne, 6 oz, saucer	$85	18
Claret, 4 oz	95	22
Cocktail, 3.5 oz	100	18
Cordial, 1 oz	250	45
Creamer and Sugar	—	95
Cup and Saucer	—	45
Goblet, 10 oz	200	25
Nut Cup	—	60
Oyster Cocktail, 3.5 oz	90	20
Pilsener	200	60
Plate, 6"	—	35
Relish, 3-part, 13"	—	35
Sherbet, 6 oz	80	15
Tumbler, juice	85	24
Wine, 3 oz	160	25

Yeoman Pattern – No. 1184

	CRYSTAL	FLAMINGO	MOONGLEAM	SAHARA
Ashtray, handled, 4"	$15	$35	$50	—
Bon Bon, 2-handled, 5.5"	20	25	30	—
Cake Salver, 10"	45	—	—	—
Candy, covered, 6"	35	70	80	—
Celery, 13"	15	22	25	$25
Champagne, 6 oz, saucer	18	20	25	20
Cheese Plate, 2-handled	18	—	—	—
Coaster	10	—	—	—
Cocktail, 3 oz	15	25	30	30
Compote, high, 5"	25	40	45	—
Compote, low, 6"	25	35	45	40
Crescent Salad, 8"	20	35	50	45
Goblet, 8 oz, water	15	25	30	25
Grill Plate, 9"	25	200	—	—
Mint, 3-part, handled, 8"	30	40	50	—
Nappy, 4.5"	12	15	20	15
Nappy, 8"	18	20	25	24
Oyster Cocktail, 2.75 oz	15	25	35	30
Parfait, 5 oz	20	30	35	30
Plate, 6"	8	12	15	15
Plate, 7"	10	15	20	18
Plate, 9"	12	18	22	20
Plate, 10.5"	40	50	60	65
Plate, 14"	25	30	40	35
Platter, oval, 12"	25	40	50	45
Platter, oval, 15"	25	30	40	35
Relish, 7" x 10"	25	40	50	45
Relish, 3-part, 13"	15	25	35	30
Sherbet, 3.5 oz	12	15	20	18
Tumbler, 8 oz	12	18	25	20

Italian Glass

Italian glass is a generic term for glassware made in Murano, the center of Italy's glass blowing industry, from the 1920s into the early 1960s. Many firms engaged the services of internationally known artists and designers.

Pezzato Vase by Fulvio Bianconi, Venini Studio, $5462 at auction. —Photo courtesy Skinner, Inc., Boston, MA.

	LOW	HIGH
Bottle, cylindrical, vertical stripes of blue and green canes, interior-ground stopper, acid-etched "Venini Murano Italia," 13.5" h, 3.25" dia	$500	$700
Bowl, disk form, blue-red centered gold on white millefiori fused to clear, Murano Studio, 5.5" dia	50	100
Bowl, sculptural, clear roundel w/ 3 blue, green, and amber cavities, Murano Studio, 2.5" h, 7.5" dia	250	400
Bowl, tapered, vertical canes, half white and yellow, half smoky gray and white, Venini, 4.75" h, 5.5" dia	600	800
Candleholders, Ercole Barovier design, heavy clear crystal w/ symmetrical protrusions overall, Barovier & Toso "Rostrato," 3" h, price for pair	300	500
Caviar Server, figural guitar, 2-piece, free-blown amber w/ stretched blue, yellow, and white murrine border belt, labeled "Vetreria La Murrina, Murano Italy," 22.5" l	500	700
Decanter, w/ stopper, squat, 4-sided, inciso, bronze-colored, acid-etched Venini Murano Italia, foil label, 7" h, 4.25" w	400	600
Dresser Set, consisting of covered powder jar, perfume flacon, and atomizer, amber w/ applied turquoise spiral decoration, partial label "in Italy 528," attributed to Venini, Murano Studio, 9" h	300	500
Figure, kneeling nude female, agate-like effect in yellow, green, blue, and brown, signed "Loredano Rosin," 5.75" h, 11" l	800	1000
Figure, owl perched on green branch, orange, yellow, blue, purple, and white feathers, inscribed "Nason Aldo," Murano Studio, 12.5" h	300	500
Vase, elongated square form, cobalt blue ground, each side etched and enameled in manner of Miro, J. Arp, Modigliani, and K. Appel in red, green, yellow, and white, marked "Aureliano Toso Murano," 19.5" h	1500	1800
Vase, flared cylinder, vertical multicolored canes, acid-etched "Venini Murano Italia," 6.75" h, 5" dia	800	1000
Vase, "Oriente" face, model #5299 design by Dino Martens, waisted vessel of brightly colored glass sections, zanfirico, mesh woven squares, gold dust and pinwheel arrangement w/ face of "Geltrude" composed abstractly w/ 2 murrine canes and 6 red rods, partial label "4835, 5299," Vetreria Artistica Aureliano, c1954, 11.5" h	15,000	20,000
Vase, ovoid w/ flared rim and tapered base, opaque white w/ black powder application cased to clear, gray spiral ribs, black rim, inscribed "Tagliapietra Angelin Effetre International Murano 1986 12/100"	400	600

Lalique

René Lalique (1860–1945) began his career as a jeweler in Paris and by 1900 had become one of the world's most celebrated Art Nouveau designers. He began to manufacture glass in 1910. Many regard him as the best glass designer of the twentieth century. The company is still in business under the direction of René Lalique's granddaughter Marie Claude Lalique. Most items produced before René Lalique's death in 1945 are marked *R. LALIQUE,* while later pieces are marked *LALIQUE.* Collectors focus on the earlier period, especially pieces in color and rare models. Many fakes and forgeries exist. They are often crude and easily recognizable. When examining Lalique never let a signature authenticate the object, let the object authenticate the signature.

For clarification we have included the MA numbers from Felix Marcilhac's *René Lalique,* Edition de L'Amateur, Paris, 1989. Dates noted in the listings refer to the year in which the model was introduced.

	LOW	HIGH
Ashtray, Caravelle, clear and frosted, center plaque molded w/ sailing ship, 1930, 2.5" h, 4" dia, MA p. 279, no. 312	$100	$200
Ashtray, Serpent, clear and frosted, center raised and molded w/ coiled snake, 1920, 4.5" dia, MA p. 269, no. 276	700	900
Bonbonnière, Cyprins, clear opalescent, molded w/ fish, purple grosgrain box, 1921, 10" dia, MA p. 230, no. 42	1400	1600
Bowl, Calypso, flaring rim, clear and frosted opalescent w/ blue stain, molded mermaids, 1930, 14" dia, MA p. 301, no. 413	5000	6000
Bowl, Dauphins, clear and frosted iridescent w/ brown stain, molded fish in rippling water, 1932, 9.25" dia, MA p. 307, no. 10-384	800	1200
Bowl, Volubilis, clear and frosted opalescent, molded blossoms, 3-footed, 1921, 8.5" dia, MA p. 293, no. 383	700	900
Box, Gui, clear and frosted w/ orange-red stain, molded mistletoe, 1920, 1.5" h, 4" dia, MA p. 234, no. 65	800	1000
Bracelet, Cerisier, clear and frosted dark blue, each link molded w/ cherries and leaves, 1928, MA p. 532, no. 1329	2000	2400
Champagne Glasses, Strasbourg, clear and frosted, standard molded w/ 2 male grape pressers, 1926, MA p. 834, no. 5086, price for set of 6	1000	1200
Chandelier, Dahlia, clear and frosted, molded w/ flowerheads, suspended from 3 chains, 1921, 11.5" dia, MA p. 671, no. 2459	2400	2800

Left to right: Baies Vase; Nanking Vase; Charmilles Vase. —Photo courtesy William Doyle Galleries.

	LOW	HIGH
Clock, Inséparables, square, clear and frosted w/ blue stain, molded w/ 2 pairs of love birds perched on flowering branches, 1926, 4.25" h, MA p. 377, no. 765	1800	2200
Clock, Marguerites, rectangular, frosted clear, molded bouquet of daisies, 1920, 5.75" h, MA p. 377, no. 762	2400	2600
Decanter, Nippon, clear, base and stopper molded w/ bubbles, 1930, 9.75" h, MA p. 846, no. 3173	700	900
Figure, Pigeon Bruges, clear and frosted, pigeon, 1931, 10.5" l, MA p. 490, no. 1204	600	800
Figure, Prinetemps Surtout Quatre Saisons, clear and frosted, kneeling nude woman amongst flowers, representing Spring, 1939, 7.75" h, MA p. 404, no. 839bis	1800	2000
Paperweight, Tête d'Aigle, clear and frosted, figural eagle's head, 1928, 4" h, MA p. 382, no. 1138	1500	2000
Paperweight, Tête de Paon, clear and frosted, figural peacock's head on black glass base, 1928, 7" h, MA p. 383, no. 1140	5500	6500
Pendant, Guêpes, clear and frosted amethyst, molded w/ wasps, 1920, 2.375" h, MA p. 578, no. 1650	1000	1200
Perfume, Calendal, clear and frosted w/ peach stain, molded nude maidens, 1937, 4.5" h, MA p. 946, no. 6	2200	2400
Perfume, Enfants, clear and frosted w/ blue stain, molded w/ frieze of putti, 1931, 3.75" h, 3.5" dia, MA p. 345, no. 610	1200	1400
Picture Frame, Rose, clear and frosted w/ silver back, open rose decoration, original box, 10.25" h, 7.25" w, similar to MA p. 260, no. J	4000	6000
Pin, Deux Figurines Dos a Dos, clear and frosted opalescent, molded w/ 2 nudes amongst flowers, 1912, MA p. 548, no. 1388	2500	3000
Sconces, Soliel, corner-mount, clear and frosted, molded w/ stylized sunbursts, 1926, 9" h, MA p. 593, no. 2018, price for pair	1800	2200
Stemware Service, Tokyo, comprising 10 goblets, 5 wines, 8 liqueurs, 5 champagnes, 7 finger bowls, 8 large plates, 8 small plates, decanter, pitcher, and cruet set, clear, beaded decoration, 1930-32, 7" h pitcher	1200	1500
Vase, Acanthes, ovoid, clear and frosted red, molded stylized acanthus leaves, 1921, 11" h, MA p. 417, no. 902	10,000	12,000
Vase, Baies, spherical, clear and frosted w/ black enamel detail, molded interlacing budding thorny branches, 1924, 10.5" h, MA p. 416, no. 894	12,000	14,000
Vase, Charmilles, spherical, clear and frosted w/ dark gray stain, molded leaves overall, 1926, 14" h, MA p. 434, no. 978	6000	8000
Vase, Davos, clear plum-brown, molded overall w/ variously sized bubbles forming geometric pattern, 1932, 11" h, MA p. 455, no. 1079	4500	6500
Vase, Esterel, clear and frosted amber, molded stylized leaves, 1923, 6.125" h, MA p. 426, no. 941	2000	2400
Vase, Formose, spherical, clear and frosted cased white, molded fish, 1924, 6.625" h, MA p. 425, no. 934	2400	2800
Vase, Fougères, squatty, frosted blue w/ white stain, molded rows of stylized leaves, 1912, 6" h, MA p. 422, no. 923	5500	6500
Vase, Lagamar, semi-ovoid, clear and frosted w/ black enamel detail, molded w/ 6 bands decorated w/ stylized geometric motif, 1926, 7.25" h, MA p. 432, no. 967	10,000	12,500
Vase, Nanking, faceted sphere, clear and frosted w/ green stain, triangular facets molded w/ concentric triangles, 1925, 13" h, MA p. 433, no. 971	7000	9000
Vase, Saint-Èmilion, cylindrical, clear and frosted w/ light green stain, sides molded w/ pairs of birds, 1942, 9.75" h, MA p. 472, no. 10-939	2400	2600
Vase, Sauterelles, ovoid, clear and frosted w/ blue and green stains, molded w/ grasshoppers on blades of grass, 1912, 10.25" h, MA p. 414, no. 888	6000	8000

Paperweights

Glass paperweights were not seen before the 1700s; they are a recent item. The most important examples were made in the nineteenth century. Millefiori weights contain arrays of small ornamental glass beads or stems arranged in a striking pattern. They are quite colorful. Sulfides are ceramic relief plaques encased in glass. Souvenir paperweights featuring some company or place are also common, though not as desirable.

The weight of the specimen is not an indication of quality. Rather, the name of the maker and the level of artistry evident determine the value of a paperweight. Clichy, Baccarat and St. Louis are important producers of artistic glass paperweights. Prices for famous makers are high, although less known craftsmen can also produce exquisite items. Although they sometimes put their initials on one of the canes in a millefiori weight, fakes are not uncommon.

See *All About Paperweights* by Lawrence H. Selman (Paperweight Press, Santa Cruz, CA, 1992), *Paperweights* by Sibylle Jargstorf (Schiffer, West Chester, PA, 1991), and *The Encyclopedia of Glass Paperweights* by Paul Hollister, Jr. (Paperweight Press, Santa Cruz, CA, 1986) for additional information.

Antique Paperweights, left to right: Baccarat, carpet ground; Saint Louis, twists and spokes; New England Glass Co., bouquet w/ double-swirl latticinio ground; Clichy, pinwheel; Baccarat, double overlay w/ garland millefiori. —Photos courtesy L. H. Selman Ltd.

Antique

	LOW	HIGH
Baccarat, 3-flower bouquet, white double clematis w/ red, white, and blue arrow/6-pointed star cane center, primrose w/ red and white stardust/bull's-eye cane center, and pansy w/ red and white stardust/bull's-eye cane center, on stems w/ spring green leaves, bottom petals of pansy formed w/ millefiori arrow canes, 3.125" dia	$8000	$10,000
Baccarat, red and white stardust carpet set w/ 6-pointed star, arrow, whorl, cog, shamrock, and trefoil canes in coral, orange, yellow, plum, cadmium green, cobalt blue, ruby, and turquoise and Gridel silhouette canes of deer, dog, 2 horses, 2 moths, goat, elephant, and rooster, and primrose portrait, B1848 signature/date cane, 3.125" dia	10,000	12,000
Bohemian, close concentric millefiori w/ complex cog and star canes in cobalt blue, ruby, turquoise, and salmon, 1.8125" dia	300	600
Clichy, alternating pinwheels in lilac and white emanating from white, watermelon, and yellow pastry mold cane, 3" dia	1900	2500
Clichy, barber pole chequer w/ pink and green rose, pink and white rose, and purple and white rose amidst complex pastry mold, stardust, moss, bull's-eye, and dog canes in pink, cadmium green, emerald, ruby, watermelon, Naples yellow, and white, divided by cables of cobalt blue and white filigree, 3.25" dia	3000	4000

	LOW	HIGH
New England Glass Co., 3-dimenstional blown yellow pear w/ peach-colored blush, pink and yellow stem, and green glass stamp on blossom end, set on round cookie base, 3" dia base	1200	1500
New England Glass Co., cruciform spoke w/ 4 spokes of ruby, pink, green, and white cog/quatrefoil canes emanating from complex ruby, white, and blue cog cane on white double-swirl latticinio ground, encircled by garland of ruby, pink, green, and white cog/quatrefoil canes, 2.875" dia	600	800
Pinchbeck, 4 men in costume of Louis XIII, on horseback near woman and child, cottage in background, 3.25" dia	1200	1500
Saint Louis, fruit bouquet, casual arrangement w/ chartreuse apple, amber apple, amber pear, and 4 ruby cherries w/ green and yellow stems, nestled on bed of spring green leaves, blossom end of apples and pear decorated w/ black stamp, arrangement set in white double-swirl latticinio funnel basket, 2.75" dia	1000	1500
Saint Louis, upright bouquet, white clematis w/ complex cog cane center atop a gathering of 4 lampwork blossoms in salmon, yellow, cobalt blue, and white, on bed of light green leaves w/ 3-dimensional stem extending to star-cut ground, inside blue and white lace filigree torsade, 6 side facets, 2.75" dia	2500	3500
Sandwich Glass Co., poinsettia w/ double tier of 5 salmon petals around Persian blue, white, red, and green complex cog/star cane in amethyst cup, stalk w/ forest green leaves, blue and white jasper ground, 3" dia	800	1200
Val Saint Lambert, pansy w/ 2 amethyst upper petals and 3 yellow-striped amethyst lower petals around yellow center, on stalk w/ green and gray leaves, over opaque black ground, arrangement encircled by pink and white spiral torsade, 3.5" dia	900	1200

Modern

Charles Kaziun II, double overlay, 15-petal yellow crimp rose w/ stamen cupped in 4 emerald green leaves, inside turquoise-over-white double overlay, 6 and 1 faceting, complex signature cane w/ millefiori hearts under flower, 2.375" dia	$4000	$4500
Chris Buzzini, blue lupine w/ 3 spikes of pink and amethyst blossoms, growing by 3 white wallflowers w/ yellow stamens, brown stems w/ 2 types of green leaves and roots, signed and dated, limited edition of 75, 1989, 3.125" dia	500	1000
Debbie Tarsitano, fantasy flower w/ alternating amethyst and white petals around blue and yellow center, stem w/ emerald green leaves and spiraling tendrils, star-cut ground, 6 and 1 faceting, signature cane, 2.75" dia	600	800
Paul Stankard, violets composed of white petals w/ delicate purple stripes around yellow center, stems w/ purple and white buds and heart-shaped yellow-green leaves, signed and dated, 1979, 3" dia	2000	2400
Paul Ysart, millefiori, heart-shaped arrangement of pink and white complex cog canes outlined in white, pink, and emerald complex cog canes, floating inside cobalt blue and emerald stave basket, signature cane, 2.8125" dia	800	1200
Rick Ayotte, Baltimore oriole w/ bright orange plumage perched on oak tree branch w/ 2 acorns and green leaves, opaque white ground, limited edition of 50, 1982, 2.625" dia	750	1000
Saint Louis, patterned millefiori w/ spaced complex canes in red, pink, chartreuse, royal blue, cadmium green, and white, divided by white filigree cables on opaque thalo blue ground, signature/date cane, limited edition of 400, 1972, 3.25" dia	600	800

Pressed Glass

Small, crude objects and feet for footed bowls were first hand-pressed in England in the early 1800s, but pressing glass with machinery appears to have originated in America. Glass companies began producing pressed glass in matching tableware sets during the 1840s.

Although identification of pieces is mainly by pattern name, there is some confusion in this area. Most of the original names have been discarded by advanced collectors who have renamed the pattern in descriptive terms. Manufacturers' marks are exceedingly rare and there are few catalogs available from the period before 1850. By studying the old catalogs that do exist, along with shards found at old factory sites, some sketchy information has been provided. But because the competition quickly copied patterns, absolute verification of the manufacturer is impossible.

Earlier pieces contain many imperfections: bubbles, lumps, impurities and sometimes cloudiness. Reproductions pose a problem to the beginning collector. Two popular patterns, Bellflower and Daisy and Button, have been reproduced extensively. With careful, informed scrutiny, collectors can detect the dullness and lack of sparkle characteristic of remakes. If the reproduction was made from a new mold (formed from an original object), the details will not possess the clarity and precision of the original article. For further information see *The Collector's Encyclopedia of Pattern Glass* by Mollie Helen McCain (Collector Books, Paducah, KY, 1982, 1998 value update) and *Standard Encyclopedia of Pressed Glass: 1860-1930* by Bill Edwards and Mike Carwile (Collector Books, Paducah, KY, 1999).

Spanish American (Admiral Dewey) Water Pitchers, ½ gal, 9.5" h, left to right: Cannonball base; Bullet base. —Photo courtesy Gene Harris Antique Auction Center, Inc.

Beveled Diamond and Star

	CLEAR	RUBY STAIN
Celery Vase	$40	$80
Compote, open, high, scalloped rim, 7.675" dia	40	150
Creamer, 5.5" h	35	125
Decanter, patterned stopper, 10.75" h	60	150
Goblet	35	60
Plate	10	20
Spoonholder, scalloped rim, footed	25	60
Sugar Bowl, covered	30	75
Toothpick Holder	25	65
Tumbler, flat, 3.75" h	15	30
Water Pitcher, scalloped rim, pressed handle, ½ gal, 7.375" h	50	150
Water Pitcher, tankard, applied handle, footed, ½ gal, 11.5" h	45	125

Deer and Pinetree

	AMBER	BLUE	CLEAR	GREEN
Butter Dish, covered, flat	$100	$120	$90	$135
Celery Vase	—	—	95	—
Creamer, 5.5" h	100	95	75	100
Goblet	—	—	50	—
Marmalade Jar, covered, plain foot, 6.25" h	—	—	140	—
Milk Pitcher, 1 qt	—	—	135	—
Pickle Dish, oblong, flat, 7.125" x 4.375"	—	—	15	35
Platter, oblong, rounded handles, 13" x 7.875"	100	100	80	100
Sauce Dish, oblong, footed, 2.625" h, 4.5" x 3.5"	—	—	25	—
Sugar Bowl, covered	—	—	100	—

Dewey

	AMBER	CHOCOLATE	CLEAR	GREEN	VASELINE
Bowl, berry, footed, 8" d	$80	$250	$60	$85	$100
Butter Dish, covered, 1/4 lb, 4" dia.	60	200	40	60	70
Butter Dish, covered, 5" dia.	100	350	60	100	100
Creamer, covered, individual size, 4" h	40	90	20	50	50
Creamer, 5" h	60	280	30	70	75
Cruet, w/ stopper	125	1000	80	150	180
Plate, footed, 7.5" dia	40	—	30	50	60
Salt and Pepper, pair	100	—	60	100	125
Sauce Dish, flat	30	60	20	40	40
Spoonholder, 5" h	40	175	30	50	60
Sugar, covered, individual size, 2.5" dia	50	100	30	60	65
Sugar, covered, 4" dia	80	400	50	95	100
Tray, serpentine	50	400	30	50	60
Tumbler, flat	50	—	40	60	65

Oregon

	CLEAR
Bowl, 7" d	$12
Bread Plate, oval, 11.25" x 7.875"	30
Butter Dish, covered, patterned scalloped rim	60
Butter Dish, covered, plain rim	40
Cakestand, high, scalloped rim, 5.75" h, 9.75" dia	50
Celery Vase	25
Compote, covered, high, 11.25" h, 8.25" dia	45
Compote, open, high, saucer bowl w/ scalloped rim, 7.25" dia	28
Goblet, 6" h	50
Jelly Compote, open, high, 5" d	25
Milk Pitcher, scalloped rim, footed, 1 qt, 9.125" h	40
Mug, pressed handle	30
Pickle Dish, boat-shaped	12
Relish	12
Syrup	60
Table Set, creamer, covered sugar, and spoonholder	80
Toothpick Holder	50
Tumbler, flat	24

Thousand Eye

	AMBER	BLUE	CLEAR	GREEN	VASELINE
Bowl, flat, 5" dia	$40	$50	$40	—	$55
Bowl, flat, 8" dia	50	60	50	—	65
Butter Dish, covered, round, footed	95	100	75	$100	125
Cakestand, high, 10" dia.	60	65	40	80	100
Celery Vase, scalloped rim, footed, 3-knob stem	50	50	45	60	65
Compote, high, scrolled stem, round foot, 6.375" h, 8" sq	45	50	40	60	60
Compote, low, scalloped rim, 3-knob stem, 2.75" h, 6" dia	45	50	35	60	70
Creamer, pressed handle, 6" h	40	60	40	80	80
Cruet, w/ stopper	50	60	40	60	65
Goblet	65	75	45	80	90
Jelly Compote, high, scalloped rim, knobbed stem, 5.5" dia	40	40	25	45	40
Milk Pitcher, covered, 7" h	100	120	80	120	125
Mug, 3.5" h, 2.625" dia	25	30	20	35	35
Pickle Dish	30	30	20	30	30
Plate, 8" sq	30	30	25	30	30
Platter, oblong, 8" x 11"	45	45	40	50	50
Platter, oval, 11" l	75	60	40	85	75
Sauce Dish, flat, 4" dia	12	15	10	20	18
Sugar Bowl, covered, 5" h	50	65	45	75	65
Syrup, pewter top	80	90	50	100	85
Toothpick Holder, hat	40	60	30	50	50
Tray, oval, 14" l	70	75	60	80	80
Tumbler, flat	30	50	20	50	45
Water Pitcher, scalloped foot, ½ gal, 8.125" h	90	100	65	90	90

Wildflower

	AMBER	BLUE	CLEAR	GREEN	VASELINE
Bowl, 2" h, 6.75" sq	$25	$30	$20	$30	$25
Bowl, 2.375" h, 7.625" sq	25	35	20	35	30
Butter Dish, covered, footed	45	55	40	50	50
Cake Basket, oblong, hinged metal handle, 5.125" h, 10.75" x 7.75"	85	95	50	95	80
Cake Stand, high, 7.25" h, 10.25" dia	50	75	45	50	50
Celery Vase, scalloped rim, footed	50	60	30	65	60
Compote, covered, high, 8" dia	80	90	45	90	75
Compote, open, high, 10.5" sq	80	90	45	90	75
Goblet	20	40	35	45	40
Platter, oblong, scalloped rim, 10.875" x 8.25"	40	45	30	50	35
Salt and Pepper, pair, pewter tops	50	75	40	125	80
Sauce Dish, footed, 4" dia	10	15	8	18	12
Spoonholder, footed	30	35	18	40	40
Syrup, applied handle, hinged tin top	100	140	80	150	125
Water Pitcher, scalloped rim, footed, ½ gal, 8.75" h	50	60	40	80	70

Sandwich Glass

In 1820, Deming Jarves founded The Boston and Sandwich Glass Company in Sandwich, Massachusetts. The company manufactured lamps, cruets and half pint jugs and was a pioneer in the glass pressing method. Up until 1840, the company specialized in "lacy glass," but moved on to incorporate colored, cut and opalescent glass into its repertoire. Striking colors are highly prized, including amethyst purple and emerald green. Be forewarned that the tiniest chips greatly affect the value. Also beware of the many high-quality reproductions available. Probably the best place to learn more about this glass is the Sandwich Glass Museum at the site of the original company on Cape Cod.

For additional information consult the multivolume sets entitled *The Glass Industry in Sandwich* and *A Guide to Sandwich Glass* by Raymond E. Barlow and Joan E. Kaiser (Schiffer, Atglen, PA). Cup Plate numbers refer to Ruth Webb Lee and James H. Rose's *American Glass Cup Plates.* Salt numbers are from L. W. Neal and D. B. Neal's *Pressed Glass Salt Dishes of the Lacy Period, 1825-1850.*

Tulip Vases, light amethyst, octagonal base, minor base chips, 10" h, price for pair, $1840 at auction. —Photo courtesy Skinner, Inc., Boston, MA.

	LOW	HIGH
Candlestick, clear, #1 lacy socket applied by wafer to solid stepped base, 1828-35, 6.5" h	$600	$1000
Candlesticks, canary yellow, petal sockets applied by wafers to bases, 1850-65, 7.5" h, price for pair	1000	2000
Cologne, w/ stopper, pressed, Panel and Star pattern, overlay, blue cut to clear, marked "23" on stopper and base, 7" h	3000	4000
Cup Plate, pressed, lacy, electric blue, 3.5625" dia, R-565-B	100	150
Cup Plate, pressed, lacy, gray-blue, 3.5" dia, R-240	500	700
Cup Plate, pressed, lacy, peacock blue, 3.375" dia, R-40	400	550
Cup Plate, pressed, opaque white, 3.25" dia, R-37	450	650
Hyacinth Vase, free-blown, silvery opaque blue w/ darker striations, tooled mouth, bulbous body, applied to base w/ folded rim and pontil, 8.75" h	1400	1800
Salt, opalescent pale blue w/ light mottling, 2.5" h, RP-2	600	1000
Salt, opaque white, rectangular, 1840-50, 2.25" h, 3" l, EE-3b	1400	1800
Salt, purple-blue, boat-shaped, 1830-40, BT-4b	1200	1600
Tulip Lamp, pressed, clambroth font applied by large wafer to blue columnar standard and square stepped base, 1845-70, 12.25" h	750	1250
Tulip Vase, violet color, made from 8-paneled tumbler, flared crimped rim, pulled body, sheared polished base, 7.75" h	500	1000

Scandinavian Glass

Scandinavian Glass is a generic term for glassware made in Denmark, Finland, and Sweden between the 1920s and the 1960s. Key manufacturers are Kosta Glasbruk and Orrefors. Highly desirable designers include Hald, Landberg, Lindstrand, Lundgren, Lundin, and Palmqvist.

Vase, heavy-walled, internally decorated w/ fish among seaweed, base inscribed "Orrefors Graal No. 558N Edvard Hald," c1940, 4.75" h, $748 at auction. —Photo courtesy Skinner, Inc., Boston, MA.

	LOW	HIGH
Bowl, cylindrical, cased glass, checkered and triangular cobalt blue and clear, acid-etched "Orrefors, Ariel no. 167H, Ingeborg, Lunden, 5.5" h, 6.5" dia	$800	$1200
Bowl, flared rim, disk foot, blue glass internally decorated w/ clear loops, base inscribed "Orrefors Graal 2109-E6 Edvard Hald," 2.25" h, 6" dia	1000	1500
Bowl, flared rim, exterior in mottled speckled violet, blue, and green, etched artist signature and number, foil label, Kosta Boda, 6.5" h, 9.5" dia	100	200
Bowl, flaring quatreform, pale blue w/ controlled bubbles throughout, acid-etched "Orrefors (artist signature)," 4" h, 6" w	400	600
Bowl, heavy-walled w/ flattened rim, ribbed w/ 14 arches between columns, clear, base inscribed "Orrefors-GL 4573-14," paper label, 5.5" h, 9.25" dia	100	250
Bowl, shallow, free-form, white, smoky amethyst, and clear spiraled ribbons, inscribed "Leerdam, M" on pontil, paper label, c1950, 1.75" h, 10" l	150	250
Bowl, wide flared rim on cylindrical body, radiating trapped bubble pattern in clear and opaque white, base inscribed "Boda afors B Vallien," 3.5" h, 7.5" dia	250	500
Tumbler, thick-walled, clear w/ interior diagonal lines, acid-etched "L. Fraucek" and number, 3" h, 3.5" dia	100	200
Vase, classic cylinder shape, flying blue ducks on white and gray ground, gold accent powders between clear surrounding glass, base inscribed "Hadeland"	200	500
Vase, gourd-shaped, clear w/ black and white vertical lines, etched "LH1257," Vicktor Lindstrand for Kosta, 10.5" h, 2.5" dia	100	200
Vase, heavy-walled flattened ovoid form, clear glass internally decorated w/ aubergine spiral lines, base inscribed "Kosta LH 1384," attributed to Vicke Lindstrom, c1955, 5.5" h	400	600
Vase, molded as stepped and ridged ice block, clear, base inscribed "Tapio Wirrkala 3429," 9.125" h	600	800
Vase, tall tapering 3-sided form, sommerso w/ green interior, acid-etched "Orrefors N U 35381," foil label, 15.25" h, 3.5" w	400	600
Vase, tapered cylinder, transparent olive w/ 6 applied free-form medallions, etched "Hadeland, 7020, S. B.," designed by Severin Brorby, 11" h, 7.5" dia	300	500
Vase, tear-shaped, 4-sided, sommerso w/ green interior, acid-etched "Orrefors N U 3538-2, 10" h, 5" w	200	400
Vase, tear-shaped, sommerso w/ cranberry interior and striated white bands, Vicktor Lindstrand for Kosta, 6.75" h, 4.5" dia	400	600

Steuben Glass

The Steuben Glass Company has concentrated on producing fine art glass since its founding in 1903. The Corning Glass Works purchased the company in 1918. Steuben pieces are marked with either the letter "S" or the entire name "Steuben" scratched neatly and in tiny letters on the underside of the base. The model number is usually scratched there as well. For more information see *Frederick Carder and Steuben Glass* by Thomas P. Dimitroff, et al. (Schiffer, Atglen, PA, 1998).

	LOW	HIGH
Basket, ruffled form, blue aurene w/ strong luster, coiled prunt at applied handle, catalog #5069, 7" h	$800	$1000
Bowl, flared scalloped rim, calcite w/ gold iridescent interior, 2" h	150	300
Bowl, grotesque, 3-lined pillar-molded floriform body w/ ruffled rim, clear, catalog #7534, 6.75" h	250	500
Bowl, scalloped rim, amethyst quartz cintra, mottled and crackled pink, blue, and frosted clear body w/ 3 applied leafy branches connecting to branching feet, fleur-de-lis mark on base, catalog #6856, 6" h, 7.25" dia	1000	1500
Basket, verre de soie, iridized silky glass w/ berry prunt at applied handle, catalog #5069, 14.25" h	800	1000
Bud Vase, stick-form, flattened disk foot, blue aurene, inscribed "Aurene," 7.75" h	250	500
Candlestick, clear decorated w/ Pomona green cintra rim wraps, disk, and 4 berry prunts, base stamped "Steuben," catalog #3374, 10.25" h	300	500
Ceiling Light, round bowl-shaped fixture, calcite etched w/ classical foliate design radiating from center, 3 sockets, 3 attached hooks, 15.75" dia	600	800
Centerpiece Figure, Kuan Yin, figural Buddhist goddess atop 2-tiered flower arranger, alabaster, catalog #6637, 9" h	400	600
Cocktail Set, consisting of jug w/ stopper and 6 handled cups, clear w/ applied mirror black threads, jug w/ fleur-de-lis mark and monogrammed "H. W. N.," catalog #7056, 9.5" h jug	300	500
Compotes, translucent green jade above applied alabaster white stems and disk feet, 1 w/ fleur-de-lis stamp, other w/ gold paper label, catalog #3234, 3" h, 7" dia, price for pair	500	700
Creamer and Sugar, crystal, John Dreves design, each inscribed "Steuben," catalog #7906 and #7907, 4" h creamer, 3.75" h sugar	200	400
Dinnerware, consisting of 6 each 7" plates, stemmed water goblets, and champagnes, Cut Star and Punty pattern w/ engraved moon and star motif, Bolas Mankowski design, bases inscribed "S" or "Steuben," c1934	500	750
Figure, fox seated w/ tail wrapped, crystal, Lloyd Atkins design, base inscribed "Steuben," catalog #8260, c1971, 8.75" h	1000	1200
Figure, owl w/ frosted eyes, crystal, Donald Polland design, base inscribed "Steuben," catalog #8064, 5.25" h	200	400
Figure, stylized Clydesdale horse, crystal, Sidney Waugh design, inscribed "Steuben," catalog #7727, 1930s, 7" h, 9.75" l	1000	1200
Figure, upright squirrel w/ extended tail, crystal, George Thompson design, inscribed "Steuben," catalog #8291, 6" h	700	900
Figures, geese, watchful gander and preening goose, crystal, Lloyd Atkins design, catalog #8519, 5.25" h gander, 4" l goose, price for pair	300	500
Figures, leaping Art Deco gazelles on molded rectangular plinths w/ stylized curvilinear waves, crystal, Frederick Carder and Sydney Waugh design, inscribed "Steuben," catalog #7399, 6.5" h, 7.5" l, price for pair	1200	1400
Goblets, flared rims, Oriental Poppy w/ swirled optic rib design, pink opalescent w/ opalescent stem and foot, 5.75" h, price for pair	600	800

	LOW	HIGH
Lamp Base, classic urn-form, purple moss agate, swirled purple, red, and blue moss agate shaft, gilt-metal lamp fitting w/ acanthus leaf decoration, purple glass jewel finial, 10" h	2400	2800
Lamp Shades, bell-form w/ 10 ribs, gold aurene, rims marked "Steuben," 4.5" h, 3.75" dia outside rim, price for 4	600	800
Lemonade Mug, Matsu Noke, optic-ribbed goblet-form, clear w/ Pomona green cintra rim, handle, and 3 fan-shaped decorations, catalog #3329, 6" h	200	400
Paperweight/Doorstop, solid crystal w/ controlled bubbles and silvered cushion centering 5-petaled bright pink cintra lily blossom, fleur-de-lis stamp on base, catalog #7257, 4" h, 4.5" dia	200	400
Vase, baluster form, delicate blue peacock feathers pulled through gold aurene ground, base inscribed "Aurene 261," catalog #261, 8" h	4000	5000
Vase, broad oval body, cluthra, rose pink, white, and clear surround, fleur-de-lis mark on base, catalog #2683, 10.5" h	1200	1500
Vase, broad oval body, yellow jade cameo-etched w/ overall blanket of flowers decoration, raised neck w/ blue aurene lava dripping over acid-etched body, catalog #7014	8000	10,000
Vase, flared rim on oval body, Black Matzu acid-etched w/ 3 full-length Ming trees under stylized cloud formations, triangular foil label on base, catalog #6391, 12" h	1000	1200
Vase, grotesque, pillar-ribbed abstract rectangular form, deep cobalt jade, fleur-de-lis mark at pontil, 6.5" h, 12.5" w, 6.25" d	3000	4000
Vase, lily-form w/ 6-scallop rim, iridized white calcite exterior, gold aurene interior, catalog #346, 8.25" h	500	700
Vase, ribbed urn-form body, lightly iridized ivrene w/ 3 applied aqua cintra handles, thin brush line of opaque white encircling widest point, base inscribed "Steuben," catalog #7568, 11.25" h	1200	1500
Vase, urn-form w/ flared rim, ribbed body, and disk foot, celeste blue, polished pontil, "Steuben" and fleur-de-lis mark at base, 7" h	300	500

Steuben Glass at Auction, left to right: Millefiore Vase, style J baluster-form, gold aurene internally decorated w/ green hearts and vines intersperced w/ cluster of white blossoms, platinum gold iridescence overall, catalog #573, 5" h, $2760; Blue Aurene Vase, 10-rib body, iridescent luster, 5" h, $1093; Gold Aurene Vase, flared rim, 6-sided, catalog #6241, 8.25" h, $690; Blue Aurene Vase, flared 10-rib body, iridescent, 5.5" h, $546; Gold Aurene Potpourri Jar, catalog #2812, 5.75" h, $633. —Photo courtesy Skinner, Inc., Boston, MA.

Hatboxes

The wallpaper decorated hatboxes of the early nineteenth century are rare finds. Those in good condition with a minimum of slight tears and no loss of original paper command high prices. The values given below are based on examples appearing in New England auctions.

	LOW	HIGH
Birds, amidst foliate and architectural view w/ swags, 19th C, 10.375" h, 16.75" l	$400	$600
Brick House, farmyard and trees in background, road in foreground, reds and browns on blue ground, c1830, 11" h	800	1000
"Castle Garden," red, brown, white, and green on blue ground, bottom signed in ink "Joel Post," 23" l	3000	4000
"Clayton's Ascent," hot air balloons in flight, labeled on underside of lid "From J. M. Hurlbert's paste board band box manufactory no. 25 Court Street, Boston," early 19th C, 12.25" h, 17.75" l, 12.5" d	1000	1200
Drapery Swag, 3 roses and vase design, c1830, 10.5" h	500	700
Eagle, top of lid w/ eagle and partially printed text above and below, sides of lid and box w/ blue and white paper w/ diamond motif and applied red, white, and green horizontal paper bands, inside lined w/ green, black, and white wallpaper, c1825, 2.25" h, 2.625" dia	500	800
Floral Design, lid w/ small blue and white flowers on brown ground, sides w/ large yellow and white flowers on blue shading to white ground, c1825, 4.5" h, 9.25" l, 6.375" d	500	800
Floral Design, red and gold on light blue ground, newspaper-lined, 5" l	300	500
Flowers, w/ bowls of fruit and foliage, white, brown, black, and faded red on blue ground, lined w/ 1835 newspaper, printed label "Warranted Nailed Band-Boxes Made by Hannah Davis, Jaffrey N.H.," 20" l	600	900
Harbor Scene, w/ eagle and foliage scrolls, green, gray, black, and white, 17.25" l	400	700
"Heraea Games," block printed, c1830, 10.75" h, 14" l	400	600
Scrolled Foliage, pink and purple on brown ground, c1825, 2.25" h, 3.125" dia	700	1000
Scrollwork, orange and white on blue ground, inside lined w/ newspapers dated 1841 and 1845, 9.5" h, 15.875" l, 10.75" d	2000	2500
Seascape, pastoral vignettes, floral background, attributed to Hannah Davis, Jaffrey, NH, c1850, 14" h	300	500
Stagecoach, amidst hunters, 11" h, 17.75" l	200	300

Left to right: Clayton's Ascent; Birds, amidst foliate and architectural view; Stagecoach, amidst hunters. —Photo courtesy Skinner, Inc., Boston, MA.

Holiday Collectibles

Holidays are special events, times when we can get together with friends and family, exchange gifts, observe religious rites or dress in outrageous costumes. Collectors of holiday items can choose from a wealth of material. Many collectors focus on one holiday, such as Christmas or Halloween. Others prefer to specialize in a type of item, such as postcards. Whatever the method, displaying your finds is great fun and collecting can be enjoyed year round. For further information we recommend *Holiday Collectables: A Price Guide* by Pauline and Dan Campanelli (L-W Books, Gas City, IN, 1997), *Christmas Through the Decades* by Robert Brenner (Schiffer , Atglen, PA, 1993), *Collectible Halloween* by Pamela E. Apkarian-Russell (Schiffer, Atglen, PA, 1997), *Romantic Valentines* by Dan and Pauline Campanelli (L-W Book Sales, Gas City, IN, 1996), and *Valentine Treasury* by Robert Brenner (Schiffer, Atglen, PA, 1997).

Christmas

Figural Light Bulbs

	LOW	AVG	HIGH
Apple, painted white milk glass	$20	$25	$30
Beach Ball, red and blue, Japan, c1940	20	25	30
Bell, w/ Santa face, painted white milk glass	15	20	25
Betty Boop, c1940	75	85	100
Bird, painted white milk glass, Japan, c1940	20	25	30
Bird House, cardinal inside	25	32	40
Candle, bubble light, c1948	8	12	15
Clown, roly-poly base, red cap and ruffled collar, blue body	90	110	130
Clown Bust, bald, yellow ruffled collar, red shoulders	25	32	40
Cottage, snowy roof, painted white milk glass, Japan, c1940	15	20	25
Dick Tracy, c1940	75	85	100
Drum, green and black, Japan, c1940	25	32	40
Dutch Girl, red scarf, green dress, white apron	50	65	80
Elephant, seated, raised trunk, painted white milk glass	40	50	60
Father Christmas, holding staff and small tree, red and white, Germany, c1915	35	42	50
Flower, painted white milk glass, Japan, c1940	30	35	40
Frog, painted white milk glass, green, Japan	75	100	125
Grape Cluster, purple, European, c1910	30	35	40
Horseshoe, horse head inside	90	110	130
Jack and Jill, c1940	200	225	250
Jackie Coogan, red cap, pants, and suspenders, white shirt	70	85	100
Japanese Lantern	10	15	20
Jester Head, sad expression, red cap, white face, paper insulator, Germany, c1910	150	165	180
Kewpie, white milk glass, painted facial features	35	42	50
Lion, holding pipe, red jacket, blue vest, green pants, Japan, c1940	45	55	65
Little Boy Blue	30	35	40
Little Jack Horner, c1950	125	140	165
Peacock	50	65	80
Pelican, painted white milk glass, Japan	75	85	100
Pinecone, European	10	15	20
Scotty Dog, seated, red	35	42	50
Stocking, green, puppy inside	75	85	100
Three Men in a Tub, painted white milk glass	100	110	125

Left: Cardboard and Honeycomb Diecut, c1910, 14.5" h, $125.

Right: Santa Sack Candy Container, diecut cardboard, 10" h, $50.

Glass Ornaments

	LOW	AVG	HIGH
Airplane, unsilvered deep pink, wire-wrapped, double wings, wire tinsel prop and tail, chalk Santa w/ paper face, c1915-20, 7.5"	$80	$100	$125
Amelia Earhart, pearly white, black, and pearly blue, c1930, 3.5"	200	275	350
Barrel, silver w/ 4 gold molded bands and 2 raised red roses w/ green leaves, wire-wrapped, c1910, 3"	85	110	130
Candle, on clip, pearly white, red flame and trim, c1920, 4"	125	150	175
Clown Head, pearly white w/ red, pink, and green, c1910-20, 2.25"	125	150	175
Cornucopia, pearly pink cornucopia w/ red and green raised flowers, pebbly back, c1920, 2"	25	35	45
Crested Bird, on clip, pearly white body w/ blue and gold wings, gold crest, and red neck, bill, and eyes, spun glass tail, c1910, 5.25" l w/ tail	20	30	40
Flapper Head, pearly white hat, blue brim, light gold hair, matte flesh face, c1920, 2.5"	175	225	275
Foxy Grandpa Head, stylized body, pearly white, gold, white frosting, silver, and pink, c1920, 5.25"	85	110	130
Frog, pearly white w/ green shading, black eyes, and red mouth, c1920, 3.25"	50	65	80
Girl in Bag, pearly white face, gold hair, red bag, c1920, 3.5"	75	95	125
House, silver w/ green shading, matte white, c1920, 2.75"	20	25	30
Jester Bell, pearly pink and white, pearly white face, c1920, 3"	75	95	125
Lady's Slipper, silver w/ gold bow and buttons, red trim, c1920, 3"	30	50	70
Lemon, unsilvered, pale yellow, c1910, 3"	20	30	40
Monkey, seated, dressed, pearly silver w/ black eyes, c1900-10, 3.25"	150	225	300
Pig, w/ clover on tummy, pearly white, red ears and mouth, black eyes, pale gold clover, c1920, 3.75"	150	200	250
Santa, red w/ silver, pink blush face, green on tree, chenille legs, composition boots, 4.25"	75	100	125
Spaniel, seated, pearly white body w/ gold shading, black eyes, and red mouth, ribbon, ears, and tail, c1930, 3"	35	45	55
Sun Face, 2-sided, pearly white w/ green shading, c1920, 2.5"	150	195	250
Turkey, full figure, pearly white w/ pink shading, c1910, 2.25"	120	145	180
Walnut, green, c1910, 1.75"	15	18	25

Miscellaneous

	LOW	AVG	HIGH
Bank, Santa at chimney, plaster, c1950s, 11" h	$60	$80	$100
Candy Container, Santa in car, celluloid	60	80	100
Crèche, 17 papier-mâché figures, wooden stable, c1930	110	140	170
Dresden Ornament, swan, embossed cardboard, 1880s-1900s	125	175	225
Garland String, glass, 1920s-30s	25	35	45
Greeting Card, "A Merry Christmas to You All," family in snowy woodland, c1880	3	4	5
Greeting Card, "Season's Greetings," mechanical, boy w/ flowers, 19th C	15	20	25
Lamp, figural Santa, hard plastic, c1955, 16" h	25	35	45
Pinback Button, "Santa Claus Gave This To Me," c1940s, 5" dia	10	12	14
Pinback Button, Santa reading a book entitled *Good Boys–Good Girls,* 1" dia	10	12	14
Plate, child's ABC, features children and snowman	80	100	120
Postcard, embossed, Santa wearing brown robe w/ gold highlights and twig crown, holding pine tree staff, angel sitting on shoulder, published by P. F. B., #9103	30	45	60
Postcard, hold-to-light, child chasing turkey, illuminated fruit, clothing, and decorative elements	100	150	200
Roly Poly Santa, composition, Schoenhut, early 1900s	250	350	450
Scrap Ornament, Father Christmas, spun glass skirt	60	90	120
Snowdome, figural Santa and reindeer w/ dome center, plastic, c1950s, 5" h	18	21	24
Stocking, cloth, Victorian	80	100	120
Tree, bottle brush, Japan, c1950	4	5	6
Tree, goose feathers, Germany, early 20th C, 58" h	400	500	600
Tree Topper, scrap angel, spun glass halo, late 1940s	30	40	50

Left: German Belsnickle Candy Container, $330 at auction. —Photo courtesy Collectors Auction Services.

Right: Celluloid Santa, 4.25" h, $45.

Easter

	LOW	AVG	HIGH
Basket, wood, painted flowers, "Made in Germany" paper label on base, 10" h w/ handle, 6" dia	$15	$20	$25
Candy Container, chick, papier-mâché, glass eyes, wire spring feet, c1930	125	175	225
Candy Container, Easter egg, cardboard, red, gold, and white, c1940	20	25	30
Candy Container, rabbit, pressed cardboard, removable head	90	110	120
Chocolate Mold, standing rabbit, 2-part mold w/ separate molds for ears and forelegs, Anton Reiche, Dresden, Germany, 18.5" h	150	200	250
Cookie Cutter, egg shape, tin, late 19th C	5	7	10
Egg Cup, figural bunny and egg, plastic, c1950s, 3" h	4	6	8
Figure, rabbit emerging from egg, composition, 6.5" h	50	65	80
Greeting Card, cross on reef in sea, by Carter & Karrick, 19th C	3	4	5
Greeting Card, girl climbing out of egg, fringed, Germany, 19th C	5	7	9
Mask, rabbit's face, heavy papier-mâché, 11" h	20	25	30
Nodder, rabbit, brown-flocked chalkware, marked "USA," 1950s, 5" h	15	20	25
Postcard, dressed rabbit family painting Easter eggs, hold-to-light illuminates eggs, lantern, and light rays	50	75	100
Postcard, embossed, divided back, Series 1520a, Germany	5	8	12
Roly Poly, rabbit on ball, celluloid, purple clothes, Japan, 4.5" h	20	25	30
Toy, rabbit, fur-covered tin, windup, hops, Japan, 5" h	50	60	75
Toy, rabbit pulling cart, tinplate, Chein	75	85	95

Halloween

	LOW	AVG	HIGH
Candleholder, devil on chicken's foot, metal, c1910	$250	$300	$350
Candy Container, jack-o'-lantern, composition, orange w/ black trim, early 20th C	50	75	100
Candy Container, witch, papier-mâché, cone-shaped, West Germany	25	30	35
Costume, gorilla, gauze mask, Collegetown Costumes, c1940s	40	45	50
Costume, Porky Pig, cloth suit and cap, plastic mask, 1950s	25	30	35
Costume, Star Trek, Mr. Spock, 1967	40	55	70
Decoration, witch and black cat dancers, accordion-fold crepe paper, 1960s, 28" l	17	19	21
Diecut, cat on moon, cardboard, © H. D. Lehrs, 14" h	28	35	45
Eyeglasses, figural hissing black cats, plastic	25	30	35
Fan, black cat, orange tissue, Germany, 1920	20	25	30
Figure, black cat w/ arched back, standing on die, celluloid, Japan, 3.5"	50	75	100
Figure, pumpkin man, wire neck, 5.5" h	20	25	30
Game, Whirl-O-Halloween Fortune and Stunt Game, card w/ spinner, 7" x 9"	30	40	50
Hat, orange and black crepe paper	8	10	12
Horn, litho tin, marked "USA"	15	20	25
Jack-O'-Lantern, papier-mâché, painted eyes and mouth, vinyl bail handle, 5.5" h	50	75	100
Lantern, devil's head, papier-mâché, 2-tone red, paper insert behind cutout eyes and mouth, wire bail handle, Germany, 7" h	75	100	125
Light Set, jack-o'-lanterns, celluloid, Noma, 1920s	650	750	850
Mask, luminous face, gauze	25	30	35
Noisemaker, cylinder, shake-type, litho tin, jack-o'-lanterns and witches, c1950, 4" dia	12	14	16

	LOW	AVG	HIGH
Noisemaker, paddle-type, litho tin, w/ jack-o'-lantern, c1940s, 10" l	25	30	35
Noisemaker, wood ratchet, small black composition cat on top, 5.5"	50	75	100
Party Favor, basket, black and orange plastic, c1950s, 3.5" dia	10	12	15
Party Favor, pumpkin, orange plastic, w/ metal bail handle, c1950s, 3.5" dia	6	8	10
Pez Container, Witch "A"	130	165	200
Postcard, embossed, child lifting top off jack-o'-lantern, design by Freixas, published by Winsch, 1914	100	125	150
Postcard, "Halloween Greetings," woman bobbing for apples, jack-o'-lantern border, E. C. Bans, 1909	12	15	18
Tambourine, litho tin, orange w/ black Halloween symbols, 1940s, 6" dia	30	35	40
Trick-or-Treat Bag, litho paper, "Happy Halloween," pumpkin head, 1940	15	20	25

Turkey Candy Container, papier-mâché, $50.

Thanksgiving

Candlesticks, pair, cornucopia shape, ceramic, 3" h	$12	$15	$18
Candlesticks, pair, pilgrims, ceramic, 2" h	10	12	14
Candy Container, cornucopia, papier-mâché, c1910	50	60	70
Candy Container, turkey, composition, c1930s	20	30	35
Centerpiece, turkey, Hallmark, c1940	10	12	14
Cornucopia, wicker	12	15	20
Platter, tom turkey design, Japan, c1935	15	18	21
Postcard, Brundage	15	23	28
Postcard, Clapsaddle	8	10	12

Valentine's Day

Valentine, children, mechanical pull-down, Germany, c1915	$6	$8	$10
Valentine, children picking heart-shaped apples from tree, "Hearts Are Ripe"	3	5	7
Valentine, cottage, mechanical pull-out and stand-up, Germany, c1910	12	15	18
Valentine, "Cupid's Temple of Love," honeycomb, c1928	6	8	10
Valentine, free-standing folding easel-back, c1900	15	18	21
Valentine, Gibson Girl photo surrounded by lace, cherub heads, Meek and Son, c1890	25	35	45
Valentine, glum-looking woman sewing hat, w/ verse, Elton and Co., NY, c1880	22	26	30

	LOW	AVG	HIGH
Valentine, heart-shaped, little girl on front, folding, Tuck	12	14	16
Valentine, lacy, heart-shaped, c1905	9	12	15
Valentine, large ship, mechanical pull-down, Germany	70	80	90
Valentine, little girl holding doll, paper doll mechanical stand-up, Gibson Art, Germany	20	25	30
Valentine, little girl holding opening parasol, mechanical stand-up, German, c1920	15	20	25
Valentine, Maggie and Jiggs, c1940	18	21	24
Valentine, Popeye, c1940	18	21	24
Valentine, silver, white, and lace, 3 layer, McLoughlin, c1880	20	25	30
Valentine, steam boiler, pull-out and stand-up, German, c1910	12	15	18
Valentine, Temple of Love, young girl and butterfly, Tuck's Betsy Beauties series	12	14	16
Valentine, "To My Valentine," 2 children and verse, Tuck's Innocence Abroad series	12	14	16
Valentine, various animals, mechanical, c1930	10	12	14
Valentine, Victorian, paper lace, fold-out	20	22	24
Valentine, white, gold, and lace, 3 layer, McLoughlin, c1880	10	12	14

Various Other Holidays

Fourth of July, postcard	$5	$8	$10
Happy Birthday, greeting card, children, 19th C	2	3	4
Happy Birthday, greeting card, floral design, blue fringe, c1880	3	4	5
Happy Birthday, greeting card, maroon floral, fringed, 19th C	3	4	5
Lincoln's Birthday, postcard	8	12	15
Memorial Day, postcard	5	8	10
Washington's Birthday, postcard	5	8	10

Holiday Postcards and Greeting Cards. —Photos courtesy Postcards International.

Jewelry

Jewelry divides into two basic groups: precious and non-precious (a.k.a., costume jewelry made after 1920). U.S. custom laws define antique jewelry as jewelry over one hundred years old. Estate or Heirloom jewelry is generally assumed to be over twenty-five years old.

For further information we recommend *Answers to Questions About Old Jewelry: 1840-1950, 5th Edition* by C. Jeannenne Bell (Krause Publications, Iola, WI, 1999), *The Official Identification and Price Guide to Antique Jewelry, Sixth Edition* by Arthur Guy Kaplan (House of Collectibles, NY, 1990), and *Warman's Jewelry, 2nd Edition* by Christie Romero (Krause Publications, Iola, WI, 1998).

Costume Jewelry

Bakelite is the trade name of the plastic marketed by the Bakelite Corporation. Leo Hendrik Baekeland invented this form of phenol formaldehyde in 1909. Since then, it has been used for everything from telephones to jewelry to the heat shield on NASA's Jupiter space probe.

Bright colors matter! A brightly colored piece will command a considerably higher price than its dark brown or black couterpart.

Bakelite

	LOW	HIGH
Bangle Bracelet, 2-tone blue and green	$60	$90
Bangle Bracelet, orange, geometric motif	50	75
Bangle Bracelet, yellow w/ colored rings	40	60
Bracelet, black and tortoise links	40	60
Earrings, pair, red loops	50	75
Necklace, white and clear beads alternating w/ fruit-shaped beads including bananas, cherries, oranges, and green grapes, w/ matching earrings	75	115
Pin, bird, blue	30	45
Pin, bow, black and white w/ rhinestones	40	60
Pin, dog, red, head moves	80	120
Pin, fan w/ berries, red, 3" h	50	75
Pin, flower on stem, purple w/ white center	50	75
Pin, man, polychrome beads, signed "Jan Carlin," 6" h	120	180
Pin, owl, yellow, winking	50	75
Pin, palm tree, green	60	90
Pin, parrot, deep yellow, rhinestone eye, signed "Buch & Deichmann, Copenhagen, Denmark," 5.25" h	100	150
Pin, parrot, shaded pink	70	100
Pin, sword, yellow blade, translucent brown hilt	200	275

Other

Bangle Bracelet, hinged, set w/ large marbleized green stones, pearls, and marquise and round yellow rhinestones, signed, Hobé, c1960	$225	$300
Bracelet, agate and silver, 6 carved amber and black agate beads w/ engraved silver heart	250	325
Bracelet, iridescent clear and topaz rhinestones set in gilt-metal, 1960s	90	120
Brooch, dragon, round and marquise gray rhinestones, 2 accent pearls, 1 faux ruby eye, marked "deposé," French, 1950s	400	500
Brooch, elaborate setting of rhinestones and colored stones surrounding large faux sapphire, signed, Jomaz, 1960s	100	150

	LOW	HIGH
Brooch, floral w/ rhinestones and aquamarine-color stone, sterling silver setting, hallmarked, 1940s	150	200
Choker, double strand of malachite and fluted lapis beads w/ gilt-metal spool-shaped spacer beads	50	75
Earrings, flat pearl flowerhead w/ clustered seed pearl and rhinestone leaves and stem, signed, Miriam Haskell, 1940s	90	120
Earrings, large diamond shape w/ floral and swirl design, signed, Eisenberg	100	150
Necklace, Art Deco, rose quartz beads and green carved glass medallion w/ marcasite frame, 1930s	150	200
Necklace, multicolor crystal beads, Austrian, 1960s	200	275
Necklace, rhinestone clusters set in gold metal filigree flowers, signed, Miriam Haskell, 1950s	300	400
Pin, flower basket, painted yellow basket w/ red and blue flowers w/ rhinestone accents, signed, Trifari, 1950s	200	275
Pin, frog, gilt-metal set w/ yellow rhinestones, Nettie Rosenstein, 1950s	100	150
Pin, lily, gilt-metal w/ pavé rhinestone petals and melon-colored stones, signed, Reja	350	500
Pin, lizard, cold cast, painted yellow, marked "Austria," early 20th C	80	125
Pin, orchid, rhinestones set in gilt-metal, unsigned, Mazer, 1970s	125	175
Pin, rooster, sterling silver set w/ marcasite and pale green stones, marked "Germany Sterling," 1940s	80	125
Pin, rope knot, blue and red enamel w/ pavé rhinestone ends, Jomaz, 1960s	100	150
Pin, spray of grasses set w/ rhinestones and centered w/ large faux aquamarine, sterling silver, signed, Coro Craft, 1940s	150	200

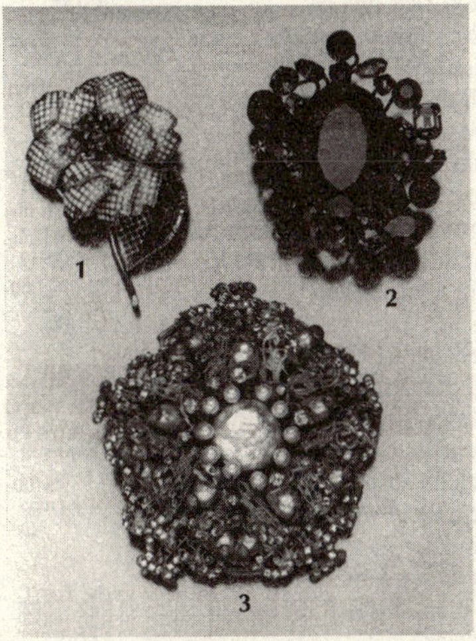

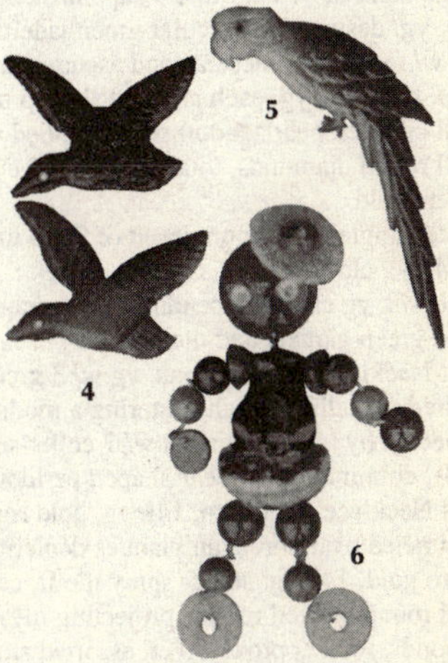

Pins: (1) Gripoix, rhinestones, white and green pâte de verre, and silver metal, c1940, $920 at auction; (2) Schiaparelli, faux amethyst and red and pink stones on bent wires, 1940s, $403 at auction; (3) Miriam Haskel, gilt filigree, faux Baroque pearl, and smaller pearls and rhinestones, 1940s, $575 at auction. —Photo courtesy William Doyle Galleries; Bakelite Pins: (4) Birds; (5) Parrot; (6) Polychrome Figure, signed "Jan Carlin." —Photo courtesy Garth's Auctions, Delaware, OH.

Estate Jewelry

Craftsmanship, aesthetic design, scarcity and current market worth of gemstones and the precious metal are principal value keys. Antique and period jewelry should be set with the cut of stone prevalent at the time the piece was made. Names (manufacturer, designer, or both) also play a major role in value.

Abbreviations: Karat *(k)*, carats *(cts)*, yellow gold *(yg)*, white gold *(wg)*, and pennyweight *(dwt)*.

	LOW	HIGH
Bangle Bracelet, 14k yg, narrow hinged band topped by 2 old mine diamonds, total approx. 1 ct	$1200	$1600
Bar Pin, platinum, filigree design set w/ 3 round diamonds at center, total approx. 1.25 cts, and 22 assorted round diamonds, total approx. 1.1 cts	1800	2400
Bar Pin, platinum, set w/ 12 round diamonds, total approx. 1.5 cts, defined by assorted calibre-cut synthetic sapphires, approx. 4.6 dwt	1000	1300
Bracelet, 14k wg, flexible band set w/ 3 navette-shaped links set w/ assorted rose-cut diamonds and centering rectangular-shaped blue stone	1300	1800
Bracelet, black and white cameo, 14k yg, designed as band of 7 square cameo plaques depicting various mythological vignettes	1700	2400
Bracelet, gold and chrysoberyl cat's-eye, flexible, 14k yg, designed as 5 spiral links each centered by small cabochon cat's-eyes, separated by figure 8 design spacers, hallmarked "FFF" for F & F Felger, Inc., Newark, NJ, retailed by Bailey Banks & Biddle, approx. 16.5 dwt	1700	2400
Bracelet, platinum, flexible band set w/ 32 box-set full-cut diamonds and 16 small single-cut diamonds, total approx. 3.5 cts, defined by step design band of 47 calibre-cut sapphires, approx. 14.1 dwt	3500	4500
Brooch, yg, designed as circular green jadeite disc, frame adorned at each side w/ red enamel accents and assorted small pearls	600	800
Earclips, pair, 18k yg, each stylized shrimp motif design clip w/ 7 rows of small cultured pearls, adorned w/ applied navette-shaped section set w/ 16 small round diamonds, total approx. .60 ct, and a cabochon ruby, sapphire, and emerald	1200	1600
Necklace, single-strand composed of 9mm uniform jade beads, fastening w/ 14k yg clasp, 17" l	1400	1800
Pendant, 18k yg chain suspending heart-shaped opal surrounded by small round green garnets and diamonds	1400	1800
Pendant Necklace, Art Nouveau, yg w/ 3 green enamel-decorated foliate-inspired medallions each centering a modified triangular-cut citrine, connected by triple chain set w/ 7 collet-set peridots and five freshwater pearls, culminating w/ pear-shaped peridot drop	2800	4000
Pendant Necklace, Victorian, 14k yg, gold rope chain suspending 3 enameled oval porcelain plaques depicting classical women	1500	2000
Pin, retro gold, 14k yg, stellar spray motif, centered by dome set w/ assorted small round faceted rubies, projecting rays set w/ 8 assorted small round diamonds, total approx. .50 ct, assorted small round faceted rubies, approx. 13.3 dwt	1600	2200
Ring, Victorian, yg, wide band supporting cabochon garnet centered by small oval opal	750	1000
Ring, yg, modified opal openwork tablet set w/ assorted rose-cut diamonds, centering upon emerald bead, approx. 6.3 dwt	500	700
Suite, pair of screwback earrings and pin, 14k red gold, each designed as budding roses, total approx. 13.6 dwt	350	500

Knives

In the 1960s, the United States government began enforcing the law requiring that knife companies mark their knives with the country of origin. This sparked a collectors craze, as dealers sought early unmarked knives. The most desirable pocketknives are those made before World War II. Collectors prefer knives in pristine condition, those neither sharpened nor cleaned.

For further information consult *The Official Price Guide to Collector Knives, Eleventh Edition* by C. Houston Price (House of Collectibles, NY, 1996) and *The Standard Knife Collector's Guide, Third Edition* by Roy Ritchie and Ron Steward (Collector Books, Paducah, KY, 1999).

	LOW	HIGH
A. Ulmer, 1869–1928	$20	$60
Baker & Hamilton, 1853–1981	15	150
Baldwin Cutlery Co., 1912–1981	15	150
Belmont Knife Co., 1920–1930	15	35
Berkshire Cutlery Co., 1890	20	45
Best English Cutlery, 1800–1860	35	130
Billings & Spencer, 1890–1914	25	150
Blue Ribbon, 1910–1950	15	65
Bridgeport Knife Co., 1904	40	150
Brown & Bigelow, 1931–1950s	25	75
Brown Camp Hardware Co., 1907–1959	25	150
Burkinshaw Knife Co., 1881–1920	35	350
Butler & Co., 1865–1952	25	120
Cameron Knife Co., 1920s	15	65
Camillus, 1902–contemp.	5	110
Canton Cutlery Co., 1879-1930	20	175
Capitol Knife Co., 1920s	15	125
Carl Klauberg & Bros., 1883–1940	10	90
Carrier Cutlery Co., 1900–1921	45	225
Car-Van Cutlery, 1911–1930	10	175
Case XX Metal Stamping Ltd., 1940s	15	75
Catskill Knife Co., 1930s	15	150
Cattaraugus, 1984–contemp.	15	50
Centaur Cutlery, 1893–1913	5	25
Challenge Cutlery Corp., 1891–1928	20	150
Clark Brothers, 1895–1929	25	125
Clauss, 1887–contemp.	10	75
Clean Cut, 1880–1912	20	95
Clearcut, 1835–1949	12	30
Clipper Cutlery Co., 1901	10	50
Colonial, 1926–contemp.	10	55
Commander, 1891–1928	65	100
Corning Knife Co., 1930s	10	50
Craftsman, 1940s–contemp.	5	65
Crescent Cutlery Co., 1917–1950	15	50
Cussins & Fearn, 1930s	25	75
Cut Sure, 1889–1962	20	150
Cutwell Cutlery Co., 1886–1945	20	200
Dame Stoddard & Co., 1901–1930	10	150
Dames & Ball, 1925–1962	65	125
Delta, 1878–1953	5	20
Depend-On-Me Cutlery Co., 1945	10	75
Dunlap, 1877–1930	25	150

	LOW	HIGH
Dunn Bros., 1927–contemp.	6	25
Dwight Divine & Sons, 1876–1941	35	175
Eagle Cutlery Co., 1883–1945	10	150
Eagle/Phila., 1883–1945	20	70
Edgemaster, 1940s	10	45
Edward Weck, 1893–1943	15	75
Enterprise Cutlery Co., 1920s	25	85
Ernest Brueckmann, 1891–1956	25	125
Esemco, 1921–1949	5	8
Fairmont Cutlery Co., 1930s	20	65
Farwell Ozmun Kirk & Co., 1881–1959	35	110
Fayetteville Knife Co., 1911	30	90
Federal Knife Co., 1920s	20	75
Fletcher Knife Co., 1863–1913	25	175
Ford & Medley, 1872–1930	20	95
Forest Master, 1934–contemp.	10	25
Fox Cutlery, 1884–1955	35	85
Frederick Westpfal, 1884–1940	25	125
Gebruder Christians, 1824–contemp.	20	150
Gebruder Krusius, 1856–1983	10	150
Gold Top, 1924–1948	10	30
Goodell Co., 1913–1948	60	90
Griffon, 1918–1966	30	125
Hammer Brand, 1936–contemp.	3	40
Hargreaves Smith & Co., 1866–1920	25	300
Hart Cutlery Co., 1920s	20	200
Heller Bros. Co., 1900–1930	25	75
Henry Sears & Son, 1878–1959	40	225
Henry Taylor, 1858–1927	25	300
Herder & Co., 1872–contemp.	10	125
Hermitage Cutlery, 1895–1927	8	25
Hollingsworth Knife Co., 1916–1930	25	200
Hudson Knife Co., 1927	20	65
Hugo Koller, 1861–1980s	15	65
Humason & Beckley, 1852–1914	20	275
Humason & Beckley Mfg. Co., 1852–1916	20	275
Indiana Cutlery Co., 1932	45	95
Jackmaster, 1938–contemp.	10	60
James Barlow & Son, 1828–1856	25	200
James Cranshaw, 1826	25	200
Jetter & Scheerer, 1880–1932	10	150
John Kenyon & Co., 1870–1920	15	150
Joseph Rodgers & Sons, 1901–1948	25	250
Judson Cutlery Co., 1900–1940	20	65
Ka-Bar, 1951–1966	25	75
Kamp King, 1935–contemp.	5	25
Keen Edge, 1901–1927	25	150
Keen Kutter, 1940–1960	25	200
Keener Edge, 1932	10	75
Keystone Cutlery Co., 1925–1938	45	200
Kingston USA, 1915–1958	15	75
Knapp & Spencer, 1895–1905	15	175
Koeller & Schmidt, 1884–1916	30	90
Koeller Bros., 1905–1927	10	100

	LOW	HIGH
Krusius B. Brothers K. B., 1888–1927	.10	150
Kutwell, 1930s	.50	300
Kwik Cut, 1921–1926	.15	60
Landers Frary & Clark, 1863–1954	.25	125
Lenox Cutlery Co., 1910	.10	25
Liberty Knife Co., 1920s	.25	60
Luna, 1903–1948	.15	75
Marshall Field & Co., 1909–1923	.15	60
Meridan Cutlery Co., 1855–1925	.25	150
Meridan Knife Co., 1917–1932	.25	150
Metropolitan Cutlery Co., 1918–1951	.10	35
Miller Bros. Cutlery Co., 1872–1926	.25	350
Morris Cutlery Co., 1882–1930	.35	200
Mumbley Peg, 1937–1948	.50	95
Nash Hdw. Co., 1873–1975	.25	150
Needham Bros., 1860–1900	.70	300
Neft Safety Knife, 1920–1930s	.65	125
Never Dull Cutlery Co., 1896–1940	.20	65
North American Knife Co., 1920s	.15	65
Northfield Knife Co., 1858–1919	.45	300
Norvell's Best, 1902–1917	.25	300
Norvell-Shapleigh Hdw. Co., 1902–1917	.15	300
Oehm & Co., 1860–1936	.15	275
Ohio Cutlery Co., 1919–1923	.40	200
Oklahoma City Hdw., 1911–1951	.25	65
Omega, 1898–1924	.5	15
Opinel, 1890–contemp.	.5	15
Orange Cutlery Co., 1923	.25	200
Othello, 1923–contemp.	.10	150
Pal Blade Co., 1929–1953	.15	90
Papes Thiebes Cutlery Co., 1903–1929	.40	200
Patton & Gallagher, 1864–1959	.25	75
Phoenix Knife Co., 1892–1916	.45	175
Press Button Knife Co., 1892–1923	.50	190
Progress, 1886–1942	.10	150
Pronto, 1926–1952	.5	75

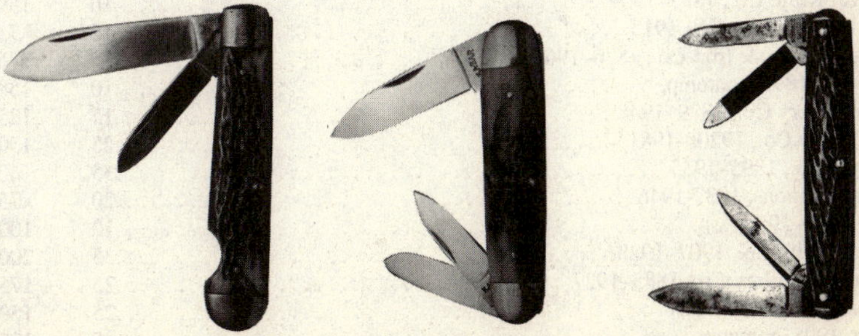

Left to right: Camillus; Ka-Bar; Schrade.

	LOW	HIGH
Providence Cutlery Co., 1890s–1980s	15	150
Queen City, 1922–1945	20	250
Quick Point, 1930s	25	75
Quick-Kut, Inc.	10	45
Rainbow, 1933–1954	5	15
Rev-O-Nov, 1905–1960	35	40
Richards & Conover Hdw. Co., 1894–1956	30	55
Rivington Works, 1900–1946	15	45
Robert Hartkopf & Co., 1855–1957	15	125
Robert Kerder, 1872–contemp.	15	175
Robert Klaas, 1834–contemp.	15	250
Robinson Bros. & Co., 1880–1925	45	300
Royal Cutlery Co., 1814–1954	10	25
Runkel Bros., 1920s	15	35
Salem Co., 1918–1935	15	60
Samuel E. Bernstein, 1890–1950s	15	125
Samuel Hague, 1830s–1950s	25	200
Samuel Hancock & Sons, 1836–1924	25	200
Samuel Wragg & Sons, 1930s–1960s	25	175
Schmachtenberg Bros. 1887–1939	20	65
Schmidt & Ziegler, 1930s	20	95
Schrade, 1973–contemp.	10	45
Seneca Cutlery Co., 1932–1942	15	65
Severing Droeschers, 1891–1924	10	18
Shapleigh, 1920–1960	15	150
Shur-Snap, 1949	20	45
Simmons Boss, 1940–1960	25	50
Simmons Hdw. Co., 1865–1960	20	300
Smith & Hemenway, 1890–1920	25	175
Smith Brothers Hdw. Co., 1903–1959	40	85
Southern & Richardson, 1846–contemp.	10	40
Southington Cutlery Co., 1867–1914	45	200
Sta-Sharp, 1927–1940	20	150
Stocker & Co., 1897–1970s	15	45
Syracuse Knife Co., 1930s	15	75
Terrier Cutlery Co., 1910–1916	45	110
Theo. M. Green Co., 1916–1920	5	60
Thornton, 1950s	5	15
Universal, 1898–1950	15	35
Universal Knife Co., 1897–1909	10	150
Valley Falls Cutlery Co., 1915	15	75
Van Camp Hdw. & Iron Co., 1876–1960	35	275
Victorinox, 1891–contemp.	10	150
Vignos Cutlery Co., 1879–1948	15	125
Voos Cutlery Co., 1920s–1981	25	150
Wallace Bros., 1895–1955	35	60
Warden Simmons, 1937-1946	20	75
Wards, 1935–1950s	10	100
Warwick Knife Co., 1907–1928	35	200
Washington Cutlery Co., 1885–1927	25	175
Watkins Cottrell Co., 1867	25	150
Wenger, 1908–contemp.	5	100
Weske Cutlery Co., 1946–1952	5	75
Western Cutlery Co., 1874–1914	20	125

Lamps

Widespread availability of electricity during the early twentieth century created a huge demand for table lamps. Examples from major manufacturers such as Handel, Pairpoint, and Tiffany are especially desirable and command top dollar for their beautifully designed shades.

The first two decades following World War II sparked a new surge in lamp production. Everyone was leaving the inner city for a slice of the American pie: Suburbia. These new homes had to be furnished and everyone needed lamps. While traditional lamps were produced, collectors prefer the kitsch, strange and sometimes downright ugly examples made between the late 1920s and the mid-1960s. Some have classic themes such as ballet dancers and Harlequin, others, such as the classic panther television lamp, are a carry-over from the Art Deco era of pre-World War II America. Futuristic designs reflect the era's obsession with technology and UFOs. Other novelty lamps used the heat emitted from the light bulb to create the illusion of moving images.

For additional reading see *Collector's Guide to Motion Lamps* by Sam and Anna Samuelian (Collector Books, Paducah, KY, 1998), *Quality Electric Lamps* edited by L-W Book Sales (L-W Book Sales, Gas City, IN, 1992, 1996 value update), *'50s TV Lamps* by Calvin Shepherd (Schiffer, Atglen, PA, 1998), and *TV Lamps* by Tom Santiso (Collector Books, Paducah, KY, 1999).

Motion

	LOW	HIGH
Bicycles, plastic, Econolite, 1959, 11" h	$130	$160
Birch Trees w/ Ducks, plastic, L.A. Goodman, 1956, 11" h	100	125
Boy Scout and Girl Scout, plastic, Rotovue Jr., Econolite, 1950, 10" h	175	250
Butterflies, plastic, Econolite, 1954, 11" h	110	150
Fireplace, plastic, Econolite, 11" h	70	80
Forest Fire, Ignition Co., 1940s, 8" h	35	55
Hawaiian Scene, palm trees, plastic, Econolite, 1959, 11" h	90	120
Indian Maiden, plaster, Gritt, Inc., 1920s, 11" h	45	60
Lighthouse/Ship, glass and paper, Scene in Action Co., 1930s, 10" h	110	140
Mill Stream, plastic, Econolite, 1956, 11" h	65	80
Niagara Falls, glass, Scene in Action Co., 1931, 10" h	100	125
Niagara Falls, plastic, Econolite, 1955, 11" h	50	65
Niagara Falls, rainbow, plastic, Econolite, oval, 1960, 11" h	60	75
Pot Belly Stove, plastic, black or silver, Econolite, 1950s, 12" h	120	150
Seattle World's Fair, plastic, Econolite, 1962, 11" h	130	160
Ships, Rev-O-Lite, 1930s, 10" h	75	95
Trains, plastic, Econolite, 1956, 11" h	100	125
Venice Grand Canal, plastic, Econolite, 1963, 11" h	125	140
White Christmas, flat front, plastic, Econolite, 1953, 11" h	120	150

Table

Abstract, pink plaster, bi-level parchment shade, 23" h	$80	$120
Abstract, turquoise and gold twist, porcelain w/ matching abstract splattered shade, 29" h	90	160
Asian Man and Woman, w/ panther, painted plaster, cloth pagoda-style shade, Continental Art, 1950, 33" h, matched pair	200	300
Ballet Dancers, painted plaster, oversized cloth shade, signed "E. Bertolozzi, Chicago," 32.5" h, matched pair	100	200
Deer and Foliage, green porcelain, pale green parchment shade w/ gold and white brush stroke design, probably Haeger, 26" h, matched pair	120	180
Harlequins, painted plaster, black and gold swirl parchment shade, Puccinni Art Co., 24" h, matched pair	175	275

Left: Reverse Painted, puffy apple tree shade, Pairpoint, $32,200 at auction.

Right: Leaded Glass, daffodil w/ dogwood border, Tiffany Studios, Favrile glass, $54,625 at auction.

—Photos courtesy William Doyle Galleries.

	LOW	HIGH
Horse, porcelain, black w/ gold accents, Venetian blind shade, 14.5" h	30	60
Hula Dancer, copper flashed white metal w/ grass skirt and matching shade, dancer's body is articulated so that she dances, 28" h	150	250
Leaded Glass, domed shade w/ radiating caramel slag glass segments, 3-socket patinated metal base w/ Art Nouveau stylized floral and linear decoration, early 20th C, 22.5" h, 17" dia shade	600	800
Mosaic, conical shade composed of multicolored glass segments arranged as blossoming red, orange, and yellow hollyhock spikes against white background above curved drop apron of lavender and granite-textured golden amber border, raised on 3-socket cast foliate-decorated base w/ locking mechanism above, attributed to Wilkinson Co., Brooklyn, NY, 30" h, 22" dia shade	5000	7000
Mosaic, "Louis XV," domed leaded glass shade w/ repeating sections of stylized floral motif separated by raised curved panels w/ green and amber glass and elaborate dore overlay, mounted on matching 4-socket gilt-bronze base w/ swirling scrolls and shell-form devices, impressed tag "The Duffner & Kimberly Co. New York," 28" h, 21.5" dia shade	20,000	25,000
Oriental Couple, stylized rocky base, tri-form Venetian blind shade, 24" h	90	130
Polka Dot, gold-colored metal base w/ 2 porcelain tumblers divided by 2 gold spheres and string and ball decoration, gold and turquoise polka-dotted parchment shade, 28" h, matched pair	120	160
Prom Queen, porcelain figure w/ layered dress, matching layered shade, 20" h	40	80
Reverse-Painted, flared domed glass shade w/ lakeside landscape w/ summer trees and distant hills, inscribed at lower edge "1972 Jefferson Co.," cast metal base, 16" h, 21" dia shade	1500	2000
Reverse-Painted, textured domed glass shade w/ maroon and green trees against blue-gray and orange clouds in blue sky, inscribed "Handel 6937" at rim, raised on 3-socket ribbed quatreform bronzed platform base, 22.5" h, 18" dia	5000	6500
Scenic, boudoir lamp, 6-sided conical glass shade w/ background blue, green, and sunset pink on interior, landscape handpainted on exterior, signed "Handel 6232," 6-sided metal base impressed "Handel," 14" h, 7.5" dia shade	2000	3000
Scenic, frosted and textured domed glass shade painted on interior and exterior w/ moonlit river landscape w/ trees and tent in shades of green, blue, brown, and yellow, 3-socket patinated and weighted baluster-shaped metal base, early 20th C, 28.5" h, 18" dia shade	3000	4000

Left: Art Nouveau, metal, Steuben gold aurene shades, $1093 at auction. —Photo courtesy Skinner, Inc., Boston, MA.

Right: Oriental Couple, red and black, red Venetian blind shade, $75-$100.

	LOW	HIGH
Slag Glass, 6 striated caramel and white bent glass panels mounted in gilt and enameled floral-decorated framework, 1-socket gilt-metal base w/ raised mistletoe decoration on stem and foot, early 20th C, 21" h, 16.5" dia shade	400	600
Slag Glass, domed shade w/ 6 panels in blue, green, purple, white, and caramel striated bent slag glass, bronze-finished metal frame w/ foliate-decorated columns, 2-socket illuminated base w/ same framework and glass panels, early 20th C, 22" h, 18.5" dia shade	800	1000
Stalking Panther, black porcelain, 3-hole planter, Venetian blind shade, 13" h	30	50
Stylized Tree Trunks, white plaster, tan and red mottled parchment shades, 27" h, matched pair	60	100
Swirling Cone, pink porcelain w/ gold trim, parchment shade, 24" h	20	40
Twin Rearing Steeds, black porcelain, Venetian blind shade, 13" x 10", matched pair	90	160

Television

Blue Birds, double, plaster tray, Lane, 11" x 13"	$50	$75
Chinese Figures, pierced gold fixtures, 13" h, pair	90	130
Chinoiserie Double Planter, green, brass surround, 7.5" x 11"	18	24
Conch Shell, pink w/ white and gold, Premco, 11" h	35	55
Cougars, double, brown and cream, 8" x 11"	30	40
Cowboy Horse, red fiberglass conical shade, 11" x 11"	25	35
Criss-Cross Sides, green shade insert, 7" x 12.5"	60	90
Dancer, leaping, gold and black plaster, 13" x 15"	40	60
Deer, porcelain w/ plaster tray, 13" x 13.5"	50	70
Deer, running, green w/ leaf and vine, 5" x 10"	15	20
Doves, white and gold, Royal Fleet Company	20	30
Farm Scene, vinyl, cylindrical, pierced gold metal base, 11.5" h	15	20
Fawn, white w/ pink planter, Electrolite, 8" h	25	35
Fish, double, gray and maroon	50	70
Flower in Basket, green, 9" h	25	35
Galleon, multicolor, 9.5" x 12"	45	55
Galleon Clock/Lamp, wooden, Gibraltor Precision, 18" x 13"	30	45
Gazelle, leaping, black, swirling base, 11" x 16"	45	65
Gazelles, leaping twins, planter, swirl plume base, 11" x 14"	35	65

Television Lamp, brown panther, $50.

	LOW	HIGH
Horse, black, 5.5" x 10.5"	20	30
Horse, on rocky plateau, white, 13" h	35	45
Horse, porcelain, on plaster rocky bluff base, Lane, 11" x 13.5"	30	40
Horse Head, brown, 14.5" h	25	35
Horse Head, knight style, gray, cutout eyes, 14" h	45	55
Leaf, green, triple frond, 5" x 13.5"	25	35
Leaf Form, 5" x 12"	25	35
Leopard in Forest, green screen, 9" h	35	45
Mallard in Flight, planter surround, 11.5" x 14.5"	35	50
Mare and Colt, brown, 8.5" x 11"	30	40
Mare and Colt, gray, 9.5" x 10"	35	45
Mermaid, deep sea background, 7.5" x 9.5"	100	150
Owl, cutout eyes, marked "Kron, Texans Inc.," 12" h	80	100
Owl, whimsical, Maddux	25	35
Panther, black planter, 22" l	25	45
Panther, black w/ rhinestone eyes, 22" l	25	45
Panther, brown planter, 22" l	25	45
Panther, cutout eyes, lime green, Royal Haeger, 20" l	35	50
Panther, gray leaf and log base, 9" x 15"	30	50
Panther, pink and gray leaf and log base, 9" x 15"	45	55
Panther, plaster w/ green screen background, 8.5" x 17"	45	65
Panther, small, black w/ gold accents, 15" l	25	30
Panther, small, green, 5" x 11"	20	30
Panther, small, pink, 6" x 9"	25	35
Panther, white screen, oval base, Royal Haeger	40	60
Pierced Metal, black, inner shade and wire legs, 13" h	12	18
Plastic Surround Landscape, 10" h	12	18
Poodles, double, pink, 10" x 13"	100	150
Rooster, crowing, maroon, 10" h	25	35
Sailboat Planter, gray waves base, 11" h	30	40
Sampan, w/ Asian couple, green, gold highlights, 6" x 16"	35	45
Ship, green stylized wave base, 10" x 11"	30	40
Siamese Cats, cutout eyes, marked "Kron, Texans Inc.," 13" h	50	70
Stag, leaping, green, 11.5" x 10.5"	20	30
Stallion, running, black, yellow, and white highlights, 11" x 15"	40	60
Swan, small, pink w/ plastic rose, 10" h	10	15
Swan, white, blue water base, Maddux, 11" h	20	30
Television Set, stylized, metal, porthole w/ scene, 7" x 11"	30	40
Tree Trunk, stylized, brown, green, and white, 10" h	20	25
Tropical Leaves, Lane, 13.5" x 10.5"	50	70

Lanterns

	LOW	HIGH
Brass, frame stamped w/ shell and grape patterns, cast brass base, fixed round globe, 19th C, 8.75" h	$400	$600
Brass, nautical lantern, pierced brass frame w/ wire guards, 2 tie-down rings, and ring handle, conical-shaped globe, brass font, bottom stamped "Wm. Porter Maker," mid-19th C, 13" h	400	600
Brass and Tin, painted tin frame w/ brass top and bell bottom, pear-shaped Drapery pattern fixed globe, base marked "H & J Sangster Patent 10 June 1851," New England, mid-19th C, 11.5" h	2500	3500
Bronze, nautical lantern, pierced frame w/ ring handle, fixed bronze lamp in base, and 2 tie-down rings, fixed onion globe, 19th C, 11" h	500	700
Tin, astronomical lantern, painted D-shaped frame w/ end handle and crimped top, frosted glass panel, interior candle socket, w/ astronomical chart, mid-19th C, 12" x 9"	400	600
Tin, barn lantern, brown-painted triangular frame w/ black highlights, 2 glass panels, 1 hinged, wire bail w/ turned wood handle, hanging loops on back, fitted w/ glass kerosene lamp and chimney, mid-19th C, 19" h	300	500
Tin, canal boat lantern, square frame painted red w/ yellow highlights and oval polychrome cartouche w/ river scene, 3 lifting glass panels beneath 2 tin closing side panels fitted w/ mirrors, mercury glass reflector, flat rectangular metal font, wick adjuster marked "Sherwoods Ltd. BHAM," wire bail w/ turned wood handle, 2 hanging loops, mid-19th C, 20" h	1000	1200
Tin, candle lantern, pierced half-round frame w/ strapwork guards and wire bail handle, glass front panel, 19th C, 11" h	400	600
Tin, lunch pail, cylindrical w/ side-attached rectangular lantern, lid w/ air vent and drinking cup, upper warming compartment, lower compartment pulls out from bottom, wire bail w/ turned wood handle, marked "Pat. Oct. 3, 1871, Dec. 18, 1877," 10.5" h, 7" dia	300	500
Tin, nautical lantern, painted and pierced hexagonal frame w/ tie-down rings and ring handle, Beaded Double Bull's-eye fixed globe, metal font, mid-19th C, 12" h	2000	3000
Tin, painted and pierced frame, round ribbed fixed globe, round iron ring handle, glass font, mid-19th C, 10" h	800	1000
Tin, painted and pierced frame w/ ring handle, bulging lighthouse-form fixed globe, glass font, mid-19th C, 11" h	500	700
Tin, painted frame w/ conical top, ring handle, upper and lower crimped bands, and wire guards, fixed barrel globe, tin font, wick adjuster marked "Holmes, Booth and Haydens Waterbury Ct.," 19th C, 3.5" h	300	500

Painted Tin, fixed etched globe, bronze ring handle, brass label reads "Great Grimsby Coal, Salt & Tanning Company Limited Maker," probably England, late 19th C, 19.5" h, $460 at auction. —Photo courtesy Skinner, Inc., Boston, MA.

Metallic Collectibles

Aluminum

Although aluminum is a basic element on the periodic table, it was extremely difficult to purify. During the nineteenth century it was a luxury metal. Not until after Charles Hill patented an inexpensive smelting method in 1886 did it become a "practical" metal. Nearly all aluminum wares on the market are twentieth century.

Aluminum can be cleaned with soap and water or even paste silver polish. Be gentle in cleaning: aluminum dents and scratches easily. Salt will corrode aluminum.

For more information read *Hammered Aluminum* by Dannie A. Woodard and Billie J. Wood (published by author, 1983) and *Hammered Aluminum, Book II* by Dannie A. Woodard (published by author, 1993).

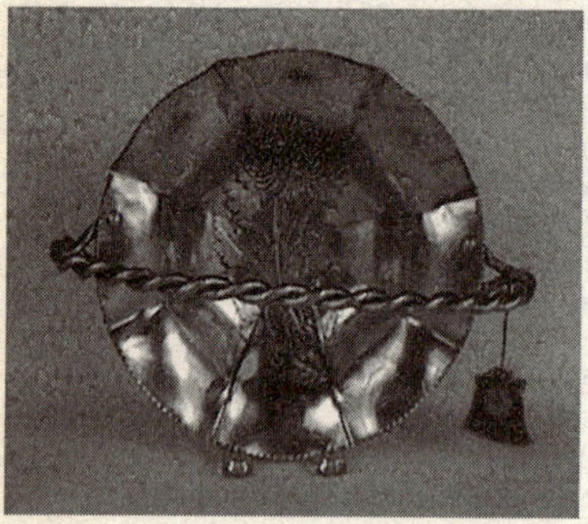

Left: Basket, chrysanthemum, Continental #868, 9" dia, $15-$30.

Right: Pan w/ attached lid, chrysanthemum pattern, Continental #505, $20-$35.

	LOW	AVG.	HIGH
Ashtray, bamboo pattern, Everlast	$20	$30	$40
Bar Tray, daisies pattern, tab handles, Everlast	25	35	45
Basket, ruby red glass insert, handle, Rodney Kent	25	35	45
Basket, sailing ship pattern, square knot handles, fluted edge, Federal	10	15	20
Beverage Set, pitcher and 8 tumblers, floral pattern, square knot handle, World	50	65	80
Beverage Set, pitcher w/ applied flower and 6 plain tumblers, World Hand Forged	70	95	120
Bowl, dogwood pattern, Wendell August Forge, 12"	50	75	100
Bowl, pierced frame, Farber	18	25	35
Bowl, pine pattern, Everlast, 10"	10	15	20
Bowl, tulip pattern, floral ribbon handle, Rodney Kent, 10"	18	25	35

	LOW	AVG.	HIGH
Bread Tray, Rodney Kent	30	45	60
Butler's Stand and Tray, Everlast	125	160	200
Butter, covered, Buenilum	20	30	40
Candelabrum, 3-lite, Continental, #833	80	125	165
Candleholder, beaded edge, wooden ball stem, Buenilum	7	10	15
Candleholders, side handles, Everlast, price for pair	25	35	45
Candleholders and Stand, pair of 2-socket candleholders, bamboo pattern 3-leg stand w/ tall rod for lifting, Everlast	140	200	260
Candlesticks, plain, Everlast, price for pair	20	30	40
Candy Dish, double bowl, rose pattern, leaf center handle, Farberware	25	35	45
Casserole Holder, bamboo pattern, Everlast	25	35	45
Casserole Holder, rose pattern, beaded knob, Everlast, 7.5"	12	20	30
Casserole Holder, twisted handles, loop finial, Buenilum, 8"	10	15	20
Cigarette Box, pine pattern, Wendell August Forge	100	150	200
Coaster, turtle pattern, Wendell August Forge, 5"	1	2	3
Coasters, daisies pattern, Everlast, price for 8	25	35	45
Coaster Set, 8 coasters and caddy, beaded edge, double loop finial, Buenilum	10	15	20
Cocktail Shaker, mum pattern, Continental	70	100	130
Coffee Urn, Continental	100	150	200
Compote, wild rose pattern, Continental, 5"	12	20	30
Creamer and Sugar, Everlast	20	30	40
Creamer and Sugar, World Hand Forged	10	15	20
Crumber and Brush, rose pattern, Everlast	18	25	35
Desk Set, bamboo pattern, Everlast, #B24, price for 3-pc. set	20	30	40
Gravy Boat, Everlast, 7"	8	12	16
Ice Bucket, chrysanthemum pattern, Continental	40	55	70
Ice Bucket, grapes pattern, Everlast	40	50	60
Ice Bucket, mum pattern, lid w/ bud finial, Continental	7	10	15
Ice Bucket, rose pattern, Everlast	30	45	60
Ladle, Argental Cellini, 14.5"	12	20	30
Lazy Susan, acorns and leaf pattern, Continental	18	25	35
Matchbox Holder, Palmer-Smith	50	65	80
Napkin Holder, Rodney Kent	18	25	35
Nut Dish, double bowl, bamboo pattern, center handle, Everlast	25	35	45
Nut Dish, ducks pattern, Wendell August Forge, 7"	25	35	45
Nut Dish, ivy pattern, Palmer-Smith	18	25	35
Pitcher, chrysanthemum pattern, Continental	35	50	65
Pitcher, pine pattern, Wendell August Forge	70	85	100
Plate, floral pattern, Laird, #444, 11.25"	12	20	30
Silent Butler, ribbon handle, Rodney Kent	18	25	35
Silent Butler, twisted handle, Buenilum	12	20	30
Tray, dogwood pattern, Wendell August Forge, #705, 6" x 11.75"	30	40	50
Tray, folding, bamboo pattern, center handle, Everlast	45	65	85
Tray, mum pattern, rectangular w/ chopped corners, Continental	25	35	45
Tray, paisley pattern, Continental, #1003	35	45	55
Tray, pansies pattern, round w/ handles, Continental	40	55	70
Tray, schooner pattern, handled, Arthur Armour	75	100	125
Tray, wheat pattern, bar handles, Arthur Armour, 6" x 14"	30	45	60
Tray, wild horses pattern, round, Arthur Armour	80	125	170
Tray, zinnia pattern, twisted handle, Farber & Shlevin	30	40	50
Tumbler, mum pattern, footed, Continental	25	35	45
Undertray, flower and fruit designs around sides, Cromwell, 17"	10	15	20
Wine Cooler and Stand, grapes pattern, Everlast	175	250	325

Brass

Brass is an alloy of copper and zinc. Early English and Continental pieces are the most valuable. Lighter-weight decorative brassware imported from Asia since the turn of the century often has intricate engraving and tooling, but is less valuable. Objects should be in excellent condition: no dents, no corrosion, even color. Brass may be polished without destroying its value (unlike bronze).

For additional reading consult *Antique Brass & Copper, Revised* by Mary Frank Gaston (Collector Books, Paducah, KY, 1992, 1996 value update) and *The Brass Book* by Peter, Nancy, and Herbert Schiffer (Schiffer, Exton, PA, 1978).

English and Continental Candlesticks. —Photo courtesy Skinner, Inc., Boston, MA.

	LOW	HIGH
Andirons, belted double lemon finial, New York, early 19th C, 20.5" h, price for pair	$700	$1000
Andirons, belted lemon finials, tapering columns, square plinths, curved billet bar w/ brass cover marked "John Molineaux Founder Boston," lemon-topped log stops, early 19th C, 18" h, price for pair	1200	1800
Andirions, double urn finials, turned shaft, spurred legs, padded snake feet, early 19th C, 15.5" h, price for pair	300	500
Andirions, Federal, elongated acorn finials above belted balls, circular molded shafts, spurred arched legs, pad feet, signed "John Molineaux," Boston, c1795, 18.75" h, price for pair	1500	2000
Andirons, ring-turned ribbed and faceted finials and shafts, spurred legs, ball feet, mid-19th C, 23.5" h, price for pair	800	1200
Barrel Stencil, round, "New York Standard A Grade, Packed By H. Haase, ATCO, Wayne Co., Pa." around border, "Min. Size" and "Inch" in center, 16.25" dia	50	100
Basin, wide flared lip, turned body and standard, stepped circular pedestal foot, Continental, 18th C, 7.75" h, 10.25" dia	400	600
Bed Warmer, engraved floral design in lid, wrought iron handle, 43.25" l	250	350
Bookends, rectangular w/ etched and embossed flower stalks outlined in green, impressed Clarence Craft mark, early 20th C, 4.75" h, 7" w, 4" d, price for pair	200	300
Bucket, spun brass, "W. A. Hayden's Patent" label, wrought iron bail handle, 13" dia	150	250
Candle Sconces, circular molded backplate, scrolled candle arm w/ circular bobeche and urn-form socket, Continental, 18th C, 4.5" h, 8" dia, price for pair	1500	2000
Candlestick, flared top w/ wide flat drip catcher around socket, 6-sided shaped and paneled shaft and base w/ stamped floral design surrounded by leaves, weighted bottom, late 19th/early 20th C, 17.125" h	40	80

	LOW	HIGH
Candlesticks, Paktong, gadrooned bobeche on Corinthian capitals, stop-fluted columns, square stepped and gadrooned base, England, c1765, 11.5" h, price for pair	3500	4500
Candlesticks, petal-form base, England, mid-18th C, 7.5" h, price for pair	800	1000
Candlesticks, pricket, turned stem, mid-drip pan, circular turned foot, Continental, late 17th/early 18th C, 15" h, price for pair	600	800
Candlesticks, push-up, beehive form, sockets w/ wide flared drip catcher, spare base, 12" h, price for pair	300	500
Candlesticks, push-up, belted shaft, circular petal base, England, late 18th C, 8.25" h, price for pair	500	700
Chamberstick, rolled rim, cylindrical shaft w/ iron ejector mechanism, rectangular saucer w/ cast brass finger ring, 4.25" h	75	125
Door Knocker, cast urn and acorn form, 19th/20th C, 7.75" h	100	200
Fire Fender, curved ends, brass molding, finials, 3 bun feet, round iron uprights, 19th C, 9" h, 48" l, 9.25" d	200	400
Fireplace Tools, coal hod and 2 shovels w/ wooden handles, repoussé decoration w/ griffins and foliage, Victorian, 19th C, 18" l	150	300
Hearth Trivet, brass shaped pierced top w/ heart handle, brass cabriole front leg, iron stretchers and 2 rear legs, England, early 19th C, 11.25" h, 13" w, 11.25" d	400	600
Inkstand, Art Nouveau, cast w/ scrollwork, butterfly, and lily of the valley, marked "7-11 VM"	75	125
Inkstand, Victorian, cast w/ relief mask and leaf decoration, square stand w/ pen rest, square crystal inkwell	100	150
Kettle Shelf, pierced brass shelf w/ turned wood handle, wrought iron stand, 12" h, 7" x 13" shelf	300	400
Mortar and Pestle, round mortar w/ flat bottom and sides flaring to rim, cast knobs on sides, shaped pestle w/ flat rounded knob-shaped ends, 4.875" h mortar, 8.125" l pestle	50	100
Sewing Bird, small pincushion on bird's back, small round red velvet pinchusion on "C" clamp base, 5" h	125	200

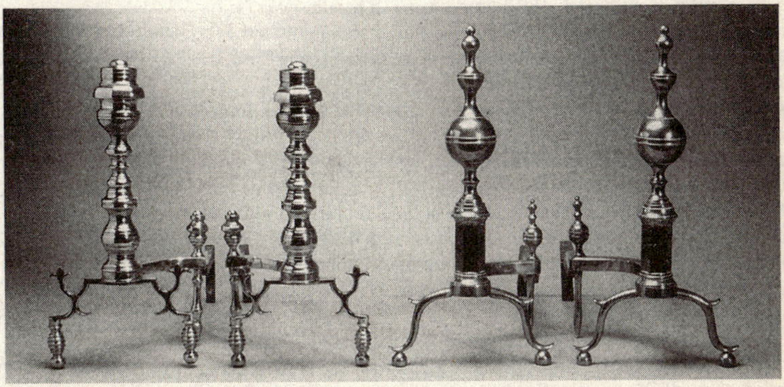

Andirons at auction, left to right: Classical form w/ faceted and ring-turned finials and shafts, and bulbous turned legs on ball feet, American, mid-19th C, 19.75" h, $489; Belted ball and urn-top finials on faceted plinths, spurred legs on ball feet, New York, early 19th C, 22" h, $1495. —Photo courtesy Skinner, Inc., Boston, MA.

Bronze

Though bronze sculpture is of ancient origin, most specimens on the market are Victorian and twentieth century. The name of the artist is the biggest factor in determining value. The name of the foundry is also important.

Don't clean a bronze sculpture with any highly abrasive cleaner. The color and condition of the "patina" is important. Vienna cold painted bronzes should have their original paint in good condition.

For more information see *Bronzes: Sculptors & Founders: 1800-1930, Vols. 1-4* by Harold Berman (Schiffer, Atglen, PA, 1994) and *Art Bronzes* by Michael Forrest (Schiffer, Atglen, PA, 1997).

Left: Desk Lamp, bronze base, lantern shade w/ textured green slag glass panels and brass strapwork, marked "Handel," 22" h, $1840 at auction.

Right: Urns, French Classical Revival, depicting Pegasus and Bellerophon, signed "Boucher," 20th C, 18" h, $2185 at auction.

—Photos courtesy Skinner, Inc., Boston, MA.

	LOW	HIGH
Altar Set, comprising crucifix and pair of pricket candlesticks, baroque style, silvered, Continental, 18" h crucifix, 16" h candlesticks, price for 3 pcs	$300	$500
Candlesticks, hammered, short baluster form, stepped circular base, early 20th C, 2.75" h, price for pair	200	300
Dagger, decorative, baroque-style designs of armor and scrolled foliage, Continental, 11.75" l	100	300
Garnitures, gilded, modeled as stylized trees, w/ slender cut glass drops, mid-19th C, 13" h, price for pair	400	600
Inkstand, Empire Revival, gilded, rectangular w/ 2 flower-form inkwells, modeled w/ flowerheads and winged beasts, 19th C, 8" l	150	250
Inkstand, Louis XV style, gilded, 2 putti atop mask-mounted base w/ scrolled candle branches, covered inkwells, shell-shaped base fitted w/ drawer, late 19th C, 9.5" h, 16" l	1000	1500
Letter Holder, gilded, Bookmark pattern, 2-tier, impressed "Tiffany Studios New York 1020," early 20th C, 5.25" h, 9.25" w, 2.25" d	400	600
Medal, depicting Leda and the Swan, Art Deco, stamped "Andre Lavrillier," c1920-30, 4" x 2.5"	100	200
Sundial, globe form, green patination, Graham, 14" h	400	600
Wall Sconces, gilded, topped by ribbon-tied wreath, 4 flat leaf down-turned arms w/ foliate sockets, ending in foliate finial, electrified, 39" h, price for pair	600	800

Sculpture

	LOW	HIGH
Allovard, Henry (French, 1844-1929), Cupid and Psyche, cire perdue, dark brown patina, foundry seal, early 20th C, 9.5" h	$300	$500
Barbedienne, portrait busts of infants, dark brown patina, late 19th C, 5" h, price for pair	300	500
Barye, Antoine-Louis (1796-1875), Senegal Elephant, signed "F(erdinand). Barbedienne," stamped "FB," base w/ incised numbers "676/44," greenish brown patina, 5.5" h	8000	12,000
Berman (c1920), Viennese cold-painted figure of a dove, painted in shades of gray and brown, 8" l	800	1200
Clara, J. (American, 20th C), seated little girl and 2 cats, greenish brown patina, signed, 11.75" h	300	500
Continental (late 19th C), Venus de Milo, Richard Eck & Durand foundry w/ reduction stamp, 34.5" h	1000	1500
Descamps, Joseph (French, 19th/20th C), The Naughty Dutch Girl, stamped "Susse Freres," base molded w/ procession of ducks, light brown patina, 13" h	1000	2000
Fremiet, Emmanuel (1824-1910), Roman Charioteer, medium brown patina, late 19th C, 16.5" h, 17" l	2500	3500
Hagenaur (Austria), stylized exotic bird w/ black finish and bronze highlights, impressed mark on base, 6.75" h	150	300
Hannaux, Emmanuel (French), bust, Young Warrior, signed, on marble socle, c1895, 23" h	3000	5000
Hundriser, Emil (German, 1846-1911), baby boy and beetle, Ernst Kraas foundry mark, red marble base, brown patina, 11" l	1000	1500
Khodarovich (Russian), figural group, peasant oxen cart, signed, foundry stamp, medium brown patina, 19th C, 14.25" h, 23" l	800	1000
Lanceray, Yevgeny-Alex (1848-1886), Cossack Rider, signed, foundry seal, light brown patina, 10" h, 10.5" l	1000	2000
Roman Bronze Works, seated man, Art Deco style, c1930, 14.5" h	1000	1500
Schaflert (German, 20th C), figure of a butcher, signed, marble base, medium brown patina, 9" h	400	600
Vidal, Louis (1831-1892), Lion Walking, signed and dated "1874," greenish-brown patina, 14.5" h, 27" l	2000	3000

Left: Carl Kauba (American, 1865-1922), St. George and the Dragon, 15" h, $5750 at auction.

Left: Emmanuel Fremiet (French, 1824-1910), Standing Hound, signed, 9.25" h, $2760 at auction.

—Photos courtesy Skinner, Inc., Boston, MA.

Copper

As the price of the metal itself has risen, so has the price for the well-crafted antiques and collectibles. Look for undented examples exhibiting good proportions and fine workmanship. Refer to *Antique Brass & Copper Revised* by Mary Frank Gaston (Collector Books, Paducah, KY, 1992, 1996 value update) for additional information.

Pawn Shop Trade Sign, 3 gilded copper balls w/ beaded detail, iron bracket, late 19th C, 13.5" dia balls, $2415 at auction. —Photo courtesy Skinner, Inc., Boston, MA.

	LOW	HIGH
Bed Warmer, punched star design on lid, turned wood handle w/ brass ferrule, 42" l	$200	$350
Bookends, triangular, hammered surface, embossed and etched sailing ship within circular rope twist border, dark patina, impressed Roycroft orb and cross mark, 20th C, 4.875" h, price for pair	200	300
Bowl, floriform, hammered surface, stamped "KLR/153," attributed to Karl Lienenen, Handicraft Shop, 2.5" h, 5.75" dia	100	200
Box, brass-banded, rectangular w/ peaked cover, Scandinavian, late 19th C, 10.25" l	100	150
Cake Mold, funnel-shaped center w/ open star design on top, rounded bottom w/ stamped floral motif, band of vertical ribbing around sides below rim, iron ring on side below rolled rim, marked "Christian Wagner, Rein-Kupfer, Made in Germany," 3.75" h, 9.375" dia	50	80
Candlesticks, flaring bobeche, cylindrical shaft, circular base, hammered surface, Roycroft orb and cross mark, incised artist's mark, 6.5" h, 3.25" dia, price for pair	600	800
Chafing Dish, supported by 3 realistically modeled rabbits, marked "Black, Starr & Forest," wood base, 11" h	400	600
Coal Hod, brass handles, 19th C, 17" h	100	200
Humidor, rectangular, hammered surface, leaf handle, riveted base, lined w/ cedar box, reddish patina, stamped "BB" for Benedict Studios, 4.5" h, 7.5" l, 5.5" d	1000	1500
Jar, hammered surface, dovetailed seams, 9" h, 11.25" dia	40	80
Jelly Mold, oval, fluted sides, tin-lined, 3.25" h, 5.875" l, 3.375" w	40	80
Jelly Mold, wide plain rim w/ ribbed arched designs around base, plain oval center, tin-lined, 4.125" h, 6.625" l, 4.375" w	50	100
Letter Holder, hammered surface w/ enameled medallion of sailing ship, inscribed "Twichell," deep patina, Gertrude Twichell, Boston Society of Arts and Crafts, 1917-26, 4.25" h, 5.5" w	300	500
Measure, cylindrical, brass rim, "Fairbanks & Co US Standard New York" label, 3.875" h, 5" dia	300	400
Measure, haystack, dovetailed seams, flange base, handle marked "J. Sykes, Cin.," 8.25" h	200	300

	LOW	HIGH
Milk Pail, stamped "1870," bail handle, 12" h	400	600
Mitten Warmer, copper pan, brass ferrule, turned wood handle, 9" l	100	200
Pan, dovetailed construction, cast steel handle, "Henry Trottman, Philada" label, 5.5" h, 8" dia, 8.5" l handle	150	250
Paper Spindle, applied bronzed eucalyptus Natural Pod and handmade leaf, hammered surface, Old Mission Kopper Kraft, 7" h	200	400
Picture Frame, Arts & Crafts, rectangular w/ warty texture and cut-out leather panels, dark patina, European, 14.25" h, 19" w	1000	1500
Pitcher, hammered surface, square strap handle, brown-green patina, impressed "A G Barton," 7.5" h	75	150
Planter, corseted, hammered surface, Gustav Stickley "Als Ik Kan" stamp, 3.25" h, 8" dia	500	700
Rocker Blotter, Zodiac pattern, impressed "Tiffany Studios New York 990" on side, early 20th C, 2" h, 5.625" l	150	250
Still, sour mash whiskey, 3-pc., consisting of boiler, extended spout, and coiled condenser	300	500
Tea Kettle, curved spout, upright swing handle w/ brass lid knob, impressed "G. Tryon" on handle, Pennsylvania, 19th C, 11.5" h	500	700
Tea Kettle, dovetailed construction, gooseneck spout, swivel handle labeled "J. Sheriff, Pittsburgh," c1837, 7" h plus handle	300	500
Tray, oval w/ rolled rim and 2 riveted handles, hammered surface, Gustav Stickley impressed mark, c1912, 23.25" l, 11.25" w	500	700
Umbrella Stand, hammered surface, cylindrical body w/ flared rim, 2 strap-work loop handles, repoussé medallion decoration, riveted flared foot, c1910, 25" h	600	800
Vase, heavy gauge hammered copper, cylindrical, band of stylized diamond-shaped flowers w/ green triangles and long stems, dark patina, impressed Roycroft mark on base, early 20th C, 7" h	800	1200
Vase, ribbed flaring oval form w/ scalloped rim, raised on oblong footed base, dark brown and green patina, inscribed "M(arie). Zimmermann maker, 1463-1915 B" and artist's cipher on base, 6.875" h, 11.5" dia	3000	5000
Vase, semi-ovoid, closed-in rolled rim, hammered leathery texture, closed box mark for Dirk Van Erp, 15" h, 11.5" dia	8000	12,000
Wall Sconces, concave crimped top, c1830, 12.25" h, price for pair	600	800
Wash Boiler, lid w/ strap handle, oval, turned wood handles, 34" l	50	150

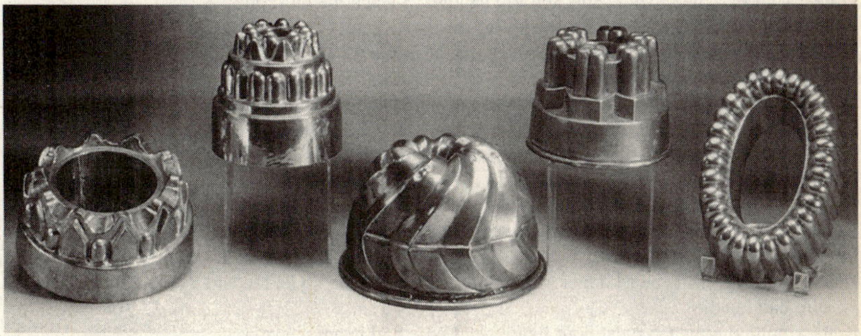

Food Molds, European, 19th C, price for 12 at auction, $1495. —Photo courtesy Skinner, Inc., Boston, MA.

Graniteware

Graniteware is metalware with an enamel coating. It often has a mottled or marbleized appearance. Most graniteware is made for kitchen use. First featured in 1876 at the Centennial Exposition in Philadelphia, graniteware quickly gained popularity. It has been manufactured from the 1870s to the present.

For more information see *The Collector's Encyclopedia of Granite Ware, Bk. 2* by Helen Greguire (Collector Books, Paducah, KY, 1993, 1997 value update).

	LOW	HIGH
Berry Pail, red and white swirl, white interior, rolled rim, flat ears, wire bail handle w/ wood grip	$1800	$2200
Bowl, black and white swirl, 4.5" h, 10.25" dia	50	100
Bowl, blue and white swirl, 2.75" h, 6" dia	25	75
Candlestick, cobalt swirl, fluted pan	150	250
Candlestick, gray, dish base, strap finger ring	50	150
Chamberstick, blue and white swirl, 5.25" dia	150	250
Chicken Feeder, gray speckled, 2-pc., cone top, 4 feed openings	150	250
Child's Bowl, white, blue rooster and rim, 6.5" dia	20	40
Child's Cereal Bowl, white, green leaf and berry decoration	20	40
Child's Mug, white, multicolor floral decoration	15	25
Child's Plate, white, red horse and rim, 8" dia	20	40
Coffee Biggin, covered, white, black rims and knob, 5 pcs., labeled "Super Quality ESCO, No. 82.2, 2 cup"	100	200
Coffeepot, covered, blue relish, tilt pot and tray w/ pewter trim	200	300
Coffeepot, covered, mauve and white mottled, nickel-plated lid, turned wood handle, 5.25" h	150	250
Colander, mottled gray, applied flattened handles, 11.5" dia	50	125
Collander, mottled gray, shallow, heavy wire handles	25	75
Cook Stove, green and black, oven on left, cooking surface on right w/ shelf above and lower shelf w/ 4 brass burners, enameled shields, temperature gauge in oven door, 48" h, 44" w, 18" d	200	400
Cream Can, gray, cylindrical w/ rounded shoulder and straight neck, arched handle, tin removable lid w/ wire loop on top, 4.75" h, 3.5" dia	150	250
Cream Can, mottled gray, tab ears, tin lid, wire bail handle w/ wood grip	75	150
Dinner Bucket, gray mottled, oblong, tab ears, matching lid w/ tin cup, wire bail handle w/ wood grip	100	200
Dinner Carrier, white, black rims and top handles, 3-stack, metal frame w/ wood handle	75	150
Dinner Carrier, white, cobalt rims, 5-stack, metal frame w/ wood handle	100	200
Dish Pan, emerald swirl, handles	150	250
Double Boiler, blue and white swirl, black rims and handles, white interior, matching lid	100	250
Food Mold, gray, melon-shaped, side w/ oval wire handle, 4.75" h, 10.5" l, 8" d	50	100
Funnel, rounded bowl, gray mottled	50	100
Kerosene Heater, shaded black and gray canister, black frame w/ gray top, Ivanhoe #110, 15" h	50	100
Kettle, blue and white swirl, black rim, white interior, Berlin style, tab ears, wire bail handle	100	175
Kettle, mottled gray, tab ears, pour handle and wire bail handle, 9" dia	25	75
Milk Can, brown and white speckled, matching lid, wire bail handle 9.75" h	75	150
Milk Can, emerald green swirl, black rim, white interior, enameled wire ears, wire bail handle w/ wood grip, matching lid, 9.25" h, 4.75" dia	1000	1250

	LOW	HIGH
Mug, blue and white swirl, black rim, white interior	25	35
Mustard Pot, covered, w/ spoon, brown and white panels, black decoration, marked "G. B. N.," 3.5" h	200	300
Pail, blue and white swirl, black rim and tab ears, white interior, matching lid, wire bail handle w/ wood grip, 7.5" h, 7" dia	150	250
Pan, end-of-day, multicolored swirl in pastel shades, cobalt rim, rectangular, 12" x 7.5"	400	600
Pie Plate, blue and white swirl, black rim, white interior	25	50
Pie Plate, brown and white swirl, black rim, white interior, 9.75" dia	75	125
Pie Plate, cobalt and white swirl, white interior, 9" dia	50	100
Pie Plate, crystolite, mottled, black rim, white interior, 9.75" dia	100	150
Pie Plate, emerald and white swirl, blue rim, white interior, 10" dia	75	125
Preserving Kettle, medium gray mottled, tin lid, tipping handle, wire bail handle w/ wood grip, 14.5" dia	75	125
Pudding Mold, gray, turk's head w/ stamped swirled design, center open cone, 3.875" h, 9.75" dia	50	100
Roaster, covered, blue and white mottled, black rims and handles, solid foot, rounded bottom inside, 17.5" l	150	250
Strainer, mottled gray, round bowl w/ decorative piercing, short handle w/ lip hook	25	75
Syrup Pitcher, gray, hinged lid, arched handle, conical shape w/ bands around base, 5.625" h, 3.875" dia base	200	300
Wash Basin, blue and white swirl, applied hanging ring, 12.75" dia	125	200
Wash Basin, cobalt, white interior, eyelet hanger, 12.5" dia	50	125
Wash Basin, cobalt and white swirl, black rim, white interior, 12" dia	75	150
Wash Basin, emerald and white swirl, blue rim, white interior, 11" dia	200	350
Wash Basin, pale gray and white mottled, white interior, eyelet hanger, 10.5" d	25	75
Wash Basin, salesman's sample, cobalt and white mottled, black rim, white interior, 1.125" h, 4.25" dia	50	100

Assortment of graniteware. —Photo courtesy Garth's Auctions, Delaware, OH.

Ironware

Marked ironware pieces have greater value. Dates do not always indicate the year made; some dates stand for the year the patent was issued. Oiling or polishing old ironware decreases its value. Many reproductions are made in Indonesia. Careless welding is a sign of modern work or fakery.

For additional reading consult *Antique Iron* by Kathryn McNerney (Collector Books, Paducah, KY, 1984, 1998 value update), *Antique Iron: Survey of American and English Forms, Fifteenth Through Nineteenth Centuries* by Herbert, Peter, and Nancy Schiffer (Schiffer, Exton, PA, 1979), and *Figurative Cast Iron* by Douglas Congdon-Martin (Schiffer, Atglen, PA, 1994). All items listed are cast iron unless noted otherwise.

Doorstops at auction. Left: Black-Eyed Susans, Hubley, 17.75" h, $1870.

Right: Rooster, 13" h, $990. —Photos courtesy Bill Bertoia Auctions.

	LOW	HIGH
Andirons, Hessian soldiers, 20" h, price for pair	$200	$400
Andirons, wrought iron, ring finials above flat shafts, arched legs w/ penny feet, 15.5" h, price for pair	150	250
Bootjack, "Naughty Nellie," painted black, late 19th C	100	150
Boot Scraper, pair of griffins standing back-to-back, wings form scraper, deep oval dish base, 10" h, 14" w, 9.5" d	200	300
Candleholder, sticking tommy, wrought iron, tooled and stamped "D. Cleaves," 9.5" l	125	175
Candlestick, wrought iron, spiral shaft, tripod base w/ penny feet, 6.5" h	100	150
Doorstop, full-bodied horse, palomino paint, 8" h	75	125
Doorstop, recumbent lion, amber glass eyes, painted black, late 19th C, 7.5" l	300	500
Doorstop, sailing ship, polychrome paint, marked "Albany Fdy. Co.," 12" h	50	150
Ember Tongs, wrought iron, 21" l	50	75
Figure, full-bodied robin w/ folded wings, mounted on iron stand, late 19th C, 6.5" h, 9.5" l	400	600
Fire Dogs, wrought iron, gooseneck finials, tooled details, penny feet, 7" h	500	700
Firemark, raised long-legged bird, 5.5" dia	50	100
Flat Iron, polychrome-painted floral decoration w/ bird on black ground, 6.5" h	50	100
Food Mold, turk's head, wire bail handle	50	100
Garden Statue, standing stag, rectangular base, painted white, 62.25" h	3000	4000
Garden Urn, scrolled handles, painted white, 34" h	250	350
Gate, wrought iron, painted black and silver, cast arrowhead finials, "Cincinnati Iron Fence Co." on shield-shaped label, 46" h, 31" w	100	150
Gypsy Kettle, covered, 3-footed, marked "1 Gal," wire bail handle, 8" h, 8" dia	50	100
Handles, cast as lion's head w/ ring handles, 1 large and 2 smaller heads joined by chain, late 19th C, price for 3 pcs	300	500

	LOW	HIGH
Herb Grinder, footed boat-shaped bowl, wheel pestle w/ wood handles, 16" l	400	600
Hitching Post, cast as tree w/ vines, painted green and white, 64" h	400	500
Hitching Post, horse head on column, painted white	200	300
Hook, figural squirrel and acorn, squirrel's tail forms hook, screw-type, 6.75" l	100	150
Kettle Shelf, wrought iron, half-round shelf, penny feet, 12" h, 15" x 17.5" shelf	200	300
Kettle Tilter, wrought iron, hanging ring, stamped label	150	200
Nutcracker, eagle's head, marked "Pat'd 1860," 10.25" l	250	350
Nutcracker, full-bodied squirrel, silver-painted, hinged tail, mounted on walnut base, late 19th C, 8" h, 7" l	200	400
Paperweight, figural cat, oval base, painted black, 4.75" l	300	400
Peel, wrought iron, ram's horn handle, 44.5" l	100	150
Rotary Broiler, wrought iron, straight and wavy lines, penny feet, heart handle	75	150
Shooting Gallery, 4 horizontal rails each w/ 8 bird targets, painted black, green, yellow, orange, and red, early 20th C, 51.5" h, 48.5" w	2000	3000
Shooting Gallery Target, running ram, painted white, 9" l	300	400
Shooting Gallery Targets, roosters, 4.5" h, price for pair	50	100
Skewer, wrought iron, ram's horn handle above twisted shaft, 11" l	30	60
String Holder, spherical w/ raised black man's face on top, string is drawn through open mouth, pedestal base, 19th C, 8" h, 6" dia	400	600
Tea Kettle, cast leaf detail on lid, molded "5," 7.25" h	200	400
Trammel, wrought iron, sawtooth, adjusts from 32" l	100	200
Trivet, wrought iron, heart-shaped, 9" l	75	125

Left to right: Gate, "Edward R. Dolan" banner above willow tree w/ doves, lambs and flowers below, painted black, green, and white, c1860, 41" h, 29" w, $1380 at auction; Settee, 3-panel back, painted black, 36" h, 48" w, $863 at auction. —Photos courtesy Skinner, Inc., Boston, MA.

Pewter

Pewter is a tin alloy, often containing copper. It is usually dark gray and soft, but can be light and shiny, almost resembling silver. Early pewter should not be used for eating, drinking or storing food, as it often contains lead, which can poison the food. Many examples contain a "touch" or hammered mark of the maker. These marks can be identified by various guides.

For additional reading consult *The American Pewterer* by Henry J. Kauffman (Astragal Press, Mendham, NJ, 1994).

	LOW	HIGH
Basin, "Hamlin" touch (Samuel Hamlin Jr. or Sr.), 7.75" dia	$300	$400
Beaker, slightly flared, unmarked, American, 3" h	75	125
Candlestick, "H. Hopper" touch (Henry Hopper, New York City), 9.5" h	200	300
Candlesticks, capstan bases, unmarked, 4.75" h, price for pair	500	700
Candlesticks, reeded detail, unmarked, 10.25" h, price for pair	200	300
Candlesticks, unmarked, attributed to Homan & Co., Cincinnati, OH, 9.875" h, price for pair	400	600
Castor Set, pewter frame holds 4 electric blue bottles w/ copper wheel engraving, 2 w/ pewter fittings and 2 w/ matching glass stoppers, unmarked	250	350
Chamber Lamp, lemon font, "R. Gleason" touch (Roswell Gleason, Dorchester, MA), whale oil burner, 4.75" h	150	250
Charger, marked "Nicholson" w/ partial eagle touch and "Robert —," engraved coat of arms on rim, 13.5" dia	250	350
Charger, rim engraved w/ folky angel, flowers, and letters "I, C, VP," faint touch marks for Richard Bache, London, 16.5" dia	250	350
Charger, "Thomas Badger, Boston" eagle touch, 13.25" dia	400	500
Charger, unmarked, 14" dia	150	250
Coffeepot, cast flower finial, gooseneck spout, spurred ear handle, marked "Homan & Co., Cincinnati," 8.75" h	75	150
Coffeepot, cast flower finial, gooseneck spout, spurred ear handle, partial mark for "Dunham" (Rufus Dunham, Westbrook, ME), 8.25" h	100	200
Communion Flagon, tankard shape, scrolled handle, hinged lid, marked "Smith & Feltman, Albany," 12" h	150	250
Ice Cream Mold, sailboat, marked "S & Co.," 5" l	75	125

Left to right: Teapot; Porringer; Candlestick; Tumbler; Teapot. —Photo courtesy Garth's Auctions, Delaware, OH.

	LOW	HIGH
Ladle, marked "J. Weeks" (New York City and Poughkeepsie), 13.25" l	150	250
Measure, bellied, cast ear handle, "B. V." (Birch & Villers) touch, Birmingham, 5" h	100	200
Pepper Pot, unmarked, 4.75" h	25	50
Plate, "Boardman & Co. New York" eagle touch (Thomas Danforth Boardman), 10.75" dia	200	300
Plate, crowned rose touch mark, "Jacob Whitmore" (Middletown, CT), 8" dia	150	250
Plate, eagle touch w/ partial name "Robert Palethorp," Philadelphia, 8.375" dia	400	500
Plates, "S. Kilbourn" eagle touch (Samuel Kilbourn, Baltimore, MD), 7.75" dia	300	400
Porringer, cast crown handle marked "IC," attributed to Boston area, 4.75" dia	150	250
Porringer, cast flowered handle, unmarked, 5.5" dia	200	300
Porringer, cast old English handle w/ eagle touch for "Hamlin" (Samuel Hamlin Jr. or Sr., Hartford and Providence), 4.25" dia	175	250
Snuff Box, shoe-shaped, simple tooling, unmarked, 3.5" l	100	200
Spoons, round bowls, 7" l, price for set of 6	100	150
Tall Pot, "F. Porter, Westbrook No. 1" touch (Freeman Porter, Westbrook, ME), 10.75" h	250	350
Tall Pot, marked "Simpson & Benham, N.Y.," 11" h	300	500
Tall Pot, "T. S. Derby" touch (Thomas S. Derby, Middletown, CT), 10.75" h	200	300
Teapot, gooseneck spout, cast spurred handle, "G. Richardson, Warranted" touch (Cranston, RI), 7.25" h	200	300
Teapot, gooseneck spout, scrolled wooden handle w/ thumbrest, marked "Atkin Brothers, Sheffield," individual size, 6.25" h	100	200
Teapot, gooseneck spout, wooden ear handle, "Hall, Boardman & Co." touch w/ "Best Britannia Metal," 8.125" h	200	300
Trade Sign, pair of rampant lions standing on shelf, supporting central crown, plaque below inscribed w/ names and dated 1713, Germany, 16" l	1500	2000
Tumbler, unmarked, 5.25" h	75	125
Water Pitcher, unmarked, 7.5" h	150	250

Left to right: Teapot; Water Pitcher; Lighthouse Coffeepot; pair of Whale Oil Lamps; 3 Porringers (front center). —Photo courtesy Skinner, Inc., Boston, MA.

Silver

Silver is alloyed with other metals for durability, as pure silver is too soft for most uses. The grade of silver is determined by the amount or percentage of alloy material contained. Sterling silver is 925 parts per 1000 pure (usually stated as .925).

The values listed are primarily for easily found items. However, some rare and valuable examples are included for comparison. Thicker, and therefore heavier, pieces are generally of better quality than lighter pieces. Although dents can be repaired by a skilled silversmith, the work is not cheap. Also beware that a faker can add new marks, new decoration (such as chasing) or even new parts (such as a new base).

For more information see *Encyclopedia of American Silver Manufacturers, Fourth Edition* by Dorothy T. Rainwater and Judy Redfield (Schiffer, Atglen, PA, 1998), *Jackson's Silver & Gold Marks of England, Scotland & Ireland* edited by Ian Pickford [Antique Collectors' Club, Woodbridge, Suffolk (England), 1989], and *The Price Guide to Antique Silver, 2nd Edition* by Peter Waldron [Antique Collectors' Club, Woodbridge, Suffolk (England), 1992].

Coin Silver

	LOW	HIGH
Beaker, barrel-form w/ reeded banding, monogrammed, marked on base, Asa Blanchard, Lexington, KY, 1818-38, 5 troy oz, 3.125" h	$3000	$5000
Butter Dish, covered, domed lid w/ floral finial and chased foliate banding, applied circular molded base w/ wide flange and pierced inset, monogrammed, base marked "Lincoln & Foss Pure Silver Coin Boston," 1848-57, 14 troy oz, 6" h, 6.125" dia	200	400
Creamer, engraved wreath w/ ribbon and initials "C. G.," maker's marks, 4.7 troy oz, 4.5" h	500	700

Auction prices for coin silver hollow ware w/ repoussé decoration, left to right: Waste bowl and ewer, William F. Ladd, New York City, 1828-45, approx. 48 troy oz, $1610; Pair of salts w/ gold-washed bowls, Ball, Black & Co., New York City, 1851-76, $288; Creamer and covered sugar, Allcock & Allen, New York City, c1820, approx. 35 troy oz, $978. —Photo courtesy Skinner, Inc., Boston, MA.

	LOW	HIGH
Creamer, Neoclassical helmet-form engraved w/ shield and swag motif, bright cut rim, square base, monogrammed, marked 4 times on base, Daniel Duprey, Philadelphia, 1785-1807, 4 troy oz, 7" h	600	800
Ladle, molded handle w/ V-slashed double-molded bowl, monogrammed and dated "1782," marked 3 times on handle, Joseph Richardson, Jr. and Nathaniel Richardson, Philadelphia, 1785-91, 7 troy oz, 13.75" l	500	800
Presentation Mug, inscribed "Wilson Sewing Machine Co." w/ portrait medallion and seal "special premium given by the Miss. Agril. Education & Mfg. Aids Ty" on base, Edward A. Tyler, New Orleans, c1860, 5 troy oz, 4" h	1400	1800
Salver, circular Rococo form w/ molded scrolled border and foliate scrolled feet, Lincoln and Reed, Boston, 1838-48, 30 troy oz, 13.5" dia	800	1000
Serving Spoon, bright cut decoration, monogrammed, marked twice, George Alexander and Peter Riker, New York, 1797-1800, 3 troy oz, 12" l	600	800
Serving Spoon, spatulate end mid-rib handle, engraved "SDS," William Homes, Boston, 1717-83, 2 troy oz, 8.25" l	150	250
Sugar, covered, 2-handled, acorn finial on domed lid, baluster-form w/ applied foliate and star banding, square molded base, monogrammed, marked twice on base, Thomas Fletcher and Sidney Gardner, Boston, 1808-25, 22 troy oz, 7" h	300	400
Sugar, covered, 2-handled, strawberry finial on molded circular lid, baluster-form body w/ acanthus leaf chasing and applied scroll and foliate banding, circular molded base w/ applied gadrooning, monogrammed, marked on base, Jonathan Stodder and Benjamin Frobisher, Boston, 1816-25, 23 troy oz, 7.75" h	400	600
Tankard, urn and flame finial on stepped domed lid, straight tapering body w/ applied molding at rim and base, applied beading above lower handle, hollow scroll handle w/ scroll thumb piece, rounded drop at upper joining, convex tip, monogrammed, marked on base, Samuel Minott, Boston, 1732-1802, 27 troy oz, 9" h	1500	1800
Teapot, basket of flowers finial on domed lid w/ foliate chasing, baluster-form body w/ applied foliate banding, ornately chased foliate and cornucopia handle, spout w/ similar chasing and open hands motif, circular molded base, Baldwin Gardiner, Philadelphia and New York, 1814-46, 43 troy oz, 10.5" h	800	1000
Teapot, basket of fruit finial on domed lid, baluster-form body w/ applied grape and foliate banding, scroll handle, oval molded base, engraved, marked on base, Henry Ball, Erastus Tompkins and William Black, New York, 1839-51, 32 troy oz, 10" h	600	800
Teapot, bird finial above domed lid w/ leaf chasing, baluster-form body w/ applied basket of fruit and flowers banding, figural serpent and fish-form handle, paneled serpent-form spout, molded circular base, marked "L. Allen," second quarter 19th C, 33 troy oz, 10.5" h	800	1000
Tea Set, Neoclassical, comprising a teapot, covered sugar, and helmet-form creamer, urn finials, applied beaded edge, monogrammed "AGL," Daniel Van Voorhis, Philadelphia and New York, 1751-1824, approx. 45 troy oz, 6.5" h teapot	4000	6000
Teaspoons, basket of flowers decoration on handles, outlined shell on bowls, monogrammed, Pelletreau, Bennett & Cook, New York, 1825-28, 3 troy oz, 5.75" l, price for set of 6	200	300
Water Pitcher, baluster-form body w/ molded circular base, chased foliate wreath centers inscription dated 1846, marked on base, Lincoln & Reed, Boston, 1838-48, 23 troy oz, 10.625" h	800	1000

Sheffield and Silver-Plated

	LOW	HIGH
Biscuit Tin, ovoid form flanked by lion mask loose-ring handles, attached conforming undertray, claw and ball feet, English, 8" h	$200	$400
Candelabra, 3-lite, scrolled candlearms on tapered standard, circular base, English, 19" h, price for pair	400	600
Candlesticks, cast-leaf standard, shaped circular base, weighted, American, 11.5" h, price for pair	600	900
Candlesticks, marked "Sheffield, E. P. N. S. Made in England," 12.25" h, price for set of 4	1000	1500
Candlesticks, telescopic w/ adjustable columnar standard, circular base, weighted, English, 7.5" h, price for pair	300	500
Coffee Set, comprising teapot, coffeepot, sugar, creamer, and tray, angular form w/ wooden handles, impressed "Made in England, T. W. + S., E. P. N. S.," 7" h, 18" l, 9.5" w	600	800
Entree Dishes, covered, oval-shaped, scroll handles, shell-edged liners, covers w/ loop handles and heraldic engraving on one side, 4 cast scroll feet, Smith, Sissons & Co., mid-19th C, 7.25" h, 13.75" l, 10.25" w, price for pair	600	800
Meat Cover, ovoid form w/ central engraved armorial crest, English, 14.25" l	100	200
Placecard Holders, each formed as coiled snake w/ inset copper-colored metal eyes and forked tongue, possibly Middle Eastern, 2.125" h, price for set of 14	500	800
Salt and Pepper Shakers, pair, engraved decoration, marked "England," 3.875" h, price for pair	200	300
Soup Tureen, full-bodied deer-form finial on lid, spherical body w/ 2 antlered deer trophy head handles, 4 deer-form legs, engraved w/ heraldic crest quartered by the Joy family arms, w/ fitted wooden box, Elkington & Co., England, mid-19th C, 13.25" h, 14" l	500	700
Tantalus, rectangular tray w/ handle w/ circular rod supports and plain ball knops and 4 bun feet, 3 glass decanters w/ inverted thistle-cut design, quadripartite plate neck collars, and circular prism-cut stoppers, marked "Grinsell's Patent," late 19th C	300	500
Tea Service, comprising teapot, sugar, and creamer, ovoid lobed form, ball feet, English, 5.5" h teapot	200	300
Tea Set, comprising teapot, covered creamer, open sugar, and waste bowl, domed lids w/ open shield-shaped finials, bodies banded top and bottom w/ stylized flowers on stippled ground, central band featuring chased and embossed bird motifs, each w/ 4 tapered feet topped by female masks, teapot w/ shell heat stops on handle, Meriden Brittania Co., late 19th C, 13.25" h teapot	300	500
Tea Tray, oval, 2-handled, gadrooned rim, engraved scrollwork bands, marked "E. P. N. S.," 30" l	150	250
Tray, oval w/ cast scroll and shell border and engraved mottoed crests, Matthew Boulton, England, late 18th C, 14.25" l, 11.25" w	200	400
Tray, shaped ovoid form w/ gallery, ball feet, American, 24" l	200	300
Tureen, ovoid w/ cast handles and reeded edge, domed lid w/ reeded edge and flower-form finial, reeded foot, monogrammed, Christofle, 20th C, 12" h, 18" l	400	600
Water Pitcher, raised floral decoration, Meriden & Co.	50	100
Waxjack, central spool w/ winder and ribbed socket, oval base w/ gadrooned rim, Old Sheffield Plate, late 18th/early 19th C, 5.75" h, 4.25" w	150	250

Sterling Silver

	LOW	HIGH
Bowl, 2-handled, open wire-work handles applied over faun's heads on foliate cartouches, tapered foot, Ball, Black & Co., 1850-75, approx. 23 troy oz, 5.25" h, 7.625" dia	$600	$800
Bowl, pierced rim and 3 handles continuing to form feet, monogrammed, Black, Starr & Frost, 18.5 oz, 10" dia	150	250
Bowl, round with anemone design, Wallace, mid-20th C, approx. 4 troy oz, 6" dia	100	200
Bowls, oval, ruffled sides and edge, applied cast scroll feet, monogrammed in center, William B. Durgin Co., retailed by Rand & Grant, approx. 31 troy oz total, 11.5" l, 8.5" w, price for pair	400	600
Castor, baluster-form body chased and embossd w/ foliate scrolls, 4 shell and scroll feet, monogrammed, American maker's mark rubbed, approx. 9 troy oz	250	350
Center Bowl, wide shaped and pierced edge w/ swirling oak leaves and acorns design, 6 scroll- and acorn-pierced feet linked w/ oak leaves, Gorham, c1901, approx. 56 troy oz, 3" h, 14.25" dia	1800	2500
Coffee and Tea Service, comprising teapot, coffeepot, covered sugar, and creamer, ovoid bodies w/ repoussé banding, teapot w/ serpentine spout, coffeepot of inverted baluster form, both w/ ivory heat stops on handles, monogrammed, Durham, 20th C, approx. 92 troy oz	1000	1500
Coffee Set, 3-part single-serving set includes covered sugar, creamer, and coffeepot, cylindrical bodies w/ 2 angled wooden handles, bulbous bases, and flaring circular foot, impressed maker's mark and "Sterling, 02741, 5 12 oz.," Lebkuecher and Co., Newark, NJ, 1896-1909, approx. 12 troy oz, 7" h coffeepot	300	500
Compotes, shell form w/ gadrooned border and reticulated edge, cast handle topped w/ caryatid above motif of fish tails, seaweed, and shells, 3 dolphin-form feet, Howard & Co., 1850-75, approx. 68 troy oz, 8.5" h, 10.5" l, 8.75" w, price for pair	4000	6000

Auction prices for sterling silver, left to right: Center Bowl, F. J. R. Gyllenberg, $633; Ladle, Mary P. Winlock, $345; Perfume, Katherine Pratt, $920; Bowl, Arthur Stone, $2645; Bowl, Katherine Pratt, $288; Center Bowl, Erickson, $1035. —Photo courtesy Skinner, Inc., Boston, MA.

Dresser Set, comprising hand mirror, hair brush, clothes brush, and nail file, Art Nouveau repoussé of women's faces and swirling florals, hair brush monogrammed, together w/ overlay perfume bottle, Wm. B. Kerr & Co., early 20th C, $518. —Photo courtesy Skinner, Inc., Boston, MA.

	LOW	HIGH
Dish, shaped sides, ribbed border on rim, monogrammed, Joseph Seymour Mfg. Co., late 19th C, approx. 14 troy oz, 2.5" h, 9.5" w	100	200
Fruit Bowl, shaped edge w/ realistically modeled and reticulated apple blossoms, monogrammed center, J. E. Caldwell & Co., late 19th/early 20th C, approx. 10 troy oz, 9.5" dia	300	400
Ladle, pierced handle w/ champleve enamel floral motif in green, purple, and white, impressed "M. P. W." and "sterling" on handle, Mary P. Winlock (member of Society of Arts and Crafts, Boston, 1901-27), 5" l	300	400
Low Bowl, circular w/ 7-sided rolled rim on circular flared footed base, hammered finish, impressed "Sterling Kalo 57" on base, Chicago, early 20th C, 2" h, 8.875" dia	400	600
Pitcher, baluster-form, tapered foot w/ ruffled edge, repoussé chased and embossed poppies on either side, cast handle w/ leaf detail, ruffled-edge spout, monogrammed, Redlich & Co., 20th C, approx. 36 troy oz, 9.25" h	2000	2500
Presentation Tea Set, Greco-Roman Revival, comprising a coffeepot, teapot, covered creamer, covered 2-handled sugar, and waste bowl, helmet-form finial w/ beading above scroll-engraved lid, elaborately engraved body centering a reserve of a locomotive (on coffeepot), reverse w/ identical engraving centering a reserve of 1868, beaded handles surmounted by neoclassical heads and ending in anthemion leaves, circular molded base, teapot inscribed "Presented to Addison Day Esq. by the Employees of the Rome, Watertown & Ogdensburg Railroad Co. Dec. 1st. 1868," 98 troy oz, 10.5" h coffeepot, 9.75" h teapot	3000	5000
Teapot, flattened spherical form w/ curved spout, upright swing handle, and hinged lid, hammered finish, raised monogram "HF," impressed "Steiu, Sterling, 186," approx. 23 troy oz, 7.25" h, 6.5" w	300	500
Trophy Cup, 2-handled, baluster form w/ angular handles, engraved "1937 Washington Handicap one mile and a quarter, Laurel, Maryland Won by War Admiral," tapered foot, Black, Starr & Frost, retailed by Schofield, Baltimore, approx. 50 troy oz, 11.5" h	600	800
Water Pitcher, paneled baluster form w/ ribbed detailing and serpentine handle, Tiffany & Co., 1875-91, approx. 31 troy oz, 7.75" h	1000	1500
Water Pitcher, vasiform body w/ tapered neck and ribbed border at top edge, angular handle, oval stepped foot, monogrammed, Gorham, late 19th C, approx. 26 troy oz, 9.75" h	400	600

Silver Flatware

Silverware includes factory merchandise and products of individual craftsmen. Chief American manufacturers include Gorham, Reed and Barton, Towle, Wallace, Rogers, Oneida, Kirk and International.

Values are given in two sections. In the first we list a large variety of tableware and serving pieces for two patterns (one sterling silver and one silver-plated). Values are for excellent condition monogrammed pieces (*M*) and excellent condition pieces with no monogram (*NM*).

In the second section, we list five key pieces for a variety of patterns listed under the name of their manufacturer: Values are for excellent condition pieces with no monogram. Dinner Fork (*DnF*), Salad Fork (*SF*), Tablespoon (*Tb*), Soup Spoon (*SpSp*) and Teaspoon (*Tsp*).

For further information see *Silverware of the 20th Century: The Top 250 Patterns* by Harry L. Rinker (House of Collectibles, NY, 1997), *Silverplated Flatware, Revised Fourth Edition* by Tere Hagan (Collector Books, Paducah, KY, 1990, 1998 vlaue update), and *Sterling Flatware: An Identification and Value Guide, Revised Second Edition* by Tere Hagan (L-W Book Sales, Gas City, IN, 1999).

Reed & Barton – Francis I Pattern

(sterling – introduced 1906)

	M	NM
Asparagus Server, 9.875"	$240	$300
Baby Fork, 4.375"	32	40
Bonbon Spoon, 4.625"	40	50
Butter Serving Knife, flat handle, 7.125"	40	50
Butter Serving Knife, hollow handle, 7"	35	42
Butter Spreader, flat handle, 5.625"	25	32
Cake Server, 9.75"	120	150
Cake Server, stainless steel blade, 10.375"	40	50
Carving Fork, stainless steel tines, 8.875"	60	75
Carving Knife, stainless steel blade	60	75
Cheese Knife, stainless steel blade, 7.25"	45	55
Cheese Plane, stainless steel plane, 9"	60	75
Cheese Server, stainless steel blade, 6.75"	45	55

Reed & Barton, Francis I pattern. —Photo courtesy William Doyle Galleries.

	M	NM
Cocktail Fork, 5.625"	32	40
Cold Meat Serving Fork, 7.875"	80	100
Cold Meat Serving Fork, 9.25"	120	150
Cream Sauce Ladle, 5.75"	45	55
Cream Soup Spoon, round bowl, 6"	35	42
Fish Server, 12"	240	300
Fork, 7.125"	40	50
Fork, 7.75"	60	75
Gravy Ladle, 6.875"	80	100
Ice Cream Server, 11.25"	240	300
Ice Cream Slicer, 12.5"	160	200
Iced Tea Spoon, 7.625"	40	50
Jelly Spoon, 6.25"	32	40
Knife, hollow handle, stainless steel blade, 8.875"	40	50
Lasagna Server, stainless steel blade, 10"	55	70
Lemon Fork, 4.875"	32	40
Macaroni Server, 10.5"	240	300
Pickle Fork, short handle, 6"	32	40
Pie Server, stainless steel blade, 9.625"	55	70
Punch Ladle, 15.5"	375	475
Salad Fork, 6.125"	40	50
Salad Serving Fork, 9.5"	135	175
Salad Serving Spoon	135	175
Soup Ladle, 11.5"	240	300
Soup Ladle, stainless steel bowl, 11"	120	150
Steak Knife, 8.875"	48	60
Sugar Spoon, 5.875"	32	40
Sugar Tongs, 4.125"	55	70
Tablespoon, 8.375"	80	100
Teaspoon, 5 o'clock, 5.5"	25	30
Toast Server, 10.125"	280	350
Wedding Cake Knife, stainless steel blade, 12.625"	45	55
Youth Knife, 7.125"	32	40

International – Vintage Pattern

(plated – patented 1904)

Butter Serving Knife, flat handle, 7.125"	$25	$35
Carving Fork, stainless steel tines, 11"	100	125
Casserole Serving Spoon, 8.875"	60	75
Cocktail Fork, 6"	15	22
Cold Meat Serving Fork, 8.25"	48	65
Cream Sauce Ladle, 5.5"	38	50
Fork, 7.75"	20	30
Fruit Spoon, 5.75"	20	30
Gravy Ladle, 7.125"	60	75
Knife, hollow handle, Old French blade, 9"	38	50
Salad Fork	45	60
Soup Spoon, oval bowl, 7.25"	25	35
Sugar Spoon, 6"	20	30
Tablespoon, 8.25"	30	40
Teaspoon, 6"	15	20
Youth Knife, 7.5"	30	40

Other Patterns

	YEAR	DnF	SF	Tb	SpSp	Tsp
ALVIN CO.						
Bridal Rose, sterling	1903	$75	$55	$155	$60	$45
Della Robbia, sterling	1922	50	40	110	45	35
Florence Nightingale, sterling	1919	40	32	85	38	23
Gainsborough, sterling	1925	35	30	75	30	25
Hamilton, sterling	1913	40	30	55	30	20
Lorna Doone, sterling	1925	35	25	70	30	22
Maytime, sterling	1936	40	30	80	30	20
Miss America, sterling	1932	30	28	75	35	20
Prince Eugene, sterling	1950	60	50	135	55	30
Rosecrest, sterling	1955	35	25	70	30	20
Spring Bud, sterling	1956	35	28	65	30	17
Winchester, sterling	1915	45	35	90	45	30
BAKER–MANCHESTER MFG. CO.						
Bridal Wreath, sterling	1919	$37	$28	$75	$33	$30
Roger Williams, sterling	1916	35	30	80	30	24
Spartan, sterling	1914	30	26	85	35	25
DOMINICK & HAFF						
Gothic, sterling	1900	$65	$50	$150	$60	$45
Marie Antoinette, sterling	1917	40	30	90	40	30
Priscilla, sterling	1916	30	25	75	35	25
Virginia, sterling	1912	35	25	70	35	20
DURGIN DIVISION OF GORHAM						
Bead, sterling	1893	$40	$30	$85	$40	$25
Colfax, sterling	1922	45	35	100	40	35
DuBarry, sterling	1901	85	75	195	90	45
Essex, sterling	1911	45	30	90	40	30
Fleur de Lis, sterling	1886	60	50	140	60	30
Hunt Club, sterling	1931	50	35	80	35	25
Iris, sterling	1900	35	25	75	35	20
Louis XV, sterling	1891	95	75	175	90	50
Medallion, sterling	1870	150	135	350	175	75

Durgin Division of Gorham, Iris pattern. —Photo courtesy Skinner, Inc., Boston, MA.

	YEAR	DnF	SF	Tb	SpSp	Tsp
New Queens, sterling	1900	75	65	170	80	40
No. 19-G, sterling	1912	40	30	75	35	20
Old Standish, sterling	1901	40	25	70	35	18
Princess Patricia, sterling	1927	38	25	65	30	15
Watteau, sterling	1891	50	40	115	50	30
FESSENDEN & CO.						
Antique, sterling	1880	$35	$27	$80	$33	$33
Greenwich, sterling	1890	50	40	110	45	30
Old Boston, hammered, sterling	1880	45	30	100	40	25
FRANK M. WHITING & CO.						
Damascus, sterling	1894	$60	$50	$130	$55	$35
Esther, sterling	1890	65	50	140	60	40
Genoa, sterling	1893	70	50	135	50	30
Georgian Shell, sterling	1948	55	45	105	40	20
Pearl, sterling	1888	50	35	105	40	30
Princess Ingrid, sterling	1945	55	40	110	50	35
FRANK SMITH SILVER CO.						
Bostonia, sterling	1914	$45	$35	$90	$35	$25
Crystal, sterling	1921	55	40	105	50	30
Ivanhoe, sterling	1915	50	40	100	45	32
M. W. Lily, sterling	1915	40	30	70	30	20
No. 2, sterling	1918	45	40	115	45	30
Oak, sterling	1912	75	65	165	70	45
Pilgrim, sterling	1909	35	30	80	35	20
Shell, sterling	1890	45	35	95	40	25
Tulipan, sterling	1933	50	40	105	45	30
GEORG JENSEN						
Acanthus, sterling	1917	$80	$75	$160	$70	$60
Acorn, sterling	1915	100	95	200	90	75
Bernadotte, sterling	1939	135	125	250	120	100
Cactus, sterling	1930	170	160	340	150	125
Pyramid, sterling	1926	60	45	90	40	35

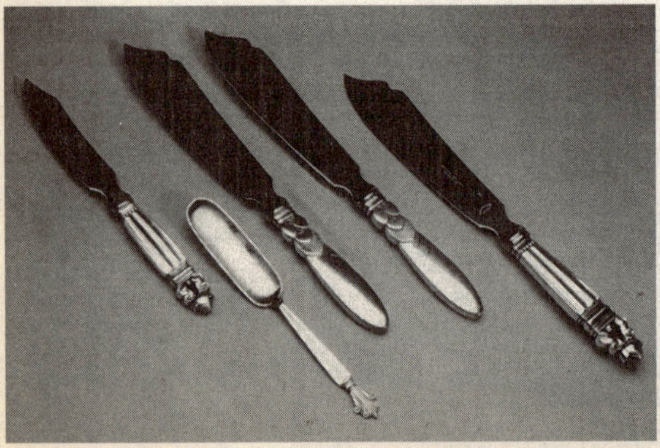

Georg Jensen patterns, left to right: Acorn, Acanthus, Cactus. —Photo courtesy Skinner, Inc., Boston, MA.

Gorham, Versailles pattern. —Photo courtesy Skinner, Inc., Boston, MA.

	YEAR	DnF	SF	Tb	SpSp	Tsp
GORHAM						
Camellia, sterling	1942	$40	$30	$60	$30	$20
Chantilly, sterling	1895	65	50	85	50	25
Chateau Rose, sterling	1963	55	35	70	30	22
English Gadroon, sterling	1939	65	50	80	35	27
Greenbrier, sterling	1938	60	35	70	30	25
Lancaster, sterling	1897	60	45	70	35	25
Lily of the Valley, sterling	1950	70	50	85	45	25
Melrose, sterling	1948	65	55	90	55	30
Old English Tipt, sterling	1870	75	50	95	65	32
Rondo, sterling	1951	75	60	100	65	30
Sea Rose, sterling	1958	60	50	80	45	25
Versailles, sterling	1888	80	90	130	80	50
INTERNATIONAL SILVER CO.						
Adoration, plated	1930	$17	$15	$27	$17	$12
Angelique, sterling	1959	40	40	50	45	25
Brocade, sterling	1950	70	50	80	60	27
Daffodil, plated	1950	17	15	27	15	10
Du Barry, sterling	1968	60	50	75	55	40
Eternally Yours, plated	1941	17	15	25	15	10
First Love, plated	1937	17	17	25	15	7
Frontenac, sterling	1903	55	70	95	60	30
Joan of Arc, sterling	1940	55	40	80	45	22
Minuet, sterling	1925	50	32	60	32	20
Orleans, plated	1964	15	15	20	15	10
Prelude, sterling	1939	50	40	85	45	20
Queen's Lace, sterling	1949	40	40	90	45	27
Remembrance, plated	1948	15	15	20	15	10
Royal Danish, sterling	1939	45	37	90	50	25
Silver Rhythm, sterling	1953	40	40	65	35	20
Spring Glory, sterling	1942	60	32	70	35	22

International Silver Co., Wild Rose pattern. *Kirk Stieff Co., Repoussé pattern.*
—Photos courtesy Skinner, Inc., Boston, MA.

	YEAR	DnF	SF	Tb	SpSp	Tsp
Wedgwood, sterling	1924	55	45	90	50	25
Wild Rose, sterling	1908	45	40	80	40	25
KIRK STIEFF CO.						
Golden Winslow, sterling, gold accent	1850	$75	$65	$120	$70	$35
Old Maryland, sterling	1850	50	40	80	35	25
Rose, sterling	1937	60	60	100	60	35
Williamsburg Queen Anne, sterling	1940	60	60	120	50	40
LUNT SILVERSMITHS						
Bel Chateau, sterling	1983	$45	$50	$80	$50	$25
Mignonette, sterling	1960	70	60	95	65	35
William & Mary, sterling	1921	55	35	65	40	25
MANCHESTER SILVER CO.						
American Beauty, sterling	1935	$55	$45	$125	$50	$30
Beaux Art, sterling	1920	40	30	90	35	25
Fleetwood, sterling	1934	45	30	90	35	25
Priscilla, sterling	1928	40	30	75	35	18
Vogue, sterling	1932	40	30	70	30	16
MOUNT VERNON CO.						
Chelsea, sterling	1920	$40	$30	$100	$35	$30
Florence, sterling	1905	60	45	130	50	35
George II, sterling	1912	45	30	90	35	25
Kenwood, sterling	1916	45	30	90	35	27
Lexington, sterling	1900	40	35	95	40	27
Medford, sterling	1905	45	35	90	35	25
Pointed Antique, sterling	1900	45	30	75	30	20
Queen Anne, sterling	1915	40	30	70	35	16
Sedgwick, sterling	1908	35	25	65	30	15
Wentworth, sterling	1905	35	25	75	30	18

	YEAR	DnF	SF	Tb	SpSp	Tsp
ONEIDA, LTD.						
Caprice, plated	1937	$15	$12	$20	$12	$7
Damask Rose, sterling	1946	50	30	65	35	25
Grenoble, plated	1938	17	15	20	15	10
Heiress, sterling	1942	40	30	60	30	20
Lady Hamilton, plated	1932	15	15	22	17	10
Modern Baroque, plated	1969	12	17	22	15	12
Queen Bess II, plated	1946	12	12	17	12	7
Virginian, sterling	1942	45	35	80	38	25
REED & BARTON						
Autumn Leaves, sterling	1957	$60	$45	$85	$40	$25
Classic Rose, sterling	1954	60	50	90	45	25
Florentine Lace, sterling	1951	60	60	110	65	35
French Chippendale, plated	1981	17	15	20	15	12
Grande Renaissance, sterling	1967	60	37	80	40	25
Lark, sterling	1960	60	50	80	50	25
Marlborough, sterling	1906	60	45	90	50	25
Savannah, sterling	1962	75	70	120	75	45
Silver Wheat, sterling	1952	60	40	70	40	25
Tara, sterling	1955	60	50	110	50	30
SAMUEL KIRK & SON, INC.						
Ellipse, sterling	1968	$45	$30	$75	$35	$20
King, sterling	1827	70	50	125	55	30
Rose, sterling	1937	60	50	130	60	35
Wadefield, sterling	1850	50	40	75	40	25
SCHOFIELD CO.						
Frabee, sterling	1936	$45	$35	$95	$40	$25
Lorraine, sterling	1900	45	40	100	45	28
Raleigh, sterling	1905	35	25	65	25	16
TIFFANY & CO.						
Century, sterling	1937	$75	$65	$90	$70	$45
English King, sterling	1885	180	130	210	150	85
Rat Tail, sterling	1958	65	55	75	60	40
Shell and Thread, sterling	1905	120	100	150	115	75
TOWLE						
Chippendale, sterling	1937	$65	$45	$85	$50	$22
Debussy, sterling	1959	60	65	100	60	32
Fontana, sterling	1957	50	40	90	50	25
King Richard, sterling	1932	60	45	90	50	25
Madeira, sterling	1948	50	32	65	40	20
Old Master, sterling	1942	40	35	85	45	25
Rambler Rose, sterling	1937	45	37	80	45	22
Spanish Provincial, sterling	1967	45	40	85	45	20
TUTTLE SILVER CO.						
Classic Antique, sterling	1926	$40	$28	$75	$35	$20
Hannah Hull, sterling	1928	45	35	100	40	27
Francis I, sterling	1906	75	50	100	42	30

	YEAR	DnF	SF	Tb	SpSp	Tsp
WALLACE SILVERSMITHS						
Carnation, sterling	1909	$75	$60	$110	$70	$35
French Regency, sterling	1986	50	40	75	45	27
Grand Colonial, sterling	1942	50	35	80	45	25
Hamilton, sterling	1911	70	60	90	65	28
La Reine, sterling	1921	75	60	110	50	35
Meadow Rose, sterling	1907	40	37	90	40	27
Old Atlanta, sterling	1975	50	37	95	45	27
Rose Point, sterling	1934	40	50	85	45	25
Silver Swirl, sterling	1955	55	45	75	50	18
Soliloquy, sterling	1963	45	40	60	45	17
St. George, sterling	1890	80	70	100	75	35
Waltz of Spring, sterling	1952	75	60	120	65	35
WATSON CO. (WALLACE)						
King Philip, sterling	1904	$45	$35	$90	$40	$25
Laurel, sterling	1917	35	30	80	30	20
Marlborough, sterling	1918	50	45	75	45	25
Mount Vernon, sterling	1907	50	40	65	45	20
Orleans, sterling	1915	65	45	105	50	25
Priscilla Alden, sterling	1923	40	30	80	35	20
Rochambeau, sterling	1919	80	65	150	70	35
Virginia, sterling	1911	70	60	100	65	30
Wedding Rose, sterling	1900	70	55	145	65	30
Windsor, sterling	1920	45	35	85	40	20
WHITING DIVISION OF GORHAM						
Alhambra, sterling	1870	$60	$50	$140	$60	$40
Colonial, sterling	1907	45	35	85	35	25
Duchess, sterling	1906	45	35	100	40	27
Eastlake, sterling	1885	40	35	80	35	20
Fruit, sterling	1876	60	55	130	60	38
Indian, sterling	1875	45	35	90	35	28
Keystone, sterling	1875	60	50	145	60	35
Laureate, sterling	1880	50	40	100	45	35
Lily, sterling	1902	95	95	155	70	60

Whiting Division of Gorham, Lily pattern. —Photo courtesy Skinner, Inc., Boston, MA.

Tinware

Often overlooked, tin collectibles can still be found at many garage sales. Look for undented pieces with little or no corrosion. For more information read *Early American Copper, Tin & Brass* by Henry J. Kauffman (Astragal Press, Mendham, NJ, 1995).

Left: Riverboat birdcage, American, 19th C, 20.5" h, $6900 at auction.

Right: Rooster, Continental, 29" h, $1035 at auction.

—Photos courtesy Skinner, Inc., Boston, MA.

	LOW	HIGH
Candle Lantern, cylindrical, inner cylinder w/ horn inserts revolves for access to candle, air vent top w/ strap ring handle, 12" h plus ring	$250	$350
Candle Lantern, pierced pyramidal top, glass on 4 sides, wire protectors on 3 sides, sliding door w/ round and square cut-out, strap ring handle, painted black, 11.5" h plus handle	250	350
Candle Lantern, square, hinged door, glass sides, wire cross guards, pierced cylinder top, wire bail handle, 10.625" h	250	350
Candle Mold, 4 tubes, strap ear handle, miniature, 5.5" h	400	500
Candle Mold, 12 tubes, 2 rows, poplar frame, wire rods for tying wicks, 15.75" h, 17.5" l, 5.5" w	600	800
Candle Mold, 24-tube, rectangular w/ 4 rows, strap handle, 8.5" h	100	150
Candle Sconces, crimped tops, circular base, 13" h, price for pair	300	400
Chamberstick, push-up, saucer base, strap ring handle, 5" h	50	75
Coffeepot, cast finial, punched design w/ Gothic arch, leaf, and flower, shiny pressed-out tin spout, 11.5" h	300	400
Colander, heart-shaped, 4.5" w	200	300
Cookie Cutter Set, 12 miniature cutters, round tin box painted green and labeled "Tala, Made in England," 4.5" dia box	100	150
Foot Warmer, mortised hardwood frame w/ turned corner posts, punched heart and circle design, 5.75" h, 9" l, 8" w	150	250
Horn, conical, wooden mouthpiece w/ reed, 24" l	100	150
Lard Lamp, diamond-shaped font on raised stem, saucer base, strap ring handle, 9" h	75	125
Matchholder, conical body, octagonal base, bail handle, 5" dia	80	120
Spice Box, covered, rectangular, embossed flower and strap handle on lid, 4 interior compartments w/ nutmeg grater in center, 5.5" l	150	250
Spice Cabinet, 2 banks of 4 drawers, stenciled labels on drawers, back labeled "Made in Germany," 11.25" h, 9" w, 3.625" d	100	150
Tinder Box, round, candle socket on lid, circular strap handle, w/ steel, flint, and damper, 4.5" dia	200	300

Toleware

Toleware is painted tinware. It ranges from the sophisticated forms produced in eighteenth-century France to the simple pieces from the backwoods of nineteenth-century America.

When buying toleware, pay attention to condition. Many pieces have flaked off much of their original paint and have been heavily restored or entirely repainted. Dents and rust also lower the value. Early American pieces are often reproduced and sometimes faked. Construction technique is often your best clue to authenticity. Modern electrical welding is often smoothed out by grinding the surfaces near the weld. Look for modern grinding marks.

All items listed are American unless noted otherwise.

Toleware at auction, left to right: Coffeepot, American, 10.5" h, $1093; Document box, dome top, American, 9.5" l, $5463; Urns, French, 19th C, price for pair, $575. —Photos courtesy Skinner, Inc., Boston, MA.

	LOW	HIGH
Bank, conical, yellow ground, green foliage decoration, black inscription in German, 3.75" h	$75	$125
Box, dome top, brown japanning w/ yellow, red, and green striping and floral decoration, bail handle, 7" l	300	400
Box, dome top, dark brown japanning w/ white band and red and yellow decoration, ring handle, 4.25" l	50	100
Coffeepot, black japanning w/ red, green, yellow, and white floral decoration, strap ear handle, 9.5" h	800	1000
Coffeepot, dark brown japanning, red, green, and yellow floral decoration, 10.5" h	300	400
Coffeepot, domed lid, dark brown japanning w/ red, green, brown, blue, and yellow floral decoration, 10.5" h	500	700
Creamer, hinged lid, dark brown japanning w/ yellow, green, red, and white floral decoration, 4.25" h	500	600
Deed Box, dome top, black japanning w/ yellow striping and stenciled flowers, 9" l	100	150
Deed Box, dome top, brown japanning w/ red, blue, white, and yellow decoration including swags and striping, brass bail handle, 12" l	700	900
Deed Box, dome top, dark brown japanning w/ yellow, red, green, and black floral decoration, white band w/ painter's mark, 8.75" l	800	1000
Food Warmer, covered, cylindrical, brown japanning w/ striping and faded floral detail, w/ burner and pans, 8.25" h	150	200

Military Memorabilia

Military memorabilia encompasses items pertaining to all branches of the military. Some hobbyists collect military memorabilia by type of item—for example, badges or swords—while others collect by military branch (Navy, Army or Air Force) or war (Civil War). For more information consult *The Official Price Guide to Military Collectibles, Sixth Edition* by Richard J. Austin (House of Collectibles, NY, 1998) and *American Military Collectibles Price Guide* by Ron Manion (Antique Trader Books, Dubuque, IA, 1995).

Warning! Federal law prohibits the sale of American military medals. There has been a crackdown at military memorabilia shows.

Civil War

The most desirable collectible in this category is that of firearms. This period in time marked a technological transition from a single-shot gun to one that would shoot several times, including the first machine gun. Other collectible areas include uniforms, buttons, belt buckles, canteens, knapsacks, insignia and personal effects, such as diaries, letters and photographs. For more information consult *The Official Price Guide to Civil War Collectibles, 2nd Edition* by Richard Friz (House of Collectibles, NY, 1995) and *The Civil War Collector's Price Guide, 8th Edition* (North South Trader's Civil War/Publisher's Press, Orange, VA, 1997).

	LOW	HIGH
Albumen Photograph, cavalryman wearing sack coat and kepi, period mat and frame, 5.25" x 7.25" image size	$100	$200
Albumen Photograph, "Major Wm. W. Anderson, 20th PA Cavalry, 181st Regt, Accidentally killed at Harpers Ferry," 5.25" x 7.375" image size	400	500
Ambrotype, cased 6th plate, seated Confederate private w/ double-breasted coat and gilt buttons, mat signed "Lanneau, Artist," 3.125" x 3.625"	200	400
Ambrotype, cased 8th plate, seated Confederate soldier holding Remington-type revolver, thermoplastic case, 2.5" x 3"	500	700
Ambrotype, cased 9th plate, Confederate lieutenant w/ shoulder strap insignia and gilt buttons, thermoplastic case marked "Peck," 2.5" x 3"	500	700
Badge, Eighth Corp., 6-pointed star w/ soldered button-type shank, 1"	25	50

Top: Confederate Bowie Knife, hand-inscribed blade w/ Confederate flag surrounded by "Our [flag] and Our RIGHTS," hand-fitted scabbard, $12,615 at auction. —Photo courtesy James D. Julia.

Bottom: Snare Drum, w/ peephole, woven carrying strap, Massachusetts Drum Manufactory paper label, $4370 at auction. —Photo courtesy Skinner, Inc., Boston, MA.

	LOW	HIGH
Book, *Hardee's Tactics,* published 1861, soft cover, inscribed "James C. Cole from his brother Dr. Whalin Cole C.S.A."	400	600
Book, *Regulations of the Army of Confederate States,* by J. W. Randolph, Richmond, published 1863, hardcover	500	600
Canteen, Model 1858, wool covering, tin spout w/ ring and cork plug, 8" dia	250	350
Carte de Visite, infantryman in front of tents, haversack reads "71 - N. Y.," period frame, 4.75" x 6.5"	150	250
Drum, red hoops, "Edward Baack, N.Y." label inside, head stenciled "D.C. Connely Stewarts Run, PA"	800	1000
Epaulets, cased pair, captain of medical staff, gilded brass and thread w/ red silk and leather lining, signed "W. H. Horstman & Sons, Philadelphia," toleware case w/ gold-stenciled eagles and stars, center compartment w/ brass tassels, 9.75" l case	1250	1500
Epaulets, cased pair, by Schuyler, Hartley & Graham, gilded finish and buttons marked "G & cie, Paris," tin box w/ japanning	150	350
Fife, rosewood, plated ends, "Geo. Cloos Crosby" stamp, 16.875" l	100	200
Hardee Hat, insignia consists of bugle and numbers "1" and "2," brass eagle and shield plate, signed "U.S. Army extra manufacture," 6" x 13.5"	1500	2000
Hat Insignia, infantry officer's, gold embroidery, tufted area in crook of horn w/ silver "18," 2" x 3.375"	100	150
Insignia, artillery, crossed cannons, embroidered, red velvet center, black velvet ground	100	150
Insignia, corps. of engineers, castle, brass, 1.5" x 1.75"	200	250
Insignia, infantry, bugle, brass, 2" x 3.5"	75	125
Insignia, infantry officer's, heavy gold thread w/ sequins around bell and mouthpiece, backing cut in oval	100	150
Insignia, ordnance, bomb, brass, 1.625"	50	100
Kepi, artillery, red wool w/ white piping and black band around base, w/ eagle "A" buttons, manufactured by "Bent & Bush-Boston,"	600	800
Pocket Surgeon's Kit, includes scalpel, various picks w/ horn or tortoiseshell handles, and probe, wooden case	150	200
Regimental Roster, "Co. B, 160th Regt., N.Y. Vols.," bright colors, shadow box frame, 21.5" x 26.5"	100	150
Salt Print, enlisted man in uniform w/ musket, cartridge box, and cap box, standing in front of camp backdrop, framed, 5.25" x 7.375"	100	150
Shoulder Strap, captain, medium blue ground w/ heavy gold border	50	100
Shoulder Strap, colonel, eagle, blue ground	150	250
Shoulder Strap, infantry lieutenant, deep blue ground	50	100
Stencil Kit, complete w/ brass alphabet stencils, pan, brush, and "N. G. Batchelder" nameplate, 8.75" x 5.5" tin case	100	200
Stereoviews, E. & H. T. Anthony's War Views series, "Burial of dead at Fredricksburg, VA" (negative by Brady), "Bomb proofs at Ft. Sedgwick," and "Grand review of the Veteran armies of Grant & Sherman at Wash.," price for 3	100	150
Tintype, cased 1/4 plate, infantry officer identified as Lt. Jesse Horton, wearing gloves and epaulets, holding a Hardee hat, paint-decorated case w/ pearl inlay, 4" x 4.875"	300	400
Tintype, cased 6th plate, soldier wearing kepi and holding telescope, 2.375" x 2.875"	200	300
Tintype, cased 6th plate, standing Union officer wearing Hardee hat, holster, and sword drawn from scabbard, gilt highlights, thermoplastic case w/ man and woman w/ palm trees, 3.25" x 3.75"	400	500
Tintype, cased 9th plate, enlisted man wearing forage cap and coat, holding musket w/ bayonet, 1/2 case, 2.5" x 3.75"	200	300

Left: Ohio National Guard fatigue cap and jacket, $330 at auction.

Right: Post-Civil War helmet and coat, $660 at auction.

Bottom center: U.S.N. Chapeau and full dress epaulets in Horstmann tin box, $743 at auction.

—Photo courtesy Gene Harris Antique Auction Center, Inc.

Uniforms

	LOW	HIGH
Aviator's Coat, U.S. Navy officer's, WWII, 3/4 length, dark brown leather w/ real fur collar, double-breasted front, satin and alpaca lining, matching belt, slash pockets, woven BuAero marked label in neck	$200	$300
Belt, German Army, WWII, black leather, pebbled aluminum body and 4-tab roundel	35	50
Beret, U.S. Army/Navy, Vietnam War, American advisor to South Vietnamese Junk Force, dark blue wool, metal Junk Force emblem, black leather band, light blue lining	80	120
Beret, U.S. Army Special Forces, Vietnam War, red beret flash on front w/ enamel and metal special forces badge	70	80
Blouse, English Army officer's, WWII, khaki cotton twill, brass artillery buttons, bronze collar insignias, 2nd lieutenant shoulder strap insignias, 3-award ribbon bar	125	175
Blouse, Polish Army non-commissioned officer's, WWII, British-pattern battle dress, khaki wool	450	550
Blouse, U.S. Army enlisted man's, 1918, light olive drab wool serge, 4 pockets, standing collar, full dark tan cotton lining, 1918 quartermaster's label, bullion overseas stripe on left cuff	60	75
Blouse, U.S. Marine Corps enlisted man's, WWII, forest green wool, 1944 USMC quartermaster's markings, 1st Marine Division patch on left shoulder, 1937 pattern Eagle, Globe, and Anchor devices, wide plastic-coated 3-place ribbon bar, trace of removed chevrons	30	40
Blouse, U.S. Navy chief petty officer's, WWII, dark tan cotton twill, removable gilt NAVY buttons and rate on left sleeve	30	40
Breeches, Soviet Union Air Force officer's, c1950, khaki wool twill, seam piping, pockets, belt loops, button calves	15	35
Breeches, U.S. Army officer's, WWI, dark tan cotton twill, zinc U.S. Army button fly and lace calves	15	25
Bush Hat, U.S. Air Force, Vietnam War, olive drab cotton, wide stitched brim snaps up on each side, red cotton lining, locally made color "Nakhon Phanom" tab sewn to front	50	75
Campaign Hat, U.S. Marine Corps, WWI, olive drab fur/felt body, brim edge folded under and double stitched, ribbed satin band, leather chinstrap, leather sweatband, dark bronze finish Eagle, Globe, and Anchor device on front of crown	175	225

	LOW	HIGH
Cap, U.S. Navy enlisted man's, WWI, navy blue melton wool w/ stiffener in wide flat crown, green cotton lining, woven clothier's label, silk-woven *U.S.S. Florida* ribbon	50	75
Cap, U.S. Navy enlisted man's, WWII, Donald Duck style, navy blue melton wool, gold leaf "U.S. Navy" ribbon	15	25
Cavalry Boots, German Army officer's, WWII, black leather, scalloped tops, 2 cloth loops, leather soles and heels w/ heavy duty horseshoes, spur tabs above heels	50	100
Cavalry Boots, U.S. Army, pre-WWII, russet brown leather, cap toes, laced fronts, leather soles, rubber heels	100	150
Combat Boots, U.S. Army, WWII, roughout brown leather, laced insteps, 2-buckle smooth leather uppers	100	150
Combat Helmet, German Army, WWII, "EF64" shell w/ original gray rough texture base paint covered w/ tan, green, and reddish camouflage paint, leather liner, steel liner band,	450	550
Combat Helmet, U.S. Army, WWI, olive drab sand finish shell w/ erratic camouflage design in shades of red, brown, and light green, 87th Division design on crown, w/ liner and leather chinstrap	75	100
Dress Tunic, German Army enlisted man's, 1942, reed-green herringbone twill, 4 patch pockets, 6 removable-button front, machine sewn-on gray bevo eagle and collar tape tabs, slip-on artillery straps, partial gray satin lining, 2 aluminum belt ramps	400	450
Fatigue Cap, U.S. Army, WWII, dark olive drab herringbone twill w/ pleated body and stitched bill	10	20
Fatigue Shirt, U.S. Marine Corps, WWII, light olive drab herringbone twill, large internal pocket each side of chest, gas flap, black-finish metal buttons, platoon sergeant chevron stenciled on each sleeve, Eagle, Globe, and Anchor stencil on chest pocket	30	60
Fatigue Trousers, U.S. Army, Vietnam War era, medium weight cotton w/ spot duck hunter camouflage pattern on light olive ground, conventional cut w/ zip fly and metal star buttons	20	30
Field Cap, U.S. Army, WWII, dark green canvas w/ dark green lining, short stitched brim, fold-down earflaps, chinstrap, 1940 quartermaster's tag	20	30
Field Jacket, South Vietnamese Army, c1967, cotton twill w/ tiger stripe camouflage pattern	100	150
Field Jacket, U.S. Army, WWII, light olive drab poplin, olive drab wool lining, zipper/button front, slash pockets, button adjustable tab at waist and cuffs, epaulets	150	175
Field Jacket, U.S. Army officer's, WWII, "Ike jacket," olive drab wool serge w/ woven maker's label, olive drab satin lining, 2nd Army patch on left shoulder, 6 overseas bars	40	65
Field Trousers, U.S. Army, 1943, light olive drab wool serge, 1943 quartermaster's label	30	40
Garrison Cap, U.S. Women's Army Corps, 1944, tan cotton twill, WAC piping, 1944 quartermaster's tag	10	20
Greatcoat, German Army enlisted man's, WWII, gray wool, large collar, partial gray lining w/ pocket	100	150
Jeep Cap, U.S. Army, WWII, light olive drab knit wool w/ fold-down earflaps and cardboard-stiffened short bill	30	50
Mittens, Arctic, U.S. Army, Korean War, dark olive drab cotton, light brown leather palms, alpaca facing, adjustable straps on wrists and gauntlets	15	25
Overcoat, U.S. Army Airborne enlisted man's, 1941, heavy olive drab wool, large gilt eagle buttons, double-breasted front, 1941 quartermaster's label, theater-made 1st Airborne Division patch on left shoulder	35	50

Above: Campaign Hat, U.S. Signal Corps.

Left: Field Jacket, U.S. Army, WWII.

	LOW	HIGH
Overcoat, U.S. Army enlisted man's, WWI, light olive drab wool, large bronze eagle buttons, double-breasted, adjustable tab on each cuff, dark tan cotton lining, oversized multipiece 76th Division patch on left shoulder, corporal chevron on right sleeve, 2 bullion overseas stripes	40	60
Overcoat, U.S. WAC, WWII, light olive drab poplin, double-breasted, button adjustable tab on each cuff, slash pockets, button-in liner, button-on hood	30	45
Overseas Cap, U.S. Army Air Force enlisted man's, WWII, tan cotton, AAF piping, small cloth-winged prop on left front	15	25
Parka, U.S. Air Force, 1950s, sage green nylon w/ woven specification label, zipper/button front, several pockets, real fur-trimmed built-in hood, sage green satin lining, faint color early USAF patch design printed on left shoulder	125	175
Peacoat, U.S. Navy, WWI, heavy navy blue serge wool, double-breasted	35	60
Peacoat, U.S. Navy WWII, navy blue melton wool, double-breasted front	20	35
Pea Jacket, German Navy, WWII, heavy navy blue wool, 2 slash pockets, wool lining w/ 2 pockets	125	160
Riding Breeches, German Luftwaffe, WWII, blue-gray, 3 pockets w/ button flaps, watch slash, belt loops, and side adjustment belts	200	275
Sack Coat, U.S. Army bandsman's, 1895, navy blue melton wool, standing collar, black woven trim, braid on cuffs, concealed button front, black cotton lining, gilt-brass lyre devices on collar	30	80
Service Coat, U.S. Army nurse's, 1942, navy blue wool, maroon trim on epaulets, woven cuff braid, matching belt, gilt-brass eagle buttons, pair of polished brass 2nd lieutenant bars, "US" and "Med/N" collar devices, quartermaster's tag dated "1942"	50	100
Visor Cap, U.S. Army, 1895 pattern, pillbox style, navy blue melton wool-covered circular top w/ black woven band, gold wire chinstrap w/ 1872 pattern domed side buttons, black visor, maker markings on black cotton lining, leather sweatband	50	75
Visor Cap, U.S. Navy chief petty officer's, WWII, white cotton top w/ CPO device on black woven band, black visor and chinstrap, gilt side buttons, "Bancroft Zephyr" brand	10	20

Weapons

Prices listed are for weapons in average condition, unless noted otherwise. For addition reading about firearms, consult *1999 Standard Catalog of Firearms, 9th Edition* by Ned Schwing (Krause Publications, Iola, WI, 1999), *The Official Price Guide to Antique and Modern Firearms, Eighth Edition* by Robert H. Balderson (House of Collectibles, New York, NY, 1996), *The Official Price Guide to Collector Handguns, Fifth Edition* by Robert H. Balderson (House of Collectibles, New York, NY, 1996) and *The Official Price Guide to Gun Collecting, 2nd Edition* by R. L. Wilson (House of Collectibles, New York, NY, 1999).

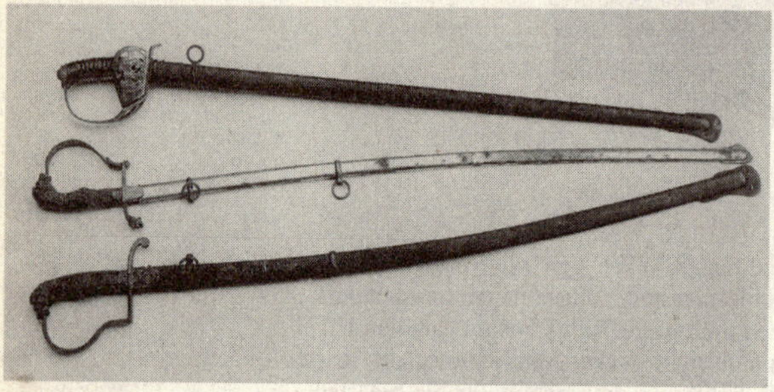

Swords, Imperial Germany, $200-$400 at auction. —Photo courtesy Sloan's Washington DC Gallery.

Edged Weapons

	LOW	HIGH
Bayonet, U.S. Army, 1898, Krag, dated "1898" on ricasso and "US" on reverse, bright steel blade, wood grips, blued scabbard	$50	$100
Bayonet, U.S. Army, c1958, Milpar, Co. M6 for M14 rifle, anodized blade, hallmarked on guard "Milpar Co.," scabbard marked "US M8A1"	25	40
Bayonet, U.S. Army, WWII, for M1 rifle, anodized blade, hallmarked "AFH/U (ordnance bomb) S" on ricasso, steel guard and pommel	30	50
Bayonet, U.S. Army, WWII, Imperial M4 for M1 carbine, blued blade, hallmarked "US M4/Imperial" on guard, USM8 scabbard	40	65
Bayonet, U.S. Army, WWII, modification of M1905 (cut from 16" l to 10" l), Bowie-point gray blade, hallmarked "SA/(ordnance bomb)/1908," black plastic grooved grips, green fiber scabbard	25	50
Dagger, German Luftwaffe, WWII, 2nd model, marked "Alcoso ACS Solingen" w/ scale trademark, gray aluminum crossguard and pommel, dark bullion wrap on orange grip, gray steel scabbard	250	350
Sword, Ames 1850, infantry officer's, 30.25" l etched and engraved blade w/ "Chicopee, Mass." address, cast hilt w/ open work, leather scabbard w/ brass bands and drag, engraved "Lt. Geo. Trembley, 174th N.Y.S.I.," 36.25" l	1500	2000
Sword, Imperial German Army artillery non-commissioned officer's, WWI, curved nickel blade marked "WK&C," engraved "Unteroffizier Dierkmann" w/ rose motif, horsehead, and military equipment, reverse has rose motif w/ 5 vignettes of military equipment, gold finish to brass fittings w/ crossed cannons on rectangular langet, P-guard w/ knight head and faces, lion hilt w/ 2 paws behind, wire-wrapped black grip, black-finished scabbard	350	450
Sword, U.S. Army officer's, c1910, model 1902, engraved bright blade, 3-strand knuckle basket, back strap blending into pommel, ferrule secures notched wood grip, scabbard w/ grip and 2 ring bands	50	100

Firearms and Accessories

	LOW	HIGH
Bandoleer, North Vietnamese Army, Vietnam War era, AK-47, khaki canvas w/ web straps, 3 magazine and 4 accessory pouches, wooden toggle closure, w/ Chinese double spout oil can	$40	$60
Cartridge Box, leather, crossed musket insignia, "E. A. Grossman & Co., N.Y."	40	60
Cup, horn w/ engraved "W. H." and iron hook, 10" h	50	75
Derringer, Moore's patent #1, .41 caliber, ornate scrollwork on grip, traces of original signature on replated barrel, #5440, 4.875" l	250	350
Flare Gun, U.S. Army, WWII, gray metal body, tip-over barrel, integral checkered grips, marked "Sklar Signal Pistol"	50	100
Grenade, U.S. Army, WWII, MK-II A1, w/ pin, arm, and fuse case	15	25
Grenade Storage Box, German Army, WWII, holds 15 M1924 "stick" grenades, hinged stamped metal body, wooden handle	75	100
Holster, German Army, 1944, breakaway style, black leather, fittings intact, marked "gxy 1944 P38"	75	100
Holster, Soviet Army, WWII, Tokarev TT 33, brown leather w/ brass fittings, compartment for extra magazine	20	30
Holster, U.S. Army, WWII, for .38 caliber Smith & Wesson or Colt M1917 revolver, tan leather w/ large flap and single belt loop in back, stamped w/ signal corps emblem over "Signal Corps"	20	25
Long Rifle, percussion, old black finish, pierced and engraved patchbox, silver half-moon and thumb piece, brass hardware and nose cap, signed "Vanmetre" (possibly J. W. Van Metre, Ross County, OH), 54" l	1200	1500
Musket, British Enfield, 1853, 2/ bayonet, 3-band model, lock marked "Tower 1857," long range rear sight, 55.125" l	800	1000
Musket, U.S. Army, 1865, percussion, Providence Tool Co., RI Model 1861, .58 caliber, maker marks on lockplate w/ U.S. Federal eagle and "1865" date, M61-style screw-in bolster	400	500
Musket, U.S. Army, Confederate States of America, Civil War, Enfield P1853, .58 caliber	350	500
Musketoon, English Army, c1857, Enfield, .577 caliber, walnut stock w/ brass buttplate, trigger guard, and endcap, iron thimble ramrod, unmarked lockplate, rack number "32 3F" on trigger guard, marked "SAS 679" on iron barrel, front sight w/ fixed rear sight, w/ bayonet lug for sword bayonet	150	250
Pistol, European, percussion, 2.75" octagon brass barrel w/ turned muzzle, added curly maple grip, 6.875" l	100	150
Pistol, French Navy officer's, c1805, flintlock blunderbuss, .62 caliber 6.75" l brass barrel w/ flared muzzle, rounded brass lockplate, varnished walnut stock w/ brass furniture and iron ramrod	2000	2500
Pistol, German Army, WWII, Browning Model GP (*aka* Model 35 or High Power), Fabrique Nationale, Belgium, 9mm automatic, Nazi proofed, checkered wooden grips	250	400
Pistol, German Army, WWII, Radom, Poland, P-35, 9mm automatic, Nazi proofed, 70% original blue, matching numbers, wartime production, no stock slot, dark reddish plastic grips w/ "FB" in triangle, w/ Nazi pattern military holster	125	200
Pistol, German Army, WWII, Walther, P38, 9mm, marked "AC041," 70% original blue, matching numbers, dark reddish brown plastic grips	350	500
Pistol, Italian Army, 1942, Beretta Model 1934, semi-automatic, 9mm, marked "M" w/ 2 bars stamped above at left rear frame, finger-rest magazine, black logo composition grips	150	250

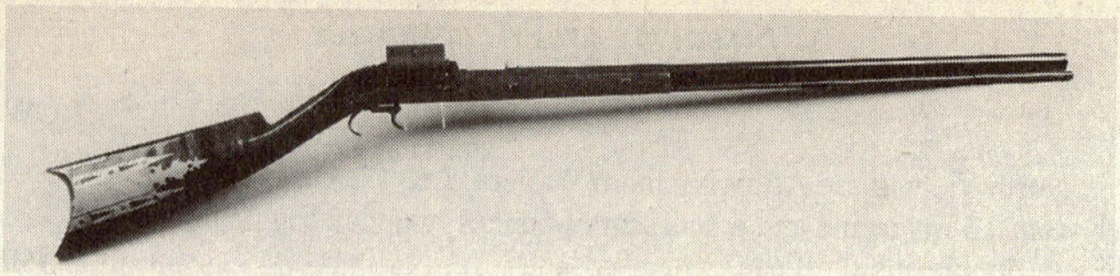

Rifle, revolving percussion underhammer, attributed to Elijah Jaquith, Brattleboro, VT, c1830, .52 caliber, 6-shot cylinder, 32" part round/octagonal barrel, figured walnut stock w/ gothic pattern brass patchbox, $6900 at auction. —Photo courtesy Skinner, Inc., Boston, MA.

	LOW	HIGH
Pistol, Japanese Army, 1943, Nagoya Arsenal, Nambu Factory, 8mm, large trigger guard version, matching numbers, dated "17,12" (Dec. 1943), 90% finish	100	200
Pistol, Japanese Army, WWII, Baby Nambu, Tokyo Gas & Electric Arsenal, 7mm, matching numbers, 90% original finish, checkered wooden grips, w/ clip	350	450
Pistol, U.S., c1852, pepperbox, percussion, underhammer, Thomas K. Bacon, Norwich, CT, .31 caliber, 6-shot, floral engraving on action, plain wooden grips, white finish	250	350
Pistol, U.S. Army, 1817-20, flintlock, Model 1816, Simeon North, Middletown, CT, .54 caliber, smoothbore, iron hardware, carved walnut stock marked "DCo" and "27," 15.5" l	800	1000
Pistol, U.S., Allen & Thurber, pepperbox, 6-shot, 4.25" barrel, scroll engraving on frame, 8.375" l	400	500
Pistols, English, percussion, double-barrel, checkered grips, engraved frames and compartment in grip, consecutive serial numbers, signed "Lang," 8.5" l, price for pair	1000	1200
Pocket Revolver, Allen & Wheelock, .31 caliber, cylinder scene w/ deer and ducks, 6" l	100	200
Pocket Revolver, Colt, 1849, traces of silver on back strap and guard, stagecoach scene, matching numbers, 11.25" l	500	700
Powder Flask, copper, embossed shell, 7.75"	40	80
Powder Flask, copper w/ embossed hunt scene, swinging measure, stamped "Boche A. Paris," 8.375"	60	100
Powder Flask, metal, fluted, 2 compartments in base, 4.375" l	125	175
Primer, horn, turned plug, 6.75" l	50	75
Revolver, French, teat fire, checkered grips, blued finish, folding bayonet, signed "Lizundia - Echaluge," 8.875" l	150	250
Revolver, knuckle duster, J. Reid, .22 caliber, engraved brass frame w/ traces of gilding, replated cylinder and hammer, #7244	300	500
Revolver, Smith & Wesson Model 1, first issue, .22 caliber short, engraved barrel and signature, ratchet on cylinder, 7"	300	400
Revolver, U.S., Civil War era, Colt, New Model Army (*aka* Model 1860), .44 caliber, 6-shot cylinder, 8" barrel, walnut grips	700	800
Revolver, U.S. Army, WWI, Colt M1917, rechambered for .45 caliber, standard issue, 5.5" barrel, parkerized finish, fixed sights, checkered walnut grips	200	300
Revolver, U.S. Navy, Civil War era, Model 1861, .36 caliber, 2-shot cylinder w/ 7.5" barrel, white finish	300	500

	LOW	HIGH
Rifle, Chinese Army, Vietnam War era, Type 56, 7.62mm, Chinese version of SKS, crude stock, refinished blade-style folding bayonet, 70% original finish	100	150
Rifle, English Army, WWI, Lee Enfield No. 1 Mark III, .303 caliber, marked w/ crest of 3 lions, 60% original finish	50	75
Rifle, German Army, 1944, Mauser M 98k, 7.92mm, laminated stock, marked Nazi eagle "H," 85% original blued finish, stamped magazine floor plate, barrel bands, w/ sight hood and sling	250	400
Rifle, Japanese Army, WWII, Type 99, Nagoya Arsenal, long version, 7.7mm, matching numbers, 90% original finish, monopod moved, w/ cleaning rod, dust cover, and aircraft sight	150	250
Rifle, North Vietnamese Army, 1950s, Vietminh handmade copy of French MAS Model 1936, smoothbore product of jungle workshops, unknown cartridge, stock w/ knot holes	700	900
Rifle, U.S. Army, 1870s, Springfield Model 1873, Springfield Armory, 45-70 caliber, trapdoor style, 70% original finish, w/ early cleaning rod	150	250
Rifle, U.S. Army, 1953, Garand M-1, International Harvester, .30 caliber, gas-operated semi-automatic, 8 rounds in block clip, dark stock, barrel dated "53," 65% original finish	175	300
Rifle, U.S. Army, WWII, Garand M-1D, Winchester, .30 caliber, sniper version w/ M-84 scope and detachable flash hider, canvas sling w/ leather cheek rest, stamped metal parts, w/ Anniston Arsenal release papers	2000	3000
Rifle, U.S. Navy, 1895-97, Winchester-Lee Model 1895, 28" l barrel, straight pull bolt action, clip-loaded 6mm (.236) caliber Lee cartridge, 65% original finish	400	600
Rifle, Winchester, 1873, 24" blued octagon barrel, .44 caliber, case colors on buttplate and trigger, 43" l	4000	6000
Scope, German Army sniper's, WWII, 4X, green painted metal storage case by "jvb," 12" blued metal body by "bek Dialytan 4x etc," ring mounts and front band stamped "1-172," brown leather lens caps marked "WaA156"	400	500
Training Pistol, U.S., WWII, M1911A, .45 automatic, cast hard rubber	65	80

Above: Colt Model 1849 Pocket Revolver, .31 caliber, 6-shot cylinder, engraved stagecoach scene, back strap engraved "Capt. R. B. Arms Co B. 16th Regt. VT. Vol.," $6325 at auction. —Photo courtesy Skinner, Inc., Boston, MA.

Above left, pistols at auction, top to bottom: English percussion target pistol, mid-19th C, $431; French 1822 cavalry percussion flint converted pistol, $345; French Charlville flintlock pistol, c1800, $805. —Photo courtesy Sloan's Washington DC Gallery.

Molds

Before ice cream producers could send the various shapes of ice cream now offered in the freezer of the corner maket, local merchants made their own ice cream and sold it in shapes they pressed into molds themselves. Homemade ice cream also found its way into these molds. Because some pewter contains lead, it is not advisable to continue the practice.

All of the chocolate molds are tin with one cavity; ice cream molds are pewter, unless noted otherwise.

Chocolate

	LOW	HIGH
Cat, sitting, #14, 3" h	$25	$50
Child, 4 cavities, tin-plated steel, hinged	100	150
Christmas Stocking	115	175
Dog Head, 4"	20	40
Eagle, #10, 4.625" h	50	75
Elephant, 3 cavities, tin-plated steel, hinged, 10" l	125	175
Girl and Rabbit, Anton Reiche #21889S, 4.25" h	75	100
Halloween Witch, 4 cavities, Germany, early 20th C	125	175
Jack-O-Lantern	25	50
Kewpies, #1980, 3-part, Germany, 6" h	75	125
Naked Child, Anton Reiche #17499, 10.875" h	155	200
Owl, #18, 4" h	20	40
Rabbit, in crouched position w/ smaller bunny riding piggy-back, 6.5" h	50	75

Assortment of chocolate and ice cream molds. —Photo courtesy Garth's Auctions, Delaware, OH.

	LOW	HIGH
Rabbit, leaping, 7" l	25	50
Rabbit, playing drum, Anton Reiche #26024, 6" h	75	125
Rabbit, riding rooster, 6"	50	75
Rabbit, standing, basket on back, marked "Made in USA," 8.25" h	50	75
Rabbit, standing, separate 2-part molds for ears and forelegs, marked "Anton Reiche, Dresden, Germany," 18.5" h	200	275
Rabbit, standing, wearing jacket, marked "Made in USA," 8.5" h	50	75
Rabbits, 2 rabbits riding motorcycle, marked "Made in Germany," 5.25" l	100	125
Rabbits and Egg on Gondola, Anton Reiche, 1.75" h	15	25
Santa, 4 cavities, Germany	200	250
Santa, in reindeer-drawn sleigh, multiple mold board w/ 15 cavities, white metal, marked "Elsreimer & Co. New York," 13.75" h, 18" w	100	150
Snowman, 4"	50	75
Teddy Bear, #2644, 11"	175	260
Turkey, 2 cavities, tin-plated steel, hinged	50	100
Turkey, Germany, 8" h	25	50
Zeppelin, Anton Reiche #25647, 2.75" h	100	150

Ice Cream

Airplane, marked "E & Co.," 5" l	$75	$125
Basket, #598, 3-part, early 20th C	25	50
Bell, Krauss #285	50	80
Blimp, marked "E & Co."	100	150
Cabin Cruiser	50	100
Child w/ Nosegay, marked "E & Co.," 4.75" h	75	125
Christmas Tree w/ Ornaments, #641K	50	80
Christmas Wreath, E. & Co. N.Y. #1146	100	150
Chrysanthemum, Krauss #313	75	100
Conch Shell, S. & Co. #270	75	125
Corn on the Cob, S. & Co. #270	50	100
Cornucopia, E. & Co. #1004	75	125
Cupid, Krauss #492	50	100
Duck, 4.25" l	75	100
Eagle w/ Shield, 5" h	100	150
Elephant, marked "E & Co."	75	100
Entwined Hearts, embossed "Love," early 20th C	25	50
Eskimo, wearing parka, marked "E & Co."	75	125
Football Player, marked "S & Co."	100	150
George and Martha Washington, full figure, 5.5" h, price for pair	200	300
Halloween Witch, 5.5" h	125	175
Jockey on Horse	100	150
Love Birds, facing pair	25	50
Man, wearing knee socks, 5" h	50	100
Native American, Krauss #458	75	125
Pumpkin, S. & Co.	40	60
Roasting Turkey, Krauss #364	50	75
Rocking Horse, E. & Co.	75	125
Rooster	50	75
Sailboat, marked "S & Co."	75	125
Stork w/ Baby, marked "Ed Hoffman, Chicago"	100	150
Train Engine, #477	75	125
Turkey	50	75

Music

Musical Instruments

For information on musical instruments consult *Antique Brass Wind Instruments* by Peter H. Adams (Schiffer, Atglen, PA, 1998).

	LOW	HIGH
Alto Saxophone, C. G. Conn, engraved "Conn 20M" at bell and "3816112," brass plated, w/ case, 20th C	$150	$300
Alto Saxophone, Cole & Dunas, engraved "The Olympian, Stands All Tests, Cole & Dunas, Music, Chicago, USA," nickel, w/ case, 20th C	150	300
Banjo, E. B. Mansfield, labeled in pot "Manufactured by E. B. Mansfield, 103 Court Street, Boston, Patent Applied For" and stamped at dowel stick "Pat Applied For," fretless, 5-string, maple pot w/ patented tension hoop device, walnut neck and peg head, w/ case, c1872, 11.625" dia. head	400	600
Bassoon, Paul Dupre, stamped "Paul Dupre, Paris, France, Conservatoire," nickel keys and fittings, w/ case, 52.375" l	500	700
Bassoon, W. Schreiber & Sohne, decal labeled "W. Schrieber & Sohne, Nauheim," stamped "18580," nickel-plated keys, w/ case	700	900
Clarinet, Bernareggy, stamped "Bernareggy, A Barcelona UT," boxwood body w/ ivory fittings, 6 round brass keys, 20.25" l	300	500
Clarinet, Gerock & Wolf, stamped "Gerock & Wolf, 79, Cornhill, London, B" and w/ maker's mark, boxwood body w/ ivory fittings, 6 brass keys w/ square covers, 19th C, 23.875" l	400	700
Clarinet, Martin Freres, stamped "Martin Freres, Lamonte, Paris" at bell and body, black wood body w/ nickel keys and fittings, plastic mouthpiece, w/ case, 26.125" l	300	400
Coronet, Boston Musical Instrument Mfg., stamped at bell "1, NE Plus Ultra, Made By The Boston Musical Instrument Manufr, 71, Sudbury St.," and "14745" on 3 piston valves, w/ case, early 20th C	250	500
Coronet, Henry Distin, engraved at bell "Superior, Henry Distin Mfg. Co. Makers, Williamsport PA, Highest Grade, 15066," stamped "17515" on piston valves, silver-plated tubing and bell engraved throughout w/ floral design, w/ multiple mouthpieces, mute, and case, c1900	600	900
Dulcimer, English, walnut case w/ oak pin and key blocks, spruce soundboard w/ brass sound hole covers, 13 chessmen bridges, c1820, 41" l	200	400
Fife, G. Butler & Sons, stamped "G. Butler & Sons, 029 Haymarket, London and Dublin" on body, single nickel key, nickel fittings	75	150
Fife, Geo. Cloos, stamped "Geo. Cloos" and "6121" on body, black wood body w/ nickel keys and fittings	100	200
French Trumpet, Henri Selmer, engraved "Henri Selmer Paris, Depose, Grand Prix, Geneve 1927 Liege 1930…" at bell, stamped "Selmer 6310" at piston, brass-plated pistons and tubing, bell engraved w/ floral motif, w/ case	700	900
Guitar, C. F. Martin, Style 000-18, stamped "C. F. Martin & Co, Nazareth PA" and "C. F. Martin & Co. Est. 1833" on peg head, mahogany body bound in faux tortoiseshell, medium to fine grain spruce top, ebony fingerboard w/ pearl eyes, 1936, 16.375" l back, 15.125" w bottom bout	5000	7500
Guitar, Vega Co., labeled "The Vega Co. 155 Columbus Ave. Boston Mass., Musical Instruments," Model C-71, arch-top, narrow curl 1-pc. maple back, broad curl sides, fine to medium grain top, mahogany neck, bound ebony fingerboard w/ pearl inlay, w/ case, c1935, 20.125" l back	2000	3000

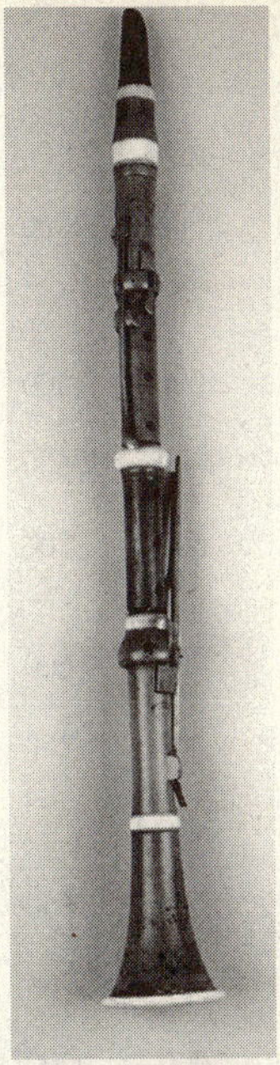

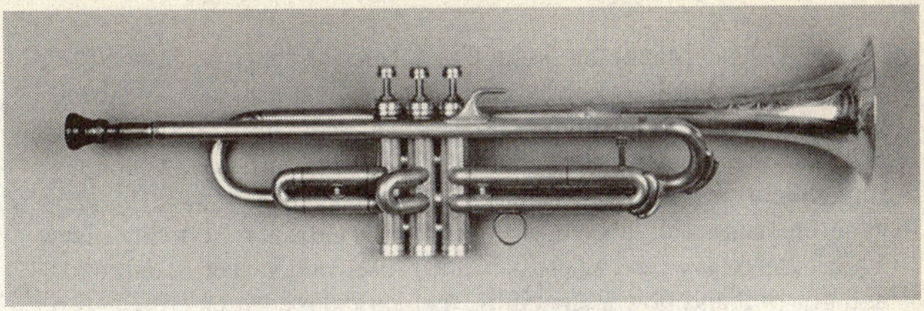

Above, top to bottom: C. G. Conn Trumpet; Henry Distin Coronet.
Left: Gerock & Wolf Clarinet.

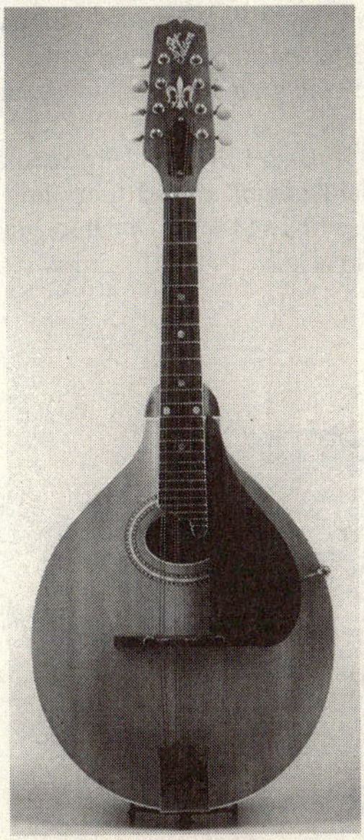

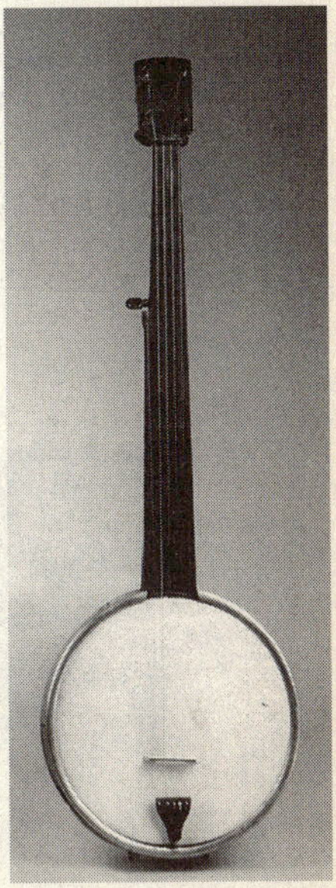

Left to right: C. F. Martin Guitar; Gibson Mandolin; E. B. Mansfield Banjo.
—Photos courtesy Skinner, Inc., Boston, MA.

	LOW	HIGH
Mandolin, Gibson Mandolin-Guitar Co., labeled "Gibson Mandolin Style A-2, Number 81158 is hereby guaranteed...," curly maple 2-pc. back, plain sides, wide to medium grain top, mahogany neck w/ snakehead peg head inlaid w/ "Gibson" and fleur-de-lis in pearl, bound ebony fingerboard w/ pearl eyes, w/ case, 1924, 13.75" l back	2500	4000
Piano Forte, Classical, labeled "Patent Thomas Gibson 61 Barclay's New York," mahogany case w/ cross-banded rosewood veneer in outline and gilt fruit and flower stenciling, leaf-carved reeded tapering legs on casters, 34.5" h, 67.5" w	1000	1500
Piccolo, Retreling, labeled "Retreling, New York," cocuswood body, nickel keys, w/ case	400	600
Piccolo, Wm. S. Haynes, stamped "Wm. S. Haynes, Boston, Mass," cocuswood body, silver keys, w/ case	500	700
Trumpet, C. G. Conn, stamped "C. G. Conn, Elkhart, Ind. USA" at bell and "308558" on 1 piston, silver-plated brass tubing, 3 piston valves, engraved Art Deco motif on bell, w/ case, c1935	400	600
Trumpet, H. & A. Selmer, engraved "By Vincent Bach, Bundy, H. & A. Selmer Inc.," stamped "198386" on piston valves, w/ case	100	250
Viola, Ernest Edler, labeled "E. Edler, Boston, 1940," narrow curl 2-pc. back, similar ribs, strong narrow curl scroll, fine to medium grain top, orange-brown varnish, w/ nickel-mounted bow and case, 1940, 16.75" l back	1200	1600
Viola, Tomaso Eberle, labeled "Tomaso Eberle, Fecit Neap 1772," irregular curl 2-pc. back, strong medium curl ribs, later carved head, fine to medium grain top w/ baleen binding, golden-brown varnish, w/ case and bow, 1772, 16.5" l back	7000	9000
Violin, Asa Warren White, labeled "By A W White, 86 Tremont Street, Boston, 1886," irregular curl 2-pc. back, medium irregular curl ribs, medium curl scroll, fine to medium grain top, red-brown varnish, w/ case, 1886, 14.125" l back	1800	2200
Violin, Leandro Bisiach, labeled "Leandro Bisiach della Scuola Cremonese, Fece in Milano 1892 Piazza del Duomo," signed "Leandro Bisiach," medium curl 1-pc. back, similar ribs and scroll, medium grain top, red varnish, w/ case, 13.875" l back	4000	6000

Piano Forte. —Photo courtesy Skinner, Inc., Boston, MA.

Records

45s

The prices below are for records in excellent condition with excellent condition sleeves. That means that the record may have small scratches that can be seen but not heard. The sleeves should be crisp and clean with only slight wear. Near mint or mint examples will command higher prices than those listed below. For further information see *Goldmine Price Guide to 45 RPM Records, 2nd Edition* edited by Tim Neely (Krause Publications, Iola, WI, 1999).

	LABEL	CAT. #	YEAR	LOW	HIGH
AC-DC, *Highway To Hell/Night Prowler*	Atlantic	3617	1979	$2	$3
Astro Jets, *Boom A Lay/Hide And Seek*	Imperial	5760	1961	12	20
Avalon, Frankie, *Venus/I'm Broke*	Chancellor	1031	1959	18	25
Baker, LaVern, *Play It Fair/Lucky Old Sun*	Atlantic	1075	1956	18	25
Bay City Rollers, *Shang A Lang*	Bell	45481	1974	2	4
Beach Boys, *Surfin' Safari/409*	Capitol	4777	1962	50	75
Beatles, *Paperback Writer/Rain*	Capitol	X6296	1980s	12	20
Berry, Chuck, *Maybellene/Wee Wee Hours*	Chess	1604	1955	28	40
Brown, Maxine, *Ask Me/Yesterday's Kisses*	Wand	135	1963	5	8
Cadillacs, *Zoom/You Are*	Josie	792	1959	18	25
Carmel Covered Popcorn, *Suzie-Q/Looking For A Place*	Vistone	2055	1968	10	15
Carpenters, *We've Only Just Begun/All Of My Life*	A&M	1183	1970	2	4
Chad & Jeremy, *You Are She/I Won't Cry*	Columbia	43807	1966	5	8
Coachmen, *Mr. Moon/Nothing At All* (blue vinyl)	MMC	010	1965	32	50
Cowsills, *You/Crystal Claps*	London	153	1972	5	8
Dee Jayes, *Bongo Beach Party/Mr. Bongo Man*	Highland	1031	1962	25	35
Deep Purple, *Hush/One More Rainy Day*	Tetragrammaton	1503	1968	7	10

Left to right: The Crickets, Great Balls Of Fire/Don't Cha Know It's Too Late, *Coral, EC-81192, $161 at auction; Buddy Holly,* Brown Eyed Handsome Man/Wishing Bo Diddley True Love Ways, *Coral, EC-81193, $316 at auction. —Photos courtesy William Doyle Galleries.*

Left to right: Carl Perkins, Pink Pedal Pushers/Jive After Five, *Columbia, 4-41131, $46 at auction; The Ronettes,* Walking In The Rain/How Does It Feel (promo), *Philles, 123, $115 at auction. —Photos courtesy William Doyle Galleries.*

	LABEL	CAT. #	YEAR	LOW	HIGH
Earth, Wind & Fire, *Evil/Clover*	Columbia	45888	1973	1	3
Exodus, *Silhouettes/You Cheated*	Wand	11248	1972	7	10
Four Imperials, *My Girl/Teen Age Fool*	Chant	10067	1958	33	50
Gentle Giant, *Word From The Wise/Spooky Boogie*	Capitol	4652	1978	3	5
Greenbaum, Norman, *I. J. Foxx/Rhode Island Red*	Reprise	0956	1970	2	4
Hollies, *Stay/Now's The Time*	Liberty	55674	1963	32	50
Jackson 5, *ABC/The Young Folks*	Motown	1163	1970	4	6
Jefferson Airplane, *Long John Silver/ Milk Train*	Grunt	0506	1971	2	4
Kai, Lani, *Beach Party/Little Borwn Girl*	Keen	2023	1958	20	30
Kingsmen, *Louie, Louie/Haunted Castle*	Wand	143	1963	12	20
Little Feat, *Willin'/Oh, Atlanta*	Warner Bros.	8420	1977	1	3
Little Richard, *Good Golly, Miss Molly/ Hey, Hey, Hey*	Specialty	624	1958	18	25
Magic Lantern, *Country Woman*	Charisma	100	1972	4	6
Mamas & The Papas, *Monday, Monday/ Got A Feeling*	Dunhill	4026	1966	5	8
McCartney, Paul, *Jet/Let Me Roll It*	Apple	1871	1974	4	6
Miller, Steve, *Swingtown/Winter Song*	Capitol	4496	1977	1	3
Monkees, *Valleri/Tapioca Tundra*	Colgems	1019	1968	7	10
Mugwumps, *My Gal/Season Of The Witch*	Sidewalk	909	1967	7	10
Nino & The Ebb Tides, *I Love Girls/ Don't Look Around*	Recorte	413	1959	75	100
Oliver & The Twisters, *Locomotion Twist/ Mother Goose Twist*	Colpix	615	1961	10	15
Ray-Vons, *Judy/Regina*	Laurie	3248	1964	50	75
Stacy, Clyde, *Hoy Hoy/So Young*	Candlelight	1015	1957	28	40

Albums

Many people who discarded their record collections in the 1980s are buying them back in the 1990s. Collectors feel that the sound quality on albums is richer and more subtle than on CDs. People also love the photos and artwork of the covers. The nostalgic appeal of records is very strong; music is often a reminder of happy moments. Many collectors remember records as their first independent purchase as a teenager.

The following is a cross-section of LPs; 45s are not covered. Each entry consists of the performer's name, the title of the LP, the company that produced it, the stock number and the date. Condition is all important for records; collectors usually grade both the record and the album cover. Scratches on the record that interfere with sound quality can destroy the price of a record. Worn, torn, or stained covers also decrease their prices. The prices below are for records in excellent condition with excellent condition covers. That means that the record may have small scratches that can be seen but not heard. The covers should be crisp and clean with only slight wear. Near mint or mint examples will command higher prices than those listed below.

For further reading see *The Official Price Guide to Records, Thirteenth Edition* by Jerry Osborne (House of Collectibles, NY, 1997), *The Official Price Guide to Country Music Records* by Jerry Osborne (House of Collectibles, New York, NY, 1996), *Goldmine Record Album Price Guide,* by Tim Neely (Krause Publications, Iola, WI, 1999).

	LABEL	CAT. #	YEAR	LOW	HIGH
Acuff, Roy, *The Voice Of Country Music*	Capitol	ST-2276	1965	$10	$15
Aerosmith, *Toys In The Attic*	Columbia	JCQ-33479	1975	7	10
Alabama, *Wild Country*	Plantation	PLP044	1981	7	10
Albert, Eddie, *September Song*	Kapp	KP-1083	1957	8	12
Allen, Steve, *Let's Dance*	Coral	CRL-57028	1956	8	12
Allman Brothers Band, *Live At Fillmore East* (2 LPs)	Nautilus	NR030	1981	20	30
Amboy Dukes, *Marriage On The Rocks*	Polydor	24-4012	1970	7	10
Ames Brothers, *Sentimental Me*	Coral	CRL-56024	1951	12	20
Andrews Sisters, *Club 15*	Decca	DL-5155	1950	10	15
Annette, *The Parent Trap* (soundtrack)	Buena Vista	BV-3309	1961	12	20
Arnold, Eddy, *Cattle Call*	RCA Victor	LPM-2578	1962	7	10
Astaire, Fred, *Shoes With Wings*	MGM	E-3413	1956	12	20
Atkins, Chet, *Class Guitar*	RCA Victor	LSP-3885	1967	3	5
Autry, Gene, *Gene Autry Sings*	Harmony	HS-7399	1968	4	6
Bachelors, *Marie*	London	LL-3435	1965	5	8
Baez, Joan, *From Every Stage* (promo)	A&M	SP-8375	1976	40	60
Ballard, Hank, *24 Hit Tunes*	King	950	1966	17	25
Band, The, *Music From Big Pink*	Capitol	SKAO-2955	1968	5	8
Bandits, *The Electric 12 String*	World Pacific	T-1833	1964	5	8
Barker, Warren, *77 Sunset Strip*	Warner Bros.	WS-1289	1959	12	20
Barracudas, *A Plane View*	Justice	JLP-143	1968	120	200
Baxter, Les, *The Sacred Idol*	Capitol	ST-1293	1960	20	30
Beach Boys, *Pet Sounds*	Capitol	T-2458	1966	10	15
Beatles, *Sgt. Pepper's Lonely Heart's Club Band*	Capitol	MAS-2653	1967	70	100
Beck, Jeff, *Wired*	Epic	HE-43849	1982	10	15
Bee, Molly, *Swingin' Country*	MGM	SE-4423	1967	7	10
Belmonts, *Summer Love*	Dot	DLP-25949	1969	8	12
Bennett, Tony, *Because Of You*	Columbia	CL-6221	1952	20	30
Benton, Brook, *Born To Sing The Blues*	Mercury	MG-20886	1964	5	8
Berry, Chuck, *Concerto In B. Goode*	Mercury	SR-61223	1969	7	10
Big Maybelle, *Got A Brand New Bag*	Rojac	RS-522	1967	12	20

	LABEL	CAT. #	YEAR	LOW	HIGH
Black Sabbath, *Paranoid*	Warner Bros.	WS4-1887	1974	7	10
Boston, *Boston*	Epic	HE034188	1981	10	15
Breedlove, Jim, *Rock 'N' Roll Hits*	Camden	CAL-430	1958	8	12
Burnette, Johnny, *Dreamin'*	Liberty	LRP-3179	1960	10	15
Calliope, *Steamed*	Buddah	BDS-5023	1968	7	10
Chad & Jeremy, *Before And After*	Columbia	CL-2374	1965	5	8
Chiffons, The, *He's So Fine*	Laurie	LLP-2018	1963	40	60
Cole, Nat "King," *Harvest Of Hits*	Capitol	L-213	1950	12	20
Couch, Orville, *Hello Trouble*	Vee Jay	LP-1087	1964	5	8
Crew Cuts, *Music Ala Carte*	Mercury	MG-20199	1957	12	20
Crosby, Bing, *Bing In Paris*	Decca	DL-8780	1958	10	15
Dan & Dale, *Batman And Robin*	Tifton	M-8002	1966	8	12
Darrin, Bobby, *Twist With Bobby Darin*	Atco	33-138	1961	10	15
Dave Clark Five, *Glad All Over*	Epic	BN-26093	1964	20	30
Davis, Skeeter, *Hand In Hand With Jesus*	RCA Victor	LSP-3763	1967	7	10
Deep Purple, *Book Of Taliesyn*	Harvest	SHVL-751	1970	40	60
Deuce Coupes, *The Shut Downs*	Crown	CLP-5393	1963	5	8
Devo, *Devo Live*	Warner Bros.	WBMS-115	1980	10	15
Diddley, Bo, *500% More Man*	Checker	LP-2996	1965	16	24
Domino, Fats, *Fats On Fire*	ABC Paramount	ABC-479	1964	5	8
Drifters, *Up On The Roof*	Atlantic	8073	1963	40	60
Dylan, Bob, *Nashville Skyline*	Columbia	CQ-32825	1973	8	12
Euphoria, *Lost In Trance*	Rainbow	1003	1970s	70	100
Everly Brothers, *The Everly Brothers' Show*	Warner Bros.	WS-1858	1970	5	8
Firesign Theatre, *Waiting For The Electrician*	Columbia	CS-9519	1968	4	6
Flatt & Scruggs, *Foggy Mountain Banjo*	Columbia	CS-8364	1961	8	12

Left to right: Bob-B-Soxx and the Blue Jeans, Zip-A-Dee Doo Dah, *Philles, PHIP-4002, $184 at auction; Billy Ward and His Dominoes,* Clyde McPhatter w/ Billy Ward and His Dominoes, *Federal, 559, $690 at auction. —Photos courtesy William Doyle Galleries.*

	LABEL	CAT. #	YEAR	LOW	HIGH
Fleetwood Mac, *Rumours*	Warner Bros.	PRO-652	1979	12	20
Frantic Freddie & The Reflections, *Music Power*	Tom Rice	—	1967	55	80
Frawley, William, *The Old Ones*	Dot	DLP-3061	1957	10	16
Fun & Games, *Elephant Candy*	Uni	73042	1968	7	10
Gaynor, Mitzi, *Mitzi*	Verve	MGV-110	1959	10	16
Genesis, *A Trick Of The Tail*	Mobile Fidelity	MFSL-062	1981	8	12
Gleason, Jackie, *Lover's Rhapsody*	Capitol	H-366	1953	8	12
Greensleeves, Eddie, *Humorous Folk Songs*	Cameo	C-1031	1963	5	8
Gryphon, *Gryphon*	—	—	1970s	18	25
Haines, Connie, *Connie Haines Sings Helen Morgan*	Tops	L-1606	1959	7	10
Haley, Bill & His Comets, *Rock Around The Clock*	Decca	DL-8225	1960	12	18
Hamilton, Roy, *Roy Hamilton's Greatest Hits*	Epic	LN-24009	1962	5	8
Harrison, George, *Dark Horse Radio Special*	Dark Horse	—	1975	125	200
Heart, *Dreamboat Annie*	Nautilus	NR-3	1980	8	12
Help, *Second Coming*	Decca	DL-75304	1971	7	10
Herman's Hermits, *Introducing Herman's Hermits*	MGM	E-4282	1965	5	8
Hi-Tones, *Raunchy Sounds*	Hi	HL-31011	1963	5	8
Holly, Buddy, *That'll Be The Day*	Decca	DL-8707	1958	750	1000
Homer & Jethro, *They Sure Are Corny*	King	639	1959	40	60
Hopkins, Lightnin', *Lightnin'*	Bluesville	BVLP-1019	1964	8	12
Howard University Choir, *Spirituals*	RCA Victor	LM-2126	1957	8	12
Husky, Ferlin, *Gone*	Capitol	T-1383	1960	8	12
Jackson, Tommy, *Popular Square Dance Music*	Dot	DLP-3015	1957	8	12
Jacobs, Hank, *So Far Away*	Sue	LP-1023	1964	28	40
James, Joni, *Irish Favorites*	MGM	SE-3749	1959	20	30
Jelly Bean Bandits, *Jelly Bean Bandits*	Mainstream	S06103	1967	12	20
Jolson, Al, *Rock A Bye Your Baby*	Decca	DL-9035	1957	7	10
Jones, George, *My Favorites Of Hank Williams*	United Artists	UAL-3220	1962	10	16
Jones, Spike, *Dinner Music For People Who Aren't Very Hungry*	Verve	MGV-4005	1957	12	20
King, B. B., *My Kind Of Blues*	Crown	CLP-5188	1961	10	16
King Crimson, *In The Court Of The Crimson King*	Mobile Fidelity	MFSL-075	1980	12	20
Kingsmen, *More Great Sounds*	Wand	WD-659	1964	7	10
Krazy Kats, *Movin' Out*	Damon	12478	1967	20	30
Leadbelly, *Take This Hammer*	Folkways	FP04	1950	55	80
Lee, Brenda, *Emotions*	Decca	DL-4104	1961	7	10
Lee, Peggy, *Benny Goodman And Peggy Lee*	Columbia	CL-6033	1949	12	20
Lennon, John, *Imagine*	Mobile Fidelity	MFSL-153	1982	7	10
Lewis, Gary & The Playboys, *This Diamond Ring*	Liberty	LRP-3408	1965	5	8
Lewis, Jerry Lee, *By Request*	Smash	MGS-27086	1966	5	8
Liberace, *Piano*	Advance	7	1951	8	12

	LABEL	CAT. #	YEAR	LOW	HIGH
Lightnin' Slim, *Lightnin' Slim's Bell Ringer*	Excello	8004	1965	70	100
Mills Brothers, *Barber Shop Ballads*	Decca	DL-5050	1950	12	20
Nelson, Willie, *Texas In My Soul*	RCA Victor	LPM-3937	1968	28	40
O'Brian, Hugh, *TV's Wyatt Earp Sings*	ABC Paramount	ABC-203	1957	20	30
Presley, Elvis, *Elvis For Everyone*	RCA Victor	LPM-3450	1965	12	20
Reese, Della, *Amen*	Jubilee	JLP-1083	1958	7	10
Righteous Brothers, *Back To Back*	Philles	PHLP-4009	1966	5	8
Rowan & Martin, *Laugh-In*	Epic	FXS-15118	1969	7	10
Scott, Tom, *Sing Of America-Gems Of American Folklore*	Coral	CRL-56-56	1952	12	20
Shangri-Las, *Leader Of The Pack*	Red Bird	20-101	1965	40	60
Simon & Garfunkel, *Bridge Over Troubled Water*	Columbia	CQ-30995	1973	8	12
Sinatra, Frank, *Fabulous Frankie*	RCA Victor	LPT-3063	1953	12	20
Sledge, Percy, *When A Man Loves A Woman*	Atlantic	8125	1966	10	16
Spiders, *I Didn't Wanna Do It*	Imperial	LP-9140	1961	200	300
Starfire, *Starfire*	Crimson	S04476/7	1974	70	100
Statler Brothers, *Flowers On The Wall*	Columbia	CL-2449	1966	7	10
Talking Heads, *Live At The Roxy*	Warner Bros.	WBMS-104	1979	10	16
Turner, Ike & Tina, *So Fine*	Pompeii	SD-6000	1968	7	10
Twitty, Conway, *Lonely Blue Boy*	MGM	E-3818	1960	28	40
Valens, Ritchie, *Ritchie*	Del Fi	DFLP-1206	1960	70	100
Von Schmidt, Eric, *Folk Blues*	Folklore	FRLP-14005	1964	8	12
Wells, Junior, *Hoodoo Man Blue*	Delmark	DL-612	1966	8	12
Wells, Kitty, *Country Music Time*	Decca	DL-4554	1964	5	8
Williams, Hank, *Honky Tonkin'*	MGM	E-242	1954	140	200
Youngbloods, *Earth Music*	RCA Victor	LPM-3865	1968	7	10

Left to right: Del Shannon, Runaway, *Bigtop, 121303, $1035 at auction; Elvis Presley,* A Date With Elvis, *RCA Victor, LPM-2011, gatefold w/ 1960 calendar on back, $173 at auction. —Photos courtesy William Doyle Galleries.*

CDs

Although they first appeared on the market only fifteen years ago, compact discs are already collector items. Music fans collect CDs for the sound they contain, often unique recordings that can't (or no longer can) be picked up by a quick visit to the local music emporium. Most of the more valuable CDs are promotional discs. Often companies only produced relatively few such promos, but not always. Although most promos have a somewhat higher value, there are enough exceptions to trip up the unwary.

When we have listed only the recording artist, the price reflects the average range for this performer. Some noteworthy exceptions for individual albums are listed as such. All prices are for near mint examples. For further information refer to *The Official Price Guide to Compact Discs* by Jerry Osborne and Paul Berquist (House of Collectibles, NY, 1994).

	LOW	HIGH
Abdul, Paula	$6	$15
AC/DC	8	10
Adams, Bryan	6	20
Aerosmith	6	25
Alice in Chains	7	10
Atlantic Starr	4	7
Baby Animals	5	12
Bad Company	5	40
Bangles	7	30
Beach Boys	8	25
Beastie Boys	7	18
Beatles	7	40
Benatar, Pat	6	15
Bennett, Tony	6	8
Black Box	8	20
Black Browes	7	15
Bowie, David	8	12
BTO	18	20
Camouflage	5	8
Carpenters	6	15
Cavedogs, The	5	10
Clapton, Eric	6	35
Crosby, Stills & Nash	5	25
Earth, Wind & Fire	4	10
Flack, Roberta	4	6
Genesis	6	20
Heart	8	40
Ice T	4	25
Indigo Girls	6	35
Jackson, Janet	8	25
Janes Addiction	20	25
Jethro Tull	6	30
Jett, Joan	5	6
Judd, Wynona	5	15
Kiss	8	20
Kool & The Gang	5	6
Kraftwerk	5	6
Kravitz, Lenny	4	15
Labelle, Patti	5	8
Lennon, Julian	5	8

	LOW	HIGH
Madonna	5	25
McCartney, Paul	6	35
Metallica	8	60
Nicks, Stevie	8	10
Oingo Boingo	4	25
Palmer, Robert	4	12
Pink Floyd	8	25
Plant, Robert	4	15
Prefab Sprout	4	7
Presley, Elvis	35	500
Pretty Poison	4	5
Prince	5	25
Prong	4	15
Psychedelic Furs	6	12
Raitt, Bonnie	5	6
Ranks, Shabba	5	6
Raves Up, The	4	10
Red Flag	5	6
Red Hot Chili Peppers	6	25
REM	5	40
Richards, Keith	6	12
Riverdogs	4	15
Rolling Stones	12	40
Ronstadt, Linda	5	6
Russell, Leon	4	12
School of Fish	4	15
Shakespears Sister	6	12
Simon, Carly	5	8
Simon, Paul	8	20
Simply Red	5	8
Simpsons, The	4	20
Sisters of Mercy	8	25
Skid Row	5	15
Slaughter	5	12
Springsteen, Bruce	5	40
Tears for Fears	4	8
They Might Be Giants	4	6
Third World	4	6
Thompson Twins	5	15
Thorogood, George	6	18
Ugly Kid Joe	5	6
Vandross, Luther	4	6
Van Halen	5	10
Vaughan, Stevie Ray	6	20
Warrant	5	6
White, Karyn	4	10
Wilson Phillips	5	10
Wire	6	8
Yes	8	30
Young, Neil	6	15
ZZ Top	6	25

Vogue Picture Records

Vogue Picture Records were the creation of Tom Saffady and manufactured by his company Sav-Way Industries in Detroit, Michigan in 1946-47. These 78 rpm records were constructed with a central aluminum core for durability. A colorful paper illustration covering the entire record was applied to the core and then sealed in clear vinyl. Regular production Vogues were issued with numbers in the R707 to R788 range and covered a wide span of music styles, including big band swing, jazz, country, Latin, and even fairy tales for children.

	NO.	LOW	HIGH
All By Myself/Sniffle Song (Did You Ever Hear A Mothball), Frankie Masters	R772	$40	$50
Atlanta, Ga./Aren't You Glad Yor're You, Shep Fields & His Orchestra	R712	35	45
Bells Of St. Mary's/Star Dust, Don Large Chorus	R710	30	40
Blue Skies/Seville, 'The Hour of Charm' All Girl Orchestra w/ Phil Spitainy	R733	25	35
Cocktails For Two/Trolley Song, Tommy Dorsey/Judy Garland	—	600	800
Don't Tetch It/Flat River, Missouri, Nancy Lee & The Hilltoppers/ Judy & Jen accompanied by The Hilltoppers	R744	50	60
Doodle Doo Doo/All I Do Is Wantcha, Art Kassel	R714	30	40
Give Me All Your Heart/I Dreamed About You Last Night, Dick LaSalle	R747	80	100
Guilty Of Love/Mucho Dinero, Enrico Madrigeura	R778	60	80
Have I Told You Lately That I Love You/I Get A Kick Off Corn, Lulu Belle & Scotty	R719	35	45
I Love You In The Daytime Too/Clementine, Sonny Dunham & Orchestra	R775	50	60
I've Been Working On The Railroad/You're Nobody 'Til Somebody Loves You, Art Mooney & His Orchestra	R713	250	350
Mean To Me/Humphrey The Singing Pig, King's Jesters and Louise	R751	50	60
More Than You Know/Go West, Young Man, Go West, Joan Edwards	R761	60	70
Muciscomania/If I Had You, Charlie Shavers Quintet	R756	60	75
Rhapsody In Blue Part 1/Alice Blue Gown, 'The Hour of Charm' All Girl Orchestra w/ Phil Spitainy	R725	30	40
Rhumba Lesson #1/Rhumba Lesson #3, Paul Shahin	R739	35	45
Sugar Blues/Basin St. Blues, Clyde McCoy	R707	20	30
Sweetheart/Little Consideration, Art Kassel	R734	25	35
Tear It Down/Put That Ring On My Finger, Clyde McCoy	R722	25	35

She's Funny That Way/Dizzy's Dilemma, *Charlie Shavers Quintet, R754, $45-$55.*

Sheet Music

Sheet music is a musical composition. It was the first way of mass merchandising popular music. Tin Pan Alley originated off-Broadway on 28th Street in New York City. It was the center of American popular music in the late nineteenth and early twentieth centuries. Publishers sought recognition for their songs. They backed shows and employed song pluggers to popularize their music. Waiters often supplemented their wages by belting out tunes.

Condition, rarity and image establish the value of sheet music. Some collectors want the music, but many others are more interested in the graphics. Sheet music represents a great area for cross-over collecting. It includes themes such as movies, WWI and WWII, Disney, character and illustration art. Winslow Homer and Norman Rockwell ("Over There") are a couple of artists that drew covers. Since sheet music was mass produced, most often in huge quantities, it is still relatively inexpensive. It can, however, be fragile, and mint examples are harder to find. Specimens are not always in top condition due to music store stamps, tape marks, staples, binder holes, and ownership signatures. Worn, incomplete copies sell for considerably less than those in mint condition described below. Garage sales are a good source for sheet music, but be prepared to sort through stacks of material. Dealers that frame sheet music realize that they have a decorative item and reflect that in the price. Sheet music is best stored in unsealed plastic containers designed for paper conservation. If framing, use acid-free backing and make sure the process is reversible, i.e., don't use methods which can damage the sheet music.

For more information consult *Collectors Guide to Sheet Music* by Debbie Dillon (L-W Promotions, Gas City, IN, 1988, 1995 value update) and *The Gold in Your Piano Bench* by Marion Short (Schiffer, Atglen, PA, 1997).

Names following the titles listed below are descriptions of the cover; a celebrity's name denotes a photo of that person. Prices listed are for sheets in very good condition.

	LOW	HIGH
Arabianna, Eastern man and woman on crescent moon, minarets below, Ray Miller Orchestra inset, 1923	$5	$8
Be My Love (The Toast of New Orleans), dark pink graphics, Mario Lanza inset, 1951	3	5
Charmaine (Sunset Boulevard), wavy line pattern, crossed musical staffs, 1926	5	8
China Boy, stylized tulip graphics at left edge, 1950	4	6
Comin' In On A Wing And A Prayer, plane in clouds, large Eddie Cantor inset, 1943	4	6

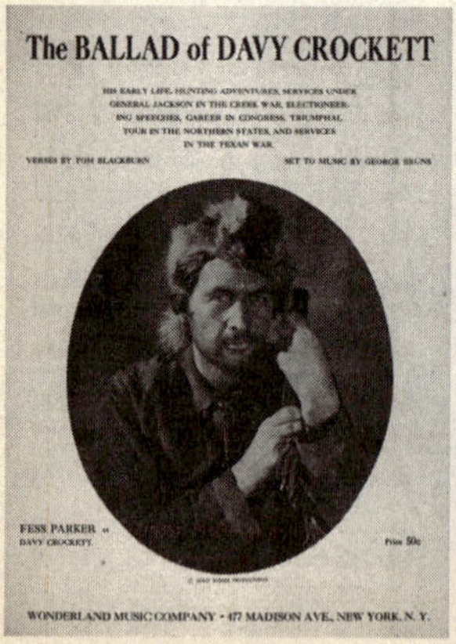

Left: The Ballad of Davy Crockett, *Fess Parker photo, $5-$8.*

Right: The Bombardier Song, *1942, $20-$28.*

	LOW	HIGH
Coquette, woman sitting on branch, Rose Valyd inset, 1928	6	8
Cuban Cabby, black and white, 1936	4	6
Dance Ballerina Dance, wavy purple shapes in background, Jefferson silhouette, Mel Torme inset, 1947	4	6
Dancing With Tears In My Eyes, border silhouettes of men and women dancing, Valle center photo, facsimile signature, 1930	4	6
Dark Eyes, Russian woman, Bernie Cummins inset, 1935	3	5
Day Dreaming, white silhouette of tree on blue background, Oliver Wallace inset, 1924	4	6
Diamonds Are A Girl's Best Friend (Gentlemen Prefer Blondes), Herschfeld characters, 1949	8	12
Don't Be Too Sure, man and woman walking by road sign w/ cupid on top, 1922	4	6
Early In The Morning Kiss Me Love Before We Part, lambs at sunrise, 1928	4	6
Enjoy Yourself, out-of-focus bubbles in background, Tommy Dorsey inset, 1949	5	8
Faded Summer Love, brown and white trees, large Georgie Shaw inset, 1931	2	3
Garden Of The Moon, movie stars' heads in stars, O'Brien, Payne, and others, 1938	6	8
Holy City, shepherd sighting angels over city, 1941	3	5
I Hadn't Anyone Til You, woman's face w/ flowers, white on red titles, 1938	4	6
I Left My Dear Old Village Home For You, green and red titles, country lane, cottage, Nellie Powers inset, 1903	5	8
I Live Alone For You, floral border, Maud Gelder inset, 1903	4	6
I'll Be Back In The Sweet By And By, soldier under tree, woman in clouds, Big City Four inset, 1912	5	8
I'll Walk Alone (With a Song In My Heart), Susan Hayward and movie scenes, 1944	7	10
I'm Afraid I'm Beginning To Love You, heart-shaped garland, cupids, Elida Morris inset photo, 1913	4	6
I'm Waiting For Your Return, woman feeding pigeons, canal scene background, 1915	4	6
I Once Had A Sweet Little Doll Dears, black on white panels, thorny flowers, drawing of children w/ dolls, 1886	6	10
Irresistible You (Broadway Rhythm), Tommy Dorsey, Ginny Simms, 1944	6	10

Left: Casey Jones, The Brave Engineer, *1909, $20-$28.*

Right: Come Josephine In My Flying Machine (Up She Goes!), *Blanche Ring photo, 1910, $25-$38.*

	LOW	HIGH
It's A Great Life (Playboy of Paris), Maurice Chevalier, 1930	8	12
It's Winter Again, snow scene w/ cottage, Benny Kyte inset, 1932	3	5
I've Had This Feeling Before But Never Like This, white on brown outline of woman, 1943	4	6
I've Waited A Lifetime For You (Our Modern Maidens), drawing of Joan Crawford in dance pose, 1929	7	10
I Want To Be There, man sitting by tree w/ dog, homestead in background, Bob Allbright inset, 1915	4	6
I Want You Georgia, woman on dock welcoming riverboat, 1916	8	12
I Was Lucky (Folies Bergere de Paris), Maurice Chevalier caricature, 1935	8	12
Jeanie With The Light Brown Hair, seated woman holding book and flowers, Dale Evans inset, 1939	4	6
Je Vous Aime (Copacabana), Groucho Marx, Carmen Miranda, Andy Russell, 1948	8	12
Keep Your Fingers Crossed (Coronado), cast on ship set, Eddy Duchin inset, 1935	10	15
La Cucaracha, Spanish and English lyrics, red graphics, Art Kassel inset, 1935	3	5
Let's Get Lost (Happy Go Lucky), Martin, Vallee, Powell, Hutton, Bracken, 1943	5	8
Lingering Lips, Wohlman woman, clock, Al Tucker and his orchestra inset, 1925	4	6
Lord's Prayer, stylized clouds, large cross, 1941	5	8
Man In A Raincoat, silhouette man and lamp post, woman in background, Priscilla Wright inset, 1955	3	5
Mia Cara (The Big Pond), Maurice Chevalier, Claudette Colbert, 1930	10	15
My Heart Sings (Anchors Aweigh), Kathryn Grayson, 1943	3	5
Romance In The Dark, Gladys Swarthout, John Boles in frame, 1938	12	18
Some Day We'll Meet Again (I'd Give My Life), Tom Brown, Frances Drake, 1936	10	15
So Nice Seeing You Again (We're In the Money), Joan Blondell and Ross Alexander photo, 1935	12	18
Sugar Plum (Thanks a Million), Dick Powell, Fred Allen, Paul Whiteman, 1935	8	12
The Cop On The Beat The Man In The Moon And You, title scene, Mark Fisher inset, 1932	5	8

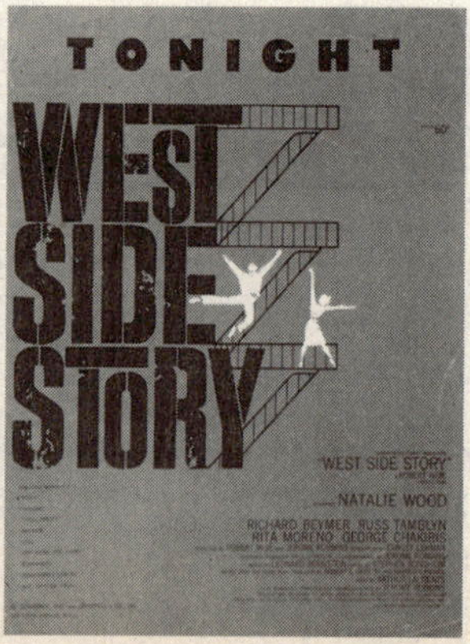

Left: In My Merry Oldsmobile, *Anna Fitzhugh photo, 1905, $25-$38.*

Right: Tonight *(West Side Story), 1957, $5-$8.*

	LOW	HIGH
The Last Long Mile (Toot Toot), man, woman, and porter w/ hatbox, 1918	8	12
Then You'll Remember Me, blue and orange diagonal panels, Herbert Foote inset, 1935	4	6
There Goes My Heart, diagonal yellow lines on blue, Doring Sisters inset, 1934	5	8
This Is No Laughing Matter, smiling mask w/ ribbons, 1941	4	6
This Time It's Love (Saturday's Millions), Robert Young and Leila Hyams, Harry Richman photo lower right, 1933	7	10
Tom's Tune, blue and white plaid background, Georgia Gibbs inset, 1951	3	5
Trolley Song, The (Meet Me in St. Louis), Judy Garland head photo, 1944	5	8
Turn Off The Moon, pink background curtain, Kenny Baker and Phil Harris orchestra center photo, 1937	5	8
Under Any Old Flag At All (The Talk of New York), blue fronds background, Cohan photo upper left, 1908	6	10
Watching My Dreams Go By (She Couldn't Say No), Winnie Lightner photo, 1929	6	10
We Belong Together (Music In the Air), blue, black, and white Deco design	5	8
Web of Love, The (The Great Gabbo), Erich Von Stroheim, Betty Compson, 1929	6	10
We Will Never Say Good Bye Again, full moon, water, and lilies, 1919	4	6
When The Little Red Roses Get The Blues For You (Hold Everything), Winnie Lightner, Joe E. Brown, 1930	10	15
Wherever You Are, stylized candle, light halos, Orrin Tucker inset, 1942	5	8
White Cliffs Of Dover, stylized title scene, Phil Brito inset, 1941	4	6
Why Stars Come Out At Night (The Big Broadcast of 1935), purple and aqua Art Deco band, Ray Noble inset, 1935	8	12
Wine Song (Caravan), Loretta Young, Charles Boyer, Jean Parker, drawing of crown, 1934	5	8
With Plenty Of Money And You (Gold Diggers of 1937), Joan Blondell, Dick Powell, chorus women, 1936	7	10
You Are My Lucky Star (Broadway Melody of 1936) Taylor, Knight, Jack Benny, red paper, 1935	5	8
You Came To My Rescue (The Big Broadcast of 1937), Jack Benny, Burns & Allen, Raye, and others around border, 1936	10	15
You Took The Words Right Out Of My Heart (The Big Broadcast of '38), Dorothy Lamour, W. C. Fields drawing, 1937	8	12

Left: Turn Back The Universe and Give Me Yesterday, *1916, $10-$15.*

Right: You're A Grand Old Flag *(Yankee Doodle Dandy), James Cagney photo, George M. Cohan inset, $10-$15.*

Native American Collectibles

American Indian artifacts range from jewelry and woven products to weapons.

Collected items date from prehistoric to contemporary times. Quality of workmanship is key to value. Artifacts may originate throughout the United States, but most items come from the Plains and the Southwest. Likewise, the majority of dealers will be found in the Southwest, particularly in the area of Santa Fe, New Mexico.

For additional reading refer to *North American Indian Artifacts, 6th Edition* by Lar Hothem (Krause Publications, Iola, WI, 1998) and *Warman's Native American Collectibles* by John A. Shuman III (Krause Publications, Iola, WI, 1998).

	LOW	HIGH
Basket, California, Pomo, gift basket, compressed globular form w/ attached carved shell discs w/ clear, pearlized, and translucent blue beads, decorative motif of hooked devices, 1900-25, 3.625" dia	$300	$400
Basket, Louisiana, double twill basket w/ square bottom and round rim, similarly constructed lid, red-brown, dark brown, and yellow split cane, early 20th C, 3" h	1500	2000
Basket, Northwest, Tlingit, rattle-top basket, twined spruce root-dyed orange, sienna, and brown, woven-in stepped motifs on body, radiating devices on lid, late 19th C, 5.25" dia	600	800
Basket, Northwest Coast, Skokomish, twine wallet form w/ indented bottom and straight sides, false embroidery of panels of brown and black spruce root geometric devices, band of trotting dogs below open-work scalloped rim, late 19th C, 7" h	1200	1600
Basket, Pacific Coast, Klamath, pictorial basket, twined globular form w/ 4 frolicking puppies, 20th C, 4.5" dia	600	800
Basketry Jar, Northwest Coast, Aleut, closed twined grass-woven jar w/ trade yarn in multicolor linear devices, lid handle finely woven of polychrome trade wool, 1900-25, 6.5" h	800	1000
Basketry Tray, Southwest, Apache, double rosette motif w/ cross and dog devices, tickled rim, 1900-25, 11" dia	400	600
Basketry Tray, Southwest, Pima, shallow coiled tray form edged in white seed beads, radiating rosette motif w/ rhombic devices, early 20th C, 7.75" dia	800	1000

Baskets, left to right: Pacific Coast, Klamath; Southwest, Pima; California, Pomo; Northwest Coast, Tlingit. —Photo courtesy Skinner, Inc., Boston, MA.

	LOW	HIGH
Belt, Central Plains, child's, harness leather strap w/ metal conchas, c1900, 22" l	150	250
Bow Case and Quiver, Central Plains, Lakota, child's, sinew-sewn hide forms w/ cotton twill binding, beaded motif of bars and boxes, light and medium blue, greasy yellow, and dull pink beadwork, late 19th C, 25" l	3000	4000
Bowl, Southwest, Hopi, pottery, shallow form w/ lug handle, interior painted in 2 panels, 1 w/ black slip feather devices on red ground, other w/ black and red slip wing or bird motif on creamy orange ground, Fred Harvey tag "Made by Nampeyo - Hopi…3628, HopiWare bought at San Diego Exposition," c1915, 9" dia	10,000	12,000
Bracelet, Southwest, Navajo, tooled silver cuff w/ large central turquoise stone, c1940, 1.5" w	100	150
Cradle Board, Southwest, Apache, wood form w/ muslin wrap, hood, and ties, hood w/ faceted bead dangler and crescent moon cut-out, 20th C, 35.5" l	300	500
Dance Wand, Central Plains, rawhide-wrapped stick roll-beaded in navy and white, red-painted joined horn head, horse hair extension wrapped w/ thread and plaited sweetgrass, late 19th C, 14.5" l	300	500
Dance Wand Mirror, probably Shoshone, salvaged carved wood handle and mirror frame, painted red and blue and tacked throughout, paper roundel mounted on back w/ period illustration of woman looking in cherub-held mirror, late 19th C, 18" l	1000	1200
Doll, Central Plains, Lakota, native-tanned hide and muslin form, face w/ faceted bead features, dress beaded at yoke in stepped geometric devices, blues, white heart reds, red, and crystal pink beads, salt and pepper leggings, c1900, 15" l	300	500
Face Mask, Northwest Coast, probably Tlingit, carved cedar form w/ white, black, red, and blue-green polychrome paint, stylized wrinkles at mouth and brow, peg remains at chin and upper lip probably held fur or hide attachments, mid-19th C, 8" l	15,000	18,000
Gauntlets, pair, Plateau, beaded hide w/ meandering floral design, amber, translucent green, and blue beads, fringed cuffs, early 20th C, 14.5" l	400	600
Hair Drop, Central Plains, Lakota, parfleche buffalo hide strip w/ trade mirrors, brass beads, and trade shells, commercially dyed quill-wrapped suspensions, and horse hair, hide strip edged in white heart red beads and beaded in repeated linear and geometric motifs, apple green, white heart red, and navy beadwork on white field, 1875-1900, 29" l	2500	3000

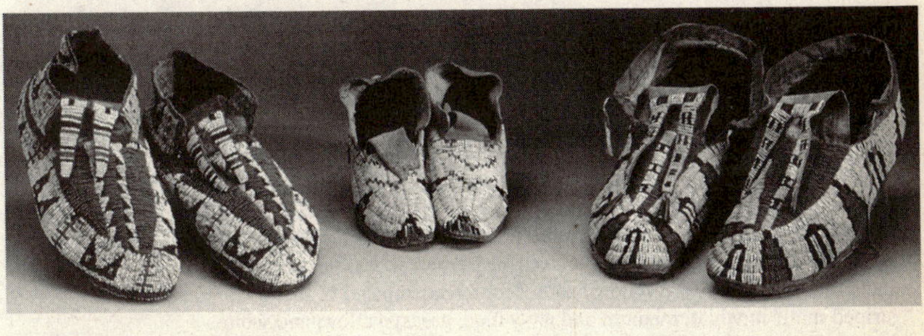

Central Plains beaded hide moccassins. —Photo courtesy Skinner, Inc., Boston, MA.

	LOW	HIGH
Jar, Southwest, Zia, pottery, globular form polychrome-painted orange and black on cream ground w/ birds in medallions, c1930-40, 6.5" h	200	400
Kachina Doll, Southwest, Wilson Tewaghaptewa (Hopi, 1843-1960), Mother Kachina, carved cottonwood form, polychrome-painted white, black, red, and dark ocher, 7" h	1000	1500
Knife Sheath, Northern Plains, sinew- and copper wire-sewn harness leather form w/ overlay of beaded buffalo hide, dull pink, white heart red, and sky, medium, and dark blue beadwork in geometric and linear devices, tin cone suspensions, c1870s, 9.5" l	1500	1800
Leggings, Central Plains, Cheyenne, child's, thread-sewn yellow-painted uppers, lower lazy stitched panel, translucent red, dark blue, and greasy yellow beads on white field, bottom finished w/ pico edge beading in translucent medium blue, early 20th C, 14" l	300	500
Leggings, Central Plains, Lakota, woman's, hide w/ red edge binding ties, lower panels beaded in rhomboid and cross devices, white heart red, translucent navy, and metallic faceted beads on white field, c1890, 15.5" l	600	800
Man's Shirt, Plains Apache, probably Mescalero, native-tanned hide, fringed, trace orange pigment at sleeves and yoke tabs, 1875-1900, 35" l	3000	4000
Moccasins, Apache, native tanned hide w/ crystal, translucent blue, and red beadwork, 1900-25, 9" l	100	200
Moccasins, Central Plains, Cheyenne, child's, sinew-sewn hard sole forms, fully beaded uppers, notched cuff, stepped geometric device decorative motif, white heart red, greasy yellow, and navy and light blue beads on white field, c1880s, 6.75" l	500	700
Moccasins, Central Plains, Lakota, sinew-sewn buffalo hide forms w/ fully beaded uppers, beaded bifurcated tongues w/ tin cone tanglers, vamp decorated w/ buffalo track device w/ stepped and linear device at toe, sides, and heel, white heart red, blues, and medium green beads on white field, c1880s, 10.5" l	800	1000
Moccasins, Southern Plains, Kiowa, sinew-sewn native-tanned hide forms, painted yellow, partially beaded w/ stylized geometric device at vamp and single lane of beadwork, c1910, 9.5" l	400	600
Pipe Bag, Northern Plains, Cree, smoked native-tanned buffalo hide, top 4 tabs and sides edge-beaded in white, tabs w/ metal tack closure, lower panel of bilateral floral motif on 1 side, slightly meandering on other side, white heart red, pumpkin, dull pink, light and medium blue, and various green beads on white field, buffalo hide fringe, c1870s, 21" l	1000	1500
Possible Bag, Central Plains, buffalo hide, commercially dyed quills across front in repeated linear motif, tied flap closure w/ beaded panel decorated w/ tin cone danglers w/ dyed horse hair suspensions, side panel of early barred devices w/ tin cone danglers and horse hair suspensions, white heart red, apple green, greasy yellow, navy, and white beads, c1880s, 19.5" l	2000	2500
Pouch, Central Plains, Lakota, sinew- and thread-sewn buffalo hide and commercial leather form, roll-beaded edges, central motif of bars and boxes design w/ stepped geometric devices, white heart red, apple green, greasy yellow, and light and medium blue beads on white field, tin cone danglers, c1880, 5.25" l	800	1000
Pouch, Oregon, Wasco, buckskin form w/ trace yellow ocher, top edge beaded in light translucent blue, drawstring closure w/ tab ties edged in medium blue and greasy yellow beads, loom-beaded panel of diagonal striped motif in white, medium and navy blue, greasy yellow, and white heart red beads, looped beaded suspensions at bottom, c1890, 7" l	900	1100
Saddle Blanket, Southwest, Navajo, commercially dyed and natural homespun wool woven in banded style, 51" x 29"	200	300

	LOW	HIGH
Sash, Prairie, probably Osage, child's, finger-woven commercial blue-green and maroon yarn woven in zigzag pattern, white beads bordering colors, drop ties w/ knotted tassel finials, late 19th C, 39" l	300	500
Skull Cracker, Central Plains, probably Lakota, sinew-sewn hide-wrapped stick w/ trace red ocher, carved quartz head, c1850-75, 31" l	300	500
Spoon, Central Plains, possibly Lakota, carved cow horn w/ remains of roll beading at handle, late 19th C, 11.5" l	300	400
Strike-a-Lite Bag, Apache, probably Mescalero, native tanned buckskin form, stepped crosses and rhomboid devices, translucent amber, navy blue, and white beads on light pony trader blue field, tin cone danglers, late 19th C, 7" l	400	600
Totem Pole, Northwest Coast, probably Haida, cedar form carved w/ concave back, front and base polychrome-painted w/ commercial pigments, pole carved in myriad of towering fantastic creatures, base constructed from commercial wood crate, late 19th C, 58" h	5000	7000
War Shirt, Northern Plains, Blackfeet, beaded hide, buckskin shirt laced at sides and sleeves, fringe at sleeves and yoke, front w/ trace yellow ocher paint in repeated dot pattern, back and sleeves w/ similar trace paint in striped motif, trace red pigment visible inside collar, front and back yoke w/ triangular tab in red and black trade cloth trimmed w/ white, navy, and light pony trader blue beads, applied buffalo hide beaded strips at sleeves and running front to back over shoulders, motifs include abstract stepped hourglass and other linear motifs, 1875-1900, 27" l	18,000	24,000
Weaving, Southwest, Navajo, Two Grey Hills, tightly woven natural shades of homespun wool, central rhombic motif on brown field w/ interlocking geometric devices, white border w/ small rhombic devices, 48.5" x 97.5"	1200	1600

Above: Beaded hide war shirt, Northern Plains, Blackfeet.

Above left: Weaving, Southwest, Navajo, Two Grey Hills. —Photos courtesy Skinner, Inc., Boston, MA.

Nautical Memorabilia

Items from the eighteenth and nineteenth centuries, the Age of Sail, are highly prized. Fine specimens command high prices. Finds can still be made in small New England auctions and estate sales. See *Nautical Antiques* by W. D. Ball (Schiffer, Atglen, PA, 1994) for more information.

	LOW	HIGH
Adze, ship builder's, steel head, wooden gooseneck-shaped handle, 19th C, 31.5" l	$100	$200
Barometer, by John W. Merrich & Co., Worcester, MA, Timby's Patent w/ printed scale, sliding brass pointer, and 1857 patent date, oak case w/ instruction label on back, 38.5" h	200	300
Binnacle Compass, brass, signed on dial "Tanaka Keiky Seisaku Sho, Osaka, Japan," w/ gimbals, lamp, and domed top, 10" h	100	200
Boat Signal Lantern, Keystoneware, black-painted tin w/ brass burner, belt clip, and wire handles, clear glass lens, 8.5" h	100	200
Caliper, beech and brass, undivided arc, spike and stylus holder, 20.5" l	100	200
Captain's Speaking Trumpet, brass, mouthpiece stamped "A. D. Richmond New Bedford," mid-19th C, 22" l	400	600
Chart Book, *Harbor Chart-Book, Boston To Bar Harbor, 1908,* authorized and published by George W. Eldridge, Vineyard Haven and Boston	600	800
Chart Box, New England, painted cherry and poplar, rectangular hinged top, dovetailed box, old green paint, early 19th C, 7" h, 33.75" w, 8" d	600	800
Chart Tube, brass, embossed "W. W. Stevens," late 19th C, 38.5" l, 2.5" dia	100	200
Chronometer, Hamilton Model 22, No. 12284, 21-jewel movement, brass gimbal, dated "1943," mahogany case w/ instruction labels and glazed inner lid and top, 6" w	300	500
Clock, Waterboy Ship's Bell No. 10, twin-train movement striking on gong, Arabic numerals, silvered dial, lacquered brass case, glazed door in form of ship's wheel, patent dates to 1910, 8.25" dia	200	400
Deck Compass, gimbal-mounted dial signed "Ritchie, Boston, USA, and Sold by Rupp & Co., New York," signed along rim "E. S. Ritchie Sons, Boston, No. 45230," in upright brass stand w/ tapered glazed 6-section top and tripod base w/ mounting feet, 32" h	400	600
Eel Fork, iron w/ wooden handle, 9' l	150	250
Merchant's Kneehole Desk, English, grain-painted pine, rectangular drop-leaf top above 2 rectangular cabinets, each w/ 3 graduated drawers w/ recessed back panels, grain-painted red umber to resemble wood, on casters, 1800-50, 31" h, 48" w, 37" d	400	600
Pilot Chart, North Atlantic Ocean, color lithograph, laid down, framed, 1887, 23" x 31.5"	200	250
Sea Chest, English, rectangular hinged top on canted dovetailed box, base painted blue, interior w/ polychrome portrait of ship, early 19th C, 17" h, 36" w, 18" d	600	800
Sextant, C. Plath, Humburg, No. 11851, black-lacquered ladder frame, silvered scale divided 160°-0°, vernier, magnifier, and accessories in fitted mahogany case w/ Kelvin White, New York and George Butler, San Francisco labels, 12" radius	200	400
Sextant, I. Mackrow, London, brass, oxidized lattice-pattern frame, lacquered arc, divided 140°-0°, vernier w/ magnifier telescope, 4 shades and detachable sight labeled "James Rahll's Patent," shaped and fitted mahogany case w/ retailer's label "Alexander Cairns, Liverpool," 12" arc radius	800	1000

	LOW	HIGH
Ship Captain's Log, for the cutter *Caroline,* August 1799, handwritten account of events at sea between the Sandwich Islands and Macao, while engaged at fur trading w/ a crew of 21, eventual arrival at Norfolk Sound on June 1st	800	1000
Shipping Clerk's Desk, New England, grain-painted pine, rectangular lift-top w/ canted sides and center gallery w/ block-turned posts, 2 short drawers and 2 long drawers, frame w/ square legs joined by straight skirt and box stretchers, old grain-painted brown to resemble mahogany, dark green-painted base, 1800-50, 59" h, 61.5" w, 41" d	600	800
Ship's Compass, by Baher, Melrose, MA, further signed "The Harris Co., Portland, Me.," w/ monochrome rose brass case and gimbal, mahogany case, 8.5" w	200	300
Ship's Lanterns, port and starboard, classes II and III, round bail handles, marked "Universal Metal Spinning and Stamping Co., New York," early 20th C, 10" h, price for pair	300	500
Ship's Signal Cannon, bronze barrel, wooden carriage, iron wheels, bronze plaque "mfg by James Gregory - 106 Cannon St - N.Y.," 1895, 19.5" h, 32" l barrel, 38" l overall	8000	10,000
Telescope, by Hayward Lumber & Inv. Co., Los Angeles, labeled "U.S. Navy Spyglass, no. 15009," tapered body tube, 2.5" object lens, oak case, 31.5" l	200	400
Wind and Current Chart, North Atlantic Seas, 8 sheets lithographed on paper, laid down on linen backing, "M. F. Maury A. M. Lieut. U. S. Navy, Superint^{dt} of U.S.N. Observatory, Washington, Compiled from materials in the Bureau of Ordnance and Hydrography, Commodore Lewis Warrington Chief of Bureau, Drawn by Lt. W. B. Whiting, U.S.N.," 1848, 70" x 96"	200	400

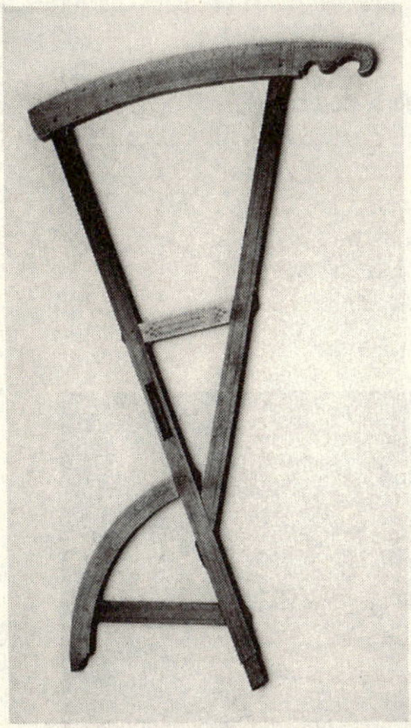

Above: Octant, ebony w/ ivory scale divided 0°-90° by 5's, vernier, brass arm and shades, 14" radius, in shaped oak case w/ Robert Merrill, NY label, $374 at auction.

Above left: Backstaff, Davis-pattern, signed "Made By Benjamin King in Newport Rh^{O} Island 1768," rosewood main limbs, boxwood greater arc divided 0°-25° by 1's and 65°-90° by 5's, reverse w/ latitude and departure chart, punched star decoration both sides, lesser arc divided 0°-60° by 10's and 0°-65° by 5's, 24.5" l, $6325 at auction. —Photos courtesy Skinner, Inc., Boston, MA.

Orientalia

Chinese Export Porcelain

The word "china," as in "fine china," derives from the time when all porcelain came from China. Before Europeans learned the secrets of kaolin clay and the firing process, kings and princes spent fortunes (literally) on their porcelain collections. Even after Western entrepreneurs cracked these secrets, merchants imported shiploads of Chinese porcelain for an ever-growing number of dinner services. The Chinese fed this demand with pieces designed for the West. Chinese Export Porcelain (CEP) developed more or less standard designs that crossed the oceans throughout the nineteenth century. Canton, Nanking and Fitzhugh are the well-known blue and white designs, while polychrome favorites are Rose Mandarin and Rose Medallion.

Pieces marked "Made in China" date after 1894. Some unscrupulous dealers have ground out this mark. Look for suspicious grinding marks or related flaws on the undersides of pieces. For further information see *Chinese Export Porcelain: Standard Patterns and Forms, 1780–1880* by Herbert, Peter and Nancy Schiffer (Schiffer, Exton, PA, 1975).

Canton

	LOW	HIGH
Bowl, cut corners, 19th C, 9.5" dia	$800	$1000
Bowl, shallow, 19th C, 2" h, 11" dia	75	150
Cider Jug, covered, double-woven strap handle w/ flower-impressed ends, foo dog finial, 19th C, 8.25" h	1500	2000
Pitcher, 19th C, 7.75" h, 6.5" dia	500	700
Platter, oblong, 19th C, 18.5" l, 15.75" w	700	1000
Platter, oval, reticulated, 19th C, 10.5" l, 9" w	200	400
Platter, rectangular, 19th C, 12" l, 9.5" w	250	500
Serving Dish, covered, rectangular base w/ shaped corners, pod finial, last half 19th C	200	400
Soup Tureen, covered, oval, 19th C, 7" h, 12" l, 9.5" w	400	600
Tea Caddy, covered, octagonal, 19th C, 5.5" h	2000	3000
Vegetable Dish, covered, rectangular, 19th C, 5" h, 9" l, 8" w	100	200
Vegetable Dishes, diamond-shaped, 19th C, 4" h, 10.5" l, 8.25" w, price for pair	500	700
Warming Dish, last half 19th C, 9.5" dia	300	500

Canton China. —Photo courtesy Skinner, Inc., Boston, MA.

Famille Rose

	LOW	HIGH
Floor Vases, applied kylins and foo dogs, hardwood stands, 24" h, price for pair	$2000	$3000
Garden Seats, 2 reserves depicting women in palace scene, 19th C, 18.625" h, price for pair	3500	4500
Jar, covered, baluster form, decorated w/ female sprite figure emerging from flower blossom, surrounded by floral devices, 19th C, 18" h	700	900
Jardinieres, Ru i borders w/ floral scrolls, decorated w/ peonies and rockery, 19th C, 12.5" h, 14" dia, price for pair	1200	1500
Plate, dragon and phoenix confronting each other on millefleur and gold ground, red Ch'ien Lung mark on base, 19th C, 9.5" dia	200	300
Vase, globular body w/ slightly flaring mouth, millefleur design on gilt ground, turquoise-glazed interior and foot, 4-character Shen Te Tang Chih mark in red on foot, 19th C, 16" h	1400	1600
Vase, Republican period, decorated en grisaille w/ iron red borders, bat-form handles, painted w/ Pu tai and children, 4-character Ch'ien Lung mark on base in light blue enamels, c1920, 13.75" h	200	300
Vases, decorated w/ birds and chrysanthemum flowers, 4-character Ch'ien Lung mark, 19th C, 9.5" h, price for pair	200	300
Wash Bowl, rim decorated w/ floral devices, interior sides w/ children surrounding the bowl, 11.5" dia	150	250

Fitzhugh

Bottle, covered, clobbered blue pattern, 19th C, 13.75" h	$500	$700
Platter, oval, blue underglaze decoration w/ gold, red, blue, and green overglaze lion crest on rim, 19th C, 12" l, 9" w	300	500
Platter, oval, gray-blue border, bright blue medallion, 19th C, 15" l, 12" w	600	800
Serving Dish, covered, rectangular w/ bamboo side handles, domed bamboo-handled cover, last half 19th C, 6.5" h, 10.5" l	300	500
Warming Dish, covered, oval, Mandarin and floral motifs, orange glaze, black and gilt highlights on white ground, 1820-30, 15.5" x 10.25"	1500	2000
Wash Bowl, clobbered blue pattern, 19th C, 16" dia	500	700

Left to right: Famille Rose Floor Vases; Fitzhugh Platters. —Photos courtesy Skinner, Inc., Boston, MA.

Nanking

	LOW	HIGH
Bowl, cut corners, 19th C, 5" h, 9.5" l, 9.5" w	$400	$600
Bowl, scalloped edge, 19th C, 9.25" dia	300	500
Garniture Set, blue and white, molded chicken skin decoration w/ gilt highlights, 19th C, 11.5" h, price for 3-pc. set	1000	1500
Platter, oval, 19th C, 8" l, 6" w	200	400
Platter, oval, 19th C, 15" l, 11.5" w	300	500
Platter, w/ pierced insert, oval, 19th C, 15.25" l, 13" w	600	800
Sauce Tureens, covered, oval, 19th C, 5.75" h, 8.5" l, 5.25" w, price for pair	500	700
Soup Tureen, oval, 19th C, 10.5" h, 15" l, 10.25" w	1200	1600
Vegetable Dishes, covered, rectangular, 5.5" h, 9" l, 7.75" w, price for matching set of 4	1000	1500

Rose Mandarin

Bough Pot, hexagonal form, applied squirrels, berry, and vine decoration, 9" h	$1000	$1500
Cider Jug, covered, woven double strap applied handle, lid w/ foo dog finial, 19th C, 9.5" h	2500	3500
Fruit Tazza, diamond-shaped, 19th C, 12.25" dia	700	900
Garden Seat, barrel-form, court scene surrounding central body w/ upper and lower bands of butterflies and floral devices, 19th C, 18.5" h	2000	3000
Pitcher, scalloped rim, 19th C, 5" h	300	500
Platter, oval, 19th C, 18.25" l, 15.25" w	800	1200
Punch Bowl, 13.5" dia	1000	1500
Punch Bowl, 19th C, 14.75" dia	2500	3500
Shrimp Dishes, shield form, floral border, 19th C, 10" l	400	500
Tea Cup and Saucer	75	150
Teapot, dome lid, gilt decorated spout and handle, 8.25" h	1000	1200
Urn, covered, baluster form w/ mask handles, dome cover w/ foo dog finial, 19th C, 16" h	1200	1500
Vase, baluster-form w/ scalloped flaring rim, decorated w/ foo dogs and kylins, 19th C, 17" h	1200	1600
Water Pitcher, paneled form w/ scalloped rim, 19th C, 7.75" h	1000	2000

Rose Mandarin Garden Seat. —Photo courtesy Skinner, Inc., Boston, MA.

Rose Medallion Bough Pots.
—Photo courtesy Skinner, Inc., Boston, MA.

Rose Medallion

	LOW	HIGH
Bough Pots, octagonal form, applied squirrel and berry devices, 19th C, 9" h, price for pair	$4000	$6000
Bough Pots, square form, 2 panels w/ court figures, 2 w/ ducks in pond, foliate handles, 19th C, 9" h, price for pair	4000	6000
Bread and Butter Plates, 19th C, 6.25" dia, price for 7 pcs.	200	400
Brush Box, rectangular, 2 compartments, 19th C, 7" x 3.5" x 2.5"	300	400
Brush Holder, cylindrical, 19th C, 4.75" h	150	250
Candlesticks, 19th C, 7" h, price for pair	1200	1600
Fruit Basket, w/ undertray, reticulated, 19th C	700	800
Garden Seats, hexagonal form, 18.25" h, price for pair	4000	5000
Platter, 19th C, 18" l	400	500
Platter, central medallion depicting family crest w/ stag, 19th C, 16.5" l	800	1000
Punch Bowl, 12.5" dia	1500	2500
Sauce Tureen, covered, gilt finial and handles, 19th C, 6" l	400	600
Shrimp Dish, 19th C, 9.5" dia	300	500
Teapot, dome lid, 19th C, 9.5" h	800	1000
Vases, baluster form, kylin handles, 10" h, price for pair	400	600
Vegetable Dish, covered, cut corners, interior decorated in Famille Rose palette, 19th C, 9.5" l	400	500
Vegetable Dish, covered, oval, interior decorated in Famille Rose palette, 19th C, 10.75" l	400	500

Miscellaneous

Basin, circular, dragon interior, flared rim w/ lattice design border w/ floral and bird reserves, landscape design on exterior, last half 19th C, 8.5" h, 27.5" dia	$1500	$1800
Bowl, Rose Canton, cut corners, 19th C, 10.5" w	1000	1200
Fruit Tazza, Rose Canton, diamond-shaped, 19th C, 14.25" dia	600	800
Garniture Set, Cabbage pattern, comprising 2 vases and 3 covered urns w/ foo dog finials, 19th C, 14.5" h vases, 13.5" h urns, price for 5 pcs.	3000	4000
Jar, Famille Verte, lion mask handles, decorated w/ birds and flowers alternating w/ scenes from novel *Hung Meng Lo,* mid-19th C	200	300
Lamps, Famille Verte colors on eggshell ground, decorated w/ warriors in brocade borders, ealy 20th C, 13" h, price for pair	200	300
Platter, oval, blue and gilt vintage border decoration, monogrammed, w/ matching pierced insert, 19th C, 17.5" l	1000	1500

	LOW	HIGH
Punch Bowl, exterior scenic decoration w/ court figures on dragon boat surrounded by warriors, interior w/ geometric border, rust and gilt scenic motifs, 19th C, 15.625" dia	2000	3000
Punch Bowl, Famille Verte palette w/ polychrome exotic birds, floral and foliate decoration, and geometric borders w/ reserves of rust-colored scrolled devices, 19th C, 14.75" dia	1500	2000
Sauceboat, polychrome and gilt decoration w/ gold edge band, interior scalloped border, floral garland motifs, mid-18th C, 3" h	200	400
Seal Paste Box, Kutani ware, underglaze blue enamels, decorated w/ birds and flowers w/ inset roundels of landscapes and flowers, underglaze blue Greek key frets for borders, interior w/ underglaze blue heraldic emblems w/ further enamel work, signed "great Japan Kutani made," 19th C	200	400
Serving Dishes, exterior decorated w/ court figures, foot w/ green grass borders w/ 4 blue flowers, 19th C, 10.5" l, price for pair	500	700
Teapot, hand painted polychrome and gilt eagle w/ wings down and shield decoration, entwined strap handle, 19th C, 5.75" h	600	800
Tea Set, partial, American Eagle pattern, sepia and gilt decoration, comprising tea caddy, 5 mugs, 3 tea cups, 1 saucer, and 1 plate, early 19th C, 5.25" h teapot	1200	1600
Tea Set, partial, comprising a teapot, cream jug, caddy, waste bowl, 6 handleless cups and saucers, and a shaped dish, hand painted grisaille floral decoration w/ gilt highlights, mid-19th C, 5.5" h teapot	300	500
Tea Set, Rose Canton, comprising teapot, sugar, creamer, and 4 cups and saucers, late 19th C, 4.5" h teapot	700	900
Umbrella Stand, cylindrical form, 3 rows of Thousand Butterfly panels surrounded by Rose Medallion bands, 19th C, 24" h	1500	2000
Vase, orange decoration w/ 2 panels w/ court scenes surrounded by floral devices and medallions w/ figures, gilt fruit-form handles, mounted as lamp, 19th C, 19" h	400	600
Vases, polychrome decorated court scenes surrounded by pink and green foliate devices, blue ground, mask handles, 19th C, 17" h, price for pair	500	700
Vegetable Dish, covered, diamond-shaped, Thousand Butterfly pattern, 19th C, 5.5" h, 12" l, 9.5" w	300	500

Above: Rose Canton Bowl and Fruit Tazza.

Left: Umbrella Stand, Thousand Butterfly panels surrounded by Rose Medallion bands.

—Photos courtesy Skinner, Inc., Boston, MA.

Cinnabar

Cinnabar is Chinese carved lacquer. Layers are built up over wood, porcelain, or metal thick enough to carve ornate designs. The color is usually deep red. Although cinnabar has been made continuously for over three hundred years, the majority of the collected pieces currently available date from the turn of the century, as do all pieces listed below.

"Good" pieces may show some wear with some minor flecks of lacquer chipped away. "Best" pieces must be in perfect condition with no chipping or cracks.

Snuff Bottle, red lapis lazuli top, late 19th C, 2.75" h, $300-$400.

	LOW	HIGH
Ashtray, 5" dia	$100	$200
Bowl, covered, pedestal foot, 6" dia	200	300
Bowl, covered, red flower design, black ground, 6" dia	175	300
Bowl, landscape, black on red, 9" dia	200	300
Bowl, scalloped rim, red, 6.5" dia	175	300
Box, covered, floral design, black on red, 6" dia	250	400
Box, covered, floral design, red on green, 6.5" dia	450	700
Box, covered, oblong, carved view, 6.5" l	250	350
Box, covered, sports scene, black on red, 15" dia	650	900
Box, melon shape, 6.5" dia	175	350
Box, scenic views, 6.5" sq	200	350
Cigarette Box, 11.5" dia	250	400
Cup, dragon handles, 4.5" dia	250	400
Cup, floral design, flared rim, 4.5" dia	300	500
Cup, footed, 5.5" dia.	200	300
Dish, floral design, 9.5" dia	300	500
Ginger Jar, landscape scene, red on cream, 8.5" h	400	600
Mirror, rust-colored landscape, 19.5" w	250	350
Plate, double dragon design, 12.75" dia	600	1000
Plate, floral design, footed base, 8" dia	250	450
Plate, floral design, red on green, 13" dia	650	1100
Plate, flower and butterfly design, 10.5" dia	400	550
Plate, geometric design, red on black, 8" dia	175	300
Pot, Taoist markings, footed, 7" dia	450	700
Stool, Greek key border, floral medallion, 18" h	1800	3000
Tray, flower and bird design, red, yellow, and green, 15" l	900	1500
Tray, flower and bird design, reddish-brown, 15" l	1000	1500
Tray, flowering tree, 12.5" l	350	500
Tray, gilded rim, 17" l	300	500
Urn, red flower, black ground, 6.5" h	100	200
Vase, dragon design, green, yellow, and red, 15" h	1500	2800
Vase, dragon design, red, 12" h	400	800
Vase, fish design, 15" h	750	1800
Vase, fish shape, red, 7.5" h	300	450

Netsukes

	LOW	HIGH
Ashinaga and Tenaga, ivory, signed "Minkoku," 19th C, 3.25" l	$700	$900
Benkei and Warrior, hauling large conch shell filled w/ demons, ivory, signed "Komin," 19th C	900	1200
Farmer w/ Hoe, wooden, signed "Yukitei" within cinnabar seal, 19th C	150	300
Four Children, trying to move immense jar, ivory, signed "Gyokuzan," 19th C	500	700
Frog, seated on conch shell, ivory w/ inlaid eyes	300	500
Fukurokuju and Stag, ivory, 19th C, 2" h	400	600
Goddess Bishamonten, playing a koto w/ 2 attendants at either side, ivory, signed "Gyokuhosai," 19th C	400	600
Group of Seven Masks, ivory, signed "Rakuosai," early 19th C	800	1000
Hankei, holding large wooden tablet w/ oni mask, wooden w/ traces of red stain, signed "Tomokazu" within oval cartouche, 18th/19th C	1500	2000
Man, peeling melon, seated on tied bundle of firewood, ivory, signed "Ko-u" for Iehijusai Kou, 19th C	800	1000
Monkey, holding chestnut, wooden, signed "Issai"	150	300
Monkey Trainer, w/ monkey pulling his ear, ivory, signed "Seiko" within cinnabar cartouche, 19th C	1000	1500
Nio Figure, fighting w/ oni demon, ivory, signed on foot "Isshu To," 19th C	700	900
Octopus, ivory w/ inlaid eyes, signed "Kogyoku," late 19th C	200	400
Ox and Calf, ivory w/ inlaid eyes, in the style of Tomotada, 19th C	2000	2500
Phallic Form, horn w/ gilt accents, Japan, early 20th C	200	300
Puppy, growling over abalone shell, ivory w/ inlaid eyes, 19th C	200	400
Shoki the Demon Queller, boxwood, signed "Minkoku," late 18th/ early 19th C	2000	2500
Sleeping Shoki, w/ dragon emerging from his robes and climbing onto his head, ivory w/ deep yellow patina, 18th/early 19th C, 2.5" l	1500	2000
Small Boy, holding tiger toy w/ movable head, ivory, signed "Masaharu" in seal form, 19th C	2000	2500
Smiling Man, holding double gourd, dressed in jewel-embroidered robe, ivory, signed "Masanao of Kyoto," 18th/19th C	2000	2500
Tiger, ivory w/ inlaid eyes, signed "Tomokazu," 19th C	600	800
Wild Boar, wooden, 19th C, 2" l	1000	1500
Wrestling Men, ivory w/ deep yellow patina, early 19th C	1000	1500

Assortment of netsukes. —Photo courtesy Skinner, Inc., Boston, MA.

Nippon Porcelain

Nippon porcelain resulted from the 1893 American tariff act requiring imports to be marked (in English) with the country of origin. "Nippon" was an accepted name for Japan at that time. Nippon ware also represents Satsuma, Noritake, Imari and other Japanese wares of that period.

The marks most frequently depict an "M" within a green wreath, and the word "Nippon" printed in curved letters underneath. There are many, many variations, however. By the late 1920s, "Japan" replaced "Nippon." Nippon ware has been faked and reproduced.

For further reading see Joan F. Van Patten's *Collector's Encyclopedia of Nippon Porcelain,* a series of five books published by Collector Books (Paducah, KY) or *The Wonderful World of Nippon Porcelain: 1891-1921* by Kathy Wojciechowski (Schiffer, West Chester, PA, 1992).

	LOW	HIGH
Bowl, bisque, walnut motif, green M mark, 9" dia	$75	$125
Bowl, blue, pink, and red floral medallions, white ground, handles, green M mark, 7" dia	15	25
Bowl, enameled, raised chestnut motif, handles, green M mark, 8" dia	25	35
Bowl, mustard color, gold jewels, rose motif, blue M mark, 9" dia	60	80
Bowl, square, green M mark and hand-painted Nippon mark, 6.5" w	40	60
Candy Bowl, palm trees and sailboat, pastel colors, beaded gold rim, pierced handles	60	75
Candy Dish, oval, scenic motif, open-work handles, hand-painted green M in wreath, 7" x 5"	50	70
Celery Dish, floral decoration and small houseboat w/ sail, satin finish, 9" x 4"	35	50
Cocoa Set, consisting of covered pot and 6 cups and saucers, rose sprays on turquoise ground	400	450
Compote, Chicago Post Office medallion, flowers, and insects, Oriental China Nippon mark	90	120
Cookie Server, floral motif, yellow ground, gold handle, M mark, 10" dia	25	50
Creamer, gold foliage motif, hand-painted Nippon mark	15	20
Cruets, oriental garden motif, M mark, 6" h, price for pair	80	125
Cup, grapevine motif, gold, green M mark, 3" h	15	25
Cup and Saucer, multicolored Art Nouveau floral motif, green M mark	10	20
Demitasse Coffee Set, consisting of covered pot and 5 cups and saucers, Art Deco black outline, Nippon mark	175	225
Dish, covered, brown and tan panel, floral motif, gold handle, rising sun mark, 8" x 6"	65	75
Egg Warmer, green M in wreath, 5" dia	140	180
Fruit Bowl, geometric designs and flowers, scalloped gold rim, handles, blue leaf mark	100	140
Jar, multicolored floral design, gold-green M mark, 4" h	25	35
Nappy, green M in wreath and hand-painted Nippon mark, 6" dia	40	50
Nut Bowl, green M in wreath and hand-painted Nippon mark, 6" dia	70	90
Nut Cup, blue maple leaf and Nippon mark, 3.5" w	25	35
Plate, Art Nouveau floral design, green M mark, 5" dia	10	20
Plate, child holding bouquet, blue M mark, 7" dia	15	25
Plate, enameled leaves, vines, and oval medallions w/ gold outline, green M mark, 8" dia	30	40
Plate, multicolored floral design, green M mark, 10" dia	20	30
Relish Dish, blue Komaru symbol, hand-painted Nippon mark, 8.25" l	45	55
Salt Dip, polychrome floral motif, gold outline, green M mark	15	25
Salt and Pepper, pair, pink floral motif, gold handles, rising sun mark, 2" h	25	35
Spoon Holder, floral motif, 2 handles, M mark	55	75
Vase, green M in wreath and hand-painted Nippon mark, 6" h	75	100

Rugs, Oriental

Oriental rugs older than fifty years have long been collected and used in fine homes throughout the United States. They originated in Persia (modern Iran), Turkey and the surrounding areas. The following representative examples show prices realized at auction (wholesale) and the corresponding retail range. "Karastan" rugs are machine made and not collected by anyone we know. All the rugs listed here are hand-woven. European examples from the nineteenth century are particularly valuable.

For further reading see *The Official Price Guide to Oriental Rugs, Second Edition* by Joyce Ware (House of Collectibles, NY, 1996) and *The Illustrated Buyer's Guide to Oriental Carpets* by J. R. Aziollahoff (Schiffer, Atglen, PA, 1998).

	LOW	HIGH
Afshar Rug, South Persia, stepped hexagonal lattice w/ quatrefoil motifs in midnight and royal blues, ivory, red, camel, and dark blue-green, several borders of similar coloration, late 19th C, 6'3" x 4'10"	$700	$1000
Anatolian Kelim, staggered rows of stepped diamonds in cochineal, sky blue, aubergine, gold, and blue-green on ivory field, sky blue eli-belinde motif border, mid-19th C, 8'9" x 5'	1000	1500
Anatolian Prayer Rug, empty red field, large blue-green spandrels, dark brown stepped polygon border, 1875-1900, 4' x 3'	2500	3500
Anatolian Yastik, diamond surrounded by 4 large serrated leaf motifs in sky blue, ivory, gold, and light aubergine on red field, multicolored border w/ gold elems, early 20th C, 2'10" x 1'8"	200	400

Left to right: Afshar Rug, South Persia, 2 stepped polygons inset w/ hooked diamonds, matching spandrels, and numerous small motifs on midnight blue field, narrow navy blue meandering border, early 20th C, 6'6" x 4'7", $1610 at auction; Bahktiari Carpet, West Persia, square grid w/ floral and geometric motifs, palmette and rosette border, early 20th C, 9'10" x 7', $4313 at auction. —Photos courtesy Skinner, Inc., Boston, MA.

	LOW	HIGH
Bahktiari Carpet, West Persia, large lobed diamond medallion and overall Herati design in ivory, red, navy blue, tan, and blue-green on midnight blue field, red spandrels, midnight blue border, 1925-50, 12' x 9'	2500	3500
Bahktiari Rug, West Persia, large circular medallion inset w/ blossoming vines in ivory, sky blue, apricot, red-brown, and sage green on black field, navy blue border, 1925-50, 7'2" x 5'2"	1000	1500
Bahktiari Rug, West Persia, large diamond medallion, stripes, and flowering vines in navy blue, ivory, rust, gold, light brown, and blue-green on midnight blue field, rust spandrels, ivory palmette and vine border, guard stripe partially missing from 1 end, early 20th C, 6'4" x 4'7"	2000	2500
Baluch Prayer Rug, Northeast Persia, rows of quatrefoil serrated leaf motifs in navy and royal blue, red, aubergine, and blue-green on camel field, black and aubergine reciprocal border, late 19th C, 4'8" x 2'9"	300	500
Baluch Rug, Northeast Persia, octagonal lattice w/ hooked squares in red, midnight blues, black, and aubergine-rust, red border, early 20th C, 5'2" x 2'10"	400	600
Bidjar Carpet, Northwest Persia, overall Herati design in royal blue, rose, camel, gold, maroon, and green on red field, narrow midnight blue turtle border, 1925-50, 12'2" x 9'	5000	7000
Bordjalou Kazak Rug, Southwest Caucasus, column of 4 octagonal Memling guls in navy blue, black, red, ivory, pale aubergine, and gold, wide ivory concentric hooked triangle border, 1875-1900, 7'2" x 4'3"	2500	3000
Chinese Rug, circular floral and fretwork medallion flanked by 6 vases in midnight blue, ivory, pale rose, and light rust on sky blue field, ivory border, late 19th/early 20th C, 4'4" x 2'6"	600	800

Left to right: Baluch Rug, Northeast Persia, large central flowering plant on camel field, stepped triangle border, late 19th C, 6'3" x 3'4", $805 at auction; Daghestan Prayer Rug, Northeast Caucasus, serrated diamond lattice w/ flowering plants on ivory field, interrupted vine border, mid-19th C, 4'2" x 3'2", $2875 at auction. —Photos courtesy Skinner, Inc., Boston, MA.

	LOW	HIGH
Chinese Silk Rug, large flowering shrub w/ animals and birds in sky blue, maroon, gold, brown, olive, green, and blue-green on midnight blue field, border of similar coloration, 20th C, 5' x 3'	300	500
Chinese Silk Rug, lobed oval medallion and delicate flowering vines in midnight and ice blues, tan, gold, light green, olive, and blue-green on rust field, large ivory spandrels, midnight blue border, 20th C, 4'8" x 3'2"	300	500
Chinese Silk Rug, overall design w/ palmettes, rosettes, flowering vines, and small cloudbands in midnight, royal, and sky blues, camel, ivory, and tan on red field, midnight blue border, 20th C, 5' x 3'	400	600
Ersari Chuval, West Turkestan, horizontal bands of geometric motifs and border designs in navy blue, ivory, gold, and dark blue-green on rust-red field, rust-brown flowering plant elems, 1850-1900, 5'4" x 3'3"	300	500
Fereghan-Sarouk Carpet, West Persia, lobed diamond medallion and delicate blossoming vines in navy, royal, and sky blues, red, rose, gold, rust, and blue-green on pale apricot field, red spandrels, navy blue border, 1875-1900, 12'2" x 8'4"	1500	2500
Gabbeh Rug, Southwest Persia, 3 concentric diamond medallions in midnight blue, gold, ivory, brown, and blue-green on red field, 3 zigzag borders of similar coloration, early 20th C, 6'4" x 3'10"	1200	1500
Hamadan Corridor Carpet, Northwest Persia, diamond medallion, matching spandrels, and Herati design in red, rose, navy blue, gold, and blue-green on midnight blue field, red border, 1925-50, 11'6" x 5'9"	1000	1500
Heriz Carpet, Northeast Persia, hooked and gabled square medallion w/ palmette pendants in black, royal blue, light red, tan, and dark green on rust field, ivory spandrels, black border, 1925-50, 10'6" x 7'4"	1500	2000

Left to right: Hamadan Rug, Northwest Persia, staggered rows of boteh and small motifs on midnight blue field, wide rosette and serrated leaf border, early 20th C, 7'4" x 4'8", $1725 at auction; Indo-Kashan Carpet, concentric diamond medallion surrounded by dense floral sprays on midnight blue field, dark red spandrels, flowerhead border, mid-20th C, 12'9" x 10', $8050 at auction. —Photos courtesy Skinner, Inc., Boston, MA.

	LOW	HIGH
Heriz Carpet, Northwest Persia, gabled square medallion surrounded by palmettes in midnight, sky, and ice blue, rose, tan, ivory, and green on rust field, ivory spandrels, midnight blue turtle border, 1925-50, 10'10" x 9'	3000	5000
Heriz Carpet, Northwest Persia, gabled square medallion surrounded by palmettes, serrated leaves, and flowering vines in midnight and sky blues, rose, gold, red-brown, and blue-green on red field, large ivory spandrels, midnight blue turtle border, 1925-50, 20' x 10'6"	7000	9000
Heriz Carpet, Northwest Persia, gabled square medallion w/ palmette pendants in navy and sky blues, rose, ivory, brown, and blue-green on red field, very large ivory spandrels, navy blue border, 1875-1900, 11'3" x 9'6"	6000	8000
Heriz Carpet, Northwest Persia, large gabled square medallion surrounded by floral motifs in midnight and royal blues, rose, tan-gold, and green on dark red field, ivory spandrels, midnight blue border, 1925-50, 12'10" x 9'4"	800	1200
Heriz Carpet, Northwest Persia, large stepped diamond medallion surrounded by floral motifs and 4 human figures in navy and royal blues, rose, ivory, wine red, tan-gold, and green on red field, multicolored spandrels, navy blue border, 1925-50, 12'2" x 8'7"	1200	1600
Heriz Rug, Northwest Persia, diamond medallion surrounded by serrated leaves and small geometric motifs in midnight and sky blues, gold, tan, ivory, and blue-green on terra-cotta red field, 3 borders of similar coloration, early 20th C, 4'3" x 3'9"	1500	2000
Indian Carpet, large lobed diamond medallion surrounded by floral sprays in red, rose, royal blue, brown, pale gold, and blue-green on midnight blue field, ivory spandrels, red cartouche border, 1925-50, 17'8" x 12'	7500	9000

Left to right: Kazak Rug, Southwest Caucasus, 2 large lobed hexagonal medallions inset w/ cloudbands on red field, ivory dragon's tooth border, 1875-1900, 7'7" x 4'10", $6900 at auction; Kuba Rug, Northeast Caucasus, 3 Lesghi stars surrounded by small star-in-octagon motifs on red field, ivory wineglass border, late 19th C, 5'6" x 3'9", $1840 at auction. —Photo courtesy Skinner, Inc., Boston, MA.

	LOW	HIGH
Indian Carpet, large lobed oval medallion and matching spandrels in cochineal, rose, ivory, and midnight blue on heavily abrashed olive-green field, cochineal border, late 19th/early 20th C, 12'8" x 8'8"	1500	2000
Indian Carpet, overall design w/ delicate palmettes, rosettes, and leaf motifs in navy and royal blues, red, rose, camel, and green on greige field, navy blue border of similar design, early 20th C, 15' x 12'	5000	6000
Isphahan Rug, Central Persia, rosette medallion surrounded by small palmettes and serrated leaves in sky blue, rust, tan, camel, and green on red field, sky blue border, 20th C, 5'4" x 3'6"	600	800
Karabagh Long Rug, South Caucasus, column of 5 notched diamond medallions flanked by hooked half-hexagons in navy blue, red, violet, ivory, gold, and abrashed blue-green on wine red field, ivory hooked square border, late 19th C, 10'10" x 4'	2000	3000
Karabagh Long Rug, South Caucasus, column of 5 octagonal medallions surrounded by small diamonds and stars in navy and sky blue, ivory, gold, aubergine, red, and light blue-green on rust field, ivory border, 1875-1900, 10'10" x 5'4"	1000	1500
Karachoph Kazak Rug, Southwest Caucasus, large octagonal medallion surrounded by 4 star-filled squares and small octagons in ivory, navy blue, gold, and blue-green on red field, blue-green wineglass border, 1850-75, 7'2" x 5'10"	2500	3500
Kashan Carpet, West Central Persia, lobed oval medallion surrounded by palmettes, curved serrated leaves, and small cartouches in midnight and royal blues, rose, gold, ivory, aubergine, light green, and blue-green on terra-cotta red field, midnight blue border, 1925-50, 12'6" x 9'	4000	6000

Left to right: Makri Rug, Southwest Anatolia, 2 elongated hexagonal medallions inset w/ groups of serrated leaves, 2 ivory and gold meandering borders, 1875-1900, 5'8" x 3'10", $3335 at auction; Marasali Prayer Rug, East Caucasus, serrated diamond lattice w/ boteh on gold field, ivory hexagon border, 1875-1900, $2185 at auction. —Photos courtesy Skinner, Inc., Boston, MA.

	LOW	HIGH
Kashan Carpet, West Central Persia, oval floral medallion surrounded by leaf-blossoming vines in royal blue, red, soft brown, and light blue-green on ivory field, similar border, 1925-50, 11'4" x 8'10"	1000	1500
Kazak Rug, Southwest Caucasus, 2 columns of 6 Memling guls in navy and sky blues, red, gold, aubergine, and light and dark blue-green on ivory field, gold hooked diamond border, early/mid-19th C, 7'2" x 3'9"	7000	9000
Kerman Carpet, Southeast Persia, overall design of floral sprays and curving blossoming vines in navy and sky blues, red, rose, tan, violet, aubergine, and light and dark greens on ivory field, wide floral border of similar coloration, 1925-50, 23' x 9'9"	6000	8000
Khamseh Carpet, South Persia, column of 4 stepped diamond medallions and overall palmette and bird motifs in royal and ice blues, red, deep rust, gold, ivory, green, and blue-green on midnight blue field, deep rust rosette, boteh, and vine border, early 20th C, 15'4" x 6'6"	8000	10,000
Kurd Bagface, Northwest Persia, diamond lattice w/ hooked diamonds in navy and sky blues, red, gold, apricot, aubergine, and dark blue-green, navy blue octagon border, late 19th C, 3'9" x 2'8"	800	1000
Kurd Rug, Northwest Persia, 2 columns of 7 ashik guls surrounded by numerous diamonds and hook motifs in navy and sky blues, red, rose, apricot, gold, and blue-green on abrashed dark brown field, red border, 1875-1900, 9' x 5'5"	5000	6000
Kurd Rug, Northwest Persia, 3 stepped polygons and flowering plant motifs in midnight and navy blues, camel, rose, brown, and blue-green on abrashed rust-red field, 4 narrow borders of similar coloration, early 20th C, 6'8" x 4'10"	1500	2000

Left to right: Mohtashem Kashan Rug, West Central Persia, lobed diamond medallion and spandrels and blossoming vines on ivory field, rosette and floral border, 1875-1900, 7'5" x 4'4", $7475 at auction; Northwest Persian Long Rug, 3 hooked and stepped medallions and matching spandrels on red field, palmette, rosette, and diamond border, early 20th C, 13'6" x 6', $2300 at auction. —Photos courtesy Skinner, Inc., Boston, MA.

	LOW	HIGH
Mahal Carpet, West Persia, overall design of wreath-like floral groups, serrated leaves, and spiraling vines in navy and ice blues, red, rose, gold, camel, ivory, and blue-green on midnight blue field, red border, early 20th C, 13'2" x 10'2"	1200	1800
Mahal Carpet, West Persia, overall design w/ rosettes, paired flowerheads, and serrated leaves in midnight and royal blues, rose, ivory, aubergine, pale gold, olive, and blue-green on dark red field, midnight blue spandrels and palmette border, 1925-50, 12' x 8'2"	2000	3000
Malayer Rug, Northwest Persia, dense staggered rows of serrated leaf motifs in light red, rust, royal blue, ivory, olive, and blue-green on midnight blue field, rust spandrels, ivory border, early 20th C, 6'7" x 5'2"	1200	1800
Malayer Rug, Northwest Persia, staggered rows of hooked square motifs in red, rose, royal blue, gold, brown, and blue-green on midnight blue field, large blue-green spandrels, ivory boteh and vine border, outer guard stripe partially missing from 1 end, early 20th C, 6'7" x 4'5"	1000	1200
Maslinghan Rug, Northwest Persia, deeply notched hexagonal medallion surrounded by serrated leaves in royal blue, camel, rose, ivory, and blue-green on red field, midnight blue rosette spandrels, ivory border, early/mid-20th C, 4' x 2'10"	200	400
Northwest Persian Rug, large diamond medallion w/ elaborate hooked pendants in camel, sky blue, rose, and blue-green on red field, navy blue spandrels, camel ashik gul and serrated leaf border, late 19th C, 5'6" x 4'	2000	2500
Northwest Persian Runner, column of 15 medallions and numerous small motifs in red, royal blue, camel, gold, ivory, rose, and dark blue-green on midnight blue field, red octagon border, early 20th C, 18'4" x 3'8"	4000	5000

Left to right: Qashqai Rug, Southwest Persia, 3 star-filled diamond medallions flanked by birds and zigzag stripes on navy blue field, diamond, boteh, and vine border, early 20th C, 6'9" x 5', $2185 at auction; Seichour Long Rug, Northeast Caucasus, 5 St. Andrew's cross motifs on abrashed blue-green field, flowering vine border, Georgian outer border, 1875-1900, 10' x 3'6", $8050 at auction. —Photos courtesy Skinner, Inc., Boston, MA.

	LOW	HIGH
Northwest Persian Runner, overall design of rosettes and flowering vines in red, ivory, sky blue, gold, and blue-green on navy blue field, red border, 1875-1900, 12' x 3'8"	600	800
Qashqai Rug, alternating rows of hooked diamonds and diagonal serrated leaves in royal and sky blue, red, ivory, gold, aubergine, and dark blue-green on midnight blue field, red octagon border, late 19th C, 9'2" x 5'8"	800	1200
Qum Silk Rug, Central Persia, large blossoming tree in midnight blue, maroon, rose, aqua, violet, caramel, and light green on ivory field, midnight blue border, 20th C, 5'2" x 3'6"	400	600
Sarouk Carpet, West Persia, overall design of vases of flowers and blossoming vines in midnight and sky blues, red, camel, tan-gold, and blue-green on deep wine red field, midnight blue border, early 20th C, 11'8" x 8'10"	2000	2500
Sarouk Carpet, West Persia, overall design w/ rosettes, large curved leaves, and flowering vines in midnight and sky blues, rose, ivory, tan, red-brown, and blue-green on terra-cotta red field, midnight blue palmette and vine border, late 19th C, 13'9" x 10'4"	8000	10,000
Sarouk Mat, staggered rows of boteh and small floral motifs in red, rose, ivory, gold, and blue-green on midnight blue field, ivory border, 1925-50, 2'6" x 1'10"	200	400
Sarouk Rug, West Persia, overall design of rosettes and floral sprays in midnight, slate, and ice blues, ivory, tan, and camel on wine red field, midnight blue border, early 20th C, 4'10" x 3'6"	400	600
Sarouk Rug, West Persia, scalloped oval medallions, matching spandrels, and flowering vines in light red, rose, sky blue, tan, and pale blue-green on ivory field, midnight blue border, 1875-1900, 6'6" x 4'6"	1200	1800

Left to right: Serapi Carpet, Northwest Persia, serrated rosette medallion surrounded by palmettes on terra-cotta red field, large ivory spandrels, rosette and serrated leaf border, 1875-1900, 13'4" x 9'6", $14,950 at auction; Shirvan Rug, East Caucasus, 7 rows of 3 peacock motifs on abrashed terra-cotta red field, ivory bird and animal motif border, 1875-1900, 4'6" x 3'7", $6325 at auction. —Photos courtesy Skinner, Inc., Boston, MA.

	LOW	HIGH
Seichour Long Rug, Northeast Caucasus, 4 vases of flowerheads w/ angular vines in dark wine red, rose, sky blue, gold, tan, ivory, and blue-green on abrashed navy blue field, dark red flowerhead border, blue and ivory Georgian outer border, late 19th C, 12'5" x 4'2"	4000	5000
Senneh Rug, Northwest Persia, elongated keyhole medallion and overall Herati design in red, navy blue, rose, ivory, gold, camel, and blue-green on midnight blue field, red border, late 19th/early 20th C, 6'2" x 4'5"	1000	1500
Serab Long Rug, Northwest Persia, overall Herati design in sky blue, rose, camel, ivory, and red-brown on midnight blue field, red border, early 20th C, 14'4" x 4'6"	500	800
Serab Long Rug, Northwest Persia, staggered rows of filigree-style boteh in red, sky blue, rust, gold, and light blue-green on abrashed midnight blue field, red border, plain camel outer border, late 19th C, 10' x 4'9"	2000	2500
Shirvan Rug, East Caucasus, 3 Lesghi stars and small geometric and floral motifs in navy and sky blue, red, gold, ivory, and blue-green on dark brown field, ivory border, 1875-1900, 4'8" x 3'	1500	2000
Shirvan Rug, East Caucasus, staggered rows of palmette motifs in midnight and royal blue, ivory, tan, and blue-green on pale gold field, tan border, 1875-1900, 4'8" x 4'	400	600
South Caucasian Long Rug, column of 5 medallions surrounded by numerous small geometric, floral, and animal motifs in red, gold, royal blue, ivory, apricot, aubergine, and blue-green on midnight blue field, ivory wineglass border, late 19th C, 11'8" x 3'6"	2500	3500

Tabriz Carpet, Northwest Persia, floral medallion w/ oval pendants, matching spandrels, and dense blossoming vines on midnight blue field, midnight blue cartouche border, early/mid-20th C, 16'10" x 11'8", $6900 at auction. —Photo courtesy Skinner, Inc., Boston, MA.

	LOW	HIGH
South Persian Bagface, central rosette w/ quatrefoil pendants flanked by 4 large serrated leaf motifs in red, ivory, navy blue, gold, and blue-green on midnight blue field, ivory meandering border, early 20th C, 2'4" x 1'7"	1000	1200
Suzani, Central Asia, 7 small flowering shrubs in red, rose, ice blue, gold, apricot, ivory, and blue-green on aubergine field, wide border of similar coloration, backed w/ printed fabric, 20th C, 5'2" x 4'	700	900
Tekke Rug, West Turkestan, 3 columns of 7 main carpet guls in midnight blue, ivory, apricot, and dark blue-green on rust field, diamond motif border and dyrnak gul elems of similar coloration, late 19th/early 20th C, 5' x 3'9"	800	1000
Ushak Carpet, West Anatolia, empty coral field, deeply serrated floral spandrels in gold, ivory, rose, and blue-green, green-gold border, narrow outer border missing from both ends, late 19th C, 11'8" x 9'2"	4000	6000
Ushak Carpet, West Anatolia, overall design w/ angular blossoming vines and cypress trees in sky blue, gold, ivory, red-brown, and green on rose field, wide green border of similar design, late 19th C, 21' x 16'	20,000	25,000
Uzbek Rug, Central Asia, 4 zigzag vertical bands surrounding paired triangles in navy blue, apricot, gold, ivory, and blue-green on dark rust-red field, blue-green dshudur border, guard stripe missing from 1 end, 1875-1900, 6' x 4'2"	3000	3500
Yomud Chuval, West Turkestan, 4 columns of 5 chuval guls in midnight blue, dark red, ivory, and blue-green on red field, compartment border and pole tree elems of similar coloration, 1875-1900, 4' x 2'10"	3000	4000

Left to right: Tabriz Rug, Northwest Persia, floral medallion and matching spandrels on terra-cotta red field, rosette and arabesque vine border, late 19th C, 5'8" x 4', $2070 at auction; Tekke Main Carpet, West Turkestan, 4 columns of 10 main carpet guls on rust-red field, stars-in-octagon border of similar coloration, early/mid-19th C, 7'2" x 6'6", $4313 at auction. —Photos courtesy Skinner, Inc., Boston, MA.

Satsuma

Satsuma is a cream-colored Japanese pottery, usually with a delicate crackled glaze, elaborately painted, and gilt. Although it dates to the seventeenth century, most pieces seen today are from the nineteenth and twentieth centuries. The following are nineteenth-century examples.

	LOW	HIGH
Bowl, covered, Meiji period, Hundred Arhats decoration w/ women and warriors within scrolls and fan-shaped medallions, interior w/ warriors, signed "Gyokuzan" w/ Satsuma mon emblem, 4.5" dia	$200	$400
Bowl, foliated edge, interior w/ peacock and peahen in garden scene of pine trees hung w/ flowering wisteria, floral border on exterior, signed "Kanzan," w/ Satsuma mon, c1900, 6.5" h, 12" dia	800	1200
Bowl, Meiji period, foliate edge w/ interior relief decoration of gods of luck in garden scene, exterior w/ same motifs, signed, w/ Satsuma mon, 5" dia	200	400
Bowl, Taisho period, foliate edge decorated w/ raised enamel floral patterns, interior w/ 3 geishas, signed, 1911-22, 10" dia	200	400
Box, covered, circular, sages in landscape decoration, 4.25" dia	100	200
Charger, Meiji period, hunt scene w/ 3 warriors and immense stag, brocade borders, signed w/ seal, c1880, 18" dia	800	1200
Incense Burner, cylindrical form, figures in landscapes and flowered panels, signed "Ryozan"	800	1000
Incense Burner, globular form, gilt bird and blossom decoration on black ground, 3.25" h	100	200
Incense Burner, Meiji period, oviform w/ 3-leg base and pierced cover, decorated w/ gods of luck and attendants, brocade borders, extensive signature "made in Great Japan" w/ Kinkozan mark w/ additional inscriptions and a Satsuma mon, c1890, 6" h	1200	1500
Plate, Meiji period, 2 dragons, 1 white and 1 gold in polychrome cloud swirls, brocade borders, signed, c1880, 9.75" dia	400	600
Teapot, bridge, pagoda, and river decoration, 6" h	200	300
Vase, cobalt blue w/ gilt phoenixes surrounding heart shape of women at dinner and boating excursion, signed "Konkozan," late 19th C, 6" h	2000	3000
Vase, cylindrical form w/ flared mouth and elephant-head handles, decorated w/ procession of various insects, mid-/late 19th C, 12.5" h	200	300
Vase, double-walled form pierced w/ floral pattern accented w/ enamels, gilt lion mask handle, butterflies borders, signed, impressed seal, 10" h	200	400
Vases, Meiji period, cobalt blue ground w/ gilt brocade patterns framing reserves of woman and small children, signed "Kinkozan," 15" h, price for pair	800	1200
Vase, Meiji period, miniature, floral borders w/ reserves of women and children and floral motifs, signed "Kyuzan," 3.5" h	400	600
Vase, Meiji period, supported on back of a shishi, 1 side decorated w/ scene of emperor Antoku at Dannoura, other w/ court scene, c1880, 8.5" h	300	500
Vase, Meiji period, trumpet mouth-form w/ reserves of people in garden scenes and fan forms, floral work borders, signed, 5.25" h	150	250
Vases, cobalt blue ground w/ brocade patterns, reserves decorated w/ warriors alternating w/ women, signed, 7" h, price for pair	600	800
Vases, cylindrical form w/ slightly indented foot and conical neck, decorated w/ butterflies on orange ground, brocade borders, signed, c1900, 12" h	300	500
Vases, square form w/ high shoulder, tapered small at base, brocade borders surrounding mirror image reserves of birds and flowers, landscapes and court scenes, signed w/ Satsuma mon, gold seal, and inscription "Great Japan Unzan," c1880, 8.5" h, price for pair	4000	6000

Snuff Bottles

Snuff bottles appeared with the growing popularity of snuff in China during the latter part of the seventeenth century. Originally a practical item, like a cigarette case, craftsmen of all sorts decorated these pieces with greater and greater sophistication. Eventually snuff bottles gained a life of their own. Collected and produced long after the fad of using snuff died out, they are still made today.

Judging snuff bottles is highly subjective. Craftsmanship and beauty are the dominant factors, but rarity of materials also plays a part. Some jade examples are valued almost solely on the quality of the piece of jade, rather than age, craftsmanship, or design.

	LOW	HIGH
Agate, tan surface skin carved in relief w/ deer, monkey, and bee, rhebus for official success, well-hollowed, Chinese, 19th C	$150	$250
Cloisonné, double bottle shape, dragon motif, c1900s	600	700
Cloisonné, yellow dragon, white cloud motifs, c1800s	400	500
Enamel, gourd shape, fruit and foliage on blue ground, c1800s	600	800
Enamel, plants and dragonfly on blue ground, c1800s	800	1000
Ivory, carved w/ woman seated on elephant and holding peony, Japan, early 20th C, 3.25" h	100	200
Ivory, lacquer inlaid designs of dragons and extensive calligraphy, 4-character Ch'ien Lung mark on base, China, late 19th C, 3" h	300	500
Jade, flattened oval form, pale celadon colored stone, well-hollowed, 19th C	200	300
Jade, streaked green and gray, toad and landscape, c1800s	600	800
Lacquer, purse-shaped, black w/ ivory rim, c1900s	700	900
Lacquer, real gourd lacquered black, c1800s	500	700
Milk Glass, enamel painting of landscape, 4-character Ch'ien Lung mark, 1735-95	400	600
Porcelain, blue and white, dragon motif, c1800s	250	400
Porcelain, blue, red, and white, courtyard scene, c1800s	400	600
Porcelain, green and white, dragon and cloud motif, c1800s	600	800
Porcelain, paneled, fish lotus motif, c1800s	500	700
Porcelain, red foo dog and pup, c1900s	400	600
Rock Crystal, clear w/ thin black lines and fish, c1800s	600	800
Rock Crystal, square, clear, basket-work motif, c1800s	1000	1500

Assortment of Snuff Bottles. —Photo courtesy Skinner, Inc., Boston, MA.

Paper Collectibles

Labels

Bottles

	LOW	HIGH
Blumers Chocolate Syrup, orange, brown palm trees, 2.375" x 7"	$0.20	$0.30
Borax Powdered, topless lady, roses, orange and black, RI, 2.625" x 4.625"	0.40	0.60
Budd, ginger ale, gilt champagne glass, NH	0.15	0.30
Camden Bock Beer, jolly man and ram guzzling beer, NJ	0.15	0.30
Colonial Checkerberry Extract, navy design and lettering on blue ground, ME, 1.5" x 3.125"	0.30	0.40
Cupid Orange Soda, whole and sliced orange, gilt, Mt. Vernon, NY, 4" x 3"	0.15	0.30
Dr. Blumers Lemon Extract, blue and white, 2" x 6.75"	0.15	0.30
Farmer's Pride, catsup, IN and IL, 2" x 2.75"	0.15	0.30
Golden Pheasant, beer, colorful flying pheasant, MI	0.40	0.60
Green Mountain Syrup, cabin, ox team, man making syrup, black family boiling cane syrup in iron kettle, 3.75" x 3.5"	0.75	1.50
Happy Day, ginger ale, rising sun and rays, sailboat on lake, PA	0.10	0.30
Haxton's Beer, sailing ship, PA	0.15	0.30
Holland, beer, Dutch girl, windmills, NJ	0.15	0.30
Jockey Club, pineapple soda, jockey and horse, NJ	0.15	0.30
Joe De Marco, fat juicy strawberries, light blue leaves, 6" sq	0.40	0.60
Kringle Ale, Santa, mantel, stockings, and tree, 1960s, PA	0.15	0.30
Lasko Brewed Birch Beer, racetrack scene, 5" dia	0.15	0.30
Myopia Club, lemon sour or cherry soda, Indian chief profile, gilt, diamond shaped, 4.5" x 3.25"	0.40	0.60
Napa Rock, Tom Collins mixer, mountain scene, conifers, stream, 2.5" x 4.25"	0.15	0.30
Old Mill, old mill and pond in silver and black, MO	0.15	0.30
Old Tyme, beer, product name on red ground, LA	0.15	0.30
Olive Oil, fancy gilt, green leaves and olives, OH, 1.75" x 3.75"	0.40	0.60
Red Medal Brand Tomato Catsup, 3 maltese crosses, gilt, NY, 3.75" x 3"	0.40	0.60
Scheidt's Lager Beer, winter country scene, homes, horse, PA	0.15	0.30
Snoboy, snowman holding peach, blue ground	0.40	0.60
Sport Beer, flying duck, goose, pheasant, men ice fishing, deer, forest, MI	0.50	1.00
Twentieth Century Ale, sunrise scene, PA	0.15	0.30
Virgil's Ginger Ale, gilt lettering, black and white, New Orleans	0.10	0.25
Wood's Violet Ink, white lettering, fancy border, purple ground, 1" x 3"	0.40	0.60

Left to right: Culmbacher Beer, India Wharf Brewing Co., NY, 3" x 4", $35 at auction; Rienzi Beer, Rochester Brewing Co., 3" x 5", $80 at auction. —Photo courtesy Cerebro.

Inner Lid Labels, left to right: American Conquest; Lone Trail. —Photos courtesy Cerebro.

Cigars

	LOW	HIGH
Band, Health Tobacco, Harmless Nicotine	$15	$25
Band, Horse Show	20	30
Band, Mark Twain	35	45
Band, Old Tom Cat	20	30
Band, Priscilla	30	40
Band, Regalia Roosevelt	20	30
Band, Seneca Chief	20	30
Inner Lid, American Conquest, #1898, Schmidt & Co.	250	300
Inner Lid, Capitolio, #51309, Hermann Shott	150	175
Inner Lid, Indian Maiden, George L. Schlegel	175	250
Inner Lid, Judge Day, Hull, Grummond	200	300
Inner Lid, Lone Trail, #1901, Schmidt & Co.	500	600
Inner Lid, Master Workman, #1884, Schumacher & Ettlinger	250	350
Outer Box, Adieu, #3836, George S. Harris & Sons	30	50
Outer Box, American Home, #1895, George S. Harris & Sons	150	200
Outer Box, Bella Vista, Louis E. Neuman	30	50
Outer Box, Blue Ring, #4156, George S. Harris & Sons	30	50
Outer Box, Byzantine, #2270, Heppenheimer & Maurer	120	140
Outer Box, Challenge Cup, #6295, Schumacher & Ettlinger	35	50
Outer Box, Clover Queen, #4031, George S. Harris & Sons	35	50
Outer Box, Club Friends, #1896, Schmidt & Co.	300	400
Outer Box, Comptroller, Heppenheimer & Maurer	40	50
Outer Box, Handicap, #6134, Schumacher & Ettinger	50	75
Outer Box, Idle Hours, #2238, Heppenheimer & Maurer	50	75
Outer Box, Jack of Hearts, #6032, Schumacher & Ettlinger	250	350
Outer Box, La Madre, #6935, Schumacher & Ettlinger	75	90
Outer Box, Little Tom, #6351, Schumacher & Ettlinger	30	50
Outer Box, Massasoit Chief, #1998, Heppenheimer & Maurer	200	300
Outer Box, Naval Cadet, #4114, George S. Harris & Sons	50	90
Outer Box, On Time, #1122, George S. Harris & Sons	250	300
Outer Box, Saturn, #1599, George S. Harris & Sons	150	200
Proof, Croaker, 5 colors	350	450
Proof, Daily Mail, W. K. Gresh & Sons	200	250
Proof, Flor de Kearney	200	300
Proof, Judge Good	350	300
Proof, The New Bachelor, Victor Thorsch Co.	100	150

Inner Lid Label, Judge Day.
—Photo courtesy Cerebro.

	LOW	HIGH
Proof, Twiddle Twaddle, George L. Schlegel	200	250
Salesmen's Sample, Beau Monde, #11090, George S. Harris & Sons	200	250
Salesmen's Sample, Bowling Club, #1374, Schmidt & Co.	700	900
Salesmen's Sample, Chief Okee, #982, Moehle Lithographic Co.	300	400
Salesmen's Sample, Conchas, #2040, O. L. Schwencke	50	75
Salesmen's Sample, Have Another, #5218, O. L. Schwencke	50	75
Salesmen's Sample, Honeyluler, #1308, Schmidt & Co.	500	800
Salesmen's Sample, Johnnie Bird, #1370, Schmidt & Co.	200	300
Salesmen's Sample, National, #1727, George S. Harris & Sons	300	350
Salesmen's Sample, Polar Light, George S. Harris & Sons	2500	3000
Salesmen's Sample, Red Hot, #1133, George S. Harris & Sons	175	200
Salesmen's Sample, Tom's Trick, #4402, George S. Harris & Sons	75	100

Cosmetics and Medical

Amber Lion, "Triple Action" germicidal dandruff remover, snarling lion's face, black ground, gilt touches, Long Beach, CA, 3.75" x 2"	$0.50	$1.00
Annette Hair Preparation For Grey Hair, white silhouette lady, green flowers, 2.625" x 4"	0.15	0.30
Columbia Greaseless Hair Cream, redheaded Columbia holding hair cream sign, 4" x 1.5"	0.50	1.00
Cream of Almond Lotion, Art Nouveau designs, trees, gilt, pointed arch shape, 3.75" x 1.5"	0.50	1.00
Crown Hair Tonic, Art Nouveau, florals, gilt, oval, 3.25" x 2.25"	0.50	1.00
Dr. Lynas Jamaica Ginger, colorful Art Nouveau designs, 3.75" x 1.125"	0.25	0.75
Eau De Cologne, fancy royal blue and white designs, 2.875" x 2.5"	0.25	0.75
Edelweiss Disappearing Cream, red roses, dark green leaves, 3.625" x 2"	0.25	0.75
Epsom Salt, topless woman, roses, yellow-gold and black, RI, 2.5" x 6.5"	0.25	0.75
Infant's & Child Croup, crying baby, Chinese writing, 3" x 2.125"	0.25	0.75
Little Fairies, "bath perfume," fairies, florals, and butterflies, 2" x 3.5"	0.50	1.25
Mentholated Cream, floral, leaves, embossed, gilt, 2" x 2.5"	0.25	0.75
Rose Almond and Benzoin Cream, silver and black Art Deco design, 1.5" x 4"	0.25	0.50
Shave-Ease Cream, Art Deco, gold and black foil w/ red, 1.5" x 2"	0.25	0.50
Superior Bay Rum, green bay leaf, gilt border, 2" x 3"	0.25	0.75
Syrup Ipecac, blue, ME, 2.75" x 1.25"	0.25	0.50
Universal Liquid Green Soap, woman, designs, orange, blue, and white, 3.5" x 1.75"	0.25	0.75
White Top Liquid Shampoo, smiling woman, green and white, PA, 3.25" x 1.5"	0.15	0.30
Wisk, shaving cream, man's face, black, blue, and silver, 3" x 5"	0.15	0.30
Witch Hazel, silver foil and flowers, black ground, 3" x 2.125"	0.25	0.75

Fruit Crates

The decorative labels that adorned the sides of wooden fruit crates are popular collectibles. The oldest and rarest date to the 1880s. Rarity and design are the important variables with fruit crate labels. California labels are usually worth more than Florida labels, and orange labels usually have more ornate designs. Label designs changed over the years, and some collectors focus on labels that have undergone design changes.

See *Fruit Box Labels: An Illustrated Price Guide to Citrus Labels* by Gordon T. McClelland and Jay T. Last (Hillcres Press, 1995) for more information.

	LOW	HIGH
All Year, lemon, orchard scene, mountains in background, cacti, desert vegetation in foreground, black border, Fillmore	$1.50	$3.00
Arbutus, cranberry, spray of pink arbutus flowers, green leaves, 7" x 10"	0.75	1.50
Athlete, lemon, 3 runners in stadium reaching finish line, Claremont	4.00	8.00
Athlete, orange, 3 runners in stadium reaching finish line, Claremont	4.00	8.00
Aunty, citrus, smiling black lady holding branch of citrus blossoms, FL, 3.5" x 8.5"	1.50	3.00
Basket, lemon, golden basket holding 5 lemons, blue ground, Lemon Cove	0.75	1.50
Ben Franklin, citrus, inset citrus, Art Deco design, 6.75" sq	1.50	3.00
Better'n Ever, citrus, half sliced grapefruit, blue ground, TX	0.25	0.75
Blue Parrot, pear, large parrot on flowering branch	0.50	1.50
Brownies, orange, several brownies preparing orange juice, yellow sun, blue ground, Lemon Cove	4.00	8.00
California Beauty, grape, bunch of roses and grapes	0.15	0.25
Channel, lemon, seacoast scene, sailing vessels, island, orchards, homes in center of label, 5 large flying seagulls, blue ground, Santa Barbara	1.00	3.00
Clipper, citrus, sailing vessel, flying gull, 6.75" sq	1.00	3.00
Corona Lily, orange, white and gold speckled lily, black ground, Corona	2.00	4.00
Daisy, big white daisy, green leaves, black ground, Covina	2.00	5.00
Dixie Boy, citrus, black boy eating half a grapefruit, FL, 9" sq	2.00	5.00
Dixie Delite, citrus, 1930s romantic dancing couple, 2 big red hearts and citrus, FL, 9" sq.	1.00	3.00
Don Juan, pear, purple mountain and orchard scene and pear	0.75	1.50
Eureka, citrus, Indian standing by river, FL, 9" sq	1.00	3.00
Fancia, orange, matador smoking, seaside ground, Rialto	4.00	8.00

Left to right: Maine Apples; Right-O-Way. —Photos courtesy Cerebro.

	LOW	HIGH
Federated, pear, bald eagle w/ wings spread, perched on shield, early	1.00	3.00
Flo, citrus, Indian woman profile, 6.75" sq	1.00	3.00
Florigold Groves, citrus, Indian profile on medallion, FL, 9" sq	1.00	3.00
Forever First, pear, red holly berries, greens, and plump juicy pears, blue ground	1.00	3.00
Futch's Choice, citrus, grove scene, palms, vertical, FL	0.50	1.50
Gladiola, orange, 2 large pink gladiola sprays on gold-tan ground, Covina	1.00	3.00
Golden Circle, orange, wreath of oranges, Redlands	1.00	3.00
Golden Hill, citrus, old packing house, old truck, red ground, FL, 9" sq	0.50	1.50
Golden Rod, orange, golden rod spray, black ground	1.00	3.00
Goleta, lemon, large sailing vessel near rocky coastline, black ground	0.50	1.50
Have One, orange, hand holding partially peeled orange, royal blue ground, Lemon Cove	1.00	3.00
Hi-Tone, orange, green musical notes, black ground, Upland	0.50	2.00
Huntsman, citrus, Indian drawing bow, flying cranes ground, FL, 9" sq	1.00	3.00
Irvale, orange, big orange in red bordered blue diamond green ground, Irvine	1.00	3.00
John & Martha, orange, small picture of oranges, white ground, Reedley	0.50	2.00
Juiciful, orange, huge orange and leaves, light blue ground, Redlands	1.00	3.00
Killdeer, citrus, killdeer wading in swamp, FL, 9" sq	1.00	3.00
Lemonade, lemon, 3 large lemons and leaves, mountains and orchards ground, Ivanhoe	0.50	1.50
Maine Apples, Indian Head Fruit Growers, Hebron, ME, 10" x 12"	30.00	40.00
Majorette, orange, majorette in red and white, maroon and green ground, Woodlake	1.00	3.00
Monmouth, cranberry, Revolutionary War scene, early 1900s, 7" x 10"	1.00	3.00
Moonbeam, citrus, full moon shining over groves and swamp scene, 7" sq	1.00	3.00
Mr. Pear, pear, cartoon pear w/ tophat and cane, blue ground	1.00	3.00
Norden, citrus, map of Florida, Art Deco designs, Lake Wales, 9" sq	0.75	1.50
Orchard King, orange, big orange wearing crown, blue ground, Covina	1.00	2.00
Pala Brave, orange, Indian chief wearing headdress, maroon ground, Placentia	3.00	5.00
Parade, lemon, drum major leading parade of drummers, Saticoy	1.00	3.00
Ponca, orange, big orange in green Art Deco arch, Porterville	2.00	4.00
Queen Esther, orange, regal queen w/ crown and turquoise jewelry, Placentia	4.00	8.00
Red Bell, cranberry, big red bell, early 1900s, 7" x 10"	0.75	1.50
Richland, citrus, white heron perched on branch by river, citrus fruit, FL, 9" sq	1.00	5.00
Right-O-Way, Stecher-Traung, sample, 1949, 7" sq	35.00	45.00
Royal Guard, citrus, knight on rearing white horse, FL, 9" sq	0.75	1.50
Royal Knight, orange, knight in armor on horseback, castle, yellow ground, Redlands	1.00	3.00
San Marcos, lemon, country scene, purple mountains, blue ground, Goleta	0.75	1.50
Sea Bird, lemon, white flying seagull, yellow letters, blue ground, Carpinteria	3.00	5.00
Shamrock, lemon, green shamrock over grove scene, Placentia	0.75	1.50
Shamrock, orange, shamrock in sky over orange groves, Placentia	0.75	1.50
Silver Medal, cranberry, Pan-Am expo scene, 1901, 7" x 10"	1.00	3.00
Snow Crest, pear, orchard scene, snowy peak, farmhouse framed by forest trees	0.75	1.50
South Mountain, orange, mountains, groves, ranch house, Santa Paula	1.00	3.00
Stardust, orange, product name in starry sky, Exeter	3.00	5.00
Sunny Heights, orange, grove and country scene, red roofed homes, snowy mountains, Redlands	1.00	3.00
Sunny Side, citrus, groves, lake, and fruit, 9" sq.	0.75	1.50
Sunshine Fruits, citrus, palms, FL	0.25	0.75
Sweetmex, citrus, smiling señorita in green, red ground, Tex & Mexico, 9" sq	0.75	1.50
Tesoro Rancho, orange, ranch home framed by palms, Placentia	2.00	4.00
Unicorn, orange, galloping pinto unicorn, E. Highlands	20.00	30.00

King Appetite Shoe Peg Sweet Corn, salesman's sample, 1928, 4" x 11", $40 at auction. —Photo courtesy Cerebro.

Tin Cans

	LOW	HIGH
Alpine, kidney beans, mountain climber, bowl of white kidney beans	$0.25	$0.50
Bess, evaporated milk, 2 images of tan cow's head	1.00	3.00
Blue Hill, white corn, house by river, conifers, early	2.00	4.00
Butterfly, Golden Sweet Corn, bowl of corn	0.50	1.25
Butterfly, sweet peas, large embossed butterfly, bowl of peas, gilt	1.00	3.00
Claudia, pizza sauce, 2 ladies, pizza, Orange, CA	0.50	1.25
Cloth of Gold, Golden Bantam Corn, large red bird, gilt, early	2.00	4.00
Cloth of Gold, succotash, red bird, bowl of succotash	0.50	1.25
Crossroads, syrup, old cabin and man making syrup in big kettle, GA	1.00	3.00
Ellendale, lima beans, forest, stream, mountains, lima beans in pods, Ellendale, DE	0.50	1.25
Fairfax Hall, apples, big white mansion and grounds, VA	0.50	1.25
Farmer's Pride, lima beans, little girl and elderly man	0.50	1.25
Forhan's Blueberry Pie, blueberries, leaves, slice of pie on plate	0.50	1.25
Gaddis, blueberries, 2 blueberries in cut glass bowl, 6.5" x 10"	1.00	3.00
Herricks, blueberries, 2 blueberry clusters on branch	0.50	1.25
Home Packed Beef, woodcut picture of Hereford cow, "T. B. Tested," black and white, NY, c1910, 12" x 4.25"	2.00	4.00
Isaacs Brand, peas, lake, woods, sail boat, tent, peas, and pods, DE	0.50	1.25
Jonesport, Fish Flakes, old lighthouse, ship, and fish, 9.875" x 4.25"	2.00	4.00
Jo Sole, grape juice, 2 images of young black boy, "So soul tasty," 1969, 13.5" x 6.5"	1.00	3.00
King's, tomatoes, stylized crowns, black ground, MD	0.50	1.25
La Perla, California olives, cute old-fashioned boy	0.25	0.75
Little Joe, crowder peas, whistling black youngster going fishing	1.00	3.00
Maryland Chief, green beans, 2 images of Indian chief	0.50	1.25
Mayfield, peas, country sunrise scene, fancy vegetable dish of early June peas, gilt, VA	0.50	1.25
Mt. Vernon, apple butter, white mansion, VA, 7 lbs., 6.5" x 8.5"	0.50	1.25
Oceana County, cherries, bunch of bright red cherries, gilt, 11" x 6.5"	0.50	1.25
Og-Na, corn, Indian chief profile, peace pipe, tomahawk, white corn, embossed, gilt, 1920s	0.50	1.25
Old Black Joe, black-eyed peas, elderly black man and cabin	1.00	3.00
Poplar, evaporated milk, 3 aqua poplar trees on hill, OH	0.50	1.2
Premier, apple butter, apple, slices of bread, apple butter, embossed, gilt, NY	0.50	1.25
Raymond, blueberries, pie w/ piece missing, cluster blueberries, embossed, gilt	1.00	3.00
Roseco, evaporated milk, cow, milking stool, and bucket, large red rose	1.00	3.00
Santa Fe, apples, apple pie and Indian in desert, KS	0.50	1.25
Shamrock, tomatoes, 2 large shamrocks, small shamrocks, tomato, gilt, MA	2.00	4.00
Squaw, peas, Indian mother and papoose	1.00	3.00
Sundrop, blueberries, cluster blueberries, 4.25" x 7.875"	0.50	1.25
Supreme Court, Fancy Red Salmon, courthouse, blue-shaded Art Deco accents, 2 salmon, Norwich, NY	4.00	6.00

Maps

Maps have a long collecting history. Those listed here are some of the earliest still available on the market. You won't find these in the glove compartment of your car, but we've seen these treasures at estate sales and small auctions throughout the country.

Maps are more valuable with original hand coloring, but beware of old maps with new hand coloring. Tears, stains, poor printing and trimmed margins all reduce value. Maps of the New World are more valuable than those of Europe, especially those of obscure Central European areas. A map is almost always more valuable when sold in the area it depicts. The more important the mapmaker, the more valuable the map.

For further information see *Mercator's World* (845 Williamette St., Eugene, OR 97401).

In the following entries, the region is listed first, followed by the map's maker, the title of the map, the date and the size.

	LOW	HIGH
Africa, John Cary, "A New Map of Africa," 24-section engraved map, hand colored, linen backed, 1826, 1330mm x 1570mm	$200	$400
Bahama Islands, Mount and Page, "A New Chart of the Bahama Islands and the Winward Passage," double page engraved map, hand colored, c1700, 445mm x 540mm	300	500
Barbadoes, Herman Moll, "The Island of Barbadoes," engraved folding map, c1732, 295mm x 370mm	50	150
British Dominions, Thomas Kitchin, "A New and Accurate Map of the British Dominions in America according to the Treaty of 1763," engraved folding map, wide margins, c1766, 535mm x 630mm	400	600
California, Benjamin Barlow, "Map of the City of Benicia," litho map, linen backed, c1851, 600mm x 875mm	400	600
California, Britton, Rey & Co., "Guide Map of the City of San Francisco… for Langley's San Francisco Directory 1875," color litho folding map, paper backed, 540mm x 660mm	50	150
California, William Brown, "Plat of the Pueblo Lands of San Francisco finally confirmed to the City of San Francisco," litho map w/ manuscript additions, printed on cloth, 1884, 680mm x 1285mm	400	600
California, William P. Humphreys, "Official Map of the City and County of San Francisco Prepared…as per Order 966 of the Board of Supervisors," 2 engraved maps, linen backed, 1878, each 1165mm x 780mm	800	1200
California, Rand McNally & Co., "Map of Coronado Beach, San Diego, California," folding litho map, 1887, 360mm x 550mm	50	150
California, U.S. Coast Survey, "City of San Francisco and its Vicinity," engraved, 1853, 775mm x 550mm	200	400
California/Nevada, Gaylord Watson, "Watson's New County, Railroad and Sectional Map, of California and Nevada," litho folding map, hand colored, 1875, 715mm x 455mm	50	150
Canada, Jonathan Carver, "A New Map of the Province of Quebec, according to the Royal Proclamation of the 7th of October 1763," double page engraved map, hand colored, 1776, 505mm x 700mm	800	1200
Canada, Thomas Jefferys, A Plan of the City of Quebec the Capital of Canada, engraved folding map, 1760, 345mm x 505mm	200	400
Cape Cod, Major J. D. Graham, "A Map of the Extremity of Cape Cod including the Township of Provincetown & Truro," set of 4 double page engraved maps, unjoined, 1836, 1500mm x 1840mm	800	1200
China, John Speed, "The Kingdome of China," double page engraved map, English text on verso, hand colored, 1626, 395mm x 515mm	2000	3000

	LOW	HIGH
Cuba/Bahama Islands, Carey & Lea, "Geographical, Statistical, and Historical Map of Cuba and the Bahama Islands," hand colored engraved map inset onto larger letterpress folio sheet, 1822, 270mm x 375mm	200	400
Denmark, William Faden, "A Map of the Kingdom of Denmark," double page engraved map, hand colored, 1790, 740mm x 535mm	200	400
England, Samuel and Nathaniel Buck, "The North East Prospect of Plymouth, in the County of Devon," engraved folding map, hand colored, 1736, 315mm x 805mm	200	400
Europe, Hartmann Schedel, "Untitled Map of Europe," extracted from Latin edition of Nuremberg Chronicle, Latin text on verso, 1493, 395mm x 580mm	2500	3500
Georgia, Emanuel Bowen, "A New Map of Georgia," engraved folding map, 1748, 365mm x 480mm	1000	2000
Germany, Edward Wells, "A New Map of Ancient Germany," double page engraved map, c1700, 370mm x 490mm	150	300
Gulf of St. Laurence, Sayer and Bennett, "A Chart of the Gulf of St. Laurence," double page engraved map, hand colored, 1775, 640mm x 515mm	200	400
Holy Land, Cornelis Le Bruyn, "A Map of Ye Holy Land," engraved folding map, 1740s, 280mm x 540mm	100	200
Holy Land, Edward Wells, "A New Map of the Land of Canaan," double page engraved map, hand colored, 1722, 375mm x 495mm	400	600
Holy Land, J. Hugh Johnson, "The Holy Land and Its Borders," color litho map, c1860, 570mm x 470mm	50	150
Iowa, H. R. Page, "Map of Iowa," folding litho map, hand colored, original 12mo cloth folder, 1879, 710mm x 1090mm	400	600
Ireland, John Cary, "A New Map of Ireland," double page engraved map, hand colored, 1799, 495mm x 555mm	100	200
Jamaica, Thomas Jefferys, double page engraved map, hand colored, 1794, 500mm x 650mm	150	300
Kansas, W. H. Holmes, "A New Map of Kansas," double page litho map, hand colored, 1859, 415mm x 690mm	2500	3500
Kansas/Nebraska, J. H. Colton, double page engraved map, hand colored, 1857, 725mm x 445mm	50	150
Kentucky, John Russell, "Map of the State of Kentucky," engraved folding map, 1795, 400mm x 475mm	200	400
Kentucky/Tennessee, J. H. Colton, "Colton's Kentucky and Tennessee," engraved folding map, hand colored, original 16mo cloth case, 1863, 350mm x 415mm	400	600
Maine, H. F. Walling and J. Chace, "Map of the State of Maine," engraved rolled wall map, hand colored, 1861, 1600mm x 1600mm	350	500
Massachusetts, Benjamin Mather, "Plan of the Town of Lowell and Belvidere Village," c1832, 530mm x 720mm	250	500
Massachusetts, J. R. Bachelder, "South View Salem Mass.," hand colored, 1856, 250mm x 400mm	200	400
Mexico, John Ogilby, "Vetus Mexico," double page engraved map, 1671, 290mm x 355mm	100	200
Michigan, A. Ruger, "Birds Eye View of the City of Marshall," Calhoun Co., 3-stone litho map, 1866, 560mm x 755mm	600	800
Milwaukee, Silas Chapman, "Map of the City of Milwaukee," hand colored litho folding map, original 16mo cloth case, 1882, 510mm x 435mm	300	500
Minnesota, G. H. Ellsbury and V. Green, "Minneapolis," MN, folding color litho map, 1874, 445mm x 775mm	1000	1500
Minnesota, G. H. Ellsbury and V. Green, "St. Paul, Minn.," folding color litho map, 1874, 445mm x 775mm	1200	1800

	LOW	HIGH
Mississippi, Lt. John Ross, "Course of the River Mississippi, from the Balisle, to Fort Chartres; Taken on an Expedition to the Illinois, in the latter end of the year 1765," engraved folding 2-sheet map joined, hand colored, 1775, 1135mm x 360mm	1500	2500
Missouri, Compton & Dry, "St. Louis," 2 litho bird's-eye views of St. Louis, each 1876, 355mm x 540mm	50	150
Montana, Baker & Harper, "Map of the Townsite of the Town of Butte, Deer Lodge Co., Montana," folding litho map, linen backed, late 19th C, 645mm x 535mm	100	250
Montana, Henry Wellge, "Perspective Map of the City of Helena, Mont.," 2-stone litho map, vignettes of factories and enterprises at bottom, 1890, 705mm x 1065mm	500	750
Netherlands, George Grierson, "The United Provinces of the Netherlands," multisheet engraved map joined, hand colored, 1730s, 580mm x 890mm	100	250
New England, Daniel Neal, "A New Map of New England according to the latest Observations 1720," engraved folding map, 1720, 235mm x 360mm	100	200
New England, Henry S. Tanner, "Map of the States of Maine, New Hampshire, Vermont, Massachusetts, Connecticut & Rhode Island," double page engraved map, 1820, 720mm x 580mm	300	500
New England, Thomas Jefferys, "The Island of Cuba w/ part of the Bahama Banks & the Martyrs," double page engraved map, 1775, 505mm x 630mm	350	500
New Jersey, John Bachmann, "Hoboken," multistone litho map, 1874, 455mm x 610mm	50	150
New Jersey/Pennsylvania/New York/New England, Emanuel Bowen, "A New and Accurate Map of New Jersey, Pennsylvania, New York, and New England," engraved folding map, hand colored, 1747, 355mm x 435mm	600	800
New York, Charles Magnus, "Central Park," color litho map, ornamental border, late 1860s, 615mm x 515mm	350	500
New York, David Burr, "Map of the State of New-York w/ parts of the adjacent Country," engraved 24-section map, hand colored, linen backed, 1834, 1205mm x 1455mm	6000	7000
New York, Hyde & Co., "Map of Long Island," 3 large folding litho maps, linen backed, 1897	500	700
New York, J. Milbert, "Falls on the Genessee Rivers-Town of Hudson," 2 litho maps, hand colored, late 1820s, 245mm x 320mm	100	200
New York, John Bachmann, "Central Park," color litho by Bien, 1865, 385mm x 535mm	300	500
New York, John Montresor, "Province de New York," engraved 4-sheet map, hand colored, 1777, 1460mm x 930mm	1500	2000
New York, John Moray, "City of Elmira," hand colored litho map, linen backed, 1884, 485mm x 670mm	400	600
New York, O. H. Bailey, "Bird's-Eye View of Seneca Falls," hand colored litho map by Parson and Atwater, 1873, 470mm x 670mm	200	350
New York, unknown maker, "A Plan of the City and Environs of New York in North America," engraved folding map, 1776, 290mm x 375mm	200	400
New York, William Bradford, "A Plan of the City of New York from an actual Survey," litho folding map, printed for Valentine's History of New York, 1853, 470mm x 595mm	50	150
North America, Herman Moll, "Map of North America according to ye Newest and Most Exact Observations," double page engraved folding map joined, hand colored, c1720, 575mm x 955mm	1800	2400
North America, William Faden, "The United States of North America," double page engraved map, hand colored, 1785, 540mm x 640mm	650	850

	LOW	HIGH
Ohio, S. Augustus Mitchell, "The Tourist's Map of the State of Ohio," hand colored engraved folding map, original 16mo roan case, 1835, 390mm x 325mm	750	1000
Oklahoma, Fowler & Kelly, "Aero View of Tulsa, Oklahoma," monotone bird's-eye view, 1918, 515mm x 1010mm	300	500
Oregon, unknown maker, "Oregon–General View of Astoria Looking Seaward," 1887, 255mm x 450mm	150	300
Pennsylvania, G. M. Hopkins, "Map of the Cities of Pittsburgh, Allegheny, and the adjoining Boroughs," hand colored litho folding map, original 12mo cloth case, 1872, 475mm x 600mm	500	700
Pennsylvania, H. J. Toudy, "Bird's-Eye View, Centennial Buildings," 3-stone litho map of U.S. Centennial Exhibition grounds, c1876, 500mm x 690mm	200	400
Pennsylvania, J. C. Wild, "Panorama of Philadelphia from the State House Steeple," 4 hand-colored litho maps on full lettered India Proof mounts, 1838, 234mm x 335mm	2000	3000
Pennsylvania, J. L. Smith, "Smith's New Map of Philadelphia and Vicinity," folding hand-colored litho map, linen backed, folds into original small 12mo cloth folder, 1881, 685mm x 1080mm	50	150
Pennsylvania, T. M. Fowler, "Harmony, Butler County, Pennsylvania, 1901," 1901, 355mm x 505mm	100	250
Persia, John Speed, "The Kingdome of Persia," double page engraved map, English text on verso, hand colored, c1627, 395mm x 510mm	650	900
Rhode Island, Des Barres, Joseph F. Wallet, "A Plan of the Town of Newport, in the Province of Rhode Island," engraved folding map, hand colored, paper backed, 1776, 745mm x 535mm	800	1200
South America/West Indies, A. Fullarton, "Dutch Possessions in South America and the West Indies," engraved map, hand colored, 1840s, 470mm x 320mm	50	150
South Carolina, Captain John Gasciogne, "A Plan of Port Royal in South Carolina," engraved double page map, 1776, 720mm x 590mm	1200	1800
Spain, John Senex, "Spain and Portugal," double page engraved map, hand colored, 1719, 495mm x 560mm	100	300
Switzerland, William Faden, "Map of the Republic of Switzeland," double page engraved map, hand colored, 1820, 575mm x 830mm	50	150
Tennessee, Mathew Carey, "A Map of the Tennessee State formerly part of North Carolina," engraved folding map, hand colored, c1796, 270mm x 530mm	200	400
Tennessee, S. Augustus Mitchell, "The Tourist's Pocket Map of the State of Tennessee," hand colored engraved folding map, original 16mo roan case, 1839, 325mm x 390mm	300	500
Texas, J. H. Young, "Map of the State of Texas from the Latest Authorities," engraved, hand colored, 1852, 335mm x 400mm	150	350
United States, Humphrey Phelps, "Ornamental Map of the United States & Mexico," wood engraved map, hand colored, 1846, 750mm x 560mm	700	900
United States, John Cary, "A New Map of Part of the United States of North America," double page engraved map, hand colored, 1811, 525mm x 580mm	200	350
United States, John Melish, "United States of America," engraved, 1829, 435mm x 650mm	300	500
United States, John Thomson, "Northern Provinces of the United States," double page engraved map, hand colored, 1817, 515mm x 620mm	100	200
United States, Joseph S. Wilson, "Map of the United States and Territories," 48-section engraved map, hand colored, linen backed, 1866, 725mm x 1440mm	200	350
United States, William Faden, "The United States of North America," double page engraved map, hand colored, 1785, 540mm x 640mm	650	900

	LOW	HIGH
United States/Canada, Rand McNally & Co., "Warner's Safe Cure Prize Map of the United States and Canada," color litho folding map, folds into original 8vo cloth case, 1887, 1000mm x 1400mm	50	150
United States/Mexico, Humphrey Phelps, "Ornamental Map of the United States & Mexico," wood engraved map, hand colored, ornamental border, 1846, 750mm x 560mm	700	900
Upper Mississippi River, J. N. Nicollet, "Hydrographical Basin of the Upper Mississippi River," folding engraved map, 1843, 965mm x 850mm	300	500
Washington D.C., Carey & Lea, "Geographical, Statistical, and Historical Map of the District of Columbia," double page engraved map, hand colored, 1822, 310mm x 295mm	100	200
Washington D.C., D. McClelland, "Map of the City of Washington," engraved folding map, 1846, 350mm x 450mm	50	150
Washington D.C., J. Russell, "Plan of the City of Washington, in the Territory of Columbia," engraved folding map, hand colored, 1795, 415mm x 530mm	250	500
West Virginia, T. M. Fowler and James Moyer, "Parkersburg, West Virginia," litho bird's-eye view, 1899, 575mm x 910mm	300	500
World, A. T. Andreas, "Western Hemisphere-Eastern Hemisphere," 2 single sheet litho maps, hand colored, 1874, 450mm x 360mm	150	250
World, John Speed, "A New and Accurate Map of the World," double page engraved double-hemispheric map, hand colored, c1627, 405mm x 510mm	2000	3000
World, Laurie & Whittle, "A New Map of the World…Second Edition," double page engraved double-hemispheric map, hand colored, 1808, 495mm x 720mm	300	500
World, R. Brookes, "A New Map of the World w/ the New Discoveries by Capt. Cook," wall map, hand colored background, 1817, 475mm x 820mm	2000	3000
World, Thomas Kitchin, "Map of the World," engraved folding map, hand colored, 1783, 360mm x 525mm	300	500

"Boston, Its Environs and Harbour with the Rebel Works Raised Against That Town in 1755," William Faden, London, 2 sheets, joined, 1778, 22" x 25", $4025 at auction; —Photo courtesy Skinner, Inc., Boston, MA.

Movie Memorabilia

In 1909, the Motion Picture Patents Company standardized the size and purpose of posters. Currently, there are seven poster sizes. "Half-sheets" (or display cards) are posters 28" x 22"; "one-sheets" are 41" x 27"; "three-sheets" are 81" x 41". Lobby cards are a set of eight photos, each 11" x 14", depicting eight different scenes from the movie. Sets that have four one-quarter-inch triangular cuts on the photos from mounting are worth 30% to 50% less. Window cards measure 22" x 14" and inserts are 36" x 14". Probably the most extensive listing of movie posters is the *Movie Poster Price Almanac* edited by John Kisch (Separate Cinema Publications in Hyde Park, NY). See also *Warren's Movie Poster Price Guide, Fourth Edition* by John R. Warren (American Collectors Exchange, Chattanooga, TN, 1997).

IMPORTANT: Movie titles and dates followed by "R" refer to a re-release of the film, not the first release.

Lobby Cards

	LOW	HIGH
Abbott and Costello Meet the Invisible Man, Universal Pictures, 1951	$15	$25
Ace in the Hole/The Big Carnival, K. Douglas, Paramount, 1951, set of 8	275	325
Across 110th Street, United Artists, set of 8	5	15
Across the Pacific, H. Bogart, S. Greenstreet, M. Astor, Warner Bros., 1942	15	25
Adventures of Martin Eden, Columbia Pictures, 1942	10	20
African Queen, The, United Artists, 1952	75	100
Alamo, J. Wayne, set of 8	150	200
Alias the Badman, K. Maynard, 1932	120	130
Alien, 1979, set of 8	70	80
Always In My Heart, K. Francis, W. Huston, Warner Bros., 1942	20	30
American Guerrilla In The Philippines, T. Power, 20th Century Fox, 1950	25	35
Andy Hardy's Private Secretary, M. Rooney, MGM, 1941	10	20
Ape, The, B. Karloff, Monogram, 1940, set of 8	500	700
Arabesque, G. Peck, S. Loren, 1966, set of 8	30	40
Armored Command, 1961, set of 8	20	30
Asphalt Jungle, The, MGM, 1950	225	275
Back to Bataan, J. Wayne, set of 8	250	300
Band Wagon, The, F. Astaire, C. Charisse, MGM, 1953, set of 8	200	300
Barbarian & Geisha, J. Wayne, set of 8	75	150
Bar C Mystery, D. Phillips	25	35
Batman, 1989, set of 8	25	35
Beau Geste, G. Cooper, R. Milland, R. Preston, 1939	150	200
Belles on Their Toes, 1952	10	20
Ben Hur, C. Heston, J. Hawkins, MGM, 1959	5	10
Berlin Express, RKO, 1948, set of 8	45	55
Big Jake, J. Wayne, set of 8	125	175
Big Jim McLain, J. Wayne, set of 8	75	150
Black Cat, The, B. Rathbone, A. Ladd, Real-Art, set of 8	200	250
Black Sleep, B. Rathbone, L. Chaney, B. Lugosi, United Artists, 1956	100	200
Black Tuesday, E. G. Robinson, United Artists, 1955	5	10
Blade Runner, 1982, set of 8	40	50
Blind Husbands, Universal Pictures, 1919	700	900
Blood Alley, J. Wayne, set of 8	250	300
Blood of Dracula, American International, 1957	5	15
Body and Soul, J. Garfield, United Artists, 1947	20	30
Border Cafe, RKO, 1937	20	30
Brannigan, J. Wayne, set of 8	125	175

	LOW	HIGH
Cabinet of Dr. Caligari, MGM, 1919	2000	2500
Cahill, J. Wayne, set of 8	125	175
Carrie, 1976, set of 8	20	30
Casablanca, Warner Bros., 1942	550	600
Cast a Giant Shadow, J. Wayne, set of 8	75	150
Charlie Chan at Monte Carlo, 20th Century Fox, 1937	40	50
Chatterbox, J. Brown, J. Canova, Republic Pictures, 1942	5	15
Check Your Guns, E. Dean	10	20
Child Is Born, A, Warner Bros., 1940	15	25
Chisum, J. Wayne, set of 8	125	175
Circus of Horrors, American International, 1960	4	8
Circus World, J. Wayne, set of 8	150	200
City Lights, C. Chaplin, United Artists, 1931	325	375
Clockwork Orange, 1972, set of 8	140	160
Colorado Sunset, G. Autry, Republic Pictures, 1939	20	30
Comancheros, J. Wayne, set of 8	150	200
Conqueror, J. Wayne, set of 8	75	125
Cross and The Switchblade, The, P. Boone, E. Estrada, 1970, set of 8	20	30
Dimension 5, 1966, set of 8	20	30
D.O.A., United Artists, luminous fluid scene, 1950	150	200
Dog's Life, A, C. Chaplin, First National, 1918, set of 6	1500	2000
Don't Fence Me In, R. Rogers, Republic Pictures, 1945	5	15
Dracula, Prince of Darkness, C. Lee, 20th Century Fox, 1966	3	6
Dr. Jekyll and Mr. Hyde, Paramount, 1920	1500	2000
Earth vs. The Flying Saucers, H. Marlowe, J. Taylor, Columbia Pictures, 1956	10	20
Empire Strikes Back, The, 1980, set of 8	40	50
Eve's Secret, B. Compson, J. Holt	15	25
Exorcist, The, 1973, set of 8	30	50
Experience, R. Barthelmess, Paramount	40	60
Fallen Sparrow, J. Garfield, M. O'Hara, RKO, 1943	20	30
Farewell to Arms, A, R. Hudson, 1963	20	30
Fighting Kentuckian, J. Wayne, set of 8	150	175
Finger of Guilt, RKO Radio Pictures, 1956, set of 8	10	20
Flight Command, R. Taylor, MGM, 1941	10	20
Flying Leathernecks, J. Wayne, set of 8	175	250

Left to right: Horse Feathers, *Marx Brothers, Paramount, 1932, $1093 at auction;* Sherlock Holmes, *J. Barrymore, Goldwyn Pictures, 1922, $920 at auction. —Photos courtesy Skinner, Inc., Boston, MA.*

	LOW	HIGH
Frenzy, 1972, set of 8	25	35
Galloping Dude, The, F. Farnum, 1920s	30	50
Gateway, D. Ameche, 1938	120	130
Gimme Shelter, The Rolling Stones, 20th Century Fox, 1970, set of 12	400	600
G-Men, First National, 1934	525	600
Going My Way, 1944	40	60
Goodbye Mr. Chips, 1939	80	90
Gorilla Ship, R. Ince, V. Reynolds, 1932	25	50
Graft, Universal, 1931	300	375
Green Berets, J. Wayne, set of 8	75	125
Guns of the Night, B. Elliott, S. Summerville	15	25
Hail to the Rangers, C. Starrett, Columbia Pictures, 1943	10	25
Hatari, J. Wayne, set of 8	150	200
Havoc, M. Bellamy, 1925	80	100
Hell Fighters, J. Wayne, set of 8	75	125
Hell On Frisco Bay, A. Ladd, E. G. Robinson, Warner Bros., 1956	10	20
High and the Mighty, J. Wayne, set of 8	75	150
High Society, B. Crosby, F. Sinatra, G. Kelly	20	30
Hindenburg, The, G. C. Scott, A. Bancroft, 1975, set of 8	25	40
His Majesty, The American, D. Fairbanks, 1919	120	130
Hondo, J. Wayne, set of 8	150	175
Hot Millions, P. Ustinov, B. Newhart, M. Smith, set of 8	10	30
House of Numbers, J. Palance, 1957	20	25
House of Wax 3-D, V. Price, F. Lovejoy, P. Kirk, Warner Bros., 1953	175	250
How the West Was Won, J. Wayne, set of 8	150	175
Hush, C. Kimball Young	20	30
Hustler, The, P. Newman, P. Laurie, 20th Century Fox, 1961	125	175
I Cover the Waterfront, C. Colbert, United Artists, 1933	25	50
I'll See You In My Dreams, D. Day	20	30
I Married A Woman, J. Wayne, set of 8	75	125
In Harm's Way, J. Wayne, set of 8	75	125
Island in the Sky, J. Wayne, set of 8	75	125
It Happened One Night, C. Gable, C. Colbert, Columbia Pictures, 1934, 14" x 17"	2400	2600
Jaws, 1975, set of 8	70	80
Jet Pilot, J. Wayne, set of 8	175	250
Kansan, The, R. Dix, J. Wyatt, 1943	10	30
Keeper of the Bees, G. Stratton-Porter	2	8
Kentuckian, The, O. Hardy, V. Ralston	20	40
Kidnapper, The, P. Lorre	140	160
King Kong, RKO, 1933	750	900
Lady Godiva, M. O'Hara, G. Nader, 1955, set of 8	20	30
Legend of the Lost, J. Wayne, set of 8	175	250
Little Miss Broadway, S. Temple, set of 8	1400	1600
Lola, Charles Bronson, 1971, set of 8	20	30
Lolita, MGM, 1962	350	400
Longest Day, The, J. Wayne, set of 8	175	250
Long Gray Line, The, Columbia Pictures, 1955, set of 8	20	30
Love Parade, M. Chevalier, Paramount, 1929	500	550
Lucky Horseshoe, T. Mix, 1925	150	200
Marked Trails, B. Steele, H. Gibson	15	25
*M*A*S*H,* D. Sutherland	2	8
McLintock, J. Wayne, set of 8	150	200
McQ, J. Wayne, set of 8	125	175

	LOW	HIGH
Men of the Night, 1934	30	40
Midnight Watch, 1930s	20	40
Mighty Joe Young, RKO, 1949	200	250
Moon Is Blue, The, W. Holden, 1960, set of 8	30	40
Mummy's Tomb, Universal Pictures, 1942	600	650
News Parade, S. Phipps, N. Stuart	15	25
Night Patrol, R. Talmadge, set of 8	125	135
North to Alaska, J. Wayne, set of 8	150	175
Not as a Stranger, United Artists, 1955, set of 8	40	50
Octopussy, 1983, set of 8	30	40
Ole Swimming Hole, The, C. Ray, color	20	30
Operation Pacific, J. Wayne, set of 8	250	300
Other Men's Women, J. Cagney, Warner Bros., 1931	600	650
Phantom From Space, United Artists, 1953, set of 8	10	20
Phantom of the Opera, Universal Pictures, 1925, set of 6	2000	3000
Psycho, 1960, set of 8	350	450
Raiders of the Lost Ark, Paramount, 1981, set of 8	140	160
Range Law, J. Mack Brown	20	30
Rawhide Rangers, J. Mack Brown, Universal Pictures	10	20
Robocop, 1987, set of 8	25	35
Room at the Top, L. Harvey, S. Signoret, 1959	15	25
Rooster Cogburn, J. Wayne, set of 8	175	250
Rough Riders, West of the Law	30	50
Rupert of Hentzau, 1920s	90	125
Sands of Iwo Jima, J. Wayne, set of 8	250	300
Sea Chase, J. Wayne, set of 8	250	300
Shampoo, W. Beatty, G. Hawn, J. Christie, 1975, set of 8	30	50
Shepherd of the Hills, J. Wayne, set of 8, R	150	175
Shine On Harvest Moon, R. Rogers, M. Hart, L. Belle	30	40
Shootist, The, J. Wayne, set of 8	175	225
Sisters, L. Gish, D. Gish, set of 8	400	600
Six of a Kind, W. C. Fields, Paramount, 1934	600	800
Soft Cushions, D. MacLean	15	25
Sonny, R. Barthelmess, color	20	30
Sons of Katie Elder, J. Wayne, set of 8	5	15
Spoilers, The, J. Wayne, M. Dietrich	75	125
Spy Who Loved Me, The, 1977, set of 8	30	50
Tank Battalion, E. G. Robinson, 1956, set of 6	30	40
Target, T. Holt, RKO Radio Pictures, 1952	15	25
Terminator, The, 1984, set of 8	30	40
Timbuktu, V. Mature, Y. DeCarlo, 1940, set of 7	20	30
Train Robbers, J. Wayne, set of 8	140	160
Trouble Along the Way, J. Wayne, set of 8	75	125
True Grit, J. Wayne, set of 8	150	250
United States Marshall, J. Wayne, set of 8	75	125
Virginia City, E. Flynn, H. Bogart, M. Hopkins, 1940	150	175
Wake of the Red Witch, J. Wayne, set of 8	175	225
Warming Up, R. Dix	10	25
War Wagon, J. Wayne, set of 8	90	110
We're No Angels, H. Bogart, A. Ray	5	15
We're Not Married, F. Allen, V. Moore, M. Monroe, 1952	20	40
Woman Condemned, The, M. Auer, L. Lane, 1934, set of 6	60	80
Young Frankenstein, 1974, set of 8	30	40

Movie Posters

	LOW	HIGH
12 Angry Men, United Artists, silkscreen, 1957, 40" x 60"	$240	$260
Africa Speaks, Columbia Pictures, paper-backed, 1-sheet	1000	1500
Alien, 20th Century Fox, linen-backed, 1979, 3-sheet	250	270
All That Heaven Allows, R. Hudson, Universal, linen-backed, 1955, 3-sheet	700	900
American In Paris, An, G. Kelly, MGM, linen-backed, 1951, 1-sheet	1200	1800
Annie Hall, W. Allen, D. Keaton, United Artists, 1977, 1-sheet	110	120
Ape, The, B. Karloff, Monogram, linen-backed, 1940, 1-sheet	300	400
Avenging Fangs, Chesterfield, linen-backed, 3-sheet	500	700
Band Wagon, The, MGM, 1953, 1-sheet	700	900
Batman, A. West, 20th Century Fox, linen-backed, 1966, 1-sheet	250	270
Big Clock, The, R. Milland, Paramount, paper-backed, 1948, half-sheet	340	350
Big Combo, The, C. Wilde, Allied Artists, paper-backed, 1955, half-sheet	240	350
Blade Runner, H. Ford, Warner Bros., 1982, 1-sheet	370	380
Blood of Dracula, American International, linen-backed, 1957, 1-sheet	110	120
Buster What's Next, Stern Brothers, 1927, 1-sheet	285	300
Caesar and Cleopatra, V. Leigh, C. Rains, CCF, paper-backed, 1946, half-sheet	300	500
Cat on a Hot Tin Roof, E. Taylor, P. Newman, MGM, linen-backed, 1958, half-sheet	340	350
China, L. Young, A. Ladd, Paramount, 1943, half-sheet	500	600
City for Conquest, J. Cagney, Warner Bros., 1940, 1-sheet	700	900
Cornered, W. Slezak, RKO, linen-backed, 1945, 1-sheet	300	500
Crossfire, R. Young, R. Mitchum, RKO, linen-backed, 1947, 1-sheet	280	300
Cry Danger, D. Powell, RKO, 1950, 3-sheet	450	470
Curse of the Cat People, The, RKO, 1944, 1-sheet	850	870
Dark Alibi, Monogram, linen-backed, 1946, 3-sheet	500	700
Debtor to the Law, A, H. Starr, Pan-American, linen-backed, 1920, 1-sheet	1100	1125
Desk Set, 20th Century Fox, silkscreen, 1957, 40" x 60"	300	400
Destry Rides Again, J. Stewart, M. Dietrich, Universal, linen-backed, 1939 1-sheet	1925	1975
Dirty Harry, C. Eastwood, Warner Bros., 1971, 1-sheet	280	300
Dragonwyck, G. Tierney, 20th Century Fox, linen-backed, 1945	170	180
Dr. Cyclops, Paramount, 1940, half-sheet	680	700
Father of the Bride, S. Tracy, MGM, linen-backed, 1950, 1-sheet	350	550
Fly, The, V. Price, 20th Century Fox, 1958, half-sheet	250	270
From Russia With Love, S. Connery, United Artists, linen-backed, 1964, 1-sheet	450	470
General Spanky, MGM, linen-backed, 1936, 1-sheet	340	350
Gimme Shelter, The Rolling Stones, 20th Century Fox, linen-backed, 1971, 1-sheet	250	270
Godfather II, Paramount, advance, 1974, 1-sheet	280	300
Goldfinger, S. Connery, United Artists, linen-backed, 1964, 3-sheet	1375	1400
Grease, J. Travolta, O. Newton-John, Paramount, advance, linen-backed, 1978, 1-sheet	315	325
Hangmen Also Die, United Artists, 1943, 1-sheet	400	600
Hell Divers, C. Gable, MGM, 1932, 1-sheet	600	800
Help, The Beatles, United Artists, 1965, 40" x 60"	220	240
Henry Aldrich, Editor, J. Lydon, Paramount, linen-backed, 1942, 1-sheet	285	300
Hollywood Gad About w/ Walter Winchell, Fox Film Corp., linen-backed, 1934, 1-sheet	1000	1500
Incredible Shrinking Man, The, Universal, 1957, half-sheet	225	240
Imitation of Life, L. Turner, Universal, linen-backed, 1959, 3-sheet	165	175

Left: Jailhouse Rock, E. Presley, MGM, 1957, 1-sheet, $1668 at auction.

Right: The Jungle Book, Disney, 1967, 1-sheet, $460 at auction.

—Photos courtesy Skinner, Inc., Boston, MA.

	LOW	HIGH
I Walk Alone, B. Lancaster, Paramount, 1-sheet, 1948	220	240
Jungle Raiders, Chapter 3: Prisoners of Fate, Paramount, linen-backed, 1945	300	400
Kiss of Death, V. Mature, 20th Century Fox, 1947, 1-sheet	1250	1275
Kiss the Boys Goodbye, D. Ameche, Paramount, linen-backed, 1941, 1-sheet	350	550
Lady Is Willing, The, M. Dietrich, Columbia, linen-backed, 1942, 3-sheet	500	700
Last Stand, The, Universal, linen-backed, 1938, 3-sheet	1125	1175
Letter From an Unknown Woman, J. Fontaine, Universal, linen-backed, 1948, 3-sheet	680	700
Little Friend, N. Pilbeam, Fox Film Corp., linen-backed, 1934, 1-sheet	500	700
Lone Ranger, The, Warner Bros., 1956, 1-sheet	250	270
Love Nest on Wheels, B. Keaton, 20th Century Fox, 1937, 1-sheet	1500	2000
Man on the Eiffel Tower, The, B. Meredith, RKO, 1949, 1-sheet	220	240
Man Who Fell to Earth, The, D. Bowie, 1976, 29" x 45"	340	350
Marnie, T. Hedren, S. Connery, Universal, linen-backed, 1964, 1-sheet	280	300
Match King, The, W. William, First National Pictures, linen-backed, 1932, 1-sheet	220	240
Melody Masters, Vitaphone, linen-backed, 1-sheet	1250	1275
MGM Cartoons, "It's Laughing Time," MGM, linen-backed, 1955, 1-sheet	400	500
Mr. Lucky, C. Grant, RKO, paper-backed, 1943, half-sheet	625	650
Mummy's Ghost, The, L. Chaney, Universal, paper-backed, 1944, half-sheet	1000	1500
Murder My Sweet, D. Powell, RKO, 1944, half-sheet	500	600
Music in My Heart, R. Hayworth, Columbia, 1939, 3-sheet	450	470
My Fair Lady, A. Hepburn, Warner Bros., 1964, 3-sheet	300	375
My Forbidden Past, R. Mitchum, RKO, linen-backed, 1951, 1-sheet	200	250
No Hands on the Clock, Paramount, linen-backed, 1941, 1-sheet	400	600
North by Northwest, C. Grant, MGM, 1959, 1-sheet	675	700
Not of This Earth, Allied Artists, 1957, half-sheet	375	450
O Henry's Full House, 20th Century Fox, 1952, 3-sheet	300	500
Once Upon a Time in the West, H. Fonda, Paramount, paper-backed, 1968, half-sheet	100	125
On the Town, G. Kelly, MGM, linen-backed, 1949, 3-sheet	450	500
Outlaw Josey Wales, The, C. Eastwood, Warner Bros., linen-backed, 1976, 1-sheet	140	150
Peachy Cobbler, The, MGM, linen backed, 1950, 1-sheet	900	1000
Porgy and Bess, S. Poitier, Columbia, linen-backed, 1959, 3-sheet	340	350
Pumping Iron, A. Schwarzenegger, White Mountain Films, 1977, 1-sheet	250	300

	LOW	HIGH
Raiders of the Lost Ark, Paramount, 1981, 40" x 60"	275	300
Reaching For the Moon, D. Fairbanks, United Artists, 1932, half-sheet	300	500
Reform School, L. Beavers, linen-backed, 1939, 1-sheet	300	350
Rock, Rock, Rock!, A. Freed, T. Weld, DCA Release, linen-backed, 1956 1-sheet	160	200
Rocky, S. Stallone, United Artists, advance, 1977, 1-sheet	200	250
Roogie's Bump, Republic, linen-backed, 1954, 3-sheet	400	500
Rosemary's Baby, M. Farrow, Paramount, linen-backed, 1968, 1-sheet	200	250
Sands of Iwo Jima, J. Wayne, Republic, paper-backed, 1950, half-sheet	900	1000
Saturday Night Fever, J. Travolta, Paramount, linen-backed, 1977, 1-sheet	170	180
Searchers, The, J. Wayne, Warner Bros., linen-backed, 1956, half-sheet	1125	1175
Sea Wolf, E. G. Robinson, Warner Bros., linen-backed, 1941, 1-sheet	275	300
Sierra, A. Murphy, W. Hendrix, B. Ives, D. Jagger, Universal, 40" x 60"	300	500
Snow White and the Seven Dwarfs, Disney, mylar version, 1-sheet, R	300	400
Song of the South, Disney/RKO, linen-backed, 1946, half-sheet	300	500
Soylent Green, C. Heston, MGM, 1973, 1-sheet	200	300
Spring Madness, M. O'Sullivan, L. Ayres, MGM, linen-backed, 1938, 1-sheet	400	600
Stooge, The, D. Martin, J. Lewis, Paramount, 1952, 1-sheet	200	400
Story of Vernon and Irene Castle, The, F. Astaire, G. Rogers, RKO, 1939, 1-sheet	1125	1175
Street of Chance, B. Meredith, Paramount, 1942, 1-sheet	200	240
Suddenly Last Summer, E. Taylor, Columbia, 1960, 1-sheet	200	240
Sun Valley Serenade, M. Berle, 20th Century Fox, linen-backed, 1941, 1-sheet	200	240
Suspect, C. Laughton, Universal, linen-backed, 1944, 3-sheet	700	800
Sweet Smell of Success, B. Lancaster, T. Curtis, United Artists, linen-backed, 1-sheet, 1957	500	525
Tail Spin, A. Faye, 20th Century Fox, 1937, 1-sheet	250	300
Terry-Toons: Much Ado About Nothing, 20th Century Fox, 1939, 1-sheet	340	360
Texas Chainsaw Massacre, The, Bryanston Pictures, linen-backed, 1974, 1-sheet	510	525
That Uncertain Feeling, B. Meredith, 1-sheet	70	90
They Drive By Night, A. Sheridan, Warner Bros., linen-backed, 1940, 1-sheet	1000	1500
Thomas Crown Affair, The, S. McQueen, F. Dunaway, United Artists, linen-backed, 1968, 1-sheet	272	325
Thunder in the City, E. G. Robinson, Astor, linen-backed, 1937, 1-sheet	280	300
THX 1138, Warner Bros., linen-backed, 1971, 1-sheet	140	150
Tingler, The, V. Price, Columbia, linen-backed, 1959, 3-sheet	340	350
Titanic, C. Webb, B. Stanwyck, R. Wagner, 20th Century Fox, 1953, 1-sheet	225	240
Tom and Jerry in "Dog Trouble," MGM, linen-backed, 1951, 1-sheet	950	1150
To Catch a Thief, C. Grant, G. Kelly, Paramount, 1955, half-sheet	280	300
Too Many Husbands, F. MacMurray, Columbia, 1940, half-sheet	200	400
Umbrellas of Cherbourg, The, American International, linen-backed, 1965, 1-sheet	200	300
Under Capricorn, I. Bergman, Warner Bros., paper-backed, 1949, half-sheet	280	300
Up In Daisy's Penthouse, The Three Stooges, Columbia, linen-backed, 1953, 1-sheet	800	1000
Winterset, B. Meredith, RKO, 1936, half-sheet	70	100
Woman on the Run, A. Sheridan, Universal, linen-backed, 1950, 1-sheet	300	500
Written on the Wind, R. Hudson, Universal, linen-backed, 1956, 3-sheet	500	600
Yellow Submarine, The Beatles, United Artists, 1968, 40" x 60"	400	500
You're in the Army Now, Gaumont, linen-backed, 1937, 1-sheet	400	600
Zaza, C. Colbert, Paramount, linen-backed, 1938, 1-sheet	300	350

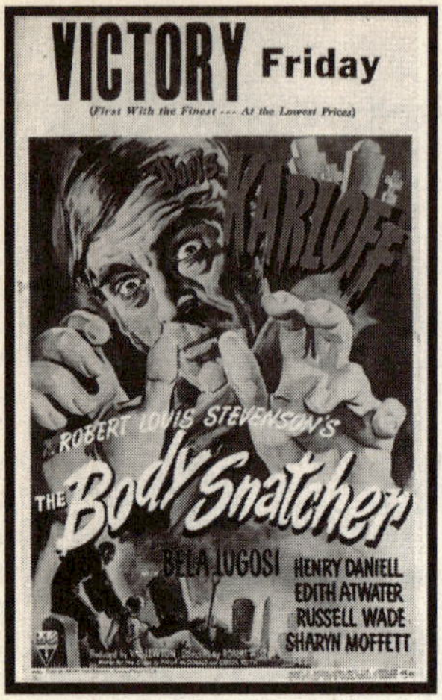

Above: It's a Wonderful Life, *J. Stewart, D. Reed, RKO, title card, 1946, $431 at auction.*

Left: The Body Snatcher, *B. Lugosi, RKO, window card, 1945, $460 at auction.*

—Photos courtesy Skinner, Inc., Boston, MA.

Other

	LOW	HIGH
3 Godfathers, MGM, insert, 1949	$250	$300
Alice in Wonderland, Disney/RKO, insert, 1951	400	600
Before I Hang, Columbia, insert, paper-backed, 1940	400	600
Blob, The, Paramount, insert, 1958	400	450
Buccaneer, Y. Brynner, pressbook, 1958	8	10
Casablanca, United Artists, daybill, linen-backed, Australia, 1970s R	300	350
Clambake, E. Presley, United Artists, window card, 1967	30	40
Country Girl, The, G. Kelly, B. Crosby, Paramount, 1954	25	35
Dancing Pirate, C. Collins, pressbook, 1936	12	16
Dog's Life, A, First National, title card, 1918	600	900
Easter Parade, MGM, insert, 1948	300	350
Fighting Heart, The, window card, linen-backed, 1926	350	400
Frankie and Johnny, E. Presley, United Artists, window card, 1966	30	40
Gilda, Columbia, window card, 1946	200	250
Glorifying the American Girl, Paramount, window card, 1929	350	400
Glory, M. O'Brien, window card, 1955	20	25
Golden Boy, Columbia, insert, paper-backed, 1939	400	600
Gold Rush, C. Chaplin, pressbook, 1973 R	8	10
Good Old Summertime, J. Garland, V. Johnson, MGM, window card, 1949	40	50
Help, United Artists, insert, 1965	300	500
Hustler, The, 20th Century Fox, insert, 1961	275	300
Imitation of Life, L. Turner, pressbook, 1965 R	8	10
Jamboree, F. Domino, pressbook, 1957	6	8
Jesse James, 20th Century Fox, insert, 1939	1000	2000
Johnny Eager, MGM, insert, paper-backed, 1941	500	600
Kid Galahad, E. Presley, United Artists, window card, 1962	30	40
Kilroy Was Here, J. Cooper, J. Coogan, Monogram Pictures, insert, 1946	20	25
Lawrence of Arabia, Columbia, window card, paper-backed, 1962	550	600
Love of Sunya, The, United Artists, window card, 1927	475	500
Maltese Falcon, The, United Artists, daybill, linen-backed, 1970s R	400	600
Manhattan Melodrama, MGM, window card, 1934	750	1000

	LOW	HIGH
Miss Sadie Thompson, R. Hayworth, Columbia, window card, 1954	35	50
Murder in Harlem, Micheaux Pictures, window card, 1934	500	600
Night at the Opera, A, MGM, window card, 1935, jumbo size	3000	5000
Pack Train, G. Autry, pressbook, 1953	12	18
Palm Beach Story, The, Paramount, window card, 1942	200	250
Prince and the Pauper, The, Warner Bros., title card, 1937	550	600
Private Detective 62/Man Killer, Warner Bros., title card, 1939	500	550
Producers, The, Embassy, insert, linen-backed, 1967	250	300
Reap the Wild Wind, Paramount, insert, 1942	300	350
Reunion, Dionne Quintuplets, 20th Century Fox, window card, 1935	30	50
Revenge of the Creature, Universal, window card, 1955	550	600
Road to Morocco, Paramount, insert, 1942	300	400
Roberta, RKO, window card, 1935, 14" x 18"	300	350
San Francisco Docks, B. Meredith, insert	50	100
Separate Tables, R. Hayworth, United Artists, pressbook, 1958	30	40
Silver Dollar, E. G. Robinson, title card, 1932	450	500
So This Is College, MGM, window card, linen-backed, 1929	100	125
Suzy, MGM, window card, 1936, jumbo size	475	500
Teacher's Pet, C. Gable, D. Day, Paramount, window card, 1958	30	40
Three Little Words, F. Astaire, V. Miles, insert, 1950	20	30
Unknown, The, MGM, window card, 1927	1000	1500
Up Goes Maisie, A. Sothern, insert, 1946	15	25
West Point Story, The, Warner Bros., window card, 1950	35	45

Above: The Phantom of the Opera, L. Chaney, Universal, title card, 1925, $920 at auction.

Left: White Heat, J. Cagney, Warner Bros., insert, 1949, $805 at auction.

—Photos courtesy Skinner, Inc., Boston, MA.

Postcards

Picture postcards in the United States were introduced in 1893 at the Columbian Exposition. By 1910 they were a national craze with nearly a billion cards being sent through the mail. In 1914, the introduction of the folding greeting card began the rapid decline of this "Golden Age" of postcards. While collectors are mainly looking for postcards from this early period, there are many wonderful cards from the 1920s through the present day that are also prized by collectors.

Postcards are roughly divided into three categories: greeting cards, view cards and real photo cards. A greeting card is any card designed by an artist. This includes all the holidays (including the popular Halloween and Santa cards), children, animals, advertising, romance, Art Nouveau, etc. Many of the better greeting cards are embossed, highly colorful and beautifully designed. Some of the best-known publishers include Tuck, Winsch and PFB. Many of these cards are "artist signed," meaning that the artist's name is on the front of the card. Some of the rarer types of greetings include hold-to-the-lights and mechanicals.

View cards are pictures of specific places, typically prints made from a photograph. They may be black and white or colored and were usually mass produced. Views are the most widely collected postcards since nearly every city, town or hamlet in the United States can be found on a postcard. Many collectors are interested in how their hometown looked at the beginning of the century. Expositions, transportation (trains, planes, autos, ships), commercial enterprises and Main Streets are among the views prized by collectors. Things that have changed little, such as monuments and waterfalls, as well as frequently visited tourist areas (Niagara Falls, Washington, D.C., national parks, etc.) are common and not very desirable.

The real photo card, our third category, has skyrocketed in value over the past decade. A real photo card is simply a photograph printed directly onto a postcard. Usually black and white, they are occasionally colored. The reason for the interest in these cards is their subject matter and scarcity. While the bigger cities had millions of published views, many small towns and villages are represented only on photo postcards. Unidentified views and family occupational photos, political and social themes (e.g. suffragettes, presidential campaign stops, criminals), postal and photographic history and any other unique subject matter is of great interest to collectors.

Condition is a major factor in determining value. A slight flaw will reduce the value considerably while a serious flaw may render the card uncollectible. For more information see *Postcard Collector* (PO Box 1050, Dubuque, IA 52004), *The Collector's Guide to Post Cards* by Jane Wood (L-W Promotions, Gas City, IN, 1984, 1997 value update), and *The Postcard Price Guide, Third Edition* by J. L. Mashburn (Colonial House, Enka, NC, 1997).

	LOW	HIGH
Advertising, Carolina White Perfume, signed "Desgranges," c1910	$125	$150
Advertising, Deshler's Patented Whalebone Barber Whisk, linen, Curt Teich	40	50
Advertising, Hershey's Ice Cream, real photo, monotone	175	200
Advertising, ICA Cameras, Art Deco woman, German	75	90
Advertising, Longines Pocket Watches	150	175
Advertising, New Departure Coaster Brakes, bears chasing Scottish scientist	75	90
Advertising, New Home Sewing Machine, c1910	85	100
Advertising, Ocean Spray Cranberry Sauce and Cranberry Cocktail, "A Cranberry Scooper and His Scoop," linen, Curt Teich	75	90
Advertising, RCA Victor, Wing Co., Pasadena, CA, linen, c1945	200	225
Advertising, Spanish Olive Oil, c1920	100	125
Advertising, The Crumperie, Greenwich Village, real photo, signed "Alletta Crump"	1000	1100
Advertising, Werner's Bowling Alleys, linen, c1940	250	275
Advertising, Yale Tires, Pure Oil Co., Maggie & Jiggs, c1912	75	100
Another Fairy Tale, Louis Wain, 1910	375	400
Christmas, Santa figure, embossed, brown robe w/ gold highlights, twig crown, and pine tree staff, w/ angel sitting on shoulder, P.F.B. #9103	40	50

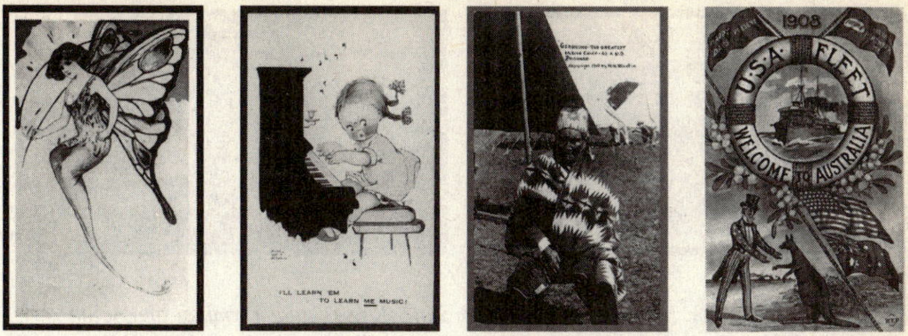

Left to right: Artist-Signed, Samuel Schmucker, Butterfly Series, Detroit Pub., 1907, $100-$150; Artist-Signed, Mabel Lucie Attwell, "I'll Learn 'Em to Learn Me Music!," $7-$10; Real Photo, "Geronimo, The Greatest Indian Chief–as a U.S. Prisoner," photo by W. H. Martin, North American Post Card Co., 1909, $150 at auction; Souvenir, "U.S.A. Fleet, Welcome to Australia," 1908, $65 at auction. —Photos courtesy Postcards International.

	LOW	HIGH
Fourth of July, firecracker, string fuse, "A Big Cracker for A Big Fourth!," 1906	200	225
Fourth of July, Miss Columbia wearing flag dress, sitting atop Liberty Bell and firecrackers, embossed	30	50
Fraternal, Knights Templar 31st Triennial Conclave, attached felt banner and metallic emblems, Chicago, 1910	50	75
Glow-In-The-Dark, 2 mermaids in moonlight, French, c1930	225	250
Halloween, child lifting lid off jack-o-lantern, embossed, Winsch, 1914	100	150
Halloween, "The Halloween Witch's Wand," witch and ghost in balloon, yellow and black checkerboard border, 1928	120	130
Hold-To-Light, "A Happy Christmas To You," child chasing turkey	125	175
Hold-To-Light, Christmas angels and stars, diecut, England, 1905	50	70
Hold-To-Light, "Easter Greeting," rabbit family painting Easter eggs	70	80
Hold-To-Light, New Year's Day, diecut, 1910	75	100
Jewish New Year, Moses and the Ten Commandments	50	100
Mechanical, Chicago Cubs, "Our Home Team," 1908	1400	1600
Mechanical, Christmas, moving bells	125	175
Mechanical, dancing couple	75	125
Mechanical, German beer stein	75	125
Mechanical, Remington Rifles	1200	1700
Military, appeal for Liberty Bonds on Liberty Day, Sat., Oct. 12, 1918, color	100	125
Military, "Army and Navy Forever," lyrics to *My Country 'tis of Thee*	30	50
Patriotic, "250th Anniversary of Kingston, New York," Uncle Sam lifting flag to see sun rising on Statue of Liberty	30	40
Patriotic, "The Yanks Are Coming!," Uncle Sam pulling teeth of Hirohito, Mussolini, and Hitler, signed "B. F. Long," black and white	30	50
Political, President Roosevelt w/ American flag	25	75
Political, President Taft, hand-drawn caricature, French	150	175
Political, President Wilson, hand-drawn caricature, signed "Garrity," 1915	30	50
Political, Standard and Standard Bearers of Working Class 1928, Presidential candidates Foster and Gitlow of the Communist Party, real photo	1750	1900
Railroad, Erie Railroad, "The Lounge of the Erie Air-Conditioned Diner Lounge Cars," black waiter serving passengers, linen	30	50

Real Photo Postcards, left to right: New York State Barge Canal Terminal and South Entrance to New Trolley and Freight Subway System, Rochester, NY, published by Rochester News Co., c1929, $5-$10; Detroit Tigers, team portrait, 1907, $600 at auction. —Photo courtesy Postcards International.

	LOW	HIGH
Railroad, Los Angeles Limited, black waiter serving man and woman	30	50
Real Photo, Alaskan warrior and squaw, Chikat, Alaska, 1912	50	70
Real Photo, "American Jazz-Band Perroni," Italian, c1920	75	100
Real Photo, Bostock circus performers, French, c1910	150	175
Real Photo, Burton's Tea Store, British, c1910	125	150
Real Photo, Charles Lindbergh arriving at France Field, Canal Zone, w/ First Air Mail U.S. to Panama, Feb. 6, 1929	250	275
Real Photo, Chief White Dog smoking pipe, Glacier National Park	50	100
Real Photo, daredevil Peggy's Famous Troupe of Diving Belles, British, c1935	150	175
Real Photo, Hallon Parker, physician of Company C, 35th New York Volunteers, c1910	75	100
Real Photo, Jewish boy in prayer shawl holding prayer book, NY	25	75
Real Photo, Larry Doby of the Cleveland Indians, signed, 1952	250	275
Real Photo, Negro baptism near Norfolk, VA, 1924, used	20	40
Real Photo, New York Giants, view of whole team and montage portraits of Wilson, McGraw, Murray, and Mathewson against stadium field background, black and white, 1912, used	550	650
Real Photo, Oneida Motor Car Co., 1915	150	175
Real Photo, salesman w/ horse and buggy, Fleischmann Co., c1908	125	150
Real Photo, Salvation Army, L. Perkoff, London, c1905	100	125
Real Photo, Shaker elder w/ horse, Mt. Lebanon, NY, c1910	300	350
Real Photo, Tommy Dorsey, King Liberty Trombone advertisement, H. N. White Co., Cleveland, OH	50	75
Real Photo, White Star Liner *Titantic* departing from Southampton, England	500	550
Souvenir, Argentina, "Greetings from Buenos Aires," views of harbor entrance, German	75	90
Souvenir, New York City, city skyline, Statue of Liberty, and Brooklyn Bridge, c1900	60	75
Souvenir, "Oh, it's all right with me, I'm in Bermuda," hand painted	30	50
Souvenir, San Francisco, CA, views of Fredericksburg Brewery, Cliff House, City Hall and Golden Gate	100	150
World's Fair, 1915 Pan Am International Exposition, San Francisco, CA, Greek woman looking down from ruins on expo site	50	100
World's Fair, 1933 Chicago, wood block design, "Greenwich Village Artist Colony. On the Midway," Century of Progress cancellation	650	700
World's Fair, 1939 New York, blue, orange and gold depictions of exhibit buildings, complete set of 6	175	225

Left to right: Kentucky/Tennessee, Ashland Flying Octanes, 1950s, $2-$5; Delaware/Maryland/Virginia/West Virginia, 1961, $2-$3.

Road Maps

At one time, local gas stations gave maps away free of charge to any customer. They are now collected as memorabilia of the post-war car culture. Folds should not be taped or worn through. Colors should be fresh and stain-free. There should be no added pen marking of routes or circled towns.

	LOW	HIGH
Arizona, 1940	$10	$20
Arizona/New Mexico, Shamrock	50	60
Boston and Vicinity Cape Cod, Shell, 3-panel, 9" h, 12" w	20	30
Colorado, 3-panel, 1955	60	70
Colorado/Utah, Sinclair, 5-panel, 9" h, 19" w	20	40
Delaware/Maryland/Virginia/West Virginia, Amoco, 3-panel, 9" h, 12" w	75	90
Florida, Sinclair, state of Florida 1 side, United States on reverse, 5-panel, c1930s, 9" h, 19.5" w	50	60
Illinois, Sinclair, family riding in automobile, 5-panel, 1934, 9" h, 19.5" w	100	300
Illinois, Sinclair, front dinosaur graphic, locomotive graphic inside, 5-panel, 1935, 9" h, 19.5" w	100	300
Indiana, Standard Oil Co., "Motor Trails are Calling," 2-panel, 9" h, 8" w	20	30
Iowa, Paraland Motor Oil, 2-panel, 9" h, 8" w	50	60
Kansas, Dixie Gasoline	50	60
Kansas, Standard Oil, 3-panel, 1934, 9" h, 12" w	20	30
Kendall, 1940	10	15
Kentucky/Tennessee, Gulf, 3-panel, 1932, 9" h, 12" w	20	30
Kentucky/Tennessee, Texaco, attendant giving directions to couple, rolling country hills background, 2-panel, 7" h, 7.5" w	5	15
Los Angeles, Standard Oil	20	30
Maryland/Delaware/District of Columbia/Virginia/West Virginia, 1-panel, 1930	20	30
Michigan, 1955	5	15
Middle Atlantic States, 2-panel, 1929, 7.75" h, 7.5" w	20	30
Minnesota, Shell, "Compliments of Jamesville Oil Co., Jamesville, Minn.," 3-panel, 1929, 9" h, 12" w	80	100
Missouri, Skelly, 3-panel, 1930	60	70
Missouri, Phillips 66, "There's a Phillips Station Ahead," 3-panel, 9" h, 12" w	70	80
Missouri, Phillips Highways of Missouri, 3-panel, pre-1928, 9" h, 11.5" w	100	300
Nevada, 1946	10	20
Ohio, Sinclair, 3-panel, 1931, 9" h, 12" w	20	40
Ohio, Shell, 1932, 3-panel, 9" h, 11.875" w	20	30
Ohio, State Highway Map, 1-panel, 1934, 8.5" h, 3.75" w	5	15
Pennsylvania, "Gulf Refining Company General Sales Offices. Pittsburgh PA U.S.A.," 1-panel, 1929, 9" h, 12" w	20	30
Pennsylvania/New Jersey, Amoco, 2-panel, 9" h, 8" w	70	80

Pens and Pencils

Pens can be either dip pens (the earliest type), fountain pens or ballpoint pens, Dip pens are the style of modern calligraphy pens: a pointed nib is dipped in ink and used quickly. Fountain pens contain their own ink supply, as do ballpoints and roller balls. Pencils are either traditional or mechanical.

The fountain pen, invented in the 1880s by Lewis Waterman, is the most collectible type. It experienced its heyday in the 1920s and 1930s. The important makers from that time are Waterman, Parker, Conklin, Sheaffer and Wahl. Rarity and condition are very important.

For further information see *Fountain Pens and Pencils* by George Fischler and Stuart Schneider (Schiffer Publishing, West Chester, PA, 1990), *The Incredible Ball Point Pen* by Henry Gostony and Stuart Schneider (Schiffer Publishing, Atglen, PA, 1998), and *Pen World International* (3946 Glade Valeey Dr., Kingswood, TX 77339).

Pens

	LOW	HIGH
Carter, hard rubber, red and black mottled, lever filler, c1920s	$125	$175
Conklin, gold filled filigree design overlay, crescent filler, c1908-18	400	600
Conklin, hard rubber, red and black mottled, crescent filler, slip cap, c1908-10	150	300
Conklin, hard rubber, red, crescent filler, c1923-26	150	300
Diamond Point, plastic, green marble, lever filler, c1929	25	75
Eversharp, ballpoint, CA model, black, gold filled cap, 1946	30	50
Eversharp, Skyline, lever filler, 1941-49	25	50
Mont Blanc, #146G, Masterpiece, plastic, green striped, twist filler, c1949-60	250	400
Mont Blanc, safety pen, silver overlay, c1915-30	400	600
Moore, Maniflex, plastic, black and pearl, lever filler, c1929-35	75	150
Moore, sterling silver, lever filler, c1922-30	125	200
Parker, #9, hard rubber, black chased, 2 gold filled bands, eyedropper fill, c1898-1918	150	250
Parker, #10, hard rubber, red and black mottled, cable chased, eyedropper filler, c1894-1905	350	500
Parker, #15, alternating pearl and abalone covered barrel, rounded gold filled filigree design overlay cap, eyedropper filler, c1905-10	750	1250
Parker, #20, Jack-Knife Safety, hard rubber, red, button filler	300	500
Parker, #30, diamond chased design overlay, gold filled, eyedropper filler, c1900-15	1250	1750
Parker, #37, sterling silver snake design overlay, eyedropper filler, c1905-18	5000	7000
Pilot, plastic and wood, black, cartridge filler, c1970	50	75
Sheaffer, 14k gold overlay, lever filler, c1922-24	1000	1250
Sheaffer, chased hard rubber, black, lever filler, c1914-22	125	200
Sheaffer, Craftsman, roseflow Radite, lever filler, c1937-45	20	35
Sheaffer, gold filled overlay, lever filler, c1917-24	100	175
Sheaffer, hard rubber, black, 2 gold filled bands, lady's, lever filler, c1914-22	40	80
Sheaffer, Lady Skripsert, gold plated, cartridge filler, 1958-64	20	35
Sheaffer, Lifetime, telephone dialer, c1929-33	100	150
Swan, #2060, plastic, black, leverless twist filler, c1947-53	35	100
Wahl-Eversharp, Boston, chased hard rubber, black, eyedropper filler, c1914-17	25	50
Wahl-Eversharp, Boston, mottled hard rubber, red and black, lady's, lever filler, c1915-17	30	60
Wahl-Eversharp, Marathon, hard rubber, red, lever filler, c1924-28	35	75
Wahl-Eversharp, sterling silver, hand engraved floral design, lever filler, 1922-32	250	400
Waterman, A. A., #8, chased hard rubber, black, eyedropper filler, c1912-15	150	250

	LOW	HIGH
Waterman, A. A., Chicago Safety Pen, sterling silver overlay, twist filler, c1921-23	75	150
Waterman, A. A., hard rubber, black, middle joint gold filled band, eyedropper filler, c1902-07	50	75
Waterman, L. E., #6, chased hard rubber, black, eyedropper fill, gold filled bands, c1800s	750	1250
Waterman, L. E., #14, red and black mottled, eyedropper filler, c1898-1922	75	175
Waterman, L. E., #24, hard rubber, black, hexagon twist, eyedropper filler, c1893-1900	350	400
Waterman, L. E., #324, 14k gold "barleycorn" design half overlay, eyedropper filler, 1900-20	500	750
Waterman, L. E., #504, 14k gold repousse design overlay, eyedropper filler, 1895-1910	2500	3500

Pencils

Cartier, sterling silver, gold mount, 1982	$30	$45
Doric, pearly lined nickel-plated trim, 1935	50	120
Eversharp, Coronet, repeater, rhodium-plated cap, 1936-41	25	65
Eversharp, plastic, black and pearl marble, 1929-32	10	20
Eversharp, repeater, dark blue, gold filled trim, 1941	40	60
Parker, burgundy and black streamline	15	35
Parker, Duofold, mechanical, 1927-29	50	75
Sheaffer, demonstrator model, mechanical, c1915-25	50	75
Sheaffer, Fineline 4000, novel point, platinum plating, 1946	30	50
Wahl, Gold Seal, lever filler pen and pencil set, plastic, burgundy and black plastic, 1930-32	125	200
Wahl-Eversharp, sterling silver, engraved case, 1924	150	200

Pen and Pencil Sets

Conklin, Endura, hard rubber, red, lever filler pen, c1924-26	$300	$400
Conklin, Nozac, 12-sided, twist filler, c1934-38	100	200
Crocker, hard rubber, red and black mottled, lever filler, c1927	150	300
Eversharp, Fifth Avenue, 14k gold cap and trim, lever filler pen	100	200
Le Boeuf, plastic, blue marble, button filler pen, c1932	75	125
Wahl, Gold Seal, plastic, burgundy and black, lever filler pen, 1930-32	125	200

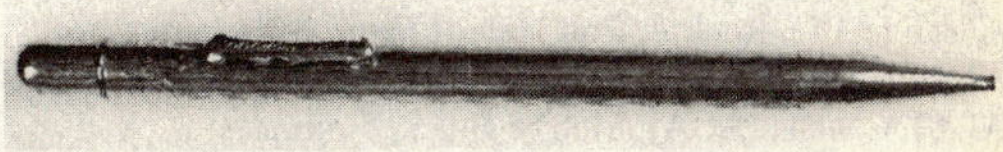

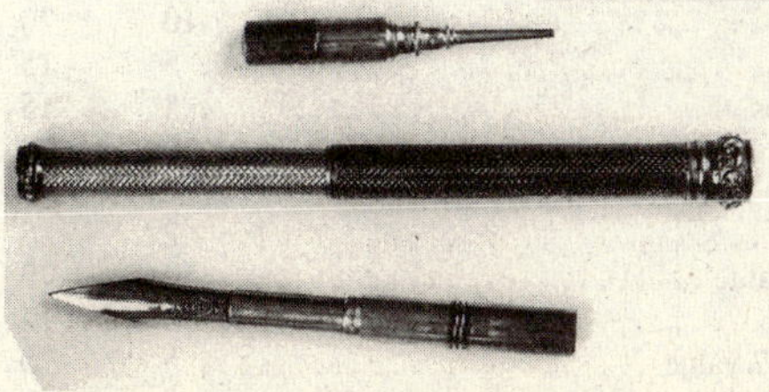

Above: Pencil, Conklin, No. 4V, rolled gold, 5.25" l, $40-$50.

Left: Pen/Pencil Combination, marked "B. T. Benton, New York, 1851," telescoping, $65-$80.

Phone Cards

Phone cards are one of the newest collectibles. They provide an easy entrance for novice collectors since many cards sell for under $10 and you can store thousands in a very small space. They appeal to a cross section of collectors because the themes are nearly endless, including sports, personalities and cartoon characters.

Phone Card.

	LOW	HIGH
Ameritech (AMT), Ameritech Yellow Pages, 5 units	$70	$80
Ameritech (AMT), Claude Monet–Water Lilies, 20 units	10	20
Ameritech (AMT), Comiskey Park, $2 value	5	10
American Express Telecom (AMX), Daisies, $20 value	15	25
American Express Telecom (AMX), Golden Gate Bridge, $5 value	5	10
AmeriVox (AVX), Cutty Sark Scots Whiskey, 5 minutes	30	50
AmeriVox (AVX), Roy Rogers & Dale Evans, $21 value	20	30
AmeriVox (AVX), Season's Greetings–Snowscape, 5 units	10	20
AmeriVox (AVX), Youth AIDS Awareness, 5 minutes	20	30
AMI Communications (AMI), First Night Game Wrigley, $15 value	15	25
Argo City Co. (ARG), After Dark, 10 units	20	30
AT&T (ATT), Apollo Lunar Module, 10 units	60	70
AT&T (ATT), AT&T Global Olympic Village, 20 units	40	50
AT&T (ATT), Democratic Convention, 10 units	200	250
AT&T (ATT), Flintstones and Rubbles, 25 units	20	30
AT&T (ATT), Florida Marlins–Andre Dawson, 5 minutes	20	30
AT&T (ATT), Gymnast Trent Dimas, 15 units	10	15
AT&T (ATT), Holiday Treats, 10 units	15	25
AT&T (ATT), Hurdler Gail Devers, 50 units	30	40
AT&T (ATT), New York Skyline, 25 units	110	125
AT&T (ATT), Pocohontas, 5 minutes	20	30
AT&T (ATT), Rock & Roll Hall of Fame, 10 minutes	5	15
AT&T Canada (ACA), Calgary Stampede, 30 minutes	20	40
AT&T Canada (ACA), Men in Black, 5 minutes	10	20
AT&T Canada (ACA), Twix, 15 minutes	10	20
ATS, Heartland Vinyl Siding, 10 minutes	5	15
ATS, Memphis Convention Bureau, 4 minutes	5	15
ATS, Olan Mills Photo Studios, 20 minutes	10	20
B&J Telecard (BJT), Rocky Allen/Piece of the Rock, $10 value	4	8
B&J Telecard (BJT), Xscape, 5 minutes	2	5
BC Tel (BCL), Chinese New Year Set, $57 value	50	70
BC Tel (BCL), Totem, $10 value	10	15
Bell Atlantic (BAT), James Earl Jones, red, $2 value	5	10
Bell Canada (BEL), Information Highway/Old Logo, $1 value	5	10
Bell Canada LePuce (LPC), Guess Jeans, $10 value	10	15
Bell Canada LePuce (LPC), Kraft Cheese, $2 value	5	10

	LOW	HIGH
Bell Canada LePuce (LPC), McDonald's, $10 value	110	20
Bell South Telecom (BST), Mobility: Beach, $10 value	15	15
Brilliant Color Cards (BCC), Telecard Man Richmond, VA, 7 units	400	500
Cable & Wireless (C&W), Beaglefest V/Christmas in July, 5 minutes	10	30
Cable & Wireless (C&W), Marcal Paper Mills, 10 minutes	5	10
Cable & Wireless (C&W), NASA–Beyond 2000, $3 value	10	20
Cable & Wireless (C&W), Walt Disney's Artistocats, 44 minutes	20	40
CallSelect (CLS), IGA Groceries/Freson, Alberta, 10 minutes	10	15
CallSelect (CLS), Just Call, 5 minutes	10	20
Canada Telecom Network (CTN), 7-11 Stores, 15 minutes	10	20
Canada Telecom Network (CTN), Catelli Pasta, $2 value	10	20
Canada Telecom Network (CTN), Greyhound Logo, 20 minutes	10	30
Capital Communications Group (CAP), Costa Rica, $25 value	10	15
Carson City King (CCK), Atlanta Peach State Coin Show, 5 minutes	15	25
Communication Design Group (CDG), Chicago at Nite is Hot, 5 minutes	5	10
Communication Design Group (CDG), Toys R Us, 50 minutes	20	30
Creative Communications (CCI), Milky Way Lite, 15 minutes	10	20
DataTel International (DAT), HBO, 5 units	10	20
DataTel International (DAT), Lizard, 180 minutes	10	15
DataTel International (DAT), Nabisco Snackwell's, 15 minutes	10	20
Destiny Communications, Inc. (DES), Alvin Harper, 10 units	5	10
Destiny Communications, Inc. (DES), Johnny Rutherford, 20 units	5	15
Destiny Communications, Inc. (DES), Seth Joyner, 10 units	5	10
EastWest Telecom (EWT), Race for the Presidency, 10 minutes	20	30
EastWest Telecom (EWT), Santa and child at fence, 10 minutes	10	15
Finish Line Racing (FIN), Bill Elliott, Series 1, $10 value	10	20
Finish Line Racing (FIN), Kyle Petty, $10 value	10	20
First Union Corp. (FUN), Gold and Silver Coins, $2 value	10	20
Frontier Communications (FRO), Beverly Hills 90210, $10 value	5	10
Frontier Communications (FRO), TGI Fridays/Jack Daniel's Grill, 5 minutes	10	30
Frontier Communications (FRO), X-Files, $10 value	5	10
GAF Telecommunications (GAF), Bud NASCAR, 5 minutes	5	15
Global Communications Network (GCN), Hard Rock Hotel Las Vegas, $10 value	10	20
Global Communications Network (GCN), Nabisco, 30 minutes	10	20
Global Communications Network (GCN), Woodstock Festival 1969, $10 value	15	25
Global Telecommunications Solutions (GTS), Incredible Hulk, $10 value	15	25
Global Telecommunications Solutions (GTS), New York Puzzle, 20 units	10	15
Global Telecommunications Solutions (GTS), Ripley's Tightrope Elephant, 20 units	10	20
Global Telecommunications Solutions (GTS), Woodstock '94, 20 units	20	40
Grapevine Telecards (GRP), Classic Rock & Other Rollers, 5 units	10	15
Grapevine Telecards (GRP), Fetzer Sundial Chardonnay, 10 units	10	15
Grapevine Telecards (GRP), Spanning the Gate, 5 units	5	15
GTE (GTE), NFL Helmets, 5 units	5	10
GTE (GTE), Pro Football Hall of Fame, 5 units	10	15
GTE Hawaii (GTH), 29th Hawaiian Open, 3 units	10	30
GTE Hawaii (GTH), Diamond Head–Sun & Fun, 3 units	75	85
GTE Hawaii (GTH), Rainbow Valley, 10 units	20	30
GTI, Dr. No, $5 value	4	8
GTI, Ralston Purina–Golden Retriever, 10 minutes	2	5
Hallmark (HAL), Dear Friend, 10 minutes	10	20
Hallmark (HAL), I Love You, 10 minutes	10	20
Hallmark (HAL), Magic Phone Card, 10 minutes	10	20
Hannibal Communications (HAN), 1917 Buick, 10 minutes	6	12

	LOW	HIGH
Hannibal Communications (HAN), Detroit–World's Motor Capital, 10 minutes	2	5
HT Technologies (HTT), Chen's Radio City Music Hall, 20 units	20	30
HT Technologies (HTT), Jensen Beach Pineapple, 10 units	5	15
HT Technologies (HTT), Smirnoff Vodka, 10 units	10	20
IDB Worldcom (IDB), Wayne Gretsky All Time Scorer, $25 value	40	60
IEM Telecom (IEM), Michael Irvin/The Ring, $3 value	5	15
Image Telecards (IMG), Junior Mints, 3 minutes	4	8
Image Telecards (IMG), Tootsie Roll 100th Anniversary, 10 minutes	15	25
Instacall Communications (INS), Tony Dorsett #33, $25 value	25	35
Interactive Telecard Services (ITS), Chicago Tribune, 10 minutes	5	10
Interactive Telecard Services (ITS), Playtex 18-Hour, 30 minutes	10	15
JAG Enterprises (JAG), Little Shop Hardware, 5 minutes	5	10
Karis Communications (KAR), Mountain Dew, 10 minutes	10	20
Karis Communications (KAR), Pepsi Time In Space, 5 minutes	15	25
Laser Radio (LSR), University of Wyoming Women's Soccer, $25 value	30	40
LDDS WorldCom (LDD), Miami Heat, 3 units	30	40
LDDS WorldCom (LDD), Michael Jordan/Hanes, 15 units	5	15
LDDS WorldCom (LDD), Oakland Bay Bridge, $5 value	5	10
LDDS WorldCom (LDD), Season's Greetings Doves, 10 units	10	20
Lifesaver Communications Inc. (LSC), Dallas Grand Prix, $5 value	5	15
Lifesaver Communications Inc. (LSC), San Francisco Marathon, $5 value	10	20
Main Street Marketing (MSM), Monday Night Football/ABC, 7 minutes	10	20
Manitoba Telephone System (MTS), Polar Bear, $20 value	20	30
Marta (MRT), October: Dave Johnson, $45 value	40	60
MCI (MCI), 1996 World Series, 5 minutes	4	8
MCI (MCI), Regular All Star Game 1985, 3 units	5	8
MCI (MCI), Rolling Stones Voodoo Lounge Tour Series, mouth logo, 10 units	15	25
Mercury Marketing (MMC), Monsters in the Mix, 40 units	4	8
Mercury Marketing (MMC), PC Expo New York, 100 units	10	15
Mercury Marketing (MMC), Speed Call: Busch Light 300, $10 value	10	20
Mercury Marketing (MMC), St. Louis/Collector's Advantage, $1 value	4	8
Metro Transit Authority (MTA), NY Rangers Stanley Cup, $5 value	5	10
Mountain America Technologies (MAT), Broadmoor Hotel, 10 units	5	15
Mountain America Technologies (MAT), Royal Gorge Bridge, 10 units	10	15
Mountain America Technologies (MAT), Taco Bell, 5 units	10	15
MT&T Technologies (MTT), Glade/White Flowers, 5 minutes	5	10
NationsBank Corp. (NBC), Visa Cash/Olympic Opening Ceremony, $5 value	75	125
North America Telephone (NAT), Bobby G's Rain Delay, 5 minutes	10	15
North America Telephone (NAT), Legendary Ladies of Baseball, 15 minutes	10	20
Nynex (NYN), Ballet Dancer, $10 value	5	15
Nynex (NYN), I Love New York, $5 value	4	10
Nynex (NYN), New York State Fair, $5 value	4	10
Nynex (NYN), U.S. Open Tennis '95, 10 minutes	20	30
OmniTel (OMN), Cam Neeley, $8 value	5	15
OmniTel (OMN), Diana Ross, 5 minutes	5	15
OmniTel (OMN), Ray Bourque, $2 value	4	8
OmniTel (OMN), Sunkist/Canada Dry, 10 minutes	10	20
OmniTel (OMN), Volvo Car, 30 minutes	10	20
Pacific Bell (PAC), Executive Forum, $10 value	20	40
Pacific Bell (PAC), Kinko's Copy Centers, $20 value	10	30
Pacific Bell (PAC), Santa & Phone, $5 value	30	50
Pacific Bell (PAC), Soccer/Cobi Jones, $20 value	10	30
Phoneline USA (PLU), Stargate/Anubis, $15 value	10	30
Precis Smart Card Systems (PSC), Inaugural OSU Athletics, $10 value	10	30

	LOW	HIGH
Precis Smart Card Systems (PSC), White Sox/Cubs Logo, $20 value	20	30
Quest Group International (QGI), Peach Bowl/Liberty, $2 value	10	15
Quest Group International (QGI), Pro Football Hall of Fame, $10 value	35	45
Quest/Liberty (QGI), Pulsar Watch, 10 minutes	15	25
Quest/Liberty (QGI), Seiko Watch, 15 minutes	20	40
Quest/Liberty (QGI), Vincent VanGogh, $5 value	10	20
Race Call (RCL), Jimmy Spencer, $3 value	2	5
Race Call (RCL), Ted Musgrave, $10 value	5	15
Sasktel (SAS), Kenosee Lake, $10 value	10	15
Sasktel (SAS), Maple Leaves, $50 value	50	60
Score Board Inc. (SBI), Barry Bonds/Talk 'N Sports, $1 value	2	8
Score Board Inc. (SBI), Cal Ripken Special Series, $10 value	15	25
Score Board Inc. (SBI), Dale Earnhardt/Classic Assets I Premier, 1 minute	2	5
Score Board Inc. (SBI), Happy Meal Guy/Hamburger, diecut, $25 value	70	80
Score Board Inc. (SBI), Shaquille O'Neal/Classic Assets I Premier, $25 value	40	60
Score Board Inc. (SBI), Troy Aikman/Classic Assets Gold, $2 value	2	5
SmarTel (SMR), Ace Ventura/When Nature Calls, 5 minutes	4	8
SmarTel (SMR), Entemann's, 10 minutes	5	10
SmarTel (SMR), Newsweek, 10 minutes	30	40
SmarTel (SMR), Norelco, 10 minutes	5	10
SmarTel (SMR), Pope John Paul II, 10 minutes	15	20
SmarTel (SMR), Wells Fargo, 5 minutes	5	10
Snet (SNT), Connecticut Huskies, 3 minutes	10	15
Sprint (SPR), Arnold Schwarzenegger, 10 units	5	10
Sprint (SPR), Baseball & Apple Pie, 100 units	80	90
Sprint (SPR), Exotic Birds/Animal Series, 100 units	20	40
Sprint (SPR), Gold Medal Waterskier, 5 units	20	30
Sprint (SPR), Monsters of the Gridiron, $3 value	5	10
Sprint (SPR), NFL Player of the Year, 5 minutes	45	55
Sprint (SPR), Norman Rockwell the Hug, 20 minutes	3	6
Strategic Telecom Systems (STS), San Diego Earth Day, 10 minutes	20	30
TekTel (TEK), Friends/Diet Coke/Umbrella, 15 minutes	10	20
Teletrading Cards (TTR), Baseball Legends/Lou Gehrig, $5 value	5	15
Teletrading Cards (TTR), Ruth & Cobb, 20 minutes	10	20
Telenova (TVA), Big Boy, 6 minutes	10	15
Telenova (TVA), Kentucky Fried Chicken, 5 minutes	5	15
Tell One Inc. (T01), Bugs Stamp Card, 10 minutes	15	20
Thunder Bay Telephone (TNB), Nordic Games/Skier, $20 value	20	30
TotalTel (TTT), Demi Moore, 10 minutes	120	130
USACard Corp. (USA), Coors Field/Field of Dreams, $20 value	20	30
USACard Corp. (USA), Cracker Jack Collector's Assoc., 5 units	15	20
USACard Corp. (USA), Pink Panther Valentine's Day, 10 units	10	20
USACard Corp. (USA), Wish You Were Here, $5 value	5	10
US West (USW), Inmate Services Keeping You in Control, $1 value	10	15
US West (USW), Seattle Space Needle, $10 value	10	15
Visa Cash–Vancouver City Savings (VCS), Visa Cash/Science World, $5 value	10	15
Vista–United (VIS), Disney Store Appreciation, 5 minutes	40	60
Wachovia Corp. (WAC), Salute to Atlanta/Gymnast, $10 value	15	25
Winston Taylor (WTA), Baton/Employee Card, $2 value	40	60
Winston Taylor (WTA), Peanuts/45 Years/Classicards, 5 units	40	50
WorldConnect Communications (WCC), 1995 PPG World Series Schedule, 3 units	5	15
WorldLink (WLC), Marilyn Monroe Laughing, $10 value	20	30
Zenex Comm. Inc. (ZEN), Mickey Mantle, 15 units	10	25

Photographs

Assorted Subjects

In the following entries, photographs are listed by type. The values quoted are the average retail price for various types of prints. Cartes de Visite average 4" x 2.5" on cardboard; Daguerreotypes generally average 4" x 3" on silver plates; Silver Prints are prints made on paper on which the image is formed by silver; Stereopticon Cards have a double image for observing in one of a variety of viewers; Tintypes generally average 3" x 2" (these values are not for the thumbnail-size variety).

The value of photographs is determined by age and subject matter. Prints made in the studios of important photographers such as Edward Cuttis, Matthew Brady, Alfred Stieglitz and Carleton Watkins command high prices.

Tintypes were invented in 1858 and declined in popularity by the 1870s. Stereographs with a revenue stamp on the back date between 1864 and 1866. In 1868, many publishers listed the views in a particular stereographic series by underlining or outlining a card number or title. After 1880, curved stereographs appeared, believed to have a more three-dimensional quality.

For more information see *Collector's Guide to Early Photographs, Second Edition* by O.Henry Mace (Krause Publications, Iola, WI, 1999) and *Stereo Views: An Illustrated History and Price Guide* by John S. Waldsmith (Wallace-Homestead, Radnor, PA, 1991). Due to the fragility of paper, *An Ounce of Preservation: A Guide to the Care of Papers and Photographs* by Craig Tuttle (Rainbow Books, Highland City, FL, 1995) is worth consulting.

Daguerrotype in wooden case.

Cartes de Visite

	LOW	HIGH
Children of the Battlefield, Wenderoth, Taylor & Brown/Philadelphia backmark	$75	$125
Doubleday, Abner, Bridgadier General, pictured seated, from waist up, in uniform, Anthony/Brady backmark	450	500
Grant, U. S., General, pictured seated, from waist up, in uniform, Gurney & Son/New York backmark	180	190
Lincoln, Abraham, pictured full standing, Anthony/Brady backmark w/ Earl's/Philadelphia label on reverse	1000	1200
Meade, George Gordon, General, pictured standing, from knees up, in uniform, Anthony/Brady backmark	170	180
Rubenstein, Anton, bust view, Gurney/New York backmark, c1870s	8	15
Sheridan, Philip, General, outdoor image, pictured seated, full length, in uniform holding sword, titled on obverse, Guille & Alles interior decorator label obscures Brady backmark	150	160

	LOW	HIGH
Stokes, W. A., Major Regular Army, pictured full standing, in uniform w/ dress epaulettes and sword, w/ Hardee hat on pillar behind, J. E. McClees/Philadelphia, image identification on reverse and dated 1862	80	90
Strauss, Johann, bust view, Gurney/New York backmark, c1870s	130	140
Whipple, William, Brigadier General, pictured standing, from knees up, in uniform, Wenderoth & Taylor backmark, signed w/ rank on reverse	200	225

Daguerrotypes

	LOW	HIGH
Boy, seated beside sleeping dog, also on wooden chair, w/ head resting on boy's legs, leather case, sixth-plate, c1850s	$1100	$1500
Gentleman, astride chestnut horse, w/ hand coloring in horse, half leather case, quarter-plate, mid-1850s	1250	1275
Gentleman, pictured from the waist up, by J. Corduan, in leather case, sixth-plate, early 1840s	500	525
Hale, John Parker, bust portrait, leather case, half-plate, mid-1850s	1380	1400
Mother and Daughter, holding posie of roses, hand colored, in claret velvet-lined case, sixth-plate, English, mid-1850s	750	850
Mother and Son, photographer E. T. Whitney's imprint in mat, half-plate, early 1850s	600	900
Two Young Sisters, 1 standing, other seated in highchair, wearing identical striped dress, w/ hand coloring in girls' cheeks, leather case, quarter-plate, mid-1850s	1000	1200
Young Woman, fixed gaze, seated, holding white rabbit, leather case, sixth-plate, c1850s	4000	4200
Young Woman, seated, holding book in hand, leather case, sixth-plate, mid-1840s	125	175
Young Woman, wearing paisley shawl, gilt highlighting, sixth-plate, 1850s	200	250

Silver Prints

	LOW	HIGH
Branches in Snow, signed by Ansel Adams in pencil on mount recto, w/ hand-editioned Portfolio II stamp on mount verso, 1959, 7" x 5.25"	$1300	$1400
Elephant, signed, dated, and editioned "2/50" by Keith Carter in pencil on verso, 1990, 15.25" x 15.25"	600	700
Enchanted Mesa, signed by William Clift in pencil on mat recto and overmat, framed, 1978, 13.25" x 19.25"	1500	1700
Esso Station, signed by Berenice Abbott in pencil on mount recto and w/ Maine handstamp on mount verso, 1960s, 13" x 10.5"	1000	1200
Flag Raising on Iwo Jima, signed and inscribed by Joe Rosenthal on recto, 1945, 12.5" x 9.75"	1200	1300
Glasses, signed by Olive Cotton in pencil on recto, title and date on verso, 1937, printed later, 11.25" x 8.25"	800	900
Indian Women, signed by Edouard Boubat in ink on recto, w/ title, date, and page number penciled on verso, 1971, printed later, 9.25" x 13.75"	700	800
Martin Luther and Coretta King, marching toward Montgomery, signed by Ivan Massar in pencil, handstamp and handwritten caption label affixed to verso, 1960, 6.75" x 10.75"	800	900
Portrait of Elizabeth McCausland at her printing press, signed by Berenice Abbott in pencil on mount recto, 1940s, 9.75" x 7.5"	75	150
Ty Cobb at Bat, flush mount, w/ title printed in negative, 1950s, 23.75" x 20"	950	950
War Came to Germany, Dmitri Baltermants, w/ photographer's handwritten title in ink in Cyrillic, handstamp on verso, 1945, printed 1960s, 17.5" x 11.5"	1100	1200

Stereopticon Cards

	LOW	HIGH
Apache Indians, bathing scene, J. C. Burge	$75	$125
Battleship *USS Brooklyn,* #2535, Griffith, 1902	5	10
Blacks Picking Cotton, #9506, Keystone	4	8
Bronx Zoo, walrus scene, #V21232, Keystone	4	8
Buffalo Bill, on horseback in New York, #1399, American Scenery	40	60
Columbian Exposition, Chicago, 1894, ferris wheel scene, Kilburn	5	15
Crow Indian, burial ground scene, #865, F. J. Hayes	15	25
Fire Engine, close view of pumpers, early 1870s	30	50
Full Moon, #2630, Kilburn	4	8
Gehrig, Lou, #32597, Keystone	200	250
Grocery Store, interior view, #18209, Keystone	10	20
Halibut, #22520, Keystone	3	8
Indian Girl, #23118, Keystone	2	5
Lincoln, Abraham, funeral scene, #2948, Anthony	40	60
Lindbergh, Charles, standing next to *Spirit of St. Louis,* #30262T, Keystone	20	40
Ruth, Babe, #32590, Keystone	200	250
Santa, coming down chimney w/ toys, #11434, Keystone	10	15
Sioux Indian, #1742, F. J. Hayes	40	60
Sunday School Class, #4262, Graves	10	30
Waikiki Beach, #10162, Keystone	5	15
Washington, Booker T., w/ Andrew Carnegie, #V11960, keystone	50	70
West Michigan State Fair, #21507, Keystone, 1908	10	20
Windsor & Whipple Circus, Olean, NY, people w/ elephant	20	40

Tintypes

African-American Girl, standing, resting arm on back of posing chair, in original wood and gesso frame, remnants of photographer's label affixed to verso, whole-plate, 1870s	$420	$440
Two Cobblers, facing each other w/ shoe lasts and leather punches, w/ hand tinting in figure's faces, in mat and preserver, half-plate, 1870s	620	640
Two Men, seated, original paper mount, quarter-plate, c1900	300	400
Two Western Men, smoking cigars, w/ pistols tucked in waistband of their chaps, sixth-plate, 1870s	170	180

Stereopticon Cards.

Wallace Nutting

At the same time he was reproducing American antique furniture, Wallace Nutting funded his many projects with money earned from selling photographs of quaint scenes. Often signed, these photographs have been collected since their first appearance. For more information consult Michael Ivankovich's *Collector's Guide to Wallace Nutting Pictures* (Collector Books, Paducah, KY, 1997).

	LOW	HIGH
Almost Ready, 9" x 12"	$60	$95
An Afternoon Tea, 13" x 16"	25	38
An Old Drawing Room, 12" x 16"	45	70
At the Fender, 16" x 20"	300	470
Auspicious Entrance, 13" x 16"	70	110
Autumn Grotto, 13" x 16"	145	225
Autumn Nook, 14" x 17"	125	200
Awaiting a Guest, 11" x 14"	150	240
Barre Brook, 11" x 14"	35	55
Barre Brook, 16" x 20"	100	160
Below the Arches, 10" x 12"	95	470
Berkshire Crossroad, 14" x 17"	215	340
Between Hill and Tree, 13" x 15"	85	130
Birch Brook, 13" x 16"	85	130
Birch Grove, 11" x 14"	40	60
Birch Strand, 13" x 16"	55	80
Bit of Paradise, 10" x 12"	150	240
Blooms at the Bend, 11" x 17"	135	215
Blossoms at the Bend, 13" x 15"	35	50
Blossom Valley, 8" x 14"	90	130
Bonnie Dale, 10" x 12"	45	70
Bonnie May, 16" x 20"	35	55
Brook and Blossoms, 14" x 17"	20	30
Call For More, 11" x 14"	175	275
Call of the Road, 11" x 14"	60	95
Canal Road, 12" x 16"	180	380
Champlain Shores, 13" x 15"	400	600
Cliff Corner, 11" x 14"	750	1175
Cluster of Zinnias, 13" x 16"	300	470
Coming Out of Rosa, 14" x 17"	90	130
Como Crest, 13" x 16"	850	1330
Concord Banks, 13" x 16"	65	100
Connecticut Blossoms, 10" x 16"	40	60
Cup That Cheers, 10" x 12"	90	130
Decked as a Bride, 16" x 20"	75	115
Dixie Creek, 14" x 17"	145	325
Durham, 14" x 17"	50	80
Early Foliage, 10" x 16"	75	120
Enticing Waters, 15" x 18"	55	85
Feminine Finery, 11" x 14"	15	25
Fine Effect, 13" x 17"	120	190
Floral Miniature, 4" x 5"	220	335
Foot Bridge and Ford, 13" x 16"	240	375
Friendly Reception, 11" x 14"	130	300
From the Mountain, 11" x 17"	130	200

	LOW	HIGH
Fruit Luncheon, 9" x 12"	170	265
Glance in Passing, 13" x 16"	150	240
Grafton Windings, 10" x 16"	40	60
Hanging Winter Herbs, 13" x 16"	280	440
Hawthorne Cottage, 12" x 20"	25	40
High Rollers, 13" x 16"	75	110
Hint of September, 15" x 22"	65	100
His First Letter, 10" x 16"	160	250
Hollyhock Cottage, 16" x 20"	40	60
Home Charm, 15" x 22"	140	220
Home Hearth, 10" x 16"	95	140
Homestead in Blossom Time, 10" x 20"	50	75
Honeymoon Drive, 10" x 12"	40	60
Honeymoon Stroll, 10" x 12"	75	110
Honeymoon Windings, 12" x 20"	15	25
Inside the Gate, 13" x 16"	190	300
In Tenderleaf, 12" x 20"	60	95
Into the West, 10" x 16"	40	60
La Jolla, 9" x 15"	125	300
Lake Brandt Birches, 13" x 16"	135	210
Lambs at Rest, 11" x 14"	170	260
Lane to Uncle Jonathan's, 10" x 17"	80	125
Langdon Door, 9" x 11"	135	210
Larkspur, 18" x 22"	150	235
Last Furrow, 13" x 16"	300	470
Lined with Petals, 14" x 17"	145	225
Litchfield Minster, 13" x 16"	170	260
Little Killarney Lake, 13" x 16"	175	275
Little River, 13" x 22"	30	85
Little River and Mt. Washington, 12" x 16"	100	190
Lost in Admiration, 12" x 15"	80	125
Maiden Reveries, 13" x 15"	115	180
Maine Coast Sky, 11" x 14"	180	280
Maple Sugar Cupboard, 12" x 16"	60	95
Mary's Little Lamb, 13" x 16"	210	325
Meandering Battenkill, 13" x 22"	45	70
Meeting of the Ways, 10" x 16"	125	200
Memories of Childhood, 12" x 16"	140	220
Mills at the Turn, 13" x 17"	200	310
Morning Duties, 10" x 12"	120	190
Mossy Stair, 16" x 20"	130	200
Nest, 13" x 16"	140	220
Nethercote, 8" x 10"	75	120
Newton October, 12" x 14"	35	55
New Vineyard House, Maine, 12" x 16"	260	400
Notch Mountain, 13" x 16"	95	150
Oak Palm Drive, 12" x 16"	350	550
October Array, 9" x 11"	55	85
October Splendors, 12" x 16"	60	95
Old Home, 12" x 20"	260	400
Old Village Street, 14" x 17"	275	430
Orchard Brook, 13" x 16"	70	110
Over the Wall, 13" x 15"	135	210
Palmetto Grace, 14" x 17"	400	625

Wallace Nutting Photograph.
—Photo courtesy Michael Ivankovich Auction Co., Inc.

	LOW	HIGH
Paradise Portal, 15" x 19"	375	585
Paradise Valley, 10" x 16"	115	180
Parlor Corner, 13" x 16"	300	470
Path of Roses, 10" x 12"	270	425
Patty's Favorite Walk, 10" x 12"	185	290
Peaceful Stretch, 10" x 16"	145	325
Petals Above and Below, 10" x 12"	55	85
Pilgrim Daughter, 14" x 16"	100	155
Pine Landing, 14" x 17"	75	115
Plymouth Curves, 14" x 17"	80	125
Porta Della Carta, 11" x 14"	275	430
Presidental Range, 7" x 9"	70	100
Purity and Grace, 13" x 16"	85	125
Quilting Party, 13" x 16"	80	125
Red Eagle Lake, 9" x 11"	95	150
Reeling the Yarn, 14" x 17"	130	200
River Meadow, 16" x 20"	120	190
Romance of the Evolution, 10" x 12"	150	240
Sewing by the Fire, 10" x 12"	115	170
Shadowy Orchard Curves, 11" x 14"	75	120
Shore Battle, 11" x 14"	135	200
Sip of Tea, 13" x 15"	135	200
Spanning the Glen, 10" x 12"	120	190
Spring in the Dell, 10" x 12"	85	125
Spring Pageant, 10" x 16"	75	115
Stamford Roadside, 10" x 12"	60	95
Stepping Stones at Bolten Abbey, 13" x 16"	575	900
Still Depths, 10" x 12"	125	195
Street Border, 12" x 16"	220	345
Swimming Pool, 16" x 20"	80	125
Tea For Two, 14" x 17"	130	200
Tea Maid, 13" x 15"	100	155
Three Chums, 10" x 12"	150	240
To the End Porch, 12" x 16"	290	450
Treasure Bag, 18" x 22"	180	380
Under the Pine, 11" x 17"	85	125
Waiting Bucket, 9" x 11"	115	180
Walk Under the Buttonwood, 14" x 17"	60	95
Walpole Road, 9" x 17"	95	150
Warm Spring Day, 12" x 16"	150	240

Nutting-Like Photos

	LOW	HIGH
Bicknell, J. C., Camp Vassar, 13" x 15"	$45	$70
Bicknell, J. C., Leafy Birches, 7" x 9"	30	50
Bicknell, J. C., View from Camp Vassar, 13" x 15"	55	85
Davidson, David, Berkshire Sunset, 12" x 15"	80	125
Davidson, David, Blossom Lane, 12" x 15"	35	55
Davidson, David, Brook's Mirror, 16" x 20"	95	150
Davidson, David, Christmas Day, 12" x 16"	160	250
Davidson, David, Easter Bonnet, 7" x 9"	50	80
Davidson, David, Elbow Pine, 9" x 16"	75	120
Davidson, David, Franconia Mirror, 7" x 9"	20	30
Davidson, David, Glory of Spring, 16" x 20"	35	55
Davidson, David, Golden Sunset, 13" x 16"	65	100
Davidson, David, Governor's Mansion, 13" x 16"	50	80
Davidson, David, Heart's Desire, 4" x 5"	30	45
Davidson, David, Her House in Order, 13" x 16"	75	120
Davidson, David, Homeward Bound, 4" x 6"	45	70
Davidson, David, Lamb's May Feast, 8" x 10"	130	200
Davidson, David, Maytime, 5" x 7"	25	40
Davidson, David, Merry Meeting River, 12" x 15"	55	85
Davidson, David, Neighbors, 14" x 16"	170	265
Davidson, David, Old Ironsides, 18" x 21"	35	55
Davidson, David, Old Mill, 10" x 16"	65	100
Davidson, David, Rosemary Club, 8" x 10"	40	60
Davidson, David, Silent Wave, 13" x 16"	35	55
Davidson, David, Snow Basin, 12" x 14"	140	210
Davidson, David, Spring Delights, 11" x 14"	45	70
Davidson, David, Tourist's Welcome, 13" x 16"	25	40
Davidson, David, Wisteria, 13" x 16"	85	130
Farini, In Her Boudoir, 10" x 16"	30	50
Garrison, J. M., Desert Verbenas & Primroses, 8" x 10"	35	55
Gibson, Mirrored Trees, 11" x 14"	10	20
Gibson, Mountain Road, 11" x 14"	20	30
Harris, A Usable Chasm, NY, 6" x 10"	25	40
Haynes, Untitled Waterfalls, 12" x 16"	20	30
Higgins, Charles, R., Apple Blossom Lane, 7" x 11"	25	40
Higgins, Charles, R., By the Fireside, 9" x 13"	90	140
Higgins, Charles, R., Lane, 9" x 12"	85	130
Higgins, Charles, R., November Sunset, 10" x 16"	10	20
Higgins, Charles, R., Untitled Old Man in Mountains, 10" x 13"	30	50
Higgins, Charles, R., Where Violets Grow, 7" x 12"	25	40
Higgins, Charles, R., Winding Stair, 7" x 14"	35	55
Hodges, Rough Pasture, 3" x 4"	40	60
Lamson, Lover's Lane, 4" x 5"	25	40
Lamson, Moonlight, 8" x 14"	40	60
Lamson, Pine Sentinel, 8" x 10"	30	50
Payne, George, S., Weekly Letter, 10" x 13"	25	40
Redden, Mildred, Perce Rache, Perce, Quebec, 12" x 15"	45	70
Sawyer, Charles, Afterglow, 7" x 9"	30	50
Sawyer, Charles, At the Bend of the Road, 4" x 5"	35	55
Sawyer, Charles, Autumnal Tapestry, 13" x 16"	70	110
Sawyer, Charles, Crystal Lake, 4" x 5"	65	100
Sawyer, Charles, Echo Lake, 10" x 13"	20	30

Charles Sawyer, "The Sea," $220 at auction. —Photo courtesy Michael Ivankovich Auction Co., Inc.

	LOW	HIGH
Sawyer, Charles, February Morning, 13" x 16"	200	310
Sawyer, Charles, Gosport Church, 4" x 5"	90	140
Sawyer, Charles, Joseph Lincoln's Garden, 16" x 20"	170	260
Sawyer, Charles, Kennebec at Madison, 12" x 20"	90	140
Sawyer, Charles, Lake Morey, 7" x 9"	30	50
Sawyer, Charles, Lake Willoughby, 4" x 5"	50	75
Sawyer, Charles, Majestic Nature, 7" x 9"	45	70
Sawyer, Charles, Meadow Stream, 12" x 20"	80	125
Sawyer, Charles, Mt. Washington and the Ammonoosic, 8" x 11"	60	95
Sawyer, Charles, Neptune's Headland, 5" x 7"	30	50
Sawyer, Charles, October Vista, 8" x 10"	60	95
Sawyer, Charles, Old Man of the Mountains, 5" x 7"	35	55
Sawyer, Charles, Rock Garden, Cape Cod, 16" x 20"	150	235
Sawyer, Charles, San Juan Capistrano Mission, 8" x 10"	60	95
Sawyer, Charles, Silver Birches, Lake George, 13" x 16"	50	75
Sawyer, Charles, Torrington Brook in May, 6" x 10"	50	75
Sawyer, Charles, Untitled California Mission, 16" x 20"	90	140
Sawyer, Charles, Winchester Bridge, 8" x 10"	210	325
Thompson, Florence, Difficult Lesson, 8" x 10"	60	95
Thompson, Florence, Ye Old Time Call, 7" x 9"	100	155
Thompson, Fred, Brook in Winter, 14" x 17"	190	300
Thompson, Fred, Calm of Fall, 9" x 14"	50	75
Thompson, Fred, Dancing Lesson, 10" x 12"	80	125
Thompson, Fred, Fireside Fancy Work, 16" x 20"	140	220
Thompson, Fred, Friendly Birches, 11" x 16"	35	55
Thompson, Fred, High and Dry, 7" x 9"	45	70
Thompson, Fred, Knitting for the Boys, 14" x 17"	160	250
Thompson, Fred, Maiden Reveries, 7" x 9"	30	50
Thompson, Fred, Nature's Carpet, 9" x 14"	50	75
Thompson, Fred, Old Toll Bridge, 10" x 16"	130	200
Thompson, Fred, Pasture Apple Blossoms, 7" x 9"	30	50
Thompson, Fred, Sunset on the Suwanee, 7" x 15"	45	70
Thompson, Fred, Toiler of the Sea, 13" x 16"	525	820
Thompson, Fred, Triple Seascape Grouping, 3" x 8"	110	170
Thompson, Fred, Whitehead, 11" x 16"	90	140
Tull, Sanford, Manchester Byway, 11" x 14"	25	40
Villar, Day Dreams, 11" x 14"	35	55
Villar, Puff or Two, 11" x 14"	75	120

Plates, Collector

Collector plates were introduced in 1895 with the issue of Bing and Grøndahl's Christmas plate. Despite much publicity about increasing values, selling a collection of plates may realize only pennies on the dollar. First and last issues within a series are generally valued higher than the other plates in the same series. As with all collectibles, buy what you love because you love it, not because it might increase in value. For more information consult Rinker Enterprises' *The Official Price Guide to Collector Plates, Seventh Edition* (House of Collectibles, NY, 1999).

The following entries are listed by company name, with series' titles indented. Original issue prices (Issue) are listed first, followed by current secondary market values for plates within that series. Issue prices have been rounded up to the nearest dollar.

	ISSUE	LOW	HIGH
American Artists			
Mares and Foals	$50	$40	$100
Noble Tribes	50	40	65
American Express Company			
American Trees of Christmas	60	40	50
Great Leaders of the World	38	20	30
American Rails & Highways			
Corvette	40	30	40
Train	33	20	30
Anna-Perenna			
Joyful Children	70	50	125
Romantic Love	95	50	95
Treasured Friends	85	60	80
Uncle Tad's Holiday Cats	75	50	70
Antique Trader			
Easter	11	5	10
Mother's Day	11	5	10
Thanksgiving	11	5	10
Armstrong's/Crown Parian			
Huggable Puppies	30	15	25
Infinite Love	25	10	20
Mischief Makers	40	20	35
Artaffects			
Adventures of Peter Pan	30	30	40
Becker Babies	30	30	45
Classic American Cars	35	15	30
Indian Bridal	25	10	20
Life of Jesus	27	10	20
Portraits of American Brides	30	20	75
Proud Young Spirits	30	20	55
Songs of Stephen Foster	60	60	70
Tribute	30	30	40
Artists of the World			
Children–Miniature	15	25	30
Floral Fiesta	40	20	40
Avondale			
Annual Christmas	90	50	90
Artistry of Almazetta Casey	70	50	70
Bayel of France			
Eagle	50	30	50
Flowers	50	30	50

	ISSUE	LOW	HIGH
Bing & Grøndahl			
American Christmas Heritage	48	25	45
Summer at Skagen	35	20	30
Boehm Studios			
Butterfly	450	200	400
Flower Series	450	450	490
Gamebirds of North America	63	40	60
Miniature Roses	40	40	45
Owl Collection	45	75	95
Tribute to Ballet	63	40	65
Water Birds	63	40	65
Bradford Exchange			
A Christmas Carol	30	20	30
A Garden of Little Jewels	35	25	35
Beary Merry Christmas	30	20	30
Bunny Tales	30	20	30
Charles Wysocki's Folktown	30	20	30
Cherubs of Innocence	30	20	30
Classic Melodies from *The Sound of Music*	30	20	30
Costuming of a Legend: Dressing *Gone With the Wind*	30	20	30
Dream of the Red Chamber	30	20	30
Escape to the Country	30	20	30
Friendship in Bloom	35	25	35
Gallant Men of the Civil War	30	20	30
Gone With the Wind: Portrait in Stained Glass	40	30	40
Heart of the Rockies	40	25	40
Heaven on Earth	30	20	30
Hideaway Lake	35	20	35
Hunters of the Spirit	30	20	30
Illusions of Nature	30	20	30
Keepsakes of the Heart	30	20	30

Armstrong's/Crown Parian
Huggable Puppies "Oh How Cute"

Artaffects
Proud Young Spirits "Protector of the Plains"

Photos courtesy Collectors News

	ISSUE	LOW	HIGH
Kindred Moments	.20	10	20
Kitten Expeditions	.30	20	30
Last Supper	.40	25	40
Light of the World	.30	20	30
Lincoln's Portraits of Valor	.30	20	30
Loving Hearts	.30	20	30
Masters of Land and Sky	.30	20	30
Mickey and Minnie Through the Years	.30	20	30
Mickey Mantle Collection	.40	20	40
Moments in the Garden	.30	20	30
Native Beauty	.30	20	30
Nesting Neighbors	.40	25	40
NFL 75th Anniversary All-Time Team	.35	25	35
Northwoods Spirit	.30	20	30
Panda Bear Hugs	.40	25	40
Picked from an English Garden	.33	20	30
Postcards from Thomas Kinkade	.35	25	35
Quiet Moments	.30	20	30
Radiant Messengers	.30	20	30
Royal Enchantments	.40	25	40
Signs of Spring	.30	20	30
Someone to Watch Over Me	.30	20	30
Soul Mates	.30	20	30
Sovereigns of the Wild	.30	20	30
Study of a Champion	.30	20	30
Thomas Kinkade's Guiding Lights	.30	20	30
Thomas Kinkade's Lamplight Village	.30	20	30
Thundering Waters	.35	20	35
Trail of the Whitetail	.35	20	35
Twilight Memories	.30	20	30
Under a Snowy Veil	.30	20	30

Bradford Exchange
Soul Mates "The Lovers"

Braymer Hall
Childhood Sonatas "Caprice"

Photos courtesy Collectors News

	ISSUE	LOW	HIGH
Untamed Spirits	30	20	30
Untamed Wilderness	30	20	30
Visions Beneath the Sea	30	20	30
Visit to Brambly Hedge	40	25	40
Winter Garlands	35	20	35
Wish You Were Here	30	20	30
Woodland Wings	35	20	35
World Beneath the Waves	30	20	30
Braymer Hall			
American Folk Art	25	10	20
Childhood Sonatas	29	15	25
Yesterday Dreams	50	30	45
Brindle Fine Arts			
Fantasy in Motion	75	50	70
Moods of the Orient	75	50	70
Calhoun's Collectors Society			
Creation	30	80	150
Four Seasons	50	20	45
Canadian Collector Plates			
Children of the Classics	78	50	70
Days of Innocence	78	50	70
Carson Mint			
Bear Feats	38	20	30
Big Top	29	15	25
Hollywood Squares	29	15	25
Littlest, The	30	15	25
Nature's Children	30	15	25
Old Fashioned Mother's Day	38	30	80
Cast Art Industries			
Dreamsicles Holiday Collection	30	20	30
Dreamsicles Sculpted Plates	37	20	35
Cavanagh Group International			
Coca-Cola American Life Heritage Collection	60	40	60
Coca-Cola Santa Claus Heritage Collection	60	40	60
Certified Rarities			
Indian Dancers	300	300	325
Postal Artists	60	40	50
Renaissance Masters	55	25	50
Christian Bell Porcelain			
American Steam	65	45	60
Canadian Pacific Last Spike Centennial (set of 2)	135	135	145
Men of the Rails	40	25	35
Count Agazzi			
Children's Hour	13	5	10
Easter	13	5	10
Creative World			
Living Dolls	50	25	45
Prize Collection	45	25	40
Crestley Collection			
Profiles of Bravery	20	10	20
Tribute to Roy Rogers	20	10	20
CUI–Carolina Collection–Dram Tree			
Coors Factory	30	20	30
First Encounter	30	20	30

	ISSUE	LOW	HIGH
D'Arceau Limoges			
Joséphine et Napoléon	30	15	25
Les Jeunes Filles des Saisons	105	100	125
Les Noels de France	29	20	50
Daum			
Famous Musicians	75	50	70
Four Seasons	150	100	125
Dave Grossman Creations			
Children of the Week	30	10	20
Magic People	65	30	50
Margaret Keane	25	20	40
Native American	45	25	45
Norman Rockwell Bas Relief II	65	30	50
Norman Rockwell Boy Scout	30	25	45
Norman Rockwell–Huckleberry Finn	40	20	35
Norman Rockwell–Tom Sawyer	26	35	40
Saturday Evening Post	25	10	20
Edwin M. Knowles			
American Journey	30	10	20
Garden Secrets	25	15	25
Home Sweet Home	40	20	30
Jessie Wilcox Smith's Not So Long Ago	25	5	15
Musical Moments from *The Wizard of Oz*	30	20	30
Notorious Disney Villains	30	20	30
Oklahoma!	20	5	15
Precious Little Ones	30	10	20
Songs of the American Spirit	30	20	65
South Pacific	25	5	15
The King and I	20	5	15
Thomas Kinkade's Enchanted Cottages	30	20	30
Tom Sawyer	28	15	20

Edwin M. Knowles
The King and I *"Shall We Dance?"*

Enesco
Happy Holidays Barbie, "1997"

Photos courtesy Collectors News

	ISSUE	LOW	HIGH
Enesco			
Barbie–Happy Holidays	30	20	30
Barbie–Hollywood Legends	35	25	35
Cherished Teddies–Easter	35	20	35
Cherished Teddies–Heaven Has Blessed This Day	10	5	10
Cherished Teddies–Mother's Day	35	20	35
Cherished Teddies–Spring Time	10	5	10
Little Bible Friends	40	20	30
Memories of Yesterday	50	35	50
Precious Moments Beauty of Christmas	50	35	50
Precious moments Christmas Collection	40	20	40
Precious Moments Inspired Thoughts	40	20	35
Precious Moments Mother's Day	50	30	50
Fairmont China			
Dreams Do Come True	30	15	25
Early Works	20	15	50
Jansen's International Beauties	55	30	40
Legend of the Gnomes	30	15	25
Ruthven Birds Feathered Friends	40	25	35
Vanishing Americana	14	5	10
Fenton Art Glass			
American Classic Series	75	50	70
Birds of Winter	40	25	35
Christmas at Home	45	25	35
Christmas Fantasy	45	25	35
Currier & Ives Limited Edition	25	10	20
Designer Series	65	40	60
Mary Gregory	65	40	60
Fine Arts Marketing			
Autumn Flights	55	25	40
Turn, Turn, Turn	50	25	40
Fleetwood Collection			
Royal Wedding	50	40	65
Tsarevich's Bride	50	50	60
Fountainhead			
Seasons	85	50	70
Twelve Days of Christmas	155	50	100
Franklin Mint			
Annual	280	280	300
Bicentennial	175	180	210
Birds	125	135	145
Butterflies of the World	240	250	275
Christmas–International	35	20	30
Game Birds of the World	55	25	45
Hometown Memories	29	10	20
Seven Seas	120	75	100
Tales of Enchantment	55	25	40
Woodland Year	55	25	40
Goebel/M. I. Hummel			
Berta Hummel Gift Collection	25	15	25
Brastoff Series	125	130	140
Native Companions	50	25	40
North American Wildlife	126	75	100
Winged Fantasies	50	25	40

	ISSUE	LOW	HIGH
Gorham			
Audubon American Wildlife Heritage	90	50	80
Cowboys	35	15	30
Four Seasons–A Helping Hand (set of 4)	100	60	80
Four Seasons–Going on Sixteen (set of 4)	75	80	100
Four Seasons–Grandpa and Me (set of 4)	60	70	90
Four Seasons–Life with Father (set of 4)	100	80	100
Four Seasons–Me and My Pal (set of 4)	70	50	70
Four Seasons–Old Buddies (set of 4)	115	80	100
Four Seasons–Old Timers (set of 4)	100	70	90
Four Seasons–Traveling Salesman (set of 4)	115	80	100
Four Seasons–Young Love (set of 4)	60	100	130
Gallery of Masters	50	30	45
Pastoral Symphony	43	40	50
Presidential Series	30	35	65
Hackett American			
Escalera's Father's Day	43	20	30
Famous Planes of Yesterday	40	20	30
Kelly's Stable	43	20	30
Landfalls	40	20	30
Little Friends	35	15	25
Ocean Stars	43	20	30
Parkhurst Annual Christmas	40	20	30
Special Moments	43	20	30
Summer Fun	40	20	30
World of Oz Franca	43	20	30
Hadley House			
Country Life	30	20	30
Country Spirit	30	20	30
Desperadoes	30	20	30
Heartland Collection	30	20	30

Hackett American
Ocean Stars "Sea Horse"

Hamilton Collection
Country Kitties "Rock and Rollers"

Photos courtesy Collectors News

	ISSUE	LOW	HIGH
Hunters Paradise	.65	50	65
Navajo Visions Suite	.50	25	40
Seasons	.30	20	30
Tranquility Suite	.50	35	50
Wildlife Memories	.65	40	60
Winner's Circle	.50	30	50
Hallmark Galleries			
Easter	.8	3	8
Family and Friends	.11	5	10
Innocent Wonders	.35	20	35
Majestic Wilderness	.35	20	30
Marjolein Bastin's Colors of Nature	.38	25	35
Hamilton Collection			
All in a Day's Work	.30	20	30
American Water Birds	.38	20	30
American Wilderness	.30	20	30
Beauty of Winter	.30	10	20
Bialosky and Friends	.30	20	30
Birds of the Temple Gardens	.30	15	25
Call of the North	.30	20	30
Cameo Kittens	.30	20	30
Child's Best Friend	.25	55	125
Child's Christmas	.30	20	30
Classic American Santas	.30	20	30
Classic Corvettes	.30	20	30
Cloak of Visions	.30	20	30
Comical Dalmatians	.30	20	30
Country Kitties	.25	25	45
Country Season of Horses	.30	20	40
Dale Earnhardt	.35	20	35
Daughters of the Sun	.30	20	30
Dolphin Discovery	.30	20	30
Dreamsicles Classics	.20	10	20
Dreamsicles Life's Little Blessings	.30	20	30
Dreamsicles Sculptural	.38	20	35
Dreamsicles Special Friends Sculptural	.38	20	35
Dreamsicles Sweethearts	.35	20	35
Easyriders	.30	20	30
Enchanted Seascapes	.30	20	30
Fairy Tales of Old Japan	.40	20	30
Familiar Spirits	.30	20	30
Fierce and the Free, The	.30	20	30
Flower Festivals of Japan	.45	30	40
Garden of Verses	.25	10	20
Gardens of the Orient	.20	5	15
Glory of the Game	.30	20	30
Golden Age of American Railroads	.30	45	90
Golden Discoveries	.30	20	30
Golden Puppy Portraits	.30	20	30
Greatest Show on Earth	.30	40	65
Growing Up Together	.30	25	35
I Love Lucy Plate Collection	.30	100	150
Japanese Blossoms of Autumn	.45	25	35
Knick Knack Kitty Cat Sculptural	.40	30	40

	ISSUE	LOW	HIGH
Legendary Warriors	30	20	30
Legend of Father Christmas	30	20	30
Little Fawns of the Forest	30	20	30
Little Ladies	30	50	100
Little Shopkeepers	30	20	45
Lore of the West	30	20	30
Love's Messengers	30	20	30
Magical World of Legends and Myths	35	20	35
Majestic Birds of Prey	55	50	65
Mickey Mantle	35	20	35
Mike Schmidt	30	20	30
Mixed Company	30	15	25
Murals from the Precious Moments Chapel	35	20	35
Nature's Majestic Cats	30	20	30
Nature's Nighttime Realm	30	20	30
Noble Owls of America	55	20	45
Nolan Ryan	30	20	30
North American Waterbirds	38	30	60
Passage to China	55	25	40
Portraits of Childhood	25	20	35
Portraits of Jesus	30	20	30
Precious Moments Bible Story	30	15	30
Precious Moments Classics	35	20	35
Precious Moments of Childhood	22	15	50
Precious Portraits	25	30	45
Princesses of the Plains	30	20	30
Proud Innocence	30	20	30
Quiet Moments of Childhood	30	20	45
Quilted Countryside: Mel Steele Signature Collection	30	20	45
Renaissance Angels	30	20	30
Rockwell Home of the Brave	35	35	75
Rockwell's *Saturday Evening Post* Baseball Plates	20	10	20
Romance of the Rails	30	20	30
Romantic Victorian Keepsake	35	20	35
Salute to Mickey Mantle	35	20	35
Scenes of an American Christmas	30	20	30
Sharing the Moments	35	20	35
Small Wonders of the Wild	30	20	60
Space, The Final Frontier	38	25	35
Sporting Generation	30	20	45
Stained Glass Gardens	55	30	50
Star Trek Generations	35	25	35
Star Trek: The Movies	35	25	35
Star Trek: The Next Generation, The Episodes	35	25	35
Star Trek: The Original Episodes	35	25	35
Star Trek: Voyager	35	25	35
Star Wars Trilogy	38	25	35
Story of Noah's Ark	45	25	40
Symphony of the Sea	30	20	30
Tale of Genji	45	20	40
Those Delightful Dalmatians	30	20	30
Treasured Days	25	30	70
Treasury of Cherished Teddies	30	20	30
Unbridled Mystery	30	20	30

	ISSUE	LOW	HIGH
Under the Sea	30	20	30
Utz Mother's Day	28	20	40
Victorian Playtime	30	20	60
Warrior's Pride	30	20	30
Winged Reflections	38	15	30
Winter Rails	30	20	30
Wizard of Oz Commemorative	25	75	100
Woodland Babies	30	20	30
World of Puppy Adventures	30	20	30
World of Zolan	30	20	75
Young Lords of the Wild	30	20	30
House of Global Art			
Blue-Button Trains Christmas	30	10	20
Christmas Morning in Dingle Dell	30	10	20
Dolly Dingle World Traveler	30	10	20
English Countryside Cats Collection	35	20	30
Hoyle Products			
Bygone Days	35	15	25
Western Series	35	15	25
Hutschenreuther			
Allegro Ensemble (set of 2)	120	120	140
Early Memories	73	40	60
Enchanted Seasons of a Unicorn	40	20	30
Love for All Seasons	125	50	100
Plate of the Month (set of 12)	324	200	300
Richard Wagner	125	50	100
Ruthven Songbirds	100	40	70
Songbirds of North America	60	30	40
Unicorns in Dreamer's Garden (set of 5)	198	100	160
Waterbabies	45	20	35
World of Legends (set of 4)	175	80	125

House of Global Art
Dolly Dingle World Traveler "Holland"

Hutschenreuther–Unicorns in Dreamer's Garden "The Smell of Roses"

Photos courtesy Collectors News

	ISSUE	LOW	HIGH
Incolay Studios			
Enchanted Moments	95	75	90
Life's Interludes	95	75	90
Judaic Heritage Society			
Great Jewish Women	35	15	25
Heritage	35	15	25
Kaiser			
America the Beautiful	50	25	40
American Cats	50	25	40
Bird Dogs	40	20	30
Classic Lullabies of the World	40	20	30
Dance, Ballerina, Dance	48	25	40
Forest Surprises	50	25	40
Four Seasons	50	25	40
Graduate	40	20	30
Happy Days	75	50	65
Little Clowns	35	20	30
Little Men	60	35	50
Stable Door Collection	30	10	20
Traditional Fairy Tales	40	20	30
Woodland Creatures	38	20	30
Kera			
Christmas	6	15	25
Moon	6	5	10
Mother's Day	6	5	10
Kern Collectibles			
Children of the Southwest	36	20	30
Horses of Harland Young	55	25	40
Kitty Cats	39	20	30
Leaders of Tomorrow	50	40	65
North American Game Birds	60	30	50
Zoological Garden	55	30	50

Kaiser–Classic Lullabies of the World, "Au Clair de la Lune"

Kern Collectibles Kitty Cats "Tattoo"

Photos courtesy Collectors News

	ISSUE	LOW	HIGH
Lance Corporation			
America's Sailing Ships	35	20	30
Mother's Day	43	35	40
Songbirds of the Four Seasons	35	20	30
'Twas the Night Before Christmas	48	30	40
Lenox			
America's Almanac	40	20	30
Arctic Wolves	30	20	30
Big Cats of the World	40	30	40
Birds of the Garden	40	30	40
Children of the Sun and Moon	40	30	40
Children's Hour	60	40	50
Christmas Trees Around the World	75	50	65
Darling Dalmatians	30	20	30
Eagle Conservation	40	30	40
Great Cats of the World	40	30	40
International Victorian Santas	40	30	40
King of the Plains	40	30	40
Magic of Christmas	40	30	40
Nature's Collage	35	20	30
Pieced Nativity	45	30	45
Lihs Linder			
Child's Christmas	40	20	30
Golden Spike Centennial	25	10	20
Lilliput Lane, Ltd.			
American Landmarks	35	20	30
Calendar Cottages of England	60	45	60
Coca-Cola Country Four Seasons	40	30	40
Limoges-Turgot			
Durand's Children	37	20	30
Quellier's Morals of Perrault	29	10	20
Lynell			
Children's Hour	25	10	20
Great Chiefs of Canada	65	30	50
Greatest Clowns of the Circus	39	20	30
Hobo Joe	50	30	40
Little House on the Prairie	45	20	30
Soap Box Derby	25	10	20
Special Celebrities	45	20	30
Michelon Enterprises			
Mistwood Designs	45	25	35
Quiet Places	75	40	65
Modern Masters			
Child's Best Friend	30	15	25
Floral Felines	55	25	40
Little Ladies	30	15	25
Through the Eyes of Love	55	25	40
Will Moses' America	45	25	40
Palisander			
Christmas	50	40	65
Presidential	50	20	40
Pemberton & Oakes			
Christmas–Miniature	17	10	15
Grandparent's Day	25	20	40

	ISSUE	LOW	HIGH
Little Girls	29	25	85
Moments Alone	29	25	45
Paintings by Donald Zolan	17	10	15
Times to Treasure, Bone China–Miniature	17	10	15
Pickard			
Children of Mary Cassatt	60	30	50
Gardens of Monet	85	50	75
Hawaiian Splendor	34	25	35
Holiday Traditions	29	20	30
Innocent Encounters	34	15	30
Legends of Camelot	63	30	50
Let's Pretend	80	50	70
Most Beautiful Women of All Time	75	50	65
Presidential	35	15	25
Sanchez Miniatures	50	25	40
Porcelaine Ariel			
Tribute to Love–The Rubaiyat of Omar Khayyam	45	25	35
Waltzes of Johann Strauss	25	10	20
Porterfield's			
Membership–Rob Anders Collectors' Society	19	10	20
Moments of Wonder–Miniature	17	5	15
Treasures of the Heart–Miniature	17	5	15
Ram			
Boston 500	30	15	25
Great Bird Heroes	8	3	5
Reco International			
Alan Maley's Past Impressions	35	20	30
Amish Traditions	30	20	30
Birds of the Hidden Forest	30	20	30
Castles and Dreams	30	20	30
Children's Garden	30	20	30

Pickard
Let's Pretend "Cleopatra"

Photo courtesy Collectors News

Reco International
Imaginary Gardens "Cowslip"

Photos courtesy Reco International

	ISSUE	LOW	HIGH
Christmas Series	.35	20	30
Christmas Wishes	.30	20	30
Days Gone By	.30	20	50
Everlasting Friends	.30	20	30
Flower Fairy Plate Collection	.30	15	25
Four Seasons	.50	50	75
Friends for Keeps	.30	20	30
Gardens of Beauty	.30	15	25
Gardens of Innocence	.33	20	30
Glory of Christ	.30	20	30
Guardians of the Kingdom	.35	15	25
Guiding Lights	.30	20	30
Imaginary Gardens	.30	20	30
In the Eye of the Storm	.30	15	25
Kittens 'n Hats	.35	25	35
Land of Our Dreams	.35	15	25
Life's Little Celebrations	.30	20	30
Little Angel Plate Collection	.30	20	30
Memories of Yesterday	.30	20	30
Moments at Home	.30	20	30
Mother's Day	.30	20	40
Noble and Free	.30	20	30
On Wings of Eagles	.30	20	30
Oscar and Bertie's Edwardian Holiday	.30	10	20
Our Cherished Seas	.38	20	30
Out of the Wild	.30	20	30
Precious Angels	.30	20	30
Premier Collection I	.95	85	125
Sandra Kuck's Mother's Day	.35	25	35
Sculpted Heirlooms	.30	20	30
Sophisticated Ladies	.30	20	30
Town and Country Dogs	.35	20	35
Trains of the Orient Express	.30	20	30
Up, Up and Away	.30	20	30
Victorian Christmas	.35	25	35
Victorian Mother's Day	.35	45	50
Wonder of Christmas	.30	20	30
Reed and Barton			
Annual	.65	30	50
Currier & Ives	.85	50	70
Founding Fathers	.65	30	50
'Twas the Night Before Christmas	.75	50	70
Ridgewood			
Little Women	.45	50	75
Tom Sawyer	.10	5	10
Wild West	.17	5	15
River Shore			
America at Work	.30	10	20
Famous American Songbirds	.20	5	15
Lovable Teddies	.22	5	15
Rockwell Good Old Days	.25	5	15
R. J. Ernst Enterprises			
Busy Bears	.20	5	15
Classy Cars	.225	30	40

	ISSUE	LOW	HIGH
Commemoratives	.40	65	145
Country Cousins	.25	10	20
Elvira	.30	25	45
Fogg and Steam	.40	25	35
Fondest Memories	.60	25	50
Little Misses Young and Fair	.60	25	50
Love Story	.25	10	20
Me and Mom	.30	15	25
Mommy and Me	.35	20	30
My Fair Ladies	.50	25	40
Narrow Gauge	.30	15	25
So Young, So Sweet	.40	20	30
Turn of the Century	.35	15	25
Rockwell Museum			
Classic Plate	.25	5	15
Elvis Presley Collection	.15	5	10
James Dean Collection	.15	5	10
Touch of Rockwell	.15	5	10
World of Children Bas-Relief	.45	20	30
Rockwell Society			
Rockwell Commemorative Stamps	.30	20	30
Rockwell on Tour	.16	10	30
Roman, Inc.			
Cats	.30	10	20
Frances Hook Collection	.25	25	75
Lord's Prayer	.25	10	20
Magic of Childhood	.25	10	20
Millennium Series, Oxolyte	.50	35	50
Precious Children	.30	20	30
Promise of a Savior	.30	20	30

R. J. Ernst
Elvira "Night Rose"

Royal Doulton
Festival Children of the World "Mariani"

Photos courtesy Collectors News

	ISSUE	LOW	HIGH
Richard Judson Zolan Collection	.30	20	30
Seraphim Classics Faro Collection	.65	45	65
Seraphim Classics Sculpted Oval Plate	.50	35	50
Visions of Our Lady	.30	20	30
Royal Copenhagen			
National Parks of America	.75	40	60
Nature's Children	.40	20	30
Royal Cornwall			
Classic Collection	.55	50	65
Courageous Few	.60	30	50
Exotic Birds of Tropique	.50	25	40
Golden Age of Cinema	.45	20	30
Golden Plates of the Noble Flower Maidens	.65	30	50
Impressions of Yesteryear	.60	30	50
Kitten's World	.45	40	80
Legend of the Peacock Maidens	.70	40	60
Little People	.35	20	30
Love's Precious Moments	.55	30	40
Most Precious Gifts of Shen Lung	.49	20	30
Promised Land	.45	20	30
Remarkable World of Charles Dickens	.60	30	50
Treasures of Childhood	.45	20	35
Two Thousand Years of Ships	.40	20	30
Royal Doulton			
Childhood Christmas	.40	20	30
Children of the Pueblo	.60	70	100
Christmas Plates	.45	30	45
Festival Children of the World	.65	30	50
Royal Orleans			
Elvis in Concert	.35	15	25
Marilyn–An American Classic	.35	20	30
Pink Panther Christmas Collection	.19	5	15
Schmid–Germany			
Ferràndiz Beautiful Bounty	.40	15	30
Ferràndiz Music Makers	.25	10	20
Schmid Pewter Christmas Plates	.50	20	35
Schmid–Japan			
Disney Four Seasons of Love	.18	5	15
Disney Valentine's Day	.18	5	15
Nature's Treasures	.45	25	40
Paddington Bear Musician's Dream	.18	10	25
Peanuts World's Greatest Athlete	.18	15	25
Seeley's Ceramic Service			
Antique French Doll Collection	.39	35	200
Old Baby Doll Collection	.43	20	30
Old German Dolls	.39	15	30
Southern Living Gallery			
Game Birds of the South	.40	20	30
Songbirds of the South	.40	20	30
Southern Forest Families	.40	20	30
Wildflowers of the South	.40	20	30
Spode			
American Songbirds (set of 12)	.350	400	765
Maritime	.150	70	120

	ISSUE	LOW	HIGH
Stratford Collection			
Famous Clowns	35	20	30
Young Wildlife	35	20	30
United States Bicentennial Society			
American Revolutionary Patriots	25	10	20
Christmas Carol	55	50	65
Great American Sailing Ships	135	130	150
Two Hundred Years of Flight	49	20	35
Vague Shadows			
Chieftains II	70	80	150
Indian Nations	35	50	85
Legends of the West	65	30	50
Masterpieces of Impressionism	35	45	60
Thoroughbreds	50	150	300
War Ponies	60	110	135
Val St. Lambert			
American Heritage	200	225	450
Annual Old Masters	50	70	90
Veneto Flair			
American Landscape	75	30	60
Christmas	55	20	40
Easter	50	50	90
Godesses	75	75	125
Mosaic	50	50	75
Viletta China			
Alice in Wonderland	25	10	20
Carefree Days	25	10	20
Christmas Annual	50	20	40
Nutcracker Ballet	20	15	40
Portraits of Childhood	25	5	15
Precious Moments	22	30	50
Women of the West	40	15	25
Western Authentics			
Guns at Sea	40	15	30
Tunes of Glory	43	15	30
Wild Wings			
Broken Silence	50	35	50
Dog Plates	50	35	50
Winston Roland			
Big Wheels Keep On Rolling	59	25	40
Canada Geese	45	25	40
Children and Pets	40	30	40
Cottage Wildlife C. W. F. Plate	45	35	45
Country Memories	27	15	25
Dodd's Annual	49	40	50
Eagles Across America	30	20	30
Extraordinary Landscapes	39	20	30
God Bless America	27	15	25
Golden Age of Flight	45	35	45
Hockey in Canada	34	15	25
Looking Back	30	20	30
Look to the Rainbow	43	25	40
Man's Best Friend	35	25	35
More Deere Memories	59	40	55

	ISSUE	LOW	HIGH
Nature's Majesty	47	30	40
Old Duffer Collection	47	30	40
Outside My Window	45	20	30
Remember When	43	20	30
Sawatsky's Steam	52	25	40
Shirley Temple Signature Series	33	20	30
The Way We Were	49	30	40
Wild and Free	39	20	30
World of Dolls	39	20	30
W. S. George			
Along an English Lane	30	20	30
Christmas Story	30	25	40
Enchanted Garden	25	15	25
Faces of Nature	30	25	45
Feline Fancy	35	20	35
Floral Fancies	35	25	35
Hometown Memories	30	20	30
Petal Pals	25	15	25
'Tis the Season	30	20	30
Touching the Spirit	30	20	30
Wild Innocents	30	20	30
Wings of Winter	30	25	40
Winter's Majesty	35	15	35
Wonders of the Sea	35	20	30
Zanobia			
African Violet Miniatures	30	15	25
Violet Portraits	35	15	25
Zolan Fine Arts/Winston Roland			
Angel Songs–Miniature	20	10	20
Country Friends	20	10	20
Symphony of Seasons	20	10	20

Viletta China
Portraits of Childhood "Friends Forever"

Photo courtesy Collectors News

Zolan Fine Arts/Winston Roland
Angel Songs–Miniature "Harp Song

Photo courtesy © Zolan Fine Arts, Ltd.

Political Memorabilia

Every political campaign from dog catcher to president produces memorabilia. In addition to the familiar campaign buttons, there is literature of all types, including posters, pictures, brochures and newpaper ads. Such variety and the number of candidates over the years create a rich and broad collecting field. Political memorabilia offers a history lesson, a chance to discover the movers and shakers of other eras. Most collectors concentrate on national elections and well-known politicians. There are others that focus on third party and more obscure candidates. Although some items are worth thousands of dollars, this collecting field offers items for every budget.

Buttons are a favorite area of specialization for many collectors. There are several types of buttons. Celluloid buttons are produced by placing a thin piece of paper over a metal disc and then sealing it with a coating of celluloid. Tin lithograph buttons are produced by printing directly onto the tin. A curious term to novices is "jugates," which are buttons picturing both the presidential and vice-presidential candidates.

For more information consult *Hake's Guide to Presidential Campaign Collectibles* by Ted Hake (Wallace-Homestead, Radnor, PA, 1992).

Assorted Memorabilia

	LOW	HIGH
Abzug, Bella, poster, cardboard, center sepia photo on white ground, "She's Done A Lot...She'll Do More," "Democrat/Liberal for Congress/Special Election, Tues., Feb. 14," 1984, 23" x 28"	$25	$50
Bryan, William, poster, "Hon. Wm. J. Bryan For President," stiff paper, full color, J. Hoover, Philadelphia, c1896, 16" x 19.5"	50	75
Cleveland, Grover, pin, diecut aluminum, figural 4-leaf clover, "Our Four Leaf Clover" in raised lettering on each petal, "Grover" on bottom segment designed like ribbon	50	75
Cleveland, Grover, tobacco tag, silvered tin frame, paper image, 1884	75	100
Cleveland/Hendricks, jugate ribbon, silk, black and white, sepia cardboard photos on shield design, 1884, 2.5" x 5.5"	100	200
Democratic National Convention, book, full page black and white photos including FDR and Henry Wallace, 184 pages, 1940, 9.5" x 13"	25	50
Democratic National Convention, watch fob, brass, raised lettering "Young Democratic Clubs of America/First National Convention Kansas City 1933"	15	25
Goldwater, Barry M., matchbook, "Goldwater in '64," black and white photo w/ red, white, and blue design on front, red and white text on blue ground on back, unused	10	15
Goldwater/Miller, license plate, plastic, yellow and blue, 1964	25	50
Hoover/Curtis, pin, figural elephant, diecut brass, red enamel lettering	15	25
Kennedy, John F., playing cards, "Kennedy Kards," complete set, boxed, ©1963 Humor House, Inc.	25	50
Kennedy, John F., ticket, Democratic nomination acceptance speech, Los Angeles, Jul. 15, 1960, "Distinguished Guest" stub, red, white, and blue, 1.75" x 7"	50	75
Landon, Alfred M., feather, "Win w/ Landon," rust-colored, yellow print, ©1935 Sport Feather, Inc., N.Y.C., 5.5" l	15	25
McKinley, William, mug, pressed glass, clear, 2 panels of same raised design and raised image of McKinley, inscribed "Protection and Prosperity/Maj. Wm. McKinley," 1896, 3.5" h	50	75
McKinley/Roosevelt, plate, milk glass, purple rim, black and white center McKinley and Roosevelt illustration, c1900, 5.25" d	50	75

	LOW	HIGH
Nixon, Richard M., ashtray, white ceramic, full color center photo of Richard and Pat Nixon, 5.5" sq.	15	25
Nixon, Richard M., poster, cardboard, black and white photo w/ "This Time Nixon," 1968, 13" x 19"	50	75
Nixon/Agnew, flicker, full color Nixon illustration, alternating bluetone photo Agnew image on blue ground	15	25
Nixon/Kennedy, magazine, *Jet,* 68 pages, Nov. 10, 1960	25	50
Reagan, Ronald, mug, ceramic, white, browntone cowboy on rearing horse illustration on 1 side, other side w/ small emblem w/ crown on top, "White House Barbeque/September 23, 1981," 4.25" h, 3.75" d	50	75
Republican National Convention, ticket, paper, Chicago, Jun. 18, 1912	25	50
Rockefeller, Nelson, bank, tin, "Rockefeller For Governor," red lettering on white ground w/ bluetone photo on 1 side, other side w/ red and blue lettering on white ground, 2.25" d	15	25
Roosevelt, Franklin D, banner, fabric, red, white, and blue, attached wooden dowel w/ gold tips	15	25
Roosevelt, Franklin D., bust, hollow white metal, dark bronze finish, first inauguration issue, base inscribed "Franklin D. Roosevelt/1933, 4" h	25	50
Roosevelt, Franklin, D., sheet music, *On With Roosevelt,* black and white FDR portrait, 4 pages, 9" x 12"	15	25
Stevenson, Adlai, ballpoint pen, plastic, shades of green, black text "Compliments of Adlai Stevenson Estes Kefauver," 1956	25	50
Stevenson, Adlai, button, red and white striped fabric, center narrow brass luster circular frame holding sheet of celluloid over black and white photo, reverse silver luster metal with shank, c1952	50	75

Political Pinback Buttons and Watch Fobs. —Photo courtesy Gene Harris Antique Auction Center, Inc.

	LOW	HIGH
Stevenson, Adlai, shoe button, "Vote Adlai," dark red on white depicting shoe sole with hole	.50	75
Taft/Sherman, postcard, oval, black and white photos of Taft and Sherman surrounded by raised flag images and gold Statue of Liberty, "Our Choice," unused, 1908, 1.5" d	.15	25
Taft/Sherman, tip tray, tin, listing Republican presidential candidates from 1856 to 1908, gold and black rim, 4" d	.75	100
Truman, Harry S., election ballot, cardboard, 2-sided, red, white, and blue, bluetone photo at top right-hand corner, Nov. 2, 1948, 2.5" x 7.5"	.100	200
Watergate, paperweight, clear glass, center red, white and blue "Watergate Circus" emblem, dated 1973, 3.5" x 4.5" x .5"	.50	75
Wilson/Marshall, campaign ribbon, red, white, and blue, inscribed "Democratic Ticket" above and below crossed flags, c1912-16, 3" x 6"	.50	75

Pinback Buttons

Agnew, Spiro, black and white Agnew photo in foreground of crowd of people, c1972	.$15	$25
Carter/Mondale, black and white photos in red, white, and blue shield, "Carter/Mondale/Democratic 1976," Trimble Co., 1.25" d	.15	25
Clinton/Gore, full color illustration on white ground, blue and red lettering, "Clinton/Gore '92"	.10	15
Coolidge, Calvin, litho tin, yellow lettering on brown ground, .3125" d	.25	50
Dewey/Bricker, jugate, litho tin, bluetone photos on white ground, white on red top and bottom accents, .8125" d	.25	50
Eisenhower/Nixon, litho tin, state of Texas in white on dark red ground, blue lettering "I'm For Eisenhower and Nixon"	.10	15
Ford, Gerald R., cartoon Republican elephant crushing peanut shell	.15	25
Humphrey/Muskie, jugate, black and white photos on white star on red ground, tiny images of 2 donkeys and date "1968"	.10	15
Landon/Knox, jugate, brown and white photo illustration in bright yellow circles, yellow elephant and sunflower accents on brown ground	.15	25
McGovern/Shriver, bluetone photos on red stripe, white ground, red lettering	.5	10
Nixon/Agnew, jugate, black and white photos against red, white, and blue eagle and shield design, on white ground, 1972	.15	25
Reagan, Ronald, black and white photo against flowing flag w/ small image of White House below	.10	15
Republican National Convention, red, white, and blue, black and white caricature of elephant wearing top hat and striped pants and holding cane, "Republican National Convention Detroit 1980"	.10	15
Roosevelt/Wallace, celluloid, jugate, brown and white photos against brown ground, red, white, and blue rim, attached red, white, and blue fabric ribbon, 1940	.15	25
Smith, Alfred E., black and white, "For President Alfred E. Smith"	.25	50
Stevenson, Adlai, litho tin, red and white, bluetone photos, "All the Way w/ Adlai"	.15	25
Truman Harry S., blue on white, inauguration date and "I'm Just Wild About Harry" accented by musical notes, 2.125" d	.400	700
Truman/Barkley, jugate, browntone photos in ovals on cream ground, red, white, and blue accents, 1.25" d	.200	400
Willkie/McNary, jugate, litho tin, red, white, and blue, bluetone photos, "The American Way of Life," 1" d	.100	200
Wilson, Woodrow, black and cream, W & H backpaper, 2.0625" d	.100	200

Pottery & Porcelain: Manufacturers

For more information on pottery and porcelain manufacturers, consult *Lehner's Encyclopedia of U.S. Marks on Pottery, Porcelain & Clay* by Lois Lehner (Collector Books, Paducah, KY, 1988).

Bauer Pottery

The J.A. Bauer Company began producing clay flowerpots in 1909. After the introduction of stoneware and art pottery, the company added colored dinnerware in 1930, which it produced until 1962. See *Collector's Encyclopedia of Bauer Pottery* by Jack Chipman (Collector Books, Paducah, KY, 1998) for additional information.

Marks: an impressed mark with *Bauer* or a combination of the words *Bauer, Los Angeles, Pottery* and *USA*. Many items are unmarked or simply stamped *Made in USA*.

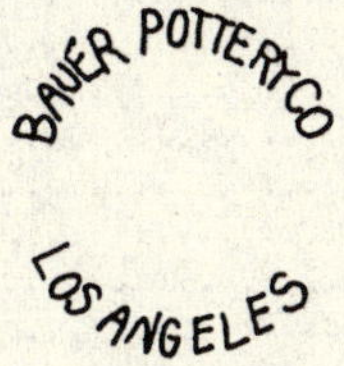

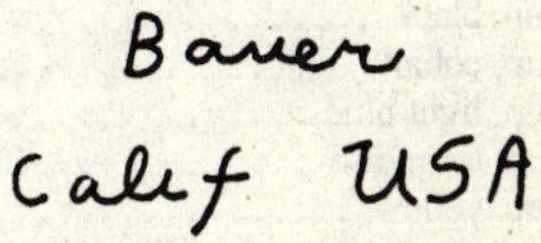

Monterey (1936-1945)

Orange-red and burgundy are the most desirable of the ten colors.

	LOW	HIGH
Berry Bowl, burgundy	$15	$25
Berry Bowl, orange-red	15	25
Beverage Server, covered, orange-red	90	160
Bread and Butter Plate, blue	7	12
Chop Plate, orange-red	35	65
Chop Plate, yellow	30	50
Coffee Server, wood handle, 8 cup, orange-red	30	50
Creamer, midget, orange-red	24	35
Creamer, midget, yellow	24	35
Dinner Plate, yellow	24	35
Fruit Bowl, footed, yellow, 13" dia	45	75
Gravy Boat, yellow	30	50
Luncheon Plate, turquoise	12	18
Platter, oval, large, yellow	32	60
Salad Plate, white	15	25
Shaker, orange-red	12	25
Soup Plate, blue	24	35
Sugar, midget, orange-red	30	50
Sugar, midget, yellow	30	50
Teapot, covered, 6 cup, yellow	60	100
Tumbler, 8 oz, orange-red	15	25
Vegetable, divided, blue	32	60
Vegetable, oval	30	45

Ring (c. 1931)

Ring is Bauer's most popular pattern. It is reputedly the line that influenced Homer Laughlin to create Fiesta. The pattern appears in many colors. Black pieces are worth more than the values quoted below.

	LOW	HIGH
Baking Dish, covered, black	$40	$60
Batter Bowl, orange-red	80	160
Bread and Butter Plate, yellow	10	20
Butter Dish, orange-red	120	180
Candlesticks, spool, cobalt, price for pair	225	375
Casserole, individual, orange-red	55	85
Casserole, metal holder, yellow	45	75
Cereal Bowl, orange-red	15	25
Cereal Bowl, turquoise	15	25
Chop Plate, orange-red, 17" dia	150	250
Chop Plate, turquoise, 12" dia	45	75
Coffee Cup, black	75	115
Coffee Cup, cobalt	25	45
Coffee Cup, light blue	20	30
Coffee Cup, turquoise	20	30
Coffee Cup, yellow	20	30
Coffeepot, 8 cup	120	200
Coffee Server, raffia-wrapped metal handle, orange-red	65	110
Creamer, orange-red	30	60
Custard Cup, orange-red	8	15
Dinner Plate, turquoise	24	38
Dinner Plate, white	20	30
Dinner Plate, yellow	60	90
Egg Cup, turquoise	60	100
Fruit Dish, green	25	40
Fruit Dish, orange-red	25	40
Fruit Dish, white	15	25
Fruit Dish, yellow	20	30
Mixing Bowl, #12, green	45	75
Mixing Bowl, #18, yellow	40	65
Mixing Bowl, #24, cobalt	35	60
Mixing Bowl, #36, ivory	45	75
Mixing Bowl, #36, orange-red	40	65
Mustard, orange-red	75	125
Pitcher, ball form, turquoise	60	90
Pitcher, ice lip, metal handle, 2 qt	70	110
Saucer, turquoise	3	8
Shaker, low, orange-red	12	25
Shaker, low, turquoise	10	20
Shaker, low, yellow	10	20
Soup Bowl, burgundy	25	35
Sugar Bowl, yellow	45	75
Teapot, wooden handle, 6 cup, yellow	45	75

Bennington Pottery

The period of true Bennington was brief, from 1842 to 1858, but this is deceiving since the output during those sixteen years was heavy. In 1842 Julius Norton (a grandson of the founder) went into partnership with Christopher Fenton. Norton and Fenton set out to duplicate the surface of Rockingham wares. From the original name of "Norton and Fenton," it became "Fenton's Works," then "Lyman, Fenton and Co." Finally, the company used the name "United States Pottery" from 1850 until its collapse in 1858.

The earliest mark of Norton and Fenton, in 1842, was a circular wording of *NORTON & FENTON, BENNINGTON, Vt.* Block lettering was used without any symbol. When the company name changed, after Norton left in 1847, the mark became *FENTON'S WORKS, BENNINGTON, VERMONT* enclosed in a rectangular decorative border. This distinctive mark was set in two styles of lettering with *FENTON'S WORKS* in slanting characters resembling italics. The address was set in standard vertical lettering. The next mark, that of Lyman, Fenton and Co., sat within a plain oval frame and read *LYMAN FENTON & CO., FENTON'S ENAMEL, PATENTED 1849, BENNINGTON, Vt.* This ushered in the era of colored glazes. Within this mark, the year (1849) is prominently displayed. The United States Pottery Co. era introduced two different marks, both reading *UNITED STATES POTTERY Co., BENNINGTON, VT.* One carries the wording in an oval frame with two small ornamental flourishes; the other is a modified diamond shape composed of decorative printer's type, but without further ornamentation.

The objects listed below are all decorated with a flint enamel "Rockingham" glaze.

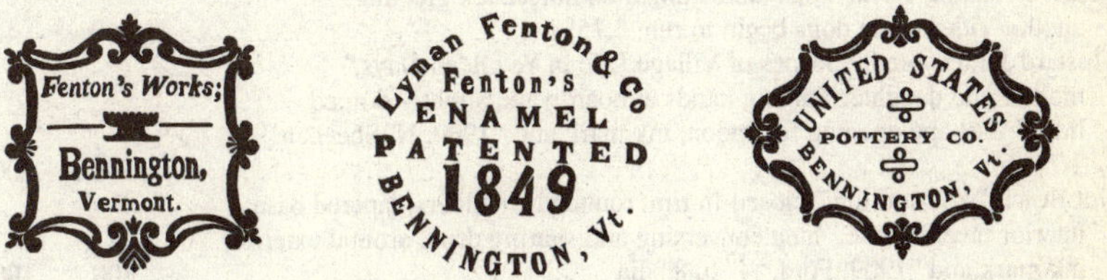

	LOW	HIGH
Bank, 2-story brick house w/ chimneys, 4.75" h	$150	$250
Book Flask, "Battle of Bennington," 6" h	400	600
Book Flask, "Departed Spirits," 5.625" h	500	700
Book Flask, "The Wonders of the Earth," blue flecks, 6.75" h	400	600
Canister, cylindrical, alternate rib pattern, impressed "1849" mark, 9.25" h	300	500
Chamber Pot, covered, molded diamond patterns, 10" dia	350	450
Coachman Bottle, impressed "1849" mark, 10.625" h	300	500
Cuspidor, paneled, impressed "1849" mark, 9" dia	100	250
Flask, molded eagle and morning glory, 7.125" h	200	400
Foot Bath, large lobed oval vessel w/ 2 handles, impressed oval mark, 8.75" h, 19.5" l, 14.5" w	3000	4000
Pie Plate, yellow flecks, impressed "1849" mark, 11.875" dia	800	1200
Pitcher, 8-panel, molded tulips and hearts, 7" h	500	700
Pitcher, alternate rib pattern, "1849" mark, 10" h	800	1200
Pitcher, molded hanging game, hound handle, 9.625" h	200	400
Soap Dish, rectangular, alternate rib pattern, domed lid w/ loop handle, strainer insert, impressed mark, 4.75" h, 5.5" l, 4.5" w	400	600
Toby Snuff Jar, "1849" mark, 4.25" h	200	400
Tulip Vase, 10" h	200	400
Violin Flask, molded flower, 7" h	100	200
Wash Bowl, molded diamond patterns, 4.5" h, 13" dia	300	500

Buffalo Pottery

Buffalo Pottery Company was established in 1901 by the Larkin Soap Company for the purpose of producing mail order premiums. Early production consisted mainly of semi-vitreous dinnerware. The company's most famous line, Deldare Ware, was produced from 1908 to 1909 and from 1921 to 1923. Emerald Deldare, which used scenes from Goldsmith's *The Three Tours of Dr. Syntax,* was made in 1911.

For more information see *The Book of Buffalo Pottery* by Violet and Seymour Altman (Schiffer, West Chester, PA, 1987).

Deldare Ware

	LOW	HIGH
Bowl, "The Fallowfield Hunt–The Death," hunter and dogs celebrating at end of hunt, still fox in background w/ birds circling above, ink mark and "1909, L. Streissel," 3.75" h, 9" dia	$500	$700
Candlesticks, "Village Scene," 6-sided pedestals and bases, 3 men engrossed in conversation, village house in background, 1 signed "D. Shuster," 9" h, price for pair	1000	1200
Card Tray, "The Fallowfield Hunt," rounded handles, feasting scene, ink mark and "1909, C. Dowlman," 8" dia	300	500
Mug, "Breaking Cover," man and woman on horseback greeting another rider while dogs begin to run, 3.75" h	300	400
Mustard Jar, covered, "Scenes of Village Life in Ye Olden Days," mother and daughter holding hands at boardwalk, slightly domed lid w/ U-shape opening for spoon, ink mark and "1909, N. Sheehan," 3.75" h	1500	2000
Nut Bowl, "Ye Lion Inn," closed-in rim, rounded shoulders, tapered base, interior tavern scene, men conversing and sharing drink around exterior, ink mark and "1909, Ford," 4" h, 8" dia	800	1000
Pitcher, "The Fallowfield Hunt–Breaking Cover," paneled form, riders greeting one another w/ pack of dogs in forefront, ink mark and "1908, E. Vanhorn," 9" h	700	900
Plate, "Ye Village Gossips," 3 men gossiping outside along boardwalk, ink mark and "1909, W. Fozter," 10.125" dia	150	200
Teapot, "Scenes of Village Life in Ye Olden Days," paneled form, embossed spout, mother and daughter holding hands while strolling along boardwalk, gentlemen conversing on back, ink mark and "1925, CB," 4.75" h	400	500
Tray, "Heirlooms," rectangular, ladies at table admiring jewelry, ink mark and "1908, L. Streissel," 13.5" l	600	800

Deldare ware. —Photo courtesy Smith & Jones, Inc. Auctions.

Emerald Deldare

	LOW	HIGH
Candlestick, hexagonal, emerald berry and vine design cascading along shaft in repeat, butterfly and floral design in repeat around base, ink mark and "1911, M. Broel," 9" h, 5" dia	$200	$400
Fruit Bowl, "Dr. Syntax Reading His Tour," interior center scene of Syntax boring his companions by reading aloud his never-ending tour, encircled by band of emerald butterflies, wide emerald band of flowers, butterflies, and geometric designs on exterior, ink mark and "1911, M. Ramlus," 9.5" dia	800	1000
Pin Tray, "Dr. Syntax Received By The Maid Instead of The Mistress," rectangular, Syntax apologizing to mistress while maid peeks out from drapery, floral and geometric border, ink mark and "1911, J. Rowley," 6.5" l	500	700
Plate, "Doctor Syntax Making A Discovery," Syntax stumbling upon affectionate Patrick making advances towards Susan, broad floral and geometric diamond border, ink mark and "1911, J. Gerhardt," 10" d	800	1000
Salt and Pepper, pair, rounded top, tapered body, micro-diamond design at top, butterfly band around neck, white flowers in repeat surrounded by stripes and geometric designs around body, signed "JG HB," 3" h	1000	1200
Tankard, "To Becky's Hand He Gave a Squeeze," wine cellar w/ large wooden barrels and stone archways in repeat, smiling Syntax squeezing hand of disinterested waitress, paunchy gentlemen dipping into spirits on back, ink mark and "1911, E. Dowlman," 12.25" h	1200	1800
Toothpick Holder, cylindrical, stylized fuschia flower drooping along base in repeat, narrow butterfly band around rim, ink mark and "1911, F. Missel," 2.25" h	1000	1500
Wall Plaque, "Dr. Syntax Sells Grizzle," Syntax trying to sell horse while gentlemen buyers ponder its condition, geometric emerald border ink mark and "1911, M. Gerhardt," 13.75" dia	1200	1500
Wall Plaque, "The Landing," large broad-winged pelican landing on grassy shore, mallards swimming in water in background, emerald and pale yellow geometric border, ink mark and "1911, 7," 12" dia	3000	4000

Emerald Deldare, left to right: Wall Plaque, "Dr. Syntax Sells Grizzle"; Tankard, "To Becky's Hand He Gave A Squeeze"; Wall Plaque, "The Landing." —Photos courtesy Smith & Jones, Inc. Auctions.

Miscellaneous

Chamberstick, Rougeware, broad curved back panel on circular base, soft pink glaze, black Buffalo Rougeware ink mark and "1930," 6.5" h, 6.25" dia	$75	$150
Child's Dish, multicolor Campbell Kids transfer on white ground, gold trim, Buffalo Pottery mark, 8" dia	100	200
Custard Cup, ring handle, pedestal foot, hand-painted hunt scene w/ hunter and dog awaiting another rider, yellow ground, Colorido mark, 3.25" h	300	500
Hot Toddy Set, comprising service bowl and 4 handled and footed cups, ivory-beige ground, dark red hand-painted devil over black transfer on each cup, dark red rings on bowl and cups, Buffalo China ink mark and "AFG," pre-1930, 9.75" dia bowl, 5" h cups	300	500
Jug, cobalt scalloped-edge rim w/ embossed foliage, embossed vine handle, and reticulated pedestal base w/ embossed leaf and bead design, gold trim, bulging mid-section painted w/ large chrysanthemums over blue transfer, vitreous mark "Chrysanthemum," 7.5" h	400	600
Plate, blue-green transfer of hunter aiming rifle while setter points at flying birds, hand-painted accents, scalloped edge w/ gold trim, vitreous ink mark, 9.25" dia	200	300
Plate, buffalo head emblem w/ monogram letters "A C," acorns and leaves in repeat border, white ground, Buffalo China ink mark, 10.25" dia	25	75
Plate, hand-painted mauve and lavender daisy-like flowers w/ cobalt blue accents on wide hunter green border, tiny gold stars scattered throughout border, ivory center, signed "Ivory Buffalo 1927," 9" dia	50	100
Plate, hand-painted stylized parrot on branch, 2-tone green rim, white ground, Ye Olde Ivory Buffalo ink mark, early 1930s, 10.75" dia	250	350
Plate, Indian transfer w/ hand-painted details on wide pale yellow border, white center, marked "Colorido ware, Lamelle," 8" dia	75	150
Platter, oblong, flow blue transfer titled "Dr. Syntax Advertisement For A Wife," prospective matrons line up trying to impress a tense Syntax while he fends them off w/ his wing chair, broad floral border, vitreous ink mark and "1909," 14.5" l	700	1000

Buffalo Pottery at auction, left to right: Rip Van Winkle Jug, $770; Pilgrim Pitcher, $770; Triumph Jug, $715; Dutch Jug, $770; Cinderella Jug, $495; Gloriana Pitcher, $523. —Photo courtesy Smith & Jones, Inc. Auctions.

Camark Pottery

The Camark Pottery Company operated from 1926 (as Camden Art and Tile Company) until 1982, but it produced few pieces for the last decade and a half. Early "Le-Camark" pieces are wheel-thrown and of the hand-decorated line. Most pieces, however, are molded. The most desired are Le-Camark pieces, animal figurals, and pitchers with figural handles. Reproductions, notably the cat with fish bowl (Wistful Kitten) are on the market. For more information consult David Edwin Gifford's *Collector's Guide to Camark Pottery* (1997), and *Bk II* (1999) published by Collector Books, Paducah, KY.

Marks: most often impressed *CAMARK*.

Impressed marks.

	LOW	HIGH
Ashtray, green	$8	$12
Ashtray, shell	15	30
Bowl, cabbage leaf	10	20
Bowl, hand-thrown, ruffled edge	40	50
Bowl, onion, large	35	45
Bowl, pumpkin, large	12	20
Bowl, pumpkin, small	8	12
Bowl, swans	12	20
Bud Vase, star	15	25
Console Bowl, floral and cones decoration	30	40
Creamer and Sugar, on stand	15	25
Dog, miniature	8	12
Flower Frog, dancer	20	30
Flower Frog, round	10	20
Flower Frog, swans	15	25
Pitcher, corn-form body	25	50
Pitcher, cornucopia	40	50
Pitcher, parrot handle	45	75
Planter, elephant	55	65
Planter, wood barrel	20	30
Vase, cornucopia	25	35
Vase, double handled	25	35
Vase, fan, black, early	60	70
Vase, flower handles	20	30
Vase, hand-thrown, rings and fluted top	45	55
Vase, leaf, large	30	40
Vase, leaf, small	25	35
Vase, mirror black, early	60	70
Vase, ribbon	30	40
Vase, twist, large	40	50

Canonsburg Pottery

The Canonsburg Pottery manufactured dinnerware for the first three quarters of this century. It is often marked by a backstamp with a cannon.

Keystone (1934)

	LOW	HIGH
Bread and Butter Plate, 6" dia	$6	$8
Casserole	15	25
Creamer and Sugar	10	20
Cup and Saucer	5	10
Dinner Plate	8	12
Platter, oval, 11" l	10	15

Priscilla (1932)

Casserole	$25	$35
Creamer and Sugar	12	18
Cup and Saucer	4	8
Dinner Plate	4	6
Salad Plate, 7" dia	2	4
Teapot	15	25

Ceramic Arts Studio

Ceramic Arts Studio is famous for its novelties manufactured between 1941 and 1955. They are usually stamped with the words "Ceramic Arts Studio" underlined or with a half circular "Madison, Wisconsin." Sometimes the piece is named. See *Ceramic Arts Studio* by Mike Schneider (Schiffer, Atglen, PA, 1994) for additional information.

Snuggles or Lap-Sitters are pairs of figures that fit together.

	LOW	HIGH
Ashtray, hippopotamus	$25	$35
Figure, Drum Girl	30	45
Figures, Gay Ninety Couple, price for pair	60	80
Figures, Manchu and Lotus, w/ lanterns, price for pair	70	90
Head Vase, Barbie	30	45
Planter, Loreli	60	75
Salt and Pepper, pair, girl and chair	30	45
Shelf Sitter, Ballet en Pose	30	40
Shelf Sitters, Maurice and Michelle, price for pair	35	50
Snuggles, doe and fawn, green, price for pair	45	60
Snuggles, Mary and lamb, price for pair	30	40
Snuggles, mother and baby kangaroos, price for pair	30	45
Snuggles, mouse and cheese, price for pair	10	15
Snuggles, native boy and crocodile, price for pair	85	150
Snuggles, Peek and Boo, Siamese cats, price for pair	30	40
Snuggles, Rep and Dem, price for pair	40	55
Snuggles, seahorse and coral, price for pair	45	60
Snuggles, Wee Piggys, price for pair	20	30
Wall Plaques, Cockatoos, price for pair	45	60

Crooksville China

The Crooksville China Company manufactured semiporcelain dinnerware and kitchenware from 1902 until 1959. Several backstamps exist.

Apple Blossom

	LOW	HIGH
Bean Pot, covered, 2-handled	$20	$30
Bread and Butter Plate	2	4
Casserole, covered, Pantry-Bak-In, 8" dia	15	20
Dinner Plate	5	8
Mixing Bowl	10	15
Pie Baker, Pantry-Bak-In, 10" dia	12	20
Platter	8	12
Soup Bowl	7	10

Petit Point House

Berry Bowl	$4	$6
Bread and Butter Plate, 6" dia	2	4
Casserole, 7" dia	15	20
Coaster, 4" dia	6	10
Coffeepot	40	60
Creamer	8	15
Cup and Saucer	8	12
Custard Cup	3	5
Dinner Plate, 10" dia	8	12
Pie Server	15	20
Platter, rectangular, 15" l	8	12
Pudding Dish	4	6
Salad Plate, 7" dia	5	8
Sugar	10	15
Syrup Pitcher	15	20
Tea Tile	15	20
Vegetable, rectangular, 9.25" l	12	18

Apple Blossom, left to right: Bean Pot; Pie Baker; Casserole.

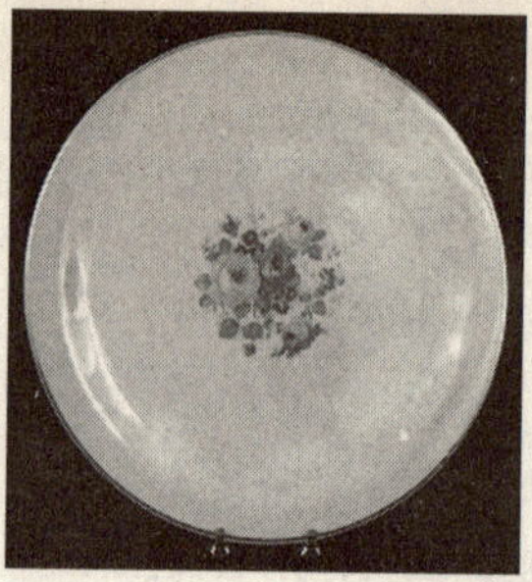

Roses, chop plate.

Roses

	LOW	HIGH
Berry Bowl	$3	$5
Bread and Butter Plate	1	2
Chop Plate, 12.375" dia	10	15
Cup and Saucer	8	12
Dinner Plate	5	7
Platter	8	12
Salad Plate	4	6
Vegetable	8	12

Silhouette

Batter Jug	$30	$50
Bread and Butter Plate, 6" dia	5	8
Cake Plate, 2-handled, 11.75" l	20	30
Cookie Jar, rattan handle	40	60
Creamer	10	15
Cup and Saucer	10	15
Dinner Plate, 10" dia	8	12
Pie Baker, Pantry-Bak-In	20	25
Pitcher	20	30
Platter, 11" l	18	25
Pudding Dish	5	8
Soup Bowl, 7.25" dia	18	25
Sugar	12	18
Tumbler, 8 oz	15	20

Vegetable Medley

Bread and Butter Plate, 6" dia	$4	$6
Casserole, 8" dia	18	25
Coffeepot	40	60
Creamer	8	12
Cup and Saucer	7	10
Custard Cup	4	6
Dinner Plate, 9.875" dia	10	15
Luncheon Plate, 9" dia	6	10
Platter, rectangular, 15.5" l	15	20
Sugar	12	18
Vegetable, rectangular, 9.25" l	18	25

Dedham Pottery

Dedham Pottery was originally founded as the Chelsea Keramicworks, but changed its name in 1895 after the company relocated to the town of Dedham, Massachusetts. The company was renowned for its gray stoneware pottery with crackle glazing and blue border designs of animals, flowers and birds.

	LOW	HIGH
Ashtray, Rabbit pattern border, flat-style rim w/ cigarette slots, stamped "Dedham Pottery registered," 6.75" dia	$200	$300
Bowl, #1, Rabbit pattern band, Maude Davenport, rebus "o" signature in band, stamped "Dedham Pottery," 3.75" h, 9" dia	300	500
Bowl, Lotus form, debossed vein design in each leaf, 5" dia	200	300
Butter Pat, floral form, pansy-style interior, stamped "Dedham Pottery registered," 3.5" w	350	450
Charger, Rabbit pattern border, stamped "Dedham Pottery," 12" dia	300	500
Dish, Azalea pattern border, 5-sided, stamped "Dedham Pottery registered," 7.25" w	300	500
Flower Holder, figural rabbit on dome-shaped holder, partial stamp, 6.75" h	1200	1500
Flower Holder, figural turtle, paneled shell w/ flower holes, blue accents, stamped "Dedham Pottery registered," 3.5" l	400	600
Gin Bottle, 4-sided, scroll-style "G" on front, stamped "Dedham Pottery," 8.5" h	400	600
Mayonnaise Bowl, Elephant & Baby pattern border, marked "Dedham Pottery, 1931," 5.5" dia	800	1200
Nappy, #3, Rabbit pattern border, stamped "Dedham Pottery," 9.25" dia	300	500
Olive Dish, Rabbit pattern border, oval w/ pointed ends, Maude Davenport, stamped "Dedham Pottery," 7.75" l	500	700
Pitcher, #2, Horsechestnut pattern band, bulbous form, stamped "Dedham Pottery," 5" h	250	350
Pitcher, #2, Rabbit pattern band, bulbous form, flat lid w/ blue band, 5.5" h	400	600
Pitcher, #6, Azalea pattern band, tapered form w/ angular handle, stamped "Dedham Pottery," 5" h	400	600
Pitcher, #6, Double Turtle pattern band, tapered body w/ angular handle, stamped "Dedham Pottery," incised "DP," 5" h	1500	2000

Left to right: Azalea Dish; Rabbit Plate w/ Coat of Arms; Horsechestnut Pitcher; Rabbit Plate; Night and Day Pitcher; Water Lily Plate; Rabbit Charger; Turtle Flower Holder. —Photo courtesy Smith & Jones, Inc. Auctions.

Left to right: Elephant & Baby Plate; Elephant & Baby Mayonnaise Bowl; Rabbit Pitcher; Butterfly Plate; Lotus Bowl; Rabbit Bowl; Chick Plate; Rabbit Salt and Pepper. —Photo courtesy Smith & Jones, Inc. Auctions.

	LOW	HIGH
Pitcher, #11, Rabbit pattern band, tankard style, stamped "Dedham Pottery registered," 7" h	400	600
Pitcher, Night and Day pattern, embossed crowing rooster w/ hens and smiling sun 1 side, owl on log and sleeping moon other side, 5" h	400	600
Plate, Butterfly pattern border, marked "Dedham Pottery reg.," 2 impressed rabbits, 9.75" dia	400	600
Plate, Chick pattern border, stamped "Dedham Pottery registered," 8.5" dia	1000	1500
Plate, Day Lily pattern, large day lilies in center, lily pods on border, Maude Davenport, rebus "o" signature on lily's stem, stamped "Dedham Pottery," 6" dia	1200	1500
Plate, Duck pattern border, raised design, Maude Davenport, rebus "o" signature in border, stamped "Dedham Pottery," impressed rabbit, 8.25" dia	200	400
Plate, Elephant & Baby pattern border, stamped "Dedham Pottery registered," 2 impressed rabbits, 8.25" dia	700	900
Plate, Moth pattern border, raised design, Maude Davenport, rebus "o" signature in border, marked "Dedham Pottery," 8.5" dia	400	600
Plate, Nasturtium motif, stamped "Dedham Pottery," impressed rabbit, 8.75" dia	4500	5500
Plate, Polar Bear pattern border, Maude Davenport, rebus "o" signature, stamped "Dedham Pottery," impressed rabbit, 10" dia	600	800
Plate, Rabbit pattern border, center coat of arms, marked "Dedham Pottery reg., 1931," 2 impressed rabbits, 8.75" dia	500	700
Plate, Rabbit pattern border, raised design, stamped "Dedham Pottery," 10" dia	200	300
Plate, Snowtree pattern border, raised design, marked "Dedham Pottery," 10" dia	200	300
Plate, Turkey pattern border, raised design, stamped "Dedham Pottery," impressed rabbit, 8.5" dia	300	400
Plate, Water Lily pattern border, raised design, Maude Davenport, rebus "o" signature, stamped "Dedham Pottery," impressed rabbit, 6" dia	100	200
Salt and Pepper, pair, Rabbit pattern band, long neck, bulbous mid-section, pedestal foot, signed "D.P.," 3.5" h	350	450
Saucer, Reverse Rabbit pattern border, stamped "Dedham Pottery," 6.25" dia	400	600

Edwin M. Knowles China

Edwin M. Knowles, son of the founder of Knowles, Taylor, Knowles, manufactured his own semiporcelain from 1901 until 1963. There are many different backstamps.

Beverly (1941)

	LOW	HIGH
Berry Dish	$2	$4
Bowl, 36s	10	15
Bowl, coupe	12	18
Bread and Butter Plate	4	6
Butter, open	20	25
Candleholders, pair	25	30
Casserole	20	25
Chop Plate	12	18
Creamer	8	12
Cup and Saucer	10	15
Dinner Plate	8	12
Gravy Boat	15	20
Platter	15	20
Salt and Pepper, pair	25	35
Soup Plate	8	12
Sugar	12	18
Teapot	30	45

Deanna (1938)

Berry Dish	$2	$4
Bowl, 36s	8	12
Bread and Butter Plate	4	6
Casserole	25	35
Chop Plate	15	20
Coaster	15	20
Creamer	12	18
Cup and Saucer	10	15
Dinner Plate	10	15
Gravy Boat	15	20
Pickle Dish	8	12
Platter	12	18
Salt and Pepper, pair	20	30
Soup, coupe	8	12
Sugar	15	20
Teapot	35	50
Vegetable	15	20

Esquire (1956)

Berry Dish	$12	15
Bread and Butter Plate	8	12
Compote	60	75
Creamer	15	20
Cup and Saucer	18	25
Dinner Plate	15	20

Yellow Trim Poppy, chop plate.

	LOW	HIGH
Gravy Boat	35	45
Pitcher, 2 qt	85	100
Platter	25	35
Salt and Pepper, pair	25	35
Server	45	60
Sugar	20	30
Teapot	100	125
Vegetable	45	60

Yellow Trim Poppy

Berry Dish	$2	$4
Bread and Butter Plate	4	8
Chop Plate	12	18
Creamer	12	18
Cup and Saucer	15	20
Dinner Plate	8	10
Gravy Boat	15	20
Pickle Dish	5	10
Platter	15	20
Salt and Pepper, pair	20	30
Soup Plate	8	10
Sugar	15	20

Yorktown (1936)

Berry Dish	$2	$4
Bread and Butter Plate	5	8
Candleholders, pair	25	35
Casserole	30	40
Chop Plate	15	20
Coaster	10	15
Creamer	15	20
Cup and Saucer	25	30
Custard Cup	4	6
Dinner Plate	10	15
Gravy Boat	15	20
Pickle Dish	8	12
Platter	12	20
Salt and Pepper, pair	25	35
Soup Plate	8	12
Sugar	15	20

Frankoma Pottery

In 1933, while working at the University of Oklahoma Ceramics Department, John Frank started Frank Potteries. By 1938, he had left the university, moved to Sapulpa, Oklahoma, and renamed his company Frankoma Pottery. Joh Frank designed all of Frankoma's dinnerware lines such as Mayan-Aztec (1945), Lazybones, Plainsman, Wagon Wheel and Westwind. Most are still in production. For further reading consult *Collector's Guide to Frankoma Pottery: 1933-1990* by Gary V. Schaum (L-W Book Sales, Gas City, IN, 1997) and *Frankoma and Other Oklahoma Potteries* by Phyllis and Tom Bess (Schiffer, Atglen, PA, 1995).

Marks: impressed *Frankoma*; some early pieces have *Frankoma* stamped in black. A mark featuring an impressed panther in front of a vase appeared from 1936 to 1938.

Frankoma impressed mark.

Miscellaneous

	LOW	HIGH
Ashtray, Dutch shoe, #914, 6" l	$18	$25
Batter Pitcher, #87	25	35
Bowl, #45, 12" dia	25	35
Bowl, #202, carved, 11" dia	25	35
Bowl, #209, swirled, 12" dia	15	25
Bud Vase, #32	8	15
Bud Vase, #43, crocus	12	18
Cornucopia, #57, 7" l	8	12
Cornucopia, #222, 12" l	15	25
Eagle Pitcher, #555, miniature	20	30
Flower Bowl	20	30
Honey Jug, #8	12	20
Lazy Susan, #838	35	45
Leaf Dish, #227	25	35
Match Holder, #89A	35	45
Mug, #C2	4	6
Pitcher, #835, 24 oz	12	20
Planter, #208A, mallard	10	15
Plate, Texas State	8	12
Rice Bowl, #F34	4	8
Vase, #6, free form	25	32
Vase, #19, fan	30	35
Vase, #23A, pedestal	6	12
Vase, #54, fan shell	35	45
Vase, #228, swan	12	20
Vase, #272, ringed	5	10
Vase, #F36, orbit	8	15

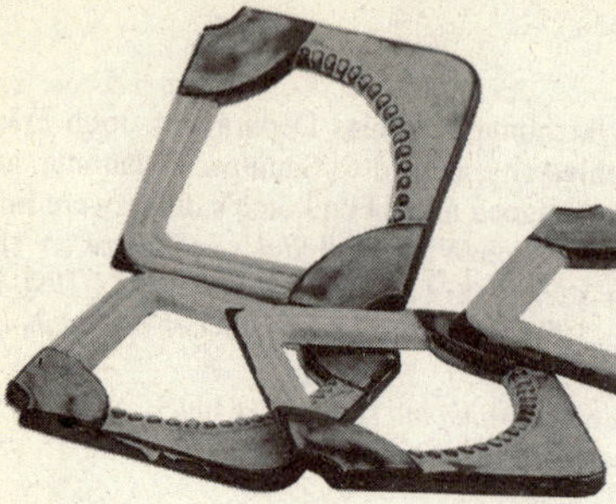

Architectural Tile Frames, glossy green, white, and bone glaze, embossed "Frankoma" and patent, Bruce Goff, 7.5" sq, price for 4, $358 at auction. —Photo courtesy David Rago Auctions, Inc.

Plainsman (1948)

	LOW	HIGH
Baker and Warmer, #5W, 3 qt	$20	$30
Creamer, #5A	4	6
Dinner Plate, #5F, 10.5" dia	10	15
Mug, #5M	8	12
Platter, #5Q, 13" l	12	18
Salad Bowl, #5X	4	6
Salad Plate, #5G, 8" dia	4	6
Salt and Pepper, pair, #5H	4	8
Sauce Boat, #5S	20	30
Teacup, #5CC, 5 oz	5	10
Tumbler, #51C	4	8

Wagon Wheel (1941)

Baker, #94W, 3 qt	$30	$50
Bean Pot, individual, #94U	30	50
Candleholder, #454	20	30
Casserole, #94V	30	40
Chili Bowl, #94XL	8	12
Creamer and Sugar, #94A&B	20	30
Creamer and Sugar, miniature, #510	15	24
Cup, #94C	8	12
Dessert Bowl, #94XO	6	10
Dinner Plate, #94FL, 10" dia	10	15
Fruit Bowl, #94XS	8	12
Luncheon Plate, #94F, 9" dia	8	13
Mug, #94M	9	15
Pitcher, #94D	20	30
Platter, #94Q, 13" l	15	25
Salad Plate, #94G, 7" dia	8	13
Salt and Pepper, pair, #94H	10	20
Saucer, #94E	5	7
Server, divided, #94QD	20	30
Serving Dish, #94N	10	18
Sugar, miniature, #510	5	12
Teapot, covered, #94T	30	42

French-Saxon China

The Sebring family of Sebring, Ohio, owned both the French China Company and the Saxon China Company. The bankruptcy of the American Chinaware Company pulled both under in 1932. W. V. Oliver bought the Saxon plant and named his company French-Saxon. It made semiporcelain kitchenware and dinnerware. Royal China bought the company in 1964.

Marks: backstamps included a knight and shield graphic backstamp and a circular Union mark. Romany and Rancho have only their names stamped.

French-Saxon backstamp.

Rosalyn (1937)

	LOW	HIGH
Berry Dish	$2	$4
Bread and Butter Plate	3	5
Casserole	9	15
Creamer	10	15
Cup and Saucer	7	11
Dinner Plate	8	10
Gravy Boat	15	20
Luncheon Plate	7	9
Salad Plate	4	6
Salt and Pepper, pair	11	18
Soup Plate, 7.75" dia	7	9
Sugar	12	18
Vegetable, 8.5" dia	16	18

Zephyr (1938)

Solid colors decorated with decals. The two solid-color lines are called Romany (red, yellow, dark blue, and green) and Rancho (maroon, gray, chartreuse, and dark green).

Berry Dish	$2	$4
Bowl, 36s	7	9
Bread and Butter Plate	3	5
Chop Plate, 13" dia	9	15
Coffeepot	36	45
Creamer	12	18
Cup and Saucer	8	12
Dinner Plate	10	12
Gravy Boat	15	21
Salad Plate	4	6
Salt and Pepper, pair	12	18
Soup Plate, 7.75" dia	8	12
Sugar	15	20
Vegetable, 8.5" dia	16	20

Fulper Pottery

The Fulper Pottery produced an Arts and Crafts-style ware from c1913 through the 1920s.

	LOW	HIGH
Bookends, Rameses, matte green and gunmetal glaze, felt bottom, 9" h, 4.25" w, price for pair	$500	$700
Bookends, Roman Mausoleum, sheer mottled ivory and white matte glaze w/ clay body showing through, rectangular ink mark, 6" h, 5.5" w, price for pair	500	700
Bud Vase, baluster form w/ flared rim and narrow neck, Leopard Skin Crystalline glaze, rectangular ink mark, 8.5" h, 3" dia	1000	1500
Bud Vase, long neck on flattened globe body, matte green and brown glaze, 7.5" h, 3" dia	400	500
Centerpiece Bowl, Ibis, shallow bowl supported by 3 ibis birds, brown flambé over mustard matte exterior, Flemington Green flambé interior, rectangular ink mark, 5.75" h, 11" w	700	1000
Chinese Lantern, leaded green slag glass windows on faceted base embossed w/ faux rivets and straps, dark blue flambé glaze, wired metal hanging fixture, remnant of original paper label, 12.75" h, 9.5" w	3000	5000
Coaster, embossed coat of arms, green crystalline on Cafe-au-Lait ground, rectangular ink mark, 4" dia	50	75
Doorstop, figural cat, Cat's Eye flambé glaze, ink racetrack mark, 6" h, 9" l	800	1200
Floor Vase, bulbous shoulder, mirrored Flemington Green flambé glaze, incised racetrack mark, 17.5" h, 9" dia	2000	3000
Flower Frog, figural frog on lilypad, green ivory, and mahogany flambé glaze, rectangular ink mark	300	400
Flower Frog, figural Indian maiden in canoe, green, mahogany, and brown matte glazes, 4" h, 7" l	400	600
Flower Frog, figural penguin on rocky base, white, blue, and brown matte glazes, rectangular ink mark, 7" h	200	300
Incense Burner, Aladdin's Lamp, glossy green over matte mustard glaze, rectangular ink mark, 3" h, 6" l	150	300
Inkwell, w/ lid, triangular, Germanic, matte green glaze, rectangular ink mark, 4" h, 5.25" w	250	500
Pilgrim Flask, 2 scrolled handles, curdled green, Mirror Black, blue, and ivory flambé glaze, rectangular ink mark, 10" h, 7.5" w	800	1200
Powder Jar, covered, flattened globe form, Famille Rose glaze, ink racetrack mark, 2" h, 4" dia	200	300
Table Lamp, trumpet-form base and mushroom shade w/ green leaded slag glass inserts, Flemington Green flambé glaze, rectangular ink marks, 16.75" h, 14" dia shade	6000	8000
Urn, 2-handled and footed, ocher, mahogany, and pale blue flambé glaze over textured body, raised racetrack mark, 9" h, 9" w	800	1000
Urn, classical shape w/ scrolled handles and rolled rim, Mirror Black glaze on hammered body, rectangular ink mark, 11" h, 5.5" dia	500	750
Vase, bulbous, 2-handled, dripping Famille Rose to matte green glaze, raised mark, 6" h, 6.5" dia	400	600
Vase, bulbous w/ flaring rim, frothy Wisteria matte glaze, ink racetrack mark, 7.5" h, 5.5" dia	300	500
Vase, classical shape, frothy cobalt and purple semi-matte glaze, ink racetrack mark, 12" h, 4.5" dia	400	600
Vase, faceted tapered cylinder, Cucumber Crystalline and ivory flambé glaze, ink racetrack mark, 10" h, 5" dia	600	800

	LOW	HIGH
Vase, faceted tapered cylinder, green, blue, mahogany, and ivory flambé glaze, incised racetrack mark, 10" h, 5" dia	600	800
Vase, gourd-shaped, Flemington Green flambé glaze, Prang mark, 5.5" h, 3.25" dia	400	600
Vase, gourd-shaped w/ 2 handles, Leopard Skin Crystalline glaze, ink racetrack mark, 7.5" h, 5.5" dia	600	800
Vase, ovoid, dark mirrored green and blue flambé glaze, raised mark, 5.5" h, 4.5" dia	300	500
Vase, ovoid, frothy Cat's Eye flambé glaze, ink racetrack mark	300	500
Vase, ovoid w/ rolled rim, Copperdust Crystalline and mahogany glaze, raised racetrack mark, 5.25" h, 5" dia	500	700
Vase, tapered bulbous form, gunmetal, mahogany, and Copperdust Crystalline glaze, raised racetrack mark, 13" h, 7.5" dia	500	750
Vase, tapered cylinder, frothy blue and green flambé glaze, rectangular ink mark, 12.5" h, 6" dia	400	600
Vessel, semi-ovoid form, purple and clear Cat's Eye glaze, rectangular ink mark, 3.75" h, 3.25" dia	200	350
Vessel, spherical, frothy Flemington Green flambé glaze, rectangular ink mark, 5.5" h, 7" dia	400	600
Vessel, squat w/ 2 angular handles, Copperdust Crystalline glaze, incised racetrack mark, 5" h, 6" dia	400	600

Fulper Pottery at auction. Top row left to right: Vessel, squat and scalloped, Mirror Black glaze, $193; Vase, corseted, 2 buttressed handles, Copperdust Crystalline over Flemington Green flambé glaze, $468; Vase, baluster form, Butterscotch Flambé glaze, $550; Urn, 2 buttressed handles, speckled matte green glaze, $825. Bottom row left to right: Vase, Cucumber Crystalline matte glaze, $825; Centerpiece Bowl, Chinese Blue flambé exterior, green crystalline glaze interior, $770; Vase, Chinese Blue over Mirror Black flambé glaze, $165; Vessel, Leopard Skin Crystalline glaze, $550; Vase, tapering, 4 buttresses, Flemington Green glaze, $523. —Photo courtesy David Rago Auctions, Inc.

George Ohr Pottery

George Ohr of Biloxi, Mississippi, designed and manufactured all pieces himself. Ohr pottery was produced between the early 1880s and 1906. Most pieces are marked "*G.E. OHR, BILOXI.*"

	LOW	HIGH
Chamberstick, deep in-body twist, ribbon handle, gunmetal and green glaze exterior, matte ocher interior, incised "G. E. Ohr," 4" h, 3.5" w	$1500	$2500
Cup, flaring w/ vertical dimples, glossy green and purple exterior, matte red interior, signed in black glaze "LG606," 3" h, 4.75" w	2000	3000
Mug, ribbed top, applied snake, ear handle, mottled gunmetal brown glaze, script signature, 4.5" h, 3" w	1500	2500
Pitcher, pinched and cut-out handle, mottled cobalt blue glaze, stamped "G. E. Ohr, Biloxi, Miss.," 4" h, 5.5" w	1200	2000
Pitcher, ribbon handle, pink, green, red, and white sponged matte glaze, impressed "G. E. Ohr, Biloxi, Miss.," 6.5" h, 4" w	6500	7500
Vase, pear-shaped w/ folded rim, raspberry, green, blue, and gray sponged glaze, stamped "G. E. Ohr, Biloxi, Miss.," 6" h, 4" w	3500	4500
Vessel, 2 pinched and folded lobes, 2 incised lines at shoulder, bisque scroddled clay, incised script signature, 5" h, 5.25" w	1500	2500
Vessel, asymmetrical bulbous form w/ torn rim and collapsed shoulder, green, mahogany, gunmetal, and ocher speckled glaze, impressed "G. E. Ohr, Biloxi, Miss.," 5" h, 4" w	4500	5500
Vessel, bulbous w/ deep in-body twist and folds, bisque, script signature, 6" h, 4.75" w	1000	2000
Vessel, deep in-body twist, matte green and light blue exterior, cobalt and green interior, script signature, 4.25" h, 4" w	3000	4000
Vessel, free-form, pinched and folded, bisque scroddled clay, incised script signature, 4" h, 6" w	2500	3500
Vessel, horizontally dimpled and folded sides, aventurine glaze, impressed "G. E. Ohr, Biloxi, Miss.," 3" h, 4" w	1500	2500
Vessel, pinched and cut-out handle, brown gunmetal glaze, impressed "G. E. Ohr, Biloxi, Miss.," 3.5" h, 5.25" w	1500	2500

George Ohr Pottery at auction, left to right: Vessel, green, raspberry, and gunmetal glaze, $7700; Vessel, spherical, mottled matte pink glaze, $2640 at auction; Vessel, whimsical face and folded rim, bisque, $7150; Vessel, bulbous, red, green, blue, and amber mottled glaze, $5225; Mug, Joe Jefferson, blue, white, and pink sponged glaze, 1896, $7150. —Photo courtesy David Rago Auctions, Inc.

Gladding, McBean

The Gladding, McBean & Company began operating as a sewer pipe manufacturer in 1875. It introduced its famous earthenware Franciscan line of dinnerware in 1934. In 1963 the company changed its name to the Interpace Corporation. Wedgwood (England) purchased it in 1979 and continued production until 1986. Franciscanware is now produced in England.

Franciscan Classics was Gladding, McBean's name for its three most popular patterns of embossed, hand-painted underglaze dinnerware. These were Apple, Desert Rose and Ivy. Both Apple and Desert Rose have seen continuous production since the early 1940s. See *Franciscan: Embossed Hand Painted* (1992) and *Franciscan: Plain & Fancy* (1996) by Delleen Enge (published by author, Ojai, CA) for additional reading.

Marks: various backstamps and decals, including *GMB* in an oval and *F* in a box for Franciscan. Contemporary pieces are backstamped *England.*

Apple (1940)

	LOW	HIGH
Bread and Butter Plate, 6.5" dia	$3	$5
Butter Dish, covered, 1/4 lb.	30	45
Cake Plate, 12.5" dia	30	40
Casserole, individual	75	90
Cereal Bowl, 6" dia	10	15
Cookie Jar, covered	200	300
Cream Soup	8	12
Cup and Saucer, jumbo	50	65
Dinner Plate, 10.5" dia	13	20
Fruit Dish	3	5
Gravy Boat, w/ liner	30	45
Milk Pitcher, 6.25" h	70	85
Platter, oval, 14" l	40	70
Salad Bowl, 10" dia	115	165
Salad Plate, 8.5" dia	9	12
Salad Plate, crescent	25	40
Salt and Pepper, pair, large	50	75
Salt and Pepper, pair, small, apple shape	15	20
Soup Bowl, 8.5" dia	15	25
Tea Cup and Saucer	8	12
Teapot	75	125
Vegetable, oval, divided, 10.75" l	40	50
Water Pitcher	100	160

Desert Rose (1941)

Bread and Butter Plate, 6.5" dia	$6	$8
Butter Pat	18	25
Cake Plate and Server, 12.25" dia plate	40	75
Candlestick, 1-lite	30	40
Cereal Bowl, 6" dia	12	16
Chop Plate, 14" dia	60	90
Coffeepot	85	110
Cup and Saucer	8	12
Demitasse Cup and Saucer	40	50
Dinner Plate, 10.5" dia	15	20
Egg Cup, single	20	35

Desert Rose pattern.

	LOW	HIGH
Gravy, w/ liner	35	50
Milk Pitcher, 1 qt	75	90
Mug	10	15
Napkin Ring	8	12
Pitcher, 6.25" h	30	40
Platter, 12.25" l	30	40
Platter, 14.5" l	35	45
Salad Plate, 8.5" dia	10	15
Salt and Pepper, pair, large	30	40
Salt and Pepper, pair, small, rosebud	20	25
Soup, footed, 5.5" dia	20	30
Vegetable, divided, 10"	35	50
Water Pitcher	100	125

Fresh Fruit (large fruit)

Bread and Butter Plate, 6.25" dia	$8	$12
Cereal Bowl, coupe, 6" w	15	20
Coffeepot, covered	100	125
Creamer	25	35
Cup and Saucer	15	20
Dinner Plate, 10.75" dia	15	20
Gravy Boat, w/ liner	70	90
Mug	25	35
Pitcher, 6.25" h	25	40
Platter, 14.5" l	30	50
Relish, 8"	25	35
Salad Bowl, 10.25" dia	60	80
Salad Plate, 7.75" dia	10	15
Soup Bowl, flat, 9.625" dia	35	45
Sugar, covered	30	40
Teapot, covered	100	125
Tray, 2-tier	80	100
Vegetable, 8.625" dia	40	65
Vegetable, covered	75	100

Grueby Pottery

Grueby Potteries operated from 1891 to 1907. After 1907 all Grueby pottery was manufactured and sold under the name of Tiffany. Grueby produced expensive, high quality vases, ornamental wares including statuettes, and decorative tiles. These usually have a factory stamp and an artist's mark, either straight-line or circular.

	LOW	HIGH
Floor Vase, semi-ovoid, tooled and applied broad leaves alternating w/ yellow buds, leathery matte green glaze, Wilhemina Post, circular pottery mark, incised "WP," 15.5" h, 10" dia	$50,000	$60,000
Floor Vase, stovepipe neck, tooled and applied yellow buds alternating w/ leaves, matte green glaze, factory label, 23.25" h, 8.5" dia	24,000	28,000
Lamp, leaded cobalt and green slag glass dome-shaped shade, gourd-shaped base w/ leathery cobalt blue matte glaze, original bronze lamp insert, Wilhelmina Post, circular pottery stamp and "228," paper label, incised "W. P.," 11" h base, 12.5" dia shade	8000	10,000
Paperweight, small scarab, matte green oatmeal textured glaze, Grueby Faience circular stamp, 2.5" l	250	350
Tile, scalloped oval shape, embossed w/ yellow, black, and white oriole on white and blue floral ground, signed "E. S." in slip, c1917, 8.5" h, 12.75" w	500	700

Grueby Pottery at auction. Top row left to right: Vase, bottle-shaped, tooled and applied leaves, medium green matte glaze, $11,000; Jardiniere, curdled matte green glaze, $1760; Vase, bulbous and tapering form, applied and tooled leaves and buds, medium green matte glaze, $5500. Bottom row left to right: Vase, bulbous, leathery matte green glaze, $1870; Cabinet Vase, squat form, leathery oatmeal matte glaze, $825; Paperweight, large scarab, matte green glaze, $523; Paperweight, medium scarab, blue matte glaze, $330; Vase, bulbous, leaf-shaped panels, matte green glaze, $3080. —Photo courtesy David Rago Auctions, Inc.

	LOW	HIGH
Tiles, horizontal 3-tile frieze, cuenca w/ ivory and yellow waterlilies and light green leaves on dark green ground, framed, stamped "Grueby Boston/63," each tile 6" x 18"	3000	5000
Vase, bottle-shaped, leathery matte green glaze, stamped pottery mark and "166," 13.25" h, 8" dia	3000	5000
Vase, bulbous w/ lobed opening, tooled and applied leaves alternating w/ buds, matte blue-green glaze, circular Faience stamp, 7.5" h, 4.5" dia	1500	2500
Vase, ovoid, full-height tooled and applied leaves, curdled ocher glaze, Ruth Erickson, circular stamp and "RE," 10" h, 6" dia	2000	4000
Vase, ovoid, tooled and applied leaves and daffodils, leathery matte green ground, Marie Seaman, pottery mark and signed "MS," 11.5" h, 5" dia	6000	8000
Vase, scrolled handles alternating w/ full-height tooled and applied leaves, curdled matte green enamel glaze, circular mark under glaze, 11.25" h, 6.25" dia	2500	5000
Vase, tooled and applied daffodils in profile, yellow, red, and green flowers w/ ocher centers, leathery matte green ground, Grueby Pottery stamp, 11.25" h, 6" dia	9000	11,000
Vase, tooled and applied leaves alternating w/ scrolled handles, feathered matte green glaze, stamped Faience mark, 11.5" h, 5" dia	6000	8000
Vessel, squat form, tooled and applied leaves alternating w/ yellow buds, pulled matte green glaze, Grueby Faience stamp, 7" h, 11.5" dia	8000	10,000
Vessel, squat form w/ rolled rim and ribbed shoulder, leathery matte green glaze, stamped circular mark, 3.25" h, 5" dia	600	900

Grueby Pottery at auction. Top row left to right: Tile, stylized waves and white flying seagulls in cuenca against sea blue ground, $1540; Vase, tooled and applied buds and leaves, leathery matte green glaze, $7150; Tile, cuenca w/ tall ship in ocher and ivory on green sea against blue sky, dead-matte leathery glazes, $990. Bottom row left to right: Vase, leathery matte green glaze, $990; Tile, cuerda seca w/ polychrome fountain and hedgerow, $330; Vase, ovoid, matte green glaze, $715; Vase, ovoid, tooled and applied leaves, light green matte glaze, $1540; Candlestick, tooled leaves, leathery dark blue matte glaze, $1650. —Photo courtesy David Rago Auctions, Inc.

Haeger China

For information on Haeger pottery refer to *Haeger Potteries* by David D. Dilley (L-W Book Sales, Gas City, IN, 1997).

Candleholder, #3068, spiral bowl, ivory, marked "Haeger U.S.A.," 1940s, 3" h, 12" dia, $45.

	LOW	HIGH
Ashtray, #127, triangular, gold tweed, 10.25" l	$15	$25
Ashtray, #2145, square leaf w/ acorns, green, 9.75" sq	12	20
Bookends, #R-475, calla lily, amber, "Royal Haeger R-475 USA" molded in base, 6.125" h, price for pair	60	75
Bookends, #R-641, figural stallions, chartreuse, 8.75" h, price for pair	50	70
Bookend/Planters, #R-638, panther, black, c1950s, price for pair	100	150
Bowl, #352, rectangular, footed, black mystique, 14.5" l	50	75
Bowl, #R-373, applied flowers, cloudy blue and white, 6.5" h, 19" x 6"	60	80
Bowl, #R-967, starfish-shaped, pearl gray drip glaze, "Royal Haeger R-967 USA" molded in base, 2.375" h, 14.5" l	40	60
Candleholder/Planter, #R-458, 2-lite, chartreuse, c1946, 7.5" l	15	30
Candleholders, #R-243, twisted stem, peach agate, c1927, 7.5" h, 4.25" w, price for pair	100	150
Candy Dish, #8044-H, 4 bowls, center handle, mandarin orange, 8.25" w	15	30
Canister, #726-H, horse decoration, "Haeger 726-H USA" molded in base, c1967, 4.25" h	35	50
Compote, #3003, white exterior, turquoise interior, 4.5" h, 12" w	20	30
Figure, #649, dove, 8.5" h	50	75
Figure, #F-17, wild goose, white matte glaze, c1941, 6.5" h, 6.25" l	15	25
Figure, #R-130, pheasant, green agate, crown foil label, 6" h, 11.25" l	30	40
Figure, elephant, chartreuse and honey, 8.25" l	35	45
Flower Frog, #57, figural swan, green, white, and beige, c1918, 4" h	25	35
Flower Frog, #R-359, 2 birds, cloudy blue, c1940s, 8.75" h	75	120
Lamp, #5190, bucking bronco, cactus finial, 26" h	200	275
Planter, #3311, cat, blue, c1946, 7" h	30	45
Planter, #8008-H, blue bird, blue crackle glaze, "Haeger-©-8008H-USA" molded in base, "H" design foil label, 7.75" h	15	25
Planter, standing horse, white, 6" h	40	60
Serving Plate, chicken-shaped, yellow and brown, "Royal Haeger 873 © USA" molded in base, 14.75" l	75	100
Table Lighter, #812-H, fish-shaped, jade blue crackle glaze, c1960, 10" h	30	50
Vase, #R-321, shell-shaped, chartreuse exterior, white interior, "Royal Haeger-USA 321" molded in base, 7.75" h	25	45
Vase, #S-447, oblong w/ thumbprint design and incised lines, "Haeger © USA" ink stamp on base, "Craftsman for a Century" label, c1952, 8" h	25	45
Wall Pocket, #R-745, grape vine, purple and green, "Royal Haeger R-745 USA" molded in base	100	150

Hall China

Robert Hall named his 1903 acquisition the Hall China Company and continued making the semiporcelain dinnerware and toiletware the old company had produced. After his death, his son experimented with firing the body and the glaze at the same time. He introduced the process in 1911. Hall still makes this vitrified hotel and restaurant ware. In 1920, the famed gold-decorated teapots appeared. In 1931, decal-decorated kitchenware and dinnerware were introduced. Hall reissues many classic designs. All are decorated in solid colors (no decal or gold decorated pieces). Many pieces are in new colors or color combinations. For more information see *The Collector's Encyclopedia of Hall China, Second Edition* by Margaret and Kenn Whitmyer (Collector Books, Paducah, KY, 1994, 1997 value update).

Early marks read *HALL'S CHINA* in a circular frame containing a mold or pattern number. *MADE IN U.S.A.* sometimes appears beneath the stamp. Later, a rectangular frame surrounded *HALL'S SUPERIOR QUALITY KITCHENWARE* or *HALL*, with a trakemark *R*.

Autumn Leaf (1933)

Produced for the Jewel Tea Company.

	LOW	HIGH
Ball Jug, #3	$20	$25
Bean Pot, covered, 1 handle	400	500
Bean Pot, covered, 2 handles	175	250
Bowl, Radiance, 9" dia	20	30
Bread and Butter Plate, 6" dia	2	5
Butter Dish, 1/4 lb	20	30
Coffeepot, rayed, w/ drip, 8 cup	50	65
Condiment Bowl, w/ liner	20	25
Cookie Jar, covered, Zeisel	100	125
Custard Cup, Radiance	3	5
Drip Jar, covered, 5" h	10	12
French Baker, 4.25" dia	10	12
Fruit Dish	6	8
Gravy Boat	18	25
Mug, conic	35	45
Platter, oval, 11.5" l	25	35
Salad Bowl, 2 qt	10	15
Salad Plate, 7" dia	3	5
Soup Bowl	12	18
Sugar, covered, ruffled	10	15
Teapot, Aladdin shape	100	150
Tidbit, 2-tier	60	80

Autumn Leaf pattern, ball jug and butter dish.

Cameo Rose (1950s)

Produced for the Jewel Tea Company.

	LOW	HIGH
Bread and Butter Plate, 6.5" dia	$5	$8
Casserole, covered, tab handles	50	75
Cereal Bowl, 6" dia	8	12
Creamer and Sugar	15	25
Cup and Saucer	15	25
Dinner Plate, 10" dia	10	15
Fruit Dish, 5.5" dia	5	8
Gravy Boat	25	35
Platter, 11" l	20	30
Platter, 13" l	25	35
Relish Dish, 9" l	20	25
Soup Plate	12	18
Teapot	60	100
Vegetable, oval	20	30
Vegetable, round, 9"	15	25

Crocus

Ball Jug	$175	$225
Cake Plate	30	40
Casserole, covered	55	70
Cup and Saucer	15	20
Dinner Plate, 10" dia	35	45
Drip-O-Lator, Medallion shape	75	100
Gravy Boat	35	45
Luncheon Plate, 9" dia	10	15
Mixing Bowl	45	60
Platter, oval, 13.25" l	35	40
Salad Plate, 8.25" dia	8	12
Soup Tureen	375	500
Teapot, Banded shape	150	200
Tidbit, 3-tier	45	60

Orange Poppy

Ball Jug, #3	$60	$75
Bowl, Radiance, 6" dia	10	15
Bread and Butter Plate, 6" dia	5	8
Cake Plate	25	30
Canister, Radiance	250	350
Casserole, covered, oval, 8" l	60	75
Casserole, covered, oval, 9" l	50	65
Drip Jar, covered, Radiance	20	25
Drip-O-Lator, Bricks and Ivy shape	30	45
Leftover	70	85
Luncheon Plate, 9" dia	12	18
Salt and Pepper, pair	60	75
Sugar, covered	20	30
Teapot, Donut shape	350	500
Teapot, Melody shape	175	250

Pastel Morning Glory (1930s)

	LOW	HIGH
Ball Jug, #3	$45	$70
Bean Pot, covered, 1 handle	100	150
Bread and Butter Plate, 6" dia	5	8
Casserole, covered, tab handles	60	85
Cereal Bowl, 6" dia	12	18
Creamer and Sugar	12	18
Dinner Plate, 9.5" dia	20	30
Drip Jar	35	50
Gravy Boat	45	65
Platter, 13" l	35	55
Salad Plate, 8.5" dia	8	12
Salt and Pepper, pair	35	55
Soup Plate, 8.5" dia	20	35
Vegetable, oval	30	45
Vegetable, round, 9" dia	25	35

Red Poppy (early 1950s)

Produced for the Grand Union Tea Company.

Ball Jug, #3	$50	$75
Berry Dish, 5.5" dia	8	12
Bread and Butter Plate, 6" dia	4	6
Cake Plate	25	35
Cereal Bowl, 6" dia	12	20
Cup and Saucer	10	15
Custard Cup	18	25
Dinner Plate, 10" dia	12	20
Drip Jar	25	35
Gravy Boat	45	65
Luncheon Plate, 9" dia	10	15
Mixing Bowl, Radiance, #5	8	12
Pie Baker	20	30
Platter, 13" l	35	55
Salad Plate, 7" dia	8	12
Salt and Pepper, pair	20	25
Soup Plate	20	35
Vegetable, round, 9" dia	40	55

Rose Parade (1940s)

Baker	$25	$40
Bean Pot, covered, tab handles	75	120
Casserole, covered, tab handles	40	55
Cereal Bowl, 6" dia	20	30
Creamer and Sugar	30	45
Custard Cup	10	15
Drip Jar	35	50
Pitcher, 5" h	40	65
Pitcher, 7.5" h	50	75
Salt and Pepper, pair	25	35
Teapot, 4 cup	40	60
Vegetable, round 9" dia	30	45

Wildfire pattern.

Wildfire (1950s)

Produced for the Great American Company.

	LOW	HIGH
Cereal Bowl, 6" dia	$10	$15
Creamer and Sugar	25	40
Cup and Saucer	15	20
Custard Cup	10	15
Dinner Plate, 9" dia	12	20
Fruit Dish, 5.5" dia	8	12
Gravy Boat	25	40
Jug, Radiance, #5	30	40
Mixing Bowl, large	45	65
Mixing Bowl, small	15	20
Pie Baker	20	30
Platter, oval, 13.25" l	25	35
Soup Plate, 8.5" dia	12	20
Tidbit, 3-tier	85	100
Vegetable, oval, 9" l	25	35

Drip-O-Lators

Ball, Bird of Paradise	$30	$45
Banded Ball, floral decal	45	60
Bricks and Ivy	20	35
Cathedral, orange, floral decal, large	15	25
Cathedral, plain, large	20	30
Crest, Minuet decal	30	45
Drape, floral decal, aluminum insert	20	30
Lattice, floral decal	30	40
Meltdown, ivory and red, platinum trim	20	35
Monarch, floral lattice design	40	55
Perk, Shaggy Tulip pattern	50	65
Rounded Terrace, floral decal, small	20	25
Rounded Terrace, plain, small	10	20
Sash, white ground, blue sash w/ white stars	60	75
Scoop, floral decal	30	40
Sweep, blue and orange tulips, aluminum insert	25	35
Target, Dutch decal	25	35
Terrace, light blue, gold flowers	20	30
Trellis, floral decal	45	60

McCormick teapot.

Teapots

	LOW	HIGH
Airflow, gold w/ gold, 8 cup	$60	$80
Aladdin, Blue Bouquet pattern	100	150
Aladdin, Wildflower pattern, oval lid and insert	125	175
Boston, brown w/ gold	40	55
Boston, cadet blue w/ gold, 2 cup	90	125
Boston, Dresden w/ gold, 6 cup	70	100
Boston, gray w/ gold, 6 cup	55	70
Boston, light green w/ gold, 2 cup	75	100
Connie, green	55	70
Flare-Ware, white w/ gold	35	50
French, avocado green w/ gold floral decoration, 12 cup	35	50
French, brown w/ gold, 6 cup	60	85
French, maroon, 4 to 6 cup	35	50
Los Angeles, cobalt blue w/ gold, 6 cup	45	60
Los Angeles, ivory w/ gold, 6 cup	35	50
Manhattan, blue	65	90
McCormick, green band, platinum stripes, white ground, 6 cup	75	100
Melody, Chinese red	175	250
Moderne, ivory, 6 cup	30	40
Moderne, marine blue w/ gold, 6 cup	100	125
Moderne, yellow, 6 cup	20	30
Moderne, yellow w/ gold, 6 cup	50	75
Newport, pink w/ floral decal, 5 cup	50	75
New York, cobalt blue w/ gold palm trees	200	275
New York, green w/ gold, 6 cup	40	55
New York, yellow rose decal	85	115
Ohio, brown w/ gold, 6 cup	175	250
Parade, canary yellow, 6 cup	45	60
Parade, canary yellow w/ gold, 6 cup	50	65
Philadelphia, brown w/ gold, 6 cup	30	40
Philadelphia, turquoise w/ gold, 6 cup	45	60
Rhythm, canary yellow w/ gold, 6 cup	100	130
Sundial, canary yellow w/ gold	125	160
Surfside, ivory w/ gold, 6 cup	100	130
Windshield, cadet blue w/ rose decals	50	70
Windshield, cobalt blue w/ gold roses, 6 cup	200	275
Windshield, Dot pattern, ivory w/ gold, 6 cup	30	40

Hampshire Pottery

	LOW	HIGH
Bowl, miniature, green matte glaze w/ streaks of light and dark gray glaze in repeat, incised "Hampshire Pottery," 2.75" h, 4.5" d	$175	$250
Bud Vase, serpent head at hollow opening w/ tail ending at opposite end, green matte glaze, black glazing along shaft, impressed "Hamshire" (missing letter "p"), 6.25" h	300	400
Candlestick, protruding lip, long shaft, broad pedestal base, lavender-pink matte glaze in sections over dove-gray throughout, incised "Hampshire Pottery," circled "M," and "78," 5.5" h, 4.5" dia	500	650
Inkwell, deep well w/ 3 round openings along perimeter, green matte glaze, unmarked, 3" h, 4" dia	200	275
Lamp Base, classic style w/ rippled mouth and Queen Anne-like feet, green matte glaze, unmarked, 6.75" h, 8" dia	600	800
Lamp Base, short neck, rounded shoulders, broad bulbous base, cerulean blue matte glaze w/ flecks of light gray and cobalt blue throughout, incised "Hampshire Pottery, 0021" and circled "M," w/ hardware, 18.5" h, 10" dia	700	900
Pitcher, classic style, curved handle, spherical body, miniature pedestal base, green matte glaze, impressed "JST & Co., Keene NH," 6" h	275	400
Pitcher, leaf-form w/ stylized stem handle extending over body into exotic-shaped leaves, rolled rim resembling leaf edge, cerulean blue matte glaze mottled throughout w/ aqua and steel gray, incised "Hampshire Pottery," circled "M," and "86," 8.25" h, 5.5" dia	1200	1600
Teapot, covered, oriental flare w/ hand-painted flowers contrasted against pale pink ground, black borders, original insert, impressed "Hampshire," 4.5" h, 8" w	600	800
Vase, hand-thrown w/ long neck, green matte glaze w/ brown flecks throughout, unmarked, 6.75" h	350	500
Vase, modeled as tied bundle, green matte glaze, impressed "Hampshire" and circled "M," 11" h	750	1000
Vase, ovoid, repeating blade-like panels w/ flowerheads at mouth, frothy mottled azure glaze w/ white accents dripping over deep cerulean blue ground, steel gray smooth mottling along base, incised "Hampshire Pottery," circled "M," and "33," 7" h	850	1200
Vase, ovoid, salmon pink matte glaze, cream-glazed rim, micro mocha brown mottling throughout, incised "Hampshire Pottery," circled "M," and "18-1," 5" h	450	600

Hampshire Pottery. —Photo courtesy Smith & Jones, Inc. Auctions.

Harker China

The Harker Pottery Company began in 1890. In 1931 it bought the E. M. Knowles plant in Chester, West Virginia, and closed its own East Liverpool, West Virginia operations. The Chester plant operated until 1972. The Cameoware line and the Hotoven Kitchenware are popular favorites. An arrow backstamp is common.

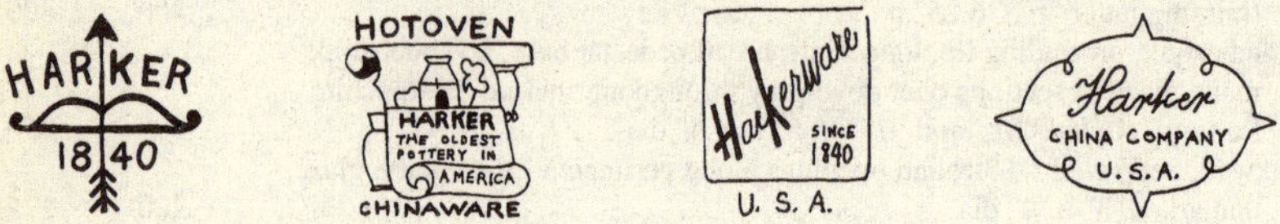

Harker backstamps.

Amy

	LOW	HIGH
Box, covered	$35	$45
Casserole, 9" dia	25	35
Casserole Tray, 10" dia	8	10
Cookie Jar	25	35
Custard Cup	4	6
Leftover, 4" dia	6	15
Mixing Bowl, 10" dia	25	30
Salt and Pepper, pair	15	20
Serving Bowl, 9" dia	10	25
Stack Set, 3-pc	35	45
Teapot, 5 cup	30	40
Tray, 10" dia	10	15

Gadroon

Berry Dish, 5" dia	$4	$6
Bread and Butter Plate, 6" dia	4	8
Chop Plate	15	20
Creamer and Sugar	25	35
Cup and Saucer	10	20
Dinner Plate, 10" dia	8	10
Dish, covered	12	18
Gravy Boat	15	20
Pickle Dish	8	12
Platter, 15" l	10	20
Salad Bowl	15	20
Salad Plate, 9" sq	6	12
Salt and Pepper, pair	10	20
Soup Bowl	8	10
Soup Plate, 8.5" dia	8	10
Teapot	30	40
Tidbit, 3-tier	20	30
Vegetable, 9" dia	20	25

Hotoven Kitchenware (1926)

	LOW	HIGH
Bean Pot, individual	$5	$8
Cake Server	15	20
Casserole, 9" dia	20	25
Cup and Saucer, 10 oz	8	12
Custard Cup	2	6
Drip Jar, Skyscraper	15	20
Leftover, paneled	15	20
Mixing Bowl, 10" dia	12	18
Pie Baker, 9" dia	6	10
Pitcher	18	25
Rolling Pin	40	50
Salad Set (fork and spoon)	30	70
Scoop	25	30
Stack Set, 4-pc	30	50
Teapot	30	35
Tea Tile, octagonal	20	25

Red Apple #1 and Red Apple #2

Berry Dish, 5" dia	$2	$4
Bread and Butter Plate, 6" dia	4	8
Creamer and Sugar	25	35
Cup and Saucer	10	20
Dinner Plate, 10" dia	10	15
Luncheon Plate, 9" dia	8	12
Platter, 11" l	12	18
Platter, 14" l	15	20
Salad Plate, 8" dia	6	10
Salt and Pepper, pair	15	25
Soup Plate	8	10
Utility Plate, 2-handled, 12" w	10	15
Vegetable	15	20

Red Apple #1

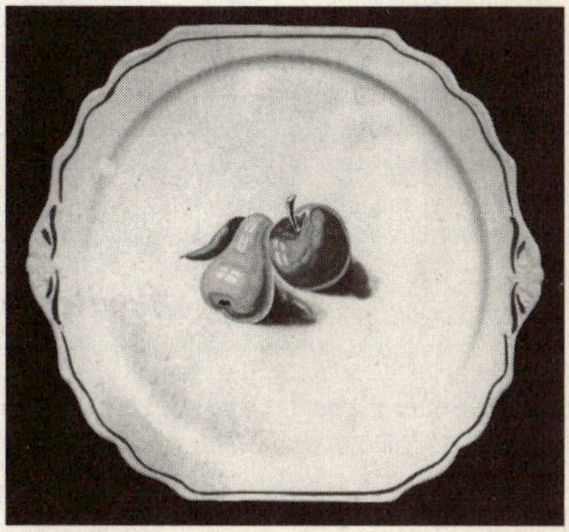

Red Apple #2

Homer Laughlin China

Founded in 1874 as the Laughlin Brothers Pottery, it became the Homer Laughlin China Company in 1896. Homer's brother, Shakespeare, withdrew in 1877. Homer Laughlin mainly produced semiporcelain. In 1959, vitreous dinnerware and institutional ware lines were introduced. The company is one of the largest still manufacturing today.

Homer Laughlin is most famous for its Fiesta dinnerware. The company is also well known because of its dinnerware designed by Frederick Rhead, head designer from 1928 to 1942, and Don Schreckengost, head designer from 1945 to 1960. Laughlin used a variety of backstamps. For more information see *The Collector's Encyclopedia of Homer Laughlin China* by Joanne Jasper (Collector Books, Paducah, KY, 1993, 1997 value update), *Homer Laughlin China: 1873-1939* by Jo Cunningham (Schiffer, Atglen, PA, 1998), and *Collector's Encyclopedia of Fiesta: Plus Harlequin, Riviera and Kitchen Kraft, Eighth Edition* by Bob and Sharon Huxford (Collector Books, Paducah, KY, 1998).

Early Homer Laughlin backstamps.

Amberstone (1967)

	LOW	HIGH
Bread and Butter Plate	$3	$5
Butter Dish	30	40
Casserole	40	50
Cereal Bowl	5	10
Creamer	8	12
Dinner Plate, 10" dia	8	12
Platter, oval	12	18
Platter, round	15	20
Salad Bowl	30	40
Salad Plate	4	6
Salt and Pepper, pair	15	20
Soup Plate, 8" dia	10	15
Sugar, covered	10	15
Vegetable	10	15
Water Pitcher	50	75

Americana (1944-56)

Berry Bowl	$5	$10
Bread and Butter Plate	3	5
Creamer	10	15
Cream Soup	50	75
Cup and Saucer	12	18
Dinner Plate, 10" dia	18	25
Platter, 11" l	15	20
Sugar, covered	15	20
Vegetable, 8" dia	20	25

Colonial Kitchen decal on Eggshell Swing.

Colonial Kitchen

Berry Bowl	$4	$6
Bread and Butter Plate, 6" dia	5	8
Casserole, covered	35	45
Creamer	12	18
Cup and Saucer	8	12
Dinner Plate, 10" dia	10	15
Luncheon Plate, 8" dia	8	12
Platter, 11" l	12	18
Salad Plate, 7" dia	6	10
Salt and Pepper, pair	15	20
Soup Plate	8	12
Sugar, covered	15	20
Utility Tray	15	20
Vegetable, 13" dia	15	20

Dogwood (1960s)

Berry Bowl, 5.75" dia	$5	$8
Bread and Butter Plate, 6" dia	4	6
Cereal Bowl, 6" dia	10	15
Creamer	12	18
Cup and Saucer	10	15
Dinner Plate, 10" dia	12	18
Gravy	20	30
Luncheon Plate, 9" dia	8	12
Mixing Bowl, Kitchen Kraft, 6.5" dia	30	35
Mixing Bowl, Kitchen Kraft, 8.75" dia	35	40
Mixing Bowl, Kitchen Kraft, 10.5" dia	40	45
Platter, 11.75" l	20	25
Platter, 13.5" l	25	35
Salad Plate, 7" dia	10	15
Soup Plate, 8" dia	10	15
Sugar, covered	10	15
Teapot	75	100
Vegetable, oval, 9.5" l	20	25
Vegetable, round, 8.75" dia	20	25

Fiesta Ware

The Homer Laughlin China Company introduced this brightly colored pottery tableware in 1935. Frederick H. Rhead's graduated ring design was one of the most widely manufactured tablewares of the twentieth century.

Colors include red, rose, dark green, medium green, light green, chartreuse, yellow, old ivory, gray, turquoise, and cobalt blue. Pieces are trademarked in the mold or with an ink hand-stamped mark. Reissued and restyled from the originals in 1986, Fiesta is still being produced. Prices are for old, not reissued pieces. Medium green is the most valued, followed by rose, gray and forest green. For additional reading on Fiesta, consult *Fiesta* by Jeffrey B. Snyder (Schiffer, Atglen, PA, 1997).

	LOW	HIGH
Bread and Butter Plate, ivory	$8	$12
Bread and Butter Plate, medium green	18	25
Bread and Butter Plate, turquoise	5	8
Candlesticks, pair, tripod, cobalt	750	1000
Carafe, turquoise	300	375
Chop Plate, cobalt	60	80
Chop Plate, ivory	40	50
Chop Plate, medium green	250	350
Chop Plate, rose	50	70
Coffeepot, light green	200	250
Creamer, cobalt	25	35
Creamer, gray	35	45
Creamer, ivory, stick handle	50	60
Creamer, medium green	75	95
Creamer, red, stick handle	60	80
Creamer, yellow	20	25
Cream Soup, light green	40	55
Cream Soup, red	75	95
Cup and Saucer, chartreuse	35	45
Cup and Saucer, cobalt	30	45
Cup and Saucer, medium green	20	30
Cup and Saucer, yellow	20	30
Deep Plate, gray	60	80
Deep Plate, ivory	45	65
Demitasse Pot, red	500	750
Dinner Plate, chartreuse	45	60
Dinner Plate, cobalt	35	45
Dinner Plate, ivory	40	50
Dinner Plate, light green	30	40
Dinner Plate, medium green	100	150
Dinner Plate, red	40	50
Dinner Plate, rose	50	60
Dinner Plate, turquoise	30	45
Dinner Plate, yellow	30	40
Disk Juice Pitcher, yellow	40	50
Disk Water Pitcher, chartreuse	300	400
Disk Water Pitcher, red	150	200
Disk Water Pitcher, cobalt	100	150
Egg Cup, yellow	45	55
Juice Tumbler, cobalt	45	60
Juice Tumbler, green	30	40
Juice Tumbler, ivory	45	55

Fiesta Pitcher and Tumblers.

	LOW	HIGH
Mixing Bowl, #1, medium green	200	275
Mixing Bowl, #1, red	225	300
Mixing Bowl, #1, turquoise	225	300
Mixing Bowl, #2, cobalt	150	200
Mixing Bowl, #4, cobalt	175	250
Mixing Bowl, #4, ivory	200	300
Mixing Bowl, #4, yellow	125	200
Mixing Bowl, #5, turquoise	175	250
Mug, ivory	70	100
Mug, medium green	60	90
Mug, turquoise	23	30
Nappy, chartreuse	30	40
Nappy, dark green	30	40
Nappy, medium green	100	150
Nappy, red	30	40
Nappy, rose	35	45
Nappy, turquoise	30	40
Onion Soup, covered, ivory	750	900
Onion Soup, covered, red	750	900
Onion Soup, covered, yellow	600	750
Pitcher, ice lip, red	200	300
Plate, divided, cobalt	40	60
Plate, divided, yellow	35	50
Platter, medium green	100	150
Salt and Pepper, pair, chartreuse	40	50
Salt and Pepper, pair, cobalt	25	35
Salt and Pepper, pair, ivory	25	34
Salt and Pepper, pair, light green	20	27
Salt and Pepper, pair, rose	40	50
Salt and Pepper, pair, yellow	20	30
Teapot, medium, turquoise	130	175
Teapot, medium, yellow	135	180
Teapot, large, cobalt	200	300
Teapot, large, rose	150	200
Tumbler, cobalt	65	80
Tumbler, ivory	75	95
Utility Tray, cobalt	25	35
Utility Tray, red	55	75

Harlequin (1938)

	LOW	HIGH
Candlesticks, pair	$100	$150
Casserole	50	100
Creamer, maroon	20	30
Creamer, yellow, individual	20	25
Cup and Saucer, dark green	20	25
Cup and Saucer, gray	15	20
Cup and Saucer, yellow	12	20
Deep Plate, chartreuse	25	35
Deep Plate, turquoise	20	25
Egg Cup, turquoise	10	15
Egg Cup, double, yellow	15	20
Gravy, rose	20	30
Gravy, yellow	20	25
Salad Plate, dark green	12	18
Salad Plate, yellow	8	12
Dinner Plate, rose	20	30
Dinner, Plate, turquoise	15	25
Platter, light green	15	20
Platter, rose	15	20
Platter, yellow	15	20
Relish Tray, 4-part	175	250
Salt and Pepper, pair	15	25
Soup Plate, chartreuse	30	40
Soup Plate, red	25	35
Soup Plate, rose	25	35
Sugar, covered, rose	20	30
Sugar, covered, turquoise	20	25
Teapot	50	75
Tumbler	25	30

Mexicana (early 1930s)

Berry Bowl, 5" dia	$6	$10
Bread and Butter Plate, 6" dia	8	12
Butter Dish, 1/2 lb	100	150
Casserole	75	100
Creamer	15	20
Cream Soup	50	75
Cup and Saucer	15	20
Cereal Bowl, 6" dia	20	25
Dinner Plate, 10" dia	20	25
Gravy Boat	25	35
Luncheon Plate, 9" dia	15	20
Platter, 11.5" l	25	35
Platter, 15" l	40	50
Salad Plate, 7" dia	10	15
Soup Plate, 8" dia	18	25
Sugar, covered	20	30
Syrup Pitcher	80	100
Teapot	125	175
Vegetable, 8.5" dia	20	30
Vegetable, 9.5" dia	25	35

Riviera

	LOW	HIGH
Batter Pitcher	$150	$225
Berry Bowl, 5" dia	12	18
Bread and Butter Plate, 6" dia	12	18
Butter Dish	150	175
Cereal Bowl, 6" dia	35	50
Creamer	10	15
Cup and Saucer	25	30
Dinner Plate, 10" dia	30	50
Gravy Boat	30	50
Platter, 15" l	40	60
Salad Plate, 7" dia	15	20
Soup Plate, 8" dia	25	30
Sugar	15	25
Syrup Pitcher	125	175
Teapot	150	200
Vegetable, 9" dia	40	50

Virginia Rose.

Virginia Rose

Virginia Rose is the name of a shape, rather than a pattern. Pieces were decorated with a variety of floral decals and trimmed in either silver or gold. For more information see *Collector's Guide to Homer Laughlin's Virginia Rose* by Richard G. Racheter (Collector Books, Paducah, KY, 1997).

Butter Dish, covered	$40	$50
Bread and Butter Plate, 6" dia	4	8
Cake Plate	15	25
Creamer	10	15
Cup and Saucer	4	8
Dinner Plate, 10" dia	10	15
Fruit Bowl, 5.25"	4	8
Gravy	5	10
Mixing Bowl, 10"	50	60
Platter, 11" dia	15	25
Salt and Pepper, pair	8	12
Soup Plate, 8" dia	8	12
Sugar	12	18
Vegetable, covered	40	55
Vegetable, open	15	25

Hull Pottery

Begun as a stoneware company, the A. E. Hull Pottery Company began producing semiporcelain dinnerware in 1907 with the purchase of the Acme Pottery Company. It slowly added various lines until the late 1930s, when Hull introduced its famous matte-finished pastel art pottery. Production continued through the 1950s when manufacturing operations ceased.

Prices for gilt pieces are higher. The listings include pattern numbers. Early marks include an impressed *H* in a circle or diamond. Later marks include *Hull, Hull Art,* or *Hull Ware* written in block or script lettering.

For further information see *The Collector's Encyclopedia of Hull Pottery* by Brenda Roberts (Collector Books, Paducah, KY, 1980, 1999 value update) and *Hull: The Heavenly Pottery, Sixth Edition* by Joan Gray Hull (published by author, Huron, SD, 1999).

Hull marks.

Bow-Knot (1949)

	LOW	HIGH
Bow Knot, Basket, B25	$200	$300
Candleholders, pair, B17	125	150
Console Bowl, B16	200	250
Cornucopia, B5, 7.5"	75	100
Cornucopia, double, B13	150	175
Creamer, B21	75	100
Ewer, B1	75	125
Teapot, B20	300	400

Calla Lily

	LOW	HIGH
Bowl, 500-32	$150	$200
Candleholders, pair, 508-39	125	175
Console Bowl, 500-32	350	450
Cornucopia, 570-33	75	100
Ewer, pink and blue, 506	500	650
Vase, 520-33	350	450
Vase, brown and tan, 530-33	600	750
Vase, cream and blue, 560-33	350	450

Ebbtide

	LOW	HIGH
Candleholders, pair, E13	$40	$50
Console Bowl, E12	125	175
Cornucopia, E3	90	125
Creamer and Sugar, E15/E16	100	150
Ewer, E10	200	325
Pitcher Vase, E1	90	120
Pitcher Vase, E10	175	300

Little Red Riding Hood

	LOW	HIGH
Batter Pitcher, 5.5" h	$200	$320
Butter Dish	500	600
Canister	800	1000
Cookie Jar, full floral skirt, closed basket	300	400
Creamer, spout on top of head	175	225
Creamer and Sugar, ruffled skirt	500	650
Creamer and Sugar, side open	250	350
Grease Jar, Wolf	800	1100
Jar, covered, basket in front, 8.5" h	400	500
Jar, covered, basket on side, 9" h	350	450
Milk Pitcher, 8" h	325	375
Mustard Jar, 4.5" h	500	600
Mustard Jar, w/ spoon, 5.5" h	400	500
Salt and Pepper, pair, 3.5" h	50	75
Salt and Pepper, pair, 5.5" h	125	150
Spice Jar	600	900
Sugar Bowl, "creeping," hands on table	175	250
Sugar Shaker, 4 holes on top	175	250
Teapot	300	400
Wall Pocket, 9.5" h	350	450

Magnolia, Glossy

Basket, H14	$200	$250
Cornucopia, H10	75	100
Creamer and Sugar, H21/H22	80	110
Ewer, H11	85	120
Ewer, H19	325	425
Teapot, H20	125	175
Vase, H-15	40	55

Magnolia, Matte (1946)

Candleholders, pair, 27	$75	$100
Console Bowl, 26	125	135
Cornucopia, 19	60	70
Creamer and Sugar, 24/25	80	100
Ewer, 14	45	55
Ewer, 18	200	260
Teapot, 23	125	150
Vase, 2	100	125
Vase, 7	80	100

Parchment and Pine

Basket, S3	$60	$90
Basket, S8	100	150
Console Bowl, S9	60	85
Cornucopia, S2	40	65
Creamer and Sugar, S12/S13	50	75
Ewer, S7	120	180
Teapot, S11	70	110

Serenade

	LOW	HIGH
Basket, S14	$250	$380
Candleholders, pair, S16	60	80
Cornucopia, S10	50	70
Creamer and Sugar, S18/S19	60	80
Ewer, S8	75	95
Ewer, S13	250	410
Fruit Bowl, footed, S15	75	125
Pitcher, S21	100	120
Pitcher Vase, S2	55	65
Window Box, S9	50	65

Woodland

Basket, W9	$225	$275
Candleholders, pair, W30	45	60
Console Bowl, W10	40	50
Console Set, W29 bowl and pair of W30 candleholders	150	200
Cornucopia, W2	35	45
Cornucopia, W10	100	150
Hanging Basket, W17	125	175
Vase, W7-5½	65	80
Vase, W9-83/4	100	150
Vase, W18	50	60
Wall Pocket, conch shell shape, W13	60	75

Above: Woodland Console Set. —Photo courtesy Collectors Auction Services.

Left: Serenade Vase.

Hummel Figurines

Hummels are ceramic figurines, usually of children. Berta Hummel, an artist and nun, created the concept and the original designs in 1935.

Each design is listed by number, followed by the title. All marks fall into seven basic categories (although variations exist):

(1) Trademark #1 / Crown Mark 1935-49
(2) Trademark #2 / Full Bee Mark 1950-59
(3) Trademark #3 / Stylized Bee Mark 1957-72
(4) Trademark #4 / Three-Line Mark 1964-72
(5) Trademark #5 / Last Bee Mark 1972-79
(6) Trademark #6 / Missing Bee Mark 1979-91
(7) Trademark #7 / New Crown Mark 1991-present

The last column lists auction prices achieved at recent auctions featuring substantial selections of Hummel figurines. The number in parenthesis following the auction price is the figure's trademark number.

For further information consult *Hummel: An Illustrated Handbook and Price Guide* by Ken Armke (Wallace-Homestead, Radnor, PA, 1995, available from Krause Publications), *Luckey's Hummel Figurines & Plates, 11th Edition* by Carl F. Luckey (Krause Publications, Iola, WI, 1997), and *The No. 1 Price Guide to M. I. Hummel: Figurines, Plates, More..., Seventh Edition* by Robert L. Miller (Bristol Park Books, New York, NY, 1998).

Above, left to right: Crown Mark; Full Bee Mark; Stylized Bee Mark.
Below, left to right: Three-Line Mark; Last Bee Mark, Missing Bee Mark.

	CM	FB	SB	3–L	LB	MB	AUCTION
1, Puppy Love	$340	$250	$170	$120	$100	$80	$116 (3)
2/I, Little Fiddler (brown hat)	670	580	300	300	180	190	—
2/II, Little Fiddler (brown hat)	1700	1480	980	850	800	660	—
2/III, Little Fiddler (brown hat)	2630	1960	1460	880	820	590	—
3/II, Bookworm	1450	1230	1180	940	790	640	—
3/III, Bookworm	2720	2200	1000	950	780	750	—
6/I, Sensitive Hunter	980	590	220	160	100	90	61 (5)
6/II, Sensitive Hunter	1460	770	420	340	300	190	—
7/I, Merry Wanderer	990	760	740	260	190	170	—
7/II, Merry Wanderer	1830	1500	1300	850	670	630	—

	CM	FB	SB	3–L	LB	MB	AUCTION
7/III, Merry Wanderer	2620	2100	1150	900	750	680	—
10/I, Flower Madonna, blue	370	240	160	130	110	100	209 (2)
10/III, Flower Madonna, white	460	210	200	150	160	160	—
10/III, Flower Madonna, blue	630	400	260	280	250	270	132 (3)
11/0, Merry Wanderer	490	250	200	190	90	70	66 (5)
11/0, Merry Wanderer, large	570	240	140	100	80	70	—
11/2/0, Merry Wanderer, large	350	200	160	100	90	80	94 (2)
12/I, Chimney Sweep	370	270	130	110	70	70	66 (5)
13/0, Meditation	290	240	190	120	80	100	99 (5)
15/I, Hear Ye, Hear Ye	520	300	200	150	120	90	—
15/II, Hear Ye, Hear Ye	1000	650	440	310	230	170	—
16/I, Little Hiker	380	260	150	120	100	80	121 (3)
21/0 ½, Heavenly Angel	350	250	160	100	90	70	—
21/I, Heavenly Angel	420	300	280	150	100	90	94 (3)
21/II, Heavenly Angel	1140	840	410	320	190	200	—
23/III, Adoration	1000	920	750	300	240	160	—
28/III, Wayside Devotion	840	660	470	400	260	210	—
45/0/W, Madonna w/ Halo	60	100	70	60	40	30	—
45/I, Madonna w/ Halo	140	110	90	60	40	30	—
45/I/W, Madonna w/ Halo	260	180	110	80	80	30	—
45/III, Madonna w/ Halo	520	390	150	140	130	90	—
45/III/W, Madonna w/ Halo	260	150	120	80	80	80	—
46/0/W, Madonna wo/ Halo	60	130	100	90	50	50	—
46/I, Madonna wo/ Halo	270	190	120	100	60	60	—
46/III, Madonna wo/ Halo	430	360	260	210	150	100	—
46/III/W, Madonna wo/ Halo	300	180	110	100	90	70	—
47/0, Goose Girl	470	390	170	120	100	90	171 (3)
47/II, Goose Girl	1000	640	400	300	240	220	—
48/II, Madonna Plaque	680	340	190	130	100	100	—
49/0, To Market	480	280	190	150	130	110	176 (2)
50/0, Volunteers	780	500	310	190	200	140	—
50/I, Volunteers	1100	830	500	360	240	230	—
51/0, Village Boy	400	300	190	150	100	100	72 (5)
51/2/0, Village Boy	150	160	100	70	60	60	33 (5)
57/I, Chick Girl	470	290	180	140	110	110	—
58/I, Playmates	500	290	200	150	110	80	—
65, Farewell	360	220	130	100	80	90	—
68/0, Lost Sheep	220	170	160	110	90	80	94 (5)
68/2/0, Lost Sheep	190	130	110	80	60	60	—
78/I, Infant of Krumbad	210	160	40	30	30	20	—
78/II, Infant of Krumbad	250	220	40	40	30	30	—
78/III, Infant of Krumbad	320	190	60	40	40	30	—
78/V, Infant of Krumbad	490	440	160	120	100	60	—
78/VI, Infant of Krumbad	750	460	260	190	190	130	—
78/VIII, Infant of Krumbad	970	750	390	350	280	230	—
81/0, School Girl	350	180	150	90	80	70	—
82/0, School Boy	350	250	160	110	90	90	61 (3)
84/V, Worship	2800	1750	880	870	710	590	—
85/II, Serenade	910	650	260	220	230	180	—
88/II, Heavenly Protection	830	750	470	260	240	230	—
89/II, Little Cellist	940	550	310	290	220	200	—
94/I, Surprise	460	300	190	120	120	90	—
98/0, Sister	180	130	140	90	80	80	99 (3)
109/II, Happy Traveler	520	600	340	290	240	210	176 (5)

Hummel Figurines. —Photo courtesy Gene Harris Antique Auction Center, Inc.

	CM	FB	SB	3–L	LB	MB	AUCTION
110/I, Let's Sing	210	230	110	100	80	70	—
111/I, Wayside Harmony	290	190	130	80	80	60	110 (2)
112/I, Just Resting	420	250	190	130	100	80	—
136/V, Friends	2000	1720	860	630	570	290	—
141/I, Apple Tree Girl	440	270	190	130	120	90	132 (2)
142/I, Apple Tree Boy	80	440	400	300	70	100	132 (5)
143/I, Boots	540	360	230	170	150	120	—
153/I, Auf Wiedersehen	1030	560	470	350	160	130	—
154/0, Waiter	410	260	180	130	110	90	—
154/I, Waiter	760	380	230	140	130	120	—
164, Worship	250	170	60	50	40	30	—
166, Boy w/ Bird	410	250	140	140	90	90	—
167, Angel Bird	220	150	60	50	30	30	—
169, Bird Duet	260	190	130	90	90	60	83 (3)
170/III, School Boys	2560	2130	1490	1360	1360	1440	—
171, Little Sweeper	240	140	120	90	70	70	143 (1)
172/II, Festival Harmony w/ Mandolin	—	1050	370	300	230	210	—
173/II, Festival Harmony w/ Flute	700	1130	360	280	210	190	—
174, She Loves Me, She Loves Me Not	370	270	150	120	80	70	88 (2)
175, Mother's Darling	400	220	150	130	100	80	121 (5)
176/0, Happy Birthday	300	290	180	130	110	100	—
176/1, Happy Birthday	690	530	340	280	170	150	—
177/III, School Girls	2660	2150	1540	1370	1460	1360	—
178, The Photographer	480	280	180	130	110	120	198 (5)
179, Coquettes	440	270	170	110	120	100	154 (3)
180, Tuneful Goodnight	420	250	140	120	98	80	—
184, Latest News (square base)	390	300	220	170	150	110	121 (3)
185, Accordion Boy	690	230	160	90	90	80	77 (3)
186, Sweet Music	730	250	150	120	100	90	88 (3)
188, Celestial Musician	740	340	190	150	140	90	—
192, Candlelight	670	690	300	130	90	80	—
193, Angel Duet	460	230	140	110	100	90	—
194, Watchful Angel	670	370	260	180	150	140	—
195/I, Barnyard Hero	370	280	230	160	140	120	132 (5)
195/2/0, Barnyard Hero	220	210	140	100	100	70	72 (5)
196/0, Telling Her Secret	430	320	220	150	160	140	132 (4)

	CM	FB	SB	3–L	LB	MB	AUCTION
196/I, Telling Her Secret	840	780	480	270	240	230	—
197/I, Be Patient	300	240	170	130	110	100	110 (6)
198/I, Home From Market	310	230	170	120	100	90	94 (5)
198/2/0, Home From Market	150	150	100	70	70	60	110 (2)
199/0, Feeding Time	310	250	170	130	100	90	—
199/1, Feeding Time	360	290	240	160	110	100	—
200/0, Little Goat Herder	250	200	180	90	90	90	—
200/1, Little Goat Herder	270	220	180	220	110	90	154 (5)
201/1, Retreat to Safety	350	380	190	170	100	100	—
201/2/0, Retreat to Safety	180	190	140	100	80	80	99 (3)
203/I, Signs of Spring	260	230	200	120	110	90	99 (4)
203/II/0, Signs of Spring	400	180	130	100	90	70	88 (5)
204, Weary Wanderer	460	320	220	150	100	100	110 (5)
206, Angel Cloud	560	440	290	90	40	30	—
207, Heavenly Angel	260	110	40	40	30	30	—
217, Boy w/ Toothache	—	170	140	100	80	80	121 (5)
218/0, Birthday Serenade	—	720	690	580	130	120	—
218/2/0, Birthday Serenade	—	460	470	400	100	80	—
220, We Congratulate	—	200	170	100	90	80	—
223, To Market	—	580	320	290	230	250	—
224/I, Wayside Harmony	—	320	240	220	200	180	—
224/II, Wayside Harmony	—	540	380	300	240	230	—
225/I, Just Resting	—	340	250	230	190	190	—
225/II, Just Resting	—	500	430	290	280	220	—
226, Mail Is Here	—	810	510	430	300	250	—
227, She Loves Me, She Loves Me Not	—	580	310	190	200	180	—
228, Good Friends	—	540	310	200	180	180	—
229, Apple Tree Girl	—	710	280	210	180	170	—

Hummel Figurines. —Photo courtesy Gene Harris Antique Auction Center, Inc.

Josef Originals

Muriel Joseph George of Arcadia, California, designed Josef Originals figurines from 1946 until 1982. (The "Josef" spelling resulted from a printing error on the labels which could not be corrected due to a lack of time.) In 1982 she sold the company to her long-time partner and representative George Good, but she continued designing figures through 1985. These pieces were produced in California through 1960, when production was moved to Japan. Examples below are from the 1940s through the 1980s. In this time period the girls were all made with black eyes and a glossy finish, the animals with a semigloss finish. Figures are now produced by Applause, which purchased the firm in 1985.

Prices are for figurines in perfect condition. All original figurines are marked on the bottom, either incised or ink-stamped "Josef Originals ©" and have a Josef oval sticker with either the California or Japan designation. Beware of copies, which have only a Josef label.

For more information see *Josef Originals, 2nd Edition,* by Jim and Kaye Whitaker (Schiffer, Atglen, PA, 1999).

	LOW	HIGH
Baby w/ Kitten, blue, pink, or yellow, Japan, 3" h	$30	$35
Birthstone Doll, colored stone in flower, Japan, 4" h	15	26
Christmas Girl, red dress w/ green front, cape, Japan, 6" h	25	35
Debby, First Love series, pink dress w/ hat, Japan, 5" h	20	30
Doll of the Month, Japan, 4" h	25	35
Doll of the Month, trimmed w/ stones, CA, 3.5" h	35	40
Elephant, flower on head, 4.5" h	35	45
Hedy, girl in pink dress w/ hat holding gift, CA, 4.25" h	40	55
Housekeepers Series, green dress w/ teapot, Japan, 3" h	25	30
Jill, Nusery Rhymes series, green dress, w/ bucket, Japan, 4" h	25	30
Kandy, blue or pink, gold trim, w/ colored stones, CA, 4.5" h	40	45
Kangaroo Mama w/ Baby in Pouch, Japan, 6" h	65	75
Lilacs, Flower Girl series, pink gown, holding lilac bouquet, Japan, 5.5" h	35	40
Little TV Cowboy, large hat, rope in hands, CA, 5.25" h	60	75
Louise, Colonial Days series, white gown, Japan, 9.5" h	95	125
Love Letter, Sweet Memories series, lavender gown, Japan, 6" h	75	80
Love Rendezvous, girl w/ light blue dress and hat, Japan, 9" h	90	125
Marie, XVII Century French series, white w/ veil, Japan, 7" h	75	90
Mary Holding Jesus, white gown, Japan, 5" h	25	35
Missy, pink, gold trim, w/ colored stones, CA, 4.5" h	35	40
Monday, Days of the Week series, pink, washing clothes, CA, 4" h	35	40
New Baby, Special Occasion series, girl holding teddy bear, Japan, 4.5" h	20	25
Penny, little girl sitting, green, CA, 4" h	40	45
Pitty Sing (first Chinese boy), large hat, CA	40	50
Poodle, Kennel Club series, Japan, 3.5" h	10	15
Portraits, Ladies of Song series, pink w/ parasol, Japan, 6" h	45	50
Prince, boy sitting w/ thumb in mouth, CA, 3.75" h	45	55
Reindeer, Christmas trim, Japan, 6" h	20	25
Robin, Musicale series, blue dress w/ harp, Japan, 6" h	55	65
Santa, w/ boy on his lap, Japan, 6.25" h	45	50
Saturday, Days of the Week series, yellow w/ pie, CA, 4" h	30	40
School Belle, yellow dress w/ apple, Japan, 3" h	20	30
Skunk, w/ perfume atomizer, Japan, 2.5" h	10	15
Sylvia, lime green, holding rose bouquet, CA, 5.75" h	55	60
Taffy, pink or green, gold trim w/ colored stones, CA, 4.5" h	30	35
Teddy, boy in gray suit holding flowers, CA, 4.5" h	40	50
Yvette, Morning-Noon-Night series, aqua gown w/ scissors, CA, 5.5" h	60	65

Limoges China

The Sterling China Company changed its name to Limoges early in this century. After WWII, legal action brought by Limoges of France forced the name change to American Limoges. Production halted in 1955. Viktor Schreckengost designed some American Limoges lines. The quality of American Limoges dinnerware is not as high as dinnerware produced by the French company of the same name. Don't pay French Limoges prices for American Limoges pieces.

For more information see *American Limoges* by Raymonde Limoges (Collector Books, Paducah, KY, 1996).

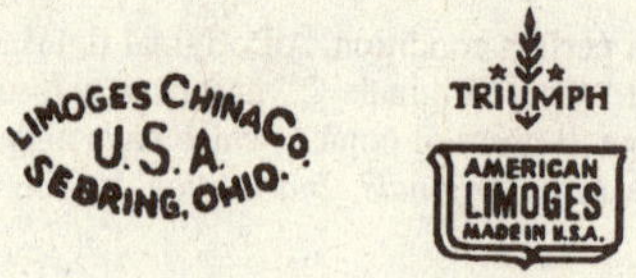

Limoges backstamps.

Casino (c. 1954)

	LOW	HIGH
Creamer and Sugar, diamond	$20	$40
Cup, club	10	20
Dish, diamond	5	10
Plate, spade	10	15
Platter, diamond	20	25
Saucer, heart	4	6

Thin Swirl

Bread and Butter Plate, 6" dia	$2	$4
Butter Dish	20	25
Casserole	20	25
Creamer and Sugar	12	18
Cup and Saucer	4	6
Dinner Plate, 9" dia	6	10
Gravy Boat	12	18
Teapot	30	40

Triumph (1937)

Berry Bowl, 5" dia	$2	$4
Bread and Butter Plate, 6" dia	2	4
Casserole	20	25
Chop Plate, 13" dia	12	20
Coffeepot	40	50
Creamer and Sugar	15	18
Cup and Saucer	4	8
Dinner Plate, 10" dia	4	8
Gravy Boat	8	12
Platter, oval, 15" l	10	18
Salt and Pepper, pair	8	12
Soup Plate, 8.25" dia	10	15
Vegetable, round, 8.75" dia	15	20

Lladró Figurines

The famous porcelain figurines made by Lladró in Labernes Blanques, Spain are popular, limited edition collectibles.

Left: I Love You Truly.
Right: Windblown Girl.
—Photo courtesy Sloan's Washington DC Gallery.

	LOW	HIGH
Afternoon Tea, #1428, 1982-99, 14.25" h	$100	$150
Aggressive Duck, #1288, 1974-96, 8.5" h	200	250
Barrow of Blossoms, #1419, 1982, 10" h	275	350
Boy on Carousel Horse, #1470, 1985, 16" h	425	500
Bridal Bell, #6200, 1995, 8.5" h	150	200
Caught in the Act, #6439, 1997, 8.5" h	100	150
Daddy's Girl, #5584, 1989-97, 8.5" h	150	200
Debutante, #1431, 1982-99, 14" h	100	150
Destination Big Top, #6245, 1996, 8" h	225	275
Dreams of a Summer Past, #6401, 1997, 9.5" h	125	175
Fawn and a Friend, 1990-97, 6" h	250	300
Fishing w/ Gramps, #5215, w/ stand, 1983, 15.5" l	500	600
Flapper, #5175, 1982-96, 13.25" h	125	175
Flower Harmony, #1418, 1982-96, 8.5" h	100	150
Flowers of the Season, #1454, 1983, 11" h	175	225
For a Perfect Performance, #7641, 1995, 10.5" h	100	150
Fragrant Bouquet, #5862, 1992, 8" h	125	175
From My Garden, #1416, 1982-98, 10" h	175	225
Gift of Love, #5596, 1989-99, 9.75" h	225	275
Grand Dame, #1568, 1987, 14" h	200	250
Guest of Honor, #5877, 1992-97, 8.5" h	75	125
Harpist, #6312, 1996, 13.5" h	375	450
Hi There, #5672, 1990-98, 6" h	250	300
How Do You Do?, #1439, 1983, 4.5" h	100	150
I Love You Truly, #1528, 1987, 13.5" h	300	375
Jesse, #5129, w/ base, 1982, 12" h	150	200
Lady of the East, #1488, w/ base, 1986-94, 9.5" h	600	700
Little Gardener, #1283, 1974, 9.5" h	400	500
Melancholy, #5542, w/ base, 1989, 12" h	200	250
Modern Mother, #5873, 1992-97, 11.5" h	100	150
My Flowers, #1284, 1974, 9" h	250	325
My Goodness, #1285, 1974-96, 9" h	150	200
Picking Flowers, #1287, 1974-99, 7" h	350	425
Socialite of the Twenties, #5283, 1985, 13.5" h	250	325
Recital, #5496, 1988, 6.5" h	100	150
Teruko, #1451, 1983, 10.5" h	200	300
Windblown Girl, #4922, 1974, 14" h	125	175

Marblehead Pottery

Most of the pottery produced at Marblehead was hand-thrown and utilized simple, classic lines and single-color glazes. First produced in 1905 by patients confined to a sanitarium in Marblehead, Massachusetts, the pottery was relocated in 1916 and ceased operations completely in 1936.

Impressed Marblehead mark.

	LOW	HIGH
Bowl, spherical, deep brown speckled glaze over soft brown matte, impressed ship, 3.25" h, 4.5" dia	$400	$600
Bowl, spherical, textured mottled glaze w/ bands of teal green over deep khaki brown, light luster finish, impressed ship, 3.25" h, 4.5" dia	300	500
Bowl, spherical w/ flat rim, midnite blue matte glaze, glossy dark brown interior, impressed ship, 3.25" h, 5" dia	200	300
Bud Vase, cylindrical shaft on spreading foot, matte gray glaze, impressed ship mark, 6" h, 3" dia	100	200
Cabinet Vase, cylindrical form w/ flat rim, dove gray matte glaze w/ cobalt speckling throughout, teal green interior, impressed ship, 3.75" h	200	300
Cabinet Vase, cylindrical w/ turned-in mouth, mocha matte brown ground w/ chocolate brown speckling throughout, glossy red mahogany interior, impressed ship, 3.5" h, 2" dia	200	300
Cabinet Vase, slightly tapered cylinder, mottled ocher over light beige matte glaze, glossy mottled ivory interior, impressed ship, 3.5" h, 2" dia	200	300
Hanging Planter, melon-shaped w/ 3 buttressed handles, matte indigo blue w/ chicory blue interior, 4.75" h, 6" dia	300	500
Monumental Vase, by Hannah Tutt, cylindrical, incised and embossed Arts & Crafts design in deep gray extending from mouth to base in repeat, matte green glaze w/ gray speckling throughout, camel high glaze interior, impressed ship and "HT.," 11.062" h, 4.5" dia	1500	2000

Marblehead Pottery. —Photo courtesy Smith & Jones, Inc. Auctions.

Marblehead Pottery.
—Photo courtesy Smith & Jones, Inc. Auctions.

	LOW	HIGH
Tile, hand-painted sailing ship scene, sails outlined in blue over beige glaze, light brown bow, clouds of powder blue, chicory blue sky, teal green and deep blue ocean, crackle finish, impressed ship, 4.5" sq	350	500
Tile, incised floral bouquet within dark brown woven basket, yellow, cobalt blue, aqua, and mocha brown tooled petals w/ luster finish, green cascading vines and leaves, matte chocolate brown ground, impressed ship, 6.125" sq	500	700
Tile, medieval theme w/ intricate border, embossed horse w/ incised war apparel, mounted knight in armor carrying circular shield burnt-orange semi-high glaze, impressed ship, 9.75" sq	250	400
Vase, classic form w/ rolled rim, full-length stylized peacock feathers in dark brown on matte dark green ground, by Hannah Tutt, impressed ship mark, incised initials "HT," 8.5" h, 4" dia	4000	4500
Vase, cylindrical w/ bulging waist and tapered base, matte dove gray exterior w/ blue speckling throughout, chicory blue glossy interior, impressed ship, 9.125" h, 5.5" dia	300	450
Vase, cylindrical w/ closed-in mouth, deeply incised butterfly and flower band below shoulder, blue butterflies w/ raised yellow spots, mulberry and rose-pink flowers surrounded by teal green foliage, speckled matte lavender ground, impressed ship, 4.75" h, 4" dia	800	1200
Vase, cylindrical w/ rolled rim and foot, teal to mint green alligator-textured exterior, aqua blue band around neck, faint mark, 5" h, 4" dia	200	300
Vase, deep mustard mottled matte glaze w/ areas of speckled reddish brown hue when held in direct light, impressed ship, 8" h, 4.5" dia	600	800
Vase, flared trumpet-form body, sky blue glaze w/ light luster finish, impressed ship, 6.5" h, 5.75" dia	200	300
Vase, pear-shaped, smooth matte blue glaze, stamped ship mark, 6" h, 5" dia	500	700
Vase, semi-ovoid w/ fine ribs, glossy olive-brown exterior, chicory blue interior, impressed ship, 4.75" h, 6" dia	150	250
Vase, tapered body, full-length stylized blossoming standard trees in blue on gray ground, by Hannah Tutt, painted artist's initials "HT," 5.5" h, 3.5" dia	1500	2000
Vessel, broad body w/ spared shoulder, deep navy blue matte glaze exterior, chicory blue interior, impressed ship, original sticker, 4.75" h, 6" dia	300	500
Vessel, flared lip, repeating oblong panels w/ grape and vine painting, dark gray panel w/ bluish lavender grapes encompassed by sage green leafy vines, matte dove gray body, by Hannah Tutt, paper label, impressed ship, signed "HT," 3.75" h, 4.5" dia	2000	2500

McCoy Pottery

The Nelson McCoy Sanitary Stoneware Company was founded by Nelson McCoy in 1910. Early products included crocks, jugs, and mixing bowls. In 1933 the company changed its name to the Nelson McCoy Pottery. Production emphasis shifted to kitchenwares and decorative novelties such as planters and vases. For additional reading see *McCoy Pottery* (1997, 1999 value update) and *Vol. II* (1999) by Bob Hanson, Craig Nissen and Margaret Hanson (Collector Books, Paducah, KY).

McCoy marks.

	LOW	HIGH
Ashtray, raised pheasant design in center, 9" dia	$30	$40
Ashtray, yellow, 8" sq	20	30
Ball Jug, yellow, 1950s	25	35
Bank, happy face	25	35
Bank, pig	45	60
Basket, Pine Cone pattern, 6.25" h, 8.5" w	35	45
Bean Pot, covered, Suburbia Ware, 1964, 2 qt	15	20
Bookends, birds, 6" h, price for pair	100	150
Bookends, lilies, 1948, price for pair	60	80
Bowl, green drip over onyx glaze, footed	35	50
Cat Dish	60	80
Cereal Bowl, brown drip glaze, 12 oz	5	8
Console Bowl, leaf shape, brown, 1960s	12	15
Console Bowl, tulips, blue, 8.75" dia	10	15
Cookie Jar, apple, red	45	60
Cookie Jar, cat, pink basketweave base	50	65
Cookie Jar, cookie kettle	25	35
Cookie Jar, ear of corn, 1969	100	150
Cookie Jar, kitten on basket, 1956-69	45	60
Cookie Jar, picnic basket	40	60
Corn Dish, brown, 9" l, 3.25" w	10	15
Creamer, brown drip glaze	5	10
Creamer, dog, green, 1950s	25	35
Dog Feeder, "Man's Best Friend," brown, 7.5" dia	45	60
Dresser Organizer, figural buffalo	15	20
Drippings Jar, covered, cabbage, 1954	30	40
Fernery, hobnail design, 1940	10	15
Figure, lamb, white	25	35
Figures, Scottie dog and cat, price for pair	45	60
Flower Holder, figural fish, yellow	50	65
Flower Holder, figural swan, yellow	60	80
Flowerpot and Saucer, paneled, flared rim, pink, 1959	8	12
Gravy Boat, rooster on nest	60	80
Hanging Basket, butterfly, white	150	200
Hanging Basket, white matte glaze	30	40

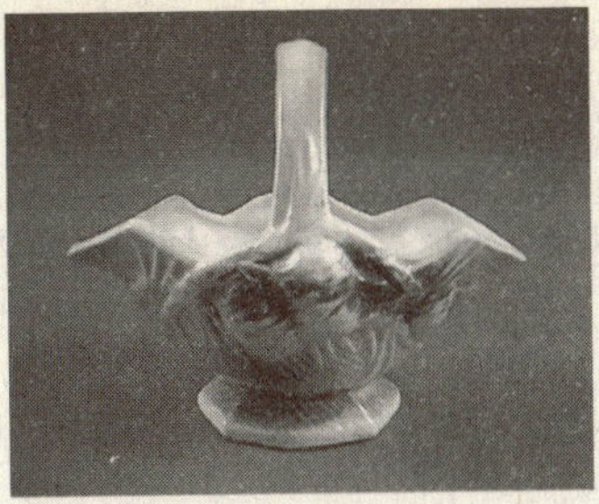

McCoy Basket, Pine Cone pattern.

	LOW	HIGH
Hanging Bird Feeder, brown, 1975	15	20
Jardiniere, flying birds motif, 7.5" h	25	35
Jardiniere, Pine Cone pattern, 6.5" h, 7.5" w	25	35
Jug, frosted blue, 1967	6	10
Lamp, cowboy boots	35	50
Mixing Bowls, nesting, both #4, 9.625" dia. green and 11.5" dia. yellow, 1926, price for pair	80	100
Mug, Vintage pattern, stoneware, green glaze, 5" h	15	20
Pitcher, vegetable design	40	55
Planter, Blossomtime, yellow	8	12
Planter, cat face, black	25	35
Planter, deer, white, 4" h	20	30
Planter, duck holding umbrella	80	100
Planter, frog	35	45
Planter, hunting dog, Sidney Cope design	80	100
Planter, lamb, white w/ blue bow	10	15
Planter, Liberty Bell, green, 10" h	175	225
Planter, quail	30	40
Planter, rabbit, ivory	8	12
Planter, rooster, gray, 1951	20	30
Planter, Springwood, pink matte glaze, white flowers, footed	10	15
Planter, stork, green	10	15
Planter, wishing well	10	15
Platter, fish, brown drip glaze, 18" l	40	55
Salt and Pepper, pair, cucumber and mango, 1954	20	30
Snack Dish, 3 leaves, rustic glaze, 1952	10	15
Soup Bowl, brown drip glaze	6	10
Spoon Rest, butterfly, 1953	35	50
Sprinkler Bottle, figural turtle	50	65
Teapot, #140, daisies, white ground	15	20
Teapot, brown drip glaze, long spout, 6 cup	25	35
Teapot, Pine Cone pattern	25	35
Vase, Blossomtime, 2-handled, 1946	25	35
Vase, Magnolia, 1953	35	50
Vase, Pink Hyacinth, 8" h	12	18
Vase, Sunflower, 1954	35	50
Wall Pocket, apple, 1953	40	55
Wall Pocket, butterfly, white	175	225
Wall Pocket, flower, rustic glaze, 1946	15	20
Wall Pocket, leaf, pink and blue	35	50
Wall Pocket, lily bud, 8" h	150	200
Wall Pocket, mailbox, blue, 1951	50	70

Merrimac Pottery

The Merrimac Ceramic Company operated between 1897 and 1908 in Newburyport, Massachusetts. Production consisted mostly of vases and other floral containers. Pieces made after 1901 were either impressed or incised with the company's sturgeon (Indian translation of "merrimac") logo.

Merrimac mark.

	LOW	HIGH
Bud Vase, trumpet neck, spherical body, jade and hunter green curdled glaze w/ black luster accents, 4" h, 3.5" dia	$300	$500
Jar, covered, paneled body w/ tapered sides, slightly domed lid w/ flattened finial, glossy speckled brown glaze, paper label, 5.25" h, 3.25" dia	400	600
Umbrella Stand, cylindrical, full-length tooled and applied leaves, leathery matte green glaze, paper label, 22.75" h, 8.5" dia	3000	5000
Vase, cylindrical neck on bulbous base, green and mirrored black mottled glaze, 10" h, 5" dia	1500	2500
Vase, semi-ovoid body w/ broad shoulder and rolled rim, dripping crystalline mustard glaze over speckled mustard matte glaze, stamped mark, 7" h, 5.5" dia	500	750
Vase, shouldered cylinder form tapering slightly to base, matte dark blue-green glaze, impressed mark, 5" h, 3.5" dia	200	300
Vase, slightly bulging cylinder form w/ flared rim, applied stylized plants repeat w/ blossoms around rim, leaves around base, and stems extending full-length, leathery semi-matte green glaze, impressed mark, 11.5" h, 6" dia	2500	3500
Vase, slightly tapered cylinder w/ narrow closed-in mouth, full-length tooled and applied marine plants all around, matte green glaze, artist signed "EB," 8" h, 4.75" dia	3000	4500
Vessel, broad squat form, matte green glaze, impressed mark, 4" h, 9" dia	1000	2000

Merrimac Vases. —Photos courtesy David Rago Auctions, Inc.

Metlox China

Metlox makes art ware, novelties, and Poppytrail dinnerware. Although solid color wares may date to 1927, decorated wares date from the 1940s through the present.

Metlox Poppytrail backstamp.

Antique Grape

	LOW	HIGH
Bread and Butter Plate, 6.375" dia	$4	$6
Butter Dish, covered, 1/4 lb	20	30
Casserole, covered, 6.75" dia	35	50
Cereal Bowl, 7.375" dia	12	18
Chop Plate, 12.25" dia	20	30
Coffeepot, covered	40	60
Creamer	8	12
Cup and Saucer	8	12
Dinner Plate, 10" dia	8	12
Fruit Bowl, 6.25" dia	5	8
Gravy, w/ liner	15	25
Pitcher, 8.25" h	35	50
Platter, oval, 9.5" l	12	18
Platter, oval, 14.375" l	15	25
Salad Bowl, 12.25" dia	30	45
Salad Plate, 7.625" dia	5	8
Salt and Pepper, pair	10	15
Sugar, covered	12	18
Vegetable, divided, 8.5" dia	12	18
Vegetable, oval, 10.25" l	15	25

California Provincial

Bread and Butter Plate, 6.375" dia	$4	$6
Bread Tray, 9.75" l	25	35
Butter Dish, covered, 1/4 lb	30	45
Cereal Bowl, 7.25" dia	8	12
Chop Plate, 12" dia	20	30
Creamer	8	12
Cup and Saucer	8	12
Dinner Plate, 10" dia	10	15
Fruit Bowl, 6" dia	6	10
Gravy	25	35
Luncheon Plate, 9" dia	8	12
Platter, oval, 11.25" l	18	25
Platter, oval, 13.625" l	20	30
Salad Plate, 7.5" dia	6	10

	LOW	HIGH
Salt and Pepper, pair	12	18
Soup Plate, 8.5" dia	8	12
Sugar, covered	15	20
Sugar Canister, 6.25" h	40	60
Vegetable, 10" dia	18	25
Vegetable, divided, rectangular, 8.625" l	20	30

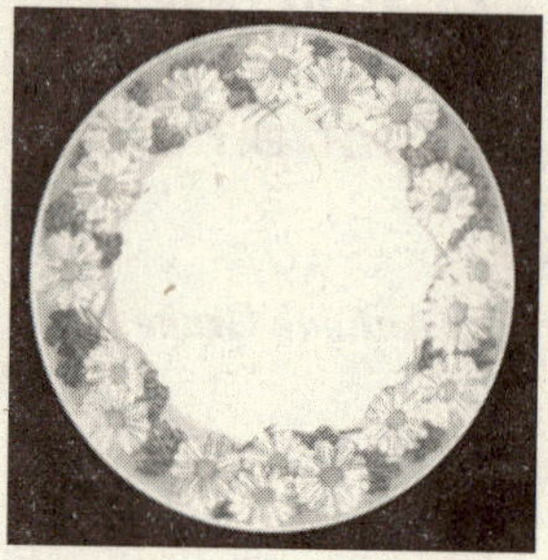

Sculptured Daisy.

Sculptured Daisy

Baker, oval, 11.125" l	$20	$30
Bread and Butter Plate, 6.25" dia	2	4
Casserole, covered, 6.625" dia	30	40
Cereal Bowl, coupe	5	8
Chop Plate, 12.25" dia	20	25
Coffeepot, covered	30	45
Creamer	6	10
Cup and Saucer	6	10
Dinner Plate, 10.625" dia	8	12
Fruit Bowl, 6.125" dia	4	6
Gravy, w/ liner	15	20
Pitcher, 8.75" h	20	30
Platter, oval, 9.75" l	10	15
Platter, oval, 14.375" l	15	20
Salad Bowl, 12.25" dia	20	25
Salad Plate, 7.625" dia	4	6
Salt and Pepper, pair	8	12
Soup Plate, 8.5" dia	6	10
Sugar, covered	10	15
Vegetable, covered, 6.375" dia	25	35
Vegetable, divided, 9.125" dia	15	25
Vegetable, open, 9.125" dia	12	20

Newcomb College Pottery

The Newcomb College Art Department in New Orleans began producing pottery for sale in 1896. Newcomb wares carry underglaze designs picturing subjects from nature. For further reading see *Newcomb Pottery: An Enterprise for Southern Women, 1895-1940* by Jessie Poesch (Schiffer, Exton, PA, 1984).

There are usually five marks on each piece: the mark of Newcomb (a white-on-black vase with the initials *N.C.*, with the *N* within the *C*, or *NEWCOMB COLLEGE* spelled out), a potter's mark, an artist's or decorator's mark, a recipe mark and a registration mark.

	LOW	HIGH
Bud Vase, transitional, flared cylinder, sprigs of white flowers on blue-green ground, Henrietta Bailey, impressed "NC/KB82/HB/212," 1915, 4.5" h, 2.5" dia	$1500	$2000
Cabinet Vase, tapered body, painted amber stylized dogs' heads in repeat around shoulder, cobalt blue ground above heads, ivory ground below, amber stripe around rim, cobalt and amber stripes around base, Sabrina, marked "NC/SEW/JM/US/Q," 1902, 4.75" h, 2.75" dia	3000	4000
Candlesticks, pink spiderwort around bobeche and base, blue ground, Sadie Irvine, marked "NC/JM/SI/NP82," paper label, 1923, 7.25" h, 4.25" dia, price for pair	1500	2500
Centerpiece Bowl, w/ flower frog, carved white and yellow flowers on blue ground, A. F. Simpson, stamped "NC/AFS/JM/265," 4" h, 11.25" dia	1500	2500
Mug, blue-green stylized landscape, glossy overglaze, Desiree Roman and Marie Delavigne, impressed "NC/DR/MD/G73X/Q/JM," 1901, 4" h, 5" w	2500	3500
Pitcher, band of carved pink nasturtium w/ green leaves, matte glaze, Sadie Irvine, incised "NC/SI/230/OB65," 1924, 8" h, 6" w	2500	4000
Pitcher, tankard form, Español pattern, dark blue ground, matte glaze, impressed "207," 5" h, 4.5" w	1000	1500

Newcomb College Pottery. —Photo courtesy David Rago Auctions, Inc.

Newcomb College Pottery. —Photo courtesy David Rago Auctions, Inc.

	LOW	HIGH
Plate, porcelain, painted border w/ white daisies on yellow band, signed "Mc/12-20-16," 8.25" dia	100	200
Toothpick Holder, vertical tab handles, ivory and green stylized triangular flowers in repeat, marked "NC/JH/A/TG39," 1931, 2" h, 3" dia	300	500
Trivet, carved wreath of stylized blossoms in blue and green on ivory ground, blue rim band, Mary Butler, marked "NC/JM/MWB/BH63," 1906, 6" dia	1500	2000
Vase, bottle-shaped w/ flared and flattened rim, lustered teal over green glaze, Leona Nicholson, incised "L.N.," stamped "NC/JM," 1918, 7.5" h, 3.5" dia	500	800
Vase, bulbous w/ slightly flared rim, semi-matte raspberry glaze exterior, periwinkle blue interior, stamped "NC," 5.25" h, 4.5" dia	400	600
Vase, classical shape, carved full-length tulips and leaves, blue tulips, green leaves, blue ground, Harriet Joor, stamped "NC/HJ/C/?-26X," c1905, 7.25" h, 4.5" dia	10,000	15,000
Vase, corseted cylinder w/ flared rim, carved full-length white and yellow narcissus w/ green leaves, pale blue ground, A. F. Simpson, marked "NC/AFS/223/NT6," 1924, 8.5" h, 3.25" dia	3000	4500
Vase, elongated cylindrical neck, tapered body, carved wreath of pink bell-shaped flowers w/ green leaves, dark blue ground, A. F. Simpson, marked "NC/AFS/JM/92/QW25," 1928, 8.5" h, 3.25" dia	3000	4000
Vase, ovoid, modeled w/ live oak trees and Spanish moss, Anna F. Simpson, impressed "NC/AFS/JH/78/SG85," 1930, 6" h, 3.25" dia	5000	7000
Vase ovoid, tooled yellow flowers and celadon leaves on ivory ground, Esther H. Elliott, stamped "NC/EHE/BB10/Q/JM," 7" h, 5" dia	20,000	25,000
Vase, ovoid, white dogwood blossom on blue-green ground, Cynthia Littlejohn, marked "NC/JM/HA82/237/CL," 1914, 5.5" h, 3" dia	1200	2000
Vase, semi-ovoid, incised w/ frieze of sailboats, glossy blue, white, and green glaze, Desiree Roman, marked "NC/W/D.R./X37/JM," 5.75" h, 5.75" dia	10,000	15,000
Vase, tapered cylinder, incised w/ stylized birch seed pods, blue-green on ivory ground, Henrietta Bailey, marked "NC/PP71/Hbailey/JM/Q," 1904, 7.5" h, 4.5" dia	10,000	15,000
Vessel, transitional, squat bulbous form, carved w/ live oak trees and Spanish moss, matte blue and green glaze, Henrietta Bailey, stamped "C/HB/70JM/HR28/49," 1915, 6.75" h, 8.5" dia	5000	7000

Niloak Pottery

Niloak Pottery is old classic redware, influenced by Greek, Roman and Native American design, but with a striking marbleized texture. Potters threw Niloak ware on a wheel. Many pieces have only an inside glaze. The word "niloak" is kaolin (the chief ingredient in porcelain) spelled backwards. Niloak pottery is completely unlike porcelain. Most successful during the 1920s, the firm survived until 1946.

The pottery had an impressed mark or a circular paper label, reading simply *NILOAK POTTERY.* Paper labels became standard in later years.

Niloak marks.

	LOW	HIGH
Candlesticks, rolled rim, stepped shaft, spreading foot, brown, blue, terra cotta, and sand scroddled clays, stamped "Niloak," 8" h, 5" dia, price for pair	$300	$500
Humidor, covered, bulbous body, marbleized shades of brown, stamped "Niloak," 5" h, 5.25" dia	300	500
Humidor, covered, bulbous body, terra cotta, cerulean blue, and ivory scroddled clays, stamped "Niloak," paper label, 6.5" h, 6" dia	500	700
Vase, baluster form, brown, blue, terra cotta, and sand scroddled clays, stamped "Niloak," 9.5" h, 5" dia	300	500
Vase, classical shape, brown, ivory, and terra cotta scroddled clays, stamped "Niloak," paper label, 12" h, 7.5" dia	500	700
Vase, conical w/ flaring foot, brown, blue, and terra cotta scroddled clays, stamped "Niloak," 8.5" h, 4.5" dia	150	300
Vase, corseted cylinder, brown, blue, and terra cotta scroddled clays, stamped "Niloak," 10" h, 4.5" dia	200	300
Vase, corseted cylinder, brown, blue, terra cotta, and purple scroddled clays, stamped "Niloak," 12.25" h, 5.5" dia	300	500
Vase, corseted w/ flaring rim and bulbous base, brown, blue, terra cotta, and purple scroddled clays, stamped "Niloak, 9.5" h, 5.5" dia	300	500
Vase, pear-shaped w/ flattened flaring rim, brown, blue, terra cotta, and sand scroddled clays, stamped "Niloak," 9.75" h, 4.75" dia	300	500
Vase, rolled rim, tapered body, brown, blue, terra cotta, and purple scroddled clays, stamped "Niloak," paper label, 14" h, 7" dia	700	900
Vase, spherical w/ closed-in rim, brown, blue, terra cotta, and sand scroddled clays, stamped "Niloak," paper label, 5.75" h, 7" dia	200	400
Vase, straight-sided cylinder w/ flaring foot, brown, blue, and terra cotta scroddled clays, stamped "Niloak," paper label, 10" h, 4.5" dia	400	600
Vessel, wide mouth, brown, beige, and terra cotta scroddled clays, stamped "Niloak," 6" h, 8" dia	400	600

North Dakota School of Mines

Pottery made at the University of North Dakota, Grand Forks, North Dakota consisted mainly of vases and novelty wares. The school taught ceramic courses from the early 1900s until 1972. Many pieces were decorated with designs carved in low relief and/or highlighted with various colored glazes. Marks include a circular ink stamp with "University of North Dakota, Grand Forks, N. D., Made at School of Mines, N. D. Clay" or incised "UND."

	LOW	HIGH
Bowl, exterior carved w/ matte green heart-shaped leaves and rim band on white ground, glossy turquoise interior, by Schnell, circular ink stamp, incised "Schnell," 4.25" h, 9" dia	$500	$750
Bowl, squat, embossed frieze of ox-drawn carts, brown and green matte glazes, by Margaret Cable, circular ink stamp, incised title "Red River Ox Cart" and artist's signature, 3.5" h, 6.5" dia	1500	2000
Cabinet Vase, spherical, carved band of prairie roses, green matte ground, by Flora Huckfield, circular ink stamp, incised title "Prairie Rose" and "Huck/51," 1951, 3" h, 3.5" dia	400	600
Charger, hand-painted dark brown flowers on burnt sienna ground, by Margaret Cable, circular ink stamp, incised "M. Cable #844/1932," 9.75" dia	900	1100
Figurine, cowboy, brick-red, black, and gold glaze, by Julia Mattson, incised "JM13/UND," 1913, 4.5" h, 3.25" w	500	750
Humidor, covered, bulbous, hand painted w/ brown and green berries and arches on matte mustard ground, by Margaret Cable, circular ink stamp, incised "MKC 1917/SM/#40," 1917, 6" h, 6.25" dia	5000	6000
Pitcher, squat form w/ embossed frieze of ox-drawn carts, glossy ivory glaze on buff clay body, by Margaret Cable, circular ink stamp, embossed signature, and "Red River Ox Carts/ 140," 5" h, 8.5" w	1000	1200
Trivet, round, carved stylized eagle in black on brick-red ground, by Julia Mattson, circular ink stamp and incised "JM 58," 1958, 4.75" dia	200	400
Trivet, round, carved w/ 2 fish in green and ocher on ivory ground, by Julia Mattson, circular ink stamp, incised "JM58," 5" dia	200	300
Vase, bulbous, carved w/ full-length daffodils, light green semi-matte glaze, by Margaret Cable, circular ink stamp, incised "M. Cable," 7.25" h, 5" dia	2000	3000
Vase, bulbous, carved w/ Indian warriors on horseback, dark brown matte ground, by Flora Huckfield, circular ink stamp, incised title "N.D. Sioux" and "151," 5.75" h, 5.5" dia	2000	2500
Vase, bulbous shoulder tapering to base, carved w/ mocha-brown narcissus on dark brown ground, by F. Cunningham, circular ink stamp, incised "F. Cunningham/12/6/50," 1950, 9" h, 5" dia	1000	1200
Vase, bulbous w/ closed-in rim, carved w/ lit lanterns in mustard yellow glaze on charcoal blue glossy ground, circular ink stamp and incised "RLH," 5.5" h, 6.5" dia	4500	5500
Vase, bulbous w/ embossed cowboy scene all around, matte chocolate brown glaze, by Flora Huckfield, circular ink stamp, artist's signature, and titled "N.D. Rodeo," 7.25" h, 5" dia	1500	2000
Vase, bulbous w/ full-length carved daffodils, mahogany matte glaze, by McCosh, circular ink stamp, incised "McCosh, '48," 8" h, 5.5" dia	1200	1500
Vase, bulbous w/ slightly flared rim, embossed w/ prairie roses under mottled green crystalline glaze, by Steen and Flora Huckfield, circular ink stamp, incised "Steen-Huck-1100," 5" h, 4.5" dia	1000	1500

	LOW	HIGH
Vase, bulbous w/ tapered neck, carved haystacks, green matte ground, by Flora Huckfield, circular ink stamp, incised "H 164," 4.25" h, 3.5" dia	500	700
Vase, classical form, incised trees, matte green glaze, by Flora Huckfield, circular ink stamp, incised title "Trees/Thorne" and artist's signature, 11" h, 6" dia	4000	6000
Vase, classical form, incised w/ stylized turquoise blossoms and green outline on beige ground, green rim, circular ink stamp, illegible artist signature, 7" h, 3.5" dia	1400	1800
Vase, ovoid, carved w/ full-length sheaves of wheat, purple-brown matte glaze, by Flora Huckfield, circular ink stamp and incised "Huck 30/ No. Dak. Wheat," 10" h, 5.5" dia	1200	1500
Vase, slightly bulging shoulder, carved full-length stylized red and blue flowers w/ green stems on blue ground, by Reinert, circular ink stamp, incised "Reinert 1938," 7.5" h, 3.25" dia	1500	2000
Vase, tapered, carved w/ frieze of bronco riders under brown shading to green matte glaze, by Julia Mattson, circular ink stamp, incised "J.M./133," 6.75" h, 4.5" dia	2000	2500
Vessel, bulging form w/ angled shoulder and tapering to base, carved panels w/ charging bison around shoulder, brown and ocher matte glazes, by Margaret Cable, circular ink stamp, incised title "Bison" and "117A/M. Cable," 5.25" h, 6" dia	2000	2500
Vessel, spherical, carved band of stylized mushrooms in blue and turquoise on white ground, circular ink stamp, incised "June/Maths(?)/May 1949," 6.25" h, 7.5" dia	1500	2000
Vessel, spherical, carved w/ frieze of cobalt coyotes in silhouette against ivory "windows," cobalt ground, by Julia Mattson, circular ink stamp, incised "JM/298," 3.5" h, 3.75" dia	500	750
Vessel, spherical, carved w/ frieze of ox-drawn Conestoga wagons under sandy brown matte glaze, by Margaret Cable, circular ink stamp, incised "M. Cable" and "Covered Wagon," 6" h, 7" dia	1500	2000
Vessel, squat bulbous form, carved w/ bands of leaves around shoulder, glossy blue glaze, circular ink stamp, 4" h, 4.5" dia	150	250
Vessel, squat w/ tapered sides, incised turkeys, matte green glaze, by Julia Mattson, circular ink stamp, incised "JM 170," 3.25" h, 3.75" dia	500	700

North Dakota School of Mines. —Photo courtesy David Rago Auctions, Inc.

Paul Revere/Saturday Evening Girls

The Paul Revere pottery operated in Boston, Massachusetts, from the early 1900s until 1942. The company was originated by a group of immigrant girls who gathered each Saturday for an evening of reading and crafts, thus the name "Saturday Evening Girls." The name was later changed to Paul Revere Pottery because of the pottery's close proximity to the Old North Church.

	LOW	HIGH
Ashtray, commemorative design w/ "1897 E.H.S. 1937" line in black glaze on chicory blue ground, navy blue perimeter band w/ light luster finish, marked "PRP/5-37," 5.25" dia	$100	$200
Bowl, broad flared rim, maroon-mauve glaze interior w/ lightly lustered finish, steel blue exterior w/ luster finish, Revere logo, 3.25" h, 5.75" dia	100	200
Bowl, flared, interior rim design of white lotus flowers surrounded by green leaves and heavily lined in black on chicory blue band, ivory outer band, buttercup yellow ground w/ light luster finish, by Rose Bacchini, 1926, marked "PRP/11-26/RB," 3.5" h, 9" dia	300	500
Bowl, midnite blue glaze w/ light luster finish, interior w/ textured buttercup yellow running glaze extending towards center over deep chicory blue drip glaze, Revere logo, 3" h, 7.5" dia	200	300
Breakfast Set, 3 pcs., comprising large mug, saucer, and plate, central design w/ white crouching rabbit, deep blue and white skyline, and sage green hills, buttercup yellow ground w/ light luster, rim band reads "Byard His Plate (...Mug, ...Saucer)," marked "SEG/7-22/L," 1922	1000	1500
Bud Vase, hand-thrown, mocha brown satin exterior, ivory-tan interior, by Sarah Galner, marked "SEG/1913/SG," 4.125" h	300	400
Centerpiece Bowl, interior perimeter band w/ wood block style design of buttercup yellow stylized tulips and green leaves in repeat, navy blue interior, powder blue white outer band, light luster finish, marked w/ Revere logo and "1-26/JMD," 1926, 2" h, 10" dia	700	900
Creamer, miniature, white lotus flowers lined in black on buttercup yellow band, white glaze ground w/ satin finish, marked "SEG/10-20/LM," 1920, 2" h	100	200
Creamer, repeating design of white squirrel outlined in black on oblong panel of chicory blue and white, ivory-white glaze ground w/ light luster finish, marked "SEG/2-7-12/EG," 1912, 3.25" h, 3.25" w	300	500
Cup and Saucer, landscape design depicting sage green tree groupings heavily lined in black against chicory blue skyline in repeat, ivory ground, light luster finish, by Eva Geneco, marked "SEG/12-19/EG/6-17," 2" h cup, 5.75" dia saucer	200	300
Cup and Saucer, narrow ivory outer rim bands lined in black, sage green ground w/ light luster finish, by Eva Geneco, marked "SEG/1913/1915/EG," 2" h cup, 5.25" dia saucer	100	200
Egg Cup, buttercup yellow hen followed by ivory chick in repeat around rim, unmarked SEG, early 1900s, 1.75" h	400	500
Egg Cup, single white chick outlined in black on chicory blue ground, light luster finish, unmarked SEG, early 1900s, 1.75" h	200	300
Inkwell, square, incised ships w/ sage green sails and deep brown bow lined in black glaze, white skyline, green hills, and chicory blue water, light luster finish, design repeats around sides, by Sarah Galner, marked "SEG/3-14/SG," 1914, 2" h, 4" w	1500	2000
Paperweight, octagonal, incised ship design, buttercup yellow wind-blown sail and deep brown bow w/ horizontal panels, outlined in black, buttercup yellow ground, satin finish, marked "SEG/JG/3-15," 1915, 2.5" w	300	400

	LOW	HIGH
Pitcher, svelte-styled body, light mocha brown band w/ miniature landscape w/ sage green and brown trees, speckled sage green matte ground, by Fannie Levine, marked "SEG/1-11-11/FL," 5" h, 3.75" dia	500	800
Plate, central design w/ rabbit wearing pink and yellow dress, cobalt blue upper sky, white, pink, and buttercup yellow skyline, and sage green field w/ pink flecks throughout, rose-pink ground, frothy white perimeter band, high glaze finish, Revere logo, 6.5" dia	1500	2000
Plate, central incised white cottage w/ deep brown roof, pale green landscaping, cottage overlooking blue water, chicory blue, white, and buttercup yellow skyline, steel blue ground, chicory blue outer band w/ light luster finish, marked "S/1922," 6.5" dia	400	600
Plate, central incised white goose w/ orange beak and feet, surrounded by sage green hills and chicory blue, white, and orange skyline, steel blue ground, broad sage green perimeter band, by Sara Galner, marked "SEG/3-14/EG," 1914, 7.5" dia	1000	1500
Plate, frothy white perimeter band w/ motto "Eate • Thy • Breade • In • Joye • And • Thankfulness" and large rosette, large central "A" inside black ring, deep rose-pink ground and outer band, satin finish, by Lillie Shapiro, signed "Paul Revere Pottery/9-36/LS," 9.5" dia	400	600
Plate, perimeter band decoration w/ light brown pinecones lined in black surrounded by green pine needles against rope design background, light lustered ivory glaze, by Eva Geneco, marked "SEG/2-17/EG," 1917, 7.75" dia	200	300
Plate, white perimeter band w/ "Nancy • Pierce • Her • Plate" and stylized rosettes, scarab blue outer band, chicory blue interior ground lined in black, light luster finish, by Fannie Levine, marked "SEG/9-21/FL," 1921, 7.75" dia	250	400
Porridge Bowl, stylized dancing rabbits design w/ white rabbits on steel blue and chicory blue band on exterior, white interior, by Tillie Block, marked "SEG/3-1-11/TB," 1911, 2.5" h, 5.5" dia	2000	3000
Tile, round, rim inscription "O Don't Bother Me, Said The Hen With One Chick" on ivory band, words alternating w/ incised pale yellow mother hen and ivory chick in repeat, pale yellow ground, high glaze finish, by Fannie Levine, marked "SEG/4-13/FL," 1913, 5.5" dia	1800	2200

Paul Revere/Saturday Evening Girls Pottery, left to right: SEG creamer; Revere plate; SEG cup and saucer; SEG plate; 2 SEG egg cups; Revere centerpiece bowl; SEG creamer; and SEG paperweight. —Photo courtesy Smith & Jones, Inc. Auctions.

Pewabic Pottery

The Pewabic Pottery was founded in 1903. Originally called the Revelation Pottery, "Pewabic" (the Chippewa translation for "clay with a copper color") was soon chosen as a more appropriate name. The earliest pieces were green-glazed vases, bowls, and jars. The pottery closed in 1961 following the death of its founder, Mary Chase Perry Stratton.

	LOW	HIGH
Cabinet Vase, broad shoulder, body tapering to base, gold, green, and ivory lustered glaze, circular stamp "Pewabic/Detroit," paper label, 2.5" h, 3.25" dia	$500	$700
Cabinet Vase, cylindrical, turquoise, green, and blue lustered dripping glaze, circular stamp "Pewabic/Detroit," 2.5" h, 2" dia	400	600
Cabinet Vase, elongated neck, semi-ovoid body, celadon and oxblood lustered glaze, stamped mark, 2.5" h, 2" dia	300	500
Cabinet Vase, semi-ovoid w/ closed-in mouth, celadon and lavender lustered glaze, unmarked, 2.25" h, 2.25" dia	300	500
Cabinet Vase, spherical, thick pink, gold, and blue lustered dripping glaze, circular stamp "Pewabic/Detroit/PP," 2.5" h, 2.75" dia	1000	1500
Plate, blue slip dragonflies positioned wing-to-wing around border w/ tails almost meeting at plate's center, white crackled ground, stamped "Pewabic," 10.75" dia	800	1200
Vase, bulbous, dripping turquoise and purple lustered glaze, stamped circular mark, 3.75" h, 3.75" dia	500	700
Vase, bulbous, lustered celadon and purple glaze, stamped cylindrical mark, remnant of paper label, 4.75" h, 4" dia	400	600
Vase, bulbous, mirrored gold glaze dripping over glossy dark blue ground, circular stamp, 4.75" h, 4" dia	1000	1500
Vase, classical shape, lustered dark blue glaze, impressed mark, 8" h, 6" dia	700	900
Vase, ovoid, gold and mauve lustered glaze, circular stamp, 4.75" h, 3.5" dia	600	800
Vase, rolled rim, sloping shoulder, tapered base, brown, green, and blue dripping matte glaze, stamped "Pewabic," 7" h, 5.25" dia	750	1000
Vessel, squat form, blue, green, and mauve semi-matte glaze, stamped mark, paper label, 3.75" h, 5" dia	600	800

Pewabic Pottery. —Photo courtesy David Rago Auctions, Inc.

Pisgah Forest Pottery

Pisgah Forest Pottery is located near Mount Pisgah, Arden, North Carolina. The company was founded by Walter B. Stephen in 1926. Although easily recognized for its cameo ware decorations featuring Conestoga wagons and rustic landscapes, the pottery also produced art pottery with fine crystalline and flambé glazes.

	LOW	HIGH
Cereal Bowl, Cameo ware, cabin in the mountains scene, 5.5" dia	$100	$200
Milk Pitcher, Cameo ware, covered wagon scene, blue ground, Ardennes mark, 1953, 3" h	150	250
Mug, Cameo ware, cabin in the mountains scene, teal blue ground, embossed "Stephen," 3.5" h, 4" dia	200	300
Vase, baluster-shape, amber flambé glaze w/ blue crystals, raised "Pisgah Forest" and date, 7.5" h, 4.75" dia	400	600
Vase, bottle-shaped, white glaze w/ white crystals, raised potter's mark and date "1941," 8" h, 5.25" dia	600	800
Vase, bulbous body w/ elongated neck, brown and amber flambé glaze w/ clusters of large blue crystals, embossed mark, 7" h, 4" dia	500	700
Vase, Cameo ware, covered wagon scene on elongated neck, glossy green bulbous base, 4.5" h, 4" dia	200	400
Vase, Cameo ware, white guitar and violin players and dancing couples, dead-matte green ground, potter's wheel mark, partial date "195-," 8.5" h, 4.5" dia	500	700
Vase, classical form, amber glaze w/ tightly packed white and blue crystals, raised potter's mark and date "1940," 6.5" h, 4" dia	500	700
Vase, classical form, blue, green, and white crystalline glaze, raised potter's mark, 1949, 7.75" h, 4.25" dia	500	700
Vase, classical form, celadon and caramel crystalline glaze, 8" h, 5.75" dia	700	900
Vase, corseted cylinder, amber glaze w/ gray crystals, raised potter's mark and date, 6.5" h, 4.5" dia	300	500
Vase, corseted cylinder, French blue and bone crystalline glaze, raised potter's mark and date "1944," 6" h, 4.5" dia	300	500
Vessel, spherical, amber flambé glaze w/ celadon crystals, raised Stephen mark and date, 3.75" h, 4.5" dia	200	350
Vessel, squat form, white crystalline glaze, raised potter's mark, 1942, 4.5" h, 6" dia	400	600
Vessel, squat w/ sloping shoulder, white and blue crystalline glaze, raised potter's mark, 1948, 4" h, 5.5" dia	400	600

Pisgah Forest, Cameo ware.

Purinton Pottery

Bernard Purinton moved the company from its 1936 home of Wellsville, Ohio, to Shippenville, Pennsylvania, in 1941. It remained there until its close in 1959. Purinton is best known for its dinnerware, kitchenware and novelties with under-the-glaze hand-painted slip decoration. Many pieces are unmarked. For more information read *Purinton Pottery* by Jamie Bero-Johnson and Jamie Johnson (Schiffer, Atglen, PA, 1997).

Apple pattern.

Apple

	LOW	HIGH
Bean Pot	$30	$40
Beer Mug	115	150
Bowl, rectangular, 14.5"	60	80
Bread and Butter Plate, 6" dia	6	10
Breakfast Plate	15	20
Butter Dish	60	80
Casserole, 9" dia	35	50
Chop Plate, 12" dia	20	30
Coffee Canister, half-oval	60	80
Coffeepot, 8 cup	55	75
Creamer	15	20
Creamer, miniature	10	15
Cup and Saucer	10	15
Dinner Plate, 10" dia	15	20
Dutch Jug, 5 pt	30	40
Fruit Bowl, 12" dia	30	40
Oil and Vinegar Cruets, round, price for pair	75	100
Oil and Vinegar Cruets, square, price for pair	55	75
Party Plate, 8.5" dia	20	30
Pitcher	35	50
Platter, 12" l	20	30
Relish, 3-part	25	35
Salad Bowl, 11" dia	40	55
Salt and Pepper, pair, range size	30	40
Salt Canister, half-oval	85	110
Sugar	18	25
Sugar, miniature	15	20
Teapot, 2 cup	20	30

	LOW	HIGH
Teapot, 6 cup	40	60
Tray, 11" l	35	50
Tumbler	10	15
Vegetable, 8" dia	25	35
Vegetable, divided	40	60

Fruit

Canister, half-oval, red trim	$15	$25
Canister, tall oval, blue trim	30	40
Creamer	10	15
Creamer, miniature	12	18
Cup and Saucer	10	15
Dinner Plate, 10" dia	8	12
Dutch Jug, 5 pt	25	35
Kent Jug, oversized	125	175
Kent Jug, regular size	15	25
Relish Tray, 3-pc	35	50
Salt and Pepper, pair, jug style	15	25
Sugar	12	18
Sugar, miniature	15	25
Sugar Canister, 9" h	60	80

Normandy Plaid

Bean Cup, individual	$30	$45
Beer Mug	35	50
Candleholder, w/ insert	475	600
Chop Plate	25	35
Coffee Cup	5	8
Coffee Mug	45	60
Coffeepot, 8 cup	50	65
Cookie Jar	65	90
Creamer	8	12
Creamer, miniature	15	20
Dutch Jug, 1 pt	30	45
Dutch Jug, 5 pt	50	65
Kent Jug	45	60
Marmalade	60	80
Oil and Vinegar Cruets, round, price for pair	75	100
Oil and Vinegar Cruets, square, price for pair	20	30
Pitcher	45	60
Platter, 11" l	45	60
Platter, 12" l	15	25
Roll Tray	25	35
Rum Jug	115	150
Spaghetti Bowl	100	130
Sugar	10	15
Sugar, miniature	20	30
Tea and Toast Set	12	18
Tumbler	8	12
Vegetable, covered	45	60
Wall Pocket	80	110

Red Wing Pottery

The Red Wing Potteries, Inc., traces its roots to 1878, although it operated under that name only from 1936 until its close in 1967. The early Red Wing stoneware and dinnerware produced from the 1930s onward are collected. Backstamps often use a wing motif. For more information see *Red Wing Dinnerware* by Ray Reiss (Property, Chicago, IL, 1997), *Red Wing Art Pottery: Including Pottery Made for Rum Rill* by Ray Reiss (Property, Chicago, IL, 1996), and *Red Wing Art Pottery* by B. L. Dollen (Collector Books, Paducah, KY, 1997).

Bob White (1955)

	LOW	HIGH
Beverage Server, covered	$80	$100
Bread and Butter Plate, 6" dia	8	12
Bread Tray, 24" l	60	80
Butter Dish	70	95
Butter Warmer, covered	45	60
Casserole, 4 qt	50	65
Cocktail Tray	30	40
Coffee Cup	20	30
Cookie Jar	40	60
Creamer	25	35
Cruet, w/ stopper	150	200
Dinner Plate, 10" dia	15	20
Dish, 5" dia	10	15
Gravy Boat, covered	45	60
Lazy Susan	90	125
Mug	50	70
Pitcher, 3.5 qt	120	160
Platter, 13" l	15	20
Platter, 20" l	30	40
Relish Tray, 3-pc	40	60
Salad Bowl, 12" dia	50	65
Salad Plate, 8" dia	10	15
Shaker, tall	25	35
Soup Plate	25	35
Sugar	30	40
Teapot	80	100
Trivet	90	110
Tumbler	175	225
Vegetable	40	60

Fondoso (1939)

Batter Pitcher	$60	$80
Batter Set Tray	45	60
Bread and Butter Plate, 6" dia	8	12
Butter Dish, large	35	45
Casserole, 8.5" dia	60	80
Chop Plate, 14" dia	30	45
Coffeepot	40	55
Coffee Server	35	50
Console Bowl	30	45
Cookie Jar	30	45

Fondoso Teapot.

	LOW	HIGH
Creamer, large	25	35
Creamer, small	12	18
Cup and Saucer	25	35
Custard Cup	25	35
Dessert Cup, footed	11	20
Dinner Plate, 10" dia	18	25
Dish, 5" dia	15	20
Mixing Bowl, 5" dia	15	25
Mixing Bowl, 9" dia	35	50
Pitcher, straight, 1 pt	40	65
Pitcher, tilt, 2 qt	60	80
Platter, oval, 12" l	25	35
Relish Tray	30	40
Salad Bowl, 12" dia	30	45
Salad Plate, 8" dia	12	20
Salt and Pepper, pair	30	45
Soup Plate, 7.5" dia	18	25
Sugar, large	30	40
Sugar, small	15	20
Syrup Pitcher	40	60
Teapot	50	75
Tumbler, 10 oz	30	40
Vegetable, round, 8" dia	25	35

Pepe

Beverage Server, covered	$80	$100
Bread and Butter Plate, 6" dia	10	15
Bread Tray, 24" l	60	80
Butter Dish	70	90
Casserole, 4 qt	50	100
Creamer	25	35
Cruet, w/ stopper	140	180
Cup and Saucer	20	25
Dinner Plate, 10" dia	15	20
Gravy Boat, covered	45	60
Lazy Susan	75	100
Mug	40	60
Pitcher, 1.5 qt	60	85
Platter, 13" l	30	45
Platter, 15" l	60	80
Relish Tray	40	55

	LOW	HIGH
Salad Bowl, 12" dia	50	65
Shaker, tall	25	35
Soup Plate	25	35
Sugar	30	45
Vegetable	45	60
Water Jar, w/ base, 2 gal	450	610

Tampico

Beverage Server, covered	$80	$100
Butter Dish, covered	70	95
Casserole, covered	50	65
Coffee Cup	20	35
Coffee Mug	20	35
Creamer	30	45
Dinner Plate, 10.5" dia	12	20
Dish, 5" dia	20	25
Gravy Boat, covered	45	60
Nappy	30	45
Pitcher, 1.5 qt	60	80
Pitcher, 3.5 qt	125	175
Platter, 13" l	30	45
Relish Dish	40	60
Salad Plate, 8.5" dia	20	30
Salt and Pepper, pair	30	45
Soup Plate	30	45
Sugar	25	35
Teapot	60	80
Vegetable	30	45
Water Jar, w/ base, 2 gal	450	600

Town and Country (1947)

Bread and Butter Plate, 6" dia	$6	$10
Casserole, individual	25	35
Creamer	12	18
Cruet, w/ stopper	40	60
Cup and Saucer	20	30
Dinner Plate, 10" dia	10	18
Milk Pitcher	50	65
Mixing Bowl, 9" dia	60	80
Mug	40	55
Mustard Jar	40	60
Platter, 9" l	20	35
Platter, 15" l	30	45
Relish Tray, 7" l	20	30
Salad Bowl, 13" dia	35	50
Salad Plate, 8" dia	8	12
Salt and Pepper, pair, large	30	45
Salt and Pepper, pair, small	20	30
Sugar	15	20
Syrup Pitcher	50	75
Teapot	100	130
Vegetable, oval, 8" l	30	45

Rookwood Pottery

Rookwood manufactured pottery from 1879 to 1967. Its heyday was from 1890 to 1930. Standard glaze pieces feature a large, bold underglaze painting. For additional information read *Rookwood* (L-W Book Sales, Gas City, IN, 1993, 1999 value update).

	LOW	HIGH
Bookends, production, figural rooks and geraniums perched on pages of open book, green, mauve, and tan glazes, flame mark and "XXVIII/227," 1928, 6.5" h, 6.5" w, price for pair	$700	$900
Centerpiece Bowl, Jewel Porcelain, polychrome decoration of abstract bird on blossoming branch, by E. T. Hurley, flame mark and "XXIX/2574C/E.T.H," 1929, 3" h, 13" dia	1200	1600
Jardiniere, heavily incised swirling band around shoulder in repeat, curdled pale sage green under olive matte glaze, by Albert Munson, flame mark and "47cz/AM," 1901, 7.5" h, 9" dia	800	1000
Loving Cup, 3-handled, carved w/ yellow clouds and 2 white-sailed galleons on waves, by Albert Pons, flame mark and "VII/659B/AP," 1907, 8.5" h, 8" w	800	1200
Mug, figural owl, vellum, tooled feathers, carved claws, surrounded by veined leaves and embossed acorns, matte green glaze w/ drip brown glaze on owl, flame mark and "VI/1171/V," 1906, 5.5" h, 5" w	700	900
Pitcher, carved w/ band of scrolled decoration under mottled mahogany matte glaze, flame mark and "I/CZ/51/AM," 1901, 6.5" h, 8" w	600	800
Pitcher, Limoges-style, sparrows in flight amidst oriental grasses, deep sage green ground w/ blended brown along base and neck, brushed gold accents throughout, by Albert R. Valentien, impressed kiln mark, "Rookwood 1883/56," and artist's cipher, 1883, 9" h	1000	1500
Plaque, scenic vellum, autumn landscape, by Lenore Asbury, flame mark and "XIV/LA," mounted in original quarter-sawn oak frame, 1914, 5" x 9.25" plaque	3500	5000
Vase, baluster form, vellum, blue-gray intertwining clovers, ground shades from deep gray to pale gray-blue to peach, by Mary Grace Denzler, flame mark and "XIII/V/1096/MGD," 1913, 5.25" h	500	700

Rookwood Pottery. —Photo courtesy Smith & Jones, Inc. Auctions.

Rookwood Pottery.
—Photo courtesy David Rago Auctions, Inc.

	LOW	HIGH
Vase, baluster form, vellum, incised stylized tulip buds finished in maroon-mauve and green in repeat, tulips attached together w/ incised leaf and vine design in deep brown, scarab blue ground, by Louise Abel, flame mark and "XIX/935D/V/LA," 1919, 8.5" h, 4.5" dia	600	900
Vase, bottle shape, heavily incised geometric design extending from neck to mid-section in repeat, watermelon pink drip glaze throughout lip and incised design, cucumber matte ground, by Rose Fechheimer, flame mark, "299/cz," and artist's cipher, 1904, 10" h, 5" dia	800	1200
Vase, bulbous, Jewel Porcelain, ivory dogwood blossoms on mottled taupe ground, by Sara Sax, flame mark, "XXVII/927D," and artist's cipher, 1927, 9.5" h, 6.5" dia	3000	4000
Vase, horizontal recessed band around shoulder w/ embossed sunflowers w/ incised circular centers in repeat, dusty pink ground, flame mark and "XLVII/2591," 1947, 5.5" h	200	300
Vase, Jewel Porcelain, bulbous, pink narcissus and green leaves on purple ground, by K. Shirayamadani, flame mark and "XLIV/6869/KS," 1944, 9" h, 5.25" dia	2000	3000
Vase, Jewel Porcelain, bulbous, yellow, pink, and blue crocus on blue-gray ground, by K. Shirayamadani, flame mark, "XXV/2831," and artist's cipher, 1925, 5.5" h, 5.5" dia	1500	2500
Vase, Jewel Porcelain, flaring rim, pink tulips on shaded gray ground, by M. H. McDonald, flame mark and "XLIII/6305/MHM," 1943, 5" h, 5.5" dia	600	900
Vase, modeled porcelain, Sung Plum, clusters of blue wisteria and green leaves on shaded celadon to burgundy ground, by K. Shirayamadani, flame mark, "XXII/120," and artist's cipher, 1922, 9.5" h, 4.25" dia	12,000	15,000
Vase, mottled wax decoration, peach flower w/ maroon accents surrounded by cucumber green broad leaves, outlined in black, mottled blue-gray around mouth, deep rose shading to pale pink ground, by Sallie E. Coyne, flame mark and "XXV11/914e/SEC," 1927, 6" h, 4.75" dia	600	900
Vase, orange rose w/ green leaves on purple ground, matte finish, by Olga G. Reed, flame mark and "VII/950E/O.G.R.," 1907, 7.25" h, 3" dia	2000	3000
Vase, paneled rectangular form, narrow panel at each corner, light chicory to scarab blue matte glaze, flame mark and "XXV/2841," 1925, 5" h	150	250
Vase, production, 3 embossed lobes rising from base to shoulder, mottled pale green and rose matte glaze, flame mark and "XI/901C/X'd," 1911, 9.5" h, 4.25" dia	500	700

	LOW	HIGH
Vase, production, fleshy poppies molded under dark red and green butterfat glaze, flame mark and "XI/1710," 1911, 11.75" h, 6" dia	1200	1500
Vase, production, ovoid, ribbed neck, embossed sky blue Art Nouveau design in repeat around shoulder, deeply incised lightning bolt design in repeat around base, caramel tan matte w/ green hue ground, flame mark and "XXXV/6537," 1935, 7" h, 5.5" dia	400	600
Vase, scenic vellum, misty landscape in blue, green, yellow, and purple, by Lenore Asbury, flame mark and "XXIII/900B/L.A.," 1923, 10.75" h, 6" dia	2500	3500
Vase, scenic vellum, smoky green trees overlooking mountainous background, sage green grassy plains in foreground, cerulean blue sky blending to creamy peach, dark gray around mouth and base, by Lenore Asbury, flame mark and "XXI/614E/V/L.A.," 1921, 9" h, 4.5" dia	2000	3000
Vase, scenic vellum, tall pines in winter landscape, by Sallie Coyne, flame mark and "XVIII/SEC/1356D," 1918, 9.25" h, 4" dia	2500	3500
Vase, spherical, carved dogwood blossoms and branches on silver-gray ground, by E. T. Hurley, flame mark and "531E/E.T.H.," 1900, 6" h, 5.5" dia	4000	5000
Vase, spherical, yellow daffodils on shaded tan ground, by Albert R. Valentien, flame mark and "I/166Z/A.R.V.," 1901, 4.5" h, 4" dia	1500	2000
Vase, vellum, shoulder decoration of white dogwood flowers w/ deep maroon accents and brown and cream centers, alternating w/ peach-colored closed buds, dark gray ground at shoulder shading to rose and peach at base, by Charles J. McLaughlin, flame mark and "XV/938/V/CJM," 1915, 7" h, 4.25" dia	600	800
Vase, vellum, slightly incised Art Deco design of mottled maroon square w/ hunter green drip streak extension, alternating w/ panels of scarab blue in horizontal black lines, salmon pink ground, by Elizabeth L. Lincoln, flame mark and "XIX/925F/V/L.N.L.," 1919, 7.25" h	700	1000

Rookwood Pottery. —Photo courtesy David Rago Auctions, Inc.

Roseville Pottery

The Roseville factory opened in 1885 in Roseville, Ohio. In 1902, the factory bought a stoneware plant in Zanesville and made art pottery there until 1954. In 1910, the Roseville arm of the company closed. Roseville called its art ware "Rozane" (the sum of *RO*seville and *ZANE*sville).

Beware of recent reproductions. They are generally easy to spot by their color and lack of quality. For further information see *Roseville In All Its Splendor* by John and Nancy Bomm (L-W Book Sales, Gas City, IN, 1998) and Sharon and Bob Huxford's *The Collectors Encyclopedia of Roseville Pottery, First Series* (1976, 1997 value update), and *Second Series* (1980, 1997 value update) published by Collector Books, Paducah, KY.

The following listings are arranged by pattern name, with individual forms indented under each pattern.

	LOW	HIGH
Basket, Apple Blossom, 309-8", green	$225	$275
Basket, Apple Blossom, 310-10", blue	175	225
Basket, Freesia, 391-8", blue	200	250
Basket, Magnolia, 384-8", brown	125	175
Basket, Ming Tree, 509-12", blue	350	400
Basket, Pinecone, 410-10", blue	800	900
Basket, Snowberry, IBK-8", green	130	175
Basket, Snowberry, 1BK-10", green	165	200
Basket, White Rose, 363-10", blue	225	275
Basket, White Rose, 363-10", pink	190	230
Basket, Zephyr Lily, 393-7", blue	165	200
Boat Dish, Wincraft, 227-10"	30	50
Bookends, pair, Bushberry, 9, orange	125	175
Bottle Vase, Wisteria, 630-6", brown	400	450
Bud Vase, Pinecone, 112-7", brown	190	250
Bud Vase, Pinecone, 748-6", blue	300	350
Candlesticks, pair, Freesia, 1161-4½", blue	150	200
Conch Shell, Magnolia, 453-6", green	100	150
Conch Shell, Magnolia, 454-8", blue	100	150
Conch Shell, Water Lily, 438-8", blue	140	170

Roseville Pottery. —Photo courtesy Smith & Jones, Inc. Auctions.

	LOW	HIGH
Console Bowl, Bleeding Heart, 382-10", green	125	175
Console Set, Bushberry, centerbowl (415-10"), flower frog (45), and pair of candlesticks (1147-C.S.), orange	200	250
Console Set, Clematis, centerbowl (1159-10") and pair of candlesticks (1159-4"), blue	125	175
Cornucopia, Pinecone, 128-8", blue	225	275
Cornucopia, Pinecone, 422-8", green	90	120
Cornucopia, White Rose, 144-3", green	90	115
Cornucopias, pair, Zephyr Lily, 204-8", green	165	200
Creamer and Sugar, Magnolia, 4S and 4C, brown	50	75
Double Bud Vase, Rosecraft Panel, 5" h	150	200
Double Wall Pockets, pair, Pinecone, 1273-8", brown	400	500
Ewer, Apple Blossom, 318-15", blue	700	800
Ewer, Bleeding Heart, 972-10", pink	250	300
Ewer, Freesia, 19-6", brown	100	150
Ewer, Zephyr Lily, 24-15", brown	200	250
Fan Vase, Bleeding Heart, 970-9", blue	225	275
Fan Vase, Pinecone, 472-6", blue	450	550
Fan Vase, Wincraft, 272-6"	65	80
Floor Vase, Magnolia, 98-15", blue or brown	300	375
Floor Vase, Peony, 70-18", green	550	600
Floor Vase, Water Lily, 85-18", blue	550	650
Floor Vase, Zephyr Lily, 142-18", green	650	750
Flower Pot, Pinecone, 633-5", green	90	115
Flower Pot and Saucer, Pinecone, 636-5", green	140	165
Hanging Basket, Zephyr Lily, 472-5", blue	275	325
Jardiniere, Freesia, 669-8", blue	275	325
Jardiniere, Fuchsia, 645-8", green	650	700
Jardiniere, Rozane, 588-10", cream	150	200
Jardiniere, Snowberry, KJ-8", pink	275	350
Pillow Vase, Pinecone, 845-8", green	225	275
Pillow Vase, White Rose, 987-9", brown	165	200
Pitcher, Bleeding Heart, 1123, green	375	450
Pitcher, Bushberry, 1325, blue	250	300
Pitcher, Freesia, 21-15", brown	200	250
Pitcher, Pinecone, 415-9", blue	715	825
Pitcher, Pinecone, 708-9", green	500	600
Planter, Pinecone, 379-9", brown	300	350
Trumpet Vase, Pinecone, 908-8", brown	400	450
Umbrella Stand, Bushberry, 779-21", orange	550	650
Urn, Clematis, 111-10", brown	65	80
Urn, Snowberry, IV-15", pink	450	525
Urn, Water Lily, 175-8", blue	100	135
Vase, Apple Blossom, 389-10", blue	125	175
Vase, Apple Blossom, 392-15", pink	275	350
Vase, Baneda, 235-5", green	600	700
Vase, Bushberry, 38-12", orange	150	200
Vase, Clematis, 107-8", blue	75	100
Vase, Clematis, 111-10", blue	75	100
Vase, Columbine, 400-6", blue	200	250
Vase, Ferella, 499-6", pink	1000	1200
Vase, Freesia, 121-8", green	100	150
Vase, Freesia, 125-10", brown	100	125
Vase, Freesia, 598-8", brown	225	250

	LOW	HIGH
Vase, Freesia, 895-7", blue	275	325
Vase, Fuchsia, 347-6", blue	400	450
Vase, Futura, 196-12", blue, sailboat	400	500
Vase, Magnolia, 91-8", green	75	100
Vase, Ming Tree, 585-14", white	450	500
Vase, Montacello, 562-7"	900	1000
Vase, Montacello, 563-8"	900	1000
Vase, Pinecone, 261-6", brown	250	300
Vase, Pinecone, 704-7", blue	275	325
Vase, Pinecone, 705-9", brown	165	200
Vase, Pinecone, 712-12", brown	650	400
Vase, Pinecone, 747-10", brown	350	425
Vase, Pinecone, 847-9", blue	400	500
Vase, White Rose, 982-7", pink	165	200
Vase, White Rose, 991-12", blue	225	275
Vase, White Rose, 992-15", pink	250	300
Vase, Wincraft, 234-10"	165	200
Vase, Wincraft, 283-8"	50	75
Vase, Wincraft, 285-10"	225	260
Vase, Wincraft, 286-12"	100	130
Vase, Windsor, 546-6", blue	400	450
Vase, Zephyr Lily, 131-7", green	100	130
Vase, Zephyr Lily, 137-10", brown	225	260
Vase, Zephyr Lily, 139-12", brown	275	325
Vessel, Blackberry, 568-4"	550	600
Vessel, Pinecone, 278-4", brown	165	200
Wall Pocket, Apple Blossom, 366-8", pink	250	300
Wall Pocket, Bleeding Heart, 1287-8", pink	375	450
Wall Pocket, Ming Tree, 566-8", white or pink	250	300
Wall Pockets, pair, Freesia, 1296-8", brown	250	350
Window Box, Wincraft, 268-12"	90	110

Roseville Pottery. —Photo courtesy Smith & Jones, Inc. Auctions.

Royal Doulton

Royal Doulton figures are ceramic works of art. Although the English company produces other items, its HN series is the best known. The company was begun in the early 1800s by John Doulton. The HN series was introduced in 1913 and named after Harry Hixon, head colorist at the time.

Besides their figurines, there are many different Royal Doulton collectibles, including Toby jugs, plates, limited editions, and bird and animal figures. Royal Doulton figures are identified by the HN prefix followed by numbers in a chronological sequence. Subjects in this series are highly diverse representing the works of many different artists at different time periods.

The earliest Royal Doulton figures (with the lower HN numbers) are usually the most desirable to collectors. For more information consult *The Charlton Standard Catalogue of Royal Doulton Beswick Figurines, Sixth Edition* by Jean Dale (Charlton Press, Toronto, Canada, 1998).

Figures

	LOW	HIGH
HN13, Picardy Peasant	$2500	$3000
HN21, Crinoline	1500	2000
HN34, Moorish Minstrel	3000	3500
HN48, Lady of the Fan	2000	2500
HN69, Pretty Lady	900	1200
HN87, Lady Anne	3500	4000
HN310, Dunce	3200	3600
HN327, Curtsey	1800	2000
HN405, Japanese Fan	2500	3000
HN456, Welsh Girl	3000	3500
HN459, Omar Khayyam and the Beloved	5500	6000
HN464, Captain MacHeath	700	1000
HN506, Marie	3000	3500
HN554, Uriah Heep, 2nd version	300	500
HN561, Fruit Gathering	3000	3500
HN570, Woman Holding Child	2500	2800
HN593, Nude on Rock	1500	2000
HN657, Mask	1800	2000
HN661, Boy with Turban	900	1200
HN678, Lady with Shawl	5000	5500
HN701, Welsh Girl	3000	3300
HN713, One of the Forty, 12th version	1500	1800
HN728, Victorian Lady	300	600
HN797, Moorish Minstrel	3500	4000
HN1201, Hunts Lady	2500	3000
HN1223, Geisha, 2nd version	1000	1500
HN1225, Boy with Turban	1000	1500
HN1233, Susanna	1200	1600
HN1272, Negligee	2000	2500
HN1292, Geisha, 2nd version	1000	1500
HN1298, Sweet and Twenty	200	400
HN1304, Harlequinade Masked	2500	3000
HN1305, Siesta	3000	3500
HN1306, Midinette	2800	3200
HN1357, Kathleen	900	1200
HN1369, Boy on Pig	4500	5500
HN1372, Darling	800	1200

Royal Doulton Figurines. —Photo courtesy Gene Harris Antique Auction Center, Inc.

	LOW	HIGH
HN1378, Fairy	700	1000
HN1380, Fairy	1200	1600
HN1390, Doreen	900	1200
HN1413, Margery	450	650
HN1453, Sweet Anne	300	500
HN1455, Molly Malone	2500	3000
HN1458, Monica	500	700
HN1502, Lucy Ann	250	450
HN1504, Sweet Maid	1200	1800
HN1506, Rose	300	500
HN1521, Eugene	900	1200
HN1523, Lisette	1200	1500
HN1616, Bookend, Tony Weller	2500	3000
HN1618, Maisie	600	800
HN1620, Rosabell	1500	2000
HN1633, Clemency	900	1200
HN1637, Evelyn	1200	1500
HN1642, Granny's Shawl	500	750
HN1656, Dainty May	500	750
HN1668, Sibell	1200	1500
HN1670, Gillian	750	1000
HN1679, Babie	75	200
HN1688, Rhoda	700	1000
HN1689, Calumet	800	1000
HN1694, Virginia	800	1200
HN1717, Diana	400	600
HN1721, Frangcon	1000	1500
HN1723, Coming of Spring	3000	3500
HN1744, Mirabel	1200	1500
HN1756, Lizana	700	1200
HN1849, Top o' the Hill	100	300
HN1853, Mirror	3000	3500
HN1858, Dawn with Headdress	2500	3000
HN1859, Tildy	1000	1500

	LOW	HIGH
HN1928, Marguerite	300	500
HN1935, Sweeting	90	250
HN1938, Sweeting	650	900
HN1940, Toinette	1500	2000
HN1949, Lady Charmain	200	400
HN1955, Lavinia	60	200
HN1962, Genevieve	325	500
HN2048, Mary Had a Little Lamb	100	250
HN2049, Curly Locks	400	600
HN2050, Wee Willie Winkie	400	600
HN2103, Mask Seller	250	350
HN2106, Linda	60	250
HN2107, Valerie	100	250
HN2157, Gypsy Dance	500	700
HN2158, Alice	100	250
HN2165, Janice	500	700
HN2173, Organ Grinder	700	900
HN2179, Noelle	400	600
HN2184, Sunday Morning	250	450
HN2203, Teenager	200	400
HN2205, Master Sweep	600	800
HN2209, Hostess of Williamsburg	100	350
HN2218, Cookie	90	250
HN2229, Southern Belle	250	400
HN2319, Bachelor	300	500
HN2338, Penny	50	200
HN2352, Stitch in Time	90	250
HN2361, Laird	250	350
HN2373, Joanne	100	250
HN2380, Sweet Dreams	175	300
HN2382, Secret Thoughts	300	450
HN2712, Mantilla	300	500
HN2713, Tenderness, white	70	200
HN2715, Patricia	50	200
HN2724, Clarinda	120	300
HN2731, Thanks Doc	300	450
HN2799, Ruth	200	450
HN2803, First Dance	200	350
HN2808, Balinese Dancer	700	1000
HN2810, Solitude	100	300
HN2811, Stephanie	200	350
HN2814, Eventide	200	350
HN2824, Harmony	100	300
HN2839, Nicola	350	500
HN2923, Barliman Butterbur	50	200
HN2937, Gail	200	400
HN2938, Isadora	175	300
HN2939, Donna	100	250
HN2954, Samantha	50	200
HN2955, Nancy	100	250
HN2956, Heather	100	250
HN2958, Amy	60	200
HN3042, Gillian	150	300
HN3045, Demure	100	250

Character Jugs

	LOW	HIGH
D5556, Jester	$100	$150
D6138, Mr. Micawber	50	100
D6251, Beefeater	100	150
D6385, Falstaff	50	100
D6517, Rip Van Winkle	50	100
D6521, Bacchus	50	100
D6534, Robin Hood	50	100
D6539, Robinson Crusoe	50	100
D6563, Gulliver	500	600
D6634, The Gardener	100	150
D6642, Henry VIII	150	200
D6710, Groucho Marx	175	225

Toby Jugs

D6070, Happy John	$75	$125
D6108, Honest Measure	100	150
D6109, Jolly Toby, blue pants	500	600
D6266, Cap'n Cuttle	200	300
D6320, The Huntsman, variation 4	125	175
D6767, Flora Fuchsia the Florist	125	175
D6910, The Jester	200	250
D6935, The Clown	175	225
D6940, Father Christmas	150	200

Character and Toby Jugs, top row left to right: Falstaff; Honest Measure; Happy John; Robin Hood; Beefeater; Bacchus. Bottom row left to right: Jester; Happy John; Mr. Micawber; The Gardener; Robinson Crusoe; Rip Van Winkle. —Photo courtesy Gene Harris Antique Auction Center, Inc.

Salem China

The Salem China Company reached its 100th year in 1968 solely as a distributor. Its semi-porcelain dinnerware, famous in the 1930s and 1940s, ceased production in 1967.

Briar Rose (c1930)

	LOW	HIGH
Berry Bowl, 5" dia	$3	$5
Bread and Butter Plate, 6" dia	3	5
Butter Dish, open	14	18
Cake Plate, 10" dia	5	8
Casserole	20	26
Creamer	6	10
Cup and Saucer	7	11
Dinner Plate, 10" dia	8	12
Gravy Boat	11	15
Luncheon Plate, 9" dia	6	10
Pickle Dish	4	6
Platter, 11" l	6	10
Platter, 13" l	8	12
Platter, 22" l	40	60
Salad Plate, 7" dia	4	8
Soup, coupe	5	8
Sugar	8	12
Vegetable, 8" dia	10	15

Tricorne (1934)

Berry Bowl, 5" dia	$3	$5
Bread and Butter Plate, 6" dia	3	5
Casserole	25	35
Comport	18	25
Creamer	12	18
Cup and Saucer	12	18
Dinner Plate, 10" dia	8	12
Nut Dish, 4" dia	6	10
Sugar	15	20

Victory (1938)

Cake Plate, 10" dia	$5	$8
Candleholder	15	20
Casserole	25	35
Cereal Bowl, 6" dia	6	10
Coffeepot	40	50
Creamer	5	10
Cup and Saucer	6	12
Dinner Plate, 10" dia	8	12
Gravy Boat	10	15
Salt and Pepper, pair	15	20
Soup Plate, 8.25" dia	5	8
Sugar	8	12
Vegetable, round, 8" dia	10	15

Sebring China

The Sebring family established the town of Sebring, Ohio, in 1899. There they consolidated their various business ventures and built the Sebring Pottery to produce semiporcelain dinnerware. Some art ware and kitchenware were made in the 1930s. The name Sebring vanished in the 1943 takeover by National Unit Distributors, although some patterns continued being manufactured.

Aristocrat (1932)

	LOW	HIGH
Bread and Butter Plate, 6" dia	$2	$4
Casserole	15	20
Coffeepot	25	30
Creamer	8	10
Cup and Saucer	6	8
Dinner Plate, 9" dia	5	8
Platter, 13" l	8	10
Salad Plate, 7" dia	3	5
Salt and Pepper, pair	10	12
Soup Plate, 7.5" dia	5	8
Sugar	6	8
Teapot	25	30

Doric (1930)

Batter Pitcher	$20	$25
Berry Bowl, 5" dia	1	2
Bread and Butter Plate, 6" dia	2	4
Creamer	8	10
Cup and Saucer	4	6
Dinner Plate, 9" dia	4	6
Gravy Boat	8	10
Platter, rectangular, 11" l	4	6
Platter, rectangular, 13" l	6	8
Salad Plate, 7" dia	3	5
Soup, coupe, 7.5 l	4	6
Sugar	6	8
Vegetable, 8" dia	8	10

Trojan

Berry Bowl, 5" dia	$1	$3
Bread and Butter Plate, 6" dia	1	3
Casserole	15	20
Chop Plate, 11" dia	6	6
Coffeepot	20	30
Creamer	8	10
Cup and Saucer	8	10
Dinner Plate, 9" dia	5	8
Egg Cup	8	10
Gravy Boat	12	16
Salad Plate, 7" dia	2	4
Sugar	6	8
Vegetable, oval, 9" l	12	15

Shawnee Pottery

The Shawnee Pottery Company produced earthenware art pottery and brightly colored dinnerware and kitchenware from 1937 through 1961. For further reading consult *The Collector's Guide to Shawnee Pottery* by Duane and Janice Vanderbilt (Collector Books, Paducah, KY, 1992, 1998 value update) and *Shawnee Pottery* by Jim and Bev Mangus (Collector Books, Paducah, KY, 1994, 1998 value update).

Marks include an embossed *USA*, and/or *Shawnee*, and/or a shape number. Some pieces are unmarked. Items trimmed in gold command a premium.

King Corn, salt and pepper shakers.

King Corn

	LOW	HIGH
Casserole, covered, #74	$75	$100
Cereal Bowl, #94	50	65
Cookie Jar	150	200
Creamer, #70	25	35
Dinner Plate, 10" dia	35	45
Dish, 6" l	10	15
Mixing Bowl, #5	35	45
Mixing Bowl, #6	35	45
Mug, #69, 8 oz	40	55
Pitcher, 1 qt	80	100
Platter, 12" l	50	70
Relish Tray, #79	35	45
Salad Plate, 7.25" dia	30	40
Salt and Pepper, pair	25	35
Teapot, 30 oz	75	100
Tumbler	30	40
Utility Jar	40	55

Queen Corn

Butter Dish, covered, #72	$25	$35
Cookie Jar, #66	125	175
Dinner Plate, 10.5" dia	8	12
Fruit Bowl, #92, 6" dia	10	15
Mixing Bowl, #5, 5" dia	12	18
Mixing Bowl, #6, 6.5" dia	15	25
Mixing Bowl, #8, 8" dia	20	30
Mug, #69, 8 oz	18	225

	LOW	HIGH
Pitcher, #7, 1 qt	40	55
Platter, #96, 12" l	20	30
Salad Plate, 7.25" dia	2	4
Shaker, #77, 5.25" h	5	8
Teapot, #75	100	150
Vegetable, #95, 9" dia	25	35

Miscellaneous

Cookie Jar, Jack, gold trim	$275	$375
Cookie Jar, Muggsy	375	475
Cookie Jar, Puss 'N Boots	175	250
Cookie Jar, Smiley, blue bib, cold paint	65	85
Cookie Jar, Smiley, shamrock	200	300
Cookie Jar, Smiley, yellow bib, gold trim	275	325
Cookie Jar, Winnie, blue collar	225	275
Planter, bird and cup, #502	10	15
Planter, boy and wheelbarrow, #750	12	18
Planter, butterfly, #524	12	18
Planter, clown, #607	30	40
Planter, cockatiel, #522	6	12
Planter, elf shoe, white, gold trim, #765	10	15
Planter, man w/ pushcart, #621	12	18
Planter, rocking horse, pink, #526	18	25
Planter, rooster, #503	15	25
Planter, windmill, blue, #715	15	25
Salt and Pepper, pair, chanticleer, large	50	60
Salt and Pepper, pair, flower pots, small	18	25
Salt and Pepper, pair, fruit, small	20	30
Salt and Pepper, pair, Jack and Jill, small	40	50
Salt and Pepper, pair, milk cans, small	15	25
Salt and Pepper, pair, Muggsy, large	125	175
Salt and Pepper, pair, owls, blue eyes, small	10	18
Salt and Pepper, pair, Puss 'N Boots, small	35	45
Salt and Pepper, pair, Smiley and Winnie, small	40	60

Shawnee, left to right: Elephant creamers; Winnie and Smiley salt and pepper shakers, small and large sizes. —Photo courtesy Gene Harris Antique Auction Center, Inc.

Southern Potteries

Southern Potteries, Inc., operated from 1920 to 1957. The company is best known for its hand-painted under-the-glaze Blue Ridge line of dinnerware, usually featuring floral designs. The pottery also produced decal-decorated hotel ware and dinnerware. For more information see *Collector's Encyclopedia of Blue Ridge Dinnerware, Vol. II* by Betty and Bill Newbound (Collector Books, Paducah, KY, 1998).

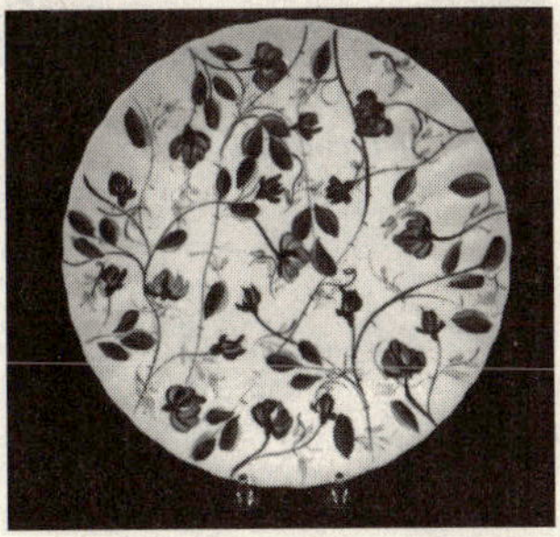

Briar Patch.

Briar Patch

	LOW	HIGH
Bread and Butter Plate, 6" dia	$4	$8
Butter Dish	25	45
Cake Plate	25	40
Cake Server	25	40
Celery	15	30
Chop Plate	25	40
Coffeepot	70	120
Creamer	15	20
Cup and Saucer	8	20
Dinner Plate, 10" dia	10	25
Dish, 5" dia	6	12
Egg Cup	25	40
Fork and Spoon	65	95
Gravy Boat	12	25
Grill Plate	30	50
Party Plate	20	30
Pickle Dish	15	25
Platter	40	60
Salad Bowl, large	25	40
Salad Plate, 8" dia	6	12
Salt and Pepper, pair	12	25
Sherbet	15	30
Soup Plate, 8" dia	12	20
Sugar	12	18
Teapot	75	125
Tidbit, 3-tier	25	40
Vegetable, covered	55	75
Vegetable, open	15	30

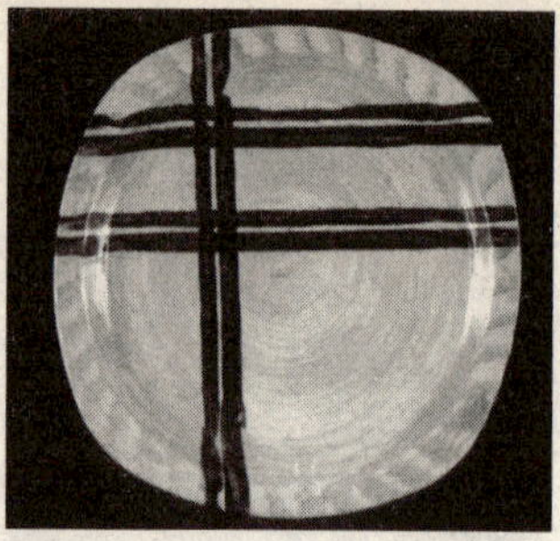

Piedmont Plaid.

Piedmont Plaid

	LOW	HIGH
Bread and Butter Plate	$5	$10
Butter Pat	18	25
Cake Plate	18	25
Chop Plate	18	25
Coffeepot	75	100
Covered Toast	85	115
Creamer	10	15
Cup and Saucer	8	12
Dinner Plate	8	15
Egg Cup	18	30
Gravy Boat	10	25
Pickle Dish	12	20
Platter	12	30
Salad Plate	6	10
Salt and Pepper, pair	10	20
Sherbet	12	18
Soup Plate	10	15
Sugar	12	18
Teapot	50	100
Tidbit, 3-tier	20	35
Vegetable, open	12	25

Trellis

Butter Pat	$35	$45
Cake Plate	35	50
Caker Server	35	55
Celery Tray	25	45
Coffeepot	150	200
Egg Cup	35	55
Fork and Spoon	100	135
French Casserole	35	60
Grill Plate	40	70
Party Plate	30	45
Pickle Dish	25	35
Plate, square	12	30
Salt and Pepper, pair	18	45
Tidbit, 3-tier	35	55
Vegetable, covered	80	135

Stangl Pottery

In 1926, John M. Stangl, acting as president of Fulper, bought the Anchor Pottery Company of Trenton and began manufacturing there as the Stangl Pottery Company. The company manufactured dinnerware and decorative accessories, including their famous bird figures, produced from 1940 until 1972. Several birds were reissued between 1972 and 1977. These versions are dated on the bottom and worth approximately one half the value of the original birds.

After Stangl's death in 1972, the Wheaton Glass Company purchased and ran the company until 1978. For more information see *Stangl and Pennsbury Birds* by Mike Schneider (Schiffer, Atglen, PA, 1994) and *Collector's Encyclopedia of Stangl Dinnerware* by Robert Runge, Jr. (Collector Books, Paducah, KY, 1999).

Birds

	LOW	HIGH
3250A, Standing Duck, 3.25" h	$125	$175
3250C, Feeding Duck, 1.375" h	75	100
3250F, Quacking Duck, 3.625" h	125	175
3275, Turkey, 3.375" h	375	500
3276, Bluebird, 5.125" h	75	100
3276D, Bluebirds, reissued, 8.25" h	200	275
3405D, Cockatoos, reissued, 9.5" h	120	160
3407, Owl, 4.5" h	200	275
3443, Flying Duck, 9" h	225	300
3444, Cardinal, 6.75" h	150	200
3446, Hen, 7.5" h	175	250
3450, Passenger Pigeon, 9.25" x 19.25"	1000	1500
3451, Willow Ptarmigan, 11" h	2500	3200
3453, Mountain Bluebird, 6.375" h	1000	1500
3454, Key West Quail Dove, wings raised, 9" h	800	1200
3490D, Redstarts, 9.5" h	200	300
3491/3492, Hen/Cock Pheasant, 6.625" h and 6.125" h	275	375
3518D, White-Crowned Pigeons, 7.875" x 12.5"	600	850
3580, Cockatoo, 8.75" h	100	150
3581, Chickadees, 5.75" x 8.25"	350	500
3582D, Parakeets, 7.5" h	250	350
3599D, Hummingbirds, reissued, 8.75" h	275	325
3627, Rivoli Hummingbird, 6.125" h	175	250
3628, Rieffers Hummingbird, reissued, 4.825" h	80	100
3635, Goldfinch, 4.5" x 12.5"	250	350
3717D, Bluejays, 13" h	3500	4500
3749S, Western Tanager, 5" h	325	425
3750D, Western Tanagers, 8" h	425	600
3752D, Red-Headed Woodpeckers, 7.75" h	325	450
3754D, White Wing Crossbills, 8.625" h	400	550
3755, Audubon Warbler, 4.5" h	425	600
3852, Cliff Swallow, 3.5" h	175	250
3853, Golden Crowned Kinglets, 5.5" h	600	750
3868, Summer Tanager, 3.625" h	425	575
3923, Vermillion Flycatcher, 5.75" h	850	1200
3924, Yellow-Throated Warbler, 5.75" h	350	500

#1902 Pattern, beverage set. —Photo courtesy Skinner, Inc., Boston, MA.

#1902 Pattern

	LOW	HIGH
Beverage Set, 2-qt pitcher w/ ice lip, 6 tumblers, and metal stand	$200	$300
Bowl, 9" dia	40	60
Jug, .5 pt	20	30
Jug, 1 pt	30	45
Jug, 1 qt	40	60
Tumbler	20	30

Ranger Pattern (Cactus and Cowboy)

Bowl, oval, 10" l	$125	$175
Bread and Butter Plate, 6" dia	75	100
Candleholders, pair	275	375
Carafe, w/ stopper, wooden handle	250	350
Charger, 14" dia	500	700
Chop Plate, 12" dia	250	350
Creamer	100	150
Cup and Saucer	100	200
Dinner Plate, 10" dia	250	350
Fruit Bowl	100	150
Luncheon Plate, 9" dia	200	300
Porridge Bowl, 6" dia	100	200
Salad Plate, 7.75" dia	200	300
Platter, oval, 12" l	250	350
Salt and Pepper, pair, figural Ranger	300	450
Salt and Pepper, pair, onion bulb shape	250	350
Sugar	125	175
Teapot	250	350

Ranger pattern. —Photo courtesy David Rago Auctions, Inc.

Taylor, Smith and Taylor China

In 1901 the Taylor, Smith and Lee Company changed its name to Taylor, Smith and Taylor. It produced semiporcelain toilet ware, dinnerware, kitchenware and specialties. Its most famous dinnerware line is Lu-Ray, produced in solid-colored pastels. Anchor Hocking bought the company in 1972. For additional information read *Collector's Guide to Lu-Ray Pastels U.S.A.* by Bill and Kathy Meehan (Collector Books, Paducah, KY, 1995, 1998 value update).

Dandelion pattern.

Dandelion

	LOW	HIGH
Berry Bowl, 5" dia	$3	$5
Bread and Butter Plate	4	6
Dinner Plate	8	12
Platter, 13.5" l	10	15
Salad Plate	6	8

Lu-Ray (1938)

	LOW	HIGH
Bread and Butter Plate	$3	$6
Butter Dish	30	40
Cake Plate, lug	25	35
Casserole	70	90
Chop Plate	20	30
Coaster	25	35
Dinner Plate	8	12
Egg Cup	12	18
Gravy Boat	15	25
Grill Plate	15	25
Mixing Bowl	45	75
Muffin Cover	60	75
Nut Dish	20	30
Pitcher, 1 qt	60	80
Pitcher, 2 qt	35	45
Platter	10	15
Relish Tray, 4 pc	75	100
Salt and Pepper, pair	8	15
Soup Plate	8	12
Teapot	45	60
Tumbler, 5 oz	20	30
Vegetable	8	12

Teco Pottery

Teco pottery is art pottery produced by the The American Terra Cotta and Ceramic Company, located in Terra Cotta, Illinois. The name was derived from the first two letters of "Terra Cotta." The company was established in 1886 and operated until about 1930, when the pottery was sold. Marks include the name Teco (tall "T" with the letters "eco" written vertically to its right) and model numbers.

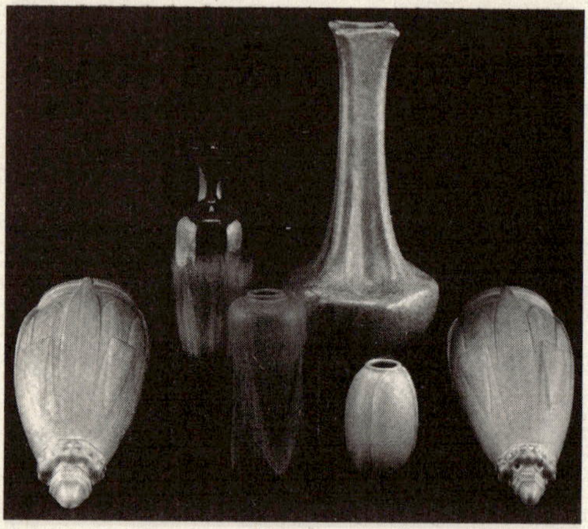

Teco Pottery. —Photo courtesy David Rago Auctions, Inc.

	LOW	HIGH
Bowl, squat w/ flared rim, matte green glaze, impressed "Teco," 2.5" h, 7" dia	$600	$800
Cabinet Vase, bulbous w/ flared rim, matte green glaze, impressed "Teco," 3.75" h, 3.25" dia	300	500
Jardiniere, slightly flared closed-in rim, matte green and charcoal glaze, impressed "Teco," 4" h, 7" dia	600	800
Vase, 4-sided, lobed rim, organic buttressed feet, medium matte green glaze, by Fernand Moreau, impressed "Teco," 13.25" h, 6" w	2000	3000
Vase, amphora shape, 2-handled, matte green glaze, impressed "Teco," 9" h, 5" w	800	1200
Vase, beaker-shaped w/ 2 buttressed handles, matte green glaze, impressed "Teco," 8" h, 5.75" w	2000	2500
Vase, bottle-shaped, mirrored black, gold, and amber microcrystalline flambé glaze, impressed "Teco," 10.5" h, 3.75" dia	2500	3500
Vase, bulbous w/ 2 long buttressed handles, dripping blue-gray over brown matte glaze, impressed "Teco," 7" h, 4" w	600	800
Vase, bulbous w/ flaring scalloped rim, matte green and charcoal glaze, impressed "Teco," 5" h, 4.5" dia	300	500
Vase, cylindrical w/ 2 long buttresses, matte green glaze, impressed "Teco," 6.5" h, 2.25" w	1200	1800
Vase, cylindrical w/ horizontal ribs, matte green glaze, impressed "Teco," 5" h, 4" dia	400	600
Vase, daffodil form w/ fluted and flaring rim, blade leaves in high-relief buttressed around base, matte green glaze, impressed "Teco," 11.5" h, 4.75" dia	7000	9000

	LOW	HIGH
Vase, double gourd-shaped w/ 4 buttresses, matte green glaze, impressed "Teco," 6.5" h, 5.5" dia	3000	4000
Vase, gourd-shaped, embossed organic decoration, dark green matte glaze, impressed "Teco," 10" h, 7" dia	3000	4000
Vase, gourd-shaped w/ buttressed handles, cut-out forms around rim, embossed oriental floral design on sides, matte green glaze, impressed "Teco/113," 6.5" h, 5.5" dia	2000	3000
Vase, Ikebana, bullet-shaped w/ reticulated blade-shaped leaves curving in to rim, embossed lotus blossoms near base, leathery matte green glaze w/ gunmetal accents, impressed "Teco," 11.5" h, 5.5" dia	7500	9500
Vase, organic form w/ tall neck on squat base, green and charcoal matte glaze, impressed "Teco," 16.5" h, 8" dia	1200	1800
Vase, ovoid w/ 4 lobes, matte green glaze, impressed "Teco," 5.5" h, 3.5"	800	1200
Vase, spherical w/ 4 flaring buttressed feet, matte green glaze, impressed "Teco/339," 12.5" h, 10.5" dia	4000	6000
Vase, squat bulbous form w/ horizontal ribs, dark matte green glaze, impressed "Teco/51," 4" h, 4" dia	300	500
Vase, tapered cylinder w/ 4 double-buttressed legs, matte blue glaze, impressed "Teco/127," 9" h, 4" dia	2000	3000
Vase, tapered cylindrical form w/ reticulated blade-shaped leaves around pedestal base, matte green and charcoal glaze, impressed "Teco," 18" h, 6" w	25,000	35,000
Vase, tulip-shaped w/ 4 long buttresses, matte cobalt glaze, by Fernand Moreau, impressed "Teco," 11.5" h, 5" w	3000	4000
Vase, tulip-shaped w/ 4 long buttresses, matte green glaze, by Fernand Moreau, impressed "Teco/463," 12" h, 5" w	3000	4000
Wall Pocket, embossed stylized leaves, matte green glaze, impressed "Teco/156A," 16.75" h, 6.5" w	1500	2500

Teco Pottery. —Photo courtesy David Rago Auctions, Inc.

Van Briggle Pottery

Artus and Anne Van Briggle founded this arts and crafts pottery in 1901. It dominated the western market with pots and vases of stylized tree limbs, cactus and other plants. Glaze colors included Mountain Craig (green to brown), Midnight (black), Moonglo (off-white), Persian Rose, Turquoise Ming and Russet.

The first and most famous mark consisted of the letters *AA*, the initials of Van Briggle and his wife, Anne. Prior to 1920, the mark often included the date of production. These are the most desirable pieces. A stock number often appeared, especially on later pieces. The words *HAND CARVED* are often found on pieces with raised decoration. For further reading consult *The Collector's Encyclopedia of Van Briggle Art Pottery* by Richard Sasicki and Josie Fania (Collector Books, Paducah, KY, 1993, 1999 value update).

	LOW	HIGH
Bud Vase, flaring rim, embossed stylized flowers, matte green glaze, impressed "AA/Van Briggle/Colo. Springs/1906," 6.5" h, 3.25" dia	$500	$700
Cabinet Vase, bulbous, dark blue and green glaze, incised "AA/Van Briggle/ 1902/101/OD/111," 1902, 4" h, 3.5" dia	900	1200
Cabinet Vase, bulbous, embossed flowers, thick dark blue glaze, incised "AA/Van Briggle/1903/III/189," 3.5" h, 3" dia	400	600
Paperweight, horned toad, matte amber glaze, matte green base, c1914, 4.75" h, 3.25" l	900	1200
Plate, embossed purple grape clusters on textured turquoise ground, marked "AA/Van Briggle/Colo. Spgs/15," 1907-11, 8.25" dia	500	750
Vase, bottle-shaped, embossed stylized papyrus, matte blue-green glaze, impressed "AA/Van Briggle/Colo Spgs/639," 8.75" h, 5" dia	1000	1500
Vase, bottle-shaped, green and charcoal matte glaze, incised "AA Van Briggle," impressed "338," c1905	200	400

Van Briggle Pottery. —Photo courtesy David Rago Auctions, Inc.

	LOW	HIGH
Vase, bulbous, embossed crocuses, matte green glaze, impressed "AA/Van Briggle/Colo Spgs/692," 1907-11, 7.5" h, 3.75" dia	700	900
Vase, bulbous, embossed green leaves and red berries, matte raspberry glaze, incised "AA Van Briggle/1904/164," 8.5" h, 7" dia	2500	3500
Vase, bulbous, embossed stylized circular flowers, matte gray-green glaze, #654, mark obscured by glaze, c1907, 4" h, 4.25" dia	400	600
Vase, bulbous, embossed stylized plants, matte green glaze, impressed "AA/Van Briggle/Colo Spgs/63," 1907-11, 7.5" h, 6" dia	800	1000
Vase, bulbous, embossed trefoils, curdled and sheer matte green glaze w/ red clay showing through, incised "AA Van Briggle/Colo. Springs," 1906-07, 5.5" h, 4" dia	800	1000
Vase, bulbous, embossed trefoils, matte green and purple glaze, incised "AA Van Briggle/Colo. Spgs. 1912/26," 5.25" h, 3" dia	1000	1500
Vase, cylindrical, embossed jonquils and stems, dark green dead-matte glaze, incised "AA Van Briggle/1902/III," 7" h, 3.5" dia	2500	3000
Vase, cylindrical, embossed stylized daisies, blue-green matte glaze, c1920, 7" h, 3.5" dia	200	300
Vase, squat, 2-handled, embossed gooseberry leaves and fruit, green glaze against raspberry ground, incised "AA Van Briggle/1905/82," 7.5" h, 9.5" w	2500	3000
Vase, tapered to rim, embossed yucca leaves, curdled brown glaze, incised "AA/Van Briggle, Colo. Spgs./162," 1907-11, 5" h, 3.5" dia	900	1100
Vessel, 2-handled, embossed desert flowers, matte green and burgundy glaze, incised "AA/Van Briggle/1904/V," 10" h, 8" dia	2000	2500
Vessel, squat, embossed mistletoe, sheer mottled mauve glaze, incised "AA/Van Briggle/1905/387," 5" h, 33" dia	3500	4500
Vessel, squat, embossed poppy pods and stems, matte green glaze, incised "AA/Van Briggle/162/190?," 1905-06, 4" h, 6" dia	1000	1200

Van Briggle Pottery. —Photo courtesy David Rago Auctions, Inc.

Vernon Kilns

Vernon Kilns was founded by Faye G. Bennison in Vernon, California, in 1932. The company produced dinnerware, Disney figurines, and commemorative items. Following its closing in 1958, Metlox Potteries bought the molds and rights to the Vernon Kilns name.

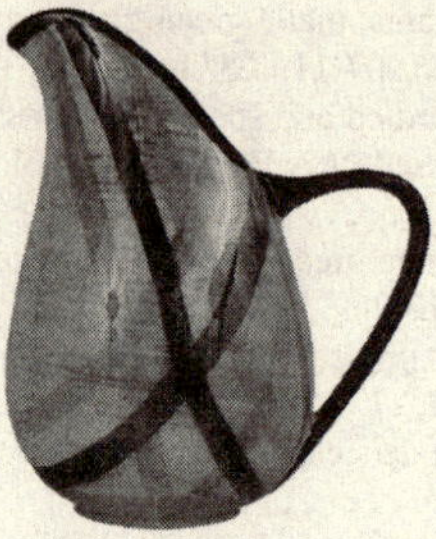

Gingham Creamer.

Gingham

	LOW	HIGH
Bread and Butter Plate	$3	$5
Butter, covered	50	75
Carafe	30	45
Casserole, covered	45	60
Chicken Pot Pie, covered	30	45
Chop Plate, 12.25" dia	12	18
Creamer	8	12
Cup and Saucer	8	12
Cup and Saucer, demitasse	40	65
Dinner Plate, 9.5" dia	10	15
Luncheon Plate, 8" dia	8	12
Mixing Bowl, 8" dia	25	35
Pitcher, 2 qt	30	40
Salad Plate, 7.5" dia	5	8
Salt and Pepper, pair, range size	40	55
Soup Plate	12	18
Teapot, covered	25	35
Tidbit, 2-tier, metal handle	30	40
Vegetable, open, 9" dia	12	20

Hawaiian Flowers

Berry Bowl	$15	$20
Bread and Butter Plate, 6" dia	8	12
Creamer	18	25
Cup and Saucer	25	35
Dinner Plate, 9.5" dia	25	35
Luncheon Plate, 8" dia	15	20
Salad Plate, 7" dia	12	18
Salt and Pepper, pair	30	40
Sugar, covered	25	35

Homespun Tidbit.

Homespun

	LOW	HIGH
Butter, covered	$55	$75
Creamer	8	12
Cup and Saucer	8	12
Cup and Saucer, demitasse	40	55
Dinner Plate, 9.5" dia	6	10
Pitcher, 2 qt	30	40
Salad Plate, 7.5" dia	5	8
Tidbit, 2-tier, metal handle	30	40
Vegetable, open, 9" dia	12	18

Organdie

Creamer	$10	$15
Cup and Saucer, demitasse	25	35
Sugar, covered	15	25
Teapot	65	90

Tam O'Shanter

Bread and Butter Plate, 6.25" dia	$6	$10
Casserole, covered, 2-handled	50	65
Dinner Plate, 7.75" dia	20	30
Salad Plate, 7.5" dia	8	12
Vegetable, 8.75" dia	25	35

Tickled Pink

Bread and Butter Plate, 6" dia	$6	$10
Butter, covered	35	45
Cup and Saucer	12	18
Dinner Plate, 10" dia	10	15
Platter, 9" l	15	25
Platter, 12" l	25	35
Relish, 3-part	25	35
Salad Plate, 7" dia	8	12
Sugar, covered	18	25

Walley Pottery

William Joseph Walley studied the pottery business at the Minton factory in England. In 1873 he returned to the United States to ply his trade. He created handmade art pottery in various locations in New England until his death in 1919. Most pieces were marked with the artist's initials "WJW."

	LOW	HIGH
Cabinet Vase, gourd-shaped, moss green and red semi-matte glaze, impressed "WJW," 4.75" h, 2.5" dia	$500	$600
Creamer, figural grotesque spout, blue cabochon bezel-set on handle, brown and gunmetal glaze, unmarked, 4" h, 4.5" w	500	600
Pitcher, ram's head spout, turquoise cabochon bezel-set on handle, mottled green and brown matte glaze, unmarked, 3.75" h, 4" w	600	800
Urn, 2 wing-shaped handles, footed, frothy multitoned glossy green glaze, mark obscured by glaze, 9.5" h, 6.75" w	1200	1500
Vase, corseted, mottled brown and green glaze, impressed "WJW," 7" h, 3.5" dia	800	1000
Vase, ovoid, applied full-length leaves, glossy green and brown flambé glaze, impressed "WJW," 8.25" h, 5.75" dia	2500	3000
Vase, ovoid, applied leaves, glossy mottled green and brown glaze, impressed "WJW," 7.75" h, 4" dia	1000	1200
Vase, spherical bottle shape, glossy leathery green and brown glaze, impressed "WJW," 7" h, 5.75" dia	2400	2800
Vessel, ovoid, impressed stylized leaves, semi-matte apple green glaze, impressed "WJW," 5" h, 4.5" dia	400	500
Vessel, spherical, collared rim, glossy mahogany glaze, impressed "WJW," 8" h, 4.5" dia	3000	3500
Vessel, squat, glossy teal and blue flambé glaze, impressed "WJW," 3.25" h, 4.25" dia	500	600
Vessel, squat, matte green glaze, impressed "WJW," 3" h, 5.5" dia	500	600

Walley Pottery. —Photo courtesy David Rago Auctions, Inc.

Watt Pottery

The Watt Pottery Company operated in Crooksville, Ohio. After producing stoneware crocks during the 1920s, the company introduced several kitchenware lines featuring simple, hand-painted decoration. Many pieces were stamped with advertising and issued as premiums. For more information see *Watt Pottery* by Sue and Dave Morris (Collector Books, Paducah, KY, 1993, 1998 value update) and *Watt Pottery* by Dennis Thompson and W. Bryce Watt (Schiffer, Atglen, PA, 1994).

Apple pattern.

Apple

	LOW	HIGH
Baker, covered, #66, 7.25" dia	$100	$130
Baker, covered, #96, 8.5" dia	75	100
Baking Dish, oblong, #85, 1 qt	50	75
Bowl, #5, 5.25" dia	50	70
Bowl, #8	60	80
Bowl, #39, 13" dia	100	130
Bowl, #60, 6.25" dia	100	140
Bowl, #66, 7.25" dia	40	55
Bowl, #74	35	50
Canister, #81, 6" h	80	125
Chop Plate, #49	300	400
Casserole, covered, #5, 5" dia	125	175
Casserole, covered, #19	200	275
Cookie Jar, covered, #503	350	500
Creamer, #62	100	125
Dinner Plate, #29	175	250
Drip Jar, #01	60	80
Ice Bucket, covered, #59, 7" dia	200	275
Mixing Bowls, nesting set of 4, #04, #05, #06, #07	175	250
Mug, #121	325	450
Nappy, covered, #05	325	450
Pie Plate, #33, 9.25" dia	100	125
Pitcher, #16, 6.5" h	90	120
Pitcher, #17, 8" h	225	300
Platter, #31	500	650
Platter, #49, 12" h	300	400
Salad Bowl, #73, 9.5" dia	60	90
Teapot, #112, 1.5 qt	300	400

Dutch Tulip

	LOW	HIGH
Bowl, #7	$100	$150
Casserole, covered, #18	250	350
Creamer, #62	350	450
Pitcher, #15	225	300
Pitcher, #16, 6.5" h	175	225

Rio Rose

Bowl, #39, 13" dia	$80	$110
Bowl, #44, 8" dia	20	30
Pie Plate, #33, 9.25" dia	125	175
Pitcher, #15, 5.25" h	200	275
Plate, 8.5" dia	20	30
Platter, #31, 15" l	90	125

Rooster

Bowl, #05, PA Dutch Days advertisement	$40	$55
Bowl, #60, 6.25" dia	90	125
Bowl, #66, 7.25" dia	80	110
Bowl, #73 dia	75	100
Casserole, #5, 5" dia	150	200
Creamer, #62, 4.25" h	200	275
Pitcher, #15, 5.25" h	100	140
Pitcher, #16, 6.5" h	100	140
Sugar, covered, #98	150	200

Starflower

Bean Cup, #75, 3.5" h	$30	$45
Bean Pot, #76	100	140
Bowl, #52, 6.25" dia	25	35
Bowl, #53, 7.25" dia	30	40
Canister, #81, 6.5" h	250	325
Cookie Jar, #21, 7.5" h	175	250
Creamer, #62, 4.25" h	200	275
Ice Bucket, cov., #59, 7" h	150	200
Mug, #501, 4.5" h	80	110
Pitcher, #15, 5.25" h	60	80
Platter, #31	150	200
Salt and Pepper, pair, barrel shape	150	200
Salt and Pepper, pair, hourglass shape	200	300

Tear Drop

Bean Pot, #76, 6.5" h	$90	$130
Bowl, #6, 6.25" dia	30	40
Bowl, #7, 7.25" dia	30	40
Bowl, #39, 13" dia	300	400
Pitcher, #15, 5.25" h	50	70
Pitcher, #16, 6.5" h	100	140
Salt and Pepper, pair, hourglass, 4" h	175	225

Weller Pottery

The Weller Pottery Company was founded in 1882 in Zanesville, Ohio, and became famous for its whimsical artware and novelty glazes. The Second Line Dickens was one of its signature collections. It was based on characters from Charles Dickens novels, decorated with animal and human figures and most frequently shaded in turquoise and light brown.

In 1903 Weller Pottery began its Jap Birdimal line based on themes incorporating Japanese landscapes. The Hudson artware line, developed in the early 1920s, is among the most desired by collectors and features pastoral scenes and floral backgrounds. The company closed in 1948. For more information see *The Collectors Encyclopedia of Weller Potter* by Sharon and Bob Huxford (Collector Books, Paducah, KY, 1979, 1998 value update).

Weller Pottery, Dickensware. —Photo courtesy Gene Harris Antique Auction Center, Inc.

	LOW	HIGH
Console Set, Silvertone, comprising 12" dia console bowl, 4" dia flower holder, and pair of 5" dia candlesticks, heavily embosed lavender and white flowers w/ brown branches and green leaves, silver-gray matte ground, price for 4-pc set	$400	$600
Flower Holder, Woodcraft, tree trunk form w/ 5 branch openings and pastel leaves and berries, intertwining roots at base, 10.5" h	100	200
Humidor, Dickensware, bisque, Turk form, incised "Dickens Weller" on cover, 7" h, 5.5" w	1000	1200
Jardiniere, Sicard, ovoid w/ tapered base, etched stylized jonquils throughout, iridescent drip glaze in repeat around base, signed "Sicard/Weller," 10.25" h, 12.25" dia	2000	3000
Jug, Dickensware, monk, 5.5" h	400	600
Jug, Etna, ovoid, clusters of smoky black grapes protruding at mid-section on both sides, soft black and gray ground, high glaze, impressed "37," 6" h, 5" w	100	200
Jug, Louwelsa, cascading grapes in varied sizes extending from vine branch in shades of brown glaze, deep brown and deep sage blended ground, high glaze, impressed "Louwelsa Weller/467/4," incised "A" (Virginia Adams), 6.25" h, 5" dia	200	300
Lamp, Bronzeware, tall vessel-form, iridescent deep violet glaze w/ green showing through, impressed "Weller," 10" h	350	450
Lamp Base, Turada, globular, footed, burnt orange, blue, and pale yellow scroll and floral design in repeat, deep brown high glaze, marked w/ half circle and "Turada/Weller/55D," 1897-98, 8" h, 10" dia	400	600
Pitcher, Dickensware, incised male deer w/ pronounced antlers beside stylized tree, blended teal, cream, and peach matte ground, tan swirl design at handle, impressed half circle and "x/17c," 11.25" h	600	800

	LOW	HIGH
Umbrella Stand, embossed stylized poppies, tulips, and daisies w/ full-length stems, smooth dark green matte glaze, Bedford Matt, 20.25" h, 10.35" dia	600	800
Vase, Aurelian, pale yellow iris w/ stamen overlay on bright yellow, deep brown ground, by William Hall, signed "Aurelian," impressed "Weller/678," incised "K" (Kappes), 9.5" h, 5.5" dia	900	1200
Vase, Coppertone, trumpet form neck on flattened spherical base, textured green glaze w/ coppertone showing through, 12.25" h	600	
Vase, Dickensware, Abe Lincoln portrait, 9" h	800	1000
Vase, Dickensware, bisque, heavily tooled monk painting, blended ocher to teal green ground, incised "A.D." (Anthony Dunlavy) on monk, impressed "Dickensware Weller/356x," 8.75" h, 5" dia	700	900
Vase, Dickensware, golfer, 9.25" h	1200	1500
Vase, Floretta, 3 embossed yellow pears on both sides, blended deep brown glaze, high glaze, impressed "Floretta (in circle)/9/Weller," 6" h, 5" dia	150	250
Vase, Hudson, bulbous form w/ long cylindrical neck and bulging base, heavy slip stylized flowers, pale pink and lavender petals, flowers accented w/ bright yellow stamens, deep blue matte ground, impressed "Weller," 9.75" h, 6" dia	400	500
Vase, Lamar, ovoid, tree landscape extending from mouth to base on both sides in metallic black glaze, mountains and sail boat scene depicted from afar, burgundy-maroon shaded ground, 6" h, 4.5" dia	200	300
Vase, La Sa, etched flowers surrounded by blades of feathered grass, iridescent ground, 8.75" h	100	200
Wall Pocket, Woodcraft, modeled as owl peering from knot hole in tree, deeply incised bark paneling, protruding leaves and branches along base, green and brown matte glaze, impressed "Weller" twice, 10.5" h	1200	1500

Weller Pottery, left to right: Louwelsa jug; Floretta vase; Lamar vase, Dickensware Monk vase; Coppertone vase, Dickensware humidor; Hudson vase; Silvertone console set. —Photo courtesy Smith & Jones, Inc. Auctions.

Wheatley Pottery Company

The Wheatley Pottery company was formed in 1903 in Cincinnati, Ohio. Thomas Jerome Wheatley, one of the company's founders, had been producing art pottery since 1879. The plant sustained major damage from a fire in 1910 and was rebuilt. Following Wheatley's death in 1917, Isaac Kahn assumed leadership and incorporated the company in 1921. Cambridge Tile and Manufacturing Company bought the pottery in 1927 and renamed it Wheatley Tile and Pottery Company. Production ceased in 1936.

Wheatley pottery was often unmarked or identified only with a paper label. Occasionally an impressed mark bearing the initials "WP" in a circle will be found.

	LOW	HIGH
Bowl, corseted, embossed leaves, thick matte green glaze, 2.5" h, 6" dia	$300	$500
Chamberstick, organic form w/ embossed leaves and scroll handle, thick leathery matte green glaze, 4" h, 6" dia	400	600
Garden Sculpture, frog, matte green glaze, 7.75" h, 11.75" l	800	1000
Jardiniere, bulbous form w/ tapered rim and incised rings at neck, frothy matte green glaze, 6" h, 8.5" dia	800	1000
Jardiniere, collared rim, frothy matte green glaze, 7.75" h, 8.25" dia	500	700
Jardiniere, double bulbous form w/ 4 buttressed handles, leathery matte green glaze, 7" h, 7.75" dia	2500	3000
Lamp Base, organic form, gourd shape w/ embossed broad leaves, matte green glaze, green leaded slag glass shade w/ row of white flowers at rim, remnants of paper label on base, 22" h, 18" dia shade	5000	6000
Pitcher, corseted, embossed grape clusters and vines, frothy matte green glaze, impressed "WP," 8" h, 7.75" w	700	900
Sculpture, bust of poet Dante, frothy matte green glaze, 11.5" h, 15" w	900	1200
Urn, bulbous, 2-handled, frothy matte green glaze, 11" h, 11" w	500	700
Vase, bulbous, modeled w/ large reptile wrapped around pot, hand-carved in high relief, matte green glaze, 10" h, 9.75" w	1500	2500
Vase, bulbous form w/ tapering rim and low pedestal foot, frothy matte green glaze, impressed "WP," 8.25" h, 5.5" dia	500	700
Vase, cylindrical neck w/ quatrefoil rim, 4 buttressed handles, frothy dripping matte green glaze, impressed "WP" and "615," 14.5" h, 10" w	3000	3500
Vase, organic form, 2-handled, frothy matte green glaze, 5.75" h, 7.75" w	2000	2500
Vase, tapered, ribbed rim, frothy matte green glaze, 9.75" h, 6" dia	500	700

Wheatley Pottery. —Photo courtesy David Rago Auctions, Inc.

W. S. George China

In 1903 William S. George bought the East Palestine Pottery Company from the Sebring brothers from whom he had leased the plant. The plant produced semiporcelain dinnerware for the next half century. The company used many different backstamps; some were unique to their shape.

Bolero pattern.

Bolero

	LOW	HIGH
Berry Bowl, 5" dia	$1	$3
Bread and Butter Plate, 6" dia	1	3
Butter Dish	12	18
Creamer	6	10
Cup and Saucer	5	8
Dinner Plate, 9" dia	4	6
Egg Cup	6	10
Gravy Boat	10	15
Salad Plate, 8" dia	2	4
Platter, 11" l	6	10
Salt and Pepper, pair	12	18
Soup Plate, 7.75" dia	4	6
Sugar	8	12
Teapot	30	50
Vegetable, 9" dia	10	15

Petalware

Bread and Butter Plate, 6" dia	$3	$5
Casserole	15	25
Creamer	6	10
Cup and Saucer	4	8
Dinner Plate, 9" dia	5	8
Gravy Boat	8	16
Pickle Dish	3	5
Platter, 16" l	8	12
Salad Plate, 8" dia	4	6
Soup Bowl	4	6
Sugar	8	12
Teapot	20	30
Vegetable, covered	18	25

Rainbow pattern.

Rainbow

	LOW	HIGH
Bread and Butter Plate, 6" dia	$2	$4
Casserole	18	25
Creamer	8	12
Cup and Saucer	5	8
Custard Cup	3	5
Dinner Plate, 10" dia	8	10
Dish, lug handle	2	4
Gravy Boat	12	18
Luncheon Plate, 9" dia	6	8
Pickle Dish	4	6
Platter, 11" l	8	12
Platter, 12" l	10	15
Relish, shell-form	8	12
Salad Plate, 8" dia	4	6
Salt and Pepper, pair	12	20
Soup Plate	5	8
Sugar	10	15
Teapot	30	40
Vegetable	10	15

Ranchero

Bread and Butter Plate, 6" dia	$2	$4
Butter Dish	15	25
Casserole	20	30
Coffeepot	35	50
Creamer	8	12
Cup and Saucer	6	10
Dinner Plate, 9" dia	6	8
Dish, 5" dia	2	4
Egg Cup	8	12
Gravy Boat	15	20
Platter	15	20
Salad Plate, 7" dia	4	6
Salt and Pepper, pair	15	20
Sugar	10	15
Teapot	25	35
Vegetable	12	18

Zsolnay Pottery

With the opening of Eastern Europe, we have seen more of the quality pottery and porcelain from that part of the world. The Zsolnay factory in Hungary originally produced cement in the middle of the nineteenth century. By the 1870s, the company produced fine art pottery. Many of the best pieces date near the turn of the century. See *Zsolnay Ceramics* by Federico Santi and John Gacher (Schiffer, Atglen, PA, 1998) for additional information.

Zsolnay Vessel, figural carp. —Photo courtesy Skinner, Inc., Boston, MA.

	LOW	HIGH
Cachepot, #5686, green and gold eosin glaze, Secession stylized floral decoration, factory mark, c1899, 9.75" h, 10.75" w	$3600	$5000
Cachepot, #5897, Secession design, metallic eosin glaze, factory mark, c1900, 4.5" h, 5" w	900	1200
Charger, #3968, historical style, factory mark, c1880, 13.5" dia	2500	3500
Figure, buffalo, #1868, rectangular base, metallic green eosin glaze, marked "Zsolnay Hungary/1868/pecs/hand-painted," 9.5" w	400	600
Goblet, #5668, Secession style, 4 flower stem handles, green and blue eosin glaze, factory mark, c1899, 6" h	1800	2500
Pitcher, #1009, yellow glaze, c1885, 10.5" h	500	600
Pitcher, #1152, rooster form, green metallic eosin glaze, factory mark, c1900, 5.5" h	1100	1600
Pitcher, #5064, maroon metallic eosin ground w/ cream and pale brown floral decoration, factory mark, c1898, 7.5" h	700	900
Pitcher, #7766, women farm workers, earth tones, c1906, 6.5" h	1100	1600
Vase, #262, yellow glaze w/ gilt highlights on relief decoration, c1873, 13" h	400	500
Vase, #359, leaf and red berry decoration, on purple ground, c1900, 3" h	1800	2500
Vase, #2289, Persian style decoration, factory mark, c1882, 4.25" h	1500	2000
Vase, #5288, landscape, rainbow metallic eosin colors, c1898, 7.75" h	5400	7500
Vase, #5330, gold Secession style decoration on maroon ground, factory mark, c1898, 4.5" h	1500	2000
Vase, #5551, organic form, blue, green and gold glaze, c1900, 9.75" h	7500	10,000
Vase, #6171, Hungarian folk design, blue and yellow stylized flowers on red ground, c1900, 9" h	2700	3800
Vase, gourd-shaped, ruby red pomegranate against nacreous eosin ground, die-stamped and wax-resist mark "Zsolnay Pecs" w/ castle, 10" h, 5" dia	1500	2000
Vessel, #683, circular, rim decorated w/ moth carved in high relief, iridescent green, gold, purple, and blue on deep red glossy ground, molded factory mark and "M," 3" h	1500	2000
Vessel, figural carp leaping from water, underpainted opaque eosin glazes, iridescent luster w/ red eyes, lips, and whiskers, marked "Zsolnay" w/ Pecs trademark, 14.75" h, 14" w	6000	8000

Pottery & Porcelain: Miscellaneous

Bookends

Dating back to before either television or the Internet, bookends were considered far more a necessity than today. But for those of us who can find no end to our books, these pottery shelf stoppers are well worth their collectors' dollars. Look for bold forms and, as always, beware of cracks and chips. Prices below are for pairs of bookends.

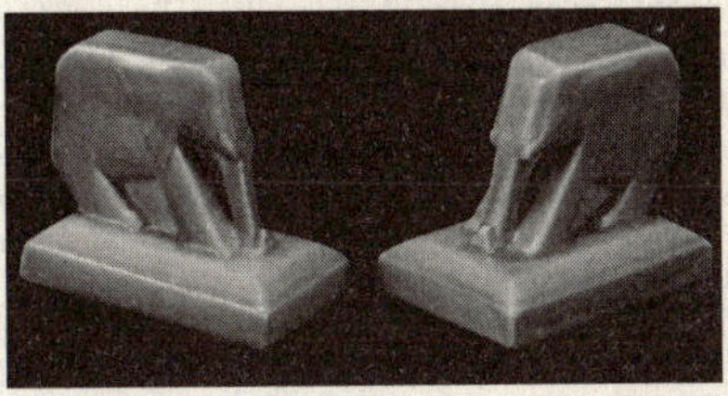

Left to right: Angular Elephants, Cowan; Roman Mausoleum, Fulper. —Photos courtesy David Rago Auctions, Inc.

	LOW	HIGH
Angular Elephants, Cowan, #840, 4.5" h	$500	$700
Boy and Girl, #519, Cowan, 6" h	600	800
Clydesdale Horse, Frankoma, 5" h	300	400
Dolphin, Abingdon, 5.5" h	20	30
Duck Head, Frankoma, 5.5" h	150	200
Eagles, Morton, 6" h	40	60
Fern Leaf, Abingdon, 5.5" h	50	75
Flying Geese, Shawnee, 6" h	30	45
Horse's Head, Abingdon, 7" h	45	75
Horse's Head, Royal Haeger, 7.5" h	30	45
Irish Setter, Frankoma, 6" h	125	175
Leopard, Frankoma, 7" h	100	150
Leopard, Royal Haeger, 15" h	60	90
Lion's Head, Royal Haeger, 7.5" h	30	45
Monk, Catalina, 7" h	400	600
Owl, Van Briggle, 6" h	275	425
Owls, wine madder, Rookwood	250	325
Panthers, wine madder, Rookwood	300	400
Parrots, Morton, 6" h	35	50
Quill, Abingdon, 8.25" h	80	110
Ramses, Fulper, 9" h	600	800
Ram's Head, Royal Haeger, 5.5" h	25	40
Roman Mausoleum, Fulper, 6" h	600	800
Rook, black matte, Rookwood	700	900
Scottie Dog, Abingdon, 6" h	50	70
Sea Gull, Abingdon, 7.5" h	70	110
Seahorse, Frankoma, 6" h	300	500
Water Lily, Royal Haeger, 5" h	20	35
Woodpeckers, Cliftwood, 6.5" h	125	185

Cookie Jars

These beloved containers of the kitchen hold the comforting treat we have pursued for years. Cookie jar collecting gained momentum in the early 1980s. Sotheby's 1988 auction of the estate of pop artist Andy Warhol catapulted figural cookie jars to national prominence. Hearing a cookie jar brought over $20,000 (it was actually for a lot of several jars), people scrambled to their kitchens and attics in hopes of striking gold. Following the sale, cookie jar collecting flourished and today many jars command hundreds, and even thousands, of dollars.

Collectors can specialize in manufacturers, themes or characters. Many times jars by one firm are referred to by the same name as similar jars by another producer. Make sure you know which jar you are purchasing. Recently, crossover interest from character memorabilia collectors fueled a rapid rise in prices of jars such as the Flintstones series (which has been reproduced), Casper the Ghost, Popeye and others. Collectors of black memorabilia seek the Mammy cookie jars.

The prices below are for jars in excellent condition, with a minimal amount of paint loss, and no chips or cracks. The amount these faults affect value depends on severity, how it alters the jar's visible appeal and personal tolerance. Cookie jar collectors are generally more tolerant of paint loss than other collectors, but top condition still brings a premium price.

For more information consult *Collector's Encyclopedia of Cookie Jars, Bk I* (1991, 1997 value update), *Bk II* (1994, 1999 value update), and *Bk III* (1998) by Fred Roerig and Joyce Herndon Roerig (Collector Books, Paducah, KY), *The Complete Cookie Jar Book, 2nd Edition* by Mike Schneider (Schiffer, West Chester, PA, 1999), and *The Wonderful World of Cookie Jars* by Mark and Ellen Supnick (L-W Book Sales, Gas City, IN, 1995, 1997 value update).

	LOW	HIGH
Albert Apple, Pitman-Dreitzer	$100	$150
Alpo Dog	45	60
Animal Crackers, McCoy	60	80
Apollo 11, McCoy	875	1150
Apple, Doranne	10	20
Apple, Hull	25	35
Apple, Metlox	35	100
Apple, yellow, McCoy	40	50
Apple in Barrel, Metlox	25	65
Asparagus Bunch, McCoy	35	75
Aunt Jemima, re-issued, McCoy	30	45
Baby Pig, Regal	400	500
Ballerina Bear, Metlox	90	130
Ball of Yarn, w/ kittens, American Bisque	90	140
Bananas, McCoy	80	100
Barefoot Boy, Hull	400	600
Barnum's Animals, McCoy	300	400
Barrel, American Bisque	25	35
Baseball Boy, McCoy	200	300
Basket of Eggs, McCoy	40	60
Basket of Fruit, McCoy	45	65
Basket of Strawberries, McCoy	40	60
Basket w/ Dog Lid, McCoy	50	70
Basket w/ Kitten Lid, McCoy	45	65
Bear, cookies in pocket, cold painted, McCoy	50	70
Bear, Maddux	150	225
Bear, w/ open eyes, American Bisque	70	90
Bear and Beehive, McCoy	30	40
Bear w/ Tie, Japan	75	120
Betsy Baker, McCoy	200	350

	LOW	HIGH
Big Bird, California Originals	60	80
Bird Feed Sack, McCoy	25	45
Bird House, Deforrest	100	150
Black Boy, w/ baseball glove, Treasure Craft	30	45
Black Cat, McCoy	300	400
Bobby Baker, McCoy	60	90
Bugs Bunny, McCoy	200	250
Butter Churn, McCoy	180	240
Calico Cat, green, Metlox	175	250
Cat, American Bisque	75	110
Chef's Head, McCoy	80	120
Chef w/ Spoon, American Bisque	90	140
Chick, wearing beret, American Bisque	60	80
Chiffonnier, McCoy	50	70
Chipmunk, McCoy	80	120
Christmas Tree, California Originals	200	300
Christmas Tree, McCoy	450	650
Circus Horse, McCoy	180	220
Clock, #653, Abingdon	70	100
Clown, American Bisque	75	110
Clown, black and white, Metlox	150	225
Clown, large, Deforrest	75	110
Clown, Pan American Art	50	75
Clown's Head, Metlox	100	270
Clown in Barrel, tan and white, McCoy	80	120
Clown on Stage, #805, American Bisque	200	425
Coalby Cat, McCoy	380	450
Coffee Grinder, McCoy	25	40
Coffee Mug, McCoy	30	40
Coffeepot, metal handle, American Bisque	30	40
Collegiate Owl, American Bisque	65	85
Cookie, girl's face w/ glasses and pigtails, Abingdon	80	100
Cookie Barn, Twin Winton	20	30
Cookie Box, McCoy	100	150
Cookie Boy, McCoy	200	300
Cookie Jug, dark brown top, white bottom, McCoy	20	25
Cookie Monster, California Originals	40	60
Cookie Time Clock, #203, American Bisque	60	80
Cookie Train, American Bisque	80	100
Cookie Truck, American Bisque	80	100
Covered Wagon, McCoy	125	175
Cow, American Bisque	70	90
Cowboy, Lane	400	700
Cowboy Boots, American Bisque	125	180
Daisy, Abingdon	50	75
Davy Crockett, American Bisque	350	500
Davy Crockett, McCoy	450	650
Davy Crockett, Regal	500	700
Davy Crockett, gold trim, Brush	500	800
Diaper Pin Pig, Regal	400	600
Dog and Basket, Brush	250	300
Dog in Doghouse, McCoy	180	220
Donald Duck on Pumpkin, California Originals	150	200
Donkey and Cart, Brush	250	450

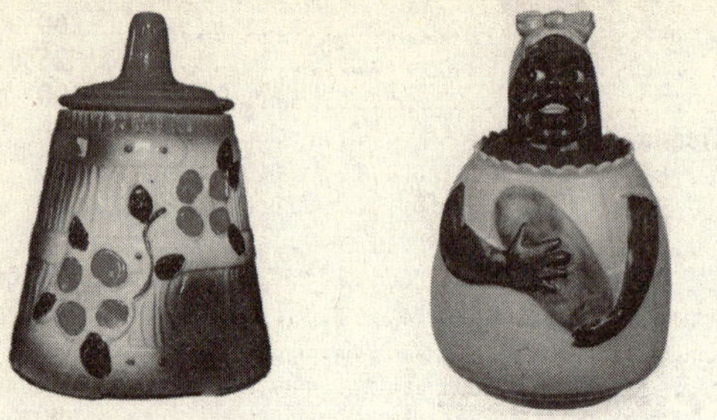

Left: American Bisque Churn, $25-$40.
Right: Weller Mammy, $1320 at auction.
—Photo courtesy Collectors Auction Services.

	LOW	HIGH
Drum, McCoy	60	80
Drum, Metlox	100	150
Drum Majorette, American Bisque	300	450
Duck, McCoy	200	300
Dutch Boy, cold painted, American Bisque	35	45
Dutch Boy, McCoy	45	55
Dutch Boy, Pottery Guild	100	150
Dutch Boy, yellow pants, gold trim, Shawnee	300	450
Dutch Girl, cold painted, American Bisque	35	45
Dutch Girl, w/ tulip, Shawnee	50	75
Dutch Girl and Boy, McCoy	100	150
Eagle Basket, McCoy	30	40
Ear of Corn, McCoy	100	150
Elephant, w/ beanie, American Bisque	90	130
Elephant, whole trunk, McCoy	300	400
Elephant, w/ ice cream cone, Brush	400	500
Elsie the Cow, Pottery Guild	350	500
Farmer Pig, American Bisque	100	150
Fat Boy, #495, Abingdon	300	400
Fire Truck, Twin Winton	25	35
Fish, Brush	400	500
Football Boy, McCoy	200	250
Formal Pig, black coat, Brush	180	220
Friar Tuck, blue, Red Wing	90	110
Frog, California Originals	30	45
Frog, Holiday	25	35
Frontier Family, McCoy	30	50
Frosty the Snowman, Robinson-Ransbottom	450	650
Gift Box, American Bisque	200	300
Goldilocks, Regal	300	400
Grandfather Clock, McCoy	50	75
Grandma, Brayton Laguna	400	500
Granny, American Bisque	125	275
Granny, Brush	300	400
Granny, McCoy	80	120
Gunfighter Rabbit, Twin Winton	75	110
Hamm's Bear, McCoy	200	250
Happy Hippo, #549, Abingdon	300	400
Hen on Nest, McCoy	70	90
Hobby Horse, McCoy	100	150
Hocus Rabbit, McCoy	40	50

	LOW	HIGH
Honey Bear, inside tree, McCoy	175	250
Honeycomb Jar, McCoy	55	75
Humpty Dumpty, Abingdon	250	385
Humpty Dumpty, in cowboy outfit, Brush	200	300
Humpty Dumpty, Regal	275	400
Humpty Dumpty, w/ beanie, Brush	200	250
Indian Head, McCoy	250	350
Jack-in-the-Box, American Bisque	100	150
Jack O' Lantern, #674, Abingdon	300	400
Jack O' Lantern, McCoy	400	600
Juggling Clown, California Originals	75	110
Kangaroo, blue, McCoy	250	300
Kangaroo, tan, McCoy	360	420
Katrina, Red Wing	150	225
Keebler Tree, McCoy	35	50
Keystone Cop, Twin Winton	75	110
Kitten on Basket, McCoy	90	110
Kitten on Beehive, American Bisque	50	75
Koala Bear, McCoy	75	95
Lady Pig, American Bisque	90	120
Lamb, "Good Little Lambs Only," Twin Winton	50	75
Lamb in Hat, American Bisque	100	150
Lamb on Basket, McCoy	100	150
Lemon, McCoy	40	60
Liberty Bell, American Bisque	90	110
Little Chef, paneled, Shawnee	25	35
Little Girl, #693, Abingdon	90	100
Little Miss Muffet, #662, Abingdon	200	250
Little Red Riding Hood, Brush	400	800
Little Red Riding Hood, gold stars, Hull	400	600
Little Red Riding Hood, Hull	225	350
Little Red Riding Hood, Pottery Guild	125	175
Log Cabin, McCoy	70	90
Lollipops, McCoy	60	80
Ma and Pa Owls, McCoy	85	105
Mammy, yellow dots, Metlox	400	600
Mickey & Minnie Mouse, Disney turnabout	150	225
Milk Can, McCoy	35	45
Money Bag, white, Abingdon	75	110
Monk, McCoy	35	45
Moose, AMC	30	45
Mother Goose, McCoy	100	150
Mouse, McCoy	35	45
Mouse on Clock, "Time for Cookies," McCoy	25	35
Mugsey the Dog, Shawnee	325	500
Nutcracker, Loomco China	20	30
Oaken Bucket, McCoy	30	40
Orange, McCoy	45	55
Oscar the Doughboy, Robinson-Ransbottom	125	175
Oscar the Grouch, California Originals	60	80
Owl, green eyes, Shawnee	250	375
Owl, McCoy	50	75
Owl, Metlox	40	60

	LOW	HIGH
Penguins, kissing, white, McCoy	60	80
Persian Kitten, Twin Winton	65	100
Picnic Basket, McCoy	55	65
Pig, Korn Top, Royal Haeger	35	50
Pineapple, McCoy	70	100
Pineapple, Metlox	125	175
Pirate Chest, McCoy	80	100
Potbelly Stove, American Bisque	30	45
Potbelly Stove, black, McCoy	30	40
Provincial Lady, Brayton Laguna	400	600
Pumpkin, Western Stoneware	30	45
Pumpkin Coach, Brush	250	300
Puppy in Blue Pot, American Bisque	45	65
Purple Cow, Metlox	350	500
Quaker Oats, Regal	100	150
Rabbit in Hat, American Bisque	55	75
Rabbit in Hat, Deforrest	125	175
Raggedy Andy, Metlox	175	225
Raggedy Ann, #859, California Originals	60	90
Raggedy Ann, colors under glaze, Maddux	150	225
Raggedy Ann, white, McCoy	25	35
Rocking Chair Dalmatians, Metlox	375	550
Rooster, McCoy	75	85
Saddle, American Bisque	200	300
Sailor Boy, white, Shawnee	90	110
Sailor Jack, Robinson-Ransbottom	200	300
Sailor Monkey, yellow hat, Deforrest	150	225
Santa, winking, American Bisque	350	550
Schoolhouse Bell, American Bisque	35	55
Sheriff Bear, Twin Winton	50	75
Smiley Pig, shamrocks, gold trim, Shawnee	425	650
Snoopy on Doghouse, Metlox	200	300
Snyder Clown, California Originals	30	45
Spaceship, American Bisque	250	350
Squash, Metlox	150	225
Squirrel on Log, Brush	200	250
Squirrel on Nut Barrel, Metlox	475	700
Strawberry, McCoy	50	75
Teapot, black, McCoy	45	55
Teepee, straight top, re-issue, McCoy	25	35
Thinking Puppy, McCoy	25	40
Tigger, California Originals	125	175
Train, #651, Abingdon	120	160
Tug Boat, American Bisque	150	250
Turkey, Morton	50	75
Walrus, California Originals	40	60
W. C. Fields, McCoy	150	250
Windmill, #678, Abingdon	200	250
Windmill, McCoy	100	150
Wise Bird, Robinson-Ransbottom	60	90
Wishing Well, McCoy	30	50
Woodsy Owl, McCoy	100	150
Wren House, McCoy	120	160

Earthenware Pottery

Using less sophisticated kilns and whatever clays were found locally, country potters produced a diverse array of beautiful and imaginative kitchenwares and tablewares. Design and coloration are key in determining values. But a crack or chip puts a major dent in the price.

Redware gets it name from the red clay used. Spatterware designs were achieved with a paint brush, often requiring several hundred touches per square inch. Spongeware decoration was applied with sponges, most commonly in blue. Yellowware gets its name from the yellow glaze in which it was dipped.

For further reading consult *Redware, 2nd Edition* and *Spongeware and Spatterware, 2nd Edition,* both by Kevin McConnell (Schiffer, Atglen, PA, 1999), *American Stonewares, 3rd Edition* by Georgeanna H. Greer (Schiffer, Atglen, PA, 1999), *Collector's Guide to Yellow Ware, Bk II* by Lisa S. McAllister (Collector Books, Paducah, KY, 1997), and *Yellow Ware* by Joan Leibowitz (Schiffer, Exton, PA, 1985).

Redware

	LOW	HIGH
Applebutter Jar, applied handle, tooled lines, brown splotches on deep orange ground, 5" h	$500	$700
Bowl, shallow, dark brown glaze, white slip decoration, 3.5" h, 14.75" dia	1800	2200
Bust, man wearing wig, wheel-thrown and hand-molded and tooled, brown glaze, 10" h	200	500
Chamberstick, saucer base w/ applied handle, brown and green on orange ground, 3" h	200	300
Creamer, applied handle, brown fleck glaze, 3" h	100	200
Dish, oblong, brown and green spots on orange ground, 11.75" l	600	800
Figure, Uncle Sam, 4" h	250	400
Flask, dark brown splotch on deep orange ground, 7" h	300	500
Flower Pot, brown running glaze on orange ground, impressed "John W. Bell, Waynesboro," 8.75" dia	500	700
Flower Pot, yellow slip "1864" within 2 wavy lines, impressed "H. Brooks," mid-19th C, 5.125" h	1000	1400

Redware. —Photo courtesy Skinner, Inc., Boston, MA.

	LOW	HIGH
Jar, covered, greenish glaze w/ mottled amber, yellow, green, and dark brown daubs, 8" h	1500	1800
Jar, ovoid, shiny glaze w/ dark brown splotches on mottled orange and green ground, galleried lip, 7.375" h	800	1000
Jug, applied strap handle, brown and green glaze w/ amber and brown spots, 9.25" h	600	800
Jug, miniature, ribbed strap handle, tooled lines, brown splotches and green mottled glaze on amber ground, 3.625" h	4000	4500
Loaf Pan, coggled rim, 4-line yellow slip decoration, 14.25" l	700	900
Mug, applied ribbed handle, brown splotches on greenish orange ground, 6.375" h	300	500
Pie Plate, coggled rim, yellow slip bird on branch design, 10" dia	3000	3500
Pie Plate, coggled rim, yellow slip seaweed design, 10.5" dia	1500	2000
Pitcher, applied handle, tooled band w/ reeded lip, marbleized w/ white slip and green, brown, and blue glaze, white slip interior, 8.125" h	500	700
Plate, slip-decorated stylized leaves, crimped edge, 19th C, 9.75" dia	400	600
Stove Leveler, brown splotches on orange ground, 2.75" h	150	250
Whistle, vasiform, dark brown glaze, unglazed spout, 19th C, 3.75" h	400	600

Spongeware

Bank, pig, bluish-green and tan sponge-spatter on cream ground, 3.75" l	$300	$450
Bowl, molded fluting, solid blue rim, blue sponge-spatter exterior, 4" h, 10.5" d	200	300
Butter Crock, stenciled label "Butter" surrounded by blue sponge-spatter decoration, wire bail w/ turned wooden handle, 6.25" h, 8.75" dia	250	400
Butter Dish, covered, w/ insert, blue sponging, 5.25" dia	150	250
Chamber Bucket, covered, green sponged bands, wire bail w/ turned wooden handle, 12" h	200	300
Inkwell, removable cone-shaped insert, pen rest on top, blue sponge-spatter decoration, 2.625" h	150	300
Jar, covered, brown, blue, and green sponge-spatter decoration, black transfer label "Spaulding's Pure Fresh Cookies," 9.25" h	200	350
Jardiniere, flared scalloped rim, molded foliage scrolls w/ gilt highlights, blue sponge-spatter exterior, 8.75" h, 10.5" dia	200	400

Spongeware. —Photos courtesy Collectors Auction Services.

	LOW	HIGH
Jug, applied strap handle, blue sponged decoration, 6.75" h	100	200
Mixing Bowl, blue sponge-spatter bands at rim and base, solid blue stripe around middle, 5" h, 11.25" dia	250	400
Mixing Bowl, blue sponge-spatter exterior, 3 solid blue bands around middle, 4" h, 9.5" dia	150	300
Mixing Bowl, blue sponge-spatter exterior, 5" h, 10" dia	200	350
Pitcher, blue sponged exterior	250	400
Pitcher, blue sponge-spatter bands at rim and base, solid blue band and 2 stripes around middle, 6.75" h	500	700
Pitcher, embossed floral designs and panels, blue sponge-spatter decoration, 8.5" h	150	300
Pitcher and Bowl, blue sponged exterior, 12.75" h pitcher	300	500
Plate, scalloped rim, allover blue sponge-spatter, 9.25" dia	200	300
Soap Dish, covered, oval, w/ insert, allover blue sponge-spatter decoration, solid blue bands around base and lid rim, 6" w	250	400
Umbrella Stand, blue and red sponging, tan salt glaze, Red Wing	1000	1500
Vase, tapered cylinder, yellow ware w/ blue sponged bands, 7" h	100	200
Water Cooler, covered, lug handles, allover blue sponge-spatter, transfer label "3," 10.5" h	150	300

Sewerpipe

Bank, pig, sitting, incised "To Pat My Godfather," 9.25" h	$200	$300
Bank, pig, standing upright, wearing bowtie and trousers, 8.375" h	150	200
Birdhouse, cylindrical, tooled bark surface, 8.5" h	500	700
Candelabra, scrolling branches w/ applied flowers, birds, and leaves, some color mixed in clear glaze, 12.375" h	75	150
Figure, bulldog puppy, seated, rectangular base, 3.75" h	150	200
Figure, bullfrog, 7" l	150	200
Figure, cat, seated, 7" h	150	200
Figure, dog, seated, Staffordshire-type, free-standing front legs, 10.25" h	200	300
Figure, lion battling serpent, realistically modeled, rectangular base, 8" h, 11" l	200	300
Figure, owl, looking to right, tooled feathers, incised "Tim Gibson," 8.25" h	125	200
Figure, raccoon, crouching, white slip details and striped tail, green eyes, incised initials "J. C.," 15" l	150	200
Figure, raccoon, crouching on log, incised "Chuck Miburn," 13" l	225	350
Figure, squirrel, climbing, drilled holes for nailing to tree, incised "E. A.," 7.5" h	150	250
Figure, squirrel eating nut, yellow slip eyes, incised "CM1980," 6.75" h	25	50
Jar, ovoid, molded Art Deco designs, 19" h	50	100
Lamp, tree trunk w/ 4 stumps, lion, and reclining naked lady in front, base incised "J. W. Moore, June 10, 1926, Uhrichsville, O. Evans Pipe Co.," 13.75" h	2500	3500
Lamp, vine-wrapped tree, bird's eggs in knothole, incised "Made by Earl F. Page," 23.5" h	500	700
Planter, basket, rectangular, tooled bark finish, 10" h	200	300
Planter, box, square, applied and tooled surface, 4 bracket legs w/ base stretcher, 11.5" h, 9" sq	300	400
Planter, tree stump, reserve on side w/ inscription "Mark Milliken, Born July 1823, Died June 22, 1879, Joanna his wife born Aug. 27, 1825, Died Jan. 25, 1908," 22.5" h	300	400
Umbrella Stand, ovoid, Art Deco designs around shoulder, 18.5" h	75	150

Stoneware

	LOW	HIGH
Apple Butter Crock, Cowden & Wilcox, impressed label, 2 qt	$50	$75
Batter Pail, Cowden & Wilcox, Harrisburg, PA, tin lids, wire bail handle, cobalt drooping bellflowers, large tulip on back, blue at ears and handle, 1 gal	2500	3500
Batter Pail, Evan R. Jones, Pittston, PA, wire bail handle, cobalt flower, 2 gal	600	800
Batter Pail, James Ryan, bulbous, wire bail handle, plain, 1.5 gal	100	150
Batter Pail, James Ryan, Pittston, plain, 4 qt	80	120
Bean Pot, covered, crown stamp, brown Albany glaze upper half, 2 qt	30	50
Bean Pot, covered, Whites, Utica, "Boston, The Home of The Bean" 1 side, "Spirit of 76 Bunker Hill" other side, fancy coggle wheel design around neck, blue at handle, 2 qt	300	450
Bedpan, cobalt decoration inside and out	1000	1500
Bottle, stamped "Hon & Winner, West Nanticoke, PA," 1 qt	150	250
Butter Churn, T. Harrington, Lyons, elaborate cobalt floral decoration, w/ dasher and guide, 3 gal	800	1200
Butter Crock, lug handles, feather decoration all around, 1 gal	300	450
Butter Crock, salt glaze, embossed "Butter," dark blue bands at top and bottom, 2 qt	100	150
Cake Crock, H. Myers, impressed label, lug handles, cobalt flowering vine all around, 7" h, 12.5" dia	2500	3500
Crock, Cowden & Wilcox, Harrisburg, PA, lug handles, large cobalt bird, 3 gal	1200	1600
Crock, G. H. Caine, script label, elaborate cobalt peacock, 12 gal	1500	2000
Crock, Hamilton & Jones, Greensboro, PA, stenciled label, 1 gal	100	150
Crock, Henry Clay, double handle, cobalt slip cup labels "Henry Clay 1844" on shoulder and "Henry Clay" on side of mouth, cobalt slip cup floral decoration	6500	8500

Cobalt-decorated Stoneware. —Photo courtesy Gene Harris Antique Auction Center, Inc.

Stoneware, jugs and crocks. —Photo courtesy Glass-Works Auctions.

	LOW	HIGH
Crock, James Hamilton & Co., Greensboro, PA, applied handles, cobalt slip cup "10" and rose, 10 gal	1000	1500
Crock, no label, lug handles, large cobalt chicken pecking corn, 3 gal	750	1000
Crock, Sipe Nichols, Williamsport, PA, large cobalt stylized flower, 1 gal	150	250
Crock, W. Roberts, Binghamton, NY, lug handles, cobalt bird, 2 gal	1200	1800
Crock w/ Spigot, covered, Red Wing stamp and "2," 2 gal	75	150
Foot Warmer, Henderson Pottery Works, Boston, Mass, dated 1912, ink stamped "Henderson, Foot Warmer" below filler plug	125	200
Harvest Jug, cobalt 3-bloom flower both sides, 1.5 gal	1000	1500
Humidor, Whites, Utica, molded bird dog at point	125	200
Jar, covered, John Young & Co., Harrisburg, PA, lug handles, elaborate cobalt floral decoration, 2 gal	4000	5500
Jar, Hamilton & Jones, Greensboro, PA, cobalt stenciled label below wavy line, 2 gal	250	400
Jug, Cortland, cobalt floral decoration, 1 gal	300	450
Jug, Cowden & Wilcox, Harrisburg, PA, cobalt fancy bellflower pinwheel, blue at handle, 4 gal	1000	1500
Jug, Cowden & Wilcox, Harrisburg, PA, gray, slip cup star, 3 gal	6000	8500
Jug, F. Stetzenmeyer, Rochester, NY, slip cup stylized flower, 1 gal	1200	1800
Jug, F. W. Farrington, Elmira, NY, strap handle, cobalt slip cup label "C. W. Skinner"	300	450
Jug, no label, brown and white, 5 gal	30	75
Jug, Warner & Ray Druggists, Utica, NY, strap handle, cobalt slip cup bird and label, 1 gal	800	1200
Jug, Whites, Utica, cobalt perky bird on branch design, 1 gal	700	1000
Milk Pan, P. Herman, Baltimore, pour lip, lug handles, cobalt brushed decoration all around, 2 gal	400	600
Mug, coggle wheel and cobalt blue bands	50	100
Pitcher, barrel-shaped, cream, green, and tan sponged decoration, 2 qt	150	250
Pitcher, J. Burger, Rochester, NY, impressed label, cobalt slip cup flower, 1 gal	800	1200
Poultry Waterer, cobalt arch, 2 gal	100	150
Rolling Pin, wood handles, cobalt foliage decoration	250	400
Salt Crock, hanging, blue and white salt glaze, grape decoration	100	150
Spittoon, cobalt flowers both sides, blue bands around	150	300
Spittoon, R. C. R. Phila., large cobalt floral decoration	300	450
Water Cooler, cobalt foliage decoration, 3 gal	100	150

Yellow Ware

	LOW	HIGH
Bank, house, molded details highlighted in black, "For My Dear Girl" on roof, 3.625" h	$600	$800
Bank, pig, black and brown sponging, amber glaze, 3.75" h	100	200
Bank, sitting dog, green and brown running glaze, rectangular base, 7.5" h	800	1200
Bottle, mermaid form, 19th C, 8.5" h	250	350
Butter Tub, pale blue glaze on molded staves, 4" h, 4.75" dia	200	300
Canning Jar, barrel-shaped, 7" h	100	150
Creamer, black stripes, white band, green seaweed decoration, 3.875" h	150	250
Creamer, molded tavern scene, brown Rockingham glaze, 4.25" h	25	75
Crock, banded	100	200
Crock, covered, blue and white bands	200	400
Crock, flat bottom w/ rounded base, sides flare slightly toward rounded rim w/ flattened top, allover blue spatter decoration, 6.5" h, 6.5" dia	25	75
Deep Dish, crimped rim, brown slip stripes, 11" x 13"	1000	1500
Deep Dish, notched rim, brown slip combed feather design, 13" x 17.5"	2000	4000
Figure, "Staffordshire" dog, Rockingham glaze, 9.875" h	100	200
Food Mold, oval, ear of corn in bottom	100	200
Food Mold, pinwheel	100	200
Grease Lamp, bluish green running glaze, marked w/ "W" in rayed circle, 14.5" h	60	100
Jar, covered, cylindrical, white band, brown stripes, 6.25" h	200	300
Milk Pitcher	75	200
Mixing Bowl, molded shoulder, brown bands, 12.5" dia	75	125
Mixing Bowls, molded scene w/ girl watering flowers below window, nesting set of 3	80	150
Pie Funnel, 2.25" h	125	200
Pie Plate, molded rim design, marked "Oven Serve," 9" dia	60	100
Pitcher, light blue and white stripes, ribbed handle w/ leaf, 5.25" h	350	500
Pitcher, squat form, Rockingham glaze, 4.5" h	75	150
Soap Dish, round, 5.5" dia	175	250

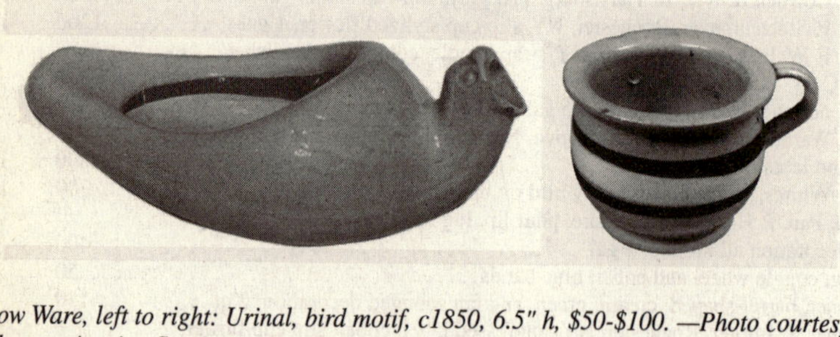

Yellow Ware, left to right: Urinal, bird motif, c1850, 6.5" h, $50-$100. —Photo courtesy Collectors Auction Services; Mug, brown and white bands, 2.375" h, $25-$75.

English and Continental Pottery and China

With few potteries of its own, the early Americans imported from Europe many tablewares. Delftware is the generic name for the tin-glazed earthenwares made in great numbers in Holland and England during the seventeenth and eighteenth centuries. The name comes from the Dutch city where many of these pieces originated. Do not confuse these pieces with those made by the modern corporation "Delft," whose wares pay tribute to the fine early pieces. The pitchers made in Liverpool, England, often called "Liverpool Jugs," sported many patriotic American themes. Lustreware is decorated in a bright metallic finish. Majolica was the tradename used by the Minton Company in England to describe wares that imitated Majolica pieces from the Italian Renaissance. Collectors now use the term to refer to similar pieces made by many English potters of the mid-nineteenth century. Mochaware was decorated in various methods that included finger-painting (to create "earthworm" designs) and spitting a tobacco juice concoction (to create "seaweed" designs).

Beware of English eighteenth-century-style earthenware pieces of various glazes, especially tortoiseshell glaze. The Dewitt Wallace Decorative Arts Gallery at Colonial Williamsburg in Virginia has documented many modern fakes including candlesticks and teapots. Some brilliant examples potted by Guy Timothy Davies have fooled many knowledgeable dealers and collectors.

For more information on pottery marks see *Kovels' New Dictionary of Marks* by Ralph and Terry Kovel (Crown, New York, NY, 1986), *Marks on German, Bohemian and Austrian Porcelain: 1710 to the Present* by Robert E. Röntgen (Schiffer, Atglen, PA, 1997), *Warman's English & Continental Pottery & Porcelain, 3rd Edition* by Susan and Al Bagdade (Krause Publications, 1998), and *Encyclopedia of British Pottery & Porcelain Marks* by Geoffrey Godden (Barrie & Jenkins, London, England, reprint, 1991).

For additional reading about majolica consult *The Collector's Encyclopedia of Majolica* by Mariann Katz-Marks (Collector Books, Paducah, KY, 1992, 1998 vlaue update), *Majolica Figures* by Helen Cunningham (Schiffer, Atglen, PA, 1997), *Price Guide to Majolica* (L-W Book Sales, Gas City, IN, 1997).

For information on Schlegelmilch porcelain see *Collector's Encyclopedia of R. S. Prussia, Fourth Series* (Collector Books, Paducah, KY, 1995, 1998 value update) and *R. S. Prussia Popular Lines* (Collector Books, Paducah, KY, 1999) both by Mary Frank Gaston and *Capers' Notes on the Marks of Prussia* by R. H. Capers (Alphabet Printing, El Paso, IL, 1996).

To learn about other types of pottery read *The Collector's Encyclopedia of Gaudy Dutch and Welsh* by John A. Shuman III (Collector Books, Paducah, KY, 1991, 1998 value update), *Quimper Pottery* by Adela Meadows (Schiffer, Atglen, PA, 1998), and *Spongeware and Spatterware, 2nd Edition* by Kevin McConnell (Schiffer, Atglen, PA, 1999).

Belleek. —Photo courtesy Skinner, Inc., Boston, MA.

Belleek

	LOW	HIGH
Basket, oval, twig handles, applied flowers on rim, impressed pad mark, c1925, 8.5" l	$1200	$1500
Teapot, covered, Thorn pattern, gilt and enamel decoration, first period black printed and impressed marks, 19th C, 7" l	1000	1200
Vase, applied flowers and floral vines, raised pedestal base w/ stepped plinth and fluted circular feet, second period black mark, late 19th/early 20th C, 16.75" h	5000	5500

Delft

Charger, allover polychrome floral decoration, mid-18th C, 13" dia	$700	$900
Charger, polychrome landscape and floral scene w/ floral border, mid-18th C, 13.5" dia	800	1200
Flower Brick, rectangular, blue floral decoration, mid-18th C, 5" l	300	500
Garniture Set, comprising 4 vases, 2 urn-shaped w/ domed lids, 2 cylindrical w/ flaring rims, all w/ scallop-framed blue-decorated landscape cartouches, 18th C, 8" h, price for 4-pc set	1500	2000

Dresden

Potpourri Urns, decorated both sides w/ harbor scene in cartouche and foliate sprigs and figures, 20th C, 16.5" h, price for pair	$1000	$2500
Punch Bowl, covered, w/ stand, sliced lemon finial, bodies enameled w/ titled figures depicting the "Punch Society," 11.75" dia bowl, 15.25" dia stand	20,000	25,000
Vase, alternating panels of figures and yellow-ground floral bouquets, Thieme factory, late 19th C, 13.25" h	200	400
Vase, covered, enamel decorated classical panels surrounded by applied flowers, insects, and fruits, bird perched on branch knop on cover, Thieme factory, 19th C, 12.75" h	600	800
Vases, domed covers, alternating panels of lovers and turquoise-ground floral bouquets, c1900, 14" h, price for pair	400	600

Delft Vases. —Photos courtesy Skinner, Inc., Boston, MA.

Gaudy Dutch

	LOW	HIGH
Cup and Saucer, handleless, Butterfly pattern	$800	$1200
Cup and Saucer, handleless, Sunflower pattern	450	650
Cup and Saucer, handleless, Urn pattern	400	600
Cup and Saucer, War Bonnet pattern	450	650
Plate, Double Rose pattern, 10" dia	1000	1500
Plate, Urn pattern, 8.25" dia	1000	1500
Plate, War Bonnet pattern, 8.125" dia	800	1200

Gaudy Ironstone

Coffeepot, paneled, blue transfer War Bonnet pattern w/ red, orange, and yellow enamel, marked "Ironstone China," 10" h	$300	$450
Cup and Saucer, handleless, seaweed in underglaze blue w/ red and green enamel	75	150
Cup and Saucer, handleless, urn in underglaze blue w/ red, pink, and green enamel	400	525
Plate, bittersweet in underglaze blue w/ red and green enamel w/ luster, impressed "Walley Paris White Ironstone," 9.625" dia	250	425
Plate, black transfer w/ 3 frogs and flowers, red, blue, green, and yellow flowers, 9.375" dia	750	1000
Plate, center flower in underglaze blue w/ red, pink, and green enamel and luster, 9.75" dia	375	525
Plate, strawberry in underglaze blue w/ red, pink, and green enamel, impressed "Elsmore Forster and Co.," 8.625" dia	300	450
Platter, black transfer w/ 8 rabbits, 4 frogs, and flowers, red, blue, green, and yellow flowers, 14.875" l	1500	2000
Platter, blue War Bonnet pattern transfer w/ red, orange, and yellow enamel, marked "Ironstone China," 14.75" l	200	325

Gaudy Staffordshire

Cup and Saucer, handleless, Adam's Rose pattern, red, green, and black, impressed "Adams"	$225	$400
Plate, Adam's Rose pattern, red, green, and black, impressed "Adams," 10.5" dia	150	275
Platter, oblong, Adam's Rose pattern, red, green, and black, impressed "Adams," 13.5" l	400	625

Gaudy Welsh

Bowl, blue transfer w/ red enameling, transfer label "Mason's Patent Ironstone China," 12" dia, 3" h	$225	$400
Cup, floral w/ oriental pagoda in underglaze blue w/ red and green enameling, 3.125" h	400	650
Pitcher, paneled, dragon handle, underglaze blue w/ red and green enamel and luster, impressed "Mason's Patent Ironstone China," 8" h	800	1200
Pitcher, paneled, snake handle, blue transfer w/ red and green enamel, marked "Mason's Patent Ironstone China," 9.75" h	375	500
Platter, blue "Amherst Japan" transfer w/ red and yellow enameling, impressed "Improved Stone China," 16.5" l	500	650
Punch Bowl, molded scrolls and beaded panels, balloon pattern in underglaze blue w/ red and green enamel and gilt, 10.75" dia, 6" h	725	1000

KPM

	LOW	HIGH
Cabinet Plate, octagonal, reticulated rim, central Frederick the Great portrait, 19th C, 9.125" w	$200	$300
Figural Grouping, 2 bacchantes and goat, 19th C, 8" l	150	250
Figural Grouping, peasant couple w/ infant, late 19th C, 12" h	300	400
Figural Grouping, seated couple facing each other, late 19th C, 5" h, 4.5" l	800	1200
Portrait Plaque, Ruth, rectangular, signed "ch. Landelle," impressed marks, 15.5" x 10"	4000	5000
Urns, multicolored floral and foliage decoration, modeled w/ lion mask and ring handles, late 19th C, 8.5" h, price for pair	300	500
Vase, double gourd form, decorated w/ figural reserves and foliate sprays, late 19th C, 14" h	500	800
Vegetable Tureen, covered, lavender and green flower-filled urns and scrolls, c1850-70, 14" l	400	700

Liverpool

Cann, "George Washington, Esq. General and Commander in Chief of the Continental Army in America," early 19th C, 4.625" h	$2000	$2500
Jug, "Seasons," spring and autumn scenes in oval reserves above related verse, framed by floral swags, scrolls, and various devices, early 19th C, 7.5" h	600	800
Pitcher, Masonic emblems 1 side, ship other side, captioned "United States" above Jefferson quote "Peace, Commerce, and Honest Friendship, with all Nations – Entangling Alliances with None – Jefferson/Anno Domini 1804," early 19th C, 11" h	3800	4500
Pitcher, "Massacre of the French King, La Guillotine, The Modern Beheading Machine at Paris, Jan'y 20th 1793" on obverse, "Marie Ann Charlotte LaCorde, assassinating Marat the French Regicide in his own House" on reverse, floral device below spout, early 19th C, 7.75" h	3000	3500
Pitcher, Herculaneum transfer, "Washington in Glory. America in Tears," and "The Mower," transfer printed Seal of the United States and "Herculaneum Pottery" below spout, 1796-1840, 9" h	2500	3500

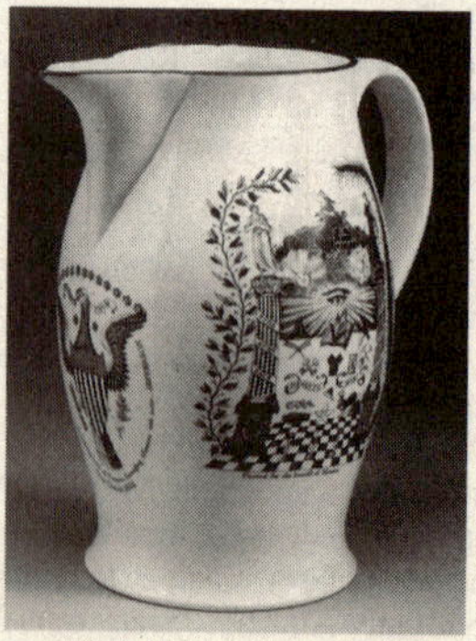

Left to right: KPM figural groups and cabinet plate; Liverpool pitcher. —Photo courtesy Skinner, Inc., Boston, MA.

Lusters

	LOW	HIGH
Creamer, canary yellow w/ silver luster resist bands w/ floral decoration, 3.75" h	$200	$300
Creamer, copper luster, canary band w/ white reserves and black transfer scenes of "Cornwallis" and "Lafayette," 4" h	800	1200
Creamer, copper luster, canary band w/ white reserves w/ purple transfer of woman and child in classical attire, polychrome enamel, 4.125" h	200	350
Cup and Saucer, canary	175	275
Punch Bowl, ships, bridge, mottos, and sailors, Sunderland, 11" dia	3500	5000
Tea Set, w/ tea plates, pink luster, house pattern, 30 pcs	700	1000

Majolica

Centerpiece, Sarreguemines, modeled as putto holding bowl formed from broad leaves and grapevines, standing on square plinth w/ molded masks at corners, c1885, 15.5" h	$3000	$4000
Cheese Stand and Cover, George Jones, dome-shaped cover molded w/ leaves and strawberry blossoms, robin's egg blue ground, impressed mark, 5" h	1200	1500
Creamer and Sugar, George Jones, strawberry blossoms, leaves, and branches, bark ground, price for pair	150	250
Compote, George Jones, pineapple, raised pad marks	300	500
Jug, George Jones, tree trunk molded body w/ leaves and blossoms in relief above grassy base w/ frogs, 4.25" h	1000	1200
Jug, Simon Fielding, modeled as branch of coral encrusted w/ shells and resting on waves, c1880, 7.75" h	325	450
Jug, William Brownfield, modeled as 2 intertwined Renaissance-style scaly fish, 1879, 11.75" h	2800	3500
Oyster Plate, Minton, green center, pale blue oyster pockets, 1872, 9" dia	1000	1200
Sardine Box, w/ lid and standard, George Jones, radiating stiff leaves, lid molded w/ 3 fish, c1872, 8.5" l base	1500	2000
Serving Dish, George Jones, pineapple, raised pad marks	200	300
Sweetmeat Dish, modeled as putto seated on conch shell, raised on dolphin and oval plinth, c1870, 7" h	2500	3000
Teapot, Minton, modeled as monkey wearing Japanese-style tunic and clutching coconut, 1874, 6" h	6500	9000
Vase, Continental, modeled as ear of corn, c1890, 10.5" h	1000	1500

Majolica, George Jones. —Photo courtesy Skinner, Inc., Boston, MA.

Meissen

Item	LOW	HIGH
Cream Jug, enamel-decorated w/ scene depicting miner at work, gilt trim, 18th C, 5.5" h	$600	$800
Cup and Saucer, enamel-decorated w/ scene depicting miner at work, gilt trim, 18th C, 5.25" dia saucer	400	600
Deep Dish, scalloped border, slip-decorated w/ raised foliate and scrolled cartouches and enameled floral sprays, early 19th C, 15.25" dia	1000	1500
Figural Grouping, allegorical, depicting partially nude females and child supporting net filled w/ sea creatures and child merman, late 19th/early 20th C, 12.75" h	1200	1500
Figural Grouping, Apple Picker, model 2229, enamel-decorated, gilt trim, late 19th/early 20th C, 9.75" h	700	900
Figural Grouping, The Good Mother, model E69, lady seated in armchair surrounded by 3 children, late 19th/early 20th C, 8.75" h	2000	2500
Figure, Beggar Cherub, model L112, standing cherub w/ crutches, enamel-decorated, gilt trim, late 19th/early 20th C, 8.25" h	800	1000
Figure, cherub, model L125, enamel-decorated, gilt trim, late 19th/early 20th C, 8" h	1000	1500
Figure, female cherub, model L111, enamel-decorated, gilt trim, late 19th/early 20th C, 8.25" h	800	1200
Figure, Lady w/ Birdcage, model E4, enamel-decorated, gilt trim, early 20th C, 5.75" h	500	700
Open Salts, figural man and woman holding bowls, 19th C, 7.25" h, price for pair	500	700
Serving Tray, oval, molded laurel leaves and grape border, gilt-framed central cartouche enamel decorated w/ figural landscape, late 18th/early 19th C, 13.375" l	1500	2000
Standish, chinoiserie figural group w/ small well, figural sander and inkwell, and scrolled base, late 19th C, 10" h, 14" w, 9.5" d	3500	4500

Meissen, Miner dinnerware. —Photo courtesy Skinner, Inc., Boston, MA.

Mocha Ware. —Photo courtesy Skinner, Inc., Boston, MA.

Mocha

	LOW	HIGH
Bowl, brown seaweed decoration on ocher ground, 3.5" h, 6.875" dia	$300	$400
Mug, blue and brown earthworm pattern, olive ground, cream and ocher sunflower pattern on dark brown ground, light blue stripes, 5.25" h	2000	2500
Mug, dark brown wavy decoration on cream ground bordered by ocher stripes, cream dot pattern on black stripe, blue impressed bands, cream handle w/ leaf-impressed ends, 4.75" h	1000	1200
Pepper Pot, baluster form w/ dome top and foot, white, cinnamon, and dark brown cat's eye pattern on blue ground, dark brown, blue, and cinnamon stripes alternating on white ground, 4.375" h	900	1000
Pitcher, cream wavy line decoration on dark brown band, light blue, cream, and dark brown cat's eye pattern on ocher ground above and below, green impressed leaf decoration on raised shoulder, light blue and cream alternating stripes, white handle w/ leaf-impressed ends, 7.25" h	3500	4000
Pitcher, open chain pattern on pumpkin ground w/ upper and lower dark brown bands, white handle w/ leaf-impressed ends, 5.375" h	1800	2000

Quimper

Bowl, geometric design, early 20th C	$450	$600
Bowl, Shield of Brittany, scalloped edge	1200	1500
Holy Water Font, Benitier, late 19th C, 5" h	250	350
Holy Water Font, Benitier, 20th C, 6" h	200	250
Platter, oval, 13" l	1500	1800
Snuff Container, baluster form, early 20th C	450	600
Snuff Container, donut form, 19th C	1200	1500
Snuff Container, frog form, early 20th C	1500	1800
Snuff Container, shield form, early 20th C	200	300
Snuff Container, butterfly form, early 20th C	1600	2000
Tray, handled, scalloped edge, late 19th C	2500	3500
Vase, baluster form, 11.5" h	1600	2000
Vase, geometric design, 9" h	1200	1500

Royal Worcester

	LOW	HIGH
Bud Vases, prismatic, trumpet form, scrolled foliate handle, pink and yellow shaded ground w/ floral decoration, c1900, 6.875" h, price for pair	$600	$800
Bud Vases, shape 854, bottle-form w/ gilt and enamel foliate designs on ivory ground, printed mark, c1888, 6.25" h	300	500
Candlestick, shape 1793, figural, modeled as woodsman by basket-molded vase, tree trunk for candlestick stem, printed mark, c1895, 11.875" h	500	700
Claret Jugs, shape 1047, enamel floral designs between gilt bands and raised blossoms, printed mark, late 19th C, 8" h, price for pair	600	800
Ewer, Chelsea-style, shape 1144, scalloped rim, satyr mask at handle terminal, gilt and enamel floral decoration on ivory ground, printed mark, c1892, 10.75" h	500	700
Ewer, shape 783, 10" h	300	500
Ewer, shape 1227, 9.5" h	300	500
Figure, Hide and Seek, shape 825, modeled as boy and girl figures hiding behind tree trunk-form vases, oval base, printed mark, c1881, 6.5" h	400	600
Inkstand, fluted well and cover supported by stand w/ 3 shell dishes alternating w/ 3 female sphinx forms, printed mark, c1877, 7.25" h	800	1000
Mortuary Vases, covered, w/ inner lid, shape 1256, scrolled handles, pierced cover, bulbous body decorated w/ gilt and enamel floral designs, printed mark, c1889, 9.25" h, price for pair	2000	2500
Urn, shape 1632, 10" h	500	700
Vase, 2-handled, cream ground, gilt and enameled fern decoration, printed mark, c1891, 9" h	300	500
Vase, double-walled, gilt jeweling on pierced cellwork body w/ lobed cartouches revealing gilt-decorated landscapes on inner wall, printed mark, c1887, 3.25" h	1000	1500
Vase, Sabrina Ware, mottled blue, iron red, and white glazes, printed mark, c1902, 8.875" h	200	400
Vase, shape 1109, 2-handled, raised foliate borders, gilt trim, enameled fern designs, printed mark, c1889, 11.75" h	500	700
Vase, shape 1431, 10" h	300	500

Royal Worcester, left to right: Ewer, shape 783; Urn, shape 1632; Vase, shape 1431; Ewer, shape 1227. —Photo courtesy Gene Harris Antique Auction Center, Inc.

Spatterware Creamer, red, green and blue spatter, blue, yellow, and black peafowl, 4" h, $5170 at auction. —Photo courtesy Garth's Auctions, Delaware, OH.

Spatterware

	LOW	HIGH
Creamer, brown and black rainbow spatter, 4.375" h	$650	$900
Creamer, green spatter, black edge stripe, black, yellow ocher, and blue peafowl, leaf handle, 3.75" h	750	1000
Cup and Saucer, handleless, blue spatter, molded panels, red, green, and black hollyberry	350	450
Cup and Saucer, handleless, blue spatter, red, green, and yellow star	450	570
Cup and Saucer, handleless, blue spatter, red, yellow, green, and black peafowl	900	1200
Cup and Saucer, handleless, green spatter, black, red, blue, green, and yellow ocher peafowl on bar	2500	3000
Cup and Saucer, handleless, green spatter, blue, yellow, red, and black peafowl	850	1000
Cup and Saucer, handleless, purple spatter, red and green thistle	800	1000
Cup and Saucer, handleless, red and purple rainbow spatter, blue, yellow ocher, red, and black peafowl	800	1200
Cup and Saucer, handleless, red spatter, blue, green, red, and black peafowl, green tree	2500	3000
Cup and Saucer, miniature, green spatter, red, blue, yellow, and black peafowl	450	575
Mug, maroon and green spatter, 2.75" h	350	475
Pitcher, blue spatter, leaf handle, 7" h	200	275
Plate, blue spatter, blue, orange, red, and black peafowl, 8.25" dia	800	1000
Plate, blue spatter, red, blue, green, and black peafowl in unusual shape, 8.75" dia	1600	2000
Plate, blue spatter, red, blue, green, and black pomegranate, 8.5" dia	450	600
Plate, blue spatter, red, green, black, and yellow peafowl, 8.25" dia	750	1000
Plate, blue spatter, red, green, yellow, and black tulip, 8.875" dia	450	575
Plate, red spatter, blue, yellow, green, and black peafowl, 8.125" dia	700	900
Platter, octagonal, red spatter, blue, yellow, green, and black peafowl, 13.5" l	1200	1800
Soup Plate, blue spatter, blue, yellow ocher, red, and black peafowl, 10.5" dia	3000	4000
Soup Plate, red spatter, green, purple, red, blue, and black columbine, 10.5" dia	450	600
Sugar Bowl, red and green rainbow spatter, 4.375" h	350	450
Teapot, blue spatter, green and black tree, molded flower finial and handle, 6" h	450	600
Toddy, scalloped rim w/ red, green, and blue rainbow spatter, impressed "Adams," 6.375" dia	250	325

Wedgwood

	LOW	HIGH
Bird Feeder, majolica, cylindrical form w/ pierced arched rectangular sides, green glaze, impressed mark, c1871, 3.875" h	$200	$400
Candlestick, black basalt, figural dolphin on raised rectangular plinth w/ shell-molded border, impressed mark, 19th C, 9.5" h	500	700
Candlesticks, jasperware, dark blue dip, columnal form, applied white bands, 19th C, 6" h, price for pair	300	500
Crocus Pot and Stand, black basalt, beehive form w/ pierced body, impressed mark, early 19th C, 7.25" h	1000	1500
Dish, majolica, argenta ground w/ floral panels on stippled ground, impressed mark, c1875, 12.25" dia	400	600
Jug, jasperware, dark blue dip, bottle-form, white relief central classical medallion of Cupid and Psyche below floral swags, impressed mark, 19th C, 9" h	500	700
Library Bust, Locke, black basalt, mounted on waisted circular socle, impressed title and mark, 19th C, 11" h	800	1000
Pie Dish, covered, caneware, oval, cover decorated w/ pastry strapwork and twig knop w/ leaves and berries, impressed mark, early 19th C, 8.5" l	600	800
Pilgrim Flask, Norman Wilson design, central embossed floral, foliate, and basketweave design, green glaze, printed mark, c1940, 8.5" h	700	900
Portland Vase, jasperware, dark blue dip, applied white classical relief, impressed mark, mid-19th C, 8" h	500	700
Sugar Bowl, covered, black basalt, "Domestic Employment" relief above engine-turned band, sibyl finial, impressed mark, late 18th C, 5" h	600	800
Sweetmeat Baskets, Queen's ware, scalloped rim, pierced body, impressed mark, early 19th C, 5" h, price for pair	2000	2500
Vase, black basalt, classical relief depicting bacchanalian boys at play, impressed mark, 19th C, 5" h	500	700
Vase, bone china, shoe-form w/ 2 hands tying lace, rectangular base w/ gilt and enameled flowers, printed mark, c1900, 5" h	600	800
Vase, caneware, applied black classical relief between floral and berry and leaf and berry bands, impressed mark, early 19th C, 7" h	600	800
Vase, Lindsay ware, 2-handled, trumpet-form neck on bulbous body, enamel-decorated butterfly design, printed mark, c1910, 6.875" h	1200	1500

Wedgwood Jasperware. —Photo courtesy Skinner, Inc., Boston, MA.

Figurines

Artisan modeled figurines in pottery and porcelain are a mainstay of the collecting market. Often, the most valuable pieces are not those produced as "limited edition." Quality of design and craft are the most important factors, but condition, rarity and size are also important.

For additional reading on individual potteries refer to *The Florence Collectibles* by Doug Foland (Schiffer, Atglen, PA, 1995), *Ceramic Arts Studio* by Mike Schneider (Schiffer, Atglen, PA, 1994), *Collectible Kay Finch* by Devin Frick, Jean Frick, and Richard Martinez (Collector Books, Paducah, KY, 1997), and *Royal Copenhagen Porcelain: Animals and Figurines* by Robert J. Heritage (Schiffer, Atglen, PA, 1997).

	LOW	HIGH
Abingdon		
Blackamoor, 7.5"	$40	$50
Fruit Girl, 10"	90	125
Goose, 5"	45	60
Gull, 5"	75	90
Heron, 5.5"	45	55
Kangaroo, 7"	90	125
Kneeling Nude, 7"	175	200
Peacock, 8"	45	60
Pelican, 5"	45	60
Penguin, 5.5"	45	60
Pouter Pigeon, 4.5"	44	60
Scarf Dancer, 13"	175	200
Shepherdess and Faun, 11.5"	90	120
Swan, 3.75"	70	100
Swordfish, 4.5"	45	60
Brayton Laguna		
Blackamoor	$30	$40
Black Girl	225	275
Emily	30	40
Female Torso, abstract, 10.5"	70	80
Frances	30	40
Geppetto (Disney)	225	275
Giraffes, pair, 18"	300	360
Hound Dog	35	45
Jon	30	40
Male, abstract	250	300
Miranda, 6.5"	30	40
Peasant Woman	30	40
Sally	20	30
Toucans, pair	225	275
Ceramic Arts Studio		
Arabesque	$30	$40
Attitude	30	40
Autumn Andy	20	30
Bali Hai	30	40
Balinese Dance Boy and Girl	100	125
Ballet en Pose	80	100

	LOW	HIGH
Bass Viola Boy	40	60
Bedtime Boy and Girl	30	40
Berty	80	100
Blythe and Pensive	100	125
Bo Peep	30	40
Boy and Girl, standing	40	50
Boy and Tiger	40	50
Boy Blue	15	25
Boy w/ Dog	40	50
Bride and Groom	60	70
Cats, Puff and Muff, pair	30	40
Chinese Boy and Girl	30	40
Chinese Couple	15	25
Chipmunk	20	30
Cinderella and Prince	40	50
Cocker Spaniel, pair	30	40
Colonial Boy and Girl	40	50
Colonial Lady and Man	40	50
Colts, Balky and Frisky, pair	50	70
Comedy and Tragedy	90	110
Cowgirl and Cowboy	50	60
Cuban Child	20	30
Cuban Woman	30	40
Dancing Dutch Boy and Girl	80	90
Dogs, Fifi and Fufu, pair	30	40
Drummer Girl	40	60
Dutch Boy and Girl	15	25
Dutch Boy and Girl, sitting	20	30
Dutch Love Boy and Girl	30	40
Fawn, standing	20	30
Fire Couple	175	225
Fishing Boy and Farmer Girl	30	40
Flame Couple	175	225
Flute Girl	40	60
Fox and Goose, pair	50	70
Gay 90s Lady and Man	40	50
Girl and Boy, sitting	40	50
Girl w/ Cat	40	50
Guitar Boy	40	60
Gypsy Girl and Boy	130	160
Hansel and Gretel	50	60
Harlequin Boy and Girl	140	180

	LOW	HIGH
Harmonica Boy	40	60
Hiawatha	20	30
Hindu Boys	40	50
King's Jester and Musicians	200	250
Kissing Girl and Boy	40	50
Lady Rowena	70	90
Little Jack Horner	15	25
Mary and Little Lamb	30	40
Mexican Boy and Girl	60	70
Minnehaha	20	30
Miss Muffet	15	25
Modern Dance Woman	60	70
Parakeets, pair	30	40
Parrots, Pete and Polly, pair	75	100
Peter Pan	50	60
Pied Piper	30	40
Pierrene and Pierrott	80	100
Pioneer Sam and Susie	40	50
Polish Boy and Girl	30	40
Rabbit	20	30
Roosters, pair	30	40
Russian Boy and Girl	60	75
Santa Claus and Evergreen Tree	20	30
Saxophone Boy	40	60
Scotties, pair	25	35
Southern Belle and Gentleman	40	50
Spanish Dance Couple	90	110
Square Dance Couple	40	50
St. Francis	80	100
St. George	90	110
Sultan and Harem	70	80
Summer Sally	20	30
Temple Dancer	170	200
Tom Tom the Piper's Son	40	60
Victorian Lady and Man	40	50
Wee Chinese	20	30
Wee Dutch	20	30
Wee Eskimos	20	30
Wee French	20	30
Wee Swedish	20	30
White Rabbit and Alice	60	70
Winney	70	90

Cliftwood Potteries

	LOW	HIGH
Billikin Doll, 7.5"	$60	$75
Billikin Doll, 11"	100	125
Cat, 1.5"	90	110
Cat, 5.75"	90	110
Cat, 6"	40	50
Cat, 8.5"	40	50
Elephant, 6"	40	60
Elephant, 9"	40	50
Lion, 14"	60	80
Lioness, 12"	60	70

Florence Ceramics

	LOW	HIGH
Ann	$50	$60
Ballerina Child	80	100
Beth	60	70
Birthday Girl	120	150
Blynken	60	70
Boy in Tuxedo	80	100
Boy w/ Fiddle	90	110
Bride	350	425
Bust	80	100
Camille	80	100
Carol	200	250
Caroline in Brocade	350	425
Catherine	150	180
Charles	90	110
Charmaine	70	90
Chinese Girl	40	50
Choir Boy	50	60
Cindy	50	60
Clarissa	50	60
Claudia	90	110
Colleen	60	75
Cynthia	200	240
Diane	90	110
Douglas	70	80
Edith	60	75
Edward	120	150
Elaine	40	50
Elisha	90	110
Elizabeth	150	175
Ellen	70	80
Ethel	60	75
Eugenia	175	210

Florence Ceramics, Julie.

	LOW	HIGH
Evangeline	50	60
Fair Lady	300	350
Fall	40	50
Gary	70	90
Genevieve	100	125
Georgia in Brocade	350	425
Girl w/ Pail	100	125
Grace	60	70
Grandmother and I	275	350
Hare	90	110
Her Majesty	70	80
Irene	50	60
Jeanette	70	80
Jennifer	130	160
Jim	50	60
Josephine	70	80
Joy	50	60
Joyce	200	250
Julie	100	125
Kay	60	70
Kiu	40	50
Lady Diana	150	180
Lantern Boy	40	50
Laura	100	120
Leading Man	150	180
Lillian	90	110
Lillian Russell	350	425
Linda Lou	70	80
Lisa	90	110
Lorry	125	150
Louis XV	200	250
Louis XVI	150	180
Louise	100	120
Madame Pompadour	200	250
Madonna Plain	50	60
Madonna w/ Child	70	80
Margot	200	250
Marie Antoinette	150	180
Marleen in Brocade	350	425
Marsie	75	80
Martin	170	200
Matilda	100	120
Melanie	70	80
Mikado	150	180
Mike	50	60
Musette	100	125
Nancy	50	60
Nita	70	80
Our Lady of Grace	50	60
Pamela	70	80
Parasol	200	250
Patricia	90	110
Peasant Girl	60	75
Prima Donna	250	300
Princess	175	200
Priscilla	60	75
Rebecca	100	125
Rhett	80	100
Rosalie	90	110
Rose Marie	90	125
Sally	60	75
Sarah	60	75
Scarlett	150	180
Shen	100	140
Sherri	150	180
Shirley	125	150
Story Hour	225	275
Sue	50	60
Sue Ellen	80	90
Susan	200	250
Taka	120	150
Victor	110	150
Victoria	200	250
Virginia in Brocade	350	425
Vivian	120	150

Frankoma

Bull, miniature	$60	$80
Cocker Spaniel, miniature	100	150
Colt, prancing, miniature	375	475
Cowboy	200	250
Elephant, miniature	80	125
English Setter	50	70
Fan Dancer	150	180
Flower Girl	70	90
Gardener Boy	90	110
Gardener Girl	75	90
Harlem Hoofer	475	575

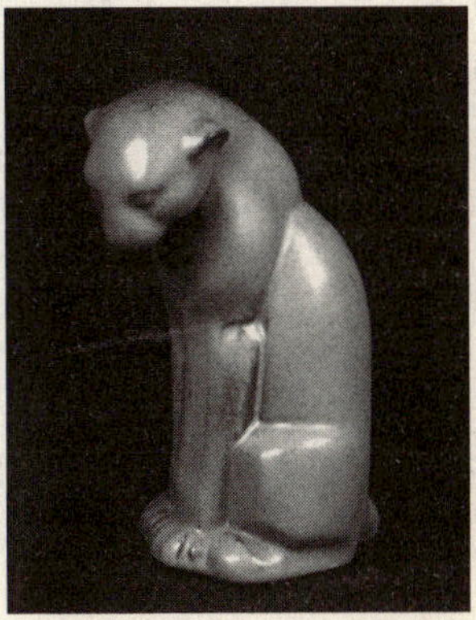

Frankoma, puma, #114.

	LOW	HIGH
Leopard, pacing, miniature	290	325
Monk	125	150
Pekingese, miniature	250	300
Puma	75	125
Swan, miniature	45	55
Torch Singer	450	550

Herend

Bears, pair, 3.5"	$350	$425
Bunny, 2.25"	100	125
Canary, 4"	125	175
Cat with Ball, 5.25"	125	175
Dog with Ball, 3.5"	100	125
Ducks, pair, 15"	900	1100
Elephant, 4.5"	250	325
Fox, 7"	325	400
Frog, 3"	75	100
Giraffes, pair, 8.25"	900	1100
Goose w/ Golden Egg, 7.5"	200	250
Hippopotamus, 4.5"	200	250
Jaguar, 6.5"	350	425
Kangaroo and Baby, 6"	350	425
Monkey, 5.125"	200	250
Mouse, 2.25"	125	175
Owls, pair, 5" and 2"	200	250
Pelican, 3.5"	125	175
Penguin, 5"	150	200
Pheasants, pair, 13"	750	900
Rabbit, 3"	125	175
Rabbits, pair, 5.25"	350	425
Ram, 4.5"	150	200
Rhinoceros, 5.125"	200	250
Seal, 7.5"	325	400
Sea Otter, 7.5"	400	500
Turkey, 4.25"	200	250
Unicorn, 5"	200	250

Herend, ducks. —Photo courtesy Sloan's Washington DC Gallery.

	LOW	HIGH

Homer Laughlin

Harlequin Cat	$125	$160
Harlequin Donkey	100	135
Harlequin Duck	100	125
Harlequin Fish	100	125
Harlequin Lamb	110	145
Harlequin Penguin	90	130

Hull

Bandanna Duck, #74	$35	$50
Bandanna Duck, #76	15	20
Dachshund, 14"	85	115
Love Birds, #93	25	35
Rabbit, 5.5"	35	55
Rooster, #951	35	50
Swan, #69, 8.5"	25	35

Kay Finch

Cat, angry, 10.25"	$80	$110
Cat, contented, 6"	40	60
Cat, Persian, 10.75"	80	100
Cat, playful, 8.5"	60	70
Chanticleer, 10.5"	100	125
Cherub Head, 2.75"	5	15
Chicken Biddy, 8.25"	30	40
Chinese Boy, 7.5"	20	30
Court Lady Ceramics, 10.5"	30	40
Elephant, 5"	20	30
Elephant, 6.75"	40	60
Elephant, 17"	350	425
Godey Lady, 7.5"	30	40
Godey Lady, 9.5"	30	40
Godey Man, 7.5"	30	40
Godey Man, 9.5"	30	40
Kitten, sleeping, 3.25"	5	15
Lamb, 2.75"	5	15
Owl, 3.75"	15	25
Owl, 8.75"	30	40
Peasant Boy, 6.75"	30	40
Peasant Girl, 6.75"	30	40
Scandie Boy, 5.25"	20	30
Scandie Girl, 5.25"	20	30

Midwest Pottery

Afghan Hound, 7"	$30	$40
Bear, 10"	25	35
Cowboy on Bronco, 7.5"	30	40
Crane, 11"	20	35
Dancing Woman, 8.5"	20	30
Deer, 8"	15	25
Deer, 12"	30	40
Female Bust	70	80

	LOW	HIGH
Female Nude, 11.5"	100	140
Fighting Cock, 6.5"	20	30
Frog, 1"	5	15
Heron, stylized, 22"	25	35
Rabbits, 2.5"	20	30
Race Horse, 7.25"	60	70
Sailing Ship, 2"	5	15
Seagull, 12"	30	40
Spaniel, 6"	40	50
Stallion, 10.75"	30	40
Turkey, wild, 11.5"	40	50

Morton Pottery

Cat, 6"	$10	$20
Deer, 4.5"	5	15
Donkey, 2"	30	40
Elephant, "GOP/candidate"	10	20
John Kennedy, Jr.	30	40
Kangaroo, 2.75"	5	15
Lamb, 3.5"	5	15
Man in Knickers, 7.5"	10	20
Oxen, 3.25"	30	40
Rabbit, 3"	5	15
Stork, 4"	5	15
Stork, 7.5"	15	25
Swordfirsh, 5"	10	20

Royal Copley

Canary, 5.5"	$20	$30
Cockatoo, 7.25"	25	35
Deer on Sled, 6.5"	20	30
Finch, #2, 5"	20	30
Hen and Rooster, #1, pair	25	40

Morton Pottery, crane.

	LOW	HIGH
Parrot, 5"	10	15
Sparrow, open beak, 5"	8	12
Teddy Bear, 5.5"	30	40
Warbler, 5"	10	15

Royal Haeger

Black Panther, 18"	$35	$50
Black Panther, 24"	100	125
Cat, Egyptian, 7.5"	15	25
Cat, sitting, 6"	25	35
Cat. sleeping, 7"	25	35
Cat, standing, 7"	25	35
Cat, tiger, 11"	30	40
Cat, tigress, 8"	30	34
Cocker Spaniel, 3"	40	55
Dachshund, 14.5"	45	60
Dove, 8.5"	40	55
Duck, 5"	20	40
Elephant, 5"	20	40
Elephant, 3.25"	40	55
Fawn, standing, 11.75"	45	60
Giraffe and Young, 13.5"	100	135
Giraffes, pair, 15"	120	140
Green Briar, 8.25"	40	55
Hen, 4"	25	35
Horse, 7"	25	35
Horse, 13"	70	90
Indian Girl w/ Basket	20	30
Macaw, 14"	35	45
Mare and Foal, 9"	65	85
Panther, 12"	15	25
Pheasant, 6"	25	35
Polar Bear, 7"	25	35
Polar Bear, 16"	65	80
Polar Bear Cub, 3"	15	20
Racing Horse, 9"	30	40
Rooster, 5"	20	40
Rooster, 11"	50	65
Russian Wolfhound, 7"	25	35
Stag, 14.5"	40	55
Wild Goose, 6.5"	20	40

Vernon Kilns

Centaur	$650	$800
Centaurette	375	450
Elephant	325	400
Hippo	325	400
Nubian Centaurette	375	450
Reclining Sprite	150	180
Satyr	140	180
Sprite	150	180
Unicorn	325	400
Winged Sprite	150	180

Flow Blue

For information on Flow Blue see *Flow Blue, 3rd Edition* by Jeffrey B. Snyder (Schiffer, West Chester, PA, 1999), *Mulberry Ironstone* by Ellen R. Hill (published by author, Madison, NJ, 1993) and Mary Frank Gaston's *The Collector's Encyclopedia of Flow Blue China* (1983, 1999 value update) and *Second Series* (1994, 1996 value update), both published by Collector Books, Paducah, KY.

Flow Blue.

	LOW	HIGH
Butter, covered, Oregon, 12-panel lid, Mayer	$450	$600
Butter, covered, w/ drain, Touraine, Stanley	200	250
Creamer, Chapoo, primary shape, Wedgwood, c1850, 5" h	400	500
Creamer, Ning Po, primary shape, Hall, c1845, 5" h	200	250
Creamer, Pelew, lighthouse shape, Challinor, c1840, 5.25" h	150	200
Cup and Saucer, Touraine, Stanley, c1898	25	50
Gravy, w/ liner, Touraine, Stanley, c1898	150	200
Milk Pitcher, Chapoo, bulbous shape, Wedgwood, c1850, 6" h	600	750
Pitcher, Cavandish, Keeling, c1910, 7" h	200	250
Pitcher, Chapoo, lighthouse shape, Wedgwood, c1850	1200	1500
Platter, Chapoo, Wedgwood, c1850, 15.75" x 12.25"	350	450
Platter, Chinese Well and Tree, Dimmock, c1845, 15.75" x 12"	350	450
Platter, Coburg, Edwards, c1860, 10" x 7.75"	100	150
Platter, Indian, Pratt, c1840, 15" x 11.5"	150	200
Platter, Jeddo, W. Adams, c1845, 18" x 14"	200	250
Platter, Oregon, T. J. and J. Mayer, 18" x 14"	500	650
Platter, Whampoa, Mellor & Venables, c1840, 21" x 17.25"	900	1100
Sauce Tureen, covered, w/ undertray, Chapoo, Wedgwood, c1850	1100	1500
Sauce Tureen, covered, w/ undertray and ladle, Oregon, Mayer, c1845	600	750
Soup Tureen, covered, white Staffordshire ladle, Hindustan, Maddock, 8" h, 14" w	600	750
Sugar, covered, Chapoo, primary shape, Wedgwood, c1850	500	650
Sugar, covered, Temple, gothic shape w/ lion head handles, Podmore, Walker & Co., c1850	300	450
Teapot, covered, Cabul, lighthouse shape, Challinor, c1847, 8.5" h	700	900
Teapot, covered, Chapoo, primary shape, Wedgwood, c1850, 9" h	400	500
Teapot, covered, Peking, primary shape w/ rosebud finial, Ridgway, c1845, 8.75" h	650	800
Teapot, Scinde, pumpkin shape, Alcock, c1840, 8.5" h	700	850
Vegetable, covered, Oregon, pedestal foot, Mayer, c1845, 9.5" sq	625	750
Vegetable, covered, Touraine, Stanley, c1898, 11" x 6.5"	225	300
Vegetable, open, Chapoo, Wedgwood, c1850, 9.5" x 7"	200	250
Wash Bowl and Pitcher, Hong Kong, bulbous pitcher w/ 6 concave panels, Meigh, c1845	650	800
Waste Bowl, Chapoo, 14-panel, Wedgwood, c1850, 3.25" h, 5.375" dia	150	200

Head Vases

Head vases are figural vases most often depicting women and young girls. They were popular in the 1950s and 1960s. Ladies with thick eyelashes, long gloves, dangle earrings and elaborate hats capture an exaggerated 1950s look. Although the United States manufactured some vases, Japan produced the majority. Identification is difficult because many were unmarked or had only paper labels.

When handling a head vase, be careful not to harm the label, the finish or delicate details such as jewelry. Beware of cracks and chips that decrease value. Watch out for reproductions or new head vases. Interest in head vases has intensified in the last five years and prices have risen accordingly. For further reading see *The World of Head Vase Planters* by Mike Posgay and Ian Warner (Antique Publications, Marietta, OH, 1992). All vases listed are female unless noted otherwise.

	LOW	HIGH
Ceramic Arts Studio, Manchu, Chinese man, 7.5"	$100	$150
Ceramic Arts Studio, Svea, pigtail, 6" h	75	100
Enesco, blue ribbons, pearl earrings, 7.25" h	300	375
Inarco, #E-1068, hair comb, pearl earrings and necklace, lashes, 1963 transfer, 10" h	350	436
Japan, #1-182, pearl necklace and earrings, hand, paper label "Brinnis, Pittsburgh, PA, Made in Japan," 7" h	225	300
Japan, #56551/A, bonnet, pearl earrings, hand, lashes, glossy finish, paper label "Fine Quality Japan," 7" h	175	250
Japan, blonde ponytail, glossy finish, faint transfer, 5.75" h	15	40
Japan, long brown hair w/ flower, lashes, jeweled, 5.25" h	75	125
Lefton, #1843, necklace, hand, lashes, luster finish, 5.75" h	50	80
Lefton, #1955, green checkered hat and bow, glossy finish, signed "Geo. Z. Lefton," 5" h	50	80
Lefton, #4228, brown gloves, eyelashes, marked "4228 Lefton," 6" h	75	125
Napco, #C4897C, blue hat w/ rose, earrings, blonde hair, lashes, 4.75" h	50	80
Napco, #C7494, blue hat, pearl necklace and earrings, paper label "National Potteries Made in Japan," 5.75" h	80	125
Relpo, #K1932, black bows in hair, earrings, paper label, 5.75" h	150	200
Rubins Original, #499, flowered dress and hat, pearl earrings, lashes, 5.75" h	75	100
Topling Imports, #50/425, black ribbon, pearl necklace, paper label, 8.5" h	200	275
Trimont Ware, pearl necklace and earrings, lashes, paper label, 7" h	125	175

Head Vases. —Photo courtesy Gene Harris Antique Auction Center, Inc.

Planters

Are planters the final frontier in figural ceramic collecting? Planter collectors think so, but something new is always being discovered. Collectors boast that planters are the perfect size; they demand less shelf space than cookie jars and display better than the smaller salt and pepper shakers. Shawnee, McCoy and other firms that produced cookie jars and salt and pepper shakers made many planters. So far, planters don't enjoy the widespread collecting base of cookie jars and salt and pepper shakers, but they're gaining momentum.

We listed style numbers of the various pieces and the manufacturer when known, and "Japan" for items so identified.

Shawnee often marked pieces with "USA," sometimes with a style number. This attribution is not foolproof because other firms also used the "USA" mark. Many planters had a paper label or were unmarked, so do your homework.

We recommend *Collector's Encyclopedia of Figural Planters & Vases: Identification & Values* by Betty and Bill Newbound (Collector Books, Paducah, KY, 1997).

Blue Bird, #4667, Lefton, 7.25" h, $20-$30. —Photo courtesy Ray Morykan Auctions.

	LOW	HIGH
Angel Fish, Japan, 3.5" h	$8	$10
Baby and Pillow, blue, Hull, #92	30	40
Baby Carriage and Lady, blue, Royal Haeger, 7.5" h	25	35
Basket Girl, 8" h	35	50
Berry and Leaf, McCoy, 8" l	12	18
Bird and Cup, Shawnee, #502	10	15
Bird on Bamboo, 5.25" h	8	12
Bird on Stump, 4.5" h	12	15
Bowling Boy, blue, Royal Haeger, 6" h	25	35
Box Car, Shawnee, #552	20	30
Boy, standing beside tall tree stump, Shawnee	8	12
Boy w/ Wheelbarrow, Shawnee, #750	15	20
Bug, metal feet, 3" h	15	20
Bulldog and Drum, 3" h	20	25
Burro, Abingdon, #673, 4.5" h	30	35
Canopy Bed, Shawnee, #734, 8" l	75	100
Cat, black, painted eyes, 15" l	30	40
Cat, blue, Haeger, #3311, 7" h	35	45
Cat, plaid, Japan, 5.25" h	5	8
Cat Playing Saxophone, Shawnee, #729	30	52
Chick w/ Cart, Shawnee, #720	15	20
Chick w/ Egg, Shawnee, #730, 3.5" h	15	20
Children on Shoe, Shawnee	15	20
Chinese Girl, Royal Copley, 7" h	25	35
Circus Wagon, Shawnee	30	35

	LOW	HIGH
Conestoga Wagon, Shawnee, #617, 3.5" h	20	30
Coolie w/ Basket and Umbrella, Shawnee, #617, 4.5" h	15	25
Cowboy Boot, Shawnee, 6.5"	10	15
Cow Skull, McCoy, 8" h	30	40
Diamond Design, McCoy, 7" l	10	15
Doe and Fawn, McCoy, 7" h	30	40
Dog Cart, McCoy, 5" h	25	30
Dog Profiles, 5" h	15	25
Donkey, Abingdon, #669, 7.5" h	40	50
Donkey w/ Basket, Shawnee, #722, 5.5" h	15	20
Duck and Logs, Occupied Japan, 3" h	15	20
Dutch Boy and Girl, 6.5" h	20	30
Dutch Boy at Wall, 5.5" h	12	18
Dutch Shoe, Abingdon, 5" l	30	50
Elephant, Hull	35	45
Elephant, Shawnee, #759	8	10
Elephant and Leaf, Shawnee, #501	50	75
Elf w/ Green Shoe, Shawnee, #765, 5.75" h, 6.5" l	30	50
Fawn, Abingdon, #672, 5" h	20	30
Fawn, Morton Pottery, #645, 6.5" h	10	20
Fish, black bass, 4.5" h	20	30
Fish in Swirling Waves, green, 7.5" h	20	30
Flamenco Dancers, 9" h	30	40
Flamingo and Foliage, 9.5" h	30	40
Flower and Bird, raised base, 4" h	15	20
Flying Bird, w/ flowers, 5" h	10	15
Gazelle, Royal Haeger, 17" l	80	125
Girl and Basket, Shawnee, #534	10	15
Gondolier, Royal Haeger, #6578, 19.5" l	30	50
Horse, rearing, 9.5" h	25	35
Igloo and Penguin, yellow, 3.25" h	10	18
Jack-in-the-Box, pink, Haeger, #3910, 8.5" h	20	30
Jaguar, rocky base, 9" l	20	25
Jalopy, Relpo, 7" l	8	12
Lady w/ Donkey Cart, Japan, 5.5" h	15	20
Lamb, Hull	45	60
Leopard, Royal Haeger, #760	25	35
Lily Pad and Frog, 3.75" h	10	15
Lovebirds on Pinecone, 4" h	20	30
Madonna, blue, Royal Windsor, 4.5" h	15	20
Madonna, white, Royal Haeger, #650, 9" h	25	35
Masks, Tragedy and Comedy, McCullogh, 3.5" h	10	15
Mexican Child, Royal Copley, 5.5" h	30	40
Motor Boat, green, 8" l	15	20
Oxcart and Dutch Girl, Japan, 3.5" h	12	18
Pelican on Bamboo Log, Japan, 9" l	65	90
Pheasant, black, gold highlights, 17" l	20	30
Piano, Shawnee, #528	20	30
Pirate, Brush, 3.5" h	25	35
Pixie, winged, Shawnee, #536, 4" h	7	10
Poodle, green, 7" h	15	20
Poodle, yellow, whimsical, 5" h	12	18
Pot and Saucer, button-tufted design, McCoy, 3.5" h	10	15
Rabbit, 7" h	10	15

	LOW	HIGH
Racing Horses, Royal Haeger, #883, 11" l	30	50
Rickshaw and Driver, Shawnee, 5" l	10	15
Rocking Horse, #526, 5.5" h	30	40
Rolling Pin, Camark, N1-51	10	15
Rooster, Camark, #501	20	30
Rooster, gray, McCoy, 1951	20	30
Santa and Chimney, Morton Pottery, 7" h	20	25
Shell, Shawnee, #2005, 4" x 7.75"	20	30
Shoe and Pup, burgundy, Shawnee	12	15
Sleeping Peasant w/ Burro, 5.75" h	30	40
Sofa, Germany, 4.5" h	8	12
Swan, black, 5.5" h	15	20
Swan, blue w/ gold floral decoration, 6" h	15	20
Swan, lime green, Hull, #69	100	150
Three-Piece Band, Napco, 7.5" h	70	100
Three Pigs, Shawnee	8	15
Top Hat, star-spangled, Shawnee, 3" h	8	15
Train Caboose, Shawnee, #553	30	40
Train Engine, Shawnee, #550	50	60
Train Set, Shawnee, #550, #551, #552, and #553	125	175
Train Tender, Shawnee, #551	25	35
Tree Stump w/ Boy, Shawnee, #533	10	14
Turkey, Morton Pottery, 5" h	10	15
Turtle, green, McCoy, 7" l	30	40
Twin Swans, yellow, cold-paint features, Brush-McCoy, 11.5" l	35	45
Two Ducks, 7.5" h	20	25
Violin, Royal Haeger, 17" l	25	35
Wishing Well w/ Dutch Boy and Girl, Shawnee, #710, 5.75" h, 8.25" w	30	50
Woman, w/ flowing skirt, 7" h	30	40

Planters, left to right: Dog, 6.75" h, $12-$18; Kitten in Basket, Royal Copley, 8.5" l, $30-$40.

Staffordshire

Staffordshire pottery refers to pottery produced in and around Staffordshire, England, from the mid-eighteenth century through the end of the nineteenth century. Originally conceived as an affordable alternative to Chinese porcelain, Staffordshire wares are now recognized in their own right. Important makers include Enoch Wood, Ridgway and Clews. With the development of the transfer decoration process, manufacturers covered dinnerware with scenes of popular landmarks and historical vignettes. "Historical Blue" had its heyday in the second half of the nineteenth century. Many popular designs are still produced.

For more information see *The Dictionary of Blue and White Printed Pottery: 1780-1880* (1982) and *Vol. II* (1989) by A. W. Coysh and R. K. Henrywood (Antique Collectors' Club, Woodbridge, Suffolk, England) and *Historical Staffordshire: American Patriots & Views* by Jeffrey B. Snyder (Schiffer, Atglen, PA, 1995). For additional reading on Staffordshire figures consult *Victorian Staffordshire Figures: 1835-1875, 2 Vols.* by A. and N. Harding (Schiffer, Atglen, PA, 1998) and *Staffordshire Animals* by Adele Kenny (Schiffer, Atglen, PA, 1998).

Soup Tureen, Holliwell Cottage, w/ ladle, dark blue, $2300 at auction. —Photo courtesy Skinner, Inc., Boston, MA.

Dinnerware

	LOW	HIGH
Basin, Landing of General Lafayette, Clews, dark blue, 12.125" l, 4.5" h	$1700	$2200
Bowl, Fair Mount Near Philadelphia, Eagle Border, Stubbs, shallow, blue, 9.25" dia	750	1000
Cup Plate, Anti-Slavery (Lovejoy/Tyrant's Foe), light blue, 4" dia	400	500
Cup Plate, Christmas Eve, no border, Wilkie series, Clews, dark blue, 3.5" dia	450	600
Cup Plate, Residence of the Late Richard Jordan, New Jersey, J. H. & Co., light blue, 3.75" dia	350	470
Gravy Boat, Catskill Mountains, Hudson River, Shell Border, Enoch Wood, dark blue, 4.75" h	500	700
Gravy Boat, Chillicothe, Cities series, Davenport, dark blue, 5.25" l	9500	12,500
Gravy Tureen Lid, Insane Hospital, Boston, Beauties of America, Ridgway, dark blue	300	400
Hot Water Plate, Death of the Bear, Indian Sporting series, Spode, medium blue, 11.5" dia	1000	1300
Mug, handled, Residence of the Late Richard Jordan, New Jersey, J. H. & Co., light purple/lavender, 3.25" h	350	450
Pitcher, States, America and Independence, Clews, dark blue, 9.75" h	3500	4500
Plate, Arms of New York, T. Mayer, dark blue, 10" dia	600	850
Plate, Arms of Rhode Island, T. Mayer, dark blue, 8.625" dia	530	720
Plate, Arms of South Carolina, T. Mayer, dark blue, 7.5" dia	800	1000
Plate, Baltimore & Ohio Railroad, Shell Border, Enoch Wood, dark blue, 10.125" dia	1400	1900

	LOW	HIGH
Plate, Beaver, Quadrupeds series, Hall, dark blue, 8.75" dia	300	400
Plate, Beehive, Stevenson & Williams, dark blue, 6.125" dia	250	320
Plate, Capitol at Washington, Shell Border, Enoch Wood, dark blue, 6.5" dia	500	650
Plate, Castle Forbes, Aberdeenshire, Grapevine Border series, Wood, dark blue, 6.625" dia	160	210
Plate, Catskill House, Hudson, Shell Border, Enoch Wood, dark blue, 6.5" dia	500	700
Plate, Chief Justice Marshall Troy, Wood, dark blue, 8.5" dia	750	900
Plate, City of Albany of State of New York, Shell Border, Enoch Wood, dark blue, 10.25" dia	900	1200
Plate, Columbia College N.Y., Acorn and Oakleaf Border, Clews, medium blue, 6.375" dia	480	650
Plate, Commodore MacDonnough's Victory, Wood, dark blue, 10.125" dia	900	1200
Plate, Esholt House, Yorkshire, Grapevine Border, Enoch Wood, dark blue, 10" dia	350	450
Plate, Fair Mount Near Philadelphia, Eagle Border, Stubbs, blue, 10.25" dia	380	500
Plate, Fair Mount Near Philadelphia, Eagle Border, Stubbs, light blue, 10.25" dia	270	350
Plate, Franklin's Morals, Davenport, dark blue, 7.625" dia	450	600
Plate, Gilpin's Mills on the Brandy, Shell Border, Enoch Wood, dark blue, 9.125" dia	1900	2500
Plate, Harvard College, Acorn and Oakleaf Border, Clews, medium blue, 10.125" dia	750	950
Plate, Highlands at West Point Hudson River, Shell Border, Enoch Wood, dark blue, 6.5" dia	1300	1600
Plate, Hospital Boston, Vine Border, Stevenson, dark blue, 9" dia	450	600
Plate, Hudson River View, Shell Border, Enoch Wood, dark blue, 5.75" dia	800	1000
Plate, India Pattern, medium blue, 8.375" dia	100	120
Plate, Landing of General Lafayette, Clews, dark blue, 8.875" dia	430	550

Staffordshire at auction, Upper Ferry Bridge over the River Schuylkill, Joseph Stubbs, Burslem, dark blue: Bowl and Pitcher, 13" dia bowl, 10" h pitcher, $1495; Platter, 19" x 15.5", $1495. —Photo courtesy Skinner, Inc., Boston, MA.

	LOW	HIGH
Plate, Nahant Hotel New Boston, Eagle Border, Stubbs, dark blue, 8.875" dia	600	800
Plate, Pass in the Catskill Mountains, Shell Border, Enoch Wood, dark blue, 7.5" dia	750	950
Plate, Pine Orchard House, Catskill Mountains, Shell Border, Enoch Wood, dark blue, 10.25" dia	850	1000
Plate, Residence of the Late Richard Jordan, New Jersey, J. H. & Co., blue, 10.375" dia	240	320
Plate, Residence of the Late Richard Jordan, New Jersey, J. H. & Co., brown, 7.75" dia	130	170
Plate, Residence of the Late Richard Jordan, New Jersey, J. H. & Co., light blue, 9" dia	240	320
Plate, Residence of the Late Richard Jordan, New Jersey, J. H. & Co., purple, 5.625" dia	100	130
Plate, Residence of the Late Richard Jordan, New Jersey, J. H. & Co., purple, 8.75" dia	110	150
Plate, Residence of the Late Richard Jordan, New Jersey, J. H. & Co., purple, 9" dia	200	250
Plate, Residence of the Late Richard Jordan, New Jersey, J. H. & Co., purple, 10.25" dia	110	150
Plate, Residence of the Late Richard Jordan, New Jersey, J. H. & Co., red, 5.625" dia	300	400
Plate, Residence of the Late Richard Jordan, New Jersey, J. H. & Co., red, 7.5" dia	130	160
Plate, Residence of the Late Richard Jordan, New Jersey, J. H. & Co., red, 10.5" dia	220	300
Plate, Rural Homes, Wood, dark blue, 7.5" dia	125	150
Plate, States, America and Independence, Clews, dark blue, 8.75" dia	400	500
Plate, States, America and Independence, Clews, dark blue, 10.5" dia	420	520
Plate, The Capitol, Washington, Shell Border, Enoch Wood, dark blue, 7.5" dia	1000	1300
Plate, Transylvania University, Lexington, Shell Border, Enoch Wood, dark blue, 9.25" dia	520	680
Plate, Union Line, Wood, dark blue, 10.25" dia	1000	1300
Plate, View Near Sandy Hill, Hudson, embossed rim, black transfer, pink luster border, 4.75" dia	300	400
Plate, View of Trenton Falls, Shell Border, Enoch Wood, dark blue, 7.5" dia	400	500
Plate, Villa in the Regent's Park, London, Regent's Park series, Adams, dark blue, 9" dia	270	360
Plate, Warwick Castle, Grapevine Border, Enoch Wood, 10" dia	240	320
Plate, Water Works, Philadelphia, Acorn and Oakleaf Border, Clews, blue, 10.125" dia	850	1100
Plate, Winter View of Pittsfield, Mass, Clews, dark blue, 8.875" dia	300	400
Plates, Cambrian, Phillips, light blue, 6.625" dia, price for set of 12	800	1000
Platter, Alms House Boston, Stevenson, dark blue, 14.5" l	2400	3200
Platter, Boston Mails...Saloon, Edwards, black, 19.875" l	480	620
Platter, Castle Garden, Battery New York, Wood & Sons, dark blue, 18.625" l	4000	5500
Platter, Fonthill Abbey, Wiltshire, Bluebell Border series, Clews, dark blue, 17" l	1400	1800
Platter, Halifax (from Dartmouth), British America series, Podmore, Walker & Co., brown, 19.25" l	950	1200

	LOW	HIGH
Platter, Lake George, State of New York, Shell Border, Enoch Wood, dark blue, 16.5" l	2300	3000
Platter, Landing of General Lafayette, Clews, dark blue, 15.25" l	2500	3300
Platter, New York from Heights Near Brooklyn, Stevenson, dark blue, 16.25" l	8000	11,000
Platter, Niagara From the American Side, Wood and Sons, dark blue, 14.875" l	3700	4800
Platter, Residence of the Late Richard Jordan, New Jersey, J. H. & Co., purple, 9.75" l	500	650
Platter, States, America and Independence, Clews, dark blue, 11.75" l	2200	3000
Platter, View of Greenwich, Grapevine Border, Enoch Wood, 14.875" l	800	1000
Sauce Boat, State House Boston, Beauties of America series, Ridgway, dark blue, 6.5" l	450	600
Soup Plate, Baltimore & Ohio Railroad, Shell Border, Enoch Wood, dark blue	1650	2200
Soup Plate, Octagon Church Boston, Beauties of America series, Ridgway, dark blue, 9.75" dia	500	650
Soup Plate, Park Theatre, New York, Acorn and Oakleaf Border, Clews, blue, 10" dia	500	650
Soup Plate, Residence of the Late Richard Jordan, New Jersey, J. H. & Co., purple, 7.75" dia	220	300
Strainer, Quebec, British America series, Podmore, Walker & Co., brown, 12.75" l	700	800
Teapot, Eagle on Urn, Clews, dark blue, 7" h	2500	3200
Undertray, Oxburgh Hall, Acorn and Oakleaf Border, openwork, dark blue, 10.625" l	1000	1250
Vegetable Dish, Quebec, Shell Border, Enoch Wood, dark blue, 9.5" sq	1100	1400
Vegetable Dish, West Point Military Academy, Shell Border, Enoch Wood, oval, dark blue, 10.75" l	1400	1900
Vegetable Dish, Winter View of Pittsfield, Mass, Clews, dark blue, 12.5" l	2500	3400
Wash Bowl, Lafayette at Franklin's Tomb, Enoch Wood, dark blue, 4.25" h, 10.75" dia	1200	1500

Staffordshire at auction, dinner service, Boston State House, John Rogers & Son, dark blue, price for 89-pc set, $14,950. —Photo courtesy Skinner, Inc., Boston, MA.

*Staffordshire Figurines.
—Photo courtesy Skinner, Inc., Boston, MA.*

Figurines

	LOW	HIGH
Baby in Cradle, 2.25" l	$90	$175
Bear w/ Cub, 3" h	215	375
Ben Franklin, holding paper titled "Freedom," black, red, and flesh tones, 15.75" h	4000	5500
Billy Goat, 2.5" h	135	200
Boy, riding rooster, wearing tricorn hat, 3.5" h	275	425
Boy, wearing blue coat, 3.25" h	215	375
Boy w/ Net, unglazed, 4" h	45	90
Boy w/ Rooster, 3.75" h	215	375
Camel, 2.75" h	125	200
Cow, 2" h, 3.5" l	150	250
Dog, sitting, 2.75" h	175	250
Dog, standing, 2.5" h	125	200
Dogs, recumbent, on mottled bases, early 19th C, 6.5" l, pair	2000	3000
Dogs, recumbent, w/ red and black markings, 4.5" l, pair	175	275
Dogs, w/ russet markings, 7" l, pair	1200	1900
Horse, reclining, 3.25" h	225	400
King Charles Spaniels, standing, 13" l, pair	3000	5000
Lamb, 2.5" h	125	200
Lamb, reclining, 3.5" h	225	400
Lion, 3.5" h	225	375
Monkey in Tree, 4" h	450	650
Ostrich, running, 4.5" h	175	300
Poodle, seated, 3.75" h	200	350
Poodles, mother w/ 3 pups on scrolled bases, 5" h, pair	775	1250
Rooster, 3.75" h	250	400
Rooster, 4.5" h	225	400
Spaniel, seated, black and white, 3" h	225	400
Spaniel, seated, orange and white, 3.5" h	275	425
Spaniels, seated, red and white, 7.5" h, pair	700	1200
Stag, reclining, 2.5" h	175	300
Turkey, 3" h	150	250
Zebra, black and green, 6.5" h	450	700

Steins

Europeans have produced steins since the thirteenth century. Collections of early steins can be very valuable. However, steins from the nineteenth and twentieth centuries are widely available. Collectors of modern steins prize those made by Villeroy & Boch Company of Mettlach, Germany. They also seek those manufactured by Merkelbach & Wick and Simon Peter Gerz. For more information see *The Mettlach Book* by Gary Kirsner, Glentiques, Ltd., Coral Springs, FL, 1994.

	LOW	HIGH
Character, Barmaid, marked "1089," by Reinhold Hanke, stoneware, .5L	$350	$500
Character, Caroline, marked "Musterschutz," by Schierholz, porcelain, .5L	500	700
Character, Cat Holding Fish, marked "420," Eckhardt & Engler, pottery, .5L	300	450
Character, Cat w/ Mandolin, by Reinhold Merkelbach, pottery, w/ working music box, .5L	400	550
Character, Devil, by E. Bohne Söhne, porcelain, .5L	500	700
Character, Football, "Yale University," Maddocks, porcelain, .5L	200	300
Character, Gentleman Dog, marked "Musterschutz," by Schierholz, porcelain, .5L	2400	3000
Character, Globe, marked "2368," by Reinhold Hanke, pottery, inlaid lid, .5L	1000	1400
Character, Knight, earthenware, .5L	350	500
Character, Monkey, by E. Bohne Söhne, porcelain, .5L	1400	1800
Character, Nürnberg Tower w/ city scenes, marked "F. & M. N. 6019," by Marzi & Remy, pottery, .25L	200	300
Character, Singing Pig, marked "Musterschutz," by Schierholz, porcelain, .3L	350	500
Character, Uncle Sam, marked "Musterschutz," by Schierholz, porcelain, .5L	6000	8000
Character, Wrap-Around Alligator, by E. Bohne Söhne, porcelain, .5L	600	800
Character, Zugspitze Mountain, marked "Martin Pauson," by Merkelbach & Wick, stoneware, .5L	600	800
Delft, landscape w/ windmill, porcelain, lithophane, porcelain inlaid lid, .5L	200	300
Faience, Bayreuth, stylized floral design, pewter lid and footring, acorn finial, c1780, 1L	700	1000
Faience, Schrezheim, cartouche w/ bird perched on tree, pewter lid and footring, orb finial, c1800, 1L	600	800
Meissen, hand-painted courting couple, gold scrollwork, porcelain, marked w/ crossed swords, 1L	2400	3200
Mettlach, #1526, coat of arms, "Seminar Bayreuth, 1901," hand painted, pewter lid, .5L	200	300
Mettlach, #1647, Alpine scene, tapestry, pewter lid, 1L	250	350
Mettlach, #2388, character Pretzel, inlaid lid, .5L	300	400
Mettlach, #2582, tavern scene, etched, inlaid lid, .5L	600	800
Mettlach, #2635, girl on bicycle, etched, inlaid lid, .5L	700	900
Mettlach, #2765, knight on horseback, etched, inlaid lid, .5L	2100	2600
Mettlach, #2891, wheat stalks, etched, inlaid lid, .5L	550	700
Mettlach, #5006, castle, faience type, pewter lid, .5L	400	500
Mettlach, Trier Cathedral, etched and print under glaze, inlaid lid, 1915, .5L	400	500
Military, "Bayer.–Hochgebirgs–Minenwerfer–Komp. 19, Weihnachten 1931," soldier and machine gun, pottery, pewter lid w/ relief helmet, .5L	400	550
Occupational, Beer Wagon Driver (Bierführer), owner's name, porcelain, pewter lid, .5L	700	900
Occupational, Glassworker (Glaser), "Glastertag, 10-18 Juli 1899, München," porcelain, owner's name on pewter lid, .5L	800	1100
Occupational, Musician (Musiker), owner's name, porcelain, pewter lid, .5L	500	700

Regimental Stein (3 views), lithophane bottom, .5L. —Photo courtesy Ray Morykan Auctions.

	LOW	HIGH
Regimental, "2. Comp., Baÿer. 1. Pionier Bataillon, München, 1912-1914," 4 side scenes, roster, lion thumblift, named to "Gefrt. Josef Hirschberger," screw-off lid w/ prism, stoneware, .5L, 11.75" h	700	900
Regimental, "2. Comp., Eisenbahn Regt. Nr. 3, Berlin, 1900-1902," 1 side scene, roster, eagle thumblift, named to "Pionier Werner," pottery, .5L, 10.5" h	900	1200
Regimental, "2. Comp., Eisenbahn Regt. Nr. 3, Berlin–Schöneberg & 2. Comp. Betriebs Abtl. Eisenbahn Brigade, 1908-10," 4 side scenes, eagle thumblift, named to "Reserv. Gestbuÿsen," 7-man roster, training area "Klausdorf, 1908-10," pottery, .5L, 11.5" h	2200	2800
Regimental, "3. Comp., Telegraph Bal. Nr. 3, Coblenz, 1900-02," roster, eagle thumblift, named to "Res. Singhof," pottery, .5L, 11" h	1200	1600
Regimental, "5. Comp., Baÿer. Inft. Regt. Nr. 5, Bamberg, 1912-1914," 4 side scenes, roster, lion thumblift, named to "Infanterist Thomas Schrenker," porcelain, .5L, 12.125" h	400	500
Regimental, "Maschinegewehr. Comp., Inft. Regt. Nr. 126, Strassburg, 1909-11," 4 side scenes, roster, Württ. thumblift, named to "Reservist Fritz," porcelain, .5L, 11" h	1800	2200
Regimental, "S.M.S. Elsass & S.M.S. Oldenburg, Wilhelmshaven, 1911-14," 4 side scenes, roster, eagle thumblift, named to "Matrose Ricok," screw-off lid w/ glass jewel, pottery, 1L, 14.625" h	1500	2000
Royal Vienna Type, scene w/ maiden and Cupid, labeled "Amor," hand-painted porcelain, porcelain inlaid lid w/ scenes inside and out, marked w/ beehive, .25L	2000	2600
Royal Vienna Type, tavern scene, labeled "Falstaff in der Schenke," hand-painted porcelain, gold-plated lid, marked w/ beehive, 1L	1300	1700
Souvenir, "Heineken's aan de Zuiderzee, New York World Fair 1939" and windmill, transfer-decorated pottery, pewter lid, 1L	400	550
Third Reich, "2. Komp., Kraftfahr Abtlg. & München, 1938," soldier on motorcycle below flag w/ swastikas, stoneware, pewter lid w/ relief helmet w/ swastika, .5L	700	900
Third Reich, "8. (M.G.) Komp., Inft. Regt. Nr. 40, 1936-1938," battle scene, pottery, pewter lid w/ relief helmet w/ swastika, .5L	400	600
Third Reich, "III Bat. Inft. Regt., Augsburg–Lindau Bodensee," battle scene, pottery, pewter lid w/ relief scene of Lindau, owner's name on lid, dated "1934-1935," .5L	400	600

Tiles

	LOW	HIGH
Copeland, modeled w/ round panel of disguised Cupid representing Winter, c1875, 8" sq	$350	$500
Grueby, 1 w/ mermaid, 1 w/ monk playing cello, red clay w/ matte mustard ground, 6" sq, pair	425	475
Grueby, 2-tile frieze, stylized Viking ship on high waves, cuenca, blues, greens, and browns, new Arts & Crafts frame, 9" x 18"	3000	3500
Grueby, 6-tile frieze spelling out in cuerda seca "Kelsey Ranch Lexington/ Supplying Waldorf Lunches" in green and ivory, Arts & Crafts frame, 3" x 30"	1000	1500
Grueby, cuenca w/ oak tree against cloud-filled sky in shades of green, blue, and white, Arts & Crafts frame, 6" sq	2000	2500
Grueby, "Pines," cuenca w/ trees in landscape in greens, blues, and brown, new Arts & Crafts frame, 6" sq	2500	3000
Grueby, stylized monk at lectern in bisque red clay against heavily curdled matte ocher ground, Arts & Crafts frame, 6" sq	500	600
Grueby, white tulip w/ green leaves on matte mustard ground, 6" sq	2000	2500
Marblehead, cluster of trees in dark green under blue overcast sky, ship mark, paper label, 4.25" sq	1000	1500
Marblehead, landscape of trees in dark green reflected in lake, ship mark, paper label, 4.25" sq	800	1000
Marblehead, large tree in forest in shades of brown and umber matte against moss green matte ground, Arts & Crafts frame, impressed ship mark, 6" sq	1500	2000
Mosaic, cuenca w/ ship on water in taupe, orange, and green against dark blue sky, company logo "MTC" on sail, Arts & Crafts frame, 6" sq	500	750
Owens, mountain landscape in cuenca in shades of green and ochre matte glazes, new Arts & Crafts frame, impressed "Owens," 11.75" sq	3000	3500
Owens/Empire, cuenca w/ ship on water in shades of ocher and brown, Arts & Crafts frame, 11.75" sq	1500	2000
Rookwood Faience, decorated in cuenca with Glasgow rose in pink w/ green leaves, new Arts & Crafts frame, impressed "Rookwood Faience/1281Y," 6" sq	1500	2000
Rookwood Faience, geometric design, matte ocher glaze, wood box frame, 6" sq	150	300
Tiffany, set of 3 w/ molded decoration blue thistle, chartreuse fleur-de-lis, and blue stylized blossoms, largest tile 3.5" sq	350	500

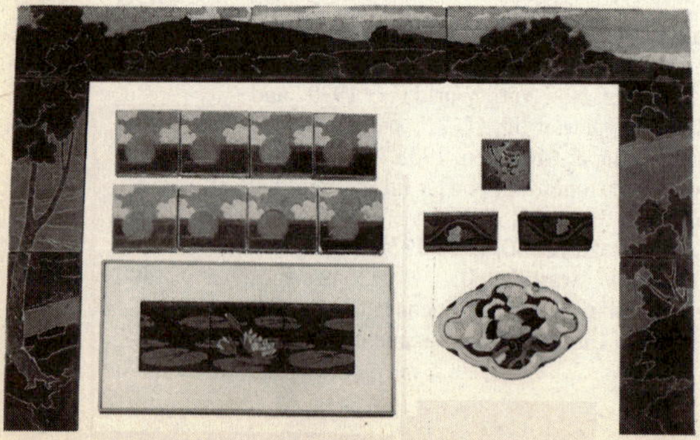

Grueby Tiles. —Photo courtesy David Rago Auctions, Inc.

Wall Pockets

For additional information see *Collector's Encyclopedia of Wall Pockets* by Betty and Bill Newbound (Collector Books, Paducah, KY, 1996) and *Collectors Guide to Wall Pockets* (1994) and *Bk II* (1997) by Marvin and Joy Gibson (L-W Book Sales, Gas City, IN).

	LOW	HIGH
Apple, Royal Copley, 6"	$20	$25
Apple and Leaves, McCoy	100	125
Aztec, moth design, Zane, 9"	85	100
Basket of Fruit, Japan, 8"	25	35
Basketweave, Catalina, 9.5"	200	250
Bird and Bamboo, Japan, 6.5"	20	25
Bird and Pineapple, Czechoslovakian	100	125
Bird at Well, Czechoslovakian	50	65
Birdhouse, Shawnee, #830	15	25
Blackamoor, holding planter above head	150	185
Book, Abingdon, #676, 6.5"	55	70
Bow, gold highlights, Shawnee, #534, 3.5"	15	25
Bucking Bronco, Brush	100	125
Butterfly, Abingdon, #601, 8.5"	30	40
Butterfly, McCoy	200	250
Calla Lily, Abingdon, #586, 9"	35	45
Camellia, Hull, #125, 8.5"	250	300
Carriage Lamp, Abingdon, #711, 10"	55	70
Cherub, Abingdon, #587, 7.5"	60	75
Chintz Pattern, red ground, Czechoslovakian, 8"	60	75
Cocker Spaniel Head, Royal Copley	20	25
Cookbook, Abingdon, #676	55	70
Cowboy Boot, Frankoma, 6.5"	20	25
Cup and Saucer, Camark, 7.5"	20	25
Cup and Saucer, Bow-Knot, Hull, #B24	100	125
Cup and Saucer, Sunglow, Hull, #80	35	45
Daisy, Abingdon, #379, 7.75"	50	70
Deer, Rosemeade	8	12
Dog in Cup, 5"	12	18
Dutch Boy Planter, Abingdon, #489, 10"	80	100
Dutch Girl Planter, #490, 10"	80	100
Dutch Shoe, Frankoma, #913, 8.5"	35	45
Egyptian, playing instrument, Rosemeade, 5.5"	150	185
Egyptian Motif, Zane, 9"	65	80
Female Mask, Abingdon, #376F, 7.5"	115	140
Fern Leaf Tri, Abingdon, #435	100	125
Fish, Brush	75	100
Fish, green and yellow, 8"	30	40
Fish, La Mirada Pottery	75	100
Frying Pan, "Them that works hard eats hardy," Cleminsons, 11.375"	25	35
Girl w/ Rag Doll, Shawnee, #810	20	30
Grape Vine, Royal Haeger, #745	20	30
Hat, wide brim, Royal Copley, 8"	25	35
Ionic, Abingdon, #457, 9"	55	70
Iron, Sunglow, Hull	40	55
Ivy Basket, Abingdon, #590, 7"	90	125
Leaf, Abingdon, #724	50	65

Wall Pockets.

Left: Roseville, Florentine, 9.5" h, $125-$150.

Right: Royal Worcester, conch shell, 11.375" h, $330 at auction. —Photo courtesy Gene Harris Antique Auction Center, Inc.

	LOW	HIGH
Lily Bud, McCoy, 8"	175	225
Little Jack Horner, Shawnee, #585	20	30
Mailbox, McCoy, 7.25"	25	35
Male Mask, Abingdon, #376M, 7.5"	115	130
Mallard Duck, DeLee Art, 7"	40	50
Mantel Clock, Shawnee, #530	20	30
Match Box, Abingdon, #675, 5.5"	35	55
Morning Glory, Abingdon, #377, 7.5"	20	30
Morning Glory, double, Abingdon, #375, 6.5"	30	40
Moss Aztec, embossed grapes, Zane	60	75
Peacock and Flowers, embossed, Czechoslovakian, 7.5"	75	100
Pear and Apple, Lefton, #3850, 7.25"	10	15
Peony, Japan, 8"	30	40
Pitcher, Bow-Knot, Hull, #B26	90	110
Pitcher, Sunglow, Hull, #81	30	40
Pitcher and 6 Mugs, red, white, and black stripes, Czechoslovakian	250	300
Pixie, sitting under tree, Treasure Craft, 5"	8	12
Poppy, Hull, #609, 9"	250	300
Rocking Horse, Royal Haeger, #724	20	25
Rosecraft Vintage, brown w/ fruit and grapevines, Roseville	90	130
Rosella, Hull, #R10, 6.5"	60	75
Scoop, embossed flowers, Camark, #N45	20	25
Scottie Dog, blue picket fence, Japan, 5.5"	25	35
Shell, Abingdon, #508, 7"	40	55
Shell, Florence Ceramics	75	90
Spanish Galleon, Japan, 7"	45	55
Telephone, Shawnee, #529	20	30
Violet, Florence Ceramics, 7"	150	200
Violin, gold trim, McCoy	150	200
Wagon Wheel, Frankoma, 7"	40	50
Wheat, Shawnee	35	45
Whisk Broom, Bow-Knot, Hull, #B27	100	125
Whisk Broom, Sunglow, Hull, #82	35	45
Woodland Glossy, Hull, 7.5"	50	65
Woodland Matte, Hull, 7.5"	100	125
Woodpecker and Tree Stump, American Art Pottery	12	18

Printed Media

Bibles

Johann Gutenberg printed the first typeset Bible in 1455. Since then, the Bible has been reprinted more than any other book. Some collectors buy only rare Bibles of the fifteenth and sixteenth centuries. Others specialize in miniature Bibles (12mo and smaller), or Bibles translated into exotic languages.

Almost everyone has an old family Bible, but most nineteenth-century examples are worth about $50; most eighteenth-century examples are worth around $100. However, there are many valuable Bibles. For an extensive listing of Bibles sold at auction consult *American Book Prices Current,* edited by Katherine and Daniel Leab, at American Book Prices Current, Box 1236, Washington, CT 06793.

Folio = 12" x 16"; 4to = 8" x 10"; 8vo = 5" x 7"; 12mo = 3" x 5".

	LOW	HIGH
1529, German, Das Gantz New Testament...Cologne: Hieronumus Fuchs for Peter Quentel	$1200	$3000
1590, Latin, Testamenta Veteris Biblia Sacra...Geneva: Jean de Tournes for the heirs of Andreas Weschel et al., 5 parts in one, old half pigskin, 4to	325	800
1616, English, The Holy Bible, Robert Barker	2000	4000
1676, John Bill and Christopher Barker, bound w/ The Book of Common Prayer and The Whole Book of Psalms, 2 parts in one, gilt-paneled morocco, over 180 engraved plates, 8vo	300	900
1682, English, The Holy Bible, Oxford & London, 1682 and 1683 Oxford and London editions of The Book of Common Prayer and The Whole Book of Psalms, folio, old calf, over 180 engraved plates	500	900
1696, English, New Testament of Our Lord, Oxford University, 12mo	130	300
1715, English, Oxford, John Baskett	100	250
1791, English, The Holy Bible, Philadelphia, W. Young, 2 volumes, 12mo	3400	8000
1796, English, Curious Hieroglyphick Bible for the Amusement of Youth, London, R. Bassam, 12mo	160	375
1800, English, London, T. Macklin, 6 volumes	500	1100
1846, English, The Illuminated Bible, NY	200	475
1856, Cherokee, Genesi, Park Hill, OK, Mission Press	200	470
1866, French, Tours, illustrated by G. Dore, 2 volumes	130	300
1910-11, English, London, Ballantyne Press, 1 of 750, 3 volumes	225	530
1915-57, Greek, The Codex Alexandrinus...Old Testament, 4 volumes, unbound, 4to	200	450
1949, English, Cleveland, 1 of 975, designed by B. Rogers	700	950
1959, English, NY, Abradale Press	70	165
1961, Latin, Paterson and NY, Pageant Books, 1 of 1000, 2 volumes, facsimile of Gutenberg Bible	1500	3500
1965, Cleveland, World Publishing Co., facsimile of first edition of King James version, 1611	340	800
1970, English, The Jerusalem Bible, Garden City, illustrated by Salvador Dali, 32 color plates, 4to	65	150

Books

Classic Books

Books were first printed around 1450, although handwritten books date back thousands of years. Many book collectors limit themselves to one or two favorite writers or a favorite subject, since the field of book collecting is vast. A collection is judged on quality rather than quantity. Books with water damage, broken bindings, or missing pages are usually worth almost nothing.

For an extensive listing of books consult *Huxford's Old Book Value Guide, Ninth Edition* (1997), *Tenth Edition* (1998), and *Eleventh Edition* (1999) published by Collector Books (Paducah, KY), *The Official Price Guide to Old Books, Third Edition* by Marie Tedford and Pat Goudey (House of Collectibles, Random House, NY, 1999), and *Collected Books* by Allen and Patricia Ahearn (Putnam, New York, NY, 1998).

Folio = 12" x 16"; 4to = 8" x 10"; 8vo = 5" x 7"; 12mo = 3" x 5".

	LOW	HIGH
Adams, H., *Education of Henry Adams*	$3500	4000
Alcott, Louisa May, *Little Men,* Boston, first American edition, cloth, 1871, 12mo	150	250
Anderson, Hans Christian, *The Complete Anderson,* New York, translated by Jean Hersholt, illustrated by Fritz Kredel, 6 volumes, cloth-backed boards, signed by Hersholt and Kredel, 1949, 8vo	50	100
Arms, Dorothy Noyes, *Hill Towns and Cities of North Italy,* New York, illustrated by John Taylor Arms, cloth, w/ 56 plates, 1932, 4to	50	100
Arnold, Lloyd R., *High on the Wild of Hemingway,* Caldwell, 1 of 950 copies signed by John Hemingway, cloth, 1969, 4to	100	150
Asimov, Isaac, *Lucky Starr and the Moons of Jupiter,* Garden City, first edition, dust jacket, 1957	250	350
Avati, Mario, *Noah's Ark,* New York, 1 of 75 copies, original wraps, w/ 10 plates, each signed, 1971, folio	800	1200
Barnes, James M., *A Guide to Good Golf,* New York, Dodd, Mead, cloth, 1925	40	70
Barnum, Phineas T., *Struggles and Triumphs...,* Buffalo, original cloth, 1882, 8vo	700	900
Bartlett, John, *Familiar Quotations,* Boston, gilt cloth, inscribed, 1892, 8vo	150	250
Bates, H. E., *Through the Woods,* London, cloth, 73 engravings by Agnes Miller Parker, 1936, 8vo	100	150
Beard, Peter Hill, *The End of the Game,* New York, cloth, 1965, 4to	50	100
Beckett, Samuel, *Nohow On,* etched plates by Robert Ryman, morocco, slipcase, 1 of 550 numbered copies signed by Beckett and Ryman, 8vo	1500	2000
Bellamy, Edward, *Looking Backward,* Boston, first edition, cloth, 1888, 12mo	200	300
Bemelmans, Ludwig, *Now I Lay Me Down to Sleep,* New York, 1 of 400 copies, 1943	25	75
Bendire, Charles Emil, *Life Histories of American Birds,* Washington, 1 volume, half morocco and marbled boards, 12 color plates, 1892, 8vo	50	100
Berger, Thomas, *Little Big Man,* New York, 1964	50	100
Bierce, Ambrose, *Black Beetles in Amber,* San Francisco, first edition, original cloth, 1892, 8vo	50	100
Biggle, Lloyd, *All the Colors of Darkness,* Garden City, dust jacket, 1963	100	150
Bourke, John Gregory, *On the Border w/ Crook,* New York, first edition, original cloth, 1891, 8vo	200	300
Bradbury, Ray, *The Anthem Sprinters and Other Antics,* New York, 1963	50	100
Bradbury, Ray, *Death Is a Lonely Business,* New York, first edition, 1985	125	175

	LOW	HIGH
Bradbury, Ray, *Fahrenheit 451,* illustated by Joe Mugnaini, aluminum boards, slipcase, 1 of 2000 numbered copies signed by Bradbury and Mugnaini, tall 8vo	350	450
Bradley, Marion Zimmer, *The Mists of Avalon,* New York, first edition, dust jacket, 1982	80	125
Briggs, Clarence Saunders, *History and Bibliography of American Newspapers, 1690-1820,* Worcester, MA, 2 volumes, cloth, 1947, 4to	200	250
Broder, Patricia J., *American West: The Modern Vision,* New York, 1 of 165 copies, half morocco, signed and numbered litho by Fritz Scholder, 1984, 4to	350	450
Bronte, Charlotte, *Jane Eyre,* first edition, 3 volumes, original cloth, signed by E. D. Mitchell on each front free endpaper, 1847, 8vo	35,000	45,000
Brown, Dee, *Bury my Heart at Wounded Knee,* New York, dust jacket, 1970	50	100
Bruce, Peter Henry, *Memoirs...,* calf gilt, 1782, 4to	150	250
Bruff, Joseph G., *Gold Rush,* New York, original half cloth, 1944, 4to	150	250
Bryant, William Cullen, *Picturesque America,* New York, 2 volumes, gilt calf, illustrated w/ steel engravings, 1872, 4to	125	175
Burnett, Frances H., *Little Lord Fauntleroy,* New York, first edition, first issue, original cloth, 1886, 4to	600	800
Burroughs, Edgar Rice, *The Bandit of Hell's Bend,* Chicago, first edition, 1925	1500	2500
Burroughs, Edgar Rice, *Tarzan of the Apes,* New York, first edition, 1912	4000	6000
Cain, James M., *The Postman Always Rings Twice,* New York, original cloth, 1934, 8vo	700	900
Canfield, Chauncey L., *The Diary of a Forty-Niner,* San Francisco, first edition, half cloth, 1906	125	175
Capek, Karel, *The Absolute at Large,* New York, dust jacket, 1927	75	125
Capote, Truman, *Breakfast at Tiffany's,* New York, first edition, 1958	125	175
Capote, Truman, *In Cold Blood,* New York, 1 of 500 copies, 1965	200	300
Carroll, Lewis, *Adventures of D'Alice au Pays des Merveilles...,* Paris, illustrated by Arthur Rackham, cloth, 1907, 8vo	50	100
Carroll, Lewis, *Through the Looking-Glass and What Alice Found There/ The Hunting of the Snark: An Agony in Eight Fits,* Berkeley, illustrated by Barry Moser, folio, cloth and wrappers within cloth chemise in publisher's cloth slipcase, 1983	200	300
Cartwright, William, *Facts and Fancies of Salmon Fishing,* cloth, 1874, 8vo	100	150
Cather, Willa, *April Twilights,* Boston, first edition, original boards, 1903	250	350
Cervantes, Miguel, *Don Quixote,* London, illustrated by Gustave Dore, half morocco, 4to	150	200
Cheever, George B., *God Against Slavery,* Cincinnati, original cloth, signed by William Goodell, c1855, 8vo	50	100
Clemens, Samuel L., *The Adventures of Huckleberry Finn,* New York, first American issue, original cloth, 8vo	8000	10,000
Clemens, Samuel L., *The American Claimant,* New York, first edition, original cloth, 1892, 8vo	30	60
Clemens, Samuel L., *A Connecticut Yankee in King Arthur's Court,* New York, first edition, original cloth, 1889, 8vo	300	400
Cody, William F., *Story of the Wild West and Camp Fire Chats,* Philadelphia, pictorial board and spine, metal lithographs, 1888	50	100
Coleridge, Samuel T., *The Rime of the Ancient Mariner,* New York, illustrated by Gustave Dore, folio, gilt cloth, w/ 38 plates, 1878	150	200
Colette, Sidonie G., *Gigi,* Paris, illustrated by Christian Berard, 1950, 4to	125	175

	LOW	HIGH
Collins, Wilkie, *The Moonstone,* New York, first American edition, original cloth, 1868, 8vo	125	175
Confucius, *The Morals,* 1724, 8vo	200	250
Conrad, Joseph, *The Arrow of Gold,* London, first edition, dust jacket, 1919, 8vo	50	100
Conrad, Joseph, *The Rover,* Garden City, original vellum gilt, dust jacket, 1923	150	250
Cooper, Bransby B., *The Life of Sir Astley Cooper,* first edition, 2 volumes, original cloth, 1843, 8vo	75	125
Coward, Noel, *Bitter Sweet and Other Plays,* Garden City, 1929	50	100
Crane, Stephen, *The Red Badge of Courage,* New York, first edition, cloth, 1895, 8vo	2500	3500
Crane, Stephen, *War Is Kind,* New York, first edition, original boards, 1899, 8vo	400	500
Darwin, Charles, *On the Origin of Species...,* London, first edition, John Murray, half morocco w/ marbled boards, gilt highlights, 1859	4000	6000
Davies, Valentine, *Miracle on 34th Street,* New York, dust jacket, 1947	50	100
Davis, Robert H., *Man Makes His Own Mask,* New York, first edition, 1932	300	400
Defoe, Daniel, *Works,* New York, 16 volumes, quarter morocco, #11 of 250 copies, 1902	250	350
Delany, Samuel R., *Nova,* Garden City, review copy, dust jacket, 1968	75	125
Denslow, William Wallace, *Denslow's Mother Goose,* NY, first edition, half cloth, 1901, 4to	1200	1500
Dickens, Charles, *Bleak House,* London, first edition in book form, half calf, gilt spine, 1853, 8vo	200	250
Dickens, Charles, *The Chimes,* first edition, cloth, 1845, 8vo	100	150
Dickens, Charles, *Hard Times,* London, first edition in book form, half morocco, Bayntun Binder, 1854, 8vo	500	600
Dickens, Charles, *Little Dorritt,* London, first edition in book form, half morocco, 1857, 8vo	100	150
Dickens, Charles, *The Posthumous Papers of the Pickwick Club,* London, first edition in book form, half morocco, illustrated by Seymour & Phiz, 1837, 12mo	200	250
Dickenson, Emily, *Single Hound: Poems of a Lifetime,* Boston, half cloth, 1914	300	400
Doyle, Sir Arthur Conan, *The Hound of the Baskervilles,* London, first edition, pictorial cloth, 1902, 8vo	400	500
Flanner, Janet, *The Stronger Sex,* Vertes, Marcel, New York, 24 mounted plates by Vertes, hand colored, 1941, folio	250	300
Fontaine, Nicolas, *History of the Old and New Testament,* London, printed by Blome, calf, w/ engravings, 1705, 4to	150	200
Frost, Robert, *Aforesaid,* New York, limited edition, gilt cloth w/ slipcase, signed and numbered 513 of 650, 1954, 8vo	200	300
Gibbon, Edward, *An Essay on the Study of Literature,* London, first English edition, printed for T. Becket and P. De Hondt, original boards, 1764, 8vo	500	600
Gibson, Charles Dana, *The Education of Mr. Pipp,* New York, pictorial boards, 1900, oblong 4to	100	150
Gould, John, *The Birds of Great Britain, Vol. II,* London, gilt morocco, 18 plates, 1873, folio	1500	1700
Grahame, Kenneth, *The Wind in the Willows,* New York, mounted color plates, slipcase, 1 of 2020 numbered copies signed by designer Bruce Rogers, 1940	400	500

	LOW	HIGH
Grey, Zane, *The Thundering Herd,* New York, pictorial boards, dust jacket, 1925, 12mo	100	150
Hammett, Dashiell, *The Maltese Falcon,* Arion Press, San Francisco, photographic illustrations, morocco w/ morocco onlay of falcon on front cover, slipcase, 1 of 400 copies, 1983, 4to	300	400
Hawthorne, Nathaniel, *A Wonder Book,* illustrated by Arthur Rackham, New York, 24 full-page color illustrations, later red morocco gilt, first American edition w/ Rackham illustrations, 1922, 4to	150	200
Hawthorne, Nathaniel, *The Marble Faun,* Limited Edition Club, 2 volumes, cloth, boxed, 1931, 8vo	100	150
Henry, O., *The Voice of the City and Other Stories,* New York, illustrated by George Grosz, cloth, slipcase, signed by Grosz, 1935, 4to	200	250
Hunter, Dard, *Paper-Making in the Classroom,* Peoria: Manual Arts Press, photo illustrations, 1931, 8vo	100	150
Huxley, Aldous, *Point Counter Point,* London, first edition, cloth, 1 of 256 copies, signed, 1928, 4to	175	225
Irving, Washington, *Life of George Washington,* New York, 5 volumes w/ 4 steel engravings, morocco, gilt, marbled boards and edges, 1856-62, 8vo	50	100
Kipling, Rudyard, *Mandalay,* New York, illustrated by Blanche McManus, 1898, 8vo	50	100
Kipling, Rudyard, *Poems, 1886-1929,* 3 volumes, first American edition, boards, one of 525, signed, 4to	300	400
Koellner, Augustus, *City Sights For Country Eyes,* Philadelphia, lithograph title and 12 plates, c1850, oblong 4to	1000	1200
Livingstone, David, *Missionary Travels and Researches in South Africa,* London, first edition, first issue, half morocco, engraved title page, 3 maps, 1857, 8vo	250	300
Maugham, Somerset, *Of Human Bondage,* New York, 16 etchings by John Sloan, 2 volumes, linen covered boards, slipcase, 1938, 8vo	200	250
Millay, Edna St. Vincent, *Huntsman, What Quarry?,* New York, cloth w/ slipcase, number 292 of 551 copies, signed, 1939, 8vo	200	250
Milton, John, *Poetical Works,* London, 6 volumes, illustrated by Turner, half calf, 1835, 8vo	150	200
Poe, Edgar Allan, *Works,* New York, Arnheim Edition, 10 volumes, half morocco, 121 of 300, 1902	200	250
Potter, Beatrix, *The Fairy Caravan,* Philadelphia: David McKay, 6 color plates, black and white illustrations, cloth, marked "Not intended for sale," 1 of 100 numbered copies signed by Beatrix Potter, 1929, 8vo	4500	5000
Rand, Ayn, *Atlas Shrugged,* New York, Tenth Anniversary Edition, cloth w/ slipcase, signed and numbered 132 of 2000, 1967	1000	1200
Rice, Alice Hegan, *Mrs. Wiggs of the Cabbage Patch,* New York, cloth pictorial cover, 1901, 8vo	30	60
Riley, James Whitcomb, *A Defective Santa Claus,* Indianapolis, gilt cloth, Dec. 1904, 8vo	75	125
Scott, Sir Walter, *Works,* London, Edition Grande Deluxe, 33 volumes, half morocco, 126 of 500, c1900	400	500
Shaw, Vero, *The Illustrated Book of the Dog,* London, 2 volumes, half morocco, 28 plates, 1881, 4to	800	1000
Stigand, Chauncey Hugh, *Hunting the Elephant in Africa,* New York, first edition, gilt cloth, photo illustrations, 1913, 8vo	150	200
Stowe, Harriet Beecher, *Uncle Tom's Cabin...,* Boston, first edition, first printing, 2 volumes, gilt cloth B variant, 1852, 8vo	750	900

	LOW	HIGH
Taplin, William, *The Sportsman's Cabinet,* London, 2 volumes, gilt tooled morocco, w/ frontispieces and 24 plates, 1803-04, 4to	600	700
Tarbell, Ida M., *The Life of Abraham Lincoln,* New York, Lincoln History Society, 4 volumes, half morocco, 1903, 8vo	75	125
Twain, Mark, *A Connecticut Yankee in King Arthur's Court,* New York, first edition, gilt pictorial cloth, 1889, 8vo	100	150
Twain, Mark, *Following the Equator,* Hartford, first edition, gilt pictorial cloth, 1897, 8vo	50	100
Verne, Jules, *Twenty Thousand Leagues Under the Sea,* Boston, half calf, steel engravings, 1874, 8vo	100	150
Verner, Elizabeth O'Neill, *Other Places,* Columbia, SC, cloth, signed, dust jacket, 1946, 4to	100	150
Voltaire, Francois, *Candide,* New York, illustrated by Clara Tice, blue morocco, w/ erotic gilt tooling, 10 colored plates, 1927	125	175
Ward, Lynd, *Wild Pilgrimage,* New York, cloth, novel in woodcuts, w/ wrapper, 1932, 8vo	75	125
Watson, William, *Orchids, Their Culture and Management,* London, original pictorial cloth gilt, 1903	100	150
Whitney, Caspar, *On Snow Shoes to the Barren Grounds,* New York, pictorial gilt cloth boards, illustrated by Frederic Remington, photo illustrations, 1896, 8vo	100	150
Wilder, Thornton, *The Bridge of San Luis Rey,* Kent, Rockwell, New York, illustrated by Rockwell Kent, pictorial cloth, 1 of 1100 numbered copies signed by Wilder and Kent, 1929, 4to	150	200

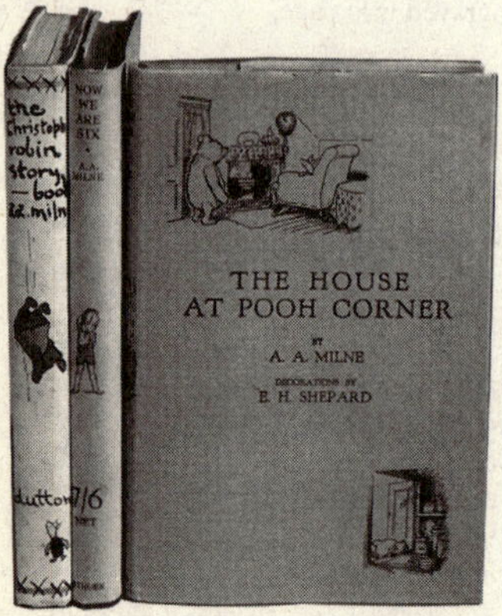

Three books written by Alan Alexander Milne and illustrated by E. H. Shepard. The Christopher Robin Story Book *(New York, 1929, 1st edition, pictorial board, dust jacket, 8vo);* The House at Pooh Corner *(London, dust jacket, 8vo); and* Now We Are Six *(London, cloth w/ gilt figure of Christopher Robin, dust jacket, 8vo). Price for 3 books at auction, $1725. —Photo courtesy Skinner, Inc., Boston, MA.*

Little Golden Books

The first twelve Little Golden Books® titles produced in 1942 sold for the bargain price of 25¢ apiece. Early books have a dust jacket and blue spine. Many titles were reprinted for years. Some books give the date and printing up front. More often the book has a code on the lower portion of the last page squeezed next to the back cover. "A" refers to a first printing, "B" to a second, and so on. Prime condition "A" printings command the highest prices. Collectors are a little more willing to accept a later printing on rare or early titles. *A Poky Little Puppy®* from the 1970s will command a fraction of the price of a first printing. Currently titles based on television series are very popular. Books with dolls, puzzles, and games are difficult to find intact; complete examples are worth several times the value of incomplete examples.

Several Little Golden Book series have been included in the listing. The prices quoted are for first printings in excellent condition showing minimal wear on the covers and pages.

For an extensive listing of Little Golden Books see *Collecting Little Golden Books, 3rd Edition* by Steve Santi (Krause Publications, Iola, WI, 1998).

	LOW	HIGH
About the Seashore, #284, 1957	$5	$10
Airplanes, #180, 1953	5	15
Albert's Stencil Zoo, #112, unpunched, 1951	75	100
Ali Baba and the Forty Thieves, #323, 1958	10	20
Alphabet From A-Z, The, #3, 1942	30	50
Animal Gym, #249, 1956	10	20
Animal Quiz, #396, 1960	5	10
Animals of Farmer Jones, The, #11, 1942	30	50
Annie Oakley and the Rustlers, #221, 1955	15	25
Baby Listens, #383, 1960	10	20
Baby's House, #80, puzzle edition, 1950	75	125
Bamm-Bamm, #540, 1963	15	25
Beany Goes to Sea, #537, 1963	15	26
Bear in the Boat, The, #397, 1972	4	8
Bedtime Stories, #364, 1942	4	8
Best of All, A Story About the Farm, The, #170, 1978	4	8
Betsy McCall, A Paper Doll Story Book, #559, 1965	50	90
Bible Stories From the Old Testament, #153, 1977	5	8
Big Brown Bear, The, #335, 1947	5	10

Left to right: Captain Kangaroo's Surprise Party, *#341, 1958, $10-$20;* The Chipmunks' Merry Christmas, *#375, 1959, $7-$12.*

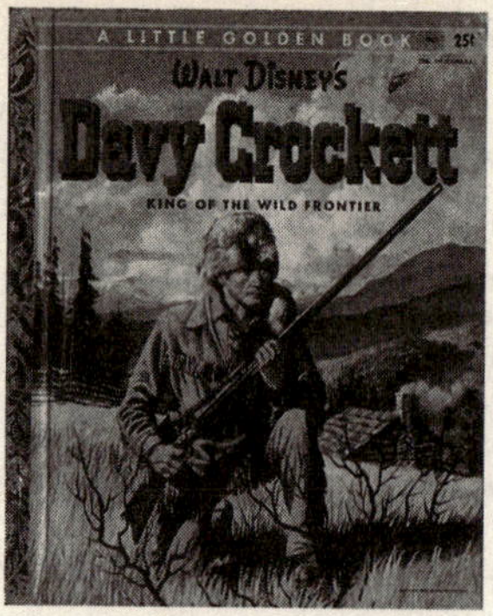

Left to right: Walt Disney's Davy Crockett 'King of the Wild Frontier,' *#D45, 1955, $10-$20;* Hopalong Cassidy and the Bar 20 Cowboy, *#147, 1952, $20-$30.*

	LOW	HIGH
Birds, #5011, Giant Little Golden Book series, 1958	10	20
Birds of All Kinds, #380, 1959	5	8
Blue Book of Fairy Tales, The, #374, 1959	10	20
Boats, #125, 1951	5	10
Broken Arrow, #299, 1957	10	20
Brownie Scouts, #409, 1961	10	20
Buffalo Bill, Jr., #254, 1956	15	25
Bugs Bunny and the Indians, #120, 1951	10	20
Busy Timmy, #50, 1948	20	40
Charmin' Chatty, #554, 1964	15	25
Cheyenne, #318, 1958	15	25
Chicken Little, #413, 1960	5	10
Child's Garden of Verses, A, #493, second cover, 1957	10	25
Chip, Chip, #28, 1947	15	35
Christmas Manger, The, #176, w/ nativity scene, 1953	15	25
Cindy Bear, #442, 1961	15	25
Circus Is in Town, The, #168, 1978	4	10
Cleo, #287, 1957	10	20
Come Play House, #44, 1948	25	35
Cub Scouts, #5022, Giant Little Golden Book series, 1959	20	30
Dale Evans and the Coyote, #253, 1956	15	25
Daniel Boone, #256, 1956	5	15
Day at the Playground, A, #119, 1951	20	30
Day at the Zoo, A, #88, 1949	10	20
Day on the Farm, A, #407, 1960	5	10
Dennis the Menace, A Quiet Afternoon, #412, 1960	5	15
Dennis the Menace and Ruff, #386, 1959	10	20
Dick Tracy, #497, 1962	15	25
Doctor Dan at the Circus, #399, 1960	90	125
Doctor Dan the Bandage Man, #295, w/ Band-Aids, 1950	75	100
Doctor Squash, #157, 1952	10	20
Dogs, #391, 1952	4	8
Dolls of Other Lands, #213, Ding Dong School series, 1954	5	15
Dr. Dan the Bandage Man, #111, 1950	90	110

	LOW	HIGH
Dumbo, #D3, Disney series, 1947	30	50
Exploring Space, #342, 1958	5	8
Farmyard Friends, #272, 1956	5	10
Fire Engines, #382, 1959	5	10
Five Bedtime Stories, #5002, Giant Little Golden Books series, 1957	10	20
Five Little Fishermen, #64, 1948	10	30
Fix It, Please, #32, 1947	15	35
Forest Hotel, #350, 1972	4	10
Friendly Book, The, #199, 1954	8	15
Fritzie Goes Home, #103, 1974	5	7
Fun with Decals, #139, complete uncut, 1952	100	150
Fury, #286, 1957	10	20
Fuzzy Duckling, The, #557, 1949	2	8
Gay Purr-ee, #488, 1962	15	26
Gene Autry, #230, 1955	15	25
Georgie Finds a Grandpa, #196, 1954	20	30
Gingerbread Shop, The, #126, 1952	15	25
Good-Bye, Tonsils, #327, 1966	5	10
Good Little, Bad Little Girl, #562, 1965	15	25
Good Morning, Good Night, #61, 1948	20	40
Growing Things, #210, Ding Dong School series, 1954	5	10
Gunsmoke, #320, 1958	15	25
Hansel and Gretel, #217, 1954	5	10
Happy Birthday, #123, 1952	30	50
Happy Family, The, #216, 1955	10	20
Heidi, #258, 1954	5	10
Helicopters, #357, 1959	5	10
Here Comes the Parade, #143, 1950	15	25
Heroes of the Bible, #236, 1955	10	20
Hi! Ho! Three in a Row, #188, 1954	20	30
Houses, #229, 1955	5	15
House That Jack Built, The, #218, 1954	8	15
How Big, #83, 1949	15	25
Howdy Doody and the Princess, #135, 1952	20	30

Left to right: The Lone Ranger, *#263, 1956, $20-$25;* Plants and Animals, *#5017, 1958, $10-$20.*

Left to right: Rin Tin Tin and Rusty, *#246, 1955, $14-$18;* Ruff and Reddy, *#378, 1959, $6-$10.*

	LOW	HIGH
Huckleberry Hound Builds a House, #376, 1959	15	25
Jack's Adventure, #308, 1958	5	15
J. Fred Muggs, #234, 1955	10	20
Jiminy Cricket Fire Fighter, #D50, Disney series, 1950	15	25
Jingle Bells, #553, 1964	4	8
Katie the Kitten, #75, 1949	10	20
Kitten's Surprise, The, #107, 1951	10	15
Kitten Who Thought He Was a Mouse, The, #210, 1954	15	25
Laddie the Superdog, #185, 1954	5	15
Lady, #D42, Disney series, 1954	10	20
Life and Legend of Wyatt Earp, The, #315, 1958	15	25
Linda and Her Little Sister, #214, 1954	65	80
Little Golashes, #68, 1949	10	30
Little Golden ABC, The, #101, 1951	5	10
Little Golden Book of Hymns, The, #34, 1947	10	20
Little Golden Holiday Book, The, #109, 1951	20	30
Little Golden Paper Dolls, The, #113, 1951	120	130
Little Mommy, #569, 1967	30	50
Little Pond in the Woods, #43, 1948	15	25
Little Red Caboose, The, #319, 1953	5	10
Little Red Hen, The, #6, 1942	35	45
Little Trapper, The, #79, 1950	10	20
Lone Ranger and the Talking Pony, The, #310, 1958	15	25
Lucky Mrs. Ticklefeather, #122, 1951	20	30
Machines, #455, 1961	5	10
Magic Compass, The, #146, 1953	15	25
Magic Wagon, The, #222, 1955	5	10
Magilla Gorilla, #547, 1964	15	20
Marvelous Merry-Go-Round, The, #87, 1949	10	20
Merry Shipwreck, The, #170, 1953	10	20
Mickey Mouse and His Space Ship, #D29, Disney series, 1952	10	20
Mister Dog, #128, 1952	20	30
More Mother Goose Rhymes, #317, 1958	5	10
Mr. Myer's Cow, 220, Ding Dong School series, 1955	5	10

	LOW	HIGH
Mr. Wigg's Birthday Party, #140, 1952	15	25
Musicians of Bremen, The, #189, 1954	5	10
My Baby Brother, #279, 1956	20	30
My Christmas Book, #298, 1957	10	20
My Christmas Treasury, #5003, Giant Little Golden Book series, 1957	10	20
My Kitten, #163, 1954	10	20
My Little Golden Dictionary, #90, 1949	10	20
My Teddy Bear, #168, 1953	20	30
My Word Book, #525, 1963	4	10
National Velvet, #431, 1961	8	15
Never Pat a Bear, #105, 1971	5	8
New Brother, New Sister, #564, 1966	10	20
New Pony, The, #410, 1961	5	15
Night Before Christmas, The, #241, 1955	20	30
Noah's Ark, #D28, Disney series, 1952	20	30
Numbers, #337, 1955	4	8
Nurse Nancy, #473, w/ Band-Aids, 1958	90	125
Our Baby, #218, Ding Dong School series, 1955	10	20
Our World, #242, 1955	5	10
Out of My Window, #245, 1955	10	20
Pal and Peter, #265, 1956	5	15
Paper Doll Wedding, #193, 1954	115	130
Party In Shariland, #360, 1958	10	20
Peek In, #209, Ding Dong School series, 1954	5	10
Peter Rabbit, #313, 1958	5	10
Pets for Peter, #82, puzzle edition, 1950	75	125
Pick Up Sticks, #461, 1962	5	15
Play With Me, #567, 1967	10	15
Prayers For Children, #205, 1952	5	10
Puff the Blue Kitten, #443, 1961	10	20
Puss In Boots, #137, 1952	10	15
Pussy Willow, #314, 1951	5	15
Quiz Fun, #5024, Giant Little Golden Books series, 1959	10	20
Rainy Day Play Book, The, #133, 1951	10	15

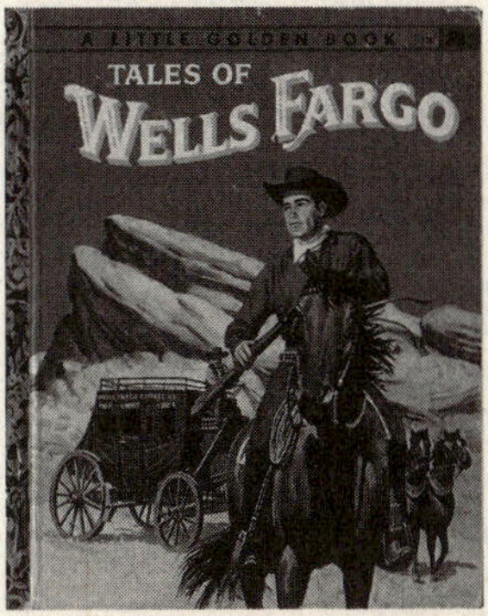

Left to right: So Big, *#574, 1968, $10-$20;* Tales of Wells Fargo, *#328, 1958, $15-$20.*

Left to right: Top Cat, *#453, 1962, $18-$24;* Walt Disney's Uncle Remus, *#D6, 1947, $10-$15.*

	LOW	HIGH
Red Little Golden Book of Fairy Tales, The, #306, 1958	10	20
Rin Tin Tin and the Lost Indian, #276, 1956	15	25
Road to Oz, The, #144, 1951	20	30
Robert and His New Friends, #124, 1951	10	15
Rocky and His Friends, #408, second cover, 1960	10	20
Romper Room Do Bees, A Book of Manners, #273, 1956	5	15
Rootie Kazootie Baseball Star, #190, 1954	25	35
Rudolph the Red-Nosed Reindeer, #331, 1958	5	10
Shazam! A Circus Adventure, #155, 1977	5	8
Shy Little Kitten, The, #248, 1956	5	10
Sly Little Bear, #411, 1960	5	10
Smokey the Bear, #224, 1955	15	25
Snow White and Rose Red, #228, 1955	10	20
Supercar, #492, 1962	20	30
Tawny Scrawny Lion, #138, 1952	10	20
Thumbelina, #153, 1953	10	20
Tiger's Adventure, #208, 1954	10	20
Tommy's Camping Adventure, #471, 1962	5	15
Topsy Turvy Circus, #161, 1953	10	20
Train Stories, #5018, Giant Little Golden Book series, 1958	10	20
Train to Timbuctoo, The, #118, 1951	15	25
Uncle Mistletoe, #175, 1953	20	30
Wally Gator, #502, 1963	10	20
We Help Mommy, #352, 1959	5	10
We Like Kindergarten, #552, 1965	4	8
We Love Grandpa, #225, Ding Dong School series, 1956	5	10
When I Grow Up, #578, 1968	2	8
When You Were a Baby, #70, 1949	10	20
Where Will All the Animals Go?, #175, 1978	5	10
Whistling Wizard, #132, 1953	15	25
White Bunny and His Magic Nose, The, #305, 1957	10	20
Wiggles, #166, 1953	20	40
Wild Animals, #5010, Giant Little Golden Book series, 1958	10	20
Wild Kingdom, #151, 1976	5	8

Comic Books

Comic book collecting enjoys a huge following. Collectors have actively pursued this area for years but it gained prominence in the early 1990s. There is an endless number of characters and new, exciting books appear each day. Because comic books (especially early ones) are fragile, condition is crucial to determining value. Grading a comic book is both an art and a science. We suggest you consult the *Overstreet* guide cited below. We list two ranges of prices. The first is loosely described as average condition (what collectors generally refer to as very good). This means the book is intact but shows wear, the color of the paper may be brownish and there may be minor inside creases or a small tear or two. Our second range is superior, although not near mint; it is what collectors consider fine condition. Near mint and, where available, mint condition books bring considerably more than the values listed below. There are reissues of many books, and some bear a striking resemblance to the original but command only a fraction of the original's price. As in any collecting area, do your homework.

For more information and extensive listings, refer to *The Overstreet Comic Book Price Guide, 29th Edition* by Robert M. Overstreet (Avon Books, New York, NY, 1999), *Comic Values Annual 2000* by Alex G. Malloy (Antique Trader Books, Dubuque, IA, 1999), and *2000 Comic Book Checklist and Price Guide: 1961 to Present, 6th Edition* by Maggie Thompson and Brent Frankenhoff (Krause Publications, Iola, WI, 1999).

	VERY GOOD	FINE
Action Comics, DC, #230, Jul. 1957	$30-$40	$110-$120
Action Comics, DC, #235, Dec. 1957	30-40	110-120
Action Comics, DC, #237, Feb. 1958	30-40	110-120
Action Comics, DC, #252, May 1958, Supergirl	300-350	900-1000
Action Comics, DC, #255, Aug. 1959, Bizarro Lois	25-35	90-100
Action Comics, DC, #275, Apr. 1961	5-10	25-35
Action Comics, DC, #283, Dec. 1961, Legion of Super-Villains	5-15	30-40
Action Comics, DC, #293, Dec. 1962, Superhorse	4-8	30-40
Action Comics, DC, #334, Mar. 1966, Supergirl	3-6	10-20
Adventure Comics, DC, #248, May 1958	30-40	110-120
Adventure Comics, DC, #258, Mar. 1959	15-25	65-75
Adventure Comics, DC, #260, May 1959, Aquaman	110-115	300-350
Adventure Comics, DC, #269, Feb. 1960, Aqualad	25-35	90-100
Adventure Comics, DC, #276, Sep. 1960, Sun Boy	5-15	40-50
Adventure Comics, DC, #282, Mar. 1961, Starboy	15-25	65-75
Adventure Comics, DC, #283, Apr. 1961, Phantom Zone	10-20	50-60
Adventure Comics, DC, #291, Dec. 1961	4-8	20-25
Adventure Comics, DC, #375, Dec. 1968, Quantum Queen	2-4	5-8
Adventures of Bob Hope, DC, #1, Feb. 1950	200-240	650-700
Adventures of Bob Hope, DC, #5, Oct. 1950	60-70	200-210
Adventures of Bob Hope, DC, #14, Apr. 1952	30-35	100-110
Adventures of Bob Hope, DC, #39, Jun. 1956	10-20	45-55
Adventures of Bob Hope, DC, #45, Jun. 1957	10-15	35-45
Adventures of Bob Hope, DC, #82, Aug. 1963, Mort Drucker	3-6	10-18
Adventures of Bob Hope, DC, #105, Jun. 1967	2-4	10-12
Adventures of Dean Martin & Jerry Lewis, DC, #1, Jul. 1952	100-150	300-400
Adventures of Dean Martin & Jerry Lewis, DC, #4, Jan. 1953	30-40	110-120
Adventures of Dean Martin & Jerry Lewis, DC, #33, Nov. 1956	10-15	30-40
Adventures of Jerry Lewis, #42, Jan. 1958	5-10	20-30
Adventures of Jerry Lewis, #47, Aug. 1958	5-10	20-30
Adventures of Jerry Lewis, #60, Sep. 1960	4-8	15-25
Adventures of Jerry Lewis, #73, Nov. 1962	3-6	15-18

Left to right: The Amazing Spider-Man, Marvel, #172, Sep. 1977, $2-$6; Casper Strange Ghost Stories, Harvey, #7, Dec. 1975, $3-$10. —Photos courtesy Ray Morykan Auctions.

	VERY GOOD	FINE
Adventures of The Fly, Archie/Red Circle, #19, May 1962	5-10	25-35
Aliens, Dark Horse, #1, May 1988, first printing	3-6	10-20
Aliens, Dark Horse, #2, Sep. 1988, first printing	2-5	10-15
Alpha Flight, Marvel, #1, Aug. 1983	1-2	3-5
Alpha Flight, Marvel, #33, Apr. 1986, Wolverine	1-2	3-5
Amazing Adventures, Marvel, #1, Aug. 1970, Inhumans	2-5	10-15
Amazing Adventures, Marvel, #18, May 1973, Killraven	3-5	6-10
Amazing Spider-Man, Marvel, #7, Dec. 1963, Vulture	100-200	500-600
Amazing Spider-Man, Marvel, #15, Aug. 1964	225-250	375-400
Amazing Spider-Man, Marvel, #49, Jun. 1967, Kraven and Vulture	5-10	20-30
Amazing Spider-Man, Marvel, #65, Oct. 1968	15-25	30-40
Aquaman, DC, #1, Feb. 1962	100-110	300-330
Aquaman, DC, #3, Jun. 1962	25-35	90-100
Aquaman, DC, #12, Dec. 1963	5-10	20-30
Aquaman, DC, #25, Feb. 1966	2-5	10-20
Aquaman, DC, #50, Apr. 1970	2-4	5-10
Astonishing Tales, Marvel, #1, Aug. 1970	2-5	10-15
Astonishing Tales, Marvel, #6, Jun. 1971	2-4	5-10
Astonishing Tales, Marvel, #25, Aug. 1974	2-5	10-15
Atom, DC, #2, Sep. 1962	55-65	100-200
Atom, DC, #7, Jul. 1973, Hawkman	40-50	125-135
Atom, DC, #13, Jul. 1964	5-10	20-30
Atom, DC, #28, Jan. 1967	2-4	10-12
Atom, DC, #38, Sep. 1968	2-5	10-15
Atom & Hawkman, DC, #40, Jan. 1969	2-5	10-20
Atom & Hawkman, DC, #45, Nov. 1969	3-6	15-18
Avengers, Marvel, #2, Nov. 1963, Space Phantom	4-6	15-20

	VERY GOOD	FINE
Avengers, Marvel, #5, May 1964	40-50	140-150
Avengers, Marvel, #9, Oct. 1964	40-50	140-150
Avengers, Marvel, #18, Jul. 1965	120-130	350-400
Avengers, Marvel, #19, Aug. 1965	5-10	20-30
Avengers, Marvel, #35, Dec. 1966	2-4	10-15
Avengers, Marvel, #75, Apr. 1970	1-2	4-6
Avengers, Marvel, #96, Feb. 1972	2-4	10-12
Avengers Annual, Marvel, #2, Sep. 1968	4-8	15-25
Avengers Annual, Marvel, #7, Nov. 1977	1-2	3-5
Batman, DC, #110, Sep. 1957	50-60	170-180
Batman, DC, #121, Feb. 1959, Mr. Freeze	40-50	125-150
Batman, DC, #129, Feb. 1960	30-40	90-100
Batman, DC, #139, Apr. 1961	15-25	65-75
Batman, DC, #155, Apr. 1963, Penguin	40-50	125-150
Batman, DC, #171, May 1965, Riddler	35-55	150-165
Batman, DC, #201, May 1968, Joker	2-5	10-15
Batman Family, DC, #1, Oct. 1975	3-5	5-8
Batman Family, DC, #6, Aug. 1976	1-2	3-5
Beware the Creeper, DC, #2, Aug. 1968	5-10	20-30
Beware the Creeper, DC, #4, Dec. 1968	5-8	10-20
Binky's Buddies, DC, #1, Jun. 1969	1-2	3-5
Blackhawk, DC, #165, Oct. 1961	3-6	10-20
Blackhawk, DC, #170, Mar. 1962	5-8	10-20
Blackhawk, DC, #194, Mar. 1964	2-4	10-12
Blackhawk, DC, #205, Feb. 1965	3-5	6-10
Blackhawk, DC, #235, Aug. 1967	2-4	6-10
Black Panther, Marvel, #1, Jan. 1977	1-3	5-8
Black Panther, Marvel, #2, Mar. 1977	1-2	3-4
Brave and the Bold, DC, #6, Robin Hood	60-70	100-200
Brave and the Bold, DC, #13, Sep. 1957	50-60	170-180
Brave and the Bold, DC, #23, May 1959	65-75	200-225
Brave and the Bold, DC, #32, Nov. 1960, Cave Carson	20-30	80-90
Brave and the Bold, DC, #40, Mar. 1962	15-25	65-75
Brave and the Bold, DC, #51, Jan. 1964, Aquaman	35-45	125-135
Brave and the Bold, DC, #74, Nov. 1967, Metal Men	2-5	10-15
Brave and the Bold, DC, #105, Feb. 1973, Wonder Woman	1-2	3-5
Captain America, Marvel, #2, Jun. 1968	2-5	10-15
Captain America, Marvel, #100, Apr. 1968	45-55	155-165
Captain America, Marvel, #110, Feb. 1969	20-30	35-45
Captain America, Marvel, #113, May 1969	5-10	20-30
Captain America, Marvel, #127, Jul. 1970	2-4	5-8
Captain America, Marvel, #137, May 1971	3-5	8-10
Captain Marvel, Marvel, #1, May 1968	10-15	35-45
Captain Marvel, Marvel, #4, Aug. 1968	2-4	5-10
Captain Marvel, Marvel, #28, Sep. 1973	2-5	10-15
Captain Savage, Marvel, #9, Dec. 1968	1-3	5-10
Captain Savage & His Leatherneck Raiders, Marvel, #1, Jan. 1968	2-4	5-10
Captain Storm, DC, #1, Jun. 1964	2-5	10-15
Captain Storm, DC, #7, Jun. 1965	1-2	4-6
Challengers of the Unknown, DC, #2, Jul. 1958	160-170	475-500
Challengers of the Unknown, DC, #12, Mar. 1960	30-40	100-120
Challengers of the Unknown, DC, #31, May 1963	10-20	50-60
Challengers of the Unknown, DC, #61, May 1968	2-4	6-8
Daredevil, Marvel, #4, Oct. 1964	40-50	130-140

Left to right: Richie Rich Gold & Silver, Harvey, #2, Nov. 1975, $3-$10; Static, DC, #3, Aug. 1993, $1-$3. —Photos courtesy Ray Morykan Auctions.

	VERY GOOD	FINE
Daredevil, Marvel, #16, May 1966	10-20	50-60
Daredevil, Marvel, #28, Jun. 1967	4-6	10-20
Detective Comics, DC, #267, May 1959	25-35	90-100
Detective Comics, DC, #297, Nov. 1961	5-10	30-40
Detective Comics, DC, #365, Jul. 1967	5-10	20-30
Doom Patrol, DC, #93, Feb. 1965	5-10	20-30
Doom Patrol, DC, #102, Mar. 1966	2-4	10-12
Fantastic Four, Marvel, #12, Mar. 1963	220-240	675-700
Fantastic Four, Marvel, #30, Sep. 1964	20-30	80-90
Fantastic Four, Marvel, #40, Jul. 1965	10-20	45-55
Fantastic Four, Marvel, #64, Jul. 1967	2-5	10-15
Flash, DC, #109, Nov. 1959	90-100	200-300
Flash, DC, #126, Feb. 1962	10-20	50-60
Flash, DC, #136, May 1963	15-20	40-50
Godzilla, Marvel, #1, Aug. 1977	2-5	6-8
Godzilla, Marvel, #11, Jun. 1978	1-2	2-4
Green Lantern, DC, #5, Apr. 1961	50-60	170-180
Green Lantern, DC, #22, Jul. 1963	10-20	50-60
Green Lantern, DC, #45, Jun. 1966	5-10	20-30
Hawkman, DC, #2, Jul. 1964	30-40	110-120
Hawkman, DC, #17, Jan. 1967	3-5	25-30
Hawkman, DC, #25, May 1968	2-5	10-15
House of Mystery, DC, #119, Feb. 1962	3-5	8-10
House of Mystery, DC, #165, Mar. 1967	6-8	10-15
House of Mystery, DC, #178, Feb. 1969	2-6	6-8
Incredible Hulk, Marvel, #104, Jun. 1968	5-8	20-25
Incredible Hulk, Marvel, #115, May 1969	2-4	6-8

	VERY GOOD	FINE
Inferior Five, DC, #1, Apr. 1967	5-10	25-35
Inferior Five, DC, #7, Apr. 1968	2-4	5-10
Iron Man, Marvel, #2, Jun. 1968	20-25	65-75
Iron Man, Marvel, #11, Mar. 1969	5-8	15-20
Iron Man, Marvel, #17, Sep. 1969, Madame Masque	2-5	10-15
Justice League of America, DC, #2, Jan. 1961	35-45	125-135
Justice League of America, DC, #8, Jan. 1962	35-45	125-135
Justice League of America, DC, #24, Dec. 1963	10-20	50-60
Justice League of America, DC, #44, May 1966	3-6	15-18
Marvel Tales, Marvel, #4, Sep. 1966	2-4	5-10
Marvel Tales, Marvel, #10, Sep. 1967	2-4	5-10
Marvel Tales, Marvel, #14, May 1968	1-2	4-6
Ms. Marvel, Marvel, #1, Jan. 1977	2-3	3-5
Ms. Marvel, Marvel, #18, Jun. 1978	3-5	6-10
Mystery In Space, DC, #53, Aug. 1959	275-300	850-900
Mystery In Space, DC, #63, Nov. 1960	25-35	90-100
Mystery In Space, DC, #94, Sep. 1964	3-5	6-10
Nick Fury, Agent of S.H.I.E.L.D., Marvel, #1, Jun. 1968	5-10	20-30
Nick Fury, Agent of S.H.I.E.L.D., Marvel, #3, Aug. 1968	2-5	10-15
Our Army At War, DC, #82, Dec. 1962	90-100	275-300
Our Army At War, DC, #138, Jan. 1964	5-8	15-20
Our Army At War, DC, #172, Oct. 1966	2-5	5-10
Our Fighting Forces, DC, #64, Apr. 1960	2-4	8-12
Our Fighting Forces, DC, #91, Apr. 1965	1-2	3-5
Our Fighting Forces, DC, #106, Apr. 1967	1-2	3-5
Phantom Stranger, DC, #1, Jun. 1969	10-12	25-35
Phantom Stranger, DC, #6, Apr. 1970	2-5	10-15
Phantom Stranger, DC, #21, Oct. 1972	2-4	6-10
Sgt. Fury and His Howling Commandos Annual, Marvel, #1, 1965	15-25	65-75
Sgt. Fury and His Howling Commandos Annual, Marvel, #6, 1970	1-2	3-5
Sgt. Rock, DC, #302, Mar. 1977	1-2	5-7
Sgt. Rock, DC, #315, Apr. 1978	1-2	3-5
Shadow, Archie, #1, Aug. 1964	5-8	10-20
Shadow, DC, #1, Nov. 1973	2-4	10-15
Shadow, DC, #10, May 1975	2-4	5-8
Showcase, DC, #1, Apr. 1956, Fire Fighters	475-500	1400-1500
Showcase, DC, #9, Aug. 1957, Lois Lane	500-550	1500-1600
Showcase, DC, #31, Apr. 1961, Aquaman	50-60	170-180
Showcase, DC, #38, Jun. 1962, Metal Men	50-60	170-180
Showcase, DC, #53, Dec. 1964, G.I. Joe	5-10	20-30
Spectre, DC, #1, Dec. 1967	10-15	35-45
Spectre, DC, #2, Feb. 1968	5-10	20-30
Spectre, DC, #5, Aug. 1968	5-8	15-25
Spectre, DC, #10, Jun. 1969	2-4	10-15
Star Spangled War Stories, DC, #90, May 1960	20-30	90-100
Star Spangled War Stories, DC, #101, Mar. 1962	5-8	15-25
Star Spangled War Stories, DC, #124, Dec. 1965	4-6	10-20
Star Spangled War Stories, DC, #144, May 1969, Enemy Ace	2-5	10-15
Star Trek, DC, #1, Feb. 1984	1-3	5-10
Star Trek, DC, #5, Jun. 1984	1-2	3-5
Star Trek, Gold Key, #1, Oct. 1967	90-100	275-300
Star Trek, Gold Key, #5, Sep. 1969	30-40	110-120
Star Trek, Gold Key, #9, Feb. 1971	90-100	140-150
Star Trek, Gold Key, #15, Aug. 1972	20-30	75-85

"Flip" Book, Brigade #4 and Youngblood #5, Image, Jul. 1993, $2-$4. —Photos courtesy Ray Morykan Auctions.

	VERY GOOD	FINE
Star Trek, Gold Key, #25, Jul. 1974	10-15	40-50
Star Trek, Gold Key, #31, Jul. 1975	5-10	20-30
Star Trek, Gold Key, #51, Mar. 1978	3-6	10-15
Star Trek, Marvel, #1, Apr. 1980	1-2	3-5
Star Wars, Marvel, #1, Jul. 1977, movie adaptation	10-15	35-45
Star Wars, Marvel, #7, Jan. 1978	2-5	10-15
Star Wars, Marvel, #22, Apr. 1979	2-4	10-15
Star Wars, Marvel, #39, Sep. 1980, *Empire Strikes Back*	3-6	10-20
Strange Adventures, DC, #125, Feb. 1961	5-10	20-30
Strange Adventures, DC, #138, Mar. 1962, Atomic Knights	5-10	20-30
Strange Adventures, DC, #180, Sep. 1965, Animal Man	5-10	20-30
Strange Adventures, DC, #205, Oct. 1967, Deadman	5-10	20-30
Strange Tales, Marvel, #89, Oct. 1961	5-10	20-30
Strange Tales, Marvel, #100, Sep. 1962	10-15	40-50
Strange Tales, Marvel, #114, Nov. 1963	40-50	140-150
Strange Tales, Marvel, #126, Nov. 1964	5-8	15-25
Sub-Mariner, Marvel, #1, May 1968	10-15	40-50
Sub-Mariner, Marvel, #3	2-4	10-15
Sugar & Spike, DC, #1, May 1956	225-250	600-700
Sugar & Spike, DC, #7, May 1957	50-60	170-180
Sugar & Spike, DC, #14, Mar. 1958	40-50	140-150
Sugar & Spike, DC, #25, Nov. 1959	30-40	110-120
Sugar & Spike, DC, #30, Sep. 1960	30-40	110-120
Sugar & Spike, DC, #38, Jan. 1962	25-35	90-100
Sugar & Spike, DC, #44, Jan. 1963	15-25	65-75
Sugar & Spike, DC, #72, Sep. 1967, Bernie the Brain	10-15	25-35
Superboy, DC, #67, Sep. 1958	5-8	15-25
Superboy, DC, #70, Jan. 1959	10-20	45-55
Superboy, DC, #83, Sep. 1960, Kryptonite Kid	5-10	15-25
Superboy, DC, #115, Sep. 1964	1-2	4-6
Superman, DC, #142, Jan. 1961	15-10	25-35

	VERY GOOD	FINE
Superman, DC, #152, Apr. 1962	5-10	20-30
Superman, DC, #160, Apr. 1963	3-5	10-15
Superman, DC, #183, Jan. 1966	2-4	20-30
Superman's Pal Jimmy Olsen, DC, #1, pre-1960	600-700	1500-2000
Superman's Pal Jimmy Olsen, DC, #2, pre-1960	300-350	900-1000
Superman's Pal Jimmy Olsen, DC, #8, pre-1960	55-65	100-200
Superman's Pal Jimmy Olsen, DC, 42, Jan. 1960	10-20	40-50
Superman's Pal Jimmy Olsen, DC, #80, Oct. 1964	3-6	10-20
Swamp Thing, DC, #1, Nov. 1972	5-10	20-30
Swamp Thing, DC, #2, Jan. 1973	2-5	10-15
Swamp Thing, DC, #7, Dec. 1973, Batman	2-5	10-15
Swamp Thing, DC, #12, Oct. 1974	1-2	3-5
Tarzan, DC, #207, Apr. 72	1-2	3-5
Teen Titans, DC, #10, Aug. 1967	3-5	8-10
Teenage Mutant Ninja Turtles, Mirage, #1, first printing	45-55	150-165
Teenage Mutant Ninja Turtles, Mirage, #2, first printing	10-15	30-40
The Tick, New England, #1, Jun. 1988	10-15	35-45
Thor, Marvel, #126, Mar. 1966, Hercules	10-20	40-50
Thor, Marvel, #128, May 1966	2-5	10-20
Thor, Marvel, #158, Nov. 1968	5-10	20-30
Thor, Marvel, #165, Jun. 1969	5-8	15-25
Thor, Marvel, #182, Nov. 1970	1-2	3-5
T.H.U.N.D.E.R. Agents, Tower, #1, Nov. 1965	15-25	65-75
T.H.U.N.D.E.R. Agents, Tower, #5, Jun. 1966	5-10	20-30
T.H.U.N.D.E.R. Agents, Tower, #12, Apr. 1967	3-6	10-20
T.H.U.N.D.E.R. Agents, Tower, #19, Nov. 1968	2-5	10-15
Tomahawk, DC, #87, Jul. 1963	5-8	10-20
Tomahawk, DC, #100, Sep. 1965	2-5	10-15
Tomahawk, DC, #121, Mar. 1969	1-2	3-5
Twilight Zone, Dell/Gold Key, #1	10-20	50-60
Twilight Zone, Dell/Gold Key, #6	5-10	15-25
Twilight Zone, Dell/Gold Key, #20	3-6	15-18
Two Gun Kid, Marvel, #72, Nov. 1964	2-4	5-10
Two Gun Kid, Marvel, #80, Mar. 1966	3-5	6-10
Uncanny X-Men, Marvel, #142, Feb. 1981	2-5	10-15
Uncanny X-Men, Marvel, #150, Oct. 1981	1-2	3-5
Uncle Scrooge, Gladstone, #210, Oct. 1986	1-2	3-5
Uncle Scrooge, Gladstone, #219, Jul. 1987, Rosa Disney story	2-4	10-15
Undersea Agent, Tower, #1, Jan. 1966	2-3	7
Unexpected, DC, #105, Feb. 1968	2-4	5--7
Unexpected, DC, #118, Apr. 1970	1-2	3-5
Warlock, Marvel, #1, Aug. 1972	4-8	15-25
Warlock, Marvel, #4, Feb. 1973	1-2	3-6
Warlock, Marvel, #10, Oct. 1975	1-3	5-10
Warlord, DC, #1, Feb. 1976	3-5	8-10
Warlord, DC, #5, Mar. 1977	1-2	3-5
Warlord, DC, #13, Jul. 1978	1-2	3-5
Weird War Tales, DC, #1, Sep. 1971	1-2	3-5
Weird Western Tales, DC, #12, Jul. 1972	1-2	3-5
Wonder Woman, DC, #112, Feb. 1960	2-4	8-12
Wonder Woman, DC, #153, Apr. 1965	1-2	3-5
World's Finest Comics, DC, #157, May 1966	2-4	5-10
X-Men, Marvel, #3, Jan. 1964, The Blob	120-130	300-400
X-Men, Marvel, #21, Jun. 1966	5-10	25-35

Magazines

Magazines are history in the first person. Few things capture the mood of the American nation as the magazines we read. Few things are as American as *Life Magazine.* But magazines, unlike books, were meant to be read and discarded. Although publishers printed large numbers, readers saved only a small percentage. These saved copies may turn up anywhere, from a church bazaar to the bottom of an auction box lot.

Collectors of magazines want clean, crisp copies. They should not be marked, torn or frayed. The best copy is an unread copy.

For more information see *The Insider's Guide to Old Books, Magazines, Newspapers, Trade Catalogs* by Ron Barlow and Ray Reynolds (Windmill Publishing, El Cajon, CA, 1995) and *Old Magazines Price Guide* (L-W Book Sales, Gas City, IN, 1994, 1997 value update). For a more extensive listing of *Life* magazines refer to *Life Magazines: 1899-1994, 2nd Edition* by Denis C. Jackson (published by author, Sequim, WA, 1998).

	LOW	HIGH
Action Packed Western, May 1950	$2	$8
Actual Detective Stories, 1930-40s	8	12
Adventure, 1930-40	5	10
Aero Digest, 1940s	4	6
Aeronautics, 1940s	1	2
Air Force, Jan. 1944	2	4
Air Force, Dec. 1944	2	4
Air Life, Mar. 1942, Vol. 1, #1	45	55
Air Progress, 1930-40	5	15
Air Progress, Nov. 1941	10	20
Alfred Hitchcock's Mystery Magazine, 1950-70s	8	12
Alfred Hitchcock's Mystery Magazine, 1971-84	3	5
Amazing Stories, Mar. 1929	25	35
Amazing Stories, Oct. 1930	15	25
Amazing Stories, Oct. 1932	15	25
American Architect, 1882	5	10
American Artist, 1930-70s	3	8
American Bee Journal, 1861, Vol. 1	140	160
American Builder, 1922-26	10	20
American Chauffeur, Aug. 1916	15	25
American Detective, 1930s	4	8
American Druggist, 1920-50s	2	6
American Family, 1952-53	4	6
American Field, 1890-1920s	3	5
American Forestry, 1910-18	10	15
American Freedman, 1866-68	140	160
American Girl, 1920s	6	10
American Heritage, 1950-70s	3	8
American Home, 1920-30s	8	12
American Lady, 1930s	6	10
American Legion Weekly, 1921, John Held, Jr. cover	10	20
American Machinist, 1912-15	10	20
American Monthly, 1830	10	20
American Printer, 1930s	5	10
American Rifleman, 1925-26	8	12
American Woodsman, 1930s	3	5
Argosy, 1880s	25	35
Argosy, Jul. & Sep. 1914	10	15

	LOW	HIGH
Arizona Highways, Feb. 1959	4	6
Arizona Highways, Jan. 1962	4	6
Art Amateur, 1892-93	20	30
Asia, Jan. 1929	25	35
Astounding Science Fiction, 1955-58	2	6
Atlantic Monthly, Jun. 1887	14	16
Atlantic Monthly, 1950-59	2	4
Atlantic Monthly, 1960-69	2	3
Atlantic Sportsman, 1932	8	12
Audio, Feb. 1966	2	3
Audio, Oct. 1967	2	3
Audio, Apr. 1975	2	3
Audio, Aug. 1975	2	3
Audio, Feb. 1976	2	3
Audubon Magazine, 1950-55	5	7
Audubon Magazine, 1956-60	4	6
Automobile Trade Journal, 1918-30	25	35
Automotive Digest, 1920s	10	20
Automotive Digest, 1930s	5	10
Aviation, 1925-27	5	7
Bachelor, Apr. 1937	40	50
Backyard Mechanic, 1976	4	6
Ballyhoo, 1934-36	8	12
Bandleaders, Jun. 1946	12	14
Barber's Gazette, Sep. 1939, gambling	35	50
Barnes & Park Family Medical Almanac, 1851-54	45	60
Baseball Magazine, 1923	12	16
Battle Stories, Feb. 1932	15	25
Beauty Parade, Mar. 1955, Bettie Page	30	40
Best of the Wrestler, Fall 1976	2	3
Best of the Wrestler, Spring 1977	2	3
Best of the Wrestler, Fall 1977, André the Giant	2	3
Better Homes and Gardens, 1920-30	6	10
Better Homes and Gardens, 1941-50	2	8
Better Roads, Jan. 1938	9	12
Billboard Magazine, 1940s	8	12
Bird Lore, 1929-43	3	6
Black Book Detective, 1940s	20	30
Black Mask, Feb. 1927	70	80
Black Mask, Jan. 1935	60	70
Black Mask, May 1936	70	80
Bliss Native Herbs Almanac, 1900-29	8	12
Booklovers, 1900-06	8	15
Boxing, 1950s	5	15
Boys' Life, 1912-35	6	12
Brides Magazine, 1930s	4	6
Broadcasting, 1930s	3	5
Bronze Thrills, Jan. 1961	2	8
Broom Maker, May 1920	20	30
Brown Book of Boston, 1903-05	7	11
Brown Herb Co. Almanac, 1908-11	10	20
Brush and Pencil Magazine, 1890s	8	15
Building Age, Mar. 1927	6	8
Business Week, 1930s	2	4

	LOW	HIGH
Camera Craft, 1940s	1	3
Camping Magazine, 1920-30s	2	4
Canadian Motorist, Aug. 1921	12	18
Car and Driver, 1960-80	2	4
Carriage Monthly, 1900, #12	50	70
Cars, Nov. 1953	3	5
Casanova, May 1957, Vol. 1, #1	15	25
Cattlemen, 1920s	2	4
Cavalier, Feb. 1961	3	4
Chase's Calendar Almanac, 1910-38	10	20
Christian Herald, 1890s	2	4
Cigar & Tobacco Journal, Jun. 1947	10	20
Clarks Almanac, 1870s	25	50
Click, 1930s	8	12
Clyde Beatty's Circus, 1940-50s	5	15
Collectibles Illustrated, 1982-85	2	4
Collier's, 1880s	8	15
Collier's, Sep. 12, 1903, Gibson illustrations	15	20
Collier's, May 5, 1906, earthquake	45	55
Collier's, Jul. 1908, Maxfield Parrish cover	25	35
Collier's, Feb. 17, 1912, N. C. Wyeth cover	20	30
Comfort, 1930s	2	6
Complete Detective Cases, Oct. 1951	8	12
Complete Sports, Jan. 1966	3	5
Connoisseur, 1900-50s	5	8
Contemporary Photographer, 1962-68	20	35
Copper Romances, Nov. 1953, Vol. 1, #1	20	50
Coronet, Jul. 1914, Christy illustrations	5	7
Coronet, Jan. 1966, Marilyn Monroe	8	12
Cosmopolitan, Aug. 1903, Rose O'Neill	15	25
Cosmopolitan, May 1953, Marilyn Monroe	25	40
Cottage Hearth, Jun. 1891	7	10
Country Gentlemen, 1926-30	8	12

Left to right: Collier's, *Feb. 1941, $12-$16;* Fortune, *Feb. 1935, $12-$16.*

	LOW	HIGH
Country Gentlemen, Nov. 1944, Wyeth cover	15	2
Crime Detective, 1940-60s	3	7
Cue Magazine, 1950s	4	6
Current History, Nov. 1925	8	12
Current Opinion, Jul. 1923	5	8
Current Opinion, Nov. 1924	8	12
Custom Rodder, Sep. 1964	3	4
Dance Magazine, 1920-50s	5	7
Daring Detective, 1930-50s	3	10
Daughters of the American Revolution, Oct. 1933	3	4
Delineator, Aug. 1922	10	20
Democratic Review, 1850s	10	30
Designer, 1910s	6	10
Detective Magazine, 1940s	6	10
Dexter Smith's Musical Journal, 1875	3	5
Discovery, 1952-55, #1-6	30	40
Disney Magazine, Jan/Feb 1966	3	5
Display World, 1920s	3	8
Doc Savage, Sep. 1933	200	240
Doc Savage, Jan. 1935	65	75
Doc Savage, Jan. 1939-48	50	60
Doc Savage, Dec. 1944	70	80
Downbeat, 1950s	3	5
Drama Magazine, 1920-30s	3	5
Dunninger's Popular Magic and Card Tricks Magazine, 1929	90	125
Dwight's Journal of Music, 1850-80s	4	8
Dynamic Science Fiction, Dec. 1952	4	6
Ebony Magazine, 1946-57	5	7
Electric Journal, Jan. 1910	4	6
Ellery Queen's Mystery Magazine, Jan. 1949	15	25
Ellery Queen's Mystery Magazine, 1956-90	2	4
Empire Almanac, 1898-1903	10	20
Esquire, 1936-39, Petty Girl	10	20
Esquire, Jul. 1934, Rockwell Kent	45	55
Esquire, Oct. 1940, Varga illustrations	35	45
Esquire, Sep. 1951, Marilyn Monroe	35	50
Esquire, Nov. 1960, Lenny Bruce	5	7
Esquire, 1970s	3	5
Etude, 1940-50s	2	5
Every Saturday, Oct. 15, 1870	10	15
Everywoman's Magazine, 1940-50s	3	6
Exclusive, 1950s	5	10
Exhibitor Magazine, 1950s	1	3
Exposed, 1950s	10	15
Eye Magazine, May 1949, Vol. 1, #1	15	25
Family Circle, 1930s	4	10
Family Circle, 1950-59	1	2
Famous Fantastic Mysteries, 1939-53	4	10
Famous Western, Feb. 1957	3	4
Fantasy & Science Fiction, 1949, Vol. 1, #1	25	50
Farm and Fireside, 1800-1930s	3	6
Farmer's Almanac, 1800s	8	15
Farmer's Wife, Jul. 1932	5	7
Farm Life, 1890s	3	8

	LOW	HIGH
FBI Detective Stories, Feb. 1949, Vol. 1	20	40
Field & Stream, Sep. 1916	8	12
Field & Stream, Nov. 1947	4	6
Filmland, Jun. 1956, James Dean	20	30
Fire Chief, May/Jun. 1930	6	10
Firehouse, Sep.-Oct. 1976	70	80
Flair, 1953, Annual	15	25
Flying, 1940-50	5	10
Flying Saucers, Aug. 1960	8	12
Focus, Apr. 1938	5	7
Follies Magazine, 1957-60	5	10
Food Magazine, 1907	20	30
Ford Times, 1920-30s	5	15
Forest & Stream, 1800s	20	30
Fortune, Mar. 1932	35	45
Fortune, Nov. 1933	10	20
Foto Parade, 1930s	8	12
Friars Fables, 1960s	5	10
Friday, Mar. 1940, Vol. 1, #1	10	20
Front Page Detective, 1940-60s	3	5
Furniture Worker, Dec. 1893	10	20
Gala, 1958-60	5	15
Gangsters, 1975, #1	5	7
Garden and Home Builder, 1920s	5	7
General Electric Review, Dec. 1912	5	8
Gent, Sep. 1956, Vol. 1, #1	25	45
Gentleman's Magazine, Jul. 1780	55	65
Gentleman's Magazine, Apr. 1792	140	160
Gentleman's Magazine, Jan. 1793	90	125
Gentleman's Magazine, Nov. 1805	75	90
Gentlewoman, 1930-73	3	5
Glamorous Models, 1950-52	5	10
Gleason's Pictorial Drawing Room Companion, May 1851	45	55
G-Men, 1930-40s	10	15
Good Furniture Magazine, Aug. 1915	10	15
Good Housekeeping, 1900-20	5	10
Good Literature, 1907	10	12
Gourmet, 1940-60s	2	4
Gray's Sporting Journal, 1976-79	1	2
Greatest Detective, 1940s	3	6
Greenbag Magazine, 1890	20	30
Grin, 1940s	3	10
Grit & Steel, 1890-1940s	2	10
Groove, 1947-49	10	12
Gun World, Apr. 1974	3	4
Ham News, Jan.-Feb. 1952	2	3
Ham News, Jul.-Aug. 1953	2	3
Ham News, Nov.-Dec. 1953	2	3
Hardware Dealer's Magazine, Jun. 1897	20	30
Harper's Bazaar, Apr. 1929	5	7
Harper's Bazaar, Aug. 1930	8	12
Harper's Monthly, 1850	7	9
Harper's Weekly, Jun. 25, 1859, Queen Victoria	10	15
Harper's Weekly, Nov. 22, 1862, Battle of Antietam	18	22

	LOW	HIGH
Harper's Weekly, Aug. 18, 1866, Mormons and Salt Lake	38	45
Harper's Weekly, Sep. 14, 1878	30	35
Harper's Weekly, Dec. 14, 1889	12	18
Harper's Weekly, 1892, World's Fair	15	25
Harvard Football News, Oct. 24, 1964	7	10
Headquarter's Detective, May 1940	5	7
Hearst's Magazine, Apr. 1960, Christy illustrations	25	35
Hearth and Home, 1868-1930s	2	10
High Fidelity, Apr. 1971	1	2
Hobbies Magazine, 1930-60s	2	6
Holiday Magazine, Mar. 1946, Vol. 1, #1	20	40
Hollywood Magazine, Jun. 1934	20	30
Hollywood Magazine, Jan. 1941	20	30
Hollywood Men, 1953, Tony Curtis	10	20
Hollywood Reporter, 1930-50s	5	15
Home Journal, 1840-1900	5	10
Horse Lover, 1951-65	2	5
Hot Rod Magazine, Sep. 1954	6	8
House and Garden, 1937-49	5	7
House Beautiful, 1919-29	7	10
House Beautiful, 1930-45	4	6
House Beautiful, 1946-60	2	4
Hunting and Fishing, 1930s	5	8
Ideal Woman, Nov. 1941, Mary Pickford	15	25
Illustrated Family Almanac, 1856-58	15	30
Illustrated London News, Sep. 16, 1871	6	8
Illustrated London News, May 15, 1937	18	25
Illustrated War News, 1898	30	50
Illustrated World, 1920s	5	8
Infinity Science Fiction, Nov. 1955	5	7
Inside Baseball, 1950s	15	30
Inside Detective, 1930-40s	3	5
Inside Detective, 1946-58	9	13
Inside Detective, 1959-70	6	8
International Studio, Jun. 1931	5	7
Jet Set, Sep. 1973, Vol. 1, #1, Jackie Onassis	12	20
Jones Family Magazine, 1893-94	15	30
Kenyon Review, 1944-45	10	20
Keyhole Detective Cases, Mar. 1942, Vol. 1, #1	15	25
Kiwanis Magazine, 1937-38	3	5
Knickerbocker, 1837	10	20
Ladies' Home Journal, 1890-10	15	22
Ladies' Home Journal, 1911-29	10	13
Ladies' Home Journal, 1930-40	5	9
Land of Sunshine, Vol. 2, #4	25	35
Liberty, Oct. 25, 1941, Hitler cover	15	25
Limelight, 1955, Vol. 1, #1, Marlon Brando	20	30
Lippincott's Monthly, 1870-1900s	5	10
Literary Digest, May 9, 1907, Leyendecker cover	15	25
Literary Digest, Apr. 27, 1918, Wyeth cover	10	20
Look Magazine, May 11, 1937, Mae West	25	35
Look Magazine, Jul. 20, 1937, Tarzan	10	20
Look Magazine, 1940-47	8	12
Look Magazine, Oct. 20, 1942, Flash Gordon	15	25

	LOW	HIGH
Look Magazine, Oct. 29, 1946, Basil Rathbone	15	25
Look Magazine, Oct. 19, 1971, last issue	5	15
Mademoiselle, 1940s	4	8
Mademoiselle, 1950s	2	4
Mad Magazine, Nov. 1979, #164, Alien	15	25
Mad Magazine, Jul. 1980, #169, Star Trek	20	30
Mad Magazine, Jan. 1981, #175, M*A*S*H	13	20
Mad Magazine, May 1981, #177, Hulk	8	12
Magazine Antiques, 1940-80s	3	8
Major League Baseball, 1948, Ted Williams	10	15
Manhunt Magazine, Jan. 1953, Vol. 1, #1	50	70
Master Detective, 1940s	3	5
Master Detective, Nov. 1960	3	5
McCall's, Oct. 1916	15	25
McCall's, Jul. 1931	15	25
McClure's Magazine, Oct. 1906, Maxfield Parrish cover	15	25
Mechanix Illustrated, 1920-30s	5	12
Men, Feb. 1947	2	3
Mentor, Jul. 1921	10	15
Merchant's Trade Journal, 1912	30	40
Merritt's Fantasy Magazine, Jul. 1950, Vol. 1, #4	5	15
Mickey Mouse Magazine, 1935, Vol. 1, #1	75	150
Mickey Mouse Magazine, Oct. 1936, Vol. 2, #1	125	200
Mickey Mouse Magazine, 1936, Vol. 2, #2, Mickey and Donald	150	250
Mickey Mouse Magazine, Jul. 1938, Vol. 3, #10	75	125
Model Railroader, 1930-50s	4	10
Modern Bride, 1960s	1	3
Modern Man, Mar. 1955, Marilyn Monroe	30	50
Modern Movies, 1937-38	20	27
Modern Romance, 1940-50s	5	15
Modern Screen, 1931-39	25	45
Modern Screen, Jan. 1943, Ronald Reagan and Jane Wyman	70	90
Modern Screen, Oct. 1953, Marilyn Monroe	45	55

Left to right: Look Magazine, *Oct. 11, 1938, $5-$10;* The Mentor, *Jun. 1929, $12-$16.*

	LOW	HIGH
Modern Screen, Jun. 1979, Elvis Presley	8	10
Mothers, Nov. 1935	3	4
Motion Picture, pre-1920	14	21
Motion Picture, Mar. 1928	20	30
Motion Picture, 1930-40	15	25
Motion Picture, Sep. 1941	15	25
Motion Picture, 1971-75	1	2
Motor, Sep. 1922, Christy cover	30	40
Motorcycling & Bicycling, Nov. 1922	15	25
Motor Guide, Mar. 1959	3	4
Motor Service, 1950s	2	4
Movieland, 1947-60	20	50
Movieland, Jan. 1945, Shirley Temple	15	25
Movie Life, 1940-50s	10	20
Movie Mirror, 1930s	10	35
Movie Mirror, Mar. 1940	10	20
Movie Mystery, Sep.-Oct. 1946	5	7
Movie People, May 1954, w/ 3-D glasses	60	70
Movies, Nov. 1944, Lucille Ball	10	20
Movie Show, 1946-48	20	25
Movie Stars Parade, 1949-58	10	20
Movie Story, 1937-49	20	35
Movie World, 1958-69	8	12
Mystique, Apr. 1973, Vol. 1, #1	15	25
National Farm Journal, 1920s	4	6
National Geographic, 1880, Vol. 1, #1	550	675
National Geographic, 1880, Vol. 1, #2	200	325
National Geographic, 1888	320	520
National Geographic, 1890-94	80	150
National Geographic, Mar. 1898	45	60
National Geographic, Mar. 1899	25	50
National Geographic, 1900-04	20	40
National Geographic, 1905-13	14	20

National Geographic, *left to right: Jun. 1932, $2-$3; Jun. 1962, $1-$2.*

	LOW	HIGH
National Geographic, 1914-19	5	8
National Geographic, 1920-29	2	4
National Geographic, 1930-49	2	3
National Geographic, 1950-95	1	2
Natural History, 1860-50s	2	10
Needlecraft, 1926-40	1	3
New England, 1830s	10	40
New Far East, Jun. 1926	4	6
New Lady's Magazine, 1788	10	20
New Movie, 1930-33	30	40
New Stars, 1940s	8	12
Newsweek, 1930s	2	8
Newsweek, Oct. 4, 1937, Hitler and Mussolini	15	25
Newsweek, Dec. 1942, Franklin D. Roosevelt	2	8
Newsweek, May 17, 1954, Grace Kelly	40	60
Newsweek, Feb. 24, 1964, The Beatles	10	30
New York Clipper, Mar. 29, 1884	10	20
New York Mirror, 1830s	8	15
Night and Day, Nov. 1954	5	10
Office Mentor, Oct. 1936, Vol. 1, #1	15	45
Official Detective, 1937-56	6	10
Oui, Oct. 1972, first issue	20	25
Our Young Folks, Nov. 1866	9	12
Outdoor America, Apr. 1931	6	8
Outdoor Life, 1910-20	2	7
Parents, 1930s	1	3
Paris Life, 1954, #17	10	15
Pearson's Magazine, 1900-10	4	8
Penthouse, 1972-74	4	8
Penthouse, 1980s, Madonna	10	30
People Magazine, 1974-77	2	4
People Magazine, Jan. 1975, Elvis Presley	5	15
People's Home Journal, 1902	3	5
Peterson's Magazine, 1844-59	4	6
Peterson's Magazine, 1860-65	6	9
Phantom Detective, 1930s	10	15
Photoplay Magazine, Sep. 1931, Barbara Stanwick	10	30
Photoplay Magazine, Nov. 1942, Ginger Rogers	10	20
Photoplay Magazine, Dec. 1945, Claudette Colbert	10	20
Photoplay Magazine, Dec. 1948, Ava Gardner	10	20
Photoplay Magazine, Apr. 1949, Betty Grable	15	25
Photoplay Magazine, Mar. 1950, Jimmy Stewart	15	20
Photoplay Magazine, Apr. 1951, Esther Williams	10	15
Photoplay Magazine, Oct. 1953, Janet Leigh	10	15
Photoplay Magazine, Dec. 1956, Natalie Wood	10	20
Pic, 1940-45	3	8
Pictorial Review, Jun. 1928	10	20
Picture Play, 1930-38	20	40
Picture Show, 1945-49	15	20
Playboy, Oct. 1958	20	30
Playboy, Mar. 1959	10	20
Playboy, Feb. 1960, Jayne Mansfield	30	40
Playboy, Oct. 1961	5	15
Poetry Magazine, Sep. 1955	2	8

	LOW	HIGH
Popular Card Tricks Magazine, c1925	90	120
Popular Imported Cars, Dec. 1965	90	110
Popular Mechanics, 1920-40s	5	7
Popular Mechanics, Jan. 1952	10	20
Popular Photography, May 1937, Vol. 1, #1	20	30
Popular Science, 1901-10	20	25
Popular Science, 1911-30	15	20
Pulse, 1954-55	1	3
Quick Magazine, 1949-59	2	4
Radio Broadcast, 1929	5	7
Radio-Electronics, Aug. 1949	2	3
Radio-Electronics, Feb. 1950	1	2
Radio-Electronics, Mar. 1952	1	2
Radio-Electronics, May 1964	1	2
Radio-Electronics, Oct. 1964	1	2
Radio News, May 1938	4	6
Radio News, Nov. 1940	4	6
Railroad Magazine, Apr. 1946	4	6
Reader's Digest, 1928-33	2	4
Reader's Digest, 1950-70s	1	3
Redbook, 1950-60s	2	4
Red Cross Magazine, Jun. 1918, Norman Rockwell cover	25	35
Richardson's Musical Hours, Feb. 1880	3	5
Ringmaster, May 1936, Vol. 1, #1	30	40
Rod & Custom, Oct. 1955	5	10
Rodding and Restyling, Mar. 1966	3	4
Saturday Evening Post, The, Aug. 12, 1912, Coles Phillips	10	20
Saturday Evening Post, The, Mar. 20, 1919, Norman Rockwell	25	40
Saturday Evening Post, The, Jul. 17, 1926, J. C. Leyendecker	5	15
Saturday Evening Post, The, Jun. 30, 1932, Norman Rockwell	25	40
Science & Invention, Dec. 1926	5	8
Science & Technology International, 1962-69	6	8

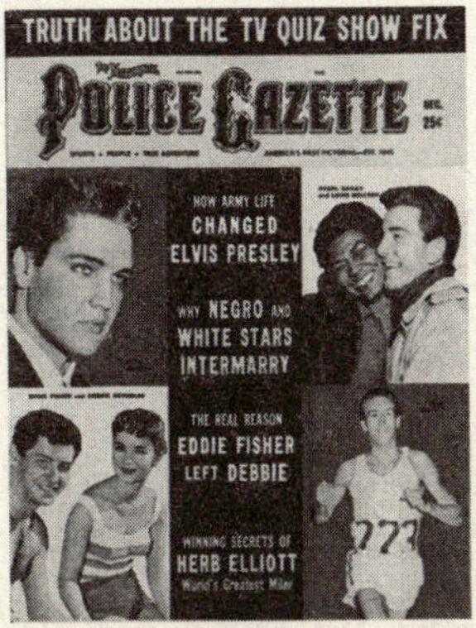

Left to right: National Police Gazette, *Dec. 1958, $30-$40;* The Saturday Evening Post, *May 11, 1901, Norman Rockwell Cover, $20-$30.*

	LOW	HIGH
Scouting, 1930s	2	4
Screen Book, 1929-39	25	50
Screen Guide, 1939-45	15	30
Screenland, 1924-32	22	32
Screenland, 1933-39	17	23
Screenland, 1940-48	12	18
Screenland, 1949-55	7	12
Screenland, 1956-65	2	6
Screen Play, Jul. 1933, Mae West	10	20
Screen Romances, Dec. 1936, Dionne Quints	40	50
Screen Stars, 1946-49	12	16
Screen Stars, 1950-57	5	10
Screen Stories, 1948-55	8	15
Screen Stories, 1956-60	5	8
Screen Stories, 1961-72	2	6
Scribner's Magazine, Dec. 1903, Maxfield Parrish illustrations	20	30
Scribner's Magazine, Oct. 1906, N. C. Wyeth illustrations	20	30
Show Magazine, 1940-60s	5	7
Silver Screen, Apr. 1960, Elvis Presley	20	30
Sky Aces, Jun. 1938	25	35
Sky Aces, Sep. 1939	10	20
Sky Devils, Mar. 1938	25	35
Song Hits, 1940s	4	6
Spinning Wheel, 1950-70s	5	15
Sporting News, 1950s	15	25
Sporting News, 1960s	10	15
Sporting News, 1970s	5	10
Sports Illustrated, 1964-65, swimsuit issue	40	60
Stage, May 1933	25	35
Stage, Aug. 1938	20	30
Successful Farming, 1940-50s	2	6
Suspense, 1951	2	8
Tab, Aug. 1966, Sophia Loren	4	6
Tempo Magazine, 1953-60	2	8
Theatre, 1910-14	25	30
Time, Jan. 20, 1936, J. P. Morgan	6	10
Time, Oct. 18, 1937, Ernest Hemingway	5	15
Time, Dec. 27, 1937, Walt Disney and Seven Dwarfs	40	50
Time, Jan. 17, 1938, Frank Lloyd Wright	20	30
Time, Mar. 28, 1938, Bette Davis	5	15
Time, Apr. 4, 1938, Einstein	10	20
Time, Jun. 19, 1939, Lindbergh	20	30
Time, Dec. 15, 1939, Vivien Leigh	70	80
Time, Mar. 3, 1941, Gary Cooper	10	20
Time, Apr. 7, 1941, Bing Crosby	10	20
Time, Nov. 10, 1941, Rita Hayworth	15	25
Time, Nov. 20, 1944, Jimmy Durante	5	15
Time, Jul. 19, 1949, Howard Hughes	10	20
Time, May 3, 1952, John Wayne	20	30
Tops, Nov. 1955	3	5
Tower Radio, Aug. 1935	12	18
Travel, 1937-38	3	8
True Confessions, 1935-50s	4	6
True Detective, 1924-39	12	20

	LOW	HIGH
True Romance, 1948-55	5	7
True's Gun Annual, 1962, #1	3	5
True's Gun Annual, 1963, #2	3	4
TV-Radio Mirror, Aug. 1975, Michael Landon	10	20
Twilight Zone, 1982-87	6	10
Vanity Fair, Apr. 1923	25	35
Vanity Fair, May 1924	30	40
Vanity Fair, Nov. 1929	35	45
Variety, 1950s	8	12
Vermont Life, 1930s	1	3
Vogue, Mar. 1917	70	80
Vogue, Oct. 1923	15	25
Vogue, Apr. 1925	35	45
Wacko, 1980, #1	25	35
Wacko, Apr. 1981, #2	23	31
Walt Disney's Magazine, 1950-60s	10	20
War Cry, 1884-90s	2	5
Weird Tales, 1920-30s	25	75
Weird Tales, Jul. 1947	25	35
Western Family, 1940-50s	2	8
Western Field Magazine, early 1900s	20	30
Whirl, 1956-59	5	10
Woman's Day, Feb. 1940	3	4
Woman's Day, Mar. 1941	3	4
Woman's Day, Sep. 1941	3	4
Worlds of Fantasy, 1968, Vol. 1, #1	40	50
Wrestling World, Jul. 1954, Vol. 1, #4	10	20
Yank, Jul. 1945	2	8
Youth's Companion, Oct. 1896	15	25
Youth's Companion, Nov. 1925	15	35

Left to right: Sports Illustrated, *Aug. 2, 1976, $1-$3;* Work and Win, *Dec. 5, 1902, $12-$16.*

Life *Magazine*

		LOW	HIGH
1936, Nov. 30	West Point Cadet	$10	$30
1937, Jan. 4	Franklin Roosevelt	15	25
1937, May 3	Jean Harlow	20	40
1937, May 17	Dionne Quintuplets, Hindenburg	40	50
1937, May 31	Golden Gate Bridge	5	10
1937, Sep. 27	Nelson Eddy	5	15
1937, Nov. 8	Greta Garbo	15	35
1938, Jun. 13	Gertrude Lawrence	7	9
1938, Jun. 20	Rudolph Valentino	10	35
1938, Oct. 4	Legionnaires Home	4	6
1938, Oct. 17	Carole Lombard	8	12
1939, May 1	Joe DiMaggio	40	50
1939, May 22	World's Fair	35	50
1939, Aug. 14	Busiest Baby	4	6
1939, Sep. 11	Benito Mussolini	5	15
1939, Nov. 13	Claudette Colbert	7	9
1939, Nov. 24	Ann Sheridan	5	7
1939, Dec. 25	Christmas Issue	12	18
1940, Jan. 29	Lana Turner	7	9
1940, Jul. 15	Rita Hayworth	10	20
1940, Oct. 7	Gary Cooper	8	20
1940, Dec. 9	Ginger Rogers	10	20
1941, Jan. 6	Katharine Hepburn	10	20
1941, May 26	Army Nurse	5	7
1941, Aug. 11	Rita Hayworth	4	6
1941, Aug. 25	Fred Astaire	4	6
1941, Nov. 10	Gene Tierney	4	6
1942, Mar. 29	Shirley Temple	15	25
1942, Apr. 27	Nelson Rockwell	6	10
1942, Jun. 1	Hedy Lamarr	10	20
1943, Jul. 12	Roy Rogers	20	35
1943, Oct. 25	Mary Martin	6	10
1944, Jan. 10	Bob Hope	3	5
1944, Apr. 17	Esther Williams	4	6
1944, Jul. 10	Admiral Chester Nimitz	5	7
1944, Oct. 16	Lauren Bacall	20	30
1944, Dec. 11	Judy Garland	6	10
1945, Apr. 30	Life's War Artists	3	8
1945, May 21	Winston Churchill	5	7
1945, Nov. 12	Ingrid Bergman	4	8
1946, Feb. 4	Bob Hope & Bing Crosby	15	25
1946, Feb. 18	Dorothy McGuire	3	5
1946, Jun. 10	Donna Reed	3	5
1946, Jul. 19	Vivien Leigh	5	15
1946, Nov. 25	10th Anniversary Issue	20	30
1947, Jul. 14	Elizabeth Taylor	10	20
1947, Sep. 1	John Cobb and Racing Car	7	11
1948, Apr. 19	Winston Churchill	4	8
1948, May 3	Israeli War	15	25
1948, Aug. 9	Marlene Dietrich	4	6
1948, Dec. 6	Montgomery Cliff	15	20
1948, Dec. 13	General Eisenhower	6	8

		LOW	HIGH
1949, Sep. 19	Arlene Dahl	4	6
1949, Oct. 10	Oppenheimer	12	18
1950, May 8	Jackie Robinson	25	40
1950, Jun. 12	Hopalong Cassidy	20	35
1950, Sep. 25	Swedish Red Cross Girls	4	6
1951, Jan. 29	Betsy VonFurstenburg, Ted Williams	5	7
1951, Mar. 12	Paul Douglas	5	7
1951, Mar. 26	Young Choir Singer, Fred Astaire	5	7
1951, Apr. 16	Esther Williams	5	15
1951, Oct. 22	Bronc Rider Casey Tibbs, Howdy Doody	8	12
1952, Apr. 7	Marilyn Monroe	15	25
1952, Apr. 14	Italian Fashions	4	6
1952, May 31	Li'l Abner & Friends	5	7
1952, Aug. 4	Adlai Stevenson	6	8
1952, Sep. 15	Rita Gam, Musial and Mantle	8	12
1953, Feb. 2	Eisenhower Inauguration	10	20
1953, Jun. 29	Cyd Charisse, Marilyn Monroe	10	14
1953, Jul. 6	Terry Moore	8	12
1953, Nov. 2	Churchill, Disney	12	18
1953, Dec. 14	Nixon, Ronald Reagan	10	15
1954, Mar. 1	Rita Moreno	2	4
1954, Mar. 8	Churchill's Granddaughter	4	6
1954, Mar. 15	Mrs. Rockefeller	4	6
1954, Apr. 26	Grace Kelly	10	20
1954, May 24	Kaye Ballard	2	4
1954, May 31	William Holden	10	15
1954, Aug. 2	Summer Show Whale	5	7
1954, Sep. 6	Dior, Rock Hudson	7	11
1954, Oct. 11	Mountain Climber	20	30
1955, Jan. 31	Spencer Tracy	2	6
1955, Feb. 28	Shelley Winters	8	12
1955, Mar. 7	Buddha, Jimmy Dean, Disney	6	10
1955, May 30	Rare Playing Cards	2	4

Left to right: Jul. 10, 1944, Admiral Chester Nimitz; Aug. 17, 1962, Marilyn Monroe.

		LOW	HIGH
1955, Jul. 11	Susan Strasberg, Girl Scouts	4	6
1955, Oct. 10	Princess Margaret	3	5
1955, Nov. 28	Carol Channing, Tyrone Power	5	7
1955, Dec. 12	Epic of Man III	5	7
1956, Jan. 30	Henry Ford II	4	6
1956, Apr. 9	Grace Kelly	3	5
1956, Apr. 23	Jayne Mansfield	8	12
1956, Jun. 25	Mickey Mantle	20	30
1956, Aug. 6	Andrea Doria	8	12
1956, Sep. 24	Janet Blair	2	4
1956, Nov. 12	Rosalind Russell	8	12
1957, Jan. 28	B-52, Wilt Chamberlain	12	18
1957, Jun. 3	Making of a Satellite	5	7
1958, Jan. 20	Lyndon Johnson	8	12
1958, Feb. 18	Queen Elizabeth	2	4
1958, Apr. 7	Sugar Ray Robinson, Elvis Drafted	15	18
1958, Apr. 28	Willie Mays	30	40
1958, Oct. 17	Satellite Camera	2	4
1958, Nov. 24	Kim Novak	2	4
1959, Apr. 20	Marilyn Monroe	15	25
1960, Jan. 11	Dina Merrill, Bobby Darin	8	12
1960, Feb. 22	Henry & Jane Fonda	2	4
1960, Mar. 7	Hypnosis, Squaw Valley Olympics	5	7
1960, Mar. 21	Billy Graham	3	8
1960, Apr. 4	Marlon Brando, Chuck Dressen	4	6
1960, Aug. 3	Kingston Trio	8	12
1960, Nov. 28	Carroll Baker, Clark Gable	4	6
1960, Dec. 26	25 Years of Life, Marilyn Monroe	18	25
1961, Jan. 13	Clark Gable	3	8
1961, Jun. 9	Kennedy, DeGaulle, Golf	3	5
1961, Aug. 11	Sophia Loren	2	4
1961, Nov. 17	Minnesota Vikings	3	5
1962, Feb. 2	John Glenn	4	6
1962, May 11	Bob Hope	4	6
1962, Aug. 10	Janet Leigh	2	4
1962, Aug. 17	Marilyn Monroe	30	40
1962, Sep. 28	Don Drysdale, Joan Crawford	25	30
1962, Nov. 2	Cuba, Natalie Wood	8	12
1962, Nov. 30	Sid Caesar	2	4
1963, Feb. 15	Lincoln's Body, Cassius Clay	7	11
1963, Mar. 8	Jean Seberg, Ted Williams	8	12
1963, May 10	Bay of Pigs, Marlon Brando	8	12
1963, Jun. 21	Shirley McLaine	4	8
1963, Dec. 13	Lyndon B. Johnson	8	12
1964, Jan. 14	Ho Chi Minh	5	7
1964, Jan. 31	Geraldine Chaplin, The Beatles	15	20
1964, May 22	Barbra Streisand	10	15
1964, Jul. 10	Oswald's Diary	10	15
1964, Jul. 17	Carroll Baker, General MacArthur	8	11
1964, Aug. 14	Lyndon Johnson	8	12
1964, Aug. 28	The Beatles	15	30
1964, Oct. 23	Leonid Brezhnev, The Beatles	8	12
1964, Dec. 25	Moses by Rembrandt	3	5
1965, Jan. 15	Ted Kennedy, The XB-70	10	14

		LOW	HIGH
1965, Feb. 26	North Vietnam Stamp	3	5
1965, Apr. 2	Gemini's Journey	2	4
1965, May 7	John Wayne	20	30
1965, Jul. 30	Mickey Mantle at 33	45	65
1966, Jan. 7	Sean Connery	15	25
1966, Apr. 15	Louis Armstrong	6	10
1966, Apr. 29	Julie Andrews	2	4
1966, May 6	Jackie Kennedy	6	10
1966, Sep. 9	LSD Art, Muhammad Ali	7	11
1966, Oct. 7	Ian Fleming, James Bond	6	10
1967, Jun. 9	Gypsy Moth, Petula Clark	5	15
1967, Jul. 14	Princess Lee Radziwill, Joe Frazier	7	11
1967, Sep. 15	Stalin's Daughter, Mark Spitz, Vietnam	5	15
1967, Sep. 22	Part II Stalin's Daughter, *Camelot*	5	15
1967, Oct. 11	Pope John, James Bond, NASA, Nixon	5	15
1967, Dec. 8	Pearl Bailey	3	5
1968, Jan. 12	Faye Dunaway	2	4
1968, Mar. 1	Georgia O'Keefe	2	4
1968, Apr. 19	Coretta Scott King	2	4
1968, Jun. 21	James Earl Ray, Sirhan Sirhan	5	7
1968, Sep. 20	Arthur Ashe	2	4
1968, Oct. 4	Deep Sea Probes, Nixon campaign	5	15
1968, Oct. 18	Paul Newman and Wife	2	4
1968, Oct. 25	Apollo 7, Mickey Mouse	5	7
1968, Nov. 1	Jackie Onassis Wedding, Apollo 7	6	10
1969, Jan. 10	The Incredible Year 1968	7	11
1969, May 23	Rowan and Martin	5	7
1969, Jul. 25	Neil Armstrong	2	4
1969, Aug. 6	Ann Margret	2	4
1969, Sep. 5	Peter Max	10	15
1969, Oct. 17	Naomi Sims	2	4
1969, Oct. 31	Marijuana, The Muppets	8	12
1969, Nov. 21	Johnny Cash	2	4
1970, Jan. 23	Johnny Carson	3	5
1970, Feb. 6	Robert Redford	4	6
1970, Mar. 13	The Great Hemline Hassle	2	4
1970, Apr. 3	Lauren Bacall	2	4
1970, Jun. 19	Dennis Hopper	2	4
1970, Jul. 24	Candice Bergen	5	7
1970, Oct. 16	Spiro Agnew	2	4
1971, Mar. 19	Ali/Frazier Fight	2	4
1971, Apr. 16	Paul McCartney	10	20
1971, Apr. 23	Jane Fonda	2	4
1971, Jul. 23	Clint Eastwood	2	4
1971, Oct. 1	The Brain	2	4
1971, Oct. 25	Disney World Opens	6	10
1971, Nov. 12	Bobby Fischer	2	4
1971, Dec. 10	Cybil Sheperd	4	6
1972, Jan. 28	John Wayne	2	4
1972, Feb. 25	Liz Taylor Turns 40	2	4
1972, Mar. 10	Marlon Brando	5	7
1972, Dec. 8	Diana Ross	2	4
1986, Fall	50 Years of *Life*	5	15

TV Guide

TV Guide is a weekly magazine that includes local television listings and articles about Hollywood stars. The nationally distributed editions began in 1953. Before 1953, there were local forerunners. Season preview issues, and issues featuring popular Hollywood stars and television shows on the cover are usually more valuable than other editions.

		LOW	HIGH
1948, Nov. 6	Howdy Doody	$65	$80
1950, Mar. 18	Marilyn Monroe	400	600
1950, Apr. 8	Easter Parade, #14	65	80
1950, May 6	Hopalong Cassidy	125	175
1950, Jul. 8	Williams/DiMaggio, All-Star Game, Comiskey Park, Chicago	75	100
1952, Jul. 18	Groucho Marx, #29	10	30
1952, Sep. 26	Roy Rogers	75	100
1952, Dec. 12	Lucy's TV Baby, #50	10	30
1952, Dec. 19	Winners of the 1952 *TV Guide* Gold Medal Awards, #51	50	85
1953, Jan. 2	Jackie Gleason, #1	15	25
1953, Jan. 23	Marilyn Monroe	75	100
1953, Feb. 13	Kukla, Fran, and Ollie, #7	40	60
1953, Mar. 5	Groucho Marx, #9	15	35
1953, Mar. 27	Charlton Heston and John Forsythe, #13	25	50
1953, Apr. 2	Charlton Heston and Red Buttons, #13	40	60
1953, Apr. 21	Hartline and Kirchner, #21	10	15
1953, May 22	Red Buttons, Howdy Doody article, #8	40	60
1953, Jun. 5	Martin & Lewis, #10	40	60
1953, Jun. 19	Ed Sullivan, #12	15	25
1953, Jul. 24	Groucho Marx and Hopalong Cassidy, #17	40	60
1953, Aug. 7	Ray Milland, #19	25	50
1953, Aug. 14	"Range Rider" stars Jack Mahoney and Dick West	25	50
1953, Sep. 4	"Back to School with Mr. Peepers," Wally Cox article, #23	15	25
1953, Sep. 18	1953-54 Fall Preview	125	175

Left to right: Oct. 16, 1953, Angie Dickinson; Aug. 1, 1959, Dave Garroway; Jun. 8, 1963, Johnny Carson.

		LOW	HIGH
1953, Sep. 25	"Superman" star George Reeves, #26	175	250
1953, Oct. 16	Angie Dickinson	20	40
1953, Oct. 30	Kukla, Fran, & Ollie, #31	15	25
1953, Dec. 11	Dragnet, #37	10	35
1954, May 21	Wally Cox	10	15
1955, Jul. 30	"The Whiting Girls With Lucy & Desi," #3	40	60
1955, Sep. 24	1955-56 Fall Preview, #39	50	75
1955, Oct. 1	Mickey Mouse Club, Walt Disney article, #40	10	15
1956, Sep. 15	Elvis Presley	150	200
1956, Sep. 29	Jackie Gleason, Elvis Presley article and photo, #39	40	60
1957, Jun. 8	Lassie, #23	15	25
1957, Sep. 14	Wagon Train, 1957-58 Fall Preview, #37	40	60
1957, Nov. 2	Lucille Ball, #4	15	35
1957, Dec. 14	Walt Disney, #5	10	15
1958, Jan. 18	Restless Gun, "How to Be a TV Cowboy" article	15	25
1958, Sep. 14	1958-59 Fall Preview	40	60
1959, Jan. 17	Maverick stars James Garner and Jack Kelly	10	15
1959, Aug. 1	Dave Garroway	7	12
1959, Sep. 5	Maverick stars James Garner and Jack Kelly	10	15
1960, May 7	Elvis Presley and Frank Sinatra, #9	15	35
1961, Jul. 1	The Flintstones, #26	15	35
1962, Nov. 10	Beverly Hillbillies, Car 54 article	5	10
1963, May 11	Andy Griffith Show, The Outer Limits article	5	20
1963, Jun. 8	Johnny Carson	5	12
1963, Sep. 14	1963-64 Fall Preview, #37	15	25
1963, Dec. 28	Patty Duke, Farmer's Daughter article	15	30
1964, Feb. 22	The Fugitive, Robert Vaughn/The Outer Limits article	15	25
1964, Sep. 19	1964-65 Fall Preview	30	50
1965, Mar. 6	The Fugitive, The Three Stooges article	10	30
1965, May 29	Bewitched, Alfred Hitchcock article	10	30
1965, Jul. 10	The Munsters, My Living Doll article	20	40
1965, Sep. 11	1965-66 Fall Preview	40	60
1965, Oct. 30	The Addams Family, #44	15	30
1965, Nov. 6	Lost In Space, Wackiest Ship article	20	40
1965, Nov. 27	Hogan's Heroes, Liza Minelli article	5	20
1966, Feb. 5	Barbara Eden, 12 O'Clock High article, #6	15	30
1966, Mar. 26	"Batman" star Adam West, #13	60	80
1966, May 21	Wild, Wild West, Dick Van Dyke article	5	15
1966, Sep. 10	1966-67 Fall Preview, #37	30	60
1966, Oct. 8	Jim Nabors, Arthur Miller article	5	15
1966, Dec. 31	Girl From U.N.C.L.E. star Stephanie Powers, Larry Hagman	5	10
1967, Mar. 4	Star Trek, #9	15	25
1967, Mar. 25	I Spy, Batman's Burt Ward article	5	15
1967, May 13	Bewitched, Mission Impossible article	15	30
1967, Jul. 22	Bonanza, Lost In Space article	20	40
1967, Sep. 15	1967-68 Fall Preview	15	35
1967, Sep. 23	The Monkees, General Custer article	15	30
1968, Jan. 6	Wild, Wild West, Your Child and TV article	10	20
1969, Nov. 22	I Dream of Jeannie	5	15
1976, Aug. 28	The Bionic Man, #35	5	10
1976, Nov. 27	Starsky & Hutch, #48	5	10
1977, Jan. 29	Wonder Woman star Linda Carter, #5	5	10
1977, Aug. 13	Starsky & Hutch star David Soul, #3	5	10

Newspapers

Valuable newspapers are those with major events in the headlines. One of the most valuable twentieth-century papers carries the premature "Dewey Defeats Truman" headline.

Prices are for whole issues, not just front pages. Front pages alone are worth less than the prices shown. The major papers of the major American cities are the most valuable, for example *The New York Times, The Chicago Tribune* and *The Washington Post.*

For further reading consult *The Insider's Guide to Old Books, Magazines, Newspapers, Trade Catalogs* by Ron Barlow and Ray Reynolds (Windmill Publishing, El Cajon, CA, 1995).

	LOW	HIGH
Albany Weekly Journal, NY, Aug. 14, 1847	$5	$10
American Federalist Columbian Centinal, Nov. 1825, local and worldwide news and ads, 4 pages	5	10
American Statesman & City Register, Boston, Jan. 30, 1827, news, commerce, and advertising, 4 pages	10	15
Army & Navy Journal, NY, Nov. 28, 1863, Gettysburg Address text	175	250
Athenian Mercury, 1694, British coffeehouse, question and answer, 2 pages	20	30
Balance (and Columbian Repository), Hudson, NY, 1802, Vol. 1, #2, Broke Gaol!, ad for $20 reward for escaped prisoner Robert Dean, 8 pages	5	15
Ballou's Pictorial, Boston, 1855	4	8
Boston Atlas Extra, Thurs., Oct. 18, 1832, electoral votes, 8 pages	15	25
Boston Daily Advertiser, Oct. 12, 1871, Chicago fire	25	40
Boston Daily Atlas, Aug. 28, 1841, UFO report	10	15
Boston Daily Globe, Sep. 20, 1881, Garfield dies, 4 pages	30	40
Boston Herald, Aug. 13, 1892, Lizzie Borden's court plea	20	30
Boston Herald, 1915, war pictorial	5	10
Boston Transcript, Sep. 17, 1849, California Gold Rush	15	20
Buffalo Evening News, May 7, 1945, War Victory issue	2	5
Canal Record, 1908, Panama Canal news, 8 pages	10	20
Charleston Daily News, 1870	3	5
Chicago America, Jun. 22, 1938, Max Schmeling vs Joe Lewis	10	30
Chicago Examiner, Jul. 3, 1938, headline "Chamberlain Warns Britain Ready For War!"	5	10
Chicago Tribune, Aug. 9, 1974, Nixon resigns	15	30
Christian Watchman, Boston, MA, Jun. 20, 1834	4	8
Cleveland Weekly Herald, Sep. 11, 1876, James Gang bank robbery	75	125
Columbian Centinel, Sep. 1, 1813, War of 1812, naval affairs on Lake Ontario	10	20
Columbian Centinel, Mar. 25, 1815, Fort Bowyer Lost, 8 pages	10	20
Commercial Appeal, Memphis, TN, Aug. 17, 1977, Elvis dies	20	30
Connecticut Herald, New Haven, CT, general news	2	5
Continental Journal, Boston, 1780	175	275
Daily Alta California, San Francisco, Apr. 20, 1865, Lincoln assassination	65	100
Daily Argus Leader, SD, Aug. 25, 1928	5	10
Daily Delta, New Orleans, Mar. 11, 1862, *Merrimac* battles	150	250
Daily Evening Bulletin, Philadelphia, Thurs., Jul. 9, 1863, Battle of Gettysburg, 8 pages	150	200
Daily Mail, Nov. 20, 1962, 16 pages	5	10
Daily National Intelligencer, Washington DC, Aug. 7, 1865, headline "Whites Fired-Blacks Hired," troops on the Rio Grande, 4 pages	10	20
Daily Nevada Tribune, Carson City, Dec. 24, 1879, Edison invents light bulb, 4 pages	10	20
Daily State Journal, Austin, TX, Sep. 17, 1870	15	25
Daily State Register, Des Moines, IA, Nov. 4, 1868, Grant elected president	60	90

	LOW	HIGH
Daily Telegraph, London, Sep. 21, 1947, 36 pages	10	20
Desert News, 1869, Mormon related news, 12 pages	20	30
Desert News, Sep. 3, 1877, Brigham Young dies	125	150
Desert News, Mar. 18, 1892, Jack the Ripper	10	20
Des Moines Register, Jan. 18, 1936, Rudyard Kipling dies	10	15
Detroit Daily Tribune, Jul. 22, 1861, first battle of Bull Run	75	120
Detroit Free Press, Nov. 7, 1858, Douglas defeats Lincoln in Illinois Senate race, Russians interfere w/ America, recruitment ad illustration	15	25
Dubuque Herald, Nov. 26, 1881, headline "Bombastic Guiteau"	40	50
Dunlap's American Daily Advertiser, Philadelphia, May 3, 1793	20	30
Eastern Argus Leader, SD, Aug. 25, 1928, saloons	5	10
Essex Gazette, Salem, MA, Nov. 22, 1774, First Continental Congress	3000	5000
Evening News, Newark, NJ, Jul. 21, 1969, moon landing	15	20
Every Saturday, Jun. 17, 1871	40	50
Examiner, London, 1712, 2 pages	20	30
Federal Gazette and Baltimore Daily Advertiser, Aug. 13, 1796	30	50
Gazette of the U.S., Philadelphia, Jan. 12, 1791	35	60
Gentleman's Magazine, London, Jul. 1815, Battle of Waterloo	60	90
Georgetown Gazette, CA, Feb. 2, 1899	8	12
Harper's Weekly, Mar. 16, 1861, Lincoln inauguration	30	50
Harper's Weekly, Dec. 28, 1861, western Missouri refugees	40	50
Harper's Weekly, Nov. 21, 1863, The Great Russian Ball at the Academy of Music, Winslow Homer illustrations	40	60
Harper's Weekly, May 13, 1865, Lincoln's funeral	40	60
Harper's Weekly, May 20, 1865, Lee surrenders to Grant, 16 pages	35	45
Harper's Weekly, Jan. 27, 1872, Ku Klux Klan	30	50
Harper's Weekly, Apr. 26, 1873, The Wreck of the Atlantic	25	35
Hartford Daily Star, Hartford, CT, 1865, Lee surrenders	40	60
Helena Weekly Herald, Jul. 21, 1892, The Dalton Gang, 8 pages	75	125
Herald of The United States, Warren, RI, national and foreign news, 4 pages	25	35
Honolulu Star-Bulletin, May 7, 1945, "EXTRA," V-E Day	35	65
Illustrated London News, May 15, 1927, King George VI crowned	10	20
Independent Chronicle & Boston Patriot, Indian battles, pirates, and politics, 4 pages	5	10
Kingsport Times, Apr. 8, 1934, Clyde Barrow sought in killing	10	30
Lancaster Daily Eagle, Lancaster, OH, Jan. 5, 1933, Coolidge dies	10	20
Lancaster Intelligencer, May 12, 1869	50	85
Liberator, 1837, 4 pages	30	40
Liberator, Jul. 13, 1860, promoting end to slavery, 4 pages	30	50
London Chronicle, 1762	6	10
London Gazette, 1694	40	60
Long Beach Press-Telegram, Dec. 8, 1941, Pearl Harbor	10	20
Los Angeles Evening Herald, Apr. 16, 1912, Sunset Edition, *Titanic* sinks	220	330
Los Angeles Evening Herald, Apr. 30, 1945, Mussolini dies	15	25
Los Angeles Times, May 7, 1945, war ends	25	35
Louisville Daily Journal, 1840-60, general news	5	10
Massachusetts Centinel, 1789	50	75
Massachusetts Spy or *Worcester Gazette,* Oct. 7, 1790	25	45
Miami Student, Miami University, Oxford, OH, Apr. 12, 1945, FDR dies	25	40
Milwaukee Sentinel, Apr. 5, 1968, Martin Luther King shot	20	30
Minneapolis Journal, Oct. 10, 1892, Lizzie Borden	20	35
Minneapolis Times Tribune, Apr. 9, 1940, Hitler seizes Norway	4	10
National Gazette & Literary Register, Oct. 2, 1823, world and national affairs, 4 pages	5	15

	LOW	HIGH
National Intelligencer, Aug. 10, 1801, Benedict Arnold dies	10	20
National Intelligencer, Jan. 29, 1829, Tennessee land bill	50	100
National Intelligencer, Nov. 4, 1868, Grant elected	30	50
Nevada Daily Transcript, Nevada City, CA, Feb. 22, 1873	8	12
New Hampshire Patriot, Sep. 23, 1817, Mississippi joins Union	15	25
New Haven Daily Palladium, Apr. 4, 1882, Jesse James killed	100	150
New Jersey State Gazette, Jul, 2, 1852, Henry Clay dies	20	30
Newport News, RI, Feb. 21, 1934, Dillinger killed	175	250
News of the World, London, Sun., Oct. 16, 1966, 24 pages	10	20
New York Daily News, Aug. 15, 1945, war w/ Japan ends	10	20
New York Daily News, Jul. 21, 1969, man lands on moon	35	55
New York Herald, Aug. 5, 1858, New Bedford Council on Negroes meeting, Lincoln/Douglas Senate race, 8 pages	15	25
New York Herald, Sep. 15, 1858, Tennessee preacher on slavery, Lincoln/ Douglas Senate race, 8 pages	10	20
New York Herald, Sep. 25, 1858, transporting blacks back to Africa, Lincoln/ Douglas Senate race in Illinois, 8 pages	20	30
New York Herald, Sep. 27, 1858, loss of steamship *Austria,* Lincoln/Douglas Senate race, 8 pages	15	25
New York Herald, Jul. 18, 1861, Fairfax Courthouse taken, 8 pages	20	30
New York Herald, Aug. 15, 1861, Battle of Wilson's Creek, 8 pages	20	30
New York Herald, Apr. 15, 1865, Lincoln's assassination, 4 pages	10	30
New York Mirror, 1830s, literature and fine arts	2	5
New York Observer, Oct. 24, 1846	10	15
New York Times, May 6, 1861, Patterson march through Baltimore, 8 pages	20	30
New York Times, Nov. 4, 1861, General Scott retires, 4 pages	20	30
New York Times, Sep. 20, 1869, San Francisco money panic, lynchings in Wisconsin, North Carolina train wreck	10	20
New York Times, Jul. 21, 1969, moon landing	25	45
New York Tribune, Apr. 6, 1865, Richmond occupied, 8 pages	40	50
New York Tribune, Apr. 20, 1865, Lincoln's funeral, 8 pages	20	30
New York Tribune, Aug. 29, 1865, Andersonville horrors detailed	30	40
New York Tribune, Sep. 18, 1865, 8 pages	10	20
Niagara Falls Gazette, Jun. 6, 1944, Normandy invasion	20	30
Niles Weekly Register, State of the Union Address, Dec. 6, 1828, 16 pages	30	40
Norwich Weekly Courier, Apr. 18, 1861, fall of Fort Sumter	50	70
Observer, London, 1686	25	35
Ogden Junction, Utah, 1873, 4 pages	25	35
Panama American, Nov. 11, 1948, Prince Charles born	10	20
Peninsula Times Tribune, Palo Alto, CA, Aug. 30, 1982, Ingrid Bergman dies	10	20
Pennsylvania Gazette, Philadelphia, Jul. 6, 1749, printed by Ben Franklin	2000	3500
Pennsylvania Gazette, Philadelphia, Jul. 3, 1766, repeal of Stamp Act	250	450
Philadelphia Inquirer, Apr. 10, 1867, Alaska purchase	100	170
Philadelphia Inquirer, Jan. 1, 1867, massacre near Fort Laramie, 8 pages	15	25
Pittsburgh Sun-Telegraph, Apr. 4, 1933, headline "Akron Breaks To Pieces: 73 Dead"	10	20
Pittston Gazette, PA, Aug. 4, 1914, WWI begins	15	20
Porcupine's Gazette, Philadelphia, Jun. 22, 1797	20	30
Portland Transcript, Apr. 14, 1877, Crazy Horse surrenders	30	50
Poulson's American Daily Advertiser, 1818, runaway slave ad, vignettes of trains, stagecoaches, and ships, 4 pages	20	40
Providence Gazette, RI, Feb. 5, 1785	30	50
Public Ledger, Philadelphia, Apr. 7, 1882, Jesse James funeral, 4 pages	100	150
Rambler, London, edited by Samuel Johnson, 1750	15	20

	LOW	HIGH
Rhode Island American, Tue., Feb. 11, 1812, William Greene sought by Navy, 4 pages	5	15
Richmond Enquirer, 1823, 4 pages	30	40
Riverside Daily Press, CA, Jun. 20, 1927, general news	4	8
Roanoke World News, Dec. 8, 1941, Pearl Harbor attack	20	30
Sacramento Bee, Nov. 22, 1963, Kennedy shot	20	30
Sacramento Daily Union, Sep. 10, 1867, general news	4	8
Sacramento Weekly Union, Jul. 11, 1863, Gettysburg	300	450
Salem Gazette, Nov. 6, 1783, U.S. Congress passed resolution	40	60
San Diego Union, CA, 1873	15	25
San Francisco Bulletin, Sep. 4, 1886, Geronimo surrenders	6	100
San Francisco Call Bulletin, Aug. 14, 1945, V-J Day	15	25
San Francisco Chronicle, Mar. 7, 1982, John Belushi dies	10	20
San Francisco Examiner, Aug. 3, 1923, Harding dies	25	40
San Francisco Examiner, Apr. 13, 1945, FDR dies	18	25
San Francisco Examiner, Jul. 27, 1956, *Andrea Doria* sinks	10	20
San Francisco Examiner, Nov. 25, 1963, Lee Harvey Oswald dies	10	20
San Francisco Examiner, Oct. 15, 1977, Bing Crosby dies	10	20
San Jose Mercury, CA, Apr. 6, 1976, Howard Hughes dies	10	20
San Jose Mercury, CA, Aug. 6, 1984, Richard Burton dies	10	20
Scientific American, NY, Mar. 2, 1895	12	20
Seattle Daily Times, Aug. 3, 1923, Harding dies	30	50
Sentinel, Richmond, VA, Jul. 27, 1863, Gettysburg, Confederate paper	750	1250
Shipping and Commercial List, NY, 1840	15	25
South Pacific Times, May 21, 1877, special edition, tidal wave and earthquake damage to Peru and Chile, 16 pages	25	40
Springfield Democrat, Apr. 13, 1945, headline "Roosevelt Dies: Pres. Truman to Continue Predecessor's Policies," 6 pages	10	20
Springfield Republican, Sep. 9, 1865, freed Negroes prosper at farming, 8 pages	10	20
St. Louis Times, May 21, 1927, headline "Lindbergh Arrives In Paris"	20	30
St. Louis Dispatch, Jan. 5, 1933, Coolidge dies	10	20
St. Louis Dispatch, Jan. 11, 1935, Emelia Earhart lost in fog	5	10
St. Paul Dispatch, Jan. 15, 1925, Lindbergh kidnapping	5	15
St. Paul Dispatch, Jan. 5, 1933, Coolidge dies	10	20
St. Paul Dispatch, Jan. 29, 1937, Mississippi flood	4	8
St. Paul Dispatch, May 8, 1945, V-E Day	5	15
St. Paul Pioneer Press, Feb. 4, 1924, Woodrow Wilson dies	10	20
St. Paul Pioneer Press, Jan. 13, 1945, Amelia Earhart lands at Oakland	5	15
Stockton Independent, CA, Jun. 29, 1926, general news	5	15
Tatler, London, 1709	15	25
The Times, London, Apr. 11, 1967, 32 pages	5	15
Toledo News-Bee, OH, Apr. 16, 1912, *Titanic* sinks	100	125
Tombstone Epitaph, Tombstone, Arizona Territory, Aug. 6, 1881, Billy the Kid dies	1250	2000
Torrence Daily Breeze, CA, Aug. 17, 1977, Elvis dies	20	35
Universal Yankee Nation, Boston, MA, Feb. 13, 1841	10	25
Vermont Watchman & State Gazette, Nov. 4, 1828, Adams and Rush presidential ticket, 4 pages	10	20
Wapakoneta Daily News, OH, Jul. 21, 1969, Neil Armstrong walks on moon	35	50
Washington Observer, Washington, PA, Feb. 15, 1929, St. Valentine's Day Massacre	120	150

Prints and Lithographs

Audubon

John James Audubon is a name synonymous with bird pictures. His "Birds of America" series is recognized worldwide. Between 1826 and 1842, Audubon traveled throughout the United States and Canada gathering material to paint this famous work. Today, experts believe there are less than 200 sets of "Birds of America" actually bound in volumes. The work was engraved by R. Havell and Son in London. There are 435 plates in a complete set. In 1971 an exact facsimile edition of 250 copies was printed in Amsterdam.

Unless noted otherwise, the prints listed are original Havel prints.

	LOW	HIGH
American Avocet, plate CCCXVIII, 14.75" x 20.4375"	$1200	$1800
American Bittern, plate CCCXXXVII, 26.375" x 31.375"	3000	5000
American Black Bear, Male and Female, plate CXLI, J. T. Bowen, 22" x 28"	2000	4000
American Crossbill, plate CXCVII, 25.8125" x 20.8125"	1200	1800
American Green-Winged Teal, plate CCXXVIII, 12.375" x 19.5"	3200	5500
American Magpie, plate CCCLVII, 25.5" x 21.5"	1200	1900
American Pied-Bill Dobchick, plate CCXLVIII, 14.8125" x 22.5625"	1500	2500
American Ptarmigan, White-Tailed Grous, plate CCCCXVIII, 16.25" x 23"	825	1200
American Redstart, plate XL, 19.375" x 12.125"	2150	2500
American Robin, plate CXXXI, 38" x 25.4375"	4500	6500
American Scoter Duck, plate CCCCVIII, 16.75" x 21.875"	1200	1800
American Snipe, plate CCXLIII, 12.25" x 19.375"	2150	3200
American Swift, plate CLVIII, 19.625" x 12.375"	500	700
American Widgeon, plate CCCXLV, 14.9375" x 19.75"	1500	2500
American Woodcock, plate CCLXVIII, 14.75" x 20.5"	2150	4500
Arctic Yager, plate CCLXVII, 30.3125" x 21.875"	1100	1500
Audubon's Warbler, Hermit Warbler, Black-Throated Gray Warbler, plate CCCXCV, 19.5" x 12.25"	825	1200
Autumnal Warbler, plate LXXXVIII, 19.5625" x 12.9375"	825	1200
Azure Warbler, plate XLVIII, 19.375" x 12.125"	825	1200
Bachman's Finch, plate CLXV, 19.5" x 12.25"	1200	1800
Bachman's Warbler, plate CLXXXV, 20.625" x 14.8125"	1100	1500
Baltimore Oriole, plate XII, 26" x 20.625"	3200	5500
Band-Tailed Pigeon, plate CCCLXVII, 29.375" x 21.75"	3200	5500
Bank Swallow, Violet-Green Swallow, plate CCCLXXXV	200	1200
Barn Owl, plate CLXXI, 39.25" x 26.5"	12,000	26,450
Barn Swallow, plate CLXXIII, 19.5625" x 12.25"	2150	3200
Barred Owl, plate XLVI, 38.25" x 25.75"	3200	5500
Bartram Sandpiper, plate CCCIII, 25" x 36"	1000	1500
Bay-Breasted Warbler, plate LXIX, 19.875" x 12.625"	1100	1800
Bay-Winged Bunting, Male, plate 94, 32.625" x 22.125"	920	1500
Belted Kingfisher, plate LXXVII, 25.75" x 20.625"	2150	4500
Bemaculated Duck, plate CCCXXXVIII, 18.4375" x 23.75"	3200	5500
Bewick's Wren, plate XVIII, 24.875" x 17.5"	350	700
Bird of Washington, plate XI, 39.875" x 26.375"	3000	4000
Black American Wolf, Male, plate LXVII, J. T. Bowen, 20" x 26"	1000	2000
Black & White Creeper, plate XC, 19.5" x 12.25"	700	925
Black & Yellow Warbler, plate CXXIII, 28" x 20"	600	800
Black-Backed Gull, plate CCXLI, 38" x 25.375"	1100	1500
Black-Bellied Plover, plate CCCXXXIV, 15.0625" x 20.9375"	400	600

Left to right: American Black Bear, Male and Female; Black American Wolf, Male.
—Photos courtesy Skinner, Inc., Boston, MA.

	LOW	HIGH
Black-Billed Cuckoo, plate, XXXII, 18.625" x 26.125"	4500	5500
Blackburnian Warbler, plate CXXXV, 19.6875" x 12.375"	1100	1500
Black-Capped Titmouse, plate CLX, 19.625" x 12.375"	825	1200
Black Guillemot, plate CCXIX, 17.625" x 20.375"	1500	2500
Black-Headed Gull, plate CCCXIV, 14.75" x 20.5"	825	1200
Black or Surf Duck, plate CCCXVII, 21.25" x 30.25"	1100	1500
Black-Poll Warbler, plate CXXXIII, 19.625" x 12.375"	825	1200
Black Skimmer or Shearwater, plate CCCXXIII, 21.125" x 21.125"	2150	3200
Black Tern, plate CCLXXX, 19.625" x 12.375"	600	825
Black-Throated Blue Warbler, plate CLV, 19.625" x 12.5"	1100	1500
Black-Throated Bunting, plate CCCLXXXIV, 19.5" x 12.3125"	700	1100
Black-Throated Diver, plate CCCXLVI, 26.25" x 38.625"	4500	6500
Black-Throated Green Warbler, Blackburnian, W. Mourning Warbler, plate CCCXCIX, 19.25" x 12.125"	825	1200
Black Warrior, plate LXXXVI, 39" x 26.375"	1200	5000
Black-Winged Hawk, plate CCCLII, 30.375" x 21.25"	825	1200
Blue-Bird, plate CXIII, 19.625" x 12.375"	1200	1800
Blue-Grey Fly-Catcher, plate LXXXIV, 19.5625" x 12.3125"	825	1200
Blue Grosbeak, plate CXXII, 26" x 20.875"	825	1200
Blue Jay, plate CII, 25.875" x 20.75"	825	1200
Blue Yellow-Backed Warbler, plate XV, 19.3125" x 12.3125"	1500	2150
Boat-Tailed Grackle, plate CLXXXVII, 35.375" x 26"	2400	3100
Bohemian Chatterer, plate CCCLXIII, 19.75" x 12.375"	825	1200
Bonapartian Gull, plate CCCXXIV, 21" x 16.875"	825	1200
Brasilian Caracara Eagle, plate CLXI, 28.5" x 25.625"	4500	6500
Broad-Winged Hawk, plate XCI, 38" x 25.25"	3500	5000
Brown-Headed Worm Eating Warbler, plate CXCVIII, 19.4375" x 12.25"	825	1200
Brown Pelican, plate CCLI, 38" x 25.25"	40,000	63,000
Brown Titlark, plate X, 12.8125" x 20.5"	5500	7000
Buffel-Headed Duck, plate CCCXXV, 14.875" x 20.5"	2150	3200
Burgomaster Gull, plate CCCXCVI, 25.5" x 38"	1500	2500
California Partridge, plate CCCCXIII, 12.25" x 19.5"	1100	1500
Canada Goose, plate, CCI, 38.5" x 26"	4500	6500
Canada Jay, plate CVII, 26" x 20.75"	1100	1500

Left to right: Canvas Backed Duck. —Photo courtesy Gene Harris Antique Auction Center, Inc.; Equimaux Dog. —Photo courtesy Skinner, Inc., Boston, MA.

	LOW	HIGH
Canada Warbler, plate CIII, 19.625" x 12.25"	850	1250
Canadian Titmouse, plate CXCIV, 19.6875" x 12.375"	500	700
Canvas Backed Duck, plate CCCI, 25.8125" x 38.3125"	600	925
Carbonated Warbler, plate LX, 19.375" x 12.125"	1200	1800
Carolina Parrot, plate XXVI, 38.125" x 25.25"	35,000	45,000
Cat Bird, plate CXXVIII, 19.5" x 12.25"	825	1200
Cedar Bird, plate XLIII, 19.375" x 12.1875"	2150	3200
Chestnut-Backed Titmouse, Black-Capt Titmouse, Chestnut-Crowned Titmouse, plate CCCLII, 19.625" x 14.375"	825	1200
Chestnut-Coloured Finch, Black-Headed Siskin, Black Crown Bunting, Arctic Ground-Finch, plate CCCXCIV, 19.375" x 12.25"	1100	1500
Children's Warbler, plate XXXV, 19.5625" x 12.25"	600	1100
Chipping Sparrow, plate CIV, 19.3125" x 12.125"	700	1100
Chuck-Will's Widow, plate LII, 25.875" x 20.5625"	2150	4500
Cock of the Plains, plate CCCLXXI, 25.125" x 38"	3000	4000
Columbian Humming Bird, plate CCCCXXV, 19.5" x 12.5"	1500	2500
Common American Swan, plate CCCCXI, 25.75" x 38.125"	13,000	19,000
Common Buzzard, plate CCCLXXII, 27.375" x 23.75"	1100	1500
Common Cormorant, plate CCLXVI, 25.625" x 38.125"	1100	1500
Common Flying Squirrel, plate XXVIII, J. T. Bowen, 27.375" x 21.5"	400	1700
Common Gull, plate CCXII, 25" x 36"	800	1500
Connecticut Warbler, plate CXXVIII, 32.375" x 22.125"	1265	1500
Cow-Pen Bird, plate XCIX, 25.25" x 38.125"	1200	1380
Crested Grebe, plate CCXCII, 20.625" x 30.3125"	2150	3200
Cuvier's Regulus, plate LV, 19.375" x 12.125"	825	1200
Double-Crested Cormorant, plate CCLVII, 37.625" x 25"	3500	2900
Dusky Duck, plate CCCII, 21.3125" x 30.375"	2150	3200
Dusky Petrel, plate CCXCIX, 12.4375" x 19.5"	600	925
Eider Duck, plate CCXLVI, 25.8125" x 38.5"	11,000	16,000
Equimaux Curlew, plate CCVIII, 25" x 37.875"	1200	1600
Equimaux Dog, plate CXIII, J. T. Bowen, 19" x 25"	800	1200
Ferruginous Thrush, plate CXVI, 38.375" x 25.125"	1500	2500
Field Sparrow, plate CXXXIX, 19.75" x 12.3125"	825	1200
Fish Crow, plate CXLVI, 38.5" x 25.875"	2150	3200

	LOW	HIGH
Fish Hawk, plate LXXXI, 38.5" x 25.625"	30,000	46,000
Florida Cormorant, plate CCLII, 19.75" x 26.5"	1500	2500
Florida Jay, plate LXXXVII, 25.75" x 20.5"	2150	3200
Foolish Guillemot, plate CCXVIII, 12.375" x 19.625"	825	1200
Fork-Tailed Flycatcher, plate CLXVIII, 19.625" x 12.5"	3200	5500
Fork-Tailed Gull, plate CCLXXXV, 12.3125" x 19.25"	825	1200
Fork-Tail Petrel, plate CCLX, 12.25" x 19.375"	825	1200
Fox-Coloured Sparrow, plate CVIII, 12.375" x 19.5625"	825	1200
Fresh Water Marsh Hen, plate CCIII, 12.9375" x 19.625"	1100	1500
Frigate Pelican, plate CCLXXI, 38.25" x 25.375"	6000	10,000
Fulmar Petrel, plate CCLXIV, 12.375" x 19.5625"	825	1200
Gadwall Duck, plate CCCXLVIII, 16.75" x 24.875"	2150	3200
Golden-Crested Wren, plate CLXXXIII, 19.5625" x 12.1875"	600	925
Golden-Crowned Thrush, plate CXLIII, 19.625" x 12.25"	700	1100
Golden-Eye Duck, plate CCCCIII, 12.25" x 19.375"	1200	1800
Golden Plover, plate CCC, 14.6875" x 20.5"	400	600
Golden-Winged Warbler, Cape May Warbler, plate CCCXIV, 20.125" x 28"	350	600
Goshawk & Stanley Hawk, plate CXLI, 38" x 25.5"	2150	3200
Gray Tyrant, plate CLXX, 19.625" x 12.5"	825	1200
Great American Shrike or Butcher Bird, plate CXCII, 26" x 20.8125"	825	1200
Great Auk, plate CCCXLI, 26.125" x 38.5625"	2150	3200
Great Carolina Wren, plate LXXVIII, 19.375" x 12.125"	2150	2500
Great-Footed Hawk, plate XVI, 25.4375" x 38.1875"	3200	5500
Great Horned Owl, plate 61, 37.875" x 25.25"	6500	10,000
Great Marbled Godwit, plate CCXXXVIII, 13.375" x 21"	1100	1500
Great Northern Diver or Loon, plate CCCVI, 25.5" x 38.25"	1500	2600
Green Black-Capt Flycatcher, plate CXXIV, 19.6875" x 12.4375"	825	1200
Green Heron, plate CCCXXXIII, 20.4375" x 22.1875"	3200	5500
Greenshank, plate CCLXIX, 14.875" x 20.625"	1200	1800
Ground Dove, plate CLXXXII, 26.0625" x 20.9375"	2600	3600
Harlequin Duck, plate CCXCVII, 20.6875" x 30.25"	1200	1800
Havell's Tern, Trudeau's Tern, plate CCCCIX, 15.25" x 24.75"	1200	1800
Hemlock Warbler, plate CXXXIV, 19.5625" x 12.625"	825	1200
Hermit Thrush, plate LVIII, 19.4375" x 12.25"	825	1200
Herring Gull, plate CCXCI, 38.1875" x 25.5"	3200	5500
Hooded Merganser, plate CCXXXII, 20.75" x 25.875"	3200	5500
Hooping Crane, plate CCLXI, 35.375" x 22.875"	8600	10,000
Horned Grebe, plate CCLIX, 14.8125" x 20.5"	1200	1900
House Wren, plate LXXXIII, 38" x 25.375"	2000	3400
Hutchins' Barnacle Goose, plate CCLXXVII, 36.75" x 24.125"	3500	6000
Hyperborean Phalarope, plate CCXV, 12.3125" x 19.625"	600	925
Iceland or Jer Falcon, plate CCCLXVI, 38.25" x 25.5"	13,000	19,000
Indigo Bird, plate LXXIV, 19.5625" x 12.25"	1200	1800
Ivory Gull, plate CCLXXXVII, 20.75" x 30.25"	1200	1800
Kentucky Warbler, plate XXXVIII, 19.5625" x 12.25"	825	1200
Kildeer Plover, plate CCXXV, 18.375" x 26"	1265	1500
Kittiwake Gull, plate CCXXIV, 12.375" x 19.5"	600	925
Labrador Falcon, plate CXCVI, 38.5625" x 25.6875"	2600	3600
Lapland Long-Spur, plate CCCLXV, 12.5" x 19.625"	500	700
Lazuli Finch, Clay-Colored Finch, Oregon Snow Finch, plate CCCXCVIII, 28" x 20.125"	800	1600
Least Bittern, plate CCX, 12.375" x 19.625"	1500	2600
Least Stormy-Petrel, plate CCCXL, 12.25" x 19.375"	600	925
Leopard Spermophile, plate XXXIX, J. T. Bowen, 21.875" x 27.75"	230	400

Left to right: Long-Haired Squirrel; Long-Tailed Deer. —Photos courtesy Skinner, Inc., Boston, MA.

	LOW	HIGH
Le Petit Caporal, plate LXXV, 19.5" x 12.25"	1100	1500
Lesser Red-Poll, plate CCCLXXV, 19.5625" x 12.25"	825	1200
Lesser Tern, plate CCCXIX, 19.5" x 12.3125"	1500	2500
Little Auk, plate CCCXXXIX, 12.375" x 19.75"	600	925
Little Sandpiper, plate CCCXX, 25.375" x 38"	1200	1850
Little Screech Owl, plate XCVII, 25.75" x 20.625"	2150	4500
Loggerhead Shrike, plate LVII, 25.875" x 20.5"	1100	1500
Long-Eared Owl, plate CCCLXXXIII, 19.625" x 12.3125"	1200	1800
Long-Haired Squirrel, plate XXVII, J. T. Bowen, 26" x 21"	800	1200
Long-Legged Avocet, plate CCCXXVIII, 14.75" x 20.4375"	1500	2500
Long-Legged Sandpiper, plate CCCXLIV, 12.375" x 19.8125"	600	925
Long-Tailed Deer, plate CXVIII, J. T. Bowen, 19" x 26"	2000	4000
Long-Tailed Duck, plate CCCXII, 21.1875" x 30.125"	1200	1800
Long-Tailed or Dusky Grous, plate CCCLXI, 25.625" x 38.375"	1500	2500
Louisiana Heron, plate CCXVII, 20.75" x 26"	16,000	27,000
Louisiana Tanager, Scarlet Tanager, plate CCCLIV, 19.75" x 12.375"	2150	4500
Louisiana Water Thrush, plate XIX, 19.5625" x 12.375"	825	1100
MacGillivray's Finch, plate CCCLV, 19.375" x 12.25"	825	1200
Mallard Duck, plate CCXXI, 25.625" x 38.875"	35,000	72,000
Mangrove Cuckoo, plate CLXIX, 19.5" x 12.375"	1500	2500
Manks Shearwater, plate CCXCV, 12.3125" x 19.5"	500	700
Maria's Woodpecker, plate CCCCXVII, 30.25" x 22.625"	2150	3200
Marsh Hare, plate XVII, J. T. Bowen, 19.875" x 26.25"	500	1500
Marsh Hawk, plate CCCLVI, 38.25" x 25.625"	4000	9750
Mississippi Kite, plate CXVII, 26.125" x 20.9375"	1500	2500
Mocking Bird, plate XXI, 33.25" x 23.6875"	4500	5500
Mountain Mocking Bird, Varied Thrush, plate CCCLXIX, 19.6875" x 14.375"	1200	1800
Musk-Rat, Musquash, plate XIII, J. T. Bowen, 20.875" x 26.875"	400	900
Nashville Warbler, plate 89, 19.4375" x 12.25"	825	1200
Night Heron or Qua Bird, plate CCXXXVI, 25.375" x 37.875"	4500	6500

Left to right: Northern Hare. —Photo courtesy Skinner, Inc., Boston, MA.; Red-Shouldered Hawk. —Photo courtesy Gene Harris Antique Auction Center, Inc.

	LOW	HIGH
Noddy Tern, plate CCLXXV, 12.25" x 19.25"	500	700
Northern Hare, plate XI, J. T. Bowen, 22" x 28"	1500	3000
Nuttalls Lesser-Marsh Wren, plate CLXXV, 19.5625" x 12.375"	600	925
Olive-Sided Flycatcher, plate CLXXIV, 38.875" x 25.625"	1200	1600
Orange-Crowned Warbler, plate CLXXVIII, 19.625" x 12.375"	500	700
Orchard Oriole, plate XLII, 37" x 24.875"	1200	4300
Painted Finch, plate LIII, 19.5" x 12.125"	2150	3200
Passenger Pigeon, plate LXII, 37.75" x 26.625"	12,000	15,000
Pewit Flycatcher, plate CXX, 19.75" x 12.375"	500	700
Pied Duck, plate CCCXXXII, 21.25" x 30.375"	1500	2500
Pied Oyster-Catcher, plate CCXXIII, 12.375" x 19.5"	1100	1500
Pigmy Curlew, plate CCLXIII, 12.3125" x 19.5"	825	1200
Pine Creeping Warbler, plate CXL, 19.375" x 12.375"	1100	1500
Pine Finch, plate CLXXX, 28" x 20.125"	700	1380
Pine Grosbeak, plate CCCLVIII, 22.25" x 16.125"	1200	1850
Pine Swamp Warbler, plate CXLVIII, 19.75" x 12.4375"	600	925
Pinnated Grous, plate CLXXXVI, 25.3125" x 38.125"	3200	5500
Pin-Tailed Duck, plate CCXXVII, 20.75" x 25.75"	5500	7750
Piping Plover, plate CCXX, 12.375" x 19.5625"	600	925
Plumed-Partridge, Thick-Legged Partridge, plate CCCCXXIII, 12.875" x 21.375"	1200	1800
Prairie Titlark, plate LXXX, 12.125" x 19.9375"	1100	1500
Puffin, plate CCXIII, 12.4375" x 19.75"	2150	3200
Purple Gallinule, plate CCCV, 12.4375" x 19.5"	2150	3200
Purple Heron, plate CCLVI, 25.625" x 38.0625"	4500	6500
Purple Martin, plate XXII, 25.8125" x 20.625"	2150	3200
Purple Sandpiper, plate CCLXXXIV, 22" x 28"	700	1000
Rathbone Warbler, plate LXV, 19.5625" x 12.25"	825	1200

Left to right: Red-Tailed Hawk; Red Texan Wolf, Male. —Photos courtesy Skinner, Inc., Boston, MA.

	LOW	HIGH
Raven, plate CI, 38.3125" x 25.75"	2150	4500
Razor Bill, plate CCXIV, 12.375" x 19.625"	825	1200
Red-Breasted Merganser, plate CCCCI, 25.25" x 38"	2150	4500
Red-Breasted Nuthatch, plate CV, 19.625" x12.375"	600	925
Red-Breasted Sandpiper, plate CCCXV, 12.375" x 19.5"	600	925
Red-Breasted Snipe, plate CCCXXXV, 12.125" x 19.5"	825	1200
Red-Eyed Vireo, plate CL, 19.5625" x 12.3125"	600	925
Red-Headed Duck, plate CCCXXII, 20.75" x 26"	2150	4500
Red-Headed Woodpecker, plate XXVII, 37.625" x 24.875"	2500	4025
Red Phalarope, plate CCLV, 15.75" x 22.5625"	825	1200
Red-Shouldered Hawk, plate 56, 38.125" x 25.5"	7000	11,500
Red-Tailed Hawk, plate 51, 38.125" x 25.0625"	1200	1800
Red Texan Wolf, Male, LXXXII, J. T. Bowen, 19" x 26"	2000	3500
Red-Winged Starling or Marsh Blackbird, plate LXVII, 25.75" x 20.625"	2150	3200
Rice Bird, plate LIV, 19.5" x 12.25"	825	1200
Richardson's Jager, plate CCLXXII, 20.625" x 25.875"	600	925
Ring Plover, plate CCCXXX, 12.125" x 19.4375"	500	700
Rock Grous, plate CCCLXVIII, 16.375" x 21.5625"	1200	1800
Rocky Mountain Plover, plate CCCL, 12.1875" x 19.4375"	500	700
Roscoe's Yellow-Throat, plate XXIV, 19.4375" x 12.125"	825	1100
Roseate Tern, plate CCXL, 19.5" x 12.25"	2150	3200
Rose-Breasted Grosbeak, plate CXXVII, 26 x 20.875"	2150	4500
Ruby Crowned Wren, plate CXCV, 19.6875" x 12.5"	825	1200
Ruby-Throated Humming Bird, plate XLVII, 25.8125" x 20.625"	11,000	16,000
Ruddy Duck, plate CCCXLIII, 16.125" x 26.25"	1500	2500
Ruddy Plover, plate CCXXX, 12.25" x 19.5"	600	825
Ruffed Grouse, plate XLI, 25.375" x 38.125"	4500	6500
Ruff-Necked Humming-Bird, plate CCCLXXIX, 19.625" x 12.3125"	3200	5500

	LOW	HIGH
Rusty Grakle, plate CLVII, 25.5625" x 20.375"	600	925
Salt Water Marsh Hen, plate CCIV, 19.5625" x 14.875"	600	825
Savannah Finch, plate CIX, 19.6875" x 12.375"	825	1200
Say's Marmot Squirrel, CXIV, J. T. Bowen, 19" x 24"	300	600
Scaup Duck, plate CCXXIX, 12.625" x 19.5"	2150	4500
Schinz's Sandpiper, plate CCLXXVIII, 12.1875" x 19.375"	600	925
Sea-Side Finch, plate XCIII, 39.25" x 26.375"	3000	4000
Selby's Flycatcher, plate IX, 20.625" x 23.9375"	825	1100
Semipalmated Snipe or Willet, plate CCLXXIV, 14.75" x 20.3125"	825	1200
Sharp-Shinned Hawk, plate CCCLXXIV, 19.5" x 14.75"	825	1200
Sharp-Tailed Grous, plate CCCLXXXII, 21.625" x 29.1875"	1200	1800
Shore Lark, plate CC, 12.3125" x 19.5625"	600	925
Small Green Crested Flycatcher, plate CXLIV, 19.3125" x 12.125"	1100	1500
Snow Bird, plate XIII, 38.875" x 25.75"	800	1150
Snow Bunting, plate CLXXXIX, 19.5" x 12.3125"	825	1200
Snow Goose, plate CCCLXXXI, 25.75" x 38"	2150	4500
Snowy Heron or White Egret, plate CCXLII, 25.75" x 20.75"	16,000	27,000
Snowy Owl, plate CXXI, 38.375" x 25.75"	27,000	37,000
Solitary Sandpiper, plate CCLXXXIX, 12.375" x 19.3125"	1200	1800
Song Sparrow, plate XXV, 19.5" x 12.25"	825	1100
Sora or Rail, plate CCXXXIII, 12.25" x 19.5"	500	700
Spotted Grous, plate CLXXVI, 25.625" x 38.0625"	3200	5500
Spotted Sandpiper, plate CCCX, 14.75" x 21.125"	825	1200
Stanley Hawk, plate XXXVI, 38.3125" x 25.625"	2150	2500
Summer or Wood Duck, plate CCVI, 38.375" x 25.8125"	10,000	13,000
Tawny Thrush, plate CLXIV, 19.5" x 12.3125"	1100	1500
Tell-Tale Godwit or Snipe, plate CCCVIII, 14.875" x 20.9375"	825	1200
Tengmalm's Owl, plate CCCLXXX, 20.5" x 15.625"	600	925
Texan Lynx, Female, XCII, J. T. Bowen, 19" x 26"	800	1200
Three-Toed Woodpecker, plate CXXXII, 26.0625" x 20.875"	2150	4500
Towhe Bunting, plate XXIX, 19.5" x 12.3125"	825	1200
Townsend's Sandpiper, plate CCCCXXVIII, 18.625" x 16"	500	700
Traill's Flycatcher, plate XLV, 19.4375" x 12.25"	600	925
Tree Sparrow, plate CLXXXVIII, 19.5" x 12.25"	700	1100
Tropic Bird, plate CCLXII, 20.75" x 30.25"	2150	4500
Trumpeter Swan, plate CCCVI, 26" x 39"	20,000	93,000
Tufted Auk, plate CCXLIX, 14.3125" x 19.5625"	1100	1500
Tyrant Fly-Catcher, plate LXXIX, 19.375" x 12.25"	1100	1500
Violet-Green Cormorant, Townsend's Cormorant, plate CCCCXII, 23.625" x 17.25"	1100	1500
Virginian Partridge, plate LXXVI, 24.75" x 38.1875"	3200	5500
Virginia Rail, plate CCV, 14.875" x 20.5"	700	1100
Wandering Shearwater, plate CCLXXXIII, 12.4375" x 19.75"	600	825
Warbling Flycatcher, plate CXVIII, 19.5625" x 12.25"	1500	2500
Western Duck, plate CCCCXXIX, 12.75" x 21.5"	825	1200
Whip-Poor-Will, plate LXXXII, 25.875" x 20.875"	1700	7000
White-Bellied Swallow, plate XCVIII, 19.5" x 12.25"	600	925
White-Breasted Black-Capped Nuthatch, plate CLII, 26.125" x 20.875"	2150	4500
White-Eyed Flycatcher or Vireo, plate LXIII, 19.5" x 12.1875"	825	1200
White-Headed Eagle, plate XXXI, 25.5" x 38.25"	3200	5500
White Heron, plate CCCLXXXVI, 25.9375" x 38.375"	13,000	19,000
White Ibis, plate CCXXII, 20.875" x 26"	20,000	30,000
White-Legged Oyster Catcher, Slender-Billed Oyster Catcher, plate CCCCXXVII, 21.5" x 27.5"	1200	1800

	LOW	HIGH
White-Winged Crossbill, plate CCCLXIV, 19.6875" x 12.375"	1100	1500
White-Winged Silvery Gull, plate CCLXXXII, 20.8125" x 26"	825	1200
Willow Grous or Large Ptarmigan, plate CXCI, 25.375" x 38"	3200	5500
Wilson's Plover, plate CCIX, 22" x 28"	450	800
Winter Hawk, plate LXXI, 25.1875" x 38.125"	2150	3200
Winter Wren, Rock Wren, plate CCCLX, 19.75" x 12.375"	700	1100
Wood Pewee, plate CXV, 19.6875" x 12.375"	600	925
Wood Wren, plate CLXXIX, 19.5625" x 12.5"	825	1200
Worm Eating Warbler, plate XXXIV, 19.625" x 12.25"	1100	1500
Yellow-Breasted Chat, plate CXXXVII, 26 x 20.75"	3200	5500
Yellow-Breasted Rail, plate CCCXXIX, 12.25" x 19.375"	600	925
Yellow-Crown Warbler, plate CLIII, 19.625" x 12.375"	1500	2500
Yellow-Poll Warbler, plate XCV, 19.3125" x12.125"	825	1200
Yellow Shank, plate CCLXXVIII, 24.75" x 37.625"	4000	8600
Yellow Throated Warbler, plate LXXXV, 19.5" x 12.375"	825	1200
Yellow-Winged Sparrow, plate CXXX, 19.5625" x 12.3125"	700	1100
Zenaida Dove, plate CLXII, 25.375" x 20.625"	825	1200

Left to right: Say's Marmot Squirrel; Texan Lynx, Female. —Photos courtesy Skinner, Inc., Boston, MA.

Currier & Ives

In 1835, Nathaniel Currier started a lithography company in New York. James Ives joined in 1852 as a bookkeeper. Currier and Ives was unique in its ability to combine artistic talent, skilled craftsmanship, appropriate technology and merchandising acumen into a successful business enterprise. It employed well-known artists of the day, including Maurer, Palmer, Tait and Worth. The finest materials were used: stones from Bavaria (where lithography was invented), lithographic crayons from France and colors from Austria. The firm invented a lithographic crayon, reputed to be superior to all others, and produced a lithographic ink of beef suet, goose grease, white wax, castile soap, gum mastic, shellac and gas black. Mass distribution and low cost were the keys to success. Uncolored prints were sold for as little as 6¢ each and even large-colored folios sold for no more than $3. Prints were sold door-to-door by peddlars and in the streets by pushcart vendors, and even overseas through agents. The firm of Currier and Ives was dissolved in 1907. Although an estimated ten million prints sold, only a small percentage survive today.

Published in various sizes, the prints are commonly grouped into folio sizes: *Very Small* (up to approximately 7" x 9"), *Small* (approximately 8.8" x 12.8"), *Medium* (approximately 9" x 14" to 14" x 20") and *Large* (anything over 14" x 20"). The sizes pertain to the image only, not the margin. Often, print owners trimmed the margins of the pictures, so an uncut print is more valuable than a pared one.

Most prints were struck in black and white and then hand colored. Because of this method, different colorings of the same print are found. Folio sizes *Very Small, Small* and *Medium* were completed in this manner. However, the *Large* folios were sometimes partially printed in color and then finished by hand, usually by only one artist. Many of these prints have been reprinted often. Beware buying a modern calendar print.

Each print is given with its Conningham number (C#), a reference to the checklist by Frederic A. Conningham, *Currier and Ives Prints: An Illustrated Check List, Revised (*Crown, NY, 1970, out of print). Photos illustrating this category are courtesy Skinner, Inc., Boston, MA.

Large Folio

C#		LOW	HIGH
23	Abraham Lincoln/The Martyr President, 1860	$300	$500
33	Across the Continent, 1868	10,000	15,000
106	American Autumn Fruits, 1865	2000	3000
155	The American Fireman, Rushing to the Conflict, 1858	690	1200
180	The American National Game of Baseball, 1866	4000	6000
183	American Prize Fruit, 1862	1800	2500
303	Attack on the Home Guard, 1864	600	1000
406	The Battle of Gettysburg, 1863	1400	1500
1145	Clipper Ship *Flying Cloud,* 1852-53	1500	3000
1171	Clipper Ship *Young America,* 1852-53	1500	3000
1336	Cutter Yacht *Bianca,* 1854	800	1200
1343	Cutter Yacht *Scud,* 1855	800	1200
1666	Eclipse and Sir Henry	1500	2500
2458	Government House	1000	1500
2596	The Great East River Suspension Bridge, 1883	630	800
3399	Lady Woodruff, Miller's Damsel, General Darcy, and Stella, 1857	1400	2600
3943	Mama's Darling	250	400
4116	Midnight Race on the Mississippi, 1860	7000	9000
4126	Mill River Scenery	2000	3500
5171	The Road–Winter, 1853	3000	5000
5264	Rush for the Pole, 1877	2000	4000
6273	Winning the Card	2000	3000
6725	Winning the Card	2000	3000

Medium Folio

C#		LOW	HIGH
92	Amateur Muscle in the Shell, 1876	$400	$500
95	The Ambuscade/Winter Scene	1500	2500
179	American Mountain Scenery, 1868	450	600
228	The Angels in the Battlefield	175	300
240	Antelope Shooting/Fatal Curiosity	1500	3000
452	Beautiful Blonde	90	150
841	Castle Howard	190	300
1023	Cherry Time, 1866	700	1200
1812	The Fairies Home, 1868	225	300
1842	The Family Photographer Register	150	300
2132	Free Lunch, 1872	350	600
2281	General James A. Garfield/20th President	175	250
2608	Great Exhibition of 1860	600	900
3364	Knocked into a Cocked Hat, 1848	200	300
3387	Lady Suffolk, 1850	1800	2500
3437	Landscape and Ruins	250	350
3534	The Lightning Express, 1855	1500	2700
3694	The Little Recruit, 1863	120	150
3717	The Little Sisters, 1862	130	175
3829	The Lucky Escape	375	500
3870	Magic Lake	175	250
3949	Mama's Rosebud, 1858	150	200
4023	Martha Washington	90	150
4127	The Mill-Stream	400	500
4132	Miller's Home	600	1000
4141	Minnehaha Falls, Minnesota	400	500
4273	The Mustang Team	450	550
4366	Napoleon Bonaparte/Emperor of France	100	200
4449	New York Pilot's Monument, 1855	250	400
4520	Now and Then	250	350
4668	Over the Garden Wall	250	400
4722	Pasture/Noontide	300	350
4733	Peace and Plenty, 1871	400	500
4744	Pennsylvania Hall, Bristol College	250	350
4774	The Pic-Nic Party	250	300
4795	Playful	150	200
4823	The Political Gymnasium	300	400
4857	The Poultry Yard, 1870	250	300
5178	Robert Burns	150	200
5441	Scottish Boarder	250	400
5531	Sinking of the Steamship *Elbe*	300	400
5582	A Snowy Morning, 1864	2250	3000
5601	The Soldier's Memorial, 1862	200	300
5613	Some Pumpkins	350	450
5623	Sophia	100	200
5690	Stag Hunt at Killarney	75	100
5815	Still Hunting on the Susquehanna	1000	1600
5878	Summer Time	400	500
5889	Sunny Morning	300	400
5896	The Sunset Tree	300	400
5958	Taking Comfort	250	350
6681	Will He Bite?, 1868	320	500

Right: #122, American Country Life. October Afternoon, large folio, $1495 at auction.

Left: #133, American Farm Scenes, large folio, $1265 at auction.

Right: #206, An American Winter Scene, small folio, $2415 at auction.

Left: #777, Camping Out, large folio, $1840 at auction.

—Photos courtesy Skinner, Inc., Boston, MA.

Small Folio

C#		LOW	HIGH
32	The Accommodation Train, 1876	$400	$600
37	Adam and Eve Drive Out of Paradise	100	200
53	An Affair of Honor/The Critical Moment	150	300
66	Agricultural Hall, 1876	200	300
187	American Railroad Scene: Snowbound, 1871	1500	3300
199	American Thoroughbreds	350	500
205	American Whalers Crushed in Ice	150	300
238	Annie	80	150
279	As He Was/A Young Man of Fashion	185	250
281	As Kind as a Kitten	225	300
343	The Bad Husband	150	250
381	Battle of Boyne	100	200
623	Boston Harbor	400	500
784	Can't Be Beat, 1880	175	250
820	Caroline	80	150
1318	The Crucifixion, 1894	20	40
1421	Darktown Sociables/A Fancy Dress Surprise, 1890	250	350
1462	Day Before the Wedding	100	200
1790	The Express Train, 1855	1200	2000
1792	The Express Train, 1870	1500	2300
1824	Falling Springs, VA, 1868	300	400
1915	Father's Pet, 1851	90	150
2146	Friendship, Love, and Truth, 1874	200	300
3140	Ivanhoe	100	200
3204	Jersey Litchfield Bull	200	300
3257	John Bull Makes a Discovery	200	300
3331	Killeney Hill, Dublin	90	150
3355	Kitties on a Frolic	150	300
3360	Kitty and Rover	220	400
3403	Lafayette at the Tomb of Washington, 1845	100	150
3449	Last Shake, 1885	120	200
3473	Learning to Ride	125	200
3503	Life and Death	100	200
3523	The Life of a Sportsman/Camping in the Woods, 1872	450	550
3539	Lilly and Her Kitty	130	200
3581	Little Boy Blue	110	150
4050	Mary Ann	80	150
4079	Mating in the Woods/Ruffed Grouse, 1871	550	600
4099	Meadowside Cottage	350	400
4133	Mind Your Lesson, Fido	125	200
4176	Moonlight in the Tropics	100	200
4356	My Three White Kittens	140	200
4414	A New England Beauty	75	200
4498	Noah's Ark	200	250
5469	Setters, 1846	300	400
5487	The Sheep Pasture	175	250
5545	The Skating Carnival	600	700
5586	Sofia, 1846	75	100
5609	Soldier's Return, 1846	150	200
5654	Spirit of '76/Stand by the Flag	250	350
5694	Star of Love	75	100
5738	Steamer *Pilgrim*/Flagship of the Fall River Line	300	350

Right: #845, Catching a Trout, large folio, $1150 at auction.

Left: #1587, A Disputed Heat, Claiming a Foul, large folio, $1035 at auction.

Right: #2800, Herb and Flora Temple, large folio, $1150 at auction.

Left: #2856, Home From the Brook, The Lucky Fisherman, large folio, $1150 at auction.

—Photos courtesy Skinner, Inc., Boston, MA.

Very Small Folio

C#		LOW	HIGH
2	The Abbey	$100	$300
177	American Landscape/Sacandaga Creek	200	300
355	The Baltimore Oriole	175	250
859	Cattskill Creek	175	250
1005	Charles O. Scott/The Prize Baby, 1855	85	150
1209	Coloring His Meerschaum, 1879	175	300
2076	Foliage	170	250
3293	The Jolly Smoker, 1880	100	200
3316	Juno	75	100
3357	Kitty	100	200
3420	Lake Winnipiseogee, New Hampshire	300	400
3538	Lilly	75	100
3866	Magic Grottoes	100	150
4025	Martha Washington	75	100
4142	Minnie	75	100
4193	Morgan Lewis	65	100
4284	My Cottage Home	200	300
4499	A Nobby Tandem	100	200
4507	Northern Scenery	120	150
4610	On the Seine	75	100
4659	Our Village Home	175	200
4962	Propagation Society/More Freedom Than Welcome, 1853	150	200
5140	A Ride to School	375	400
5148	Ripe Fruits	180	250
5346	St. Mary's Abbey/Highland Falls	100	200
5386	Sappho	80	120
5682	Squirrel Shooting	300	350

Trade Cards

94	Amateur Muscle in the Shell, 1880	$70	$100
512	Between Two Fires, 1879	70	100
541	A Bite All Around, 1880	70	100
548	Black Duck Shooting, 1879	70	100
572	Blood Will Tell, 1879	70	100
588	Bolted	65	90
616	The Boss of the Road, 1880	80	100
730	Bull Dozed, 1877	70	100
790	A Capital Cigar	70	100
863	Caught Napping, 1879	80	100
1209A	Coloring His Meerschaum, 1879	75	100
1287	Crack Trotter in the Harness of the Period, 1880	75	100
1456	Dawn of Love	70	100
1464	The Deacon's Mare, 1880	75	100
1832A	Falsetto, 1881	85	150
2366	Getting a Hoist, 1879	75	100
2755	Hattie Woodward, 1881	85	150
3132	Iroquois–Winner of the Derby, 1881	85	150
4586	The Old Suit and the New Suit, 1880	80	120
4747	People's Evening Line, 1881	100	200

Right: #3514, Life in the Woods, Starting Out, large folio, $1495 at auction.

Left: #4870, Preparing for Market, large folio, $1150 at auction.

Right: #4974, The Pursuit, large folio, $690 at auction.

Left: #6170, 'Trotting Cracks' on the Snow, large folio, $1093 at auction.

—Photos courtesy Skinner, Inc., Boston, MA.

Louis Icart

Louis Icart's works demonstrate a mastery of dry point, line etching, aquatint, and their variations. Icart produced up to 500 prints each of over 1,000 subjects. However, his works are scarce because many have been lost or destroyed.

Most prints bear his hallmark near the edge of the print. His signature is also easily identifiable, although subject to fogery and sometimes found on lithographic reproductions of his prints. Earlier works will have his signature but may not bear the hallmark. Most will, however, bear the stamp of his gallery, an oval shape with the letters EM for "estampe moderne." It is possible to have an original Icart with no hallmark at all, but this is rare. Icart often pulled two editions, one for Europe and one for American distribution. Sometimes the number is preceded by the letter "A" for an American edition, for example "A 75/120." Not all prints were numbered.

For more information see *Icart: The Complete Etchings, 3rd Edition* by William R. Holland, Clifford P. Catania and Nathan D. Isen (Schiffer, Atglen, PA, 1998).

	LOW	HIGH
Awakening, 1925, 15.5"	$800	$1000
Before Christmas, 1922, 15" x 10.25"	3000	6000
Belle Rose, 1933, 16.75" x 21.25"	1500	2000
Bubbles, 1930, 17.25" x 13"	5750	6500
Coursing, 12" x 16.5"	8500	11,500
D'Artagnan, 1931, 20.75" x 14"	1200	1500
Delilah, 1929, 20.5" x 13"	1000	1200
Don Juan, 21" x 14"	1200	1700
Faust, 20.25" x 12.75"	2200	3000
Favorite, 1936, 14.5" x 14.5"	1800	2000
Fountain, 1936, 21" x 8.875"	2000	3000
Four Dears, 1929, 21.25" x 15"	2000	2500
Frolicking, 14.75" x 19"	1600	2200
Gay Señorita, 1939, 18.5" x 22"	1500	2000
Grande Eve, 1934, 31" x 20.25"	15,000	20,000
Green Robe, 13.75" x 17.5"	1200	1700
Guardians, 1936, 14.5" x 14.5"	1700	2000
Hydrangeas, 1929, 16.75" x 21.25"	1500	2000
Jeunesse, 1930, 24.5" x 16"	1800	2000
Joan of Arc, 1929, 22.5" x 15.125"	1200	1500
Kiss of Motherland, 22" x 13.75"	1700	2400
La Cachette, 1927, 18.75" x 15.25"	1200	1500
Lampshade, 1948, 15.625" x 19.25"	1000	1500
Laziness, 15" x 19.25"	1900	2600
L'Elan, 1928, 20" x 15"	800	1200
Lilies, 1934, 28.375" x 19.5"	2000	3500
Little Bo Peep, 20.25" x 13.5"	1600	2200
Lovers, 1930, 21" x 14.125"	1000	1500
Love's Blossom, 1937, 17.5" x 25.25"	2500	3000
Masks, 1926, 19" x 15"	1000	1500
Mealtime, 1927, 18.25" x 14"	1250	1500
Mignon, 1928, 20.25" x 13.5"	800	1000
Miss America, 1927, 21" x 17"	2300	2500
Mon Chien, 1929, 10" x 10.5"	1400	1800
Moquerie, 1928, 15.8975" x 19"	800	1200
Old Yarn, 17" x 21.25"	1100	1500
On the Beach, 1925, 11" x 16"	1300	1800
Orange Cellar, 19" x 14.5"	2800	3900

	LOW	HIGH
Orchids, 1937, 28" x 19.5"	2100	2500
Pink Slip, 1939, 19.5" x 11.625"	1000	1500
Poem, 1928, 19" x 22.75"	1700	2000
Rainbow, 1930, 25.125" x 17.25"	2500	3000
Recollections, 1928, 12.5" x 17.125"	1000	1500
Red Gate, 1925, 17.75" x 13"	750	1200
Repose, 1934, 19.5" x 46"	11,000	15,000
Sheep Dog, 1925, 15 x 18"	1200	1500
Sleeping Beauty, 15.5" x 19.25"	1900	2600
Snack, 1927, 18.375" x 14"	1200	1500
Spanish Dancer, 21.25" x 14"	1700	2400
Storyteller, 1926, 15" x 18"	1000	1500
Tsar, 10.5" x 8.25"	1200	1700
Two Beauties, 1931, 17.5" x 25.5"	20,000	25,000
Unmasked, 12" x 8"	1200	1700
Waltz Echoes, 19" x 19"	2900	4100
Wisteria, 1940, 18" x 21.75"	1500	2000
Young Mother, 1929, 19.75" x 25.5"	3000	6000
Youth, 1930, 24.25" x 15.875"	2500	3000

Left: Moquerie.
Right: Mon Chien.

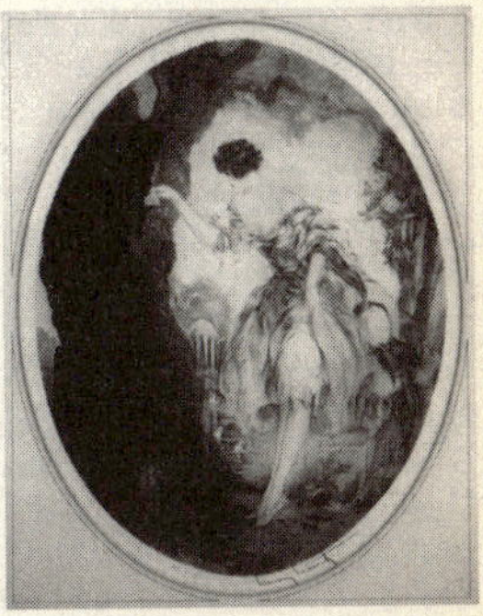

Left to right: Jeunesse; L'Elan; La Cachette. —Photos courtesy Skinner, Inc., Boston, MA.

Maxfield Parrish

Maxfield Parrish illustrated magazines and advertisements for various national companies during the early 1900s. He also created many limited edition prints. There are many reproductions on the market. See *Maxfield Parrish, 3rd Edition* by Erwin Flacks (Colectors Press, Portland, OR, 1998) for additional information.

Old King Cole, smoking tobacco package, unopened, $220 at auction. —Photo courtesy Wm. Morford.

	LOW	HIGH
A Dark Futurist, *Life* magazine cover, Mar. 1, 1923	$75	$125
American Water Color Society, poster, 1899, 14" x 22"	1500	2500
An Ancient Tree, calendar, Brown & Bigelow, small	250	450
And Night Is Fled, playing cards, Edison Mazda, 1918	300	400
Arizona, thermometer, Thomas D. Murphy Co. 1940s	100	200
Aucassin Seeks For Nicolette, print, Charles Scribner's Sons, 1903, 11.5" x 17"	500	550
Autumn, print, P. F. Collier & Son, 1905, 10" x 12"	150	250
Boboli Garden, print, The Century Co., 1915, 5" x 7.75"	50	80
Broadmoor, The, brochure	75	150
Cadmus Sowing the Dragon's Teeth, print, P. F. Collier & Son, 1909, 9.25" x 11.5"	125	175
Canyon, The, print, House of Art, 1924, 12" x 15"	250	300
Cassim, print, P. F. Collier & Son, 1906, 9" x 11"	125	185
Christmas Morning, print, Brown & Bigelow, 1949	200	325
Circe's Palace, print, 1908, 9.25" x 11.5"	150	225
City of Brass, print, P. F. Collier & Son, 1905, 9" x 11"	120	160
Cleopatra, print, House of Art, 1917, 6.25" x 7"	200	300
Comical Toy Soldiers, game, Parker Bros., 1921	1500	2000
Contentment, playing cards, Edison Mazda, 1928	200	300
Daybreak, print, House of Art, 1923, 10" x 18"	250	450
Dream Garden, print, Curtis Publishing Co., 1915, 14" x 24.5"	550	1000
Dreaming, calendar, Thomas D. Murphy, 1939, small	300	500
Dreamlight, calendar, Edison Mazda, 1925, small	1200	1800
Dust Jacketer-Kiss Cosmetics, poster, girl in swing, 1916	800	1500
Dust Jacketer-Kiss Waltz, sheet music, 1925	125	200
Dutch Boy, poster, Colgate & Co., 1897	2000	3000
Easter, print, P. F. Collier & Son, 1905, 8" x 10"	125	200
Ecstasy, calendar, Edison Mazda, 1930, large	1500	2000
Enchantment, calendar, Edison Mazda, 1926, small	1500	2000
Evening, calendar, Brown & Bigelow, 1947, small	250	350
Evening, Early Snow, *Yankee* magazine cover, Dec. 1979	25	45
Evening Shadows, calendar, Brown & Bigelow, 1962	200	300

Garden of Allah, print, 1918, 20.5" x 35", $575 at auction. —Photo courtesy Wm. Morford.

	LOW	HIGH
Fisk Tire, poster, The Magic Circle, 1919, 5" x 10.75"	1000	2000
Fountain of Pirene, The, Charles Scribner's Sons, 1907, 9.25" x 11.5"	150	200
Gardener, The, *Yankee* magazine cover, May 1977	15	35
Garden of Allah, Crane's Chocolate Box, 1918	400	700
Garden of Opportunity, print, Curtis Publishing Co., 1915, 10.75" x 20.5"	500	700
Glen, The, print, Brown & Bigelow, small	250	350
Harvest, print, Dodge Publishing Co., 1905, 8" x 10"	225	300
Haverford College Athletic Assoc., poster, 1891, 4" x 6.5"	1000	2000
Her Window, *Life* magazine cover, Aug. 24, 1922	75	125
Hilltop, print, House of Art, 1927, 12" x 20"	350	550
History of the Fisherman and the Genie, print, P. F. Collier & Son, 1906, 9" x 11"	100	150
Hornby's Oatmeal, poster, 1896, 28" x 42.5"	2000	3000
Humpty Dumpty, *Life* magazine, Mar. 17, 1921	225	400
Interlude, print, House of Art, 1924, 12" x 15"	250	350
Jack and the Beanstalk, poster, D. M. Ferry Co., 1923, 19" x 27"	1500	2000
Jack Frost, print, P. F. Collier & Son, 1936, 12.5" x 13"	250	450
Jack Sprat, poster, Swift Premium Ham, 1919, 15" x 20"	1000	1500
John Cox–His Book, bookplate	60	90
Kiddies' Komical Kut Out, jigsaw puzzle, Parker Bros., 1913	750	1500
Lampseller of Baghdad, calendar, Edison Mazda	650	1050
Landing of the Brazen Boatman, The, print, P. F. Collier & Son, 1907, 9" x 11.125"	150	250
Land of Make-Believe, calendar, Sunlit Road, 1925	100	150
Lights of Welcome, calendar, Brown & Bigelow, 1952	200	300
Morning, print, House of Art, 1922, 12" x 15"	300	400
My Homeland, print, Brown & Bigelow, 1964	75	125
New Moon, calendar, Brown & Bigelow, 1958, medium	375	450
Only God Can Make a Tree, calendar, Thomas D. Murphy, 1938	200	400
Our Beautiful America, calendar, Brown & Bigelow, 1942	100	175
Our Boys, playbill, West Chester Cricket Club, 1891	300	400
Page, The, print, House of Art, 1925, 9.75" x 12"	200	300
Pandora, print, P. F. Collier & Son, 1909, 9" x 11"	150	250
Peter, Peter Pumpkin Eater, poster, D. M. Ferry Co., 1918	1000	1500
Pied Piper, postcard, 1915	100	150
Pied Piper, print, P. F. Collier & Son, 1909, 6.75" x 21"	750	1200
Polly Put the Kettle On, *Vanity Fair* magazine cover, Feb. 1922	65	125
Prince Codadad, print, P. F. Collier & Son, 1906, 9" x 11"	125	200
Reveries, print, House of Art, 1928, 6" x 10"	100	150
Romance, print, House of Art, 1925, 23.5" x 14.25"	1000	1400

	LOW	HIGH
Rubaiyat, House of Art, 1917, 2" x 8.5"	150	250
Search for the Singing Tree, Calendar of Friendship, 1922	75	125
Sherman, The, cigar box label, 1927	800	1200
Shower of Fragrance, print, Curtis Publishing Co., 1912	225	275
Sinbad Plots Against the Giant, print, P. F. Collier & Son, 1907, 9" x 11"	125	200
Solitude, calendar, Edison Mazda, 1932, small	1200	1600
Spirit of Dust Jacketer-Kiss, The, calendar, 1925	350	550
Spirit of the Night, calendar, Edison Mazda, 1919, small	2000	3000
Spring, print, P. F. Collier & Son, 1905, 9.75" x 11.75"	100	150
Sterling Cycle Works, catalog cover, 1897	325	450
Sugar-Plum Tree, print, Charles Scribner's Sons, 1905, 11" x 16"	225	300
Summer, print, Charles Scribner's Sons, 1905, 11" x 16"	150	250
Tea? Guess Again, *Life* magazine cover, Jul. 20, 1922	75	125
Tempest, The, print, P. F. Collier & Son, 1909, 7" x 7"	100	150
Thanksgiving, print, P. F. Collier & Son, 1909, 9" x 11"	225	300
Three Shepherds, print, P. F. Collier & Son, 1904, 11" x 13.25"	200	300
Twilight, calendar, Brown & Bigelow, 1937, small	75	95
Twilight Hour, The, calendar, Brown & Bigelow, 1951	200	300
Valley of Diamonds, print, P. F. Collier & Sons, 1907	125	175
Venetian Lamplighter, calendar, Edison Mazda, 1924, large	3000	4000
Village Brook, The, calendar, Brown & Bigelow, 1941, small	225	350
Wassail Bowl, print, P. F. Collier & Son, 1909, 3.5" x 2.5"	75	125
White Birch in Winter, *Yankee* magazine cover, Dec. 1935	45	75
Wild Geese, *Spinning Wheel* magazine cover, Nov. 1973	30	50
With Trumpet and Drum, print, Charles Scribner's Sons, 1905, 11.25" x 16.5"	250	350
Wynken, Blynken, and Nod, print, Charles Scribner's Sons, 1905, 10.25" x 14.5"	225	300
You and Your Work, *Tranquility* magazine cover, May 13, 1944	55	125

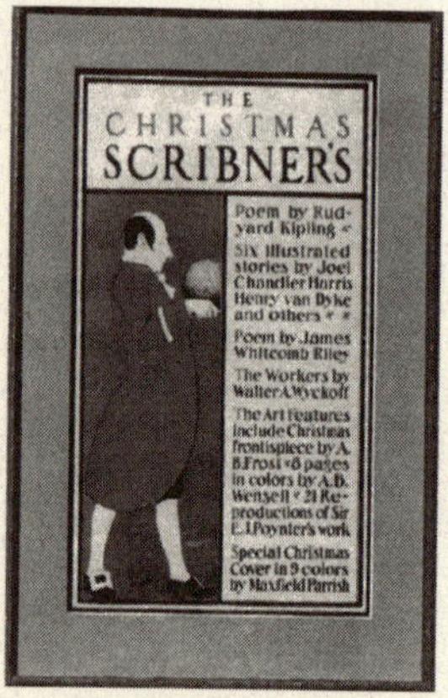

Left to right: Butler Carrying Christmas Pudding, poster advertising Scribner's *magazine Christmas issue, c1897, 27.5" x 19.625", $1925 at auction; Waterfall, playing cards, Edison Mazda, 1931, $468 at auction. —Photos courtesy Wm. Morford.*

Radios

The following section encompasses several areas of radio collecting. Included are early examples from the 1920s, Catalin plastic case radios from the 1930s and 1940s, later Cold War-era radios from the 1950s and 1960s, early transistor radios from the same era and novelty and advertising radios.

Catalin radios are the beautiful marbleized or mottled-look radios. They are often mistakenly called Bakelite. Catalin refers to a clear plastic that can be colored, first developed by the Catalin Corporation. The prices of Catalin radios shot up dramatically in the late 1980s to early 1990s. Interest has cooled but they still draw great interest. In the case of Catalin radios many collectors suggest "don't touch that dial" because heat can crack the cases. Catalins have also been known to shrink, crack and fade.

There are those who prefer the early wooden case models. Many new collectors, however, or those frustrated by Catalin's prices, have turned to what we call the dashboard-type radios, due to their ultrasleek "techno" designs. Others pursue newer advertising radios.

We suggest these books: *Guide to Old Radios, Second Edition* by David and Betty Johnson (Wallace-Homestead, Radnor, PA, 1995); *Collector's Guide to Antique Radios, Fourth Edition* by Marty and Sue Bunis (Collector Books, Paducah, KY, 1997); and *Collector's Guide to Novelty Radios* (1995) and *Bk II* (1998) by Marty Bunis and Robert F. Breed (Collector Books, Paducah, KY).

Baldwin, "Baldwinette," table model, tombstone shape, wooden case w/ arched top and scalloped grill, 1930, $125-$150. —Photo courtesy Gene Harris Antique Auction Center, Inc.

	LOW	HIGH
Admiral, 4B24, portable, beige plastic, 1954	$30	$40
Admiral, 5A32, clock radio, brown plastic, 1952	30	40
Admiral, Y2998, table, turquoise plastic, 1961	20	35
Admiral, YH302-GP, transistor, red, 1966	20	25
Air Castle, 10002, table, plastic, 1949	40	50
Air Castle, G-521, portable, leatherette, tambour top, 1949	40	50
Air King, 9209, table, plastic, right front vertical slide rule dial	50	60
Air King, A511, table, plastic, right front dial, left lattice grille knobs, 1947	40	50
Airline, 25BR-1542A, table, plastic, 1953	40	50
Airline, 84BR-1517A, table, brown Bakelite, push-button, 1947	50	60
American Bosch, 604, table, wood, 1935	30	40
Apex, 60, console, walnut, 7 tubes, AC	110	130
Apex, 106, console, wooden, highboy, inner window dial, fold-down front, 3 knobs	130	150
Arvin, 240P, portable, plastic, center vertical slide rule dial, checkered grille, 1949	35	45
Arvin, 842J, table, metal, 4 tubes, 1954	60	75

Left: Arvin, Model 840T, table model, green metal case w/ plastic knobs and trim, 1954, $60-$80. —Photo courtesy Gene Harris Antique Auction Center, Inc.

Right: Channel Master, Model 6511 "All Transistor Home Super," table model, green plastic case, $40-$60.

Left: RCA Victor, Model 96-X-1, table model, Art Deco style white plastic case, 1939, $150-$200.

RCA Victor, Model 40X-56, table model, pressed wood case w/ 1939 New York World's Fair motif, $900-$1000.

	LOW	HIGH
Atwater Kent, 82Q, cathedral, wood, 7 tubes, battery, 1931	375	425
Automatic, table, wood, 3 knobs, AC, 1975	35	45
Barbie, novelty, ©1974 Mattel, made in Hong Kong	35	50
Bendix, 65P4, table, plastic, 3 knobs, 1949	35	45
Bendix, 626C, table, plastic, 3 knobs, rear hand-hold, AC/DC, 1947	45	55
Bulova, 360, table, plastic, upper right window dial, metal perforated grille, 1961	20	25
Clarion, 14601, table, plastic, right square dial, left checkerboard grille, AC/DC, 1949	40	50
Clinton, 254, portable, leatherette, fold-open front door, handle, 1937	60	75
Coronado, 43-6951, console, wood, upper slanted slide rule dial, cloth grille area, 4 knobs, AC, 1948	70	80
Crosley, 5-38, table, wooden, high rectangular case, slanted front panel w/ 3 dials, 5 tubes, battery, 1926	175	200
Crosley, 11-301U, portable, plastic, flip up semi-circular front w/ crest, inner dial, handle, AC/DC, battery, 1951	40	55
Crown, TR-830, transistor, coat pocket-style, 1959	20	30
Delco, R-1127, table, wood, right front airplane dial, 3 bands, 1937	65	85
DeWald, 565, portable, leatherette, inner slide rule dial, cloth grille, 1941	30	40
DeWald, K412, table, plastic, right front dial, checkered grille, 1957	25	30
Dr. Pepper, advertising, AM/FM	20	30
Emerson, 25A, table, wood, curved top, right front dial, center cloth grille, 1933	80	100
Emerson, 505, portable, leatherette, right front dial, perforated grille, handle, 1946	30	40
Evel Knievel, novelty, made in Hong Kong	35	50
Eveready, 1, table, gumwood w/ maple finish, center front dial, 3 knobs, AC, 1927	110	130
Fada, 44, table, plastic, right front dial, wrap-around louvers, 2 knobs	45	55
Fada, 260D, table, plastic, black, chrome trim, right front dial, cloth grille w/ Art Deco bars, 2 knobs, 6 tubes, AC/DC, 1936	230	250
Fada, C34, portable, leatherette, inner dial, vertical grille bars, flip-open front, 5 tubes, AC, 1939	55	65
Farnsworth, CT-43, table, 2-tone mahogany plastic, right front dial, 4 tubes, 1941	35	40
Farnsworth, GP-350, portable, metal and leatherette, metal grille, AC/DC	30	40
Firestone, 4-A-21, table, wood, right front slide rule dial, cloth grille, 1947	45	55
General Electric, 143, portable, plastic, lower front slide rule dial, AC/DC, battery, 1949	30	40
General Electric, 522, clock radio, ivory plastic, brown knob and dial, 1954	30	40
General Electric, ER-753, crystal	200	250
General Electric, K-41, table, metal, right front dial, cloth grille, 2 knobs, AC, 1933	80	90
General Electric, T-115A, table, plastic, raised upper front slide rule dial, lattice grille, 2 knobs, 6 tubes, AC/DC, 1958	15	20
Grantline, 501-7, table, white plastic, 1948	45	55
Hallicrafters, 611, table, brown plastic, beige knobs, 1954	30	35
Hershey's Instant Chocolate, advertising	35	50
Hitachi, WH-761, transistor, 1961	25	30
Hoffman, P-410, transistor, large dial, 1957	55	65
Kiss, novelty, ©1977 Aucoin	50	75
Knight, 5F-525, table, plastic, 1949	35	45
Lloyds, TR-10K, transistor, 1965	15	20
Magnavox, AM-62, portable, 1962	10	20

Telefunken, Model TR-1, transistor, 1955, $3197 at auction. —Photo courtesy Auction Team Köln.

	LOW	HIGH
Majestic, 511, table, white Bakelite, blue Catalin grille, 1938	300	350
Martian, Big 4, crystal	100	150
Midget, crystal, blue	45	50
Mitchell, 1257, clock radio, ivory, 1952	30	35
Motorola, 41A, table, brown Bakelite, 1940	75	85
Mr. and Mrs. T. Bloody Mary Mix, advertising	30	45
Norelco, L3X76T-01, transistor, 1961	20	25
Old Crow, advertising, made in Japan	350	400
Olympic, 402, table, blue, gold dial, 1955	20	30
Pabst Blue Ribbon, advertising	20	35
Philco, 48-206, table, leatherette, ivory grille, 1948	30	40
Philco, T-7, transistor, black and white, painted metal grill, 1956	50	60
Philmore, 336 Blackbird, crystal	50	75
Polaroid 600 Plus, novelty, AM/FM, made in China	20	30
Quick Quaker Oats, advertising	100	125
RCA, 6-X-7-B, table, black plastic, 1956	20	25
Regal, 7251, table, plastic, 1948	40	50
Silvertone, 11, clock radio, white, 1951	30	40
Sony, TR-630, transistor, 1963	40	60
Sparton, 7-46, console, wooden, 1946	75	100
Strawberry Shortcake, novelty, purse-style, ©1983 American Greetings	25	35
Stromberg-Carlson, 1500, table, red plastic, 1950	40	50
Sylvania, 4P14, transistor, 1961	15	20
Telechron, 8H59, clock radio, red, 1948	50	60
Temple, G-419, table, metal, 1947	50	60
Toshiba, 6TP-357, transistor, 1961	20	25
Truetone, D-2418A, clock radio, black plastic, 1954	25	30
Westinghouse, H-147, brown Bakelite, 1947	30	40
Westinghouse, H-331P4U, portable, green plastic, 1952	20	25
Wilson Tennis Balls Can, novelty	30	45
Winston Tote Bag, advertising, made in China	25	35
Zenith, G-725, table, Bakelite, FM/AM, 1950	30	40
Zenith, R-640, transistor, 1966	10	15

Salt and Pepper Shakers

Salt and pepper shakers are on most dinner tables (very few of us use salt cellars). Although people obtain shakers to match table settings, we listed shakers that are considered novelty or figural shakers; some even advertise products. Collectors are drawn to the strange forms and bright colors. Many shakers match a more expensive cookie jar by the same manufacturer such as Shawnee or Regal. Shakers draw collectors not only from the cookie jar field but from the fields of black Americana, comic character and advertising memorabilia. With so many shapes and themes, crossover collecting is nearly endless. Collectors talk about sets such as one piece (one container), nodders (which sit in a base and rock back and forth), nesters (which sit one inside the other), or huggers (which fit together).

Sometimes a pair of salt and peppers aren't really a pair, but two different forms that share a theme, such as a cow jumping over the moon or a bowling ball and pin. Many times there are other pieces, such as a condiment jar, a tray or a bench, that are required in order to complete the set. Be alert to reproductions of expensive shakers and missing pieces. Prices listed are for excellent condition examples—no chips, cracks, flaking finish, or missing parts.

The shakers below usually range from 1" to 5" in height, so nearly everyone has room for two or three...hundred. Many common shakers can be purchased for less than $10.

For further reading we recommend *The Complete Salt and Pepper Shaker Book* by Mike Schneider (Schiffer, Atglen, PA, 1993) and *Salt and Pepper Shakers, Vols. I–IV* by Helene Guarnaccia (Collector Books, Paducah, KY, 1998-99 value updates).

Left: Plastic advertising shakers, pair of Philgas tanks and Phillips 66, $55 at auction.

Below: Auction prices for plastic gas pump advertising shakers w/ original boxes. Left to right: Sunoco, blue, $210; Texaco, 1 red, 1 blue, $319; and Shell, yellow and orange, $193.

—Photos courtesy Collectors Auction Services.

Left to right: Cats, Puss 'n Boots, Shawnee, 3.25" h, $30-$35; Cows, Elmer and Elsie, Borden advertising, 4" h, $99 at auction. —Photo courtesy Collectors Auction Services.

	LOW	HIGH
African Head, carved wood	$8	$10
African Head, ceramic, black, gold, white, and red accents, 4.125" h	15	20
Alarm Clock, comical face, Japan, 3.25" h	10	15
Amish Woman, painted pot metal	8	10
Andy and Min Gump, ceramic	100	200
Bagpiper, Norcrest	10	15
Ballantine Beer, aluminum, rubber stopper, c1940s, 2.25" h	25	50
Begging Scottie, gold trim, ceramic	8	10
Billiard Ball, plastic	25	30
Bird, Bakelite	40	60
Blender, plastic, 3.75" h	15	20
Bluebird, Rosemeade	45	55
Book, bone china, Japan, 2" h	5	10
Bride and Groom, Sorcha Boru	75	85
Bugs Bunny, ceramic, Warner Bros., 1960s, 4.375" h	75	100
Bulldog Head, Rosemeade	25	30
Bullfighter and Bull, ceramic	20	25
Cabbage, McCoy	20	30
Camel, brown and yellow, Ceramic Arts Studio	115	125
Campbell's Kids, range	10	15
Canning Jar, plastic, made in Hong Kong, 3.75" h	2	5
Chef and Mammy, china, cork stopper, c1940s	50	75
Collie, ceramic	20	25
Colonel and Mrs. Sanders, plastic, 1960s, 4" h	65	85
Diamond Crystal Salt, cardboard	8	10
Dog, glass	15	20
Donald Duck and Ludwig Von Drake, ceramic, ©1961 Dan Breschner, 5" h	75	100
Donkey Head, metal	10	15
Donkey Head, Rosemeade	30	35
Don Winslow and Red Pennington, hand-painted plaster, 1940s	50	75
Elephant, Frankoma	60	70
Elmer and Elsie, ceramic, Borden	85	100
Fantasia's Hop Low, ceramic, Vernon Kilns, 3.25" h	200	400
Ferdinand the Bull	35	45
Figaro the Cat, yellow	35	45

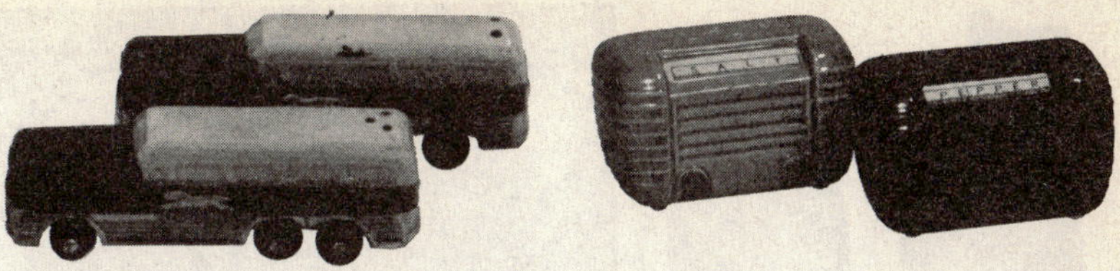

Left to right: Greyhound Buses, metal w/ rubber tires, 3.25" l, $94 at auction. —Photo courtesy Collectors Auction Services; Radios, plastic, 1 blue, 1 black, $10-$15.

	LOW	HIGH
Fish, Grindley, 2.25" x 3.5"	10	15
Fish and Creel, ceramic	15	20
Flamingos, Rosemeade	50	60
Flower Pot, gold trim, Shawnee, 3.75" h	35	45
Fred and Wilma Flintstone, Vandor	30	40
Giraffe, ceramic, Ceramic Arts Studio	65	75
Giraffe Head, ceramic	10	15
Greyhound Bus, metal	40	70
Grinder and Spinning Wheel, Enesco	10	15
Gumball Machine, plastic	15	20
Hamm's Beer, ceramic, 5" h	125	150
Heinz Catsup Bottle, plastic	10	15
Indian Brave, copper plated	15	20
Kermit and Miss Piggy, ceramic, Sigma, 1980s, 4.25" h	75	100
Kewpie, hand-painted white china, marked "M/K Hand Painted/Japan," 2.25" h	75	100
Kissing Bunnies, Ceramic Arts Studio	30	40
Kissing Indians, Napco, 3.75" h	15	20
Liberty Bell, metal, 1.75" h	20	25
Mermaid, Enesco	15	20
Mickey Mouse Head, white, ceramic	20	25
Milk Can, McCoy, 3.75" h	8	15
Minehaha and Hiawatha, Ceramic Arts Studio	150	165
Mobilgas, shield shaped, ceramic	40	50
Mormon Temple, ceramic, Japan	15	20
Mouse, Rosemeade, 1.75" h	75	90
Mr. Peanut, red plastic, 3" h	10	15
Mushroom, Bakelite	40	60
Mountain Lion, Rosemeade, 4.25" l	90	110
Nabisco Blue Bonnet Sue	10	15
New Era Potato Chip Cans, metal	25	45
Noritake Azalea, 2.75" h	30	40
Oil Lamp, glass	15	20
Orange Tree, made in Taiwan	15	20
Owl and the Pussycat, Fitz and Floyd	80	120
Palomino Horse Head, Rosemeade	60	70
Parakeet, blue and yellow, Ceramic Arts Studio, 4" h	50	60
Pelican, metal	30	35
Penguin, metal	20	25
Pillsbury Doughboy and Girl, ceramic, 1988	15	25
Pluto, Leeds China, 1949, 3" h	25	50

Left to right, Penguins, Millie and Willie, Kool advertising, plastic, 3.25" and 3.5" h, $55 at auction. —Photo courtesy Collectors Auction Services; Tulips, ceramic, Mikasa, Japan, 2.875" h, $10-$15.

	LOW	HIGH
Popeye and Olive Oyl, bisque-type	15	20
Quail, Rosemeade, 1.5" h	30	40
Rabbit Head, painted wood	8	10
RCA Nipper, ceramic, 3.375" h	45	55
Reclining Nude and Dog, painted hollow plaster, 1950s	25	50
Rocketship, plastic, 4.25" h	25	50
Roly Poly, plastic	15	20
Santa Claus, Holt-Howard	20	25
Schmoo, ceramic, c1948, 3.5" h	75	100
Seahorse, Ceramic Arts Studio, 3.75" h	45	55
Sealtest Milk Bottles	25	35
Seated Devil, painted plaster, 1940s, 2.5" h	50	75
Skunk, Goebel, marked "WDP"	100	125
Smiley Face, yellow and black composition, Japan, c1970s, 3" d	25	50
Smokey Bear, ceramic, Norcrest, 1960s, 3.5" h	75	100
Snowman, painted wood	12	15
Spaceship and Creature, Vallona Star	45	50
Squirrel, metal	10	15
Squirrel and Stump, ceramic, Japan, 2.75" h	10	15
Steam Iron, plastic	8	12
Steamship, ceramic, 1950s, 5.5" l	50	75
Stylized Cat, light brown, Ceramic Arts Studio	65	75
Tappan Range, glass, 1940s	25	50
Trader Vic Tiki's, ceramic	5	10
Transistor Radio, glazed bisque, brass wire handle, Enesco, 1960s, 4" h	50	75
Trylon and Perisphere, 1939 New York World's Fair, marked "J. B."	75	100
Turkey, ceramic, Japan, 3.5" h	15	20
Washington Monument, Bakelite	40	50
Wee French Girl, Ceramic Arts Studio	25	30
Windmill, Occupied Japan	15	20
Woodsy Owl, Japan, 4" h	40	50
WWII Bomber Plane, painted plaster, gray, red accents, cork stopper	75	100

Scrimshaw

Scrimshaw is artwork done on bone. It can be carved or painted. Carved scrimshaw, which seldom has any painted decoration, is mostly in the nature of little trinkets, boxes, pins, or forks, for example. Painted scrimshaw is done directly on the tooth or bone. It is accomplished by scratching the design into the surface with needles, then working India ink into the scratches. Whalebone is the most commonly found material, followed by walrus tusk. Occasionally a low-grade ivory such as whale tooth is used.

The age, size, artistic quality, subject matter and state of preservation all go into determining the value of scrimshaw. Beware of fakes made from polymers (see *Fakeshaw: A Checklist of Plastic "Scrimshaw"* by Stuart Frank, Kendall Whaling Museum, Sharon, MA, 1988). Also beware of various endangered species laws. Differences in federal and state regulations make this a tricky topic. Check with local authorities before buying or selling scrimshaw.

For more information see *Scrimshaw* by Martha Lawrence (Schiffer, Atglen, PA, 1993).

	LOW	HIGH
Box, baleen and ivory, checkerboard design on lid w/ floral engraving, fitted interior lift-out tray w/ ivory edging, 3.75" x 5" x 10"	$1500	$3000
Busk, decorated w/ whaling scene, flanked by hearts bearing portraits of sweethearts, vignettes of cityscape and country scene flanked by hearts, anchor, inscription "on Board Brig Bruce," 19th C, 13" l	2500	4500
Busk, engraved whaling scenes, black and red highlights, 19th C, 14.75" l	1200	2000
Busk, scalloped end, engraved w/ whaling vignettes enclosed by vine borders, flanked w/ wreaths, 19th C, 13.125" l	500	700
Busk, whalebone w/ polychrome decoration depicting floral bouquet, potted plant, ship at sea, basket of fruit and foliage, initialed "H. D. R.," red, blue, yellow, and green highlights, 19th C, 13.125" l	900	1100
Cribbage Board, Eskimo, engraved salmon, walrus, and "Nome Alaska," several pins, 9" l	330	650

Inset View.

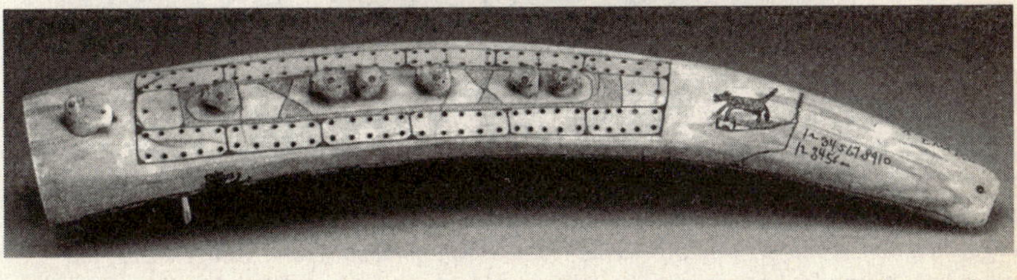

Cribbage Board, tusk engraved w/ horse pulling sled, sea monster threatening hunter, dog in leg-hold trap, and hunter using telescope to examine caribou, signed "A Lamka," 19" l, $1093 at auction. —Photo courtesy Skinner, Inc., Boston, MA.

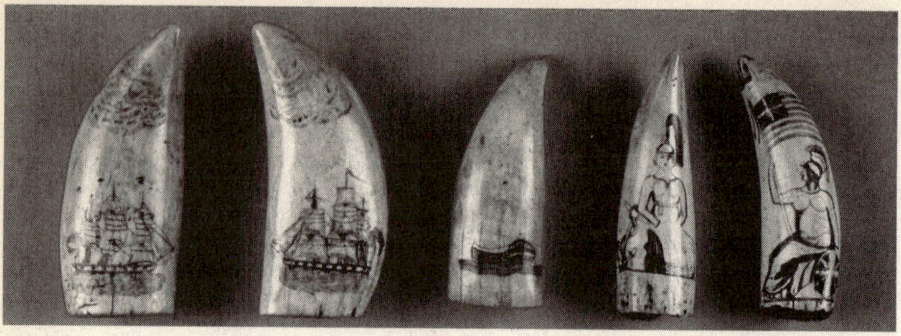

Above and below: Scrimshaw Whale's Teeth.

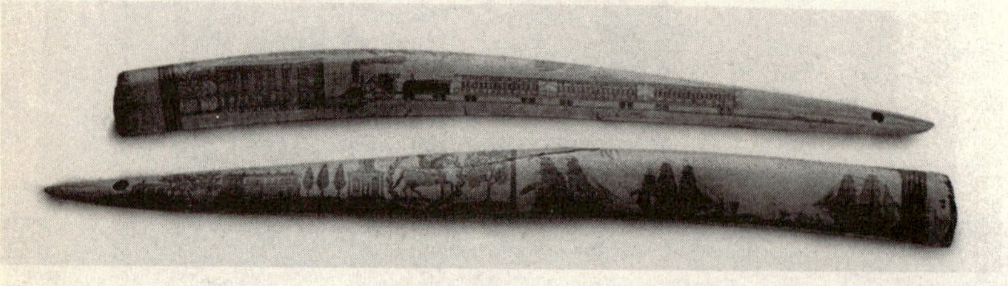

Walrus Tusks, 1 engraved w/ steam train, coal car, and 3 passenger cars being chased by 2 dogs and pulling up to 3-story brick and clapboard building w/ willow tree at left, reverse vertically decorated w/ palm tree, crusader on horseback, willow tree, memorial urn, leafy branch w/ birds, potted plant, vines, and various animals. The other tusk decorated on obverse w/ whaling scene, crusader on horseback, and village scene, on reverse w/ mermaid, horse-taming scene framed by leafy vine, and floral devices. Both tusks have geometric borders, 19th C, 34" l, price for matched pair, $13,800 at auction.

—Photos courtesy Skinner, Inc., Boston, MA.

Whale's Tooth, polychrome decorated, Elizabeth London *whaling ship on 1 side, whales in ocean on other side, by Edward Burdett (1805-33), $20,125 at auction. —Photo courtesy James D. Julia.*

	LOW	HIGH
Dolphin Jawbone, engraved w/ whaling scene, 2 whaleships, 19th C, 16" l, 10.5" w	1610	1900
Jagging Wheel, ships, hearts, flowers, stars, and compass rose, 20th C, 4.75" l	400	800
Paperweight, Inuit, carved ivory, block form w/ inked caribou, salmon, and insect motifs, 3.125" l	350	550
Powder Horn, engraved map of fort and roads, stag hunt scene, and "JR," 18th C, 10.5" l	2750	5200
Sailors Horn, whale, kettle, harpoons, hooks, engraved "M. Pyne of New Bedford," early wrought iron hook, 1848, 8.25" l	550	1200
Snuff Box, engraved crossed British flags and anchor above full-rigged sailing ship, rural village scene, brass lid, 5" l	550	950
Walrus Tusks, engraved polychrome vignettes depicting flowering branches, patriotic symbols of eagles, star, basket of flowers, Scottish warrior and his lady w/ harp, bordered by flowering leafy vine, red and black highlights, 19th C, 15.25" l	1500	3000
Walrus Tusks, vignettes of women, ships, walrus, and penguin, each marked "Susan," 13" l, price for pair	550	950
Whale's Teeth, engraved w/ Victorian ladies in elegant dress, 19th C, 3.75" l, price for pair	490	850
Whale's Tooth, engraved eagle in oval, seated Liberty figure, compass rose, and initials "TN," anchor and rope, ocean waves and geometric border, carved mahogany base inset w/ 4 round ivory inlays, 20th C, 5.5" h	1500	2750
Whale's Tooth, engraved framed vignette of whaling scene, American whaleship, 19th C, 9" l	1700	3250
Whale's Tooth, engraved w/ British vessel under sail w/ bird and shoreline background, basket of flowers, 19th C, 4.5" l	250	550
Whale's Tooth, engraved whale scene, crossed lances and 2 leafy branches, 20th C, 4.5" l	200	400
Whale's Tooth, engraved whaling scene depicting vessel working on pod of whales, 19th C, 8" l	2400	4500
Whistle, whalebone, decorated w/ whaling scene, border of stars, ivory finial, early 20th C, 2.5" l	800	1200

Shaker Collectibles

The Shakers formed a socioreligious organization in England in 1747. Their doctrines advocated simplicity and celibacy. They were nicknamed "Shakers" because of their devotional dancing in religious services. Ann Lee led a group to America in 1776 and attracted many converts. Known for their fine quality, Shakers made products that symbolized beliefs of purity and utility from the early nineteenth century to the twentieth century. Although the Shakers made furniture for their own use, much was made for commercial sale.

Identifying Shaker pieces can be difficult. Pieces are worth more if the collector can identify the Shaker community of origin.There are large numbers of fakes and countless reproductions. For further information see *Shaker Woodenware: Vol. 1* by June Sprigg and Jim Johnson (Berkshire House, Great Barrington, MA, 1991) and *The Complete Book of Shaker Furniture* by Timothy D. Rieman and Jean M. Burks (Harry N. Abrams, New York, NY, 1993).

Wash Tub, projecting handles continuing to body w/ iron staves, chamfered inside edge, painted blue exterior and ivory interior, 20" h, 27.5" dia, $3680 at auction. —Photo courtesy Skinner, Inc., Boston, MA.

	LOW	HIGH
Alarm, walnut, figure-8 shaped sounding board, turned maple handle w/ attached octagonal hammer, 19th C, 10" l	$150	$250
Basket, buttocks, woven splint, Eye of God design at bent twig handle, 12" x 14", 6.5" h plus handle	80	100
Basket, cloverleaf form, woven straw, openwork top, attached lid, late 19th C, 5" h, 4.5" l	75	100
Blanket, woven charcoal gray wool w/ white and gray stripe, fringed, Sabbathday Lake, ME, 64" x 134"	425	525
Bonnet, miniature, woven straw w/ gray silk ruffle cape and ribbons, late 19th/early 20th C	200	300
Bonnet, woven poplar splint, natural and black, beige silk ribbons and trim, paper label "5," 9.5" l	125	140
Brush, horse hair, turned handle, 11" l	30	40
Bucket, stave construction, old blue paint w/ black on metal bands, black stenciled "28" on lid, side and bottom, worn light green interior, wooden handle, wire bale w/ diamond attachments, 11" h	2600	2860
Candlestand, cherry, old dark red finish, tripod base, cut-out feet, turned tapered column and turned block w/ rounded 1 board top, Mount Lebanon, NY, 24.25" h, 16.5" d	2400	3000
Chair, revolving, maple curving crest above raking tapered spindles, hollowed-out pine seat, cast iron swiveling mechanism above tapered stem, maple double-arched spider base, New Lebanon, NY, 1860-70, 21" h, 14.75" dia seat	6000	8000
Cheese Colander, tin, rim handles, 22" d	55	75
Cheese Ladder, hickory, old patina and worn white paint, 25" l	460	575

	LOW	HIGH
Chest of Drawers, walnut, poplar secondary wood, old mellow refinishing, cut-out feet and scalloped apron, 5 dovetailed overlapping drawers and wide 1 board ends and top, replaced turned pulls and top refastened w/ screws, 49.5" h	1320	1650
Child's Cloak, blue wool, machine sewn, 25" l	385	470
Child's Rocker, #1, dark finish, turned detail, mushroom cap arms, replaced red tape seat and back, Mount Lebanon, NY, 28.5" h	450	550
Chimney Cupboard, pine, old worn white repaint exterior, original orange paint on interior, old pumpkin repaint on inside of doors, old replaced latches on raised panel doors, Enfield, NH, 80" h, 21.25" w, 7.5" d	4200	5280
Chip Carrier, rectangular, pine, dovetailed, added tin corner braces, bentwood handle w/ copper rivets, Mount Lebanon, NY, 12.25" x 18.5", 7" h	270	330
Cloak Cabinet, refinished walnut, pine secondary wood, cut-out feet w/ scalloped apron, paneled doors, chamfered corners and flat board top, interior shelves w/ worn gray repaint, Union Village, OH, 77" h, 37" w, 13.5" d	2200	2750
Cloak Hanger, pine and poplar, attributed to Harvard, MA, 36.5" l	150	190
Coffeepot, tin, side spout, pewter finial, 12.25" h	80	100
Corner Cupboard, 1-pc., walnut, poplar secondary wood, high cut-out feet w/ scalloped apron, paneled doors, applied molding between sections and cove molded cornice, Union Village, OH, 27" w, 49.5" w at cornice, 86.5" h	970	1210
Cricket Stool, original dark finish, Mount Lebanon, NY, 11.375" x 11.625", 6.5" h	200	250
Crutches, oak and ash, late 19th C, price for pair	300	400
Drying Rack, poplar, folding 3 sections, old worn graying-yellow repaint, each section 35" x 56"	160	200
Drying Rack, poplar, old brownish-red paint, ladder style w/ cross frame, Mount Lebanon, NY, 43.5" h, 16.5" d, 30.5" w	110	140
Drying Rack, walnut, mortised construction, shoe feet, 39" h, 28" w	130	165
Fly Swatter, turned wooden handle, 18.5" l	50	60
Footstool, slanted top, 4 turned swelled legs joined by stretchers, Mount Lebanon, NY, late 19th C, 5.5" h, 12" w	300	400

Assortment of Shaker items. —Photo courtesy Skinner, Inc., Boston, MA.

	LOW	HIGH
Foot Warmer, oval, tin, wooden base and top, punched pinwheel designs, old tag "Leavitt Collection," Enfield, NH, 11" l	650	800
Handkerchief Caddy, brown leather, brown silk trim, red silk lining, ribbon closure, 5 hankies, 8" x 8.5"	65	85
Harvest Table, walnut, square tapered legs, mortised and pinned apron, 2 board top, Union Village, OH, 24" x 77", 28.5" h	2000	2530
Hooked Rag Rug, multicolored, yellow, blue, red, beige, and black border stripes, 25" x 41"	175	225
Jug, brown-glazed stoneware, partial paper label "Corbett's Shakers' compound concentrated Syrup of sarsaparilla prepared at Shaker Village…," late 19th C, 6.5" h	100	200
Knife Box, bentwood, ash and chestnut, turned handle, 8.5" x 13"	110	140
Line Winder, carved and turned maple and ash, mortised and pinned construction, mid-19th C, 10.5" l	150	250
Measuring Stick, walnut, old patina, 39" l	130	165
Nutmeg Grater, turned mahogany, brass fittings, 7.625" l	300	385
Pie Lifter, wire, wooden handle, 16" l	45	55
Rag Rug, multicolored, red and olive border, Canterbury, NH, 23" x 38"	175	220
Rocker, #0, 3 slats, turned finials and arm posts, shaped arms w/ mushroom caps, replaced woven tape seat, Mount Lebanon, NY, 23" h	600	770
Rocker, #7, 2 tapering back posts, shaped arms, replaced orange and beige tape seat, New Lebanon, NY, 1880-1930, 42.5" h	700	850
Rocker, dark worn finish, gold stenciled label "Shakers Trade Mark, Mt. Lebanon, NY. No. 6," 4 slats w/ replaced shawl bar, new woven tape seat, Mount Lebanon, NY, 40" h	265	330
Rocker, maple, 4 arched slats flanked by tapered stiles topped by turned and shaped pommels, shaped arms w/ down-scrolled terminals, caned seat, double row of turned stretchers, shaped rockers, Harvard, MA Community, 1840-50, 49" h	10,000	12,000
Scoop, oval chamfered pine scoop w/ iron tacks, turned maple handle attached w/ rivet, mid-19th C, 11" l	300	400

Chest, 6-board construction w/ recessed panels, lidded till, turned feet, Pleasant Hill or South Union Communities, KY, mid-19th C, 23.5" h, 46" w, $575 at auction. —Photo courtesy Skinner, Inc., Boston, MA.

	LOW	HIGH
Sewing Box, 2-tier, mahogany and maple, pincushion finial above top compartment fitted w/ 8 spool holders and ivory eyelets, lower compartment w/ drawer, paper label "Sabbathday Lake Shakers, Maine," late 19th/early 20th C, 6" h, 7" w	200	400
Sewing Box, oval, 4 fingers on base, 1 on lid, copper tacks, original reddish-tint varnish, interior lined w/ pale blue silk w/ woven straw needle case and strawberry shaped pincushion, brass monogram medallion added to lid, Mount Lebanon, NY, 11.5" l	700	880
Sewing Box, oval, swing handle, silk-lined interior, late 19th C, 7" l, 4.75" w	200	400
Sewing Carrier, oval, swing handle, punched holes to attach implements, stamped "Sabbathday Lake Shakers, Maine," 20th C, 11" l, 7.625" w	500	600
Sewing Case, black leather, purple knit binding, black pompons and ribbon tie, blue silk lining, 7.5" l	45	60
Side Chair, maple, 3 arched slats, stiles w/ turned finials, woven cloth seat, turned legs joined by double stretchers, refinished, Enfield, NH, c1800, 41" h	500	700
Spice Rack, hanging, birch, 6 drawers, wire nail construction, plywood back, old varnish finish, 12.75" h, 12.75" w	200	250
Spool Holder, maple and chestnut, wooden spools on pins, red velvet pincushion, 5.75" h	110	140
Stool, revolving, green-painted pine seat mounted on metal screw shaft, turned and tapering natural maple shaft on spider base w/ 2 maple arches, New Lebanon, NY, 1860-70, 17" h, 14.5" dia seat	1000	1500

Shaker Furniture. —Photo courtesy Skinner, Inc., Boston, MA.

Ship Models

There are four main types of ship models. Wright's models were made by a shipwright (a ship builder) as a working model for an actual ship. Sailor's models were made while the sailor served on a ship. Collector's models were made after the ship was constructed, often after it ceased to exist, using photographs or drawings in books. Kit models are built from components and directions furnished in a commercially sold kit.

Wright's models are the most desired and expensive. Sailor's models may be crude, but they are often highly regarded. The value of a collector's model is determined by age, size, intricacy of detail and state of preservation. Models of steamships are generally not as valuable as sailing vessels.

Schooner Bluenose, *fully rigged, cotton sails, 1/20 scale, 58" h, 80" l, $1265 at auction. —Photo courtesy Skinner, Inc., Boston, MA.*

	LOW	HIGH
Clipper Ship, hand-carved and painted wood, rigged w/ canvas sails, 50" l	$1000	$1500
Clipper Ship *Young America,* case ebonized w/ inlaid nautical motifs, 20th C, 11.5" h, 16" w, 6" deep	1000	1500
Frigate *U.S. Constitution,* copper clad hull, incised plaque reads "U.S. Frigate Constitution Built in Boston Mass. 1797...," cased, 20th C, 1/8" scale, 30" h, 43" l, 43" deep	800	1200
Prisoner of War, french ivory, 3-masted, fully rigged, on wooden base, 19th C, 13.25" h, 15.5" l	3000	5000
R.M.S. Queen Mary, 5-level rounded deck overlooking bow marked "Queen Mary," red and black funnels, cream deck, black hull, red below waterline, c1948	17,000	20,000
Schooner *Traviata,* original rigging, lifeboat, captain's gig, and sailing kayak, above lead keel on stand monogrammed "CA," brass plate engraved "R. Lincoln Lippitt," c1875, 74" h, 100.5" l	3000	5000
S.S. Manhattan, metal, cream deck, blue hull, red below waterline, top decks lift off to reveal ribbed interior for housing lighting equipment, 72" l	8000	10,000
Three-Masted Man-of-War, bone, 76 cannons and carved figurehead, balleen detailing and chequer inlaid wood plinth, modern plexiglass case, 19th C, 8" h, 9.75" l	7000	9000
Three-Masted Ship, whalebone and ivory, wooden stand, 19th C, 9.5" h, 13.5" l	1000	1500
Three-Masted Ship *Agusta,* full sail, shadowbox, painted and decoupage ground, 19th C, 16.5" h, 24.375" l	800	1200

Silhouettes

Silhouettes are profiles cut out of one color paper and mounted to a contrasting-colored background. Sometimes detail is added in chalk, pen or watercolor. Most collected silhouettes date to the first half of the nineteenth century. Value depends on age, quality and size of the specimen. The fame of the subject is also very important. Modern and semimodern silhouettes have little or no value.

	LOW	HIGH
Gentleman, books in hand, cut, replaced background paper, ogee frame, 14.5" h, 10.25" w, price for pair	$400	$800
Gentleman, cut, gilded detail and embossed gilded paper oval liner, black lacquered frame w/ gilded fittings, 5.5" h, 4.75" w	200	500
Gentleman w/ Whip, seated, hollow-cut, watercolor and pen and ink on paper, unsigned, framed, 5.375" x 6.25"	300	600
Lady, cut, w/ ornate hat, marked on back of wavy paper "Mrs. Norman" and on back of backing paper "Mrs. Norman, Henley on Thames," black lacquered frame w/ gilded fittings, 5.75" h, 4.875" w	200	500
Man and Woman, Spencer Stafford (Albany, NY pewterer) and his wife, full-length, ink and pencil, gold-painted frames, 10.5" x 7", price for pair	300	700
Man in Top Hat, hollow-cut, full figure, molded pine frame, 8.125" h, 5.125" w	200	500
Man in Top Hat, w/ cane, cut, full figure, black and white litho background, signed "M. Socke, fecit 1844," framed, 12.5" h, 8.625" w	500	1000
Woman, hollow-cut, black cloth backing, ink inscription "Edith Butler," black molded frame, 6" h, 4.875" w	200	500
Woman, w/ baby and child, cut, full length, ink wash ground, ogee frame, 12.625" h, 10.5" w	400	800
Young Lady, hollow-cut, black litho dress detail w/ blue watercolor, black cloth backing, old gilt frame, 5.125" h, 4.125" w	500	1000
Young Lady, hollow-cut, painted highlights, unsigned, period frame, 4.375" x 3.5"	200	500
Young Lady, ink and watercolor, blue dress, gilt highlights, marked "H46," ogee bird's-eye veneer frame w/ gilded liner, 9.625" h, 8.125" w	500	1000
Young Man, cut, gilt detail, inscription on back "A college friend of G. H. Nurse's 1858," matted and framed, 5.875" h, 4.375" w	150	250

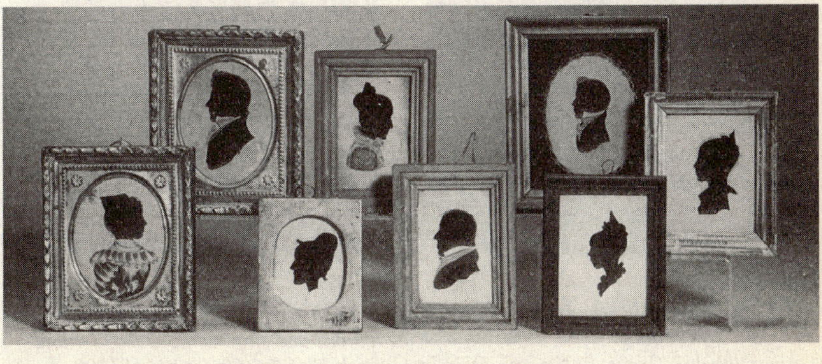

Hollow-Cut Silhouettes. —Photo courtesy Skinner, Inc., Boston, MA.

Textiles

Coverlets

Coverlets are bedspreads woven on a loom. They fall into two categories: geometrics and Jacquards. The geometrics generally date earlier and have small simple designs such as the star, diamond or snowball. The Jacquards, produced using a loom device made by Frenchman Joseph Jacquard, have curving, ornate designs such as flowers, birds and trees.

The early geometric coverlets were woven at home usually by women. The Jacquards were more often made by professional male weavers. The Jacquard device enabled the weaver to put his name on his work; the simple loom didn't. Two threads are used in weaving. The warp threads (vertical) are usually cotton, and the weft threads (horizontal) are usually wool. Red and blue dye was primarily used until the middle of the nineteenth century when synthetic dyes brought a greater color variety. The development of the power loom brought an end to most manual loom weaving.

Most collected coverlets date to the middle of the nineteenth century. Jacquards are more popular with collectors than the geometrics. Expect higher prices for the rare all-cotton or all-wool coverlets. The listings are identified as geometric or Jacquard. Following the identification are color, description and dates, when available.

For more information see *American Star Works Coverlets* by Judith Gordon (Design Books, Lyons & Burford, New York, NY, 1995).

Geometric

	LOW	AVG.	HIGH
Blue and White, cross pattern, c1835, 68" x 84"	$350	$525	$750
Blue and White, wavy stripes border, blue fringe, c1840, 74" x 86"	150	275	350
Blue, Red, and White, c1849, 74" x 86"	150	250	350

Left to right: Overshot woven 2-pc. coverlet w/ geometric design, $385 at auction; Jacquard 2-pc. double weave coverlet, rose medallions and stars w/ floral border and corners labeled "Wove at Newark, Ohio by G. Stich 1846," price for pair, $1100 at auction. —Photos courtesy Garth's Auctions, Delaware, OH.

Jacquard coverlets are often labeled and dated at the corner. —Photo courtesy Garth's Auctions, Delaware, OH.

	LOW	AVG.	HIGH
Blue, Rust, and White, double weave, c1835-40, 72" x 76"	150	275	350
Navy Blue and White, double weave, 70" x 84"	100	150	200
Navy Blue and White, 4 rose pattern, double weave, 78" x 88"	150	200	250
Red and White, c1840, 60" x 60"	300	350	400
Red, White, and Blue, double weave, c1830-35, 58" x 92"	150	175	350

Jacquard

Navy Blue and Light Blue, 4 rose medallions, bird and flower borders and baskets of flowers in corners, 70" x 82"	$100	$140	$175
Navy Blue and White, floral medallions, seaweed and floral border, "1848," 71" x 88"	290	385	485
Navy Blue and White, peacocks feeding young, vintage and floral border, "Made 1868," single weave, 67" x 81"	250	330	410
Navy Blue and White, peacocks, turkeys, trees, and houses, Christian and Heathen border, double weave, 68" x 84"	325	300	375
Navy Blue and White, stars and 4 rose medallions, bird and tree borders, "Made by D. L. Meyers, Bethel Township for James Spence 1850," single weave, 80" x 96"	620	825	1025
Navy Blue, Red, and White, vining floral design, eagle borders, double weave, "Cadiz, Ohio"	410	550	690
Navy Blue, Sage Green, Red, and White, center medallion w/ 4 eagles, floral border, "Henry Gabriel, Allentown, F.," 74" x 90"	275	360	450
Navy Blue, Salmon Pink, Olive Yellow, and White, tulip medallions, Christian and Heathen and bird borders, "A. Henning, Sugarcreek, T. Stark County, Ohio 1845," single weave, 72" x 81"	290	385	485
Pink, Navy Blue, and White, oak leaf and bellflower, "By James Pearson, Chatham, Medina, Ohio," single weave, 76" x 82"	165	220	275
Red, Blue, Green, Brown, and White, center medallion w/ angels in spandrels, floral border, double weave, 72" x 80"	165	220	275
Red, Green, Blue, Brown, and White, floral medallion, single weave, 74" x 80"	70	90	110
Red, Navy Blue, and White, floral, bird borders, "G. Stich, Newark, Ohio 1838," double weave, 73" x 83"	415	440	465
Red, Navy Blue, Green, and White, floral medallions and border, single weave, 73" x 81"	415	440	465
Salmon Pink, Navy Blue, and White, floral, vintage border, corners labeled "Samuel Neily, Mansfield, Richland, Ohio 1846," 72" x 86"	290	385	485
Salmon Pink, Navy Blue, and White, floral medallions and scrolled borders, "Samuel Meily Mansfield, Ohio 1852," 70" x 86"	110	150	190

Hooked Rugs

Hooked rugs made from discarded rags or scraps from the cutting room show a wealth of American imagination. The best are nineteenth-century examples with scenes and/or figures, but those are difficult to find in good condition. Collectors can find fine examples from the early twentieth century more easily. Watch out for rotted and unraveled examples. They may look good from the back of the auction hall, but restoring them can cost more than the value of the rug itself.

For additional information see *Hooked Rugs* by Jessie A. Turbayne (Schiffer, West Chester, PA, 1991).

	LOW	HIGH
Black Dog, gray ground w/ green, white, black, and tan borders, 30" x 54"	$600	$800
Floral Design, multicolor flowers on gray ground, red and dark brown borders, 37" x 78"	75	150
House, blue, white, and yellow, red roof, beige sky, 2-tone brown ground, 8.5" x 10.5"	250	350
Leaping Deer, gold, brown, light blue, shades of green, tan, and black, 27" x 45"	200	300
Multicolored Stripes, brown buggy rope binding, 33" x 53"	150	250
Owl on Tree Branch, silhouetted by moon, shades of brown, gray, green, and black on gray ground, blue border, 19" x 33.5"	200	300
Stylized Landscape, deer and white birch, blue, gray, green, beige, white, and black, 26" x 39"	300	450
Stylized Landscape, dogs and fawns, 19" x 40.5"	250	350
Three Bears, multicolored, beige ground, black border, 24" x 40"	500	700
Three Cats, white and gray cats playing w/ yarn, magenta ground, blue and white borders, cats named on border "Skeeks," "Shasta," and "Minnie," 21" x 33.5"	400	550
Winter Landscape, house in snow, blue, green, brown, black, and white, rebacked, 25.5" x 34.5"	200	300

Left: Noah's Ark w/ inscription "I Hope He Don't Miss Any," American, 20th C, 52" x 33", $1380 at auction.

Right: Repeating geometric design w/ striated borders, initialed and dated "BF 1963-4," 12'3" x 8'10", $5175 at auction.

—Photos courtesy Skinner, Inc., Boston, MA.

Needlework

Embroidery or decorative needlework uses diverse threads such as silk, gold, wool, or cotton stitched into any type of fabric including cloth or leather. The most valuable and rarest embroidery work is from the 1700s. Embroidery pieces from the 1800s and 1900s are more readily available. The condition, workmanship, materials, design and age of a piece are equally important in determining value. Many hobbyists collect all types of embroidery while others collect by motif, stitch, or country of origin.

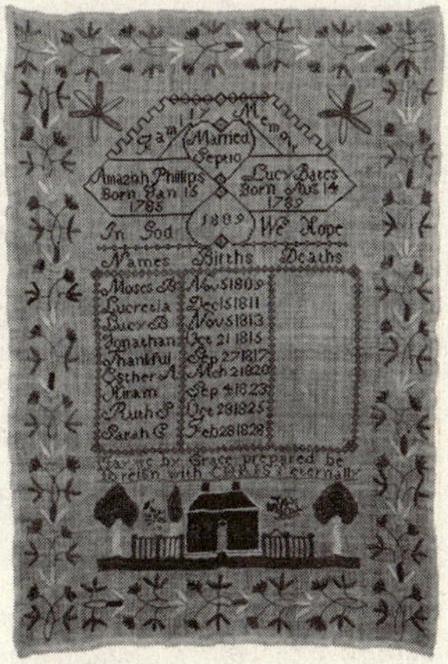

Family Register "Amaziah Phillips born Jan 15, 1785, Lucy Bates born Aug 14, 1789 Married Sept 10, 1809...," genealogical data above pious verse and cottage flanked by trees and potted plants, foliate border, 25" x 17", $4600 at auction. —Photo courtesy Skinner, Inc., Boston, MA.

	LOW	HIGH
Handkerchief, sheer white linen, small flowers and vines border, c1935-40, 12" x 12"	$25	$50
Memorial, for William Weston, by Caroline Weston, 1837, 16" x 13"	1000	2000
Memorial, young girl at 3 neoclassical urn-form memorials, New England, early 19th C, 17.625" x 21"	5000	6500
Panel, crochet and appliqué, stylized flowering tree, cotton on linen light blue, pink, red, and yellow, beveled frame, 20th C, 12.5" x 16.5"	50	100
Panel, silk on woven cotton, cherub by tree w/ medallion and "BCB," framed, 8.25" x 9.75"	50	100
Panel, wool on linen, cattle, tree, and shepherd, green, gold, brown, and white, 16.5" x 17.375"	350	500
Panel, wool on linen, teal, purple, red, white, shades of green, embroidered border, framed, early 20th C, 27" x 35"	450	600
Petit Point, silk on linen, flowers in yellow, brown, and green, mid-19th C, 7" x 2"	25	50
Piano Throw, woven silk, white, white flowers and green leaves, silk fringe, c1910-30, 90" x 90"	250	450
Picture, silk, "Edgar & Matilda," signed by Sally Aldrich, watercolor and sequin highlights, early 19th C, 16" d	800	1000
Pillow Case, cotton, embroidered flowers, bow ribbons, and swirls, c1910-20, 28" x 28"	25	75
Pocketbook, "John Clark, 1757," flame-stitched	400	500
Sampler, "Martha James Aged 11, 1814," verse above animal and floral motifs, geometric floral border, framed, 16" x 12.75"	500	650

	LOW	HIGH
Sampler, "Mary Ann Shaner," alphabets, flowers, couple holding hands, and stag, brown, yellow, and blue, framed, 23.5" x 13.25"	250	400
Sampler, "Sarah Eliza Baker, Aged—, 1840," multicolored alphabets, flowers, and birds, mounted on gold board in gilt frame, 27.25" x 20.75"	400	600
Sampler, stylized flowers, birds, and house, vining strawberry border, signed "E. Butler 1815," green, tan, black, and cream, 13.75" x 18"	300	450

Above, left to right: Memorial to George Washington, American, early 19th C, 18.25" x 16.25", $1955 at auction; Needlework, women standing before Slatersville Textile Mill in Cumberland, RI, "...Wrought in 1810 by Miss Alpha Bishop, Cumberland RI. Married to Rev. VR Osborn 1815," 21" x 23.75", $1093 at auction.

Below, left to right: Sampler, "Mary I. Spearght aged 12 years," alphabets and pious verse w/ foliate and geometric motifs, 17" x 16.5", $1495 at auction; Sampler, Lydia Ritter aged 11 Years," pious verse, baskets of fruit, foliate sprays, hearts, birds, geometric devices, and flowering vine border, 20.25" x 23.75", $3265 at auction.

—Photos courtesy Skinner, Inc., Boston, MA.

Quilts

Amish quilts are the leaders in hobbyist appeal, and usually, though not always, the most valuable.

Centennial, pieced and printed cotton, reserves w/ various exhibition halls, flag, star, and stripe borders in red, white, blue, and black on white ground, c1876, 83" x 74.5", $748 at auction. —Photo courtesy Skinner, Inc., Boston, MA.

	LOW	HIGH
Airplanes, pieced, 20 pink airplanes on white ground, 71" x 84"	$250	$400
Album or Friendship Design, pieced and appliquéd, 49 squares, w/ initials, Odd Fellow insignia, animals, embroidery, Masonic device, etc., 80" x 80"	500	700
American Flag, pieced, red, white, and blue cotton, counter-striped border, white cotton ground, late 19th/early 20th C, 76" x 76"	2000	3000
Bars, pieced, mauve, navy, aqua, rust, and other colors in crêpe, twill, knit, etc., Garnett, KS, 52" x 80"	60	125
Basket, pieced, tan, green, and pink calico, 76" x 78"	100	200
Cotton Crêpe, pieced, black, light blue, beige, and brown, 4 different designs, dated "Jan 2, 1946," 72" x 84"	500	700
Crazy Quilt, pieced, velvet, dark colors, w/ colorful embroidery, knotted, 56" x 63"	350	500
Crazy Quilt Top, pieced, silk and satin, bright colors, w/ embroidery, 70" x 92"	150	250
Diamond in Square, pieced, maroon, pink, gray, blue, and purple crêpe, floral quilting, Amish, Bucks County, PA, 82" x 84"	100	200
Flower Baskets, appliquéd, vining floral border, red, green, and goldenrod, 87.5" x 89"	800	1000
Geometric, pieced, pink calico and white, 71" x 85"	250	400
Geometric, pieced, red and white, 72" x 82"	200	300
Irish Chain, blue and white, 72" x 82"	200	300
Irish Chain, pieced, green calico, red, hand sewn, some machine work on piecing and binding, 63" x 79.5"	400	600
Log Cabin, pieced, wool, red, black, blue, and gray, Amish, 20" x 70"	250	400
Mountains, pieced, red, yellow, and green calico, back w/ pink and gray bar pattern, 76" x 80"	800	1000
Nine Patch, pieced, colored prints, 76" x 82"	125	250

	LOW	HIGH
Occupational, Irish Chain, pieced and embroidered, red on white ground, red, white, purple, and green embroidery, dated 1885, 96" x 79"	1500	2500
Quilt Top, appliquéd, rose and bud pattern, pink calico, green, and red on white ground, 90" x 73"	450	650
Red Diamond, blue border, wide geometric border in red and shades of blue on white ground, Amish, 90" x 108"	250	400
Rising Sun, appliquéd, potted plant border, red, blue, and green calicos on white ground, 103" x 85"	250	400
Rose of Sharon, appliquéd, stylized pink calico floral medallions, red and teal green calico, trapunto wreaths in center, 67.5" x 82.5"	750	1000
Rose Wreath, appliquéd, red and teal green, mid-19th C, 84" x 82"	200	350
Stylized Floral Medallions, appliquéd, swag and flower border, red and green print, 83" x 86"	500	770
Sunburst and Eagle, appliquéd, green, terra-cotta, and red on white field, 88" x 90"	200	350
Star, pieced, red and white, 64" x 74"	125	200
Star, pieced, youth, lavender, yellow, coral, and blue on pale green ground, machine sewn binding, 48" x 64"	250	400
Sunshine and Shadow, pieced, multicolored design in wool, crêpe, knit, etc., purple border, Amish, 1930, 80" x80"	350	500

Left to right: Sawtooth Design, pieced silk and glazed cotton, blue, white, and amethyst on khaki field, signed and dated on reverse "Mary Anne Wisner 1841," Quaker, PA, 95.5" x 100.5", $690 at auction; Sunburst and Rose of Sharon w/ Birds, appliquéd, red, green, and terra cotta on white ground, mid-19th C, 83.5" sq, $2415 at auction. —Photos courtesy Skinner, Inc., Boston, MA.

Thermometers

	LOW	HIGH
Coca-Cola, tin, emb, "Drink Coca-Cola In Bottles/Quality Refreshment," 1950s, 3" x 9"	$800	$1000
CSC Hi-D Ammonium Nitrate, tin, Pam Clock Co, 12" d	100	150
Dr. Pepper, tin, "Drink Dr. Pepper/Good For Life" and bottle, 1930-40s	700	900
Dr. Pepper, tin, "When Hungry, Thirsty or Tired Drink Dr. Pepper Good For Life!," c1940s, 10" x 26"	300	400
Mail Pouch Tobacco, porcelain, "Chew Mail Pouch Tobacco/Treat Yourself To The Best," c1920-30s, 19" x 74"	600	750
Mason's Root Beer, tin, "Enjoy Mason's Root Beer/Bold Refreshing Flavor," 12" d	200	250
Mobil Car-Care, tin, "At All Temperatures," 11.75" d	325	400
Nature's Remedy, porcelain, "To-Night Tomorrow Alright/Come In/If you get it here/It's good," 1920-30s, 7" x 27"	400	525
Orange Crush, tin, bottle cap, 6" x 16"	100	150
Pepsi-Cola, painted metal, embossed bottle cap, "Pepsi-Cola/The Light Refreshment," 7.5" x 27.5"	100	150
Sunbeam Bread, Miss Sunbeam, "Reach For Sunbeam Bread/Let's Be Friends," 1950-60s, 12" d	800	1000
Sun Crest, tin, "Get Tingleated with Sun Crest" and bottle, round	200	300
Taylor, wood, "Taylor Thermometers Sold Here," 7.625" x 29"	50	100
Thermo Royal, tin, glass and porcelain face, antifreeze can, 17.625" h	250	350

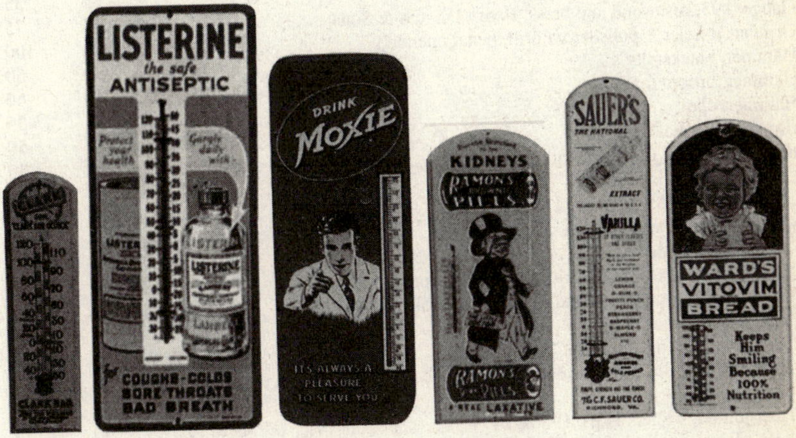

Advertising Thermometers at auction, left to right: Clark Bar, wood, c1930, 19" h, $165; Listerine, porcelain, 30" h, $880; Moxie, tin, 1952, 26" h, $1320; Ramon's, wood, 1930s-40s, 21" h, $198; Sauer's, wood, c1910, 24" h, $550; Ward's, porcelain, c1920s, 21" h, $688. —Photos courtesy Gary Metz's Muddy River Trading Co.

Tools

Hand tools of the eighteenth, nineteenth and twentieth centuries often represent fine craftsmanship and engineering. Values vary with quality, rarity and also usability. Many craftsmen prefer the high quality of some antique tools over those now available. Watch out for missing parts.

"Good" pieces show wear but no damage and are still capable of use. "Best" pieces are in perfect condition with superior quality manufacture. For further information see *The Antique Tool Collector's Guide to Value, Third Edition* by Ronald S. Barlow (Windmill Publishing, El Cajon, CA, 1991), *Collecting Antique Tools* by Herbert P. Kean and Emil S. Pollak (Astragal Press, Morristown, NJ, 1990), and *Town-Country Old Tools* by Jack Wood (L-W Book Sales, Gas City, IN, 1990, 1999 value update).

	GOOD	BEST
Axe, cast steel, bent handle, C. Hammond	$50	$75
Brace, brass trimmed chucks, Millers Falls, 1800s	20	60
Calipers, solid brass, hook and leg style, Vernier, 5" l	50	125
Chisel, corner, socket handle, 1" w	30	40
Chisel, shipbuilder's, socket handle	35	50
Chisel, V-shape, socket handle, Ohio Tool Co., 1"	10	25
Cobbler's Bench, straddle, plank style, no seat, 3 legged, 5 drawers	125	175
Cobbler's Pliers and Hammer	20	30
Compass, primitive, solid walnut wing dividers, 13" l	125	175
Drawing Knife, Keen Kutter, 8" l	30	40
Drill, bow, Eclipse #3, J. Neill & Co.	50	100
Drill, breast, Goodell-Pratt, #477	25	40
Drill, hand, #370, jointed handle, adjustable, Proto Mfg. Co.	30	50
Drill Press, unmarked, table top	25	35
Gauge, #93, rosewood and brass, Henry Disston & Sons	50	75
Grinder, jeweler's, polisher w/ drill, pedal operated	65	100
Hammer, blacksmith's	30	50
Hammer, broom maker's	40	60
Hammer, claw	25	35
Hammer, jeweler's	30	50
Hatchet, lathing, C. Hammond	20	30
Level, machinist's, cast iron, 7.5"	30	50
Level, mason's, M. Lennon, 42"	75	100
Mallet, tinsmith's, hickory	15	25
Plane, basket maker's, 28" l	250	350
Plane, block, cast iron, American Tool & Foundry, 4.5" l	20	30
Plane, compass, coffin shaped, flexible iron sole, J. Mosley	80	120
Plane, coping, John Bell, .75" w	25	50
Plane, fore, beech, Ohio Tool Co., 22" l	30	50
Plane, horn, laminated rosewood sole, French, 3" x 8"	40	60
Plane, jack, Bailey Tool Co.	300	500
Plane, jointer, Millers Falls, 1930s, 24" l	50	75
Plane, plow, boxwood, D. R. Barton	200	300
Plane, scraper, rosewood handle and knob, 12"	125	200
Pliers, leather worker's	10	20
Plumb Bob, mason's, brass, turnip shaped	50	100
Plumb Bob, wooden, acorn finial	20	50
Protractor, brass, 6" beveled bottom edge	20	40
Router, carriage maker's	450	600
Router, nickel plated, Ohio Tool Co.	40	80
Rule, blacksmith's, brass, folding	60	125

	GOOD	BEST
Rule, hat maker's, boxwood, brass extension slide, 5" l	50	100
Saw, bow	75	125
Saw, buck	40	80
Saw, combination jigsaw and lathe, cast iron, c1886	200	300
Saw, compass, center mounted pivot handle, Charles Bush	75	100
Saw, hack	50	80
Saw, hand, Wells W. Awyer & Co.	50	75
Screwbox, oak, homemade, 2" x 5.5"	30	50
Screwdriver, gripper style, C. A. Munn & Co.	10	20
Screwdriver, gunsmith's	15	25
Sharpening Stone	10	20
Soldering Iron, shepherd's crook shape, 12"	25	35
Soldering Iron, solid copper head, wooden handle	5	15
Spokeshave, iron, wood handles	75	125
Square, Stanley, 46.5" maple board	50	75
Square, Universal, 5"	5	10
Surveying Compass, A. Leitz Co., 4" d	40	65
Tool Cabinet, oak, wall hung, Keen Kutter, 19" x 27.5" x 8"	100	250
Tool Chest, machinist's	75	150
Vise, cast iron, Columbian	5	15
Vise, Sargent, #95, c1925	5	15
Wrench, bicycle, adjustable, 5" l	5	10
Wrench, buggy, brass adjustable collar, 1883	40	60
Wrench, monkey	10	20
Wrench, pipe, wheel-shaped lower jaw, Craftsman, 12"	30	50
Wrench, pocket	10	25

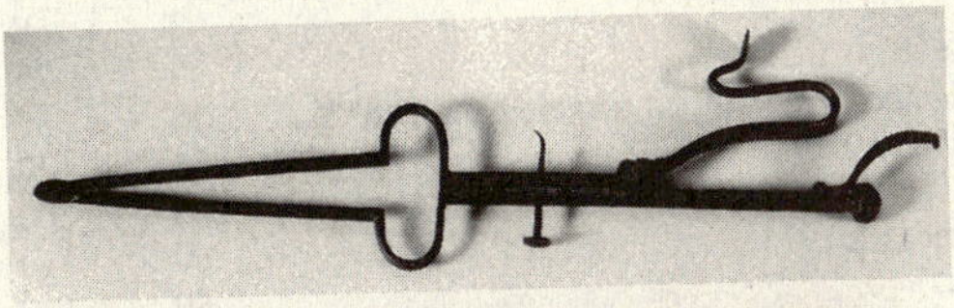

Left: Pipe Tongs, wrought steel, inscribed "Fort W. M. Henry Capt. B. Williams 1756," $9200 at auction.

Left: Silversmith's Tool Chest and Tools, dovetailed walnut chest w/ molded rim and base raised on low round feet, upper locking interior fitted w/ 2 removable trays above single locking drawer containing stamps, gouges, files, and treading tools, American, mid-19th C, 11" x 15" x 11" chest, $2760 at auction.

—Photos courtesy Skinner, Inc., Boston, MA.

Toys and Playthings

Baby Rattles

Baby rattles are a universal toy. Almost every culture in the world has its own traditions and superstitions surrounding them. Available examples range from Georgian coral-and-bells to the plastic ones of today. Rattles can be made of gold, silver, ivory, tin, celluloid, paper and plastic. Collectors must compete with silver collectors and toy collectors for the prime examples, but flea markets, antique shows and some auctions are still good resources.

For more information see *Collecting Baby Rattles* by Marcia Hersey (Krause Publications, Iola, WI, 1998).

	LOW	HIGH
Bakelite and Celluloid, Humpty Dumpty, c1940	$85	$150
Bone, 4 bells, whistle handle, 4" l	150	175
Celluloid, black boy, yellow shorts and shoes, marked "Canada"	40	55
Celluloid, clown playing lute, pink, brown highlights, 4.5"	35	45
Celluloid, dumbbell, ivory grained, some blue paint, 6" l	25	35
Celluloid, Santa Claus, Occupied Japan	75	125
Celluloid, stork, white, black highlights, made in Japan, 6.25"	55	65
Celluloid, turtle shell, green, yellow celluloid handle	8	15
Gold, mother-of-pearl handle, French, c1800	3500	4500
Leather and Wood, Japan, c1900	50	75
Litho Tin, girl, cat, boy, and dog, soldered, 4.5" l	150	175
Nickel Plated, bells, leatherized white cloth straps w/ red zigzag, black painted turned handle, 6" l	125	175
Plastic, bunny, yellow, white apron, pink hat, Knickerbocker	5	10
Plastic, dog in bubble, red handle	3	8
Plated Brass, urn shaped, ivory handle, 6" l	35	75
Rubber, pacifier, 2 bells on replaced leather strap, turned whistle handle, 6" l	15	35
Silver, Art Nouveau, ivory ring, French, c1910	85	140
Silver, butterfly, German, c1905	200	300
Silver, child reaching for moon, American, c1925	60	110
Silver, fish, ivory handle, Portugese, c1940	80	120
Silver, jester, mother-of-pearl handle, English, c1900	250	350
Silver, mallet, Indian, c1900	50	75
Silver, repoussé child's head and 4 bells, ivory handle, 6" l	175	225
Silver, rooster, pearl handle, 3.25" l	50	75
Silver-Gilt, carnelian handle, Dutch, c1850	450	650
Silver Plate, bell, bone ring handle	50	75
Silver Plate, London bobby, English, c1920	40	75
Silver Plate, whistle, English, c1930	40	75
Stuffed Cloth, Disney's Minnie Mouse	50	100
Tin, 4 bells, worn japanning, turned wooden black handle, 8.25" l	150	200
Tin, 12 bells on leatherized cloth straps, turned handle, worn white paint, 6.75" l	138	165
Tin, boy's head, painted, c1900	140	200
Tin, barrel rattle w/ embossed eagle and "For A Good Child," 5.5" l	45	75
Wood, carved handle, 5.75" l	45	75
Wood, ice cream sandwich, hand carved, c1991	20	30
Wood, paper litho covering, 4.625" l	45	75
Wood, Wire, and Tin, 8 bells attached to wires on twisted wire rod fitted in round japanned tin rattle, turned wood handle	150	200

Banks

The values indicated for mechanical banks in this section reflect prices realized at private sales and recent public auctions. When evaluating a bank, one must consider market trends, subject matter, personal taste, and condition. Prices are given for banks in working condition and with original paint.

Still banks are aptly named since there are no mechanical actions required to make the deposit. When collecting still banks, beware of rust, reproductions and repaints. Prices are for examples with no major cracks, repairs, or repaints. Such faults decrease the value of a bank.

Many banks have been reproduced and most of these are poor quality and easy to detect. Beware of banks that are badly rusted and look like they have been buried in someone's backyard, since that may have been done in order to simulate age. Banks that bear the mark "The Book of Knowledge" are 1950s reproductions that are handsome but worth only a fraction of the value of the originals.

For further reading we recommend *The Bank Book: The Encyclopedia of Mechanical Bank Collecting* by Bill Norman (Accent Studios, San Diego, CA, 1984), *The Penny Bank Book: Collecting Still Banks, Revised* by Andy and Susan Moore (Schiffer, Exton, PA, 1997), and *Penny Lane: A History of Antique Mechanical Toy Banks* by Al Davidson, Longs Americana, Mokelumne Hill, CA, 1987.

Mechanical Banks

	LOW	HIGH
Acrobat, blue base, swinging acrobat causes clown to spin and coin to fall, J. & E. Stevens Co., 7.25" l	$6000	$8000
Artillery Bank, Union soldier w/ moving arm mortar fires coin into tower, J. & E. Stevens Co., 8" l	3000	5000
Bear and Tree Stump, moving tongue, black, Judd Mfg. Co., 5" h	400	600
Boy on Trapeze, red shirt, blue trousers, lattice base, J. Barton & Smith Co., 9.5" h	1000	1500
Boys Stealing Watermelon, 1 boy's arm moves as coin disappears and dog runs out of house, standing boy in yellow shirt and trousers, lying boy in red shirt and trousers, tan dog house, Kyser & Rex Co., 6.5" l	2500	5000
Bulldog, sitting, tail lever, dog tosses coin placed on his nose, catches it in mouth, and swallows, J. & E. Stevens Co.	1200	1500
Bulldog, standing, moving tongue and tail, Judd Mfg. Co., 6.5" l	600	800
Cabin, yellow walls, pivoting man kicks coin through roof, J. & E. Stevens Co., 4.25" h	600	800
Chief Big Moon, frog jumps at fish being cooked by Indian squaw at tent, J. & E. Stevens Co.	1500	2000

Left to right: Mule Entering Barn; 'Spise a Mule. —Photo courtesy Garth's Auctions, Delaware, OH.

	LOW	HIGH
Clown on Globe, clown and globe turn, clown does headstand, red and orange costume, yellow base, J. & E. Stevens Co., 9" h	1000	1500
Creedmoor, red trousers, firing rifle, bell, stamped "Bowden Series," marked on base, J. & E. Stevens Co., 10" l	800	1200
Eagle and Eaglets, mother eagle feeds coin to crying baby eagles in nest, J. & E. Stevens Co.	600	1000
Elephant and 3 Clowns, red blanket, elephant's trunk knocks coin into base as mounted clown turns, J. & E. Stevens Co., 5.75" h	2500	4000
Elephant Pull-Tail, moving trunk and tail, gray, gold, and black, Hubley, 9" l	300	600
Elephant w/ 3 Stars, moving trunk and tail, 9" l	400	700
Elephant w/ Pop-up Man, wood figure pops out of elephant's trunk as it moves, gold, black, and red, Enterprise Mfg. Co., 6.5" l	700	1000
Ferris Wheel, orange and black wheel w/ 6 yellow gondolas each carrying 2 male riders, base w/ clockwork motor, coin slot, on/off lever, and red and black highlights, marked "Bowen's Pat Apd For" on base, 22" h	8000	12,000
Frog on Lattice Base, green and white base, foot lever operates frog's mouth and eyes, J. & E. Stevens Co., 4.5" dia	600	800
Frog on Lattice Base, red and yellow base, foot lever operates frog's mouth and eyes, J. & E. Stevens Co., 4.5" dia	400	600
Giant in Tower, circular tower w/ red bricks and yellow trim, giant pops up, uses English penny, J. Harper & Co., England	4500	6000
Hall's Liliput, pivoting cashier, white building, J. & E. Stevens Co., 4.5" h	4000	6000
Hen and Chick, brown hen opens its mouth, chick pops up to deposit coin, J. & E. Stevens Co., 9.75" l	4000	6000
Humpty Dumpty, multicolored, moving arm, tongue, and eyes, Shepard Hardware Co., 7.5" h	1200	1600
Indian and Bear, Indian w/ moving head shoots coin into white bear's opening mouth, J. & E. Stevens Co., 10.25" l	2500	5000
Jolly Nigger, moving eyes and tongue, bronze finish, 5.5" h	250	500
Jolly Nigger, moving eyes and tongue, red shirt and collar, yellow butterfly tie and buttons, 4.625" l	200	300
Jonah and Whale, man in boat tosses Jonah, coin slides from Jonah's head into whale's mouth, whale nods head, Shepard Hardware Co.	2500	3500
Leap-Frog, 1 boy leaps over another to hit lever which causes coin to fall into tree, Shepard Hardware Co., 7.5" l	2500	3500
Lion and Monkeys, monkey drops coin in lion's mouth while baby monkey jumps up to watch, Kyser & Rex Co., 9.125" l	1500	2500
Lion Hunter, rifle fires, head moves, lion rears, J. & E. Stevens Co., 11" l	6000	8000
Little Moe, wearing straw hat, moving arm deposits coin in mouth, Chamberlin & Hill, Ltd., England	2000	2500
Mammy and Child, red dressed mother tilts her hand and nods her head, baby's legs raise when coin is deposited through apron, Kyser & Rex Co., 7.5" h	2000	3000
Monkey and Coconut, moving hand, mouth, and eyes, opening coconut, J. & E. Stevens Co., 8.25" h	3000	5000
Mosque, black w/ blue wipe, rotating gorilla, Judd Mfg. Co., 6.75" h	1000	1500
Mule Entering Barn, mule tosses coin into barn, dog springs from kennel, J. & E. Stevens Co.	800	1000
New Creedmoor, firing rifle, bell, moving head, J. & E. Stevens Co., 10" l	600	900
Organ and Monkey, monkey on barrel organ, hand-turned mechanism, monkey deposits coin and tips hat, bell rings, Kyser & Rex Co., 6.5" h	1000	1500
Organ and Monkey, w/ boy and girl figures, barrel organ w/ hand-turned mechanism, monkey drops coin into top and tips his cap, children dance, bell rings, 7.75" h	3000	4000

Left: Elephant Pull-Tail.
Right: Elephant w/ 3 Stars.

Left: Humpty Dumpty.
Center: Stump Speaker.
Right: Monkey and Coconut.

Left: Clown on Globe.
Center: Shoot the Chute.
Right: Boy on Trapeze.

Left: Teddy and the Bear.
Right: Indian and Bear.

Left: Trick Pony.
Center: Speaking Dog.
Right: Lion and Monkeys.

—Photos courtesy Skinner, Inc., Boston, MA.

	LOW	HIGH
Organ and Monkey, w/ dog and cat figures, barrel organ w/ hand-turned mechanism, monkey drops coin into top and tips his cap, dog and cat dance, bell rings, 7.75" h	600	800
Organ Grinder and Bear, house w/ organ grinder and bear on lawn, organ grinder plays organ and deposits coin as bear performs tricks, Kyser & Rex Co.	1200	1500
Organ Grinder and Monkey, place coin in monkey's mouth, monkey jumps and deposits coin in organ grinder's box, Hubley	300	500
Owl, coin deposited in slot in book under wing causes owl's eyes to move, 5.75" h	250	350
Owl, glass eyes, white owl turns head and deposits coin in base, J. & E. Stevens Co.	1200	1800
Paddy and the Pig, pig kicks coin into Paddy's opening mouth, J. & E. Stevens Co.	1800	2500
Pay Phone, maroon, black, and silver, w/ 5-, 10-, and 25-cent slots, handle-operated bell, J. & E. Stevens Co., 7.25" h	2500	3500
Peg Leg Beggar, off-white face, nodding head, Judd Mfg. Co., 5" h	600	800
Pig in Highchair, nickeled and cast w/ floral and foliate motifs, pig lifts tray, swallows coin, and moves his tongue, J. & E. Stevens Co., 6" h	1200	1600
Pineapple Head, moving arm deposits coin in mouth, commemorates Hawaii's becoming 50th state, 9" h	400	600
Punch and Judy, puppet stage w/ large letters, Judy turns and deposits coin, Punch rushes forward brandishing club, Shepard Hardware Co.	1000	1500
Rooster, moving head and beak, Kyser & Rex Co., 6.25" h	700	1000
Shoot the Chute, nickel-plated, Buster Brown and Tige in boat, J. & E. Stevens Co., 9.75" l	6000	10,000
Speaking Dog, maroon base, girl moves arm holding coin on plate, depositing coin through opening trap door in bench, dog opens mouth and wags tail, Shepard Hardware Co.	600	800
'Spise a Mule, bench, mule turns and kicks boy, causing coin to be deposited, J. & E. Stevens Co.	700	900

Left: Ferris Wheel Bank.

Below, left to right: Owl; Jolly Nigger.

—Photos courtesy Skinner, Inc., Boston, MA.

	LOW	HIGH
'Spise a Mule, jockey, kicking mule, pivoting rider, John Harper & Co., Ltd., England, 10" l	800	1200
Squirrel and Tree Stump, squirrel leaps to drop coin into stump, Mechanical Novelty Works, 7" l	1000	2000
Stump Speaker, moving urn, opening mouth and carpet bag, Shepard Hardware Co., 9.5" h	3000	5000
Tabby, sitting on egg w/ moving chick's head	500	800
Tammany, black jacket, gray trousers, 5.5" h	500	800
Tammany, dark blue jacket, brown trousers, moving head and arm, J. & E. Stevens Co.	400	700
Teddy and the Bear, brown tree, Teddy shoots bull's eye, raises his head, bear pops out of tree, J. & E. Stevens Co., 10.25" l	2500	3500
Toad on Stump, green, mouth opens, J. & E. Stevens Co., 4" l	400	500
Trick Dog, yellow and red base, dog jumps through clown's hoop and deposits coin in red barrel, Hubley, 8.75" l	500	800
Trick Pony, pony lowers its head to deposit coin in trough which opens and closes to receive coin, Shepard Hardware Co., 7" l	1200	2500
Tricky Pig, cast brass, tail lever causes figure to emerge from pig's back, 8.5" l	600	800
Uncle Sam, coin drops in opening satchel, beard moves, Shepard Hardware Co., 4.75" l	1000	1500
Uncle Sam, moving hand, opening mouth and satchel, Shepard Hardware Co., 11.5" h	1500	1800
Watchdog Safe, dog opens mouth, sides cast w/ classical head, J. & E. Stevens Co., 5.75" h	500	700
William Tell, figure shoots apple off boy's head into tower and strikes bell, J. & E. Stevens Co., 10.5" l	600	1000
World's Fair, Indian chief appears and hands Columbus a peace pipe as Columbus salutes, "Columbus" cast in base, J. & E. Stevens Co., 8.25" l	1200	1600

Still Banks

Arabian Safe, door and sides cast w/ Middle Eastern scenes, Kyser & Rex, 4.5" h	$100	$150
Bank Building, black w/ gold highlights, 5.5" h	150	250
Bank of Industry, nickel-plated, combination lock door cast w/ blacksmith, top cast w/ tools, instruments, and other technological motifs, Kenton, 5.5" h	50	100
Baseball Player, gold and red, 5.625" h	75	150
Bear, begging, 5.25" h	75	150
Bear w/ Honey Pot, brown w/ polychrome, 6.25" h	25	50
Billiken, gold and red, 6.5" h	50	100
Billiken Good Luck, gold w/ green hair, A. C. Williams, 4" h	300	600
Black Boy, 2-face, black, gold, and silver, 3.25" h	200	300
Boston Terrier, brown, white, and black, 5.25" h	150	250
Boxer Dog, seated, gold and red, 4.5" h	40	80
Buffalo, traces of gold	75	150
Campbell Kids, 4" l	150	250
Cat, seated, black, 4.25" h	100	200
Cat on Tub, gold repaint, 4.125" h	75	150
Clock, Big Ben style, black and gold, 3.5" h	50	100
Clown, crooked hat, 6.875" h	300	400
Clown, red, blue, and gold, 6.25" h	200	300

	LOW	HIGH
Counting House–Fidelity Trust Vaults, ornate bank kiosk, front w/ coin slot and Little Lord Fontleroy-style "Cashier," sides w/ bulldog "Paying Tellers," rear w/ unmarked clock-type combination dial w/ 2 indicator arms, brown w/ gilt highlights, J. Barton Smith, 7" h	400	600
Cupola Bank, red roof, gray-blue walls, yellow and red details, J. & E. Stevens Co., 4.25" h	1000	1200
Elephant, trunk down, gray, 4" l	50	80
Elephant on Tub, 5.375" h	75	150
Elephant w/ Howdah, gray and silver w/ gold highlights, 5" l	75	125
Flat Iron Building, triangular, silver finish, Kenton, 5.75" h	300	500
General Butler, J. & E. Stevens Co., 6.75" h	3000	4000
G.O.P. Elephant, red and gold, 4" h	250	350
Hall's Excelsior, maroon walls, string-pull mechanism, wood figure, paper "Cashier" label, J. & E. Stevens Co., 5.25" h	400	600
Home Savings Bank, dog's head finial, J. & E. Stevens Co., 6" h	500	700
Horse, rearing, gold, 5" h	75	150
House, gold, 3.325" h	50	80
House, gold and green, 3" h	50	80
House, red and silver, 4" h	75	125
Independence Hall, removable tower, cast legends "Birthplace of American Independence" and "Liberty Proclaimed July.4.1776," tied reed plinth w/ gilt finish, Enterprise Mfg. Co., 10.25" h	800	1000
Ironmaster's House, combination trap, Kyser & Rex Co., 4.5" h	2000	3000

Above, left to right: Clown; Radio; U.S. Mail; Liberty Bell; North Pole; U.S. Treasury; Radio; Sailor.

Below, left to right: Billiken; Rabbit; Flat Iron Building; Elephant on Tub; St. Bernard; Lion.—Photos courtesy Garth's Auctions, Delaware, OH.

	LOW	HIGH
Jewel Chest, hinged lid, combination lock, bronzed foliate decoration, 6.5" l	200	400
Key Lock Safe No. 50, nickel-plated, cast w/ floral and geometric motifs and "Security Safe Deposit," inner and outer alphabetic combination knobs, J. & E. Stevens Co., 4.5" h	100	150
Liberty Bell, wooden base, labeled "Bailey's Centennial Money Bank," gold and black, 4.75" h	50	100
Lion, gold, 5.125" h	50	100
Lion on Tub, gold, blue, and red, 5.5" h	100	200
Mailbox, green and gold, 3.75" h	40	80
Mailbox, red and gold, 5.25" h	50	80
Mammy, hands on hips, gold, 5.25" h	200	300
Mulligan, blue, pink, red, and black, 5.75" h	175	275
Multiplying, cream, red, and brown Gothic-style building, J. & E. Stevens Co., 6.5" h	4000	6000
Mutt and Jeff, gold finish, A. C. Williams, 5.25" h	125	175
North Pole, yellow and red, 4.25" h	175	275
Old South Church, green roof, white walls and spire, 9.5" h	4000	5000
Puppo, polychrome, 4.75" h	75	150
Puppo on Pillow, Hubley, 4.25" h	150	250
Rabbit, begging, gold and red, 5" h	100	200
Rabbit, standing, red and gold, 6.625" h	150	250
Radio Bank, blue and gold, 3.375" h	100	200
Radio Bank, nickel finish, 3.375" h	75	150

Left to right: Mulligan; G.O.P. Elephant; Sea Lion; Sesquicentennial Liberty Bell; Billiken; Aunt Jemima.

Left to right: Bear w/ Honey Pot; State Bank; Liberty Bell; Boxer Dog; Rabbit; Puppo. —Photos courtesy Garth's Auctions, Delaware, OH.

	LOW	HIGH
Roof Bank, mansard roof, gilt highlights, J. & E. Stevens Co., 5.5" h	300	500
Roof Bank, triangular shingles, gilt highlights, Grey Iron Casting Co., 5.5" h	200	400
Safe, black and green, 3.625" h	254	50
Safe, nickel plated, 3.375" h	25	50
Sailor, silver, 5.5" h	75	150
Savings Chest, nickeled steel, w/ key, 6.25" l	200	300
Sea Lion, black w/ red highlights, 3.375" h	300	400
Security Safe Deposit, inner and outer lettered combination knobs, gilt highlights, 4.75" h	100	200
Sesquicentennial Liberty Bell, 3.75" h	50	100
Sharecropper, no paint, 5.25" h	50	75
Spitz Dog, gold finish, Grey Iron Castings Co., 4.5" l	300	400
State Bank, cupola dormer windows, locking door, Kenton, 8.75" h	1200	1500
Statue of Liberty, gold, 6.25" h	75	150
St. Bernard w/ Pack, black w/ gilt details, A. C. Williams, 7.75" l	100	200
St. Bernard w/ Pack, brown japanning w/ gilt highlights, 5.5" h	100	200
Tank Bank U.S.A., gold, 5.75" l	150	250
Thrifty Pig, white and polychrome, 6.625" h	75	125
Time Safe, nickel plated, cast w/ eagle motif above clock face w/ legend "What Time Does it Open," clock hand-operated opening mechanism, w/ original instruction sheet, E. M. Roche Novelty Co., Bloomfield, NJ, 7.25" h	500	700
Tower Bank 1890, inner and outer alphabetic combination door lock, Kyser & Rex Co., 7" h	800	1200
Trick Buffalo, removable head, 9.5" l	500	800
U.S. Mail, silver and red, 4.25" h	75	150
U.S. Treasury, white and red, 3.125" h	50	100
Villa Bank 1882, gabled roof w/ Gothic windows, Kyser & Rex Co., 5.5" h	400	600

Left to right: Old South Church; Flat Iron Building; Home Savings; Ironmaster's House.

—Photos courtesy Skinner, Inc., Boston, MA.

Left to right: Counting House-Fidelity Trust Vaults; State Bank; Independence Hall.

Character Clocks and Watches

Mention "character watches" and you will invariably hear the reply, "You mean like a Mickey Mouse watch?" It was Mickey who ushered in the first comic character watch in 1933 and the market has been thriving ever since. Prices for watches in their original, colorful boxes have skyrocketed due to scarcity and increasing demand. Promotional watches requiring boxtops or proof of purchase and acquired by mail have gained in popularity.

The prices listed in the MNP column are for mint condition working watches, without their packaging or original boxes; the second price range (MIP) is for working, mint in the package examples. MIP for promotional watches means that they come with their original mailing material. We have substituted AC for alarm clock, PW for pocket watch and WW for wristwatch.

The following are our codes for manufacturers: *BR*–Bradley; *BY*–Bayard; *GO*-Goober Time Company; *IG*–Ingraham; *IN*–Ingersol; *K*–Kellogg's; *LW*–Lafayette Watch Company; *M*-Marx; *NH*–New Haven Clock Co; *P*-Picco; *SH*-Sheffield Watch, West Germany; *SM*–Smith's, England; *UK*–Unknown; *UST*–U.S. Time.

Hopalong Cassidy WW, UST, $65-$75.

	COMPANY	CIRCA	MNP	MIP
Aladdin WW, animated second hand magic lamp, blue velvet pouch, Nestle promotion, ©Disney Limited Edition	UK	1993	$185-$250	$250-$325
Annie WW, red leather band, 3.5" h hard plastic dome package	P	1982	35-55	75-95
Batman AC, talking alarm, plastic	UK	1974	75-100	125-155
Betty Boop PW, silvered brass, engraved portrait of Betty and Bimbo on back	UK	1930s	560-750	940-1125
Bugs Bunny AC, animated	IG	1951	200-300	375-470
Bugs Bunny WW, "It's Bugs Bunny Time," vinyl strap	LW	1974	55-75	100-125
Buster and Tige PW, Buster Brown Shoes, gold numerals, black hands and text, red Buster and Tige image	NH	1930s	200-400	500-625
Captain Marvel WW, green vinyl strap	UK	1958	200-400	500-625
Captain Midnight WW, battery operated, flying plane image, simulated brown alligator strap	UK	1970s	35-55	75-95
Captain Midnight 30th Anniversary WW, Ovaltine premium, original letter and ad offer, quartz numbers, vinyl strap, bubble pack packaging	UK	1988	55-75	100-125
Cinderella WW, white vinyl strap, blue hard plastic case	BR	1973	55-75	100-125
Dale Evans WW, brown strap w/ hand-tooled design	IG	1940s	150-300	400-500
Davy Crockett WW, brown leather strap	UST	1955	300-525	700-875
Dick Tracy WW, new black leather strap	NH	1948	200-400	500-625
Disneyland Canoe Races WW, employee's, blue velvet pouch	UK	1993	75-150	200-250

	COMPANY	CIRCA	MNP	MIP
Flash Gordon WW, black leather strap	BR	1979	75-100	125-155
Fred Flintstone AC, ceramic, figural, wind-up	SH	1960s	200-400	500-625
Howdy Doody WW, animated eyes, glow-in-the-dark hands, red leather strap	UK	1948-51	200-400	500-625
Jimmy Carter WW, Carter caricature, "Original Jimmy Carter From Peanuts To President" dial face, red, white, and blue fabric strap	GO	1976	35-55	75-95
Li'l Abner WW, animated flag	UK	1951	100-200	250-325
Lone Ranger PW, miniature metal gun and leather holster strap fob	NH	1940	275-325	450-560
Lone Ranger WW, dark brown leather strap w/ tooled design, plastic case	BR	1980	55-75	100-125
Mary Marvel WW	UK	1948	75-100	125-155
Mickey Mouse AC, wind-up	BY	1965	115-150	200-250
Mickey Mouse WW, 5" h plastic figure	IG/UST	1958	150-300	400-500
Mickey Mouse WW, animated, plastic case	BR	1970s	50-75	100-125
Mickey Mouse WW, leather strap	IN	1933	200-400	500-625
Mickey Mouse WW, yellow vinyl strap	M	1973	25-50	75-95
Popeye AC, wind-up, animated Swee' Pea	SM	1967	115-150	190-240
Popeye PW, animated Wimpy	NH	1934	340-450	550-700
Popeye WW, animated Wimpy	NH	1935	275-300	375-470
Roy Rogers AC, wind-up, animated	IG	1950s	200-400	500-625
Smitty	NH	1935	110-150	200-250
Snoopy WW	UST	1974	35-50	65-85
Spiro Agnew WW, blue suede strap	SH	1970	50-75	100-125
Superman WW, brown leather strap	NH	1939	200-400	500-625
Superman WW, yellow strap	BR	1962	100-200	250-325
Three Little Pigs PW, animated Wolf	IN	1934	700-1000	1250-1550
Three Little Pigs WW, Fiddler Pig image	UST	1947	100-200	250-325
Tony the Tiger WW, leather strap	K	1989	35-55	75-95
Wizard of Oz WW, Macy's 50th anniversary of original movie, black rubber strap, black plastic buckle, plastic display case	UK	1989	55-75	100-125

Left to right: Hopalong Cassidy AC, UST, $200-$300; Little Black Popeye AC, ©1937, 5.25" h, $100-$200. —Photo courtesy Collectors Auction Services; Mickey Mouse WW, IG, $345 at auction. —Photo courtesy Skinner, Inc., Boston, MA.

Character Toys

Character toys and memorabilia charm children and adults alike. They are based on familiar faces seen in the comics, heard on the radio or seen on a movie screen or TV. The following items range from the Yellow Kit (turn of the century) to Pee Wee Herman (1980s). Since there is such a diversity of materials, collecting criteria varies a bit. Most of the keywind tinplate character toys have a lithographed or printed finish while cast-iron toys are usually painted. Overall the condition reported below is for excellent and better. Prices are given for the item and in many cases a separate range is listed for the item in its original box or package. We do not give a range for toys that are unlikely to be found with their original box nor do we give a price for items that have little value without their packaging, such as records.

For futher information about character and other toys we suggest *Hake's Price Guide to Character Toys, 2nd Edition* by Ted Hake (Gemstone Publishing, Timonium, MD, 1998), *The Official Price Guide to Action Figures* by Stuart Wells III and Jim Main (House of Collectibles, New York, NY, 1997), *O'Brien's Collecting Toys, 9th Edition* edited by Elizabeth Stephan (Krause Publications, Iola, WI, 1999), *Schroeder's Collectible Toys: Antique to Modern, Sixth Edition* by Sharon and Bob Huxford (Collector Books, Paducah, KY, 1999), and *Toys & Prices 2000, 7th Edition* edited by Sharon Korbeck and Elizabeth Stephan (Krause Publications, Iola, WI, 1999).

There are also character items in the following sections of this book: Advertising, Comic Books, Comic Character Watches, Dolls, Games, Little Golden Books, Premiums, Radios, Robots, Space Toys and Viewmaster.

	UNBOXED	BOXED
Addams Family, Tru-Vue Set w/ Viewer, set of 3 film cards, yellow plastic viewer, ©1965 Filmways TV Productions, Inc.	$75-$100	—
Alfred E. Neuman, record, *Musically Mad,* RCA Victor	—	$25-$50
Allen Funt, game, The Allen Funt Candid Camera Game, Lowell, 1963	—	25-50
Amos 'N' Andy, Amos wind-up, litho tin, Marx, 1930, 11.25" h	500-750	—
Andy and Miranda Panda, lunch box, leather, ©Walter Lantz Productions, Inc., c1970s, 7.25" h	200-400	—
Andy Gump, figure, wood, jointed, black shirt, white sleeves and collar, green pants, black shoes, c1930, 5.5" h	100-200	—
Annette Funicello, game, Annette's Secret Passage, Parker Brothers, 1956	—	50-75
Annie Oakley, View-Master set, "Annie Oakley In Indian Water Hole," 3 reels, w/ envelope and story booklet, 1958	—	25-50
A-Team, game, The A-Team Game, Parker Brothers, 1984	—	15-25
A-Team, slot car, van, hard plastic, black, red and white accents, Tyco, 1984, 2.75" l	25-50	—
Bambi, bud vase, ceramic, underside incised "DIS 42B," full bee mark, Goebel, 1950s, 5.5" h	200-400	—
Banana Splits, frame tray puzzle, snowmobiling at North Pole, Whitman, ©1969 Hanna-Barbera Productions, Inc., 11.5" x 14.5"	25-50	—
Banana Splits, tattoo vending machine card, Fleer Dubble Bubble Gum, 1969	15-25	—
Barney Google, sheet music, *Barney Google Fox Trot,* ©1923 King Features Syndicate	15-25	—
Batman, bank, painted composition, figural Batman w/ hands on hips, white base w/ reed name decal on front, marked "Lego, Japan," ©1966 National Periodical Publications, Inc., 6.75" h	100-200	—
Batman, Batmobile, diecast metal and plastic, Corgi, 1966, 5.25" l	—	200-400
Batman, Batmobile Magic Car, diecast, w/ plastic figure, Triang, England, 1966, 5" l	—	400-500

Left to right: Baby Sandy Pull Toy, 1930s-40, $300-$350; Batmobile, "Piston," Taiwan, 1970s, $200-$300.

	UNBOXED	BOXED
Batman, Colorforms, 1966	—	50-75
Batman, figure, Sky Diving Parachutist, Ahi, 1973, 4.5" h	—	50-75
Batman, marionette, plastic head and feet, cloth outfit, Hazell/NPPI, 1966, 15" h	—	150-165
Batman, Mystery Action Batmobile, litho tin, battery operated, 1970s, 4" x 9.5" x 3"	—	200-400
Batman, pencil case, hard plastic, gun shaped, clear lid, green bottom, marked "Made In U.S.A.," 1966, 4.75" x 8.5"	50-75	—
Batman, poster, "Bring Back Adam West as Batman," 1986, 14" x 22"	75-100	—
Batman, record, *The Official Adventures of Batman & Robin,* 33⅓ rpm, Leo the Lion Records, ©1966 National Periodical Pub., Inc.	—	25-50
Beaky Buzzard, bank, cast metal, figural, 1940s, 4.25" h	100-200	—
Beaky Buzzard, pencil holder, metal, figural, 1940s, 4.25" h	75-100	—
Beany and Cecil, lunch box, vinyl, ©1949-50 Robert Clampett, c1960s, 8.5" h	100-200	—
Beany and Cecil, musical toy guitar, black plastic, red wooden handle, Mattel, 1961, 14" l	50-75	—
Betty Boop, doll, wooden, 1930s, 4.25" h	100-200	—
Betty Boop, guitar, images of Betty, Bimbo, and Ko Ko, 21" l	725	—
Betty Boop, pin, enamel and silvered brass, 1930s, 1.5" l	75-100	—
Beverly Hillbillies, punch-out book, Whitman, 1964, 10" x 14"	75-100	—
Blondie and Dagwood, paint set, litho tin, ©1952 King Features Syndicate, Inc., The American Crayon Co., Ohio, NY, 4.5" x 5.625 x .625"	25-50	—
Buck Rogers, Sunday comics, *Syracuse Herald,* Aug 30, 1931, 4 pages	175-185	—
Bugs Bunny, doll, cloth and vinyl, 1950s, 21" h	50-75	—
Bullwinkle, bank, vinyl, figural, ©1970 P.A.T. Ward, Hong Kong, 2.25" x 4" x 10"	50-75	—
Bullwinkle, cup, white milk glass, smiling Rocky and Bullwinkle, 1960s, 3.125" h	50-75	—
Captain Action, headquarters carrying case, vinyl, Ideal, 12" x 13"	—	75-85
Captain America, Cosmic Ray Light Gun, Larami Corp., 1974, 3" l	—	25-50
Captain America, Jetmobile, diecast metal and plastic, Corgi, 1979	—	50-75

Left to right: Captain Marvel Puzzle, "One Against Many," c1941, $60-$75; Dick Tracy's 2 in 1 Mystery Puzzle, Jaymar, 1948, $50-$75.

	UNBOXED	BOXED
Captain Hook, marionette, Peter Puppet Playthings, 1950s, 16.5" h	75-100	—
Captain Kangaroo, flicker cup, plastic, 1950s, 3.5" h	25-50	—
Captain Marvel, Magic Membership Card, 1940s, 2.5" x 3.75"	75-100	—
Captain Midnight, ring, adjustable brass bands, eagle and shield on each side, raised Marine Corps emblem, 1942	200-400	—
Captain Video, vehicle, hard plastic, Lido, 1950s, 3.5" l	50-75	—
Casper the Friendly Ghost, figure, vinyl, Sutton & Sons, Inc., 1972, 6.5" h	—	50-75
Casper the Friendly Ghost, push puppet, Kohner Bros., 1960s, 4" h	—	50-75
Charlie McCarthy, pencil sharpener, catalin, c1938	50-75	—
Charlie's Angels, Beauty Set, Fleetwood, ©1977 Spelling-Goldberg Productions	—	50-75
Cindy Bear, push puppet, Kohner Bros., 1960s, 3.75" h	50-75	—
Courageous Cat, record, 33⅓ rpm, *Simon Says,* Cosmo Recording Co., NY, c1967	75-100	—
Crusader Rabbit, book, *Crusader Rabbit In Bubble Trouble,* Whitman Top Tales, 1960	25-50	—
Daffy Duck, pull toy, wooden, Brice Toy Novelty, Inc.	100-200	—
Davy Crockett, 620 Snapshot Camera, black plastic, attached vinyl carrying strap, Herbert George Co., mid-1950s, 3" x 3" x 3.875"	75-100	—
Davy Crockett, cup, white milk glass, brown image of Crockett leading wagon train, Fire-King Oven Ware, c1955, 3.375" h	15-25	—
Davy Crockett, game, Davy Crockett Adventures, Gardner & Co., 1955	—	75-100
Davy Crockett, lamp, painted plaster, figural, "©1955 Premco Mfg. Co., Chicago" incised on base, 14" h	100-200	—
Davy Crockett, Official Davy Crockett Frame Tray Puzzle, Jaymar, c1955, 9.75" x 12.75"	25-50	—
Davy Crockett, peace pipe, wood body, orange plastic mouthpiece, Disney copyright on shaft, c1955, 11" l	50-75	—
Davy Crockett, pocketknife, Imperial Knife Co., c1955, 3.5" l	50-75	—
Davy Crockett, soap bubbles, Chemical Sundries, 5" h	75	—
Davy Crockett, TV tray, litho tin, 1955, 12.5 x 17.25	50-75	—
Deputy Dawg, Prairie Pinball Game, Larami, 1972	—	25-50
Dick Tracy, Candid Camera, w/ instruction booklet, Seymour Prod./New York News	—	75-120

Left: Disneyland Ferris Wheel, Chein, wind-up, mid-1940s, 17" h, $400-$600. —Photo courtesy Gene Harris Antique Auction Center, Inc.

Right: Felix Soakie, 10" h, $30-$40.

	UNBOXED	BOXED
Dick Tracy, car, battery operated, pressed steel, rubber tires, Linemar, 1949, 8.5" l	200-400	—
Dick Tracy, Crime Stoppers Detective Set, News Syndicate Co.	—	110-125
Dick Tracy, Military Set Hair Brush, wooden grip, 1940s	75-100	—
Dick Tracy, Secret Service Phone Set, Quaker premium, 1938-39	75-100	—
Don Adams, record, *Don Adams Get Smart,* 33⅓ rpm, United Artists, 1960s	—	25-50
Donald Duck, camera, hard plastic, Herbert George Co., 1950s	—	100-200
Donald Duck, dime register bank, litho tin, 1939	400-700	—
Donald Duck, drinking glass, "Full/Going/Going/Gone," 1950s, 4.625"	75-100	—
Donald Duck, music box, Schmid, 1970s, 4.25" h	50-75	—
Donald Duck, ramp walker, plastic, Marx, 1950s, 3" h	25-50	—
Donald Duck, sprinkling can, litho tin, Ohio Art, 1938, 3" h	75-100	—
Donald Duck, View-Master set, 3 reels and story booklet, 1960s	25-50	—
Donald Duck, wind-up, Donald on hand car, litho tin, missing key, Lionel Corp., c1936, 3.5" x 10.5" x 6.75"	700-1000	—
Donald Duck, wind-up, Donald the Drummer, litho tin, Linemar, 1950s, 6" h	200-400	—
Dr. Kildare, bobbing head, painted composition, head mounted on spring, MGM copyright sticker, 1960s, 6.5" h	200-400	—
Dukes of Hazzard, Electric Slot Racing Set, ©1981 Warner Bros., Inc.	—	25-50
Dumbo, doll, stuffed, plush, Regal Toy Ltd., Canada, 1970s, 14" h	25-50	—
Dumbo, puzzle, Dumbo Picture Puzzle, Jaymar, 1950s	—	25-50
Dyno Mutt, game, The Dyno Mutt Dog Wonder Game, Milton Bradley, 1977	25-50	—
Evel Knievel, Evel Knievel Funny Car, diecast metal, Ideal, 1977	—	50-75
Farrah Fawcett, rug, full color photo image of Farrah from waist up, facsimile signature, ©1976 Pro Arts, Inc., 20" x 29"	25-50	—
Fat Albert, pinback button, "Hey, Hey, Hey!," 3" d	15-25	—
Felix the Cat, figure, celluloid, stamped "Jap" on right side, 1920s, 1.75" h	100-200	—
Ferdinand the Bull, hand puppet, painted composition head, felt body, fabric flowers attached to hand, Crown Toy Mfg. Co., 1938, 10" h	100-200	—

Left to right: Gumby's Pal Pokey Hand Puppet, Lakeside, 1965, $30-$40; Harold Lloyd "Funny Face," wind-up walker, Marx, 1929, 11" h, $500-$700. —Photo courtesy Gene Harris Antique Auction Center, Inc.; Happy Hooligan Bell Ringer, Hill Brass, c1900s, 5.75" h, $2000-$3000.

	UNBOXED	BOXED
Ferdinand the Bull, wall plaque, wood, silkscreen design, 1938, 4.25" x 6 x .25"	50-75	—
Fess Parker, record, *Fess Parker Cowboy and Indian Songs,* 33⅓ rpm, 1969	—	25-50
Figaro, figurine, ceramic, American Pottery Co., c1947, 3.5" h	100-200	—
Flash Gordon, Medals and Insignias, set of 5 plastic pins, Larami Corp., 1978	—	25-50
Flash Gordon, Saucer Launcher, M. Shimmel Sons, Inc., 1970s, 6" l	—	25-50
Flipper, thermos, metal, red cup, King-Seeley, 1966, 6.5" h	50-75	—
Flying Nun, paper dolls, Artcraft, 1969	50-75	—
Foghorn Leghorn, figure, Dakin, 8.5" h	25-50	—
Foxy Grandma, doll, stuffed, blue suit, red tie, black hat, 10.75" h	100-200	—
Fred Flintstone, bank, vinyl, 1970s, 13" h	50-75	—
Fred Flintstone, camera, plastic, figural, Hong Kong, 1976	—	50-75
Fred Flintstone, model, Fred Flintstone's Rock Cruncher, AMT, 1974	—	50-75
Garfield, telephone, figural, molded plastic, eyes open and close, original orange wire and phone jack, Tyco, 1988, 5" h, 9.375" w	50-75	—
Gene Autry, Repeating Cap Pistol, cast iron, plastic grips, facsimile signature above trigger, Kenton, 8.5" l	—	250-275
Godzilla, figure, hard plastic, Mattel, 1977, 18" h	100-200	—
Godzilla, ring, brass, c1970s	50-75	—
Green Hornet, Pez dispenser w/ 2 Pez candies and booklet, 1960s	—	200
Green Hornet, record, 33⅓ rpm, features 2 episodes and theme song, Leo the Lion Records, 1966	—	25-50
Green Hornet, walkie-talkies, plastic, Remco, 1966	—	500-600
Grumpy, mask, starched linen, wearing green hat, name in black, marked "Apon Novelty Co.," 1938, 8" x 10" x 3"	25-50	—
Gumby, charm, plastic, made in Hong Kong, 1970s, 1.875"	10-15	—
Gumby, Fireman Adventure Costume, red hat, fire extinguisher, axe, flashlight, belt, and gray ladder, Lakeside Toys, 1965	—	25-50
Happy Hooligan, bank, hand-painted bisque, mid-1900s, 3.5" h	75-100	—

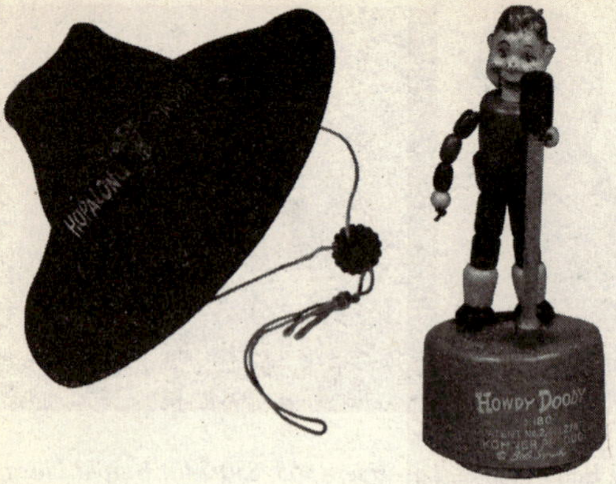

Left: Hopalong Cassidy Hat, black felt, $100-$200.

Right: Howdy Doody Push-Puppet, Kohner Products No. 180, $25-$35.

	UNBOXED	BOXED
Happy Hooligan, figure, painted plaster, c1905, 11" h	100-200	—
Happy the Wonder Dog, push puppet, wood, black leather ears, green base, late 1940s, 4.5" h	—	75-100
Hee Haw, coloring book, 80 pages, Saalfield, 1970, 8.5" x 11"	25-50	—
Herman Munster, doll, hard plastic body, soft vinyl head, Remco, 1964, 6.5" h	50-75	—
Hopalong Cassidy, Auto-Magic Filmstrip Gun, gray metal, battery operated, 1950s, 3.75" x 5.75"	75-100	—
Hopalong Cassidy, binoculars, black painted metal, Galter Prod. Co., Sport Glass, Chicago, IL, 1950s	75-100	—
Hopalong Cassidy, hand puppet, soft vinyl head, cloth body, felt hands, 8.75" h	100-200	—
Hopalong Cassidy, pencil case, leatherette, w/ insert photo page, 1950s	75-100	—
Hopalong Cassidy, Repeater Cap Pistol, nickel-finished white metal, ivory white incised grips w/ image of smiling Hoppy and facsimile signature on each side, name in relief on both sides below handle, Wyandotte, 1950s, 8.5" l	200-400	—
Hopalong Cassidy, Sparkler, plastic, metal plunger, c1950	250-275	—
Howdy Doody, flicker picture key fob, 1.375" x 2"	50-75	—
Howdy Doody, Flub-A-Dub/Dilly Dally Figurine Painting Kit, ©Bob Smith, Hadley Co., Elizabeth, NJ, c1950	—	100-200
Howdy Doody, Flub-A-Dub Flip-A-Ring, ©Kagran Corp., 1950s	—	25-50
Howdy Doody, Little Golden Book #135, *Howdy Doody and the Princess,* first edition, ©1952 Kagran Corp.	15-25	—
Howdy Doody, Secret Combination Safe, plastic, 1950s	—	140-160
Howdy Doody, spoon, smiling image on handle, Crown Silver Plate, ©Kagran, 1950s, 6.875" l	25-50	—
Huckleberry Hound, badge, "Huckleberry Hound For President," 1960	25-50	—
Huckleberry Hound, wind-up, litho tin, Linemar, 1962, 3.5" h	400-700	—
I Dream of Jeannie, doll, poseable, Remco, 1977, 6.5" h	—	100-200
Incredible Hulk, action figure, Mego, 1979, 8" h	—	25-50
Jackie Coogan, pencil case, litho tin, red, Coogan portrait on lid, c1920s, .75" x 2" x 7.75"	25-50	—
James Bond, Action Figure Disguise Kit, complete set, c1966	—	25-50
James Bond, model, Moonraker Space Shuttle, Revell, 1979	—	25-50

Above: Mickey Mouse Hand Car, Lionel, 1930s, $1300-$1500. —Photo courtesy Gene Harris Antique Auction Center, Inc.

Left: Li'l Abner Frame Tray Puzzle, Jaymar, 14" x 11", $20-$30.

	UNBOXED	BOXED
James Bond, Multi-Buster Machine Gun, cap firing plastic rifle, 19" l	—	600-700
James Bond, Secret Agents Car, plastic, advances, 9.5" l	—	150-200
Jerry Lewis, Kook Bath Soap container, 1964, 10.5" h	—	50-75
Jetsons, Somersaulting Turnover Tank, litho tin, China, 1960s	—	100-125
Jetsons, spinning top, litho tin, Japan, 6" d	200-250	—
Jimmie Allen, Official Jimmie Allen Secret Signal Brass Whistle, 1930s, 1.5" l	100-200	—
Joe Palooka, wristwatch, smiling, boxer image, brown leather band, c1948	100-200	—
Julie Andrews, paper dolls, Saalfield, 1957	50-75	—
Kewpies, game, Kewpie Doll Game, Parker Brothers, 1963	—	50-75
King Kong, Jim Beam decanter, "Commemorating the New Paramount Pictures Release," 1976, 10" h	25-50	—
King Louie, Disneykin figure, Marx, c1967, 1.25" h	25-50	—
Kojak, Buick Corgi Junior, diecast metal and plastic, ©1977 Universal City Studios	—	15-25
Krazy Kat, clip, enamel and brass, Krazy Kat playing mandolin, "So's Your Old Man," c1920s, 1.25" l	100-200	—
Lassie, doll, stuffed, plush, vinyl head, plastic eyes, Smile Novelty Toy Co., Inc., 1950s, 8.5" h	50-75	—
Laurel and Hardy, model, '25 T Roadster, AMT, 1970s	—	50-75
Little Lulu, Dinner At 8 Jewelry Set, Larami, 1970s	—	25-50
Little Lulu, perfume gift set, ©1958 M. H. Buell House of Tre-Jur	—	25-30
Little Lulu and Tubby, car display, full set of 12 plastic cars, Spain/ Western Publishing, 1984, 12" x 17"	—	175-200
Lone Ranger, costume, size small, Ben Cooper, 1980	—	25-50
Lone Ranger, target, litho tin, Marx, c1938, 9.5" x 9.5" x .25"	75-100	—
Lone Ranger, The Lone Ranger Hi-Yo Silver Clicker Gun, litho tin, ©1938 The Lone Ranger, Inc., 7.75" l	75-100	—
Maggie and Jiggs, figures, hand-painted plaster, 9.75" h Maggie, 8.25" h Jiggs, 1920s	200-400	—
Maggie and Jiggs, paperweight, glass, black and white image of Maggie standing over Jiggs w/ "You Sarcastic Insect-When I Think of the Men I Could Have Married," c1920s	50-75	—

Left to right: Mickey Mouse Safety Patrol, Fisher-Price #733, $300-$400; Mickey Mouse Puzzle, Jaymar, 1950s, $20-$30.

	UNBOXED	BOXED
Man From U.N.C.L.E., accessory outfit, binoculars, bazooka, targets, and jacket, Gilbert, 1965	—	65-75
Man From U.N.C.L.E., accessory outfit, tommy gun, parachute, and outfit, Gilbert, 1965	—	75
Man From U.N.C.L.E., View-Master Set, set of 3 reels, booklet, and catalogue, ©1966 MGM	—	25-50
Matt Mason, Major Matt Mason Satellite Locker, Mattel, 1967	—	100-200
Mickey Mouse, Acrobatic Clown Trapeze Toy, c1960s, 5" h	—	25-50
Mickey Mouse, condiment set w/ tray, ceramic, 2" h salt and pepper shakers, 4" h mustard jar, and serving spoon, Germany	—	750-825
Mickey Mouse, doll, stuffed, composition shoes, oilcloth eyes, felt ears, Knickerbocker, 1930s, 12" h	400-700	—
Mickey Mouse, doll, stuffed, felt, oilcloth eyes, string whiskers, 4 glass buttons on pants, missing rubber tail, original Steiff fabric tag in ear and diecut cardboard chest tag, 1930s, 4.75" h	700-1000	—
Mickey Mouse, ferris wheel, litho tin, Chein, 17" h	—	400-600
Mickey Mouse, figure, celluloid, movable head and arms, original label "Mickey Mouse Corp. 1928. 1930 By Walter E. Disney," complete w/ original string tail, professionally restrung, 2.25" x 2.375" x 5"	400-700	—
Mickey Mouse, game, Mickey's Fun Fair Card Game, Castell Brothers Ltd., 1938	—	100-200
Mickey Mouse, gloves, brown leather hands, brown suede cuffs, matching fringe trim, felt patch of Mickey as cowboy wrestling steer attached to cuffs, 6.5" x 10"	400-700	—
Mickey Mouse, Glow-in-the-Dark Calendar, 1979, 10.5" x 13"	25-50	—
Mickey Mouse, Mickey Math Educational Ruler, plastic, 1970s	—	25-50
Mickey Mouse, Mickey Mouse Club Medical Kit, Hasbro, 1950s	—	75-100
Mickey Mouse, Mickey Mouse Club News Reel, Mattel, 1950s	—	100-200
Mickey Mouse, Mickey Mouse Target Game, Chad Valley, 1930s	200-400	
Mickey Mouse, pencil box, paper covered cardboard, snap closure, Dixon, 1930s	75-100	—
Mickey Mouse, sand pail, litho tin, attached handle, Mickey and Minnie building sand castle as Pluto watches, Ohio Art, 1930s, 4.25" h	200-400	—

Right: Pinocchio the Acrobat, tin, wind-up, Marx, 1939, $500-$700. —Photo courtesy Gene Harris Antique Auction Center, Inc.

Below: Minnie Mouse Marionette, Pelham Puppets, wood, composition, and cloth, 9.5" h, $150-$200.

	UNBOXED	BOXED
Mickey Mouse, sweeper, litho tin, wood side panels and wheels, Ohio Art, 1930s, 4" x 6" x 2"	100-200	—
Mickey Mouse, Twirly Tail Toy, Marx, 7.5" l	—	275-300
Mickey Mouse, wind-up, plastic, Gabriel, 1978, 9.25" h	75-100	—
Minnie Mouse, bank, painted composition, Minnie sitting on brown stool, Korea, 1970s, 7.5" h	50-75	—
Minnie Mouse, Fun-E-Flex figure, wood body, flexible metal arms and legs, original cardboard ears, missing rubber tail, 1930s, 2.5" x 6 x 7"	700-1000	—
Miss Piggy, teapot, ceramic, Sigma, 1980s, 10" h	100-200	—
Morocco Mole, soaky, Purex, late 1960s, 6.75" h	—	75-100
Mr. Jinks, doll, stuffed cloth, vinyl, Knickerbocker, 1959, 12" h	50-75	—
Mr. Magoo, flicker picture keychain, GE logo and Magoo image, Vari-Vue, ©1961 UA Pictures, 1.5" x 1.875"	25-50	—
Mrs. Beasley, paper dolls, Whitman, 1972, 10" x 13"	25-50	—
Mrs. Beasley, sticker book, Whitman, 1972, 10.25" x 12"	25-50	—
Mushmouse, figure, vinyl, Ideal, 1960s, 7.5" h	75-100	—
Pac-Man, doll, "Pac-Man Hungry For You," yellow cloth, blue shirt, Knickerbocker, 7.25" h	10-15	—
Paddington Bear, centerpiece, Paper Art Co., Inc., 10" x 14.75"	—	25-50
Pee-Wee Herman, talking doll, Matchbox, 1987, 18" h	—	50-75
Peter Pan, lunch box, vinyl, Aladdin, c1969	100-200	—
Peter Potamus, figure, vinyl, c1960s, 7.75" h	75-100	—
Pinocchio, doll, composition, movable arms and head, original outfit, Knickerbocker, 1940, 10.5" h	200-400	—
Pinocchio, figure, "Bendables," rubber, Durham Industries, 1970s	—	25-50
Pinocchio, lunch pail, litho tin, black and white on red ground, c1940, 4" h	200-400	—
Pinocchio, wind-up, litho tin, Marx, 1939, 8.5" h	400-700	—
Planet of the Apes, candy box, Phoenix Candy Co., 1967	—	25-50
Planet of the Apes, Inter-Planetary Ape Phones, Larami Corp.	—	50-75

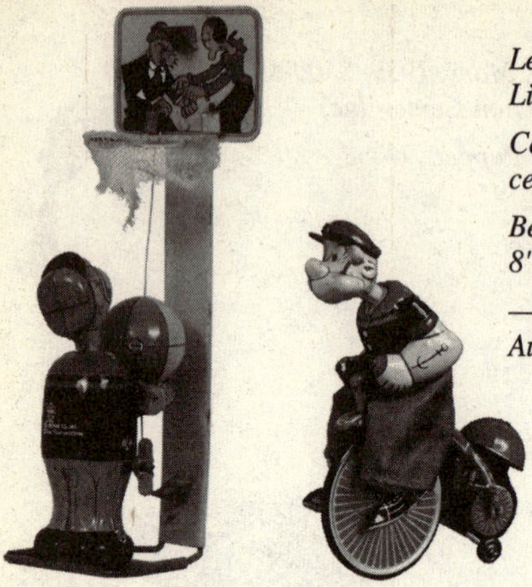

Left: Popeye Basketball Player, tin, wind-up, Linemar, 1950s, $800-$1200.

Center: Popeye on Tricycle, metal and celluloid, wind-up, Linemar, $500-$600.

Below: Wise Pluto, tin, wind-up, Marx, 1939, 8" l, $275-$375.

—Photos courtesy Gene Harris Antique Auction Center, Inc.

	UNBOXED	BOXED
Pluto, bank, hard vinyl, Animal Toys Plus, Inc., 1970s, 8.5" h	—	25-50
Pluto, candle, figural, Pluto on green base w/ dog dish, 1960s, 3.5" h	15-25	—
Pluto, ramp walker, plastic, Marx, 1950s, 4.25" l	25-50	—
Pongo, push puppet, plastic, Kohner Bros., 1960s, 2.5" h	25-50	—
Popeye, bubble set, 2 wooden bubble pipes, molded soap image of smiling Popeye w/ name on top of hat, Transogram, ©1936 King Features Syndicate	—	75-100
Popeye, Comic Department Ink Stamping Set, Stamperkraft, 1935	—	100-200
Popeye, keychain flashlight, yellow plastic case, litho paper sticker, 1950s	25-50	—
Popeye, palm puzzle, "Popeye's Bingo," litho tin, Bar Zim Toy Co., 1929, 3.5" x 5.5"	100-200	—
Popeye, ring, Post Toasties Corn Flakes premium, litho tin, 1949	25-50	—
Popeye and Olive Oyl, salt and pepper shakers, pair, ceramic, Japan, 3" h	100-200	—
Prince Valiant, book, *Prince Valiant in the New World,* #6, 96 pages, Hastings House, ©King Features Syndicate, 1956	50-75	—
Quick Draw McGraw, wind-up, litho tin, Linemar, 1962, 4" h	400-700	—
Radio Orphan Annie, mask, diecut paper, full color, tabs marked "Orphan Annie/Compliments of Ovaltine," 1933, 7.5" x 9"	75-100	—
Radio Orphan Annie, Secret Society Manual, Ovaltine premium, 12 pages, 1935, 5" x 7.5"	75-100	—
Radio Orphan Annie, Shake-Up Mug, Beetleware, Ovaltine premium, c1938, 5" h	75-100	—
Raggedy Andy, pencil holder, figural, hand-painted plaster, 1970s, 5.5" h	25-50	—
Raggedy Ann, bank, plaster, figural, 1970s, 9.25" h	50-75	—
Rin-Tin-Tin, coloring book, "The Adventures of Rin-Tin-Tin," Whitman #1195, 1956	25-50	—
Rin-Tin-Tin, Fort Apache Playset, litho tin, Marx, 1957	100-200	—

	UNBOXED	BOXED
Rin-Tin-Tin, skill puzzle, Nabisco Shredded Wheat Juniors premium, blue, white, and yellow portrait on red ground, 1956, 1.375" d	15-25	—
Robin, action figure, Mego, 1973, 8" h	—	100-200
Robin, doll, stuffed, plush, vinyl head, felt outfit, Commonwealth Toy and Novelty Co., Inc., 1966, 15" h	200-400	—
Roy Rogers, Better Little Book, *Roy Rogers and the Deadly Treasure,* Whitman #1437, ©1945, 1947 by Roy Rogers	50-75	—
Roy Rogers, guitar, wooden, Range Rhythm Toy, Tupelo, MI, 1950s	100-200	—
Roy Rogers, neckerchief, silk, smiling Roy in lariat design, cow brands and name at bottom on each end, 5.25" x 34 x 4"	50-75	—
Roy Rogers, Repeater Cap Pistol, nickel finish white metal, dark brown grips w/ stag horn pattern and "RR" initial at top, c1950s, 10" l	100-200	—
Schmoo, figural planter, ceramic, 1940s, 4.625" h	100-200	—
Scooby Doo, van, diecast metal, LJN, 1975	—	25-50
Sergeant Preston, game, The Sergeant Preston Game, Milton Bradley, 1956	—	50-75
Shari Lewis' Hush Puppy, doll, soft vinyl, movable head, squeak sound, Alan Jay Clarolyte Company, ©1962 Tarcher Productions, Inc., 13.5" h	50-75	—
Six Million Dollar Man, See-A-Show Viewer, Kenner, 1976	—	15-25
Smokey Bear, bank, ceramic, seated Smokey holding bucket in right hand, 1960s, 6" h	100-200	—
Smokey Bear, jeep, battery operated, litho tin, Japan, 10" l	—	1000-1120
Smokey Bear, mug, figural, "Prevent Forest Fires!," 1960s, 3.25" h	75-100	—
Sniffles, pencil holder, metal, ©1947 W.B.C., 4.5" h	100-200	—
Snoopy, Joe Cool bobbing head, composition, ©1958, 1966 United Features Syndicate, c1980s, 4" h	25-50	—
Snoopy and Woodstock, telephone, plastic, figural, simulated wood plastic base, American Telecommunications Corp., 1976	75-100	—
Snow White, bowl, clear glass, red image, 1938, 4.75" d	75-100	—
Snow White, Castille Soap, original storybook box, 8" x 13"	—	100-110
Snow White, Disneykin Playset, hand-painted hard plastic figures w/ accessories, 1960s	—	50-75
Snow White, figurine, Hagen-Renaker, 2.25" h	100-200	—
Snow White, frame tray puzzle, Whitman, 1950s, 9.25" x 11.5"	25-50	—
Snow White, lamp, painted plaster, figural, La Mode Studios, Inc., 1938, 3" x 5" x 8"	200-400	—
Soupy Sales, Mini-Board Card Game, Ideal, 1965	—	50-75
Spark Plug, figure, wooden, painted gray, wooden head, "Made In Czechoslovakia" paper label, mid-1920s, 1.25" x 3.75" x 3.25"	200-400	—
Spider-Man, action figure, The Amazing Spider-Man, Mego, 8" h	—	50-75
Spider-Man, license plate, embossed litho tin, Marx, 2.25" x 4"	25-50	—
Spider-Man, The Amazing Spider-Man Communications and Code Set, H. G. Toys, 1978	—	75-1
Spider-Man, The Amazing Spider-Man Playset, complete, unused, Ideal, 1973, 6" x 16" x 1.5"	75-100	—
Stan Laurel, doll, soft vinyl, flexible legs over wire, cloth outfit, Knickerbocker, c1970s, 9.5" h	—	50-75
Superman, belt, brown leather, metal buckle, raised name and repeated Superman image, 1940s, 28" l	100-200	—

Above: Three Little Pigs Musical Top, Ohio Art, litho tin, 1962, 9.5" dia, $40-$60.

Left: Top Cat Frame Tray Puzzle, Whitman #4457, 1961, $20-$30.

	UNBOXED	BOXED
Superman, booklet, "With Superman at the Gilbert Hall of Science," A. C. Gilbert, 1948, 6" x 9"	175-200	—
Superman, Crusader Ring, Kellogg's premium, adjustable silvered brass band, 1940s	100-200	—
Superman, Flip Flashlite, hard plastic, Bantamlite, ©1966 National Periodical Publications, Inc.	—	100-200
Superman, movie viewer, hard platic, complete w/ films, Chemtoy Corp., 1965	—	25-50
Superman, radio, hard plastic, figural, ©1973 National Periodical Publications, Inc.	—	100-200
Superman, record, *The Official Adventures of Superman,* $33\frac{1}{3}$ rpm, Leo the Lion Records, 1966	—	25-50
Superman, valentine, diecut stiff paper, full color, young boy and girl at fence w/ full figure image of flying Superman in diecut heart design, ©1940 Superman Inc., 4.5" x 6.5"	50-75	—
Tarzan, book, *Jungle Tales of Tarzan,* #2915, 318 pages, 1940s, Grosset & Dunlap	50-75	—
Tarzan, coloring book, Ron Ely as Tarzan on front and back covers, 96 pages, Whitman, ©1966 Edgar Rice Burroughs, Inc., 8" x 11.5"	25-50	—
Tarzan, Flicker Ring Set, Vari-Vue, c1966, complete set of 6	75-100	—
Tarzan, Golden Record, 78 rpm, *Tarzan Song/Jungle Dance,* ©1952 Edgar Rice Burroughs, Inc.	25-50	—
Three Little Pigs, matchbox holder, enameled brass, 1930s, 1.125" x 1.625" x .5"	100-200	—
Thumper, figurine, Hagen-Renaker, 1950s, 1.25" h	50-75	—
Tom Mix, RCA Victor Miniature Television Film Viewer, brown plastic, complete w/ 5 films and original white envelope	—	50-75
Touché Turtle, tile puzzle, plastic, Roalex Co., 1960s, 2.5" x 2.5"	50-75	—
Ultraman, figure, Baltan, Bandai, 1984, 15" h	—	100-200
Underdog, Little Golden Book, *Underdog and the Disappearing Ice Cream,* 1975	15-25	—
Wacky Races, Nutty Dragster Car, Larami, 1971	—	25-50
Waltons, action figure, Pop, Mego, 1974, 8" h	—	50-75

Left: Yellow Kid Figure, cast iron, $150-$250.

Below: Topo Gigio Figure, Ed Sullivan Show, $12-$20.

	UNBOXED	BOXED
W. C. Fields, record, *W. C. Fields Famous Lectures,* 78 rpm, Variety Records/United Artists, 1946	—	50-75
Wild Bill Hickok and Jingles, coloring book, Saalfield, 1953, 11" x 14"	25-50	—
Wilma Flintstone, friction car, litho tin, Marx, 1962	200-400	—
Winnie the Pooh, lunch box, vinyl, Aladdin, 1964	200-400	—
Winnie the Pooh, music box, ceramic, Eeyore pulling circus wagon w/ Tigger and Winnie the Pooh inside, "Made in Japan" sticker, 1960s, 7.25" h	200-400	—
Winnie the Pooh, squeeze toy, vinyl, Holland Hall Pro., 1966, 5.5" h	50-75	—
Wonder Woman, Color-A-Deck Card Game, Russell Mfg. Co., ©1977 DC Comics, 6" x 8"	—	25-50
Wonder Woman, marionette, Madison Ltd., 1977	—	75-100
Woody Woodpecker, Door Knocker Assembly Kit, Kellogg's premium, complete w/ instruction sheets in French and English, 4.25" h	—	50-75
Yogi Bear, gloves, brown cotton, red simulated suede cuffs, Yogi profile image on each side, Boxx, ©Hanna-Barbera Productions, 1959, 4.5" x 7"	25-50	—
Yogi Bear, Play Fun Jellystone Park Coloring Set, Whitman, 1964	—	75-100
Yogi Bear, slippers, moccasin-style, soft vinyl, simulated white fur around top, smiling Yogi face and name on top, early 1960s	—	50-75
Yogi Bear and Boo Boo, clothes tree w/ height marker, diecut wood, 1970s, 47.5" overall	75-100	—
Zorro, hat/mask, black starched felt hat w/ white chinstrap, black and white fabric patch attached to front, Benay Albee, 1950s, 12" x 13" x 3"	50-75	—
Zorro, punch-out book, Giant Funtime Book, Pocket Books, Inc., 1958, 7.25" x 13"	100-200	—
Zorro, wallet, brown vinyl, tooled design, Croyden, 1950s	—	75-100
Zorro, wind-up, plastic, Durham Industries, Inc., 1975, 4.25" h	50-75	—

Cracker Jack

F. W. Ruckenheim and his brother developed this famous mixture of popcorn, peanuts and molasses. In 1893 they sold it at the Columbian Exposition in Chicago where it was an overnight sensation. In 1896 it was named Cracker Jack and soon after prizes were introduced. At first coupons were used which the customer could trade for various prizes. The company began putting the actual prize in each box by 1912. Cracker Jack prizes have been made of lead, paper, porcelain, plastic, tin, paper and wood. The little sailor, Jack, is based on the founder's grandson Robert (for trivia fans, the dog's name is Bingo).

The following prices are for items in excellent to mint condition; dates are approximate. For more information see *Cracker Jack Collectibles* by Ravi Piña (Schiffer, Atglen, PA, 1995) and *Cracker Jack: The Unauthorized Guide to Advertising Collectibles* by Larry White (Schiffer, Atglen, 1999).

Delivery Truck, litho tin, 1930s, 1.375" l, $75-$100.

	LOW	HIGH
Air Corps Wings Stud, metal, late 1930s	$75	$100
Bookmark, litho tin, brown dog, 1930s	15	25
Figure, Andy Gump, bisque, 2.125" h	50	75
Figure, Chester Gump, bisque, 2" h	50	75
Figure, Herby, bisque, 2" h	50	75
Lapel Stud, Cracker Jack Air Corps, metal, 1920-30s	50	75
Lapel Stud, Cracker Jack Police, metal, 1920-30s	25	50
Lapel Stud, "Me For Cracker Jack," metal, 1920s	50	75
Painting Book, paper, ©APT Litho Co., 1920s	50	75
Palm Puzzle, 1920s	75	100
Pinback Button, "I'm For Cracker Jack," c1916	200	400
Play School Magic Speller, paper, ©1946 C. Carey Cloud	50	75
Pocket Watch, litho tin, black and white dial face, gold flashing, 1930s	50	75
Premium Catalogue Order Coupon, printed cardboard, unused, 1930s	25	50
Rubber Face Push Pictures, set of 37, cardboard frames, unused, 1950s	200	400
Service Cap, paper, white, red lettering, blue trim, 1930s	75	100
Slide Cards, set of 27, full color, 1964	400	700
Spinner, paper, 1930-40s	75	100
Spinner Top, litho tin, wooden dowel, red, white, and blue, 1930s	50	75
Standup, Kayo, litho tin, 1930s	75	100
Standup, lion, litho tin, 1930s	50	75
Standup, Long May It Wave, litho tin, 1940s	15	25
Standup, Smitty, litho tin, 1930s	75	100
Standup, Stars and Stripes Forever, litho tin	25	50
Tape Canister, Angelus Marshmallows, celluloid, late 1920s-30s	25	50
Tilt Card, cardboard, sailor passing ball from hand to hand, "Tilt Card To And Fro," 1950-60s	15	25
Train Set, litho tin, 3 passenger cars and streamliner engine, c1940s	75	100
Whistle, tin, single barrel, 1930s	15	25
Wiggle Wag Duck Toy, paper	25	50

Dollhouses and Furnishings

Dollhouses and dollhouse furniture are difficult areas to evaluate because of their diversity. Quality craftsmanship and attention to detail are important considerations for wooden items. Because most earlier dollhouses are hand crafted, price is often determined by a collector's individual taste. Collectors of paper on wood examples rely on manufacturer, style and condition. Tinplate dollhouses made by Marx and other firms are worth more money if unassembled in the original box with all accessories intact. Dollhouse furniture and accessories have similar criteria; elaborate, well-crafted early items in excellent condition command the highest prices. Many items have been reproduced or created in the style of earlier periods; these items are not worth as much as similar period pieces. Color variations can occasionally affect the prices of plastic dollhouse accessories; prices listed are for more common colors.

For further reading see *Doll Furniture: 1950s-1980s* by Jean Mahan (Hobby House Press, Grantsville, MD, 1997) and *Antique and Collectible Dollhouses and Their Furnishings* by Dian Zillner and Patty Cooper (Schiffer, Atglen, PA, 1998).

Mystery Doll House, painted wood, glass windows, 8 rooms, early/mid-20th C furniture including some Tyne-Toy pieces, late 19th C, 46" h, 49" w, 25" d, $27,600 at auction. —Photo courtesy Skinner, Inc., Boston, MA.

	LOW	HIGH
Baby Carriage, wheelbarrow, carpet sweeper, step ladder, and Star kitchen range, cast iron, early 20th C, 1" scale	$200	$350
Biedermeier Secretary, rosewood finish, gold stenciled details, fall-front, mirrored interior, 5 drawers, mid-19th C, 7.5" h	350	500
Bungalow, yellow w/ red gambrel roof, 2 rooms first floor, 1 room second floor, front dormer, opens either end, 1920s, 18.75" h, 19.25" w, 10.5" d	700	1150
Chairs, Saxony, early Empire style, painted red, printed cotton upholstered seats, braid trim, c1850, 3.0625" h, 1" scale, price for set of 4	115	150
Grocery Store, German, painted wood, wall shelf and telephone, tin wall box, 2 cans, dust pan, set of scales, ceramic containers, glass bottle, c1900, 9" h	600	1600
House, Japanese, soft wood, 1 room, sliding glass and cloth solji screen doors, 20th C, 28" h, 36.75" w, 27.25" d	300	450
House, Marx, 2-story, litho tin, w/ Disney nursery, 1950	150	200
House, Meritoy, clapboard and gray stone, litho tin, red roof, 3 dormers, 5 windows, chimney, 1949, 21" h, 15" w	200	350
House, Ohio Art #95, litho tin, w/ 28 pcs. plastic furniture, 8.5" h, 5.25"w	75	100
House, Rich, replica of Colleen Moore's dollhouse, painted and stenciled, hard board, electric, wiring diagram sheet, Colleen Moore's Dollhouse booklet, mid-1930s, 18" h, 23.75" w, 13.75" d	375	400

	LOW	HIGH
House, Saxony, German or Austrian villa style, litho paper on wood, 2 rooms first floor, 1 room second floor, separate front steps, original interior papers, Gottschalk blue roof, 1870s, 31" h, 26.5" w	8000	9200
House, Stirn & Lyon, stenciled wood building sections decorated w/ crayons, litho paper illustration on cover, some paper loss, patented 1881, 15" h	170	175
House, T. Cohn, Spanish 2-story, litho tin, w/ patio, 1948	150	200
House, yellow with white trim, second and third floors, glass windows, paneled interior doors, side porch and chimney, unmarked, c1900, 60" h, 51" w with porch, 23" d	1000	1600
Parlor Set, Adrian Cooke, metal, settee and 2 chairs, velvet seats, boxed, c1895, 1" scale	60	75
Townhouse, Handcrafted Wood, 4 rooms, front opens, faux red brick, gray trim, front stoop, c1906, 49" h, 33.5" w, 20.5" d	145	300
Victorian Cottage, wood, yellow with red trim, green shingled roof, 2 rooms first floor, 1 room second floor, .75 to 1" scale, wood, pressed board, and Tootsietoy furniture and accessories, chimney and finial missing, early 20th C, 23" h, 26" w, 23.75" d	460	500
Victorian Mansion, mansard roof and belvedere, square lawn, mustard yellow with brown trim, gray roofs with accents, 2 rooms first floor, 1 room second floor, attic, staircases, cast iron fence and lions on wood plinths, wood outhouse, late 19th C, 36" h, 25" w, 49" sq base	2800	2875

Left to right: Bliss, paper on wood, hinged front, 2 rooms w/ printed carpeting and wallpaper, celluloid windows, electric lights, 16.5" h, $1725 at auction; Schoenhut, Daggle 2-Story, No. 5/50, wood and fiberboard, embossed siding and roof, 8 rooms and attic w/ litho paper walls, Tootsietoy furniture, 1923, 27.625" h, $2415 at auction. —Photos courtesy Skinner, Inc., Boston, MA.

Dolls

Doll collecting has grown remarkably in the last twenty-five years to become one of the top hobbies in the United States. It rivals stamps and coins. Individual appeal seems to be the magic ingredient which drives the marketplace. The prices of dolls cover such a wide range that any collector can find a category to fit his budget. Interesting and varied collections can be assembled by specializing in dolls of a certain era, made from a specific material or all the various dolls produced by a single manufacturer.

In doll collecting, condition is all important. Prices given here are for dolls in excellent condition. Dolls with original or true period clothes will carry an incrementally higher value depending on quality. Deductions must be made for any missing or replaced parts, worn-out or faded clothes and wigs, and most importantly, broken, chipped or cracked heads.

For further reading see Dawn Herlocher's *200 Years of Dolls* (1996) and *Doll Makers & Marks* (1999), both published by Antique Trader Books (Dubuque, IA), *14th Blue Book Dolls & Values* by Jan Foulke (Hobby House Press, Grantsville, MD, 1997), and *Doll Values: Antique to Modern, Third Edition* by Patsy Moyer (Collector Books, Paducah, KY, 1999.

Antique

	LOW	HIGH
Alt, Beck, and Gottschalck, 698, bisque turned shoulder head, brown glass fixed eyes, closed mouth, chestnut human hair wig, kid body, cloth lower legs, composition hands, late 19th C, 22" h	$750	$1000
American Character, Sally, composition, painted sleep eyes, molded or wigged hair, original outfit, 1930, 12" h	225	250
American Character, Toodles, hard rubber, 1956, 18.5" h	225	250
Armand Marseille, 370, bisque head, blue glass sleep eyes, open mouth, original blonde mohair wig, kid body, bisque hands, cotton lower legs, 21" h	175	300
Armand Marseille, 390, bisque head, blue glass sleep eyes, open mouth, blonde human hair wig, fully jointed composition body, 23" h	320	400
Armand Marseille, 1894, bisque head, brown glass sleep eyes, open mouth, original blonde mohair wig, fully jointed composition body, 26" h	250	400
Armand Marseille, American Indian Squaw, tinted bisque, brown glass fixed eyes, open mouth, original black mohair wig, composition body and limbs, jointed at shoulders and hips, fringed brown mohair dress, 12.5" h	200	300
Armand Marseille, Dream Baby, bisque head, blue glass fixed eyes, cloth body and limbs, composition hands, 20" h	175	350
Armand Marseille, Our Pet, bisque head, blue glass sleep eyes, open mouth, original blonde mohair wig, bent limb composition body, 7.5" h	200	250
Arranbee, Little Angel Baby, composition, 1940s, 16"-18"	275	300
Arranbee, Nancy Lee, composition, original outfit, 18" h	350	400
Art Fabric Mills, Topsy Doll, printed cotton, uncut and shrink-wrapped, 1900, 19" h	345	500
Bahr and Proschild, 585-4, bisque head, blue sleep eyes, open mouth with 2 teeth, composition body, 12" h	375	500
Bahr and Proschild, 620-3, bisque head, brown glass sleep eyes, open mouth, replaced human hair wig, fully jointed composition toddler body, 12.5" h	550	600
B. J. & Co., My Sweetheart, bisque head, brown sleep eyes, open mouth with 4 teeth, wood and composition body	175	180
Bruno Schmidt, bisque head, sleep eyes, open mouth, jointed composition body, 18"-20" h	550	650
Cameo, Bye-Lo Baby, composition head, brown steel sleep eyes, closed mouth, cloth body and legs, composition hands, 1924, 14" h	175	300

	LOW	HIGH
Carl Harmus, Character Toddler, bisque head, brown glass sleep eyes, open mouth, original blonde wig, straight wrist composition toddler body, 11.5" h	115	250
C. M. Bergmann, bisque head, blue glass sleep eyes, open mouth, strawberry blonde human hair wig, fully jointed composition body, impressed 1916 mark, 30" h	550	700
C. M. Bergmann, bisque head, brown glass sleep eyes, open mouth, original dark brown mohair wig, fully jointed composition body, 23" h	230	300
China Head, black hair, cloth and china body, lace dress, 15.5" h	50	75
China Head, black hair, pink luster, cloth and china body, 13.5" h	60	75
China Head, blonde hair, jeweled chest, cloth and china body, new clothing, 16" h	75	150
Dressel, Germany, Uncle Sam, bisque head, fixed eyes, original outfit, jointed body, 13" h	400	500
Effanbee, American Children, composition head and body, straight limb, 20" h	200	250
Effanbee, Belle-Telle, vinyl head, rooted hair, sleep eyes w/ lashes, hand painted features, says 11 sentences, battery operated, 1962, 18" h	65	100
Effanbee, Patsy Ann, composition, steel sleep eyes, closed mouth, molded hair, jointed at head, arms, and legs, complete with wardrobe and trunk of clothes, 1930s, 18.75"	250	350
Effanbee, Patsyette, composition, jointed at neck, shoulders, and hips, period silk outfit, 1931, 9.25" h	300	500
Effanbee, Patsy Lou, composition head and body, 22" h	325	350
Effanbee, Saucy Walker, composition, green sleep eyes, 18.5" h	70	100
E. I. Horsman, Rene Ballerina, vinyl, rooted hair, fully jointed, 19" h	150	175
Ernest Heubach, 275, bisque shoulder head, brown glass sleep eyes, open mouth, original light brown mohair wig, kid body, bisque hands and feet, 18" h	175	300

Effanbee Dolls.

Above, left to right: Patsy Lou; American Children. —Photo courtesy Gene Harris Antique Auction Center, Inc.

Left: Belle-Telle.

	LOW	HIGH
Ernest Heubach, 320-1, bisque head, blue glass fixed eyes, open mouth, replaced wig, fully jointed composition body, 19" h	200	300
Ernest Heubach, Character Boy, bisque head, molded and painted hair and features, intaglio eyes, closed mouth, fully jointed composition body, impressed sunburst mark, 13.5" h	400	500
Freundlich, Red Riding Hood, Grandmother, and Wolf, molded and painted heads, jointed at head, shoulders, and hips, wolf head on human body, cotton outfits, original box, 1934	800	1000
Gebrüder Heubach, 5777, Dolly Dimple, 19-22" h	3000	3200
Gebrüder Heubach, Laughing Boy, 1912, 15.75" h	1400	1900
Gebrüder Krass, 165, bisque head, brown glass sleep eyes, open mouth, original brown mohair wig, fully jointed composition body, 23" h	200	350
Gems & Seyfarth, Germany, 120-11, bisque head, blue/gray sleep eyes, open mouth with 4 teeth, jointed wood and composition body, 24" h	300	350
George Borgfeldt, bisque head, blue sleep eyes, open mouth with 4 teeth, jointed wood and composition body, 24" h	250	350
George Borgfeldt & Co., Gladdie, biscaloid head marked "Germany, Gladdie, copyright by Helen W. Jensen," brown eyes, light brown brows, open teeth, molded light brown hair, stuffed body, composition arms and legs, original pink dress, 1929, 21" h	1200	1600
Georgine Averill, Little Lulu, pressed cloth face with painted features, yarn hair, red dress, 1930s, 36" h	200	300
German, bisque shoulder head, brown glass fixed eyes, open/closed mouth, pierced ears, original blonde mohair wig, jointed kid body and limbs, original silk taffeta and satin dress, wool broadcloth coat, cotton morning coat and nightdress, French brown kid boots, 14.5" h	865	1200
Grace Storey Putnam, Bye-Lo Baby, bisque head, blue glass sleep eyes, closed mouth, cloth body and legs, celluloid hands, original christening gown with cloth label, 10.75" h	400	500

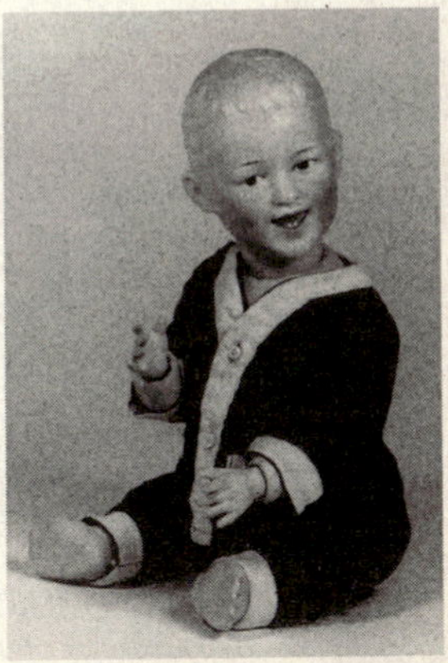

Left to right: George Borgfeldt & Co., Gladdie; Gebrüder Heubach, Laughing Boy. —Photo courtesy Auction Team Köln.

	LOW	HIGH
Grace Storey Putnam, Bye-Lo Baby, bisque head, blue glass sleep eyes, cloth body and legs, celluloid hands, original christening gown with cloth label, 1920s, 13" h	375	450
Gregor, vinyl, blue eyes, blonde hair, original navy sweater and blue jeans, brown shoes, wrist tag, 1965-86, 16" h	115	200
Hamburger & Co., Viola, bisque head, open blue glass fixed eyes, open mouth, original blonde mohair wig, fully jointed composition body, 22" h	145	300
Handwerck, 110.13, bisque head, brown glass sleep eyes, open mouth, pierced ears, blonde human hair wig, fully jointed composition body, impressed mark, complete w/ dresses, shoes, socks, and bedding, 26" h	575	600
Handwerck, 119, bisque head, brown glass sleep eyes, open mouth, pierced ears, original blonde mohair wig, fully jointed composition body, 18.5" h	550	650
Handwerck, bisque head, blue glass sleep eyes, open mouth, pierced ears, original blonde human hair wig, fully jointed composition body, 18" h	575	600
Handwerck, Simon, and Halbig, bisque head, brown glass sleep eyes, open mouth, pierced ears, original dark blonde mohair wig, fully jointed composition body, 24" h	300	350
H. D. Lee Mercantile Co., Buddy Lee, composition, molded and painted features, jointed at shoulders and hips, original blue denim engineer's outfit with cloth label, 1920s, 13" h	300	350
Hermann Steiner, Character Baby, jointed composition body, 10" h	300	500
Hertel & Schwab, bisque head, brown glass sleep eyes, open mouth, pierced ears, original strawberry blonde wig, fully jointed composition body, 28" h	900	1000
Ideal, Baby Snooks, composition head, hands, and torso, flexible metal cable arms and legs, wooden feet, cotton outfit, 1938, 12.75" h	145	250
Ideal, Buster Brown, composition head, cloth body, composition lower arms, original red suit with hat, 1929, 17" h	325	375
Ideal, Shirley Temple, composition, crazed sleep eyes, original mohair wig, body jointed at shoulders and hips, original yellow, green, and tan plaid outfit from "Bright Eyes," original pin and paper tag, mid-1930s, 13" h	500	600

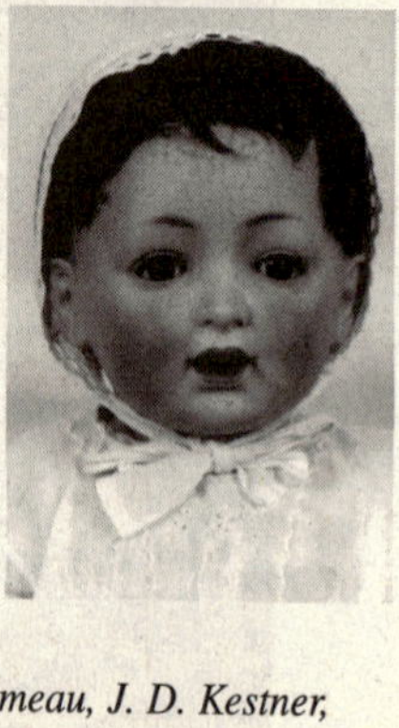

Above left to right: Jumeau, Tête Jumeau, J. D. Kestner, Character Baby.

Left: Jumeau, #12-758.

—Photos courtesy Gene Harris Antique Auction Center, Inc.

	LOW	HIGH
Ideal, Shirley Temple, composition, crazed sleep eyes, open mouth, original blonde mohair wig, body jointed at shoulders and hips, marked "Shirley Temple" on head and back, original button, 1936, 17.75" h	200	300
Ideal, Shirley Temple, composition, hazel sleep eyes, open mouth, original blonde mohair wig, body jointed at shoulders and hips, mid-1930s, 14.5" h	450	500
Ideal, Shirley Temple, composition, hazel sleep eyes, open mouth, original blonde mohair wig, jointed at shoulders and hips, original light blue organdy dress with pink ribbons, original underwear, shoes, socks, and pin, marked on head and back, 1934, 18" h	400	630
Japanese, Character Baby, bisque head, brown glass sleep eyes, open mouth, original blonde mohair wig, bent limb composition body, impressed F. Y. Nippon mark, 14" h	140	250
J. D. Kestner, 14, bisque head, blue glass sleep eyes, open mouth, fully jointed composition body, 26" h	375	500
J. D. Kestner, 143, bisque head, gray glass sleep eyes, open mouth, original blonde mohair wig, composition body, arms jointed at shoulders, legs jointed at hips and knees, 7.75" h	230	600
J. D. Kestner, 149, blue glass fixed eyes, open mouth, brown human hair wig, fully jointed composition body, 17.25" h	400	450
J. D. Kestner, 151, bisque head, gray/blue fixed eyes, open mouth with molded tongue and teeth, bent limb composition body, 14" h	300	400
J. D. Kestner, 154, bisque shoulder head, blue glass sleep eyes, open mouth, replaced wig, jointed kid body, bisque hands, 16.5" h	260	300
J. D. Kestner, 168, bisque head, brown glass sleep eyes, open mouth, red human hair wig, fully jointed composition body, 18.5" h	345	60
J. D. Kestner, 169, bisque head, brown glass sleep eyes, closed mouth, original blonde mohair wig, fully jointed composition body, 13.5" h	2000	2185
J. D. Kestner, 171, bisque head, blue glass sleep eyes, open mouth, original blonde mohair wig, fully jointed composition body, 18" h	750	1000
J. D. Kestner, 214, bisque head, brown glass fixed eyes, open mouth, strawberry blonde human hair wig, fully jointed composition body, 23" h	250	430

Left to right: Hermann Steiner, Character Baby; Jules Steiner, A-13 Bebe le Parisien.
—Photos courtesy Gene Harris Antique Auction Center, Inc.

Kämmer & Reinhardt, 117X. —Photo courtesy Auction Team Köln.

	LOW	HIGH
J. D. Kestner, 260, bisque head, glass sleep eyes, open mouth, original blonde mohair wig, fully jointed composition body, 21.75" h	550	600
J. D. Kestner, Character Baby, 20" h	800	1200
Jules Steiner, A-13 Bebe le Parisien, 22" h	8000	9000
Jumeau, 7, "Tête Jumeau," brown fixed eyes, closed mouth, pierced ears, jointed body, 16.5" h	2000	2500
Jumeau, 8, "Tête Jumeau," blue fixed eyes, closed mouth, pierced ears, jointed body, 19" h	3000	3500
Jumeau, 12-758, bisque head, blue set eyes, open mouth w/ 6 teeth, pierced ears, jointed wood and composition body, 27" h	2000	2500
Jumeau, 13 "Tête Jumeau," gray/blue fixed eyes, open mouth w/ 6 teeth, pierced ears, large chunky limbed body, 28.5" h	2500	3500
Jumeau, 230, Character Child, bisque socket head, open mouth, fixed or sleep eyes, wig, jointed composition body, original outfit, c1910, 16" h	1500	2000
Jumeau, 1907, "Tête Jumeau," bisque head, open mouth, 14" h	2000	2200
Jumeau, Princess Elizabeth, bisque socket head, flirty glass eyes, incised "Jumeau Paris Princess," 18"-29"	1600	1800
Kamkins, 114, Cloth Girl, molded mask face, painted features, original dark blonde mohair wig, cloth body and limbs, original cotton dress and bloomers, stamped mark back of head, 1919-28, 19" h	860	1500
Kämmer & Reinhardt, 55, blue glass sleep eyes, open mouth, pierced ears, original henna mohair wig, fully jointed composition body, 19" h	300	400
Kämmer & Reinhardt, 117X, 1912, 11" h	1800	2200
Kämmer & Reinhardt, Hans, bisque head, painted intaglio eyes, closed mouth, blonde mohair wig, fully jointed composition body, period blue cotton sailor suit, black broad brimmed sailor hat, blue romper suit, shoes and socks missing, 19.5" h	5175	6000
Kämmer & Reinhardt, Marie, bisque head, painted features, closed mouth, original blonde mohair wig, fully jointed composition body, original velveteen and cotton German costume, 1909, 10" h	1150	1200
Karl Hartmann, Germany, Globe Baby, bisque head, blue sleep eyes, open mouth with 4 teeth, original body, 8" h	275	350
Käthe Kruse, molded and painted face, blonde human hair wig, cloth body and limbs, 1940-50s, 17.5" h	350	600
Kewpie, Cameo, composition, jointed at shoulders and hips, original cotton sunsuit, shoes, and socks, paper label, 13" h	140	300
Kewpie, Rose O'Neil, bisque, farmer, holding wooden rake, impressed "O'Neil," paper label, c1913, 5.5" h	500	550

	LOW	HIGH
Kewpie, Rose O'Neil, bisque, guitar player, red and navy cloth ribbons on guitar, paper label, 3.625" h	300	500
Kewpie, Rose O'Neil, bisque, seated, with black cat, paper label, 3.25" h	550	600
Kewpie, Rose O'Neil, bisque, seated soldier, on black, red, and gold German helmet, jointed at shoulders, impressed on bottom "9876," c1913, 3.5" h	1000	1150
Kewpie, Rose O'Neil, bisque, sitting in wicker armchair, c1913, 3.5" h	300	400
Kley & Hahn, Walküre, 12, bisque head, brown glass sleep eyes, open mouth, pierced ears, original dark brown human hair wig, fully jointed composition body, 24" h	250	350
König & Wernicke, 99, bisque head, brown glass sleep eyes, open mouth, pierced ears, original blonde mohair wig, fully jointed composition body, 31" h	600	700
Lanternier, Cherie, bisque head, fixed eyes, open mouth, pierced ears, original wig, papier-mâché body, 16"-18"	700	800
Leibe & Hoffman, bisque shoulder head, blue glass fixed eyes, open mouth, pierced ears, brown mohair wig, kid body, bisque hands, late 19th C, 23" h	140	350
Lenci, felt head, surprised glass eyes, ash blond hair, felt body, green dress, yellow hat, holding wooden cage, 1920s, 20" h	2500	3500
Lenci, Henriette, pressed felt head with painted features, side-glancing fixed eyes, swivel head, jointed shoulders and hips, original clothes, 1930s, 25" h	800	1000
Lenci-Type, felt, molded and painted features, blonde hair, felt and velveteen Bavarian costume, 1930s, 12" h	100	150
Louis Wolf, 48, Character Baby, bisque head, blue glass fixed eyes, open mouth with tongue, bent limb composition body, impressed mark, 23" h	375	600
Madame Alexander, Alice, cloth, molded felt or flocked mask face, painted side-glancing eyes, 19"-20"	650	750
Madame Alexander, Lissy, 2051, Portrait Series, vinyl, Coco face, red hair, pink dress	2200	2600
Madame Alexander, Little Colonel, composition, 13" h	600	650

Left to right: Lenci Doll; Kewpie, Cameo Doll Products Co.

Madame Alexander Dolls.
Left: Scarlet
Right: Lissy.

	LOW	HIGH
Madame Alexander, Margot Ballerina, hard plastic, 14" h	400	500
Madame Alexander, Scarlet, #2061, Portrait Series, vinyl, Coco face, brunette hair, white tulle dress	2000	3000
Madame Alexander, Smarty, vinyl, 12" h	200	250
Martha Chase, yellow hair, blue eyes, cotton sateen body with trademark, early 20th C, 25" h	250	300
Mary Hoyer, plastic, blue sleep eyes, red mohair wig, jointed at head, shoulders, and hips, hand-knit 3-pc. raspberry snow suit, 1950s, 14" h	260	600
Moramuri, Character Baby, bisque head, blue glass sleep eyes, open mouth, original mohair wig, bent limb composition body, c1920, 11" h	115	200
Moramuri, Character Baby, bisque head, blue glass sleep eyes, open mouth, original mohair wig, bent limb composition body, c1920, 15" h	200	300
Papier-Mâché, Lady Doll, molded and painted hair and features, kid body with wooden limbs, 1830s, 9.5" h	200	520
Queen Louise, Germany, bisque head, blue glass sleep eyes, open mouth, fully jointed composition body, 23" h	230	500
Recknagel, 31, Max, molded hair, painted features, 8" h	650	700
Recknagel, Character Baby, bisque head, painted or glass eyes, cloth body or composition bent limb body, 7"-8" h	300	350
Rempel & Breitung, 117, bisque head, brown glass sleep eyes, open mouth, original blonde mohair wig, fully jointed composition body, period navy wool flannel sailor dress, early 20th C, 20" h	200	630
Sandra Sue, hard plastic, molded eyelashes, Saran wig, 8" h	100	150
Schoenau and Hoffmeister, Character Baby, bisque socket head, sleep eyes, open mouth, original wig, composition bent limb body, 13"-15" h	400	500
Schoenau and Hoffmeister, Pouty Baby, bisque dome head with painted hair, sleep eyes, closed pouty mouth, cloth body, composition arms and legs, original outfit, c1925, 11"-12" h	750	800
Schoenhut, Jiggs, wood, jointed at head, shoulders, and hips, original felt shirt and trousers, 1924, 7" h	200	375
Schoenhut, Sober Face Character Girl, wood, blue intaglio eyes, open/closed mouth, blonde mohair wig, original union suit, period cotton dress, 15" h	500	800
Schoenhut, Sober Face Character Girl, wood, brown eyes, original blonde mohair wig, 18.5" h	375	500

Simon & Halbig, 1892.
—Photo courtesy Auction Team Köln.

	LOW	HIGH
SFBJ, 60, papier-mâché head, fully jointed body, 22" h	400	500
SFBJ, 227, Character Doll, bisque head, 17" h	1850	2000
SFBJ, 251, Toddler, 20" h	1500	2000
Simon & Halbig, 17, Evelyn, brown glass sleep eyes, open mouth, pierced ears, original blonde mohair wig, fully jointed composition body, impressed S&H 17 mark, 42" h	2000	2500
Simon & Halbig, 719, blue glass sleep eyes, open mouth, pierced ears, original light brown mohair wig, fully jointed composition body, 23.75" h	1500	2000
Simon & Halbig, 1009, bisque head, blue glass sleep eyes, open mouth, pierced ears, original blonde human hair wig, fully jointed composition body, impressed mark, with wicker lawn swing, 18.5" h	800	1000
Simon & Halbig, 1079, blue glass sleep eyes, open mouth, pierced ears, original blonde mohair wig, fully jointed composition body, 17.5" h	400	500
Simon & Halbig, 1428, Character Baby, bisque head, blue glass fixed eyes, open/closed smiling mouth, original blonde mohair wig, bent limb composition body, impressed mark, 13" h	1035	1500
Steiff, Dutch Girl, center face seam, black steel eyes, light brown hair, original costume, missing button, c1913, 13.75" h	1000	2000
Steiner, Clockwork Doll, bisque head, blue glass fixed eyes, open mouth, pierced ears, original blonde lambskin wig, cloth-covered torso, kid lower body and upper legs, composition arms and legs, 1880s, 20" h	1000	1200
Steiner, Crying/Moving Doll, bisque head, blue glass fixed eyes, open mouth, pierced ears, original blonde mohair wig, papier-mâché body, kid lower body and upper legs, composition arms and legs, late 19th C, 23.5" h	950	1000
Terri Lee, hard plastic, white hair, yellow sweater, 16" h	60	75
Uneeda, Dollikin, hard plastic, fully jointed, 1957, 8" h	30	40
Uneeda, Toddler, composition, original outfit, c1940, 13" h	225	250
Vogue, Ginny, hard plastic, painted eyes, original wig and outfit, 1940s, 7"-8" h	350	400
Welsch & Co., bisque head, brown glass sleep eyes, open mouth, original strawberry blonde mohair wig, fully jointed composition body, impressed MOA 200 mark, 29" h	250	400
Wisleizenus, bisque head, blue glass sleep eyes, open mouth, fully jointed composition body, impressed A.W. mark, 24" h	260	300

Barbie

Barbie was born in 1959, arriving as a svelte, young woman. Mattel founders Elliot and Ruth Handler had already bought out their partner Harold Matson when they introduced the doll named after their daughter. She was modern and little girls could role play with her, dressing her in countless costumes. Barbie had elegant gowns, mirroring many of the best designers of the day, as well as work togs and casual clothes. Barbie was advertised on "The Mickey Mouse Club." Barbie rapidly became the "must have" doll of the baby-boomer generation. Ken (named after the Handler's son) and a group of friends soon joined Barbie. The doll is still going strong after forty years. Many adults who adored her as a child now collect her today. Her thirtieth birthday in 1989 was a gala event covered by news services around the world.

Collectors look for condition. The most desirable Barbies are pristine examples from the 1950s and 1960s. Collectors shy away from much of the 1970s material because there is a perception of inferior quality.

The prices below are based on items in near mint to mint condition. Since the same item can be bought at a variety of locations and prices, and many dolls are no longer in their original boxes, we have devised a double range system. The low range (MNP) includes items that are near mint to mint without packaging. The higher end range (MIP) reflects the prices of near mint to mint items in near mint to mint original boxes. Therefore, prices below are for the best items available; scratched, chipped, or altered examples are not included. Cut hair, missing clothes and cracked or stained plastic greatly reduces Barbie's value. Each entry lists the approximate year of introduction and the item number.

For further reading consult *The Collectors Encyclopedia of Barbie Dolls and Collectibles* by Sybil DeWein and Joan Ashabraner (Collector Books, Paducah, KY, 1977, 1996 value update), *The Barbie Doll Years: 1959-1996, Third Edition* by Patrick C. Olds (Collector Books, Paducah, KY, 1999), and *The Ultimate Barbie Doll Book* by Marcie Melillo (Krause Publications, Iola, WI, 1996). For information on Barbie fashions see *Barbie Fashion, Vol. I: 1959-1967* (1990, 1998 value update) and *Vol. II: 1968-1974* (1997) by Sarah Sink Eames (Collector Books, Paducah, KY).

Barbie and Friends

	YEAR	NO.	MNP	MIP
Allan, bendable legs	1965	1010	$150-$175	$550-$650
Allan, painted reddish-brown hair	1963	1000	35-55	100-135
Barbie #1, blonde	1959	850	3500-4000	5000-6000
Barbie #2, brunette	1959	850	3500-4000	5000-6000
Barbie #3, brunette	1959	850	500-800	750-1000
Barbie #4, brunette	1960	850	300-400	500-600
Barbie #5, brunette	1961	850	200-300	300-400
Barbie #6 and #7, blonde	1962	850	100-200	200-300
Bubblecut Barbie	1961	850	100-175	250-350
Bubblecut Barbie	1962	850	200-400	500-800
Busy Francie	1971	3313	100-125	150-250
Busy Ken, painted brown hair	1971	3314	25-50	75-100
Busy Talking Barbie, blonde	1971	1195	100-125	175-250
Busy Talking Ken, painted brown hair	1971	1196	50-100	100-175
California Midge	1971	1196	50-100	100-175
Color Magic Barbie, blonde	1967	1150	750-1000	1500-2500
Dramatic New Living Barbie, blonde	1969	1160	100-125	175-250
Fashion Queen Barbie, painted hair	1962	870	100-150	400-500
Free Moving Cara	1974	7745	20-30	50-65
Gold Medal Olympic Barbie, blonde	1974	7233	20-30	50-65
Happy Meal Whitney	1993	11476	5-10	10-15
Island Fun Skipper	1987	4064	5-10	10-15
Ken, bendable legs	1965	1020	75-150	375-450

	YEAR	NO.	MNP	MIP
Ken, flocked hair	1961	750	50-60	100-150
Ken, painted hair	1962	750	30-40	100-125
Live Action Barbie, blonde	1970	1155	50-75	100-150
Live Action P. J., blonde	1970	1156	65-75	100-150
Living Barbie, brunette	1970	1116	100-125	175-250
Living Skipper	1970	1117	25-50	75-150
Magic Moves Barbie, blonde	1985	2126	10-25	25-50
Midge, bendable legs	1964	1080	200-325	500-650
Newpory Barbie, blonde	1973	7807	50-65	150-175
Peaches 'n Cream Barbie	1984	7926	10-15	30-45
Pose 'n Play Tiff	1971	1199	50-75	150-175
Ricky, painted red hair	1965	1090	45-55	100-135
Skipper, bendable legs	1964	1030	100-125	250-350
Skooter, straight legs	1965	1040	35-45	75-125
Sun Gold Malibu P. J., brunette	1983	1187	5-10	15-25
Sun Set Malibu Ken, painted yellow hair	1970	1088	10-15	40-50
Superstar Ken, black version	1988	1550	5-10	25-50
Swirl Ponytail Barbie, blonde	1962	850	200-300	350-400
Talking Barbie, blonde	1968	1115	125-150	300-375
Talking Barbie, brunette, side ponytail	1962	850	250-300	350-400
Talking Christie	1967	1126	100-125	200-250
Talking Ken, painted hair	1968	1111	75-80	150-175
Talking Stacey, side ponytail	1968	1125	150-175	350-400
Todd, painted black hair, groom outfit	1982	4253	10-20	25-35
Tutti	1965	3550	50-75	100-150
Twist & Turn Barbie, blonde	1966	1160	150-175	400-450
Twist & Turn Barbie, blonde	1969	1160	150-175	400-500
Twist & Turn P. J.	1969	1118	50-100	200-275
Twist & Turn Skipper	1968	1105	50-100	300-350
Twist & Turn Stacey	1969	1165	100-150	350-400
Walk Lively Barbie	1971	1182	50-60	125-145

Above: Barbie and Ken Gift Set, c1962, $1050 at auction. —Photo courtesy Jackson's Auctioneers & Appraisers.

Above left: Ken #1020, wearing #1401 Special Date Outfit; Ponytail Barbie #850, wearing #971 Easter Parade Coat; Ken #750, wearing #0779 American Airlines Captain's Outfit.

Clothing

	YEAR	NO.	MNP	MIP
After Five	1962	934	$60-$75	$100-$125
Altogether Elegant	1970	1242	40-50	65-75
Barbie in Hawaii	1964	1605	65-75	75-100
Barbie Learns to Cook	1965	1634	75-100	100-150
Bloom Bursts	1967	1778	75-100	100-150
Bloom Zoom	1970	1239	25-50	50-75
Brunch Time	1965	1628	75-100	100-150
Culotte-Wot?	1968	1214	40-50	65-75
Disc Dates	1965	1633	50-75	75-100
Dogs 'n Duds	1964	1613	75-100	120-150
Firelights	1968	1481	40-50	65-75
Fraternity Dance	1965	1638	100-150	150-200
Friday Night Date	1960	979	50-60	80-90
Fun at the Fair	1965	1624	65-75	75-100
Garden Tea Party	1964	1606	25-35	55-65
Golden Girl	1959	911	20-30	40-50
Graduation	1963	795	65-75	100-125
Great Coat	1970	1459	40-50	65-75
Hooray For Leather	1969	1477	40-50	65-75
Ice Breaker	1962	942	65-75	75-100
It's Cold Outside	1964	0819	40-50	65-75
Junior Designer	1965	1620	50-75	100-125
Junior Prom	1965	1614	175-200	200-250
Ken in Switzerland	1964	0776	75-100	100-150
Little Leaguer	1965	1504	40-50	65-75
London Tour	1966	1661	65-75	85-100
Masquerade	1963	794	65-75	100-125
Midnight Blue	1965	1617	175-200	200-250
Mood For Music	1962	948	30-40	65-75
Mood Matchers	1970	1792	40-50	65-75
Night Scene	1971	1496	40-50	65-75
Outdoor Life	1965	1637	50-75	75-100
Peachy Fleecy Coat	1959	915	30-40	50-60
Poodle Parade	1965	503	200-250	300-325
Sleeping Pretty	1965	1636	40-50	65-75
Sorority Meeting	1962	937	40-50	65-75
Striped Types	1970	1243	40-50	65-75
Sweet Dreams	1959	973	40-50	65-75
Wedding Day	1959	972	85-100	125-150

Gift Sets and Accessories

Action Accents Barbie Gift Set	1969	1585	$350-$400	$450-$500
Barbie & Ken Camping Out	1983	4984	20-35	75-95
Furry Friends Jamie Gift Set	1969	1584	350-400	450-500
Little Theatre Gift Set	1964	1018	600-700	750-1000
Pep Rally Gift Set	1964	1022	350-400	450-500
Perfectly Plaid Talking Barbie Gift Set	1971	1193	300-350	400-450
Stacie & Butterfly Pony Gift Set	1993	10227	5-10	15-25
Swingin' in Silver P. J. Gift Set	1970	1588	125-150	150-200
Twirly Curls Barbie Gift Set	1982	4097	65-75	75-100

G.I. Joe

Joe is thirty-five and still going strong. Hasbro introduced him in 1964. The Irwin Company produced some of Hasbro's early vehicles for Joe. Plastic and 11.5" tall, Joe was marketed as a fighting or action figure and not as a doll. Thus the action figure toy was created. A huge success with boys, girls often substituted him for Ken, to act as Barbie's date. Joe has changed with the times. In 1977 Hasbro reduced his height to 8.5". Following the enormous success of the *Star Wars* action figure line, Joe was reintroduced in the 3.75" size in 1982, and is still being produced. Collectors are beginning to seek these smaller figures. The following list, however, focuses on the earlier 11.5" figures.

The prices below are based on items in excellent or mint condition. Since the same item can be bought at a variety of locations at different prices we devised a range system. The low range (MNP) covers complete, near mint to mint items without the original box or packaging. The higher range (MIP) reflects the prices of complete, near mint to mint items in near mint to mint boxes. Prices below are for complete "like new" items. Completeness is an important factor for G.I. Joes.

The Complete Encyclopedia of G.I. Joe, 2nd Edition by Vincent Santelmo, Krause Publications, Iola, WI, 1997, describes in great detail what each set contained.

The year listed is the year of introduction, unless it's a reissue or update. Following the date is the series: Action Marine–*AM*; Action Girl–*AG*; Action Sailor–*ASL*; Action Soldiers of the World–*ASW*; Action Solder–*ASD*; Action Pilot–*AP*; Adventure Team–*ADT*. Words are abbreviated to conserve space. Following the series is the product number.

G.I. Joe, Man of Action, #7500.—Photo courtesy New England Auction Gallery.

Action Figures

	YEAR	SERIES	NO.	MNP	MIP
Action GI Nurse, with green medic bag	1967	AG	8060	$2000-$2500	$3000-$3300
Action GI Nurse, with white medic bag	1967	AG	8060	3000-3500	4000-4500
Action Marine	1964	AM	7700	200-300	350-450
Action Pilot	1964	AP	7800	300-375	400-500
Action Sailor	1964	ASL	7600	100-200	300-400
Action Soldier	1964	ASD	7500	150-200	250-350
Air Adventurer	1970	ADT	7403	50-100	100-200
Annapolis Cadet Set	1967	ASL	7624	200-400	500-900
Black Talking Commander	1973	ADT	7406	200-300	400-500
British Commando	1966	ASW	8100	1000-1500	2000-2500
German Soldier	1966	ASW	8100	1000-1500	2000-2500
Man of Action	1970	ADT	7500	50-100	100-200
Sea Adventurer	1970	ADT	7402	50-100	100-175
Talking Action Marine	1967	AM	7790	250-450	650-750

	YEAR	SERIES	NO.	MNP	MIP
Talking Action Pilot	1967	AP	7890	1000-1300	1500-1600
Talking Action Sailor	1967	ASL	7690	500-1000	1000-1200
Talking Action Soldier	1967	ASD	7590	50-100	200-500
Talking Astronaut	1970	ADT	7405	150-250	300-400

Action Figure Accessories

	YEAR	SERIES	NO.	MNP	MIP
Action Sea Sled, JC Penney	1970	ADT	—	$5-$15	$25-$50
Adventure Pack: Army Bivouac Series	1968	ASD	7549.83	500-800	1000-1200
Adventure Pack: Marine Medic Series	1968	AM	7733.83	1000-1200	1500-1800
Adventure Pack: Navy Scuba Series	1968	ASL	7643.83	1500-2000	2500-2800
Adventure Team Vehicle Set	1970	ADT	7005	200-250	300-350
Air/Sea Rescue Set	1967	AP	7825	750-1000	1200-1500
Amphicat, Sears	1970	ADT	59158	5-15	25-50
Beachhead Field Pack Set	1964	AM	7712	150-250	300-400
Breeches Buoy Set	1967	ASL	7625	200-400	600-650
British Commando Set	1966	ASW	3304	100-200	300-400
Combat Rifle/Helmet Set	1967	ASD	7510	50-100	200-250
Communications Flags Set	1964	AM	7703	150-250	400-500
Crash Crew Set	1966	AP	7820	75-150	250-350
Danger of the Depths Set	1970	ADT	7412	25-75	50-100
Deep Freeze Set	1967	ASL	7623	200-400	500-700
Deep Sea Diver Set	1965	ASL	7620	300-500	600-700
Drag Bike Set	1971	ADT	7364	10-20	30-40
Dress Parade Set	1964	AM	7710	150-200	300-400
Flying Rescue Set	1971	ADT	7361	5-15	25-50
Frogman Scuba Top Set	1964	ASL	7603	25-75	100-125
Green Beret	1966	ASD	7536	75-125	150-200
Japanese Imperial Soldier Set	1966	ASW	8201	1000-1200	1500-2000
Jungle Fighter Set	1867	AM	7732	750-1000	1200-1500
Landing Signal Officer Set	1966	ASL	7621	200-300	400-450
Marine Basics Set	1966	AM	7722	25-75	100-150
Marine Mortar Set	1967	AM	7725	50-100	200-300
Mobile Support Vehicle Set	1972	ADT	7499	50-100	200-300
Motorcycle and Sidecar	1967	ASD	5651	10-20	30-40
M. P. Duffle Bag Set	1964	ASD	7523	25-75	50-100
Navy Basics Set	1966	ASL	7628	50-75	100-150
Navy Machine Gun Set	1965	ASL	7618	25-50	100-125
Official Sea Sled and Frogman Set	1966	ASL	8050	200-300	550-650
Paratrooper Parachute Pack Set	1964	AM	7705	150-200	300-400
Radiation Detection Set	1971	ADT	7341	10-20	30-40
Recovery of the Lost Mummy Adventure Set, Sears	1970	ADT	—	100-200	250-350
Scramble Set	1964	AP	7807	100-200	300-400
Secret Mission to Spy Island Set	1970	ADT	7411	50-75	100-125
Shore Patrol Set	1967	ASL	7612	400-800	1000-1500
Ski Patrol Set	1965	ASD	7531	100-200	400-500
Sonic Rock Blaster Set	1972	ADT	7312	5-15	20-30
Special Forces Set	1966	ASD	7532	200-400	650-750
Survival Life Raft	1964	AP	7802	25-75	100-200
Talking Adventure Pack and Shore Patrol Equipment	1968	ASL	90612	1000-1500	2000-2500
Talking Adventure Pack and Tent Set Equipment	1968	AM	90711	400-800	1000-2000

Paper Dolls

Paper dolls date to the 1400s and appeared as children's toys in the late 1700s. Collectors usually specialize either in antique examples or in specific types such as celebrity, advertising or works of favorite artists or companies. Dolls based on movie and TV stars attract collectors from other areas.

A paper doll's collectibility depends upon artist, subject, age, construction, condition and size. Prices below are for uncut near mint condition examples. Near mint, cut dolls may command prices only 20% to 50% of the value of the same uncut dolls. Prices listed are for paper doll books and sets in unused condition.

For more Information see *America's Early Advertising Paper Dolls* by Lagretta Metzger Bajorek (Schiffer, Atglen, PA, 1999).

	LOW	HIGH
Airline Stewardess, Lowe, 1957	$25	$50
Alive-Like Baby Elizabeth, Lowe, 1963	20	40
Ann Blythe, Merrill, 1952	35	50
Ann Sothern, Saalfield, #4407, 1956	35	50
Archies, Whitman, 1969	30	50
Arlene Dahl, Saalfield, 1953	25	50
Ava Gardner, Whitman	15	25
Baby Brother, Saalfield, 1959	5	15
Baby Dears, Saalfield, #4418	10	20
Baby Doll, Samuel Lowe, 1957	15	25
Baby Sandy, Merrill, 1941	40	50
Baby Sparkle Plenty, Saalfield, #1510, 1940s	50	75
Badgett Quadruplets, Saalfield, 1941	40	50
Barbara Britton, Saalfield, 1954	25	50
Barbie and Ken, Whitman, 1960s	25	50
Barbie Country Camper and Paper Dolls, Whitman, #4347, 1973	15	25
Barbie Friend Ship, Whitman, 1973	25	50
Beauty Queen, Saalfield	10	15
Betsy McCall, Artcraft, 1965	25	50
Betty Field, Saalfield, 1943	25	50
Beverly Hillbillies Punch-Out Book, Whitman, 1964	75	100
Bewitched, Samantha, Magic Wand, 1965	65	75
Bob and Betty, Saalfield, 1945	15	25
Bride and Groom, Merrill, 1949	20	40
Buffy, Whitman, 1968	50	75
Bobbsey Twins, Lowe, #1254, 1952	50	75
Candy Stripers, Saalfield, 1973	8	15
Carmen Miranda, Saalfield, #1558	15	20
Caroline Kennedy, large	50	75
"Charlie's Angels" Jill, The Toy Factory, 1977	50	75
Children of America, Saalfield, #2335, 1941	10	25
Chitty Chitty Bang Bang, Whitman, 1968, 10" x 13"	25	50
Cinderella Steps Out, Lowe, 1948	10	20
Connie Darling and Her Dolly, Saalfield, #6092, 1964	10	15
Cowboys and Cowgirls, Lowe, #1296, 1950	20	40
Curiosity Shop, Saalfield, 1971	5	15
Cynthia Pepper Featured on the Margie Television Show, Watkins-Strathmore, 1963	50	75
Daddy's Girl, Saalfield, 1974	5	10
Daisy Mae and Li'l Abner, Saalfield, #1549, 1951	75	100
Debs and Sub-Debs, Saalfield, 1941	10	25

	LOW	HIGH
Disneyland Punch-Out Book, Golden Press, 1963	200	400
Dodie From "My Three Sons," Artcraft, 1972	25	50
Dollies Go 'Round the World, Lowe, #2714, 1971	5	10
Donna Reed, Saalfield, 1959	15	25
Doris Day, Whitman, 1952	30	50
Double Date, Whitman, #962, 1949	35	50
Dr. Kildare and Nurse Susan, Lowe, 1960s	75	100
Dutch Treat, Saalfield, 1961	15	25
Esther Williams, Merrill, 1953	35	50
Eve Arden, Saalfield, 1953	25	50
Evelyn Rudie, Saalfield, 1958	10	20
Fashions of the Modern Miss, Saalfield, 1957	5	10
Faye Emerson, Saalfield, 1952	15	25
Finian's Rainbow, Saalfield, 1968	10	15
Flying Nun, Artcraft, 1969	50	75
Gilda Radner, Avon Books, 1979	25	50
Girl Scouts, Brownies, Dolls of 39 Nations, c1950	65	75
Giselle MacKenzie, Saalfield, 1957	15	25
Gloria Jean, Saalfield, 1941	50	75
Grace Kelly, Whitman	30	40
Green Acres, Whitman, 1967	50	75
Happiest Millionaire, Saalfield, 1967	10	15
Happy Bride, Whitman, 1967	15	25
Harry the Soldier, Lowe, #1074	10	25
Hee Haw, Artcraft, 1971	75	100
Heidi and Peter, Saalfield, 1957	10	15
Here's the Bride, Whitman, #1948, 1960	25	50
Honeymooners, Lowe, #2560, 1952	50	75
Hootenanny, Saalfield, 1964	10	15
Hot Looks, Whitman, #1541, 1988	5	10
Ice Festival, Saalfield, 1957	10	25
Jane Russell, Saalfield, 1955	20	40
Janet Leigh, Abbott, 1958	50	75
Joan Caulfield, Saalfield, 1953	15	25
Joanne Woodward, Saalfield, 1958	15	25
Judy Doll—Miss Teenage America, Saalfield, 1964	10	25
Judy Holliday, Saalfield	15	25
Julia, Saalfield, 1969	50	75
Julie Andrews, Saalfield, 1957	50	75
Juliet Jones, Saalfield, 1955	20	35
June and Stu Erwin, Saalfield, 1954	15	25
June Bride, Stephens Co., 1946	15	25
Karen Goes to College, Merrill, 1955	5	10
Kathy, Lowe, #9986, 1962	35	45
Kathy and Sue, Saalfield, #6117, 1958	15	25
Kewpie-Kin Paper Dolls, Artcraft, 1967	40	50
Kim Novak, Saalfield, 1957	20	30
Kitty Goes to Kindergarten, Merrill, 1956	5	10
Lana Turner, Whitman, 1947	75	100
Laraine Day, Saalfield, 1953	15	25
Laugh-In, Saalfield, 1969	50	75
Lennon Sisters, Whitman, 1957	40	50
Lilac Time, Saalfield, 1959	5	10
Linda Darnell, Saalfield, 1953	15	25

	LOW	HIGH
Little Ballerina, Whitman, 1969	10	25
Little Family and Their Little House, Merrill, 1949	15	25
Little Girls, Lowe, #2784, 1969	5	10
Little Miss America, Saalfield, #2358	50	75
Lucille Ball, Saalfield, 1944	50	75
Lydia, Whitman, 1977	25	50
Malibu Skipper, Whitman, #1952, 1973	10	20
Marie Osmond, Saalfield, 1973	50	75
Martha Hyer, Saalfield, 1958	15	25
Mary, Mary, Quite Contrary, Saalfield, 1972	5	10
Miss Piggy, Colorforms, 1980	25	50
Moon Dreamers, Whitman, #1542, 1987	5	10
Mrs. Beasley, Whitman, 1972	25	50
Munsters, Whitman, 1966	75	100
My Fair Lady, Standard Toykraft, 1960s	50	75
My Little Margie, Saalfield, 1954	15	25
Nanny and the Professor, Artcraft, 1970	50	75
Natalie Wood, Whitman, 1957	50	75
Once Upon a Wedding Day, Saalfield, #9619	10	25
One Hundred and One Dalmatians, Whitman, 1960	75	100
Ozzie and Harriet, Saalfield, 1954	20	35
Paper Dolls Around the World, Saalfield, 1964	15	25
Papoose, Saalfield, 1949	10	15
Partridge Family, Artcraft, 1971	50	75
Partridge Family Susan Dey as Laurie, Artcraft	50	75
Patti Page, Abbott, 1958	35	50
Patty Duke, Whitman, 1965	50	75
Pert and Pretty, Saalfield, 1954	10	15
Petticoat Junction, Whitman, 1964	50	75
Piper Laurie, Merrill, 1953	35	50
Polly Bergen, Saalfield, 1958	15	25
Playhouse Dolls, Stephens Co., 1949	15	25
Playtime Fashions, Stephens Co., #135, 1946	10	15
Princess Diana, Golden Book, 1985	20	35
Punky Brewster, Whitman, #1532, 1986	5	10
Queen Holden's Nursery School Dolls, Whitman, 1953	40	50
Rhonda Fleming, Saalfield, 1954	25	50
Rosemary Clooney, Bonnie Book, 1958	55	75
Roy Rogers and Dale Evans, Whitman, 1950	75	100
Sabrina and the Archies, Whitman, 1971	25	50
Sandra Dee, Saalfield, 1959	15	25
Santa's Workshop, Whitman, 1960	50	75
School Friends, Merrill, 1955-60	15	25
Shari Lewis, Saalfield, 1958	15	25
Sheree North, Saalfield, 1957	15	25
Shirley Temple, Whitman, 1976	25	50
Snow White and the Seven Dwarfs, Whitman, 1960s	50	75
Sports Time, Whitman, 1952	15	25
Square Dance, Lowe, #968, 1950	5	10
Story of the Ballet, Saalfield, #9568	10	15
Teen Time Dolls, Whitman, #4401, 1959	15	25
That Girl Starring Marlo Thomas, Saalfield, 1967	10	15
Thumbelina, Whitman, 1969	25	50
Waltons, Whitman, 1975	50	75

Games

Board games are a part of practically everyone's lives. Beginning in the 1840s, mass-produced games have offered hours of fun and provided glimpses of their eras. A large number of those listed below are based on television shows, a theme that dominates post-war collecting. There are also examples of card, skill and target games included. The majority are by American companies.

The following prices are for games ranging from the 1880s to the 1980s. There are differences between post-WWII and pre-war collecting but condition and quality are sought by all collectors. Prices for post-war games are for *near mint complete.* These examples must have no tears, stains, broken corners, or missing pieces. Prices of the pre-war games, particularly for those dating before 1920, are a bit more lenient on condition due to age. They reflect examples that are complete with no stains or tears on the box or board image, but may have minor flaws: repaired inner corner or small skirt tears, and some dirt but nothing that affects the illustrations.

For further reading see *Antique Trader's Guide to Games & Puzzles* by Harry L. Rinker (Antique Trader Books, Dubuque, IA, 1997), and *Board Games* by Desi Scarpone (Schiffer, Atglen, PA, 1995).

Aero-Chute Target Game.

	LOW	HIGH
ABC Monday Night Football, Aurora, 1972	$35	$45
ACME Checkout Game, Milton Bradley, 1959	30	40
Across the Board Horse Racing Game, MPH, 1975	10	30
Across the USA, Hasbro, 1966	10	20
Addiction, Createk, 1968	5	15
Adventures of Tom Sawyer and Huck Finn, Stoll & Edwards Co., 1925	70	80
Aero-Chute Target Game, American Toy Works, c1930s	60	70
Aeroplane Race, No. 60 "Mac" Whitling, McDowell Mfg. Co., 1930s	80	90
Air Ship Game, McLoughlin Brothers, 1904	325	375
Alfred Hitchcock Presents Why, Milton Bradley, 1958	30	40
All-Pro Baseball, Ideal, 1967	35	45
Alumni Fun, Milton Bradley, 1965	15	25
American History, The Game of, Parker Brothers, c1890	40	50
American Pachinko, Pressman, 1970s	15	25
Amoco Mileage, The, Cadaco, 1976	20	30
Amusing Game of Innocence Abroad, The, Parker Brothers, 1888	275	325
Animal Talk Game, Mattel, 1963	20	30
Animal Trap Game, Multiple Products Corp., 1950s	15	25
Annie Oakley Game, Game Gems/T. Cohn, 1965	35	45
Anti, National Games, 1977	15	25
Antiquity, Terri Heit, 1984	10	20
Apple's Way, Milton Bradley, 1974	15	20
Aquanauts, Transogram, 1961	30	40

The Air Ship Game.

Auctioneer.

	LOW	HIGH
Arbitrage, H. C. Jacoby, Inc., 1986	5	15
Archie Bunker's Card Game, Milton Bradley, 1972	10	20
Arm Chair Quarterback, Novelty Mfg. Co., 1955	20	30
Arnold Palmer's Inside Golf, The David Bremson Co., 1961	45	55
Around the World in 80 Days, Transogram, 1957	30	40
Art Linkletter's Game of "People Are Funny," Whitman, 1968	20	30
Assembly Line, The Game of, Selchow & Righter, 1950s	55	65
As The World Turns, Parker Brothers, 1966	15	25
Atom Ant, Transogam, 1966	45	55
Auctioneer, Ideal, 1972	20	30
Authors, Game of, J. Ottmann Lith. Co., c1900	30	40
Authors Illustrated, Clark & Sowdon, Tokalon Series, 1893	30	40
Auto Bridge, The Auto Bridge Co., 1948	5	15
Auto Game, The, Milton Bradley, c1906	275	325
Avalanche, Parker Brothers, 1966	5	15
Avilude or Game of Birds, West & Lee Game Co., 1873	30	40
"Babe" Ruth's Baseball Game, Milton Bradley, c1926-28	725	775
Babes In Toyland, Walt Disney's, Parker Brothers, 1961	25	35
Babes In Toyland, Walt Disney's, Whitman, 1961	25	35
Bamm Bamm Color Me Happy Game, Transogram, 1963	55	65
Bandersnatch, Mattel, 1968	10	20
Bang, Game of, McLoughlin Brothers, 1903	150	200
Bantu, Parker Brothers, 1955	15	25
Barbie Game, The "Queen of the Prom," Mattel, 1964	50	60
Barbie's Little Sister Skipper Game, Mattel, 1864	45	55
Barnabas Collins Dark Shadows Game, Milton Bradley, 1969	70	80
Barney Miller, Parker Brothers, 1977	10	20
Barrel of Monkeys, Giant, Lakeside, 1969	10	20
Baseball, Transogram, 1969	25	35
Bash!, Milton Bradley, 1965	10	20
Batman Game, Milton Bradley, 1966	70	80
Battle, Game of, or Fun for Boys, McLoughlin Brothers, 1889	475	525

Avalanche.

The Black Cat Fortune Telling Game.

	LOW	HIGH
Battle-Cry, American Heritage, Command Decision Series, Milton Bradley, 1961	35	40
Battle Line Game, Ideal, 1964	35	40
Battle Stations!, John E. Burleson, 1952	25	35
Battleship, Milton Bradley, 1967	35	45
Bazaar, The Trading Game, 3M, 1967	5	15
Beat the Clock Game, Lowell, 1954	55	65
Ben Casey M.D. Game, Transogram, 1961	25	35
Benny Goodman Swings Into a Game of Musical Information, Toy Creations, 1940s	70	80
Beverly Hillbillies Game, The, Standard Toykraft, 1963	45	55
Bewitch, Selchow & Righter, 1964	15	20
Bewitched, Game Gems, 1965	70	80
Bible Characters, Game of, Zondervan Publishing House, 1939	15	25
Bicycle Race, McLoughlin Brothers, 1891	950	1025
Big Apple, Rosebud Art Co., 1938	45	55
Big Business, Transogram, 1954	10	20
Big League Baseball, 3M, 1966	20	30
Big Six: Christy Mathewson Indoor Baseball Game, 1922	550	625
Bild-A-Word, Educational Card & Game Corp., 1929	10	20
Billy Bump's Visit to Boston, George S. Parker & Co., c1887	30	40
Bing Crosby's Game, Call Me Lucky, Parker Brothers, 1954	50	60
Bingo, Deluxe, Whitman, 1957	6	10
Bingo or Beano, A Game, Parker Brothers, 1930s	10	20
Black Cat Fortune Telling Game, The, Parker Brothers, 1897	75	85
Black Sambo, Game of, Samuel Gabriel Sons & Co., c1939	225	275
Blockhead!, Parker Brothers, 1976-77	15	25
Boake Carter's Star Reporter Game, Parker Brothers, 1937	100	150
Bobby Shantz's Baseball Game, Realistic Games Mfg. Co., 1954	125	175
Bonanza, Parker Brothers, 1964	35	45
Boundary, Mattel, 1970	5	15
Bowl Em, Parker Brothers, 1950s	10	15
Boy Hunter, The, Parker Brothers, c1925	85	95
Bradley's Telegraph Game, Milton Bradley, c1905	125	150
Bradley's Toy Town Post Office, Milton Bradley, 1910	150	200

Break the Bank.

Cities.

	LOW	HIGH
Brady Bunch Game, The, Whitman, 1973	60	75
Break the Bank, Bettye-B, 1955	40	50
"Brownie" Kick-In Top, M. H. Miller Co., c1910	70	80
Bucket of Fun, Milton Bradley, 1968	15	25
Buffalo Bill, Game of, Parker Brothers, 1898	70	80
Bugs Bunny Adventure Game, Milton Bradley, 1961	30	35
Bull In a China Shop, Milton Bradley, 1906	45	55
Bulls and Bears, Parker Brothers, 1936	75	125
Bunny Rabbit Game, Parker Brothers, 1961	20	30
Burke's Law, Transogram, 1964	40	50
By the Numbers, Milton Bradley, 1962	5	15
Calling All Cars, Parker Brothers, 1938	40	50
Call Kelly, Game for Industry, 1966	20	35
Call My Bluff, Milton Bradley, 1965	25	35
Camelot, Parker Brothers, 1950s	25	35
Camp Granada (Alan Sherman's), Milton Bradley, 1965	45	55
Candid Camera, Lowell, 1963	45	55
Caper, Parker Brothers, 1970	30	45
Captain Kangaroo, Milton Bradley, 1956	70	80
Captain Kidd Junior, Parker Brothers, 1926	70	80
Cargo For Victory, All-Fair, 1943	40	50
Carol Burnett's Card Game–Spoof, Milton Bradley, 1964	20	35
Car Travel Game, Milton Bradley, 1958	15	25
Cat and Mouse, Game of, Parker Brothers, 1964	10	20
Cavalcade, Selchow & Righter, 1950s	35	45
Charlie McCarthy Question and Answer Game, Edgar Bergen's, Whitman Publishing Co., 1938	45	55
Children's Hour, Parker Brothers, 1950-60s	25	35
Chiromagica, McLoughlin Brothers, c1870	445	560
Chivalry, George S. Parker & Co., 1888	90	110
Choo Choo Charlie Game, Milton Bradley, 1969	35	45
Chug-A-Lug, Dynamic Games, 1969	5	15
Chuggedy Chug, Milton Bradley, 1955	40	50
Chutzpah, What-Cha-Ma-Call-It, Inc., 1967	45	55
Cities, Alderman-Fairchild, 1932	30	40
Cities, The Game of, Parker Brothers, 1898	35	45
Click, Akro Agates, 1930s	40	50

The Game of Cities.

Defenders of the Flag.

	LOW	HIGH
Clue, "Parker Brothers Detective Game," 1963	5	15
Clue, "The Great Detective Game," Parker Brothers, 1949	35	45
Comical Game of Whip, The, Russell Mfg. Co., 1930-32	15	25
Comical Game: Sir Hinkle Funny-Duster, The, Parker Brothers, 1903	20	30
Conflict, Parker Brothers, 1940	85	95
Construction Game, Wilder Mfg. Co., 1925	80	90
Contack, Parker Brothers, 1939	6	10
Coon Hunt Game, The, Parker Brothers, 1903	370	380
Corn & Beans, E. G. Selchow & Co., 1875	40	50
County Fair, The, Parker Brothers, 1891	45	55
Cribbage Board, Milton Bradley, 1960s	10	15
Crosby Derby, The, H. Fishlove & Co., 1947	100	120
Cuckoo, J. H. Singer, 1891	30	40
Davy Crockett Frontierland Game, Walt Disney's Official, Parker Brothers, 1955	50	60
Defenders of the Flag, Noble and Noble Publishers, Inc., c1922	35	45
Derby Day, Parker Brothers, c1900	30	40
Derby Steeple Chase, The, McLouglin Brothers, 1890	90	100
Dewey's Victory, Parker Brothers, 1900	275	325
Dick Tracy Crime Stopper Game, Ideal, 1963	85	95
Dick Tracy Playing Card Game, Whitman Publishing Co., 1937	40	50
Diner's Club Credit Card Game, The, Ideal, 1961	40	50
Disk, The Madmar Quality Co., c1900	30	40
Diver Dan, Milton Bradley, 1961	40	50
Doc Holliday Wild West Game, Transogram, 1960	40	50
Doctors and the Quack, The, Parker Brothers, 1887	35	45
Dog Race, Toy Creations, 1937	25	35
Dondi Prairie Race, Hasbro, 1960	30	40
Down and Out, Milton Bradley, c1928-30	30	40
Down You Go, Selchow & Righter, 1954	15	25
Dude Ranch Game, Gene Autry's, Built Rite, 1956	45	55
Dunce, Schaper, 1955	15	25
Ed Wynn, The Fire Chief, Selchow & Righter, c1937	20	30
Election '68, Createk, 1967	20	25
Electronic Detective, Ideal, 1979	20	30
Elementaire, Theodore Presser, 1896	15	25
Engineer, Selchow & Righter, 1957	20	25
Errand Boy or Failure and Success, The, McLoughlin Brothers, 1891	375	425

The Errand Boy.

The House That Jack Built.

	LOW	HIGH
Exports and Transportation, Game of, Mills Games Mfg. Co., 1936	10	15
Fairies' Cauldron Tiddledy Winks Game, The, Parker Brothers, c1925	25	35
Fairyland Game, Milton Bradley, c1880s	45	55
Famous Men, Game of, George S. Parker & Co., c1887	15	25
Fan-Tel, O. Schoenhut, Inc., 1937	15	20
Fascination, Remco, 1961	25	35
Fascination, Selchow & Righter, c1890	20	30
Feeley Meeley, Milton Bradley, 1967	10	20
Fish Pond, The Game of, McLoughlin Brothers, 1890	120	130
Flags, Game of, Cincinnati Game Co., 1896	40	50
Flight 'Round the World, A, Spears, 1928	40	50
Flinch, Flinch Card Co., 1913	5	15
Flinch, Parker Brothers, 1951	2	8
Foolish Questions, Wallie Door Co., 1924-26	15	20
Frisko, The Embossing Co., 1937	20	30
Gavitt's Stock Exchange, W. W. Gavitt Printing and Publishing Co., 1903	12	18
George Washington's Dream, Parker Brothers, c1899	15	25
Goat, Game of, Milton Bradley, 1916	10	20
Go Bang, Milton Bradley, c1890s	30	40
Going Hollywood, Hollywood Game Co., 1943	30	40
Gold Hunters, The, Parker Brothers, 1902	185	200
Gusher, Carrom Industries, 1946	70	85
Halma, The Famous Game of, Parker Brothers, 1915	25	35
Hands Up Harry, Transogram, 1964	40	50
Have-U "It?," Selchow & Righter, 1924	20	25
Hendrick Von Loon's Wide World Game, Parker Brothers, 1933	40	50
Hidden Titles, Parker Brothers, c1910s	10	20
History Up to Date, Parker Brothers, c1904	20	25
Home Games, The Martin Co., c1900-05	135	145
House That Jack Built, The, McLoughlin Brothers, c1890	20	30
Hurdle Race, Milton Bradley, 1905	90	110
Intercept, Lakeside, 1978	10	20
Intrigue, Milton Bradley, 1955	30	40
Ivanhoe, George S. Parker & Co., 1890	15	25

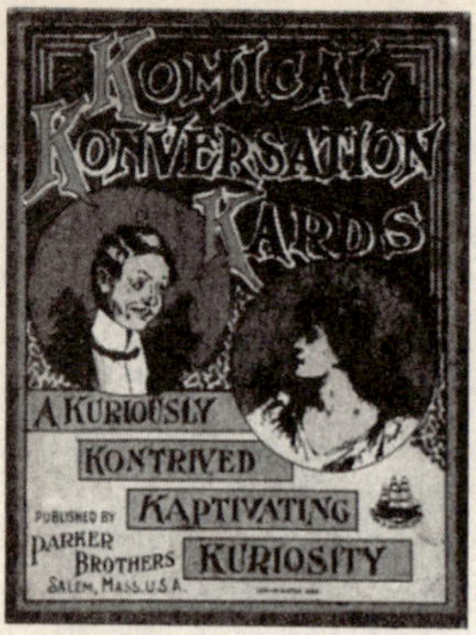

Komical Konversation Kards.

The Little Soldier.

	LOW	HIGH
I've Got A Secret, Lowell, 1956	35	45
Jack Straws, Milton Bradley, c1900	10	20
James Bond 007 Thunderball Game, Milton Bradley, 1965	25	35
J. Fred Muggs 'Round the World Game, Gabriel, 1955	55	65
Jig Chase, Game Makers, 1940s	25	35
Jingo, Cadaco-Ellis, 1941	15	20
Jolly Faces Game, The, Ideal Book Builders, 1912	30	40
Junior Combination Board, Milton Bradley, 1905	45	55
Ka-Bala, Transogram, 1967	70	80
Kate Smith's Own Game America, Toy Creations, 1940s	50	60
Kings, Akro Agates, 1931	30	40
Komical Konversation Kards, Parker Brothers, 1893	20	30
Leaping Lena, Parker Brothers, 1920s	90	100
Let's Drive, Milton Bradley, 1967	10	20
Life, The Game of, Milton Bradley, 1960s	10	15
Literary Salad, Parker Brothers, 1890	15	25
Little Boy Blue, Cadaco-Ellis, 1955	10	20
Little Soldier, The, United Games Co., c1900	45	55
London Game, The, Parker Brothers, 1898	750	825
Magnificent Race, The, Parker Brothers, 1975	10	20
Mandinka, E. S. Lowe, 1978	5	15
Mask, Parker Brothers, 1985	2	8
Mastermind, Invicta, 1972	5	10
Mob Strategy, Hasbro, 1969	10	20
Mother's Helper, Milton Bradley, 1969	15	25
Musingo, Mattel, 1962	15	25
Nations, Game of, Milton Bradley, 1908	15	25
New Frontier, Colorful Products, 1962	25	35
Northwest Passage!, Impact Communications, 1969	20	25
Old Glory, Parker Brothers, 1899	35	45
"Ole" Thousand Faces, Cardboard Products Co., c1925	15	25
Ouija, Parker Brothers, 1970s	5	15
Over the Garden Wall, Milton Bradley, 1937	10	20
Pac-Man Game, Milton Bradley, 1980	10	15

The Professional Game of Base Ball.

Say When!!

	LOW	HIGH
Park and Shop, Milton Bradley, 1950s	35	45
Park and Shop, Milton Bradley, 1960	20	30
Peanuts, Selchow & Righter, 1959	15	25
Petticoat Junction, Standard Toykraft, 1964	40	50
Politics, Game of, Parker Brothers, 1952	20	30
Prince Valiant, Transogram, 1955	30	40
Professional Game of Base Ball, The, Parker Brothers, 1889	75	100
Quiz of the Whiz, The, H. J. Phillips Co., Inc., 1921	15	25
Radio Game, Milton Bradley, c1926	70	80
Raiders of the Lost Ark, Kenner, 1981	15	20
Ranger Commandos, Parker Brothers, 1942	30	40
Rex Morgan, M.D., Ideal, 1972	20	30
Ring My Nose, Milton Bradley, c1926-28	40	50
Road Runner Game, The, Whitman, 1969	20	30
Rose Ball, E. S. Lowe, 1966	10	20
Say When!!, Parker Brothers, 1961	15	25
"Screwball" A Mad Mad Game, Transogram	45	55
Sea Battle, Lido Toy Co., 1940s	20	30
Secrecy, Universal Games, 1965	20	30
Seven-Up Game, Transogram, 1961	10	20
Shindig, Remco, 1965	30	40
Shopping Center Game, Whitman, 1957	15	20
Siege Game, Milton Bradley, 1966	20	30
Silly Sidney, Transogram, 1963	30	40
Sinking of the Titanic, The, Ideal, 1976	25	35
Skirmish, American Heritage, Milton Bradley, 1975	15	25
Skudo, Parker Brothers, 1949	10	20
Sleeping Beauty, Walt Disney Presents, Parker Brothers, 1958	20	30
Smokey Bear Game, Milton Bradley, 1973	25	35
Snake Game, McLoughlin Brothers, c1888	25	35
Sonar Sub Hunt, Mattel, 1961	40	50
Sorry!, "Parker Brothers Slide Pursuit Game," 1958	10	15
Space Pilot, Cadaco-Ellis, 1951	25	35
Special Agent, Parker Brothers, 1966	5	15
Spot, Game of, Milton Bradley, c1925	35	45
Square Mile, Milton Bradley, 1962	20	30
Star Reporter, Parker Brothers, 1950-60	35	45
States, The Game of, Milton Bradley, 1960	10	15

Video Village.

Whirlpool Game.

	LOW	HIGH
Step Lively Shuffleboard, Marx, 1972	10	20
Steve Scott Space Scout, Transogram, 1952	45	55
Superstition, Milton Bradley, 1977	10	20
Sweeps, All-Fair, 1940s	20	30
Thinking Man's Golf, 3M, 1969	15	25
Three Musketeers, Milton Bradley, 1950	35	45
Ticker Tape, Cadaco, 1963	15	25
Toll Gate, A Game of, McLoughlin Brothers, c1890	425	475
Tom Sawyer, The Game of, Milton Bradley, c1937	70	80
Toonin Radio Game, Alderman-Fairchild, c1910s	90	100
Topsy Turvy, The Game of, McLoughlin Brothers, 1899	475	525
Totopoly, Waddington, 1949	25	35
Touring, Wallie Dorr Co., 1926	20	30
Town Hall, Milton Bradley, 1939	15	25
Trade Winds, Parker Brothers, 1960	20	30
Traffic Hazards, Trojan Games, c1930s	40	50
Transatlantic Flight, Game of the, Milton Bradley, c1924	135	145
Trial Lawyer, James N. Vail, 1977	10	15
Turbo, Milton Bradley, 1981	8	12
TV Guide's TV Game, Trivia, Inc., 1984	8	12
Twenty-One, Lowell, 1956	25	35
Twiggy, Milton Bradley, 1967	30	40
Twilight Zone, The, Ideal, 1964	45	55
Tycoon, Wattson Games, 1976	8	12
Uncle Sam's Mail, Game of, McLoughlin Brothers, 1893	175	225
Undercover, Cadaco-Ellis, 1960	20	30
Uranium, Saalfield, 1955	25	35
Vegas, Milton Bradley, 1973	8	12
Video Village, Milton Bradley, 1960	20	30
Wacky Races Game, The, Milton Bradley, 1969	15	25
Waltons Game, The, Milton Bradley, 1974	8	12
W. C. Fields How to Win At Bridge, The Game Keepers, 1972	8	12
Weird-Oh's Game, Ideal, 1963-64	35	45
Wendy the Good Little Witch, Milton Bradley, 1966	40	50
What Shall I Be?, Selchow & Righter, 1966	10	20
When My Ship Comes In, George S. Parker & Co., 1888	20	30
Whirlpool Game, McLoughlin Brothers, 1899	20	30

Hess Trucks

Every year around Thanksgiving Hess gas stations announce the arrival of the latest Hess toy. Since 1964, these vehicles have been sold for a limited time only during the Christmas season. Collectors pay top prices for earlier toys or rare variations. We have listed price ranges for mint in box (MIB) examples. Boxes and packaging materials are crucial in determining value. The MIB prices listed are for items that are practically in the same condition as they were when purchased. Assessing value is tricky because sometimes the same truck is used two different years with only minor changes to the truck but with different boxes. The box therefore becomes the determing factor in dating an item.

On June 1, 1998, Hess issued its first miniature truck (Matchbox scale). This white tanker truck, similar to the 1990 truck, sold for $3.99 at stations. It sold out in one day. The miniature truck was billed as a "promotional offering being test marketed." Chances are that future promotions of miniatures will be offered.

	LOW	HIGH
1964, Model B Mack Tanker Truck, w/ funnel	$2000	$2500
1965, Model B Mack Tanker Truck, w/ funnel	2000	2500
1966, Voyager Tanker Ship, w/ stand	2000	3000
1967, Split Window Tanker Truck, w/ red velvet base box	2400	2800
1968, Split Window Tanker Truck, wo/ red velvet base, Perth Amboy, NJ	650	750
1969, Amerada Hess Split Window Tanker Truck (not issued to the public)	2000	3000
1969, Split Window Tanker Truck, Woodbridge, NJ on box	700	800
1970, Red Pumper Fire Truck	700	800
1971, Red Pumper Fire Truck in Season's Greetings box	2500	3000
1972, Split Window Tanker Truck	300	400
1974, Split Window Tanker Truck	300	400
1975, Box Truck, w/ 3 unlabeled oil drums, 1-pc. cab, made in Hong Kong	300	400
1976, Box Truck, w/ 3 Hess labeled oil drums, 2-pc. cab, made in Hong Kong	300	400
1977, Tanker Truck, w/ large rear label	180	220
1978, Tanker Truck, w/ slightly smaller label than 1977 version	180	220
1980, GMC Training Van	350	450
1982, '33 Chevy, "The First Hess Truck," red switch	80	120
1983, '33 Chevy, "The First Hess Truck," bank	80	120
1984, Hess Tanker Truck Bank, similar to 1977 truck	80	120
1985, '33 Chevy, "The First Hess Truck," bank, reissue of 1983 truck	90	120
1985, Hess Tanker Truck Bank, reissue of 1984 truck	90	120
1986, Red Aerial Ladder Fire Truck	100	150
1987, White Box Truck, w/ 3 labeled oil drums	60	90
1988, Slant Bed Truck, w/ race car	75	95
1989, White Ladder Fire Truck	45	65
1990, White Tanker Truck	40	50
1991, Slant Bed Truck, w/ race car, similar to 1988 truck	30	40
1992, Race Car Hauler, car inside	30	50
1993, Patrol Car, w/ 2 sirens and flashing lights	25	30
1993, Premium Diesel Tanker Truck (not issued to the public)	900	1200
1994, Rescue Truck	20	25
1995, Truck and Helicopter	25	35
1996, Emergency Truck	18	30
1997, Toy Truck and Racers	18	30
1998, Hess Miniature Tanker Truck (for children 4 years and older), 1st mini	30	60
1998, Recreation Van w/ Dune Buggy and Motorcycle	18	35

Hot Wheels

Hot Wheels burst onto the toy scene in 1968 as Mattel's answer to Matchbox Toys. Their popularity soared because the product lived up to its name:

- The design of the axles and wheels produced a smooth fast ride
- They emulated the souped-up drag racing cars popular at the time
- The metallic paint was attractive

The amazing aspect of collecting Hot Wheels is the number of variations possible for what seems to be the same model. Most differences in value are due to the different paint jobs or details such as wheels, applied logos and decoration. Many times a model is introduced in a more desirable paint color. Early vehicles finished in metallic pink seem to command higher prices, as the color was discontinued after a short production run. Conversely, common colors produced in huge quantitites or for several years often deflate the price of a vehicle. The same model (with slight changes such as color) was introduced over the years but age doesn't necessarily constitute value. The year 1973 was disastrous for Mattel. Trying to cut costs, the company removed the button from the package and changed the paint from the metallic Spectra Flame finish to less costly enamels. Sales plummeted. Although terrible for the company, it was a boon for collectors. The 1973 line is more difficult to find than other years, thus prices are consistently higher. Collectors can be fickle; what is thought rare and sought after one year may be displaced by something else the next.

Since the same item can be bought at a variety of locations and because condition and color variations further complicate pricing, we have devised a range system. The low range includes items that are in excellent to mint condition without packaging (MNP). The higher end price reflects the prices of excellent to mint items in excellent to mint boxes (MIP). Therefore prices below are for the best items available; scratched, chipped or altered examples are not included. We have seen poor condition Hot Wheels ranging from $1 to the prices listed below and beyond. In our opinion, bad condition models are worth little unless extremely rare. On the other hand, some special colors (frequently metallic pink) are rare and worth considerably more than the general prices listed here. Because of the many variations, exact identification can be tricky.

For more information see *The Complete and Unauthorized Book of Hot Wheels, 3rd Edition* by Bob Parker (Schiffer, Atglen, PA, 1999) and *Tomart's Price Guide to Hot Wheels, 3rd Edition* by Thomas Strauss (Tomart Publications, Dayton, OH, 1998).

	DATE	NO.	MNP	MIP
'31 Doozie, orange	1977	9649	$15-$25	$20-$30
'56 Hi-Tail Hauler, orange	1977	9647	20-30	20-40
'57 T-Bird, metallic red	1978	2013	15-25	20-30
AMX/2, metallic pink	1971	6460	35-45	60-80
Army Funny Car, white	1978	2023	10-20	15-25
Auburn 852, red	1979	2505	5-8	10-15
Backwoods Bomb, light blue	1975	7670	30-40	60-80
Baja Breaker, green	1978	2022	5-8	10-15
Baja Bruiser, orange	1974	8258	30-40	45-55
Bubble Gunner, light green	1979	2511	5-8	10-15
Buzz Off, blue	1974	6976	35-45	70-90
Bywayman, light blue	1979	2509	5-10	10-15
Captain America, white	1979	2879	5-10	15-25
Captain America Van, white	1979	2851	20-30	30-40
Carabo, light green	1974	7617	30-40	50-60
Carabo, pink	1970	6420	60-70	90-110
Classic Machines, 6-pack	1981	9885	10-20	30-40
Corvette Stingray, red	1976	9241	30-40	55-70

Left: '35 Classic Caddy, #1543, metalflake silver w/ purple plastic fenders, beige plastic interior, 1989, $10-$15.

Right: School Bus, #1795, yellow and black, 1989, $4-$6.

—Photos courtesy Bill Bertoia Auctions.

	DATE	NO.	MNP	MIP
Custom Continental Mark III, red	1969	6266	10-20	30-40
Custom Corvette, metallic gold	1968	6215	30-50	100-200
Custom Fleetside, metallic purple	1968	6213	35-45	100-130
Custom Volkswagen, metallic blue	1968	6220	5-10	20-40
Custom Volkswagen, metallic pink	1968	6220	50-70	75-100
Ferrari 312P, metallic red, white interior	1970	6417	100-150	180-220
Fire Chief Cruiser, red	1970	6469	10-14	18-22
Fire Eater, red	1977	9640	10-15	20-30
Formula 5000, white	1976	9119	10-20	20-30
Formula P.A.C.K., black	1976	9037	15-25	30-40
Fuel Tanker, white enamel	1971	6018	50-70	100-150
Funny Money, gray	1972	6005	50-60	180-220
Funny Money, magenta	1974	7621	30-40	40-60
GMC Motor Home, orange	1977	9645	200-400	500-600
Go Team, 4-pack	1971	6428	200-300	400-500
Grass Hopper, engine on hood, green	1974	7622	35-45	40-50
Gremlin Grinder, green	1975	7652	25-35	40-50
Gun Slinger Jeep, olive	1975	7664	25-35	40-50
Heavy Chevy Silver Special, chrome	1970	6189	40-50	90-110
H.E.L.P. Machines, 6-pack	1976	9031	50-100	150-200
Highway Patrol, white	1978	2019	5-8	10-15
Hood, metallic pink	1971	6175	60-80	60-80
Hot Heap, metallic magenta	1968	6219	10-15	20-40
Indy Eagle, gold chrome	1969	6263	50-70	160-200
Inferno, yellow	1976	9186	20-40	45-50
Jack Rabbit Special, white	1970	6421	10-15	35-45
Jaguar XJS, gray	1978	2012	10-15	20-30
Khaki Kooler, olive	1976	9183	15-25	30-35
Large Charge, orange, purple and white tampo	1975	8272	10-15	15-20
Letter Getter, white	1977	9643	10-15	20-25
Lickety Six, dark blue	1978	2017	10-15	20-25
Light My Firebird, metallic blue	1970	6412	10-15	20-25

	DATE	NO.	MNP	MIP
Light My Firebird, metallic brown	1970	6412	20-25	40-45
Lowdown, light blue	1976	9185	25-35	40-50
Mantis, metallic yellow	1970	6423	10-15	35-45
Maserati Mistral, aqua	1969	6277	35-45	75-90
Maxi Taxi, yellow	1976	9184	25-35	20-40
Mighty Maverick, metallic blue	1970	6417	25-35	50-70
Mighty Maverick, metallic magenta	1970	6417	20-40	50-75
Mod Quad, metallic gold	1970	6456	10-20	25-35
Mongoose II, metallic blue	1971	5954	60-90	200-300
Mongoose and Snake Dragster Pak, 2-pack	1981	5935	200-400	500-600
Mongoose Funny Car, red	1970	6410	50-60	120-160
Motocross, red and black	1975	7668	50-80	150-160
Moving Van, metallic aqua	1970	6455	20-40	50-60
Mustang Stocker, yellow, blue and red tampo	1975	7644	100-200	200-400
Neet Streeter, light blue	1976	9244	15-25	25-35
Nitty Gritty Kitty, metallic green	1970	6405	25-35	40-45
Odd Job, red	1973	6981	75-85	200-250
Odd Rod, plum	1977	9642	100-200	300-400
Packin' Pacer, orange	1978	2015	5-10	15-20
Paddy Wagon, dark blue	1970	6402	9-12	25-35
Paramedic, white	1975	7661	25-35	45-55
Peepin' Bomb, metallic green	1970	6419	10-20	25-35
Poisin Pinto, light green	1976	9240	10-20	30-40
Police Cruiser, white	1973	6963	50-75	250-275
Power Pad, metallic blue	1970	6459	30-40	65-75
Prowler, plum	1973	6965	150-200	300-400
Python, metallic brown	1968	6216	15-25	40-50
Race Bait 308, red	1978	2021	10-20	25-35
Racer Rig, white or red	1971	6194	70-90	250-350
Ramblin' Wrecker, white, blue-tinted windshield	1975	7659	10-25	30-40
Ranger Rig, green	1975	7666	25-35	40-50
Rash I, dark blue, white interior	1974	7616	100-200	300-500
Rear Engine Mongoose, blue	1972	5699	140-180	300-500
Rear Engine Snake, yellow	1972	5856	140-180	300-500
Red Baron, red, black interior	1970	6400	20-30	30-40
Road King Truck, yellow	1974	7615	400-600	700-800
Rock Buster, yellow	1976	9088	10-20	25-30
Rodger Dodger, plum, chrome plastic base	1976	8259	35-45	70-80
Rolls Royce Silver Shadow, green	1969	6276	35-45	40-50
Rolls Royce Silver Shadow, pink	1969	6276	75-100	125-150
Sand Crab, metallic magenta	1970	6403	10-15	25-35
Sand Drifter, green	1975	7651	125-150	250-350
Sand Witch, fluorescent pink	1973	6974	50-80	100-200
Science Fiction, white	1978	2018	5-8	8-10
S'Cool Bus, yellow	1971	6468	100-150	600-700
Second Wind, white	1977	9644	25-35	40-45
Shelby Turbine, blue	1969	6265	10-15	30-35
Show Hoss II, yellow	1977	9646	300-325	350-400
Show Off, red	1973	6982	75-100	200-250
Silhouette, metallic pink	1968	6209	65-75	100-110
Sir Sidney Roadster, yellow, red flame tampo	1974	8261	30-40	50-60

	DATE	NO.	MNP	MIP
Sizzlin' Six Set, 6-pack	1970	6431	75-100	200-250
Snake II, white	1971	5953	50-60	200-250
Snake Funny Car, yellow	1970	6409	50-80	200-250
Snake Rail Dragster, white	1971	5951	70-90	500-600
Special Delivery, blue	1971	6006	40-60	150-200
Spoiler Sport, green	1977	9641	10-20	25-30
Stagefright, brown	1978	2020	8-10	10-15
Steam Roller, white, red and blue tampo	1974	8260	25-35	50-60
Street Eater, yellow	1975	7669	30-50	80-100
Street Machines, 4-pack	1976	9032	75-100	150-200
Street Rodder, black	1976	9242	30-40	45-55
Super Van, black	1975	7649	30-40	40-60
Talking Service Center	1969	5159	40-70	80-120
Team Trailer, white or red	1971	6019	60-80	150-200
Thrill Drivers Torino, white	1977	9793	50-70	75-100
Torero, gold	1969	6260	5-10	25-35
Torero, pink	1969	6260	60-70	80-100
Torino Stocker, red	1975	7647	30-40	40-60
Tough Customer, olive	1975	7655	14-20	40-60
Twin Mill II, orange	1976	8240	18-22	25-30
Vega Bomb, orange	1975	7658	35-45	70-90
Volkswagen Bug, orange, bug on roof	1974	7620	30-40	50-60
Volkswagen Bug, orange w/ stripes	1974	7620	140-180	300-400
What 4, gold	1971	6001	80-100	180-220
Winnipeg, yellow	1974	7618	60-90	95-135
Z Whiz, gray	1977	9639	20-25	30-40

Playset, U.S.A. Builder Set, dock, ferry, tollgate, bridge, classic auto dealer and fast food restaurant, MIB, $20-$30.

Japanese Automotive Tinplate Toys

Two decades before Japan threatened Detroit for the auto market they dominated the post-war tinplate toy industry. Ford, GM and American Motors refined the art of the automobile in the 1950s and Japan replicated their efforts in toys. A score of Japanese toy companies produced these toys. Even four decades later, very little is known about these firms.

Collectors of post-war Japanese automotive toys favor those models in the 10" to 16" category, followed by the 8" category. Many oversized models are less popular because of the amount of shelf space they require. The *créme de la créme* of this area is the 16" 1962 Chrysler Imperial, a car any collector will find space for.

When collecting these vehicles examine them carefully and make sure there are no missing parts, including mirrors and trim. Make sure there is no restoration; battery boxes should be examined closely for corrosion. Never leave a battery in a toy; it can leak and cause damage. The prices below are for mint without box (MNB) and mint in the box (MIB) examples. Rust, scratches and restoration will lower these prices. All dates refer to the year the vehicle most closely resembles; production is usually around the same time. These are toys and not exact replicas, so there are differences between them and their real life counterparts. In the cases where a model looks the same for several years, we used *c.* Abbreviated company names are unidentified firms, as in *UK* (unknown). Regarding power, *BT* stands for battery operated, *BR* for battery operated with remote control, *BL* is battery operated with lights, and *F* is friction powered.

An excellent source of information on this subject is *Collecting the Tin Toy Car 1950–1970* by Dale Kelly (Schiffer, Exton, PA, 1984).

MODEL	YEAR	CO.	SIZE	POWER	MNB	MIB
Airport Limousine, blue	c1960	UK	6"	F	$75-$100	$100-$150
Atom Jet Car	c1950	Y	30"	F	500-1000	1200-1500
BMW 600 Isetta, 4 wheels	c1950	Bandai	9"	F	500-700	600-800
Buick Century	1958	Yonezawa	12"	F	600-1000	1200-1500
Buick Emergency Car	1961	T.N.	14"	F	75-100	100-125
Buick Roadmaster	1955	Yoshiya	11"	F	175-400	500-700
Buick Station Wagon	1954	UK	8"	BT	150-200	300-400
Buick Wildcat	1963	Ichiko	15"	F	400-800	1000-1200
Cadillac	c1960	Bandai	10.5"	BT	50-75	100-200
Cadillac, 4-door	1959	Bandai	11"	F	300-400	500-700
Cadillac, 4-door	1965	Ichiko	22"	F	700-900	1200-1400
Cadillac Convertible	1952	Alps	11.5"	F	1800-2200	2200-2500
Cadillac Convertible	1959	Bandai	12"	F	100-200	250-300
Cadillac Convertible	1960	Bandai	11"	F	400-600	600-800
Cadillac El Dorado	1967	Ichiko	28"	F	400-800	1000-1200
Cadillac Fleetwood	1961	S.S.S.	17.5"	F	300-400	500-700
Champion Racer	c1954	Yonezawa	18"	F	1200-1500	1400-2000
Chevrolet	1960	Marusan	11.5"	F	300-600	700-800
Chevrolet Bel Air	1961	A.T.C.	10"	F	75-100	150-200
Chevrolet Camaro	1967	Taiyo	9.5"	F	20-30	50-75
Chevrolet Camaro Rusher	1971	Taiyo	9.5"	BT	20-30	45-55
Chevrolet Corvair Van, white	1962	K.T.S.	8"	F	100-200	250-400
Chevrolet Corvette	1963	Bandai	8"	F	300-350	400-500
Chevrolet Corvette	1968	Taiyo	9.5"	BT	150-200	250-300
Chevrolet Impala	1963	UK	18"	F	300-400	500-600
Chevrolet Impala Sedan	1961	Bandai	11"	F	200-400	500-600
Chevrolet Pickup Truck	1958	Bandai	8"	F	70-90	100-125
Chevrolet Red Cross Ambulance	1958	Bandai	8"	F	30-50	75-125
Chevrolet Sedan	1954	Linemar	11.25"	F	750-1000	1300-1350
Chevrolet Wagon	c1960	Bandai	7"	F	50-70	75-100

Left: Broadcasting Co. TV Bus, Cragstan, friction, 6.25" l, $99 at auction.

—Photos courtesy Collectors Auction Services.

Right: Bus, I. Y. Metal Toys, friction, 16.5" l, $149 at auction.

MODEL	YEAR	CO.	SIZE	POWER	MNB	MIB
Chrysler	1955	Yonezawa	8"	F	200-300	400-500
Chrysler Imperial	1962	Asahi	16"	F	800-1000	1200-1500
Chrysler New Yorker	1957	Alps	14"	F	800-1000	1200-1500
Citroen DS 19 Convertible	1960	UK	12"	F	600-900	1000-1200
Corvair Bertone	1963	Bandai	12"	BT	150-200	250-300
Corvette, red, white, and blue	c1960	Taiyo	10"	BT	50-75	75-100
Datsun 280Z	1976	Alps	19"	F	300-350	450-550
Datsun Bluebird 1200	c1960	Bandai	8"	F	75-125	150-200
DeSoto	c1930	Masudaya	8"	F	400-800	900-1100
Dodge	1958	Nomura	11"	F	600-800	700-800
Dodge Pickup	1959	UK	18.5"	F	500-800	900-1000
Dodge Yellow Cab	1968	T.N.	12"	F	200-400	500-700
Dream Car Buick Phantom	c1950	Tipp & Co.	12"	F	400-600	800-1000
Edsel Convertible	1958	Haji	10.25"	F	1200-1500	1500-2000
Edsel Wagon	1958	Haji	10.5"	F	300-400	500-700
Ferrari	1958	Bandai	11"	BT	150-300	400-500
Ferrari 250G Convertible	1957	Asahi	9.5"	F	500-600	600-800
Fiat Hardtop Sedan	1955	Nomura	15"	F	200-300	300-500
Fire Engine	c1960	Usagiya	7.5"	F	50-70	75-100
Ford	1957	Ichiko	12"	F	800-1200	1000-1400
Ford Ambulance	1958	UK	8.5"	F	100-150	175-185
Ford Convertible	1955	Bandai	12"	F	500-600	700-800
Ford Convertible	1964	Rico	17"	F	400-600	750-1000
Ford Country Sedan Station Wagon	1961	Bandai	10.5"	F	800-900	900-1200
Ford Fairlane Convertible	1957	Ichiko	10"	F	400-600	900-1200
Ford Falcon	c1960	Bandai	8"	F	30-50	75-100
Ford Flower Delivery Wagon	1955	Bandai	12"	F	1000-1200	1500-2000
Ford Good Humor Ice Cream Truck	1950	K.T.S.	10.75"	F	200-400	500-700
Ford Gyron	c1968	Bandai	10"	BT	400-600	500-700

Right: Sedan, "B," friction, 10" l, $75-$100.

Left: Rolls-Royce Silver Cloud, friction, 11.5" l, $83 at auction. —Photo courtesy Collectors Auction Services.

MODEL	YEAR	CO.	SIZE	POWER	MNB	MIB
Ford Mustang, blue	c1960	Bandai	7"	F	50-70	75-100
Ford Pickup	1955	Bandai	12"	F	250-300	400-500
Ford Station Wagon	1955	Bandai	12"	F	250-300	400-500
Ford Thunderbird	1956	Nomura	11"	BL	600-700	700-800
Ford Thunderbird, cream	c1960	Bandai	8"	BT	75-100	125-145
Ford Torino	1968	S.T.	16"	F	300-500	600-800
Hi-Speed Racer	c1960	UK	12"	BT	50-70	75-100
Hot Rod	c1950	T.N.	10"	BT	75-100	150-185
International Cement Mixer	c1950	S.S.S.	19"	F	600-800	1000-1200
International Grain Hauler	c1950	S.S.S.	23"	F	600-800	900-1000
Jaguar 3.4 Sedan	c1960	Bandai	8"	F	50-100	150-200
Jaguar Coupe	1960s	Bandai	9.5"	F	200-300	350-360
Jaguar XKE	c1960	Bandai	10"	BT	125-200	250-350
Jaguar XKE Convertible	c1960	T.T.	10.5"	F	125-175	200-300
Jeepster Station Wagon	1966	Daiya	10.5"	F	150-250	300-400
Jet Race	c1960	Yonezawa	11.5"	F	500-600	675-775
Land Rover	1960	Bandai	7.5"	F	400-600	600-700
Land Rover 88 Station Wagon	c1960	Bandai	8"	F	50-60	75-100
Lincoln	1964	UK	10.5"	F	200-300	400-500
Lincoln Futura	1956	Alps	11"	BT	600-800	800-1000
Lincoln Hardtop Convertible	1960	Yonezawa	11"	F	150-300	400-600
Lincoln Mark II	1956	Linemar	12"	B	2500-3000	3000-3500
Lincoln Sedan	1955	Yonezawa	12"	F	350-500	600-700
Lotus Elan, red	c1960	Bandai	8.5"	F	50-70	75-100
Lotus Elite	c1958	Bandai	8.5"	B	150-200	200-250
Mercedes Benz	1962	S.S.S.	12"	BT	250-350	400-500
Mercedes Benz 220	c1960	Bandai	10"	F	75-100	125-150
Mercedes Benz 250S	c1960	Daiya	13.5"	F	100-200	250-275
Mercedes Benz Racer	c1950	Linemar	9.5"	F	150-200	250-300
Mercury Cougar	1967	Taiyo	10"	BT	400-600	500-800
Messerschmitt	1957	Bandai	8.5"	F	500-600	700-1000
Mitsubishi Auto Tricycle	c1950	Bandai	11"	F	150-300	400-500
MG, red	c1950	UK	4"	F	50-75	100-150
MG TF	1955	Bandai	8"	F	300-400	400-600
Nash	c1950	M.S.K.	8"	BT	75-100	150-200

Right: Shell Truck, San, friction, 13.5" l, $105 at auction.

Left: Esso Truck, friction. 6.5" l, $39 at auction.

—Photos courtesy Collectors Auction Services.

MODEL	YEAR	CO.	SIZE	POWER	MNB	MIB
Oldsmobile Convertible	1961	Yonezawa	12"	F	125-175	200-300
Oldsmobile Sedan	1958	A.T.C.	12"	F	300-400	500-800
Oldsmobile Toronado	1968	Ichiko	17.5"	F	400-500	600-800
Opel	c1955	Yonezawa	11.5"	BL	500-600	600-700
Packard Convertible	1953	Alps	16"	F	5000-7000	7000-10,000
Packard Sedan	1953	Alps	16"	F	4000-6000	5000-8000
Pan Am Airport Service Car ...	c1960	Kyoei	9.5"	F	25-45	50-75
Patrol Jeep	c1950	T.N.	7.5"	F	25-50	75-100
Plymouth Ambulance	1961	Bandai	12"	F	600-700	700-800
Plymouth Fury	1958	Bandai	8"	F	100-150	175-200
Plymouth Fury Hardtop	1957	Y	1.5"	F	400-600	700-900
Plymouth Sedan	1961	Ichiko	12"	F	250-350	400-500
Plymouth Valiant Sedan	1963	Bandai	8.25"	F	75-85	100-125
Pontiac Firebird	1967	Bandai	10"	F	55-75	100-125
Porsche Rally 911	c1965	Alps	9.5"	BT	300-500	400-600
Porsche Speedster	c1950	Distler	10.5"	BT	300-500	700-900
Rambler Station Wagon	1959	Bandai	11"	—	400-500	500-700
Renault 750	1958	Masudaya	7"	F	400-600	500-700
Rolls Royce	1960	UK	10.5"	F	1000-1200	1200-1500
Rolls Royce Convertible	c1955	Bandai	12"	F	400-600	500-700
Saab 93B	c1960	Bandai	7"	F	75-100	150-200
Speed Racer	c1950	Yonezawa	6"	F	200-400	525-550
Studebaker Avanti	c1960	Bandai	8"	F	175-300	400-500
Stutz Bearcat	c1950	UK	6.5"	F	25-45	50-75
Suburu 360	c1960	Bandai	7"	F	100-125	150-200
Toyopet Crown	c1960	Bandai	9"	F	50-75	100-150
Toyota	c1960	Ichiko	16"	F	200-275	300-325
Toyota 2000 GT	1967	A.T.C.	15"	F	300-350	375-400
U.S. Army Jeep	c1960	Yone	6.25"	F	25-45	50-75
Vespa	c1960	Bandai	9"	F	75-125	150-200
Volkswagen, metallic blue	c1960	Bandai	7"	F	75-100	125-150
Volkswagen Convertible	c1960	Bandai	7.5"	BT	75-100	150-200
Volkswagen Pickup Truck	c1960	Bandai	8"	F	60-75	100-150
Volkswagen Police Car	c1970	S.H.	7"	BT	25-45	50-75
Volkswagen Television Truck ..	c1960	UK	7"	BR	200-350	375-385
Zuendapp Janus	c1950	Bandai	8"	F	150-200	250-350

Lionel Trains

Joshua Lionel Cohen founded America's best-known toy train producer, Lionel, in 1901. In the following descriptions we give the numbers and titles of various locomotives and cars. Descriptions of locomotives contain the wheel configuration, such as 4-4-4 (four forward wheels, four wheels in the middle and four in the back). Locomotive descriptions contain engine type, steam or electric. This describes the style of the locomotive, not the power that runs the toy. Unless otherwise noted, electricity is the power source. Gauge, which refers to track width, for cars and locomotives is listed. Although specific years are not listed, *post-war* and *pre-war* indicate if an item was produced before WWII (pre) or after WWII (post).

The following prices are given in a double range format. The first range is for items in good condition, having scrapes and many scratches and/or some light corrosion. The second range is for items in excellent or like-new condition.

There are many variations of Lionel trains. Color and stylistic differences can dramatically influence prices. The prices below, unless otherwise specified, are for the most common variations. We strongly recommend you consult the large Greenberg Guides for information on variations.

For further information we recommend *Greenberg's Pocket Price Guide to Lionel Trains* edited by Kent J. Johnson (Kalmbach Books, Waukesha, WI, 1998) and *Greenberg's Guide to Trains, 1901–42, Volumes I–IV* and *Greenberg's Guide to Trains, 1945–69, Volumes I–VII* (Kalmbach Books, Waukesha, WI).

Set No. 267W, "Flying Yankee" Streamliner, O gauge, comprising 616W locomotive, two 617 coaches, 618 observation car, and 65 whistle controller, w/ instructions and boxes, $1495 at auction. —Photo courtesy Skinner, Inc., Boston, MA.

NO.		GOOD	EXCELLENT
2	Trolley, 4 wheel, standard gauge, pre-war	$550-$650	$1300-$1550
4	Locomotive 0-4-0, electric, O gauge, pre-war	200-400	500-1000
7	Locomotive 4-4-0, standard gauge, pre-war	1200-1500	1750-3000
8	Locomotive 0-4-0, electric, standard gauge, pre-war	1250-1750	1800-3500
8E	Locomotive 0-4-0, red, standard gauge, pre-war	75-100	140-280
9E	Locomotive 0-4-0, electric, standard gauge, pre-war	250-500	700-1400
10E	Locomotive 0-4-0, electric, standard gauge, pre-war	75-100	140-275
11	Flat, standard gauge, pre-war	25-50	55-110
12	Gondola, standard gauge, pre-war	25-45	50-100
13	Cattle, standard gauge, pre-war	25-70	75-150
18	Pullman, orange, standard gauge, pre-war	250-500	600-1200
19	Combine, standard gauge, pre-war	200-300	400-600
27	Station, standard gauge, pre-war	200-300	400-500
29	Day Coach, maroon, standard gauge, pre-war	100-200	300-600
30	Water Tank, black, post-war	50-75	80-150
33	Locomotive 0-6-0, electric, pre-war	200-300	400-800

Set No. 269E, O gauge, comprising 261E 2-4-2 steam locomotive, 2611 tender, 654 oil tank, 655 box car, 659 dump car, and 657 caboose, w/ instructions and boxes, $978 at auction. —Photo courtesy Skinner, Inc., Boston, MA.

NO.		GOOD	EXCELLENT
35	Lamp Post, post-war	10-15	25-50
42	Locomotive 0-4-4-0, electric, standard gauge, pre-war	400-500	800-1200
48	Whistle Station, litho, O gauge, pre-war	10-20	25-55
50	Locomotive 0-4-0, electric, standard gauge, pre-war	50-75	150-300
53	Locomotive 0-4-0, standard gauge, pre-war	400-500	600-1200
54	Locomotive O-4-4-0, electric, standard gauge, pre-war	800-1000	1250-2500
60	Telegraph Poles, O gauge, pre-war, set of 6	35-50	55-65
62	Semaphore, pre-war	10-15	20-40
79	Flashing Signal, pre-war	50-75	100-120
100	Trolley, standard gauge, pre-war	500-600	1000-2000
104	Tunnel, standard gauge, pre-war	25-50	75-100
111	Trolley, standard gauge, pre-war	600-800	1000-2000
112	Gondola, standard gauge, pre-war	20-35	40-80
116	Ballast, standard gauge, pre-war	50-75	100-180
122	Station, standard gauge, pre-war	50-75	100-125
128	Newsstand, O gauge, post-war	150-200	250-350
132	Station, O gauge, post-war	25-45	50-70
150	Locomotive 0-4-0, electric, O gauge, pre-war	50-75	100-200
153	Locomotive 0-4-0, electric, O gauge, pre-war	50-75	100-200
156	Locomotive 4-4-4, electric, O gauge, pre-war	300-400	450-850
157	Hand Truck, standard gauge, pre-war	10-20	25-50
162	Dump Truck, standard gauge, pre-war	20-40	50-100
164	Lumber Loader, electric, O gauge, post-war	150-250	350-500
190	Observation, standard gauge, pre-war	200-300	400-600
203	Locomotive 0-6-0, steam, O gauge, pre-war	225-325	400-500
204	Locomotive 2-4-2, steam, O gauge, pre-war	25-60	75-150
211	Flat, standard gauge, pre-war	30-50	60-120
216	Hopper, standard gauge, pre-war	75-150	200-300
249E	Locomotive 2-4-2, O gauge, pre-war	75-150	200-300
251E	Locomotive 0-4-0, electric, O gauge, pre-war	50-100	170-340
253	Locomotive 0-4-0, electric, blue, O gauge, pre-war	80-100	150-200
253E	Locomotive 0-4-0, electric, O gauge, pre-war	100-150	200-400
259	Locomotive 2-4-2 and 4-wheel Tender, O gauge, pre-war	55-100	150-250
282	Gantry Crane, O gauge, post-war	160-200	250-300
309	Pullman, standard gauge, pre-war	25-50	75-150
310	Baggage, standard gauge, pre-war	25-50	70-140
322	Observation, standard gauge, pre-war	20-40	50-100

Station No. 124A, w/ 1 interior and 2 exterior lights and 2 arrival signs, $288 at auction. —Photo courtesy Skinner, Inc., Boston, MA.

NO.		GOOD	EXCELLENT
337	Pullman, standard gauge, pre-war	40-60	70-130
341	Observation, standard gauge, pre-war	20-40	50-100
348	Culvert Unloader, manual, O gauge, post-war	25-50	75-150
362	Barrel Loader, O gauge, post-war	15-25	50-75
380	Locomotive 0-4-0, electric, standard gauge, pre-war	200-300	350-650
385E	Locomotive 2-4-2, steam, standard gauge, pre-war	300-400	500-1000
392E	Locomotive 4-4-2, steam, standard gauge, pre-war	400-500	650-1300
420	Pullman, standard gauge, pre-war	250-350	400-800
445	Operating Switch Tower, O gauge, post-war, set of 2	50-100	150-200
455	Oil Derrick and Pumper, O gauge, post-war	150-180	200-250
497	Coaling Station, O gauge, post-war	100-200	275-325
515	Tank, standard gauge, pre-war	50-75	100-180
517	Caboose, standard gauge, pre-war	25-45	50-100
530	Observation, O gauge, pre-war	5-10	15-25
600	Pullman, O gauge, pre-war	75-100	150-200
615	Baggage, O gauge, pre-war	100-125	150-250
624	C&O Switcher, O gauge, post-war	100-150	220-250
628	Tonner Switcher, O gauge, post-war	50-60	75-100
637	Coach, O gauge, pre-war	35-55	60-75
665	Locomotive 4-6-4, steam, O gauge, post-war	55-75	80-100
671	Locomotive 6-8-6, steam, O gauge, post-war	75-100	120-220
700	Locomotive 0-4-0, electric, O gauge, pre-war	200-300	400-800
710	Pullman, O gauge, pre-war	75-100	150-250
753	Streamliner Coach, O gauge, pre-war	50-70	75-140
803	Hopper, O gauge, pre-war	10-20	25-50
806	Cattle, O gauge, pre-war	20-40	50-100
0045	Tank, O gauge, pre-war	10-15	25-50
0017	Caboose NYC, O gauge, pre-war	15-25	30-50
1105	Handcar, Santa, pre-war	400-425	1300-1400
1107	Handcar Donald Duck, pre-war	350-375	1000-1100
1515	Tank, O gauge, pre-war	15-25	30-50
1517	Caboose, pre-war	5-10	15-25
1651E	Locomotive 0-4-0, electric, O gauge, pre-war	70-75	140-150
1666	Locomotive 2-6-2, steam, O gauge, post-war	50-55	125-135
1691	Observation, pre-war	10-15	20-40
1722	Caboose, O gauge, pre-war	15-25	30-60
1866	Baggage, post-war	20-40	50-100
1872	Locomotive 4-4-0, steam, post-war	75-125	150-300
1887	Flat Car, O gauge, post-war	50-75	100-120
1910	Pullman, standard gauge, pre-war	900-1000	2000-2100
1911	Locomotive 0-4-4-0, electric, standard gauge, pre-war	1200-1300	2500-2700

Set, O gauge, comprising 253 engine, two 607 Pullmans, and 608 observation car, w/ 81 controlling rheostat and original box, $825 at auction. —Photo courtesy Collectors Auction Services.

NO.		GOOD	EXCELLENT
1912	Locomotive 0-4-4-0, electric, standard gauge, pre-war	2000-2200	4750-5000
2023	Locomotive Union Pacific AA Diesel, yellow and gray, O gauge, post-war	50-100	150-200
2056	Locomotive 4-6-4, steam, O gauge, post-war	70-75	140-150
2401	Observation, post-war	50-75	100-120
2411	Flat, post-war	25-35	40-80
2412	Illuminated Vista Dome, blue stripe, O gauge, post-war	50-75	100-120
2414	Pullman, post-war	35-50	60-120
2421	Pullman, post-war	25-40	50-100
2452	Gondola Pennsylvania, O gauge, post-war	5-10	15-25
2461	Transformer, O gauge, post-war	50-75	100-120
2521	Observation President McKinley, O gauge, post-war	75-100	130-160
2555	Tank, O gauge, post-war	15-25	30-50
2631	Observation, O gauge, pre-war	25-50	75-100
2810	Derrick, O gauge, pre-war	140-150	375-395
2812	Gondola, O gauge, pre-war	20-30	50-70
2954	Box Car, O gauge, pre-war	150-175	200-300
3366	Box Car Circus, O gauge, post-war	70-100	150-250
3409	Helicopter Car, O gauge, post-war	40-45	110-120
3413	Mercury Capsule Car, O gauge, post-war	60-65	145-155
3472	Automatic Milk Car, O gauge, post-war	25-30	70-80
3510	Satellite Car, O gauge, post-war	40-45	150-160
3512	Fireman and Ladder Car, O gauge, post-war	20-40	70-120
6065	Tank, O gauge, post-war	8-10	15-25
6284	Switcher Burlington SW-1, post-war	50-100	150-200
6361	Timber, O gauge, post-war	10-20	60-80
6465	Tank, O gauge, post-war	5-10	15-25
6822	Searchlight Car, O gauge, post-war	15-25	35-45
6824	Caboose First Aid, O gauge, post-war	60-75	100-200
6830	Submarine Car, O gauge, post-war	30-60	75-125
8369	Locomotive Erie Lackawanna GP-20, diesel, post-war	60-90	100-140
8676	Locomotive J. C. Fairbanks Morris, diesel, post-war	50-75	100-200
9672	Box Car, Mickey Mouse 50th Anniversary Hi-Cube, post-war	100-200	250-350

Lunch Boxes

Steel lunch boxes produced from the 1950s to the 1980s were one of the last holdouts of the lithographed metal process once prevalent in the production of toys. In order to deter sandlot warriors from injuring each other, steel boxes were discontinued in the 1980s. Soon after, they burst onto the collecting scene. Buying back a box from their youth, collectors relived grade school memories and the late summer ritual of shopping for school supplies. Collectors also love the diversity of topics represented. Many of the boxes are based on classic TV shows, and they frame their topics like small screens. Steel boxes are not the only ones sought by collectors; some of the vinyl examples are among the costliest. After a meteoric rise, the market cooled in the early '90s. However, today's growing interest in TV memorabilia is bringing in a new group of collectors.

We devised a range system for pricing. Since bottles often become separated from the box, we have given estimates for boxes and bottles separately. The prices below reflect items that are in excellent to mint condition. Rust and dents decrease the value of boxes and bottles.

For more information consult *The Illustrated Encyclopedia of Metal Lunch Boxes, 2nd Edition* by Allen Woodall and Sean Brickell (Schiffer, Atglen, PA, 1999), and Larry Aidins' *Pictorial Price Guide to Metal Lunch Boxes & Thermoses* (1992, 1999 value update) and *Pictorial Price Guide to Vinyl & Plastic Lunch Boxes & Thermoses* (1992, 1995 value update), both published by L-W Book Sales, Gas City, IN.

We used several abbreviations in this listing. "The" was removed from titles such as "The Munsters." We have listed distinguishing features such as embossed and domed lid. All boxes are steel, unless "vinyl" appears in the description. Dates reflect our best approximation.

	BOX	BOTTLE
Addams Family, King Seeley Thermos, 1974	$75-$100	$25-$50
All American, Universal, Landers, Frary & Clark, 1954	200-400	100-200
Alvin and The Chipmunks, vinyl, King Seeley Thermos, 1963	200-400	100-200
Americana, Thermos, 1958	200-400	100-200
Annie, embossed, Aladdin, 1981	50-75	25-50
Archies, embossed, Aladdin, 1969	50-75	25-50
Astronauts, Aladdin, 1969	25-50	15-25
Astronaut Space, dome, Thermos, 1960	100-200	50-75
Batman and Robin, embossed, Aladdin, 1966	100-200	50-100
Beany and Cecil, vinyl, King Seeley Thermos, 1960s	100-200	50-100
Beatles, embossed, Aladdin, 1966	300-350	90-110
Beverly Hillbillies, embossed, Aladdin, 1963	100-200	75-100
Black Hole, embossed, Aladdin, 1980	35-45	8-12
Boating, Thermos, 1959	200-400	100-200
Bonanza, embossed, Aladdin, 1963	100-200	75-100
Bond XX, Ohio Art, 1967	100-200	75-100
Bozo, dome, Aladdin, 1963	200-400	100-200
Bread Box, Aladdin, 1968	100-200	75-100
Bullwinkle, vinyl, Thermos, 1962	300-600	200-400
Campbell Kids, Ohio Art, 1975	200-400	100-200
Can of Flowers, vinyl, Aladdin, 1968	25-50	25-50
Captain Kangaroo, vinyl, King Seeley Thermos, 1964	75-100	50-75
Casper the Friendly Ghost, vinyl, King Seeley Thermos, 1960s	200-400	100-200
Chan Clan, Thermos, 1973	20-50	10-20
Charlie's Angels, embossed, Aladdin, 1978	50-75	25-50
Chuck Wagon, dome, Aladdin, 1958	120-180	60-80
Circus Wagon, dome, Thermos, 1958	200-400	100-200
Close Encounters, King Seeley Thermos, 1978	60-80	10-12
Cyclist Dirt Bike, Aladdin, 1979	20-50	10-20
Daniel Boone, Aladdin, 1955	100-200	75-100

Roy Rogers and Dale Evans Double R Bar Ranch, $72 at auction. —Photo courtesy Collectors Auction Services.

	BOX	BOTTLE
Dark Crystal, King Seeley Thermos, 1982	25-50	10-20
Davy Crockett, Adco Liberty Corp., 1955	200-400	100-200
Davy Crockett, Thermos, 1955	100-200	75-100
Deputy Dawg, vinyl, Thermos, 1961	200-400	100-200
Dick Tracy, embossed, Aladdin, 1967	100-200	75-100
Disneyland, Aladdin, c1960	100-200	75-100
Doctor Dolittle, embossed, Aladdin, 1968	75-95	30-40
Dog and Flowers, dome, Aladdin, 1975	50-75	25-50
Double Deckers, Aladdin, 1975	50-75	25-50
Drag Strip, Aladdin, 1975	25-50	15-25
El Chapulin Colorado, Aladdin, 1979	50-75	25-50
E. T., embossed, Aladdin, 1982	25-50	15-25
Fess Parker/Daniel Boone TV Show, King Seeley Thermos, 1965	100-200	75-100
Flintstones, Aladdin, 1971	100-200	75-100
Flying Nun, vinyl, Aladdin, 1968	200-400	100-200
Fraggle Rock, King Seeley Thermos, 1966	10-15	5-8
Gene Autry, Universal, Landers, Frary & Clark, 1954	250-300	90-110
Get Smart, King Seeley Thermos, 1966	75-100	50-75
Globe-Trotter, dome, Aladdin, 1959	150-250	75-100
Grizzly Adams, dome, Aladdin, 1977	50-75	25-50
Guns of Will Sonnett, King Seeley Thermos, 1968	100-200	75-100
Hair Bear Bunch, King Seeley Thermos, 1972	30-40	15-20
Happy Pow Wow, vinyl, Bayville, c1970	100-200	75-100
Have Lunch With Snoopy, dome, Thermos, 1968	25-50	15-25
Hector Heathcote, Aladdin, 1964	100-200	75-100
Howdy Doody, Adco Liberty, c1954-55	75-100	50-75
How the West Was Won, King Seeley Thermos, 1978	50-75	25-50
Huckleberry Hound and Friends, Aladdin, 1961	40-60	25-35
I Love a Parade, vinyl, Bayville, c1970	100-200	75-100
Jim Henson's Muppet Movie, King Seeley Thermos, 1979	25-50	15-25
Julia, King Seeley Thermos, 1969	50-75	25-50
Knight Rider, King Seeley Thermos, 1983	25-50	15-25
Kroft Supershow, Aladdin, 1971	40-60	25-35
Land of the Giants, embossed, Aladdin, 1968	100-200	75-100
La Petite Cafe De Paris, vinyl, dome, Universal, Landers, Frary & Clark, 1960s	200-400	100-200
Lawman, Thermos, 1961	100-200	75-100
Little Red Riding Hood, Ohio Art, 1982	50-75	25-50
Magic of Lassie, Thermos, 1978	25-50	15-25
Man From U.N.C.L.E., Thermos, 1966	80-120	50-75

	BOX	BOTTLE
Masters of the Universe, embossed, Aladdin, 1983	10-15	2-5
Mickey Mouse Club, embossed, Aladdin, 1963	25-50	25-50
Model Rockets, vinyl, Ardee, 1960s	200-400	100-200
Moon Landing, vinyl, Ardee, c1970	100-200	75-100
Mork and Mindy, Thermos, 1980	15-20	10-15
Munsters, King Seeley Thermos, 1971	150-200	50-80
Nancy Drew Mysteries, King Seeley Thermos, 1977	50-75	25-50
Partridge Family, King Seeley Thermos, 1971	50-75	25-50
Peanuts, King-Seeley Thermos, 1980	50-75	25-50
Pebbles and Bamm Bamm, Aladdin, 1971	50-100	25-50
Peter Pan, vinyl, Aladdin, 1969	100-200	75-100
Planet of the Apes, embossed, Aladdin, 1975	80-100	20-30
Police Patrol, Aladdin, 1978	100-200	75-100
Popeye, embossed, Aladdin, 1980	25-50	15-25
Porky's Lunch Wagon, dome, King Seeley Thermos, 1959	300-350	50-80
Punky Brewster, plastic, Deka, 1984	15-25	10-15
Racing Wheels, King Seeley Thermos, 1977	50-75	15-25
Rat Patrol, Aladdin, 1967	75-100	50-75
Rifleman, Aladdin, 1960	200-400	100-200
Rough Rider, Aladdin, 1972	25-50	15-25
Roy Rogers Chow Wagon, dome, Thermos, 1958	75-100	50-75
Scooby Doo, Thermos, 1973	15-25	10-15
Sesame Street, embossed, Thermos, 1979	25-50	15-25
Shari Lewis and Her Friends, Aladdin, 1963	100-200	75-100
Skateboarder, embossed, Aladdin, 1977	50-75	25-50
Sleeping Beauty, vinyl, Aladdin, 1970	100-200	75-100
Space: 1999, King Seeley Thermos, 1975	50-75	25-50
Space Explorer, Aladdin, 1960	300-350	60-80
Sport Goofy, embossed, Aladdin, 1983	25-50	15-25
Star Trek The Motion Picture, King Seeley Thermos, 1979	75-100	50-75
Star Wars, Thermos, 1977	50-75	25-50
Stewardess, vinyl, Aladdin, 1962	300-500	40-60
Superman, Universal, 1954	200-400	100-200
Tom Corbett Space Cadet, Aladdin, 1954	200-400	100-200
Transformers, Aladdin, 1986	25-50	15-25
Twiggy, vinyl, Aladdin, 1967	150-250	100-125
Underdog, Ohio Art, 1974	75-100	100-150
Universal's Movie Monsters, embossed, Aladdin, 1979	100-200	75-100
U.S. Mail, dome, Aladdin, 1969	75-100	50-75
Voyage to the Bottom of the Sea., Aladdin, 1967	75-100	50-75
Walt Disney School Bus, dome, Aladdin, 1960s	75-100	50-75
Welcome Back Kotter, embossed, Aladdin, 1977	50-75	25-50
Wild Bill Hickok & Mingles, Aladdin, 1956	75-100	100-200
Wild Wild West, embossed, Aladdin, 1969	100-200	75-100
Winnie the Pooh, vinyl, Aladdin, 1964	200-400	100-200
Wonder Woman, vinyl, Aladdin, 1977	75-100	50-75
World of Dr. Seuss, vinyl, Aladdin, 1970	50-75	25-50
Wrangler, vinyl, Aladdin, c1962	200-400	100-200
Yankee Doodles, Thermos, 1975	25-50	15-25
Yogi Bear, vinyl, Aladdin, 1960s	350-650	250-350
Zorro, embossed, Aladdin, 1966	100-200	75-100

Matchbox Toys

Leslie Smith and Rodney Smith (no relation) started Lesney Toys in England in 1947. They produced their first toys in 1948 and had a huge success with a coach produced in 1952 for the Queen's coronation in 1953. In 1953 they started producing small diecast vehicles packed in what appeared to be matchboxes. These toys are known as the 1-75 Series. They range from approximately 1.5" to 3". Lesney has produced other series over the years but the list below refers mainly to the 1-75 Series. Exceptions are the early toys which have no product number, and the Yesteryear Series, denoted by Y as the first letter in the product code. Cars in both these series are larger than those in the 1-75 series. Matchbox toys are still produced, but the Lesney name was removed in 1982.

Since the same item can be bought at a variety of locations at different prices, we devised a range system. The low range *(MNB)* covers complete, near mint to mint items without the original package. The higher range *(MIB)* reflects the prices of complete, near mint to mint items in the original near mint to mint boxes. Prices below are for complete like-new examples. Prices of scratched, chipped or altered examples are not included. Beware of high prices for poor quality. We have seen many poor condition Matchbox vehicles ranging in price from $1 to the prices listed below. In our opinion these poor condition models are worth very little unless they are extremely rare.

To battle Hot Wheels Lesney developed super fast wheels and axles. For the most part, collectors prefer the regular wheels. The numbering system is not foolproof; sometimes a model produced for this country has a different number than the same vehicle originally sold exclusively in England. The letters that precede a number refer to a system designed by collectors to distinguish different models with the same number; the earlier the letter, the earlier the model. Because there are so many variations, exact identification can be tricky. For more information we suggest *The Encyclopedia of Matchbox Toys: 1947-Present, 2nd Edition* by Charlie Mack (Schiffer, Atglen, PA, 1997) and *Matchbox Toys: 1947-1998, Third Edition* by Dana Johnson (Collector Books, Paducah, KY, 1999).

	YEAR	NO.	MNB	MIB
1908 Grand Prix Mercedes, cream	1958	Y-10-A	$45-$55	$65-$80
1909 Opel Coupe	1967	Y-4-B	15-20	25-30
1910 Benz Limousine, cream	1966	Y-3-B	20-30	40-50
1913 Mercer Raceabout, yellow	1961	Y-7-B	10-15	20-35
Allis-Chalmers Earth Scraper	1961	K-6-A	10-20	25-40
Aston Martin, blue	1958	52-B	15-20	25-40
Atlantic Trailer, tan	1957	16-B	20-30	35-50
Austin A-55 Cambridge Sedan, black plastic wheels	1961	29-B	10-15	20-25
Austin Taxi Cab, gray plastic wheels	1960	17-C	20-30	35-50
Bedford Evening News Van	1957	42-A	20-30	35-50
Bedford Lowloader, dark green cab	1956	27-A	10-20	25-40
Bedford Wreck Truck	1955	13-A	20-30	35-50
Boat and Trailer	1966	9-D	5-10	12-15
Cadillac Sixty Special, green	1960	27-C	100-200	250-350
Case Bulldozer	1969	16-D	2-5	8-12
Caterpillar Bulldozer, black plastic rollers	1964	18-D	25-50	75-110
Caterpillar DW20 Earth Scraper	1957	M-1-A	25-50	75-110
Caterpillar Tractor	1964	8-D	5-10	15-18
Cement Mixer, blue	1953	3-A	10-20	25-35
Claas Combine Harvester	1967	K-9-B	5-15	18-25
Concrete Truck, silver grille	1956	26-A	10-20	25-40
Curtis Wright Rear Dumper	1961	K-7-A	10-20	25-40
Daimler Ambulance, cream, metal wheels	1956	14-A	10-20	25-40
Dodge Cattle Truck	1966	37-C	4-6	8-12

Left: Caterpillar DW20 Earth Scraper M-1-A.

Right: Ford Mustang Fastback #8-E.

Left: Ford Thunderbird #75-A.

Right: Massey Harris Tractor #4-A.

Left: Ford Escort XR31 Cabriolet #17-1.

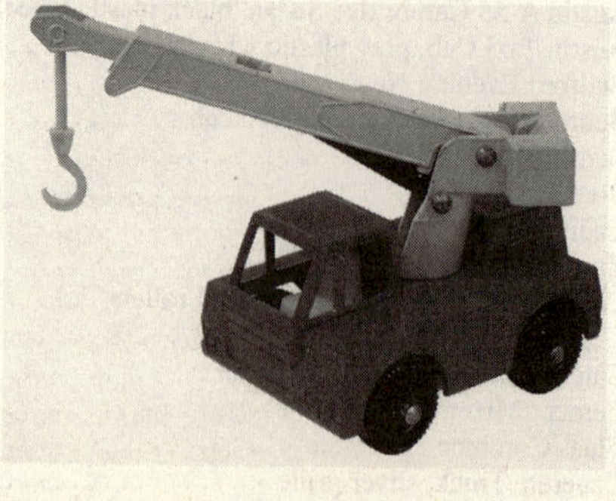

Right: Iron Fairy Crane #42-C.

Left: Road Tanker #11-A.

	YEAR	NO.	MNB	MIB
Dodge Stake Truck	1967	4-D	20-45	50-75
Dumper	1957	2-B	20-30	35-40
Dunlop Van	1956	25-A	10-20	25-40
Ferrari Berlinetta, light green	1965	75-B	5-8	10-15
Ferret Scout Car	1959	61-A	5-10	12-18
Fiat 1500, turquoise	1965	56-B	3-5	8-12
Ford Anglia, light blue, gray plastic wheels	1961	7-B	5-10	15-20
Ford Escort XR31 Cabriolet	1985	17-1	4-6	8-12
Ford Kennel Truck	1969	50-C	3-4	5-8
Ford Mustang Fastback	1966	8-E	5-10	12-15
Ford Station Wagon, metal wheels	1957	31-A	10-20	30-40
Ford Thunderbird, silver plastic wheels	1960	75-A	20-40	45-60
General Service Lorry	1959	62-A	20-40	35-50
Greyhound Bus, clear windows	1967	66-C	20-45	50-75
Hatra Tractor Shovel	1965	K-3-B	8-15	20-30
Honda Motorcycle & Trailer	1967	38-C	10-20	25-40
Horse Box	1969	17-E	2-4	5-8
Horse Drawn Milk Float	1954	7-A	20-40	50-75
Iron Fairy Crane	1969	42-C	2-4	5-8
Jaguar 3.4 Litre Saloon, gray plastic wheels	1962	65-B	10-20	25-40
John Deere Trailer, black plastic tires	1964	51-B	10-15	20-30
Lamborghini Muira, yellow, red interior	1969	33-C	2-4	5-8
Land Rover, olive green	1959	12-B	55-65	75-90
London Bus	1954	5-A	40-50	50-65
London Bus, metal wheels	1954	5-B	30-40	45-60
Long Distance Coach, metal wheels	1958	21-B	20-30	35-50
Lotus Racing Car, green	1966	19-D	5-10	15-20
Mack Dump Truck	1968	28-D	3-5	8-12
Massey Harris Tractor	1954	4-A	20-30	35-50
Massey Harris Tractor, metal wheels	1957	4-B	20-30	35-50
Mercedes Benz Lorry	1968	1-E	3-5	8-12
Mercedes Coach, turquoise	1965	68-B	20-40	50-75
Mercedes Trailer	1968	2-D	3-6	8-12
Mercury Cougar, metallic lime green	1968	62-C	2-4	5-8
Mercury Police Commuter	1969	K-23-A	5-10	12-18
Merryweather Fire Engine	1964	K-15-A	8-15	18-25
MG Sports Car, white	1956	19-A	35-50	55-75
Muir Hill Dumper	1960	K-2-A	10-20	25-40
Pipe Truck	1967	K-10-B	10-15	18-25
Pontiac Gran Prix Sports Coupe	1964	22-C	5-10	12-15
Pony Trailer	1968	43-C	2-4	5-8
Quarry Truck	1957	6-B	10-15	20-30
Readymix Concrete Truck	1963	K-13-A	10-20	25-40
Road Roller	1955	1-B	25-35	40-60
Road Tanker	1955	11-A	30-40	45-60
Safari Land Rover, blue	1965	12-C	3-5	8-12
Scaffold Truck	1969	11-D	2-4	5-8
Scammell Crane Truck	1969	K-12-B	5-10	15-20
Sentinel Steam Wagon, black plastic wheels	1956	Y-4-A	125-150	175-225
Triumph Motorcycle & Sidecar	1960	4-C	20-30	35-50
Vauxhall Cresta	1956	22-A	10-20	25-40
Volkswagen 1600TL, red	1967	67-B	5-8	10-15
Volkswagen Camper	1968	34-D	3-5	7-10
Weatherhill Hydraulic Shovel	1960	K-1-A	20-40	50-75

Pez Dispensers

Pez is so American, a part of growing up from the 1950s to present day. Like most of us, Pez has its roots in a different country. Eduard Haas introduced it in 1927 in Austria. It takes its name from the German word for peppermint, *pfefferminz.* Originally sold as a breath mint/candy, it came with a handy dispenser with grip (called regulars). Pez redesigned its product for the American market in 1952. They added character heads and introduced fruit flavors. Pez became a kids' candy.

In recent years, Pez collecting has been very active. Christie's auction house even included a section of Pez in one of its sales. Collectors tend to concentrate on the head of a Pez dispenser; most do not collect based on stem or container differences. That is because heads can be switched from stem to stem. There is a feet versus no-feet controversy. Most containers have a rounded base. Some people call them shoes but they are more often referred to as no feet. Feet are the bases that appeared on figures beginning around 1987. They are thin, flat, and have a stylized "V" indentation. Many collectors prescribe to the "only the head matters" theory, while others place a higher value on no-feet examples. Collectors contend that packaging for the most part does not matter since early Pez containers came in unattractive bags or boxes. The matter is harder to determine when evaluating Pez sold on blisterpacks or blistercards. We feel that original packaging will increase the value of an item, especially the more elaborate and interesting packaging. Most notable is the Stand-By-Me Pez, which must have the original packaging, including the movie poster, or it is just a Pez Pal Boy.

The prices below are for mint nonpackaged examples except where noted differently. Pez dispensers are hard to date, so the decades we suggest are only our best guess. For further reading we recommend *PEZ Collectibles, 3rd Edition* by Richard Geary (Schiffer, Atglen, PA, 1999) and *Collecting PEZ* by David Welch (Bubba Scrubba Publications, Murphyboro, IL, 1994).

	LOW	HIGH
Air Spirit, soft head	$150	$265
Angel, no feet	50	90
Arlene, feet, 1980s	3	5
Astronaut, aqua	150	200
Bambi, feet, 1980s	6	12
Barney Bear, feet	30	40
Baseball Glove	200	300
Batgirl, soft head, no feet	125	170
Batman, w/ cape, no feet	100	125
Big Top Elephant, flat hat, no feet, 1960s	50	60
Blonde Stewardess, "Coffee, Tea or ...Me?!"	175	235
Bouncer Beagle	3	6
Brutus, no feet, 1950s	90	150
Bullwinkle, brown stem	450	535
Candy Shooter Gun, black	100	125
Captain America, blue mask	75	100
Casper, no feet, 1960s	60	80
Clown w/ Chin, no feet	50	75
Cockatoo, green or blue	50	75
Cool Cat, feet	50	75
Cow, blue face/horns	75	95
Cow, orange	75	120
Cowboy, no feet, 1960s	220	350
Creature from the Black Lagoon	375	425
Daffy, plastic eyes, feet	10	20
Dalmatian, feet	35	55
Daniel Boone	250	275

	LOW	HIGH
Dog Whistle, feet	15	25
Dog Whistle, no feet	20	40
Donald Duck, diecut face, no feet, 1960s	90	120
Droopy Dog, feet	15	25
Dumbo, blue, feet	25	35
Eerie Spectres Diabolic, no feet, 1980s	35	50
Elephant, gray, red hair	155	255
Elephant, pink, black trunk	15	25
Engineer	175	235
Fireman Pez Pal, no feet	50	75
Foghorn Leghorn, feet	65	95
Frog Whistle, feet	25	45
Gorilla, brown face	85	115
Green Hornet, no feet, 1960s	200	300
Henry Hawk, feet	50	85
Icee Bear, feet	3	6
Incredible Hulk, no feet	25	50
Indian Chief, blue headdress	150	225
Indian Maiden, no feet, 1970s	50	80
Joker, soft head, no feet	75	150
King Louie, feet	15	25
King Louie, no feet	20	40
Koala Whistle, feet	20	40
Lamb Whistle, no feet	8	15
Li'l Bad Wolf, feet	8	15
Mary Poppins, no feet, 1960s	325	525
Merlin Mouse, feet	10	20
Mickey, no feet	6	12
Mowgli, feet	15	25
Mowgli, no feet	20	40
Mr. Ugly, green, feet	35	65
Octopus, orange, no feet	45	95
Olympic Snowman	350	625
Orange, no feet, 1970s	60	90
Papa Smurf, feet	2	5
Peter Pan	125	235
Petunia Pig, feet	15	35
Petunia Pig, no feet	29	40
Pig Whistle, feet	25	55
Pineapple, no feet, 1970s	700	1100
Pink Panther, feet, MOC	2	4
Pirate, no feet	30	60
Pony, orange head, no feet	50	100
Practical Pig, feet	25	45
Rabbit, feet	10	15
Rabbit, no feet	15	25
Raven, no feet	25	55
Road Runner, feet, MOC	15	25
Rooster, white, feet	20	35
Rooster, yellow, no feet	20	40
Rooster Whistle, feet	25	45
Rudolph the Red-Nosed Reindeer, no feet	50	75
Sailor Pez Pal, floppy head, no feet	70	140
Santa, full body, 1950s	150	200

	LOW	HIGH
Scrooge, feet	15	25
Sheik, red	25	55
Smurfette, blue, yellow stem	4	7
Snowman, orange face, feet, MOC	15	25
Space Trooper, full body, 1950s	300	400
Speedy Gonzalez, feet	8	15
Snow White, dark turquoise collar/bow	300	450
Snow White, white collar/bow	175	300
Snow White, yellow collar/bow	175	300
Space Gun, orange, 1980s	70	120
Space Gun, red	50	90
Spook, soft head	175	265
Sylvester, no feet, 1980s	2	4
Thumper, feet	25	45
Tinkerbell, feet	200	300
Uncle Sam	175	275
Vamp, soft head	200	300
Wile E. Coyote, no feet	30	50
Winnie the Pooh, feet	45	85
Witch, no feet	150	175
Wolfman, no feet, 1960s	200	300
Wonderwoman, soft head, no feet	70	130
Yappy Dog, feet	50	75
Yappy Dog, no feet	45	85

Pez Dispensers.

Playing Cards

Over the past fifteen years, interest in collecting playing card decks has grown considerably.

Since their introduction in Europe some six centuries ago, many thousands of different designs have adorned playing cards. But because most decks of cards get used and tossed away, complete packs of some issues are exceedingly rare.

The 52-card pack of spades, hearts, diamonds and clubs, introduced by French printers, has become the international standard. Other deck arrangements, still being published today, are the Italian and Spanish traditional suits (swords, batons, cups and coins), and the German-suited packs (leaves, hearts, acorns and bells). Rare and desirable packs of all traditions command quite high prices.

Earliest packs were cut with square corners, and usually lacked any design on their cardbacks. After 1875, cards with rounded corners became the norm, as back designs became elaborate. Corner symbols, known as indexes (or indices), became standard about 110 years ago. Even today, packs are usually undated. However, the spade ace and joker cards may yield useful information.

Besides innovative design variants, card decks have cultural relevancy: Advertising, souvenir, entertainment, commemorative, political and transportation-related packs are a few examples.

Maximum value goes to packs that are complete, including Joker (first introduced about 125 years ago) and still with original box or wrapper. Except for the rarest of packs, value seriously declines when cards are damaged, soiled or missing. Among older packs, "wide" (2.5" x 3.5") is valued over "narrow" or "bridge" size (2.25" x 3.5").

In purchasing playing cards, you'll find prices fluctuate greatly. For the lucky and knowledgeable buyer, valuable decks can still be found at small cost. Reproductions of interesting old packs will have a bit of value, but don't mistake them for the real thing.

	LOW	AVG.	HIGH
52 Selected Views of Ireland, Irish Tourist Assoc., C. T. Co. Ltd., 1930s	$15	$25	$50
101 Pipers Scotch By Seargram, black and gold bagpipers on red ground, gold edges	10	15	20
1893 Columbian Exposition, World's Fair souvenir	150	225	300
1901 Pan Am Exposition, wide size, 52 photos	50	75	100
1933/34 Century of Progress, Chicago World's Fair	20	60	100
Antique Liqueur, Scotland, green advertising back, c1932	50	100	150
Army & Navy 303, U.S. Playing Card Co., blue angel back, fortune telling writing on each card, c1885	20	60	100
Art for the Earth, tropical rainforest	20	60	100
Baraja Taurina, Casero, 52 portraits of bullfighters, 1965	15	20	30
Bezique, Samuel Hart, 32 cards, square corners, 1865	100	200	300
Bicycle 808, U.S. Playing Card Co., cupid, red back, c1910	25	35	50
Bicycle 808, U.S. Playing Card Co., emblem, c1895	20	30	40
Boca Raton Club, double deck, Brown & Bigelow, 1947	25	35	50
Boron Motor Oil, can shaped	5	10	15
Bowl Up, Creative Sales Co., St. Louis, 1954	15	25	30
Brown Derby–City of Hope, caricatures on 44 cards, Brown Derby photos on Aces, Hollywood entertainers	20	35	50
Buffalo & Niagara, red riverbank back, sepia toned photos, c1905	135	150	175
C&O Railroad, wide size, oval souvenir photos on each card (several versions), 1900	50	100	150
California, Bullock's Orange Grove back, 1927	50	100	150
Canada, 53 views Montreal and Quebec	10	20	30
Canary Islands, Fournier, Spain, souvenir photos on each card, 1959	20	30	40
Capital Airlines Viscount, inscription "Powered By Rolls-Royce," 1950-60s	15	25	50

Hard-A-Port Tobacco, 52 cards, c1890s, $523 at auction. —Photo courtesy Wm. Morford.

	LOW	AVG.	HIGH
Capitol 188, U.S. Playing Card Co., four leaf clover back, c1886	70	95	120
Chessie & Peake, double deck, 1950s	35	50	75
Cir-Q-Lar, Waddington's, London, round cards, 1930	10	15	25
Cleveland Car Specialty, advertising back, 1907	95	125	150
Coca-Cola, girl in water holding Coke, 1950s	50	75	100
Concordia Line, dark blue and black and white design centered by symbol "H" flag above sponsor title, inscription "Christian Haaland/Haugesnund, Norway," 1930s	25	35	50
Congress 606, U.S. Playing Card Co., Berenice, nude woman and lion back	20	30	40
Congress 606, U.S. Playing Card Co., Laughing Water, c1919	35	50	65
Congress 606, U.S. Playing Card Co., The Silvery Moon, 1919	35	50	65
Cornell University, double deck, 1935	20	30	40
Cuba, 53 views of Cuba, black and yellow photo back, 1915	50	75	100
Culbertson's Own, Russell, NY, bridge tips in card margins, 1932	15	25	30
Dallas Cowboys Cheerleaders, 1982	5	10	15
Dante & Beatrice, Italy, historical aces, Renaissance figures, gold edges, c1924	120	150	175
Edison Mazda Lamp, blue and gold back, "His Only Rival," c1912	80	100	125
Esquire, double deck, canasta	20	30	40
Fauntleroy, U.S. Playing Card Co., miniature cards, 1910-30	10	25	35
Fitzgeralds Casino, Reno, NV, c1979	5	10	15
Flying "A" Service, black and white basset hound next to logo, 1950s	15	25	50
Gaiety 54 Models, made in Hong Kong, 1960s	15	25	50
GM Electro-Motive, double deck, diesel back	30	45	60
Gold Medal Flour, medallion back, 1913	40	50	60
Green Spade Tarot, August Petryl, 78 cards, Native American theme, 1922	250	775	1200
Hyatt Roller Bearing, painting of old car back, c1917	80	100	125
John F. Kennedy/Air Force One, double deck, presidential seal and plane	200	400	700
Johnnie Walker Black Label Scotch, "12 Years Old," gold and black	5	10	15
Johnson's Gulf Service, nude w/ hatbox, early 1950s	10	15	20
Kelly Springfield Tires, "Lotta Miles" back, 1916	40	50	75
Laugh-In, Stancraft, MN, TV's Rowan and Martin and wisecracks, 1969	25	40	50
Maxfield Parrish, Edison Mazda, 1930-40	100	350	600
Missouri, "Gateway Arch Saint Louis," city view and mule	8	10	15

	LOW	AVG.	HIGH
Missouri Pacific Railroad, The Sunshine Special, 1930	80	100	125
Modern Woodmen of America, red and green logo back, 1931	35	50	75
National-Aladdin 1001, red pattern back, c1910	75	95	125
New York Central, double deck, morning on the Hudson	20	30	40
Nile Fortune Telling	15	30	45
North American Van Lines	7	10	15
Old English Pipe Tobacco, wide size, 1906	30	40	50
Ozark Airlines, World's Fair 1984, white print	7	10	15
Patent Cereals Co., "Old Man Rex" back	20	35	50
Portina Cigars, pinochle, early 1900s	25	35	50
Put & Take, novelty deck, overprint instruction on each card, 1920	30	50	75
Queen High Equality, 1971	30	40	50
Reynolds Wrap, use for product on each card, 1964	20	40	65
Rocky Mountain, Tom Jones, bouquet of columbines back, c1900	175	200	225
Royal Revelers, double deck, anti-prohibition, Mr. Bluenose Joker, Merry Cards, 1932	100	200	300
Russell, New York Girl, pinochle	25	50	75
Russell, red pattern back, Statue of Liberty	10	25	50
Singapore Air, "California Here We Come"	5	10	15
Springmaid Fabrics, double deck, special Queens and Aces, colorized Jokers, 1956	40	50	65
SS Mardi Gras, "Cruise the Fun Ship" back	18	22	30
Swedish America Line, double deck, 1930s	30	50	65
Trans Caribbean, purple toned photo of DC-8, 1960s	18	25	40
Tydol, Flying Gasoline, double deck, late 1940s	30	50	75
United States Lines, *SS Leviathan,* shield and ship back	18	25	40
University of Michigan, center gold logo on blue ground, gold edges, 1928	30	45	60
Vanity Fair, U.S. Playing Card Co., first transformation pack, 1895	225	455	700
Vargas Pin-ups, double deck, made in Italy, 1950s	75	100	200
Vermont, Chosolm Bros., 52 views of state, 1910	50	75	125
Vulcan Iron Works, double deck, locomotive back, 1949	20	40	55
Win, Lose or Draw, MacPherson pin-ups, 1940s	50	75	100

Planters Peanuts, linen finish, complete w/ Joker and box, c1920s, $1375 at auction. —Photo courtesy Wm. Morford.

Premiums

The excitement of getting a prize or an extra gift is a temptation for consumers. Combining this with a child's favorite radio, comic book or television hero creates a powerful inducement to purchase. Premiums gained momentum in the radio days of the Great Depression. Cereal, soap and other companies hosted programs; in turn radio Orphan Annie, Captain Midnight, the Lone Ranger and others promoted the host's product. When television replaced radio, many programs made the switch as well. These personalities induced young viewers with mail-in offers for membership packages, decoder rings, books, badges and toys. Other premiums were included with the package and occasionally offered at the store.

Collectors actively seek these items. They collect a range of items basing their collection on characters or types of items like decoders or rings. In recent years astounding prices have been paid for rare premium rings. Collectors are also seeking newer premiums from the 1960s and 1970s. Quisp and Quake items are currently very popular. The presence of original packaging and instructional materials increases the prices of premiums, so don't throw them away. Premiums are still used as sales inducements, mainly by the cereal industry. Prices below are for items in excellent to near mint condition. Each entry contains the character who promoted the product, a brief description of the premium, the date of issue and the company who made the product.

For further reading see *Hake's Price Guide to Character Toys, 2nd Edition* by Ted Hake (Gemstone Publishing, Timonium, MD, 1998) and *Overstreet Premium Ring Price Guide, Third Edition* by Robert M. Overstreet (Gemstone Publishing, Timonium, MD, 1997).

	LOW	HIGH
Amos 'N Andy, radio script, "Amos' Wedding," Pepsodent, 1935, 8.375" x 11"	$75	$100
Amos 'N Andy, standees, diecut, scowling Andy holding smoking cigar in left hand and cane in right hand, smiling Amos petting kneeling dog, Pepsodent, 1930, 4.25" x 8.5"	75	100
Aunt Jenny, fan photo w/ mailer, black and white photo of smiling Jenny at CBS microphone, white facsimile signature, Lever Brothers Co., 1930s	25	50
Bazooka Joe, doll, w/ mailing bag, cloth, stuffed, Bazooka Bubble Gum, 1973	20	25
Bazooka Joe, Magic Circle Club membership certificate, black and white, orange accent, smiling Bazooka Joe image in each corner, facsimile signature at bottom, Bazooka Bubble Gum, 1960s, 5.25" x 8"	25	50
Bobby Benson, H-Bar-O Ranger drinking glass, Force Toasted Wheat Flakes, 1930s, 4.75" h	10	15
Bobby Benson, H-Bar-O Ranger H-O Holster, w/ cartridge belt, brown leather, simulated cowhide pocket, w/ matching brown leather belt and metal belt buckle, H-O Cereals, 1933	100	200
Boo Berry, door knocker, vinyl, General Mills, 1970s, 3.375" h	25	50
Buck Rogers, Ring of Saturn, white plastic glow-in-the-dark bands w/ folded image of crocodile w/ opened jaws, Post Corn Toasties, 1946	400	700
Buck Rogers, Space Ranger Kit, punch-out, Sylvania, 1952, 11.5" x 15"	200	400
Buffalo Bee, bowl hanger, yellow vinyl, figural, Nabisco Cereal, c1961, 2" h	25	50
Buster Brown, Nature Scope, clear plastic, relief image on top of Buster and Tige, Buster Brown Shoes, 1960s, 2.25" h	25	50
Cap'n Crunch, bank, vinyl, figural, name on reverse, Quaker, 1972, 6.5"	50	75
Captain Midnight, mug, red plastic, "Hot Ovaltine," 1953, 3" h	50	75
Captain Midnight, Secret Squadron Manual, w/ mailer, 16 pages, full color, Ovaltine, c1950	100	200
Captain Midnight, Secret Squadron Patch, w/ premium offer sheet, cloth, full color, Ovaltine, c1950	20	25
Captain Midnight, Spy-Scope instruction folder, 4 pages, Ovaltine, 1947	50	75

	LOW	HIGH
Captain Midnight, Whirlwind Whistling Ring, brass, siren whistle on top, adjustable bands w/ wing design on each side, Ovaltine, 1941	200	400
Captain Tim Healy, photo, full color image of Capt. Tim Healy in uniform smiling at NBC microphone, reverse w/ biographical data and stamp collecting activities, Dixie Ice Cream, c1939, 8" x 10"	25	50
Captain Video, Flying Saucer Ring, w/ instruction sheet, Power House Candy Bars, 1951	75	125
Captain Video, tab, litho tin, Purity Bread, 1950	40	70
Chandu, booklet, "Chandu Book of Magic," 16 pages, Rio Grande Cracked Super Anti-Knock Gasoline, 1932, 5.25" x 7.5"	150	350
Charlie McCarthy, ring, brass, figural, Chase & Sanborn, 1938	100	200
Choo-Choo Cherry, Funny Face mug, purple, Pillsbury, 1969, 3" h	15	25
Count Chocula, figure, vinyl, dark brown, General Mills, 1970s, 2.5" h	25	50
Dick Darling, book, *Dick Darling's New Bag of Tricks,* paperback, Quaker Oats, ©1934 Reilly & Lee Co., 5" x 7.5"	50	75
Dick Tracy, Good Luck Secret Compartment Ring, brass, four-leaf clover and horseshoe on sides, relief portrait of Tracy surrounded by crescent moon and stars on top, Quaker, 1938	200	400
Dig 'Em, cup, full figure frog on front, reverse image on back, attached to blue base in design of large pair of shoes, Kellogg's, 1981, 4.5" h	15	25
Don Winslow, League For Defense Membership Card, red, white, and blue, Winslow image and facsimile signature, Fleer's Dubble Bubble Gum, 1940, 2.25" x 4"	100	200
Don Winslow, Official Squadron of Peace Manual, 24 pages, text, art, and photos, Kellogg's, 1939, 4.75" x 6.25"	75	100
Eddie Cantor, folder w/ envelope, "How to Make a Quack-Quack," Chase & Sanborn, 1933	25	50
Eddie Cantor, photo folder w/ mailer, "Eddie Cantor's Picture Book," photos, cartoons, and text, Chase & Sanborn, 1933, folder opens to 18.25" x 23"	25	50
Flash Gordon, comic book, issue #1, full color, 16 pages, ©1951 King Features Syndicate, Harvey Publications, Gordon's Bread, 6.75" x 10.25"	15	25
Frank Buck, Adventurer's Club Manual, full color, 24 pages, blue text, red accent art, Pepsodent, 1930s, 5" x 7"	100	200
Franken Berry, Spooky Shape Maker, vinyl, General Mills, 1970s	25	50
Gabby Scoops, Junior Press Club Membership Card, Milky Way, 1954, 2.375" x 3.875"	15	25
George Burns & Gracie Allen, folder, "George Burns/Gracie Allen/They're on the Air for Grape-Nuts," Grape-Nuts Flakes, early 1930s, 3.5" x 6.25"	50	75
Goofy Grape, Funny Face pitcher, purple, Pillsbury, 1974, 9" h, 5.25" d	50	75
Hopalong Cassidy, comic book, full color newsprint, 24 pages, "A Present From Grape-Nuts Flakes, Hoppy's Favorite Cereal," c1950, 6" x 9"	75	100
Hopalong Cassidy, ring, silver luster, raised portrait surrounded by horseshoe on top, adjustable band w/ Hoppy's initials and "XX," Popsicle, c1950	50	75
Hopalong Cassidy, William Boyd Hopalong Cassidy Rubber Band Gun Punch-out, stiff paper, full color, Pillsbury Farina, 1940	400	700
Howdy Doody, fudge bar wrapper, w/ talking pin offer, textured glassine paper white wrapper w/ orange and black front design of smiling Howdy, talking pin offer on back, membership card, and prize booklet, Standard Ice Cream Co., Detroit, MI, 1950s	25	50
Howdy Doody, spoon, figural, Crown Silver Plate ©Kagran, Welch's, 1950s, 6.875" l	25	50
Huckleberry Hound and Friends, game sheet, w/ mailer, 33" x 44" yellow vinyl board, red vinyl diecut spinner, 4 diecut vinyl figural playing pieces, red and black plastic checkers, illustrated instruction sheet, Kellogg's, 1962	50	75

	LOW	HIGH
Jack Armstrong, Egyptian Whistle Ring instruction sheet, black and yellow text, images of Jack, Betty, Uncle Jim, and Billy w/ hieroglyphic around borders, Wheaties, 1937, 3" x 4"	50	75
Jack Armstrong, Explorer Telescope, black cardboard tube, gray metal extension, Jack Armstrong Explorer name in relief on side, Wheaties, 1938, 6.75" l	50	75
Jack Armstrong, Hike-O-Meter Treasure Hunt Game, w/ instruction folder, Wheaties, 1938	50	75
Jack Armstrong, picture set w/ mailer, real photo images of smiling Jack wearing varsity sweat w/ facsimile signature, smiling Betty Fairfield w/ facsimile signature, and All-American Team showing Jack, Betty, and husky in snow, Wheaties, 1934	75	100
Jack Armstrong, Secret Bomb Sight, black wood, litho paper, green wood sight and dial on bottom, w/ 2 of 3 red wooden bombs, Wheaties, 1942	200	400
Jack Armstrong, Sky Ranger Plane, Wheaties, 1940s	100	200
Joe E. Brown, ring, adjustable brass band, raised portrait and symbolic bow tie w/ "B" on top, Grape-Nuts, 1936	75	100
Keebler Elf, ring, 1.5" h white elf figure on flexible prong base, 1970	50	75
King Vitamin, Magni Viewer, 1970s	15	25
Lefty Lemonade, cloth patch, w/ instruction envelope, oval, colorful cartoon image of Left Lemon w/ name in black at bottom, Pillsbury, 1980s, 2.5" d	15	25
Little Orphan Annie, "Good Luck" coin, w/ instruction envelope, brass medal picturing Annie within wishbone flanked by "Good Luck" and "Radio Orphan Annie's Secret Society/Ovaltine 3 Times A Day" rim lettering w/ cloverleaf, same rim inscription and "Make A Wish-Good Luck" on reverse, Ovaltine, 1934	75	100
Lone Ranger, Atomic Bomb Ring, bomb shaped top, adjustable brass band w/ lightning bolt and starburst design, removable red plastic end cap, Kix, 1940s	100	200
Lone Ranger, Hi-Yo Silver Rubber Band Gun, w/ targets, Morton's Salt, 1938	75	100
Lone Ranger, photo, "The Lone Ranger Safety Club," full color, Lone Ranger and Tonto on horseback in desert w/ mountains in background, reverse text promotes Merlita Bread & Cake and radio show, 1942	50	75
Mandrake the Magician, club kit card, Taystee Bread, 1934, 3" x 5"	75	100
Melvin Purvis, Junior G-Man Corps Ring, eagle and shield design on top, adjustable brass band, Post, 1936	50	75
Milton the Toaster, card, vinyl, orange, black text, 3 diecut holes, Kellogg's, 1973, 3" x 5"	10	15
Og, Son of Fire, figure, metal, painted green, white mouth, "Libby Rex" in relief on chest, Lincoln Logs, Libby's Food, 1935, 2.25" h	75	100
Omar the Mystic, bookmark, 2-sided, Taystee Bread, c1936, 2" x 5.75"	75	100
Phantom, ring, litho tin, Phantom color portrait on front, red accents to side, yellow bands w/ black lettering, Post Toasties Corn Flakes, 1949, 2.5" l	100	200
Popsicle Pete, Magical Pencil, green, orange, and blue point, image of Popsicle Pete as band leader on side, Popsicle, 1950s, 6.5" l	15	25
Quisp, Gyro Trail Blazer, blue hard vinyl motorcycle w/ Quisp image driver, Quisp Cereal, 1960s, 2" l	25	50
Ronald McDonald, ring, plastic, yellow full figure Ronald on orange plastic base, McDonald's, 1970s	25	50
Rootin' Tootin' Raspberry, Funny Face walker, w/ plastic weight, Pillsbury, 1971, 3.25" h	50	75
Roy Rogers, Roy Rogers Model Ranch Punch-Out Kit, Post Cereal, 1950s, 3.875" x 8.5" folder opens to 18.75" h	200	400

	LOW	HIGH
Seymour, ring, orange plastic, raised image, expandable band, Burger Chef, c1970	75	100
Sgt. Preston, comic book, "Sgt. Preston How He Found Yukon King," full color newsprint, 16 pages, Quaker Cereal, 1956, 2.5" x 7"	25	50
Sgt. Preston, pedometer, aluminum, 1952, 2.375" d	50	75
Shadow, matchbook, diecut Shadow image w/ skull on front, skeleton holding bloody knife on back w/ "The Shadow Radio's Thrilling Mystery Drama/ Brought To You" and printed name and address, 1940s, Blue Coal	100	200
Sky King, magic kit, w/ mailer and instruction sheet, 8 pages, includes 3 diecut cards and 2 coins, Peter Pan Peanut Butter, c1949	25	50
Snap, Crackle, & Pop, stencil, green vinyl, diecut images, Kellogg's, 1970	10	15
Sugar Bear, comic book, "Sugar Bear in the Race for Outer Space," 16 pages, Post, 1970s, 2.5" x 4.375"	10	15
Today's Children, sheet music, *Lonely Heart,* front cover shows black and white cast photo and "Elaine's Wedding Party," back cover shows "Eilene's Wedding Cake," 6 pages, Pillsbury, 1936, 9" x 12"	15	25
Tom Corbett, Space Academy Certificate, Kellogg's, 1950s, 5" x 6.75"	75	100
Tom Mix, book, "Tom Mix Straight Shooters Album," black and white, 24 pages, Ralston, 1940s, 6" x 9"	75	100
Tom Mix, Look-Around Ring, w/ mailer and instruction folder, Ralston, 1946	100	200
Tony the Tiger, mug, plastic, figural, F & F Mold Co., Kellogg's, c1964, 3.5" h	50	75
Tony the Tiger, postcard, full color, "Hi! It's Gr-r-reat Here at Camp," Kellogg's, mid-1960s, 3.625" x 5.625"	15	25
Trix Rabbit, figure, vinyl, smiling full figure w/ hands clasped at chest, General Mills, 1978, 8.5" h	50	75
Trix Rabbit, ramp walker, vinyl, orange, General Mills, 1970s, 3" h	15	25
Uncle Don, booklet, "Terry and Ted on the Trail of the Secret Formula by Uncle Don," 16 pages, illustrated, ©1936 General Baking Co., 5" x 7.25"	20	25
Wild Bill Hickok, treasure map, full color map of U.S., images around borders and on states, lower corner w/ image of Wild Bill Hickok and Jingles on horseback and text referring to secret treasure guide, ©1952 Rand McNally & Co., Chicago, issued by Kellogg's Sugar Corn Pops, 25" x 36" open size	75	100

Radio Orphan Annie, brass decoder badges at auction, left to right: 1935, 1.25" dia, $33; 1936, w/ secret compartment, 1.25" x 1.75", $33; 1939, Mysto-Magic, 1.75" dia, $55.
—Photos courtesy Past Tyme Pleasures.

Robots and Space Toys

The word robot is derived from "robata" for forced labor. Robot first appeared in the 1921 play *R.U.R.* by Czechoslovakian playwright Karl Capek. It was not until the futuristic 1950s that robots really hit their stride, when toy robots and spacecraft started to appear. Although some were made in the United States (by firms such as Marx, Remco and Ideal) and Germany, the majority were produced in Japan. Friction drives and keywind mechanisms were employed but battery power increased the complexity of the toy. With batteries, metal monsters and spaceships could twirl, spin, light up, roll backwards, change directions and perform a multitude of other tricks. Collectors call this "action" and it attracts them to these toys.

When collecting these toys beware of condition; make sure there are no missing parts, including remote controls, battery boxes or antennas. Make sure there is no restoration; battery boxes should be checked closely. Never leave a battery in a toy; it can leak and cause damage. The prices below are for mint without box (MNB) and mint in the box (MIB) examples. Rust, scratches and restoration will lower these prices.

In recent years astronomical prices achieved for rare items (over $25,000 at auction for a Robby Space Patrol car) have encouraged people to create new robots such as the Robby Space Patrol, Mr. Atomic and the Rosko Astronauts. Some of these toys are incredible reproductions of the original toy, right down to the box. Other robots are old style new products. Be sure of what you are buying. Robots are listed either by the name that appears on the original box or the name coined by collectors. Different robots often have the same or similar names.

Refer to *Vintage Toys, Vol. I: Robots & Space Toys* by Jim Bunte, Dave Hallman and Heinz Jueller (Antique Trader Books, Dubuque, IA, 1999) for additional information.

Left: Cragstan Robot, battery operated, tin, 10.5" h, $1725 at auction.

Right: Space Patrol Car, IN, battery operated, litho tin, 9.5" l, $1265 at auction.

—Photo courtesy Skinner, Inc., Boston, MA.

	MNB	MIB
Answer Game Machine Robot, Idnida, battery operated, tin, 14.5" h	$300-$400	$525-$550
Antique Robot R-35, Masudaya, keywind, litho tin and hard plastic, metallic blue, 1984, 4.5" h	10-15	25-50
Apollo 11 Eagle Lunar Module, Daishin, for Mego, 7 automatic actions, 8" h	80-140	220-320
Apollo 11 Moon Rocket, Ashai, friction, 14" h	40-60	90-130
Astro Scout 3 Robot, Yoshiya, keywind, drum body, cylindrical domed metallic blue helmet, red arms, collar, and feet, astronaut face behind plastic panel, 1950s, 9.25" h	1500-2000	2500-3100
Atom Robot, KO, friction, litho tin, 6.5" h	500-600	600-650
Attacking Martian, Amico Toy, battery operated, litho tin, moves forward as arms swing, stops as door panels on chest open and double-barrelled gun pops out producing firing noise and flashing lights, 1960s, 11" h	100-150	200-400

	MNB	MIB
Blink-A-Gear Robot, Taiyo, battery operated, tin, plastic arms and feet, strides w/ swinging arms, lighted blinking eyes, working light behind clear plastic chestplate, 15" h	800-1000	1200-1285
Blue Rosko Astronaut, Rosko Toys, litho tin, 13" h	900-1300	1500-2200
Cap't Astro Spaceman, Mego, keywind, hard plastic body, litho tin chest, face, and panels on legs, 1972, 6" h	50-75	100-200
Circus 8 Car, Ashai, litho tin, clown robot driving Circus 8 Mercedes, 8" l	600-900	1200-1600
Colonel Hap Hazard, Marx, astronaut in white NASA spacesuit w/ whirling copter blade, 11" h	800-1000	1200-1800
Cragstan's Mr. Robot, Yonezawa, red body, litho chest panel, swiveling domed head, 11" h	450-650	800-900
Dalek, Marx, battery operated, plastic, 1960-70s, 6.5" h	50-100	200-225
Driving Robot, keyind, robot-driven auto swing, 6" h	300-500	600-900
Dux Astroman, Western Germany, battery operated, remote control, green plastic astroman w/ radar antenna over clear dome, white head w/ red features, rock crushing action, 14" h	1200-1500	2000-3000
Earth Man, Nomura, litho tin, yellow, moves forward, lifts gun w/ lighting barrel and fires, 1950s, 9.5" h	700-850	900-975
Engine Robot, Horikawa, chest pan w/ swiveling gun and litho circuitry, 12" h	100-150	200-300
Fighting Robot, Japan, battery operated, plastic, double firing machine guns in torso, 1970s, 9.5" h	80-120	150-200
Fighting Spaceman, SH, battery operated, tin, moves forward w/ swinging arms, light on helmet blinks, stops as gun in chest fires while moving back and forth w/ gun noise, litho chest plate, 12" h	180-220	300-500
Firebird Space Patrol, Masudaya, litho tin, green and red, 14" l	300-400	500-700
Flying Jeep, Linemar, friction, litho tin, moves forward as visual engine spins, 6" l	100-150	200-250
Flying Saucer, Haji, friction, litho tin, 2 astronauts under clear plastic dome, 7" d	180-220	300-350
Forklift Robot, Horikawa, yellow w/ red cap, plastic forklift and crate, 11.5" h	1000-1500	1800-2400
Friendship 7-Space Capsule, SH, friction, litho tin, transparent plastic windows over cockpit, plastic front tip and exhaust jets, 1960s, 4.25" h	50-75	100-200
Gear Chest Robot, Japan, battery operated, tin, full view gear in chest, slow and stop dial on head, 2 antennas on shoulders, 11.5" h	50-100	125-175
Godaikin Sun Vultan Super Robot, Bandai, diecast metal and plastic, 1982, 10" h	25-50	75-100
Golden Gear Robot, SH, battery operated, tin, moves forward with moving legs and arms, flashing light atop head, transparent chest reveals moving gears, flashing bullet shaped plastic eyes, 9" h	350-450	500-575
Great Garloo, Marx, battery operated, remote control, hard plastic, moves forward and backward, upper body moves up and down, arms open and close, complete w/ medallion around neck, chain around wrist, and fabric loincloth, 1960s, 18" h	400-600	700-1000
Happy Harry the Hysterical Robot, Straco/Japan, plastic, movable arms and mouth w/ large white teeth, bump-and-go action, produces loud laughing sound, 1969, 13" h	150-250	350-400
High-Bouncer Moon Scout, Marx, battery operated, plastic, remote control, moves forward w/ swinging arms as blade on helmet spins, trap-door on chest opens to shoot out super balls, 1968, 11.5" h	1200-1800	2000-3000

	MNB	MIB
High-Wheel Robot, KO, windup, tin, plastic hands, moves forward while sparking in chest and 6 plastic gears revolve, 10" h	400-550	650-750
Hysterical Robot, plastic, laughs and grins, 13" h	100-150	250-350
Interplanetary Space Fighter, Nomura, tinplate, retractable side fins, 12" l	200-300	500-700
Jupiter Robot, Yoshiya, keywind, plastic, Robbie-style, 1960s, 7" h	200-275	375-425
Krome Dome, Yonezawa, plastic, multicolored, clam-shaped head and accordion torso, 10" h	60-80	120-180
Lost in Space Robot, Ahi, battery operated, hard plastic, moves forward as red light shines inside dome, stops as light blinks and clicking noise is produced, 1977, 10" h	100-150	200-400
Lost in Space Robot, Remco, battery operated, hard plastic, 12" h	100-150	200-400
Lunar Spaceman, Japan, battery operated, plastic, hinged torso panels open to reveal firing gun, 1980s, 12" h	200-275	375-400
Man in Space, Alps, battery operated, remote control, tinplate and celluloid astronaut	100-200	600-900
Mars King, SH, battery operated, litho tin, moves forward on black rubber treads, stops, raises arms, and screeches as TV screen in chest lights and shows Mars landscape, 10" h	200-300	400-465
Martian Supersensitive Radar Patrol, Jeep, friction, 9" l	700-900	1400-2000
Marvelous Moon Man, Yone, keywind, plastic, 5" l	50-100	150-175
Mechanical Sparking Robot, Yonezawa, keywind, plastic, red	70-90	120-170
Mechanical Walking Spaceman, Yoshiya, keywind, metallic blue litho, flat arms, red feet, start/stop lever at front, 1960-65, 7.5" h	200-300	400-450
Mighty Midget Walking Robot, Kent, Hong Kong, keywind, hard plastic, 1970s	20-40	50-75
Mighty Robot, N, keywind, litho tin, moves forward as sparks appear behind red plastic chest window, 5.5" h	75-125	150-200
Mirror Man, Bullmark, keywind, litho tin, movable vinyl head, moves forward w/ arms moving in unison, 9.5" h	250-350	500-575
Moon Capsule, Horikawa, friction, 6" l	50-70	80-120
Moon Creature, Marx, keywind, litho tin, vinyl feelers, 1968, 6" h	100-150	250-275
Moon Detector, Yonezawa, cylindrical space vehicle, bubble dome front and astronaut, 10" l	400-600	700-900
Moon Doctor, Japan, keywind, litho tin, plastic glasses and arms, moves forward on feet marked "X-25," 7" h	450-550	700-900
Moon Explorer, KO, keywind, tin, moves forward w/ crank action, litho tin face under clear plastic dome, 7.5" h	500-700	900-1200
Moon Man 001 Walking Astronaut, OK, Hong Kong, battery operated, hard plastic, 1960s, 5.75" h	50-75	100-200
Moon Orbiter, Yone, keywind, soft plastic capsule w/ attached vinyl astronaut, 1960s, 3" x 6" x 4"	40-60	75-100
Moon Patrol Helicopter, Marx, keywind, litho tin, moves forward w/ spinning propellers, NASA logo on tail fin, 10.5" l	50-75	100-150
Moon Patrol Space Division, Nomura, blue, star and satellite motif, astronaut driver and bubble-covered astro globe, 12" l	2000-3000	4000-6000
Moon Ranger, Japan, friction, litho tin, moves forward w/ spinning saucer blade and plastic rear weapon attachments, 2 drivers under tinted dome cockpit, 11" l	25-45	50-60
Moon Space Ship, Nomura, light blue, bubble-encased radar mechanism, 13" l	1200-1800	2500-3500
Mr. Atomic, Cragstan, Yonezawa, blue and red w/ yellow feet, flashing lights in domed head, 11" h	2500-4000	5000-7000

	MNB	MIB
Mr. Brain the Tru-Smoke Robot With a Memory, Remco, battery operated, hard plastic, complete w/ 6 memory disks, empty tube of Tru-Smoke, and instruction sheet, 1969, 13" h	50-75	150-250
Mr. Machine, Ideal, keywind, plastic, 1977, 16" h	60-80	100-150
Mr. Robot the Mechanical Brain, Alps, keywind and battery operated, remote control, boilerplate style, 8.5" h	900-1300	1800-2200
Mystery Space Ship, Marx, plastic, 1962, 7.5" d	80-120	150-200
New Fighting Robot, Horikawa, light-up dome, guns in chest, 12" h	100-130	200-300
Patrol Disk Saucer, Japan, friction, litho tin, 1950s, 2.5" d	30-40	50-75
Piston Robot, SJM, battery operated, litho tin lower body, clear plastic head and upper body, silver eyes and ears, advances as clicking noise is produced and pistons move and light, 1970s, 11" h	60-80	100-200
Planet Explorer, Masudaya, tinplate vehicle w/ bubble front and astronaut, 9.5" l	80-120	200-250
Planet Robot, KO, battery operated, tin, remote control, metal claw hands, moves forward, antenna spins, radar dish inside mask revolves and lights, 9" h	500-750	1000-1500
Planet Y Space Station, Nomura, 8" d	100-150	200-300
R-7 Flashy Jim, Ace/S.N.K., battery operated, remote control, silver boilerplate style, red headphones, 6.5" h	900-1300	1800-2200
R-35 Robot, Japan, battery operated, litho tin, remote control, moves forward and back, working lighted eyes, 9" h	400-500	700-865
Radar Scope Space Scout, battery operated, gray, TV screen torso displays space scene, 1965-70, 9.5" h	150-250	350-400
Ranger Robot, Daiya, ribbed clear plastic, smoking action, 13" h	600-900	1000-1500
Robby Robot Bulldozer, Marusan, friction, litho tin, 1960s, 4.5" h	75-100	200-400
Robby the Robot, Masudaya, battery operated, hard vinyl, jointed arms and legs, clear plastic canopy for head, 1984, 14.5" h	50-75	125-175
Robbie the Roving Robot, Japan, keywind, gray, hinged arms, antenna on head, 1950s, 7.5" h	450-650	750-800

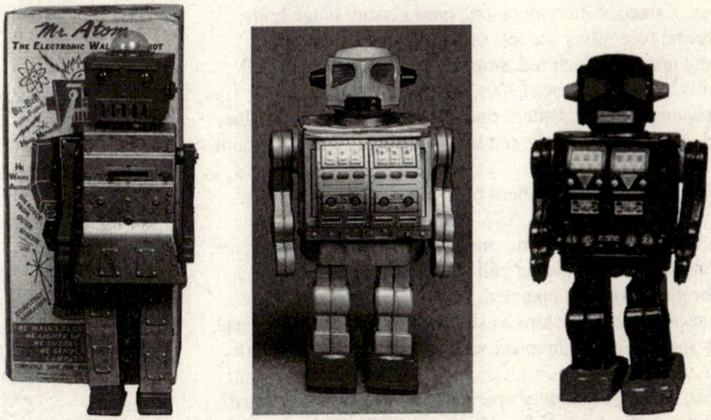

Robots at auction, left to right: Mr. Atom Walking Robot, Advance Doll & Toy Co., battery operated, plastic, 18" h, $495; Large Robot, Japan, battery operated, litho tin, 16" h, $605; Super Robot, Japan, battery operated, litho tin, 11.5" h, $138. —Photos courtesy Bill Bertoia Auctions.

	MNB	MIB
Robert the Robot/The Mechanical Man, Ideal, battery operated, remote control, hard plastic, manually movable arms, talking action, 1950s, 13.5" h	100-150	200-400
Robodachi Robot, Japan, diecat metal and plastic, 3.5" h	55-65	75-100
Robot 2500, Durham Industries, battery operated, red light on torso, 10" h	30-50	70-80
Robot Captain, Yone, keywind, litho tin body, plastic arms and legs, dials and gauges on chest, small diecut opening for viewing sparking mechanism, advances w/ sparking action, 5.5" h	50-75	100-200
Robot Commando, Ideal, battery operated, remote control, plastic, blue body, red dome and accents, voice activated, 1961, 15" h	200-300	400-450
Robot ST-1, Strenco, Germany, boilerplate-style w/ coil and diamond-shaped antennas, 6.5" h	500-700	800-1200
Robotank-Z Space Robot, TN, battery operated, litho tin body, hard plastic arms and cover over top of head, travels in erratic fashion as arms rapidly move levers while rotating light is visible on top of head, stops as 2 guns on front pop out producing loud firing noise and flashing action, 1960s, 10.5" h	100-150	200-400
Rocket Car X, MT, friction, litho tin, 6" l	100-200	300-350
Rocket w/ Sparks, Linemar, friction, litho tin, 6" l	75-125	150-250
Rotate-O-Matic Super Astronaut, Horikawa, battery operated, astronaut moves forward, body rotates as guns fire from chest, 1980s, 11.75" h	75-150	175-200
Roto Robot, SH, battery operated, litho tin and plastic, moves w/ realistic stride, rotates body 360 degrees, shoots w/ sound and flash action, 9" h	100-150	275-325
Rototrac Bulldozer, Linemar, battery operated, red and yellow, propulsion levers, light on head, rolls forward, horn sounds when objects hit, 1950, 9.5" h	300-500	600-650
Satellite Fleet, TPS, keywind, litho tin, embossed details, mother ship w/ radar screen pulling 3 smaller ships on rod, 11" l	75-150	250-350
Satellite X-107, flying saucer w/ floating astronaut, 8" d	50-70	90-140
Saturn Robot, Kamco, battery operated, hard plastic, black body, red hands and feet, silver accents on head, moves forward as arms swing and eyes flash red, stops as chest lights up w/ full color revolving space scene, 1980s, 12.5" h	50-65	75-100
Smoking Spaceman, Marx, battery operated, tin, gray or light blue, red shoes, rivet detailed body, red light bulb eyes, chrome mouth, 1950s, 12" h	900-1300	1500-2000
Son of Garloo, Marx, keywind, hard plastic body, painted tin legs, complete w/ necklace, 1960s, 5.75" h	100-150	200-400
Space Dog, KO, keywind, litho tin, moves forward w/ flapping ears, opening/closing mouth, plastic ball tail end	500-700	1000-1150
Space Explorer, SH, battery operated, litho tin body, plastic arms and feet, moves forward, stops as screen on chest lights to reveal revolving space scenes, complete w/ removable antenna, 1960s, 13" h	100-150	200-400
Space Fighter, Horikawa, battery operated, brown, moves forward, hinged doors at chest reveal firing guns, 1965-70, 9" h	100-150	200-250
Space Jumper, Blue-Box, remote control, hard plastic, 1980s, 5.5" h	15-35	50-75
Spaceman, Linemar, litho tin, battery operated, remote control, 1950s, 7.5" h	200-300	400-500
Space Patrol Vehicle, ATC, battery operated, litho tin, plastic fins, moves forward w/ blinking light, 8.5" l	400-500	650-750

Space Whale PX-3 "Pioneer," KO (Kanto), Japan, wind-up, litho tin, 1950s, 9" l, $200-$300. —Photo courtesy Auction Team Köln.

	MNB	MIB
Space Rocket Car X, MT, friction, litho tin, 6" l	50-75	100-225
Space Rocket w/ Detonation, MT, friction, litho tin, vinyl headed driver behind windscreen, produces loud engine sound, 13" l	100-200	300-400
Space Scout, SH, battery operated, litho tin and plastic, moves forward, body rotates 360 degrees, shoots w/ sound and flash action, 9.5" h	50-75	100-150
Space Ship 1, MT, battery operated, litho tin, moves forward w/ sound and flashing lights	400-500	800-900
Space Ship X-5, Modern Toys, battery operated, remote control, 8" d	50-75	100-125
Sparkling Super Robot, Hiro, keywind, hard plastic body, litho tin inserts on face, chest, and outside of each leg, dials and gauges on chest w/ diecut slot at top center, advances forward as sparks are visible through chest area, 1960s, 6" h	50-75	100-200
Sparky Robot, KO, keywind, litho tin, metallic green body, red transparent plastic panel on chest, moves forward as sparks are visible through chest area, 5" h	50-75	100-200
Star Mission Robot, Durham Industries, keywind, hard plastic, blue body, black arms, red hands, silver and clear plastic accents on head, color panel chest sticker, rotating head and movable arms, 1978, 10" h	20-40	50-75
Star Strider, Japan, battery operated, gray, astronaut advances forward, body rotates as gun fires from chest, 1970s, 12.5" h	50-100	150-175
Super Robot, Japan, battery operated, litho tin, dark gray, chest doors open to reveal shooting guns, 11.5" h	50-75	100-140
Super Space Capsule, SH, battery operated, tin and plastic, 9" h	50-75	100-200
Swivel Robot, unknown maker, keywind, hard plastic, 1970s, 4.25" h	45-65	75-100
Talking Dalek, Tomy, battery operated, hard plastic, silver body, raised blue dots on lower half of body, blue transparent insert inside head, w/ 3 removable attachments, 1970s, 6" h	55-75	100-200
Venus Robot, Yoshiya, plastic, red and black, 1965-70, 5.5" h	100-200	300-350
Video Robot, SH, battery operated, litho tin body, hard plastic head, arms, and legs, metallic blue, red feet, white plastic screen on chest, moves forward as screen lights up w/ full color revolving lunar landscape scene, 1970s, 9.5" h	25-50	100-200
Voltron Giant Commander, LJN, battery operated, remote control, soft plastic and vinyl, w/ large removable sword, 1984, 26" h	25-50	75-100
X-1 Explorer Space Ship, MT, battery operated, litho tin, advances w/ flashing lights, inner cockpit under bubble spins separately from outer shell as astronaut simulates working the controls	50-100	150-225
Zeroid Alien, Ideal, battery operated, hard plastic body, soft rubber arms, 6" h	20-40	50-75
Zoomer the Robot, TN, battery operated, tin, 8" h	700-900	1000-1050

Schoenhut

Albert Schoenhut began production of the Humpty & Dumpty Circus at his Philadelphia toy company in 1903. Advertised as "The World's Most Popular Toy," the animals and people are valued today for their lively representations and charm.

In the following listings the designation *NA* means that the animal was not produced in that style. Collectors look for pieces whose condition is as close to original as possible; some paint or fabric wear and missing ears or tails are considered minor flaws, but repaints, touch-ups or replaced clothing affect the prices more significantly.

Left: Teddy Roosevelt, $880 at auction.

Right: Kangaroo, painted eyes, $1320 at auction.

—Photo courtesy Gene Harris Antique Auction Center, Inc.

Animals

	PAINTED EYES			GLASS EYES			REDUCED SIZE		
	Fair	Good	Exc.	Fair	Good	Exc.	Fair	Good	Exc.
Bear, brown	$125	$250	$400	$300	$400	$600	$125	$275	$400
Buffalo, cloth mane	—	NA	—	450	575	650	—	NA	—
Burro	200	300	350	300	375	450	—	NA	—
Camel, 2 humps	300	425	500	700	1100	1400	200	300	375
Cat	800	1100	1500	1500	2000	2500	—	NA	—
Cow	300	400	500	400	650	850	—	NA	—
Deer	200	400	600	300	600	900	—	NA	—
Donkey	50	75	100	75	125	200	—	NA	—
Elephant	50	100	150	100	150	200	65	90	125
Gazelle	400	800	1500	1000	1500	2500	—	NA	—
Giraffe	100	200	300	200	350	500	275	350	400
Goat	150	250	300	250	275	350	—	NA	—
Goose	175	375	500	—	NA	—	—	NA	—
Gorilla	2000	2800	3400	—	NA	—	—	NA	—
Hippopotamus	125	275	400	300	500	800	400	450	500
Horse, white	125	150	200	125	200	300	100	175	200
Hyena	1100	1500	1800	1800	2800	3800	—	NA	—
Leopard	150	300	450	300	500	800	200	250	400
Lion, cloth mane	200	400	500	200	400	600	—	NA	—
Ostrich	225	300	450	300	600	900	150	300	425
Pig	250	400	450	500	725	800	250	350	425
Polar Bear	500	700	900	800	1000	1200	—	NA	—
Poodle, carved mane	150	200	250	600	900	1200	300	400	450
Poodle, cloth mane	—	NA	—	200	275	350	—	NA	—
Rabbit	500	650	800	2000	3000	3500	—	NA	—

	PAINTED EYES			GLASS EYES			REDUCED SIZE		
	Fair	Good	Exc.	Fair	Good	Exc.	Fair	Good	Exc.
Rhinoceros	400	500	600	625	750	1000	275	325	400
Sea Lion	400	500	700	600	900	1200	—	NA	—
Sheep	300	400	600	450	600	750	—	NA	—
Tiger	275	375	450	400	550	700	200	275	325
Wolf	1000	1500	1800	1800	2500	3500	—	NA	—
Zebra	225	300	400	400	550	700	225	325	425
Zebu	500	900	1400	1400	2100	3000	—	NA	—

People

	1-PART HEAD			BISQUE HEAD			REDUCED SIZE		
	Fair	Good	Exc.	Fair	Good	Exc.	Fair	Good	Exc.
Chinaman	$300	$450	$600	—	NA	—	—	NA	—
Clown	75	100	150	—	NA	—	$75	$110	$135
Gent Acrobat	—	NA	—	$300	$450	$600	—	NA	—
Hobo	200	300	400	—	NA	—	325	400	450
Lady Acrobat	300	400	450	300	450	550	—	NA	—
Lady Circus Rider	225	300	350	275	375	450	175	225	275
Lion Tamer	300	450	600	300	450	600	—	NA	—
Negro Dude	325	400	500	—	NA	—	375	450	500
Ring Master	300	375	450	350	425	550	175	225	27

Humpty Dumpty Circus, includes tent, ring w/ flags, trapeze and rings, curtain, 17 full- and reduced-size figures, 2 chairs, and pedestal, $2300 at auction. —Photo courtesy Skinner, Inc., Boston, MA.

Star Trek Memorabilia

Star Trek first appeared on NBC on September 8, 1966 but lasted only three seasons. When NBC canceled it, enraged fans bombarded the network with over one million letters of protest. Ironically, the show became even more popular in syndication. Reruns spurred the production of books, pins, fanzines and toys. "Trekkie" fan clubs and conventions evolved. Speculation regarding the series' return was surpassed only by rumors of a Beatles reunion.

Star Trek: The Motion Picture spawned a lot of material, but the 1979 film was a disappointment. Less material was produced for *Star Trek II: The Wrath of Khan.* That film re-established *Star Trek* and it has been followed by five movies and several new TV shows. The films and programs have created a new generation of fans and collectors.

For more information see *The Official Price Guide to Star Trek Collectibles, Fourth Edition* by Sue Cornwell and Mike Kott (House of Collectibles, NY, 1996) and *Greenberg's Guide to Star Trek Collectibles, Vol. 1* (1991), *Vol. 2* (1992), and *Vol. 3* (1992) by Chris Gentry and Sally Gibson-Downs (Greenberg Publishing, Sykesville, MD, now available from Kalmbach Publishing, Waukesha, WI).

Action Figures

	MNP	MIP
Arcturian, *Star Trek: The Motion Picture,* 1979, 12.5" h	$65	$75
Captain Janeway, *Star Trek Voyager,* Playmates, 1995, 5" h	5	10
Captain Kirk, *Star Trek: Generations,* Playmates, 1994, 9" h	50	60
Captain Kirk, *Star Trek: The Motion Picture,* Knickerbocker, 1979, 13" h	40	60
Captain Kirk, *Star Trek: The Motion Picture,* Mego, 1979, 3.75" h	15	20
Captain Kirk, *Star Trek V: The Final Frontier,* Galoob, 1989, 8" h	30	40
Captain Kirk, Star Trek TV series, Mego, 1974, 8" h	25	60
Captain Picard, *Star Trek: First Contact,* Playmates, 1996, 6" h	5	8
Captain Picard, *Star Trek: Generations,* Playmates, 1994, 9" h	15	20
Captain Picard, *Star Trek: The Next Generation,* Playmates, 1992, 5" h	15	25
Commander Deanna Troi, *Star Trek: Generations,* Playmates, 1994, 5" h	10	15
Commander Gul Dukat, *Star Trek: Deep Space Nine,* Playmates, 1994, 5" h	15	25
Commander Kruge, *Star Trek III: The Search for Spock,* Playmates, 1995, 5" h	5	10
Commander Riker, *Star Trek: First Contact,* Playmates, 1996, 6" h	5	8
Commander Riker, *Star Trek: The Next Generation,* Galoob, 1988, 3.75" h	10	15
Commander Riker, *Star Trek: The Next Generation,* Playmates, 1992, 5" h	20	25
Commander Sisko, *Star Trek: Deep Space Nine,* Playmates, 1994, 5" h	8	12
Dr. Beverly Crusher, *Star Trek: The Next Generation,* Playmates, 1993, 5" h	10	15
Dr. Bones McCoy, *Star Trek: The Motion Picture,* Playmates, 5" h	5	8
Dr. Bones McCoy, *Star Trek V: The Final Frontier,* Galoob, 1989, 8" h	30	40
Dr. Bones McCoy, Star Trek TV series, Mego, 1974, 8" h	50	150
Ferengi, *Star Trek: The Next Generation,* Galoob, 1988, 3.75" h	50	75
General Chang, *Star Trek VI: The Undiscovered Country,* Playmates, 1995, 5" h	5	10
Guinan, *Star Trek: The Next Generation,* Playmates, 1992, 5" h	10	15
Ilia, *Star Trek: The Motion Picture,* Mego, 1979, 12.5" h	40	50
Klaa, *Star Trek: The Final Frontier,* Galoob, 1989, 8" h	30	40
Klingon, *Star Trek: The Motion Picture,* Mego, 1979, 3.75" h	20	25
Klingon, *Star Trek: The Motion Picture,* Mego, 1979, 12.5" h	50	60
Klingon, *Star Trek III: The Search for Spock,* Ertl, 1984, 3.75" h	15	25
Lieutenant Commander Data, *Star Trek: Generations,* Playmates, 1994, 5" h	10	15
Lieutenant Commander LeForge, *Star Trek: Generations,* Playmates, 1994, 9" h	25	30
Lieutenant Sulu, *Star Trek: The Motion Picture,* Playmates, 1995, 5" h	5	8
Lieutenant Tuvok, *Star Trek Voyager,* Playmates, 1995, 5" h	3	6
Lieutenant Uhura, Star Trek TV series, Mego, 1974, 8" h	45	100

	MNP	MIP
Lieutenant Worf, *Star Trek: The Next Generation,* Galoob, 1988, 3.75" h	.15	20
Lieutenant Worf, *Star Trek: The Next Generation,* Playmates, 1992, 5" h	.20	25
Martia, *Star Trek VI, The Undiscovered Country,* Playmates, 1995, 5" h	.5	10
Megarite, *Star Trek: The Motion Picture,* Mego, 1979, 3.75" h	.125	150
Mr. Spock, *Star Trek: The Motion Picture,* Mego, 1979, 3.75" h	.20	25
Mr. Spock, *Star Trek: The Motion Picture,* Mego, 1979, 12.5" h	.40	50
Mr. Spock, *Star Trek V: The Final Frontier,* Galoob, 1989, 8" h	.30	40
Mr. Spock, Star Trek TV series, Mego, 1974, 8" h	.25	60
Pavel A. Chekov, *Star Trek: Generations,* Playmates, 1994, 5" h	.30	40
Sybok, *Star Trek V: The Final Frontier,* Galoob, 1989, 8" h	.30	40
Zaranite, *Star Trek: The Motion Picture,* Mego, 1979, 3.75" h	.125	15

Greeting Card, bi-fold, Random House Greetings, 1976, 5.75" x 7.75", $20-$35.

Miscellaneous

	LOW	HIGH
Book, *Devil's World,* Gordon Eklund, Bantam, 1979	.$10	$15
Book, *I Am Not Spock,* Leonard Nimoy, Celestial Arts, 1975	.35	60
Book, *Letters to Star Trek,* Susan Sackett, Ballantine, 1977	.15	20
Book, *Making of Star Trek II,* Asherman, 1982, paperback	.14	18
Book, *Official Star Trek Cooking Manual,* Ann Piccard, 1978	.40	60
Book, *Shatner: Where No Man Has Gone Before,* William Shatner, Ace, 1979	.40	60
Book, *Starfleet Technical Manual,* Franz Joseph, Ballantine, 1975	.35	85
Book, *Star Trek Memories,* William Shatner and Chris Kreski, Harper, 1993	.8	10
Book, *Star Trek: Voyage to Adventure,* Michael J. Dodge, Archway, 1984	.5	10
Book, *Trek or Treat,* T. Flanaghan and E. Ehrhardt, Ballantine, 1977	.3	5
Book, *Trouble with Tribbles,* David Gerrold, Ballantine, 1973	.10	15
Classic Trek Bridge Set, Playmates	.50	75
Communicator Walkie-Talkie, Playmates, 1993	.35	45
Costume, Captain Kirk, *Star Trek: The Motion Picture,* Collegeville, 1979	.30	40
Costume, Klingon, *Star Trek: The Next Generation,* Ben Cooper, 1988	.10	20
Enterprise, Star Trek: The Motion Picture, Mego, 1980	.125	200
Enterprise Bridge Playset, *Star Trek: The Next Generation,* Playmates	.50	75
Ferengi Fighter, *Star Trek: The Next Generation,* Galoob, 1988	.50	60
Frame Tray Puzzle, Transporter scene, Whitman, 1978, 8.5" x 11"	.10	15
Game, *Star Trek: The Motion Picture,* Milton Bradley, 1979	.50	75
Greeting Card, "The Captain and I both wish you a very happy birthday," Kirk holding rose, Random House, 1976	.2	4
Kite, *Star Trek: The Motion Picture,* Spock, 1979	.15	25

	LOW	HIGH
Klingon Attack Cruiser, Playmates, 1993	40	50
Klingon Bird-of-Prey, *Star Trek III,* Ertl, 1984	10	20
Klingon Cruiser, *Star Trek: The Motion Picture,* 1980	125	200
Magazine, *Time,* Nov. 28, 1994, Kirk and Picard on cover	15	20
Model Kit, *Enterprise,* Ertl, 1989	15	20
Phaser, plastic, Star Trek logo, Azrak-Hamway, 1976	25	35
Phone Card, *Star Trek: Deep Space Nine,* TEC, 10 units, 1995	10	15
Pinback Button, Captain Kirk, *Star Trek III: The Search for Spock, 1984,* 1.5" d	1	2
Playing Cards, *Star Trek: The Motion Picture,* Aviva, 1979	25	35
Poster, *Star Trek III: The Search for Spock, Enterprise* and logo, Lever Bros., 1984, 16" x 22"	6	10
Rapid-Fire Tracer Gun, Ray Plastic, Inc., ©1967 Desilu Prod.	50	75
Record, *The New World of Leonard Nimoy,* LP, Dot Records	30	50
Romulan Warbird, *Star Trek: The Next Generation,* Playmates, 1993	40	50
Runabout Orinoco, *Star Trek: Deep Space Nine,* Playmates, 1994	15	20
Sheet Music, *A Star Beyond Time (Ilia's Theme), Star Trek: The Motion Picture,* Famous Music, 1979	3	5
Shuttlecraft Galileo, *Star Trek: The Next Generation,* Galoob, 1988	50	60
Shuttlecraft Goddard, *Star Trek: The Next Generation,* Playmates, 1992	20	25
Starfleet Communicator, Playmates, 1994	6	10
Star Trek Phaser Gun, Remco, 1975	75	150
Star Trek Super Phaser II Target Game, Mego, 1976	35	50
Transporter Playset, *Star Trek: The Next Generation,* Playmates	30	40
Tricorder, Mego, 1976	100	200
Tricorder, Playmates, 1993	50	60
View-Master Reel Set, *Star Trek: The Motion Picture,* GAF, 1979	10	15
Watch, *Star Trek: Deep Space Nine,* digital, Hope Industries, 1993	10	15
Watch, *Star Trek: The Motion Picture,* Bradley, analog, 1979	100	150
Wrist Communicator, *Star Trek: The Motion Picture,* Mego, 1980	200	350
Yo-Yo, *Star Trek: The Motion Picture,* Aviva, 1979	15	25

Snow Globe, U.S.S. Enterprise *suspended on lucite rod, marked "Hallmark Authorized User/Willitts Designs, Item No. 47051, NCC 1701 Lighted Star Globe," 1992, 7" h, $50-$65.*

Star Wars Memorabilia

Star Wars burst onto movie screens in 1977. Stunning special effects made it an instant success. Two equally successful sequels followed, *The Empire Strikes Back* in 1980 and *Return of the Jedi* in 1983. *Star Wars* not only revolutionized special effects, it also introduced a smaller sized action figure. Although sizes vary they are generally 3.75" or smaller. Most of the following toys are the 3.75" figures and the vehicles made for them. Kenner made the figures and most of the toys listed below.

Dating carded *Star Wars* figures is relatively easy. The back of each card pictures each figure in the product line; as the line grows so do the number of illustrations. The original 12 figures are referred to as 12 backs. Packaging is more important in *Star Wars* items than any other area. The same figure on a *Star Wars* card is worth more than on an Empire Strikes Back or Return of the Jedi card and an Empire Strikes Back carded figure is worth more than an Return of the Jedi carded figure. Power of the Force, produced in 1985, is a series of figures that usually includes a collector coin. These figures are generally more valuable than Return of the Jedi or Empire Strikes Back. The other factor affecting price is condition. The first price quoted (MNP) is for mint complete figures with no package. The other range is for mint items mint in package (MIP). Many times figures came with weapons or clothing. Loose figures are devalued if they are lacking this original equipment. Because Kenner marketed *Star Wars* toys worldwide, there is an incredible range of packaging variations.

The demand for toys and *Star Wars* products continues. The sharpest increases are for early small figures, produced for the first movie, in mint condition on mint cards. Another area that has seen significant increases is the large figure category. For more information see *The Official Price Guide to Star Wars Collectibles, Fourth Edition* by Sue Cornwell and Mike Kott (House of Collectibles, NY, 1997) and *The Galaxy's Greatest Star Wars Collectibles Price Guide, 1999 Edition* by Stuart W. Wells III (Antique Trader Books, Norfolk, VA, 1998).

Action Figures

	MNP	MIP
4-LOM, *The Empire Strikes Back,* 1982	$50	$100
8-D8, *Return of the Jedi,* 1984	10	20
Admiral Ackbar, *Return of the Jedi,* 1983, 3.75" h	10	20
Amanaman, *The Power of the Force,* 1985, 5" h	80	160
Anakin Skywalker, *The Power of the Force,* 1984, 3.75" h	300	600
AT-AT Commander, *The Empire Strikes Back,* 1982	12	25
AT-AT Driver, *The Empire Strikes Back,* 1981	15	25
A-Wing Pilot, *The Power of the Force,* 1985	40	80
Barada, *The Power of the Force,* 1985, 3.75" h	45	75
Ben Obi-Wan Kenobi, *Star Wars,* 12 back, 1978	100	200
Bespin Security Guard, *The Empire Strikes Back,* 1980	25	50
Bespin Security Guard, *The Empire Strikes Back,* 1982	20	40
Bib Fortuna, *Return of the Jedi,* 1983, 3.75" h	10	20
Biker Scout, *Return of the Jedi,* 1983, 3.75" h	15	25
Boba Fett, *Star Wars,* 1977	225	550
B-Wing Pilot, *Return of the Jedi,* 1983, 3.75" h	8	15
C-3PO, *Star Wars,* 12 back, 1978	65	125
C-3PO, *The Empire Strikes Back,* 1980	15	30
Chewbacca, *Star Wars,* 12 back, 1978, 4.25" h	85	175
Chief Chirpa, *Return of the Jedi,* 1983, 3.75" h	10	20
Cloud Car Pilot, *The Empire Strikes Back,* 1982	15	35
Darth Vader, *Star Wars,* 12 back, 4.25" h	100	200
Dash Rendar, *Shadows of the Empire,* 1986, 3.75" h	4	8
Death Squad Commander, *Star Wars,* 12 back, 1978	100	200

Left to right: Tauntaun, Empire Strikes Back, *Kenner, $5-$8; Structors Action Walker, All Terrain Scout Transport, MPC, wind-up, $10-$15.*

	MNP	MIP
Death Star Droid, *Star Wars,* 1978	75	150
Dengar, *The Empire Strikes Back,* 1980	15	30
Emperor, *Return of the Jedi,* 1983, 3.75" h	15	25
Emperor's Royal Guard, *Return of the Jedi,* 1983, 3.75" h	15	25
EV-9D9, *The Power of the Force,* 1985, 3.75" h	50	110
FX-7, *The Empire Strikes Back,* 1980	20	40
Gamorrean Guard, *Return of the Jedi,* 1983, 3.75" h	8	15
General Madine, *Return of the Jedi,* 1983, 3.75" h	10	20
Greedo, *Star Wars,* 1978	75	150
Hammerhead, *Star Wars,* 1978, 4" h	65	125
Han Solo, *Return of the Jedi,* 1983, 3.75" h	20	40
Han Solo, *Star Wars,* 12 back, 1978	300	500
Han Solo, *The Empire Strikes Back,* 1980	25	50
Imperial Dignitary, *The Power of the Force,* 1985, 3.75" h	20	50
Imperial Gunner, *The Power of the Force,* 1985	60	120
Imperial Stormtrooper, *The Empire Strikes Back,* 1980	20	40
Imperial Tie Fighter Pilot, *The Empire Strikes Back,* 1982	25	50
Jawa, *Star Wars,* 12 back, cloth cape, 1978	100	200
Klaatu, *Return of the Jedi,* 1983, 3.75" h	10	20
Lando Calrissian, *Return of the Jedi,* 1980, 3.75" h	15	30
Lando Calrissian, *The Empire Strikes Back,* 1980	20	40
Lando Calrissian, *The Power of the Force,* 1985, 3.75" h	45	90
Lobot, *The Empire Strikes Back,* 1980	15	30
Logray, *Return of the Jedi,* 1983, 3.75" h	10	20
Luke Skywalker, *Return of the Jedi,* 1983, 3.75" h	30	60
Luke Skywalker, *Shadows of the Empire,* 1986, 3.75" h	4	8
Luke Skywalker, *Star Wars,* 12 back, 1978, 3.75" h	200	300
Luke Skywalker, *The Empire Strikes Back,* 1980	50	100
Luke Skywalker, *The Power of the Force,* 1985, 3.75" h	35	75
Lumat, *Return of the Jedi,* 1984	15	30
Nien Nunb, *Return of the Jedi,* 1983, 3.75" h	15	25
Nikto, *Return of the Jedi,* 1984	8	15

	MNP	MIP
Paploo, *Return of the Jedi,* 1984	15	30
Power Droid, *Star Wars,* 1977, 2.5" h	60	60
Princess Leia Organa, *Return of the Jedi,* 1983, 3.75" h	20	40
Princess Leia Organa, *Star Wars,* 12 back, 1978, 3.75" h	200	300
Princess Leia Organa, *The Empire Strikes Back,* 1980, 3.75" h	50	100
Prune Face, *Return of the Jedi,* 1984	8	15
R2-D2, *Star Wars,* 12 back, 1978, 2.25" h	65	125
R2-D2, *The Power of the Force,* 1985, 3.75" h	75	150
R5-D4, *Star Wars,* 1977, 2.5" h	65	130
Rancor Keeper, *Return of the Jedi,* 1983, 3.75" h	10	20
Rebel Commando, *Return of the Jedi,* 1983, 3.75" h	10	20
Rebel Commando, *The Empire Strikes Back,* 1980	10	20
Rebel Soldier, *The Empire Strikes Back,* 1980	15	30
Ree-Yees, *Return of the Jedi,* 1983, 3.75" h	10	20
Romba, *The Power of the Force,* 1985, 3.75" h	20	40
Sand People, *Star Wars,* 12 back, 1977	100	225
Squid Head, *Return of the Jedi,* 1983, 3.75" h	10	20
Stormtrooper, *Star Wars,* 12 back, 1978	100	200
Teebo, *Return of the Jedi,* 1984	10	20
Ugnaught, *The Empire Strikes Back,* 1980	15	30
Walrus Man, *Star Wars,* 1977	75	150
Weequay, *Return of the Jedi,* 1983, 3.75" h	8	15
Wicket W. Warrick, *Return of the Jedi,* 1983, 3.75" h	10	20
Yak Face, *The Power of the Force,* 1985	300	650
Yoda, with orange snake, *The Empire Strikes Back,* 1981	25	50
Zuckuss, *The Empire Strikes Back,* 1982	15	30

Miscellaneous

	LOW	HIGH
Artoo Detoo's Activity Book, *Star Wars,* 1979	$10	$15
AT-AT All Terrain Armored Transport, *The Empire Strikes Back*	250	300
Bank, Jabba the Hutt, *Star Wars,* ceramic, 1983, 6.25" h	50	75
Biker Scout Laser Pistol, 1983	75	125
Book, *Art of Star Wars, The,* Ballantine, paperback, 1983	30	40
Book, *Star Wars Blueprints,* Ballantine, 1977	15	25
C-3PO Collector's Case, 1983	20	40
Cake Pan, Boba Fett, aluminum, Wilton, 1980	40	50
Calendar, 1978, *Star Wars,* Ballantine	25	30
Cantina Adventure Set, *Star Wars,* Sears, 1978	400	600
Cloud City Playset, *The Empire Strikes Back,* 1981	200	400
Coloring Book, *Star Wars,* Chewbacca cover, 1977	5	10
Coloring Book, *The Empire Strikes Back,* Chewbacca and Leia cover, 1980	5	10
Comic Book, *The Empire Strikes Back Annual,* Grandreams, 1980	25	35
Costume, Boba Fett, Ben Cooper	25	50
Creature Cantina, *Star Wars,* 1977	50	100
Dagobah Action Playset, *The Empire Strikes Back,* 1981	40	75
Darth Vader's Star Destroyer, *The Empire Strikes Back,* 1980	85	200
Darth Vader's TIE Fighter, *Star Wars,* 1977	100	150
Death Star Space Station, *Star Wars,* 1978	80	300
Death Star Space Station, *Star Wars,* Palitoy, 1978	300	800
Dixie Cups, *The Empire Strikes Back,* box of 100 five-ounce cups	10	15
Droid Factory, *Star Wars,* 1977	750	150

	LOW	HIGH
Droid Factory, *The Empire Strikes Back,* 1979	100	200
Ewok Assault Catapult, *The Return of the Jedi*	25	50
Ewok Battle Wagon, *The Power of the Force*	30	80
Ewok Village Action Playset, *The Return of the Jedi,* 1983	75	125
Figurine, Luke Skywalker, Jedi Knight, *Return of the Jedi,* Sigma, 1983	50	60
Game, Hoth Ice Planet Adventure Game, *The Empire Strikes Back,* Kenner, 1977	10	15
Greeting Card, *Star Wars,* "That's Droid Talk for Happy Birthday!," full color, diecut, R2-D2, Drawing Board, 1977	4	6
Hand Puppet, Yoda, vinyl, original box, Kenner, 1980, 8" h	50	75
Hoth Ice Planet Adventure Set, *The Empire Strikes Back,* 1980	65	175
Imperial Attack Base, *The Empire Strikes Back,* 1980	60	120
Imperial Shuttle, *The Empire Strikes Back,* 1984	175	400
Imperial Sniper Vehicle, *The Power of the Force,* 1984	50	125
Imperial Troop Transporter, *Star Wars*	65	125
Jabba the Hutt Action Playset, *Return of the Jedi,* 1983	40	80
Jigsaw Puzzle, *Star Wars,* Artoo-Deetoo/See-Three Pio, #40100, diecut cardboard, 140 pcs., Kenner, 1977, approx. 14" x 18"	5	15
Kite, Darth Vader, Spectra Star, 1983	15	25
Land of the Jawas Action Playset, *Star Wars,* 1977	75	200
Landspeeder, *Star Wars,* 1977	35	75
Laser Pistol, *Return of the Jedi*	75	125
Lightsaber, *The Power of the Force*	40	60
Limited Edition Plate, Han Solo, The Hamilton Collection, T. Blackshear, 1987	125	175
Magazine, *Time, "Star Wars III: The Return of the Jedi,"* May 23, 1983, Vol. 121, #21	6	12
Mask, Wicket W. Warrick, latex rubber, Don Post, 1983, 8" x 8" x 11"	50	75
Millennium Falcon, *Star Wars*	100	300
Model Kit, Star Destroyer, MPC, 1980	20	30
One Man Sand Skimmer, *The Power of the Force,* 1984	40	100
Paint-By-Number Set, "The Battle on Hoth," *The Empire Strikes Back,* Craft Master, 1980	25	35
Radio, *Star Wars,* Luke Skywalker AM Headset Radio, Kenner, 1978	200	300
Rebel Armored Snow Speeder, *The Empire Strikes Back,* 1982	65	150

Left to right: Trading Card, C-3PO (Anthony Daniels) No. 207, ©1977 20th Century-Fox Film Corp., $1-$2; Lobby Cards, Star Wars, *1977, price for set of 8 at auction, $345. —Photo courtesy Skinner, Inc., Boston, MA.*

Movie Poster, Star Wars, *half-sheet, style A, art by Tom Jong, 1977, framed, $2300 at auction. —Photo courtesy Skinner, Inc., Boston, MA.*

	LOW	HIGH
Record, *The Empire Strikes Back* soundtrack, set of 2 LP's, John Williams and the London Symphony Orchestra, RSO Records, 1980	30	35
Robot, R2-D2, *Star Wars,* remote control, hard plastic, moves forward and backward, head turns, eye lights up, produces beep sound, original box, Kenner, 1978, 8" h	100	200
Security Scout, *The Power of the Force,* 1984	50	100
Speeder Bike, *Return of the Jedi,* 1983	20	40
Talking Alarm Clock, R2-D2 and C-3PO, battery operated, Bradley Time, 1980	75	100
Tatooine Skiff, *The Power of the Force,* 1985	200	800
TIE Interceptor, *Return of the Jedi,* 1983	60	120
Toothbrush Holder, ceramic, figural Snowspeeder, Sigma, 1981, 7" l	75	125
Tri-Pod Laser Cannon, *The Empire Strikes Back*	20	30
Turret & Probot Playset, *The Empire Strikes Back,* 1980	100	200
Wall Clock, *The Empire Strikes Back,* Darth Vader, Stormtroopers and Empire logo, Welby Elgin, 1981	50	75
Watch, Darth Vader, analog, Bradley, 1977	75	100
X-Wing Fighter, *The Empire Strikes Back,* 1983	75	200
Y-Wing Fighter, *Return of the Jedi,* 1983	100	200

Movie Posters

	AUCTION	RETAIL	
		Low	High
"A long time ago in a galaxy far, far away…Star Wars," white lettering on blue ground, third and final advance poster, 20th Century Fox, 1-sheet, 1977, framed	$460	$500	$700
"Luke Skywalker," art by Chaykin, signed, first poster for title distributed at 1976 fan club convention, Star Wars Corp., 20" x 29", mounted and framed	2300	3000	4000
"Star Wars: Return of the Jedi" above 2 hands raising lightsaber, style A, 20th Century Fox, 1-sheet, 1983	175	200	300
"Star Wars: The Empire Strikes Back" and Luke Skywalker riding Tauntaun superimposed over large "10," art by Dayna Stedry, 10th Anniversary poster, 20th Century Fox, 1-sheet, 1990, framed	920	950	1200
"*The Empire Strikes Back,* coming soon to a radio near you," Yoda and other creatures, art by Ralph McQuarrie, distributed by National Public Radio to stations airing the ESB drama, 1982, 17 x 28", framed	2530	3000	4500

Steiff

For information on Steiff refer to Margaret Fox Mandel's *Teddy Bears and Steiff Animals* (1984, 1997 value update) and *Second Series* (1987, 1996 value update), and *Teddy Bears, Annalee Animals & Steiff Animals, Third Series* (1990, 1996 value update), all published by Collector Books, Paducah, KY).

Pony, beige and white, horsehair mane and tail, $1000-$1500. —Photo courtesy William Doyle Galleries.

	AUCTION	RETAIL Low	RETAIL High
Airedale, "Jack," mohair, straw stuffed, glass eyes, floss nose and mouth, working squeaker, c1926-34, 6" h	$500	$600	$850
Badger, "Diggy," mohair, glass eyes, chest tag, 1960-70s, 6.375" l	100	200	450
Brontosaurus, "Brosus," gray and yellow mohair, orange felt back bone, glass eyes, c1960, 11.5" h	300	400	650
Bulldog, blonde plush, brown and black spots, poseable wire ears, articulated head, wrinkled forehead over wooden eyes, stitched snout, dewlap jaws, blonde mane surrounding collar, c1958, 24" h, 35" l	630	800	950
Cat, golden mohair, fully jointed, straw stuffed, green glass eyes, floss nose, mouth, and claws, horsehair whiskers, felt pads with cardboard innersoles, stiff tail, 9.5" h	150	200	400
Dog, seated, yellow mohair, glass eyes, black embroidered nose, mouth, and claws, 1913, 5.5" h	175	250	400
Dog on Wheels, cream and ginger mohair, embroidered nose and mouth, cast iron frame and wheels, c1910, 10" h, 13" l	85	150	300
Elephant on Wheels, gray mohair, glass eyes, white felt tusks, steel frame, rubber-tired metal wheels, red leather harness, red and yellow felt blanket, mid-20th C, 24.5" l	430	600	950
Frog Foot Rest, green and tan plush, brown spots, 4-legged metal composition, with button on flipper, c1958, 12" h, 22" l	1380	2000	2600
German Shepherd on Wheels, off-white and tan, glass eyes (1 missing), embroidered nose and mouth, cast iron wheels, ear button, c1910, 8" l	175	250	400
Giraffe, orange and tan plush, glass eyes, articulated neck and roached mane, post 1945, 59" h	1500	2000	2500
Guinea Pig, "Swinny," synthetic fur, plastic eyes, felt feet, ear button and chest tag, 1960-70s, 4.5" l	100	200	450
Mallard Drake, "Stanic," airbrushed Dralon fur, black plastic eyes, yellow felt bill, button wing, c1973, 10.5" h, 13.5" l	230	300	500
Okapi, velveteen, airbrushed coat, glass eyes, mohair mane, accents on ears and tail, ear button, 1960s, 11" h	300	475	600

Teddy Bears at auction.
Left: Yellow mohair, c1906, $5462.
Right: Curly blonde mohair, c1905, 20" h, $9200.
—Photos courtesy Skinner, Inc., Boston, MA.

	AUCTION	RETAIL Low	RETAIL High
Pony, felt, straw stuffed, glass eyes, painted dapple highlights, c1937, 10.5" h, 11.5" l	550	700	950
Rabbit, orange and white mohair, straw stuffed, jointed head, glass eyes, black floss nose and mouth, pre-1930s, 7" h	1200	1500	2000
Rocking Horse, plush, red saddle and reins, pull ring "whinny" mechanism, button in ear, mounted on wooden platform glider, post 1945, 36" h, 48" l	1600	2000	2500
Snail, multicolored velvet, vinyl shell, rubber antennae, button, cloth tag and paper tag, 1960s, 6.5" l	320	500	750
Spider, mohair, multicolored plush back, black glass eyes, gold furry underbody, legs, antennae, and mouth, 1960s, 9" l	400	550	750
Spitz Dog on Wheels, white mohair, glass eyes, excelsior stuffing, embroidered nose and mouth, steel frame and spoke wheels, 1908, 18.5" h, 22" l	700	1000	1500
St. Bernard Rocking Dog, dark brown and white synthetic fur, plastic eyes, black embroidered nose, steel frame and rocker base, ear button, mid-20th C, 23" h, 50" l	175	200	400
Stegosaurus, "Dinos," yellow mohair belly, blue, emerald green, brown, magenta, and yellow airbrushed, green and black glass eyes, pink felt open mouth, green, blue, and orchid felt back plates, yellow felt ears, 1960, 11" l	400	600	800
Teddy Bear, beige mohair, fully jointed body, black bead eyes, embroidered nose and mouth, ear button, c1905, 3.5" h	800	1200	1500
Teddy Bear, ginger mohair, fully jointed, excelsior stuffing, center seam, black steel eyes, embroidered nose, mouth, and claws, c1905, 19" h	8050	10,000	12,000
Teddy Bear, golden mohair, fully jointed, excelsior stuffing, black steel eyes, black embroidered nose, mouth, and claws, felt pads, ear button, growler, c1905, 17" h	3000	4000	5000
Teddy Bear, honey beige mohair, fully jointed, glass eyes, embroidered nose, mouth, and claws, felt pads, 13" h	230	300	450
Twin Teddy Bears, light yellow mohair, fully jointed, excelsior stuffing, black steel eyes, tan embroidered nose, mouth, and claws, cream pads, spotty fur loss, ear buttons missing, c1905, 10" h, price for pair	2530	3000	4500

Tonka Toys

Tonka toys became the post-war symbol of the well-crafted American toy. In an industry turning increasingly to plastic and smaller sizes, Tonka's large, light, pressed steel vehicles ruled sandbox construction sites. The firm began as Mound Metal Works in 1946. The Tonka name came with the move to Minnetonka, Minnesota.

Since children used the vehicles for heavy duty projects and often left them outside (moms often banished the heavy toys from the house), the condition of Tonka toys is often poor. In the following listing we give two price ranges: excellent (EXC) for toys with some light wear but no significant rust or major paint loss and near mint (NM) for toys with only traces of wear and in excellent original boxes. Keep in mind that collectors often pay a hefty premium for mint in mint box examples. Such toys may bring more than prices quoted below. Rusty, damaged pieces will bring significantly less than those in excellent or better condition.

For further information we recommend *Collectors Guide to Tonka Trucks, 1947-63* by Don and Barb DeSalle (L-W Book Sales, Gas City, IN, 1994).

	EXC	NM
AAA Wrecker Truck, black boom, 1956	$250-$275	$550-$575
Aerial Ladder Truck, #48, 1958	100-125	150-200
Army Jeep & Trailer, 1964, #384	75-100	100-125
Army Troop Carrier, #380, 1964	50-100	225-250
Big Mike Dual Hydraulic, 1958	400-500	600-650
Bulldozer, #300, 1963	25-50	50-75
Carnation Milk Van, 1955	150-175	300-350
Carry-All-Trailer, #170, w/ #150 crane and clam, 1949	175-275	400-450
Cement Truck, #620, 1963	50-75	150-200
Coast to Coast Utility Truck, 1952	100-150	250-300
Doughboy Feeds, 1961	225-250	350-375
Dump Truck w/ Sand Loader, #616, 1964	50-100	125-175
Eibert Coffee Van, 1954	225-250	425-450
Ferry Brothers Stake Truck, 1959	325-350	450-500
Fire Jeep, #425, 1963-64	50-100	200-250
Fisherman Pickup, #136, w/ houseboat, 1961	300-350	500-525
Gasoline Tanker, #16, 1957	525-550	700-750
Gas Truck, #16, 1957	550-600	850-900
Giant Bulldozer, #118, 1961	75-100	200-225
Grading Service, #134, 1961	75-100	150-175
Grain Hauler, #550, 1952-53	50-100	150-180
Green Giant Rack Truck, 1961	225-250	375-400
Green Giant Utility Truck, #175, 1954	150-200	350-400
Hi-Way Grader, #12, 1959-60	50-75	100-125
Hi-Way Pickup, 1958-59	50-100	150-200
Hi-Way Side Dump, 1959	150-175	200-275
Holsum Bread Van, 1956	350-400	600-675
Hormel Meats Semi, 1954	525-550	700-800
Hydraulic Aerial Ladder Truck, #48, 1957	150-175	250-300
Hydraulic Dump Truck, 1960	100-125	225-250
Jeep Wrecker, #375, 1964	50-75	150-175
Land Rover Hydraulic Dump Truck, 1959	650-700	900-950
Livestock Van, #500, 1952-53	50-100	125-175
Log Hauler, #14, 1954-57	100-150	200-250
Log Hauler, #575, 1953	50-100	125-175
Lumber Truck, #0850-5, 1955	150-175	250-300
Marshall Field and Company, 1952	300-350	550-650

	EXC	NM
Minute Maid Semi, 1955	850-1000	1750-2000
Mobile Clam, #942, 1963	100-125	200-225
Our Own Hardware, dual axle, 1953	300-350	400-450
Parcel Delivery Van, #10, 1957	150-200	400-475
Powerlift Truck and Trailer, #200, 1948	150-225	250-300
Rescue Van, #105, 1960-61	50-75	175-225
Sportsman Pickup, #5, w/ boat mounted on camper shell, 1959	50-100	250-275
Standard Tanker, 1961	500-550	700-750
Star-Kist Utility Truck, cans on sides, 1954	150-200	350-400
Steam Shovel, #50, 1949	50-100	125-150
Steel Carrier, #145, 1950-53	50-100	125-175
Stock Rack Farm Truck, #32, 1959	150-275	150-375
Suburban Pumper, #46, grab bar on back, 1956	100-150	250-275
Terminix Van, red, 1959	300-350	550-650
Tonka Air Express, #16, 1959	150-200	400-450
Tonka Express, #185, 1950	175-250	300-400
Tonka Farms Rack Truck, #04, 1957	125-150	250-300
Tonka Farms Stake Truck, #04, 1959	50-75	125-150
Tonka Tanker, #145, 1960-61	150-200	325-350
Tonka Toy Transport, #140, red roof, 1950-52	150-175	200-250
Tractor and Carry-All, #120, 1949-50	75-150	200-275
Trencher, #534, 1963	25-50	50-75

Tonka Trucks.

Toy and Miniature Soldiers

The soldiers in the following section are lead. Of the various producers of toys and miniature soldiers, we chose Britains, Mignot and Courtenay.

In 1893 William Britain, founder of a London toy firm, and his sons developed hollow-cast lead toy soldiers. They were cheaper to produce and ship than earlier solid figures. They were packaged in distinctive red boxes with elaborate labels. They established 54mm (2.125") as a standard size, and by the early 1900s were outproducing their German and French competitors. Britains production reached a peak between the two world wars and in the 1950s. Pre–World War II sets usually command a premium price and are listed as pre-war in the descriptions below. Production of hollow-cast lead figures ceased in 1966. The company now produces a new line of metal toy soldiers and plastic figures. Because Britains improved designs and updated uniforms over the years, there can be many variations of the same set. For further information see *Collecting Foreign-Made Toy Soldiers* by Richard O'Brien (Krause Publications, Iola, WI, 1997).

Three French toy makers founded C.B.G. Mignot in the 1820s. The firm is known for fine quality 55mm toy soldiers representing the French army, with special emphasis on the Napoleonic Wars and World War I. Although still in existence, production is limited, and figures are made for collectors rather than children. The sets listed below were made in the 1970s and 1980s. Dates following descriptions refer to the period of the unit represented rather than the year of production.

Although Richard Courtenay began by producing a line of toy figures in the 1920s, he is best known for his line of high quality, miniature medieval knights, produced from 1938 to 1963. These spectacular figures are now highly sought by connoisseur collectors. The figures represent knights of the 100 Years War, specifically, the Battle of Poitiers (1356). Courtenay assigned numerical designations according to the position of the knight, e.g. a knight lunging with battle ax is position 7. We have listed position numbers in the descriptions below. Courtenay signed many of his figures but not all. An unsigned figure will bring approximately 20% less than the prices listed.

We list two price ranges for Britains and Mignot sets: one for excellent unboxed sets, the second for excellent to near mint condition sets in the original boxes. Courtenay figures are listed with one range for excellent to near mint condition, no box. Set numbers and the number of figures are included for Britains. Prices are based primarily on recent auction results.

Britains

	# FIGS.	SET #	UNBOXED	BOXED
4th Queen's Own Hussars	5	8	$50-$75	$100-$150
5th Dragoon Guards, pre-war	5	3	200-250	300-350
16th Century Knights in Armour	9	1307	50-75	75-125
16th Queen's Lancers, pre-war	5	33	100-125	150-175
Arabs of the Desert	5	164	50-75	100-115
Arabs of the Desert, pre-war	5	193	200-300	350-450
Arabs of the Desert, pre-war	13	223	175-225	250-350
Band of the Coldstream Guards	21	37	500-600	650-750
Band of the Life Guards	12	101	150-200	250-350
Beefeaters, Outriders, and Footmen of the Royal Household	18	1475	100-150	200-300
Belgian Army–Le Regiment Des Grenadiers	8	2009	50-75	100-125
Belgium Army–Infantry of the Line	14	1383	50-100	125-185
Bersaglieri and Italian Cavalry, pre-war	13	1368	500-750	1000-1035
Bikanir Camel Corps, pre-war	3	123	250-350	450-550
Black Watch Colour Party	6	2111	200-300	400-500
British Infantry	8	1858	15-30	35-50
British Infantry	25	1614	75-100	125-150
British Machine Gun Section, pre-war	12	198	20-40	50-70

	# FIGS.	SET #	UNBOXED	BOXED
Bulgarian Infantry, pre-war	8	172	500-650	700-800
Capetown Highlanders	8	1901	125-175	200-230
City Imperial Volunteers	10	104	1250-1300	1300-1380
Coldstream Guard Band	21	37	150-175	200-250
Coldstream Guards	8	120	50-65	75-95
Colour Party of the Scots Guards, pre-war	7	460	125-150	175-230
Cowboys Mounted, pre-war	6	179	20-40	50-70
Cowboys on Foot	9	1252	125-150	200-250
Cuirassiers, pre-war	5	138	150-175	200-300
Devonshire Regiment 11th Foot, pre-war	7	110	75-100	120-140
Drums and Bugles	6	30	75-125	150-175
Egyptian Cavalry	5	115	50-75	100-150
French Army Cuirassiers	5	138	75-100	125-160
French Foreign Legion	7	1711	90-120	150-200
General Staff Officers	4	201	100-125	150-175
Gordon Highlanders, pre-war	8	77	75-100	120-150
Governor-General's Foot Guards	8	1634	50-75	75-100
Grenadier Guards	3	1283	25-50	75-95
Gun Detachment	8	1730	75-90	100-120
Highlanders Light Infantry, pre-war	8	213	400-450	500-550
Historical Series Set	10	1874	400-500	700-900
Historical Series Yeoman of the Guard	9	1257	30-40	50-80
Indian Army (13th Duke of Connaught's Own Lancers)	5	66	50-75	100-115
Indian Army Service Corps, pre-war	15	1893	200-250	300-400
Infanterie De Ligne, pre-war	8	1410	30-40	50-60
Irish Free State Infantry, pre-war	8	1603	150-175	200-230
Italian Carabinieri, pre-war	8	1437	200-250	300-350
Knights of the Middle Ages	11	1308	90-120	150-200
Life Guards, pre-war	5	1	100-125	150-175
Life Guards, pre-war	5	400	150-200	240-280
Los Rurales De La Federacion, Mexico's Pride	8	186	350-450	500-700
Mobile Howitzer Unit	4	1727	200-300	400-500

U.S. Army Military Band, Active Service Dress, No. 1301, c1940, $2000-$2500.

Above: Britains, Royal Marines, No. 35, pre-war, boxed set of 8, $150-$200.

Above: Britains, United States of Soviet Russia Infantry, No. 133, pre-war, boxed set of 8, $431 at auction

Below: Britains, Corps of Madras Pioneers, No. 67, pre-war, boxed set of 8, $431 at auction. —Photos courtesy William Doyle Galleries.

	# FIGS.	SET #	UNBOXED	BOXED
Mountain Artillery Team, pre-war	11	28	200-300	400-600
New Zealand Infantry	7	1542	90-120	150-200
Ninth Lancers, pre-war	5	24	200-300	450-550
North West Mounted Police	5	1349	50-75	100-125
Officers of the General Staff	4	201	75-100	125-150
Pilot's of the Royal Air Force	8	1894	200-250	275-320
Queen's Own Cameron Highlanders, pre-war	8	114	200-300	350-450
Red Army Infantry Guards	8	2027	90-120	150-175
Royal Army Medical Corps/Doctors and Nurses, pre-war	7	320	225-250	325-375
Royal Army Medical Corps Stretcher Party	8	2132	80-100	150-200
Royal Artillery Mountain Battery	7	28	150-200	200-300
Royal Horse Artillery, pre-war	13	39	300-350	500-600
Royal Horse Guards, pre-war	5	2	80-100	150-175
Royal Navy Landing Party	11	79	75-100	125-150
Russian Cavalry	5	136	200-225	250-275
Scots Guards and 1st Life Guards in Winter Dress	8	429	225-250	325-375
Sons of the Empire-Our Indian Army, pre-war	13	64	1700-1800	1900-2000
South African Mounted Infantry, pre-war	5	38	900-1000	1100-1150
Sovereign's Standard	7	2067	200-250	300-400
Spanish Infantry, pre-war	8	92	900-1000	1100-1150
Staff Officers	5	1907	125-150	180-230
State Coach	11	1470	200-250	275-320
Swedish Army–Svea Livgarde	7	2035	75-100	125-150
Turcos, light blue, pre-war	8	191	70-100	130-160
Turkish Cavalry, pre-war	5	71	800-850	900-975
Uruguayan Infantry, pre-war	8	222	575-625	650-700
U.S. Marines, pre-war	8	228	70-100	130-160
U.S. Military Band, pre-war	12	1301	80-100	150-200
U.S. West Point Cadets	8	229	50-75	100-125
Zouaves, pre-war	8	192	150-175	200-250
Zulus	8	147	125-150	175-220

Courtenay

	SINGLE FIGURE
Boy Prince Philip "Le Hardi," position 21	$300-$350
Erie of Armagnac, position Z-5	350-450
Erle of Rochechouaret, position 12	350-450
Fallen Knight, Sieur de la Rosay, position 13	350-450
French Knight Matthew de Rouvray, position 7	350-450
King John of France, position 3	350-450
Lord de Chargny, position 6	600-800
Lord de la Warr, position 15	300-350
Pierre, Sieur de Loigny, position 15	600-800
Sieur de Basentian, position 14	300-400
Sieur John de Landis, position Z-2	300-400
Sir Bartholomew Burghursh, position H-1	500-700
Sir John de Clinton, position H-2	600-800
Sir John Treffrey, position X-2	350-450
Sir Nele Loring, K. G., position H-6	700-900
Sir Thomas Warenhale, position H-3	600-800

Mignot

	FIG. #	UNBOXED	BOXED
British Grenadiers of the 33rd Regiment (1776)	12	$200-$220	$220-$320
Garde Imperiale De Russe, #228	6	200-250	250-350
Mounted Grenadier Guards	6	100-200	300-500
New England Regiment (1775)	12	175-220	225-350
New York Regiment, with officer, flag bearer, and drummer (1775)	12	100-200	200-350
Royal Deux Ponts Regiment (1779)	12	175-220	225-350
World War I German Triplane	2	150-200	200-350

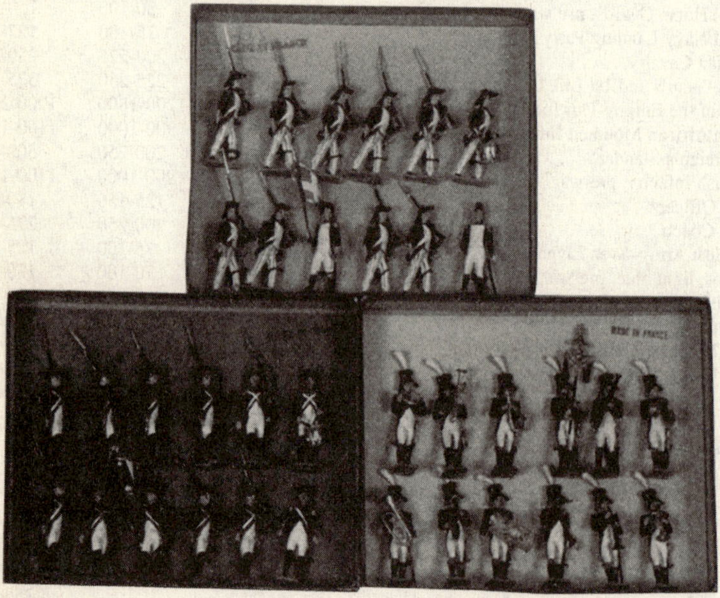

Mignot Soldiers at auction, top: Infantry of the Ligne, boxed set of 12, $287. Bottom, left to right: Band of the Imperial Guard of Honor of Strasbourg (1805), boxed set of 12, $488; Band of the Imperial Guard of Honor of Strasbourg (1805), boxed set of 12, $488. —Photo courtesy William Doyle Galleries.

Trolls

Do you have trolls? You may have them or remember them from the mid-1960s to the early 1970s. Although trolls have existed in folklore for hundreds of years, the trolls we are addressing trace their roots to the late 1950s in Denmark, when Thomas Dam made a troll for his daughter. By the mid-1960s Dam produced and exported the dolls with crazy hair and scrunched-up faces. They were a sensation which, in turn, created a troll-collecting frenzy and competition for Dam from Scandia House (they later joined forces) and Uneeda Doll Company, who called their trolls "Wishniks." There were also lower-quality imitators. The following listing focuses on Dam and Wishniks. In the 1990s another wave of troll mania hit, introducing trolls to a younger generation. After their burst of success, the Dam toys were not available in the United States for many years. They are now marketed here as Norfins. Wishniks never really left the scene, with its company repackaging and releasing trolls over the years. Dam Trolls were the standard of the troll world, just as their successors, Norfins, are today. The troll market also boasts Russ Trolls, Magic Trolls and Treasure Trolls, and again a host of lower-quality imitators.

The following are just a few of the thousands of trolls produced. Since trolls are still manufactured and identification is an art rather than a science, do some research. Compare new and old, high quality and cheap imitators. The Dam Animals, some of the most widely sought trolls, were recast from the original molds by Norfin in 1990. They were limited to a run of 500, sold for $50 and comprise the large horse, the large cow, the large elephant and the lion. Since the edition was so limited, it probably will have little or no effect on the price of the originals. Dam Trolls may bear a variety of "Dam" markings, and Wishniks may bear the double horseshoe mark or "Uneeda Wishnik" or "Uneeda Dolls."

The prices below are based on items in excellent to mint condition with original clothing, accessories and tags. Packaging is not as important as in other areas but it always adds value and desirability. Permanent marks and stains on the trolls themselves, as well as damaged hair and clothes, adversely affect value. Clothing and accessories are an important factor in determining value. Many times trolls are redressed or missing part of their original ensemble. Replacement clothes may add some value to an otherwise undressed troll, but crisp, bright original clothes with original accessories demand the highest values. The following descriptions list what is currently known as outfits and accessories for the specific troll.

For further information refer to *Trolls: Identification and Price Guide* by Debra Clark, Hobby House, Cumberland, MD, 1993 and *Collector's Guide to Trolls* by Pat Peterson, Collector Books, Paducah, KY, 1995. See also the newsletter *Troll Monthly*, 216 Washington St., Canton, MA 02021.

	LOW	HIGH
Baseball Player, blonde hair, blue eyes, black and white striped outfit, black felt cap, Wishnik, 6.5" h	$25	$50
Bride-Nik, red hair, cotton and lace gown, Wishnik, 6" h	10	25
Cave Girl, blonde hair, soft flannel leopard skin outfit with matching hair ribbon, Dam, 3" h	15	30
Caveman, yellow hair, green eyes, leopard skin outfit, Dam, 12" h	110	150
Cowboy, blonde hair, brown eyes, Wishnik, 6.5" h	25	50
Cowboy, yellow hair, amber eyes, red checked shirt, tulip motif scarf, light blue jeans, flocked thin plastic hat, Wishnik, 3.5" h	10	20
Good Night-Nik, pink hair, amber eyes, yellow felt nightshirt, Wishnik, 5" h	15	25
Indian, black hair, amber eyes, brown cotton costume with yellow zig-zag stitching, Dam, 3" h	10	20
Rock-Nik, black hair, amber eyes, 1-pc. red and blue costume with sequins, Wishnik, 6" h	10	20
Sock-It-To-Me, white hair, Wishnik, 6" h	40	60
Tartan Girl, black hair with plaid ribbons, plaid shirt with black apron skirt, Dam, 12" h	110	170

View-Master

Visitors to the 1939 World's Fair were treated to many spectacular new inventions, including the View-Master, which was introduced there by Sawyer. The invention of Harry Gruber, View-Master produced reels for the war effort. Pre-1945 single reels were either dark blue with a gold sticker or blue and tan. These early reels command a premium price among collectors. After the war, Sawyer did numerous travel site and National Parks reels. In 1952 they purchased their competitor, Tru-Vue, thereby acquiring the licensing rights to Disney productions. Some of the most sought after reel packs are those depicting classic TV shows and cartoons from the 1950s and 1960s. There is a lot of cross-over collecting from the television memorabilia field. The firm stopped selling three-packs in 1980 but are still in business. Having been owned by five different companies, including Sawyer and GAF, they are now owned by Tyco. Collectors love the frozen-time aspect of View-Master, this century's stereoscope.

The prices below are based on items in near mint to mint condition, which means no damage to the reels or package, including all flaps (4). If the package states that instructions were enclosed they should be present. Blister packs should display virtually no signs of wear. We removed "The" from several titles in order to make the listings easier to use. Dates are approximate and the number of each pack is listed after the date.

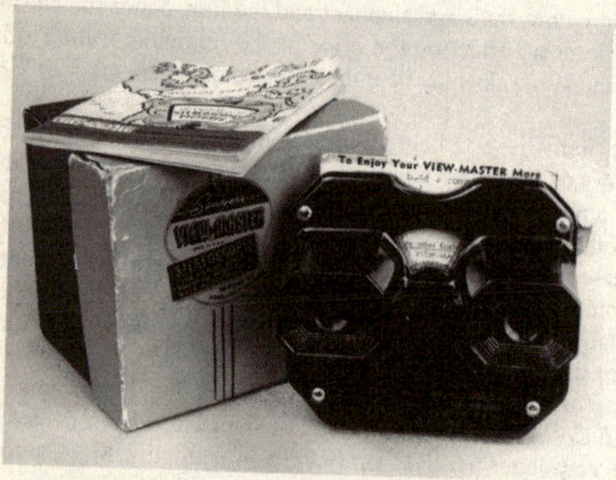

Sawyer's De Luxe Stereoscope, black Bakelite, original box, instruction card, and catalog, 1948, $25-$50.

Reels

	LOW	HIGH
A Day at the Circus I, Ringling Bros. and Barnum & Bailey, 702	$2	$4
Adventures of Tom Sawyer, "Sam Flies to the Moon," SAM-1	3	5
Alaska Bound, 301	2	6
Antigua and Lake Atitlan, Guatemala, 553	8	12
Baseball Stars of the Major Leagues III, 725	10	20
Beautiful Caverns of Luray I, VA, SP-9026	2	5
Berthoud Pass, Highway 40, Rocky Mountains, SP-237	2	5
Bird Sanctuary, Bonaventure Island, Quebec, Canada, 1951, SP-9067	5	10
Calcutta, India, 1949, 4305	2	4
Carlsbad Caverns National Park, 251	2	6
Cathedral of St. John the Divine, A6631	5	15
Cedar Breaks National Monument, UT, SP-231	5	10
Cinderella and the Glass Slipper, FT5	2	4
City of Canberra, Australia, 5025	8	15
Corn Palace, Mitchell, SD, M501	2	6
Festivals of Japan, 4873	3	5

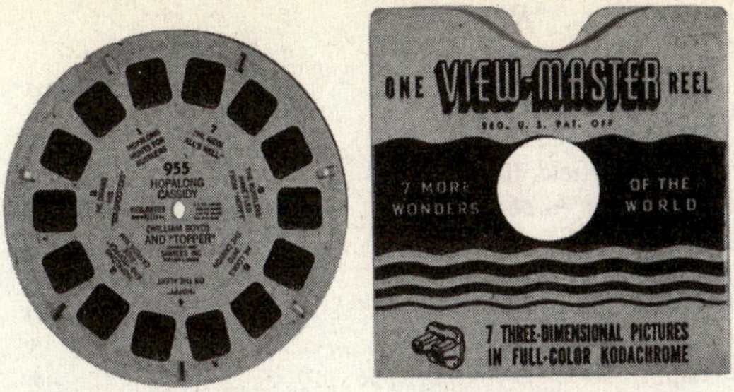

Hopalong Cassidy, #955, $5-$10.

	LOW	HIGH
Fresisland Beauty Spots, Holland, 1944	6	10
Garden of the Gods, Colorado, 51	2	4
Gettysburg National Military Monument, PA, 348	5	10
Goldilocks and the Three Bears, FT6	2	4
Highland Scenes, Scotland, 1210	8	15
H.M.S. *Queen Mary*, England	15	25
Home of Santa's Workshop, North Pole, NY, 9058	2	6
Jerusalem, The Old City, Palestine, 1948, 4000	2	5
Kangaroo Hunt with Aborigines of Australia, 5020	2	5
Kenora and Lake of the Woods, Ontario, Canada, 1951, SP-9069	2	5
Kew Gardens, London, England, 1009	12	20
Key West and Overseas Highway, 170	5	10
Lassie and Timmy in "The Runaway Mule," B4721	10	20
Marine Studios, St. Augustine, 166	2	4
Melbourne, Australia, 5043	10	15
Movie Stars, Hollywood I, 740	10	20
National Museum of Western Colorado, 1949, SP-9043	2	5
Partridge Family, B5924	10	20
Peak District, Derbyshire, England, 1065	10	20
Pinky Lee 7-Day Reel, 750	20	30
Prehistoric Cliff Dwellers of Mesa Verde, CO, 1950, SP-9055	2	5
President Kennedy's Visit to Ireland, June 1963, 1305	50	80
Prime Minister Nehru's United States Visit, India, 4360	40	60
Rhineland I, Germany, 1515	8	15
Rock City Gardens, Lookout Mountain, TN, SP-9024	2	5
Santiago, Chile, 641	2	6
Southern Alps, South Island, New Zealand, 5301	2	5
Statue of Liberty National Monument, 87	8	10
St. Louis, MO, SP-9059	2	5
St. Paul's Cathedral, England, 1006	12	20
Tower of London, England, 1012	2	6
Trees of Mystery, Requa, CA, SP-9002	2	5
Tweetsie Railroad, Blowing Rock, NC, A8931	20	30
Tyrol, Austria	2	4
Waltzing Waters, Fort Myers, FL, J518	2	5
Waterton Lakes National Park, Canada, 321	2	4
Wedding of Princess Alexandra, England, 1120	25	50
White Sands National Monument, NM, SP-287	4	8
Wild Flowers, Rocky Mountain Region, 276	5	10
Woody Woodpecker in "The Bill Collector," 821	2	4
World's Fair Brussels, 1959, B7604	10	20

Reel Sets

	LOW	HIGH
1960 Ghent Flower Show, C353	$30	$40
Abe Lincoln's New Salem and Springfield, Ill. 1950, 298	4	6
Air Force Academy, Colorado Springs, A326	5	10
Airplanes of the World, B773	10	20
American Ballet Theater, B777	25	35
Animals of Our National Parks, H6	10	15
Badlands National Monument, SD, A489	5	8
Barbie's Around the World Trip, B500	8	15
Batman, B492	10	20
Bazooka Joe, B563	10	20
Bedknobs and Broomsticks, Disney's, B366	5	15
Bermuda, B029	10	15
Bonanza, 1971, B487	30	40
Brady Bunch, B568	10	20
Busch Gardens, #2, A143	10	15
Captain America, H43	2	5
Cat From Outer Space, Disney's, J22	2	5
Central Scotland, C329	15	25
Cheap Trick, L33	10	20
Corsica, I'lle de Beaute	15	25
Dale Evans "Queen of the West," B463	20	30
Dark Shadows, B503	15	25
Detroit Zoo, MI, A581	5	10
Dukes of Hazzard, #2, M19	2	5
Dutch Wonderland, A634	5	8
Elektra Woman, H3	5	10
Era of the Space Shuttle, M36	10	20
Fangface, K66	2	5
Flipper, B485	5	10
Garden of the Gods, CO, A336	5	10
Gay 90's Melody Museum, St. Louis, MO, A452	25	35
Golden Book Favorites, H14	2	5
Hearst Castle, A190	5	8
Horses, H5	10	15
Hydroplane Races, B945	20	30
Insect World–Entomology, B688	20	30
Japanese Village and Deer Park, A232	10	15
Knott's Berry Farm and Ghost Town, A235	12	20
Kodak Hula Show, A122	8	12
Kong, B557	5	8
Lassie and Timmy, B474	5	15
Laverne and Shirley, J20	2	6
Lion Country Safari, Kings Island, Kings Mills, OH, A603	10	20
Magic Mountain, Valencia, CA, A204	5	5
Maritime Provinces, A030	8	12
Matter and Energy–Physics, B682	5	10
Mickey Mouse in Clock Cleaners with Donald Duck and Goofy, B551	4	8
Minnesota State Parks, A511	10	20
Modern Philadelphia, A631	5	15
Monkees, B493	20	30
NASA's Lyndon B. Johnson Space Center, Houston, TX, A425	5	15
National Wax Museum, A638	5	15

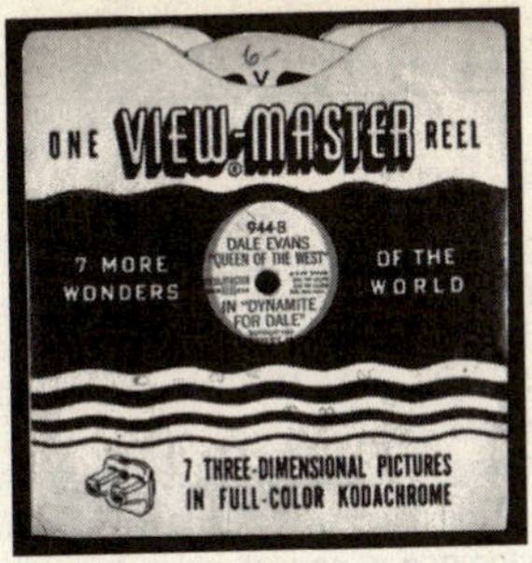

Reel Set, Dale Evans "Queen of the West," #944A, B, & C, $25-$35.

	LOW	HIGH
North and Central Wales, C338	15	25
Northern England, C340	10	20
Painted Desert and Petrified Forest, A363	2	5
Pennsylvania Dutch and Amish Country, A633	5	10
Pete's Dragon, Disney's, H38	2	6
Planet of the Apes, B507	15	20
Queen Elizabeth Visits Nigeria, B114	40	50
Rin-Tin-Tin, B467	5	15
Rowan and Martin's Laugh-In, B497	15	25
Roy Rogers "King of the Cowboys," B462	15	25
San Diego Zoo II, A197	10	15
Santa's Village, A135	10	20
Secrets of the Sea, D118E	20	30
Secret Squirrel and Atom Ant, 1966, B535	25	50
Six Flags Over Mid-America, St. Louis, A458	5	10
Sleeping Beauty, B308	2	5
Snoopy and the Red Baron, B544	2	5
Television Shows at Universal City, B477	20	30
Vacation Kingdom, Disney World, H20	2	5
Venezuela, B050	5	10
Voyage to the Bottom of the Sea, B483	10	20
West Virginia, A835	4	8
Winchester Mystery House, CA, A220	10	15
Winnie the Pooh and the Blustery Day, K37	2	5
Woody Woodpecker, Andy Panda, and Chilly Willy, B510	10	20
Woody Woodpecker Show, B508	2	5
Yosemite National Park, A171	5	8

Transportation Collectibles

Automobiles

The antique car market is coming back. Cars from the 1960s and early 1970s show increased prices even for ordinary models. Flashy cars from the late 1950s are extremely popular, especially those with big fins. However, the cars of the 1980s, even the high end models, have yet to see a return on investment for their buyers.

The cars listed in this section are divided into three categories: Good: drivable original or good amateur restoration, Fine: well-restored or well-maintained original with minimal wear, and Excellent: professional quality restoration or perfect original.

For further information see *The Official Price Guide to Collector Cars, Eighth Edition* by Robert H. Balderson, House of Collectibles, New York, 1996, and *2000 Standard Guide to Cars and Prices, 12th Edition,* edited by James T. Lenzke and Ken Buttolph, Krause Publications, Iola, WI, 1999.

Austin

	GOOD	FINE	EXC
1928, Chummy, 4 cyl.	$2000	$3000	$7088
1949, Model A90 Convertible, 4 cyl.	6000	7000	14,000
1959, Model A95 Sedan, 6 cyl.	2000	4000	10,000

Bentley

1958, Model S1 Convertible, 6 cyl.	$12,000	$36,000	$50,000
1962, Model S2 Saloon, 2-door, black	5000	10,000	15,225
1966, Mulliner-Park Ward Flying Spur, 8 cyl.	15,000	30,000	45,000
1967, Model T1 Sedan, V-8	5000	10,000	28,000
1979, Corinche Coupe, V-8	15,000	20,000	30,000

B.M.W.

1954, Model 501 Sedan, 6 cyl.	$3000	$5000	$8000
1958, Isetta 300 Coupe, 1 cyl., red	5000	7000	9550
1961, Sedan, 8 cyl.	4000	6000	10,000
1969, Model 2800 Sedan, 6 cyl.	2800	4500	7000
1974, 530i Sedan, 6 cyl.	3500	5400	8000
1988, Model 325 I Convertible, 6 cyl., black	2000	4000	6300

Buick

1911, Touring Convertible, 2-door, 4 cyl., red	$7500	$12,000	$18,250
1919, High Top, 6 cyl., 4-door, black	6000	10,000	15,000
1928, Deluxe Roadster, 6 cyl., orange	3000	5000	10,000
1940, Century Convertible, 8 cyl., maroon	6000	10,000	29,000
1948, Super Convertible, 8 cyl., black	10,000	22,000	33,500
1949, Roadmaster Sedan, 4-door, 8 cyl., black	2500	5000	8250
1963, Riviera Hardtop, 2-door, V-8, white	1500	2500	7000
1965, Riviera Gran Sport, V-8, yellow	1500	3500	7850
1969, Electra 225 Convertible, V-8, gold	2000	4500	6800
1973, Riviera Boattail, V-8, black	1500	3000	4800

Cadillac

	GOOD	FINE	EXC
1931, Sedan, 4-door, V-8, black	$5000	$15,000	$23,600
1938, LaSalle Convertible, 8 cyl., cream	15,000	25,000	32,500
1941, Model 62 Convertible Coupe, 8 cyl., black	10,000	35,000	67,000
1954, Model 62 Covertible, V-8	3500	8500	17,300
1960, Eldorado Biarritz Convertible, V-8, rose	15,000	25,000	50,000
1963, Eldorado Convertible, V-8	2500	5000	10,700
1967, Deville Convertible, V-8	2000	4000	10,200
1976, Eldorado Convertible, V-8, gold	3000	6000	13,100
1976, Seville Sedan, 4-door, V-8, silver	1000	2000	4000
1977, Custom Pickup, V-8, maple	2000	4500	8000

Chevrolet

	GOOD	FINE	EXC
1929, Cabriolet, 2-door, 6 cyl., blue	$3000	$8000	$16,000
1933, Master Roadster, 6 cyl., tan	10,000	25,000	40,000
1940, Super Deluxe Sedan, 4-door, V-6, black	3500	7500	14,200
1951, Club Coupe, V-6, gray	2500	5500	7500
1955, Bel Air Hardtop, 2-door, V-8, red	7500	12,000	17,500
1956, Nomad Station Wagon, V-8, black	3000	8000	17,500
1957, Bel Air Fuelie Convertible, V-8, red	8500	18,000	27,500
1958, Impala Convertible, V-8, blue	10,000	25,000	50,000
1959, Corvette Convertible, V-8, red	6000	12,000	23,600
1961, Corvette Convertible, V-8, red	5000	10,000	20,750
1963, Corvette, 2-door, V-8, black	10,000	18,000	36,000
1963, Impala Convertible, V-8, red	3000	6000	10,500
1964, Biscayne, 2-door, V-8, black	5500	10,000	22,500
1966, Nova, 2-door, V-8, turquoise	3000	8000	15,500
1968, Camaro Z28 Super Sport, V-8, red	10,000	15,000	30,000
1969, Nova SS Hardtop, 2-door, V-8, green	2000	5000	11,000
1970, Pickup, V-8, orange	900	2000	3500
1972, Chevelle SS, 2-door, V-8, black	2000	6000	14,000
1972, Corvette Coupe, V-8, yellow	1200	3500	7500
1973, Camaro Z28 Coupe, V-8, dark blue	1000	3000	6500

Chevrolet, 1957 Nomad Bel Air Station Wagon, V-8, black, $22,313 at auction. —Photo courtesy Kruse International.

Chrysler

	GOOD	FINE	EXC
1928, Series 62 Sedan, 2-door, 6 cyl.	$5200	$7500	$10,000
1931, Imperial CG Coupe, 8 cyl.	22,000	32,000	43,000
1935, Airstream Sedan, 6 cyl.	6200	9000	13,000
1937, Royal Convertible, 6 cyl.	14,000	18,000	25,000
1940, Thunderbolt Convertible, 8 cyl.	62,000	90,000	120,000
1942, Royal Sedan, 6 cyl.	3000	4000	7000
1942, Saratoga Coupe, 8 cyl.	3000	4000	7000
1949, New Yorker Club Coupe, V-8	4000	5500	9000
1950, Royal Station Wagon, V-8	8000	12,000	20,000
1953, Windsor Convertible, V-8	9000	12,000	18,000
1959, Town & Country Station Wagon, 8 cyl.	2500	4000	6000
1962, Imperial LeBaron Hardtop, 4-door, V-8	4000	6000	9000
1964, 300-K Hardtop, 2-door, V-8	10,000	16,000	24,000

Dodge

	GOOD	FINE	EXC
1917, Model 30 Sedan, 4 cyl.	$2200	$4000	$5700
1925, Roadster, 2-door, 4 cyl.	3000	5000	7000
1926, Model 124 Sport Phaeton, 6 cyl.	3000	5000	10,000
1928, Model 130 Victoria Sedan, 2-door, 6 cyl.	2500	4000	7000
1929, Rumble Seat Roadster, 6 cyl.	4000	6500	13,800
1935, Model DU Sedan, 2-door, 6 cyl.	1500	2100	5500
1940, Model D17 Cabriolet, 6 cyl.	5000	12,000	22,000
1949, Wayfarer Roadster, 6 cyl.	4000	8000	20,000
1952, Coronet Convertible, 6 cyl.	4000	10,000	18,000
1962, Dart 440 Station Wagon, 8 cyl.	850	2000	3300
1965, Monaco Hardtop, 2-door, V-8	1200	2500	4600
1966, D200 Fleetside, V-8, white	1500	2200	3500
1966, Polara Hardtop, 2-door, V-8	900	1500	2800
1969, Dart Swinger, 8 cyl.	1200	2500	4200
1970, Superbird Hardtop, 2-door, V-8	7000	14,000	24,500
1973, Challenger Rallye, 8 cyl.	3000	5000	10,000

Chrysler, 1960, 300F Convertible, maroon, $63,000 at auction. —Photo courtesy Kruse International.

Ford

	GOOD	FINE	EXC
1911, Model T Runabout, 4 cyl.	$2500	$5000	$10,000
1920, Model T, 3-door, 4 cyl.	1000	2500	4500
1927, Rumbleseat Roadster, 4 cyl.	2000	3500	5750
1928, Model AR Phaeton, 4 cyl.	2000	5000	11,000
1929, Model AA Good Humor Ice Cream Truck, 4 cyl.	3500	6000	10,000
1929, Roadster Street Rod, V-8	4000	8000	20,000
1931, Model A Mail Truck, 4 cyl.	6500	10,000	21,000
1932, Cabriolet, V-8	4000	8000	16,500
1932, Victoria, V-8	4000	8000	23,000
1934, Phaeton, V-8	8000	15,000	27,500
1936, Pickup Truck, flathead V-8, 3-speed transmission	3500	7000	14,805
1940, Convertible, 8 cyl.	7500	15,000	32,000
1941, Convertible, V-8	4500	10,000	19,500
1949, Deluxe Club Coupe, V-8	2500	4000	7000
1950, Custom Convertible, V-8	2500	5000	12,200
1952, Crestliner Convertible, V-8	2000	7000	15,000
1955, Crown Victoria Hardtop, 2-door, V-8, white	5000	10,000	24,250
1956, Thunderbird Convertible, V-8, red	8000	12,000	20,000
1957, Fairlane Convertible, V-8, blue	7000	15,000	28,000
1957, Skyliner Retractable, V-8, green	4000	8000	15,000
1957, Thunderbird Convertible, V-8, black	6000	10,000	18,000
1959, Galaxie Retractable Hardtop, V-8, red	5000	10,000	24,000
1960, Sunliner Convertible, V-8, red	1800	4000	10,000
1962, Galaxy 500 Hardtop, 2-door, V-8, black	2500	5000	8000
1963, F100 Pickup, 4 cyl., red	1000	2500	5000
1965, Mustang Convertible, V-8, blue	3000	6000	13,200
1966, Mustang Coupe, V-8, beige	2500	5000	8500
1966, Mustang GT Convertible, V-8, red	3000	5500	12,100
1967, Mustang Shelby GT Fastback, V-8, red	4000	8000	16,900

Ford, 1931, Model A, green and black, $8800 at auction. —Photo courtesy Collectors Auction Services.

Jaguar

	GOOD	FINE	EXC
1954, Mark VII, 4-door, 6 cyl., black	$2000	$5000	$10,600
1954, XK 120 M Roadster, 4-door, 6 cyl., dark blue	10,000	18,000	23,750
1969, XKE Series II Coupe, 6 cyl., yellow	4000	5500	14,250
1986, XJSC Cabriolet, V-12, blue	2500	6000	12,800

Lincoln

1928, Model L Sedan, 4-door, V-8, green	$5000	$8000	$11,500
1939, Zephyr Convertible Sedan, green	12,000	20,000	58,000
1940, Brunn Town Car, V-12, black	10,000	25,000	45,000
1947, Continental Coupe, V-12, maroon	4200	7000	14,000
1951, Sedan, 4-door, V-8, blue	1000	2500	4500
1956, Continental Mark II Coupe, V-8, red	5000	10,000	26,250
1956, Continental Mark II Hardtop, 2-door, V-8, blue	8000	15,000	30,000
1962, Continental Convertible, V-8, white	1000	2500	4500
1966, Continental Convertible, V-8, white	2000	3500	6000
1971, Continental Mark III Hardtop, 2-door, V-8, blue	500	800	1500
1972, Continental Limousine, V-8	2500	5000	9000
1976, Continental Mark IV Coupe, 2-door, V-8, white	1000	2500	4500

Mercedes-Benz

1933, Model 380 K Cabriolet C, 8 cyl., red	$35,000	$95,000	$130,000
1957, Model 180 Sedan, 4 cyl.	3000	5000	8000
1959, Model 220 S Coupe, 6 cyl.	4000	10,000	22,000
1967, Model 280 SL Convertible, 6 cyl.	8000	15,000	30,000
1973, Model 220 Sedan, 8 cyl.	2000	4000	8500

Mercury

1970, Marquis Convertible, V-8, green	$1500	$3000	$5000
1971, Cougar Convertible, V-8, maroon	2000	3500	8500

Lincoln, 1957, Continental Mark II Hardtop, 2-door, V-8, blue, $31,500 at auction. —Photo courtesy Kruse International.

M.G.

	GOOD	FINE	EXC
1957, Model A Roadster, 4 cyl., red	$2000	$4500	$9000
1967, Model B GT, 4 cyl., green	1000	2000	4000
1972, Model MGB, Roadster, 4 cyl.	1500	3500	7000
1976, Model MG-Midget Roadster, 4 cyl.	1250	3000	4700

Nash

1919, Model 680 Sedan, 6 cyl.	$2000	$4500	$10,000
1932, Model 960 Sedan, 6 cyl.	1000	3200	8000
1935, Ambassador Sedan, 8 cyl.	1500	3000	6000
1936, LaFayette Sedan, 6 cyl.	1100	2100	6000

Oldsmobile

1932, Model F-32 Rumble Seat Coupe, 6 cyl.	$3200	$6100	$11,000
1957, Model 88 Hardtop, 2-door, V-8, white	1500	4000	7000
1968, Toronado, 2-door, V-8, maroon	900	2500	4800
1974, Delta Royale Convertible, V-8, black	3500	6500	9800
1977, Cutlass Supreme Brougham Coupe, V-8, black	2500	4500	6800

Packard

1924, Roadster, 2-door, 6 cyl., orange	$7500	$11,000	$21,500
1925, DW Phaeton, 6 cyl., silver	7000	10,000	23,000
1930, Model 740 Rumble Seat Coupe, 8 cyl., cream	7500	15,000	25,500
1941, Coupe Convertible, 8 cyl., maroon	10,000	18,000	32,000
1949, Custom 8 Sedan, 4-door, 8 cyl., beige	3000	5000	10,000

Plymouth

1937, Roadking Coupe, 6 cyl.	$2000	$4000	$7000
1948, Deluxe Coupe, black	2000	4000	7500
1949, Special Deluxe Convertible, 6 cyl.	7000	14,000	22,000
1957, Plaza Coupe, V-8	2000	3000	5000
1965, Belvedere Hardtop, 4-door, V-8, white	800	1200	2000
1967, Barracuda Coupe, V-8	6000	10,000	16,000
1970, Super Bird Hardtop, 2-door, V-8	10,000	20,000	45,000

Pontiac

1935, Deluxe Coupe, 8 cyl.	$2000	$5500	$11,000
1954, Star Chief Hardtop, 2-door, V-8	3000	7000	15,000
1965, GTO Coupe, V-8, teal	3500	7500	12,500
1967, GTO Convertible, V-8, white	6000	12,000	21,750
1967, GTO Hardtop, 2-door, V-8, white	1000	2500	6000
1972, Grand Prix Hardtop, 2-door, V-8, gold	2000	4000	6200
1974, Grand Am Hardtop, 2-door, V-8	1200	3000	4500

Automobilia

Automobilia is a catch-all category consisting of anything relating to automobiles, other than the vehicle itself. Listings include advertising and promotional items, car parts and accessories, and decorative objects fashioned either in the shape of or with an image of an automobile. For more information see *The Official Price Guide to Automobilia* by David K. Bausch (House of Collectibles, New York, 1996).

Bulb Kit, Packard, tin box, 6 bulbs, 4" l box, $303 at auction. —Photo courtesy Collectors Auction Services.

	LOW	HIGH
Air Pump Stand, cast iron, fluted pedestal base, Gilbert & Barker Gilbarco Air Meter #4-6598X, restored, 41" h, 12" w	$250	$300
Ashtray, Champion Ford Spark Plug, ceramic, center spark plug, bottom stamped "Champion Sill-Manite," 3.5" h, 5" d	100	150
Ashtray, Phillips 66, tire shaped, rubber, glass tray, "Miller's Super Service Oakland, Iowa," original box, 6.5" d	100	125
Attendants' Cap, Mobil Service, cloth, plastic rim, 5" h, 10" w, 11" l	100	150
Badge, Highway Trailer Co., silvered metal, depicts truck trailer centered by "362" serial number, inscription "Hazleton, Pa.," c1950	15	25
Badge, Shell Oil Co., "Approved Shell Service," metal, bronze luster finish, c1930s	100	200
Badge, United Valets Corporation, celluloid, c1930s	25	50
Bank, Phillips 66, glass, "Phill-up with Phillips 66/See what you save," 4.75" h, 4.75" w	100	150
Blotter, Gargoyle Lubricants, leather, gilt lettering, 6.75" h, 3.25" w	50	75
Book, *With Jack and Jill in Motor-Car-Land,* "The History of the Packard: Ask the Man Who Owns One," c1933	65	75
Bottle Rack, Mobiloil Gargoyle, metal frame, 2 porcelain 1-sided signs on sides, 24.5" h, 30" l	1000	1200
Brochure, Firestone, 1939 New York World's Fair, "Firestone Builds Today the Tire of Tomorrow"	10	20
Brochure, Franklin, H. H. Franklin Mfg. Co., Syracuse, NY, 1906	275	300
Brochure, International Body Works, Chicago, IL, "Distributors of custom built bodies for Fords and Chevrolets," c1925	20	40
Calendar, 1913, Marble City Garage, litho scene of woman w/ roses climbing into automobile	500	600
Calendar, 1920, Chevrolet Motor Cars	140	150
Calendar, 1930, Goodyear Tires, baby in tub	10	20
Calendar, 1937, Mobilgas, "Along the Magnolia Trail," 11.5" x 13"	100	200
Calendar, 1938, Gilmore Gasoline, litho paper graphic of girl w/ Scottie dogs tangled around her legs, Slugren/Botkins Gilmore Service San Diego, CA, 15.25" h, 7" w	20	40
Can, Hy-Grade Phillips Motor Oil, tin, .5 gal, 6.25" h, 8" w, 3.25" l	150	200

	LOW	HIGH
Can, Pep Boys Lighter Fluid, tin, "1934 The Pep Boys Manny, Moe, and Jack" at bottom, 5.25" h, 2.5" d	175	200
Can, Phillips 66 Motor Oil, tin, "Phillips Petroleum Company, Bartlesville, Oklahoma," 1 gal, 11.5" h, 8" w	300	500
Chalkboard Thermometer, "Nor'way Reliable Service Anti-Freeze," self-framed tin, 22.25" h, 15.25" w	100	150
Change Purse, leather and metal, "Compliments of Studebaker Bros. Co., Portland, Oregon"	25	50
Clicker, Benzo-Gas, litho tin, "Does What Gasoline Can't," 1930s	50	75
Clock, wind-up, Packard Motor, metal, porcelain cloisonné, slug plate inscribed "J. E. Land" under "Master Salesman 1926," Seth Thomas, 4 jewels, 5.25" h, 4" w	2000	3000
Club Kit, Jaguar Drivers Club, includes metal license plate attachment #5301, Jaguar Drivers Club decal, and Jaguar plastic license holder, original box, 5" h, 3.5" w	60	80
Credit Card, Texaco, paper, #66574, May, Jun., Jul., and Aug., 1949, purchase coupons attached	125	175
Desk Accessory, Bennett Gasoline & Oil, cast metal truck mounted on woodbase, 3" h, 7.25" l	125	175
Desktop Accessory Box, Comfort Tires, pressed glass, tire shaped, worn black and silver paint, 3.5" h, 3" d	200	250
Display, GE Mazda Lamps, litho tin, electric, w/ bulbs, "How Are You Fixed For Lamps?," 22.5" h, 27.5" w, 25.5" l	450	500
Display, Leader Spark Plugs, cardboard, wood top and base, label on top marked "This cabinet and contents is the property of Leader Products Corporation, New York, N.Y.," 10.25" h, 15" w, 4" l	300	400
Display, Rusco Fan Belts, metal, wood base, w/ 2 belts, marked "The Russell Mfg. Co. Middletown, Conn.," 16.75" h, 12.5" w, 22" l	150	200
Fan, flapper girl seated in 1920s car, Marrell Inns advertisement	25	30
Flange Sign, "Houdaille Shock Absorber Service," painted metal, marked "Made in U.S.A.," 19.75" h, 26.25" w	70	90
Flange Sign, "Oldfield Tires," porcelain, 2-sided, 16.5" h, 21.25" w	700	900
Flange Sign, "Replace with a Delco/The Original Equipment Battery," painted metal, 2-sided, marked "AM 9-55 Made in U.S.A. From A 353," 18" h, 22.5" w	125	175
Flange Sign, "Stop Here for Silver Edge Raybestos Brake Service," metal, 2-sided, Shank Sign Co., NY, 14" h, 18.5" w	400	450
Game, Champion Spark Plug, 1935, 21" x 12" fold-out size	60	75
Game, Get That License, Selchow & Righter, 1955	20	40
Game, Taxi, Selchow & Righter, 1960	10	20
Game, The Auto Game, Milton Bradley, c1906	250	350
Gas Globe, Holiday Regular 94 Octane, glass body, metal base, 2 lenses, 13.5" d	500	700
Gas Globe, National White Rose Ethyl, glass body, 2 lenses, 13.5" d	350	400
Gear Shift Knob, onyx, variegated white and rust swirl, metal insert, 1" h, 1.75" d	20	40
Instruction Manual, Volkswagen, for sedan and convertible, black and white, blue insert, soft cover, 88 pages, 5.625" x 7.875"	10	15
Jigsaw Puzzle, 60's Chevys: For 1960 Chevy's Got 'Em All!, 12 pcs., cardboard, 1960 Corvair in front of U.S. Capitol, Shilling Chevrolet Co. advertising on back of flap, original package	20	40
Jigsaw Puzzle, Dunlop Circular Picture Puzzle, 600 pcs., 19" d, original box, c1970	20	40
Keychain Flicker Tag, Chevron Supreme Gasoline, cardboard, 1960s	50	75

License Plate, Oklahoma, 1957, $28 at auction. —Photo courtesy Collectors Auction Services.

	LOW	HIGH
Keychain Fob, Chevrolet, celluloid, local service station name on back panel, c1930s	15	25
Keychain Fob, Yellow Cab Co., figural, diecut brass profile image of taxi cab, reverse engraved "Phone 8800 Gaspee" and "653" serial number, 1930s	75	100
Keychain Holder, Sinclair H-C Gasoline, yellow plastic tube, removable cap, red and green logo w/ name and address of local Sinclair Oil Products dealer in Hanover, PA, 1930-40s	25	50
Key Holder, Gulf Oil, plastic, orange and blue logo w/ "Ask The Pro From Gulf," c1950s	15	25
Lap Blanket, fur front, wool backing, 53.5" h, 71" w	30	50
License Plate, Arizona, Apache #YD, 1936	20	40
License Plate, Connecticut, #4123, 1934	10	15
License Plate, Kentucky, Boone #37635, 1935	10	30
License Plate, Maine, #37518, 1942	2	8
License Plate, New Hampshire, #A34, commercial, 1960	10	20
License Plate, New Hampshire, #2434, tractor, 1968	5	10
License Plate, New York, #S9580, 9A, 1936	10	30
License Plate, Pennsylvania, tractor, 1915	100	125
License Plate, Vermont, #35787, 1929	10	20
License Plate, Wisconsin, #VET 423, disabled vet, 1976	2	8
License Plate Attachment, "C.S.E.A.," porcelain, metal stand, reverse stamped "Irvine & Jachens S.F. 6838," 5.5" h, 3.5" w	20	40
License Plate Attachments, Phillips 66, diecut tin, 6" h, 6" w, price for pair	250	300
Lighter, metal, Chevy logo and tinted color image of Chevy passenger car, 1960s	15	25
Magazine, *Rambler,* 1908	100	125
Magazine Tear Sheet, Packard, *Ladies Home Journal,* 1930s	5	10
Magazine Tear Sheet, Rambler, *Country Life,* c1905	5	10
Map, Chevron, 1938	10	20
Map, Michigan, 1955	5	15
Map, Standard Oil of Indiana, 1936	5	15
Map, Trailways Bus Time Tables, Florida West Coast, 1945	10	20
Notepad, Columbus Buggy Co., Columbus, OH, 1903-13	35	40
Operator Badge, taxicab driver, silvered brass, inscribed "1963-64 Taxicab Driver/City of Flint," w/ engraved "339" operator number	25	50
Paperweight, brass, embossed car and "Ask the Man Who Owns One/ Packard Motor Car Co. Detroit, Mich.," 3.5" w	300	350
Photograph, Ford, Bell Telephone Model T service truck, mounted on trimmed card, c1913, 7" x 5"	65	75
Pinback Button, Chevrolet, "Baltimore Zone Jamboree 1937," celluloid, blue on white ground	15	25
Pinback Button, "Chevrolet/Try It," 1930s	15	25
Pinback Button, Knox Motor Car, oval photo of touring car w/ "Touring New England/1909 Models," c1900-13	25	50

	LOW	HIGH
Pinback Button, Maxwell Motor Car, celluloid, green and black open coupe w/ spoked wheels on gold ground, "Perfectly Simple–Simply Perfect," c1910	75	100
Pinback Button, Pyro-Action Spark Plugs, "Crusade Against Spark Plug Paralysis–Sponsored By Robert Bosch," c1920s	15	25
Pinback Button, Studebaker, celluloid, wheel motif, Bastian Bros., .875" d	50	70
Pocket Watch, Swiss, silver case, 1900 automobile w/ driver and passenger in relief, 2" d	275	300
Salt and Pepper Shakers, pair, Phillips 66, plastic, 2.75" h	40	75
Sheet Music, *The Little Ford Rambled Right Along,* C. R. Foster and Byron Gay, c1915	20	25
Sign, "Approved Western Motor Association Inc. Motor Court," porcelain, 2-sided, 27.5" h, 29" w	40	50
Sign, "Cadillac Certified Craftsman," aluminum, 1-sided, 12" h, 10" w	150	200
Sign, "Chevrolet," diecut porcelain, 1-sided, 12" h, 36" w	800	1000
Sign, "Ford/Deary Garage, Sales, Service, Deary Idaho," 6.5" h, 28.125" w	300	350
Sign, "Fortune Ethyl Gasoline, painted metal, 1-sided, 9" h, 12" w	400	600
Sign, "Gargoyle Mobiloil Certified Service," porcelain, 1-sided, 19.5" h, 19.5" w	200	300
Sign, "GMC Trucks," porcelain, 2-sided, 24" h	500	550
Sign, "Member Portland Automotive Trades Association," porcelain, 2-sided, 19" h, 17.25" w	250	400
Sign, "OK Used Cars," tin, 1-sided, wood frame, 20" h, 96" w	300	400
Sign, "Wings Regular Gasoline," porcelain, 1-sided, 6" h, 7" w	1500	2000
Soap Dispenser, Phillips, stainless steel, plastic window	150	200
Spark Plug, Autolite, BT6, 18mm	75	125
Spark Plug, Champion, C10S, shielded plug	2	5
Spark Plug, Hitachi	5	7
Spark Plug, Mosler Spit Fire, green letters	10	20
Spark Plug, Moto Meter	30	40
Stickpin, brass, 5-pointed star w/ inscription "Studebaker" in center, c1900-20s	50	75
Stickpin, brass, Ford emblem w/ inscription and Becker Auto Co.," c1920s	50	75
Stickpin, brass, image of rabbit running at full speed w/ "Apperson Motor Car," c1920-26	50	75
Stickpin, sterling silver, miniature horseless carriage w/ inscription "Olds Motor Works, Detroit Mich. U.S.A.," late 1890s	50	75
Tape Measure, Chevrolet, white celluloid canister, 1 side w/ black emblem and "For Economical Transportation," reverse w/ local dealership in Chicago, c1920-30s	25	50
Thermometer, "Call A Lincoln/Lincoln Cab Co.," wood, glass tube, metal holders, 15" h, 4" w	70	90
Thermometer, "Shell Gasoline/Shell Motor Oil, pat. Mar. 16, 1915," porcelain, 27" h, 7.25" w	1700	2000
Tin, Pep Boys Handy Bulb Kit, depicts Manny, Moe, and Jack, advertises Cornell Tires and Cadet Batteries on sides, 2.5" h, 4" w	50	75
Trophy, metal and silver plate, Chicago Automobile Club 1914, Frank E. Rose Trophy presented to Joseph Eliot Callender, 10" h, 7" w, 4.75" l	125	150
Watch Fob, National Motorcycle Gypsy Tour, silvered brass, depicts driver and passenger in sidecar motorcycle within patriotic shield design, reverse inscription "Perfect Score/Federation Of American Motorcyclists/ National Tour 1918"	200	400
Whistle, litho tin, double reed, "Whistle For A Yellow Cab Or Dial 5441," 1930s	25	50

Aviation

Aviation memorabilia ranges from the era of early flight—in balloons, bi-planes and airships—through the period of early scheduled commercial transcontinental Clipper flight and World War II combat flight, to the present day of commercial jets and space exploration. As with other commercial enterprises, those offering service to the public distinguished their particular operations by the type and design of objects used in passenger service, such as dining china and silver, in-flight giveaways and flight badges and uniforms. These items, together with passenger timetables, promotional photographs of aircraft, early calendars, airport-related objects (e.g., ashstands with metal aircraft figures, restaurant and earlier souvenir china), and crash fragments are highly collectible.

Advertising Tin, transportation motif w/ airplane, zeppelin, train, and car in country setting, 7" h, $44 at auction. —Photo courtesy Collectors Auction Services.

	LOW	HIGH
Address Book/Telephone Note Pad, blue and white, Charles Lindbergh, the *Spirit of St. Louis,* and "New York/Paris," Peoples National Bank, Delta, PA advertisement, 3.25" x 4.25"	$150	$250
Ashtray, British Overseas Airways Corp., white china, Spode China by Copeland of England, 6" d	50	100
Ashtray, Mexicana Airlines, stainless steel	4	6
Ashtray, Piper Planes, aluminum tray w/ embossed rim inscription "Fly Piper Planes" and center image of single engine passenger aircraft, 1950s, 4.5" d	15	50
Baggage Sticker, TWA, paper, full color portrait of saluting stewardess by George Petty, blue and red "Keep 'Em Flying," unused, 1940s, 3.5" x 5.5"	15	50
Book, *Airplanes in Action,* Whitman, 40 pages, ©1938, 5.25" x 6.5"	25	75
Book, *American Racing Planes and Historic Air Races,* Reed Kinert, Wilcox & Follet Co., 130 pages, hardcover, ©1952, 9.5" x 12.25"	25	75
Book, *Byrd Antarctic Expedition,* Tide Water Oil Co. premium, 32 pages, sepia photos from 1927-30 expedition, ©1930, 8.5" x 11.5"	25	75
Booklet, "From Travel Air To Tristar, The First Fifty Years of Delta Air-Lines, 1929-1970"	4	6
Booklet, "Lindbergh's Decorations and Trophies," multicolored, soft cover w/ *Spirit of St. Louis* over ocean waves, pictures of awards and trophies, ©1935, 7.5" x 10.5"	20	60

	LOW	HIGH
Bookmark/Letter Opener, blade and shield emblem, "Duralumin Used In The Airship 'Akron' Made By The Goodyear Zeppelin Corporation/ Akron, Ohio" below image of airship in flight, 1920-30s, 1.25" x 5"	25	75
Brochure, Piedmont Airlines, F-27 on front and back, "F-27 New Pacemakers Coming Soon on Piedmont Airlines," 9.75" x 4"	10	30
Calendar, TWA, 1950	10	30
Cap Badge, TWA	25	50
Card Game, Around the World w/ the Graf Zeppelin, J. W. Spear & Sons, NY	100	300
Coffeepot, Pan Am, International Silver Co., 1940s	100	300
Compact, Lindbergh photo, "Lindy" powder puff label, 2" d	300	400
Cup, American Airlines, silver plated, black wood handle, relief "AA" eagle emblem, 1930s, 2.25" h, 2.5" d	50	100
Cup and Saucer, United Airlines, white china, swirl pattern, gold rim and logo	20	50
Drinking Glass, Eastern Airlines, blue and red painted logo w/ Rickenbacker top hat symbol and facsimile signature, "New Type Constellation" and "Compliments of Eastern Air Lines" perimeter inscriptions, 1930s, 4.75" h	25	75
Flight Bag, Northwest Airlines, gray nylon, zipper top and side pocket, grab handles, red and white logo on sides	10	30
Flight Map, Northwest Airlines, Northwest Passage Coast-to-Coast Air Map and Flight Log, 20 pages, maps and photos, 1945	10	25
Flight Map, TWA Air Routes in the United States, 1956	5	10
Fork, United Airlines, silverplate, "United" engraved near handle tip w/ stylized emblem, Silver Co., 1930s	50	100
Handkerchief, cotton, black and white image of Lindbergh and "Lindy–So this is Paris!–Compliments of the Multistamp Co of NY"	100	200
Lapel Pin, Chicago Airport, stylized "V" w/ airplane diving in center, gilt w/ black enamel highlights, J. O. Pollack Co.	10	30
Lighter, silver plate, criss cross pattern designs on sides w/ "Fly JAL," Crown, 2.5" h	10	30
Magazine, *Air Trails,* 3 issues, May, June, July 1938, 8.5" x 11.5"	25	75
Magazine, *Model Airplane News,* 3 issues, July, Aug., Sept. 1941, 8.5" x 11.5"	25	75
Magazine, *Time,* Jan. 2 1928, Charles Lindbergh "Man of the Year," 8" x 11"	15	50
Match Holder, metal, oval celluloid insert w/ image of Lindbergh and "Farmers & Merchants National Bank, Baltimore," 2" x 2.75"	400	500
Needle Book, Trans-Atlantic Aeroplane, diecut cardboard, full color art, 1920-30s, 2.25" x 3.25"	50	100
Nut Dish, TWA, silver plated, scalloped, TWA logo, International Silver Co., 9" d	20	60
Pennant, La Guardia Airport, NY, felt, picture of TWA 4-engine passenger plane, 1940s, 5" x 10.5"	25	75
Pin, figural airplane, wood, w/ mechanical propeller, "*Spirit of St. Louis*/ NX211" on wing, 2.5" l	250	350
Pinback Button, "Cleveland National Air Races," red, white, and blue, 1930s	25	75
Pinback Button, image of Amelia Earhart w/ "Amelia Earhart Putnam," and "1st Woman Trans-Atlantic Solo Flight–May 21, 1932	15	30
Pinback Button, image of Lindbergh above U.S. shield, red, white, and blue, off-center, 1.25" d	50	70
Plaque, *Spirit of St. Louis* and NY Statue of Liberty above "Lindbergh 1927," embossed gold and white painted metal, back has label w/ flight information and "Printed in England," 4.75" x 6"	150	200
Playing Cards, Capital Airlines Viscount	25	75

	LOW	HIGH
Pocket Watch, silvered metal case, Lindbergh flight commemorative, dial face depicts aircraft above inscription "New York to Paris Air Plane Model," bezel rim design is floral pattern w/ repeated images of aircraft and image of Statue of Liberty and Eiffel Tower, 2" d	300	500
Poster, "Fly TWA," full color image of western woman under "Arizona," 1940s	50	100
Radiator Ornament, pot metal, figural airplane, "Lucky Lindy–Our Hero/ New York to Paris in 33½ Hours" on wing, "*Spirit of St. Louis*" on tail, 5" l, 4.75" w	450	500
Sheet Music, *Lucky Lindy,* ©1927, 9.25" x 12.25"	25	75
Shot Glass, Southern Airways, 1952-55	25	50
Spoon, Pacific Northern, silver plated, 1950s	10	15
Sticker, Airship Hindenburg/American Airlines, oval paper, promoting "Exclusive Connecting Service," unused, 3.75" x 5.5"	25	75
Swizzle Stick, Piedmont	1	3
Timetable, American Airlines, 1951	10	20
Timetable, German Zeppelin Transport Co., "2 Days to Europe," 1937	50	150
Timetable, Pan American, 1930s	25	50
Tray, silver plated, embossed American Airlines eagle flying to right and "AA" in center, original box, lid marked "The Captain's Flagship American Airlines, Inc.," 6" d	25	75
Wings, plastic, "Goodyear Airship," 3" l	10	30
Wings, plastic, "JFK International Airport/Gateway To The USA," 1960s, 2.5" w	15	50

Left to right: Poster, Imperial Airways, 1937, 43" h, 28" w, $880 at auction. —Photo courtesy Collectors Auction Services. Postage Stamps, #C13-15 Graf Zeppelins, postmarked, $489 at auction. —Photo courtesy Skinner, Inc., Boston, MA.

Bicycles

Bicycles fall into four categories. Running machines, known as hobby-horses, the precursor to the bicycle, were introduced in 1817 and do not have pedals. The addition of cranks and pedals to the front driving wheel in the early 1860s created the first bicycle, generally known as the velocipede or boneshaker. Enlarging the front driving wheel for greater speed created the high wheel bicycle (c. 1870–1892). The rear wheel size was reduced to save weight and facilitate mounting the machine. As these bicycles were quite dangerous to ride, safer versions called high wheel safeties were developed. High wheel tricycles fall into this category and became quite popular in the 1880s. Finally, the bicycle with chain drive to the rear wheel was introduced in 1885. These were called, quite simply, safeties. The addition of pneumatic tires in the early 1890s led to the "golden age" of the bicycle. In the 1920s, bicycles began assuming a motorized look, with tanks and balloon tires. In the 1930s they became streamlined. Balloon-tire bicycles are known as Classic bicycles. For more information see *Evolution of the Bicycle* (1991, 1994 value update) and *Vol. 2* (1994) edited by Neil S. Wood (L-W Book Sales, Gas City, IN).

Prices vary depending on model, year and condition. The prices listed below are for complete machines with original parts.

Antique Bicycles

	LOW	HIGH
Boneshaker, c1860	$2500	$3500
Colson Adult Tricycle, c1900	500	800
Columbia Century, lady's, pneumatic safety, 19th C	1000	2000
Columbia Century, man's, split frame pneumatic safety, 19th C	500	900
Columbia Light Roadster, 50", c1890–91	1500	2500
High Wheel Bicycle, St. Nicholas, 19th C	1500	2500
High Wheel Bicycle, Star, c1880	1200	1600
Pneumatic Safety, Crawford, lady's, wooden fender and chain guard, c1898	400	750
Pneumatic Safety, Griffith's Corp., 19th C	200	400
Pneumatic Safety, Indian, c1920	800	1500
Scorcher Safety, c1894	1000	1800
Tandem, Lozier Mfg. Co., c1897	1000	1500
Tandem, Rover, c1900	300	450
Tandem Safety, Columbia Model 43, c1900	200	400
Velocipede Tricycle, child's size, c1870	300	400
Velocipede Tricycle, Montpelier Mfg. Co., Vermont, 19th C	500	800

Classic (Balloon-Tire) Bicycles, post-1920

Elgin Deluxe, girl's, 1940	$100	$300
Firestone Bullnose, c1939	800	1200
Firestone Streamline, 1937	3000	4000
Hawthorn Flo-Cycle, c1936	2000	3500
J. C. Higgins, boy's, c1957	1000	2500
Monark Silver King 26-X, 1939	1800	3000
Raleigh Chopper, 1970s	300	500
Schwinn Corvette, 3-speed, 1960s	350	600
Schwinn D97XE, boy's, 1939	1500	3000
Schwinn Jaguar Mark 2, 1955	500	800
Schwinn Panther, boy's, 1960s	200	400
Shelby Speedline Airflow, lady's, c1939	1000	1500
Silver King Racing Bicycle, restored, c1935	1500	2500
Silver King Wingbar, girl's, c1939	600	800

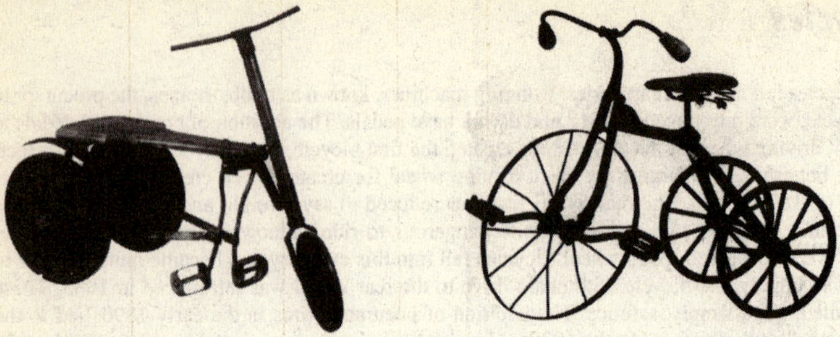

Tricycles, above left to right: Metal handles, pedals, and rims w/ hard rubber tires, wooden seat, 19" h, $110 at auction; Metal frame, wooden handles, leather seat, rubber rear tires, 21" h, $121 at auction.

Left: Gene Autry Monark Silver King, rodeo brown, jewel-studded fenders and chain guard, attached cap pistol in leather holster, w/ original papers, $2420 at auction.

Right: Schwinn Girl's, battery-operated head light and horn, $446 at auction.

Photos courtesy Collectors Auction Services.

Railroad Memorabilia

Some collectors of railroad memorabilia concentrate on lines that once ran through their hometowns or region. This fosters regional differences of what people collect and how much they pay for items. Other collectors concentrate on a topic, or type of item, regardless of region. The following prices are for items in excellent condition.

Beware of items with no identifying marks or provenance. Some railroads used stock china patterns, with or without custom top or back marks. If special markings are documented to a railroad, authentic pieces are most often required to have these markings. Some railroad china patterns have been reproduced, but not all are clearly and permanently labeled as such. "Fantasy pieces" are china patterns never made for any railroad but which are produced with actual railroad logos and colors. These are often produced in smaller, less common shapes, such as butter pats, teapots, and mustard pots. Be particularly wary of overglaze decoration, as the manufacturers of originals ordinarily applied all but metallic coloring under the glaze. If the glaze over an important part of a piece is more yellowed than the glaze overall, it could indicate applied fraudulent additions. Fake glass signs purportedly used in railroad stations are on the market, as well as expertly manufactured, fraudulent badges. Very small rubber stamps with a railroad logo, which may or may not be authentic, have been offered for sale, and could of course have been illegitimately used. Finally, beware of items with interchangeable parts. Lanterns, in particular, have appeared as marriages of fraudulent intent.

For more information refer to *Railroad Collectibles, 4th Edition* by Stanley Baker (Collector Books, Paducah, KY, 1990, 1999 value update).

	LOW	HIGH
Ashtray, Chesapeake & Ohio, white, 4 rests, outer blue band, Chessie kitten logo at center, Syracuse China, 4" d	$75	$90
Ashtray, Pullman, brown Bakelite, 4.25" d	15	20
Badge, Baldwin Locomotive Works Workmen's Safety Committee, silvered brass, 1930s	25	75
Badge, Chesapeake & Ohio Special Police Officer, nickel finish, eagle top, embossed steam locomotive on center disc	200	275
Badge, Pennsylvania Railroad Fire Department, silvered brass, firefighting symbols left and right, raised relief "13," 1930s	50	100
Badge, Railway Express Agency, #49031, cloisonné	15	50
Blotter, Burlington Route, 100th Anniversary 1849-1949, 4" x 9"	5	10
Bond, Western & Atlantic, 50 cents, Mar. 15, 1862	5	7
Book, *The Rector Cook Book, Compliments of the Milwaukee Road,* 5th ed., George Rector, 173 pages, hard cover, 1928, 5" x 8"	50	80
Brochure, Burlington Zephyr, Wings to the Iron Horse, foldout, 1933	20	60
Brochure, California Zephyr, large format, 1949	45	90
Brochure, Illinois Central Green Diamond, foldout, 1936	40	80
Brochure, Pullman's Diamond Jubilee, large format, 1934	20	60
Butter Knife, Northern Pacific, hollow handle, stainless blade	15	25
Calendar, Burlington Route, 1934, single sheet	35	50
Calendar, Chesapeake & Ohio, 1938, complete	100	175
Calendar, Chicago Milwaukee & St. Paul, 1928, Yellowstone National Park scenes, complete	50	75
Calendar, Pennsylvania Railroad, 1956, framed	200	275
Calendar, Pennsylvania RR, 1954, tri-month, complete	90	150
Cap Badge, conductor's, Chicago Great Western	125	175
Cap Badge, porter's, Lackawanna	50	100
Carafe, SOO Line, etched logo, 9" h	150	225
Celery Dish, Erie, Buffalo China, 1928, 4.75" x 10"	100	150
Cereal Bowl, Union Pacific Railroad, Challenger pattern, 6.25" d	15	30

Above: Matchcover, Crusader and Blue Comet advertising on front, New Jersey Central Terminal Restaurant on back, $5-$8.

Left: Uniform, Chesapeake and Ohio Railway hostess, navy blue, white blouse, navy blue shoes, late 1940s, $150-$200.

	LOW	HIGH
Chocolate Mold, tin, hinged, 6-wheel locomotive, 4.25" x 6"	50	75
Chop Plate, Chicago, Rock Island & Pacific, El Reno pattern, Shenango China, 11.25" d	350	400
Cigar Box, SOO Line, S. A. Cutter, c1880s	20	40
Cigar Box, Union Pacific, wooden	20	60
Claret, New York Central, white frosted, "20th Century Limited"	30	40
Coal Shovel, Atchison Topeka & Santa Fe	35	65
Coffeepot, Chicago, Burlington & Quincy, Reed & Barton, 14 oz	50	75
Dinner Plate, Baltimore & Ohio, Shenango China, 9.25" d	50	100
Dinner Plate, Delaware & Hudson, Adirondack pattern, Syracuse China, 9.5" d	75	90
Head Rest, Illinois Central, 15" x 15.5"	10	15
Lantern, Boston & Albany, bell bottom	175	250
Lantern, C.R.R. (Concord Railroad), cylindrical ruby-flashed fixed globe w/ etched "C.R.R.," ring handle, mid-19th C, 11.25" h	600	800
Lantern, Rock Island Lines	75	150
Lantern Globe, Wabash, clear, Corning-style	60	90
Lapel Stud, Brotherhood Railroad Trainmen, gold letters, red border	15	45
Lapel Stud, Lehigh Valley Veterans Association, Lehigh Valley Railway flag within gold wreath on white ground, 625" d	15	40
Lighter, Chicago Great Western Railway	75	125
Magazine, *Railroad Trainmen's Journal,* Vol. XX, #5, May 1903	5	7
Map, Union Pacific, roll-down wall-type, Rand McNally, 40" x 62"	15	25
Match Holder, Iowa Central, Easter 1901, wooden, hanging	80	150
Mechanical Pencil, Burlington Northern	15	40
Mechanical Pencil, Santa Fe logo, "The World's Largest Fleet of Diesel Drawn Trains"	10	30
Menu, Great Northern, Western Star, luncheon, 1957, 6.5" x 10"	20	40
Milk Bottle, Northern Pacific Railway Dairy & Poultry Farm, Kent, WN, half pint, 5.5" h	125	175
Napkin, Pullman, white linen, floral design, 21" x 22"	5	15
Napkin, Union Pacific, cloth, winged streamliner motif, 11" x 16"	5	15
Paperweight, Burlington, Cedar Rapids & Northern Railway, reverse lists railroad stop signs, Alberta Lea Route	100	150

	LOW	HIGH
Pass, Baltimore & Ohio, ornate, brown train vignette, 1773	25	75
Pass, Burlington, Cedar Rapids & Minnesota, 1871, map on back	35	50
Pass, Lehigh Valley, violet, 1942	5	10
Pass, Minneapolis & St. Louis Railway, 1894	10	40
Pass, Wabash, red flag logo, map on back, 1896	15	20
Pinback Button, Canadian Northern Railway, black, white, and red	15	50
Pinback Button, Chesapeake & Ohio Railway, litho Chessie and "Chessie C & O RY," 1950s	25	75
Pinback Button, National Railway Employees Protective Association, red, white, and blue shield symbol at lower center, 1900s, .875" d	25	75
Pinback Button, New York Central Lines, celluloid, oval	15	50
Pinback Button, Northern Pacific Railroad, "Yellowstone Park Line"	15	50
Pinback Button, North Western Line, red, black, and white logo on olive green ground, "Alfalfa/The Great Wealth Producer," 1900s	15	75
Pinback Button, Railroad Men's Reliance/The Travelers Insurance Company, image of oncoming steam engine in blue on white ground, 1900s	25	75
Pinback Button, Reading Lines, blue and white, red rim, 1940s	25	75
Plate, Union Pacific, Circus Series, 8.24" d	75	150
Playing Cards, Amtrak	5	15
Playing Cards, Chicago Great Western, Cornbelt Route	25	65
Playing Cards, New York, Haven & Hartford, double deck	40	60
Playing Cards, Waterloo Cedar Falls & Northern, Waterloo, IA	20	60
Pocket Watch, Illinois, Santa Fe Special, 21j	250	300
Print, Chicago Great Western, "April Showers"	20	50
Rule Book, Waterloo Cedar Falls & Northern, 1947	20	55
Sheet Music, *Casey Jones, The Brave Engineer,* Seibert and Newton, 1909	20	30
Shot Glass, Union Pacific, frosted decoration	5	15
Sign, "Fast Dependable Through Service/Order and Ship by Railway Express Agency Incorporated," tin, 1-sided, "H. D. Beach Co. Coshocton, O. U.S.A.," 13.25" h, 19.25" w	100	150
Sign, "Missouri Pacific Lines," round, tin, 1-sided, 48" d	50	75
Sign, "Railway Express," porcelain, mounted on plywood, 13" h	75	150
Soup Plate, Baltimore & Ohio, Derby pattern, 9" d	75	90
Spittoon, Atchison Topeka & Santa Fe	120	150
Spittoon, Southern Pacific	50	100
Stamp, Brookville Street Railway Co., cast iron and brass, painted gold, black, and red, "Brookville Street Railway Company Incorpor. Nov. 9th, 1906," red repaint, 11" h, 6.5" l	30	55
Stickpin, North Western Line, "Best of Everything," red accents, 1920s	25	75
Stock Certificate, Baltimore & Ohio, 100 shares, 1903	10	20
Stock Certificate, Chicago & North Western, 3 shares, 1958	8	12
Stoneware Jug, Atchison Topeka & Santa Fe, 1 gal.	100	160
Stoneware Jug, Chicago & North Western, 11.25" h	250	300
Sugar Packet, Northern Pacific, red and black logo	3	6
Switch Key, Burlington, Cedar Rapids & Northern, brass	175	200
Switch Key, Chicago Rock Island & Pacific, nickel plated	30	55
Switch Lock, Chicago, St. Paul, Minneapolis & Omaha, brass	80	110
Switch Lock, Delaware, Lackawanna & Western, brass	75	90
Switch Lock, Erie, steel	10	20
Swizzle Stick, Union Pacific, plastic, red	1	3
Table Cloth, Union Pacific, cotton, "UPRR" woven in bottom border w/ 2 flowers, 42" x 50"	40	50
Tag, Chicago Great Western Railway, brass	10	30

	LOW	HIGH
Teapot, covered, Chicago, Rock Island & Pacific, Buffalo China, 4.5" h	400	600
Thermometer, Great Northern, metal, 10" h	40	60
Ticket, Central Vermont, 1886	10	20
Ticket, Chicago & North Western, coupon booklet, 1886	25	40
Ticket, Ridge Avenue Railway Company, Philadelphia, paper, late 1800s/ early 1900s, 1.125" x 1.75"	25	75
Ticket, Wabash Railroad, 1904	5	10
Timetable, Baltimore & Ohio South Western, 1911	10	15
Timetable, Burlington Northern, 1970	2	4
Timetable, Chicago & North Western, 1942	5	15
Timetable, Delaware & Hudson, 1907	15	20
Timetable, Des Moines & Fort Dodge, 1874	25	45
Timetable, Great Northern, 1926	10	15
Timetable Holder, Chicago & North Western, metal, wall type	55	75
Tip Tray, Burlington Northern, glass	50	70
Tip Tray, Southern Pacific, silver, Reed & Barton, 1929	125	175
Token, Union Pacific, aluminum, souvenir, 1940, 1.25" d	8	12
Tumbler, Chicago Milwaukee St. Paul & Pacific, etched logo, 4.75" h	15	30
Tumbler, Union Pacific, frosted shield logo, 4.5" h	10	15
Utility Box, Northern Pacific, tin	10	20
Wall Lamp, Union Pacific, 2.5" h	50	75
Watch Fob, Northern Pacific, enamel on bronze, leather strap	75	100
Watch Fob, Railway Signal Association, brass, train and semaphores in center, leather strap, F. H. Noble & Co., Chicago	40	60
Watering Can, Burlington Route, galvanized, embossed logo, 9.5" h	30	50
Whiskey Glass, Burlington Route	55	70
Wine Glass, Chicago, Milwaukee, St. Paul & Pacific, etched logo	60	75

Safety Poster, © 1923 American Railway Assoc., engraved and printed by Sales Printing Corp., New York City, 14" x 22", $303 at auction. —Photo courtesy Collectors Auction Services.

Watches

Pocket Watches

Fine watches contain a varying number of jewels, usually synthetic ruby which is second in hardness only to diamond, within the movement mechanism to reduce friction and wear. They improve the accuracy of the watch and generally increase its value.

We abbreviate "jewel" as "j" (e.g., 17j means 17 jewels). American pocket watch movements are described in standard sizes (abbreviated as "s" in this book), ranging from popular sizes including 16s (1.7"), 12s (1.566"), 10s (1.5"), 0s (1.166") and 000s (1.1").

For purposes of simplicity we have given three value levels. Low: rough, serviceable, but needs repair or restoration. These watches are priced as needing a minimum of $100 in parts or repair. You must decide whether the cost to repair outweighs any possible profit. Average: normal to extended wear depending on age. Minor cost for parts or repair. High: in fine condition with minimum of wear, needing only possible cosmetic touch-ups.

Numerous fakes are circulating on the open market including 24j examples of Illinois and Rockford watches as well as original Rolex and Piaget movements in bogus cases. As always, it pays to do your homework prior to any purchase. If it looks too good to be true, it probably is.

For further information, see *Complete Guide to Watches, Nineteenth Edition* by Cooksey Shugart, Tom Engle and Richard E. Gilbert (Cooksey Shugart Publications, Cleveland, TN, 1999).

	LOW	HIGH
American, 18s, Appleton, Tracy & Co., #1857, key wind, 15j	$175	$300
American, 18s, Appleton, Tracy & Co., thin model, key wind, 11j	350	500
American, 18s, Crescent Street, #1870, stem wind, 15j	135	265
American, 18s, Dennison, Howard, Davis, #1857, key wind, original case, 7j	1000	1500
American, 18s, P. S. Bartlett, #1879, key wind, 11j	85	150
American, 18s, thin model, key wind, ¾ plate, 11 j	200	500
American, 20s, #1862, key wind, adjusted, 19j	2500	3500

Left to right: Ami Bourquin, Locle, #30993, key wind, 18k case w/ rose-cut diamonds, $1093 at auction; American, Maximus, 18k hunter case, 21j, $1150 at auction. —Photos courtesy Skinner, Inc., Boston, MA.

Left to right: Elgin, key wind, 18k hunting case signed "D & Co.," 15j, $403 at auction; Geneve, #37752, 18k case, $5175 at auction. —Photos courtesy Skinner, Inc., Boston, MA.

	LOW	HIGH
American, 20s, Appleton, Tracy & Co., key wind, 19j	600	1,000
Ansonia Clock Co., Guide	50	75
Ansonia Clock Co., Sesqui-Centennial	250	400
Appleton Watch Co., 16s, 3/4, stem attached, 7-11j	550	850
Aurora Watch Co., 18s, key wind, key set, gilded, hunter case, 17j	200	300
Ball-Hamilton, 18s, Brotherhood of Locomotive Engineers, open face, 21j	1800	2500
Chicago Watch Co., 18s, key wind, 11j	200	450
Cornell Watch Co., 18s, J. C. Adams, key wind, 11j	350	575
E. Howard & Co., K size (14), X, nickel, horse, side wind, open face, 14k, 15j	1000	1300
E. Ingraham Co., Allure	40	55
E. Ingraham Co., Beacon	45	65
E. Ingraham Co., The Pal	45	50
E. Ingraham Co., Pony	45	50
E. Ingraham Co., Sentry	45	50
Elgin, 18s, Overland, nickel plated, key wind, hunter case, 17j	125	225
Elgin, 18s, G. M. Wheeler, key wind, gilded, hunter case, 11j	100	200
Elgin, 16s, WWII model, open face, 21j	150	200
Elgin, 12s, 922 MP, gold filled, Hamilton case	425	600
Elgin, 6s, Atlas, hunter case, 7j	60	125
Hamilton, 12s, 17-19j	100	150
Hamilton, 16s, Official Standard, open face, 17j	300	500
Hamilton, 18s, 922, open face, 15j	500	650
Hampden Watch Co., 000s, Molly Stark, pin set, open face, 7j	100	150
Hampden Watch Co., 18s, Dueber W. Co., open face, 16j	70	150
Illinois Watch Co., 12s, Ariston, open face, 11-17j	70	150
Illinois Watch Co., 13s, 19j	90	175
Illinois Watch Co., 14s, 22j	150	375
Illinois Watch Co., 16s, Ariston, open face and hunter case, 15j	100	150
Illinois Watch Co., 16s, B & O Standard, 21j	900	1200
Illinois Watch Co., 16s, Burlington, open face, 17j	125	200

Left to right: Hampden, 14k hunting case w/ engraved floral motif and bezel-set ruby, diamond, and sapphire, $748 at auction; Patek Philippe, Geneve #78478, repoussé sterling silver case, $1093 at auction. —Photos courtesy Skinner, Inc., Boston, MA.

	LOW	HIGH
Illinois Watch Co., 16s, Getty Model #4 and #5, 17j	125	150
Illinois Watch Co., 18s, America, #1-2, key wind, 7j	100	200
Illinois Watch Co., 18s, Baltimore & Ohio Railroad Special, gold jewel settings, adjusted, 24j	1800	2500
Illinois Watch Co., 18s, Forest City, key wind/side wind, gilded, 17j	175	225
Illinois Watch Co., 18s, Stuart Special, adjusted, 17j	175	200
Ingersoll, Dollar type, American Pride	100	125
Ingersoll, Dollar type, Chancery	75	125
Ingersoll, Dollar type, Fancy Dials	150	300
Ingersoll, Dollar type, George Washington	175	275
Ingersoll, Dollar type, Waterbury	60	90
International Watch Co., Mascot, open face	90	200
J. P. Stevens & Co., Waltham, 11-15-17j	450	625
Keystone Standard Watch Co., 8s, dust proof, 11j	125	175
Lancaster Watch Co., 18s, Elberon, dust proof, 7j	70	95
Lancaster Watch Co., 18s, Keystone, adjusted, gilded, gold jewel settings, dust proof, 15j	90	175
Lancaster Watch Co., West End, Sidney, nickel plates, dust proof, 15j	125	150
Manistee Watch Co., 16s, open face, 17j	250	400
Newark Watch Co., Arthur Wadsworth, stem wind	525	850
New England Watch Co., Alden	50	65
New England Watch Co., Excelsior, 7j	70	95
New Haven Clock and Watch Co., Ford Special	75	100
New Haven Clock and Watch Co., Jerome U.S A.	50	75
New York Springfield Watch Co., E. W. Bond, 3/4, 15j	600	700
Philadelphia Watch Co., 16s, key wind, key set, 15j	175	225
Rockford, 16s, Commodore Perry, adjusted, 15-17j	125	175
Rockford, 16s, Herald Square, 3/4, open face, 7j	200	350
Rockford, 18s, #970, open face, 7j	75	100
San Jose Watch Co., 16s	1500	2500
Seth Thomas, 0s, #1, open face, 7j	50	125

Left to right: Racine Perrot, #37207, key wind, 18k hunting case w/ rose-cut diamonds, $690 at auction; Tiffany & Co., #90409, 18k case, dated 1898, $3450 at auction. —Photos courtesy Skinner, Inc., Boston, MA.

	LOW	HIGH
Seth Thomas, #3, hunter case, 15j	75	150
Seth Thomas, 6s, Edgemere, 7-11j	50	100
Seth Thomas, 6s, Republic U.S.A., 7j	50	100
Seth Thomas, 18s, Chautauqua, #5, gold jewel settings, 15j	150	300
South Bend, 12s, #160; hunter case, 11j	50	150
South Bend, 16s, #347, open face, nickel plates, 17j	100	150
Trenton Watch Co., 0s, 3 Finger Bridge, 15j	25	75
Trenton Watch Co., 6s, 3 Finger Bridge, 7j	20	50
Trenton Watch Co., 16s, Peerless, side wind, lever set, 7j	50	80
Trenton Watch Co., 18s, Trenton, key wind, key set, 7j	250	500
U.S. Watch Co., 10s, R. F. Pratt, Swiss, 1/4 plate, key wind, 15j	100	250
U.S. Watch Co., 16s, Edwin Rollo, key wind, 15j	400	550
U.S. Watch Co., 18s, Fayette Stratton, gilded, 11j	250	425
U.S. Watch Co. of Waltham, 16s, #110, 3/4, open face, 7j	50	125
U.S. Watch Co. of Waltham, 18s, Washington Square, hunter case, 15j	175	300
Waterbury Watch Co., Oxford	50	100
Waterbury Watch Co., Series Z	60	100
Westclox, Anniversary	35	60
Westclox, Boy Proof	60	80
Westclox, Coronado	15	25
Westclox, Dewey	10	20
Westclox, Farm Bureau	65	100
Westclox, Glory Be	20	30
Westclox, Lighted Dial	25	40
Westclox, Mascot	20	30
Westclox, Monitor	15	25
Westclox, Sceptor	20	30

Wristwatches

	LOW	HIGH
Alpina, 17j, Alpha, auto wind, 18k, 1950s	$175	$250
Alpina, 17j, Alsta, gold-filled, wrist alarm	85	150
American Waltham, 15j, Masonic, 14k, c1925	500	700
American Waltham, 17j, Duxbury, gold-filled	75	100
American Waltham, 17j, Oberlin, gold-filled	50	100
American Waltham, 17j, w/ hackset, stainless steel	50	75
American Waltham, 21j, Albright, 14k	125	175
Angelus, 17j, stainless steel, c1955	175	250
Audemars Piguet, 17j, diamond bezel, center lugs, 18k	2000	2400
Ball W. Co., 25j, auto wind, stainless steel	250	325
Baume & Mercier, 18j, tachometer, stainless steel, black dial, 1940	400	500
Benrus, 15j, enamel bezel, 14k, 1930	200	300
Benrus, 17j, dial-o-rama, gold-filled, 1958	150	225
Benrus, 17j, Sky Chief, stainless steel, 1940s	400	575
Benson, 17j, curved, rhinestones, hooded lugs, 14k	200	275
Berg, 25j, auto wind, 14k, 1959	125	175
Bulova, 7j, gold-filled, 1945	45	75
Bulova, 17j, The Governor, 14k	125	200
Bulova, 21j, plain bezel, curved, gold-filled	75	100
Bulova, Accutron, wood bezel, day/date, gold-filled	75	150
Bulova, Spaceview Alpha, 14k, 1960	500	750
Cartier, 18j, Santos, lady's, 18k and stainless steel case and band	600	800
Cartier, 18j, sapphire crown and bezel, 18k, 1970	2500	3500
Cortebert, 15j, gold-filled, 1940s	30	55

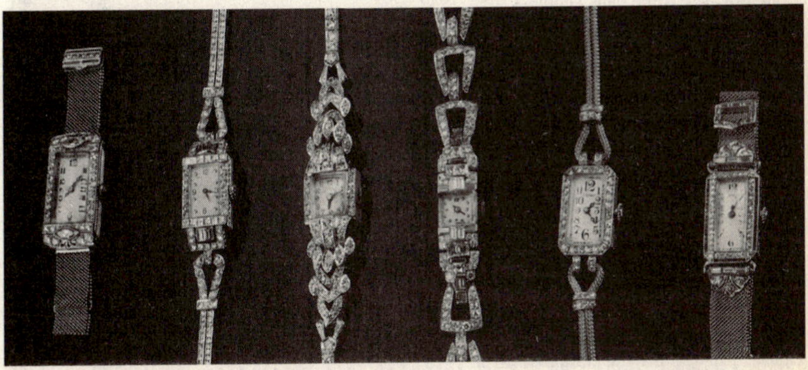

Lady's Art Deco Wristwatches at auction, left to right: Smith Patterson #404031, 17j, white gold and diamond-set, 1.40 cts, $1620; Agassiz #300096, 17j, diamond-set bracelet, 2.70 cts, $2645; Hamilton #7725683, 17j, diamond-set bracelet, 2.38 cts, $1265; Movado, diamond links, 3.40 cts, $5175; International Watch Co. #833376, Cartier, diamond-set bezel, white metal and platinum strap, Cresaux hallmark, .56 cts, $2415; C. H. Meylan #39462, 18j, Tiffany & Co., diamond- and emerald-set bezel, platinum bracelet, $2990. —Photo courtesy Skinner, Inc., Boston, MA.

Men's Wristwatches at auction, left to right: Blancpain #527, 18k, $9200; Patek Philippe Geneve, silvertone, c1960, $2415; Patek Philippe Geneve, goldtone, c1950, $2990; Bulgari Automatic International Edition 1100/3300, 25j, $1725. —Photo courtesy Skinner, Inc., Boston, MA.

	LOW	HIGH
Corum, 17j, rope style bezel, 18k case and band	1000	1500
Crawford, 17j, triple date, stainless steel, 1942	40	80
Croton, 7j, driver's style, gold-filled, 1938	150	250
Driva, 17j, double teardrop lugs, 14k, 1945	200	275
Duodial, 15j, 9k, 1934	900	1200
Eberhard, 17j, wire lugs, enamel dial, waterproof case, 1928	700	900
E. Borel, 17j, cocktail style, gold-filled, 1960s	60	90
E. Gubelin, 15j, triple date, stainless steel, 1945	300	400
E. Gubelin, 19j, curvex, 2-tone, 18k	1000	1200
E. Huguenin, 17j, Black Star, 14k, 1940	300	500
Elgin, 7j, Avigo, 1929	55	80
Elgin, 15j, Art Deco style, gold-filled, 1928	25	45
Elgin, 15j, Legionnaire, gold-filled, 1929	30	55
Elgin, 17j, Adonis, gold-filled, 1929	40	75
Elgin, 17j, stepped case, gold-filled, 1935	55	80
Elgin, 21j, Lord Elgin, gold-filled	100	150
Enicar, 15j, egg shaped, compass, silver, 1918	400	500
Eska, 17j, multicolored enamel dial, 18k	2000	2700
Eterna, 17j, gold jewel settings, 14k, 1935	125	200
Frey, 15j, engraved case, 1933	30	55
Gallet, 15j, wire lugs, silver, 1925	75	135
Girard-Perregaux, 17j, date, gold-filled, 1960	55	85
Glycine, 17j, 15 diamond dial, 14k, 1945	500	700
Gruen, 17j, alarm, date, stainless steel, 1964	125	175
Gruen, 17j, Citadel, curvex, gold-filled, 1943	125	200
Gruen, 17j, Curvex Precision, gold-filled, 1945	185	275
Gruen, 17j, day/date/month, stainless steel, 1948	150	225

Men's Wristwatches at auction, left to right: Rolex Oyster Perpetual, GMT-Master, date, stainless steel, 1981, $1610; Rolex Oyster Perpetual, date, gold and stainless steel, $1150; Tag Heuer, date, stainless steel, $546; Patek Philippe Cushion, 18k, $2875. —Photo courtesy Skinner, Inc., Boston, MA.

	LOW	HIGH
Gruen, 17j, double dial, gold-filled	900	1100
Gruen, 17j, driver's watch, gold-filled, 1938	250	350
Gruen, 21j, Precision, gold-filled, 1945	75	125
Hafis, 15j, luminous dial, gold plate	30	50
Hafis, 15j, Queen Marie, 26 diamonds, 18k	200	300
Hamilton, 17j, Greenwich, gold-filled	100	175
Hamilton, 19j, Cedric, gold-filled, 1951	60	80
Hamilton, 22j, auto wind, stainless steel, 1970	40	80
Hamilton, Everest II, electric, gold-filled	75	100
Hamilton, Nautilus 402, electric, gold-filled	40	60
Hamilton, Polaris, electric, diamond dial, 14k	300	400
Hamilton, Skip Jack, electric, stainless steel	40	60
Helbros, 7j, Federal, base metal, 1929	20	40
Helbros, 7j, Fortress, gold plate, 1929	20	40
Illinois, 15j, Ensign, gold-filled	225	400
Illinois, 17j, Cavalier, gold-filled	200	300
Illinois, 17j, Tuxedo, engraved bezel, 14k, 1920	300	450
Illinois, 19j, Beau Brummel, 18k	700	950
Imperial, 17j, stainless steel	30	55
Ingersoll, 7j, radiolite dial wire lugs, original band	30	55
International Watch Co., 17j, date, auto wind, waterproof, 18k	700	900
International Watch Co., 17j, Tiffany on dial, 14k, 1942	600	700
Invicta, 17j, auto wind, waterproof, stainless steel	50	70
J. Jurgensen, 17j, recessed crown, fancy lugs, 14k, 1952	200	250
Junghans, Electronic Auto Chron, 14k, 1978	90	125
Juvenia, 17j, stainless steel	40	60
Kelton, 7j, Drake, gold-filled	30	40
Kingston, 17j, day/date/month, moon phase, gold-filled	225	325

Ladies' Wristwatches at auction, left to right: Boucheron #B908247, 18k, $2875; Piaget, tiger's-eye dial and bezel, 18k, $805. —Photo courtesy Skinner, Inc., Boston, MA.

	LOW	HIGH
Le Coultre, 17j, alarm, date, auto wind, 14k	400	500
Le Coultre, 17j, ruby dial, alarm, gold-filled, 1960	350	500
Le Coultre, 17j, triple date, moon phase, fancy lugs, gold-filled	800	1000
Le Phare, 17j, triple date, moon phase, waterproof, 18k	600	850
Longines, 15j, metal dial, gold jewel settings, 14k, 1925	250	400
Longines, 17j, diamond bezel, gold-filled	150	250
Longines, 17j, double dial, stainless steel, 1937	700	1000
Longines, 17j, Flagship,14k	200	300
Longines, 17j, Weems, revolving bezel, stainless steel, 1940	475	650
Longines, 19j, Conquest, auto wind, 14k	700	900
Mars, 17j, Dateur, hinged back, gold-filled, 1934	250	400
Mido, 17j, auto wind, stainless steel, 1960s	40	65
Mimo, 17j, De Frece, 14k, 1935	150	225
Minerva, 17j, center second, auto wind, gold-filled	40	60
Movado, 14j, fancy lugs, 14k, 1947	300	400
Movado, 17j, diamond bezel, 18k	200	300
Movado, 28j, Kingmatic, center second, 14k	250	350
National, 15j, day/date/month, gold-filled	20	40
New Haven, 7j, Duchess, lady's, etched case, gold plate	5	15
New Haven, 7j, engraved bezel, base metal	20	35
Nivada, 25j, waterproof, 14k, 1940	500	625
Omega, 15j, wire lugs, 14k	350	450
Omega, 17j, Seamaster, date, waterproof, 18k	400	500
Orvin, 17j, day/date, stainless steel, 1945	30	50
Patek Philippe, 18j, hinged back, 18k, 1920s	4000	5000
Piaget, 17j, 18k, 1957	500	700
Porta, 17j, antimagnetic, gold plate, 1955	20	40
Rado, 17j, date, gold plate, 1960	20	40
Record, 17j, triple date, moon phase, auto wind, 18k	1000	1200
Regina, enamel dial, center lugs, silver, 1929	95	150
Roamer, 17j, auto wind, gold-filled	20	35
Rockford, 17j, Iroquois, gold train, gold-filled	200	350
Rolex, 15j, Railway, stepped case, 18k, 1930s	7000	9000

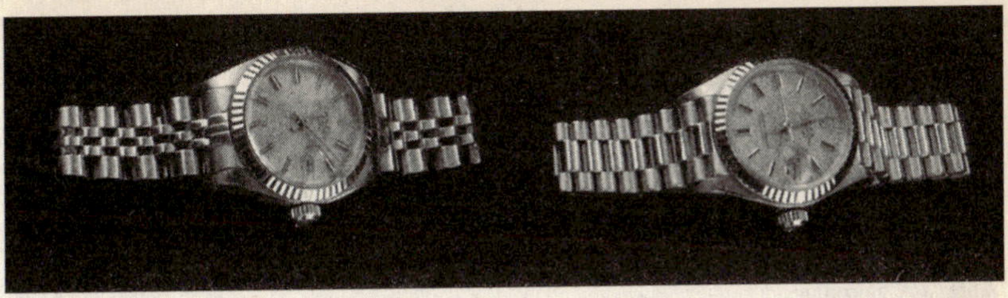

Ladies' Wristwatches at auction, left to right: Rolex "Lady President" Oyster Perpetual Datejust, 18k, $6038; Rolex Oyster Perpetual, goldtone, $1265. —Photo courtesy Skinner, Inc., Boston, MA.

	LOW	HIGH
Rolex, 17j, Century Club, 18k, 1960s	1400	1800
Rolex, 17j, Precision, gold-filled	400	550
Rolex, 17j, Precision, stainless steel	500	650
Rolex, 17j, Skyrocket, gold-filled, 1944	500	700
Rolex, 25j, Air King, stainless steel, 1959	400	600
Rolex, 25j, stainless steel, 1963	600	800
Rolex, 26j, Sea-Dweller, stainless steel	1200	1600
Tavannes, 15j, enamel dial, flip top, silver, 1915	300	400
Technos, 17j, Sky Diver, auto wind, stainless steel, 1970	50	75
Tiffany, 15j, enamel dial, silver, 1930s	500	600
Tissot, 17j, Navigator, auto wind, stainless steel, 1972	150	225
Tissot, 17j, Stadium, tachymeter, gold plate, 1960	150	200
U. Nardin, 17j, center second, auto wind, 18k	400	625
Universal, 17j, Cabriolet, stainless steel, 1930s	3500	4500
Universal, 17j, day/date/month, moon phase, 18k	1200	1500
Universal, 28j, center dial, date, 18k, 1958	300	400
Vacheron, 17j, day/date/month, 18k, 1940s	3000	4000
Vacheron, 17j, textured bezel, 18k	1300	1800
Vacheron, 17j, triple date, moon phase, 18k, 1945	8000	10,000
Vacheron, 29j, center second, auto wind, date, 18k	2200	2750
Vulcain, 17j, Cricket, alarm, stainless steel, 1948	50	75
Vulcain, 17j, Minstop, stainless steel	50	75
Warwick, 6j, hinged back, gold plate, 1930s	20	40
West End, 17j, Keepsake, silver, 1925	150	225
Wittnauer, 17j, alarm, gold-filled, 1960	50	85
Wittnauer, 17j, auto wind, base metal, 1960	40	60
Wittnauer, 17j, Professional, 18k, 1955	600	725
Wyler, 17j, center second, stainless steel	50	75
Yale, 15j, calendar, 14k, 1939	200	300
Zenith, 15j, enamel dial, wire lugs, silver, 1918	250	350
Zenith, 36j, El Primero, triple date moon phase, 18k, 1970s	2500	3000
Zodiac, 17j, 14k	100	150
Zodiac, 21j, Olympos, date, auto wind, stainless steel, 1965	40	60

Swatch Watches

Swatch™ watches appeared out of nowhere (Switzerland) to become an instant hot collectible. Their brightly colored flashy plastic dials are seen on chic and trendy (and other) wrists around the world. Original bands are a must! Although occasionally showing up at auction, they're more often found on the Internet.

	LOW	HIGH
Abraxas/Caterpillar	$100	$125
Antibea/Chic 'n' Marine	80	100
Aqua Club/Sea Tales	75	100
Artic Star/Giro del Mondo	40	65
Black Divers/Waikiki Surf	250	300
Black Dots/City Line	75	100
Black Magic/Paris Costes	115	135
Blue Bay/Color Tech	90	120
Blue Racer/Malibu Beach	200	240
Chrono-Tech/Aspen	350	400
Classique/Meet Me at the Carlyle	400	450
Coca-Cola/Comet	150	175
Don't Be Too Late/Memphis	675	725
Eclipse/True Stories	300	325
Fire Signal/Classic Line	100	150
Flumotions/Neospeed	300	350
Gengis Khan/Mongolic Dreams	70	90
Heart Break/Heavy Metal	75	100
Hearthstone/Heavy Metal	175	225
High Beam/Night Vision	65	90
Hula/Beach Graffiti	45	75
Little Jelly/Clear Tech	40	55
Mezza Luna/Morgans	250	300
Miss Pinstripe/Carlton	100	125
Passion Flower/Tropical Fiesta	80	110
Ping Pong Blue/Devil's Run	125	150
Pink Cassita/Candy	150	175
Pink Drip/Alfresco	90	100
Plutella/Caterpillar	80	100
Red Island/Scuba	75	100
Red Zebra/Zebra Time	75	95
Rising Star/Aqua Fun	40	65
Robin/Comic Heroes	80	100
Seventeen-Seven/Kids Collection	100	125
Silver Circle/Cool Chic	1000	1200
Sir Swatch/Coat of Arms	325	375
Sputnik/Space Heroes	75	95
St. Catherine Point/Signal Corps	300	400
Stiffy/Cold Fever	40	65
Strawberry Fields/Bright Flags	40	60
The Boss/Rock-Oco Dream	60	90
Touch Down/Top Flight	150	175
Turbine/Sky Walker	80	110
Vasily/Calypso Beach	200	250
White Window/Wall Street	150	175
World Record/Sprint	65	90

Weathervanes

The most valued weathervanes are those handmade of sheet copper before 1850. These are quite rare. In the nineteenth and early twentieth centuries factory workers made weathervanes of copper hammered in iron molds. Important makers include Cushing and White of Waltham, Massachusetts, and the J. Howard Company of East Bridgewater, Massachusetts. Many reproductions have been made from original molds. For more information see *The Art of the Weathervane* by Steve Miller (Schiffer, Exton, PA, 1984).

American Flag Weathervane. —Photo courtesy Skinner, Inc., Boston, MA.

	LOW	HIGH
American Flag, sheet metal, gilded and silver-painted, silhouette flag w/ molded arm and hand holding hammer, New England, 1850-75, 25.5" h, 65" l	$32,000	$36,000
Arrow, steel, cut-out sections, ornate feathered back w/ 20 pierced feathers, middle section w/ scrolls and pierced steelwork, shaft w/ 4 directionals on large copper housing, 74" l	2000	4000
Banneret and Arrow, sheet metal, "God Is Love" message in banneret, late 19th C, 38" h, 56" l	1500	2500
Banneret and Sun, sheet copper, scrolled banner w/ sun terminal, traces of verdigris, attributed to Howard, Bridgewater, MA, late 19th C, 23.25" h, 20.75" l	2000	3000
Blackhawk, trotting horse, molded and gilded copper, allover verdigris, late 19th C, 18.5" h, 33" l	6000	8000
Butterfly, molded copper, perched in frame w/ upper and lower crossbars and decorated w/ stylized flowers, traces of gilt paint, allover patination, attributed to J. W. Fiske, late 19th C, 35" h, 36" w	4000	6000
Centaur, sheet metal, cut silhouette figure w/ molded drawn bow and arrow, outlined in molded zinc beading, mounted on molded shaft and horizontal bar, old gray weathered surface, Manchester, NH, late 19th C, 61" h, 76" l	5000	8000
Cow, molded copper, full-bodied, weathered gilt verdigris surface, Harris and Co., Boston, late 19th C, 21" h, 33" l	20,000	25,000
Cow, molded copper, narrow full-bodied cow w/ horns, curved ears, and broom-type tail, gilt and green verdigris surface, 15" h, 28" l	3000	5000
Dexter Horse and Jockey, molded copper horse and rider w/ cast zinc heads, tag on shaft reads "Cushing & White Patent Applied For Waltham Mass," traces of gilding, c1868-72, 28" l	10,000	12,000
Eagle, copper w/ cast head and feet, dark finish w/ some green verdigris, bullet hole in wing, A. L. Jewell & Co., 12" h, 24" l	3000	5000
Eagle, gilt copper, embossed, full-bodied, perched on ball w/ arrow, late 19th C, 21" h, 25" l	300	500

Weathervanes.

Above: Molded cow; molded Bbackhawk; fish; 2 silhouette scrolled banners.

Below: Molded eagle; molded running horse; silhouette peacock; molded rooster.

—Photos courtesy Skinner, Inc., Boston, MA.

	LOW	HIGH
Eagle, molded and gilded copper, full-bodied, perched on ball, arrow crossbar above directionals, early 20th C, 21" h, 24.5" l	1500	2500
Eagle, molded copper, full-bodied, poised in flight, A. L. Jewell & Co., Waltham, MA, 1855-67, 21" h, 25.5" l	3000	4000
Eagle and Quill, molded copper, full-bodied eagle perched on ball, quill crossbar, remnants of gold paint, fine verdigris surface, late 19th C, 36.5" h, 45" l	2000	3000
Fox, running, iron, long bushy tail, 7.5" h, 33" l	6000	8000
Fox, running, molded and gilded copper, L. W. Cushing & Sons, Waltham, MA, c1883, 22" l	5000	7000
Horse, running, sheet iron, red glass eye, late 19th C, 25" l	400	600
Horse, standing, molded copper body w/ cast zinc head, identified as "Washington," mounted on wooden plinth, attributed to J. W. Fiske, late 19th C, 31" h, 33" l	6000	8000
Horse, trotting, molded and gilded copper, w/ directionals, East Concord, NH, 19th C, 65.5" h, 33.5" l	2000	3000
Horse, trotting, molded copper, full-bodied, gilt, 6 bullet holes, 15" h, 32" l	800	1000
Horse, trotting, molded metal, mounted on diagonally braced support w/ sheet metal broom-form terminal, ME, late 19th C, 22" h, 47" w	2000	4000
Horse and Sulky, molded and gilded copper, St. Julian model, full-bodied horse and driver, attributed to J. W. Fiske & Co., late 19th C, 24.5" h, 45.25" l	25,000	30,000
Hunter, taking aim, sheet iron silhouette, painted black, late 19th/early 20th C, 26.5" h, 25" w	1000	1500
Lightning Rod, 5-pronged finial on twisted shaft w/ gilt-painted molded metal trotting horse on cast directional, white glass ball, tripod base, Cretzer, St. Louis, MO, c1900, 69" h	400	600
Lightning Rod, gilded sunburst finial on spiral shaft w/ molded black-painted cow on cast directional, turquoise blue glass ball, tripod base, Midwestern America, c1900, 69" h, 22.5" w	200	400
Lightning Rod, molded zinc trotting horse figure on cast directional, celadon green molded glass ball, tripod stand, Midwestern America, c1900, 54" h, 28" w	300	500
Lightning Rod, painted cast shaft on cast scrolled directional w/ etched ruby-flash glass panel, translucent white glass ball, tripod base, Midwestern America, c1900, 48" h	500	700
Lightning Rod, tapering shaft w/ arrow and star banner directional, star and crescent white glass base, tripod stand, Midwestern America, c1900, 54" h	300	500
Rooster, cast zinc full-figure body, sheet copper tail, verdigris surface, J. Howard, Bridgewater, MA, late 19th C, 26.75" h, 25" l	2500	3500
Schooner, 2-masted sailing ship in full sail w/ full-bodied hull and rigged sail and mast construction, flying flags, gilt decorated, 59" h, 64" l	5000	7000
Ship, carved wood hull, zinc sails, attributed to Frank Adams, Martha's Vineyard, MA, c1930, 21" h, 37.75" l	1000	2000
Stag, leaping over bush, molded and gilded copper, on cast iron stand w/ cardinals, attributed to Harris & Co., Boston, late 19th C, 26" h, 29.5" l	14,000	18,000
Sulky & Driver, molded copper, 4-wheeled sulky, full-bodied horse and driver, mounted on wooden base, attributed to J. W. Fiske, Boston, late 19th C, 19.5" h, 50" l	15,000	20,000
William Tell, molded and painted metal, full-bodied figure w/ raised arms, wearing plumed hat w/ red and blue feathers, blue, red, and yellow ruffled shirt, and red pantaloons, missing bow, 19th C, 32" h, 17" w	15,000	20,000

Windmill Weights

Bull, standing silhouette, silver paint, lettered "Fairbury Nebr.," early 20th C, 18" h, 24.5" l	$800	$1000
Crescent Moon, marked "Eclipse, A18," early 20th C, 9" h, 10" l	200	300
Horse, bob-tailed, embossed mark no. "58," late 19th/early 20th C, 21.5" h, 17.5" l	300	500
Horse, bob-tailed, embossed mark no. "586," painted brown and white, late 19th/early 20th C, 16.5" h, 17" w	400	600
Horse, standing, cast features, long tail, Demster Mfg. Co., Beatrice, NE, 20th C, 18.5" h, 19.75" l	1000	1200
Horse, standing, full-figured w/ cast features, impressed "58G," painted white, early 20th C, 16.5" h, 17" l	800	1000
Horse, standing on plinth, embossed mark no. "58," traces of white and black paint, late 19th/early 20th C, 18.5" h, 17.5" l	300	500
Letter "W," w/ hexagonal serifs, side mounting, early 20th C, 9" h, 16.5" w	400	600
Rooster, full-bodied w/ rainbow tail, Elgin Co., late 19th C, 15" h, 19" l	1800	2200
Rooster, full-tailed, cast features, marked "10 FT No. 2," rectangular iron base, early 20th C, 15.5" h, 16.5" l	1500	2000
Rooster, full-tailed, embossed mark "10 ft. no. 2," painted white w/ red comb and wattle, late 19th/early 20th C, 15" h, 17" l	600	800
Rooster, full-tailed, painted black w/ red comb and wattle, late 19th/early 20th C, 15.5" h, 16.5" l	600	800
Rooster, molded features, rectangular base, early 20th C, 15.5" h, 17" l	1000	1500
Rooster, painted white w/ red trim, Elgin Wind, Power & Pump Co., Elgin, IL, 18" h	800	1000
Rooster, rainbow-tailed, traces of red comb and wattle, late 19th/early 20th C, 19" h, 17" w	1200	1500
Star, 5-pointed, silver paint, late 19th C, 15" h, 15" w	900	1100

Left to right: 58G Horse; Fairbury Bull; Full-Tailed Rooster; Rainbow-Tail Rooster. —Photo courtesy Skinner, Inc., Boston, MA.

Woodenware

While many types of wood items are highly sought-after collectibles, this section lists miscellaneous wooden items including tools and kitchen utensils. Wooden utensils are most commonly made of maple. Other woods used include cedar, pine, hickory, ash and oak. Prices vary depending on item and type of wood.

Left: Goblet, treenware, incised decoration, English, late 18th/early 19th C, 8.25" h, $9200 at auction.

Right: Covered Bowl, painted red and green feather design on ocher ground, OH, 1800-50, 7" h, 6" dia, $2645 at auction.

—Photos courtesy Skinner, Inc., Boston, MA.

	LOW	HIGH
Apple Peeler, hard and soft wood, Shaker, old patina, w/ table clamp, 17" h	$400	$650
Baby Rattle, wood, wire, and tin w/ bells, worn japanning	150	200
Bowl, ash burl, worn patina, 3.25" h, 17.25" h	450	750
Bowl, covered, turned burl w/ incised top and sides, 19th C, 3.5" h, 5.5" dia	300	
Bowl, hardwood, w/ hand work, natural patina, 10" x 17.5"	75	150
Bucket, stave construction, worn red graining, white interior, black steel bands, wooden handle w/ wire bale and diamond attachments, 6" h, 7.5" d	175	275
Buck Saw, Shaker, old patina, 26" l	250	410
Burl Butter Paddle, maple, chamfered handle, old finish, 10.5" l	125	200
Butterprint, cow and tree, hardwood, turned 1-pc. handle, 4.25" l	100	160
Butterprint, primitive tulip and leaves, poplar, old black finish, handle dated "1796," attributed to Ephrata, PA, 4.5" x 5"	400	700
Candle Box, curly maple, hanging, 14.5" l	400	700
Candle Box, pine, sliding lid, red, 6" l	350	550
Candle Sconce, pine, worn patina, 15.75" h	125	200
Candy Mold, pine, 2-part, carved fish, hinged, 11.75" l	225	375
Carousel Figure, running horse, raised head, carved animal saddle pad, attributed to C. W. Parker Co., Abilene, KS, late 19th/early 20th C, 53" h, 70" l	3000	5000
Carousel Figure, setter, painted brown w/ black, red, and yellow studded collar and shaped saddle, attributed to Herschell Spillman Co., Tonowanda, NY, late 19th/early 20th C, 28" h, 58" l	7000	9000
Carrier, octagonal, painted red, central square compartment surrounded by 4 hexagonal compartments, shaped fixed handle, late 19th C, 4" h, 12.5" w	500	700
Checkerboard, pine, old brown stain, black painted squares, white-detailed back, gallery edge, 20" x 29"	400	700
Cheese Ladder, hickory, Shaker, old patina, worn white paint, 25" l	450	700
Coffee Bin, wood, worn old red paint, black stenciled label "Use Capital Coffee," slant lid w/ stenciled label "Agents," 32.75" h	375	625
Coffee Grinder, poplar, dovetailed, pewter hopper, cast iron crank, 8" h	75	100

Left to right: Canns, turned maple, incised banding, late 18th C, 4.75" h, price for pair, $1380 at auction; Goblets, Lehn ware, painted floral decoration on pink ground, red, green, and black bands on feet, yellow interiors, c1849-92, 3" and 2.75" h, price for pair, $1150 at auction. —Photos courtesy Skinner, Inc., Boston, MA.

	LOW	HIGH
Cookie Board, beech, 5 carved scenes, 3.5" x 28"	175	275
Cookie Board, cherry, bear print, old patina, branded "B.R." and inscribed in ink "B. Raber," 5" x 8"	150	250
Dipper, bentwood, hard and soft woods, old brown finish, copper tacks, 7.5" d, 8" turned handle	150	250
Dipper, curly maple, round bowl, old worn finish, 10" l	75	125
Dipper, hardwood, natural burl growth bowl, 12.5" l	100	200
Dish, burl, carved animal handle, 4.375" d, 4.5" h plus handle	550	950
Drying Rack, poplar, attributed to Shakers, folding, 3 sections, old worn grayish-yellow repaint, each section 35" x 56"	150	250
Drying Rack, walnut, 2-part, Shaker, mortised bars, brass hinges, 18" x 29"	125	200
Duster, pine, old dark patina, 24" l	75	150
Egg Carrier, bird's-eye maple, Shaker, old patina, wire fasteners and wire spring clip, 11" h	1000	1700
Firkin, painted red, stenciled "Gran. Sugar," 14.5" h, 15" dia	300	500
Flour Sifter, poplar, old finish, 8" h	275	450
Foot Warmer, pine, old red paint, compass star relief carving w/ drilled holes, wire bale handle, 7.25" h	100	150
Gameboard, painted, dark brown, orange, and red, w/ gold and colored decals, 17.5" x 17.75"	350	600
Grain Measure, set of 5, bentwood, galvanized metal bands, stenciled "1 qt.," "2 qt.," "4 qt.," and "½ Bu."	275	450
Ice Skates, wood, wrought iron blades, worn leather straps, old blue repaint, 14.75" l	40	70
Jug, wire bale w/ wooden handle, bottom marked "Mrs. Theobald," old soft finish, minor age cracks, Pease, 8.25" h, 8.5" h	600	1000
Knife Box, ash and chestnut, bentwood, turned handle, 8.5" x 13"	100	175
Knife Box, mahogany, dovetailed w/ scalloped detail, pine bottom, old worn finish, 6.75" h	300	500
Knife Box, walnut, single compartment, cutout bale handle, 6" x 12"	75	125
Lamp, carved pine draped lady base, old alligatored varnish, 13.5" h	75	150
Match Holder, treen, wine glass shaped, turned rings, black striping, 3.5" h	40	70
Mortar and Pestle, primitive, attributed to Indians, worn gray patina, 23" h	75	125
Nutmeg Grater, turned mahogany, brass fittings, 7.625" l	300	500

	LOW	HIGH
Picture Frame, carved w/ columns, trees, and the letters "B" and "G," dark brown finish, 19th C, 10" x 7.5"	300	500
Pull Toy, stern wheel steamship, wood and wire, old brown paint, 24" l	350	550
Rolling Pin, w/ double rollers, birch w/ walnut colored patina, 20.25" l	75	150
Scoop, wooden, cut-out handle, natural patina	35	55
Sieve, wood, hinged corners change shape from diamond to square, old patina, 18.5" x 18.5"	200	300
Spice Box, walnut, dovetailed, sliding reeded lid, old finish, 10" l	350	550
Spice Rack, hanging, birch, old varnish finish, wire nail construction, plywood back, 12.75" x 12.75"	150	250
Spool Holder, maple and chestnut, turned, Shaker, old finish, wooden spools on pins and red velvet pincushion, 5.75" h	100	170
Stocking Stretcher, child size, old patina, 16" h	35	55
Sugar Bucket, walnut, 2-tone, pine staves w/ wooden bands, wooden handle w/ wire bale, 6.625" h	150	250
Vessel, curly maple, tumbler shaped, old finish, 3.125" h	45	75
Vise, chestnut and leather, old patina, Union Village, OH, 28" h	75	150
Wheelbarrow, child's, red striping and black stenciled squirrel on sides, wooden wheel w/ iron rim, iron hardware, stenciled label "made by Paris Mfg. Co. South Paris ME U.S.A., no. 2," early 20th C, 38" l	200	400
Whirligig, Indian squaw, horsehair wig, wide-open eyes, open mouth w/ carved and painted teeth, wearing leather bustier, skirt, boots, and copper cross necklace, standing on painted floor, 19th C, 24" h	20,000	30,000
Whirligig, soldier, painted, red shirt, blue cap and pants, tan blades, 9" h	700	900

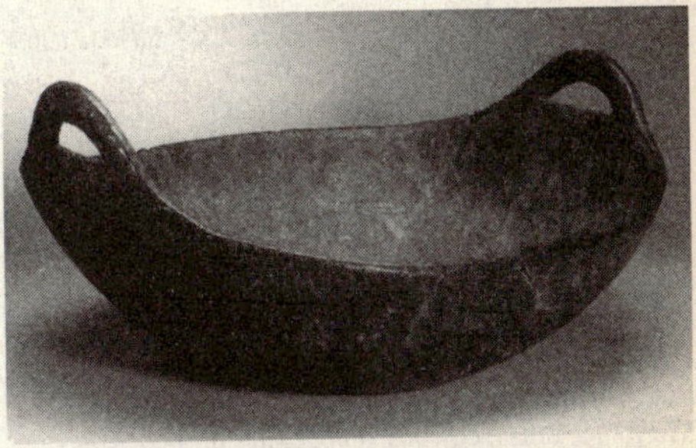

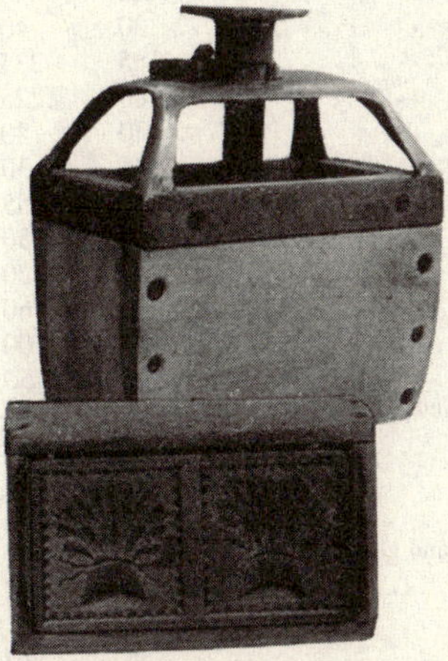

Above: Burl Bowl, hand-tooled "Indians' Bowl," 18th C, 6.5" h, 24.5" x 21.5", $13225 at auction. —Photo courtesy Skinner, Inc., Boston, MA.

Left: Butter Mold, sheath of wheat pattern on bottom, 7" h, 6" w, $121 at auction. —Photo courtesy Collectors Auction Services.

Zippo Lighters

The first Zippos appeared in 1932. One of the most active areas in this market is the "Vietnam Zippos." American G.I.s used these lighters during the Vietnam War. Although made in Bradford, Connecticut, G.I.s commissioned a variety of decorations ranging from the patriotic to the absurd. In some cases they decorated the lighters themselves. There are two types of reproductions in this area: old, undecorated lighters sometimes acquire a new decoration; other reproductions are entirely new, made in Asia.

For further information on Zippo lighters see *The Viet Nam Zippo: 1933-1975* by Jim Fiorella (Schiffer, Atglen, PA, 1999).

Windproof, 1940, $420 at auction. —Photo courtesy Auction Team Köln.

	LOW	HIGH
Ace Sugar Cones, "Ace Cone Co., Green Bay, Wis.," 1955	$45	$55
AMP Special Industries, brushed stainless, enamel etched logo, 1973	30	40
ATCO, Dallas, 1962	20	25
B & L Machine Co., Inc., Houston, TX, unused, 1969	30	40
Beechcraft Model 76 Duchess, 1977	30	40
Buick, "Buick Suggestion Winner 1953," 1952	185	235
Charlie the Tuna, "Think Safety," 1988	180	225
Cinderella Frocks For Girls, slim style, 1958	30	40
D-Day, "D-Day Normandy 50 Years 1944-1994," black crackle finish, 1994	25	30
Eaton Truck Axles, 1975	45	55
Elvis, "50 Years with Elvis," 1989	65	80
Frolich Bros. Marine Divers Inc., 1979	55	70
John Weitzel, Inc., engraved jet airplane logo, 1961	50	60
Lee, sterling silver case, 1950s	80	100
Marlboro, brass, cowboy on bucking bronco, 1993	40	50
Packers of Castle Brand Meats, Rose City Packing Co., Inc., New Castle, IN, 1965	55	65
Pittsburgh Paints, peacock logo, 1973	50	60
Reddy Kilowatt, 1968	185	235
Rudy Fick Ford, Ford emblem and dealer address	45	55
Slim Lighter, polished finish, engine turned line design, white and gold box, 1973	25	35
Smith Furnace Co. Jobbers, New Castle, PA, 1962	20	25
Tampa Bay Buccaneers, slim style, 1975	90	105
Thompson Pumps Precision Oil Well Pumps, 1967	65	80
United Commercial Travelers of America, 1958	20	25
US Naval Station Bermuda, BWI, 1956	25	30
USS Biddle DLG-34, 1967	20	25
USS Essex E Navibus Pugnissima, 1959	75	95
Westinghouse, 1958	45	65
York Air Conditioning Refrigeration Heating, 1964	25	45

Auction Houses

The following auction companies and dealers generously supply Rinker Enterprises, Inc., with copies of their auction/sales lists, press releases, catalogs and illustrations, and prices realized. In addition, the auction houses in **bold** typeface graciously provide Rinker Enterprises, Inc. with photographs, digital images, and/or permission to scan images from their catalogs.

Action Toys, PO Box 102, Holtsville, NY 11742; (516) 563-9113; Fax: (516) 563-9182.

Sanford Alderfer Auction Co., Inc., 501 Fairgrounds Road, Hatfield, PA 19440; (215) 393-3000; Fax: (215) 368-9055; e mail: auction@alderfercompany.com; web: www.alderfercompany.com.

American Social History and Social Movements, 4025 Saline Street, Pittsburgh, PA 15217; (412) 421-5230; Fax: (412) 421-0903.

Apple Tree Auction Center, 1616 West Church Street, Newark, OH 43015; (740) 344-4282; Fax: (740) 344-3673; web: www.appletreeauction.com.

Arthur Auctioneering, 563 Reed Road, Hughesville, PA 17737; (800) ARTHUR-3.

Auction Team Köln, – Breker –The Specialists, Postfach 50 11 19, D-50971 Köln, Germany; Tel: -/49/221/38 70 49; Fax: -/49/221/37 48 78; Jane Herz, International Rep USA; (941) 925-0385; Fax: (941) 925-0487; e mail: auction@breker.com; web: www.breker.com.

Aumann Auctions, Inc., 20114 Illinois Route 16, Nokomis, IL 62075; (888) AUCTN-4U; Fax: (217) 563-2111; e mail: aumannauct@ccipost.net.

Robert F. Batchelder, 1 West Butler Avenue, Ambler, PA 19002; (215) 643-1430.

Bill Bertoia Auctions, 1881 Spring Road, Vineland, NJ 08361; (609) 692-1881; Fax: (609) 692-8697; e mail: bba@ccnj.net; web: bba.ccc.nj.net.

Wayland Bunnell, 199 Tarrytown Road, Manchester, NH 03103; (603) 668-5466; e mail: wtarrytown@aol.com.

Butterfield & Butterfield, 220 San Bruno Avenue, San Francisco, CA 94103; (415) 861-7500; Fax: (415) 861-8951; e mail: info@butterfields.com; web: www.butterfields.com.

Butterfield & Dunning, 441 West Huron Street, Chicago, IL 60610; (312) 377-7500; Fax: (312) 377-7501; e mail: info@butterfields.com; web: www.butterfields.com.

Cards From Grandma's Trunk, The Millards, PO Box 404, Northport, IN 49670; (616) 386-5351.

Cerebro, PO Box 327, East Prospect, PA 17317; (800) 69-LABEL; Fax: (717) 252-3685; e mail: cerebro@cerebro.com; web: www.cerebro.com.

Christie's East, 219 East 67th Street, New York, NY 10021; (212) 606-0400; Fax: (212) 452-2063; web: www.christies.com.

Christie's Inc., 502 Park Avenue, New York, NY 10022; (212) 546-1000; Fax: (212) 980-8163; web: www.christies.com.

Christmas Morning, 1806 Royal Lane, Dallas, TX 75229-3126; (972) 506-8362; Fax: (972) 506-7821.

Cobb's Doll Auctions, 1909 Harrison Road, Johnstown, OH 43031-9539; (740) 964-0444; Fax: (740) 927-7701.

J. M. Cohen, Rare Books, 2 Karin Court, New Paltz, NY 12561; (914) 883-9720; Fax: (914) 883-9142; e mail: jmcrb@ulster.net; web: www.kiwiclub.org/jmcrb/.

Collectors Auction Services, RR 2, Box 431 Oakwood Road, Oil City, PA 16301; (814) 677-6070; Fax: (814) 677-6166; e mail: manderton@mail.usachoice.net; web: www.caswel.com.

Collector's Sales and Services, PO Box 6, Pomfret Center, CT 06259; (860) 974-7008; Fax: (860) 974-7010; e mail: collectors@antiquechina.com; web: www.antiquechina.com, www.antiqueglass.com.

Copake Auction, Inc., 226 Route 7A, PO Box H, Copake, NY 12516; (518) 329-1142; Fax: (518) 329-3369; e mail: copakeauction@netstep.net; web: www.usi-ny.com/copakeauction.

Robert Coup, PO Box 348, Leola, PA 17540; (717) 656-7780; Fax: (717) 656-8233; e mail: polbandwgn@aol.com.

Dawson's, 128 American Road, Morris Plains, NJ 07950; (973) 984-6900; Fax: (973) 984-6956; e mail: dawson1@idt.net; web: www.dawsonsauction.com.

The Doctor's Bag, 397 Prospect Street, Northampton, MA 01060; (413) 584-1440.

William Doyle Galleries, Inc., 175 East 87th Street, New York, NY 10128; (212) 427-2730; Fax: (212) 369-0892; e mail: info@doylegalleries.com; web: www.doylegalleries.com.

Dunbar's Gallery, 76 Haven Street, Milford, MA 01757; (508) 634-8697; Fax: (508) 634-8698; e mail: Dunbar2bid@aol.com.

Early American History Auctions, Inc., 7911 Herschel Avenue, Suite 205, La Jolla, CA 92037; (619) 459-4159; Fax: (619) 459-4373; e mail: auctions@earlyamerican.com; web: www.earlyamerican.com.

Early Auction Co., Roger and Steve Early, 123 Main Street, Milford, OH 45150; (513) 831-4833; Fax: (513) 831-1441.

Ken Farmer Auctions & Estates, LLC, 105A Harrison Street, Radford, VA 24141; (540) 639-0939; Fax: (540) 639-1759; e mail: auction@usit.net; web: www.kenfarmer.com.

Fink's Off the Wall Auction, 108 East 7th Street, Lansdale, PA 19446; (215) 855-9732; Fax: (215) 855-6325; e mail: lansbeer@finksauctions.com; web: www.finksauctions.com.

Flomaton Antique Auction, 277 Old Highway 31, Flomaton, AL 36441; (334) 296-3059.

Frank's Antiques & Auctions, Box 516, 2405 North Kings Road, Hilliard, FL 32046; (904) 845-2870; Fax: (904) 845-4000; e mail: franksauct@aol.com.

Freeman\Fine Arts of Philadelphia, Inc., 1808 Chestnut Street, Philadelphia, PA 19103; (215) 563-9275; Fax: (215) 563-8236; web: www.auctions-on-line.com/Freeman.

Chuck Furjanic, Inc., PO Box 165892, Irving, TX 75016; (800) 882-4825; Fax: (972) 257-1785; e mail: furjanic@onramp.net.

Garth's Auctions, Inc., 2690 Stratford Road, PO Box 369, Delaware, OH 43015; (740) 362-4771; Fax: (740) 363-0164; web: www.garths.com.

Lynn Geyer's Advertising Auctions, 300 Trail Ridge, Silver City, NM 88061; (505) 538-2341; Fax: (505) 388-9000.

Glass–Works Auctions, PO Box 180, East Greenville, PA 18041; (215) 679-5849; Fax: (215) 679-3068; e mail: glswrk@enter.net; web: www.glswrk-auction.com.

Greenberg Shows and Auctions, 7566 Main Street, Sykesville, MD 21784; (410) 795-7447; Fax: (410) 549-2553; e mail: auction@greenbergshows.com.

Green Valley Auctions, Inc., Route 2, Box 434-A, Mount Crawford, VA 22841; (540) 434-4260; Fax: (540) 434-4532; e mail: gvai@shentel.net; web: www.greenvalleyauctions.com.

Marc Grobman, 94 Paterson Road, Fanwood, NJ 07023-1056; (908) 322-4176; e mail: mgrobman@worldnet.att.net.

GVL Enterprises, 21764 Congress Hall Lane, Saratoga, CA 95070; (408) 872-1006; Fax: (408) 872-1007; e mail: jlally@kpcb.com.

Gypsyfoot Enterprises, Inc., PO Box 5833, Helena, MT 59604; (406) 449-8076; Fax: (406) 443-8514; e mail: Gypsyfoot@aol.com.

Hakes' Americana and Collectibles, PO Box 1444, York, PA 17405-1444; (717) 848-1333; Fax: (717) 852-0344; e mail: hake@hakes.com.

Gene Harris Antique Auction Center, Inc., PO Box 476, 203 South 18th Avenue, Marshalltown, IA 50158; (515) 752-0600; Fax: (515) 753-0226; e mail: ghaac@marshallnet.com; web: www.marshallnet.com/ghaac.

Norman C. Heckler & Co., Bradford Corner Road, Woodstock Valley, CT 06282; (860) 974-1634; Fax: (860) 974-2003.

Horst Auction Center, 50 Durlach Road, Ephrata, PA 17522; (717) 859-1331; Fax: (717) 738-2132.

Michael Ivankovich Antiques, Inc., PO Box 2458, Doylestown, PA 18901; (215) 345-6094; Fax: (215) 345-6692; e mail: wnutting@comcat.com; web: www.wnutting.com.

Jackson's Auctioneers & Appraisers, 2229 Lincoln Street, Cedar Falls, IA 50613; (319) 277-2256; Fax: (319) 277-1252; web: jacksonsauction.com.

S. H. Jemik, PO Box 753, Bowie, MD 20715; (301) 262-1864; Fax; (410) 721-6494; e mail: Shjemik@aol.com.

James D. Julia, Inc., PO Box 830, Route 201, Skowhegan Road, Fairfield, ME 04937; (207) 453-7125; Fax: (207) 453-2502; e mail: jjulia@juliaauctions.com; web: www.juliaauctions.com.

Gary Kirsner Auctions, PO Box 8807, Coral Springs, FL 33075; (954) 344-9856; Fax: (954) 344-4421.

Charles E. Kirtley, PO Box 2273, Elizabeth City, NC 27906; (252) 335-1262; Fax: (252) 335-4441; e mail: ckirtley@coastalnet.com.

Kruse International, PO Box 190, 5540 County Road 11-A, Auburn, IN 46706; (800) 968-4444; Fax: (219) 925-5467.

Henry Kurtz, Ltd., 163 Amsterdam Avenue, Suite 136, New York, NY 10023; (212) 642-5904; Fax: (212) 874-6018.

Lang's Sporting Collectables, Inc., 14 Fishermans Lane, Raymond, ME 04071; (207) 655-4265; Fax: (207) 655-4265.

Leland's, 36 East 22nd Street, 7th Floor, New York, NY 10010; (212) 545-0800; Fax: (212) 545-0713.

Los Angeles Modern Auctions, PO Box 462006, Los Angeles, CA 90046; (213) 845-9456; Fax: (213) 845-9601; e mail: peter@lamodern.com; web: www.lamodern.com.

Howard Lowery, 3812 West Magnolia Boulevard, Burbank, CA 91505; (818) 972-9080; Fax: (818) 972-3910.

Majolica Auctions, Michael G. Strawser, 200 North Main, PO Box 332, Wolcottville, IN 46795; (219) 854-2859; Fax: (219) 854-3979.

Manion's International Auction House, Inc., PO Box 12214, Kansas City, KS 66112; (913) 299-6692; Fax: (913) 299-6792; e mail: collecting@manions.com; web: www.manions.com.

Joel Markowitz, Box 10, Old Bethpage, NY 11804; (516) 249-9405; e mail: smctr@sheetmusiccenter.com; web: www.sheetmusiccenter.com.

Mastro Fine Sports Auctions, 1515 West 22nd Street, Suite 125, Oak Brook, IL 60523; (630) 472-9551; Fax: (630) 472-1201; web: www.mastrofsa.com.

Ted Maurer, Auctioneer, 1003 Brookwood Drive, Pottstown, PA 19464; (610) 323-1573; web: www.maurerail.com.

Mechantiques, 26 Barton Hill, East Hampton, CT 06424; (860) 267-8682; Fax; (860) 267-1120; e mail: mroenigk@aol.com; web: www.Mechantiques.com.

Gary Metz's Muddy River Trading Co., PO Box 1430, 251 Wildwood Road, Salem, VA 24153; (540) 387-5070; Fax: (540) 387-3233.

Charles F. Miller, 708 Westover Drive, Lancaster, PA 17601; (717) 285-2255; Fax: (717) 285-2255.

Wm. Morford, RD 2, Cazenovia, NY 13035; (315) 662-7625; Fax: (315) 662-3570; e mail: morf2bid@aol.com.

Ray Morykan Auctions, 1368 Spring Valley Road, Bethlehem, PA 18015; (610) 838-6634; e mail: dmorykan@enter.net.

Harold R. Nestler, 13 Pennington Avenue, Waldwick, NJ 07463; (201) 444-7413.

New England Absentee Auctions, Inc., 16 Sixth Street, Stamford, CT 06905; (203) 975-9055; Fax: (203) 323-6407; e mail: NEAAuction@aol.com.

New England Auction Gallery, Box 2273, West Peabody, MA 01960; (978) 535-3140; Fax: (978) 535-7522; e mail: dlkrim@star.net; web: www.old-toys.com.

Norton Auctioneers, Pearl at Monroe, Colwater, MI 49036-1967; (517) 279-9063; Fax: (517) 279-9191; e mail: nortonsold@cbpu.com; web: www.nortonauctioneers.com.

Nostalgia Publications, Inc., 21 South Lake Drive, Hackensack, NJ 07601; (201) 488-4536.

Ingrid O'Neil, PO Box 60310, Colorado Springs, CO 80960; (719) 473-1538; Fax: (719) 477-0768; e mail: auction@ioneil.com.

Richard Opfer Auctioneers, Inc., 1919 Greenspring Drive, Timonium, MD 21093; (410) 252-5035; Fax: (410) 252-5863.

Ron Oser Enterprises, PO Box 101, Huntingdon Valley, PA 19006; (215) 947-6575; Fax: (215) 938-7348; e mail: RonOserEnt@aol.com; web: members.aol.com/RonOserEnt.

Past Tyme Pleasures, PMB #204, 2491 San Ramon Valley Boulevard #1, San Ramon, CA 94583-1601; (925) 484-4488; Fax: (925) 484-2551; e mail: pasttyme1@aol.com.

Pettigrew Auction Co., 1645 South Tejon Street, Colorado Springs, CO 80906; (719) 633-7963; Fax: (719) 633-5035.

Phillips New York, 406 East 79th Street, New York, NY 10021; (212) 570-4830; Fax: (212) 570-2207; web: www.phillips-auctions.com.

Cordelia and Tom Platt, 2805 East Oakland Park Boulevard #380, Fort Lauderdale, FL 33306; (954) 564-2002; Fax: (954) 564-2002; e mail: ctplatt@ctplatt.com; web: www.ctplatt.com.

Postcards International, 2321 Whitney Avenue, Suite 102, PO Box 185398, Hamden, CT 06518; (203) 248-6621; Fax: (203) 248-6628; e mail: quality@vintagepostcards.com; web: www.vintagepostcards.com.

Poster Mail Auction Co., PO Box 133, 40189 Patrick Street, Waterford, VA 20197; (703) 684-3656; Fax: (540) 882-4765.

Ken Prag, PO Box 14817, San Francisco, CA 94114; (415) 586-9386; e mail: Kprag@planeteria.net.

Provenance, PO Box 3487, Wallington, NJ 07057; (973) 779-8785; Fax: (212) 741-8756.

David Rago Auctions, Inc., 333 North Main Street, Lambertville, NJ 08530; (609) 397-9374; Fax: (609) 397-9377; web: www.ragoarts.com.

Lloyd Ralston Gallery, 109 Glover Avenue, Norwalk, CT 06850; (203) 845-0033; Fax: (203) 845-0366.

Red Baron's Antiques, 6450 Roswell Road, Atlanta, GA 30328; (404) 252-3770; Fax: (404) 257-0268; e mail: rbaron@onramp.net.

Remmey Galleries, 30 Maple Street, Summit, NJ 07901; (908) 273-5055; Fax: (908) 273-0171; web: www.remmeygalleries.com.

Ken Schneringer, 271 Sabrina Court, Woodstock, GA 30188; (770) 926-9383; e mail: trademan68@aol.com; web: old-paper.com.

L. H. Selman Ltd., 123 Locust Street, Santa Cruz, CA 95060; (800) 538-0766; Fax: (831) 427-0111; e mail: selman@paperweight.com; web: www.paperweight.com.

Skinner, Inc., Boston Gallery, The Heritage on the Garden, 63 Park Plaza, Boston, MA 02116; (617) 350-5400; Fax: (617) 350-5429; web: www.skinnerinc.com.

Sloan's Washington DC Gallery, 4920 Wyanconda Road, North Bethesda, MD 20852; (800) 649-5066; Fax: (301) 468-9182; web: www.sloansauction.com.

Bill Smith, 56 Locust Street, Douglas, MA 01516; (508) 476-2015.

Smith & Jones, Inc. Auctions, 12 Clark Lane, Sudbury, MA 01776; (978) 443-5517; Fax: (978) 443-2796; e mail: smthjnes@gis.net; web: www.smithandjonesauctions.com.

R. M. Smythe & Co., Inc., 26 Broadway, Suite 271, New York, NY 10004-1701; (800) 622-1880; Fax: (212) 908-4047; web: www.rm-smythe.com.

SoldUSA, Inc., 6407 Idlewild Road, Building 2, Suite 207, Charlotte, NC 28212; (877) SoldUSA; Fax: (704) 364-2322; web: www.soldusa.com.

Sotheby's London, 34-35 New Bond Street, London, England W1A 2AA; 0 (171) 293-5000; Fax: 0 (171) 293-5074.

Sotheby's New York, 1334 York Avenue, New York, NY 10021, (212) 606-7000; web: www.sothebys.com.

Stanton's Auctioneers, 144 South Main Street, PO Box 146, Vermontville, MI 49096; (517) 726-0181; Fax: (517) 726-0060.

Steffen's Historical Militaria, PO Box 280, Newport, KY 41072; (606) 431-4499; Fax: (606) 431-3113.

Streamwood, Inc., Chris R. Jensen, PO Box 1841, Easley, SC 29641-1841; (864) 859-2915; Fax: (800) 453-0398; e mail: cjensen@streamwood.net; web: www.streamwood.net.

Susanin's, Gallery 228, Merchandise Mart, Chicago, IL 60654; (312) 832-9800; Fax: (312) 832-9311; web: www.theauction.com.

Swann Galleries, Inc., 104 East 25th Street, New York, NY 10010; (212) 254-4710; Fax: (212) 979-1017.

Theriault's, PO Box 151, Annapolis, MD 21404; Fax: (410) 224-2515.

'Tiques Auction, RR 1 Box 49B, Old Bridge, NJ 08857; (732) 721-0221; Fax: (732) 721-0127; e mail: tiquesauc@aol.com; web: www.tiques.com.

Tool Shop Auctions, Tony Murland, 78 High Street, Needham Market, Suffolk, England, 1P6 8AW; Tel: (01449) 722992; Fax: (01449) 722683; e mail: tony@toolshop.demon.co.uk; web: www.toolshop.demon.co.uk.

Toy Scouts, Inc., 137 Casterton Avenue, Akron, OH 44303; (330) 836-0668; Fax: (330) 869-8668; e mail: toyscout@akron.infi.net.

Toy Soldiers Etcetera, 732 Aspen Lane, Lebanon, PA 17042-9073; (717) 228-2361; Fax: (717) 228-2362.

Tradewinds Antiques, PO Box 249, 24 Magnolia Avenue, Manchester-by-the-Sea, MA 01944-0249; (978) 768-3327; Fax: (978) 526-3088; e mail: taron@tiac.net; web: www.tradewindsantiques.com

Victorian Images, PO Box 284, Marlton, NJ 08053; (609) 953-7711; Fax: (609) 953-7768; e mail: rmascieri@aol.com; web: www.tradecards.com/vi.

Tom Witte's Antiques, PO Box 399, Front Street West, Mattawan, MI 49071-0399; (616) 668-4161; Fax: (616) 668-5363.

York Town Auction, Inc., 1625 Haviland Road, York, PA 17404; (717) 751-0211; Fax: (717) 767-7729; e mail: yorktownauction@cyberia.com.

If you would like to be included on this list, contact Rinker Enterprises at 5093 Vera Cruz Road, Emmaus, PA 18049; (610) 965-1122; e mail: rinkeron@fast.net.

INDEX